5/02

WHAT DO
CHILDREN
READ
NEXT?

A Reader's Guide to
Fiction for Children

ISSN 1525-3740

WHAT DO
CHILDREN
READ
NEXT?

A Reader's Guide to Fiction for Children

VOLUME 4

JANIS ANSELL

GALE GROUP

THOMSON LEARNING

Detroit • New York • San Diego • San Francisco
Boston • New Haven, Conn. • Waterville, Maine
London • Munich

Janis Ansell

Contributor: Carrie Ansell

Coordinating Editor: Dana Ferguson
Editor: Kathleen Meek
Associate Editor: Prindle LaBarge

Managing Editor: Debra M. Kirby

Manager, Composition and Electronic Prepress: Mary Beth Trimper
Assistant Manager, Composition Purchasing and Electronic Prepress: Eveline Abou-el-Seoud
Manufacturing Manager: Dorothy Maki
Buyer: Stacy L. Melson
Graphic Artist: Michael Logusz

Manager, Data Capture Services: Ronald D. Montgomery
Project Administrator, Data Capture: Beverly Jendrowski
Data Capture Associate: Nancy Sheridan

Manager, Technical Support Services: Theresa Rocklin
Programmer/Analyst: Magdalena Cureton, David J. Mosorjak

ISBN 0-7876-6617-3
0-7876-4799-3 (set)
ISSN 1525-3740

Printed in the United States of America

10 9 8 7 6 5 4 3 2 1

Contents

Preface

What Do Children Read Next? is a reader's advisory tool designed to match readers from Preschool through Grade 5 with books that reflect their interests and concerns. It guides both reluctant and avid readers to new authors and titles for further reading. *What Do Children Read Next?* allows readers quick and easy access to specific information on recent juvenile titles. In addition, each entry provides alternate reading selections, giving children, parents, and librarians the answer to the frequently asked question: "What do I read next?"

Highlights

• Compiled by Janis Ansell, educator, former school psychologist, and former children's book review writer for *ForeWord Magazine*.

• Overview essay describes recent trends in children's literature.

• "Other books you might like," included in each entry, leads to the exploration of additional authors or titles.

• Eleven indexes help locate specific titles or offer suggestions for reading in favorite time periods or geographic locales, about special subjects or characters, or for a particular age level.

• All authors and titles listed in entries under "Other books by the author" and "Other books you might like" are indexed, allowing easy access to thousands of books recommended for further reading.

Details on 1,100 titles

What Do Children Read Next? contains entries for 1,100 books published from 1999-2000 aimed at young readers. Titles have been selected on the basis of their currency, appeal to readers, and literary merit. The entries are listed alphabetically by author. Books by authors with more than one entry are then subarranged by title. The following information is provided where applicable:

• Author's name and real name if a pseudonym is used. Co-author, editor, and illustrator's names also given.

• Book title.

• Date and place of publication; name of publisher.

• Series name.

• Age Range: Indicates the grade levels for which the title is best suited.

• Subject(s): Up to three themes or topics covered in the story.

• Major character(s): Names of up to three featured characters and brief descriptions of them.

• Time Period(s): Tells when the story takes place.

• Locale(s): Tells where the story takes place.

• What the book is about: A brief plot summary.

• Page Count: Indicates the title's specific page count. Located at the end of the plot summary.

• Where it's reviewed: Citations to reviews of the book, including the source of the review, date of the source, and page on which the review appears. Reviews are taken from general reviewing sources such as *Kirkus Reviews* and *Publishers Weekly*, as well as from sources which specialize in materials for younger readers, such as *School Library Journal* and *Horn Book*.

• Awards the book has won.

• Other books by the author: Titles and publication dates of other books the author has written, for those wanting to read more books by a particular writer.

• Other books you might like: Titles by other authors written on a similar theme or in a similar style. A one sentence description of each of these titles whets the reader's appetite for additional titles.

Indexes Answer Reader's Questions

The eleven indexes in *What Do Children Read Next?* are the heart of the book.

Used separately or in conjunction, they create many pathways to the featured titles, answering general questions or locating specific titles. For example:

"What are the best books for children?"

The AWARDS INDEX lists awards and citations given by experts in the field of children's literature. These titles are especially noteworthy.

"Do you know of any books set during the Civil War?"

The TIME PERIOD INDEX is a chronological listing of the time settings in which the main entries take place.

"Are there any books set in Australia?"

The GEOGRAPHIC INDEX lists titles by their locale, helping readers pinpoint a geographic area in which they may have a particular interest.

"I like stories with animals in them. What do you suggest?"

The SUBJECT INDEX lists books by what they are about. Topics include such things as fiction genres (e.g. Fantasy, Ghost Stories, Mystery and Detective Stories), life and relationships (e.g. Family Life, Friendship, School), and subjects of interest to today's children (e.g. Dinosaurs, Magic, Sports).

"Do you have any books with kids whose name is the same as mine?"

The CHARACTER NAME INDEX lists the characters named in the entries, helping readers who remember some information about a book, but not an author or title.

"Do you have any books with cowboys or cowgirls in them?"

The CHARACTER DESCRIPTION INDEX identifies the major characters by occupation (e.g. Astronaut, Doctor) or persona (e.g. Cat, Toy, Twin).

"Which books are good for third graders?"

The AGE LEVEL INDEX lists titles by grade levels for which they are best suited. The ability of individual readers may not necessarily reflect their actual age; the wide variety of age ranges allows the user to select titles for slower or more advanced readers.

"I need to write a report on a 100 page book. What do you suggest?"

The PAGE COUNT INDEX groups titles according to their page count ranges, allowing readers to select individual titles with specific page counts.

"Which books have pictures by Chris Raschka?"

The ILLUSTRATOR INDEX is an alphabetical listing of the illustrators of the main entry titles.

"What has Marc Brown written recently?"

The AUTHOR INDEX contains the names of all authors featured in the entries and those listed under "Other books you might like."

"Are there any books like Peggy Parish's Amelia Bedelia?"

The TITLE INDEX includes all main entry titles and all titles recommended under "Other books by the author" and "Other books you might like" in one alphabetical listing. By searching for a specific title, the reader can find out what other books are similar to a title they like.

The indexes can also be used to narrow down or broaden choices. A reader interested in 50 page stories set in England during World War II would consult the PAGE COUNT, SUBJECT, and GEOGRAPHIC indexes to see which titles appear in all three. Someone interested in detective stories set during the 1930s could compare titles in the TIME PERIOD and CHARACTER DESCRIPTION indexes. And with the AUTHOR and TITLE indexes, which include all books listed under "Other books by the author" and "Other books you might like," it is easy to compile an extensive list of titles for further reading, not only with the titles recommended in a main entry, but also by seeing other titles to which the main entry or its recommended titles are similar.

About the Author

As a school psychologist, teacher of young children, and board member, Janis Ansell wrote numerous psychological studies, lesson plans, student evaluations, and reports for meetings. But seldom did she have an opportunity to write book reviews until she began collaborating with Pam Spencer on *What Do Children Read Next?*

Ansell's writing for *What Do Children Read Next?* reflects her life-long interest in reading and her ability to adapt knowledge gained in one subject area to another. Her interest in reading isn't just personal; she aims to help children share her love of reading and develop their reading skills. Janis and her husband Charles, a self-employed architect, have brought up three enthusiastic readers--their children Jonathan, Carrie, and Laurie.

Professional expertise and affiliations and volunteer participation in libraries and classrooms augment her natural interest in books, especially those for children. Ansell is a former children's book reviewer for *ForeWord Magazine*. Professionally affiliated with the Randolph-Macon Woman's College Alumnae Association Board, Ansell has been named an Honorary Life Member of the Virginia Congress of Parents and Teachers and Volunteer of the Year at Alanton Elementary School. She has served on the Lynnhaven Middle School Planning Council and is a past board member of the Tidewater Association of Hearing Impaired Children and of the Alanton PTA. Ansell is a member of the American Library Association (ALA) and the Association of Library Service to Children (ALSC). Ansell is a library volunteer at Virginia Beach Friends School and she looks forward to being an involved parent volunteer at the Model Secondary School for the Deaf during the next four years.

Janis Ansell's psychological insight into young children, her love of books, and her practical experience as a professional, a parent, and a volunteer make her entries in *What Do Children Read Next?* exceptionally informative and useful.

Acknowledgements

To all those who contributed to the completion of the fourth volume of *What Do Children Read Next?* I am grateful. The cooperative support of many people has been invaluable and I offer appreciation to my family: my husband, Charles; my son Jonathan; daughters Carrie and Laurie; my sister, Pam Spencer; my parents Boyd and Jane Gustafson. My thanks go also to the Virginia Beach (VA) Public Library for upgrading their computer system so I could submit reserve requests from home. Many publishers graciously sent review copies of their 1999-2000 titles. Editor Dana Ferguson is a joy to work with--thanks for your patience, your feedback and your good humor. To my alma mater, Randolph-Macon Woman's College, introduced the concept of lifelong learning leading to the "vita abundantior" of the college's motto--the life more abundant--and gave the me confidence to pursue it.

Also Available Online

The entries in *What Do Children Read Next?* can also be found in the online version of *What Do I Read Next?* on GaleNet. This electronic product encompasses over 96,000 books, including genre fiction, mainstream fiction, and nonfiction. All the books included in *What Do I Read Next?* Online are recommended by librarians or other experts, award winners, or appear on bestseller lists. The user-friendly functionality allows users to refine their searching by using several criteria, while making it easy to identify similar titles for further research and reading. The online version is updated with new information two times a year. For more information about *What Do I Read Next?* Online or GaleNet, please contact Gale Group, Inc.

Suggestions Are Welcome

The editors welcome any comments and suggestions for enhancing and improving *What Do Children Read Next?* Please address correspondence to:

Editor
What Do Children Read Next?
Gale Group, Inc.
25700 Drake Road
Farmington Hills, Michigan 48331-3535
Phone: 248-699-GALE
Toll-free: 1-800-347-GALE
Fax: 248-699-8054

Introduction

Volume 4 of *What Do Children Read Next?* comprises titles published during the years 1999 and 2000 and could perhaps be subtitled "The Millennium Edition" or "The Harry Potter Years." While either trite phrase would limit a discussion of children's literature during this time period, both events have shaped what writers are writing, publishers are publishing, and, of course, what children are reading. The arrival of a new century inspired reissues of a variety of classic works and numerous articles listing the "best" books and most memorable characters of the last century as well as those predicting future classics. In Robbie Hewitt's reflections on the momentous advent of 1900 in Katherine Paterson's coming-of-age story *Preacher's Boy*, winner of the 2000 Jefferson Cup award and a 1999 *Booklist* Editors' Choice selection, readers find a glimpse of what the dawn of a new age might have been like for those facing the arrival of the 20th century.

The phenomenal popularity of J.K. Rowling's Harry Potter books thrust both the author and her work into the limelight. The titles have so dominated the *New York Times* Best Seller List that a separate category for children's books was established for the first time. Another first garnered by Rowling's books was their designation as the most challenged books of 1999 and 2000 in a report of written complaints filed in schools and libraries. Many others saw the books in a different light, including *Publishers Weekly* which, in the August 2, 1999 issue, notes the broad impact of Rowling's work on children's books in general by "showing them in an extremely positive light and silencing criticisms about the dearth of good contemporary writing." Harry Potter has been pictured on the cover of *Time* magazine and featured on numerous talk shows—and we still haven't seen the movie! Many librarians, teachers, and parents think the interest in Harry Potter has inspired children who might not otherwise pick up a book to join the ranks of readers. As children eagerly await the release of the fifth book about Harry and his friends, they are turning to other authors and exploring other genres. The fictional Hogwarts is not only a school for educating wizards and witches but also a real-life launching pad for readers, even the "Muggle" ones.

1999

For the 80th annual observance of National Children's Book Week, the Children's Book Council chose the theme "Plant a Seed . . .Read!" A Chinese-American girl's mother literally plants seeds that sprout into *The Ugly Vegetables*, an inaugural work for author/illustrator Grace Lin that harvested recognition as a Notable Social Studies Trade Book for Young People. Another title designated a Notable Social Studies Trade Book for Young People also received the *Booklist* Editors' Choice award for its depiction of *Love as Strong as Ginger*, an intergenerational story of a Chinese immigrant grandmother's hard work in a crab factory to assure a better life for her granddaughter. Other first–time authors planting the seeds of future reading by producing award-winning books for very young readers include author Trudi Braun, whose picture book *My Goose Betsy* was recognized as a *Booklist* Editors' Choice, and author/illustrator Caroline Uff with *Hello, Lulu*, one of *Smithsonian*'s Notable Books for Children this year. Two other debut works honored with *Smithsonian*'s Notable Books for Children awards are Carmen T. Bernier-Grand's *In the Shade of the Nispero Tree*, set in Puerto Rico in the early '60's and *A Boy Named Giotto* by Paolo Guarnieri, the fictionalized account of a talented young Italian shepherd who becomes a famous 14th-century artist. A far-fetched bedtime tale by debut author/illustrator team Kate Lum and Adrian Johnson entitled *What! Cried Granny: An Almost Bedtime Story* garnered multiple awards, including *School Library Journal* Best Books, ALA Notable Books for Children, *Horn Book* Fanfare and IRA/CBC Children's Choice. Morning travails for a working mother whose imaginative daughter's choice of attire conflicts with mom's practicality are realistically portrayed in *Lottie's Princess Dress* by first-time author Doris Dorrie and illustrator Julia Kaegel, winner of a *Bulletin of the Center for Children's Books* Blue Ribbon. Three works of historical fiction received recognition as Notable Social Studies Trade Books for Young People: *Goodbye, Walter Malinski*, an immigrant story set during the Depression, by Helen Recorvits; Jennifer L. Holm's *Our Only May Amelia*, a Pacific Northwest immigrant tale set in 1899; and *When the Soldiers Were Gone* by Vera W. Propp. In addition, Propp's fictionalized account of post-World War II adjustment for a young Jewish boy hidden from the Nazis on a Dutch farm and returned to his family when the soldiers were finally gone was named a *Booklist* Editors' Choice. *Our Only May Amelia* does not meet her stern Finnish father's expectations for proper "girl" behavior but the literary version of her exploits received accolades, including commendations as a 2000 Newbery Honor book, an ALA Notable Book for Children in 2000, and a *Publishers Weekly* Best Book for 1999. A third grader's move from California to Massachusetts, described in *Morgy Makes His Move*, gained first-time author Maggie Lewis recognition in the *Horn Book* Fanfare Fiction category. Two other debut works selected as Notable Social Studies Trade Books for Young People were Grace Tseng's *White Tiger, Blue Serpent*, which retells a Chinese folktale, and *Gowanus Dogs* by Jonathan Frost. The latter title also received a 2000 Marion Vannett Ridgway Honor designation. A humorous first effort set in Napoleonic France, *I, Crocodile* by author/illustrator Fred Marcellino, was named to the following lists: *Publishers Weekly* Best Books, *New York Times* Best Illustrated Children's Books, and ALA Notable Books for Children. The Coretta Scott King/John Steptoe Award for new talent in illustration was given to Eric Velasquez, illustrator of *The Piano Man*, written by Debbi Chocolate.

Established authors were also honored for their work with multiple awards. Jon Scieszka, author of many titles, including the *Time Warp Trio* series and *The Stinky Cheese Man and Other Fairly Stupid Tales*, received the 1999 Jo Osborne Award for Humor in Children's Literature presented by the Ohio State University Children's Literature Conference. Posthumously, Marguerite Henry, author of 60 children's books, including Newbery-winner *King of the Wind*, was named to the Milwaukee Public Library's Wisconsin Writers Wall of Fame. The Children's Services Division of the Oregon Library Association presented its 1999 Evelyn Sibley Lampman Award to Oregon resident Tom Birdseye for his "significant contribution in the area of literature" to the children of his state. Birdseye is the author of numerous works, including *A Regular Flood of Mishap*, *Tarantula Shoes*, and *Just Call Me Stupid*. The School Library Media Specialists of Southeastern New York named James Howe, creator of such characters as good friends Pinky and Rex and Bunnicula, a vampire rabbit, as the recipient of the 1999 Rip Van Winkle Award for his contributions to children's literature. Vera Williams received the 1999 Empire State Award from the Youth Services Section of the New York Library Association, recognizing the significance of her contributions to literature for young people. The New York Public Library and the Ezra Jack Keats Foundation presented the 1999 Ezra Jack Keats New Writer Award to Stephanie Stuve-Bodeen for her picture book, *Elizabeti's Doll*. In May, Britain named its first children's laureate, Quentin Blake, illustrator of more than 200 books, to a two-year term. The 1999 David McCord Children's Literature Citation recog-

nized the contributions made by Kevin Henkes to the genre. Eve Bunting and Lois Lenski received the 1999 Kerlan Award, given "in recognition of singular attainments in the creation of children's literature" and for their contributions to the University of Minnesota's Kerlan Collection. Author Natalie Babbitt was named one of the 1999 winners of the Hope S. Dean Memorial Award by the Foundation for Children's Books in appreciation of her many literary creations.

At the American Library Association's midwinter meeting, the major awards presented by the organization's divisions to books published during 1998 were announced. The Caldecott Medal went to Mary Azarian for her illustration of the picture book biography *Snowflake Bentley*. Four works were designated as Caldecott Honor Books: *Tibet Through the Red Box* by author/illustrator Peter Sis; David Shannon's *No, David!*; *Snow* by Uri Shulevitz; and Brian Pinkney's *Duke Ellington: The Piano Prince and His Orchestra*, written by Andrea Davis Pinkney. The latter title also received notice as a Coretta Scott King Illustrator Honor Book along with Floyd Cooper's *I Have Heard of a Land* and E.B. Lewis's *The Bat Boy and His Violin*. Louis Sachar was honored with the Newbery Medal for *Holes* while *A Long Way from Chicago* by Richard Peck was named the only Newbery Honor Book of the year.

In the year that *Horn Book* magazine turned 75 and Newbery Medal recipient Phyllis Reynolds Naylor published her 100th book, Ramona returned after a 15-year absence to star in Beverly Cleary's novel, *Ramona's World*. Another character readers met first in 1955, Eloise, created by Kay Thompson, reappeared with the first reissues of the sequels to the original *Eloise*. Virginia Lee Burton's beloved picture book *Mike Mulligan and His Steam Shovel* celebrated 60 years of hard-working Mary Anne helping Mike fulfill his promise to dig the cellar of the new town hall in only one day. Also, Simon & Schuster recognized the 20th anniversary of the publication of Deborah and James Howe's *Bunnicula: A Rabbit-Tale of Mystery* by issuing a special anniversary edition. And Jon Scieszka's *The True Story of the 3 Little Pigs by A. Wolf*, illustrated by Lane Smith, reappeared in a 10th anniversary issue from Viking with a "Special A. Wolf Update." Dr. Seuss's mischievous "Cat in the Hat" appeared on stamps issued by the U.S. Postal Service as part of a "Celebrate the Century" series.

Sadly, 1999 also saw the end of the writing careers of several authors, including 87-year-old William H. Armstrong, winner of the 1970 Newbery Medal for his book *Sounder*, who passed away during the year. In May, Shel Silverstein succumbed to a heart attack at the age of 66. Silverstein is remembered for his classic title *The Giving Tree* and his popular collections of children's poetry, such as *A Light in the Attic* and *Where the Sidewalk Ends*. Cancer took the life of 56-year-old author Sherley Anne Williams in July. Williams was a poet and playwright as well as an author that children remember for her picture book *Working Cotton*, winner of both a Caldecott Honor and a Coretta Scott King Honor for illustration in 1993. Eighty-nine-year-old Leo Lionni, creator of the Caldecott Honor Books *Swimmy*, *Inch by Inch*, *Frederick*, and *Alexander and the Wind-Up Mouse*, died in October.

2000

Sixty-five years before the dawn of the new millennium Holiday House became the first to publish exclusively for children. Despite the current trend in publishing toward mergers, growth, and diversification, Holiday House continues with its mission to produce good books for young readers. The centennial of the publication of Baum's *The Wizard of Oz* was recognized with four books: Simon & Schuster's commemorative pop-up by illustrator Robert Sabuda; a reissue of Holt's 1982 version illustrated by Michael Hague; a facsimile of the original for HarperCollins' Books of Wonder series; and an anniversary compilation of various authors' and illustrators' comments on the classic, also issued by HarperCollins. One of the amazing finds of 1999 was published in 2000, 60 years after H.A. and Margret Rey smuggled the original manuscript out of Paris. Readers have long been familiar with the Reys' *Curious George* and now they can meet another endearing and indomitable character with the posthumous publication of *Whiteblack the Penguin Sees the World*. To honor the 30th anniversary of Margaret K. McElderry Books, an imprint of Simon & Schuster, the publisher established the McElderry Picture Book Prize to be presented for the first time in April 2001 to an unpublished author/illustrator. This year also marked the celebration of the 25th anniversary of the publication of *Tuck Everlasting* by Natalie Babbitt. The publisher, Farrar, Straus & Giroux, issued an anniversary edition of the popular novel, which was also one of 23 unanimous selections for inclusion on the list of "One Hundred Books That Shaped the Century" by *School Library Journal* (January 2000). Penguin Putnam, publisher of over 90 books about Spot, the lovable pooch created 20 years ago by Eric Hill, marked the event with a special edition of *Spot's Birthday Party*. Another character celebrating a 20th anniversary this year was Cam Jansen, the amateur detective with the photographic memory, who stars in a series by David Adler.

The passage of time was also marked by the conclusion of some careers. In January, renowned and prolific illustrator Leonard Weisgard died at the age of 83 in his Copenhagen home. Weisgard received the Caldecott Medal in 1947 for *The Little Island*, written by Margaret Wise Brown, an author with whom he frequently collaborated, under the pseudonym of Golden MacDonald. The life of noted author and illustrator Barbara Cooney, 1992 recipient of the Kerlan Award, ended in March at the age of 83. During her career, Cooney illustrated 110 books for children and was twice honored with the Caldecott Medal: for *Chanticleer and the Fox* in 1959 and in 1980 for *Ox-Cart Man* by Donald Hall. Her final project, illustrations for *Basket Moon* by Mary Lyn Ray, was published in 1999. Also in March, 86-year-old Beatrice Schenk de Regniers, author of many children's books, including the Caldecott Medal winner *May I Bring a Friend?* passed away. In May, Verna Aardema, author of *Why Mosquitoes Buzz in People's Ears: An African Tale*, for which illustrators Leo and Diane Dillon received the 1976 Caldecott Medal, died at the age of 88. Another recipient of the Caldecott Medal (in 1974 for *Hosie's Alphabet*) 77-year-old Leonard Baskin, passed away in June. Three-time Newbery Honor winner Eloise Jarvis McGraw died in November at 84 years of age. Her most recently honored book was her last one, *The Moorchild*, awarded the Newbery Honor in 1997. The other two titles were *Moccasin Trail* in 1953 and *The Golden Goblet* in 1962. As the year drew to a close, 91-year-old Mirra Ginsburg passed away on December 26th. Ginsburg was an award-winning translator of Russian and Yiddish books into English as well as an author and adaptor of folktales.

The 2000 Caldecott and Newbery Medals as well as the Coretta Scott King Awards were presented to books published during 1999 at the midwinter meeting of the American Library Association. Simms Taback claimed the Caldecott for *Joseph Had a Little Overcoat*. Four illustrators recognized with a Caldecott Honor were: Molly Bang for *When Sophie Gets Angry—Really, Really Angry*; Trina Schart Hyman for *A Child's Calendar* by John Updike; Jerry Pinkney for his retelling of Hans Christian Andersen's *The Ugly Duckling*; and David Wiesner for *Sector 7*. For his Depression-era novel about spirited *Bud, Not Buddy*, Christopher Paul Curtis was awarded the Newbery Medal. Curtis also received the 2000 Coretta Scott King Author Award for *Bud, Not Buddy*, his second book. Jennifer Holm's first novel, *Our Only May Amelia*, was one of three Newbery Honor books. Brian Pinkney received the Coretta Scott King Illustrator Award for *In the Time of the Drums*, written by Kim Siegelson. CSK Honor Awards went to illustrators E.B. Lewis for *My Rows and Piles of Coins* by Tololwa M. Mollel and Christopher Myers, author/illustrator of *Black Cat*.

The International Board on Books for Young people presents the biannual Hans Christian Andersen Awards to an author and illustrator whose works have made a "lasting contribution to children's literature." In 2000, the awards were given to Brazilian author Ana Maria Machado and British illustrator Anthony Browne. The Ezra Jack Keats New Writer Award for 2000 went to Soyung Pak for the picture book *Dear Juno*. For "outstanding writing in a picture book" Molly Bang received the Charlotte Zolotow Award for *When Sophie Gets Angry—Really, Really Angry*. The Sydney Taylor Award for younger readers recognizing an "outstanding children's book with Jewish content" went to *Peddler's Gift* by Maxine Rose Schur and Kimberly Bulcken Root. Patricia Lauber, author of more than 80 titles, many of them nonfiction books about nature, received the 2000 Kerlan Award "in recognition of singular attainments in the creation of children's literature." In October, Jan Spivey Gilchrist, artist, author, and award-winning illustrator of 47 children's books, was inducted into the International Literary Hall of Fame for Writers of African Descent. Jack Prelutsky, author of such popular books of poetry as *The Dragons Are Singing Tonight* and *The New Kid on the Block*, received the David McCord Children's Literature Citation. The Jo Osborne Award for Humor in Children's Literature went to William Steig, author/illustrator of numerous books for children, including the 1970 Caldecott Medal winner *Sylvester and the Magic Pebble* and the 1977 Caldecott Honor title *The Amazing Bone*. In 1977, Steig also received a Newbery Honor for *Abel's Island*, one of two Newbery Honor titles to his credit. Steig's other Newbery Honor was received in 1983 for his humorous depiction of the dentist *Dr. DeSoto* outwitting a fox with a toothache and a penchant for mice.

First-time authors have also been recognized for their work. *Because of Winn-Dixie*, a dog found at the grocery store, lonely 10-year-old Opal finds friends and a greater understanding of herself, her father, and her absentee mother. Because of her writing, debut author Kate DiCamillo received at least seven awards, including the title's selection as a 2001 Newbery Honor book. Three picture books by first-time authors also captured multiple awards. For *Olivia*, the simple story of a pig with a personality reminiscent of fictional characters Geraldine or Lilly, author/illustrator Ian Falconer received six awards, including a 2001 Marion Vannett Ridgway Honor as a new picture book author. Numerous awards were also given to Doreen Cronin's humorous look at labor relations on a farm, *Click, Clack, Moo: Cows That Type*, with illustrations by Betsy Lewin, and author/illustrator D.B. Johnson's contemplative tale, *Henry Hikes to Fitchburg*, based on Thoreau's *Walden*. Illustrator Marie-Louise Fitzpatrick's first published effort as a writer/illustrator of a picture book, *Lizzy and Skunk*, received recognition as a *School Library Journal* Best Book as did author/illustrator Manya Stojic's simple cumulative tale about the arrival of *Rain* as sensed by animals on the African savanna. A lost cat down to the last of her nine lives becomes *The Good Luck Cat* in an award-winning debut by Joy Harjo with illustrations by Paul Lee.

Fuel Your Mind

The theme for the 81st National Children's Book Week suggests using books and reading as fuel for the mind. Indeed, current research shows that literary activities help to sustain mental agility as we age. The cost of this fuel continues to rise, just as the cost of fossil fuels to propel our cars to the library and bookstore has risen. According to figures reported in *School Library Journal*, the average price for a children's hardcover book in 1998 was $15.92 (in 1999 the cost was $16.66); and in 2000 it rose to $17.57. Although library budgets do not seem to grow as rapidly, books are still readily available to satisfy the preferences of a diverse population.

Recognizing the importance of literacy, publishers are meeting the needs of the growing numbers of beginning readers by providing the fuel that will propel them on to chapter books and novels. Demographically, this age of too-old-for-picture-books-but-not-quite-ready-for-a-full-length-novel is a growing segment of the population. HarperCollins continues the "I Can Read" series first introduced in 1957 with Else Holmelund Minarik's *Little Bear*, still in print. Random House's Beginner Books were also first published in 1957; and the next decade saw the arrival of Dial's Easy-to-Read and Macmillan's Ready to Read titles. These original hardcover series have been joined by paperback lines such as Random House's "Step into Reading" series, Grosset and Dunlap's "All Aboard Reading" and Scholastic's "Hello Reader." Newer series include "Green Light Readers" from Harcourt Children's Books, Candlewick's "Brand New Readers," Golden's "Road to Reading" and Scholastic's "JumpStart." When children move beyond the beginning reader level, they can turn to early chapter book genres that provide the bridge to the next level of reading. These popular series include the Captain Underpants books by Scholastic; Little, Brown's Arthur Chapter Books series; The Magic Tree House books from Random House; and the newly launched "Ready-for-Chapter" series from Aladdin Paperbacks.

Whether a child is being read to, taking that first solo journey into a book, or confidently navigating the range of genres in children's literature, the succeeding pages of this fourth volume of *What Do Children Read Next?* offer 1,100 books to spark their interest and fuel their minds. Ready . . .Set . . .Go!

A

1

ALMA FLOR ADA
LORI LOHSTOETER, Illustrator

Friend Frog
(San Diego: Gulliver Books/Harcourt, Inc., 2000)

Subject(s): Animals/Frogs and Toads; Animals/Mice; Friendship
Age range(s): Grades K-2
Major character(s): Field Mouse, Mouse, Friend; Frog, Frog, Friend
Time period(s): Indeterminate
Locale(s): Earth

Summary: Field Mouse desperately wants a friend and he doesn't see much potential in the pebbles and grass that he talks to sometimes. One day, while searching for a friend he hears a croaking sound and seeks the source of the strong voice. Field Mouse finds Frog sitting on a rock and asks if she'll be his friend. Frog's agreeable and invites Field Mouse to croak with her, but Field Mouse can't croak. The next day Field Mouse tries again but this time he's invited to jump and he can't jump as well as Frog. Field Mouse envies Frog's abilities but fears their differences will keep them from having a friendship. Then, as Field Mouse sits beside Frog's pond he recognizes the sudden shadow that covers them and calls for Frog to jump into the pond. Frog is grateful that Field Mouse saved her from a falcon and the two realize they can build a friendship by sharing their differences. (32 pages)

Where it's reviewed:
Horn Book Guide, Fall 2000, page 260
School Library Journal, May 2000, page 126

Other books by the same author:
The Malachite Palace, 1998
Yours Truly, Goldilocks, 1998
Jordi's Star, 1996

Other books you might like:
Laurie A. Jacobs, *So Much in Common*, 1994
    Although Philomena and Horace seem to have little in common, it is enough to build a friendship.
Arnold Lobel, *Frog and Toad Are Friends*, 1970
    In several brief stories, Frog and Toad share some of the difficulties as well as the pleasures of friendship.
John Schindel, *I'll Meet You Halfway*, 1993
    Titus and Fuller plan special gifts for each other, but learn that the best gift of all is their friendship.

2

ALMA FLOR ADA
REG CARTWRIGHT, Illustrator

The Three Golden Oranges
(New York: Atheneum Books for Young Readers, 1999)

Subject(s): Folklore; Fairy Tales; Brothers
Age range(s): Grades 2-4
Major character(s): Santiago, Brother (oldest); Tomas, Brother; Matias, Brother (youngest)
Time period(s): Indeterminate Past
Locale(s): Spain

Summary: Three brothers searching for wives seek assistance from the old woman who lives on the cliff by the sea. The old woman gives the brothers explicit advice to stay together and follow her instructions to retrieve three golden oranges and return them to her. Impatiently, Santiago sneaks off in the night to fulfill the quest alone and is soon imprisoned in the castle dungeon. Then, Tomas abandons Matias and meets the same fate as Santiago. Only Matias completes the task, but when he returns to the old woman, she cannot immediately fulfill his desire for a wife because of his selfish brothers. Patient Matias returns home to his mother and in due time he is able to break a sorcerer's spell and find the wife he is seeking. (32 pages)

Where it's reviewed:
Booklist, May 15, 1999, page 1698
Horn Book Guide, Fall 1999, page 322

Publishers Weekly, May 31, 1999, page 93
School Library Journal, July 1999, page 83

Other books by the same author:
The Malachite Palace, 1998
Yours Truly, Goldilocks, 1998
Jordi's Star, 1996
The Gold Coin, 1991

Other books you might like:
Cynthia DeFelice, *Three Perfect Peaches: A French Folktale*, 1995
   A humorous retelling depicts the kind country lad who outwits the king and marries the princess. Mary DeMarsh, co-author.
Andrej Dugin, *Dragon Feathers*, 1993
   To win his true love, a young man plucks three feathers from a dragon. Olga Dugina, co-author.
Eric A. Kimmel, *Three Sacks of Truth: A Story from France*, 1993
   A humble, but clever peasant bests a greedy, unscrupulous king seeking the perfect peach in exchange for his daughter's hand in marriage.

3

JEAN EKMAN ADAMS, Author/Illustrator

Clarence Goes Out West and Meets a Purple Horse

(Flagstaff, AZ: Rising Moon, 2000)

Subject(s): Animals/Pigs; Vacations; Ranch Life
Age range(s): Grades K-2
Major character(s): Clarence, Pig; Smoky, Horse
Time period(s): Indeterminate
Locale(s): United States (out west)

Summary: After a long bus ride Clarence arrives Out West for an eagerly anticipated vacation. At first he's a little homesick because he forgot to pack his special pillow, but soon he meets Smoky, the horse assigned to him for the week. With Smoky, Clarence learns to ride, line dance, play cards and perform on the washtub in a cowboy band. Clarence is having a wonderful vacation until he learns, just prior to his departure, that Smoky is to be sold because he's too old to work the ranch. Clarence feels sad when he hears the news and he cashes in his bus ticket home to buy Smoky. It might take a while but Clarence plans to just ride Smoky all the way home. This is the first picture book for the author. (32 pages)

Where it's reviewed:
Booklist, April 1, 2000, page 1466
Children's Book Review Service, April 2000, page 95
Horn Book Guide, Fall 2000, page 260
Publishers Weekly, March 6, 2000, page 109
School Library Journal, June 2000, page 100

Other books you might like:
Betsy Byars, *The Golly Sister Go West*, 1986
   In six short stories, two intrepid sisters head out west to try life on the frontier.
Sharon Phillips Denslow, *On the Trail with Miss Pace*, 1995
   Miss Pace begins her long-anticipated summer vacation

from school on a dude ranch, surprised to discover two students following her everywhere.
Mark Teague, *How I Spent My Summer Vacation*, 1995
   Imaginative Wallace tells his class about an exciting summer vacation when cowboys kidnapped him and taught him the life of a cowboy.

4

DAVID A. ADLER
WILL HILLENBRAND, Illustrator

Andy and Tamika

(San Diego: Gulliver Books/Harcourt Brace & Company, 1999)

Series: Andy Russell. Book #2
Subject(s): Babies; Brothers and Sisters; Family Life
Age range(s): Grades 3-4
Major character(s): Andy Russell, 4th Grader, Animal Lover; Tamika Anderson, 4th Grader, Friend; Rachel Russell, Sister (older)
Time period(s): 1990s (1999)
Locale(s): United States

Summary: Daydreamer Andy spends his time in class thinking of a name for his new sibling rather than learning fractions. At lunch he feeds part of his food to a stray cat; for the fourth grade carnival he donates baby gerbils as prizes. This time it's not Andy's fault that some of the gerbils escape in the school gym. With Rachel's help he plans a welcoming celebration for Tamika who is moving in with the Russells temporarily. Rachel follows the recipe and bakes delicious cookies; creative Andy comes up with interesting, but inedible shapes. (129 pages)

Where it's reviewed:
Booklist, March 1, 1999, page 1211
Horn Book Guide, Fall 1999, page 287
School Library Journal, May 1999, page 79

Other books by the same author:
School Trouble for Andy Russell, 1999
The Many Troubles of Andy Russell, 1998
Cam Jansen and the Scary Snake Mystery, 1997

Other books you might like:
Judy Blume, *Superfudge*, 1980
   In the sequel to *Tales of a Fourth Grade Nothing*, Peter contends with his irrepressible younger brother, Fudge.
Ann Cameron, *More Stories Julian Tells*, 1986
   Julian describes typical childhood activities in this award-winning sequel to *The Stories Julian Tells*.
Patricia Hermes, *Nothing but Trouble, Trouble, Trouble*, 1994
   Alex's attempts to prove that she is growing into a responsible person seem to end in nothing but trouble.
Johanna Hurwitz, *Make Room for Elisa*, 1993
   Russell and his younger sister Elisa prepare for the arrival of a baby brother and a move to a bigger apartment.

5

DAVID A. ADLER
TERRY WIDENER, Illustrator

The Babe & I

(San Diego: Gulliver Books/Harcourt Brace & Company, 1999)

Subject(s): Depression (Economic); Sports/Baseball; Fathers and Sons
Age range(s): Grades 1-4
Major character(s): Jacob, Paperboy, Friend; Unnamed Character, Son, Paperboy; Babe Ruth, Baseball Player
Time period(s): 1930s (1932)
Locale(s): New York, New York (the Bronx)

Summary: When a young boy sees his father, dressed in his business suit, selling apples on the street corner he feels sad to realize his father is out of work and too proud to admit it to his family. He is also determined to help the family and begins selling newspapers with Jacob. Jacob has a successful system: he stands outside Yankee Stadium and shouts out the headlines about Babe Ruth. One day, an injured Babe Ruth purchases a paper as he enters the stadium, paying with a five-dollar bill and allowing the paperboy to keep the change. Excitedly, the boy buys two tickets so he and Jacob can go to the game. The paperboy feels a kinship with Babe as if the Babe is part of the team helping him sell papers just as the boy and his dad are a team helping to support the family. (32 pages)

Where it's reviewed:
Booklist, March 15, 1999, page 1327
Horn Book, March 1999, page 182
Publishers Weekly, May 10, 1999, page 67
Riverbank Review, Summer 1999, page 28
School Library Journal, May 1999, page 79

Awards the book has won:
Notable Social Studies Trade Books for Young People, 2000
Smithsonian's Notable Books for Children, 1999

Other books by the same author:
Chanukah in Chelm, 1997
Lou Gehrig: The Luckiest Man, 1997
Lucky Stars, 1996

Other books you might like:
Ron Cohen, *My Dad's Baseball*, 1994
   Max's discovery of an autographed baseball in his grandparents' attic prompts his dad to tell the story behind the ball.
Gavin Curtis, *The Bat Boy & His Violin*, 1998
   A father expects his son to work as a baseball team's bat boy rather than practice his violin until he sees the team's response to violin music.
Donald Hall, *When Willard Met Babe Ruth*, 1996
   In 1917, a young baseball fan and his farmer father unexpectedly meet Babe Ruth when his car goes into the ditch while avoiding their flock of geese.
Helen Ketteman, *I Remember Papa*, 1998
   Audie's joy at attending a Cincinnati Reds game with his dad is dampened when he loses the money he's saved to buy a baseball glove.

Mary Kay Kroeger, *Paperboy*, 1996
   In 1927, Willie hawks newspapers to earn money for his large family. Co-author Louise Borden.

6

DAVID A. ADLER
SUSANNA NATTI, Illustrator

Cam Jansen and the Barking Treasure Mystery

(New York: Viking, 1999)

Series: Cam Jansen. Number 19
Subject(s): Animals/Dogs; Boats and Boating; Mystery and Detective Stories
Age range(s): Grades 2-4
Major character(s): Jennifer "Cam" Jansen, Detective—Amateur, Friend (Eric's); Eric Shelton, Friend (Cam's); Little Treasure, Dog
Time period(s): 1990s (1999)
Locale(s): United States

Summary: A sightseeing cruise of the harbor provides another opportunity for Cam to use her photographic memory to solve a mystery. When a wealthy passenger smuggles her poodle aboard the boat, Cam is the first to notice that Little Treasure is not in the large handbag the woman carries. With Eric's help, Cam strolls the decks trying to locate the dog. Although Little Treasure reappears, her jewel-studded collar is missing. Cam's photographic memory goes back into action until the case is solved and the thief apprehended. (55 pages)

Where it's reviewed:
Booklist, October 15, 1999, page 441
Horn Book Guide, Spring 2000, page 63
School Library Journal, December 1999, page 87

Other books by the same author:
Cam Jansen and the Catnapping Mystery, 1998 (Cam Jansen, Number 18)
Cam Jansen and the Scary Snake Mystery, 1997 (Cam Jansen, Number 17)
Cam Jansen and the Ghostly Mystery, 1996 (Cam Jansen, Number 16)

Other books you might like:
Duncan Ball, *Emily Eyefinger*, 1992
   Emily solves mysteries with the assistance of a third eye on the end of her finger.
Lucinda Landon, *The Meg Mackintosh Series*, 1986-
   In a series of solve-it-yourself mysteries, Meg Mackintosh is a winner any way you read the story.
Marjorie Weinman Sharmat, *The Nate the Great Series*, 1972-
   Nate copies the style of Sherlock Holmes as he follows the clues in this mystery series for beginning readers.

7

DAVID A. ADLER
WILL HILLENBRAND, Illustrator

Parachuting Hamsters and Andy Russell
(San Diego: Gulliver Books/Harcourt, Inc., 2000)

Subject(s): Behavior; City and Town Life; Aunts and Uncles
Age range(s): Grades 2-5
Major character(s): Andy Russell, Friend (Tamika's); Tamika Anderson, Friend, Niece; Mandy Taylor, Aunt (Tamika's); Jason Collins, Neighbor, Child
Time period(s): 2000s (2000)
Locale(s): New York, New York

Summary: The more Andy hears about Tamika's Aunt Mandy and her expectations of children, the less sure he is about visiting someone who enjoys art museums and lives in an apartment with no TV. While Andy and Tamika wait in the building's lobby they discover hamsters, attached to colorful silk handkerchief parachutes, floating from one of the upper level apartments. Pet-lover Andy is outraged and adopts a detective mindset for the weekend in his determination to find the person responsible. Andy also tries to be a polite guest, but even his best intentions sometimes go awry. For a day's excursion to a museum and the ballet, Aunt Mandy invites Jason, a neighbor two floors above them. Sneaky Jason is a non-stop troublemaker who tries to make his vandalism appear to be Andy's doing. Eventually Jason is caught in his own deceit and Andy figures out that he's also the person responsible for the parachuting hamsters. Aunt Mandy learns that Jason lacks the etiquette to be one her guests in the future, but she'll invite Andy and Tamika back again. (112 pages)

Where it's reviewed:
Booklist, November 1, 2000, page 536
School Library Journal, October 2000, page 110

Other books by the same author:
Andy and Tamika, 1999
School Trouble for Andy Russell, 1999
The Many Troubles of Andy Russell, 1998

Other books you might like:
Johanna Hurwitz, *Aldo Applesauce*, 1979
   One outcome of Aldo's move to the big city of New York is a new friend and the other is a new nickname.
Bonnie Pryor, *Toenails, Tonsils, and Tornadoes*, 1997
   A dreaded visit from his Great Aunt Henrietta has an unexpectedly positive impact on Martin.
Gina Willner-Pardo, *Spider Storch's Fumbled Field Trip*, 1998
   Joey "Spider" Storch has good intentions, but trouble seems to follow him even on a class field trip.

DAVID A. ADLER
WILL HILLENBRAND, Illustrator

School Trouble for Andy Russell
(San Diego: Gulliver Books/Harcourt Brace & Company, 1999)

Series: Andy Russell. Book 3

Subject(s): Schools; Teachers; Behavior
Age range(s): Grades 3-5
Major character(s): Andy Russell, 4th Grader, Daydreamer; Stacy Anne Jackson, 4th Grader, Friend (Andy's); Cory Davis, 4th Grader
Time period(s): 1990s (1999)
Locale(s): United States

Summary: Imaginative Andy uses his class time to plan his future instead of listening to the math lesson and receives extra homework from his teacher. Could school get any worse? It does when Andy's teacher becomes ill and the substitute blames the creative underachiever for mishaps that are actually inspired by Cory. Even perfect student Stacy Anne finds herself sitting with Andy outside the principal's office because of Cory's misdeeds. Andy's regular teacher is strict, but even he is wishing she recovers quickly and returns to class. (118 pages)

Where it's reviewed:
Booklist, January 1, 2000, page 920
Horn Book Guide, Spring 2000, page 73
School Library Journal, November 1999, page 108

Other books by the same author:
Andy and Tamika, 1999
The Many Troubles of Andy Russell, 1998
Lucky Stars, 1996

Other books you might like:
Patricia Reilly Giff, *Pet Parade*, 1996
   Beast's inattentiveness in class is also obvious at home as he prepares for Pet Week by forgetting his fish at the park and accidentally letting the dog out.
Becky Thoman Lindberg, *Thomas Tuttle, Just in Time*, 1994
   Thomas, a procrastinator at heart, tries to improve his school performance by completing his work by the due date.
Susan Shreve, *Joshua T. Bates in Trouble Again*, 1997
   Distracted with worry about a class bully, fourth-grader Joshua makes some unwise decisions.

DAVID A. ADLER
SUSANNA NATTI, Illustrator

Young Cam Jansen and the Baseball Mystery
(New York: Viking, 1999)

Series: Young Cam Jansen. Number 5
Subject(s): Mystery; Sports/Baseball; Lost and Found Possessions
Age range(s): Grades 1-2
Major character(s): Jennifer "Cam" Jansen, Detective—Amateur, Friend; Rachel, Child, Friend; Eric Shelton, Child, Friend
Time period(s): 1990s (1999)
Locale(s): United States

Summary: Rachel brings her ball to the park, Cam and Eric bring mitts and their other friends bring bats. They divide into teams and begin playing until a hard hit ball soars over the outfielder's head and vanishes. Everyone begins looking for the ball, but with no luck. They find two balls, but not the Rachel's. It's Cam's photographic memory that solves the mystery and helps them find the right one so the game can resume. (31 pages)

Where it's reviewed:
Booklist, October 1, 1999, page 364
Horn Book Guide, Fall 1999, page 272
School Library Journal, June 1999, page 85

Other books by the same author:
Young Cam Jansen and the Ice Skate Mystery, 1998 (Young Cam Jansen, Number 4)
Young Cam Jansen and the Lost Tooth, 1997 (Young Cam Jansen, Number 3)
Young Cam Jansen and the Missing Cookie, 1996 (Young Cam Jansen, Number 2)

Other books you might like:
Matt Christopher, *The Dog That Stole Home*, 1996
    The dog in this baseball story doesn't run off with the ball, but he does steal home.
Emily Arnold McCully, *Grandmas at Bat*, 1993
    Two competitive grandmothers with good intentions complicate things for Pip's baseball team in this easy reader.
Megan McDonald, *Beezy at Bat*, 1998
    In this beginning reader Beezy's team has a ball, but they need to find one more player in order to start the game.
Peggy Parish, *Play Ball, Amelia Bedelia*, 1972
    In her usual, literal way, Amelia learns to play baseball, leading to a humorous game as she misunderstands the meaning of baseball terms.

10

PATRICE AGGS, Author/Illustrator

The Visitor

(New York: Orchard Books, 1999)

Subject(s): Animals/Cats; Animals/Giraffes; Difference
Age range(s): Grades K-1
Major character(s): Cosy Redcat, Cat; Posy Redcat, Cat; Giraffe, Giraffe
Time period(s): Indeterminate
Locale(s): England

Summary: In the first book both written and illustrated by the author, Cosy and Posy learn from their mother that Giraffe is coming to dinner. Feeling anxious about this strange visitor, Cosy and Posy ask several neighbors for more information about giraffes. A mouse describes the giraffe as having a long neck while a goose says a giraffe has spots. Each neighbor identifies a different feature of the giraffe so that Cosy and Posy have a very scary looking image in mind. However, after the kittens meet Giraffe they realize that the dinner guest is quite nice and nothing to be scared of at all. (32 pages)

Where it's reviewed:
Booklist, February 1, 1999, page 478
Horn Book Guide, Fall 1999, page 243
Kirkus Reviews, January 15, 1999, page 142
Publishers Weekly, April 12, 1999, page 74
School Library Journal, April 1999, page 85

Other books you might like:
Sheena Knowles, *Edward the Emu*, 1998
    Tired of being an emu, Edward imitates the other animals at the zoo, only to decide he likes being an emu best.
Rafik Schami, *Albert & Lila*, 1999
    Albert, the pig, and Lila, the hen, are farmyard outcasts, but together they gain the respect of the other animals.
Janet Morgan Stoeke, *A Friend for Minerva Louise*, 1997
    Minerva Louise, a hen, tries to deduce who the new addition to her household is.

11

JOAN AIKEN

Dangerous Games

(New York: Delacorte Press, 1999)

Subject(s): Adventure and Adventurers; Fantasy; Mystery
Age range(s): Grades 4-7
Major character(s): Dido Twite, Sailor; Lord Herodsfoot, Adventurer; Tylo, Guide
Time period(s): Indeterminate Past
Locale(s): Aratu, Pacific Islands

Summary: The captain of the ship on which Dido is sailing sends her to the island of Aratu to locate Lord Herodsfoot so that he can be returned to London to entertain the king with his knowledge of unusual games. Dido is apprehensive about searching an island known for the fatal bites of its pearl snakes and sting monkeys, but the competent Tylo, one of the native Forest People, soon eases her concerns. Dido and Tylo find Lord Herodsfoot with help from the Forest People, but realize that completing the mission may not be possible as political intrigue and an attempted overthrow of the king put their lives in danger. (251 pages)

Where it's reviewed:
Booklist, March 1, 1999, page 1211
Horn Book, January 1999, page 57
Kirkus Reviews, December 1, 1998, page 1730
Publishers Weekly, January 11, 1999, page 73
School Library Journal, January 1999, page 124

Other books by the same author:
Cold Shoulder Road, 1996 (ALA Notable Book)
Is Underground, 1992
The Wolves of Willoughby Chase, 1987

Other books you might like:
Lloyd Alexander, *The Iron Ring*, 1997
    After losing his kingdom to Jaya in a dice game, Tamar is honor bound to comply with the command to journey to Jaya's palace and face his fate.
L. Frank Baum, *The Wizard of Oz*, 1900
    Dorothy searches for a way out of Oz and back to her home in Kansas.
Gail Carson Levine, *Ella Enchanted*, 1997
    This Newbery Honor Book describes Ella's dangerous search for the fairy whose gift of obedience is actually Ella's curse.
Margaret Mahy, *The Pirate's Mixed-Up Voyage*, 1993
    To fulfill his dream of being a pirate, Lionel sails away to

the Thousand Islands intent on kidnapping a wealthy inventor.

J.R.R. Tolkien, *The Hobbit*, 1938

In the first book of a fantasy trilogy, the Hobbit finds himself on a journey that grows more and more treacherous.

12

JEZ ALBOROUGH, Author/Illustrator

Duck in the Truck

(New York: HarperCollins Publishers, 2000)

Subject(s): Stories in Rhyme; Humor; Animals
Age range(s): Grades K-1
Major character(s): Duck, Duck, Driver; Frog, Frog
Time period(s): Indeterminate
Locale(s): Fictional Country

Summary: Duck drives merrily along in his bright red truck until—yuck—he's stuck in muck. Helpful Frog offers to join Duck as he tries to push the truck out of the muck, but the truck stays stuck. Sheep driving his jeep beeps and beeps because he can't get by the truck stuck in the muck. Frog suggests that reluctant Sheep push with them, but the truck stays stuck in the muck. A contented goat boating by ties a rope to the truck to pull it from the muck and just as the truck pulls free the knot breaks and goat flips out of his boat. Duck drives away in his unstuck truck leaving Frog, Sheep and the goat still stuck and covered with muck in a title first published in the United Kingdom in 1999. (32 pages)

Where it's reviewed:
Booklist, December 15, 1999, page 788
Children's Book Review Service, March 2000, page 83
Five Owls, January 2000, page 65
Kirkus Reviews, December 1, 1999, page 1880
Publishers Weekly, January 10, 2000, page 66

Other books by the same author:
My Friend Bear, 1998
Watch Out! Big Bro's Coming!, 1997
It's the Bear!, 1994
Cuddly Dudley, 1993
Where's My Teddy?, 1992

Other books you might like:
Lynn Plourde, *Pigs in the Mud in the Middle of the Rud*, 1997
    Grandma needs to get down the road, but first the pigs and other animals have to move out of the muddy way.
Mary Lyn Ray, *Mud*, 1996
    No one becomes stuck in this title celebrating mud, a seasonal medium perfect for fun.
Nancy Shaw, *Sheep in a Jeep*, 1986
    A group of exuberant sheep take off in a jeep and, as usual, find themselves in a bit of a predicament.

13

JEZ ALBOROUGH, Author/Illustrator

Hug

(Cambridge, MA: Candlewick Press, 2000)

Subject(s): Animals; Parent and Child; Love
Age range(s): Preschool
Major character(s): Bobo, Child, Chimpanzee; Mommy, Mother, Chimpanzee
Time period(s): Indeterminate
Locale(s): Earth (jungle)

Summary: A young chimp's initial pleasure at seeing a mother elephant hug her baby gradually changes to sorrow as the chimp walks past different species hugging their children. The elephant mom gives the chimp a ride and they walk past many hugs but none seem to offer what the chimp is seeking. Finally, the chimp hears "Bobo" and responds "Mommy." The resulting hug from his own mother is just what Bobo wants and he gives the mommy elephant a hug of thanks too. (32 pages)

Where it's reviewed:
Horn Book Guide, Spring 2001, page 11
Publishers Weekly, November 20, 2000, page 67
School Library Journal, December 2000, page 94

Other books by the same author:
Watch Out! Big Bro's Coming!, 1997
It's the Bear!, 1994
Cuddly Dudley, 1993
Where's My Teddy?, 1992

Other books you might like:
Jonathan London, *Snuggle Wuggle*, 2000
    Animal mothers cuddle their infant offspring in unique ways.
Dave Ross, *A Book of Hugs*, 1999
    Hugs come in many varieties as this book explains.
Rosemary Wells, *Read to Your Bunny*, 1998
    While hugging your bunny, read a book too and one day your bunny will be able to read to you.

14

ARLENE ALDA
EVE ALDRIDGE, Illustrator

Hurry Granny Annie

(Berkeley, CA: Tricycle Press, 1999)

Subject(s): Grandmothers; Surprises
Age range(s): Grades K-3
Major character(s): Granny Annie, Grandmother; Ruthie, Child, Fisherman; Joe, Brother, Baseball Player
Time period(s): 1990s (1999)
Locale(s): United States

Summary: When Granny Annie hurries past Ruthie on her way to "catch" something great, Ruthie, still clutching her fishing pole, runs with her. Then Joe, baseball mitt in hand, joins them as does a neighbor boy with a butterfly net. Each time Granny Annie gets ready to tell the children what she plans to catch, she sneezes so the secret is not revealed until she reaches the ocean shoreline—just in time to catch the sunset. Initially disappointed not to catch a fish, a ball or a butterfly, the children do admit that the colors of the sky make the race to catch the sunset worthwhile. (32 pages)

Where it's reviewed:
Booklist, August 1999, page 2062
Horn Book Guide, Spring 2000, page 26
Kirkus Reviews, August 1, 1999, page 1222
Publishers Weekly, July 12, 1999, page 93
School Library Journal, January 2000, page 92

Other books by the same author:
Pig, Horse, or Cow, Don't Wake Me Now, 1994
Arlene Alda's ABC, 1993
Matthew and His Dad, 1983

Other books you might like:
Kathryn Lasky, *The Gates of the Wind*, 1995
  Desiring to experience a more adventurous life, Gamma Lee moves out of her snug valley home to a windy mountaintop.
Margaret Mahy, *A Busy Day for a Good Grandmother*, 1993
  Mrs. Oberon, grandmother extraordinaire, overcomes unusual obstacles in a mad dash to reach and soothe her teething grandson.
Margaret Wild, *Our Granny*, 1994
  In an award-winning look at the diversity of grandmothers and their activities, two children remember the granny who lives with them.

15

BRIAN ALDERSON
FRITZ WEGNER, Illustrator

The Tale of the Turnip

(Cambridge, MA: Candlewick Press, 1999)

Subject(s): Traditional Stories; Greed; Folk Tales
Age range(s): Grades K-2
Major character(s): Unnamed Character, Farmer; Unnamed Character, Royalty; Unnamed Character, Squire
Time period(s): Indeterminate Past
Locale(s): England

Summary: When a poor, humble farmer grows an enormous turnip he recognizes that such a turnip is destined as a gift for the king and so the farmer hauls it to him. The king is so impressed with the turnip that he gives the farmer a wagonload of gold as reward. The farmer's neighbor, a greedy squire, is furious to think that the king would offer gold in exchange for a turnip. Sure that he has horses worth much more than turnips, the squire presents the king with his finest horse. The king, impressed with the gift, knows that gold is not sufficient reward and so he gives the surprised squire his prized turnip. (32 pages)

Where it's reviewed:
Horn Book, November 1999, page 747
Kirkus Reviews, August 15, 1999, page 1306
Magpies, September 1999, page 22
Publishers Weekly, August 2, 1999, page 83
School Library Journal, October 1999, page 130

Other books by the same author:
Stories for Me!, 1998
The Swan's Stories, 1997

Other books you might like:
Marcia Brown, *Dick Whittington and His Cat*, 1950
  In a Caldecott Honor Book a poor boy seeking his fortune in London achieves it by trading his beloved cat for gold, jewels and a title.
Walter De La Mare, *The Turnip*, 1992
  A poor farmer's wealthy brother is envious of the fortune the kind framer reaps from the enormous turnip he grows.
Eric A. Kimmel, *Onions and Garlic*, 1996
  When Getzel's greedy brothers learn he has traded onions for diamonds they offer the same king garlic and receive his most precious crop in exchange.

16

SUE ANN ALDERSON
ARDEN JOHNSON, Illustrator

Wherever Bears Be: A Story for Two Voices

(Berkeley, CA: Tricycle Press, 1999)

Subject(s): Animals/Bears; Food; Imagination
Age range(s): Grades 1-3
Major character(s): Belinda, Child; Samantha, Child
Time period(s): 1990s (1999)
Locale(s): Canada

Summary: Belinda and Samantha head up a mountain to fill their pails with blueberries. As they go they make up a song to keep away the hungry bears they imagine are everywhere. They're sure each sound they hear must be a bear, but instead it's a squirrel or a raccoon or a deer. Just as they finish picking Samantha spills her pail and her berries. Belinda helps her fill it again before they trip lightly down the mountain singing a song of farewell to the bears. (32 pages)

Where it's reviewed:
Children's Book Review Service, July 1999, page 145
Children's Bookwatch, April 1999, page 3
Horn Book Guide, Fall 1999, page 243
Resource Links, June 1999, page 1
School Library Journal, June 1999, page 85

Other books by the same author:
Hurry Up, Bonnie!, 1990
Ida and the Wool Smugglers, 1987
Bonnie McSmithers Is at It Again!, 1980

Other books you might like:
Jez Alborough, *It's the Bear!*, 1994
  Remembering the bear he met on his last walk in the woods, Eddie is afraid to return there for a picnic with his mom.
Ann Dixon, *Blueberry Shoe*, 1999
  While a family picks berries on Ptarmigan Mountain a baby loses a shoe that many animals find useful before it's found again the next year.
Robert McCloskey, *Blueberries for Sal*, 1948
  While picking blueberries Sal loses her mom but finds a lost bear cub searching for his mother.

17

LLOYD ALEXANDER

Gypsy Rizka

(New York: Duttons Children's Books, 1999)

Subject(s): Gypsies; Orphans; Humor
Age range(s): Grades 4-8
Major character(s): Rizka, Gypsy, Orphan
Time period(s): Indeterminate Past
Locale(s): Greater Dunitsa, Fictional Country

Summary: Although Rizka lives with her cat on the outskirts of town she still manages to involve herself in the town's business. Rizka stays busy aiding runaway lovers, healing various health ailments, beating the various laws created in order to run her out of town, and dealing with the problems of the Zipple, the continuous breeze that goes through town in the spring making the residents ornery. Despite the attempts of the town elders to oust her and the willingness of the returning gypsies to take her with them, Rizka remains in town. (144 pages)

Where it's reviewed:
Booklist, March 15, 1999, page 1327
Horn Book, March 1999, page 205
Publishers Weekly, March 15, 1999, page 60
School Library Journal, March 1999, page 206
Smithsonian Magazine, November 1999, page 54

Awards the book has won:
Booklist Editors' Choice, 1999
Smithsonian's Notable Books for Children, 1999

Other books by the same author:
The Iron Ring, 1997
The Arcadians, 1995
The Remarkable Journey of Prince Jen, 1991

Other books you might like:
Roald Dahl, *Matilda*, 1988
  Matilda takes revenge on her less-than-brilliant parents and on her cruel schoolmistress.
Michael Ende, *Momo*, 1985
  Independent Momo, who lives alone in the town amphitheater, protects her town from swindlers in this novel originally published in German.
Astrid Lindgren, *Pippi Longstocking*, 1950
  Pippi sets up house with a monkey and a horse for companions and with a unique approach to life.

18

LLOYD ALEXANDER
JUDITH BYRON SCHACHNER, Illustrator

How the Cat Swallowed Thunder

(New York: Dutton Children's Books, 2000)

Subject(s): Animals/Cats; Behavior; Fantasy
Age range(s): Grades 2-4
Major character(s): Mother Holly, Aged Person; Cat, Cat
Time period(s): Indeterminate Past
Locale(s): Fictional Country

Summary: Before Mother Holly leaves for a day of errands she gives Cat specific chores to complete during her absence. Not one for working, Cat finds the sweeping so tiring that he thinks about napping before making Mother Holly's bed. Cat also feels hungry so before he sleeps, Cat stirs the soup as Mother Holly asked him to do and thus begins an unforeseen sequence of events. Cat spills some soup on the floor and, in cleaning it, inadvertently unleashes April showers from Mother Holly's magical watering can. While cleaning up that problem Cat unwittingly releases March winds from Mother Holly's bellows, and subsequently endures thunder from her bag of corn and a blizzard from the goose feathers of her bed. Although Cat thinks he's successfully cleaned the many messes, as Mother Holly comes up the path he spots a bit of corn on the floor and quickly swallows it. Mother Holly is impressed with the neat cottage and the amusing sound that comes from previously purr-less Cat. (40 pages)

Where it's reviewed:
Booklist, July 2000, page 2037
Bulletin of the Center for Children's Books, September 2000, page 4
Horn Book Guide, Spring 2001, page 27
Publishers Weekly, July 3, 2000, page 70
School Library Journal, October 2000, page 110

Other books by the same author:
The House Gobbaleen, 1995 (School Library Journal Best Books)
The Fortune Tellers, 1992 (ALA Notable Book)
The Truthful Harp, 1967

Other books you might like:
Verna Aardema, *How Ostrich Got Its Long Neck*, 1995
  When Ostrich ignores Fish Eagle's warnings and tries to help Crocodile pull out a tooth he escapes with his life and a very long neck.
Marguerite W. Davol, *How Snake Got His Hiss*, 1996
  Round and self-absorbed, snake rolls along not thinking of others and causes the hyena's spots, the lion's mane and his own slender shape.
Mary-Joan Gerson, *How Night Came from the Sea: A Story from Brazil*, 1994
  A folk tale describes the origins of darkness long ago at a time of relentless daylight.
Beatrice Orcutt Harrell, *How Thunder and Lightning Came to Be: A Choctaw Legend*, 1995
  Unwittingly, two clumsy birds devise a method of forewarning people of approaching storms that pleases the Great Sun Father.
Michael Rosen, *How the Animals Got Their Colors: Animal Myths From Around the World*, 1992
  Nine retellings of folktales and myths explain the coloration of various animals.

19

MARTHA ALEXANDER, Author/Illustrator

And My Mean Old Mother Will Be Sorry, Blackboard Bear

(Cambridge, MA: Candlewick Press, 2000)

Subject(s): Runaways; Animals/Bears; Parent and Child
Age range(s): Grades K-1
Major character(s): Anthony, Child, Son; Blackboard Bear, Bear, Friend (imaginary)
Time period(s): Indeterminate Past
Locale(s): United States

Summary: Revised and reissued with full color illustrations the 1969 title explores Anthony's reaction to being sent to his room for making a mess in the house at the end of a long day. Anthony's so angry with his mean old mother that he thinks Blackboard Bear's idea to run away is a good one. Out the window the two climb in search of a cave. Living in the woods is more appealing to Blackboard Bear than to Anthony who, after a dinner of blueberries and honey, would like to find a hamburger. After sleeping in a cave Anthony agrees to Blackboard Bear's suggestion that he take Anthony home because his mean old mom isn't mean all the time. (40 pages)

Where it's reviewed:
Booklist, November 15, 2000, page 645
Publishers Weekly, November 6, 2000, page 93

Other books by the same author:
You're a Genius, Blackboard Bear, 1995
Good Night, Lily, 1993
Where Does the Sky End, Grandpa?, 1992
We're in Big Trouble, Blackboard Bear, 1980

Other books you might like:
Betsy Everitt, *Mean Soup*, 1992
  After a bad day, Horace helps his mother make Mean Soup and he begins to feel better.
Lynne Jonell, *Mommy Go Away!*, 1997
  Christopher deals with his frustration about being the littlest and being told what to do by treating his mother the same way.
Maurice Sendak, *Where the Wild Things Are*, 1963
  Max is angry to be sent to his room and takes an imaginary, temporary journey to the Land of the Wild Things.

20

ALIKI, Author/Illustrator

All by Myself!

(New York: HarperCollins Publishers, 2000)

Subject(s): Independence; Growing Up; Self-Reliance
Age range(s): Grades K-1
Major character(s): Peter, Student, Son; Unnamed Character, Mother; Unnamed Character, Father
Time period(s): 2000s
Locale(s): England

Summary: Peter is happily self-sufficient. With a little nudge from his cat he's out of bed in the morning to wash, brush, dress and comb. Following a quick hug from dad at the schoolhouse door, Peter's on to a day of paint, play, build and fun. His mother greets him when school lets out though he doesn't need her help to select library books, set the table or help prepare dinner. Peter can get ready for bed all by himself too, but having his mom read a bedtime story is a comfort at the end of a busy day. (32 pages)

Where it's reviewed:
Booklist, November 1, 2000, page 544
Horn Book Guide, Spring 2001, page 11
Horn Book, September 2000, page 545
Publishers Weekly, August 21, 2000, page 71
School Library Journal, September 2000, page 184

Other books by the same author:
Those Summers, 1996
Best Friends Together Again, 1995
I'm Growing!, 1992

Other books you might like:
Ivan Bates, *All by Myself*, 2000
  A young elephant is determined to gather the breakfast leaves all by herself—and she does with only a little help from mom.
Arthur Howard, *When I Was Five*, 1996
  Jeremy reviews the accomplishments of his fifth year of life from the wise perspective of a just turned six-year-old.
Daniel Kirk, *Bigger*, 1998
  A young boy recounts his physical growth as well as his other achievements throughout his short life.
Mercer Mayer, *All by Myself*, 1983
  Little Critter demonstrates the many things he's learned to do on his own—tying shoes, riding a bike—and one that he can't do alone.

21

DEBBIE ALLEN
KADIR NELSON, Illustrator

Dancing in the Wings

(New York: Dial Books for Young Readers, 2000)

Subject(s): Ballet; Self-Confidence; Teasing
Age range(s): Grades K-2
Major character(s): Sassy, Dancer, Sister (younger); Hughie, Brother; Uncle Redd, Uncle, Aged Person
Time period(s): 2000s
Locale(s): Inglewood, California; Washington, District of Columbia

Summary: Sassy can see that she's taller than the other girls in dance class and the constant teasing from the other students and Hughie make her self-conscious about her height and her big feet. Sassy's so much taller than the others that she's never included in a performance so she contents herself dancing in the wings. Still, after some words of encouragement from Uncle Redd she signs up to audition for a summer dance festival and arrives in a bright yellow leotard rather than the required black one. The audition is a long day of exercises with the number of dancers gradually dwindling until only Sassy remains—winner of the summer opportunity in Washington, D.C. No longer dancing in the wings, Sassy earns a spot on stage for the summer concert. (32 pages)

Where it's reviewed:
Booklist, November 15, 2000, page 646
Horn Book Guide, Spring 2001, page 27
Kirkus Reviews, August 15, 2000, page 1190
Publishers Weekly, September 25, 2000, page 116
School Library Journal, September 2000, page 184

Other books by the same author:
Brothers of the Knight, 1999

Other books you might like:
Mary Hoffman, *Amazing Grace*, 1991
   Grace learns she can achieve her goal of starring in *Peter Pan* if she has the courage and determination to persevere.
Rachel Isadora, *Lili on Stage*, 1995
   A sequel to *Lili at Ballet* finds young Lili performing in *The Nutcracker* for the first time.
Jane O'Connor, *Nina, Nina, Star Ballerina*, 1997
   In a performance of *Night Sky* Nina is one of the stars dancing around Eric who portrays the moon.

22

LINDA JACOBS ALTMAN
CORNELIUS VAN WRIGHT, Illustrator
YING-HWA HU, Illustrator

The Legend of Freedom Hill
(New York: Lee & Low Books Inc., 2000)

Subject(s): Gold; Freedom; Slavery
Age range(s): Grades 2-4
Major character(s): Sophie, Child, Friend; Rosabel, Child, Slave (former); Miz Violet, Mother, Slave (runaway)
Time period(s): 1850s
Locale(s): Freedom Hill, California

Summary: As two outsiders in a gold rush town African American Rosabel and Jewish Sophie strike up a friendship. When a slave catcher tracks down Miz Violet and locks her in his wagon, Rosabel runs to Sophie's house for help. While Sophie's family provides shelter, Sophie and Rosabel figure out the only way to free Miz Violet is to buy her freedom. The fastest source of income in town is gold mining and the girls try their hand at it without too much initial success. They get some helpful suggestions from the town's assay office and soon locate a vein of gold in a very small cave. The nugget they dislodge is enough to purchase Miz Violet's freedom, but when they see the other four slaves that have been captured they sign their claim over to the slave catcher to buy the freedom of the others too. (32 pages)

Where it's reviewed:
Booklist, November 1, 2000, page 537
Horn Book Guide, Spring 2001, page 27
School Library Journal, August 2000, page 144

Awards the book has won:
Notable Social Studies Trade Books for Young People, 2001

Other books by the same author:
Forever Outsiders: Jews and History from Ancient Times to August 1935, 1998

Small Dogs, 1998
Amelia's Road, 1993

Other books you might like:
Pamela Duncan Edwards, *Barefoot: Escape on the Underground Railroad*, 1997
   A runaway slave finds food, water and a safe house by observing the animals along a trail.
Michael J. Rosen, *A School for Pompey Walker*, 1995
   With help from a white friend, Pompey Walker uses slavery to achieve his goal of educating black children.
Jeanette Winter, *Follow the Drinking Gourd*, 1988
   Escaped slaves use a song about the Big Dipper for the information they need to find a safe route to the North.
Courtni C. Wright, *Journey To Freedom: A Story of the Underground Railroad*, 1994
   Eight-year-old Joshua tells how Harriet Tubman safely leads his family and other escaped slaves to Canada.

23

RUDOLFO ANAYA
DAVID DIAZ, Illustrator

Roadrunner's Dance
(New York: Hyperion Books for Children, 2000)

Subject(s): Animals; Deserts; Fear
Age range(s): Grades K-3
Major character(s): Snake, Snake, Bully; Desert Woman, Deity; Roadrunner, Bird
Time period(s): Indeterminate Past
Locale(s): Southwest

Summary: An original tale explains the origins and unusual appearance of Roadrunner. Snake blocks the road and refuses to allow people to pass so they complain to Desert Woman who gives Snake rattles for his tail so people will know when he is nearby. Snake becomes an even bigger bully after he receives the rattles and the animals complain to Desert Woman. Unable to take away something she's given, Desert Woman requests the animals' help in creating a new animal to teach a lesson to Snake. Using clay from Sacred Mountain, and contributions from different animals, Desert Woman creates an odd-looking bird with long, thin legs. Desert Woman instructs Roadrunner to dance about Snake to distract him so others can use the road. With practice Roadrunner becomes agile and courageously he confronts Snake who no longer blocks the road. (32 pages)

Where it's reviewed:
Booklist, December 15, 2000, page 823
Children's Book Review Service, September 2000, page 6
Kirkus Reviews, July 15, 2000, page 1034
Publishers Weekly, August 21, 2000, page 73
School Library Journal, September 2000, page 184

Awards the book has won:
Americas Award for Children's and Young Adult Literature, 2000

Other books by the same author:
Farolitos for Abuelo, 1999
Maya's Children: The Story of La Llorona, 1997
The Farolitos of Christmas, 1995

Other books you might like:

Te Ata, *Baby Rattlesnake*, 1989

In a retelling of a folktale a baby rattlesnake is not sure what to do with the rattle it's given.

Gerald McDermott, *Coyote: A Trickster Tale from the American Southwest*, 1994

Overly confident Coyote's rude, boastful behavior contributes to his failed attempt to learn to fly with the crows and changes his appearance.

Sheila White Samton, *Tilly and the Rhinoceros*, 1993

When a cantankerous rhinoceros lies down in the road and refuses to move Tilly, a kind goose solves the problem so the road can reopen.

24

LAURIE HALSE ANDERSON
DOROTHY DONOHUE, Illustrator

No Time for Mother's Day

(Morton Grove, IL: Albert Whitman & Company, 1999)

Subject(s): Holidays; Gifts; Mothers
Age range(s): Grades K-3
Major character(s): Charity Chatfield, Student—Elementary School, Daughter; Mom, Mother; Fred, Cousin
Time period(s): 1990s (1999)
Locale(s): United States

Summary: When Charity's teacher announces that Mother's Day is only two days away she begins to worry about what to give Mom. A trip to the mall with obnoxious Fred does nothing to help her find a gift, but it does help her start thinking in a new way. Her father decides that his gift will be to paint the kitchen and suggests that Charity draw a picture. While tossing and turning late at night, Charity hears the clock chime and realizes what her gift to her very busy mom will be. She secretly unplugs every buzzing, beeping or ringing piece of equipment in the house and gives Mom the perfect present—a day of peace and quiet. (32 pages)

Where it's reviewed:
Booklist, February 15, 1999, page 1073
Bulletin for the Center for Children's Books, April 1999, page 271
Horn Book Guide, Fall 1999, page 243
Kirkus Reviews, March 1, 1999, page 372
School Library Journal, April 1999, page 85

Other books by the same author:
Ndito Runs, 1996
Turkey Pox, 1996

Other books you might like:

Diane Goode, *Mama's Perfect Present*, 1996

Two children search the shops of Paris to find just the right gift for Mama's birthday.

Mary Ann Hoberman, *The Seven Silly Eaters*, 1997

A mother's seven children, each one a picky eater, surprise her by creating a cake for her birthday that all the family enjoys.

Pat Mora, *A Birthday Basket for Tia*, 1992

Cecelia plans a very special birthday surprise for beloved Great-Aunt Tia.

Robin West, *My Very Own Mother's Day: A Book of Cooking and Crafts*, 1996

For children less inventive than Charity, this nonfiction title offers directions for making simple gifts and includes the history of Mother's Day.

25

LAURENCE ANHOLT
CATHERINE ANHOLT, Illustrator

Billy and the Big New School

(Morton Grove, IL: Albert Whitman & Company, 1999)

Subject(s): Schools; Animals/Birds; Fear
Age range(s): Grades K-1
Major character(s): Billy, Child, Student—Elementary School
Time period(s): 1990s (1997)
Locale(s): England

Summary: Knowing that Billy loves birds, his mother compares his excitement mixed with nervousness about the start of school to the feeling a baby bird has when it's time to leave the nest. Billy thinks he'd prefer to be a bird and not have to tie shoes or attend school. The day before school opens, Billy finds an immature sparrow in the yard, too young to fly and care for itself. Billy brings the sparrow inside, warms it and talks to it all day. The next morning, the sparrow is so much better that Billy knows it's time to let it go. It's also time for Billy to start school and he does—all by himself! (32 pages)

Where it's reviewed:
Booklist, March 1, 1999, page 1218
Horn Book Guide, Fall 1999, page 228
Publishers Weekly, February 9, 1999, page 213
School Library Journal, March 1999, page 162
Smithsonian Magazine, November 1999, page 46

Awards the book has won:
Smithsonian's Notable Books for Children, 1999

Other books by the same author:
Camille and the Sunflowers, 1994
The New Puppy, 1994
The Forgotten Forest, 1992

Other books you might like:

Miriam Cohen, *Will I Have a Friend?*, 1967

First day of school jitters have Jim wondering if he will find a friend in his class.

Jonathan London, *Froggy Goes to School*, 1996

Although he feels nervous about the first day of school, Froggy not only survives, he also enjoys the day.

Amy Schwartz, *Annabelle Swift, Kindergartner*, 1988

Annabelle is not sure that school will be as much fun as she has anticipated.

Rosemary Wells, *Timothy Goes to School*, 1981

A friend assists Timothy when a bully almost spoils the first day of school.

26

LAURENCE ANHOLT
CATHERINE ANHOLT, Illustrator

Harry's Home

(New York: Farrar Straus Giroux, 2000)

Subject(s): Farm Life; Animals; City and Town Life
Age range(s): Grades K-1
Major character(s): Harry, Child, Son; Grandad, Grandfather; Unnamed Character, Mother
Time period(s): 1990s (1999)
Locale(s): England

Summary: Harry loves the busy streets and varied activities in the city where he lives with his mom. Most of all Harry likes to watch the lights of the city twinkle outside his window as he drifts off to sleep. A birthday gift from Grandad who lives far from the city near some mountains on a farm with animals gives Harry the opportunity to experience another type of home. Life in the country is quiet and so dark that Harry has difficulty falling asleep and wants to return to his city home. Then, Grandad introduces him to a lamb in need of feeding and Harry soon becomes so acclimated to farm life that by the end of his weeklong visit he's reluctant to leave. As Harry travels back to the city with his mother he notices the many different homes they pass and he realizes that the home for Harry is his own. First published in Great Britain in 1999. (32 pages)

Where it's reviewed:
Booklist, May 1, 2000, page 1675
Horn Book Guide, Fall 2000, page 244
Kirkus Reviews, April 15, 2000, page 55
Publishers Weekly, May 8, 2000, page 220
School Library Journal, April 2000, page 90

Other books by the same author:
Sophie and the New Baby, 2000
Billy and the Big New School, 1999
A Kiss Like This, 1997

Other books you might like:
Margaret Wise Brown, *Big Red Barn*, 1995
　A description of one day in the life of a big red barn introduces the many animals that live inside.
Carol Carrick, *Valentine*, 1995
　Helping Grandma care for a weak baby lamb helps Heather forget how much she misses her mom.
Kay Chorao, *Little Farm by the Sea*, 1998
　Farmer Brown and his family stay busy with work of the farm in every season of the year.
Alice Provenson, *The Year at Maple Hill Farm*, 1978
　As the seasons change so too do the activities on the farm. Martin Provenson, co-author.

27

LAURENCE ANHOLT
CATHERINE ANHOLT, Illustrator

Sophie and the New Baby

(Morton Grove, IL: Albert Whitman & Company, 2000)

Subject(s): Babies; Brothers and Sisters; Seasons
Age range(s): Grades K-1
Major character(s): Sophie, Daughter, Sister (older); Winter Baby, Brother, Son
Time period(s): 1990s
Locale(s): England

Summary: During a spring walk in the woods Sophie's parents tell her that by winter their family will include a new baby and Sophie will become a big sister. Through all the seasons as Sophie waits and waits she plays with her doll, caring for it as if it were her new sibling. Finally, during the first snowfall her brother is born. Winter Baby is not what Sophie expected. He cries, eats and needs changing with no waiting. Only Sophie has to wait for everything because her parents are too busy with Winter Baby. Sophie is so angry she wants to send him back! By the time the first signs of spring become visible Sophie has grown accustomed to Winter Baby so she gives her doll to him because she doesn't need it anymore. Originally published in Great Britain in 1995. (32 pages)

Where it's reviewed:
Booklist, September 15, 2000, page 247
Horn Book Guide, Spring 2001, page 11
Kirkus Reviews, October 1, 2000, page 1418
School Library Journal, November 2000, page 110
Smithsonian, November 2000, page 62

Awards the book has won:
Smithsonian's Notable Books for Children, 2000

Other books by the same author:
Here Come the Babies, 1995
Toddlers, 1993
Twins: Two by Two, 1992

Other books you might like:
Martha Alexander, *Nobody Asked Me If I Wanted a Baby Sister*, 1977
　Despite the fact that his baby sister receives too much attention, a little boy begrudgingly admits to feeling some affection for her.
Russell Hoban, *A Baby Sister for Frances*, 1964
　Frances is not sure about the new addition to the family, but her understanding parents help her adjust to the arrival of a baby sister.
Holly Keller, *Geraldine's Baby Brother*, 1994
　It takes some time for Geraldine to adjust to her noisy baby brother and all the attention he receives.
Clara Vulliamy, *Ellen and Penguin and the New Baby*, 1996
　There's a new baby brother in the family and Ellen agrees with her toy Penguin that having one is not such a good idea.
Susan Winter, *A Baby Just Like Me*, 1994
　Martha is disappointed that her baby sister is unable to be her playmate immediately.

28

LAURENCE ANHOLT
LYNNE RUSSELL, Illustrator

Summerhouse
(New York: DK Ink/DK Publishing, Inc., 1999)

Subject(s): Grandmothers; Imagination; Winter
Age range(s): Grades K-3
Major character(s): Grandma, Grandmother; Ella, Child; Grandpa, Grandfather
Time period(s): 1990s (1999)
Locale(s): United States

Summary: Many years before Ella's birth, Grandma and Grandpa leave their island home for America. As a reminder of what they've left behind Grandpa builds a summerhouse in the garden for Grandma. Now, on a snowy winter day, Grandma hands overly-serious Ella the key and sends her to the summerhouse to find the happiness inside. When Ella enters the summerhouse she is startled to be surrounded by warmth, flowers, and the sound of the surf. She frolics in the water, plays on the sand, and when it is time to go, bundles up in her jacket and boots to walk back to Grandma and share the laughter of the sunshine she's found within. (32 pages)

Where it's reviewed:
Booklist, February 15, 1999, page 1074
Horn Book Guide, Fall 1999, page 243
School Library Journal, May 1999, page 79

Other books by the same author:
The New Puppy, 1995
Camille and the Sunflowers: A Story about Vincent Van Gogh, 1994
The Forgotten Forest, 1992

Other books you might like:
Arthur Dorros, *Isla*, 1995
  Abuela is such a gifted storyteller that, as she listens, Rosalba feels she's been transported to her mother's childhood island home.
Lynn Joseph, *Coconut Kind of Day: Island Poems*, 1990
  Poems describe the daily life of a young girl in the Caribbean.
Audrey Wood, *The Flying Dragon Room*, 1996
  Patrick borrows tools from Mrs. Jenkins to create a fantastic subterranean realm that he willingly shares with his parents.

29

NANCY ANTLE
S.D. SCHINDLER, Illustrator

Sam's Wild West Christmas
(New York: Dial Books for Young Readers, 2000)

Series: Dial Easy-to-Read
Subject(s): Christmas; Santa Claus; Robbers and Outlaws
Age range(s): Grades 1-2
Major character(s): Sam, Cowboy, Entertainer; Rodeo Rosie, Cowgirl, Entertainer
Time period(s): Indeterminate Past

Locale(s): West

Summary: Sam and the performers from his Wild West Show are heading home on Christmas Eve when the sounds of crying draw them to a train stopped on the tracks with its doors sealed shut with taffy. The passengers have been robbed of all their Christmas presents, but the eager thieves left a trail of wrapping paper that Sam and Rosie follow to a small log cabin. There they discover the thieves are two jail escapees who have also tied up a fellow in a red suit that they found on the roof. Rosie distracts the thieves with one of her tricks while Sam lets the prisoner free to resume his work. Sam then ties up the thieves with ribbon and they haul the prisoners and the rewrapped gifts back to the train. Looks as if everyone will be home in time for Christmas, except the thieves who will be back in jail. (40 pages)

Where it's reviewed:
Booklist, September 1, 2000, page 126
Bulletin of the Center for Children's Books, October 2000, page 52
Horn Book Guide, Spring 2001, page 55
Kirkus Reviews, September 1, 2000, page 1278
School Library Journal, October 2000, page 56

Other books by the same author:
Staying Cool, 1997
Sam's Wild West Show, 1995
Beautiful Land: A Story of the Oklahoma Land Rush, 1994

Other books you might like:
Betsy Byars, *The Golly Sisters Go West*, 1986
  Six stories trace the amusing travels of two comical sisters on the frontier.
Eleanor Coerr, *Buffalo Bill and the Pony Express*, 1995
  A beginning chapter book tells of Buffalo Bill who, while delivering mail for the Pony Express, escapes from wolves and outwits outlaws.
Roy Gerrard, *Rosie and the Rustlers*, 1989
  A story in rhyme describes how Rosie catches the rustlers who have stolen her cattle.
Frank Remkiewicz, *The Bone Stranger*, 1994
  When outlaws steal the strongbox containing the orphans' bedtime treats Boney and Wolfgang go into action to nab the scoundrels.
Diane Stanley, *Saving Sweetness*, 1996
  A sheriff trying to catch an orphanage escapee is actually rescued by the runaway.

30

KATHI APPELT
BARRY ROOT, Illustrator

Cowboy Dreams
(New York: HarperCollins Publishers, 1999)

Subject(s): Dreams and Nightmares; Bedtime; Stories in Rhyme
Age range(s): Grades K-1
Major character(s): Unnamed Character, Child, Cowboy
Time period(s): Indeterminate
Locale(s): West

Summary: Night is falling as cowpokes settle in at the end of a long day. Under the silver moonlight a young cowboy brushes his pony and joins the others around the campfire. As the last song is sung he closes his eyes, ready for cowboy dreams. (32 pages)

Where it's reviewed:
Booklist, January 1, 1999, page 885
Horn Book Guide, Fall 1999, page 243
Publishers Weekly, January 18, 1999
School Library Journal, February 1999, page 77

Other books by the same author:
A Red Wagon Year, 1996
Watermelon Day, 1996
Bayou Lullaby, 1995

Other books you might like:
Kate Banks, *And If the Moon Could Talk*, 1998
   Parents lovingly prepare a young child for bed as a brilliant moon shines down on all that it would tell us—if the moon could talk.
Sue Heap, *Cowboy Baby*, 1998
   It takes ingenuity for Sheriff Pa to convince Cowboy Baby and his sidekicks to go to bed.
Christine Loomis, *Cowboy Bunnies*, 1997
   After riding their rocking horses all day, cowboy bunnies are ready to say good night to their cowboy mamas and papas.

31

KATHI APPELT
JANE DYER, Illustrator

Oh My Baby, Little One
(San Diego: Harcourt, Inc., 2000)

Subject(s): Parent and Child; Love; Stories in Rhyme
Age range(s): Preschool
Major character(s): Baby Bird, Bird, Student; Mama Bird, Mother, Bird
Time period(s): Indeterminate
Locale(s): Fictional Country

Summary: The love of Mama Bird for Baby Bird is the invisible bond that links them while they are apart. After a final hug and wave good-bye Mama Bird reassures Baby Bird that her love is as constant as the sun in the sky and as near as the breeze holding a kite aloft. While Mama Bird works she is aware of the love that is always with her. The end of the school day brings a joyful reunion of mother and child. (32 pages)

Where it's reviewed:
Booklist, March 1, 2000, page 1249
Horn Book Guide, Fall 2000, page 244
Publishers Weekly, February 14, 2000, page 196
School Library Journal, April 2000, page 90

Other books by the same author:
A Red Wagon Year, 1996
Bayou Lullaby, 1995
Elephants Aloft, 1993

Other books you might like:
Margaret Wise Brown, *The Runaway Bunny*, 1942
   Mother bunny loves her baby too much to let him run away so she finds him each time he escapes.
Barbara M. Joosse, *I Love You the Purplest*, 1996
   Mama's responses to her sons' many questions affirm her love for each of them.
Sam McBratney, *Guess How Much I Love You*, 1995
   Little Nutbrown Hare enjoys playing a game with his father in which each professes the magnitude of his love for the other.

32

MARGOT APPLE, Author/Illustrator

Brave Martha
(Boston: Houghton Mifflin Company, 1999)

Subject(s): Animals/Cats; Fear; Bedtime
Age range(s): Grades K-1
Major character(s): Martha, Child; Sophie, Cat
Time period(s): Indeterminate Past
Locale(s): United States

Summary: Martha and Sophie are a team. They play together by day and at night their bedtime routine includes a "monster check" by Sophie. Each night when Sophie emerges unscathed from under the bed, Martha knows it is safe to go to sleep. The evening that Martha's parents have guests who arrive with their dog, Sophie vanishes. Poor Martha! Bedtime arrives and her father doesn't know how to do a proper monster check so Martha lies in bed listening to a scratching sound and trying to bravely find and dispose of the monster. When the "monster" finds Martha, she is relieved to discover that the shining eyes and scratching sounds belong to Sophie and they both settle contentedly into bed. (32 pages)

Where it's reviewed:
Booklist, September 15, 1999, page 264
Horn Book Guide, Spring 2000, page 26
Kirkus Reviews, September 15, 1999, page 1496
School Library Journal, September 1999, page 174

Other books by the same author:
Blanket, 1990

Other books you might like:
Russell Hoban, *Bedtime for Frances*, 1960
   Frances imagines so many scary things in her room that she is unable to sleep.
Betsy James, *Flashlight*, 1997
   Grandpa gives Marie a flashlight to help her control the shadows by illuminating their scary shapes in the dark room.
Mercer Mayer, *There's a Monster under My Bed*, 1968
   Sometimes inviting monsters out of the closet helps them seem less scary.
Polly Powell, *Just Dessert*, 1996
   While sneaking into the dark kitchen to get more dessert Patsy is so terrified by the dangers lurking in her path that she forgets the cake.

33

JENNIFER ARMSTRONG
SUSAN GABER, Illustrator

Pierre's Dream
(New York: Dial Books for Young Readers, 1999)

Subject(s): Dreams and Nightmares; Circus; Conduct of Life
Age range(s): Grades 1-3
Major character(s): Pierre, Unemployed
Time period(s): Indeterminate Past
Locale(s): Apt, France

Summary: Pierre lacks the ambition to do anything more than find the next shady spot for a quick snooze. One day while napping he notices a circus in the field near the olive trees. Since the field had been empty when he went to sleep, Pierre decides that he must be dreaming. Believing that he is dreaming, he's also confident that all things are possible in a dream so he confronts an escaped lion, walks a tightrope and takes over for the ailing ringmaster of the circus. Pierre is a little surprised that his dream is continuing for such a long time because he's feeling tired from all the activity so he returns to his spot under the olive tree and sleeps. When morning comes, the field is again empty, but Pierre remembers dreaming about the circus. He also finds evidence that perhaps his dream was more real than he originally thought. (32 pages)

Where it's reviewed:
Booklist, August 1999, page 2062
Bulletin of the Center for Children's Books, July 1999, page 379
Kirkus Reviews, May 1, 1999, page 718
Publishers Weekly, May 31, 1999, page 92
School Library Journal, June 1999, page 85

Other books by the same author:
Sunshine, Moonshine, 1997
Wan Hu Is in the Stars, 1995
Chin Yu Min and the Ginger Cat, 1993 (ALA Notable Book)

Other books you might like:
Demi, *Liang and the Magic Paintbrush*, 1980
   A Chinese boy's dreams come to life with the help of his paintbrush.
Laura McGee Kvasnosky, *What Shall I Dream?*, 1996
   Though he receives many dream suggestions, Prince Alexander realizes he must select his own dreams.
Roni Schotter, *Dreamland*, 1996
   Theo sketches ''dream machines'' that Uncle Gurney turns into amusement park rides in sunny, southern California.
Chris Van Allsburg, *The Sweetest Fig*, 1993
   A dentist is offered magical figs that, when eaten, can make dreams come true.

34

MARSHA DIANE ARNOLD
BRAD SNEED, Illustrator

The Bravest of Us All
(New York: Dial Books for Young Readers, 2000)

Subject(s): Courage; Sisters; Weather
Age range(s): Grades K-3
Major character(s): Ruby Jane, Sister (younger); Velma Jean, Sister (older); Elsie June, Sister (younger)
Time period(s): Indeterminate Past
Locale(s): United States

Summary: Everyone in a large farm family knows that Velma Jean is the bravest of all the siblings. Why, Velma Jean can walk through the bull's pasture, meet strangers, break a colt, and cross the sandbur patch barefoot. Ruby Jane admires her sister and wishes she could be recognized for something more exciting that best kitchen helper. While Velma Jean is outside doing brave deeds on hot days, Ruby Jane sometimes seeks the coolness of the root cellar to play with little Elsie June. When a tornado approaches and the family races to the protection of the root cellar, Velma Jean cannot be found. Ruby Jane sees her by the horse tank and races out to get her. Then Ruby Jane learns that brave Velma Jean is afraid of underground spaces and it is up to Ruby Jane to assure their safety. (32 pages)

Where it's reviewed:
Booklist, May 1, 2000, page 1676
Bulletin of the Center for Children's Books, June 2000, page 350
Horn Book Guide, Fall 2000, page 260
School Library Journal, May 2000, page 126

Other books by the same author:
The Chicken Salad Club, 1998
The Pumpkin Runner, 1998
Heart of a Tiger, 1995 (Marion Vannett Ridgeway Award)

Other books you might like:
Darleen Bailey Beard, *Twister*, 1999
   Protected in a cellar, frightened siblings endure the terror of a tornado passing over while their mom tries to help a neighbor.
Betsy Byars, *Tornado*, 1996
   While sheltered in a storm cellar, a farmhand tells a family about a dog blown into his life by a tornado.
Georgia Graham, *The Strongest Man This Side of Cremona*, 1998
   Matthew and his father are working in the fields when a tornado appears suddenly forcing them to race to a culvert where they weather the storm.
Marc Harshman, *The Storm*, 1995
   Facing a tornado alone, Jonathan finds the courage to save himself and the family's animals.
George Ella Lyon, *One Lucky Girl*, 2000
   A tornado sweeps away Nick's baby sister as she sleeps in her crib and miraculously drops her unharmed and still asleep in a field.

35

TEDD ARNOLD, Author/Illustrator

Huggly Takes a Bath

(New York: Cartwheel/Scholastic, 1999)

Series: Monster under the Bed
Subject(s): Monsters; Behavior; Humor
Age range(s): Grades K-2
Major character(s): Huggly, Monster
Time period(s): 1990s (1999)
Locale(s): United States

Summary: After ''people'' go to bed, Huggly crawls out from his home under the bed and goes exploring for a snack. He heads into the bathroom where he finds some tasty toothpaste and some not-so-tasty soap. He cleans his toes with the soft brushes he finds and explores the ''big bowl with a lid.'' The best discovery, however, is the bathtub, which Huggly turns into a slippery, slimy swamp. (24 pages)

Where it's reviewed:
Booklist, February 1, 1999, page 978
Horn Book Guide, Fall 1999, page 228
Publishers Weekly, December 7, 1998, page 58
School Library Journal, April 1999, page 85

Other books by the same author:
Huggly's Pizza, 2000 (Monster under the Bed)
Huggly and the Toy Monster, 1999 (Monster under the Bed)
No More Water in the Tub, 1995 (Monster under the Bed)

Other books you might like:
Jackie French Koller, *No Such Thing*, 1997
　　Just as Howard's mother refuses to believe his claim that there is a monster under his bed, so Monster's mother will not accept that a boy is in the bed.
Betty Paraskevas, *Maggie and the Ferocious Beast: The Big Scare*, 1999
　　Maggie and Hamilton try to help the ferocious beast overcome his fears.
Phyllis Root, *The Hungry Monster*, 1998
　　The Hungry Monster, new to earth, searches for something to eat.
Jeanne Willis, *The Monster Bed*, 1987
　　Dennis, a monster, is afraid to sleep because there might be humans under his bed.

36

FRANK ASCH, Author/Illustrator

Baby Bird's First Nest

(San Diego: Gulliver Books/Harcourt Brace & Company, 1999)

Subject(s): Animals/Birds; Animals/Frogs and Toads; Problem Solving
Age range(s): Grades 1-2
Major character(s): Baby Bird, Bird, Baby; Little Frog, Frog; Mama Bird, Bird, Mother
Time period(s): Indeterminate
Locale(s): Fictional Country

Summary: Baby Bird falls from her nest before she is able to fly. Mama Bird does not hear the frightened bird's cries for help, but Little Frog does. Baby Bird rejects Little Frog's first suggestion to simply wait until morning, but she likes his idea to build a nest. Together the duo fashion a nest on the ground that make them easy prey for a wandering raccoon. For safety, Little Frog leaps into the pond while Baby Bird, in desperation, hops to the lowest branch of a nearby tree. When Little Frog finds her there, he shows Baby Bird that she is capable of solving her own problem. (32 pages)

Where it's reviewed:
Horn Book Guide, Fall 1999, page 244
Publishers Weekly, May 24, 1999, page 77
School Library Journal, June 1999, page 85

Other books by the same author:
Ziggy Piggy and the Three Little Pigs, 1998
Moonbear's Pet, 1997
Moondance, 1993

Other books you might like:
Janell Cannon, *Stellaluna*, 1993
　　Accidentally separated from her mother, Stellaluna falls into a bird's nest where she is treated like one of the family.
Joyce Dunbar, *Baby Bird*, 1998
　　A baby bird learning to fly falls to the ground where dangers surround the fledgling.
P.D. Eastman, *Are You My Mother?*, 1986
　　After falling from the nest, a baby bird tries to find its mother.

37

FRANK ASCH, Author/Illustrator

Moonbear's Dream

(New York: Simon & Schuster Books for Young Readers, 1999)

Subject(s): Animals/Bears; Animals/Birds; Dreams and Nightmares
Age range(s): Preschool
Major character(s): Bear, Bear, Friend; Bird, Bird, Friend
Time period(s): 1990s
Locale(s): Fictional Country

Summary: While playing marbles in the yard, Bear and Bird see a kangaroo hop past. Convinced that they must be dreaming, they decide to enjoy the dream completely by eating their supply of food, breaking dishes and making a big mess in their house. Then they go for a swim, knowing that when they wake up from the dream, everything will be as it was before they ''fell asleep.'' While Bear and Bird are swimming an escaped kangaroo is found inside Bear's house by the zookeeper who assumes the kangaroo has made the mess. Diligently, the zookeeper cleans up everything, repairs the broken dishes and replaces the eaten honey and birdseed. When Bear and Bird return they pinch themselves before opening the door and, as expected, everything is just as it was before they began dreaming. The dream experience is so exhausting that they both need a nap. (32 pages)

Where it's reviewed:
Booklist, September 15, 1999, page 264
Horn Book Guide, Spring 2000, page 12
Publishers Weekly, September 20, 1999, page 89

School Library Journal, October 1999, page 102

Other books by the same author:
Moonbear's Pet, 1997
Moondance, 1993
Mooncake, 1982

Other books you might like:
Naomi Shihab Nye, *Benito's Dream Bottle*, 1995
    Benito believes that the source of dreams is a bottle within each person that must periodically be refilled.
Francesca Simon, *Spider School*, 1996
    Kate's first day of school is so horrid that she is relieved to discover it's all been a bad dream.
Audrey Wood, *Sweet Dream Pie*, 1998
    When Ma bakes her sweet dream pie she must be ready to sweep up the inevitable dreams that overtake the neighborhood so everyone can sleep peacefully.

38

JEANNINE ATKINS
TAD HILLS, Illustrator

A Name on the Quilt: A Story of Remembrance

(New York: Atheneum Books for Young Readers, 1999)

Subject(s): AIDS (Disease); Grief; Aunts and Uncles
Age range(s): Grades 2-4
Major character(s): Lauren, Niece, Sister (older); Bobby, Brother (younger), Nephew
Time period(s): 1990s (1999)
Locale(s): United States

Summary: Family members gather at Lauren's home to create a quilt in memory of her recently deceased uncle. Using his old clothes, each person cuts out a letter of her uncle's name reminiscing as they work of the activities they enjoyed doing with him. Too young to sew, Bobby annoys Lauren with his behavior until he appears with a pair of red socks given to him by their uncle. Kindly, Lauren adds them to the quilt. An author's note describes the NAMES Project AIDS Memorial Quilt and includes photographs of some of the panels. (32 pages)

Where it's reviewed:
Booklist, January 1, 1999, page 885
Horn Book Guide, Fall 1999, page 275
Kirkus Reviews, December 15, 1998, page 1794
Publishers Weekly, January 11, 1999, page 72
School Library Journal, March 1999, page 162

Other books by the same author:
Mary Anning and the Sea Dragon, 1999
Get Set! Swim!, 1998
Aani and the Tree Huggers, 1995

Other books you might like:
Mary Kate Jordan, *Losing Uncle Tim*, 1989
    Though he grieves for the loss of his beloved Uncle Tim, Daniel finds comfort in the legacy of joy and courage left by his favorite relative.

Margaret Merrifield, *Morning Light*, 1996
    A nonfiction work explores the changes in Max and Maggie's lives after they learn their mother has AIDS.
Leslea Newman, *Too Far Away to Touch*, 1995
    Uncle Leonard takes Zoe to a planetarium to explain that, if he dies, he will be just like the stars—too far away to touch, but close enough to see.
Patricia Quinlan, *Tiger Flowers*, 1994
    After his uncle's death, Joel consoles himself and his little sister with memories of their shared activities.

39

DEBBIE ATWELL, Author/Illustrator

River

(Boston: Houghton Mifflin Company, 1999)

Subject(s): Pollution; Rivers; Environment
Age range(s): Grades K-2
Time period(s): Multiple Time Periods
Locale(s): United States

Summary: A river provides nourishment to fish and animals before the first human discovers it and settles on its wooded shores. Over time many more people come, but the newer arrivals do not live in harmony with the river. They cut down the forests on the surrounding hillsides and build towns on the shore. Factories appear, steamboats ply the river, and trains and cars travel its banks. Soon the river can no longer sustain life, the fish vanish, and no animals drink from the water. Some inhabitants remember the river of old and work to restore the trees and repair the damage from the polluting factories. As the people learn to share with the river, the river comes to life again. (32 pages)

Where it's reviewed:
Booklist, November 1, 1999, page 537
Horn Book Guide, Spring 2000, page 27
Kirkus Reviews, July 1, 1999, page 1050
Publishers Weekly, September 6, 1999, page 102
School Library Journal, November 1999, page 108

Other books by the same author:
Barn, 1996

Other books you might like:
Nancy White Carlstrom, *Raven and River*, 1997
    An Alaskan river and the animals dependent on it gradually awaken from winter's chill to welcome spring as the river springs to life.
Donald Hall, *Old Home Day*, 1996
    The cycle of growth, decline and renewal of a New England town is described through the history of its settlers.
Jacqueline Briggs Martin, *Washing the Willow Tree Loon*, 1995
    A community effort following an oil spill enables the rescue, treatment and rehabilitation of an oil-soaked loon.
Jane Yolen, *Letting Swift River Go*, 1992
    When a dam is built across the Swift River, the waters quickly cover Sally Jane's home, village and the simple country life that she knows.

40

MARY JANE AUCH, Author/Illustrator

The Nutquacker

(New York: Holiday House, 1999)

Subject(s): Animals/Ducks; Christmas; Determination
Age range(s): Grades K-3
Major character(s): Clara, Duck
Time period(s): Indeterminate
Locale(s): Fictional Country

Summary: Clara, the newest addition to the barnyard, is determined to discover this "Christmas" about which all the animals are whispering. When none of the animals will help her find Christmas, she sets out in a snowstorm to locate it for herself. Along the way she bravely faces down a large-eyed monster (a tractor) and a big animal with horns (a deer), but she meets her nemesis when a small soft creature (a fox) tries to take a bite out of her tail. Seeing a light in the distance, Clara hurries to the warmth and safety of the barn where her friends are celebrating Christmas with dancing and gifts. (32 pages)

Where it's reviewed:
Booklist, November 1, 1999, page 537
Horn Book Guide, Spring 2000, page 27
Kirkus Reviews, October 15, 1999, page 1638
Publishers Weekly, September 27, 1999, page 59
School Library Journal, October 1999, page 65

Other books by the same author:
Bantam of the Opera, 1997
Eggs Mark the Spot, 1996
Hen Lake, 1995

Other books you might like:
Roger Duvoisin, *Petunia the Silly Goose Stories*, 1985
   The five stories of a confident, but rather silly goose are gathered in one volume.
Pat Hutchins, *Rosie's Walk*, 1968
   Unaware that she is being followed Rosie enjoys her walk around the farmyard, unintentionally leading a fox from one accident to another.
Janet Morgan Stoeke, *Minerva Louise*, 1988
   A confident and very independent hen explores the house with the red curtains.
Ellen Stoll Walsh, *You Silly Goose*, 1992
   Knowing that a fox has been reported in the neighborhood, Lulu panics and sounds the alarm when she spots George—who is really only a mouse.

41

SYLVIE AUZARY-LUTON, Author/Illustrator

1, 2, 3, Music!

(New York: Orchard Books, 1999)

Subject(s): Music and Musicians; Family; Talent
Age range(s): Grades K-2
Major character(s): Annie, Child, Musician; Grandpa, Grandfather, Musician; Grandma, Grandmother
Time period(s): 1990s (1997)
Locale(s): France

Summary: Annie loves music so much she listens to it through earphones all the time as her feet dance to the rhythm of the sound in her ears. Of course, Annie's style creates some problems since she can't hear anyone speaking to her and sometimes her dancing feet knock over laundry baskets or break things. When Grandma takes away her headset and sends her out to play, Annie hears music from a street band and races to watch them, but her joy fades quickly when her cousins laugh at her. Annie retreats to the attic and stumbles upon an old trunk of Grandpa's, containing instruments from his days in a band. Now music seems more appealing to the cousins and they join Annie and Grandpa to try making their own band. The author's first book was originally published in France in 1997. (36 pages)

Where it's reviewed:
Horn Book Guide, Spring 2000, page 27
Publishers Weekly, September 13, 1999, page 83
School Library Journal, December 1999, page 87

Other books you might like:
Dayle Ann Dodds, *Sing, Sophie!*, 1997
   During a thunderstorm Sophie sings her little sister to sleep even though no one else appreciates her voice.
Leah Komaiko, *I Like the Music*, 1987
   A grandmother escorts her music-loving granddaughter to an outdoor symphony concert.
George Ella Lyon, *Five Live Bongos*, 1994
   Five lively children create the "Found Sound Band" with everyday household items and discards.
Lloyd Moss, *Zin! Zin! Zin! A Violin*, 1995
   Playful rhymes and zany illustrations introduce the instruments of the orchestra.
Brian Pinkney, *Max Found Two Sticks*, 1994
   Max uses two sticks he finds near his urban home to musically imitate and answer the sounds of the city.

42

AVI

DON BOLOGNESE, Illustrator

Abigail Takes the Wheel

(New York: HarperCollins Publishers, Inc., 1999)

Series: I Can Read Chapter Books
Subject(s): Historical; Ships; Fathers and Daughters
Age range(s): Grades 2-4
Major character(s): Abigail Bates, Daughter, Sister (older); Tom Bates, Son, Brother; Captain Bates, Father, Sea Captain
Time period(s): 1880s
Locale(s): Old Port, New Jersey; New York, New York; *Neptune*, At Sea (New York Harbor)

Summary: The Bates family lives aboard the *Neptune*, making it easy for Tom and Abigail to travel the 20 nautical miles into New York for school each day as their father makes deliveries with the freight boat. On one such trip, while traversing the crowded harbor, Captain Bates observes a collision between two sailing vessels and takes the disabled one in tow. To do so, Captain Bates must board the disabled vessel, leaving his first mate in charge of the *Neptune*. When the first mate becomes ill and leaves the helm, Abigail takes over with Tom shouting instructions to the crew in the engine room. Despite some tense moments and near misses, Abigail safely brings the *Neptune* and her tow to the pier in time for the children to hurry off to school. A concluding author's note gives the historical basis for the story. (64 pages)

Where it's reviewed:
Booklist, April 1, 1999, page 1424
Horn Book Guide, Fall 1999, page 275
Horn Book, March 1999, page 206
School Library Journal, May 1999, page 85

Other books by the same author:
Poppy and Rye, 1998
Finding Providence: The Story of Roger Williams, 1997
Poppy, 1995

Other books you might like:
Richard Berleth, *Mary Patten's Voyage*, 1994
   With her husband bed-ridden and the first mate in the brig, Mary Patten takes the helm and safely brings the *Neptune Car* to port.
Louise Borden, *The Little Ships: The Heroic Rescue at Dunkirk in World War II*, 1997
   A young, but seaworthy daughter sails with her father in his fishing boat to assist in the evacuation of soldiers from Dunkirk.
Deborah Hopkinson, *Birdie's Lighthouse*, 1997
   With her father ill, 10-year-old Birdie tends the lighthouse alone during a northeaster.
Thomas P. Lewis, *Clipper Ship*, 1978
   When Jamie's father, captain of a clipper ship, falls ill his mother must take over and bring the ship safely to port.
Marissa Moss, *True Heart*, 1999
   After working as a freight loader for the Union Pacific, Bee finally achieves her dream of being a railroad engineer.

43

AVI (Pseudonym of Avi Wortis)
BRIAN FLOCA, Illustrator

Ereth's Birthday
(New York: HarperCollins Publishers, 2000)

Series: Tales from Dimwood Forest
Subject(s): Animals; Parent and Child; Fantasy
Age range(s): Grades 3-6
Major character(s): Erethizon "Ereth" Dorsatum, Porcupine; Poppy, Mouse, Friend
Time period(s): 2000s (2000)
Locale(s): Dimwood Forest, Fictional Country; Long Lake, Fictional Country

Summary: Ereth awakens on his birthday expecting Poppy to be waiting with birthday greetings. When she's not, Ereth feels forgotten and wanders off through the forest in a snowstorm to find his own birthday treat—salt. Instead Ereth finds humans in the cabin at Long Lake and a dying fox caught in one of their traps. Before she dies, the fox begs Ereth to care for her three kits and directs him to the den. Thus, curmudgeonly, but kind-hearted Ereth becomes the caretaker

of three boisterous, meat-eating youngsters. Finding food is difficult for the vegetarian porcupine with no hunting skills. The snow-covered traps complicate the quest for food, but together the animals survive. Ereth is so focused on the kits, his search for salt and his hurt feelings that he is unaware that Marty the fisher is patiently stalking him, waiting for the moment that Ereth is alone without the kits. Marty seizes the first opportunity and Ereth wonders if he will ever see Poppy and his hollow log home again. (180 pages)

Where it's reviewed:
Booklist, April 1, 2000, page 1461
Five Owls, September 2000, page 17
Horn Book, May 2000, page 306
Publishers Weekly, May 8, 2000, page 222
School Library Journal, May 2000, page 166

Other books by the same author:
Ragweed, 1999 (Tales from Dimwood Forest)
Poppy and Rye, 1998 (Tales from Dimwood Forest)
Poppy, 1995 (Booklist Editors' Choice)
The Barn, 1994 (ALA Notable Book)

Other books you might like:
Brooks Hansen, *Caesar's Antlers*, 1997
   Caesar carries a sparrow and her baby-filled nest in his antlers as he helps Bette search for her lost mate Piorello.
Dick King-Smith, *Three Terrible Trins*, 1994
   Three mice set out to avenge their father's death and make the house safe by ridding it of cats.
Cynthia Rylant, *Gooseberry Park*, 1995
   After an ice storm breaks the tree home of a squirrel her dog friend rescues the babies and then is stuck babysitting until the mother can be found.

44

AVI

Midnight Magic
(New York: Scholastic Press, 1999)

Subject(s): Magicians; Kings, Queens, Rulers, etc.; Mystery
Age range(s): Grades 5-8
Major character(s): Teresina, 10-Year-Old, Royalty (princess); Fabrizio, 12-Year-Old, Servant; Mangus, Magician, Aged Person
Time period(s): 15th century (1491)
Locale(s): Pergamontio, Italy

Summary: At midnight on a dark stormy night, Mangus is summoned to the castello for an audience with the king. Accompanied by Fabrizio, Mangus learns that he is charged with the task of ridding Princess Teresina of a ghost that visits her in the castle halls. While Fabrizio snoops, Mangus reasons and both fear for their lives. They quickly realize that they are caught in the intrigue of the king's evil advisor who plans to take control of the kingdom by marrying Teresina. Despite the danger, Fabrizio and Mangus succeed in revealing the advisor's plans, saving Teresina from an unwanted marriage and vanquishing the ghost. (247 pages)

Where it's reviewed:
Booklist, September 15, 1999, page 256
Five Owls, November 1999, page 46

Horn Book, November 1999, page 733
Publishers Weekly, November 8, 1999, page 68
School Library Journal, October 1999, page 144

Other books by the same author:
Perloo the Bold, 1998
What Do Fish Have to Do with Anything? And Other Stories, 1997
The Barn, 1994

Other books you might like:
Sid Fleischman, *The Whipping Boy*, 1986
  A Newbery Medal winner relates the tale of an orphan selected as the whipping boy for Prince Brat and the unexpected reversal of their roles.
Dian Curtis Regan, *Princess Nevermore*, 1995
  Bored in Mandria, Princess Quinn unintentionally receives her wish to travel to Earth; unprepared, she arrives by way of a botched magic spell.
Barbara Brooks Wallace, *Cousins in the Castle*, 1996
  Kidnapped orphans, lost heirs, and criminals determined to get rich at the children's expense combine to make a thrilling adventure.

45

AVI
BRIAN FLOCA, Illustrator

Ragweed
(New York: Avon Books, Inc., 1999)

Subject(s): Animals/Mice; Fantasy; Animals/Cats
Age range(s): Grades 3-6
Major character(s): Ragweed, Mouse, Adventurer; Silversides, Cat; Clutch, Mouse, Musician
Time period(s): Indeterminate
Locale(s): Amperville, Fictional Country

Summary: In the prequel to *Poppy* and *Poppy and Rye* Ragweed, ever adventurous, leaves his comfortable home in the Brook and hops a train for the city. He reaches Amperville, home of Silversides, recently displaced in her owner's affections by a pet mouse and vowing revenge against all mice. Ragweed finds himself in the middle of hostilities that are as foreign to him as the city streets. Not a mouse to run from danger, Ragweed declares to his new friend Clutch his intentions to overcome the cats and make the town safe for mice. Rallying the fearful mice, Ragweed leads the charge, repelling the cats' attack and then moves onto to explore other new territories. (178 pages)

Where it's reviewed:
Booklist, May 15, 1999, page 1690
Horn Book Guide, Fall 1999, page 287
Publishers Weekly, May 10, 1999, page 68
School Library Journal, July 1999, page 92

Other books by the same author:
Poppy and Rye, 1998
Poppy, 1995 (Booklist Editors' Choice)
The Barn, 1994 (ALA Notable Book)

Other books you might like:
Brian Jacques, *Redwall*, 1987
  The evil rat Cluny destroys the peace of ancient Redwall Abbey as he and hordes of villains attempt to seize control.
Dick King-Smith, *Three Terrible Trins*, 1994
  Three mice set out to avenge their father's death and make the house safe by ridding it of cats.
Robert C. O'Brien, *Mrs. Frisby and the Rats of NIMH*, 1971
  Needing help, a widowed mouse bravely visits rats, retired from laboratory experiments that have made them wise and long-lived. Newbery Medal winner.

46

JIM AYLESWORTH
BARBARA MCCLINTOCK, Illustrator

Aunt Pitty Patty's Piggy
(New York: Scholastic Press, 1999)

Subject(s): Folklore; Animals/Pigs; Problem Solving
Age range(s): Grades K-2
Major character(s): Nelly, Child, Niece; Pitty Patty, Aunt; Farmer Brown, Farmer
Time period(s): Indeterminate Past
Locale(s): England

Summary: In this retelling of a cumulative folktale, the pig Aunt Pitty Patty buys at the market refuses to go through the gate so Nelly is left with the pig while her aunt cooks supper. Nelly seeks help from a dog, a stick, fire, water, an ox, a butcher, a rope and a mouse, but receives no support until she pleads with a cat. The cat has a request in return and when Nelly is able to comply with that, thanks to some help from Farmer Brown, a sequence of events is set in place that sends piggy through the gate and Nelly, with Farmer Brown, into the house for supper. (32 pages)

Where it's reviewed:
Booklist, September 15, 1999, page 258
Horn Book, September 1999, page 618
Publishers Weekly, August 2, 1999, page 83
School Library Journal, October 1999, page 132

Other books by the same author:
The Gingerbread Man, 1998
Teddy Bear Tears, 1997
My Sister's Rusty Bike, 1996

Other books you might like:
Byron Barton, *The Wee Little Woman*, 1995
  A wee little cumulative tale tells of a wee little woman whose wee little cat has hurt feelings when chastised for drinking the wee little milk.
Aubrey Davis, *The Enormous Potato*, 1998
  A farmer's potato grows so large that the cooperation of many is needed to pull it out of the ground.
Rosanne Litzinger, *The Old Woman and Her Pig*, 1993
  When an old woman's newly purchased pig refuses to go over the stile, the woman calls for help in a lively retelling of a traditional cumulative tale.
Laura Joffe Numeroff, *If You Give a Pig a Pancake*, 1998
  When a little girl gives a pancake to a pig that crawls in the

kitchen window, she creates one unexpected problem after another.

Ann Tompert, *Just a Little Bit*, 1993

Mouse receives help from many animals in order to successfully seesaw with his friend Elephant.

47

JIM AYLESWORTH
WENDY ANDERSON HALPERIN, Illustrator

The Full Belly Bowl

(New York: Atheneum Books for Young Readers, 1999)

Subject(s): Fairy Tales; Folklore; Magic
Age range(s): Grades K-3
Major character(s): Angelina, Cat; Unnamed Character, Aged Person; Unnamed Character, Benefactor
Time period(s): Indeterminate Past
Locale(s): Fictional Country

Summary: With his sweet cat Angelina a kind, but poor old man lives in a small house near a forest. While searching for food one day, the old man rescues a wee man from the jaws of a hungry fox. The very old man cares for the tiny man in his home for four days and then the wee man is gone without a trace. Several days later, a beautiful bowl appears on the old man's doorstep along with a note explaining the use of the "Full Belly Bowl." Gradually, the old man learns the true value of the bowl and the way in which to use it so it is a blessing and not a burden. When the old man formulates a plan to use the bowl to become rich, he also becomes careless and, in the resulting chaos, the "Full Belly Bowl" shatters leaving the old man wiser but no less content with his life. (40 pages)

Where it's reviewed:
Booklist, November 1, 1999, page 524
Horn Book Guide, Spring 2000, page 27
Publishers Weekly, November 8, 1999, page 67
School Library Journal, October 1999, page 102

Awards the book has won:
Booklist Editors' Choice, 1999

Other books by the same author:
The Gingerbread Man, 1998
Through the Night, 1998
Teddy Bear Tears, 1997

Other books you might like:
Teresa Bateman, *Leprechaun Gold*, 1998
After rescuing a leprechaun from a stream, Donald refuses the traditional gift of gold so the clever leprechaun delivers a more valuable reward.
Tomie DePaola, *Strega Nona*, 1975
Oh no! Strega Nona has left Big Anthony alone with her magic pot and he's cooking pasta in it.
Paul Galdone, *The Magic Porridge Pot*, 1976
This magic pot cooks porridge and more porridge because the words that tell it to stop are forgotten.
Lily Toy Hong, *Two of Everything*, 1993
In an award winning retelling of a Chinese folktale a poor farmer finds a magic pot and must learn to live with the unexpected consequences of his good fortune.

B

48

LINDA BAILEY
WENDY BAILEY, Illustrator

When Addie Was Scared

(Buffalo, NY: Kids Can Press, 1999)

Subject(s): Fear; Farm Life; Courage
Age range(s): Grades K-3
Major character(s): Addie, Child; Babcha, Grandmother
Time period(s): 1930s
Locale(s): Prairie Provinces, Canada

Summary: Fearful Addie feels frightened of the family's turkey gobbler, the unseen creatures that make sounds in the bushes as she brings in the cows each evening, and the cry of wolves on a winter's night. Every Saturday Addie walks an extra mile to Babcha's house rather than walk past the pasture of a bull. One day, when returning home from Babcha's a sudden thunderstorm sends Addie racing back to the comfort of Babcha's arms. It is at Babcha's house during another visit that Addie also finds the courage to chase away a chicken hawk determined to dine on one of Babcha's chickens. Although Addie still has times when she feels fearful, the experience teaches her that she also has courage within her to call upon when needed. (32 pages)

Where it's reviewed:
Booklist, November 15, 1999, page 632
ForeWord Magazine, October 1999, page 61
Horn Book Guide, Spring 2000, page 27
Quill & Quire, October 1999, page 43
School Library Journal, November 1999, page 110

Other books by the same author:
Petula, Who Wouldn't Take a Bath, 1998
Gordon Loggins and the Three Bears, 1997

Other books you might like:
Frances Arrington, *Stella's Bull*, 1994
  Frightened Mary goes without her new spelling book for three days before finding the courage to retrieve it from a ferocious bull's pasture.

Betsy James, *Flashlight*, 1997
  Grandpa recognizes Marie's fear of sleeping in a strange place and gives her a flashlight to illuminate the shadows.
Bill Martin Jr., *The Ghost-Eye Tree*, 1985
  As they walk down a dark road on a family errand, a brother and sister argue about who is afraid of the Ghost-Eye tree. John Archambault, co-author.
Jacqueline Briggs Martin, *Grandmother Bryant's Pocket*, 1996
  Grandmother's gift of an embroidered pocket filled with herbs helps Sarah overcome her fears.
Marilynn Reynolds, *The Prairie Fire*, 1999
  As a prairie fire threatens his family's homestead, Percy must conquer his fears in order to calm the livestock and douse errant sparks.

49

BARBARA BAKER
KATE DUKE, Illustrator

One Saturday Afternoon

(New York: Dutton Children's Books, 1999)

Series: Dutton Easy Reader
Subject(s): Family Life; Animals/Bears; Parent and Child
Age range(s): Grades 1-3
Major character(s): Papa, Bear, Father; Rose, Bear, Sister; Jack, Bear, Brother (younger)
Time period(s): Indeterminate
Locale(s): Fictional Country

Summary: In the sequel to *One Saturday Morning* each of six brief stories tell the activities of a particular family member. While Mama takes a quiet walk, Papa enlists the children's help to bake bread. Rose becomes upset when her older sister will not let her have a turn to be teacher when the four siblings play school. Young Jack ignores everyone else while focusing his attention on a red crayon that he alternately nibbles on or uses to color pictures on the walls. (48 pages)

Where it's reviewed:
Booklist, May 15, 1999, page 1704

Horn Book Guide, Fall 1999, page 272
Horn Book Guide, Fall 1999, page 272
Kirkus Reviews, June 15, 1999, page 960
School Library Journal, August 1999, page 124

Other books by the same author:
One Saturday Morning, 1995
Staying with Grandmother, 1994
Digby and Kate Again, 1989

Other books you might like:
Franz Brandenberg, *A Fun Weekend*, 1991
    A family of bears enjoys a weekend trip that includes ice cream, swimming and shopping.
Arnold Lobel, *Frog and Toad Together*, 1972
    This Newbery Honor book is one of four titles describing the adventures and misadventures of loyal friends Frog and Toad.
Else Minarik, *Father Bear Comes Home*, 1959
    When Father Bear returns from his fishing trip, the family has a picnic and tries to overcome the hiccups.
Marjorie Dennis Murray, *Saturday with Live Rabbit*, 1993
    Five brief chapters describe the activities of Little Rabbit and his friends Woodchuck and Raccoon.

50

LESLIE BAKER, Author/Illustrator

Paris Cat
(Boston: Little Brown and Company, 1999)

Subject(s): Animals/Cats; Lost and Found Possessions; Pets
Age range(s): Grades K-2
Major character(s): Alice, Cat; Annie, Child; Isabella, Aunt (great aunt)
Time period(s): 1990s
Locale(s): Paris, France

Summary: Just as Annie and Alice arrive at Great Aunt Isabella's home, Alice spots a mouse in the garden and dashes out an open door in pursuit. Annie races after her, but loses sight of her pet. After Alice loses the mouse she is unable to find Annie although she searches all over Paris. Finally, exhausted by her adventures, Alice falls asleep in a bed of flowers at a park and awakens surrounded by onlookers, including Annie and Great Aunt Isabella. (32 pages)

Where it's reviewed:
Booklist, May 1, 1999, page 1597
Horn Book Guide, Fall 1999, page 244
Publishers Weekly, May 3, 1999, page 76
School Library Journal, June 1999, page 85

Other books by the same author:
The Antique Store Cat, 1992
The Third-Story Cat, 1987

Other books you might like:
Ludwig Bemelmans, *Madeline's Rescue*, 1953
    When Madeline's rescuer, Genevieve vanishes, all the orphans help search the streets of Paris for the lost dog. Caldecott Medal winner.
Mary Calhoun, *Henry the Sailor Cat*, 1994
    Stowaway Henry proves to be a capable sailor who knows just what to do when Man falls overboard.

Tad Hardy, *Lost Cat*, 1996
    A rhyming tale describes the problems caused by a lost cat who wanders into a restaurant.
Tim Wynne-Jones, *Zoom at Sea*, 1993
    Zoom is a cat that likes water so much that he goes on a fantastic ocean adventure.

51

MOLLY BANG, Author/Illustrator

When Sophie Gets Angry—Really, Really Angry
(New York: The Blue Sky Press/Scholastic, Inc., 1999)

Subject(s): Anger; Problem Solving; Family
Age range(s): Grades K-2
Major character(s): Sophie, Child, Sister; Unnamed Character, Sister (Sophie's), Child; Gorilla, Toy
Time period(s): 1990s (1999)
Locale(s): United States

Summary: Sophie plays contentedly until her sister grabs Gorilla causing Sophie to fall over a truck. Sophie's mother agrees that it is her sister's turn to play with Gorilla and Sophie begins to seethe. Her tantrum explodes in a roar and she runs out of the house, slamming the door behind her. Sophie runs until her anger is spent and then she begins to cry. Gradually growing calmer, Sophie climbs her favorite tree and allows the branches and the view to soothe her before she returns home to the welcome of her family. (36 pages)

Where it's reviewed:
Booklist, February 1, 1999, page 978
Kirkus Reviews, December 15, 1998, page 1795
Publishers Weekly, January 18, 1999, page 337
Riverbank Review, Spring 1999, page 33
School Library Journal, January 1999, page 79

Awards the book has won:
Caldecott Honor Book, 2000
ALA Notable Children's Books, 2000

Other books by the same author:
Common Ground: The Water, Earth, and Air We Share, 1997 (Giverny Book Award)
Goose, 1996 (Horn Book Fanfare)
One Fall Day, 1994

Other books you might like:
Betsy Everitt, *Mean Soup*, 1992
    After a bad day, Horace helps his mother make Mean Soup and he begins to feel better.
Dorothea Lachner, *Andrew's Angry Words*, 1995
    When Andrew shouts angry words at his sister he learns just how far-ranging the impact of such an outburst can be.
Mercer Mayer, *I Was So Mad*, 1983
    A child tries different techniques to dissipate angry feelings.

52

KATE BANKS
TOMEK BOGACKI, Illustrator

The Bird, the Monkey, and the Snake in the Jungle

(New York: Frances Foster Books/Farrar, Straus and Giroux, 1999)

Subject(s): Animals; Trees; Dwellings
Age range(s): Grades K-3
Time period(s): Indeterminate
Locale(s): Fictional Country

Summary: Identified only by their pictures or rebus symbols, three animals share a tree home in the jungle. The monkey complains because the bird's singing wakes him, the snake complains because the monkey drops shells on him and the bird complains because the snake's nightly dancing is too noisy. When heavy rains cause their tree to fall over, the three animals search for separate trees to call home. Other creatures live in the first three trees they find so the bird, the monkey and the snake are forced to spend a scary night in the jungle without shelter. During the night, each animal comes to the aid of one of the others when a spider, a crocodile and a tiger threaten. In the morning they find a tree that is home to a cooperative frog that agrees to share with the bird, the monkey and the snake and they all live happily ever after without changing anything except their attitudes. (32 pages)

Where it's reviewed:
Booklist, March 1, 1999, page 1206
Horn Book Guide, Fall 1999, page 244
Kirkus Reviews, January 1, 1999, page 62
Publishers Weekly, March 8, 1999, page 67
School Library Journal, March 1999, page 162

Other books by the same author:
And If the Moon Could Talk, 1998 (Boston Globe/Horn Book Award)
Baboon, 1997 (Booklist Editors' Choice)
Spider Spider, 1996

Other books you might like:
Lynne Cherry, *The Great Kapok Tree: A Tale of the Amazon Rain Forest*, 1990
    A man changes his plans to cut down a kapok tree after he dreams about the animals that depend on the tree.
Libba Moore Gray, *Is There Room on the Feather Bed?*, 1997
    During a storm, the farm animals seek shelter in the teeny, tiny house of the wee fat woman and her wee fat husband.
Betsy Lewin, *Chubbo's Pool*, 1996
    When the pool he claims as his own dries up Chubbo realizes that he has been wrong to be so selfish.
Leo Lionni, *It's Mine!*, 1986
    Three selfish frogs argue about ownership of their pond and island until a storm threatens their safety and they begin to work together.
Bernard Waber, *Bearsie Bear and the Surprise Sleepover Party*, 1997
    On a cold winter night, Bearsie Bear's friends come knocking at the door asking to share his warm bed.

53

KATE BANKS
ISAAC MILLMAN, Illustrator

Howie Bowles and Uncle Sam

(New York: Frances Foster Books/Farrar Straus and Giroux, 2000)

Subject(s): Schools; Family Life; Humor
Age range(s): Grades 2-4
Major character(s): Howie Bowles, 3rd Grader, Brother (older); Toby, 3rd Grader, Friend; Mrs. Beagle, Teacher
Time period(s): 2000s (2000)
Locale(s): Connecticut

Summary: Howie is doomed! The very fact that he was born on Friday the 13th assures that he is the unluckiest person in the world and destined to a life of misfortune. Events seem to confirm Howie's idea—he loses his best marble, he's in trouble with Mrs. Beagle for not doing his math homework and he gets a letter from Uncle Sam advising that he could go to jail if he doesn't pay the $112.15 he owes. Howie doesn't remember having an Uncle Sam or borrowing money from him, but he now appreciates the emphasis his parents and teacher place on being careful with numbers. Afraid to tell his parents about his possible imprisonment Howie confides only in Toby who suggests applying for a bank loan. Before the payment deadline arrives, Howie's mother finds the form letter in his room and takes him to the IRS office. There they learn that the problem resulted from a social security number being written incorrectly. Once again, Howie is reminded of the importance of numbers—every single one—and he's relieved that his luck turned just in time. (85 pages)

Where it's reviewed:
Booklist, October 15, 2000, page 437
Horn Book Guide, Spring 2001, page 59
Kirkus Reviews, August 1, 2000, page 1112
Publishers Weekly, August 7, 2000, page 97
School Library Journal, December 2000, page 94

Other books by the same author:
Howie Bowles, Secret Agent, 1999
The Bunny Sitters, 1991

Other books you might like:
David A. Adler, *The Many Troubles of Andy Russell*, 1998
    Try as he might, Andy's plans seem to go awry and problems crop up everywhere for him.
Betsy Duffey, *Spotlight on Cody*, 1998
    Nothing goes right for Cody as he tries to find some "talent" to perform for the school's talent show.
Stephanie Greene, *Owen Foote, Second Grade Strongman*, 1996
    Owen's small stature doesn't prevent him from standing up for his friend.
Suzy Kline, *Herbie Jones*, 1985
    Herbie and his friend Raymond face the challenges of third grade with determination.

54

KATE BANKS
ISAAC MILLMAN, Illustrator

Howie Bowles, Secret Agent

(New York: Frances Foster Books/Farrar Straus Giroux, 1999)

Subject(s): Moving, Household; Schools; Identity
Age range(s): Grades 2-3
Major character(s): Howie Bowles, 3rd Grader; Mrs. Beagle, Teacher
Time period(s): 1990s (1999)
Locale(s): Washington (Palmer Elementary)

Summary: After two moves in one year, Howie doesn't seem to have the energy to adjust to one more new school. So, he becomes Secret Agent Bean Burger and suddenly other students are interested in befriending him. Then, Mrs. Beagle assigns him the task of determining who is putting chewing gum in the water fountains and Howie begins to lose sight of who he is. He also notices that his classmates like his secret agent persona, but don't really know him as Howie. After solving the case, Howie "retires" Secret Agent Bean Burger so he can find his own way in the classroom. (89 pages)

Where it's reviewed:
Booklist, December 15, 1999, page 784
Horn Book, November 1999, page 733
Publishers Weekly, October 25, 1999, page 81
School Library Journal, October 1999, page 102

Other books you might like:
Betsy Duffey, *Hey, New Kid!*, 1996
　　To impress classmates in his new school, Cody makes up interesting stories about his life and ends up creating problems for himself.
Patricia Reilly Giff, *Shark in School*, 1994
　　Matthew approaches a new school with memories of his friends at the Polk Street School and concerns about making new ones.
Johanna Hurwitz, *Roz and Ozzie*, 1992
　　Roz's adjustment to a new school is more complicated than she expected.
Susan Richards Shreve, *Zoe and Columbo*, 1995
　　When Zoe and Columbo enter a new school, Columbo feels insecure and left out so he embellishes the true story of his life.

55

KATE BANKS
GEORG HALLENSLEBEN, Illustrator

The Night Worker

(New York: Frances Foster Books/Farrar Straus Giroux, 2000)

Subject(s): Work; Construction; Fathers and Sons
Age range(s): Grades K-2
Major character(s): Alex, Son, Child; Papa, Father, Engineer
Time period(s): 2000s (2000)
Locale(s): United States

Summary: Most nights Papa says good night, dons his hard head and goes to work as Alex goes to sleep, but one night Papa has a hard hat for Alex, too and together they go out into the dark city streets. Papa points out some of the other night workers—police and street sweepers. When they reach the construction site Alex watches the machines digging an enormous hole in the ground for the building. Papa lifts Alex onto the seat of one machine and Alex helps dump dirt into a truck. When the work crew stops for a break, Papa takes Alex home to sleep and dream of being a night worker. (40 pages)

Where it's reviewed:
Booklist, August 2000, page 2134
Bulletin of the Center for Children's Books, July 2000, page 389
Horn Book Guide, Spring 2001, page 28
Publishers Weekly, June 26, 2000, page 74
School Library Journal, August 2000, page 144

Awards the book has won:
Booklist Editors' Choice, 2000
ALA Notable Children's Books, 2001

Other books by the same author:
And If the Moon Could Talk, 1998 (Boston Globe/Horn Book Award)
Baboon, 1997 (Booklist Editors' Choice)
Spider Spider, 1996

Other books you might like:
Karen Ackerman, *By the Dawn's Early Light*, 1994
　　Mom works the graveyard shift at a box factory, arriving home "by the dawn's early light."
Patricia Grossman, *The Night Ones*, 1991
　　On the night bus people who work while others sleep travel to their various jobs and return home on the morning bus.
Eileen Spinelli, *Night Shift Daddy*, 2000
　　A story in rhyme describes a tender ritual; Daddy tucks his daughter in bed before leaving for work and in the morning she does the same for him.

56

LYNNE REID BANKS

Alice-by-Accident

(New York: HarperCollins Publishers, 2000)

Subject(s): Single Parent Families; Mothers and Daughters; Grandmothers
Age range(s): Grades 4-6
Major character(s): Alice Elizabeth Williamson-Stone, 9-Year-Old, Daughter; Rita "Mum" Stone, Single Mother; Gene Williamson, Grandmother, Actress
Time period(s): 2000s (2000)
Locale(s): London, England

Summary: Alice knows that she's born "by accident" to her unmarried mother and, though she's never met her father, she enjoys knowing his mother Gene. In both her private journal and school essays, Alice uses creative writing to explore her feelings about Mum, her relationship with Gene and how she fits into this accidental family. Thanks to Gene, Alice enjoys private school, plays, and travel. Mum, though grateful, is also resentful of Gene and what she sees as attempts to direct Alice's life. Mum thinks Alice deserves the money Gene spends on her as compensation for the father's failure to voluntarily pay support. When Mum has a row with Gene that effectively ends her contact with Alice and then develops a chronic illness, Alice is frightened of being left alone and contacts Mum's estranged mother. Soon after Alice falls ill with meningitis and, while she struggles to live, Gene, her father and her other grandmother visit her in the hospital, beginning some reconciliation between her proud, stubborn Mum and the extended family Alice longs to know. (140 pages)

Where it's reviewed:
Booklist, June 2000, page 1890
Horn Book, May 2000, page 306
Kirkus Reviews, June 1, 2000, page 790
Publishers Weekly, June 19, 2000, page 80
School Library Journal, June 2000, page 138

Other books by the same author:
Maura's Angel, 1998
The Key to the Indian, 1998
Angela and Diabola, 1997 (IRA/CBC Children's Choices)
The Magic Hare, 1993
The Mystery of the Cupboard, 1993

Other books you might like:
Adele Griffin, *Split Just Right*, 1997
    Although Danny feels satisfied with her life with a single mom, she still fantasizes about the father she's never knows.
Patricia Hermes, *Someone to Count On*, 1993
    Sam, daughter of unconventional Elizabeth, experiences a brief period of stability while living with her grandfather who is someone she can count on.
Jacqueline Wilson, *Double Act*, 1998
    In a notebook twin sisters record their thoughts about unpopular changes in their single-parent family life.
June Rac Wood, *A Share of Freedom*, 1994
    Freedom tries to unlock the secrets of her past, including her father's identity.

57

SARA HARRELL BANKS

Abraham's Battle: A Novel of Gettysburg
(New York: Anne Schwartz/Atheneum Books for Young Readers, 1999)

Subject(s): American History; Civil War; African Americans
Age range(s): Grades 4-7
Major character(s): Abraham Small, Worker, Slave (former); Ladysmith Lightly, 10-Year-Old; Lamar Cooper, Military Personnel (Confederate Army), 16-Year-Old
Time period(s): 1860s (1863)
Locale(s): Gettysburg, Pennsylvania

Summary: Since his escape from slavery with the help of the Underground Railroad, Abraham has worked for Ladysmith's father. As troops gather in the Gettysburg area a chance encounter with Lamar, a poor farmer from Georgia who has never before seen a "colored" person, convinces Abraham that he must join the Union Army. With his mule, he offers his services as an ambulance driver and while searching for wounded after one of the battles finds Lamar. Fearful of crossing the Confederate lines, Abraham carries the severely

wounded youth to the Union field hospital for treatment. The book concludes with the dedication of the National Cemetery at which the Gettysburg Address was given. (88 pages)

Where it's reviewed:
Booklist, March 1, 1999, page 1214
Kirkus Reviews, February 15, 1999, page 296
Publishers Weekly, March 22, 1999, page 93
School Library Journal, July 1999, page 92

Other books by the same author:
Under the Shadow of Wings, 1997
Remember My Name, 1993
Tomo-Chi Chi: Gentle Warrior, 1993

Other books you might like:
Paul Fleischman, *Bull Run*, 1993
    Sixteen characters offer their accounts of the Civil War, from its beginning to the first battle of Bull Run.
Patricia Polacco, *Pink and Say*, 1994
    The senseless tragedy of war is eloquently portrayed through the brief friendship of two young Union soldiers, one a former slave.
G. Clifton Wisler, *Mr. Lincoln's Drummer*, 1994
    Willie's service as a drummer boy in the Union Army is rewarded when he meets President Lincoln.

58

LYNNE BARASCH, Author/Illustrator

Radio Rescue
(New York: Frances Foster Books/Farrar Straus Giroux, 2000)

Subject(s): Radio; Communication; Perseverance
Age range(s): Grades 2-5
Major character(s): Robert Marx, 10-Year-Old; Bill Irwin, Teenager
Time period(s): 1920s (1923-1926)
Locale(s): New York, New York

Summary: Fascinated by wireless radio communication, Robert is eager to master Morse code so he can acquire his ham radio license. Until he passes the test, Robert is able to listen to the transmissions of others and so learns of an operator who lives near his apartment. Bill encourages Robert and, when Robert passes the licensing test, Bill helps him purchase the materials to build his radio. Robert's skill increases and, by the time he's twelve, while monitoring reports from Florida following a hurricane he is able to notify the Coast Guard of a family in need of rescue. An Author's Note gives the historical basis for the story based on the life experience of her father. (40 pages)

Where it's reviewed:
Booklist, September 15, 2000, page 239
Horn Book, September 2000, page 546
Publishers Weekly, October 16, 2000, page 76
School Library Journal, October 2000, page 110
Smithsonian Magazine, November 2000, page 68

Awards the book has won:
School Library Journal Best Books, 2000
Smithsonian's Notable Books for Children, 2000

Other books by the same author:
Reluctant Flower Girl, 2001
Old Friends, 1998
A Winter Walk, 1993
Rodney's Inside Story, 1992

Other books you might like:
Louise Borden, *Good-bye, Charles Lindbergh: Based on a True Story*, 1998
  In 1929 young Gil meets Charles Lindbergh when he lands his plane in a neighbor's field.
Sara Hoagland Hunter, *The Unbreakable Code*, 1996
  Grandfather tells John of his work during World War II when the Navajo used their language to develop a code the enemy could not decipher.
Mary Kay Kroeger, *Paperboy*, 1996
  Willie earns extra money for his large family by selling papers on the Cincinnati streets in 1927. Louise Borden, co-author.
Martin Schwartz, *Mastering the Morse Code*, 1987
  A nonfiction title gives specific information about Morse code and how to learn it.

59

SUSAN BARTLETT
TRICIA TUSA, Illustrator

Seal Island School
(New York: Viking, 1999)

Subject(s): Teachers; Schools; Islands
Age range(s): Grades 2-4
Major character(s): Miss Sparling, Teacher; Pru Stanley, 3rd Grader, Friend; Nicholas Lansing-Ross, 4th Grader, Friend
Time period(s): 1990s (1999)
Locale(s): Seal Island, Maine

Summary: Each year a different teacher comes to the small one-room schoolhouse on Pru's island home. This year, Pru hopes that Miss Sparling will like it enough to stay because she's the best teacher Pru's ever had. To surprise their teacher, Pru and Nicholas secretly save money to purchase a dog when they learn she's looking for a Newfoundland as a companion. The six children in the school also begin a correspondence with a girl on the mainland after Pru finds a bottle on the shore with a note inside. By the end of the school year, it's Pru who finds herself surprised, but happy at changes on the island. (69 pages)

Where it's reviewed:
Horn Book Guide, Fall 1999, page 276
Kirkus Reviews, February 15, 1999, page 296
Publishers Weekly, February 22, 1999, page 95
School Library Journal, May 1999, page 85

Other books you might like:
Paula Danziger, *Amber Brown Is Not a Crayon*, 1994
  Third Grade is a confusing and sad time for Amber because her best friend is moving.
Suzy Kline, *Mary Marony and the Chocolate Surprise*, 1995
  Eager to win a special pizza lunch with the teacher, Mary

manipulates the contest outcome and is stuck with a guilty conscience.
Maud Hart Lovelace, *Betsy-Tacy and Tib*, 1941
  Best friends Betsy and Tacy invite Tib to join them for more fun.
Janice Lee Smith, *The Kid Next Door and Other Headaches: Stories about Adam Joshua*, 1984
  Adam Joshua does not agree with the kid next door about many things, but they are able to remain friends.

60

FRANCINE BASSEDE, Author/Illustrator

A Day with the Bellyflops
(New York: Orchard Books, 2000)

Subject(s): Animals/Pigs; Working Mothers; Brothers and Sisters
Age range(s): Grades K-2
Major character(s): Lilly Bellyflop, Pig, Sister; Wiggly Bellyflop, Pig, Sister; Peter Bellyflop, Pig, Brother; Mrs. Bellyflop, Pig, Mother
Time period(s): Indeterminate
Locale(s): Fictional Country

Summary: Mrs. Bellyflop settles into her new "at-home" office in the refurbished tool shed in the garden to complete only two hours work. Lilly, Peter and Wiggly promise to play quietly while their mother works so she'll have time to make apple pie with them later. After a few minutes of play Lilly interrupts Mrs. Bellyflop's work to complain about Peter and Wiggly playing with the hose and messing up her tutu. Then Peter eats all the apples they were saving for the pie and Wiggly dives into the mud so all the children need a bath. By the time the day is over and the children are sleeping Mrs. Bellyflop still has two hours of work to do in her new office. Originally published in Great Britain in 1998. (28 pages)

Where it's reviewed:
Children's Bookwatch, May 2000, page 5
Horn Book Guide, Fall 2000, page 261
Kirkus Reviews, March 1, 2000, page 298
Publishers Weekly, March 20, 2000, page 91
School Library Journal, March 2000, page 178

Other books by the same author:
George Paints His House, 1999
George's Store at the Shore, 1998

Other books you might like:
Arthur Geisert, *Oink, Oink*, 1993
  Illustrations and the repetition of one word tell the story of eight piglets who wander away from their sleeping mother.
David McPhail, *Pigs Aplenty, Pigs Galore*, 1993
  A man's plans for a quiet evening change when uninvited pigs arrive, order pizza and make a mess of his home.
Jill Murphy, *A Quiet Night In*, 1994
  Parents' plans for an evening free of children fail when the bedtime story they read the children puts the parents and not the children to sleep.

61

FRANCINE BASSEDE, Author/Illustrator
DOMINIC BARTH, Translator

George Paints His House

(New York: Orchard Books, 1999)

Subject(s): Animals; Housing; Dwellings
Age range(s): Grades K-1
Major character(s): George, Duck, Friend; Mary, Cat, Friend
Time period(s): Indeterminate
Locale(s): Fictional Country

Summary: Mary agrees to help George paint his house but first he must choose a color. Nearby animals have opinions to share. The lizard prefers yellow while a ladybug thinks red is best. The bluebird definitely agrees with blue but the butterfly thinks purple is the way to go. Mary likes orange to match her fur but George recalls that she also likes the color pink. The horse thinks white and the bull demands black but the magpie thinks both colors should be used. The frog is happy when George and Mary agree on green. To thank the others for their help, they have a party with foods in all the colors they considered. (24 pages)

Where it's reviewed:
Booklist, February 15, 1999, page 1074
Horn Book Guide, Fall 1999, page 229
Kirkus Reviews, January 15, 1999, page 142
Publishers Weekly, February 1, 1999, page 83
School Library Journal, June 1999, page 91

Other books by the same author:
A Day with the Bellyflops, 2000
George's Store at the Shore, 1998

Other books you might like:
Bill Martin Jr., *Brown Bear, Brown Bear, What Do You See?*, 1967
   The rhyme and repetition in this color concept book make it a favorite read-aloud.
David McPhail, *Big Brown Bear*, 1999
   While painting Big Brown Bear and the ladder on which he's standing are accidentally knocked over and he becomes covered in blue paint.
Daniel Pinkwater, *The Big Orange Splot*, 1977
   One can of orange paint dropped by a seagull onto the roof of Mr. Plumbean's neat house inspires an idea that changes the neighborhood.

62

IVAN BATES, Author/Illustrator

All by Myself

(New York: HarperCollins Publishers, 2000)

Subject(s): Animals/Elephants; Mothers and Daughters; Independence
Age range(s): Grades K-1
Major character(s): Maya, Elephant, Daughter; Unnamed Character, Mother, Elephant
Time period(s): 1999
Locale(s): Earth

Summary: With stubborn determination Maya attempts to change the morning routine she and her mother follow. Maya refuses to allow her mother to pick leaves from the tree for breakfast, insisting that she can do it without help. Patiently, her mother watches as Maya tries to knock the leaves off with a stick, blast them off with water from her trunk, and shake them off by head-butting the tree. Each failed attempt attracts the attention of another forest animal that offers to help, but Maya is no more willing to accept help from a lion, a bird and a snake than she is from her mother. Finally, Maya's mother offers a suggestion that Maya agrees to and she picks the juicy leaves—all by herself. This first book for the children's book illustrator was originally published in England. (32 pages)

Where it's reviewed:
Booklist, April 1, 2000, page 1466
Horn Book Guide, Fall 2000, page 245
Kirkus Reviews, December 1, 1999, page 1880
Publishers Weekly, January 3, 2000, page 74

Other books you might like:
Syd Hoff, *Bernard on His Own*, 1993
   Bernard's parents assure him that one day he'll be able to climb a tree, catch a fish and gather honey on his own.
Arnold Lobel, *Owl at Home*, 1975
   Owl likes to be helpful; unfortunately his attempts are not always successful.
Jan Wahl, *Little Gray One*, 1993
   On the African plain, under the guidance of his loving mother, Little Gray One learns how to find water and to choose the sweetest plums.

63

GWENDOLYN BATTLE-LAVERT
COLIN BOOTMAN, Illustrator

The Music in Derrick's Heart

(New York: Holiday House, 2000)

Subject(s): Music and Musicians; African Americans; Aunts and Uncles
Age range(s): Grades K-3
Major character(s): Derrick, Child; Booker T., Musician, Aged Person
Time period(s): 1990s
Locale(s): United States

Summary: With the beginning of summer vacation Derrick eagerly awaits the arrival of Uncle Booker T. who has promised to teach him how to play the harmonica. During the daily lessons the duo travel about the neighborhood visiting relatives as Uncle Booker T. plays the genre of music each one requests. Every evening Derrick practices, but his progress does not satisfy the impatient pupil. Uncle Booker T. reminds him that he needs to go slowly, waiting for the music to be in his heart for a true musician depends on more than skill. Derrick tries many strategies including taping the harmonica to his heart as he sleeps, but the final test comes on the first cool morning of fall when Uncle Booker T. does not appear for the daily lesson. Derrick finds him with hands too crippled by arthritis to play. Derrick puts his heart into a tune, finally understanding the wisdom of his uncle's instruction as the soothing music moves Uncle Booker T. to relinquish the harmonica to Derrick to carry on the tradition. (32 pages)

Where it's reviewed:
Booklist, February 15, 2000, page 1104
Five Owls, March 2000, page 97
Publishers Weekly, January 24, 2000, page 310
School Library Journal, March 2000, page 178

Other books by the same author:
The Shaking Bag, 2000
Off to School, 1995
The Barber's Cutting Edge, 1994

Other books you might like:
Mary Brigid Barrett, *Sing to the Stars*, 1994
   A young violinist and a blind pianist perform at a neighborhood concert in the park.
Gavin Curtis, *The Bat Boy & His Violin*, 1998
   Papa, manager of a Negro League baseball team, develops an appreciation for his son's musical talent when he drafts Reginald as the team's batboy.
Alice Faye Duncan, *Willie Jerome*, 1995
   On his beloved trumpet, Willie Jerome plays "red hot bebop" from the apartment house roof.
Libba Moore Gray, *Little Lil and the Swing-Singing Sax*, 1996
   When her uncle pawns his sax to buy medicine for her sick mother, Little Lil knows she must get it back so her mother can hear the healing music.
Brian Pinkney, *Max Found Two Sticks*, 1994
   With two twigs as drumsticks, Max uses every available surface as a drum, tapping out the rhythms of the city.

64

MARION DANE BAUER

An Early Winter

(New York: Clarion Books, 1999)

Subject(s): Old Age; Grandfathers; Fishing
Age range(s): Grades 4-7
Major character(s): Leo "Granddad" Palmer, Grandfather, Veterinarian (retired); Timothy Palmer, 11-Year-Old; Paul, Construction Worker, Stepfather
Time period(s): 1990s (1999)
Locale(s): Sheldon, Wisconsin

Summary: Timothy thought it was a good idea for his mother to marry Paul, but he didn't realize it would mean moving away from Sheldon. Now that they are returning for a visit, Timothy is sure that Granddad will be all right. He hears the grown-ups talking about Alzheimer's disease, but he knows Granddad is just feeling sad because Timothy's been gone. In his determination to protect Granddad and prove to everyone that Granddad is fine, Timothy secretly plans a fishing trip to their favorite lake that endangers both of them. Although Granddad's mental confusion is frightening to Timothy, his conversation about past events answers some questions Timothy has had for a long time. (120 pages)

Where it's reviewed:
Booklist, December 1, 1999, page 703
Bulletin of the Center for Children's Books, October 1999, page 46

Kirkus Reviews, July 1, 1999, page 1050
Publishers Weekly, August 23, 1999
School Library Journal, October 1999, page 144

Other books by the same author:
A Question of Trust, 1994
A Taste of Smoke, 1993
On My Honor, 1986 (Newbery Honor Book)

Other books you might like:
Carolyn J. Gold, *Dragonfly Secret*, 1997
   Although Gramps is growing older, Nathan and Jessie do not agree with Aunt Louise's idea to put him in a nursing home.
Richard Graber, *Doc*, 1986
   It is difficult for Brad to accept the fact that his beloved grandfather, once a successful doctor, is suffering from Alzheimer's.
Jerry Spinelli, *Crash*, 1996
   After his beloved grandfather suffers a stroke, Crash begins to reconsider his priorities and the way he acts toward others.
Carol Lynch Williams, *If I Forget, You Remember*, 1998
   Elyse and her sister Jordan learn to adjust to life with an Alzheimer's victim when Granny moves into their home.

65

MARION DANE BAUER
JO ELLEN MCALLISTER STAMMEN, Illustrator

Sleep, Little One, Sleep

(New York: Simon & Schuster Books for Young Readers, 1999)

Subject(s): Bedtime; Sleep; Animals
Age range(s): Preschool
Major character(s): Unnamed Character, Father; Unnamed Character, Daughter
Time period(s): 1990s (1999)
Locale(s): United States

Summary: A father compares the preparations for sleep to the cradle spun by a spider and the feathery wings of a mother bird enveloping its young in warmth and safety. The father assures his daughter that, with patient waiting, sleep will come to cuddle her as if it were a wooly lamb. Sleep does come, first to the father dozing in the rocking chair, and finally to the daughter snug in her bed, dreaming. (32 pages)

Where it's reviewed:
Booklist, August 1999, page 2062
Horn Book Guide, Spring 2000, page 12
Publishers Weekly, August 23, 1999, page 56
School Library Journal, September 1999, page 174

Other books by the same author:
Bear's Hiccups, 1998
If You Were Born a Kitten, 1997
When I Go Camping with Grandma, 1995

Other books you might like:
Kathi Appelt, *Bayou Lullaby*, 1997
   A rhyming lullaby about the animals of the bayou soothes a little girl at bedtime.

Kate Banks, *And If the Moon Could Talk*, 1998
  Following a bedtime ritual with her parents a child, wrapped in love, sleeps while the silent moon watches over all.
Margaret Wise Brown, *Little Donkey Close Your Eyes*, 1995
  Animals throughout the world are bid good night in this gentle poem.
Mem Fox, *Time for Bed*, 1993
  Mothers all over the world are putting their kittens, lambs, fawns and children to sleep.
Mirra Ginsburg, *Asleep, Asleep*, 1992
  Animals are quietly bid good night until only the sleepy child and the wind are awake.

66

STEVEN BAUER
BRAD SNEED, Illustrator

The Strange and Wonderful Tale of Robert McDoodle: The Boy Who Wanted to Be a Dog

(New York: Simon & Schuster Books for Young Readers, 1999)

Subject(s): Animals/Dogs; Stories in Rhyme; Self-Acceptance
Age range(s): Grades K-3
Major character(s): Robert McDoodle, 6-Year-Old
Time period(s): 1990s (1999)
Locale(s): United States (Jellicoe Dog School)

Summary: As Robert's sixth birthday approaches he bemoans the fact that a boring, human life in school lies ahead of him. What Robert longs to become when he grows up is a dog and so he runs away from home and finds the Jellicoe Dog School. After rigorous training in digging, scratching and drinking from bowls, Robert decides that dogs don't have as easy a life as he originally thought. Before he can escape and return to his life as Robert McDoodle, the dogs lead him to a surprise birthday party where his parents wait to drive him—and his puppy—home. This is the first children's book for this author of adult novels. (32 pages)

Where it's reviewed:
Booklist, September 1, 1999, page 137
Horn Book Guide, Spring 2000, page 28
Kirkus Reviews, September 1, 1999, page 1424
Publishers Weekly, September 13, 1999, page 82
School Library Journal, October 1999, page 102

Other books you might like:
Betsy Byars, *Ant Plays Bear*, 1997
  Ant annoys his older brother when he insists on pretending to be a dog.
Jane Cutler, *No Dogs Allowed*, 1992
  Allergies prevent two brothers from having pets so 5-year-old Edward decides to ''become'' a dog.
Carol Diggory Shields, *I Wish My Brother Was a Dog*, 1997
  A young boy imagines how much better life would be if only the new baby was his pet dog and not his little brother.

67

DARLEEN BAILEY BEARD
NANCY CARPENTER, Illustrator

Twister

(New York: Farrar Straus Giroux, 1999)

Subject(s): Weather; Fear; Brothers and Sisters
Age range(s): Grades K-3
Major character(s): Lucille, Sister; Natt, Brother
Time period(s): Indeterminate
Locale(s): United States

Summary: Lucille and Natt are spending a relaxing summer day on their front porch swing, eating orange popsicles and pretending to be royalty. Suddenly, the weather changes and Natt, Lucille, and their mother realize that a tornado is coming so they hurry to the storm cellar. Once Natt and Lucille are safely inside, their mother goes to help an elderly neighbor. The children are scared when their mother does not return, but after the tornado passes, they find their mother and the neighbor are unharmed. (32 pages)

Where it's reviewed:
Booklist, February 1, 1999, page 979
Kirkus Reviews, January 15, 1999, page 142
Publishers Weekly, March 22, 1999, page 92
Riverbank Review, Fall 1999, page 33
School Library Journal, March 1999, page 162

Other books by the same author:
The Flimflam Man, 1998
The Pumpkin Man from Piney Creek, 1995

Other books you might like:
Georgia Graham, *The Strongest Man This Side of Cremona*, 1998
  Matthew and his dad head for shelter when a tornado hits.
Marc Harshman, *The Storm*, 1995
  When he faces a tornado alone, Jonathan finds the courage to save himself and the family's animals.
Stephen Kramer, *Tornado*, 1992
  This nonfiction book explains how tornadoes are formed and how to stay safe when one hits.
Jonathan London, *Hurricane!*, 1998
  A young boy and his family go to a community shelter when a hurricane hits their home in Puerto Rico.

68

LISZE BECHTOLD, Author/Illustrator

Buster: The Very Shy Dog

(Boston: Houghton Mifflin Company, 1999)

Subject(s): Animals/Dogs; Shyness; Pets
Age range(s): Grades 1-3
Major character(s): Buster, Dog (younger); Phoebe, Dog (older); Roger, Child
Time period(s): 1990s (1999)
Locale(s): United States

Summary: In the author's first book, three stories introduce Buster, a shy puppy who grows into a shy dog in the shadow of outgoing, talented Phoebe. Buster demonstrates his sensitivity by befriending an equally shy guest at Roger's birthday party. In the second story, Buster finds his true talent of listening when his acute hearing locates Roger's lost hamster. While trying to catch the animals raiding the garbage cans, Buster's good hearing, but not too good eyesight put him in the line of fire from a skunk. Finally, the two pets agree to cooperate and with Phoebe's good vision and Buster's hearing they catch the three guilty raccoons with their paws in the garbage cans. (48 pages)

Where it's reviewed:
Booklist, May 15, 1999, page 1704
Horn Book, July 1999, page 462
Kirkus Reviews, February 15, 1999, page 297
Publishers Weekly, January 18, 1999, page 339
School Library Journal, May 1999, page 85

Other books you might like:
Janice Boland, *A Dog Named Sam*, 1996
    Sam's enthusiasm for fetching, water play and nighttime activity create problems for his family.
Patricia Reilly Giff, *Good Luck, Ronald Morgan!*, 1996
    Ronald Morgan's attempts to train his new dog are complicated when a girl with a pet cat moves in next door.
Megan McDonald, *Beezy Magic*, 1998
    In the second book in a series for beginning readers Beezy's dog, who is not shy at all, tries to join a class field trip.
Sara Swan Miller, *Three Stories You Can Read to Your Dog*, 1995
    This read-aloud for dogs includes three short stories about typical dog antics such as digging, barking and sleeping.
Cynthia Rylant, *The Henry and Mudge Series*, 1987-
    The adventures of Henry and his lovable, slobbery dog Mudge entertain beginning readers.

69

ANDREA BECK, Author/Illustrator

Elliot Bakes a Cake

(Buffalo, NY: Kids Can Press, 1999)

Series: Elliot Moose Story
Subject(s): Cooks and Cooking; Birthdays; Surprises
Age range(s): Grades K-1
Major character(s): Elliott Moose, Moose, Stuffed Animal; Socks, Stuffed Animal, Friend (Elliott's); Lionel, Lion, Stuffed Animal
Time period(s): 1990s (1999)
Locale(s): Canada

Summary: Elliot gathers Socks and other friends to bake a surprise birthday cake for Lionel. Lacking experience, the friends have some difficulty following the recipe's directions to separate the eggs and cream the butter, but finally they produce a batter to bake. Now they wait for the cake to spontaneously "spring" back and indicate that it is done. The cake becomes overcooked and black as they wait but Elliot comes up with a plan that saves the day. Lionel is surprised to receive the small, but beautifully decorated cake and happily shares it with his friends. (32 pages)

Where it's reviewed:
Booklist, October 1, 1999, page 360
Horn Book Guide, Spring 2000, page 28
Publishers Weekly, September 20, 1999, page 89
Quill & Quire, July 1999, page 51
School Library Journal, December 1999, page 87

Other books by the same author:
Elliot's Shipwreck, 2000 (Elliot Moose Story)
Elliot's Emergency, 1998 (Elliot Moose Story)

Other books you might like:
Eileen Christelow, *Don't Wake Up Mama!*, 1992
    Five little monkeys are trying to quietly bake a surprise birthday cake for Mama before she awakens.
Cynthia Rylant, *Mr. Putter and Tabby Bake the Cake*, 1994
    Neither inexperience or a lack of cake pans will deter Mr. Putter from his plan to bake a light and airy cake for his neighbor's Christmas present.
Janet Stevens, *Cook-a-Doodle-Doo!*, 1999
    Not all of Big Brown Rooster's friends are willing to help make strawberry shortcake and the ones that volunteer have no experience in the kitchen.
Rosemary Wells, *Bunny Cakes*, 1997
    Max and Ruby, as usual, have different ideas about the kind of cake to bake for Grandma's birthday and Max is determined to have his way.

70

ANN KEAY BENEDUCE
GENNADY SPIRIN, Illustrator

Jack and the Beanstalk

(New York: Philomel Books, 1999)

Subject(s): Folklore; Fairy Tales; Giants
Age range(s): Grades 1-4
Major character(s): Jack, Child, Son; Mother, Mother, Widow(er)
Time period(s): Indeterminate Past
Locale(s): England; Fictional Country

Summary: When Jack learns that there is no food in the house he decides to sell the family's cow. Mother is so unhappy when Jack returns home with the ten "magic" bean seeds he received as payment that she throws the seed out the cottage window. By morning the bean seeds have grown so high their tops are lost in the clouds and curious Jack decides to climb them. At the top he meets a fairy that explains that he is in the land of a giant who killed Jack's father and stole his wealth. Jack manages to get into the giant's home not once, but three times and each time he steals gold or treasures to provide for his mother. On the third trip, the giant chases him, but Jack descends the beanstalk first and chops it down, causing the giant to plummet to the ground. A concluding author's note gives background to the story and the oral legend on which it is based. (32 pages)

Where it's reviewed:
Booklist, November 1, 1999, page 532
Horn Book Guide, Spring 2000, page 109
Kirkus Reviews, October 1, 1999, page 1574
Publishers Weekly, November 1, 1999, page 83

School Library Journal, November 1999, page 134

Other books by the same author:
Snow White and Rose Red, 1997
Gulliver's Adventures in Lilliput, 1996
The Tempest, 1996

Other books you might like:
Susan Cooper, *The Silver Cow: A Welsh Tale*, 1991
   The magic people reward a boy's harp playing with a silver cow and then seek revenge against the boy's greedy father.
Steven Kellogg, *Jack and the Beanstalk*, 1991
   In one of many retellings of the 1889 English tale, Jack outsmarts the giant and his wife in order to save himself and provide for his mother.
Fiona Moodie, *The Boy and the Giants*, 1993
   Kind Thomas rescues his beloved Kate from the giant who kidnaps her with help from the many animals he's befriended in the past.

71

CHERIE BENNETT

Zink
(New York: Delacorte Press, 1999)

Subject(s): Cancer; Self-Perception; Antebellum South
Age range(s): Grades 5-7
Major character(s): Becky Zaslow, 6th Grader, Cancer Patient; Zink, Zebra (imaginary)
Time period(s): 1990s
Locale(s): United States; Serengeti National Park, Tanzania

Summary: At the culminating activity for her middle school's study of Tanzania, Becky faints. Thus begins her first hospital stay, the diagnosis of leukemia and chemotherapy treatments. Becky compares her battle against the leukemia to wild animals protecting themselves against predators. During her first treatment three zebras, visible and audible only to Becky, visit her to offer comfort and to take her on an adventure to the Serengeti. While visiting the herd she hears the story of Zink, an unusual zebra covered in polka dots rather than stripes. During their visits to Becky the zebras make suggestions to help her cope with her illness. An afterword gives factual information about acute lymphocytic leukemia and its treatment. (230 pages)

Where it's reviewed:
Booklist, August 1999, page 2058
Bulletin of the Center for Children's Books, November 1999, page 83
Kirkus Reviews, October 15, 1999, page 1639
Publishers Weekly, October 25, 1999, page 81
School Library Journal, February 2000, page 117

Other books by the same author:
Life in the Fat Lane, 1998
Searching for David's Heart: A Christmas Story, 1998
The Accident, 1996

Other books you might like:
Virginia Hamilton, *Bluish*, 1999
   Dreenie reaches out to the frail student in the wheelchair who is known for the blue cast to her skin and the knit cap on her head.

Kathryn Lance, *Going to See Grassy Ella*, 1993
   Determined to take control of her cancer treatment, Peej travels from Ohio to New York to meet a psychic healer.
Lurlene McDaniel, *Too Young to Die*, 1991
   Melissa accepts the fact that she has leukemia.
Sally Warner, *Sort of Forever*, 1998
   Nana's diagnosis of leukemia makes Cady wonder how long the best friends will be together.

72

EDNA COE BERCAW
ROBERT HUNT, Illustrator

Halmoni's Day
(New York: Dial Books for Young Readers, 2000)

Subject(s): Grandmothers; Korean Americans; Schools
Age range(s): Grades 1-3
Major character(s): Jennifer, Student—Elementary School, Daughter; Halmoni, Grandmother; Mom, Mother (Jennifer's), Daughter (Halmoni's)
Time period(s): 2000s (2000)
Locale(s): United States

Summary: Halmoni's first visit in four years coincides with Grandparent's Day in Jennifer's class and Jennifer wonders what will happen when Halmoni, in her native dress, comes to the classroom. Because Halmoni cannot speak English Mom also comes to translate the afternoon's activities. As each grandparent receives an award prepared by their grandchild they also share a story with the class. Halmoni's story touches Jennifer's heart and makes her realize that, although her language and dress is different, this day is truly Halmoni's. (32 pages)

Where it's reviewed:
Booklist, November 1, 2000, page 545
Horn Book Guide, Spring 2001, page 29
Kirkus Reviews, July 1, 2000, page 954
School Library Journal, August 2000, page 144
Tribune Books, October 8, 2000, page 4

Awards the book has won:
Notable Social Studies Trade Books for Young People, 2001

Other books you might like:
Sook Nyul Choi, *Halmoni and the Picnic*, 1993
   Yunmi worries about the students' reaction to the traditional Korean food Halmoni prepares for the class picnic.
Yumi Heo, *Father's Rubber Shoes*, 1995
   As a recent immigrant, Yungsu is lonely for his friends in Korea and hopeful of adjusting to a new country.
Frances Park, *My Freedom Trip: A Child's Escape from North Korea*, 1998
   A biographical picture book describes young Soo's nighttime escape from North Korea to South Korea and freedom. Ginger Park, co-author.

73

CARMEN T. BERNIER-GRAND

In the Shade of the Nispero Tree

(New York: Orchard Books, 1999)

Subject(s): Prejudice; Friendship; Schools
Age range(s): Grades 4-6
Major character(s): Teresa Giraux, 4th Grader, Friend; Ana, 4th Grader, Friend; Mami, Mother (Teresa's), Seamstress
Time period(s): 1960s (1961)
Locale(s): Ponce, Puerto Rico

Summary: The friendship between Teresa and Ana that began in first grade is threatened when Mami, seeking higher social status, insists that her daughter take advantage of a scholarship and attend a private school. For the first time Teresa becomes aware of the color of people's skin and realizes that Mami does not like Ana because her skin is so dark. Despite her father's objections, Teresa acquiesces to Mami's ambitions. Her brief experience at the private school subjects Teresa and Mami to discrimination from the wealthier, privileged families whose children attend the school and then Mami and Teresa realize how hurtful their treatment of Ana and her family has been. This is the first children's novel written by this author of adult fiction. (186 pages)

Where it's reviewed:
Booklist, April 1, 1999, page 1412
Horn Book Guide, Fall 1999, page 288
Kirkus Reviews, February 15, 1999, page 297
Publishers Weekly, March 15, 1999, page 59
School Library Journal, March 1999, page 206

Awards the book has won:
Smithsonian's Notable Books for Children, 1999

Other books you might like:
Alma Flor Ada, *My Name Is Maria Isabel*, 1993
    When Maria's family moves to a ''better'' neighborhood, Maria misses her many friends.
Vaunda Micheaux Nelson, *Mayfield Crossing*, 1993
    When the children of Mayfield Crossing are sent to larger Parkview Elementary they are treated as outsiders and judged by the color of their skin.
Vicki Winslow, *Follow the Leader*, 1997
    Jackie and Amanda's friendship suffers when Jackie's parents enroll her in a segregated private school rather than the newly integrated public school.
Ronder Thomas Young, *Learning by Heart*, 1993
    In the 1960s Rachel becomes aware of racial prejudices and their impact on friendships in her small southern town.

74

MARGERY BERNSTEIN
DOROTHY HANDELMAN, Illustrator

My Brother, the Pest

(Brookfield, CT: The Millbrook Press, 1999)

Series: Real Kids Readers. Level 2
Subject(s): Sibling Rivalry; Playing; Stories in Rhyme
Age range(s): Grades K-2
Major character(s): Unnamed Character, Sister (older); Unnamed Character, Brother (younger)
Time period(s): 1990s (1999)
Locale(s): United States

Summary: A young girl complains about her pesky little brother who takes her markers, draws in her book and suffers no consequences because of his youth. While she pouts and ponders how horrid he is, the little brother enters the room with a stack of books and a request that she read to him. The positive interaction and the brother's willingness to play student to her teacher lead to begrudging admittance that he may not be so bad after all. (32 pages)

Where it's reviewed:
Booklist, May 15, 1999, page 1704
School Library Journal, August 1999, page 124

Other books by the same author:
That Cat!, 1998 (Real Kids Readers, Level 2)

Other books you might like:
Martha Alexander, *Nobody Asked Me If I Wanted a Baby Sister*, 1977
    Despite the fact that too much attention is paid to his baby sister, a little boy reluctantly admits to feeling some affection for her.
Angela Johnson, *Do Like Kyla*, 1990
    Kyla's younger sister follows her all day, imitating every behavior.
Holly Keller, *Geraldine First*, 1996
    Big sister Geraldine is annoyed by Willie's copycat ways, until she thinks of something he will not imitate.
Rosemary Wells, *Max's Dragon Shirt*, 1991
    While shopping, Max becomes separated (accidentally?) from bossy big sister Ruby and her control.

75

CARI BEST
DIANE PALMISCIANO, Illustrator

Last Licks: A Spaldeen Story

(New York: DK Ink/DK Publishing, Inc., 1999)

Subject(s): Playing; Neighbors and Neighborhoods; Games
Age range(s): Grades 1-4
Major character(s): Annie Ellis, Child, Neighbor; Miss Hatchett, Teacher; S. Paul ''Super'' Dean, Manager (super of Sycamore Gardens)
Time period(s): Indeterminate Past
Locale(s): New York, New York (Queens)

Summary: The allure of Annie's lucky Sky-High Super Pinkie is so great that she cannot resist the urge to throw the ball at the blackboard while Miss Hatchett is writing spelling words on the board. Miss Hatchett gives Annie a warning and a note to her parents, but Annie is happy to still have the ball she loves so much that she sleeps with it in her pocket. Although the lucky ball has been lost many times, she's always found it. Her friends are not as lucky. The super collects the balls that hit his window and displays them in his collection. By Sunday only Annie has a ball for the weekly punchball game. Annie willingly shares the soft rubber ball for everyone to enjoy the sport until the call to dinner signals the end of the game. Then

Annie gets off one last punch, sending the ball high over everyone's heads in the most fantastic punch ever seen in the neighborhood. (32 pages)

Where it's reviewed:
Booklist, May 1, 1999, page 1598
Bulletin of the Center for Children's Books, May 1999, page 308
Horn Book Guide, Fall 1999, page 245
Publishers Weekly, January 25, 1999, page 95
School Library Journal, May 1999, page 85

Other books by the same author:
Getting Used to Harry, 1996
Red Light, Green Light, Mama and Me, 1995
Taxi! Taxi!, 1994 (Ezra Jack Keats Award)

Other books you might like:
Dale Gottlieb, *My Stories by Hildy Calpurnia Rose*, 1991
    In her diary, Brooklynite Hildy records the details of life in her apartment building.
Eloise Greenfield, *Night on Neighborhood Street*, 1991
    The joys of an inner city neighborhood come to life in poems depicting the feelings of the people as well as the sights and sounds of the environment.
Amy Hest, *How to Get Famous in Brooklyn*, 1995
    A sudden wind blows Janie's notebook pages with observations about her neighbors all over the streets, giving her unexpected notoriety.
Barney Saltzberg, *Mrs. Morgan's Lawn*, 1998
    Well-known for her sour disposition and perfect lawn, Mrs. Morgan keeps the stray balls that end up in her yard.

76

CARI BEST
DIANE PALMISCIANO, Illustrator

Montezuma's Revenge
(New York: Orchard Books, 1999)

Subject(s): Animals/Dogs; Vacations; Pets
Age range(s): Grades K-2
Major character(s): Montezuma "Monty", Dog; Wild Bill, Dog (stray)
Time period(s): 1990s (1999)
Locale(s): United States

Summary: When Montezuma's family makes vacation plans they never seem to include him. Once again they pack their bags and leave Monty in the care of a hated dog-sitter. This time, Monty leaves home, meets Wild Bill at the park and, as he listens to the adventures of the stray's traveling life, comes up with a plan to get invited on the next trip. The day his family returns, Monty hides in the bushes, while Wild Bill takes over the house. One whiff of Wild Bill and the sight of his indoor demolition derby convinces Montezuma's family that their pet is now a vacationing dog. (32 pages)

Where it's reviewed:
Booklist, November 15, 1999, page 632
Horn Book Guide, Spring 2000, page 28
Instructor, September 1999, page 25
School Library Journal, November 1999, page 110

Other books by the same author:
Last Licks: A Spaldeen Story, 1999
Getting Used to Harry, 1996
Taxi! Taxi!, 1994 (Ezra Jack Keats Award)

Other books you might like:
William Maxwell, *Mrs. Donald's Dog Bun and His Home Away from Home*, 1995
    After Bun refurbishes an old playhouse for his use he is so crowded by visitors that he goes back to sleeping on an old carpet in the house.
Susan Meddaugh, *Martha Calling*, 1994
    Martha makes the most of the vacation she wins in a radio call-in contest despite the resort's "No Dogs Allowed" policy.
Danny Shanahan, *Buckledown the Workhound*, 1993
    As president of a large corporation, Buckledown is "dog tired" so he plans a vacation at Shirttail Wagon Farm where he learns to lead a dog's life.
Maggie Smith, *Argo, You Lucky Dog*, 1994
    While Argo's owners are out of town he wins the lottery and uses the proceeds to redecorate the house.

77

CARI BEST
GISELLE POTTER, Illustrator

Three Cheers for Catherine the Great!
(New York: DK Ink, 1999)

Subject(s): Grandmothers; Birthdays; Gifts
Age range(s): Grades 1-4
Major character(s): Sara, Child; Grandma "Catherine the Great", Grandmother (Russian American); Mama, Mother
Time period(s): Indeterminate Past
Locale(s): United States

Summary: For her birthday when she is "as old as all the numbers on the clock added together," Grandma announces that she wants no presents. Sara doesn't know how they can have a birthday party with no presents until Mama explains that a "no present" can be something such as a hug, a kiss or a kind gesture. Then Sara tries to think of the very best "no present" for her wonderful Grandma, Catherine the Great. Although Grandma immigrated to America when Mama was a little girl, Grandma still speaks Russian. Sara's interest in writing poetry—in English—and her desire to understand Grandma's writing give her an idea for the perfect "no present" for a great Grandma. (32 pages)

Where it's reviewed:
Booklist, September 15, 1999, page 258
Horn Book, November 1999, page 727
Publishers Weekly, July 19, 1999, page 194
Riverbank Review, Fall 1999, page 32
School Library Journal, August 1999, page 125

Awards the book has won:
Booklist Editors' Choice, 1999
Publishers Weekly Best Books, 1999

Other books by the same author:
Last Licks: A Spaldeen Story, 1999
Getting Used to Harry, 1996

Taxi! Taxi!, 1994

Other books you might like:

Amy Hest, *Nana's Birthday Party*, 1993
Cousins Maggie and Brette work together to create a special birthday gift for Nana.

Pat Mora, *A Birthday Basket for Tia*, 1992
Cecelia makes a special present for her family's celebration of Great Aunt Tia's 90th birthday.

Jeri Hanel Watts, *Keepers*, 1997
As a birthday gift for his grandmother, Kenyon compiles her oft-told family stories in a book.

78

FRANNY BILLINGSLEY

The Folk Keeper

(New York: Atheneum Books for Young Readers, 1999)

Subject(s): Fantasy; Folklore; Orphans
Age range(s): Grades 5-8
Major character(s): Corinna ''Corin'' Stonewall, 15-Year-Old, Orphan; Finian Hawthorne, Gentleman, Sailor; Edward Merton, Gentleman, Nobleman
Time period(s): Indeterminate Past
Locale(s): Rhysbridge, England; Cliffsend, England (Marblehaugh Park)

Summary: To spare herself a life of drudgery as an orphan girl, Corinna cuts her hair, burns her skirts and arrives, with a shipment of orphans, at Rhysbridge masquerading as a Folk Keeper named Corin. To the inexplicable magical powers inherent in her, Corin adds information she gleans from the market, kitchen gossip and tips from others experienced at keeping the ''other folk'' happy so that life will run smoothly at the orphanage. When a dying nobleman locates Corinna and convinces her to become the folk keeper for his estate, she begins an unexpected and dangerous journey of self-discovery. Along the way Corinna finds an ally in Finian, an enemy in Sir Edward, the answer to her identity and the explanation for her remarkable traits. She also must face a choice that will change her life forever. (162 pages)

Where it's reviewed:
Booklist, September 1, 1999, page 126
Five Owls, March 2000, page 100
Horn Book, November 1999, page 734
Kirkus Reviews, October 15, 1999, page 1639
School Library Journal, October 1999, page 144

Awards the book has won:
Publishers Weekly Best Books, 1999
School Library Journal Best Books, 1999

Other books by the same author:
Well Wished, 1997 (School Library Journal Best Book)

Other books you might like:

Susan Cooper, *The Selkie Girl*, 1986
The illustrated retelling of a Scottish tale introduces readers to the selkie—a seal that can shed its skin and take on human form.

Berlie Doherty, *Daughter of the Sea*, 1997
A fisherman and his wife raise a foundling as their child, but in time the sea calls her home.

Kenneth Lillington, *Selkie*, 1985
When Cathy's father loses his job, the family moves to a dilapidated Cornish cottage where they observe a mysterious girl swimming with the seals.

Jenny Nimmo, *Griffin's Castle*, 1997
Wild animals spring forth from stone carvings on the walls of a Welsh castle, threatening Dinah's life and the secure future she seeks.

79

GAVIN BISHOP, Author/Illustrator

Stay Awake, Bear!

(New York: Orchard Books, 2000)

Subject(s): Animals/Bears; Sleep; Seasons
Age range(s): Grades K-1
Major character(s): Old Bear, Bear, Neighbor; Brown Bear, Bear, Neighbor
Time period(s): 2000s
Locale(s): Fictional Country

Summary: Old Bear declares that sleeping is a waste of time so when his neighbors prepare for their annual hibernation, he prepares to stay awake all winter. He keeps busy reading, watching videos and playing the banjo. Although Old Bear is wide-awake he's a little restless so he's pleased when he hears a knock at the door. Brown Bear is also unable to sleep so the two neighbors spend the winter together and plan their summer vacation. When the snow melts, Old Bear and Brown Bear depart on their trip. They fall asleep on the train and sleep through the seashore, the mountains and the plains. They arrive home just as the snow begins to fall, refreshed from the vacation and looking forward to staying awake for another winter. (32 pages)

Where it's reviewed:
Horn Book Guide, Fall 2000, page 245
Publishers Weekly, March 20, page 90
School Library Journal, March 2000, page 178

Other books by the same author:
Little Rabbit and the Sea, 1997
Maui and the Sun: A Maori Tale, 1996
The Three Little Pigs, 1989
Mrs. McGinty and the Bizarre Plant, 1983

Other books you might like:

Hans De Beer, *Bernard Bear's Amazing Adventure*, 1994
Rather than hibernating alone, Bernard Bear tries a sparrow's advice to head south for the winter.

Denise Fleming, *Time to Sleep*, 1997
Bear passes the word on through the animal grapevine that it's time to settle in for the winter; eventually the news comes back to awaken Bear.

Don Freeman, *Bearymore*, 1976
Rather than plan his new circus act, Bearymore settles down for his winter's hibernation.

Paul Stewart, *A Little Bit of Winter*, 1999
While Hedgehog hibernates Rabbit finds a way to ''save'' a little bit of winter for him so he'll know what he misses every year.

80

CHRISTINA BJORK
INGA-KARIN ERIKSSON, Illustrator
PATRICIA CRAMPTON, Translator

Vendela in Venice

(New York: R&S Books/Farrar Straus Giroux, 1999)

Subject(s): Travel; Fathers and Daughters; Vacations
Age range(s): Grades 4-7
Major character(s): Vendela, Child
Time period(s): 1990s (1999)
Locale(s): Venice, Italy

Summary: Vendela, a young Swedish girl, is excited to be visiting Venice with her father. She sees the horses of St. Mark's Cathedral, the Isle of the Dead, and Murano where the glass is made. One of Vendela's adventures begins when she gets a fish bone stuck in her throat and has to go to an Italian hospital. During her visit to the city, Vendela meets many interesting people including a glass blower who creates a glass unicorn for her. Vendela's week in Venice slowly comes to an end, leaving her with many happy memories. (96 pages)

Where it's reviewed:
Booklist, November 15, 1999, page 624
Horn Book, November 1999, page 734
Publisher's Weekly, November 8, 1999, page 68
School Library Journal, January 2000, page 128

Awards the book has won:
Batchelder Honor Book, 2000

Other books by the same author:
Big Bear's book, 1994
The Other Alice: The Story of Alice Liddell and Alice in Wonderland, 1993
Linnea in Monet's Garden, 1987

Other books you might like:
Anni Axworthy, *Anni's Diary of France*, 1994
    While on a summer trip to France, Anni keeps a diary of her impressions and experiences.
Rosalie Seidler, *Grumpus and the Venetian Cat*, 1979
    Grumpus the mouse outwits, Furfantello.
Marilyn Tolhurst, *Italy*, 1988
    The language, culture, and geography are introduced through text and illustrations.

81

ROBERT J. BLAKE, Author/Illustrator

Fledgling

(New York: Philomel Books, 2000)

Subject(s): Animals/Birds; City and Town Life; Growing Up
Age range(s): Grades K-2
Major character(s): Fledgling, Bird (kestrel)
Time period(s): 2000s (2000)
Locale(s): New York, New York (Brooklyn)

Summary: Four kestrels must learn to fly today and Fledgling, as the oldest, is chosen to go first. She stands fearfully on the edge of a tall building before jumping into space and fluttering to a ledge. Trying again Fledgling feels the air currents beneath her wings and realizes that she can fly! She's also aware that something is following her and she tries to evade the hawk. Frightened, Fledgling races into a crowded subway car, but quickly realizes that's not the right place. By the time she's back in the open air she's become lost. As she soars over the city Fledgling hears the call of her family and contentedly returns to her home. A concluding artist's note gives information about the inspiration for the story, facts about kestrels and the development of the story and its pictures. (32 pages)

Where it's reviewed:
Booklist, December 15, 2000, page 824
Horn Book Guide, Spring 2001, page 29
Horn Book, January 2001, page 82
Kirkus Reviews, October 1, 2000, page 4
School Library Journal, October 2000, page 112

Other books by the same author:
Akiak: A Tale from the Iditarod, 1997 (School Library Journal Best Book)
Spray, 1996
Dog, 1994

Other books you might like:
Judy Allen, *Eagle*, 1994
    Initially fearful of an eagle hunting nearby, Miguel learns to respect the bird when it saves his life by consuming a threatening snake.
Laurence Anholt, *Billy and the Big New School*, 1999
    Watching a young sparrow as it learns to fly convinces timid Billy that he can go to school without his mother too.
Eric Rohmann, *Time Flies*, 1994
    A wordless story shows a bird trapped in a museum who flies through the dinosaur exhibit and back to the time of live, hungry dinosaurs.
Nick Williams, *How Birds Fly*, 1997
    A nonfiction title explains how the shape of bird's bodies makes flight possible.

82

BECKY BLOOM
PASCAL BIET, Illustrator

Mice Make Trouble

(New York: Orchard Books, 2000)

Subject(s): Magic; Animals/Mice; Behavior
Age range(s): Grades K-3
Major character(s): Henry, Child, Brother
Time period(s): 1990s (1999)
Locale(s): England

Summary: Secretly, curious Henry borrows the colored pencils that his sister claims are magic. Henry's too young to read the warning label on the box or he could avoid the mischief that he inadvertently creates. After drawing a truck that comes to life, Henry uses the pencils to draw a mouse to ride in it. Not satisfied with his mice after six attempts Henry draws a hedgehog that pleases him, but all seven animals come to life. The hedgehog has good manners, but the mice are a problem as they keep drawing toys until Henry's room is mess. Finally, Henry draws one more mouse and when it comes to life as a teacher, she organizes the mischief-makers to clean up and return to class with her. In 1999 this book was published in Great Britain with the title *Six Mice and a Hedgehog*. (32 pages)

Where it's reviewed:
Booklist, April 1, 2000, page 1467
Horn Book Guide, Fall 2000, page 245
Kirkus Reviews, March 1, 2000, page 299
School Librarian, Winter 1999, page 184
School Library Journal, March 2000, page 189

Other books by the same author:
Wolf!, 1999
Mr. Cuckoo, 1998

Other books you might like:
Martha Alexander, *You're a Genius, Blackboard Bear*, 1995
  With help from Blackboard Bear, Anthony builds a spaceship to the moon.
Anthony Browne, *Bear Goes to Town*, 1989
  Using his magic pencil, Bear is able to create all that he needs and come to the assistance of other animals too.
Judith Heide Gilliland, *Not in the House, Newton!*, 1995
  When Newton sees that his new red crayon creates drawings that become real he quickly hops on his paper airplane and flies out the window.
Crockett Johnson, *Harold and the Purple Crayon*, 1955
  Using his magic purple crayon, Harold draws himself into and out of adventure.
Daniel Lehan, *Wipe Your Feet!*, 1993
  Animals in a painting come to life and leave footprints all over the house.

83

BECKY BLOOM
PASCAL BIET, Illustrator

Wolf!

(New York: Orchard Books, 1999)

Subject(s): Animals/Wolves; Books and Reading; Literacy
Age range(s): Grades K-3
Major character(s): Wolf, Wolf
Time period(s): Indeterminate
Locale(s): France

Summary: Wolf, hungry and newly arrived in town, visits a nearby farm to find a meal. The animals take little notice of Wolf because they are too intent on reading. Shocked, Wolf decides to learn more about this engrossing activity by going to reading class. When his reading still fails to impress the animals, Wolf checks books out of the library, and buys a book at the bookstore. Soon Wolf is welcomed on the farm, not as a scary brute but as an excellent reader. (32 pages)

Where it's reviewed:
Booklist, February 15, 1999, page 1074
Horn Book Guide, Fall 1999, page 245
Kirkus Reviews, February 1, 1999, page 220
Publishers Weekly, February 8, 1999, page 212
School Library Journal, May 1999, page 85

Other books by the same author:
Mice Make Trouble, 2000

Mr. Cuckoo, 1998

Other books you might like:
Sara Fanelli, *Wolf*, 1997
  Friendly Wolf's intentions are misunderstood by the fearful townspeople who chase Wolf away from their city.
Carol Jones, *What's the Time, Mr. Wolf?*, 1999
  Mr. Wolf plans an elaborate dinner party for his barnyard friends. Should they be nervous about his intentions?
Colin McNaughton, *Suddenly!*, 1995
  A wolf keeps barely missing his target, Preston the pig.
Jon Scieszka, *The True Story of the Three Little Pigs*, 1989
  The wolf finally tells his version of the tale of the three little pigs.

84

JOAN BLOS
ANN BOYAJIAN, Illustrator

Hello, Shoes!

(New York: Simon & Schuster Books for Young Readers, 1999)

Subject(s): Growing Up; Grandfathers; Lost and Found Possessions
Age range(s): Preschool
Major character(s): Unnamed Character, Child; Unnamed Character, Grandfather
Time period(s): 1990s
Locale(s): United States

Summary: Although he's not yet capable of fastening the buckles on his sandals, a little boy still likes his sandal shoes better than his everyday shoes or his dress-up shoes. So, when his grandpa is ready to take the boy outside, he insists on wearing the sandal shoes. Together they search the house, finding green boots and one caboose, but no sandal shoes. When they finally sit to rest in their respective rocking chairs, the difficulty the boy has in rocking leads to the discovery of the sandals. Confidently, the little boy puts them on his feet and buckles them himself for the very first time. Then he and his grandpa head outside. (32 pages)

Where it's reviewed:
Booklist, October 15, 1999, page 450
Horn Book Guide, Fall 1999, page 229
Publishers Weekly, May 31, 1999, page 91
School Library Journal, July 1999, page 61

Other books by the same author:
Bedtime!, 1998
The Hungry Little Boy, 1995
The Grandpa Days, 1989
Old Henry, 1987
Martin's Hats, 1984

Other books you might like:
Niki Daly, *Not So Fast, Songololo*, 1986
  A slow-moving boy finds a new speed when he laces up a pair of red sneakers.
Mem Fox, *Shoes from Grandpa*, 1992
  A rhyming tale describes the clothes a family offers a rapidly growing girl to go with her shoes from Grandpa.

Johanna Hurwitz, *New Shoes for Silvia*, 1993
  Silvia finds many uses for her new red shoes while she waits to grow into them.
Ann Morris, *Shoes, Shoes, Shoes*, 1995
  Photographs illustrate a rhyming description of many types of shoes worn around the world.
Denise Lewis Patrick, *Red Dancing Shoes*, 1993
  Grandma's gift of red shoes sets her granddaughter's feet to dancing around the neighborhood.

85

ODDS BODKIN
BERNIE FUCHS, Illustrator

Ghost of the Southern Belle: A Sea Tale
(Boston: Little, Brown and Company, 1999)

Subject(s): Shipwrecks; Ghosts; Sea Stories
Age range(s): Grades 2-5
Major character(s): Captain LeNoir, Sea Captain (of the *Southern Belle*); Father, Sea Captain (of the *Candace*), Father; Unnamed Character, Son, Sailor
Time period(s): Indeterminate Past
Locale(s): Gloucester, Massachusetts; *Candace*, At Sea

Summary: Captain LeNoir's reputation for recklessness on the seas is well known. When a young boy asks him why he chooses to race he suggests that perhaps he's waiting to be beaten. LeNoir shows the boy two magical spheres he carries and tosses the one named "Luck" to the boy. Soon after, while racing *Candace* in a storm, the *Southern Belle* crashes onto the rocks. Father refuses to endanger his crew by turning back or lowering a boat to seek survivors and when the boy pulls LeNoir's orb from his pocket it is foggy and dripping sea water. He hides it from Father who does not believe in superstitions, but each time a ship sinks inexplicably the boy sees the ball drip salt water. Tales of a ghost ship are heard in the streets of town and the youth realizes that LeNoir is angry no effort was made to save his crew. He tells Father of his suspicions and they take the ship out to await a storm so they can recreate the race with the *Southern Belle* and bring an end to its haunting of the seas. (32 pages)

Where it's reviewed:
Booklist, September 15, 1999, page 256
Bulletin of the Center for Children's Books, October 1999, page 47
Kirkus Reviews, July 15, 1999, page 1130
Publishers Weekly, August 16, 1999, page 85
School Library Journal, September 1999, page 176

Other books by the same author:
The Crane Wife, 1998 (Booklist Editors' Choice)
The Banshee Train, 1995

Other books you might like:
Laura Cecil, *A Thousand Yards of Sea: A Collection of Sea Stories and Poems*, 1992
  This illustrated collection includes poems and stories about the sea written by many authors.
Eric Jon Nones, *Caleb's Friend*, 1993
  During a storm a mer-boy befriended by orphaned Caleb guides Caleb's ship to safety.

Joan Skogan, *The Good Companion*, 1998
  Despite objections by the ship's superstitious captain the crew rescues a young woman; months later she appears again during a storm and saves them.
Elvira Woodruff, *The Ghost of Lizard Light*, 1999
  Jack solves a 150-year-old misconception about a shipwreck so a ghost can rest in peace.

86

TOMEK BOGACKI, Author/Illustrator

Cat and Mouse in the Snow
(New York: Frances Foster Books/Farrar Straus Giroux, 1999)

Subject(s): Animals/Cats; Animals/Mice; Winter
Age range(s): Grades K-1
Major character(s): Cat, Cat, Friend; Mouse, Mouse, Friend
Time period(s): Indeterminate
Locale(s): Fictional Country

Summary: Cat and Mouse return to the green meadow to play only to discover the ground covered with something white and the meadow missing. The friends search up the hill, slip and slide down the hill, but still cannot find the green meadow. Their siblings come out to play with them, but instead find two strange white creatures and no green meadow. In time, the animals realize that the meadow and Cat and Mouse are simply covered in snow and they enjoy their day of play in the white meadow. (32 pages)

Where it's reviewed:
Booklist, October 1, 1999, page 360
Hungry Mind Review, Winter 1999, page 53
Kirkus Reviews, October 15, 1999, page 1640
Publishers Weekly, December 13, 1999, page 85
School Library Journal, September 1997, page 176

Other books by the same author:
Cat and Mouse in the Night, 1998
Cat and Mouse in the Rain, 1997
Cat and Mouse, 1996

Other books you might like:
Judith Ross Enderle, *Six Snowy Sheep*, 1994
  Six sheep enjoy a winter day playing in the snow. Co-author Stephanie Gordon Tessler.
Mick Inkpen, *Kipper's Snowy Day*, 1996
  Kipper and his friend Tiger play happily together all day in the snow.
Steve Sanfield, *Snow*, 1995
  A young boy marvels at the beauty of the newly fallen snow dotted with the tracks of passing animals.

87

TOMEK BOGACKI, Author/Illustrator

My First Garden
(New York: Frances Foster Books/Farrar Straus Giroux, 2000)

Subject(s): Gardens and Gardening; Family Life; Neighbors and Neighborhoods
Age range(s): Grades 1-3

Major character(s): Unnamed Character, Child, Son; Unnamed Character, Father, Businessman
Time period(s): Indeterminate Past
Locale(s): Poland

Summary: While commuting through the countryside by train a businessman's view of a town in the distance triggers memories of his childhood. He remembers how large his hometown seemed to him until he was given a bicycle. On the bike he learns his way around the town and the surrounding country, meeting his father each week at the train station. On one excursion a field of wildflowers inspires him to create a garden in the cobblestone courtyard of his home. Now, the businessman's reverie ends as his train ride brings him to his own town where his son awaits his arrival and the son's first garden greets him as they walk home together. (40 pages)

Where it's reviewed:
Booklist, February 15, 2000, page 1117
Publishers Weekly, February 7, 2000, page 85
School Library Journal, April 2000, page 90

Other books by the same author:
The Story of a Blue Bird, 1998
I Hate You! I Like You!, 1997
Cat and Mouse, 1996

Other books you might like:
Pat Brisson, *Wanda's Roses*, 1994
    Wanda transforms a litter-strewn vacant lot into a neighborhood garden.
Lois Ehlert, *Planting a Rainbow*, 1988
    A mother and child plant a family garden, carefully planning the placement of the flowers to create a rainbow of color.
Lynne Rae Perkins, *Home Lovely*, 1995
    Tiffany's beginning efforts at gardening are noticed and nurtured by a friendly letter carrier.
Sarah Stewart, *The Gardener*, 1997
    Lydia Grace uses her gift for gardening to transform her temporary home and her dour uncle.

88

JO ELLEN BOGART
LAURA FERNANDEZ, Illustrator
RICK JACOBSON, Illustrator

Jeremiah Learns to Read

(New York: Orchard Books, 1999)

Subject(s): Literacy; Determination; Schools
Age range(s): Grades K-3
Major character(s): Jeremiah, Aged Person, Farmer; Juliana, Spouse, Aged Person; Mrs. Trumble, Teacher
Time period(s): Indeterminate Past
Locale(s): Canada

Summary: Jeremiah has many skills, but reading is not one of them. Determined to learn, he accompanies the other children down the lane to the schoolhouse. Mrs. Trumble welcomes her new student and Jeremiah's education begins. As Jeremiah tackles the fundamentals of reading, he shares his knowledge of birds, whistling and whittling with his classmates and Mrs. Trumble. When Jeremiah is comfortable with his new skill, he borrows a book of poetry from the school to read to Juliana and inspires her to seek literacy. The book was originally published in Canada in 1997. (32 pages)

Where it's reviewed:
Booklist, September 15, 1999, page 265
Quill & Quire, January 1998, page 37
Resource Links, February 1998, page 100
School Library Journal, October 1999, page 102

Awards the book has won:
Ontario Library Association's Best Bets, 1997

Other books by the same author:
Gifts, 1996
Daniel's Dog, 1990
Dylan's Lullaby, 1988

Other books you might like:
Eve Bunting, *The Wednesday Surprise*, 1989
    Every Wednesday while Grandma cares for her, Anna teaches her to read as a surprise for Papa's birthday.
Dolores Johnson, *Papa's Stories*, 1994
    Papa's inability to read creates interesting stories that change with every telling.
Tony Johnston, *Amber on the Mountain*, 1994
    With no school near her isolated mountain home, Amber is unable to read until Anna comes into her life, determined to teach her.
Vashanti Rahaman, *Read for Me, Mama*, 1997
    Mama finally admits to Joseph that she is unable to read to him and enrolls in an adult literacy class.

89

REBECCA BOND, Author/Illustrator

Bravo, Maurice!

(Boston: Megan Tingley/Little, Brown and Company, 2000)

Subject(s): Family Life; City and Town Life; Individuality
Age range(s): Grades K-3
Major character(s): Maurice Duncan Marcela, Son; Mama, Mother, Writer; Papa, Baker, Father
Time period(s): 2000s (2000)
Locale(s): United States

Summary: Maurice's relatives each see a resemblance between one of his features and one of their own and decide that means he's destined to follow their career path. Papa thinks that with Maurice's big hands he'll take after his father and become a baker. Mama sees Maurice as being observant, a trait useful to anyone who becomes a writer as she is. Maurice accompanies Mama and Papa as well as an uncle and grandmother to their jobs and, while he enjoys all he sees, he prefers simply hearing the different sounds unique to each workplace. The sounds he hears in a variety of places become part of his experience of family and urban life and contribute to what Maurice most wants to become—a singer. (32 pages)

Where it's reviewed:
Booklist, September 15, 2000, page 247
Horn Book Guide, Spring 2001, page 29
Publishers Weekly, September 18, 2000, page 111
School Library Journal, December 2000, page 96

Other books by the same author:
Just Like a Baby, 1999

Other books you might like:
Melrose Cooper, *I Got a Family*, 1993
A young girl describes the unique affection she receives from each individual in her caring family.
Karla Kuskin, *I Am Me*, 2000
Although each family member sees a part of themselves in a little girl's features she knows she is no one other than a person named ''me.''
Marilyn Singer, *The One and Only Me*, 2000
To a little girl, having teeth like her uncle or a nose like grandma means nothing because she knows that she is completely unique.
Mary Whitcomb, *Odd Velvet*, 1998
Velvet doesn't mind being different from others in her class and gradually her classmates come to appreciate her originality.

90

REBECCA BOND, Author/Illustrator

Just Like a Baby

(Boston: Little, Brown and Company, 1999)

Subject(s): Babies; Family; Love
Age range(s): Grades K-2
Major character(s): Father, Father; Mother, Mother
Time period(s): 1990s (1999)
Locale(s): United States

Summary: In the author's first book, Father prepares for the arrival of a child by building a cradle that looks so comfy Father immediately lies down in it and sleeps—just like a baby. As each family member contributes something—paint, a quilt, the hanging mobile—the relative naps in the cradle. Mother provides a view of the sky for the cradle before her daughter comes home to sleep—just like a baby-in the new cradle. (32 pages)

Where it's reviewed:
Booklist, September 15, 1999, page 265
Bulletin of the Center for Children's Books, September 1999, page 6
Kirkus Reviews, July 1, 1999, page 1051
Publishers Weekly, July 12, 1999, page 94
School Library Journal, September 1999, page 176

Other books by the same author:
Bravo, Maurice!, 2000

Other books you might like:
Melrose Cooper, *I Got a Family*, 1993
A young girl describes the unique affection she receives from each individual in her caring extended family.
Karen Katz, *Over the Moon: An Adoption Tale*, 1997
Long before the baby they eventually adopt is born, her future parents dream and plan for her arrival.
Phyllis Root, *What Baby Wants*, 1998
While Mama naps, everyone in the family tries to determine what will soothe the crying baby.

Amy Schwartz, *A Teeny Tiny Baby*, 1994
The many needs of a teeny tiny baby are immediately met by doting parents and grandparents.

91

SUSAN BONNERS, Author/Illustrator

Edwina Victorious

(New York: Farrar Straus Giroux, 2000)

Subject(s): Aunts and Uncles; Letters; Social Issues
Age range(s): Grades 3-5
Major character(s): Edwina ''Eddy'' Osgood, Niece, Student—Elementary School; Edwina Osgood, Aunt (great grandaunt), Aged Person; Roger Bailey, Student—Elementary School, Friend
Time period(s): 2000s (2000)
Locale(s): United States

Summary: Inspired by a box of old letters found in Aunt Edwina's attic, shy Eddy writes letters to the mayor complaining about various problems in the town. Realizing that the mayor might not pay attention to a child, Eddy borrows some of Aunt Edwina's phrases, uses Aunt Edwina's return address and traces her signature when she signs the letters. Then, she gets Roger to mail them for her so they'll have the same postmark as Aunt Edwina's nursing home. Eddy is surprised that her letters actually do some good. The swings at the park are repaired and the town cleans up a vacant lot. After two successes Eddy enlists Roger's help with more than mail deliveries and the summer becomes filled with the identification of projects needing the mayor's attention. All goes well until the mayor contacts Aunt Edwina for financial assistance with a pet project of his own and Eddy has to reveal the truth behind the letters. (131 pages)

Where it's reviewed:
Bulletin of the Center for Children's Books, October 2000, page 54
Horn Book Guide, Spring 2001, page 70
Publishers Weekly, November 13, 2000, page 104
School Library Journal, October 2000, page 112

Other books by the same author:
The Silver Balloon, 1997 (Christopher Award)
Hunter in the Snow: The Lynx, 1994
The Wooden Doll, 1991

Other books you might like:
C. Coco De Young, *A Letter to Mrs. Roosevelt*, 1999
The fear of losing her home during the depression prompts Margo to write to Mrs. Roosevelt for help
Peg Kehret, *My Brother Made Me Do It*, 2000
The relationship between Julie and Mrs. Kaplan begins as a school project to write to a pen pal.
Kate Klise, *Regarding the Fountain: A Tale in Letters of Liars and Leaks*, 1998
When a principal requests a catalog to guide selection of a new water fountain he's surprised the designer takes a personal interest in the project.

92

LOUISE BORDEN
TED LEWIN, Illustrator

A. Lincoln and Me

(New York: Scholastic Press, 1999)

Subject(s): Birthdays; American History; School Life
Age range(s): Grades 1-3
Major character(s): Unnamed Character, Student—Elementary School; Mrs. Giff, Teacher; A. Lincoln, Historical Figure
Time period(s): 1990s
Locale(s): United States

Summary: Sharing a birthday with a historical figure gives a young boy a special interest in Lincoln. When awkwardness and his gangly appearance bother the boy, Mrs. Giff reminds him that Lincoln was also tall and thin and often teased for his clumsiness. The youngster uses his knowledge of Lincoln to help him ignore the laughter of classmates and maintain his self-confidence. (32 pages)

Where it's reviewed:
Booklist, November 15, 1999, page 622
Children's Book Review Service, January 2000, page 53
Kirkus Reviews, October 1, 1999, page 1574
Publishers Weekly, November 1, 1999, page 83
School Library Journal, October 1999, page 109

Other books by the same author:
Good-bye, Charles Lindbergh: Based on a True Story, 1998
The Little Ships: The Heroic Rescue at Dunkirk in World War II, 1997
Just in Time for Christmas, 1994

Other books you might like:
Ingri D'Aulaire, *Abraham Lincoln*, 1939
    The Caldecott Medal winning illustrated biography of Lincoln is a classic. Edgar D'Aulaire, co-author.
Cheryl Harness, *Abe Lincoln Goes to Washington, 1837-1865*, 1997
    The picture book biography continues the story of the life of Lincoln begun by Harness in *Young Abe Lincoln*.
Karen B. Winnick, *Mr. Lincoln's Whiskers*, 1996
    Based on an actual event, the story tells of a letter written to Lincoln by a young girl suggesting that a beard would make him more electable.

93

LOUISE BORDEN
ADAM GUSTAVSON, Illustrator

Good Luck, Mrs. K.!

(New York: Simon & Schuster/Margaret K. McElderry, 1999)

Subject(s): Teachers; Cancer; Schools
Age range(s): Grades 1-4
Major character(s): Mrs. Kempczinski "Mrs. K", Teacher; Ann Zesterman, 3rd Grader; Mrs. Dodd, Teacher (substitute)
Time period(s): 1990s
Locale(s): United States

Summary: Ann loves the rhythm of her 3rd grade teacher's name. She says it brings her good luck when she plays basketball. Mrs. K. makes 3rd grade interesting by sharing her travels around the world and doing her famous homework dance when everyone turns their homework in on time. The students soon grow accustomed to doing things the "3rd grade way" and are saddened when the principal announces that Mrs. K. has cancer and Mrs. Dodd will take over the class for the remainder of the year. Ann and her classmates try to be good teachers so Mrs. Dodd will learn the "3rd grade way" to do things too and Mrs. K. will be proud of them all when she returns. (32 pages)

Where it's reviewed:
Booklist, July 1999, page 1942
Publishers Weekly, May 17, 1999, page 79
Riverbank Review, Fall 1999, page 31
School Library Journal, May 1999, page 86

Other books by the same author:
Good-bye, Charles Lindbergh: Based on a True Story, 1998
The Little Ships: The Heroic Rescue at Dunkirk in World War II, 1997
Just in Time for Christmas, 1994
Albie the Lifeguard, 1993

Other books you might like:
Judy Finchler, *Miss Malarkey Won't Be in Today*, 1998
    Miss Malarkey worries about her students when a fever keeps her out of class for the day.
Marilyn Hafner, *Mommies Don't Get Sick*, 1995
    The routine at home is disrupted when Mommy gets sick just as the classroom routine changes when Mrs. K becomes ill.
Ferne Sherkin-Langer, *When Mommy Is Sick*, 1995
    A nonfiction bibliotherapeutic offering tells about a young girl whose mother is hospitalized and how she and Dad cope at home without her.

94

LOUISE BORDEN
ROBERT ANDREW PARKER, Illustrator

Sleds on Boston Common: A Story from the American Revoluton

(New York: Margaret K. McElderry Books/Simon & Schuster, 2000)

Subject(s): Historical; Revolutionary War; American Colonies
Age range(s): Grades 3-5
Major character(s): Henry Price, 9-Year-Old, Brother (youngest); Kate Price, Sister (older); Thomas Gage, Military Personnel (general)
Time period(s): 1770s (1774-1775)
Locale(s): Boston, Massachusetts

Summary: The British occupation of Boston is never more annoying to the Price children than on Henry's birthday when he wants to try out his new sled. During the brother's lunch break from school, Kate joins them and the four siblings with their sleds head straight for the hills surrounding Boston Common. The British troops are not only camped all over the common, but they have also blocked the best sled runs and broken the ice on the ponds. As they wander incredulously through the British camp Henry spies General Gage and bravely approaches him to describe the dilemma he faces. General Gage listens attentively and then instructs the soldiers to clear the sled runs and leave one pond frozen for skating. Though Henry dislikes the British presence, he appreciates General Gage's actions and enjoys using his new sled. A concluding author's note gives factual information about Boston Common and General Gage. (40 pages)

Where it's reviewed:
Booklist, July 2000, page 2028
Horn Book Guide, Spring 2001, page 59
Horn Book, November 2000, page 743
Publishers Weekly, August 14, 2000, page 355
School Library Journal, December 2000, page 97

Other books by the same author:
Good-bye, Charles Lindbergh: Based on a True Story, 1998
The Little Ships: The Heroic Rescue at Dunkirk in World War II, 1997 (Notable Social Studies Trade Books for Children)
Just in Time for Christmas, 1994

Other books you might like:
Katherine Kirkpatrick, *Redcoats and Petticoats*, 1999
   The role of the Strong family of Long Island in conveying secret messages to the American forces is described in a picture book for older readers.
Henry Wadsworth Longfellow, *Paul Revere's Ride*, 1990
   The illustrated edition of Longfellow's 1861 poem describes the midnight ride of a colonist Revere in 1775 to alert American troops.
Connie Roop, *Buttons for General Washington*, 1986
   A teen uses his coat buttons to carry messages secretly to General Washington.
Karen B. Winnick, *Sybil's Night Ride*, 2000
   The teenaged daughter of an American Colonel rides all night to alert her father and his troops of a British attack on a nearby town.

95

PAULETTE BOURGEOIS
SHARON JENNINGS, Co-Author
BRENDA CLARK, Illustrator

Franklin's Class Trip

(Buffalo, NY: Kids Can Press, 1999)

Subject(s): Animals; Schools; Museums
Age range(s): Grades K-1
Major character(s): Franklin, Turtle, Student—Elementary School; Snail, Snail, Student—Elementary School; Beaver, Beaver, Student—Elementary School
Time period(s): Indeterminate
Locale(s): Fictional Country

Summary: Franklin is looking forward to the class field trip to a natural history museum until Beaver announces that the museum houses real dinosaurs. Snail, riding on Franklin's back, is equally nervous as the two visit the museum's exhibits. When they finally approach the dinosaur exhibit, Franklin and Snail are startled but relieved to discover that the

dinosaurs are real skeletons, and not living creatures. (32 pages)

Where it's reviewed:
Booklist, March 1, 1999, page 1218
Horn Book Guide, Fall 1999, page 245
Resource Links, June 1999, page 2
School Library Journal, May 1999, page 86

Awards the book has won:
IRA/CBC Children's Choices, 2000

Other books by the same author:
Franklin and the Baby, 1999
Franklin Goes to School, 1998
Franklin's Bad Day, 1996
Franklin's Blanket, 1995
Franklin in the Dark, 1986

Other books you might like:
Wolfram Hanel, *Lila's Little Dinosaur*, 1994
   After visiting a museum Lila notices that a rainbow-colored dinosaur has followed her home.
Syd Hoff, *Danny and the Dinosaur*, 1958
   A dinosaur follows Danny out of the museum in order to continue playing with him.
James Mayhew, *Katie and the Dinosaurs*, 1992
   When Katie visits a natural history museum she finds herself surrounded by real dinosaurs.
Trinka Hayes Noble, *The Day Jimmy's Boa Ate the Wash*, 1987
   What should be an educational field trip to a farm becomes a most unusual adventure for Jimmy's class when his pet boa gets loose.

96

LYNEA BOWDISH
NANCY CARPENTER, Illustrator

Brooklyn, Bugsy, and Me

(New York: Farrar Straus Giroux, 2000)

Subject(s): Grandfathers; Moving, Household; City and Town Life
Age range(s): Grades 3-5
Major character(s): Sam, 9-Year-Old; Gramps ''Bugsy'', Grandfather; Tony, 4th Grader, Friend
Time period(s): 1950s (1953)
Locale(s): West Virginia; New York, New York (Brooklyn)

Summary: West Virginia is the only home Sam knows so after his mother loses her job and is unable to find another, he's disappointed when they pack everything, including his father's ash-filled urn, and take the train to Brooklyn. Sam is frightened by the big city, silent Gramps, unfamiliar street games, and the threat of gangs. Boredom finally drives him as far as the front stoop of Gramps' apartment where he meets Tony who seems to have learned a great deal about Sam by talking to someone named Bugsy. Tony introduces Sam to the neighborhood, the Brooklyn culture and to another side of Gramps. By summer's end, Sam is adjusting to his new home and learning to appreciate why the community calls his grandfather Bugsy. (84 pages)

Where it's reviewed:
Booklist, February 15, 2000, page 1110
Horn Book, May 2000, page 306
Kirkus Reviews, January 15, 2000, page 118
Publishers Weekly, February 14, 2000, page 200
School Library Journal, June 2000, page 102

Awards the book has won:
Notable Social Studies Trade Books for Young People, 2001

Other books by the same author:
Living with My Stepfather Is Like Living with a Moose, 1997
This Is Me, Laughing, 1996

Other books you might like:
Betsy Duffey, *Hey, New Kid!*, 1996
Cody is so unhappy to be entering a new school that he makes up a new identity rather than tell people the truthful, boring story of his life.
Amy Hest, *The Private Notebook of Katie Roberts, Age 11*, 1995
Katie keeps a record of her thoughts and feelings when her widowed mother remarries, moving them from New York to Texas.
Andrea Davis Pinkney, *Solo Girl*, 1997
When Cass moves to a new neighborhood her math skills help her gain a friend and a teacher of double dutch jump roping technique.
Vera B. Williams, *Scooter*, 1993
When Lanny, her scooter and her mother move to a new apartment in the city, Lanny's out-going personality helps her make new friends.

97

MARIE BRADBY
CHRIS K. SOENTPIET, Illustrator

Momma, Where Are You From?

(New York: Orchard Books, 2000)

Subject(s): Family; African Americans; Mothers and Daughters
Age range(s): Grades K-2
Major character(s): Momma, Mother; Unnamed Character, Child, Daughter
Time period(s): 2000s (2000); Indeterminate Past
Locale(s): United States

Summary: Helping Momma in the kitchen, a young girl asks where she's from. Momma responds, not with a place, but with a description of a bygone lifestyle. Momma says she's from a time of wringer washers, hanging clothes out to dry, and putting irons to heat on a stove. Momma comes from the days of ice deliveries, selling old clothes to the ragman, chickens in the yard, ball games on the radio, and long bus rides to segregated schools. Momma's daughter wants to go back to that place and Momma promises to take her on a trip through her memory of days gone by so she'll know where she's from too. (32 pages)

Where it's reviewed:
Booklist, February 15, 2000, page 1117
Bulletin of the Center for Children's Books, March 2000, page 240

Horn Book Guide, Fall 2000, page 262
Publishers Weekly, April 3, 2000, page 79
School Library Journal, April 2000, page 92

Awards the book has won:
Notable Social Studies Trade Books for Young People, 2001

Other books by the same author:
The Longest Wait, 1998
More than Anything Else, 1995 (ALA Notable Children's Book)

Other books you might like:
Sandra Belton, *May'naise Sandwiches & Sunshine Tea*, 1994
Big Mama shares with her granddaughter the story of a childhood friendship.
Valerie Flournoy, *Tanya's Reunion*, 1995
Helping Grandma prepare for a family reunion, Tanya visits and learns about the Virginia farm where Grandma lived as a child.
Jan Spivey Gilchrist, *Indigo and Moonlight Gold*, 1993
Secure in her mother's love, Autrie imagines her future even as she wishes time could stand still.
Margaree King Mitchell, *Uncle Jed's Barbershop*, 1993
Sarah Jean recalls the challenges Uncle Jed had to overcome in order to save enough money to open his own barbershop.

98

KIMBERLY BRUBAKER BRADLEY

One-of-a-Kind Mallie

(New York: Delacorte Press, 1999)

Subject(s): Twins; Individuality; Gypsies
Age range(s): Grades 3-5
Major character(s): Matilda ''Mallie'' Graber, 10-Year-Old, Twin; Hannah ''Hallie'' Graber, 10-Year-Old, Twin; Ruthie Hawk, 10-Year-Old, Friend
Time period(s): 1910s (1917)
Locale(s): Cedarville, Indiana

Summary: As Mallie struggles to find a way to be seen as an individual she asks her family to call her Matilda, tries to dye a new dress so she will not be identical to Hallie and finds a way to barter for piano lessons from the mail-order bride on a nearby farm. Initially, Hallie does not understand Mallie's search for her own identity, but her dislike of the piano helps her decide not to follow Mallie along the musical path. Best friend Ruthie is caught in the middle as she tries to remain friends with each of the girls. By summer's end, Mallie revises her romantic notions about the Gypsies camped on the Hawk farm, masters a difficult piano piece as a surprise for her mother and gladly accepts the offer to select her own fabric for the next year's school dress. A concluding author's note gives the historical basis for the story. (150 pages)

Where it's reviewed:
Booklist, August 1999, page 2055
Bulletin of the Center for Children's Books, September 1999, page 6
Kirkus Reviews, June 15, 1999, page 960
Publishers Weekly, August 2, 1999, page 85
School Library Journal, September 1999, page 176

Other books by the same author:
Ruthie's Gift, 1998

Other books you might like:
Carol Ryrie Brink, *Magical Melons*, 1990
   The sequel to the Newbery winner *Caddie Woodlawn* continues the story of the Woodlawn family's life on the frontier.
Patricia Hermes, *Everything Stinks*, 1995
   In the second entry in The Cousin's Club series, 10-year-old twins Jennifer and Amy are frustrated by a day when nothing goes as they plan.
Jacqueline Wilson, *Double Act*, 1998
   When Garnet receives the only scholarship to a school Ruby had hoped to attend the twins face their need to be individuals with different interests.

99

KIMBERLY BRUBAKER BRADLEY

Weaver's Daughter

(New York: Delacorte Press, 2000)

Subject(s): Frontier and Pioneer Life; Asthma; Medicine
Age range(s): Grades 4-6
Major character(s): Elizabeth "Lizzy" Baker, 10-Year-Old, Sister; Hezzy Baker, 12-Year-Old, Sister (oldest); Sarah Beaumont, Gentlewoman, Neighbor (temporary)
Time period(s): 1790s (1791-1792)
Locale(s): Southwest Territory

Summary: Lizzy and her family dread the approach of fall for that is the time each year that Lizzy becomes ill. When the sickness begins again, Lizzy's family takes her to a doctor in Jonesborough, selling the coverlet from her parents' bed to pay for his services. The doctor's treatment does little to help Lizzy breathe but the local midwife with her herbal remedies keeps Lizzy alive until the first killing frost brings relief. Lizzy is so sure she will not live through the next sick spell that during the winter she cards a fleece, spins the wool, and prepares a weaving project to leave as her legacy to the family. As winter ends, childless Mistress Beaumont asks to take Hezzy back to Charleston with her family. Hezzy, having heard of the healing properties of sea air, sacrifices the opportunity to live in finery to assure Lizzy's life and requests that Lizzy go in her place. Lizzy who has no desire to leave her home must decide if she will choose life. A concluding author's note gives historical background for the story and the medical knowledge of diseases at that time. (166 pages)

Where it's reviewed:
Booklist, August 2000, page 2138
Horn Book Guide, Spring 2001, page 70
Kirkus Reviews, October 15, 2000, page 1480
Publishers Weekly, October 23, 2000, page 75
School Library Journal, October 2000, page 155

Other books by the same author:
One-of-a-Kind Mallie, 1999
Ruthie's Gift, 1998

Other books you might like:
Cynthia De Felice, *The Apprenticeship of Lucas Whitaker*, 1996

As the apprentice to a doctor Lucas hopes to learn about diseases, especially the one that took the lives of his family members in the mid-1800s.
Louise Erdrich, *The Birchbark House*, 1999
   In the mid-1840s the folk medicine of the Ojibwa is not enough to combat the smallpox carried to the tribe's village by a visitor.
Kathleen V. Kudlinski, *Facing West: A Story of the Oregon Train*, 1994
   As his family departs Missouri for Oregon, Ben wonders if the journey or his asthma poses the greatest danger in the months ahead.

100

HENRIETTA BRANFORD

White Wolf

(Cambridge, MA: Candlewick Press, 1999)

Subject(s): Animals/Wolves; Survival; Wilderness
Age range(s): Grades 4-6
Major character(s): Snowy, Wolf, Captive; Jesse, Child, Captive; Drums-Louder, Indian
Time period(s): Indeterminate Past
Locale(s): Northwest Territories

Summary: As a cub, Snowy is captured and raised as a pet for Jesse whose trapper father believes the white wolf offers protection from Native Americans. The Indians, however, consider the white wolf sacred and kill Jesse's father when they capture Jesse and his pet. Snowy escapes from the ceremonial sacrifice intended as his fate and joins a pack of wolves in the wild, learning to hunt and eventually mating and forming his own pack. At times Snowy's path crosses that of "the barefoot people" and once his mate is saved from a trap by Drums-Louder. After several seasons, Jesse stumbles into Snowy's den as he runs from the tribe intent on killing him for stealing game and finds temporary sanctuary with the white wolf. (95 pages)

Where it's reviewed:
The Book Report, November 1999, page 59
Booklist, August 1999, page 2055
Books for Keeps, January 1999, page 24
Publishers Weekly, March 29, 1999, page 105
School Library Journal, June 1999, page 126

Other books by the same author:
Fire, Bed and Bone, 1998 (Guardian Award for Children's Fiction)
The Theft of Thor's Hammer, 1996

Other books you might like:
Jean Craighead George, *Julie of the Wolves*, 1974
   In a Newbery Award winning title, a pack of wolves comes to Julie's rescue during her trek across the Alaskan wilderness.
Jack London, *Call of the Wild*, 1903
   Stolen from his home and treated cruelly in the Klondike Gold Rush, Buck, a mixed breed dog, becomes leader of a wolf pack.

Dorothy Hinshaw Patent, *Return of the Wolf*, 1995
  After she is banished from her pack, a wolf attracts a new mate with whom to establish a new territory and pack.

101

TRUDI BRAUN
JOHN BENDALL-BRUNELLO, Illustrator

My Goose Betsy

(Cambridge, MA: Candlewick Press, 1999)

Subject(s): Animals/Geese; Growing Up; Spring
Age range(s): Grades K-2
Major character(s): Betsy, Goose, Mother; William, Goose (gander)
Time period(s): 1990s
Locale(s): England

Summary: Carefully Betsy collects the materials to build a nest in the corner of the goose house. After lining it with down plucked from her breast, she lays her first egg. Eventually Betsy sits, warming a nest of eight eggs, patiently waiting for them to develop and the goslings to hatch. William guards the goose house, hissing at anyone who ventures near. Finally, Betsy struts out of the goose house leading the parade of goslings into the farmyard. The author's first book, originally published in England in 1998, concludes with factual information about geese and an age-appropriate, user-friendly index. (32 pages)

Where it's reviewed:
Booklist, April 1, 1999, page 1408
Horn Book, May 1999, page 311
Publishers Weekly, April 12, 1999, page 73
School Library Journal, April 1999, page 85

Awards the book has won:
Booklist Editors' Choice, 1999

Other books you might like:
June Crebbin, *Danny's Duck*, 1995
  Through his artwork, Danny shows his teacher the progression of events in a duck's nest.
Robert McCloskey, *Make Way for Ducklings*, 1941
  In this Caldecott Medal winner a mother duck and her ducklings stop traffic while crossing a busy Boston street on their way to a pond.
John Schoenherr, *Rebel*, 1995
  One of a clutch of five Canada Goose eggs hatches into a gosling with a mind of his own.
Jane Yolen, *Honkers*, 1993
  While visiting her grandparents, Betsy watches daily for three abandoned goose eggs to hatch.

102

ANN BRAYBROOKS
SCOTT MENCHIN, Illustrator

Plenty of Pockets

(San Diego: Harcourt, Inc., 2000)

Subject(s): Cleanliness; Lost and Found Possessions; Problem Solving

Age range(s): Grades K-2
Major character(s): Henry Bunch, Father, Spouse; Henrietta Bunch, Mother, Spouse; Junior Bunch, 7-Year-Old, Son
Time period(s): 2000s (2000)
Locale(s): United States

Summary: The Bunch family lives in a small house so cluttered that one day Henry cannot find his toothbrush and Henrietta cannot find Junior. Henry's solution to the problem is to sew pockets on his overalls—as soon as he finds them. Into the many pockets Henry stuffs Junior and his pet hedgehog, toys, pots and pans, books and chairs. Henry thinks his idea is so successful that he sews pockets on Henrietta's favorite dress too. By the time they finish, their house is uncluttered but they cannot find the sofa. They go into the yard to unload their pockets and inadvertently attract the neighbors who assume they are having a yard sale. At the end of the day Henry and Henrietta move the remaining possessions back into their neat, uncluttered house. The pockets are still useful for storage until Junior's birthday party when their home once again becomes cluttered with more stuff than the pockets can hold. (32 pages)

Where it's reviewed:
Booklist, July 2000, page 2037
Bulletin of the Center for Children's Books, June 2000, page 352
Horn Book Guide, Fall 2000, page 262
School Library Journal, May 2000, page 130

Other books by the same author:
No More Mess!, 2000
A Hunny, Funny, Sunny Day!, 1999
Bounce Around Tigger!, 1998

Other books you might like:
Emmy Payne, *Katy No-Pocket*, 1973
  A mother kangaroo without a pocket has a real problem until a sympathetic carpenter gives her his work apron.
James Stevenson, *Yard Sale*, 1996
  At the conclusion of their yard sale the residents of Mud Flat have a party and share their new purchases.
Rosemary Wells, *Max Cleans Up*, 2000
  Each time Ruby hands Max some trash from his room to throw away he stuffs it in his overall pocket.

103

BERKELEY BREATHED, Author/Illustrator

Edwurd Fudwupper Fibbed Big: Explained by Fannie Fudwupper

(Boston: Little, Brown and Company, 2000)

Subject(s): Honesty; Brothers and Sisters; Stories in Rhyme
Age range(s): Grades K-3
Major character(s): Edwurd Fudwupper, Child, Brother; Fannie Fudwupper, Child, Sister (younger)
Time period(s): Indeterminate
Locale(s): Earth

Summary: The fib Edwurd tells to explain the broken ceramic pig is overheard by someone who thinks the story of alien pigs is true and calls in the military to save the town. Overwhelmed by the impact of one fib too many, Edwurd cowers on his roof in the shadow of the chimney as a huge alien atop a spaceship shouts for quiet and threatens to swat the fibber who started the commotion. Though all fingers in town point to Edwurd, Fannie bravely takes the blame to protect the brother that never notices her. The alien is so stunned by Fannie's kindness that he goes home to his sisters leaving Edwurd and Fannie to face their parents with the truth. Edwurd seems to be cured of his lying habit and Fannie is grateful to finally have his attention. (48 pages)

Where it's reviewed:
Children's Bookwatch, October 2000, page 6
Five Owls, September 2000, page 16
Horn Book Guide, Spring 2001, page 33
Publishers Weekly, August 28, 2000, page 82
School Library Journal, November 2000, page 110

Other books by the same author:
Red Ranger Came Calling, 1994
Goodnight Opus, 1993
A Wish for Wings that Work: An Opus Christmas Story, 1991

Other books you might like:
Marc Brown, *Arthur and the True Francine*, 1996
   Muffy's willingness to let Francine take the blame for a cheating incident at school damages their friendship.
Bill Cosby, *My Big Lie*, 1999
   Little Bill's explanation as to why he is late for dinner is not truthful and he suffers the consequences.
Patricia C. McKissack, *The Honest-to-Goodness Truth*, 2000
   Comments Libby makes while attempting to always be truthful offend her friends.
Al Newman, *Fibber E. Frog*, 1993
   Boastful Fibber tells lies to boost his self-esteem.

104

JAN BRETT, Author/Illustrator

Gingerbread Baby

(New York: G.P. Putnam's Sons, 1999)

Subject(s): Cooks and Cooking; Food; Problem Solving
Age range(s): Grades K-2
Major character(s): Matti, Child, Cook; Gingerbread Baby, Runaway
Time period(s): Indeterminate Past
Locale(s): Switzerland

Summary: Impatient Matti peeks into the oven to check the progress of the gingerbread boy he is baking with his mother and a gingerbread baby hops out and runs away. Through the snowy village Gingerbread Baby races with Matti's parents, cat and dog in pursuit. More people and animals, including a fox, join the chase, but not Matti. He stays home cooking up a plan to catch Gingerbread Baby. (32 pages)

Where it's reviewed:
Booklist, November 15, 1999, page 633
Horn Book Guide, Spring 2000, page 30
Publishers Weekly, September 20, 1999, page 88
School Library Journal, November 1999, page 110

Other books by the same author:
The Hat, 1997 (ABBY Children's Prize)
Comet's Nine Lives, 1996

The Mitten: A Ukranian Folktale, 1989

Other books you might like:
Jim Aylesworth, *The Gingerbread Man*, 1998
   The many people and animals that have run after Gingerbread Man look on in frustration as the fox devours him.
Richard Egielski, *The Gingerbread Boy*, 1997
   Set in New York City, the Gingerbread Boy in this award winner successfully runs from a rat, street musicians and a construction crew but not the fox.
Paul Galdone, *The Gingerbread Boy*, 1975
   This book is one of many retellings of the runaway cookie whose speed evades everyone's hunger except that of a clever fox.
Eric A. Kimmel, *The Gingerbread Man*, 1993
   The setting is contemporary, but the gingerbread man still leads the chase while proclaiming his invincibility. The fox has his own ideas.

105

JAN BRETT, Author/Illustrator

Hedgie's Surprise

(New York: G.P. Putnam's Sons, 2000)

Subject(s): Animals/Chickens; Animals/Hedgehogs; Problem Solving
Age range(s): Grades K-2
Major character(s): Henny, Hen; Hedgie, Hedgehog; Tomten, Mythical Creature, Thief
Time period(s): Indeterminate Past
Locale(s): Scandinavia

Summary: Every morning Henny lays an egg and every morning Tomten steals it for his breakfast. Tomten's thievery becomes more than an annoyancy to Henny after she sees a goose with goslings and realizes that her eggs could hatch into chicks too if only she could keep Tomten from taking them every day. Hedgie, silent observer of Tomten's daily raid, approaches Henny with a plan to trick Tomten. Now, before Tomten arrives each day, Hedgie takes Henny's egg to a secret hiding place and replaces it with another edible item. Gradually the substitute increases in size from an acorn to a strawberry, a mushroom and a potato. While Tomten enjoys the new and varied foods, none are as filling as an egg and he awakens hungry from his daily nap. Finally, Tomten insists that he must have Henny's egg the next morning so Hedgie prepares his final surprise—one that is sure to keep Tomten out of the hen house forever. (32 pages)

Where it's reviewed:
Booklist, September 1, 2000, page 120
Publishers Weekly, July 17, 2000, page 192
School Library Journal, September 2000, page 184

Other books by the same author:
The Hat, 1997 (ABBY Children's Prize)
Armadillo Rodeo, 1995
Christmas Trolls, 1993
The Trouble with Trolls, 1992
The Mitten: A Ukranian Folktale, 1989

Other books you might like:

Erin Douglas, *Get That Pest!*, 2000

In order to apprehend the thief responsible for the disappearance of their hens' eggs a farmer and his wife try increasingly complex traps.

Ingrid Schubert, *Bear's Eggs*, 1999

When Bear finds three eggs Hedgehog helps him care for the eggs and the geese that hatch from them.

Betty Jo Stanovich, *Hedgehog Surprises*, 1994

The adventures Hedgehog shares with his friend Woodchuck include a surprise birthday party.

106

PAT BRISSON

DIANA CAIN BLUTHENTHAL, Illustrator

Bertie's Picture Day

(New York: Henry Holt and Company, 2000)

Subject(s): Beauty; Brothers and Sisters; Schools

Age range(s): Grades 2-3

Major character(s): Eloise, Sister (younger); Bertie, Brother, 2nd Grader; Howard, Friend, Student—Elementary School

Time period(s): 2000s (2000)

Locale(s): United States

Summary: School picture day is Monday and Bertie plans to follow his teacher's instructions and come to school looking "spiffy." Howard helps rid him of a bothersome loose tooth by throwing a ball in his face so now Bertie has a nice square hole in the middle of his smile that he's eager to display. While playing kick ball with Howard, Eloise and other friends, Bertie races to make a play at first when he and Eloise collide headfirst. Eloise loses her first two teeth and Bertie's on the way to his first shiner. Later, when Bertie falls asleep while reading a book Eloise (whose current ambition is to be a hair stylist) tries her hand at her first haircut—on Bertie! By the time Bertie arrives at school Monday in his good clothes and bow tie, he knows he's ready for a memorable, "spiffy" picture. (69 pages)

Where it's reviewed:

Booklist, December 1, 2000, page 703

School Library Journal, September 2000, page 184

Other books by the same author:

Little Sister, Big Sister, 1999

The Summer My Father Was Ten, 1998

Hot Fudge Hero, 1997 (Parents' Choice Honor Book)

Wanda's Roses, 1994

Other books you might like:

Judy Blume, *Superfudge*, 1980

Peter's life is filled with the unexpected as the family tries to stay one step ahead of little brother Fudge.

Ann Cameron, *The Stories Julian Tells*, 1981

Six episodes of happy family interaction are told from the perspective of Julian in the first award-winning book about his family.

Johanna Hurwitz, *Russell and Elisa*, 1989

Most of second grader Russell's problems are with his little sister who is challenging.

Lois Lowry, *See You Around, Sam!*, 1996

Life with a younger brother is full of surprises for Anastasia. The latest is Sam's decision to run away to Alaska.

107

PAT BRISSON

WENDELL MINOR, Illustrator

Sky Memories

(New York: Delacorte Press, 1999)

Subject(s): Mothers and Daughters; Cancer; Grief

Age range(s): Grades 4-6

Major character(s): Emily, 10-Year-Old, Daughter; Mom, Single Mother, Cancer Patient; Vicki, Aunt, Waiter/Waitress

Time period(s): 1990s

Locale(s): United States

Summary: When Emily and Mom see a memorable sky they hold hands and make a picture in their minds. They continue sharing their tradition during Mom's treatment for cancer. As Mom's condition weakens, Aunt Vicki moves into their apartment where she stays to care for Emily after Mom dies. All summer Emily grieves for her mother and when she is finally able to make her own sky memory, Emily knows the truth of Aunt Vicki's statement that one day the hurting will go away. (71 pages)

Where it's reviewed:

Booklist, May 15, 1999, page 1695

Horn Book Guide, Fall 1999, page 276

Publishers Weekly, June 14, 1999, page 71

School Library Journal, August 1999, page 125

Other books by the same author:

The Summer My Father Was Ten, 1998

Hot Fudge Hero, 1997

Wanda's Roses, 1994

Kate on the Coast, 1992

Other books you might like:

Arno Bohlmeijer, *Something Very Sorry*, 1996

Rosemyn and her family are seriously injured in an automobile accident; her mother dies of her injuries compounding the family's pain.

Patricia Hermes, *You Shouldn't Have to Say Good-bye*, 1982

Sarah tries to forget the fact that her mother is dying of cancer because it is so hard to consider life without her.

Mary Jo Valley, *Please Don't Go*, 1996

While her mother undergoes treatment for breast cancer, a young girl often finds herself taking on her mother's role at home.

108

NANCY STEELE BROKAW

Leaving Emma

(New York: Clarion Books, 1999)

Subject(s): Friendship; Self-Reliance; Family Life

Age range(s): Grades 4-7

Major character(s): Emma Coleman, 5th Grader, Friend; Sirat ''Tem'' Temiyasathit, 5th Grader, Friend
Time period(s): 1990s
Locale(s): Champaign, Illinois

Summary: As Brokaw's debut novel opens Emma receives two pieces of bad news. First Tem, her very best friend since forever, announces that her father has accepted a teaching position in another city and at the end of the school year she'll be moving. As soon as Emma announces the sad news to her parents, her father tells her that he must go on a five-month work-related trip to Turkey. Emma knows that her father's trips turn her mother into a couch potato who can't be counted on for anything, including dinner, so she has only loneliness to look forward to during his trip. On Christmas, it becomes obvious to Emma that everyone is leaving when her mother announces that she is going on a five-week trip to Turkey to visit Emma's dad. Emma realizes reluctantly that she can count on only herself. (137 pages)

Where it's reviewed:
Booklist, March 1, 1999, page 1211
Horn Book Guide, Fall 1999, page 289
Publishers Weekly, March 8, 1999, page 69
School Library Journal, May 1999, page 122

Other books you might like:
Paula Danziger, *Amber Brown Is Not a Crayon*, 1994
  Amber's best friend Justin announces that his father has a new job and his family will soon move out of state.
Susan Patron, *Maybe Yes, Maybe No, Maybe Maybe*, 1993
  Eight-year-old PK feels overwhelmed by the rapid changes in her life and unhappy about her family's move to a new apartment.
Susan Shreve, *Ghost Cats*, 1999
  For Peter, the problems begin when his family stops moving all the time and he's unable to adjust to life in one place.

109

ERIK BROOKS, Author/Illustrator

The Practically Perfect Pajamas
(New York: Winslow Press, 2000)

Subject(s): Animals/Bears; Individuality; Peer Pressure
Age range(s): Grades K-3
Major character(s): Percy, Bear; Aurora, Fox
Time period(s): Indeterminate
Locale(s): Arctic

Summary: To Percy his footed pajamas are perfect for keeping him warm during naps, protecting his fur from spills and preventing ice from forming between his toes during walks. The other bears tease Percy when they see him in his beautiful pajamas so Percy realizes the attire is not completely perfect. The laughter of the other polar bears and the Arctic foxes makes Percy feel so alone that he decides to pack away his pajamas and join his peers wearing only his white fur coat. Aurora, who secretly watches and admires Percy in his pajamas, follows him when she sees him without his usual garb. Unfortunately, even without his distinctive attire, Percy is still the brunt of the other bears' jokes and miserable without the

comfort of his pajamas. Forlornly he retires to his den, but Aurora approaches with an idea. Percy agrees and soon all the bears—and Aurora—are able to adopt Percy's style as the author's first picture book ends with a positive fashion statement. (32 pages)

Where it's reviewed:
Booklist, May 15, 2000, page 1747
Horn Book Guide, Fall 2000, page 262
Publishers Weekly, May 8, 2000, page 221
School Library Journal, May 2000, page 132

Other books you might like:
Mary Blackwood, *Derek, the Knitting Dinosaur*, 1990
  Green, gentle Derek prefers knitting to ferocious dinosaur activities, a trait appreciated by the others when he has warm clothes to offer.
Helen Lester, *Three Cheers for Tacky*, 1994
  Despite his teammates efforts to mold him into a ''perfect'' cheerleader, Tacky remains true to himself and proves to be a winner.
Ellen Stoll Walsh, *Hop Jump*, 1993
  A blue frog decides she is tired of hopping and learns to dance, setting a new trend for other frogs also.

110

KEN BROWN, Author/Illustrator

Mucky Pup's Christmas
(New York: Dutton Children's Books, 1999)

Subject(s): Animals/Dogs; Christmas; Family
Age range(s): Grades K-1
Major character(s): Mucky Pup, Dog
Time period(s): 1990s (1998)
Locale(s): England

Summary: Mucky Pup thinks he's being helpful when he rearranges the tree in the house so he's hurt when his family is upset and sends him to the barn with the other animals. No one except the cat seems to know what Christmas is so Mucky Pup cannot understand what he has done wrong. When he awakens the next morning, the ground is covered with snow and Mucky Pup and the pig run out to play. Mucky Pup slips and rolls down the hill right into the snowman that the children are making. Overjoyed to see their pet, the children hurry into the house with him so he can enjoy Christmas too in a book first published in Great Britain in 1998. (32 pages)

Where it's reviewed:
Booklist, September 15, 1999, page 265
Horn Book Guide, Spring 2000, page 12
School Library Journal, October 1999, page 65

Other books by the same author:
Mucky Pup, 1997
Nellie's Knot, 1993

Other books you might like:
Louise Borden, *Just in Time for Christmas*, 1994
  As the family members gather for Christmas, Will is relieved to see his dog Luke, who's been missing for five days, appear too.
Eileen Christelow, *Not Until Christmas, Walter!*, 1997
  After Walter opens the presents prior to Christmas morn-

ing Louise sets up a booby trap to keep her pet from doing it again.

Marc McCutcheon, *Grandfather's Christmas Camp*, 1995
Grandfather's dog vanishes into the snowy woods, but reappears by Christmas morning.

111

MARC BROWN, Author/Illustrator

Arthur's Underwear

(Boston: Little, Brown and Company, 1999)

Series: Arthur Adventure
Subject(s): Animals/Aardvarks; Schools; Dreams and Nightmares
Age range(s): Grades K-2
Major character(s): Arthur Read, Aardvark, Student—Elementary School; Binky Barnes, Bear, Student—Elementary School; Buster, Rabbit, Student—Elementary School
Time period(s): 1990s (1999)
Locale(s): Fictional Country

Summary: While working problems at the board, Binky Barnes bends down to pick up a piece of dropped chalk and splits the seat of his pants much to the amusement of his classmates. Seeing his embarrassment makes such an impression on Arthur that he begins dreaming that he will have a similar embarrassing moment. His friend Buster suggests that Arthur stop sleeping in order to stop the dreaming. Unfortunately, Buster also tells just a few people about Arthur's problem hoping someone will offer a better suggestion for dealing with it. Soon Arthur hears giggles wherever he goes but none as loud as the laughter in the cafeteria when his pocket catches on something causing his pants to rip. Oh well, at least the bad dreams stop—for Arthur. (32 pages)

Where it's reviewed:
Booklist, January 1, 2000, page 935
Horn Book Guide, Spring 2000, page 30
School Library Journal, December 1999, page 88

Other books by the same author:
Arthur's Family Treasury, 2000 (Arthur Adventure)
Arthur's Perfect Christmas, 2000 (Arthur Adventure)
Arthur Lost and Found, 1998 (Arthur Adventure)

Other books you might like:
Kathryn Lasky, *Lunch Bunnies*, 1996
    The night before school starts Clyde dreams about having problems in the cafeteria.
Jonathan London, *Froggy Goes to School*, 1996
    Froggy's so nervous about the first day of school that he dreams he goes in his underwear.
Francesca Simon, *Spider School*, 1996
    Kate has such a horrible first day of school that she's relieved to know she was only dreaming.

112

MARC BROWN, Author/Illustrator

D.W., Go to Your Room!

(Boston: Little, Brown and Company, 1999)

Subject(s): Sisters; Family Life; Animals/Aardvarks
Age range(s): Grades K-1
Major character(s): Dora Winfred "D.W." Read, Sister (older); Kate Read, Baby, Sister; Mother, Mother
Time period(s): 1990s (1999)
Locale(s): United States

Summary: D.W.'s resentment of Kate grows as the baby takes the blocks with which D.W. is trying to build a castle. When the friction escalates Mother sends D.W. to her room where the time crawls and each of D.W.'s attempts to leave the room are thwarted. Just as she's packing her bags to move out, Mother asks her to care for Kate for a few minutes. Kate turns on her baby charms and all is soon forgiven between the sisters. (32 pages)

Where it's reviewed:
Booklist, June 1999, page 1838
Horn Book Guide, Fall 1999, page 246
School Library Journal, July 1999, page 61

Other books by the same author:
D.W.'s Lost Blankie, 1998
D.W. Rides Again!, 1996
D.W. Flips!, 1991

Other books you might like:
Russell Hoban, *A Baby Sister for Frances*, 1964
    Frances is unsure about the new addition to the family, but her patient, understanding parents help her adjust to the arrival of a baby sister.
Holly Keller, *Maxine in the Middle*, 1989
    To Maxine, being the "middle" bunny in the family is the worst place possible, so she leaves and soon her siblings realize they miss her.
Clara Vulliamy, *Ellen and Penguin and the New Baby*, 1996
    Ellen agrees with her stuffed Penguin's observation that having a new baby in the house is not such a good idea.

113

MARGARET WISE BROWN
CHRIS RASCHKA, Illustrator

Another Important Book

(New York: Joanna Cotler Books/HarperCollins Publishers, 1999)

Subject(s): Growing Up; Stories in Rhyme; Self-Awareness
Age range(s): Preschool
Time period(s): Indeterminate
Locale(s): Earth

Summary: No matter their race or ethnicity, children share certain characteristics as they grow from age one to six. Rhythmic descriptions relate all that two can do and the importance to three of being me. Ones have just begun while four is bigger than before. Each day children grow and learn and by ages five and six they have many tricks, but none more important than just being who you are. (32 pages)

Where it's reviewed:
Booklist, October 15,1999, page 450
Horn Book, September 1999, page 593
The New Advocate, Spring 2000, page 187
Publishers Weekly, October 25, 1999, page 80
School Library Journal, September 1999, page 176

Awards the book has won:
School Library Journal Best Books, 1999

Other books by the same author:
The Important Book, 1949
Goodnight Moon, 1947
The Runaway Bunny, 1942

Other books you might like:
Trish Cooke, *When I Grow Bigger*, 1994
    Leanne and her friends quibble about what they can or will
    do when they grow bigger.
Heidi Goennel, *While I Am Little*, 1993
    A young boy revels in the pleasures that are uniquely his
    because he's young enough and small enough to do them.
Martin Waddell, *Once There Were Giants*, 1989
    A girl describes her growth from infancy when everyone
    around her is a giant to motherhood when she becomes one
    of the giants in her baby's life.

114

RUTH BROWN, Author/Illustrator

Holly: The True Story of a Cat
(New York: Henry Holt and Company, 2000)

Subject(s): Animals/Cats; Family; Pets
Age range(s): Grades K-2
Major character(s): Holly, Cat
Time period(s): 2000s
Locale(s): England

Summary: Christmas is approaching when a family receives
an abandoned kitten so they name her Holly in honor of the
season. Fearful at first, Holly becomes more confident as she
matures. In time she has two kittens of her own who always
seem to find her when she sneaks away for a little peace and
quiet. All in all, Holly is a contented cat, loved by her family.
Originally published in the United Kingdom in 1999. (28
pages)

Where it's reviewed:
Horn Book Guide, Spring 2001, page 12
Kirkus Reviews, October 15, 2000, page 1481
Publishers Weekly, November 13, 2000, page 103
School Library Journal, October 2000, page 57

Other books by the same author:
Cry Baby, 1997
Toad, 1997
Copycat, 1994
The Picnic, 1993

Other books you might like:
Patricia Casey, *My Cat Jack*, 1994
    A well-loved pet, Jack is a stretching, yawning, playful cat.
Denise Fleming, *Mama Cat Has Three Kittens*, 1998
    Two of Mama Cat's kittens follow her lessons carefully,

but Boris sleeps during "class" and tries to play while the
others are napping.
Ann M. Martin, *Leo the Magnificat*, 1996
    A fluffy black and white cat wanders into a churchyard and
    makes himself at home for the rest of his long life.

115

ANNE BROYLES
LEANE MORIN, Illustrator

Shy Mama's Halloween
(Gardiner, ME: Tilbury House, Publishers, 2000)

Subject(s): Halloween; Emigration and Immigration; Family
Life
Age range(s): Grades 2-4
Major character(s): Anya, Daughter, Sister (oldest); Mama,
Immigrant, Mother; Dimitrii, Son, Brother (youngest)
Time period(s): Indeterminate Past
Locale(s): United States

Summary: With help from a neighbor who has a sewing
machine and scraps of fabric, Anya, Dimitrii and their sisters
have costumes for their first Halloween in America. Although
they plead with Mama to take them trick-or-treating Mama
gives the task to their father. On Halloween night, the children
sit, ready in their costumes, when their father arrives home
late from work too ill to go out again. Anya prepares her
siblings for the inevitable disappointment when Mama unexpectedly appears in her baboushka, ready to take her children
out. The experience of so many costumed people whose
identities are hidden just as hers is makes Anya feel a sense of
belonging to this new country. The magical evening cannot go
on forever and reluctantly the tired children return to their
home to do what all Americans do after trick-or-treating—
count their treats. The story concludes with two pages of
suggestions for sharing the book with children. (40 pages)

Where it's reviewed:
Booklist, November 15, 2000, page 646
Horn Book Guide, Spring 2001, page 31
Publishers Weekly, September 25, 2000, page 64
School Library Journal, January 2001, page 91

Awards the book has won:
Notable Social Studies Trade Books for Young People, 2001

Other books you might like:
Elisa Bartone, *American Too*, 1996
    When immigrant Rosie is chosen as the Queen of the San
    Gennaro feast she makes it clear that she is American too
    by dressing as the Statue of Liberty.
Brett Harvey, *Immigrant Girl, Becky of Eldridge Street*, 1987
    With her family 10-year-old Becky lives in a New York
    tenement, adjusting to a new and different life.
Lillian Hammer Ross, *Sarah, Also Known as Hannah*, 1994
    After her father's death, shy, reluctant Sarah is sent, in
    place of her sister Hannah, to live with her aunt and uncle
    in America.

116

JOSEPH BRUCHAC
S.D. NELSON, Illustrator

Crazy Horse's Vision

(New York: Lee & Low Books Inc., 2000)

Subject(s): Indians of North America; Conduct of Life; Biography
Age range(s): Grades 2-4
Major character(s): Curly, Indian (Lakota), Son; Tashunka Witco, Indian (Lakota), Father
Time period(s): 19th century
Locale(s): Black Hills, Great Plains

Summary: The son of Tashunka Witco is given the name Curly at his birth in recognition of his curly hair. Although quiet, Curly's leadership ability is apparent to playmates and other members of his tribe. Always courageous eleven-year-old Curly tames a wild horse and earns the right to claim it as his own. After witnessing a massacre of innocent Lakotas, Curly heads into the hills in a quest for a vision without following the rituals of his tribal culture. When he's found, he keeps his vision to himself for three years until the time is right to share it with Tashunka Witco. His father helps him to interpret the vision and confers his name upon his son so that Curly is now the one known as Tashunka Witco-Crazy Horse. Concluding notes by the author and illustrator give the historical basis for the story and the illustrative style. (36 pages)

Where it's reviewed:
Booklist, May 15, 2000, page 1747
Horn Book, July 2000, page 433
Kirkus Reviews, May 1, 2000, page 628
Publishers Weekly, May 29, 2000, page 83
School Library Journal, July 2000, page 68

Awards the book has won:
Notable Social Studies Trade Books for Young People, 2001

Other books by the same author:
The Boy Who Lived with the Bears: And Other Iroquois Stories, 1995 (ALA Notable Book)
A Boy Called Slow, 1994
Fox Song, 1993
The First Strawberries: A Cherokee Story, 1993 (Book Links Good Book)

Other books you might like:
Leigh Casler, *The Boy Who Dreamed of an Acorn*, 1994
   With two other boys from his village a young boy goes on a spirit quest seeking the dream that will explain his destiny.
Caron Lee Cohen, *The Mud Pony: A Traditional Skidi Pawnee Tale*, 1988
   Mother Earth transforms a poor boy's mud pony into a real one but to be a great leader the youth must find his own strength.
Kathryn Lasky, *Cloud Eyes*, 1994
   Cloud Eyes, a visionary, fulfills his destiny by learning the dance of bee and making peace with the bear so his people can harvest honey.
Virginia A. Stroud, *Doesn't Fall Off His Horse*, 1994
   Saygee's elderly great grandfather recalls the events of his

youth that earned him the name "Doesn't Fall Off His Horse."

117

JOSEPH BRUCHAC
GREG SHED, Illustrator

Squanto's Journey: The Story of the First Thanksgiving

(San Diego: Silver Whistle/Harcourt, Inc., 2000)

Subject(s): Indians of North America; Survival; Historical
Age range(s): Grades 2-5
Major character(s): Squanto, Indian
Time period(s): 17th century (1610s-1620s)
Locale(s): New England, American Colonies; Spain; England

Summary: Squanto, a man of honor and a leader of his people, is kidnapped in 1614 and sold into slavery in Spain. Freed with the help of Friars, Squanto travels to England to find a ship that can return him to his homeland. After sailing to New England, Squanto learns that his family and friends have died because of a sickness brought by the English. Using his knowledge of English and native languages Squanto attempts to act as a peacemaker between the groups and is taken prisoner by one of the tribes. Several months after the *Mayflower* pilgrims reach shore Squanto is freed to act as an intermediary in hopes that the different peoples can coexist in this land. He teaches the English about hunting and farming in the new world and with them celebrates their first bountiful harvest. (32 pages)

Where it's reviewed:
Booklist, September 1, 2000, p. 127
Horn Book Guide, Spring 2001, page 31
Kirkus Reviews, October 15, 2000, page 1481
Publishers Weekly, September 25, 2000, page 65
School Library Journal, November 2000, page 110

Awards the book has won:
Notable Social Studies Trade Books for Young People, 2001

Other books by the same author:
The Arrow Over the Door, 1998
Children of the Longhouse, 1996
The Boy Who Lived with the Bears: And Other Iroquois Stories, 1995

Other books you might like:
Gary Bowen, *Stranded at Plimoth Plantation 1626*, 1994
   A fictional diary describes the difficult living conditions for the Pilgrims in the Massachusetts colony.
Barbara Greenwood, *A Pioneer Thanksgiving: A Story of Harvest Celebrations in 1841*, 1999
   The Robertson family prepares for and celebrates a successful harvest.
Jackie French Koller, *Nickommah: A Thanksgiving Celebration*, 1999
   The Native American celebration of the Narragansett people for the annual harvest precedes the Pilgrim's Thanksgiving.

118

JEFF BRUMBEAU
GAIL DE MARCKEN, Illustrator

The Quiltmaker's Gift
(Duluth, MN: Pfeifer-Hamilton Publishers, 2000)

Subject(s): Quilts; Kings, Queens, Rulers, etc.; Conduct of Life
Age range(s): Grades 1-4
Major character(s): Unnamed Character, Seamstress (quiltmaker); Unnamed Character, Royalty
Time period(s): Indeterminate Past
Locale(s): Fictional Country

Summary: A talented quiltmaker refuses to sell her creations, but generously gives them away to anyone in need of warmth, comfort or shelter. The greedy king, however, thinks one of her quilts is just what he needs to be happy. When the king refuses the quiltmaker's demand that he give away all his possessions before he can receive a quilt, the king orders his soldiers to take one by force. Quickly, the quiltmaker throws her creation out the window where a breeze carries it away. Imprisonment does not change the quiltmaker's mind and finally the frustrated, unhappy king tries her plan. As the king gives away his possessions he begins to realize that giving is more pleasurable than receiving and by the time he's eligible to receive his quilt he's so happy that he really doesn't need it. (48 pages)

Where it's reviewed:
Booklist, January 1, 2000, page 935
ForeWord, November 1999, page 54
Kirkus Reviews, October 1, 1999, page 1575
Publishers Weekly, October 11, 1999, page 75
School Library Journal, February 2000, page 92

Awards the book has won:
Notable Social Studies Trade Books for Young People, 2000
Parents' Choice Silver Honor, 2000

Other books by the same author:
The Man-in-the-Moon in Love, 1992

Other books you might like:
Dick Gackenbach, *Barker's Crime*, 1996
    Stingy Mr. Gobble not only refuses to share a morsel with a hungry dog but he also has the dog arrested for stealing the aroma of the food.
Angela McAllister, *The King Who Sneezed*, 1988
    When King Parsimonious searches for the source of the draft in his castle he finds the outcome of his lack of concern for others.
Ruth Sanderson, *Papa Gatto: An Italian Fairy Tale*, 1995
    Greedy stepsister Sophia tires to trick Papa Gatto in order to claim a diamond bracelet, but he discovers her ruse.

119

QUINT BUCHHOLZ, Author/Illustrator
PETER F. NEUMEYER, Translator

The Collector of Moments
(New York: Farrar, Straus, Giroux, 1999)

Subject(s): Artists and Art; Music and Musicians; Friendship
Age range(s): Grades 3-6
Major character(s): Max, Artist, Friend; Professor, Child, Musician (violinist)
Time period(s): Indeterminate Past
Locale(s): Europe (an island)

Summary: When Max moves into the top-floor apartment the life of the boy who lives two flights below is transformed. Dubbed ''Professor'' by Max, the boy finds refuge in Max's red easy chair where he sits silently watching Max at work. In the evening, when Max puts his drawings aside to sing, Professor accompanies him on the violin. Each time Max completes a drawing he faces it to the wall so the boy never sees any of Max's work until Max goes on a long trip and leaves an exhibition just for him around the walls of the apartment. During the months of Max's absence the boy studies the art, considering the moment in time that is captured in each one, pondering the meaning of the surreal elements Max inserts into each drawing, and listening for the music revealed to him in the art. (48 pages)

Where it's reviewed:
Booklist, November 15, 1999, page 622
Five Owls, November 1999, page 43
Kirkus Reviews, October 1, 1999, page 1575
Publishers Weekly, November 22, 1999, page 55
School Library Journal, October 1999, page 109

Awards the book has won:
Batchelder Honor Book, 2000
New York Times Best Illustrated Children's Books, 1999

Other books by the same author:
Sleep Well, Little Bear, 1994

Other books you might like:
Christina Bjork, *Linnea in Monet's Garden*, 1987
    Mr. Bloom introduces Linnea to impressionist art and the artist Monet.
Joan MacPhail Knight, *Charlotte in Giverny*, 2000
    In 1892 Charlotte records in a journal her travels with her artist parents from Boston to Monet's artist colony.
Chris Van Allsburg, *The Mysteries of Harris Burdick*, 1984
    An award-winning title includes fourteen captioned drawings that challenge the reader's imagination to interpret the meaning.

120

NOLA BUCK
R.W. ALLEY, Illustrator

Hey, Little Baby!
(New York: Harper Festival/HarperCollins Publishers, 1999)

Series: Harper Growing Tree
Subject(s): Family Life; Growing Up; Stories in Rhyme

Age range(s): Preschool
Major character(s): Unnamed Character, Child, Sister (older); Unnamed Character, Baby, Brother (younger)
Time period(s): 1990s (1999)
Locale(s): United States

Summary: An energetic big sister happily boasts to her baby brother of all that she can do. Her accomplishments include counting to three, getting dressed herself and blowing her nose. She can also hop, slide, splash and twirl. Best of all, she promises to teach her brother all that she knows as soon as he grows a little bigger. (24 pages)

Where it's reviewed:
Booklist, February 1, 1999, page 978
Horn Book Guide, Fall 1999, page 230
Kirkus Reviews, January 1, 1999, page 62
Publishers Weekly, March 1, 1999, page 71
School Library Journal, March 1999, page 164

Other books by the same author:
Oh, Cats!, 1997
Sid and Sam, 1996
Gotcha!, 1994

Other books you might like:
Judith Caseley, *Mama, Coming and Going*, 1994
    Jenna is a big help to Mama after baby Mickey is born.
Holly Keller, *Geraldine's Baby Brother*, 1994
    Gradually, Geraldine becomes more accepting of her noisy baby brother and all the attention he receives.
Brigitte Weninger, *Will You Mind the Baby, Davy?*, 1997
    As the youngest in the family until his sister's birth, Davy realizes he has a lot to teach her as she grows.
Susan Winter, *A Baby Just Like Me*, 1994
    Martha is disappointed that her baby sister is not able to be her playmate immediately.

121

HELEN E. BUCKLEY
JAN ORMEROD, Illustrator

Where Did Josie Go?

(New York: Lothrop, Lee & Shepard Books, 1999)

Subject(s): Family; Games; Stories in Rhyme
Age range(s): Preschool
Major character(s): Josie, Child, Sister
Time period(s): 1990s
Locale(s): United States

Summary: In an updated, newly illustrated edition of a story first published in 1962, Josie hides from one place to another in her house and yard as her family searches. Josie's brother, father, pregnant mother and the family pets look for Josie, following a trail of strewn flowers from spot to spot until the trail leads back to the hammock. This time it is Josie, not her napping father in the hammock, but there's room for everyone. (24 pages)

Where it's reviewed:
Booklist, May 15, 1999, page 1701
Horn Book Guide, Fall 1999, page 230
Horn Book, July 1999, page 451
School Library Journal, May 1999, page 86

Other books by the same author:
Moonlight Kite, 1997
Someday with My Father, 1985
Josie's Buttercup, 1967
Josie and the Snow, 1964

Other books you might like:
Linda Berkowitz, *Alfonse, Where Are You?*, 1996
    When Little Bird does not find Alfonse the gander a concerned Alfonse becomes the seeker.
Paulette Bourgeois, *Franklin Is Lost*, 1993
    Not listening to his parents and becoming lost is not a game to frightened Franklin.
Dale Gottlieb, *Where Jamaica Go?*, 1996
    Cheerful Jamaica goes downtown, to the beach and for a ride in daddy's van.
Marisabina Russo, *Where Is Ben?*, 1990
    While Ben's mother is busy in the kitchen he tries to get some attention by engaging her in a game of hide-and-seek.
William Steig, *Toby, Where Are You?*, 1997
    Toby's parents play along with his game of hiding from his family.

122

EVE BUNTING

Blackwater

(New York: Joanna Cotler Books/HarperCollins Publishers, 1999)

Subject(s): Accidents; Death; Guilt
Age range(s): Grades 5-8
Major character(s): Brodie Lynch, 13-Year-Old, Son (of a minister); Alex, 12-Year-Old, Cousin (Brodie's)
Time period(s): 1990s (1999)
Locale(s): Rivertown, California

Summary: Unhappy to be stuck entertaining Alex who is visiting for the summer from Los Angeles, Brodie plans an early morning swimming lesson at a swimming hole formed by a bend in the treacherous Blackwater River. When Alex and Brodie arrive they see a couple on the large rock at the far side of the pond and Brodie plays a foolish prank on them that accidentally causes both teens to fall into the rushing waters of the Blackwater. Brodie's desperate but unsuccessful attempts to save the teens cause the townspeople to consider him a hero, an opinion supported by Alex's lying account of the tragedy. Recovering from a head injury suffered during the rescue attempt, Brodie finds his initial attempts to speak the truth are not heard and soon he is caught in the web of Alex's lies, racked by guilt and tormented with the shame of his actions. (146 pages)

Where it's reviewed:
Bulletin of the Center for Children's Books, September 1999, page 7
Kirkus Reviews, July 15, 1999, page 99
Los Angeles Times Book Review, December 12, 1999, page 6
Publishers Weekly, August 16, 1999, page 86
School Library Journal, August 1999, page 152

Other books by the same author:
Spying on Miss Mueller, 1995

The In-Between Days, 1994
For Always, 1993
Sharing Susan, 1991
A Sudden Silence, 1988

Other books you might like:
Marion Dane Bauer, *On My Honor*, 1986
Good friends Jore and Tony swim in a forbidden river; when Tony drowns, Jore is afraid to tell either set of parents.
Dorothy Reynolds Miller, *The Clearing: A Mystery*, 1996
While visiting relatives, Amanda becomes involved in the unsolved mystery of a youth's disappearance.
Katherine Paterson, *Preacher's Boy*, 1999
Robbie wrestles with his conscience when he realizes that his foolish actions could lead to the death of an innocent man.
Susan Beth Pfeffer, *The Year without Michael*, 1987
Michael sets off for a softball game and never returns. His family is left wondering if he was kidnapped or has run away.

123

EVE BUNTING
GREG SHED, Illustrator

Butterfly House
(New York: Scholastic, 1999)

Subject(s): Animals/Insects; Grandfathers; Nature
Age range(s): Grades K-3
Major character(s): Young girl, Child; Grandfather, Grandfather
Time period(s): Indeterminate
Locale(s): United States

Summary: After a young girl saves a caterpillar from a hungry bird, Grandfather helps her make a box in which to keep it. The girl decorates the box, placing twigs and leaves inside for the caterpillar. Soon, the caterpillar completes its metamorphosis and the time comes for the butterfly to be released. The girl is sad to part with the butterfly, but butterflies continue to visit her, thanking her for her kindness. (32 pages)

Where it's reviewed:
Booklist, June 1999, page 1838
Horn Book Guide, Fall 1999, page 246
Publishers Weekly, May 24, 1999, page 78
Reading Teacher, December 1999, page 346
School Library Journal, April 1999, page 91

Awards the book has won:
Notable Social Studies Trade Books for Young People, 2000

Other books by the same author:
I Have an Olive Tree, 1999
Some Frog!, 1998
Smoky Night, 1994 (Caldecott Medal winner)

Other books you might like:
Nancy Markham Alberts, *Elizabeth's Beauty*, 1997
Elizabeth helps an injured butterfly to fly again.
Deborah Heligman, *From Caterpillar to Butterfly*, 1996
In this nonfiction book, a child narrates the metamorphosis from caterpillar to butterfly.

Virginia Kroll, *Butterfly Boy*, 1997
Emilio learns about the habitat of the butterflies enjoyed by his invalid grandfather to assure they will be attracted to his yard annually.
Cynthia Rylant, *The Bird House*, 1998
A homeless girl finds a home surrounded by the birds who helped her.

124

EVE BUNTING
LEUYEN PHAM, Illustrator

Can You Do This, Old Badger?
(San Diego: Harcourt, Inc., 2000)

Subject(s): Animals/Badgers; Grandfathers; Love
Age range(s): Grades K-2
Major character(s): Old Badger, Badger, Grandfather; Little Badger, Badger
Time period(s): Indeterminate
Locale(s): Fictional Country

Summary: Although Old Badger may have lost the speed and agility needed to jump as high as Little Badger the grandfather proves that he still has knowledge worth sharing. After being shown where to find juicy worms following a rain or the best way to extract honey from a hive without being stung, Little Badger understands the value of what Old Badger can still do. The grandfather and grandson enjoy a loving day as Old Badger patiently teaches Little Badger to fish and then they settle down together to rest. (32 pages)

Where it's reviewed:
Booklist, March 15, 2000, page 1385
Horn Book Guide, February 2000, page 246
Kirkus Reviews, March 15, 2000, page 377
School Library Journal, March 2000, page 189

Other books by the same author:
Ducky, 1997
Twinnies, 1997 (IRA/CBC Children's Choices)
Secret Place, 1996
A Day's Work, 1994 (CLASP Commended Book)

Other books you might like:
Gillian Heal, *Grandpa Bear's Fantastic Scarf*, 1997
A young bear listens to Grandpa Bear's stories as he weaves, selecting colors to convey the significance of events in his life.
Amy Hest, *Baby Duck and the Bad Eyeglasses*, 1996
With her new glasses Baby Duck can read her name on the rowboat Grampa gives her.
Keiko Kasza, *Grandpa Toad's Last Secret*, 1995
From Grandpa Toad, Little Toad learns the secrets of survival in a world of hungry enemies—and just in time, too!
Helen Ketteman, *The Year of No More Corn*, 1993
Ole Grampa may be too old to help plant the corn crop but he's not too old to entertain his young grandson with a tall tale.

125

EVE BUNTING
BEN F. STAHL, Illustrator

Dreaming of America: An Ellis Island Story

(Mahwah, NJ: Troll/BridgeWater Books, 2000)

Subject(s): Voyages and Travels; Emigration and Immigration; Brothers and Sisters
Age range(s): Grades 2-4
Major character(s): Annie Moore, Immigrant, Sister (older); Anthony Moore, Immigrant, Brother; Phillip Moore, Immigrant, Brother
Time period(s): 1890s (1891-1892)
Locale(s): Cork, Ireland; SS Nevada, At Sea; New York, New York (Ellis Island)

Summary: A fictionalized account of the experience of the first immigrant to be processed through Ellis Island on January 1, 1892 begins as Annie and her brothers bid a poignant goodbye to their homeland. Three years earlier their parents had sailed to America and now third class tickets have been purchased for their children to join them. As Annie, Phillip and Anthony watch Ireland vanish in a cold mist, they meet a Russian immigrant who befriends them during the voyage. The siblings endure cramped living quarters and seasickness during a storm. By Christmas, opening the gifts their aunt sent along helps to cheer them and only a week later, on Annie's birthday they arrive to the excitement of the opening of Ellis Island and their reunion with their parents. An "Afterword" gives the historical basis for the story. (32 pages)

Where it's reviewed:
Booklist, April 1, 2000, page 1478
Publishers Weekly, February 21, 2000, page 87
School Library Journal, May 2000, page 132

Other books by the same author:
So Far from the Sea, 1998
Going Home, 1996 (CLASP Commended Book)
Train to Somewhere, 1996 (Booklist Editors' Choice)
Cheyenne Again, 1995
A Day's Work, 1994 (CLASP Commended Book)
Smoky Night, 1994 (Caldecott Medal)

Other books you might like:
Amy Hest, *When Jessie Came Across the Sea*, 1997
 Thirteen-year-old Jessie receives the gift of a ticket to America. After three years of work she's able to purchase a ticket for her grandmother.
Riki Levinson, *Soon, Annala*, 1993
 Anna and her parents eagerly await the arrival of the ship bringing Anna's two younger brothers to join the family in America.
Edith Tarbescu, *Annushka's Voyage*, 1998
 Two sisters leave their grandparents in Russia to meet their father in America.

126

EVE BUNTING
KAREN BARBOUR, Illustrator

I Have an Olive Tree

(New York: Joanna Cotler Books/HarperCollins Publishers, 1999)

Subject(s): Greek Americans; Family; Grandfathers
Age range(s): Grades 1-3
Major character(s): Sophia, 8-Year-Old; Mama, Mother; Grandfather, Grandfather
Time period(s): 1990s
Locale(s): California; Greece

Summary: Before Grandfather dies, he hands Sophia the beads of his deceased wife and asks Sophia to hang them on the olive tree he gave her a year earlier as a birthday gift. In order to fulfill Grandfather's request, Sophia and Mama must travel to the Greek island on which Grandfather and Mama once lived as the olive tree grows near their former home. Only after she makes this pilgrimage does Sophia come to appreciate the birthday gift that she initially considered disappointing. Placing the beads in the tree helps Sophia feel connected to her heritage and assures her that she will one day return. (32 pages)

Where it's reviewed:
Booklist, May 15, 1999, page 1702
Horn Book, July 1999, page 452
Publishers Weekly, May 24, 1999, page 78
School Library Journal, May 1999, page 86

Other books by the same author:
So Far from the Sea, 1998
December, 1997 (Book Links Lasting Connections)
Going Home, 1996 (CLASP Americas Commended Book)
Smoky Night, 1995 (Caldecott Medal)
A Day's Work, 1994 (CLASP Americas Commended Book)

Other books you might like:
Sherry Garland, *The Lotus Seed*, 1993
 An award-winning story portrays an immigrant's connection to her birthplace through a lotus seed and the sharing of her heritage with her descendants.
Jirina Marton, *You Can Go Home Again*, 1994
 After hearing stories of now-deceased relatives in the old country, Annie is eager to accompany her mother on a visit to her homeland.
Allen Say, *Grandfather's Journey*, 1993
 A grandson completes his grandfather's journey between homeland and adopted land, memory and desire. Caldecott Medal winner.
Mary Watson, *The Butterfly Seeds*, 1995
 As Grandpa promises, his gift to Jake, when planted, produces the plants that attract butterflies to remind Jake of Grandpa.

127

EVE BUNTING
NANCY CARPENTER, Illustrator

A Picnic in October

(San Diego: Harcourt Brace & Company, 1999)

Subject(s): Emigration and Immigration; Italian Americans; Relatives
Age range(s): Grades 1-3
Major character(s): Tony, Child, Narrator; Grandma, Grandmother, Immigrant
Time period(s): 1990s (1999)
Locale(s): New York, New York

Summary: Annually on October 28th Grandma insists that the entire family picnic at the base of the Statue of Liberty in celebration of Lady Liberty's birthday. Tony is annoyed to attend a picnic on a cold day and embarrassed by his family's public display of appreciation of the statue. To Grandma it is an important reminder of the freedom she enjoys in America. When Tony sees a family of recent immigrants viewing the statue reverently he begins to understand the importance of this symbol to those who have journeyed far to freedom. (32 pages)

Where it's reviewed:
Booklist, October 15, 1999, page 450
Horn Book Guide, Spring 2000, page 30
Kirkus Reviews, November 1, 1999, page 1739
Publishers Weekly, November 29, 1999, page 70
School Library Journal, October 1999, page 109

Awards the book has won:
Notable Social Studies Trade Books for Young People, 2000

Other books by the same author:
So Far from the Sea, 1998
Train to Somewhere, 1996 (Booklist Editors' Choice)
A Day's Work, 1994 (CLASP Commended Book)

Other books you might like:
Elisa Bartone, *American Too*, 1996
    When Rosina is chosen as Queen of a feast day in her neighborhood of Italian immigrants, she dresses as Lady Liberty to show she is American too.
Arthur Dorros, *Abuela*, 1991
    A glimpse of the Statue of Liberty reminds Rosalba of her arrival in the United States.
Betsy Maestro, *Coming to America: The Story of Immigration*, 1996
    A factual account explains the immigrant experience from its beginning to the present day.

128

EVE BUNTING
JO ELLEN MCALLISTER STAMMEN, Illustrator

Swan in Love

(New York: Atheneum Books for Young Readers, 2000)

Subject(s): Animals/Swans; Boats and Boating; Difference
Age range(s): Grades 2-3
Major character(s): Swan, Swan; Dora, Swan (boat)
Time period(s): Indeterminate
Locale(s): United States

Summary: Swan is enamored with a swan-shaped boat named Dora. During summers when the swan boat is used to give rides about the lake Swan swims right beside his beloved, ignoring the mockery of other swans. Even the fish and frogs think Swan is foolish to love something so different from his kind, but Swan is not troubled by difference. In the winter, when Dora is pulled onto shore, Swan stays beside it, refusing to migrate despite offers of help from other migrating fowl. Over time as the boat becomes older and begins showing signs of wear and tear, Swan also notices signs that he is aging. Still, he is horrified when the boat's owner announces plans to break her up because Dora can no longer float. Then the magical power of love overtakes Swan and his beloved and they are transformed together into a new state of being. (32 pages)

Where it's reviewed:
Booklist, April 1, 2000, page 1467
Horn Book Guide, Fall 2000, page 263
Kirkus Reviews, April 1, 2000, page 472
Publishers Weekly, May 15, 2000, page 116
School Library Journal, June 2000, page 102

Other books by the same author:
So Far from the Sea, 1998
December, 1997 (Book Links Lasting Connections)
I Am the Mummy Heb-Nefert, 1997 (Notable Children's Trade Books in the Field of Social Studies)
On Call Back Mountain, 1997 (Notable Children's Trade Books in the Field of Social Studies)
Secret Place, 1996
Smoky Night, 1994 (Caldecott Medal)

Other books you might like:
Michael Morpurgo, *The Silver Swan*, 2000
    A farm boy watches lovingly over a swan pair with nest and cygnets and grieves when a fox kills the pen in order to feed her cubs.
Jerry Pinkney, *The Ugly Duckling*, 1999
    In a retelling of Andersen's classic tale, the ugly outcast matures into a graceful swan and finally understands where he belongs.
Brenda Seabrooke, *The Swan's Gift*, 1995
    His family is starving yet Anton is unable to kill a beautiful swan that he sees while hunting; in thanks the swan magically bestows diamonds upon him.

129

EVE BUNTING
TIMOTHY BUSH, Illustrator

Wanna Buy an Alien?

(New York: Clarion Books, 2000)

Subject(s): Aliens; Science Fiction; Space Travel
Age range(s): Grades 3-5
Major character(s): Ben, 11-Year-Old, Friend; Jason Liebowicz, Friend; Paloma, Friend
Time period(s): 1960s
Locale(s): California

Summary: As Ben unpacks the unusual contents of the birthday gift he received from Jason he begins to wonder about this present. Paloma comes over and admits she was in on the idea, but insists that it's intended as a joke. Jason answered an ad to ''buy an alien'' thinking it would be a cool present for his friend, but Ben and Paloma both think that pictures of an alien with Ben, strange, warm rocks, audio tape with the alien's voice and a letter suggesting a meeting in two days are a little bit creepy. The three friends arrange to sneak out during a sleepover to the field suggested as the meeting spot and set up the rocks to guide the spaceship to a landing. They are astonished when an alien craft actually arrives and the alien tries to entice Ben aboard for a visit to Cham. Suddenly, the joke doesn't seem very funny. (92 pages)

Where it's reviewed:

Bulletin of the Center for Children's Books, June 2000, page 352

Horn Book Guide, Fall 2000, page 291

Publishers Weekly, April 3, 2000, page 81

School Library Journal, August 2000, page 177

Other books by the same author:

Some Frog!, 1998

Your Move, 1998

Night of the Gargoyles, 1994 (School Library Journal Best Books)

The In-Between Days, 1994

Other books you might like:

Herbie Brennan, *The Mystery Machine*, 1995
  Hubert discovers that his neighbor is not the witch everyone suspects but an alien with plans to take over Earth.

Jostein Gaarder, *Hello? Is Anybody There?*, 1998
  An alien baby from the planet Eljo falls from the sky and becomes stuck in a tree where Joe finds it.

Gery Greer, *Jason and the Escape from Bat Planet*, 1993
  In a series entry, Jason and his alien friend Coop rescue an absent-minded professor imprisoned in outer space. Coauthor Bob Ruddick.

Stephen Manes, *It's New! It's Improved! It's Terrible!*, 1989
  He looks like a boy, talks like a television commercial and is really an alien who's making Arnold and his friends feel crazy.

Daniel Pinkwater, *Ned Feldman, Space Pirate*, 1994
  Ned discovers Captain Lugo, an alien pirate, under the kitchen sink and accompanies him on a trip through space.

130

MELVIN BURGESS
RICHARD WILLIAMS, Illustrator

The Copper Treasure

(New York: Henry Holt and Company, 2000)

Subject(s): Treasure, Buried; Friendship; Adventure and Adventurers

Age range(s): Grades 4-6

Major character(s): Jamie, 11-Year-Old, Friend; Davies, Orphan, Friend; Ten Tons, Orphan, Friend

Time period(s): 1850s

Locale(s): London, England (River Thames)

Summary: Ten Tons, Davies and Jamie work together scrounging dropped coal, bits of iron and pieces of rope from the mud flats at low tide to sell. Sometimes they steal from ships at anchor awaiting repairs. While the boys are aboard one such ship the anchor rope breaks and a huge roll of copper on deck rolls into the dirty water. Clever Ten Tons proposes a plan to Davies and Jamie to raise the copper from the river bottom, float it downstream, sell it and have enough money to live without a care in the world. Luck seems to be on their side as they gather the rope and timber needed for the plan. At low tide, under cover of darkness, they set their plan in motion and soon realize just how dangerous their adventure is. A concluding glossary defines Victorian terms in this book first published in England in 1998. (104 pages)

Where it's reviewed:

Booklist, June 2000, page 1890

Horn Book Guide, Fall 2000, page 300

Horn Book, July 2000, page 451

School Library Journal, July 2000, page 100

Other books by the same author:

The Earth Giant, 1997

An Angel for May, 1995

Burning Issy, 1994

Other books you might like:

Will Hobbs, *Ghost Canoe*, 1997
  In 1874 suspicious circumstances after a shipwreck lead Nathan on a dangerous search for a murderer and a missing treasure.

Jill Paton Walsh, *A Chance Child*, 1978
  Searching for proof of the existence of a half brother, Christopher discovers papers describing working conditions during the Industrial Revolution.

Barbara Brooks Wallace, *Cousins in the Castle*, 1996
  Kidnapped orphans, lost heirs, and criminals determined to get rich at the children's expense combine to make a thrilling adventure.

131

ROBERT BURLEIGH
JOANNA YARDLEY, Illustrator

It's Funny Where Ben's Train Takes Him

(New York: Orchard Books, 1999)

Subject(s): Trains; Imagination; Bedtime

Age range(s): Grades K-3

Major character(s): Ben, Child

Time period(s): 1990s (1999)

Locale(s): United States

Summary: Ben doesn't want to go to bed yet, so he draws a picture of a train, and goes for a ride. His train takes him past hills, a farm, into a tunnel, over a river, through a town, and finally arrives at the station—in his bed. (32 pages)

Where it's reviewed:

Booklist, February 1, 1999, page 979

Horn Book Guide, Fall 1999, page 230

Kirkus Reviews, January 15, 1999, page 143

Publishers Weekly, March 1, 1999, page 67

School Library Journal, April 1999, page 91

Other books by the same author:
Home Run: The Story of Babe Ruth, 1998
Flight: The Story of Charles Lindbergh, 1997
Hoops, 1997

Other books you might like:
Jim Aylesworth, *Country Crossing*, 1991
On a summer night, an old man and a young boy wait for a freight train to pass.
Judith Heide Gilliland, *Not in the House, Newton!*, 1995
With his magical red crayon Newton makes an airplane and flies right out the window.
William H. Hooks, *The Mighty Santa Fe*, 1993
On Christmas Eve, eccentric Granny Blue takes sleepless William for a fantastic train trip.
Crockett Johnson, *Harold and the Purple Crayon*, 1958
Harold has a magic purple crayon, a vivid imagination, and a talent for drawing himself into and out of trouble.
David McPhail, *The Train*, 1977
One night, when his parents think he's sleeping, Matthew's train comes to life and takes him for a ride.
Charlotte Voake, *Here Comes the Train*, 1998
A family makes a trip to the local train tracks.

132

ROBERT BURLEIGH
BARRY ROOT, Illustrator

Messenger, Messenger

(New York: Atheneum Books for Young Readers, 2000)

Subject(s): Work; Bicycles and Bicycling; Stories in Rhyme
Age range(s): Grades K-3
Major character(s): Calvin Curbhopper, Worker (bicycle messenger)
Time period(s): 2000s
Locale(s): United States

Summary: Calvin Curbhopper begins his day by waking early, donning his cycling gear, carrying his bike down the apartment stairs and hurrying off to his job as a bicycle messenger in a large city. Across bridges, through traffic, up and down elevators and in and out of buildings Calvin pursues his responsibility with energy. With no time to stop for lunch, he dines while riding, waves to friends he passes, calls his dispatcher for more orders, tries to ignore the cold and the unsafe neighborhoods that he sometimes must visit. His last delivery is after dark on the 95th floor of an office building but then he goes home to the tiny studio he shares with a cat and his bike. (32 pages)

Where it's reviewed:
Booklist, May 15, 2000, page 1742
Horn Book Guide, Fall 2000, page 263
Publishers Weekly, June 19, 2000, page 79
Riverbank Review, Summer 2000, page 33
School Library Journal, June 2000, page 102

Awards the book has won:
Booklist Editors' Choice, 2000

Other books by the same author:
Hercules, 1999
It's Funny Where Ben's Train Takes Him, 1999

Home Run: The Story of Babe Ruth, 1998
Hoops, 1997

Other books you might like:
Jim Aylesworth, *My Sister's Rusty Bike*, 1996
A rhyming tale describes a boy's tour of the small towns of America astride his sister's rusty bicycle.
Eve Bunting, *Summer Wheels*, 1992
Bicycle Man repairs old bikes for use by the neighborhood kids.
Allen Say, *The Bicycle Man*, 1982
At the conclusion of school sports day two American soldiers borrow a bike and impress the Japanese students by doing tricks.
Audrey Wood, *The Red Racer*, 1996
Before Nona can demonstrate a need for the coveted Deluxe Rocket Racer in the store window she has to somehow get rid of her old bike.

133

JOHN BURNINGHAM, Author/Illustrator

Whaddayamean

(New York: Crown Publishers, Inc., 1999)

Subject(s): Problem Solving; God; Environmental Problems
Age range(s): Grades 1-5
Major character(s): God, Deity
Time period(s): Indeterminate
Locale(s): Earth

Summary: After creating the planet Earth, God rests. When God awakens to view the paradise that is Earth, the conditions are sad and alarming. God instructs the two children who journey with him to tell the groups responsible for the pollution, war, poverty and destruction of natural resources to stop their harmful practices. The adults will not listen to the children until they hear that the children are complying with God's request. Miraculously, the people of world take steps to change the destruction they have wrought and soon God's world becomes a paradise again. (32 pages)

Where it's reviewed:
Booklist, September 1, 1999, page 138
Kirkus Reviews, June 15, 1999, page 961
Magpies, May 1999, page 22
Publishers Weekly, July 16, 1999, page 83
School Library Journal, July 1999, page 67

Other books by the same author:
Cloudland, 1996
Courtney, 1994
Hey! Get Off Our Train, 1990

Other books you might like:
Sheila MacGill Callahan, *And Still the Turtle Watched*, 1991
Sadly, a turtle carved into a rocky promontory observes the disappearance of native peoples and the pollution of the land and river.
Dr. Seuss, *The Lorax*, 1971
The environmental changes that come with "progress" are recounted with sadness by the Lorax.
Chris Van Allsburg, *Just a Dream*, 1990
A dreamlike vision of the future gives Walter a new per-

spective on the importance of recycling and respect for the environment.

134

BETSY BYARS
BILL CIGLIANO, Illustrator

Me Tarzan

(New York: HarperCollins Publishers, 2000)

Subject(s): School Life; Plays; Animals
Age range(s): Grades 3-5
Major character(s): Dorothy, Student—Elementary School; Dwayne Wiggert, Classmate; Herb Mooney, Teacher
Time period(s): 2000s (2000)
Locale(s): United States

Summary: Dorothy's a relatively new student in her school, but she has the chance to make a name for herself and get back at her enemy Dwayne when Mr. Mooney holds try-outs for a class play about literary characters. When Dwayne auditions for the role of Tarzan with an anemic yell, Dorothy steps up and roars so convincingly that she gets the part. Dorothy is pleased with her Tarzan yell, but each time she yells the urge is stronger, the yell is louder and more animals are attracted by the sound. Mr. Mooney becomes so concerned that he fears losing his teaching position if Dorothy is Tarzan during the actual performance so he changes her lines. On the night of the program in front of a parent-filled auditorium Dorothy cannot control her urge and yells so loudly that the animals from a visiting circus stampede the school. Only Dorothy can get them back where they belong if she can just muster up one more cry of the jungle. (87 pages)

Where it's reviewed:
Booklist, March 15, 2000, page 1376
Horn Book, May 2000, page 309
Kirkus Reviews, May 15, 2000, page 711
Publishers Weekly, May 22, 2000, page 93
School Library Journal, July 2000, page 68

Other books by the same author:
Tornado, 1996
The Seven Treasure Hunts, 1991
Hooray for the Golly Sisters!, 1990
Beans on the Roof, 1988

Other books you might like:
Diane DeGroat, *Annie Pitts, Artichoke*, 1992
  Annie's class play about nutrition holds surprises that were not part of the teacher's plan.
Stephen Krensky, *Francine the Superstar*, 2000
  By striving for perfection in her school play, Francine instead almost ruins the production.
Marilyn Singer, *Twenty Ways to Lose Your Best Friend*, 1990
  Emma loses the friendship of a classmate when she doesn't support her friend's campaign to win the lead role in the class play.

135

BETSY BYARS
BETSY DUFFEY, Co-Author
LAURIE MYERS, Co-Author
LOREN LONG, Illustrator

My Dog, My Hero

(New York: Henry Holt and Company, 2000)

Subject(s): Animals/Dogs; Heroes and Heroines; Contests
Age range(s): Grades 3-5
Time period(s): Multiple Time Periods
Locale(s): United States

Summary: The first collaboration of mother and daughter authors, includes eight stories about heroic dogs selected as finalists in a fictional newspaper contest for the My Hero award. The young owner of a Newfoundland nominates Bear for his courage in leaping into an icy river to save a neighbor's dog. An elderly resident of a nursing home recommends Little Bit, a pet therapy dog, for the loving companionship that saved a depressed old woman. Blue receives a nomination for saving his owner's life after the man is seriously injured in a chain saw accident. Old Dog is a stray adopted by a young resident of a Georgia trailer park; he locates first his owner and then the other buried survivors of a tornado in the wreckage of their homes. (48 pages)

Where it's reviewed:
Booklist, January 1, 2001, page 954
Horn Book Guide, Spring 2001, page 70
Publishers Weekly, October 16, 2000, page 78
Riverbank Review, Winter 2000-2001, page 40

Other books you might like:
Joanna Cole, *Give a Dog a Bone: Stories, Poems, Jokes, and Riddles about Dogs*, 1996
  The illustrated compilation concludes with factual information explaining why dogs bark at "nothing." Stephanie Calmenson, co-compiler.
Fred Gipson, *Old Yeller*, 1956
  This Newbery Medal winner is a classic story of a boy and his dog.
Martin H. Greenberg, *A Newbery Zoo: A Dozen Animal Stories by Newbery Award-Winning Authors*, 1995
  A diverse collection of realistic, fantastic and adventurous animal stories. Charles G. Waugh, co-editor.
Margo Lundell, *Lad to the Rescue*, 1997
  While saving an invalid child from a poisonous snake Lad is bitten and almost dies.
Rosemary Wells, *Lassie Come Home*, 1995
  The picture book adaptation of Eric Knight's classic story tells of the power of love binding pet to owner and Lassie's determination to return to Joe.

136

JANIE BYNUM, Author/Illustrator

Otis

(San Diego: Harcourt, Inc., 2000)

Subject(s): Individuality; Animals/Pigs; Cleanliness

Age range(s): Grades K-1
Major character(s): Otis, Pig, Son; Little Frog, Frog, Friend
Time period(s): Indeterminate
Locale(s): Fictional Country

Summary: A clean pig who dislikes mud is a pig searching for a friend. Otis's parents assure him that he will develop a liking for mud, but he disagrees. While his siblings wallow, slide and play tag in the mud, Otis counts buttercups and tries to remain pristine. When Otis happens upon Little Frog who is unable to retrieve his ball from the mud because he refuses to touch the icky stuff Otis knows he's found a kindred spirit. Together Otis and Little Frog devise a way to both recover the ball and stay clean thus beginning a truly neat friendship. (36 pages)

Where it's reviewed:
Booklist, March 15, 2000, page 1385
Horn Book, July 2000, page 434
Publishers Weekly, April 17, 2000, page 78

School Library Journal, April 2000, page 92

Other books by the same author:
Altoona Baboona, 1999

Other books you might like:
Janice Boland, *Annabel*, 1993
    Dissatisfied with being a pig, Annabel tries to become some other kind of animal, but learns to accept herself as she is.
Dick King-Smith, *The Spotty Pig*, 1997
    Peter dislikes his spots and tries a variety of tactics to remove them until he meets Penny, a beautiful spotted pig.
Phyllis Root, *Mrs. Potter's Pig*, 1996
    Neat Mrs. Potter's daughter has so little interest in staying clean that she joins a pig that, unlike Otis, likes mud.
Ellen Stoll Walsh, *Hop Jump*, 1993
    Other frogs may hop, but an independently minded blue frog learns to dance instead.

C

137

MARY CALHOUN
ERICK INGRAHAM, Illustrator

Blue-Ribbon Henry

(New York: Morrow Junior Books, 1999)

Subject(s): Animals/Cats; Fairs; Pets
Age range(s): Grades K-2
Major character(s): Henry, Cat; The Kid, Child; Buttons, Dog
Time period(s): 1990s (1999)
Locale(s): United States

Summary: The Kid and his family take Henry and Buttons to the fair with plans to enter them in the small pet competition. Although overwhelmed by the large animals and crowds of people, Henry is still able to follow his instincts and save a lost girl who wanders into the horse ring. He returns the toddler to her appreciative family just in time to parade with Buttons and The Kid. Buttons is awarded a 2nd place ribbon in the dog class and Henry receives a special blue ribbon to recognize his heroism. (40 pages)

Where it's reviewed:
Booklist, June 1999, page 1838
Horn Book Guide, Fall 1999, page 246
School Library Journal, August 1999, page 131

Other books by the same author:
Henry the Sailor Cat, 1994
High-Wire Henry, 1991
Hot-Air Henry, 1981

Other books you might like:
Ruth Brown, *Copycat*, 1994
    Buddy is a cat that likes to mimic the actions of other animals, including the family dog.
Sheryl McFarlane, *Going to the Fair*, 1996
    Friends and neighbors eagerly prepare for the fair and dream of winning blue ribbons.
Tasha Tudor, *The County Fair*, 1940
    The events of a typical county fair of long ago are beautifully illustrated and simply related.

138

STEPHANIE CALMENSON
JOANNA COLE, Co-Author
LYNN MUNSINGER, Illustrator

Gator Halloween

(New York: Morrow Junior Books, 1999)

Subject(s): Animals/Alligators; Friendship; Halloween
Age range(s): Grades 2-4
Major character(s): Amy Gator, Alligator, Friend; Allie Gator, Alligator, Friend
Time period(s): 1990s
Locale(s): Fictional Country

Summary: Amy and Allie are so determined to win the Halloween costume contest that they visit a fortuneteller to help them come up with a costume idea. Though the fortuneteller isn't helpful with costume ideas, she does give the Gator Girls the confidence to tackle the job themselves. Unfortunately, their compassion for a lost lizard sidetracks them. By the time the lizard is rescued, the contest is finished, but as the fortuneteller predicted, Amy and Allie feel as if they are winners even if someone else has the crown and the glory. (64 pages)

Where it's reviewed:
Booklist, September 1, 1999, page 145
Horn Book Guide, Spring 2000, page 64
Publishers Weekly, September 27, 1999, page 48
School Library Journal, September 1999, page 176

Other books by the same author:
Get Well, Gators!, 1998
Rockin' Reptiles, 1997
The Gator Girls, 1995

Other books you might like:
Marion Dane Bauer, *Alison's Fierce and Ugly Halloween*, 1997
    Alison's attempt to be scary on Halloween creates friction with her friend Cindy.
Robin Michal Koontz, *Chicago and the Cat: The Halloween Party*, 1994

On Halloween night nothing seems to go the way Chicago and the cat have planned.

Dav Pilkey, *Dragon's Halloween*, 1993

In the fifth tale about Dragon, the kindly creature scares himself with the pumpkin monster he makes and then with the sounds from his hungry stomach.

139

ANN CAMERON
LIS TOFT, Illustrator

Gloria's Way

(New York: Frances Foster/Farrar, Straus, Giroux, 2000)

Subject(s): Friendship; Parent and Child; African Americans
Age range(s): Grades 2-4
Major character(s): Gloria Jones, Child, Friend; Mr. Bates, Businessman, Father; Julian Bates, Son, Friend
Time period(s): 2000s (2000)
Locale(s): United States

Summary: Gloria faces the trials and tribulations of childhood with support from friends and family. When a new girl moves into the neighborhood the dynamics are rearranged, but some quiet advice from her mother helps Gloria learns to overcome her jealousy and enjoy the friendship she has with Julian as they both try to include the new neighbor in their play. Frequently, Mr. Bates helps solve small problems that arise such as encouraging Gloria to make a new valentine for her mom to replace one that was accidentally damaged. While Gloria struggles with fractions, her dad works patiently to help her understand them. (96 pages)

Where it's reviewed:
Booklist, February 15, 2000, page 1110
Bulletin of the Center for Children's Books, February 2000, page 204
Horn Book, March 2000, page 193
Publishers Weekly, March 20, 2000, page 92
School Library Journal, March 2000, page 189

Other books by the same author:
More Stories Huey Tells, 1997
More Stories Julian Tells, 1986
The Stories Julian Tells, 1981

Other books you might like:
Malorie Blackman, *Girl Wonder and the Terrific Twins*, 1993
  Maxine and her twin brothers have great plans to help their mother but their ideas seem to create work not reduce it.
C.B. Christiansen, *Sycamore Street*, 1993
  Best friends Angel and Chloe try to ignore the obnoxious new kid, but eventually learn that he has something to offer in the way of friendship.
Beverly Cleary, *Ramona Quimby, Age 8*, 1981
  Spirited Ramona continues to keep her family guessing about her next adventure as she enters third grade in this Newbery Honor book.
Angela Shelf Medearis, *The Adventures of Sugar and Junior*, 1995
  When Sugar moves into the apartment building Junior is happy to finally have a playmate his age nearby.

Philippa Pearce, *Here Comes Tod!*, 1994
  The episodic beginning chapter book features a lively six-year-old and his loving family.

140

LINDSAY CAMP
TONY ROSS, Illustrator

Why?

(New York: G.P. Putnam's Sons, 1999)

Subject(s): Fathers and Daughters; Aliens; Fantasy
Age range(s): Grades K-3
Major character(s): Lily, Child, Daughter; Unnamed Character, Father
Time period(s): 1990s
Locale(s): Earth

Summary: Lily has a one-word response, ''Why?'' to everything her father says. Patiently, he tries to answer her question, but some days he becomes frustrated when each reply prompts the same response from Lily. While playing in the park, Lily, her father and other families are stunned when a large spaceship lands and the inhabitants come out to announce their intention to destroy the planet. Everyone is speechless, except Lily whose one-word question causes such discussion among the aliens that they eventually board their spaceship and leave. (32 pages)

Where it's reviewed:
Booklist, July 1999, page 1949
Horn Book Guide, Fall 1999, page 246
Publishers Weekly, June 14, 1999, page 69
School Library Journal, July 1999, page 67

Other books by the same author:
Dinosaurs at the Supermarket, 1993
Keeping Up with Cheetah, 1993

Other books you might like:
Frank Asch, *Insects from Outer Space*, 1995
  A spaceship of friendly alien insects lands just in time to take part in the annual Bug Ball before returning to their own planet.
Anita Jeram, *Contrary Mary*, 1995
  Mary is having an uncooperative day. She puts her shoes on the wrong feet, refuses to use the umbrella in the rain and reads books upside down.
Colin McNaughton, *Here Come the Aliens!*, 1995
  Rhyming descriptions match the pictures of aliens on an invasion path until stopped by an orbiting picture of a group of 4-year-olds.
Anne F. Rockwell, *No! No! No!*, 1995
  Nothing is going the way a little boy plans and all he can say is ''No! No! No!''

141

JANELL CANNON, Author/Illustrator

Crickwing

(San Diego: Harcourt, Inc., 2000)

Subject(s): Animals/Cockroaches; Animals/Ants; Animals

Age range(s): Grades 1-4
Major character(s): Crickwing, Cockroach, Artist; Eartha, Ant
Time period(s): Indeterminate
Locale(s): Earth

Summary: His escape from a toad's sticky tongue results in Crickwing's twisted wing and his despised nickname. Crickwing's interest is in sculpture and he'd prefer to be alone to transform the leaves, roots, and petals of the forest floor into figures that he then eats for dinner. More accurately, larger creatures seem to be the ones that eat them for dinner, after stealing them from Crickwing. When Crickwing happens upon a colony of leaf-cutting ants and, in frustration, bullies the smaller insects, the small, but numerous ants take him prisoner, intending to sacrifice him to the army ants. Eartha convinces the others to free Crickwing and, in gratitude, he enlists their help creating the grandest sculpture he's ever made, saving the colony from invasion by the army ants. Concluding notes give factual information about cockroaches and ants. (48 pages)

Where it's reviewed:
Booklist, October 15, 2000, page 434
Children's Bookwatch, September 2000, page 5
Kirkus Reviews, September 15, 2000, page 1352
Publishers Weekly, August 7, 2000, page 95
School Library Journal, November 2000, page 110

Other books by the same author:
Verdi, 1997 (IRA/CBC Children's Choice)
Trupp: A Fuzzhead Tale, 1995
Stellaluna, 1993 (California Young Reader Medal)

Other books you might like:
Richard Egielski, *Jazper*, 1998
    Jazper uses the magic he learns while house sitting for five moths to protect himself and his father when the moths attack the insects.
William Joyce, *The Leaf Men and the Brave Good Bugs*, 1996
    Summoned by the Doodle Bugs, the Leaf Men battle the Spider Queen and retrieve Long-Lost Toy.
Kevin O'Malley, *Leo Cockroach. . .Toy Tester*, 1999
    Unappreciated by the CEO of a toy company, Leo seeks employment with a rival, soon regrets his decision and creatively finds a way to return.

142

KATHY CAPLE, Author/Illustrator

The Friendship Tree
(New York: Holiday House, 2000)

Series: Holiday House Reader. Level 2
Subject(s): Animals/Sheep; Trees; Friendship
Age range(s): Grades 1-2
Major character(s): Blanche, Sheep, Friend; Otis, Sheep, Friend
Time period(s): Indeterminate
Locale(s): Fictional Country

Summary: As Blanche helps Otis rake the leaves in his yard she laments the fact that her pine tree does not provide the pleasure of colorful falling leaves. Otis plans a surprise for Blanche by placing the leaf bags in her pine tree and rigging

them to make the leaves fall. During a storm, the wind topples the big tree in Otis's yard so Blanche gives him a living tree to decorate for Christmas with the promise to help him plant it in the spring. At first Otis worries that his newly planted tree is cold and lonely, but when birds build a nest in the tree he's sure the tree is fine. Blanche builds two chairs from the wood of Otis's fallen tree and the two neighbors sit in them to enjoy watching the new tree. (32 pages)

Where it's reviewed:
Booklist, February 15, 2000, page 1123
Horn Book, July 2000, page 453
Kirkus Reviews, February 15, 2000, page 241
Publishers Weekly, February 14, 2000, page 197
School Library Journal, April 2000, page 92

Other books by the same author:
Hillary to the Rescue, 2000
Well Done, Worm!, 2000
Starring Hillary, 1999

Other books you might like:
Arnold Lobel, *Frog and Toad Together*, 1972
    The Newbery Honor Book is one of four titles describing the friendship of Frog and Toad in five brief chapters.
James Marshall, *George and Martha*, 1972
    The first book in a series about George and Martha uses several brief, humorous stories to describe the antics of two hippo buddies.
Cynthia Rylant, *Poppleton Forever*, 1998
    Poppleton's friend and neighbor Cherry Pie is one of his supportive friends who suggest solutions to Poppleton's many little problems.

143

ALYSSA SATIN CAPUCILLI
PAT SCHORIES, Illustrator

Happy Birthday, Biscuit!
(New York: HarperCollins Publishers, 1999)

Subject(s): Animals/Dogs; Birthdays; Pets
Age range(s): Preschool
Major character(s): Biscuit, Dog; Unnamed Character, Child (girl)
Time period(s): 1990s (1999)
Locale(s): United States

Summary: Biscuit's owner carefully plans for the celebration of his first birthday. Two of his animal friends join in for the party. Biscuit seems confused by the party hat and the candle in his food, but he knows how to open the presents. A new collar is nice, but the best present is the box of dog biscuits. (24 pages)

Where it's reviewed:
Booklist, June 1999, page 1838
Horn Book Guide, Fall 1999, page 231
School Library Journal, June 1999, page 85

Other books by the same author:
Bathtime for Biscuit, 1998
Biscuit Finds a Friend, 1997
Biscuit, 1996

Other books you might like:

Norman Bridwell, *Clifford's Birthday Party*, 1990
  Emily Elizabeth gives Clifford a very special party complete with a pinata and birthday cake.
Alexandra Day, *Carl's Birthday*, 1995
  Madeleine's mother thinks she is preparing a surprise party for Carl but she doesn't know that Carl and Madeleine are not really napping.
Eric Hill, *Spot Goes to a Party*, 1992
  Popular pup, Spot, attends a costume party at Helen's house.
Mick Inkpen, *Kipper's Birthday*, 1993
  A misunderstanding threatens the careful plans Kipper makes for his birthday party.

144

ERIC CARLE, Author/Illustrator

The Very Clumsy Click Beetle
(New York: Philomel Books, 1999)

Subject(s): Animals/Insects; Determination; Animals
Age range(s): Grades K-2
Major character(s): Unnamed Character, Insect (click beetle)
Time period(s): Indeterminate
Locale(s): Fictional Country

Summary: A young click beetle walks from morning until night up and down a flower, through a pile of pebbles and among blades of grass. Tired, the click beetle climbs up a tree to rest when it falls to the ground and lands on its back. In the morning an older and wiser click beetle shows the young one how to flip over. The young click beetle tries but each time he flips, he lands on his back again. A succession of animals encourages him and he keeps trying with the same results until two very large feet approach and a boy bends down as if to grab the beetle. This time when the young beetle clicks he flips three times and lands on his feet! The author includes factual information about the many species of click beetle and their unique flip technique. (32 pages)

Where it's reviewed:
Booklist, October 1, 1999, page 360
Horn Book Guide, Spring 2000, page 13
Publishers Weekly, August 23, 1999, page 56
School Library Journal, November 1999, page 112
Teacher Librarian, February 2000, page 49

Other books by the same author:
The Very Lonely Firefly, 1995
The Very Quiet Cricket, 1990
The Very Busy Spider, 1985
The Very Hungry Caterpillar, 1969

Other books you might like:
Jerry Booth, *Big Bugs*, 1994
  A factual look at many bugs describes habitats and characteristics.
Mick Inkpen, *Billy's Beetle*, 1992
  When Billy loses his beetle he receives a lot of help with his search for it.

Megan McDonald, *Insects Are My Life*, 1995
  A new classmate seems to share Amanda's interest in insects.

145

MARGARET CARLSON
KIMANNE SMITH, Illustrator

The Canning Season
(Minneapolis: Carolrhoda Books, Inc.)

Series: A First Person Book
Subject(s): African Americans; Prejudice; Friendship
Age range(s): Grades 2-5
Major character(s): Peggy Nolan, Friend (Peggie's), Child (Caucasian); Peggie, Child (African American), Friend (Peggy's); Mom, Mother (Peggie's)
Time period(s): 1950s (1959)
Locale(s): Minneapolis, Minnesota

Summary: In the August heat, Peggie's mother, aunt and grandmother are busy canning beans while Peggie looks forward to having her friend, also named Peggy, sleep over as she's done many times before. When Peggy says she's no longer allowed to stay at Peggie's house because Peggie has brothers and the family is Negro, Peggy angrily makes up an excuse about Peggy's white brothers as the reason she cannot go to Peggy's house. Mom notices how upset Peggie is when she arrives home and offers what solace she can to Peggie's broken dreams. A concluding author's note gives factual information about racism and includes discussion questions. (40 pages)

Where it's reviewed:
Booklist, February 15, 1999, page 1067
Kirkus Reviews, January 1, 1999, page 63
Publishers Weekly, February 1, 1999, page 85
School Library Journal, March 1999, page 171

Other books you might like:
Sandra Belton, *From Miss Ida's Front Porch*, 1993
  The stories told by neighbors gathered on Miss Ida's porch include those of famous African Americans who faced prejudicial treatment.
K. Scott Conover, *Can I Play Too?*, 1998
  New to the neighborhood, a young boy in orthopedic braces must convince the other children to let him join in their games.
Vaunda Micheaux Nelson, *Mayfield Crossing*, 1993
  When the children of Mayfield Crrossing are bused to a larger school, they are treated as outsiders and judged by the color of their skin.
Jerdine Nolen, *In My Momma's Kitchen*, 1999
  A young African-American girl shares the experiences of her family from the perspective of her mother's kitchen.

146

NANCY CARLSON, Author/Illustrator

Look Out Kindergarten, Here I Come!

(New York: Viking, 1999)

Subject(s): Schools; Education; Mothers and Sons
Age range(s): Grades K-1
Major character(s): Henry, Mouse, Student—Elementary School; Mom, Mother, Mouse; Ms. Bradley, Pig, Teacher
Time period(s): 1990s
Locale(s): Fictional Country

Summary: Henry is so excited when the first day of school arrives that he wants to leap out of bed and hurry out the door. Patiently, Mom suggests that he get dressed and eat breakfast first. As they walk to school, Henry asks many questions about what he can expect to do all day. When they arrive at the building, Henry's eager anticipation changes to anxious apprehension and he considers returning home with Mom. Ms. Bradley greets Henry at the classroom door and invites him to look around the room. That's all the convincing Henry needs to decide to stay. (32 pages)

Where it's reviewed:
Booklist, June 1999, page 1838
Horn Book Guide, Fall 1999, page 246
The New York Times Book Review, November 21, 1999, page 39
School Library Journal, July 1999, page 67

Other books by the same author:
It's Going to Be Perfect!, 1998
ABC, I Like Me!, 1997
Sit Still!, 1996

Other books you might like:
Holly Keller, *Harry and Tuck*, 1993
    Inseparable twins Harrison and Tucker discover that being placed in different kindergarten classrooms is less difficult than they expected.
Kathryn Lasky, *Lunch Bunnies*, 1996
    Apprehensive Clyde is terrified by his brother's stories about the school cafeteria yet he finds an equally nervous friend and both enjoy lunch.
Jonathan London, *Froggy Goes to School*, 1996
    Despite feeling nervous about the first day of school, Froggy manages to overcome his fears and enjoy the day.
Amy Schwartz, *Annabelle Swift, Kindergartner*, 1988
    The shared experiences of Annabelle's big sister help Annabelle have a successful first day of kindergarten.
Mary Serfozo, *Benjamin Bigfoot*, 1993
    Benjamin's reservations about beginning kindergarten vanish after a visit to the teacher.

147

NANCY WHITE CARLSTROM
BRUCE DEGEN, Illustrator

What a Scare, Jesse Bear

(New York: Simon & Schuster Books for Young Readers, 1999)

Subject(s): Animals/Bears; Halloween; Stories in Rhyme

Age range(s): Preschool
Major character(s): Jesse Bear, Bear, Son; Mama, Bear, Mother; Papa, Bear, Father
Time period(s): Indeterminate
Locale(s): Fictional Country

Summary: Selecting and carving a pumpkin with Papa's help is fun, but also a little scary for Jesse Bear. Searching the attic with Mama and Papa for just the right costume is exciting until Jesse Bear looks in the mirror while wearing a monster mask. What a scare! Mama and Papa, in costume, walk with Jesse around the neighborhood as he trick-or-treats and feels a little frightened by some of the costumes. Finally, they return home, sneaking in the back door to give Jesse's grandparents a scare, too. (32 pages)

Where it's reviewed:
Booklist, September 1, 1999, page 147
Horn Book Guide, Spring 2000, page 13
Kirkus Reviews, August 15, 1999, page 1307
Publishers Weekly, September 27, 1999, page 48
School Library Journal, October 1999, page 110

Other books by the same author:
Guess Who's Coming, Jesse Bear, 1998
Let's Count It Out, Jesse Bear, 1996
Jesse Bear's Yum Yum Crumble, 1994

Other books you might like:
Abby Levine, *This Is the Pumpkin*, 1997
    Max wears his Halloween costume to school and then comes home to carve a pumpkin and trick-or-treat with his family.
Dav Pilkey, *The Hallo-Weiner*, 1995
    Oscar's bravery on Halloween night wins him some respect despite the embarrassing costume his mother has made.
Kay Winters, *The Teeny Tiny Ghost*, 1997
    A very small ghost is also so timid that he has trouble doing his haunting homework because he scares himself.

148

JAN CARR
ROBERT BENDER, Illustrator

Swine Divine

(New York: Holiday House, 1999)

Subject(s): Animals/Pigs; Photography; Farm Life
Age range(s): Grades K-2
Major character(s): Rosie, Pig; Luke, Farmer; Mr. Porkpie, Photographer
Time period(s): 1990s
Locale(s): United States

Summary: Rosie's perfect morning sprawled in the mud comes to an abrupt end when Luke blasts her with the hose to prepare her for a visit to Mr. Porkpie. Luke's promise to Mr. Porkpie that Rosie will "ham it up" makes Rosie feel a little nervous about the purpose of this visit. As it turns out, Mr. Porkpie dresses Rosie in one outrageous outfit after another to photograph her. The tutu proves to be the final straw. Rosie darts from the studio through the town and back to the farm where Luke finds her asleep in the mud. (32 pages)

Where it's reviewed:
Booklist, March 1, 1999, page 1218
Children's Book Review Service, April 1999, page 97
Kirkus Reviews, March 1, 1999, page 373
Publishers Weekly, March 8, 1999, page 68
School Library Journal, June 1999, page 91

Other books by the same author:
Dark Day, Light Night, 1996 (Smithsonian's Notable Books for Children)
The Nature of the Beast, 1996
Beauty and the Beast, 1993

Other books you might like:
Karen Beaumont Alarcon, *Louella Mae, She's Run Away!*, 1997
  Family members and farm animals join a frantic search for their pig Louella Mae.
Janice Boland, *Annabel Again*, 1995
  After searching for a residence more exciting than a mud puddle, Annabel discovers that there is no place like home.
William Mayne, *Lady Muck*, 1997
  Lady Muck's attempt to elevate her station in life fails when she eats the truffles before they can be sold at the market.
Abigail Pfizer, *Penelope Pig*, 1988
  Tired of a muddy pigsty for a home, Penelope decides to move into the farmhouse.

149

CAROL CARRICK
DAVID MILGRIM, Illustrator

Patrick's Dinosaurs on the Internet
(New York: Clarion Books, 1999)

Subject(s): Dinosaurs; Computers; Space Travel
Age range(s): Grades K-2
Major character(s): Hank, Child, Brother (older); Patrick, Child, Brother; Flato, Dinosaur, Spaceship Captain
Time period(s): 1990s
Locale(s): Earth; Planet—Imaginary

Summary: Hank and Patrick are researching dinosaurs on the Internet when Hank tires and goes to bed. Patrick lies awake looking at the screensaver when the image of a dinosaur appears. Soon, the same dinosaur, introducing himself as Flato, arrives in a spaceship and carries Patrick back to his planet where he is scheduled to be Flato's show-and-tell offering for the day. After answering questions from Flato's classmates and playing with the herbivores at recess, Patrick is frightened by an approaching Tyrannosaurus Rex and eagerly enters the space ship for a ride home. (32 pages)

Where it's reviewed:
Booklist, December 1, 1999, page 709
Publishers Weekly, September 6, 1999, page 102
School Library Journal, September 1999, page 178

Other books by the same author:
Valentine, 1995
Big Old Bones: A Dinosaur Tale, 1992
What Happened to Patrick's Dinosaurs?, 1986
Patrick's Dinosaurs, 1983

Other books you might like:
Lois G. Grambling, *Can I Have a Stegosaurus, Mom? Can I? Please?*, 1995
  To convince Mom to accept a stegosaurus as a family pet, a child lists the dinosaur's positive attributes.
James Mayhew, *Katie and the Dinosaurs*, 1992
  When Katie visits a natural history museum, she finds herself surrounded by real dinosaurs.
Mark Alan Weatherby, *My Dinosaur*, 1997
  A little girl rides through the moonlit woods atop her dinosaur and then goes home to sleep, clutching her green stuffed dinosaur.

150

LEWIS CARROLL (Pseudonym of Charles Lutwidge Dodson)
HELEN OXENBURY, Illustrator

Alice's Adventures in Wonderland
(Cambridge, MA: Candlewick Press, 1999)

Subject(s): Fantasy; Dreams and Nightmares; Humor
Age range(s): Grades 3-6
Major character(s): Alice, Child; Queen of Hearts, Royalty; White Rabbit, Rabbit
Time period(s): Indeterminate Past
Locale(s): Fictional Country

Summary: Oxenbury's illustrated edition of Carroll's classic story, originally published in 1865 includes the complete text. Curious Alice, who has charmed readers for years, once again follows White Rabbit into a hole beneath a tree and tumbles into a fantastic world. With her sense of adventure, Alice overcomes many unexpected obstacles, attends a very strange tea party, and matches wits with a Queen determined to cut off her head. Just as it appears that the Queen of Hearts will have her way, Alice wakes up on the grassy bank beside her sister where she first saw the White Rabbit and tells her sister about her curious dream. (207 pages)

Where it's reviewed:
Booklist, January 1, 2000
Horn Book, January 2000, page 72
Publishers Weekly, November 1, 1999, page 84
School Library Journal, January 2000, page 93
Times Educational Supplement, April 23, 1999, page 11

Awards the book has won:
ALA Notable Children's Books, 2000
Horn Book Fanfare, 2000

Other books you might like:
L. Frank Baum, *The Wizard of Oz*, 1900
  Dorothy and Toto, after being hurled into a strange land by a tornado, finally find a way home to Kansas.
Roald Dahl, *James and the Giant Peach*, 1961
  Finding a giant peach in his yard, James leaves his unhappy home to travel in the peach with an assortment of fantastic creatures.
Kenneth Grahame, *The Wind in the Willows*, 1908
  Mole, Ratty, Badger and Mr. Toad are involved in many adventures in a classic story set in the English countryside.
Norton Juster, *The Phantom Tollbooth*, 1961
  The tollbooth Milo receives provides him with an opportu-

nity to travel to a land where he learns to appreciate the importance of words and numbers.

C.S. Lewis, *The Lion, the Witch, and the Wardrobe: A Story for Children*, 1950

The first of the seven volumes of the Narnia chronicles introduces three children to a magical land entered through their wardrobe.

151

ALDEN R. CARTER
DAN YOUNG, Illustrator
CAROL S. CARTER, Illustrator

Dustin's Big School Day

(Morton Grove, IL: Albert Whitman & Company, 1999)

Subject(s): Down Syndrome; Schools; Mentally Handicapped
Age range(s): Grades K-2
Major character(s): Dustin Apfel, 2nd Grader, Mentally Challenged Person; Lexi Morgan, 2nd Grader, Friend (Dustin's); Dave Parker, Entertainer (ventriloquist)
Time period(s): 1990s (1998)
Locale(s): Marshfield, Wisconsin

Summary: An exciting day for everyone at Grant Elementary School is more so for Dustin because Dave Parker, a friend of Dustin's dad, will perform with his wooden puppet for all the students. Before the afternoon assembly, Lexi and Dustin still must complete their work in Language Arts, Math and Science. Dustin also goes to speech class and the occupational therapist while eagerly awaiting the performance. Finally the show begins and Dustin's biggest school day comes to an end. (32 pages)

Where it's reviewed:
Booklist, April 15, 1999, page 1534
Bulletin of the Center for Children's Books, March 1999, page 234
Horn Book Guide, Fall 1999, page 247
Horn Book Guide, Fall 1999, page 247
School Library Journal, June 1999, page 92

Other books by the same author:
Big Brother Dustin, 1997
I'm Tougher than Asthma, 1996

Other books you might like:
Virginia Fleming, *Be Good to Eddie Lee*, 1993
Although Christy tries to avoid playing with Eddie Lee, her neighbor with Down Syndrome, his insight into nature provides a basis for shared activities.
Helen Lester, *Hooway for Wodney Wat*, 1999
Rodney Rat becomes the class hero when he uses his speech impediment and a game of Simon Says to outsmart a bullying classmate.
Patricia Polacco, *Thank You, Mr. Falker*, 1998
For years Trisha feels dumb in school until Mr. Falker recognizes her artistic ability and the way to solve her reading problem.

152

ANNE CARTER
DAVID MCPHAIL, Illustrator

Tall in the Saddle

(Custer, WA: Orca Book Publishers, 1999)

Subject(s): Fathers and Sons; Imagination; Fantasy
Age range(s): Grades K-3
Major character(s): Dad, Father, Cowboy; Unnamed Character, Child, Son
Time period(s): Indeterminate
Locale(s): Fictional Country

Summary: A curious young boy mounts his tricycle one morning to follow his dad as he leaves for work, still wearing the cowboy boots he donned for their early morning play. Dad doesn't walk far before he clambers onto a bicycle that changes into a cowboy's horse, as the city streets become dusty trails. All day, Dad rides with a herd of cattle, leading them to water and green grass and protecting them from rustlers. The author's first book concludes as Dad arrives home with the setting sun to the waiting arms of his son. (32 pages)

Where it's reviewed:
Booklist, September 1, 1999, page 138
ForeWord, October 1999, page 61
Publishers Weekly, August 16, 1999, page 83
School Library Journal, September 1999, page 178

Other books you might like:
Tricia Gardella, *Casey's New Hat*, 1997
Casey's outgrown her cowgirl hat, but she has a hard time finding a new one that suits her.
David McPhail, *Moony B. Finch, the Fastest Draw in the West*, 1994
Moony's imaginative talent for drawing has him looking down the barrel of Wild Willie's gun so he defends himself with pencil, eraser and wits.
Mark Teague, *How I Spent My Summer Vacation*, 1995
On the way to Aunt Fern's house, Wallace is kidnapped by cowboys and spends the summer learning cowboy tricks.

153

DOROTHY CARTER
HARVEY STEVENSON, Illustrator

Wilhe'mina Miles After the Stork Night

(New York: Farrar Straus Giroux, 1999)

Subject(s): Babies; Brothers and Sisters; Courage
Age range(s): Grades K-3
Major character(s): Wilhe'mina Miles, Sister (older), 7-Year-Old; Mama, Mother; Mis' Hattie, Midwife
Time period(s): Indeterminate Past
Locale(s): South (rural area)

Summary: Wilhe'mina's father is working up north the night Mama goes into labor. Although Wilhe'mina is afraid of the dark, she obeys her mother's request to hurry to Mis' Hattie's house for help. Mis' Hattie goes into the night to Mama's aid, leaving Wilhe'mina in the care of her sister. In the morning, when Mis' Hattie returns, she sends Wilhe'mina home to meet her baby brother. (32 pages)

Where it's reviewed:
Booklist, February 15, 1999, page 1074
Horn Book, March 1999, page 185
Kirkus Reviews, January 15, 1999, page 143
Publishers Weekly, March 15, 1999, page 58
School Library Journal, June 1999, page 92

Other books by the same author:
Bye Mis' Lela, 1998

Other books you might like:
Ezra Jack Keats, *Peter's Chair*, 1967
    Peter's baby sister takes over his cradle and his crib, but Peter's not going to let his favorite chair get painted pink.
Norma Simon, *The Baby House*, 1995
    A young girl awaits the birth of her baby brother, as well as kittens and puppies.
Mildred Pitts Walker, *My Mama Needs Me*, 1983
    When his baby sister is born, Jason wants to help Mama care for her.

154

MARY CASANOVA
ED YOUNG, Illustrator

The Hunter: A Chinese Folktale

(New York: Atheneum Books for Young Readers, 2000)

Subject(s): Folklore; Folk Tales; Courage
Age range(s): Grades 1-3
Major character(s): Hai Li Bu, Hunter
Time period(s): Indeterminate Past
Locale(s): China

Summary: Hai Li Bu is the hunter for his small village and a good one too. Even a skilled hunter struggles during a drought when the crops wither and animals are scarce. When Hai Li Bu hears a snake call for help, he complies and the snake later thanks the hunter for saving her life by taking him to her father's palace beneath the sea. Offered any reward, the hunter chooses to be able to understand the language of animals. Hai Li Bu's wish is fulfilled with the condition that he must never reveal the secret of the gift or he will turn to stone. As he hopes, he becomes a better hunter and his village prospers. The gift enables Hai Li Bu to hear the animals speak of an impending natural disaster that will destroy his village and he hurries to warn his people. The warning is so dire that the villagers will not believe him and in order to save them he chooses to divulge the secret knowing it means his death. (32 pages)

Where it's reviewed:
Booklist, May 15, 2000, page 1754
Children's Bookwatch, September 2000, page 4
Five Owls, March 2001, page 90
Kirkus Reviews, June 15, 2000, page 881
School Library Journal, August 2000, page 168

Awards the book has won:
Booklist Editors' Choice, 2000
ALA Notable Children's Books, 2001

Other books you might like:
Linda Fang, *The Ch'i-lin Purse: A Collection of Ancient Chinese Stories*, 1995
    The collection includes illustrated retellings of nine folktales from China.
Julie Lawson, *The Dragon's Pearl*, 1993
    In a retelling of a Chinese folktale, a poor boy swallows a magical pearl in order to protect it from robbers and turns himself into a river dragon.
Laurence Yep, *City of Dragons*, 1995
    With a caravan of kind giants, a young outcast journeys beneath the sea to the City of Dragons.

155

DENYS CAZET, Author/Illustrator

Minnie and Moo and the Musk of Zorro

(New York: DK Ink/Dorling Kindersley Publishing, Inc., 2000)

Subject(s): Animals/Cows; Animals/Chickens; Heroes and Heroines
Age range(s): Grades 1-3
Major character(s): Moo, Cow; Minnie, Cow
Time period(s): 2000s (2000)
Locale(s): United States

Summary: Moo's reading a book about Zorro and lamenting the demise of heroes. Minnie recognizes the signs of trouble that result when Moo begins reading and thinking. Inspired by the story, Moo leads Minnie to the farmer's attic to rummage through a trunk of old clothes. Properly attired and renamed ''Juanita del Zorro del Moo'' and ''Dolores del Zorro del Minnie'' the intrepid duo tape a found lipstick to a sword so that Moo can make the ''Z'' of their hero. A spray can in the trunk yields the musk of Zorro scent they're seeking and Minnie and Moo are in the hero business. They begin by ''saving'' the bewildered chickens from a fox and leave behind a stunned rooster with lipstick streaks and the scent of deodorant. Next they tackle two figures in the farmer's backyard; the bad guys are actually the farmer's long underwear. As Minnie and Moo smugly retire to their tree to begin another book the farmer and his wife try to comprehend the meaning of the ''P'' and the ''U'' on the stinky underwear. (48 pages)

Where it's reviewed:
Booklist, December 1, 2000, page 725
Horn Book Guide, Spring 2001, page 56
Horn Book, September 2000, page 565
Kirkus Reviews, July 15, 2000, page 1036
School Library Journal, November 2000, page 112

Other books by the same author:
Minnie and Moo Go to Paris, 1999
Minnie and Moo Save the Earth, 1999
Minnie and Moo Go Dancing, 1998
Minnie and Moo Go to the Moon, 1998

Other books you might like:
Jean Marzollo, *Hockey Hero*, 1998
    In a Level 3 ''Hello Reader'' Hal experiences more pleasure on the ice when he plays with his new teammates rather than trying to be a solo star.

Kate McMullan, *Fluffy Saves Christmas*, 1998

Fluffy the classroom guinea pig dreams that he saves Christmas when Santa becomes ill and asks Fluffy to substitute in a level 3 "Hello Reader" title.

Toby Speed, *Two Cool Cows*, 1995

Maude and Millie, two cool cows in borrowed boots and sunglasses, jump to the moon to frolic with their bovine buddies.

156

DENYS CAZET, Author/Illustrator

Minnie and Moo and the Thanksgiving Tree

(New York: DK Ink/Dorling Kindersley Publishing, Inc., 2000)

Subject(s): Animals/Cows; Farm Life; Humor
Age range(s): Grades 1-2
Major character(s): Minnie, Cow, Friend; Moo, Cow, Friend; Mrs. Farmer, Spouse, Cook
Time period(s): 2000s (2000)
Locale(s): United States

Summary: As Minnie and Moo sit in their lawn chairs, eating cream puffs and considering the changing of the seasons, their turkey friends appear and ask the cows to hide them, preferably on the moon, until Thanksgiving is over. Although Minnie and Moo try to reassure the birds that Mrs. Farmer has not cooked a turkey in years, the turkeys are not placated until they are hidden in a tree. No sooner are the turkeys out of sight than the chickens arrive also seeking shelter from their feared place on the menu as substitutes for the missing turkeys. On the heels of the chickens are other farm animals with the same request. Soon the entire barnyard is safely sequestered, as Mrs. Farmer sets up a picnic complete with a tofu turkey beneath this bountiful Thanksgiving tree. (48 pages)

Where it's reviewed:
Booklist, September 1, 2000, page 127
Horn Book, September 2000, page 565
Publishers Weekly, September 25, 2000, page 65
School Library Journal, September 2000, page 186

Other books by the same author:
Minnie and Moo and the Musk of Zorro, 2000
Minnie and Moo Go Dancing, 1998
Minnie and Moo Go to the Moon, 1998

Other books you might like:
Eve Bunting, *A Turkey for Thanksgiving*, 1991

Mr. and Mrs. Moose change to a vegetarian menu after the live turkey they buy causes them to have second thoughts about the Thanksgiving meal.

Joy Cowley, *Gracias, the Thanksgiving Turkey*, 1996

Rather than fatten the turkey for Thanksgiving dinner, Miguel names it Gracias, treats it as a pet and asks his family to eat chicken for the holiday.

Alison Jackson, *I Know an Old Lady Who Swallowed a Pie*, 1997

A dinner guest swallows everything in sight, including the turkey, when she arrives to share Thanksgiving dinner with a family.

157

MARSHA WILSON CHALL
WENDY ANDERSON HALPERIN, Illustrator

Bonaparte

(New York: DK Ink, Dorling Kindersley Publishing, Inc., 2000)

Subject(s): Animals/Dogs; Pets; Schools/Boarding Schools
Age range(s): Grades 1-3
Major character(s): Jean Claude Jean, Student—Boarding School, Son; Bonaparte, Dog
Time period(s): 2000s
Locale(s): Montrouge, France; Paris, France (La School d'Excellence)

Summary: Jean Claude's parents will not allow Bonaparte to ride along as they drive Jean Claude to boarding school. Not willing to be separated from his boy, Bonaparte departs for Paris to find him. Unfortunately, La School d'Excellence does not allow dogs on the premises so in order to locate Jean Claude, Bonaparte dons a different disguise each day. Some gain the determined pooch more entry than others but he cannot find Jean Claude in the band room, the dining hall or even his bed. When Bonaparte and the school officials realize that Jean Claude is missing, Bonaparte extends his search beyond the school grounds and he finds Jean Claude near his village trying to find his pet. The two are happily reunited and, with a change in school policy, both return to school. (32 pages)

Where it's reviewed:
Booklist, October 15, 2000, page 444
Horn Book, September 2000, page 548
Publishers Weekly, August 7, 2000, page 94
School Library Journal, September 2000, page 186
Smithsonian, November 2000, page 64

Awards the book has won:
Smithsonian's Notable Books for Children, 2000

Other books by the same author:
Happy Birthday, America!, 2000
Sugarbush Spring, 2000
Rupa Raises the Sun, 1998
Mattie, 1992
Up North at the Cabin, 1992

Other books you might like:
Ludwig Bemelmans, *Madeline's Rescue*, 1951

Madeleine and the other orphans search the streets of Paris for Genevieve when the dog that rescued her from the river is banished from the orphanage.

Wende Devlin, *The Trouble with Henriette!*, 1995

Joie almost loses her pet Henriette when the dog's hay fever keeps her from earning her keep by locating truffles.

Susan Meddaugh, *Martha Calling*, 1994

With clever disguises, talking dog Martha makes the most of the vacation she wins despite the resort's "No Dogs Allowed" policy.

Danny Shanahan, *Buckledown the Workhound*, 1993

As president of a large corporation, Buckledown is "dog tired" so he plans a vacation at a farm where he learns to lead a dog's life.

158

MARSHA WILSON CHALL
GUY PORFIRIO, Illustrator

Happy Birthday, America!

(New York: HarperCollins Publishers, 2000)

Subject(s): Family Life; Holidays; Reunions
Age range(s): Grades K-3
Major character(s): Kay, 8-Year-Old, Narrator; Dad, Father; Betsy, Cousin, Child
Time period(s): 2000s (2000)
Locale(s): United States

Summary: Relatives gather at Kay's home for the annual Fourth of July family reunion. Well-established traditions determine who brings the various contributions to the picnic lunch that is served right after the town's parade. Kay loans her younger cousin Betsy a decorated two-wheeler to ride in the parade while Kay, dressed as Princess Kay of the Milky Way, rides in a decorated wheelbarrow float pushed by another cousin. After lunch the children all leap into the cold lake for a swim and then enjoy a watermelon seed-spitting contest. As the sun sinks in the sky Dad takes a boatload of family onto the lake to watch the evening fireworks. The day concludes with sparklers on the beach and choruses of "Happy birthday, America!" from everyone. (32 pages)

Where it's reviewed:
Booklist, May 1, 2000, page 1676
Horn Book Guide, Fall 2000, page 264
Publishers Weekly, June 5, 2000, page 94
School Library Journal, June 2000, page 102

Other books by the same author:
Sugarbush Spring, 2000
Rupa Raises the Sun, 1998
Mattie, 1992
Up North at the Cabin, 1992

Other books you might like:
Holly Keller, *Henry's Fourth of July*, 1985
  Family and friends join Henry for a Fourth of July celebration.
Kathryn Lasky, *Fourth of July Bear*, 1991
  Rebecca's summer vacation on a Maine island feels a little lonely until she meets Amanda who invites her to join the Fourth of July parade.
Jane Resh Thomas, *Celebration!*, 1997
  On the Fourth of July relatives gather at Maggie's house for swimming, games, a picnic and sparklers.
Wendy Watson, *Hurray for the Fourth of July*, 1992
  A small town's observance of America's birthday includes a parade, picnic and fireworks.
Harriet Ziefert, *Hats Off for the Fourth of July!*, 2000
  A rhyming tale describes the annual Fourth of July parade in a small Cape Cod town.

159

MARGARET CHANG
RAYMOND CHANG, Co-Author
LORI MCELRATH-ESLICK, Illustrator

Da Wei's Treasure: A Chinese Tale

(New York: Margaret K. McElderry Books/Simon and Schuster, 1999)

Subject(s): Folklore; Conduct of Life; Treasure
Age range(s): Grades 1-4
Major character(s): Da Wei, Orphan; Lian Di, Maiden, Seamstress
Time period(s): Indeterminate Past
Locale(s): China (northern)

Summary: Despite poverty, Da Wei lives happily with his widowed father tending the fields and giving a large part of the harvest to the magistrate as payment. Prior to his death, Da Wei's father cautions him to guard the family "rock," a gift from a fisherman that was presented with the promise that it would one day show the way to treasures beneath the sea. Indeed, the rock does bring Da Wei treasures, because through attentiveness to the rock, Da Wei finds Lian Di who becomes his wife and the mother of his children. Da Wei lives to have treasures greater than anything he ever imagined. (32 pages)

Where it's reviewed:
Booklist, May 15, 1999, page 1699
Horn Book Guide, Fall 1999, page 322
Kirkus Reviews, May 1, 1999, page 720
Publishers Weekly, June 14, 1999, page 70
School Library Journal, June 1999, page 112

Other books by the same author:
The Beggar's Magic: A Chinese Tale, 1997
The Cricket Warrior: A Chinese Tale, 1994
In the Eye of War, 1990

Other books you might like:
Demi, *The Greatest Treasure*, 1998
  For Li, a poor farmer, the sound of his children singing is a greater treasure than the bag of coins given to him by a wealthy neighbor.
Laurence Yep, *The Dragon Prince: A Chinese Beauty & the Beast Tale*, 1997
  To save her father's life his youngest daughter marries a dragon and travels with him to his underwater kingdom where he transforms into a prince.
Ed Young, *The Lost Horse: A Chinese Folktale*, 1998
  A Chinese peasant doubts the common wisdom about just what comprises good luck or bad luck and events support his novel approach.

160

BECKY CHAVARRIA-CHAIREZ
ANNE VEGA, Illustrator

Magda's Tortillas: Las Tortillas de Magda

(Houston, TX: Pinata Books, 2000)

Subject(s): Grandmothers; Cooks and Cooking; Birthdays
Age range(s): Grades K-3

Major character(s): Magda Madrigal, 7-Year-Old; Abuela, Grandmother, Cook
Time period(s): 2000s (2000)
Locale(s): United States

Summary: At last, Magda has reached her seventh birthday and Abuela will allow her to roll out the tortillas for the family's afternoon celebration of her birth. Magda can imagine the perfectly round tortillas she will produce—just like her grandmother makes. The surprised disappointment Magda feels when her first attempt creates a heart rather than a circle quickly changes to despair as each little ball she rolls ends up with a new shape. Magda rolls stars, flowers, clouds, a football, but not one circle. Abuela cooks Magda's tortillas right along with the round ones that Abuela makes. When they are served, Magda's embarrassment quickly vanishes as her family admires her creative shapes and recognizes her artistic talent. The author's first book is written in both English and Spanish. (32 pages)

Where it's reviewed:
Booklist, May 1, 2000, page 1676
Children's Book Review Service, August 2000, page 155
School Library Journal, October 2000, page 119

Other books you might like:
Jama Kim Rattigan, *Dumpling Soup*, 1993
    As her extended family gathers to celebrate the Hawaiian New Year, Marisa helps to make the dumplings for the first time.
Gary Soto, *Too Many Tamales*, 1993
    Maria's attempt to help her mother prepare the tamales for their traditional Christmas Eve meal leads to a dilemma with a humorous solution.
Leyla Torres, *Saturday Sancocho*, 1995
    Maria Lili and Mama Ana visit the market to barter their eggs for the ingredients needed to make the Saturday Sancocho.

161

EMMA CHICHESTER CLARK, Author/Illustrator

I Love You, Blue Kangaroo!

(New York: Doubleday Book for Young Readers, 1999)

Subject(s): Love; Toys; Gifts
Age range(s): Preschool
Major character(s): Lily, Child, Sister (older); Blue Kangaroo, Kangaroo (stuffed animal), Toy; Unnamed Character, Baby, Brother (younger)
Time period(s): 1990s (1998)
Locale(s): England

Summary: As Lily snuggles into bed she reminds Blue Kangaroo just how much she loves her one and only special toy. As Lily receives more stuffed animals as gifts from relatives and friends, her bed becomes crowed. Blue Kangaroo worries so much that sleep is difficult so when he accidentally rolls out of the overcrowded bed he walks down the hall to sleep with Lily's baby brother. The next morning, when Lily finally finds Blue Kangaroo playing with her brother, she trades all her other stuffed animals for her one and only special Blue

Kangaroo. The title was first published in Great Britain in 1998. (32 pages)

Where it's reviewed:
Horn Book Guide, Fall 1999, page 247
Publishers Weekly, January 4, 1999, page 89
Riverbank Review, Summer 1999, page 29
School Library Journal, March 1999, page 171

Other books by the same author:
Across the Blue Mountains, 1993
Lunch with Aunt Augusta, 1992
The Bouncing Dinosaur, 1990

Other books you might like:
Nancy White Carlstrom, *Barney Is Best*, 1994
    Facing a trip to the hospital, a young boy decides that Barney, his toy elephant, is the best one to provide comfort.
Shirley Isherwood, *Something for James*, 1995
    When a mysterious, rustling box arrives the other toys help James learn what is inside.
Shulamith Levey Oppenheim, *I Love You, Bunny Rabbit*, 1995
    Micah's well-worn Bunny Rabbit, soiled from years of loving attention, is irreplaceable to Micah.
Margery Williams, *The Velveteen Rabbit*, 1926
    A toy rabbit is so loved by a little boy that the rabbit, in time, becomes real.

162

LAUREN CHILD, Author/Illustrator

Clarice Bean, That's Me

(Cambridge, MA: Candlewick Press, 1999)

Subject(s): Family Life; Brothers and Sisters; Sibling Rivalry
Age range(s): Grades 1-3
Major character(s): Clarice Bean, Daughter, Sister; Minal Cricket, Brother (younger), Child; Marcie, Sister (older), Teenager
Time period(s): 1990s (1999)
Locale(s): United States

Summary: In Clarice Bean's crowded home, finding a little peace and quiet is a challenge. Marcie can go to her room as can Clarice's older brother, but Clarice is stuck sharing a room with that pest, Minal Cricket. Clarice's grandfather finds peace napping in a chair all day, her father goes to the office and her mother soaks in the bathtub. Clarice can't even find a space for herself in the yard because when she goes out seeking solitude a neighbor climbs over the fence to play with her. Clarice is at the end of her patience when she dumps a bowl of spaghetti on Minal Cricket's head and inadvertently earns herself a three-hour time out in her room—and she savors every minute. (32 pages)

Where it's reviewed:
Books for Keeps, September 1999, page 24
Horn Book Guide, Spring 2000, page 31
Kirkus Reviews, August 15, 1999, page 1308
Publishers Weekly, August 30, 1999, page 83
School Library Journal, December 1999, page 88

Other books by the same author:
I Will Never Not Ever Eat a Tomato, 2000
I Want a Pet, 1999

Other books you might like:
Marc Brown, *D.W., Go to Your Room!*, 1999
    To D.W. a ten-minute time out in her room seems like a punishment that will last forever, or at least until she starves.
Patricia Lee Gauch, *Christina Katerina and the Time She Quit the Family*, 1987
    Rebelling against the constraints of family life, Christina Katerina "quits" her family for a week.
Jill Murphy, *Five Minutes' Peace*, 1986
    Mrs. Large is hoping for just five minutes of quiet in a warm bath, away from the demands of her family.

163

LAUREN CHILD, Author/Illustrator

I Want a Pet

(Berkeley, CA: Tricycle Press, 1999)

Subject(s): Animals; Pets; Parent and Child
Age range(s): Grades K-2
Major character(s): Mom, Mother; Dad, Father; Granny, Grandmother
Time period(s): 1990s (1999)
Locale(s): England

Summary: A little girl desperately wants a pet but has some difficulty choosing one that meets the requirements of her family. Mom doesn't want anything with too much fur or the dirty footprints of an octopus or a bat dangling in the closet. Dad says boa constrictors hug too tightly and howling wolves would give him a headache. An animal that buzzes is out of the question because buzzing bothers Granny's hearing aids. Finally the pet shop lady shows the girl a pet that has the potential to be everything she's seeking, though she won't know for sure until it hatches. (24 pages)

Where it's reviewed:
Booklist, April 15, 1999, page 1534
Children's Book Review Service, April 1999, page 98
Horn Book, May 1999, page 312
Publishers Weekly, February 15, 1999, page 106
School Library Journal, May 1999, page 88

Awards the book has won:
IRA/CBC Children's Choices, 2000

Other books by the same author:
Beware of the Storybook Wolves, 2001
I Will Never Not Ever Eat a Tomato, 2000
Clarice Bean, That's Me, 1999

Other books you might like:
Troon Harrison, *Aaron's Awful Allergies*, 1998
    Poor Aaron is forced to give up his many furry pets because they contribute to his illness.
Holly Keller, *Furry*, 1992
    Allergies to a variety of animals narrow Laura's choice of pets until she's left with a chameleon.
Mary Packard, *The Pet That I Want*, 1995
    In the rhyming text of a book in the "My First Hello

Reader" series a young boy visiting a pet store describes the pet he seeks.
Tres Seymour, *I Love My Buzzard*, 1994
    A young boy who loves his buzzard as well as his squid, slugs and warthog reconsiders his priorities when his mom moves out to escape the menagerie.
Dan Yaccarino, *An Octopus Followed Me Home*, 1997
    As a young girl explains to her overwhelmed dad, the octopus simply followed her home just as the crocodile, seals and penguins did previously.

164

YANGSOOK CHOI, Author/Illustrator

New Cat

(New York: Farrar Straus Giroux, 1999)

Subject(s): Animals/Cats; Pets; Friendship
Age range(s): Grades K-3
Major character(s): Mr. Kim, Businessman; New Cat, Cat
Time period(s): 1990s (1999)
Locale(s): New York, New York (The Bronx)

Summary: After moving from Korea to New York, Mr. Kim adopts New Cat to keep mice out of his tofu factory. New Cat is also allowed to sample tofu in her bowl, but she is never allowed in the production room. When New Cat sees a mouse in the production room, she enters to chase it. Although she is not successful in her search for the mouse, New Cat does spot a fire in time to save the factory from destruction. (32 pages)

Where it's reviewed:
Booklist, February 1, 1999, page 979
Horn Book, March 1999, page 186
Kirkus Reviews, January 1, 1999, page 63
Publishers Weekly, March 15, 1999, page 58
School Library Journal, March 1999, page 171

Other books by the same author:
The Sun Girl and the Moon Boy, 1997

Other books you might like:
Jennifer Armstrong, *Chin Yu Min and the Ginger Cat*, 1993
    Chin Yu Min, a greedy widower, learns the gift of generosity through her cat.
Janet Gill, *Basket Weaver and Catches Many Mice*, 1999
    In this book, illustrated by Yangsook Choi, Catches Many Mice helps her owner win a basket-weaving contest.
Joseph Kennedy, *Lucy Goes to the Country*, 1998
    Lucy helps her owners prepare for a dinner party.

165

KAY CHORAO, Author/Illustrator

Pig and Crow

(New York: Henry Holt and Company, 2000)

Subject(s): Animals/Pigs; Animals/Birds; Conduct of Life
Age range(s): Grades K-2
Major character(s): Pig, Pig, Cook, Friend; Crow, Bird, Trickster; Goose, Bird, Friend
Time period(s): Indeterminate
Locale(s): Fictional Country

Summary: Pig depends on the satisfaction of baking for relief from the monotony of his lonely life. Sly Crow enjoys the products of Pig's hard work in the kitchen so he offers Pig ''magic'' items in exchange for the baked goods. Each time Pig realizes the trade is not fair, but he agrees anyway. With Pig's positive attitude and careful attention to the instructions Crow attaches to each magic trade item, the token trades of seeds, a worm and an egg actually do become magic for Pig. The egg hatches into Goose who becomes Pig's constant companion. The two friends share skills—Pig teaches Goose to cook and Goose teaches Pig to swim. Sometimes they share dinner with Crow. (36 pages)

Where it's reviewed:
Booklist, July 2000, page 2032
Children's Bookwatch, May 2000, page 4
Horn Book, May 2000, page 291
Publishers Weekly, June 5, 2000, page 93
School Library Journal, June 2000, page 102

Other books by the same author:
Little Farm by the Sea, 1998
The Cats Kids, 1998
Annie and Cousin Precious, 1994

Other books you might like:
Erica Silverman, *Don't Fidget a Feather*, 1994
  The competitiveness between Duck and Gander almost leads to both becoming Fox's dinner before one sacrifices victory for friendship.
Janet Stevens, *Cook-a-Doodle-Doo!*, 1999
  Big Brown Rooster gets help from some willing, but inexperienced friends as he tries his great grandmother's cookbook. Susan Stevens Crummel, co-author.
Jan Wahl, *Mrs. Owl and Mr. Pig*, 1991
  When a lonely widowed owl agrees to take in Mr. Pig as a boarder both must adjust their style of living in order to get along.

166

MATT CHRISTOPHER
DANIEL VASCONCELLOS, Illustrator

The Captain Contest

(Boston: Little Brown and Company, 1999)

Series: Soccer 'Cats. Book #1
Subject(s): Sports/Soccer; Competition; Contests
Age range(s): Grades 2-3
Major character(s): Dewey London, 10-Year-Old, Soccer Player; Bundy Neel, 10-Year-Old, Soccer Player; Don Bradley, Coach
Time period(s): 1990s (1999)
Locale(s): United States

Summary: Best friends Dewey and Bundy eagerly sign up for a summer soccer league. Anyone wanting to be team captain submits an entry in a contest and the team members select the team name and logo design they like best. As a natural leader, everyone agrees Bundy should be the team captain so no one else plans to submit an entry. Dewey, who has no interest in being captain, is a talented artist who wants the team to have a recognizable design on their shirts. A conflict of conscience

and friendship brews during the first week of practice with Coach Bradley. When the contest results are announced after the team's first game, Bundy and Dewey realize they'll be able to stay friends and teammates. (58 pages)

Where it's reviewed:
Booklist, June 1999, page 1828
Horn Book Guide, Fall 1999, page 276
Publishers Weekly, March 22, 1999, page 92
School Library Journal, August 1999, page 131

Other books by the same author:
Operation Baby Sitter, 1999 (Soccer 'Cats #2)
The Catcher's Mask, 1998
All-Star Fever, 1997

Other books you might like:
Mary Jane Auch, *Angel and Me and the Bayside Bombers*, 1989
  Brian has the desire, but not the skill, to play soccer and stoops to bribery to gain a place on a team.
Stephanie Greene, *Owen Foote, Soccer Star*, 1998
  Owen finds the confidence to help the team bully learn to be a team player.
Elizabeth Levy, *Rude Rowdy Rumors: A Brian and Pea Brain Mystery*, 1994
  With help from sister Penny, Brian tries to determine which of his soccer teammates is starting the rumors about him.
Jean Marzollo, *Soccer Cousins*, 1997
  While visiting his cousin, David takes the field during an important soccer game and proves to himself that he can play under pressure.

167

MATT CHRISTOPHER
DANIEL VASCONCELLOS, Illustrator

Secret Weapon

(Boston: Little, Brown and Company, 2000)

Series: Soccer 'Cats. Number 3
Subject(s): Sports/Soccer
Age range(s): Grades 2-4
Major character(s): Lisa Gaddy, Soccer Player, Twin; Ted Gaddy, Twin, Soccer Player
Time period(s): 2000s (2000)
Locale(s): United States

Summary: Shorter than her teammates, including her twin brother, Lisa thinks she'll never be good with throw-ins unless she grows two inches. As a fullback she's often in position to handle throw-ins for her team but she's simply too short to get it over the defenders. What Lisa may lack in size she makes up for in agility and courage. Her coach uses a little known rule, Lisa's gymnastic ability and her willingness to practice to develop a ''secret weapon'' for the team—Lisa doing a flip throw rather than a standing throw to put the ball back into play. (56 pages)

Where it's reviewed:
Horn Book Guide, Fall 2000, page 291
School Library Journal, April 2000, page 94

Other books by the same author:
Heads Up, 2001 (Soccer 'Cats, Number 6)
Hat Trick, 2000 (Soccer 'Cats, Number 4)
Operation Baby Sitter, 1999 (Soccer 'Cats, Number 2)
The Captain Contest, 1999 (Soccer 'Cats, Number 1)
The Catcher's Mask, 1998 (Peach Street Mudders)

Other books you might like:
Stephanie Greene, *Owen Foote, Soccer Star*, 1998
　　Despite his experience, Owen feels intimidated by the
　　bigger players when he moves up to a different soccer
　　league.
Elizabeth Levy, *Rude Rowdy Rumors: A Brian and Pea Brain
　　Mystery*, 1994
　　With help from sister Penny, Brian tries to determine how
　　the rumors about him are starting on his soccer team.
Jean Marzollo, *Soccer Cousins*, 1997
　　Visiting a cousin in Mexico, David takes the field during
　　an important soccer game and proves that he can play
　　under pressure.

168

ELAINE CLAYTON, Author/Illustrator

The Yeoman's Daring Daughter and the Princes in the Tower

(New York: Crown Publishers, Inc., 1999)

Subject(s): Kings, Queens, Rulers, etc.; Letters; Historical
Age range(s): Grades 1-4
Major character(s): Jane, Child, Daughter (of the yeoman);
　　Edward, Royalty (prince), 13-Year-Old; Richard, Royalty
　　(prince), 10-Year-Old
Time period(s): 15th century (1483)
Locale(s): London, England (Tower of London)

Summary: After their father's death, Prince Edward and
Prince Richard are brought to the Tower of London for protection as they await Edward's coronation. They begin corre-
sponding with Jane by using her pet raven to carry messages
to her. When Jane overhears plans to assassinate the princes
and the order for the coronation robe that she is helping sew is
changed from size small to size large, Jane warns the princes
and tries to help them escape from the tower. A concluding
author's note gives historical background to the tale. (40
pages)

Where it's reviewed:
Booklist, April 1, 1999, page 1429
Horn Book Guide, Fall 1999, page 247
Publishers Weekly, March 22, 1999, page 92
School Library Journal, June 1999, page 92

Other books by the same author:
Ella's Trip to the Museum, 1996
Pup in School, 1993

Other books you might like:
Leon Garfield, *The Saracen Maid*, 1994
　　Captured by pirates and imprisoned in a foreign land,
　　Gilbert escapes to England with the brave Saracen maid
　　who rescues him.

Marilyn Singer, *In the Palace of the Ocean King*, 1995
　　Marianna dives into the ocean that she fears in order to
　　save her beloved Sylvain from the Ocean King.
Mark Twain, *The Prince and the Pauper*, 1999
　　In a picture book retelling by Marianna Mayer of Twain's
　　classic, Prince Edward VI switches clothes with a street
　　beggar.

169

BEVERLY CLEARY
ALAN TIEGREEN, Illustrator

Ramona's World

(New York: Morrow Junior Books, 1999)

Subject(s): Schools; Family Life; Friendship
Age range(s): Grades 3-5
Major character(s): Ramona Quimby, 4th Grader, Sister;
　　Daisy Kidd, Friend (Ramona's), 4th Grader; Beezus
　　Quimby, Sister (older)
Locale(s): Oregon

Summary: Ramona enters 4th grade with the confidence that
comes from learning to tolerate the educational process. Her
biggest wish of the year comes true when Daisy moves to
town, joins the class, and becomes Ramona's friend. With the
birth of her little sister, Ramona is now the middle child and
she often wishes that her parents didn't have so many girls.
Her mother seems to be too busy with the baby to pay
attention to Ramona and Beezus is so interested in friends,
parties and high school that she has no time for Ramona
either. At least on her tenth (or ''zeroteenth'' as Ramona says)
birthday, she's the center of attention for most of the day, not
perfect, but close enough to please Ramona. (192 pages)

Where it's reviewed:
Booklist, June 1, 1999, page 1824
The New York Times Book Review, November 21, 1999, page
　　28
Publishers Weekly, June 7, 1999, page 83
School Library Journal, August 1999, page 131
Smithsonian Magazine, November 1999, page 48

Awards the book has won:
IRA/CBC Children's Choices, 2000
Smithsonian's Notable Books for Children, 1999

Other books by the same author:
Ramona Forever, 1984
Ramona the Brave, 1975
Ramona the Pest, 1968
Beezus and Ramona, 1955

Other books you might like:
Judy Blume, *Tales of a Fourth Grade Nothing*, 1976
　　Peter's stereotypically terrible, two-year-old brother com-
　　plicates his life.
Paula Danziger, *Amber Brown Is Feeling Blue*, 1998
　　When Kelly Green joins Amber Brown's 4th grade class
　　Amber loses her special status as the kid with the colorful
　　name.
Johanna Hurwitz, *Spring Break*, 1997
　　Cricket suffers an unlucky break of her ankle and ruins her
　　plans for a spring-break trip with a friend.

Marissa Moss, *Amelia's Notebook*, 1995

In a journal, 9-year-old Amelia records her thoughts about friends, school and family.

170

ANDREW CLEMENTS
SUE TRUESDELL, Illustrator

Circus Family Dog
(New York: Clarion Books, 2000)

Subject(s): Animals/Dogs; Circus; Loyalty
Age range(s): Grades K-3
Major character(s): Grumps, Dog; Red the Clown, Entertainer (clown); Sparks, Dog
Time period(s): 2000s
Locale(s): United States

Summary: Grumps has been a part of the circus family for a very long time. He's a one-trick dog, but his act with Red the Clown always draws laughter from the children in the audience. When Sparks joins the act with his many tricks, he steals the limelight from Grumps and makes the old dog determined to prove his worth one last time. Daily Grumps secretly practices until he can jump through the flaming hoop and on the last night of the show, after Sparks leaps through the hoops to wild applause, Grumps gets up and leaps through also for the first and last time. Red the Clown understands the message Grumps sends with the action and from then on he and Sparks make sure that Grumps receives his share of the applause. After all, Grumps is still part of the circus family. (32 pages)

Where it's reviewed:
Booklist, June 1, 2000, page 1905
Horn Book Guide, Fall 2000, page 264
School Library Journal, August 2000, page 144
Smithsonian, November 2000, page 62

Awards the book has won:
Smithsonian's Notable Books for Children, 2000

Other books by the same author:
Workshop, 1999
Double Trouble in Walla Walla, 1997
Temple Cat, 1996

Other books you might like:
Lois Ehlert, *Circus*, 1992
Colorful collages communicate the excitement of a circus performance.
Lisa Campbell Ernst, *Ginger Jumps*, 1990
For a lonely pooch like Ginger, the circus is a place of work and travel with no home to call her own.
Leslie McGuirk, *Tucker Over the Top*, 2000
Tucker, a daredevil terrier, tries to apply his skateboarding skills to a circus act.

171

ANDREW CLEMENTS

The Janitor's Boy
(New York: Simon & Schuster Books for Young Readers, 2000)

Subject(s): Fathers and Sons; Work; Schools
Age range(s): Grades 4-6
Major character(s): John Philip ''Jack'' Rankin Jr., Son, 5th Grader; John Philip Rankin, Father, Maintenance Worker; Mr. Ackerby, Principal
Time period(s): 2000s
Locale(s): Huntington, Minnesota

Summary: With the completion of a new middle school a year away, Jack and other fifth graders are temporarily assigned to the old high school, vacated when the new high school opened. Jack is mortified to be in the same building where his father works as head custodian and does his best to keep the relationship secret. Before long two bullies discover the connection and begin to torment Jack who plans revenge against the person he considers responsible for his humiliation—John Rankin. The ''perfect'' crime he carefully plots backfires and the punishment Mr. Ackerby assigns is suited to the crime— three weeks of assisting the janitor by scraping chewing gum from the underside of desks and tables. Gradually, through the work experience and some secret snooping after hours, Jack learns to respect his father and his work. (140 pages)

Where it's reviewed:
Booklist, March 1, 2000, page 1243
Horn Book, July 2000, page 454
Publishers Weekly, May 1, 2000, page 71
Riverbank Review, Summer 2000, page 38
School Library Journal, May 2000, page 170

Other books by the same author:
The Landry News, 1999
Frindle, 1996 (Christopher Award)

Other books you might like:
Lynea Bowdish, *Living with My Stepfather Is Like Living with a Moose*, 1997
Athletic Matt is embarrassed by his inept stepfather until he tries to participate in one of Frank's hobbies and realizes how challenging it is.
Carol Fenner, *The King of Dragons*, 1998
Ian and his Vietnam vet father together live in a deserted courthouse until Ian's father vanishes and Ian continues to survive alone.
Katherine Paterson, *Preacher's Boy*, 1999
Being the son of a preacher is challenging to mischievous Robbie whose behavior never seems to match the community's expectations.
Mildred Pitts Walker, *Suitcase*, 1999
Xander begrudgingly participates in sports in order to win his father's approval when he'd prefer to pursue his love of art.

172

ANDREW CLEMENTS
SALVATORE MURDOCCA, Illustrator

The Landry News

(New York: Simon & Schuster Books for Young Readers, 1999)

Subject(s): Newspapers; Teachers; Schools
Age range(s): Grades 4-6
Major character(s): Cara Landry, 5th Grader, Child of Divorced Parents; Karl Larson, Teacher; Joey DeLucca, 5th Grader, Computer Expert
Time period(s): 1990s (1999)
Locale(s): Carlton, Illinois

Summary: Mr. Larson's unique approach to teaching—ignore the students and they will learn—gives Cara plenty of time to pursue her primary interest of journalism. The first edition of "The Landry News" inspires Joey to offer his computer skill so more copies can be printed and a weekly paper begins. As more students become involved, Mr. Larson emerges from his doldrums and begins teaching again, using the newspaper project to explore the meaning of the First Amendment with his class. When the school principal tries to use an "inappropriate" article in "The Landry News" as a means of disciplining Mr. Larson, the class begins another paper that is published privately with no use of school funds, thus circumventing the principal's control. Cara deftly uses the media to organize support for Mr. Larson prior to and during the disciplinary hearing with the School Board. The First Amendment is a winner! (123 pages)

Where it's reviewed:
Booklist, June 1999, page 1828
Bulletin of the Center for Children's Books, June 1999, page 346
Horn Book, July 1999, page 462
Publishers Weekly, June 7, 1999, page 83
School Library Journal, July 1999, page 95

Awards the book has won:
School Library Journal Best Books, 1999

Other books by the same author:
The Janitor's Boy, 2000
Frindle, 1996 (Christopher Award)

Other books you might like:
Ralph Fletcher, *Flying Solo*, 1998
    Students in a classroom without a teacher use the absentee sub's plans to conduct class for a day and suffer the consequences.
Stephen Krensky, *The Printer's Apprentice*, 1995
    As a printer's apprentice in Colonial America, Gus learns the skills of the trade and an appreciation for the freedom to print the truth.
Claudia Mills, *Standing Up to Mr. O.*, 1998
    Maggie puts her principles before her grade point average and refuses to participate in the dissection lab planned by Mr. O'Neill.
Barbara Robinson, *The Best School Year Ever*, 1994
    In a sequel to *The Best Christmas Pageant Ever* the inimitable Herdmans are back for a school year of mayhem and disaster.

173

SHIRLEY CLIMO
ROBERT FLORCZAK, Illustrator

The Persian Cinderella

(New York: HarperCollins Publishers, 1999)

Subject(s): Fairy Tales; Folklore; Princes and Princesses
Age range(s): Grades 1-4
Major character(s): Settareh, Stepdaughter; Mehrdad, Royalty (prince)
Time period(s): Indeterminate Past
Locale(s): Persia

Summary: Settareh grows up lonely and hungry after her mother's death. Mistreated by her stepmother and jealous stepsisters in the women's quarters of the home, Settareh rarely sees her father. When Settareh's father gives each of the women in his household a gold coin with which to buy fabric for a New Year's celebration held by Prince Mehrdad, Settareh spends her money on food, an old beggar woman and a cracked jug. Settarah soon learns that the little blue jug contains a "pari" or fairy that grants wishes and so she is able to go to the palace where, of course, she meets the prince. Their plans to marry are briefly foiled by the stepsisters who try to use Settareh's "pari" to get rid of her. Although Settareh is changed into a dove that visits Prince Mehrdad, the prince's kindness breaks the spell and Settareh regains her human form so the marriage can take place as planned. (32 pages)

Where it's reviewed:
Booklist, July 1999, page 1948
Horn Book Guide, Fall 1999, page 323
Kirkus Reviews, April 15, 1999, page 628
Publishers Weekly, June 7, 1999, page 82
School Library Journal, July 1999, page 84

Other books by the same author:
The Irish Cinderlad, 1996
The Little Red Ant and the Great Big Crumb: A Mexican Fable, 1995
The Korean Cinderella, 1993
The Egyptian Cinderella, 1989

Other books you might like:
Rebecca Hickox, *The Golden Sandal: A Middle Eastern Cinderella Story*, 1998
    Maha's loss of a golden sandal after a party leads to her discovery by a well-to-do villager interested in marrying her.
Charles Perrault, *Cinderella*, 1954
    In a classic tale of love and inner beauty, Cinderella survives years of torment from her stepmother and stepsisters to win the Prince's hand in marriage.
Robert D. San Souci, *Sootface: An Ojibwa Cinderella Story*, 1994
    In a retelling of an Ojibwa Cinderella Story, Sootface, who is mistreated by her two older sisters, is chosen as the bride of a legendary hunter.
Alan Schroeder, *Smoky Mountain Rose: An Appalachian Cinderella*, 1997
    The Cinderella Story of Rose, an orphan in the Smoky

Mountains, tells how she marries the "rich feller" who is her neighbor.

174

MARYANN COCCA-LEFFLER, Author/Illustrator

Bus Route to Boston

(Honesdale, PA: Boyds Mills Press, 2000)

Subject(s): Transportation; Mothers and Daughters; Shopping
Age range(s): Grades K-3
Major character(s): Bill, Driver (bus); Mom, Mother; Unnamed Character, Daughter, Sister
Time period(s): Indeterminate Past
Locale(s): Woodlawn, Massachusetts; Boston, Massachusetts

Summary: Daily games played in the street come to a halt when the bus drives past every twenty minutes but for two sisters, the real fun comes on Saturdays when they travel with Mom to Boston for a day of shopping. They look for bargains in Filene's basement, buy chops at the butchers and devour ice cream sundaes at Bailey's. Their favorite bus driver is Bill and they make sure to buy enough cannelloni to share with him when they stop at the bakery before boarding his bus for the trip home. (32 pages)

Where it's reviewed:
Booklist, February 1, 2000, page 1028
Children's Book Review Service, May 2000, page 108
Kirkus Reviews, February 15, 2000, page 241
Publishers Weekly, February 21, 2000, page 87
School Library Journal, April 2000, page 94

Other books by the same author:
Clams All Year, 1996
Ice-Cold Birthday, 1992
Wednesday Is Spaghetti Day, 1990

Other books you might like:
Cari Best, *Read Light, Green Light, Mama and Me*, 1995
   Lizzie rides the subway with Mama all the way to her job at the downtown library.
Bruce McMillan, *Grandfather's Trolley*, 1995
   On a breezy summer day, a little girl patiently waits to ride her grandfather's trolley to the end of the line and back again.
Mary Quattlebaum, *Underground Train*, 1997
   A little girl enjoys a subway ride with her mother.

175

MARYANN COCCA-LEFFLER, Author/Illustrator

Mr. Tanen's Ties

(Morton Grove, IL: Albert Whitman & Company, 1999)

Subject(s): Clothes; Schools; Individuality
Age range(s): Grades K-2
Major character(s): Mr. Tanen, Principal; Mr. Apple, Administrator; Alex, Student—Elementary School
Time period(s): 1990s
Locale(s): Saugus, Massachusetts (Lynnhurst Elementary School)

Summary: Students depend on Mr. Tanen's ties to tell them the lunch menu, the weather and the holidays. He stores his extensive collection in his office closet so he can change ties during the day to suit any occasion. Staid Mr. Apple thinks the silly ties are inappropriate for a role model to wear at school and presents Mr. Tanen with a basic blue tie and the instruction to wear no other at school. The students are unhappy and Mr. Tanen is so depressed that Mr. Apple is called on to substitute as the principal for one week. Observing Mr. Apple's interests in birds gives Alex an idea that lightens up Mr. Apple's mood and restores Mr. Tanen's neckties to their proper place—unless Mr. Apple is borrowing one. (32 pages)

Where it's reviewed:
Booklist, May 15, 1999, page 1702
Horn Book Guide, Fall 1999, page 248
School Library Journal, March 1999, page 171

Other books by the same author:
Missing: One Stuffed Rabbit, 1998
Clams All Year, 1996
Ice-Cold Birthday, 1992
Wednesday Is Spaghetti Day, 1990

Other books you might like:
Harry Allard, *Miss Nelson Is Back*, 1985
   When the students learn that their teacher will be away for one week, they make plans to enjoy their time during her absence.
Ivon Cecil, *Kirby Kelvin and the Not-Laughing Lessons*, 1998
   Ever-cheerful Kirby is sent to the principal's office to receive "not-laughing" lessons from Mr. Gloomsmith.
Stephen Krensky, *My Teacher's Secret Life*, 1996
   A student imagines what happens after hours at his school and is astonished to discover that teachers and the principal have private lives.
Peggy Parish, *Teach Us, Amelia Bedelia*, 1977
   When the principal mistakes literally minded Amelia Bedelia for the substitute teacher, the students have an interesting day.

176

CARON LEE COHEN
CHRISTOPHER DENISE, Illustrator

Digger Pig and the Turnip

(San Diego: Harcourt, Inc., 2000)

Series: Green Light Readers. Level 2
Subject(s): Folklore; Animals; Food
Age range(s): Grades 1-2
Major character(s): Digger Pig, Pig, Cook
Time period(s): Indeterminate Past
Locale(s): Fictional Country

Summary: After digging up a very large turnip Digger Pig seeks help from some of the other animals to chop it and mash it so she can make a pie. No one is willing to help her so Digger Pig does all the work herself. When the pie is ready the animals that refused to help earlier are eager to help eat the pie, but Digger Pig sends them away and she and her children enjoy the entire pie. (20 pages)

Where it's reviewed:
Booklist, February 15, 2000
Horn Book Guide, Fall 2000, page 339
Publishers Weekly, March 27, 2000, page 83
School Library Journal, July 2000, page 93

Other books by the same author:
How Many Fish?, 1998 (I Can Read Book)
Three Yellow Dogs, 1997
Where's the Fly?, 1996
Pigeon, Pigeon, 1992

Other books you might like:
Byron Barton, *The Little Red Hen*, 1993
    A little red hen seeks but receives no help with her work.
Margaret Hillert, *Not I, Not I*, 1981
    Little Red Hen's lazy friends refuse to help her plant, harvest or grind the wheat but all are willing to eat the bread she bakes from it.
Philemon Sturges, *The Little Red Hen (Makes a Pizza)*, 1999
    In this retelling of the traditional tale the friends refuse to help, but Little Red Hen doesn't hold it against them and they do offer to clean up.

177

MIRIAM COHEN
THOMAS F. YEZERSKI, Illustrator

Mimmy & Sophie
(New York: Farrar Straus Giroux, 1999)

Subject(s): Sisters; Emigration and Immigration; Family Life
Age range(s): Grades K-3
Major character(s): Mimmy, 6-Year-Old, Sister; Sophie, 4-Year-Old, Sister
Time period(s): 1930s
Locale(s): New York, New York (Brooklyn)

Summary: In a series of four vignettes, Mimmy and Sophie do everything together, from eating popsicles to drawing on the sidewalk. While visiting their grandparents, immigrants from Russia, they learn a little about the hardship of life in Tzarist Russia. When the other kids in their neighborhood go on vacation, Mimmy and Sophie are disappointed until their parents plan a picnic "vacation" for the family on the Brooklyn Bridge. Then, Mimmy and Sophie decide they are the luckiest family of the neighborhood. (40 pages)

Where it's reviewed:
Booklist, August 1999, page 2066
Horn Book Guide, Fall 1999, page 276
Kirkus Reviews, January 15, 1999, page 144
Publishers Weekly, April 5, 1999, page 241
School Library Journal, March 1999, page 173

Other books by the same author:
Down in the Subway, 1998
Don't Eat too Much Turkey!, 1996
When Will I Read?, 1996

Other books you might like:
Aliki, *Those Summers*, 1996
    Memories of family vacations at the seashore remind siblings and cousins of their carefree younger years.

Barbara Cooney, *Hattie and the Wild Waves*, 1991
    Hattie, a young girl from Brooklyn, enjoys her summer at the beach.
Lisa Westberg Peters, *The Hayloft*, 1995
    Two sisters share many activities during an memorable summer on their farm.
Jean Van Leeuwen, *Two Girls in Sister Dresses*, 1994
    Molly and her older sister, Jennifer, enjoy a day at the beach, a visit with a neighbor, and the arrival of their baby brother.

178

BABETTE COLE, Author/Illustrator

Bad Habits!
(New York: Dial Books for Young Readers, 1999)

Subject(s): Behavior; Conduct of Life; Problem Solving
Age range(s): Grades K-3
Major character(s): Lucretzia Crum, Child, Daughter; Mr. Crum, Father, Scientist; Mrs. Crum, Mother
Time period(s): 1990s (1998)
Locale(s): England

Summary: Lucretzia Crum is proud of her obnoxious behavior. The kids in her class are so fascinated by her revolting habits that they all begin imitating her. The other parents confront Mr. and Mrs. Crum with the demand that something be done to keep Lucretzia under control. Mr. Crum comes up with inventions to handle each of Lucretzia's bad habits, but as soon as the gadget is removed, her behavior is worse than ever. Finally Lucretzia's birthday arrives. Her monstrous friends enjoy helping her misbehave at the party until some really big monsters crash the party. After Lucretzia and her friends get a taste of their own medicine they decide to learn some manners in this title originally published in Great Britain in 1998. (32 pages)

Where it's reviewed:
Booklist, July 1999, page 1950
Horn Book Guide, Fall 1999, page 248
Kirkus Reviews, June 1, 1999, page 881
Publishers Weekly, May 31, 1999, page 92
School Library Journal, August 1999, page 131

Awards the book has won:
IRA/CBC Children's Choices, 2000

Other books by the same author:
Drop Dead, 1997
Dr. Dog, 1994
Winni Allfours, 1994
Princess Smartypants, 1987

Other books you might like:
Diane Cuneo, *Mary Louise Loses Her Manners*, 1999
    When Mary Louise's manners run away she needs help to find them quickly.
Jack Gantos, *Not So Rotten Ralph*, 1994
    Sarah's pet is a cat with deplorable behavior, but she loves Ralph anyway.
Russell Hoban, *Dinner at Alberta's*, 1975
    Arthur Crocodile has difficulty learning proper table manners.

William H. Hooks, *Rough, Tough, Rowdy: A Bank Street Book about Values*, 1992
  Rowdy doesn't understand his siblings' annoyance with his behavior until he's treated in the same way that he's been treating others.
Suzanne Williams, *My Dog Never Says Please*, 1997
  Ginny Mae envies the family dog because he has no chores and never is told to mind his manners.

179

BROCK COLE, Author/Illustrator

Buttons

(New York: Farrar Straus and Giroux, 2000)

Subject(s): Fathers and Daughters; Humor; Problem Solving
Age range(s): Grades 1-4
Major character(s): Unnamed Character, Daughter (eldest); Unnamed Character, Daughter (second), Sister; Unnamed Character, Daughter (youngest), Sister
Time period(s): Indeterminate Past
Locale(s): Fictional Country

Summary: After their portly father pops his trouser buttons into the fire, three sisters devise what they consider to be foolproof plans for acquiring more buttons. None of the plans works out as expected, but at least the youngest daughter manages to get some buttons with her foolish scheme. The eldest daughter and the second daughter snare husbands, but completely forget their father's need for buttons. The youngest daughter not only brings home buttons, but also a husband whose pants are held up by a string, an endearing quality that seems peculiar to her family. (32 pages)

Where it's reviewed:
Booklist, February 15, 2000, page 1104
Horn Book, March 2000, page 182
Publishers Weekly, January 3, 2000, page 75
Riverbank Review, Spring 2000, page 28
School Library Journal, April 2000, page 96

Awards the book has won:
Boston Globe/Horn Book Honor Book, 2000
School Library Journal Best Books, 2000

Other books by the same author:
The Giant's Toe, 1986
Nothing but a Pig, 1981
The King at the Door, 1979

Other books you might like:
Cynthia DeFelice, *Three Perfect Peaches: A French Folktale*, 1995
  A humorous retelling depicts the kind country lad who outwits the king and marries the princess. Mary DeMarsh, co-author.
Crescent Dragonwagon, *Brass Button*, 1997
  Unbeknownst to Mrs. Moffatt a button falls off her new red coat and begins a journey about town until she finds it, months later, on her sidewalk.
Uri Shulevitz, *The Golden Goose*, 1995
  A retelling of a Grimm tale explains how a kind, but simple woodsman unwittingly wins the hand of a princess in marriage.

180

MICHAEL COLEMAN
GWYNETH WILLIAMSON, Illustrator

One, Two, Three, Oops!

(Waukesha, WI: Little Tiger Press, 1999)

Subject(s): Animals/Rabbits; Babies; Problem Solving
Age range(s): Grades K-1
Major character(s): Mr. Rabbit, Rabbit, Father; Mrs. Rabbit, Rabbit, Mother
Time period(s): Indeterminate
Locale(s): Fictional Country

Summary: Surrounded by his large family, Mr. Rabbit stubbornly undertakes the task of counting his active offspring despite Mrs. Rabbit's suggestion that he wait. Playful bunnies never slow down enough until they collapse for a nap. Then, Mr. Rabbit is finally able to complete his census—or so he thinks until Mrs. Rabbit reminds him of the roomful of babies that he's overlooked. The book was first published in England in 1998. (32 pages)

Where it's reviewed:
Booklist, January 1, 1999, page 886
ForeWord, March 1999, page 55
Kirkus Reviews, January 1, 1999, page 64
Publishers Weekly, February 15, 1999, page 106
School Library Journal, March 1999, page 173

Other books by the same author:
Hank the Clank, 1996
Ridiculous!, 1996
Lazy Ozzie, 1996

Other books you might like:
Nancy White Carlstrom, *Let's Count It Out, Jesse Bear*, 1996
  Jesse Bear practices counting to twenty in his usual rhyming style.
Michael Foreman, *Dad! I Can't Sleep*, 1995
  Little Panda counts animals to help him fall asleep and they all want one last drink of water.
Sam McBratney, *Guess How Much I Love You*, 1995
  Little Nutbrown Hare enjoys playing a game with his father in which each professes the magnitude of his love for the other.
Sue Porter, *My Little Rabbit Tale*, 1994
  Little Rabbit enjoys an active, fun-filled day with his supportive parents.
Cindy Szekeres, *I Can Count Bunnies: And So Can You*, 1999
  Wilbur's many relatives come to meet his baby sister and the reader is invited to help him count them all.
Rick Walton, *So Many Bunnies: A Bedtime ABC and Counting Book*, 1998
  Old Mother Rabbit uses an alphabetical system to put her twenty-six children to bed, but not necessarily to sleep.

181

BRYAN COLLIER, Author/Illustrator

Uptown

(New York: Henry Holt and Company, 2000)

Subject(s): African Americans; City and Town Life
Age range(s): Grades K-3
Major character(s): Unnamed Character, Child, Narrator
Time period(s): 2000s
Locale(s): New York, New York (Harlem)

Summary: To a young boy, Uptown is rows of brownstones, the Apollo stage, and the winding Metro-North Train. It's an urban environment of jazz, the community gathering of a barbershop, the art of photography and a summer of basketball. In this boy's experience, Uptown is girls going to church, boys singing in the choir, and his world, his home. (32 pages)

Where it's reviewed:
Booklist, June 1, 2000, page 1906
Horn Book Guide, Fall 2000, page 264
Kirkus Reviews, June 1, 2000, page 793
Publishers Weekly, June 19, 2000, page 78
School Library Journal, July 2000, page 70

Awards the book has won:
Coretta Scott King Illustrator Award
Notable Social Studies Trade Books for Young People, 2001

Other books you might like:
William Low, *Chinatown*, 1997
    A young boy's daily walk with his Grandma provides a tour of the attractions of New York's Chinatown neighborhood.
Walter Dean Myers, *Harlem*, 1997
    A Caldecott Honor book explores the people, the places, and the essence of Harlem in a picture book for older readers.
Faith Ringgold, *Tar Beach*, 1991
    In an award-winning book, Cassie soars over the rooftops of Harlem, viewing familiar sites from a new perspective.
Chris K. Soentpiet, *Around Town*, 1994
    On a summer day, a girl and her mother share a day in New York City, enjoying all that a vibrant city has to offer.
Jacqueline Preiss Weitzman, *You Can't Take a Balloon into the Metropolitan Museum*, 1998
    A museum guard chases an errant balloon through the streets of New York.

182

PETER COLLINGTON, Author/Illustrator

Clever Cat

(New York: Alfred A. Knopf, 2000)

Subject(s): Animals/Cats; Pets; Resourcefulness
Age range(s): Grades K-3
Major character(s): Tibs, Cat; Mrs. Ford, Businesswoman, Spouse; Mr. Ford, Businessman, Spouse
Time period(s): 2000s (2000)
Locale(s): England

Summary: Tibs grows impatient of his daily wait for breakfast as his family hurries to leave for work and school with no time for their pet. Finally, Tibs begins feeding himself—on a plate, with a spoon, while standing on two legs. His family is amazed to see what the clever cat can do. Mrs. Ford gives Tibs a house key and her cash card so he can shop for himself. Tibs gets a little carried away with his new freedom and begins dining in restaurants, going to movies and shopping for toys. When their clever cat becomes an expensive one Mr. and Mrs. Ford retrieve the cash card and demand that Tibs get a job and pay rent. Working is so tiring that when Tibs loses his job, rather than get another as Mr. and Mrs. Ford demand, he joins the other neighborhood cats that spend their days sleeping—now that's a clever cat! (32 pages)

Where it's reviewed:
Booklist, August 2000, page 2144
Horn Book, September 2000, page 549
New York Times Book Review, May 14, 2000, page 21
Publishers Weekly, July 17, 2000, page 192
School Library Journal, August 2000, page 146

Other books by the same author:
A Small Miracle, 1997
The Tooth Fairy, 1995
The Midnight Circus, 1993

Other books you might like:
Andrew Clements, *Temple Cat*, 1996
    Tired of his pampered life as a temple cat, the creature runs away to live the life of a family pet.
Garrison Keillor, *Cat, You Better Come Home*, 1995
    When Jack ignores his pet's complaints about food Puff leaves home despite Jack's pleas for her to stay.
Lensey Namioka, *The Loyal Cat*, 1995
    A cat rescued by a poor priest uses magical powers to gain recognition for the priest and his temple.
Danny Shanahan, *Buckledown the Workhound*, 1993
    As president of a large corporation, Buckledown is ''dog tired'' so he plans a vacation at a farm where he learns to lead a dog's life.

183

ELLEN CONFORD
RENEE W. ANDRIANI, Illustrator

Annabel the Actress Starring in Gorilla My Dreams

(New York: Simon & Schuster Books for Young Readers, 1999)

Subject(s): Actors and Actresses; Humor; Careers
Age range(s): Grades 2-4
Major character(s): Annabel, Child, Actress (aspiring); Maggie, Friend (Annabel's), Child; Lowell Boxer, Bully, Child
Time period(s): 1990s (1999)
Locale(s): United States

Summary: The first casting call Annabel receives to her advertising flier is to play the part of a gorilla at a 5-year-old's birthday party. Disappointed not to receive a part for which she already has a costume, Annabel enlists Maggie as her costume designer and gives her the lining to an old raincoat to transform into a gorilla. Because the furry fabric is too thick for Maggie to sew, Annabel's gorilla suit is held together with safety pins that do not stay closed for long. The gorilla mask borrowed from Maggie's brother completes the costume and Annabel is feeling confident until Lowell steals the mask. Believing that the show must go on, Annabel makes the most of what she has and brings joy to the birthday boy with her acting talents. (64 pages)

Where it's reviewed:
Booklist, July 1999, page 1945
Horn Book Guide, Fall 1999, page 276
The New Advocate, Spring 2000, page 182
Publishers Weekly, June 21, 1999, page 68
School Library Journal, July 1999, page 67

Other books by the same author:
Get the Picture, Jenny Archer?, 1994
Can Do, Jenny Archer, 1993
What's Cooking, Jenny Archer?, 1989

Other books you might like:
Beverly Cleary, *The Ramona Series*, 1952-1999
   Irrepressible Ramona endures school problems and sibling squabbles with a sense of humor.
James Howe, *Pinky and Rex and the Bully*, 1996
   Pinky decides to ignore bully Kevin's teasing about his name, his interests and his friendship with a girl.
Johanna Hurwitz, *The Adventures of Ali Baba Bernstein*, 1985
   Changing his boring name is only of many adventures for 8-year-old David.
Susan Wojciechowski, *Don't Call Me Beanhead!*, 1994
   Beany is a worrier; her worries lead to plans and then the fun begins!

184

ELLEN CONFORD
TOM NEWSOM, Illustrator

Diary of a Monster's Son
(Boston: Little, Brown and Company, 1999)

Subject(s): Monsters; Fathers and Sons; Diaries
Age range(s): Grades 2-4
Major character(s): Bradley Fentriss, Son, Child; Mr. Fentriss, Father, Monster
Time period(s): 1990s (1999)
Locale(s): United States

Summary: Bradley's dad is not like other dads. He is large. He is hairy. He has sharp, pointy teeth, and his shirt sometimes pops buttons when he gets excited. From school shopping to meeting Bradley's friends, Bradley's dad gets noticed. However, Bradley and his dad make a good family, and that is what is most important in the end. (76 pages)

Where it's reviewed:
Booklist, July 1999, page 1946
Horn Book Guide, Fall 1999, page 277
School Library Journal, July 1999, page 68

Other books by the same author:
Annabel the Actress Starring in Gorilla My Dreams, 1999
The Frog Princess of Pelham, 1997
And This Is Laura, 1987

Other books you might like:
Debbie Dadey, *The Monsters Next Door*, 1998
   Annie, Ben, and Jane are quite surprised when they see their new neighbors.
Marcia Thornton Jones, *Kilmer's Pet Monster*, 1999
   Kilmer Hauntley's pet is unlike any Bailey City has ever seen.
Dian Curtis Regan, *Monster of the Month Club*, 1997
   Rilla thinks that the Monster of the Month Club is a joke, until her first package arrives.

185

PAM CONRAD
RICHARD EGIELSKI, Illustrator

The Tub People's Christmas
(New York: A Laura Geringer Book/HarperCollins Publishers, 1999)

Subject(s): Christmas; Toys; Santa Claus
Age range(s): Grades K-2
Major character(s): Tub Grandfather, Toy, Grandfather; Tub Child, Toy, Son
Time period(s): Indeterminate
Locale(s): United States

Summary: Tub Child is sleepy and wants to go to bed, but obediently he stands guard with the other Tub People on a table near the fireplace. Tub Grandfather seems to have some experience with standing guard and gives Tub Child a silver hook for use later in the evening. Suddenly, an unidentified man comes down the chimney knocking all the Tub People off the table with his large pack and the tree that he pulls into the room. He does notice the small toys on the floor and hangs each one on the tree where they continue standing guard over the toys, gifts, lights and candy that the man sets up before vanishing up the chimney. (32 pages)

Where it's reviewed:
Booklist, September 1, 1999, page 147
Children's Bookwatch, December 1999, page 1
Kirkus Reviews, October 1, 1999, page 1577
Publishers Weekly, September 27, 1999, page 59
School Library Journal, October 1999, page 66

Other books by the same author:
Call Me Ahnighito, 1995
Molly and the Strawberry Day, 1994
The Tub Grandfather, 1993
The Tub People, 1989

Other books you might like:
Diana Kimpton, *The Bear Santa Claus Forgot*, 1995
   When a little bear falls out of Santa's sack onto Maddie's roof, he must find his way into the house so Maddie will have a gift on Christmas morning.
Mariana, *Miss Flora McFlimsey's Christmas Eve*, 1949
   With help from Timothy Mouse, an angel, and her own belief, Miss Flora has a joyful Christmas that proves wishes do come true.
Jan L. Waldron, *Angel Pig and the Hidden Christmas*, 1997
   Angel Pig reminds a houseful of pigs that money is not necessary for a memorable Christmas holiday.

186

TRISH COOKE
SHARON WILSON, Illustrator

The Grandad Tree

(Cambridge, MA: Candlewick Press, 2000)

Subject(s): Grandfathers; Death; Trees
Age range(s): Grades 1-3
Major character(s): Grandad, Grandfather; Vin, Child, Brother (older); Leigh, Child, Sister (younger)
Time period(s): 2000s (2000)
Locale(s): United States

Summary: Vin and Leigh remember playing under the blossoming apple tree with Grandad in the spring. On summer days they listen to Grandad play his fiddle in the shade of the tree and they harvest apples in the fall as Grandad watches. Though the tree lives on, Grandad dies and Vin and Leigh are left with memories, a photo album and a fiddle. Leigh plants a seed in memory of Grandad and Vin assures her that it will grow and change and serve well to represent their undying love for Grandad. (32 pages)

Where it's reviewed:
Booklist, June 1, 2000, page 1896
Horn Book Guide, Fall 2000, page 265
Kirkus Reviews, March 15, 2000, page 378
Magpies, March 2000, page 28
School Library Journal, June 2000, page 104

Other books by the same author:
Mr. Pam Pam and the Hullabazoo, 1994
When I Grow Bigger, 1994
So Much, 1994 (Booklist Editors' Choice)

Other books you might like:
Halina Below, *Chestnut Dreams*, 2000
    Anya and her grandmother watch the seasonal changes of a tree growing in the park and Anya plants some seeds in her yard.
Eve Bunting, *Someday a Tree*, 1993
    Carelessly dumped chemicals kill an oak tree that holds a special place in a family's memories making Alice grateful for her acorn collection.
Mem Fox, *Sophie*, 1994
    Because Grandpa has always been part of Sophie's life his death leaves a sense of emptiness that, in time, is filled.
Karen Hesse, *Poppy's Chair*, 1993
    Leah's grandmother helps her to understand her grandfather's death and to appreciate the items that serve as reminders of him.
Marisabina Russo, *Grandpa Abe*, 1996
    Grandpa Abe dies leaving 9-year-old Sarah with memories and the ability to perform his magic thumb trick.
Janice May Udry, *A Tree Is Nice*, 1956
    The Caldecott Medal winner celebrates the many simple pleasures that a tree offers.
Jane Yolen, *Grandad Bill's Song*, 1994
    With support from family and friends, a young boy begins to accept his feelings following his grandfather's death.

187

HELEN COOPER, Author/Illustrator

Pumpkin Soup

(New York: Farrar Straus Giroux, 1999)

Subject(s): Cooks and Cooking; Friendship; Animals/Ducks
Age range(s): Grades K-2
Major character(s): Cat, Cat; Squirrel, Squirrel; Duck, Duck
Time period(s): Indeterminate
Locale(s): England

Summary: Cat, Squirrel, and Duck are friends who live together, each doing part of the routine. When making pumpkin soup, Cat cuts up the pumpkin, Squirrel stirs in the water, and Duck adds just the right amount of salt. One day Duck decides that he wants to stir the soup, but Squirrel refuses to give up his job so Duck runs away. His friends soon realize how much they miss him, and when he returns, they allow Duck to stir the soup. (32 pages)

Where it's reviewed:
Booklist, September 1, 1999, page 147
Children's Book Review Service, October 1999, page 181
Kirkus Reviews, October 1, 1999, page 1577
Publishers Weekly, November 1, 1999, page 83
School Library Journal, September 1999, page 179

Awards the book has won:
Kate Greenaway Medal, 2000

Other books by the same author:
The Bear under The Stairs, 1997
The Boy Who Wouldn't Go to Bed, 1997 (Winner of the Kate Greenaway Award)
The Tale of Bear, 1995

Other books you might like:
Karen English, *Just Right Stew*, 1998
    Victoria observes her family members making her grandmother's famous stew.
Karen Gray Ruelle, *The Thanksgiving Beast Feast*, 1999
    Harry Cat and his family prepare a Thanksgiving feast for their friends and neighbors.
Teri Sloat, *Patty's Pumpkin Patch*, 1999
    Patty plants her pumpkins and watches them grow in this alphabet story.

188

SUSAN COOPER

King of Shadows

(New York: Margaret K. McElderry Books/Simon & Schuster, 1999)

Subject(s): Time Travel; Actors and Actresses; Theater
Age range(s): Grades 5-8
Major character(s): Nathan "Nat" Field, Actor, Time Traveler; Richard "Arby" Babbage, Director; Will Shakespeare, Actor, Writer
Time period(s): 1990s (1999); 16th century (1599)
Locale(s): Cambridge, Massachusetts; London, England (Globe Theater)

Summary: Orphan Nat uses acting as a refuge so he's pleased to be selected to join Arby's Company of Boys for a performance of *A Midsummer Night's Dream* at the newly reconstructed Globe Theatre. After preliminary rehearsals in Cambridge, the group travels to London where Nat falls ill with a high fever. When he awakens he's in Elizabethan England, cast in the same role as Puck for a performance commanded by the Queen at the original Globe Theatre. Nat's experience of working directly with Will Shakespeare provides some healing for the pain of his father's suicide three years earlier, but when Nat abruptly returns to the present day he grieves for the loss of Will. Arby offers some perspective and the performance gives Nat a focus for and a distraction from his confused feelings. (186 pages)

Where it's reviewed:
Booklist, October 15, 1999, page 4442
Horn Book, November 1999, page 735
Publishers Weekly, September 27, 1999, page 106
Riverbank Review, Spring 2000, page 38
School Library Journal, November 1999, page 156

Awards the book has won:
Booklist Editors' Choice, 1999
Boston Globe/Horn Book Honor Book, 2000

Other books by the same author:
The Boggart and the Monster, 1997
The Boggart, 1993
The Grey King, 1975 (Newbery Award Winner)
The Dark Is Rising, 1973

Other books you might like:
Gary L. Blackwood, *The Shakespeare Stealer*, 1998
  As part of a scheme to steal Shakespeare's latest play, Orphan Widge feels caught between the friendly cast and his devious master.
Pamela Melnikoff, *Plots and Players: The Lopez Conspiracy*, 1989
  Shakespeare writes *The Merchant of Venice* to help his young friend Robin.
Jane Yolen, *Boots and the Seven Leaguers*, 2000
  Gog and his pal sign on to work with their favorite band, but then Gog's brother disappears and they may miss the band's show while looking for him.

189

SHANA COREY
CHESLEY MCLAREN, Illustrator

You Forgot Your Skirt, Amelia Bloomer!

(New York: Scholastic Press, 2000)

Subject(s): Clothes; Women's Rights; Conduct of Life
Age range(s): Grades 1-4
Major character(s): Amelia Bloomer, Feminist, Editor (newspaper); Elizabeth Cady Stanton, Feminist, Friend (Amelia's); Libby, Feminist, Cousin (Elizabeth's)
Time period(s): 1850s (1851)
Locale(s): Seneca Falls, New York

Summary: Amelia Bloomer is proud that she is considered an improper lady because, as a married woman, she chooses to work. Amelia founds *The Lily*, a newspaper that promotes

women's right to vote and to work. Society's fashion demands also draw Amelia's attention. Though she refuses to don corsets and hoops, until Elizabeth brings her cousin Libby to visit her, Amelia hasn't found an alternative to long dresses. Libby is wearing an outfit modified from European fashions with a short dress over billowy pants. Immediately Amelia sews similar clothes and revels in the freedom of her new attire. Derisively, the townspeople call the outfit "bloomers" and mock Amelia for her appearance. After the pattern for bloomers appears in *The Lily*, independently minded women everywhere thank Amelia for starting the trend. A concluding "Author's Note" gives the historical basis for the story. (40 pages)

Where it's reviewed:
Booklist, February 1, 2000, page 1018
Bulletin of the Center for Children's Books, February 2000, page 205
Kirkus Reviews, January 15, 2000, page 119
Publishers Weekly, January 31, 2000, page 106
School Library Journal, March 2000, page 190

Awards the book has won:
Booklist Editors' Choice, 2000
Publishers Weekly Best Books, 2000

Other books by the same author:
Brave Pig, 1999 (Step into Reading)
Babe: Oops, Pig!, 1998 (Early Step into Reading)

Other books you might like:
Faye Gibbons, *Mama and Me and the Model T*, 1999
  When Mama hears her husband explaining the workings of the new Model T to the boys of the family she shows him that a woman can also drive a car.
Betsy Hearne, *Seven Brave Women*, 1997
  Seven generations of women in one family live their lives in a way that has a positive impact on those around them.
Kathryn Lasky, *She's Wearing a Dead Bird on Her Head!*, 1995
  Founders of the Audubon Society work to stop the killing of birds for fashion.
Emily Arnold McCully, *The Ballot Box Battle*, 1996
  By fighting for women's suffrage, Elizabeth Cady Stanton makes a difference in the lives of women.
Pam Munoz Ryan, *Amelia and Eleanor Go for a Ride*, 1999
  Two independent women ignore convention and leave a dinner party at the White House for a night flight over the city.

190

BILL COSBY
VARNETTE P. HONEYWOOD, Illustrator

My Big Lie

(New York: Cartwheel Books/Scholastic Inc., 1999)

Series: Little Bill Books for Beginning Readers
Subject(s): Parent and Child; Dishonesty; Trust
Age range(s): Grades 2-3
Major character(s): Little Bill, Child, Son; Mom, Mother; Dad, Father
Time period(s): 1990s (1999)

Locale(s): United States

Summary: To ease the trouble Little Bill knows he is in for being very late for dinner he fabricates a story that actually causes even more trouble for him. When Dad starts to call the police, Little Bill quickly admits that he's not telling the truth and Mom and Dad send him to his room to read "The Boy Who Cried Wolf." He's relieved when his parents talk with him later and assure him of their continuing love and their belief that he'll never lie again. (40 pages)

Where it's reviewed:
Booklist, October 15, 1999, page 441
Horn Book Guide, Fall 1999, page 277
School Library Journal, August 1999, page 132

Other books by the same author:
The Worst Day of My Life, 1999 (Little Bill Books for Beginning Readers)
Shipwreck Saturday, 1998 (Little Bill Books for Beginning Readers)
The Treasure Hunt, 1997 (Little Bill Books for Beginning Readers)

Other books you might like:
Eve Bunting, *A Day's Work*, 1994
    The value of honesty is learned by a young boy when his efforts to help his immigrant grandfather backfire.
Bernice Chardiet, *The Best Teacher in the World*, 1990
    Bunny is too timid to admit to her teacher that she didn't deliver a note as requested until her guilty conscious gives her a sleepless night.
John Himmelman, *Honest Tulio*, 1997
    Tulio has an unexpected adventure when he tries to return a man's copper coin.

191

BILL COSBY
VARNETTE P. HONEYWOOD, Illustrator

One Dark and Scary Night

(New York: Cartwheel Books/Scholastic, Inc., 1999)

Series: Little Bill Books for Beginning Readers
Subject(s): Fear; Grandmothers; African Americans
Age range(s): Grades 1-2
Major character(s): Little Bill, Child, Son; Alice the Great, Grandmother (great grandmother); Mom, Mother
Time period(s): 2000s (2000s)
Locale(s): United States

Summary: Little Bill hears thumps and sees lights on his wall and he knows the things in his closet are coming to get him so he races to his parents room. Mom walks Little Bill back to bed and checks the closet, but the comfort of her presence is short-lived for as soon as she leaves, those things in the closet start threatening Little Bill again. Now he races for Alice the Great's room and she not only walks him back to his room and checks the closet, but she sits in the dark in the closet with Little Bill waiting for the thumping things. When nothing comes she puts Little Bill back in bed, smoothes his covers in a magic way and assures him he'll be able to sleep. Again Little Bill hears the thump of a branch falling on the roof and sees the lights of a passing car on the wall, but his time he

knows the magic will protect him and he sleeps until morning. (32 pages)

Where it's reviewed:
Horn Book Guide, Fall 1999, page 277
School Library Journal, July 1999, page 68

Other books by the same author:
Hooray for the Dandelion Warriors!, 1999 (Little Bill Books for Beginning Readers)
Super-Fine Valentine, 1998 (Little Bill Books for Beginning Readers)
The Treasure Hunt, 1997 (Little Bill Books for Beginning Readers)

Other books you might like:
Stan Berenstain, *The Berenstain Bears in the Dark*, 1982
    After hearing Brother Bear's scary library book, Sister Bear begins to imagine frightening things in the darkened bedroom.
Russell Hoban, *Bedtime for Frances*, 1960
    Frances imagines so many scary things in her room that she is unable to sleep.
Mercer Mayer, *There's a Nightmare in My Closet*, 1985
    Sometimes inviting monsters out of the closet helps them seem less scary.

192

BRUCE COVILLE
TONY SANSEVERO, Illustrator

I Was a Sixth Grade Alien

(New York: A Minstrel Book/Pocket Books, 1999)

Series: I Was a Sixth Grade Alien. Book 1
Subject(s): Aliens; School Life; Humor
Age range(s): Grades 3-6
Major character(s): Tim Tompkins, 6th Grader, Friend; Pleskit Meenom, Alien (from Planet Hevi-Hevi), 6th Grader
Time period(s): 1990s
Locale(s): Syracuse, New York

Summary: Tim has always been interested in extraterrestrial life so when a real alien is assigned to his classroom, Tim is eager to meet Pleskit and become his friend. Although Pleskit has attended "training module" to learn the Earth culture, he makes many innocent mistakes and creates an embarrassing situation for himself, his ambassador father and their mission. Anti-alien sentiment is growing in the community and the superiors from Hevi-Hevi threaten to recall the mission. When Pleskit invites Tim to visit the embassy, the new friends discover that Pleskit's training was deliberately sabotaged in order to remove his Fatherly One as ambassador so others could profit from trade with Earth. (169 pages)

Where it's reviewed:
Booklist, October 15, 1999, page 443
Publishers Weekly, August 2, 1999, page 87
School Library Journal, October 1999, page 148

Other books by the same author:
The Attack of the Two-Inch Teacher, 1999 (I Was a Sixth Grade Alien, Book 2)
The Skull of Truth, 1997

Space Brat 4: Planet of the Dips, 1994
Aliens Ate My Homework, 1993

Other books you might like:
Betsy Byars, *The Computer Nut*, 1984
  Kate has met some interesting people via computer but BB-9 is the first alien.
Mark J. Harris, *Solay*, 1993
  Melissa's ho-hum existence changes drastically when a space ship, thinking it's in New York, drops off Solay in her California neighborhood.
Pamela F. Service, *Stinker from Space*, 1988
  An alien takes the form of a skunk to disguise his presence on Earth.

193

BRUCE COVILLE

Song of the Wanderer

(New York: Scholastic Press, Inc., 1999)

Series: Unicorn Chronicles. Book 2
Subject(s): Unicorns; Fantasy; Heroes and Heroines
Age range(s): Grades 5-8
Major character(s): Cara Diane Hunter, 12-Year-Old; Ivy Morris, Grandmother
Time period(s): Indeterminate
Locale(s): Luster, Fictional Country; Earth

Summary: Cara has made it to Luster, the land of the unicorns, but now she must go back to earth to rescue Ivy, known to the unicorns as the Wanderer. Cara and her unicorn friends begin a long and perilous journey to find the gate that will allow them to cross to Earth and bring the Wanderer back. Unicorn hunters try to stop their journey, but Cara and Ivy succeed in returning to Luster together. (330 pages)

Where it's reviewed:
The Book Report, January 2000, page 64
Booklist, March 1, 2000, page 1243
New York Times Book Review, December 19, 1999, page 30
School Library Journal, December 1999, page 130

Other books by the same author:
A Glory of Unicorns, 1998
Fortune's Journey, 1995
In the Land of Unicorns, 1994 (Unicorn Chronicles, Book 1)

Other books you might like:
Gail Carson Levine, *Ella Enchanted*, 1997
  In the Newberry Honor book, Ella is cursed with obedience and must go on a quest to save herself and those she cares about.
Patricia C. Wrede, *Dealing with Dragons*, 1990
  In the first book of the Enchanted Forest Chronicles, Princess Cimorene runs away from home to become the princess of a dragon.
Jane Yolen, *Here There Be Unicorns*, 1994
  This collection of stories and poems features unicorns.

194

CRESSIDA COWELL, Author/Illustrator

Don't Do That, Kitty Kilroy!

(New York: Orchard Books, 2000)

Subject(s): Mothers and Daughters; Behavior; Parent and Child
Age range(s): Grades 1-2
Major character(s): Kitty Kilroy, Daughter, Child
Time period(s): 1990s (1999)
Locale(s): England

Summary: All day long Kitty hears her mother call, "Don't do that, Kitty Kilroy!" if she puts her feet on the couch or eats candy or makes a mess. Kitty is so tired of hearing the same admonition that she tells her mother to go away and let her do what she wants to do. So, her mother picks up the baby and goes away. Kitty has a wonderful day wearing pajamas, watching TV, eating cereal and ice cream and playing with her friends. By the time her mother reappears, Kitty and her friends are feeling a little sick and tired so Kitty's mom sends the friends home, gives Kitty some medicine to settle her stomach and washes her up for bed. Kitty is happy to be tucked into bed, but she goes to sleep dreaming of her plans for tomorrow. (32 pages)

Where it's reviewed:
Horn Book Guide, Fall 2000, page 246
Kirkus Reviews, January 15, 2000, page 119
Publishers Weekly, March 6, 2000, page 110
School Library Journal, March 2000, page 190

Other books by the same author:
Hiccup, the Seasick Viking, 2000
What Shall We Do with the Boo-Hoo Baby?, 2000
Little Bo Peep's Library Book, 1999

Other books you might like:
Lynne Jonell, *Mommy Go Away!*, 1997
  Tired of being too small to make decisions, Christopher tells his mother to go away and provides her with the necessary transportation.
Barbara M. Joosse, *Mama, Do You Love Me?*, 1991
  A young girl seeks reassurance that her mother will continue to love her if she misbehaves.
Lisa McCourt, *I Love You, Stinky Face*, 1997
  A girl imagines becoming a succession of nasty animals and is comforted to know that her mother would love and care for each one.

195

CRESSIDA COWELL
INGRID GODON, Illustrator

What Shall We Do with the Boo-Hoo Baby?

(New York: Scholastic Press, 2000)

Subject(s): Babies; Animals; Problem Solving
Age range(s): Preschool
Major character(s): Unnamed Character, Baby
Time period(s): 2000s (2000)

Locale(s): Fictional Country

Summary: Four animals try to satisfy a crying baby, but none of their initial efforts have a lasting effect. The duck offers a toy and the dog suggests feeding. Each animal carries food to the baby—most of it not on a baby's diet—but the baby soon begins crying again. The cat thinks a bath is in order but that only calms the baby for a few moments. The cow thinks playing with the baby is a good idea and it is, but not for long. Finally, the duck puts the baby to bed and that plan seems to work. The animals are soon snoring in a heap on the floor while the baby, smiling, sits in the crib. (32 pages)

Where it's reviewed:
Booklist, January 1, 2001, page 967
Horn Book Guide, Spring 2001, page 13
Kirkus Reviews, October 1, 2000, page 1421
Publishers Weekly, November 6, 2000, page 89

Other books by the same author:
Don't Do That, Kitty Kilroy!, 2000
Hiccup, the Seasick Viking, 2000
Little Bo Peep's Library Book, 1999

Other books you might like:
Kate McMullan, *Papa's Song*, 2000
   Lullabies from Granny, Grandpa and Mama Bear are nice, but only Papa Bear's song lulls Baby Bear into sleep.
Phyllis Root, *What Baby Wants*, 1998
   While Mama naps everyone in the family tries to determine what will soothe the crying baby.
Frieda Wishinsky, *Oonga Boonga*, 1990
   Baby Louise wails and her only consolation is brother Daniel's catchy phrase ''Oonga boonga.'' Unfortunately for her parents, it only works for Daniel.

196

JOY COWLEY
JENNIFER PLECAS, Illustrator

Agapanthus Hum and the Eyeglasses

(New York: Philomel Books, 1999)

Subject(s): Behavior; Parent and Child; Humor
Age range(s): Grades 1-3
Major character(s): Agapanthus, Child (energetic), Daughter; Mommy, Mother; Daddy, Father
Time period(s): 1990s (1999)
Locale(s): United States

Summary: Active Agapanthus hums as she whizzes about so her parents call her Agapanthus Hum. Fortunately, Agapanthus has a very patient Mommy and Daddy because her energy tends to lead to accidents, frequently involving her eyeglasses. When Agapanthus, who aspires to be an acrobat, does hand stands, her glasses slip off and she lands on them when she falls. Mommy and Daddy treat Agapanthus to an acrobatic show and Agapanthus learns that Mommy is right; acrobats put their glasses in their mother's pocket while they perform. (48 pages)

Where it's reviewed:
Horn Book Guide, Fall 1999, page 277
Kirkus Reviews, December 1, 1998, page 1732
Publishers Weekly, December 21, 1998, page 68

School Library Journal, April 1999, page 91

Awards the book has won:
Publishers Weekly Best Books, 1999

Other books by the same author:
Nicketty-Nacketty, Noo-Noo-Noo, 1998
Singing Down the Rain, 1997
Gracias, the Thanksgiving Turkey, 1996
The Mouse Bride, 1995

Other books you might like:
James Howe, *Pinky and Rex*, 1990
   Pinky and Rex, inseparable friends, embark on the first of many shared adventures in this initial book in the series.
Megan McDonald, *Beezy Magic*, 1998
   Three stories tell of events in active Beezy's life with her dog and grandmother.
Phyllis Reynolds Naylor, *I Can't Take You Anywhere!*, 1997
   Amy Audrey is so prone to clumsiness that her parents prefer to stay home rather than risk mishaps in public.
Cynthia Rylant, *The Henry and Mudge Series*, 1987-
   The adventures of Henry and his lovable, slobbery dog Mudge entertain beginning readers.

197

JOY COWLEY
OLIVIER DUNREA, Illustrator

The Rusty, Trusty Tractor

(Honesdale, PA: Boyds Mills Press, 1999)

Subject(s): Farm Life; Grandfathers; Seasons
Age range(s): Grades K-2
Major character(s): Micah, Child; Mr. Hill, Salesman (farm equipment); Granpappy, Grandfather, Farmer
Time period(s): Indeterminate
Locale(s): United States

Summary: Granpappy's tractor may not look like much, but for fifty years it's helped plow the fields, plant the crops and bring in the harvest. Micah does not understand why Granpappy isn't interested in the shiny new, air-conditioned tractors at Mr. Hill's store. Mr. Hill wonders too and wagers Granpappy a box of jelly donuts that the tractor won't make in through another season. With just a little coaxing from Granpappy, the tractor plows, sows, and harvests the field without stopping. When Mr. Hill delivers the jelly donuts to Micah and Granpappy, the rusty, trusty tractor has enough energy left to haul his car out of the mud. (40 pages)

Where it's reviewed:
Booklist, March 15, 1999, page 1332
Horn Book Guide, Fall 1999, page 248
Publishers Weekly, March 1, 1999, page 68
School Library Journal, May 1999, page 88

Other books by the same author:
Agapanthus Hum and the Eyeglasses, 1999
Big Moon Tortilla, 1998
Gracias, the Thanksgiving Turkey, 1998

Other books you might like:
Virginia Lee Burton, *Mike Mulligan and His Steam Shovel*, 1939

Age does not prevent Mike Mulligan's steam shovel Mary Anne from doing the work that the newer power shovels cannot.

Libba Moore Gray, *The Little Black Truck*, 1994

A young man finds and restores an abandoned pick-up truck that reminds him of the one his grandfather drove for many years.

Watty Piper, *The Little Engine That Could*, 1930

The Little Engine proves that gumption is more important than size if there is a job to be done.

Sue Porter, *Parsnip and the Runaway Tractor*, 1999

Parsnip, a lamb, accidentally starts the farmer's shiny, new tractor and goes for quite a ride.

Miryam Yardumian, *The Happy Man and His Dump Truck*, 1999

A man takes a group of farm animals for a ride in his dump truck.

198

JOY COWLEY
GAVIN BISHOP, Illustrator

The Video Shop Sparrow

(Honesdale, PA: Boyds Mills Press, 1999)

Subject(s): Animals/Birds; Animals, Treatment of; Problem Solving

Age range(s): Grades 1-4

Major character(s): George, Child; Harry, Child

Time period(s): 1990s (1999)

Locale(s): New Zealand

Summary: When George and Harry try to return their video, they discover the video shop is closed and a sparrow is trapped inside. They try to get help from the waitress next door, their parents, and finally the police, but no one will help them because the bird is "only a sparrow." Finally, the boys enlist the aid of the mayor and, at last, the sparrow is saved. (32 pages)

Where it's reviewed:

Booklist, December 1, 1999, page 709
Horn Book Guide, Spring 2000, page 32
Kirkus Reviews, October 15,1999, page 1641
Magpies, July 1999, page 7
School Library Journal, December 1999, page 90

Other books by the same author:
The Rusty, Trusty Tractor, 1999
Big Moon Tortilla, 1998
Gracias, the Thanksgiving Turkey, 1996

Other books you might like:

Caroline Arnold, *House Sparrows Everywhere*, 1992

This nonfiction book describes the habitat and physical characteristics of the sparrow.

Leyla Torres, *Subway Sparrow*, 1993

Passengers on a subway train work together to try to help a trapped sparrow escape.

Charlotte Zolotow, *Peter and the Pigeons*, 1993

After touring the zoo's collection of birds, Peter decides he prefers the everyday variety of pigeons.

199

JUDY COX
CYNTHIA FISHER, Illustrator

Mean, Mean Maureen Green

(New York: Holiday House, 1999)

Subject(s): Bullies; School Life; Fear

Age range(s): Grades 2-4

Major character(s): Lilley Nelson, 3rd Grader, Child of Divorced Parents; Adam Levy, 3rd Grader, Friend (Lilley's); Maureen Green, 4th Grader, Bully

Time period(s): 2000s (2000)

Locale(s): United States

Summary: Due to a change in bus routes Maureen rides Lilley's bus this year. From the moment she hears the news Lilley is terrified because she's heard the stories about mean, mean Maureen Green. Adam, a new kid in class, is not at all intimidated by bullies and actually plays a trick of Maureen. Now, timid Lilley knows she's doomed to be Maureen's next victim so rather than ride the bus she walks to school. Walking is too slow and Lilley is late because of an encounter with a loose, vicious dog. The desire to avoid Maureen is so strong that Lilley finally overcomes her fear of falling and learns to ride a two-wheeler without training wheels. Now she and Adam can ride their bikes to school together and not worry about the bus trip again. The book concludes with bicycle safety tips. (89 pages)

Where it's reviewed:

Booklist, December 1, 1999, page 703
Bulletin of the Center for Children's Books, February 2000, page 206
Horn Book Guide, Fall 2000, page 292
Kirkus Reviews, December 1, 1999, page 1881
School Library Journal, March 2000, page 192

Other books by the same author:
Weird Stories from the Lonesome Cafe, 2000
Rabbit Pirates: A Tale of the Spinach Main, 1999
Third Grade Pet, 1998

Other books you might like:

Debbie Dadey, *King of the Kooties!*, 1999

When a mean 4th grader teases Nate's new friend they devise a plan to stop her bullying.

Stephen Krensky, *Louise Takes Charge*, 1998

Putting an end to Jasper's bullying requires cooperative effort for Louise and her classmates.

Kirby Larson, *Cody and Quinn, Sitting in a Tree*, 1996

After being teased because he has a girl for a friend, Cody considers several ways to respond to his tormentor.

Elizabeth Levy, *Third Grade Bullies*, 1998

Sally's introduction to a new school suffers when she tries to help a classmate deal with two bullies.

Louis Sachar, *Marvin Redpost: Why Pick on Me?*, 1993

Marvin fears that a small problem at recess could be used to make him the third grade class outcast.

C. Anne Scott, *Lizard Meets Ivana the Terrible*, 1999

When third grader Lizzie moves in with her grandmother and enters a new school she worries about making friends.

Carol Sonenklar, *Mighty Boy*, 1999
Howard develops the confidence to deal with the class bully.

200

JUDY COX
EMILY ARNOLD MCCULLY, Illustrator

Rabbit Pirates: A Tale of the Spinach Main

(San Diego: Browndeer/Harcourt Brace, 1999)

Subject(s): Pirates; Restaurants; Animals/Rabbits
Age range(s): Grades 1-4
Major character(s): Monsieur Lapin, Pirate, Rabbit; Monsieur Blanc, Pirate, Rabbit; Reynard, Fox
Time period(s): Indeterminate Past
Locale(s): Provence, France

Summary: Monsieur Lapin and Monsieur Blanc have a shared past as pirates, but now own and run a restaurant together. Their restaurant is successful until Reynard starts coming and scaring away customers. What Reynard really wants to eat is not the customers but Monsieur Lapin and Monsieur Blanc. The friends decide not to respond with force to Reynard's intimidations. Instead they bake life-sized bunnies that are hot and spicy. In the dark, Reynard mistakes them for Monsieur Lapin and Monsieur Blanc. One bite and Reynard is never seen again. (32 pages)

Where it's reviewed:
Booklist, October 15, 1999, page 451
Publishers Weekly, August 2, 1999, page 83
School Library Journal, October 1999, page 110

Other books by the same author:
Mean, Mean Maureen Green, 1999
The West Texas Chili Monster, 1998
Third Grade Pet, 1998

Other books you might like:
Tim Egan, *Friday Night at Hodges' Cafe*, 1994
Three tigers that ignore the "No Tigers" sign on the door of Hodges Cafe learn new dinner ideas from chef Hodges and his pet duck.
Vivian French, *Red Hen and Sly Fox*, 1995
A clever hen outwits a fox who had hoped to enjoy her for dinner.
Julia Noonan, *Hare and Rabbit: Friends Forever*, 2000
Hare and Rabbit remain friends through all their adventures.
Kathy Tucker, *Do Pirates Take Baths?*, 1994
A story in rhyme provides details of the daily life of pirates.
Brigitte Weniger, *Why Are You Fighting, Davy?*, 1999
Davy and Eddie fight, and then make up again.

201

JUDY COX
DIANE KIDD, Illustrator

Weird Stories from the Lonesome Cafe

(San Diego: Browndeer Press/Harcourt, Inc., 2000)

Subject(s): Restaurants; Aunts and Uncles; Humor
Age range(s): Grades 2-4
Major character(s): Clem, Uncle, Writer, Restaurateur; Sam, 10-Year-Old, Nephew
Time period(s): 2000s (2000)
Locale(s): Nevada (Lonesome Cafe)

Summary: Seeking quiet and inspiration for his writing career Uncle Clem packs his belongings and heads for the desert of Nevada where he intends to operate a restaurant with help from his visiting nephew Sam. Although the Lonesome Cafe has few customers other than the Channel 54 news crew in search of a story, Sam and Uncle Clem are busy enough that Uncle Clem has no time to write. Uncle Clem puts out a "Help Wanted" sign and soon he's hired a cook, a delivery person, a handyman, a waitress and a dishwasher. To Sam, each of the employees bears a striking resemblance to a legendary character whose sighting has recently been reported in *Weird and Amazing Tales*. Unimaginative Uncle Clem doesn't see any similarity between his employees and Bigfoot, Elvis, Santa Claus, Dorothy or ET and he bemoans the lack of inspiring material for his book in this isolated desert. Sam, however, is eager to begin a school assignment about his summer's activities. (72 pages)

Where it's reviewed:
Booklist, April 15, 2000, page 1542
Horn Book Guide, Fall 2000, page 292
Publishers Weekly, April 24, 2000, page 91
School Library Journal, June 2000, page 104

Other books by the same author:
Mean, Mean Maureen Green, 1999
Rabbit Pirates: A Tale of the Spinach Main, 1999
The West Texas Chili Monster, 1998
Third Grade Pet, 1998

Other books you might like:
Roald Dahl, *The Wonderful Story of Henry Sugar and Six More*, 1977
Seven fantastic short stories include Henry Sugar's tale as well as one about a hitchhiker and another about a boy who talks to animals.
Margaret Mahy, *The Girl with the Green Ear: Stories about Magic in Nature*, 1992
Trickle is a magical town; nine stories tell of the wondrous events that happen there.
Daniel Pinkwater, *Wallpaper from Space*, 1996
Steve's new space ship wallpaper not only glows in the dark but also carries him aboard a space ship on a journey to outer space.
Cynthia Rylant, *The Van Gogh Cafe*, 1995
Cynthia and her father believe the magical things that happen in their restaurant are more than coincidences.

202

JOHN COY
LESLIE JEAN-BART, Illustrator

Strong to the Hoop
(New York: Lee & Low Books, Inc., 1999)

Subject(s): Sports/Basketball; Brothers; Competition
Age range(s): Grades 2-5
Major character(s): James, 10-Year-Old, Brother (Nate's); Nate, Brother (older), Basketball Player; Marcus, Basketball Player
Time period(s): 1990s (1999)
Locale(s): United States

Summary: Although James and Nate walk together to the basketball courts in their urban neighborhood, James knows his place is on the sidelines while Nate plays on one of the teams in a pick-up game. When one of Nate's teammates is injured, James is drafted as the replacement and assigned to guard Marcus. The size and strength of Marcus makes James question his readiness to play with the bigger boys. What James lacks in size and experience he makes up for in determination and skill, proving to be a valuable contributor to the game. (32 pages)

Where it's reviewed:
Booklist, December 15, 1999, page 784
Children's Book Review Service, January 2000, page 56
Kirkus Reviews, August 1, 1999, page 1224
Publishers Weekly, September 27, 1999, page 105
School Library Journal, October 1999, page 112

Awards the book has won:
ALA Notable Children's Books, 2000
Notable Social Studies Trade Books for Young People, 2000

Other books by the same author:
Vroomaloom Zoom, 2000
Night Driving, 1996 (Marion Vannett Ridgway Award)

Other books you might like:
Barbara E. Barber, *Allie's Basketball Dream*, 1996
    The basketball Allie receives for her birthday will help her achieve her dream of mastering the sport.
Robert Burleigh, *Hoops*, 1997
    An illustrated prose poem expresses the intensity of the game, the drive of the players and the joy of basketball.
Eloise Greenfield, *For the Love of the Game: Michael Jordan and Me*, 1997
    A poem describes the basketball maneuvers of Michael Jordan.
Bill Martin Jr., *Swish!*, 1997
    On the final play of a basketball game, teamwork scores the winning goal for the Cardinals. Michael Sampson, co-author.

203

JOHN COY
JOE CEPEDA, Illustrator

Vroomaloom Zoom
(New York: Crown Publishers, 2000)

Subject(s): Automobiles; Imagination; Bedtime
Age range(s): Grades K-2
Major character(s): Carmela, Child, Daughter; Daddy, Father
Time period(s): 2000s (2000)
Locale(s): Earth

Summary: Daddy grabs the car keys and Carmela brings her blankie to the big yellow car. Buckled up and ready on a hot evening Daddy begins driving, hoping that when they reach the countryside Carmela will be ready to sleep. Carmela's not ready yet so she instructs Daddy to keep driving and he does—through woods, up mountains, across streams, around waterfalls, sideways, backwards and in circles. The sun sinks below the horizon, the sky's colors change from orange to purple, darkness deepens and Carmela's eyes close, but not for long—keep driving Daddy. (32 pages)

Where it's reviewed:
Booklist, December 1, 2000, page 717
Horn Book Guide, Spring 2001, page 33
Publishers Weekly, November 6, 2000, page 90
School Library Journal, October 2000, page 119

Other books by the same author:
Strong to the Hoop, 1999 (ALA Notable Children's Book)
Night Driving, 1996 (Marion Vannett Ridgway Award)

Other books you might like:
Helen Cooper, *The Boy Who Wouldn't Go to Bed*, 1997
    When a young boy hears bedtime announced he races away in his toy car, intending to stay awake all night.
Michael Foreman, *Dad! I Can't Sleep*, 1995
    Dad's going-to-sleep suggestions fail to produce the desired effect.
Laurence Pringle, *Octopus Hug*, 1993
    Active pre-bedtime play with Dad encourages the children to settle into bed before Mom comes home.

204

CHARLOTTE CRAFT
K.Y. CRAFT, Illustrator

King Midas and the Golden Touch
(New York: Morrow Junior Books, 1999)

Subject(s): Legends; Mythology; Gold
Age range(s): Grades 1-4
Major character(s): King Midas, Royalty, Father; Aurelia, Royalty, Daughter; Unnamed Character, Spirit
Time period(s): Indeterminate Past
Locale(s): Fictional Country

Summary: In this retelling of the Greek myth, King Midas loves only one thing more than gold—his daughter. Every morning Aurelia brings roses from the garden to grace the breakfast table she shares with her father. After King Midas is granted his wish, the roses become gold and no longer are fragrant. Aurelia becomes more concerned when she notices that her father is unable to eat because his food turns to gold before he can put it into his mouth. When Aurelia hurries to comfort him, his touch changes his beloved Aurelia into a golden statue. The apparition that first granted the king his wish returns with a plan to reverse the spell and King Midas hurries to complete the task and restore his daughter. (32 pages)

Where it's reviewed:
Booklist, April 15, 1999, page 1532
Horn Book Guide, Fall 1999, page 323
The New York Times Book Review, November 21, 1999, page 50
Publishers Weekly, May 10, 1999, page 68
School Library Journal, March 1999, page 191

Other books by the same author:
Cupid and Psyche, 1996

Other books you might like:
John Warren Stewig, *King Midas*, 1999
A lively, illustrated retelling of the classic tale brings a touch of humor to the tragic story.
Rosemary Wells, *Max and Ruby's Midas: Another Greek Myth*, 1995
In this story of Midas, told to curb Max's appetite, everything the prince looks at turns to food.
Marcia Williams, *Greek Myths for Young Children*, 1992
Eight Greek myths are presented in an illustrated format accessible to elementary age students.

205

SHARON CREECH
CHRIS RASCHKA, Illustrator

Fishing in the Air

(New York: Joanna Cotler Books/HarperCollins Publishers, 2000)

Subject(s): Fathers and Sons; Fishing; Imagination
Age range(s): Grades K-3
Major character(s): Unnamed Character, Father; Unnamed Character, Son
Time period(s): Indeterminate
Locale(s): United States

Summary: A Saturday fishing trip becomes an imaginative journey beyond the river and into an exploration of family history and intergenerational connections. The trip begins early with the important task of digging worms and loading poles into the car but the boy's father sets the tone when he describes their journey as being one to a secret place to "catch the air." As his father metaphorically describes passing street lamps, trees and birds the boy imagines them as the compared objects. While the father fishes in the river, his son casts his line into the air to catch the breeze just as his father did as a youth. The day together fishing links father and son, memory and present experience. (32 pages)

Where it's reviewed:
Booklist, November 1, 2000, page 546
Horn Book Guide, Spring 2001, page 33
Kirkus Reviews, July 1, 2000, page 957
Publishers Weekly, July 10, 2000, page 63

School Library Journal, September 2000, page 193

Awards the book has won:
Publishers Weekly Best Books, 2000

Other books by the same author:
Ruby Holler, 2001
Pleasing the Ghost, 1996

Other books you might like:
John Coy, *Night Driving*, 1996
An all-night drive to reach their camping spot near the mountains is a special time for a father and son.
Patricia Lakin, *Dad and Me in the Morning*, 1994
Jacob and his father enjoy some special, private time together watching the sunrise.
Jane Yolen, *Owl Moon*, 1987
A father shares a memorable time with his young daughter during a moonlit walk through the snowy woods in search of an owl. Caldecott Medal winner.

206

ANN HOWARD CREEL

A Ceiling of Stars

(Middleton, WI: American Girl/Pleasant Co., 1999)

Series: AG Fiction
Subject(s): Homeless People; Letters; Diaries
Age range(s): Grades 5-7
Major character(s): Vivien Manell, 12-Year-Old, Abandoned Child; Mama, Widow(er), Alcoholic; Locket, Streetperson, Friend (Vivien's)
Time period(s): 1990s (1999)
Locale(s): Denver, Colorado

Summary: Through letters to family members and diary entries, Vivien tells of her life since her father's accidental death. With her mother she is traveling from Ohio to Oregon, camping along the way. They make it as far as Colorado before the money runs out and Mama heads to Denver to look for work. When Mama doesn't return, Vivien tries to find her. After living on the street, Vivien seeks shelter at a home for youth where she meets Locket, a street-smart 16-year-old. Together the friends return to the streets and Vivien receives word that her mom is hospitalized for treatment of alcoholism. Eventually, Vivien returns to the shelter, and then goes to a group home until Mama's treatment is completed and she can care for Vivien again. (85 pages)

Where it's reviewed:
The Book Report, November 1999, page 59
Horn Book Guide, Spring 2000, page 76
Kirkus Reviews, September 1, 1999, page 1415
School Library Journal, January 2000, page 128

Other books by the same author:
Water at the Blue Earth, 1998

Other books you might like:
Barthe DeClements, *No Place for Me*, 1987
With her mom in treatment for alcoholism, Copper is sent to live with one relative after another and learns that she must stand up for herself.

Paula Fox, *Monkey Island*, 1991
 Coping with the difficulties of homelessness in New York City presents challenges for 11-year-old Clay.

Patricia Hermes, *Someone to Count On*, 1993
 Sam's unconventional widowed mother leaves her daughter at her father's ranch while she pursues her own interests.

June Rae Wood, *A Share of Freedom*, 1994
 Freedom struggles to keep her family together while her alcoholic mother undergoes treatment.

207

GAEL CRESP
DAVID COX, Illustrator

The Tale of Gilbert Alexander Pig

(New York: Barefoot Books, 2000)

Subject(s): Animals/Pigs; Folklore; Music and Musicians
Age range(s): Grades 1-3
Major character(s): Gilbert Alexander Pig, Pig, Musician; Wolf, Wolf
Time period(s): Indeterminate Past
Locale(s): Fictional Country

Summary: Gilbert Alexander is one little pig determined to make his musical way in the world. After bidding farewell to his mother, Gilbert Alexander, toting his trumpet, walks until thirst and fatigue force him to stop along the banks of a river. There he sets up camp, roasts fish for dinner and nightly plays his trumpet to the stars. His idyllic life abruptly ends when Wolf, attracted by the smell of the roasting fish, makes a threatening visit. Gilbert Alexander is not turning over his trumpet to anyone so he flees to a mountaintop and sets up camp in a twig hut until the Wolf appears once again. Gilbert's third refuge is a home of bricks built in a city. When Wolf locates him this time Gilbert tries a new strategy. Rather than fleeing, he negotiates an agreement with Wolf and the two become companions who camp on the river in the summer, live on the mountain in the fall and seek shelter in their brick city home in the winter. This take-off of a traditional tale was originally published in Australia in 1999. (32 pages)

Where it's reviewed:
Booklist, March 15, 2000, page 1386
Children's Bookwatch, May 2000, page 5
ForeWord, April 2000, page 52
Publishers Weekly, April 17, 2000, page 79
School Library Journal, August 2000, page 146

Other books you might like:
Steven Kellogg, *The Three Little Pigs*, 1997
 The pigs in this humorous retelling face a tough-looking hungry wolf trying to order piglet from their waffle wagon.
James Marshall, *The Three Little Pigs*, 1989
 In a traditional retelling of the folktale, three pigs survive a wolf's attacks because one brother uses his wits to outsmart the wolf.
Jon Scieszka, *The True Story of the Three Little Pigs*, 1989
 A humorous retelling of a classic tale with a different look at just what happened with those three little pigs.
Eugene Trivizas, *The Three Little Wolves and the Big Bad Pig*, 1993

A familiar tale takes a new turn when the big, bad pig tries to outmaneuver the three little wolves and ends up surprising himself.

208

CAROLYN CRIMI
LYNN MUNSINGER, Illustrator

Don't Need Friends

(New York: A Doubleday Book for Young Readers, 1999)

Subject(s): Behavior; Friendship; Animals
Age range(s): Grades K-2
Major character(s): Possum, Opossum, Friend (Rat's); Rat, Rat; Dog, Dog
Time period(s): 1990s
Locale(s): United States

Summary: After Rat's best friend Possum moves to another junkyard, Rat decides he doesn't need friends and becomes a crabby loner. He rebuffs the offers from other junkyard residents to share food or attend parties so often that the overtures stop and Rat lives a solitary, friendless life. When a dog with a similar temperament moves into a vacant barrel at the junkyard, Dog and Rat become best enemies. Rat is curious about Dog's nightly howling at the moon but he makes no inquiries until the cold winter night that Dog doesn't howl. Peeking in on Dog the next day, Rat notices that he is not feeling well. Rat's next action speaks kindness although his words say otherwise, as do Dog's in return, but a friendship forms in spite of each animal's intentions to the contrary. (32 pages)

Where it's reviewed:
Booklist, November 15, 1999, page 634
Horn Book, November 1999, page 728
Publishers Weekly, November 8, 1999, page 67
School Library Journal, January 2000, page 93

Other books by the same author:
Outside, Inside, 1995

Other books you might like:
Patience Brewster, *Two Bushy Badgers*, 1995
 Arthur and Ollie learn to value their friendship, put aside their anger and resolve their differences.
Jennifer Brutschy, *Celeste and Crabapple Sam*, 1994
 Young Celeste ignores reclusive Sam's grumpiness, pets his dog, gathers mussels with him and, finally, wins his friendship.
Jean Jackson, *Thorndike and Nelson: A Monster Story*, 1997
 Intent on their argument, two monsters are slow to notice that Nelson's dog is choking; fortunately, the friendship and the dog survive.
Hiawyn Oram, *Badger's Bad Mood*, 1998
 Secretly Mole plans a surprise that he hopes will cheer up his good friend Badger.

209

CRAIG CRIST-EVANS
BONNIE CHRISTENSEN, Illustrator

Moon over Tennessee: A Boy's Civil War Journal

(Boston: Houghton Mifflin Company, 1999)

Subject(s): Civil War; Fathers and Sons; Diaries
Age range(s): Grades 4-7
Major character(s): Unnamed Character, 13-Year-Old, Son; Pa, Father, Farmer
Time period(s): 1860s (1863)
Locale(s): Tennessee; Fredericksburg, Virginia; Gettysburg, Pennsylvania

Summary: Although he doesn't claim to understand this war, Pa feels duty bound to leave his family and farm and join the Confederate Army. His son travels with him, recording his thoughts, as Pa undergoes some training in Virginia. Eventually they make their way to Gettysburg where, after 3 days of fighting, Pa is killed. Sadly, the son retraces their recent journey, making his lonely way back to his mountain home to keep a promise to his father. An Afterword gives the factual basis for the story. (63 pages)

Where it's reviewed:
The Book Report, November 1999, page 59
Booklist, May 15, 1999, page 1695
Horn Book Guide, Fall 1999, page 290
Publishers Weekly, May 24, 1999, 80
School Library Journal, August 1999, page 155

Other books you might like:
Sara Harrell Banks, *Abraham's Battle: A Novel of Gettysburg*, 1999
  The Battle of Gettysburg is seen through the eyes of a former slave who volunteers as an ambulance driver for the Union Army.
Paul Fleischman, *Bull Run*, 1993
  Sixteen characters offer their accounts of the Civil War from its beginning to the first battle of Bull Run.
George Ella Lyon, *Cecil's Story*, 1991
  A boy considers the consequences for the family if his father leaves to fight in the Civil War.
Gary Paulsen, *Soldier's Heart*, 1998
  Not wanting to be left out, 15-year-old Charley lies about his age and joins the Union Army, but after being wounded dies of "soldier's heart."
Patricia Polacco, *Pink and Say*, 1994
  The senseless tragedy of war is eloquently portrayed through the brief friendship of two young Union soldiers.

210

DOREEN CRONIN
BETSY LEWIN, Illustrator

Click, Clack, Moo: Cows That Type

(New York: Simon & Schuster Books for Young Readers, 2000)

Subject(s): Animals/Cows; Farm Life; Humor
Age range(s): Grades K-3

Major character(s): Farmer Brown, Farmer, Aged Person
Time period(s): Indeterminate Past
Locale(s): United States

Summary: Clever cows come upon an old typewriter in the barn and, after some "click, clack, moo" practice, deliver a polite letter to Farmer Brown requesting electric blankets because the barn is so cold. Farmer Brown is a bit of a traditionalist and he doesn't take orders from cows, even ones that go on strike and refuse to deliver milk. The next day the hens send the same request and stop egg production until Farmer Brown agrees to the demands. The neutral duck mediates the dispute by carrying letters and responses between labor and management. Finally, an agreement is reached. Farmer Brown leaves electric blankets outside the barn door and the typewriter, in exchange, is given to the duck to deliver to Farmer Brown. As the cows and hens snuggle under the warm blankets the no longer neutral ducks are learning to type in the humorous ending to the author's first book. (32 pages)

Where it's reviewed:
Booklist, April 1, 2000, page 1468
Horn Book, March 2000, page 183
Publishers Weekly, February 21, 2000, page 86
Riverbank Review, Summer 2000, page 29
School Library Journal, March 2000, page 192

Awards the book has won:
School Library Journal Best Books, 2000
Publishers Weekly Best Books, 2000

Other books you might like:
Chris Babcock, *No Moon, No Milk!*, 1993
  Martha refuses to give her owner any milk until she fulfills her dream to be a "cowsmonaut" and walk on the moon.
Amy Ehrlich, *Parents in the Pigpen, Pigs in the Tub*, 1993
  When Ma allows Bossy the cow to move into the house, she doesn't realize she's starting a trend.
Paul Brett Johnson, *The Cow Who Wouldn't Come Down*, 1993
  Miss Rosemary resorts to an ingenious scheme to convince her flying cow Gertrude to land and resume more typical cow behavior.
Tres Seymour, *Hunting the White Cow*, 1993
  An independent, crafty white cow is able to evade all attempts to capture her and bring her home.
David Small, *George Washington's Cows*, 1994
  According to this tale Washington's outlandish animals are the reason he gave politics a try.
Martin Waddell, *Farmer Duck*, 1992
  Farm animals decide to take over from the lazy farmer who does nothing but sleep while Farmer Duck does the work.

211

SUSAN STEVENS CRUMMEL
JANET STEVENS, Illustrator

Tumbleweed Stew

(San Diego: Harcourt, Inc., 2000)

Series: Green Light Readers. Level 2
Subject(s): Animals/Rabbits; Trickster Tales; Food
Age range(s): Grades 1-2

Major character(s): Jack Rabbit, Rabbit, Trickster; Armadillo, Armadillo, Rancher
Time period(s): Indeterminate Past
Locale(s): Texas

Summary: Jack Rabbit wakes up hungry on a beautiful day with a plan for dining on tumbleweed stew. He hops on over to a nearby ranch where Armadillo tries to send him on his way. Quickly, Jack offers to cook a pot of tumbleweed stew for her and before she can say no again he has the fire started, the water boiling and the tumbleweed in the pot. Armadillo throws in some carrots and various other animals happen by with contributions. By the time the stew is finished potatoes, onions, carrots, corn and celery have been added to the tumbleweed and the stew makes mighty fine eating for all the animals. The next morning Jack Rabbit wakes up hungry for cactus pie. (20 pages)

Where it's reviewed:
Booklist, October 1, 2000, page 351
Horn Book Guide, Spring 2001, page 56
School Library Journal, January 2001, page 92

Other books by the same author:
Cook-a-Doodle-Doo, 1999 (Janet Stevens, co-author)
Shoe Town, 1999 (Janet Stevens, co-author)
My Big Dog, 1999 (Janet Stevens, co-author)

Other books you might like:
Marcia Brown, *Stone Soup*, 1986
    In one of many retellings of the tale, three hungry soldiers claiming to make soup from water and a stone outwit villagers hoarding food.
Paul Brett Johnson, *A Perfect Pork Stew*, 1998
    Baba Yaga's poor eyesight allows Ivan to get away with her pig while making pork stew from a load of dirt and all Baba Yaga's vegetables.
Tony Ross, *Stone Soup*, 1987
    A hen cleverly avoids becoming a wolf's dinner by offering him a taste of her stone soup.

212

TONY CRUNK
MARGOT APPLE, Illustrator

Big Mama

(New York: Farrar, Straus, Giroux, 2000)

Subject(s): Grandmothers; Playing; Family Life
Age range(s): Grades K-2
Major character(s): Billy Boyd, Orphan, Child; Big Mama, Grandmother (Billy's); Papa, Grandfather
Time period(s): Indeterminate Past
Locale(s): Kentucky

Summary: All the neighborhood kids want to play at Billy Boyd's house because his grandparents share their unconditional love with all children. Big Mama encourages their imaginative play and joins them for a game of kickball. She gives them jars for catching fireflies and Papa gives a nickel to the child who catches the most. Big Mama will give each child fifty cents for ice cream and walk with them to the store, but on the way she sees that they perform a little community service. Together they pull weeds from a neighbor's garden

and help another close up her vegetable stand for the day. Then Big Mama makes sure the ice cream orders are just right before walking all the children home again. The author bases his first picture book on memories from his childhood. (32 pages)

Where it's reviewed:
Booklist, February 15, 2000, page 1104
Children's Book Review Service, April 2000, page 96
Kirkus Reviews, January 15, 2000, page 119
Publishers Weekly, February 21, 2000, page 86
School Library Journal, May 2000, page 133

Other books you might like:
Betty G. Birney, *Pie's in the Oven*, 1996
    When Grandma bakes pies with the apples picked by Grandpa and their grandson the aroma of the baking pies attracts family and friends to the house.
Kathleen Hershey, *Cotton Mill Town*, 1993
    A little girl visits her grandmother and learns to enjoy the simply pleasures of lazy summer days in a small southern town.
William Low, *Chinatown*, 1997
    Daily, a young boy and his grandmother walk through the crowded streets of Chinatown past stores and delivery trucks.
Shulamith Levey Oppenheim, *Fireflies for Nathan*, 1994
    While visiting with Nana and Poppy, Nathan learns to catch fireflies just as his father did as a child.
Margaret Wild, *Our Granny*, 1994
    In an award-winning look at the diversity of grandmothers and their activities, two children remember their own granny who lives with them.

213

PAT CUMMINGS, Author/Illustrator

Angel Baby

(New York: Lothrop, Lee & Shepard Books, 2000)

Subject(s): Babies; Brothers and Sisters; Stories in Rhyme
Age range(s): Grades K-2
Major character(s): Amanda Lynne, Sister (older), Daughter; Unnamed Character, Baby, Brother
Time period(s): 2000s (2000)
Locale(s): United States

Summary: Amanda Lynne tries to be the expected, helpful daughter but her little brother's behavior does not fit his mother's image of his angelic nature. Amanda Lynne sees her little brother spill juice, chase the cat and slosh water out of the tub. Without complaining, Amanda Lynne does all she's asked and prevents further calamity by catching falling lamps and reading stories until her brother falls asleep. Then she gets a little rest until a new day begins when her brother climbs into her bed. (24 pages)

Where it's reviewed:
Booklist, June 1, 2000, page 1906
Horn Book Guide, Fall 2000, page 247
Kirkus Reviews, May 15, 2000, page 712
Publishers Weekly, June 12, 2000, page 71
School Library Journal, June 2000, page 111

Other books by the same author:
Purrrrr, 1999
My Aunt Came Back, 1998
Carousel, 1994
Clean Your Room, Harvey Moon!, 1991
C.L.O.U.D.S., 1986
Jimmy Lee Did It, 1985

Other books you might like:
Jennifer Armstrong, *That Terrible Baby*, 1994
    The havoc caused by a crawling baby sibling annoys Eleanor and Mark but they rush to the rescue when the baby crawls out the cat door.
Judith Caseley, *Mama, Coming and Going*, 1994
    Jenna helps her busy and distracted mother after the birth of her baby brother.
Carol Snyder, *One Up, One Down*, 1995
    Katie is kept busy helping her parents care for her twin brothers.
Nancy Van Laan, *Little Baby Bobby*, 1997
    Perhaps if Baby Bobby had a helpful big sister to watch his stroller he would not have rolled down the hill leaving a trail behind him.

214

DIANE CUNEO
JACK E. DAVIS, Illustrator

Mary Louise Loses Her Manners
(New York: Random House, 1999)

Subject(s): Behavior; Human Behavior; Humor
Age range(s): Grades K-3
Major character(s): Mary Louise, Child
Time period(s): 1990s (1999)
Locale(s): United States

Summary: In the author's debut, Mary Louise loses her manners one morning at breakfast. Instead of "Thank you" she says, "Spank you," and that's only the beginning. Deciding that she has neglected her manners so they have run away, Mary Louise searches the town for them. As Mary Louise follows the route her neighbors say her manners have followed her rude behavior continues from the street to a doctor's office to the library where she finds her manners curled up sleeping. Mary Louise brings her manners home, saying please and thank you to anyone she meets. (32 pages)

Where it's reviewed:
Booklist, November 1, 1999, page 537
Publishers Weekly, May 31, 1999, page 92
School Library Journal, September 1999, page 180

Other books you might like:
Caralyn Buehner, *It's a Spoon Not a Shovel*, 1995
    In question and answer format, this book portrays good manners with humor.
Babette Cole, *The Bad Good Manners Book*, 1996
    This wacky book shows what manners are good and which are bad.
Babette Cole, *Bad Habits!*, 1999
    Lucretzia Crum's parents work to curb her bad habits.

Russell Hoban, *Dinner at Alberta's*, 1975
    Arthur Crocodile learns polite table manners when his sister brings a friend to dinner.

215

MARY LOUISE CUNEO
PAM PAPARONE, Illustrator

Mail for Husher Town
(New York: Greenwillow Books/HarperCollins Publishers, 2000)

Subject(s): Toys; Animals; Imagination
Age range(s): Grades K-1
Major character(s): Julia, Child
Time period(s): Indeterminate
Locale(s): Husher Town, Fictional Country

Summary: Julia has a bedtime ritual that brings together her stuffed animals and the family cat on Husher Town, a mountain made from Julia's bed covers. The toy bear becomes the deliverer of the mail that Julia creates from homework papers used as letters and toys in her room that she wraps as packages. Receiving mail adds to the fun of Husher Town because the animals have some unusual ideas about what to do with their mail. Soon, everyone is happy—and asleep. (24 pages)

Where it's reviewed:
Booklist, July 2000, page 2038
Children's Book Review Service, June 2000, page 121
Horn Book Guide, Fall 2000, page 265
School Library Journal, June 2000, page 111

Other books by the same author:
What Can a Giant Do?, 1994
How to Grow a Picket Fence, 1993
Inside a Sand Castle and Other Secrets, 1979

Other books you might like:
Holly Berry, *Busy Lizzie*, 1994
    An active bedtime ritual helps Lizzie prepare for slumber.
Mordicai Gerstein, *Bedtime, Everybody!*, 1996
    Daisy has difficulty convincing her stuffed animals to settle down for the night.
Penelope Lively, *Good Night, Sleep Tight*, 1995
    Although Mary Ann is tired after a day of play her stuffed animals and doll are not so they make plans for a bedtime adventure.
Kate McMullan, *Good Night, Stella*, 1994
    Stella is not sleepy at bedtime so she plays with her toys, comforts her bears and, unexpectedly, falls asleep.

216

ANNA CURREY, Author/Illustrator

Truffle's Christmas
(New York: Orchard Books, 2000)

Subject(s): Animals/Mice; Christmas; Santa Claus
Age range(s): Grades K-1
Major character(s): Truffle, Mouse, Brother; Santa, Mythical Creature, Aged Person
Time period(s): Indeterminate
Locale(s): Fictional Country

Summary: Truffle really wants a hula-hoop for Christmas, but his conscience says he should ask Santa for a new blanket so his younger siblings will be warmer. The letter he sends to the "Norf Pol" asks for the hula-hoop, but on Christmas Eve Truffle begins to feel guilty about his selfish request and sits up to wait for Santa and request the needed blanket. Truffles falls asleep on the cold snowy hillside near his home, but Santa's reindeer awaken him and Santa understands not only what Truffle wants, but what he needs. On Christmas morning Truffle and his brothers and sisters find their hearts' desires under the tree. (32 pages)

Where it's reviewed:
Booklist, September 15, 2000, page 247
Horn Book Guide, Spring 2001, page 33
Publishers Weekly, September 25, 2000, page 68
School Library Journal, October 2000, page 58

Other books by the same author:
Tickling Tigers, 1996

Other books you might like:
Toby Forward, *Ben's Christmas Carol*, 1996
  Mice are the characters in this abbreviated retelling of Dicken's Christmas classic.
Katharine Holabird, *Angelina's Christmas*, 1985
  When mouse Angelina discovers that Mr. Bell is alone for Christmas she makes plans to brighten his holiday.
Clyde Watson, *How Brown Mouse Kept Christmas*, 1980
  While human residents are sleeping, mice hold their own Christmas celebration.

217

CHRISTOPHER PAUL CURTIS

Bud, Not Buddy

(New York: Delacorte Press, 1999)

Subject(s): Depression (Economic); African Americans; Runaways
Age range(s): Grades 4-7
Major character(s): Bud Caldwell, 10-Year-Old, Orphan; Herman E. Calloway, Musician
Time period(s): 1930s (1936)
Locale(s): Flint, Michigan; Grand Rapids, Michigan

Summary: Before her death when Bud was six, Bud's mother imparted memorable words of wisdom, including the admonition that he should never allow anyone to call him Buddy. For four years Bud has been in and out of the "Home" and various foster homes, surviving with his self-made set of rules for "Having a Funner Life and Making a Better Liar Out of Yourself." As Bud totes a battered suitcase containing the few belongings left him by his mother wherever he goes, the seed of an idea grows in him that his father is the man, Herman E. Calloway, pictured on the band posters in his suitcase. After running away from a particularly disagreeable foster home, Bud plans to walk to Grand Rapids and find Herman E. Calloway. With a little help along the way, Bud reaches Grand Rapids and discovers that Mr. Calloway is an old, grumpy man. Though Bud wishes they were not related, and Mr. Calloway denies they are, Bud does have the sense that he's finally at home. . .and he's right. (236 pages)

Where it's reviewed:
Booklist, September 1, 1999, page 131
Five Owls, November 1999, page 44
Horn Book, November 1999, page 737
Riverbank Review, Fall 1999, page 35
School Library Journal, September 1999, page 221

Awards the book has won:
Newbery Medal, 2000
Publishers Weekly Best Books, 1999

Other books by the same author:
The Watsons Go to Birmingham—1963, 1995 (Newbery Honor Book)

Other books you might like:
Michael Dorris, *The Window*, 1997
  When 11-year-old Rayona meets her father's family for the first time, she discovers long-held family secrets that help her understand herself.
Virginia Hamilton, *Plain City*, 1993
  An award-winning title explores Buhlaire's search for her long-absent father and answers to questions about her identity.
Richard Peck, *A Long Way from Chicago*, 1998
  A Newbery Honor Book tells of seven summers a brother and sister spend with their "no-nonsense" grandmother during the depression years.
June Rae Wood, *A Share of Freedom*, 1994
  Freedom's efforts to avoid foster care and keep her family together lead to surprising answers about her father's identity.

218

DOUG CUSHMAN, Author/Illustrator

Inspector Hopper

(New York: HarperCollins Publishers, 2000)

Series: An I Can Read Book
Subject(s): Mystery and Detective Stories; Animals/Insects; Humor
Age range(s): Grades 1-3
Major character(s): Inspector Hopper, Detective—Private, Insect; McBugg, Insect, Sidekick; Skeet, Mosquito, Client
Time period(s): Indeterminate
Locale(s): Fictional Country

Summary: With confidence, Inspector Hopper, Private Bug, tackles the problems of other insects in his community. Thanks to McBugg's complaints of hunger, Inspector Hopper locates the missing spouse of a ladybug that failed to respond to the call, "Ladybug, Ladybug fly away home." By following a trail of leaf parts Inspector Hopper and McBugg locate Skeet's missing boat that looks remarkably like a leaf because it is a leaf. The caterpillar that devoured the leaf/boat agrees to help the Skeet find a new, less tasty leaf for his next boat. In the third and final story Inspector Hopper and McBugg receive help in tracking down a thief from the moon that intermittently blocks its light with a cloud. Inspector Hopper sees potential in the detective business for the moon as soon as it learns to follow suspects a little more unobtrusively. (64 pages)

Where it's reviewed:
Booklist, April 15, 2000, page 1555
Horn Book, July 2000, page 454
Kirkus Reviews, April 15, 2000, page 558
School Library Journal, July 2000, page 70

Awards the book has won:
Horn Book Fanfare, 2001

Other books by the same author:
The Mystery of the Monkey's Maze, 1999
Aunt Eater's Mystery Halloween, 1998
The Mystery of King Karfu, 1996
The ABC Mystery, 1993
Aunt Eater's Mystery Vacation, 1992

Other books you might like:
Crosby Bonsall, *The Case of the Cat's Meow*, 1965
    The four members of the Private Eyes Club solve the
    mystery of a missing cat.
Eth Clifford, *Flatfoot Fox and the Case of the Missing
    Whoooo*, 1993
    Detective Flatfoot Fox and his trusted assistant, Secretary
    Bird, locate Owl's missing whoooo.
Robert Quackenbush, *Detective Mole and the Circus Mystery*,
    1980
    On the day of her wedding, Melba the cow vanishes from
    the circus. Detective Mole finds her in time for the cere-
    mony.
Marjorie Weinman Sharmat, *The Nate the Great Series*, 1972-
    In a series for beginning readers, Nate follows one clue
    after another in the style of Sherlock Holmes.
Robyn Supraner, *Sam Sunday and the Mystery at Ocean
    Beach*, 1996
    Investigating a case at the Ocean Beach Hotel, Detective
    Sam Sunday discovers there's more to the case than he was
    originally told.

219

DOUG CUSHMAN, Author/Illustrator

The Mystery of the Monkey's Maze

(New York: HarperCollins Publishers, 1999)

Subject(s): Mystery and Detective Stories; Humor; Animals
Age range(s): Grades K-3
Major character(s): Seymour Sleuth, Detective—Private; Ab-
    bott Muggs, Sidekick, Mouse; Irene A. Tann, Explorer,
    Scientist
Time period(s): 1990s
Locale(s): Singapore, Malaysia; Indonesia (Borneo)

Summary: While preparing for the Great Curry Cooking Contest in Singapore, Detective Sleuth and Muggs are visited by
Dr. Tann's son who seeks their assistance in solving the
mystery of anonymous threats to his mother that demand she
cancel her search for the Black Flower of Sumatra. Upon
arriving at Dr. Tann's camp deep in the jungle, Abbot Muggs
begins his job of photographing evidence while Detective
Sleuth interviews the others participating in the search. With
his customary logic and a bit of luck Seymour Sleuth identifies the culprit and helps Dr. Tann find the legendary black
flower. (32 pages)

Where it's reviewed:
Booklist, June 1999, page 1838
Horn Book Guide, Fall 1999, page 249
School Library Journal, May 1999, page 88

Other books by the same author:
The Mystery of King Karfu, 1996
Aunt Eater's Mystery Christmas, 1995
The ABC Mystery, 1993

Other books you might like:
Eth Clifford, *Flatfoot Fox and the Case of the Bashful Beaver*,
    1995
    Detective Flatfoot Fox gives his assistant, Secretary Bird,
    an opportunity to solve the mystery of Bashful Beaver's
    stolen button bag.
Elizabeth Levy, *The Something Queer Series*, 1971-
    Gwen, Jill and basset hound Fletcher have many adven-
    tures while they solve mysterious occurrences.
Ursel Scheffler, *The Return of Rinaldo, the Sly Fox*, 1993
    Tricky Rinaldo eludes Detective Bruno, but ends up being
    outfoxed by a clever cat.
Marjorie Weinman Sharmat, *The Nate the Great Series*, 1972-
    Nate follows one clue after another in the style of Sherlock
    Holmes in this mystery series for beginning readers.

220

JANE CUTLER
TRACEY CAMPBELL PEARSON, Illustrator

'Gator Aid

(New York: Farrar Straus Giroux, 1999)

Subject(s): Animals/Alligators; Animals, Treatment of;
    Neighbors and Neighborhoods
Age range(s): Grades 3-4
Major character(s): Edward Fraser, 2nd Grader, Brother
    (younger); Jason Fraser, 5th Grader, Brother
Time period(s): 1990s (1999)
Locale(s): United States (Shaw Park Lake)

Summary: While trying out his teacher's new binoculars,
Edward spots a baby alligator in the neighborhood lake. Jason
attributes the sighting to Edward's active imagination. Two of
Edward's friends believe him and spread the word so convincingly that the media picks up the story and soon rumors
about the reptile's size have the lakeshore crowded with
reporters, zookeepers, animal rescue groups and entrepre-
neurs. Only Edward sits quietly enough to see the small
alligator, but still no one believes him. By the time Edward's
week of spring vacation is almost over the alligator has been
rescued so at least everyone knows it wasn't his imagination
in the lake. (134 pages)

Where it's reviewed:
Booklist, August 1999, page 2056
Bulletin of the Center for Children's Books, September 1999,
    page 9
Horn Book, September 1999, page 609
Kirkus Reviews, July 15, 1999, page 1131
School Library Journal, September 1999, page 180

Other books by the same author:
Spaceman, 1997

Rats!, 1996
No Dogs Allowed, 1992

Other books you might like:
David A. Adler, *The Many Troubles of Andy Russell*, 1998
  One of Andy's many troubles is capturing his pet gerbils
  that have escaped from their cage—again.
Beverly Cleary, *Ramona Quimby, Age 8*, 1981
  This book, one of several about energetic Ramona and her
  family, is a Newbery Honor award winner.
Jean Craighead George, *The Missing 'Gator of Gumbo
  Limbo: An Ecological Mystery*, 1992
  An algae-eating alligator keeps an Everglades spring free
  of pollutants.
Suzy Kline, *Song Lee and the Hamster Hunt*, 1994
  When Song Lee brings her hamster to school the animal
  becomes lost in the classroom.

221

JANE CUTLER
GREG COUCH, Illustrator

The Cello of Mr. O.

(New York: Dutton Children's Books, 1999)

Subject(s): Music and Musicians; War; Courage
Age range(s): Grades 1-4
Major character(s): Mr. O, Musician, Aged Person; Unnamed
  Character, Child, Neighbor; Elena, Child, Friend
Time period(s): Indeterminate Past
Locale(s): Earth

Summary: Despite the hardships imposed by a war that has
taken her father off the fight, closed the schools and left her
family with little food, a young girl tries to maintain some
semblance of normalcy by playing with Elena and other
friends. The only thing to look forward to each week is the
Wednesday arrival of the relief truck. Even that small diversion is taken from the residents when a rocket destroys the
truck and the relief organization refuses to enter the community with supplies. The following Wednesday, precisely at
four o'clock, Mr. O sets up a chair at the truck's stopping spot
and begins to play the cello. He returns daily, offering hope
and inspiration with his courage as well as his music. (32
pages)

Where it's reviewed:
Booklist, December 15, 1999, page 782
Five Owls, November 1999, page 41
Publishers Weekly, August 16, 1999, page 84
Riverbank Review, Winter 1999/2000, page 26
School Library Journal, November 1999, page 112

Awards the book has won:
Booklist Editors' Choice, 1999
Notable Social Studies Trade Books for Young People, 2000

Other books by the same author:
Mr. Carey's Garden, 1996
Darcy and Gran Don't Like Babies, 1993

Other books you might like:
Jean-Louis Beeson, *October 45: Childhood Memories of the
  War*, 1995
  The author's memories of World War II, beginning when

he was seven years old, give a child's observations of the
shortages, air raids and invading troops.
Luis Garay, *The Long Road*, 1997
  Political unrest threatens Jose and his mother forcing them
  to seek refuge in another country.
Elizabeth Fitzgerald Howard, *Papa Tells Chita a Story*, 1995
  Although she knows the story by heart, Chita loves to hear
  Papa tell of his bravery during the Spanish-American War.
Patricia Polacco, *Pink and Say*, 1994
  The senseless tragedy of war is eloquently portrayed
  through the brief friendship of two young Union soldiers.
James Stevenson, *Don't You Know There's a War On?*, 1992
  In a nonfiction picture book the author recalls his child-
  hood during World War II when his brother joins the Navy
  and gas and food are rationed.

222

MARGERY CUYLER
ARTHUR HOWARD, Illustrator

100th Day Worries

(New York: Simon & Schuster Books for Young Readers, 2000)

Subject(s): Schools; Mathematics; Collectors and Collecting
Age range(s): Grades K-2
Major character(s): Jessica, 1st Grader, Daughter; Mom,
  Mother; Mr. Martin, Teacher
Time period(s): 2000s (2000)
Locale(s): United States

Summary: First grade provides worrywart Jessica with many
things to worry about—missing the bus, forgetting lunch
money or making errors on her homework. When Mr. Martin
assigns his students the task of bringing in a collection of 100
items for display on the 100th day of school, Jessica has five
days to fret about what to collect. Some students complete
their collections early and when Jessica sees them she wonders why she didn't think of five bags of twenty peanuts each
or 100 paper clips in groups of ten or 100 peppermints in bags
of twenty-five. On the morning of the 100th day, Jessica is
still trying to decide on the items for her collection. Her
family hurriedly offers Jessica a variety of odds and ends as
she dashes for the bus. When Jessica has time to count them
she realizes she is short ten items, but the ten kisses Mom adds
to the note in her lunch box completes the collection of 100
things given to Jessica by her family. (32 pages)

Where it's reviewed:
Booklist, November 1, 1999, page 537
Bulletin of the Center for Children's Books, February 2000,
  page 206
Kirkus Reviews, December 1, 1999, page 1882
Publishers Weekly, December 13, 1999, page 81
School Library Journal, January 2000, page 93

Other books by the same author:
The Biggest, Best Snowman, 1998
That's Good! That's Bad!, 1991
Fat Santa, 1987

Other books you might like:

Trudy Harris, *100 Days of School*, 1999
   A rhyming picture book shows a variety of number combinations of various objects that all add up to one hundred.

Angela Shelf Medearis, *The 100th Day of School*, 1996
   The Level 2 entry in the Hello Reader series presents the activities of one class celebrating the culmination of 100 days of school.

Joseph Slate, *Miss Bindergarten Celebrates the 100th Day of Kindergarten*, 1998
   Miss Bindergarten's students have no time to worry because they have only one night to gather collections of 100 items for school.

Rosemary Wells, *Emily's First 100 Days of School*, 2000
   Beginning on the first day of school, as Emily and her classmates learn a new number each day, they record it in their number book.

223

MARGERY CUYLER
ARTHUR HOWARD, Illustrator

The Battlefield Ghost

(New York: Scholastic Press, 1999)

Subject(s): Ghosts; Revolutionary War; Haunted Houses
Age range(s): Grades 3-4
Major character(s): Lisa Perkins, 10-Year-Old, Sister; John Perkins, Brother, 4th Grader; Hans Koehler, Spirit
Time period(s): 1990s (1999)
Locale(s): Princeton, New Jersey

Summary: John doesn't share his parents' excitement about moving into the old stone house that is rumored to be haunted. When he and Lisa feel invisible hands touching them and hear piano music from the empty house, they are both convinced that the legendary ghost is real. John's teacher knows a lot of history and local lore that seems to confirm the presence of the ghost of a Hessian soldier. When Lisa's riding instructor boards his horse in the old barn temporarily, the reason for the ghost's desire to get the children's attention begins to emerge. On the anniversary of the Battle of Prince Town, Hans Koehler appears to ask for John and Lisa's help so he can be reunited with his horse and finally rest in peace. (103 pages)

Where it's reviewed:
Booklist, November 15, 1999, page 626
Horn Book Guide, Spring 2000, page 64
Kirkus Reviews, August 1, 1999, page 1225
Publishers Weekly, September 27, 1999, page 106
School Library Journal, December 1999, page 90

Other books by the same author:
Invisible in the Third Grade, 1995
Weird Wolf, 1989

Other books you might like:
Elaine Marie Alphin, *Ghost Cadet*, 1991
   Benjy helps a ghost find a pocket watch lost during the Battle of New Market in the Civil War.
Eileen Dunlop, *The Ghost by the Sea*, 1996
   Robin and her cousin John try to solve the mystery of the

ghost haunting her grandparents' home so the family can have some peace.
Betty Ren Wright, *The Ghost of Popcorn Hill*, 1993
   When Peter and Martin's family moves into an old cabin they have to solve the problem of visits from a lonely ghost so they can all get some sleep.

224

MARGERY CUYLER
YU CHA PAK, Illustrator

From Here to There

(New York: Henry Holt and Company, Inc. 1999)

Subject(s): Self-Acceptance; Mexican Americans; Geography
Age range(s): Grades K-2
Major character(s): Maria Mendoza, Child, Sister
Time period(s): 1990s (1999)
Locale(s): Splendora, Texas

Summary: Maria writes a letter introducing herself, her family, and her town as she relates the place of each in the larger universe. Her perspective moves from her family to the family's place in their town, county and state to the state's context in the country, continent, hemisphere, planet, solar system, galaxy and universe, home of Maria Mendoza. (32 pages)

Where it's reviewed:
Booklist, June 1999, page 1838
Horn Book Guide, Fall 1999, page 249
Publishers Weekly, March 8, 1999, page 56
School Library Journal, May 1999, page 88

Other books by the same author:
The Biggest, Best Snowman, 1998
That's Good! That's Bad!, 1991
Baby Dot: A Dinosaur Story, 1990

Other books you might like:
Robin Hirst, *My Place in Space*, 1992
   As Henry Wilson gives his address in this award-winning title he also reveals an awareness of his place in the universe. Co-author Sally Hirst.
David Milgrim, *Here in Space*, 1997
   A young boy and his dog explore the wonderful, strange and mysterious place that is the planet earth, floating in space.
Joan Sweeney, *Me and My Place in Space*, 1998
   A young astronaut travels from earth past the planets of our solar system.

225

JAN M. CZECH
FRANCES CLANCY, Illustrator

An American Face

(Washington, D.C.: Child and Family Press, 2000)

Subject(s): Adoption; Korean Americans; Self-Esteem
Age range(s): Grades K-2
Major character(s): Jessie, Adoptee, Kindergartner; Carolyn Cheung, Judge
Time period(s): 2000s (2000)

Locale(s): United States

Summary: A mirror is all Jessie needs to be reminded that his face is very different from his parents and the faces of the children in his class, but he also endures unkind comments from shoppers and students. Jessie knows he hasn't much longer to wait until he gets his American face. As Jessie counts down the days until he goes to court to officially become an American citizen he imagines what his new face will look like. He wonders about his new eye and hair color and happily anticipates a day without prejudicial comments because he's sure he'll look just the same as all other Americans. Not until he's sitting in the courtroom and voices his imaginings aloud do his parents realize his misconception. Though their words do little to console him, the arrival of the Honorable Carolyn Cheung to the bench to preside over the ceremony gives him a face with which he can identify and he begins to accept that his face can be a fine American face just the way it is. (32 pages)

Where it's reviewed:
Booklist, May 15, 2000, page 1747
School Library Journal, August 2000, page 153

Other books you might like:
Edna Coe Bercaw, *Halmoni's Day*, 2000
    Grandparents' Day at Jennifer's school begins with a fear of embarrassment, but Jennifer sees acceptance and understanding during Halmoni's visit.
Maggie Rugg Herold, *A Very Important Day*, 1995
    Despite a severe snowstorm, immigrants from 32 countries make their way to downtown New York to be sworn in as U.S. citizens.
Rose Lewis, *I Love You Like Crazy Cakes*, 2000
    An American mother expresses her love for her adopted Chinese daughter.
Carol Antoinette Peacock, *Mommy Far, Mommy Near: An Adoption Story*, 2000
    An adopted Chinese girl wonders why a country as large as China could not contain the many babies that were adopted by Americans.
Nina Pelligrini, *Families Are Different*, 1991
    As an adopted Korean girl gets to know her classmates she discovers many variations in American families and feels less ''different.''

D

226

DEBBIE DADEY

Cherokee Sister

(New York: Delacorte Press, 2000)

Subject(s): Indians of North America; Indian Removal; Friendship
Age range(s): Grades 4-6
Major character(s): Allie MacAllister, 12-Year-Old, Friend; Papa, Father; Leaf Sweetwater, Indian (Cherokee), Friend
Time period(s): 1830s (1838)
Locale(s): Georgia

Summary: Strong-willed and independent Allie doesn't understand Papa's insistence that she stay away from Leaf. The reason becomes obvious when Allie sneaks out of church to visit Leaf's home on the morning the soldiers come to round up the Cherokees to remove them from their land. Allie is mistaken for a Cherokee and forced to join Leaf and the others from the village. The harsh treatment makes Allie angry with the white people who mistreat the Cherokee and sad at the needless death and misery of people who have been kind to her. As Leaf's grandmother lies dying in the mud of the enclosure that imprisons them, Allie promises to take care of Leaf. When Papa finds her, he willingly takes Leaf and her grandmother's body to return them to their homeland. (119 pages)

Where it's reviewed:
Booklist, April 1, 2000
Children's Bookwatch, August 2000, page 4
Horn Book Guide, Spring 2001, page 71
Kirkus Reviews, March 1, 2000, page 300
School Library Journal, April 2000, page 134

Other books by the same author:
King of the Kooties, 1999
Will Rogers: Larger than Life, 1999
Triplet Trouble and the Runaway Reindeer, 1995 (Marcia Thornton Jones, co-author)

Other books you might like:
Sara Harrell Banks, *Remember My Name*, 1993
   To avoid the Trail of Tears Annie Rising Fawn Stuart and Righteous Cry secretly leave Georgia to seek refuge in the Cherokee mountain homelands.
Elisabeth Jane Stewart, *On the Long Trail Home*, 1994
   Separated from her family during the forced march to Oklahoma territory, 9-year-old Meli finds her brother and the two escape the Trail of Tears.
Gloria Whelan, *Night of the Full Moon*, 1993
   Libby is visiting her Indian friend Fawn when soldiers arrive, forcing the Indians and Libby farther west.

227

DEBBIE DADEY
KEVIN O'MALLEY, Illustrator

King of the Kooties!

(New York: Walker & Company, 1999)

Subject(s): Teasing; Bullies; Schools
Age range(s): Grades 2-4
Major character(s): Nate Nelson, 4th Grader, Friend (Donald's); Donald, 4th Grader, Friend (Nate's); Louisa Albertson, 4th Grader, Bully
Time period(s): 1990s (1999)
Locale(s): United States

Summary: On the first day of school, Nate is pleased to learn that his new friend Donald is in his class. He is not happy to see Louisa's name on the class list and even more upset when she decides to name Donald the "King of the Kooties." Nate and Donald think that they can deter Louisa's bullying behavior by "killing her with kindness." The homemade cookies and Nate's compliments don't win her over so they try a new plan. Nate and Donald greet Louisa at recess with a "Princess of the Kooties" t-shirt and an offer to join the kootie club. (84 pages)

Where it's reviewed:
Booklist, September 15, 1999, page 256

Bulletin of the Center for Children's Books, November 1999, page 89
Kirkus Reviews, July 15, page 1131
Publishers Weekly, October 4, 1999, page 75
School Library Journal, November 1999, page 112

Other books by the same author:
Goblins Don't Play Video Games, 1999
Ghouls Don't Scoop Ice Cream, 1998
Mummies Don't Coach Softball, 1996

Other books you might like:
Patricia Reilly Giff, *The Beast in Ms. Rooney's Room*, 1984
    One of many titles about the antics of students at Polk Street School, this one features Richard "Beast" Best.
Suzy Kline, *Horrible Harry in Room 2B*, 1988
    Although Harry, a student in Room 2B, seems to frequently be in trouble he is capable of changing his behavior.
Virginia Scribner, *Gopher Takes Heart*, 1993
    Gopher finds a way to work with Fletcher to end the bully's harassment of him.

228

ANDRE DAHAN, Author/Illustrator

Squiggle's Tale
(San Francisco: Chronicle Books, 2000)

Subject(s): Animals/Pigs; Vacations; Behavior
Age range(s): Grades K-2
Major character(s): Squiggle, Pig, Vacationer; Snook, Pig, Cousin; Puddin, Pig, Cousin
Time period(s): Indeterminate Past
Locale(s): Paris, France (Luxembourg Park)

Summary: To reassure his parents that he is fulfilling his promise to be on his best behavior while visiting Puddin and Snook, Squiggle writes a long letter describing their visit to a park. Squiggle's letter describes the activities in terms acceptable to parents while the illustrations show what actually happened as the cousins' true behavior has gendarmes in pursuit most of the day. At closing time Puddin, Snook and Squiggle leave the park promptly, but on their way out they pick some flowers "left" by the gardener as the present. Squiggle's letter home was originally published in French in 1998. (40 pages)

Where it's reviewed:
Booklist, April 1, 2000, page 1468
Children's Book Review Service, April 2000, page 96
Horn Book Guide, Fall 2000, page 265
Publishers Weekly, February 14, 2000, page 197
School Library Journal, April 2000, page 97

Other books you might like:
David Martin, *Five Little Piggies*, 1998
    The author interprets the familiar nursery rhyme to show what really happens with each of those pigs.
David McPhail, *Pigs Aplenty, Pigs Galore*, 1993
    A quiet evening becomes a noisy free-for-all when a man's home is invaded by pigs intent on enjoying pizza.
Janet Morgan Stoeke, *Minerva Louise at School*, 1996
    Independent Minerva Louise interprets what she finds in a

"big red barn" in her own unique way while the pictures show a different story.

229

JUDE DALY, Author/Illustrator

Fair, Brown & Trembling: An Irish Cinderella Story
(New York: Farrar Straus Giroux, 2000)

Subject(s): Fairy Tales; Folklore; Sisters
Age range(s): Grades 1-4
Major character(s): Fair, Sister (older); Brown, Sister (older); Trembling, Sister
Time period(s): Indeterminate Past
Locale(s): Ireland

Summary: Three daughters of a widower live in a castle but only Fair and Brown go to church each week in new dresses. Trembling stays home to work and cook for her sisters who fear that their beautiful sister will marry before they do if others see her. The old henwife uses her magic to provide clothes for Trembling and a mare to ride to church. The terms of the enchantment require that Trembling not enter the church and return home as fast the mare can run when the service is over. Trembling does this for two weeks, standing outside the church's doorway as everyone strains to see the beautiful maiden in her finery. On the third Sunday, suitors from many lands assemble near the church to see and woo the mysterious girl. It is difficult for Trembling to get away and one prince grabs a shoe as she leaps onto her horse. Using the shoe, the prince identifies Trembling and they live happily ever after with their fourteen children. The sisters were not as lucky. (32 pages)

Where it's reviewed:
Booklist, September 1, 2000, page 120
Horn Book Guide, Spring 2001, page 99
Publishers Weekly, August 21, 2000, page 71
Riverbank Review, Winter 2000-2001, page 31
School Library Journal, September 2000, page 214

Other books you might like:
Jewell Reinhart Coburn, *Domitila: A Cinderella Tale from the Mexican Tradition*, 2000
    In a variant based on Mexican folklore the mystery girl is the former cook at the governor's home who's sought by the governor's son.
Oki S. Han, *Kongi and Potgi: A Cinderella Story from Korea*, 1996
    Kongi's ability to treat others kindly, despite mistreatment by her stepmother and stepsister, is eventually rewarded.
Charles Perrault, *Cinderella*, 1954
    In a retelling of a classic tale of love and inner beauty, Cinderella survives years of torment from her stepfamily to marry a prince.

230

NIKI DALY, Author/Illustrator

The Boy on the Beach

(New York: Margaret McElderry Books/Simon & Schuster, 1999)

Subject(s): Beaches; Summer; Playing
Age range(s): Grades K-1
Major character(s): Joe, Child; Mom, Mother; Dad, Father
Time period(s): 1990s (1999)
Locale(s): South Africa

Summary: Joe's joy at seeing the wide expanse of sand and ocean is tempered by the sight of the large waves. Coaxed by Mom and Dad and tightly gripping their hands he goes into the water. The first wave is more than enough for him and Joe returns to frolic on the beach, walking past a lifeguard stand and into the dunes where he finds the relic of a boat. Joe lets his imagination guide his play until fear creeps in again and he calls for Mom and Dad. A lifeguard locates him and reunites him with his parents who treat everyone to ice cream. (32 pages)

Where it's reviewed:
Booklist, May 15, 1999, page 1702
Horn Book Guide, Fall 1999, page 249
Publishers Weekly, May 10, 1999, page 66
School Library Journal, June 1999, page 92

Awards the book has won:
Bulletin of the Center for Children's Books Blue Ribbon, 1999

Other books by the same author:
Bravo, Zan Angelo!, 1998
My Dad, 1995
Not So Fast, Songololo, 1986

Other books you might like:
Nancy Cote, *Flip Flops*, 1998
    When Penny and Mom go to the beach, Penny's solo flip-flop comes in handy for everything but walking.
Douglas Florian, *A Beach Day*, 1990
    A family enjoys a relaxing day at the beach looking for sea shells.
Troon Harrison, *The Long Weekend*, 1994
    For his birthday, Michael chooses to spend three days playing at the beach with his mom.

231

NIKI DALY, Author/Illustrator

Jamela's Dress

(New York: Farrar Straus Giroux, 1999)

Subject(s): Clothes; Blacks; Africa
Age range(s): Grades K-2
Major character(s): Jamela, Child, Daughter
Time period(s): 1990s (1999)
Locale(s): South Africa

Summary: Jamela is put in charge of looking after the beautiful fabric her mother purchased to make a dress for her sister's wedding. Jamela just cannot resist the attractive cloth and soon drapes herself in the fabric and parades around town. Although the fabric becomes torn and dirty, one of the villagers takes a picture of Jamela that wins first prize in a photography contest. The prize money is enough to buy her mother some more fabric, and a dress for Jamela. (32 pages)

Where it's reviewed:
Booklist, March 15, 1999, page 1333
Horn Book Guide, Fall 1999, page 231
Horn Book, July 1999, page 453
Publishers Weekly, May 10, 1999, page 67
School Library Journal, August 1999, page 132

Awards the book has won:
ALA Notable Children's Books, 2000

Other books by the same author:
The Boy on the Beach, 1999
Bravo, Zan Angelo!, 1998
My Dad, 1995

Other books you might like:
Rachel Isadora, *Over the Green Hills*, 1992
    Zolani, who lives in rural South Africa, travels to meet his grandmother.
Hugh Lewin, *Jafta and the Wedding*, 1981
    Jafta tells of the weeklong festival in his South African village to celebrate his sister's marriage.
Elinor Batezat Sisulu, *The Day Gogo Went to Vote*, 1996
    After black South Africans are given the right to vote, Thembi's great-grandmother goes to the polls.
Andrea Spalding, *Sarah May and the New Red Dress*, 1999
    All Sarah May wants is a red dress, so she is disappointed when her mother buys dark blue material.

232

CLAIRE DANIEL
LISA CAMPBELL ERNST, Illustrator

The Chick That Wouldn't Hatch

(San Diego: Harcourt Brace & Company, 1999)

Series: Green Light Readers. Level 2
Subject(s): Animals/Chickens; Animals; Farm Life
Age range(s): Grades 1-2
Major character(s): Hen, Chicken, Mother
Time period(s): Indeterminate
Locale(s): United States

Summary: Five of Hen's eggs hatch, but the sixth one rolls out of the nest and across the barnyard with Hen in hot pursuit. As she goes, Hen calls, ''Stop that egg!'' to each animal she passes and soon a pig, a duck, and a horse are also running after the egg. The chase ends when the egg hits a wall, cracks and the chick emerges. (20 pages)

Where it's reviewed:
Booklist, December 1, 1999, page 716
Horn Book Guide, Spring 2000, page 61
School Library Journal, November 1999, page 112

Other books by the same author:
Short and Long Vowels, 1997

Other books you might like:

Antonia Barber, *Gemma and the Baby Chick*, 1993

Gemma warms a rejected egg until it hatches and then returns the baby chick to its sleeping mother.

Julia Hoban, *Quick Chick*, 1989

Eventually, Jenny Hen's youngest chick lives up to his Quick Chick nickname.

Mary Wormell, *Hilda Hen's Search*, 1994

Hilda Hen confidently searches until she finds a perfectly original spot for her nest.

233

TERI DANIELS
TRAVIS FOSTER, Illustrator

The Feet in the Gym

(New York: Winslow Press, 1999)

Subject(s): Schools; Cleanliness; Stories in Rhyme
Age range(s): Grades K-2
Major character(s): Handy Bob, Maintenance Worker
Time period(s): 1990s (1999)
Locale(s): United States (Lakeside School)

Summary: Handy Bob is diligent about keeping Lakeside School clean. No space requires more attention than the gym floor. Handy Bob cannot stand footprints on the floor so he stands ready with mop and bucket to clean up as students, a Brownie troop, an art class, and dancers use the space in rapid succession. Finally, two marching bands practice in the facility and as they leave, all the dirt and goo from the floor sticks to their shoes and goes out the door to the football field. As the author's first book concludes, Handy Bob cleans up one last spot and leaves the gym with the floor shining, or so he thinks. (32 pages)

Where it's reviewed:

Booklist, July 1999, page 1950
Bulletin of the Center for Children's Books, June 1999, page 348
Kirkus Reviews, May 1, 1999, page 720
Publishers Weekly, May 24, 1999, page 78
School Library Journal, June 1999, page 92

Other books you might like:

Lisa Campbell Ernst, *Duke the Dairy Delight Dog*, 1996

Darla's Dairy Delight is too neat a place for a stray, dirty dog until one slips into the new Scrubber-Buffer-Waxer machine and emerges transformed.

Patricia C. McKissack, *Messy Bessy's School Desk*, 1998

When Bessy cleans her very messy desk she inspires the class to clean the room in this beginning reader.

Lisa Westberg Peters, *When the Fly Flew In. . .*, 1994

More quietly than marching bands, a fly enters a child's cluttered room, disturbing the pets that restore some order as they try to catch the fly.

234

TERI DANIELS
TRACEY CAMPBELL PEARSON, Illustrator

G-Rex

(New York: Orchard Books, 2000)

Subject(s): Brothers; Dinosaurs; Sibling Rivalry
Age range(s): Grades K-2
Major character(s): Gregory, Brother (younger); Mark, Brother (older); Fanny, Aunt
Time period(s): 2000s (2000)
Locale(s): United States

Summary: Gregory wishes he were big enough to have some of the privileges that Mark has such as riding in the front seat of the car, controlling the remote and the sofa and sleeping in the best bed. Gregory's frustration and anger take over one night at dinner and he transforms into a meat-eating dinosaur. When he's devoured all the meat in the house the g-rex threatens to eat Mark. For a week Mark and his parents try to cope with Gregory's new behavior and then they move next door to Aunt Fanny's house leaving Gregory alone. Gregory's lonely and unhappy in his empty house and he envies the fun he sees Mark having with Aunt Fanny. When his g-rex tail accidentally knocks over and breaks Mark's best trophy Gregory begins to cry because his dinosaur hands are too big to fix it. The tears change Gregory from a dinosaur back to a boy and Gregory views his ''big'' brother in a different way. (32 pages)

Where it's reviewed:

Horn Book Guide, Spring 2001, page 34
Kirkus Reviews, September 15, 2000, page 1354
Publishers Weekly, September 11, 2000, page 90
School Library Journal, October 2000, page 119

Other books by the same author:

Just Enough, 2000
The Feet in the Gym, 1999

Other books you might like:

Laurie Krasny Brown, *Rex and Lilly Family Time*, 1995

Dinosaur siblings help plan Mom's birthday surprise, contend with an overeager robot helper and select a family pet.

Betsy Byars, *Ant Plays Bear*, 1997

The sequel to *My Brother Ant* continues the story of Ant and his sympathetic older brother.

Patricia Polacco, *My Rotten Red-Headed Older Brother*, 1994

Patricia's one wish is to be able to best her older brother at something—anything!

Judith Viorst, *I'll Fix Anthony*, 1969

Look out Anthony! Your little brother is making plans to get even with you.

235

JULIE DANNEBERG
JUDY LOVE, Illustrator

First Day Jitters

(Watertown, MA: Whispering Coyote/Charlesbridge Publishing, 2000)

Subject(s): Schools; Teachers; Fear

Age range(s): Grades K-3
Major character(s): Sarah Jane Hartwell, Spouse, Teacher; Mr. Hartwell, Spouse; Mrs. Burton, Principal
Time period(s): 2000s (2000)
Locale(s): United States

Summary: Sarah Jane Hartwell has multiple excuses for staying in bed on the first day of school, but Mr. Hartwell is insistent that she get up for breakfast before she is late. He assures Sarah that the children will be nice and she will make new friends. Mr. Hartwell makes Sarah's breakfast, packs her lunch and drives her to school where Mrs. Burton finds her cowering in the car, leads her to her classroom and introduces her to her students—for this is Mrs. Sarah Jane Hartwell's first day teaching in a new school. (32 pages)

Where it's reviewed:
Booklist, March 15, 2000, page 1386
Horn Book Guide, Fall 2000, page 265
Kirkus Reviews, March 15, 2000, page 379
School Library Journal, May 2000, page 133

Other books by the same author:
Margaret's Magnificent Colorado Adventure, 1999

Other books you might like:
Nancy Bo Flood, *I'll Go to School If—*, 1997
    A frightened little boy offers conditions under which he will go to school for the first time, but his practical mom suggests alternatives.
Nancy Poydar, *First Day, Hooray!*, 1999
    Students, teachers, bus drivers and other school employees prepare for the beginning of a new school year.
Joseph Slate, *Miss Bindergarten Gets Ready for Kindergarten*, 1996
    Miss Bindergarten's preparations for the opening of school including matching her students' names with a letter of the alphabet.
Jean Van Leeuwen, *Amanda Pig, School Girl*, 1997
    Amanda is so eager to begin school that she's able to help a less enthusiastic girl she meets on the bus.

236

PAULA DANZIGER
TONY ROSS, Illustrator

I, Amber Brown

(New York: G.P. Putnam's Sons, 1999)

Subject(s): Self-Esteem; Divorce; Parent and Child
Age range(s): Grades 3-5
Major character(s): Amber Brown, 4th Grader, Child of Divorced Parents; Philip Brown, Father, Divorced Person
Time period(s): 1990s (1999)
Locale(s): New Jersey

Summary: Now that Philip Brown is living in New Jersey again Amber is experiencing the reality of joint custody and she doesn't like it at all. Because her friends are getting their ears pierced and Amber is tired of feeling "owned" by her parents, she decides that she has custody of her ears and manipulates a visit with her dad into a trip to the mall for an ear piercing. Amber knows she's causing trouble, but she's so overwhelmed by conflicting emotions that she goes ahead,

comforted by the fact that she has at least achieved the goal of getting her ears pierced. When her mother's discovery leads to the inevitable argument, the experience allows both parents and Amber to establish some realistic ground rules for the shared custody. Amber still has conflicting feelings, but she's claiming her own identity. (140 pages)

Where it's reviewed:
Booklist, October 15, 1999, page 443
Horn Book Guide, Spring 2000, page 77
Publishers Weekly, October 18, 1999, page 85
School Library Journal, November 1999, page 112

Other books by the same author:
Amber Brown Is Feeling Blue, 1998
Amber Brown Sees Red, 1997
Forever Amber Brown, 1996
Amber Brown Goes Fourth, 1995
Amber Brown Is Not a Crayon, 1994

Other books you might like:
Beverly Cleary, *Strider*, 1991
    As Leigh Botts learns to accept his parents' divorce he finds the confidence to join the track team.
P.J. Petersen, *I Want Answers and a Parachute*, 1993
    Matt and his younger brother reluctantly fly from Arizona to California to visit their dad and meet his new wife and her daughter.
Susan Richards Shreve, *The Formerly Great Alexander Family*, 1995
    Liam is so crushed when his parents separate that he isolates himself from his friends while he adjusts to the changes in his life.
Jacqueline Wilson, *The Suitcase Kid*, 1997
    When her parents divorced Andy refused to choose one over the other so she divides her time between each of her new stepfamilies.

237

SHARON DARROW
KATHRYN BROWN, Illustrator

Old Thunder and Miss Raney

(New York: DK Ink/Dorling Kindersley Publishing, Inc., 2000)

Subject(s): Contests; Fairs; Weather
Age range(s): Grades K-3
Major character(s): Old Thunder, Horse; Raney Cloud, Cook, Farmer
Time period(s): Indeterminate Past
Locale(s): Washita County, Oklahoma

Summary: In the author's first children's book, Raney is certain that, this year, she'll win a blue ribbon at the County Fair for her Sooner Biscuits. In her haste, she accidentally burns the first batch of biscuits and has to hurry to town to buy more flour in order to compete. Speed is not one of Old Thunder's attributes and, by the time Raney has her flour in the wagon, she, Old Thunder and the flour are caught in a storm. When they are swept up by a tornado, Raney loses the flour briefly, but locates it again when the wind stops and they all tumble back to the ground. The wind-sifted flour produces light-as-air biscuits, but they do not impress the judges enough to win the blue ribbon. Disappointed, Raney feeds some of the biscuits to Old Thunder and prepares to return home. Old Thunder has his own ideas and joins a plow horse race, speeds past the competition and earns a blue ribbon. The judges are so amazed by Old Thunder's transformation that they award a special blue ribbon to Miss Raney Cloud for best horse feed—her Sooner Biscuits. (32 pages)

Where it's reviewed:
Booklist, November 1, 2000, page 547
Horn Book, September 2000, page 549
Publishers Weekly, August 21, 2000, page 72
School Library Journal, October 2000, page 119

Other books you might like:
Marguerite W. Davol, *The Loudest, Fastest, Best Drummer in Kansas*, 2000
   The townspeople don't appreciate Maggie's drumming until she uses it to drive a tornado away from town.
Anne Isaacs, *Swamp Angel*, 1994
   In an award-winning original tall tale Angelica Longrider saves settlers in Tennessee before moving to Montana to continue her heroic exploits.
Sonia Levitin, *Boom Town*, 1998
   While Pa mines for gold in the nearby hills Amanda establishes a business baking pies that becomes more profitable than panning for gold.
Nancy Van Laan, *With a Whoop and a Holler: A Bushel of Lore from Way Down South*, 1998
   An award-winning folklore collection includes stories designed for read-aloud pleasure.

238

SALLY J.K. DAVIES, Author/Illustrator

When William Went Away

(Minneapolis: Carolrhoda Books, Inc., 1999)

Subject(s): Friendship; Moving, Household; Shyness
Age range(s): Grades K-3
Major character(s): Matthew, Student—Elementary School, Brother (younger); William, Friend (Matthew's); Mary T., Neighbor (new), Child
Time period(s): 1990s
Locale(s): Canada

Summary: Since William moved Matthew has been without a friend in his neighborhood. Although he tries to make other friends at school there is no one nearby to play with Matthew and he certainly doesn't want to play with his pesky older sister. When Matthew arrives home from school on a snowy day and sees a moving truck containing a bike and hockey stick in front of William's old house and a two-headed snow monster in the yard, he's sure the perfect playmate has arrived. Matthew shrugs off his shyness and bravely rings the doorbell. He's surprised when Mary T. who claims to be the creator of the snow monster answers and is interested in playing. Could the perfect playmate be a girl? (32 pages)

Where it's reviewed:
Booklist, August 1999, page 2063
Horn Book Guide, Spring 2000, page 32
Kirkus Reviews, June 1, 1999, page 881

School Library Journal, July 1999, page 68

Other books by the same author:
Why Did We Have to Move Here?, 1997

Other books you might like:
Aliki, *Best Friends Together Again*, 1995
   Robert faces Peter's visit with mixed emotions—eager to see his friend, yet wondering if Peter's move has changed their relationship.
Kevin Henkes, *Chester's Way*, 1988
   Chester and Wilson do everything together in exactly the same way until Lilly moves in and shows them that friends can do things differently.
Nette Hilton, *Andrew Jessup*, 1993
   After Andrew Jessup moves away nothing is the same for the saddened best friend left behind until Madeleine Havenblower moves into the neighborhood.

239

KATIE DAVIS, Author/Illustrator

I Hate to Go to Bed!

(San Diego: Harcourt Brace & Company, 1999)

Subject(s): Bedtime; Dreams and Nightmares; Parent and Child
Age range(s): Grades K-2
Major character(s): Unnamed Character, Child, Daughter; Mommy, Mother; Daddy, Father
Time period(s): 1990s (1999)
Locale(s): United States

Summary: A little girl is so sure that her parents have a party in the evening after she goes to bed that she devises one plan after another to find a way to join them. Each time Mommy and Daddy catch their daughter sneaking out of bed they shout, "Go to bed!" Since the little girl hates to go to bed, she keeps trying to crash the parent's party until she discovers that there is no party. Dejected, the little girl climbs back into bed determined to have her own fantastic party—in her dreams. (36 pages)

Where it's reviewed:
Booklist, October 15, 1999, page 451
Horn Book Guide, Spring 2000, page 32
Kirkus Reviews, August 15, 1999, page 1309
Publishers Weekly, August 23, 1999, page 57
School Library Journal, March 2000, page 194

Awards the book has won:
IRA/CBC Children's Choices, 2000

Other books by the same author:
Who Hoots?, 2000
Who Hops?, 1998

Other books you might like:
Bill Harley, *Nothing Happened*, 1995
   Jack stays awake all night to see if his brother's exciting stories about a secret party room are true.
Russell Hoban, *Bedtime for Frances*, 1960
   Frances is a master at avoiding sleep, but her patient parents have a response for every problem.

Jill Murphy, *A Quiet Night In*, 1994

A bedtime story has the desired soporific effect—on the parents and not the kids—leaving the children to put themselves to bed.

Peggy Rathmann, *10 Minutes till Bedtime*, 1998

A hamster's guided tour of a child's nightly routine begins when the child's father announces "10 minutes till bedtime."

Elizabeth Winthrop, *Asleep in a Heap*, 1993

While waiting for Julia to finish her bath, Daddy falls asleep on the bathroom floor. Mama, sister Molly, a dog, four cats and finally Julia join him.

240

PATRICIA A. DAVIS
LAYNE JOHNSON, Illustrator

Brian's Bird

(Morton Grove, IL: Albert Whitman & Company, 2000)

Subject(s): Pets; Blindness; Brothers
Age range(s): Grades 1-3
Major character(s): Brian Johnson, 8-Year-Old, Blind Person; Kevin Johnson, Brother (older); Scratchy, Bird (parakeet)
Time period(s): 1990s
Locale(s): Baltimore, Maryland

Summary: For his eighth birthday Brian receives a parakeet from his family. Patiently Brian learns to care for Scratchy, to seek help from family members when Scratchy gets out of his cage and to teach Scratchy to talk. In time, all his efforts are rewarded. Scratchy first learns to greet him with "Hello Brian," before acquiring several other phrases. When Kevin startles Brian and Scratchy by coming into the room too loudly, Scratchy takes off quickly. Kevin has forgotten to close the front door and Scratchy flies out of the house. Brian enlists Kevin's assistance to tell him where Scratchy is so he can stand outside and hold his finger near the tree until Scratchy flies to him. For all the trouble Kevin causes, as least he's willing to help out too so Brian decides maybe he's not so bad after all. (32 pages)

Where it's reviewed:
Booklist, February 15, 2000, page 1117
Horn Book Guide, Fall 2000, page 266
School Library Journal, May 2000, page 133

Other books you might like:
Estelle Condra, *See the Ocean*, 1994

Nellie is the first to sense the nearness of the ocean as the fog along the coast prevents the sighted members of her family from seeing it.

Virginia Kroll, *Naomi Knows It's Springtime*, 1993

Naomi doesn't need to see a rainbow; she knows it's spring by the warm breeze and the taste of seasonal foods.

Patricia McMahon, *Listen for the Bus: David's Story*, 1995

Photographs enhance a factual account of a young blind boy's first day at school.

241

MARGUERITE W. DAVOL
CAT BOWMAN SMITH, Illustrator

The Loudest, Fastest, Best Drummer in Kansas

(New York: Orchard Books, 2000)

Subject(s): Music and Musicians; Conduct of Life; Tall Tales
Age range(s): Grades K-3
Major character(s): Maggie, Daughter, Musician (drummer); Mama, Mother; Mayor Plogg, Political Figure
Time period(s): Indeterminate Past
Locale(s): Serena, Kansas

Summary: Even Maggie's doctor can tell you that she's born drumming. Maggie rattles out so many tunes on her crib that the slats break and Maggie uses them for drumsticks so she can continue playing on the floor. By the time Maggie is six she has a real drum so she can become the loudest, fastest, best drummer in Kansas. When the constant drumming gets to be too much for Mama, Maggie just strolls outside and into town with her big bass drum. Mayor Plogg is not blessed with Mama's patience and quickly issues an ordinance forbidding drumming. The town's citizens are willing to find other solutions to the noise pollution because the forceful sound waves from Maggie's drumming successfully protect the town from a wasp invasion and even destroy a tornado. Maggie may yet reach her goal. (32 pages)

Where it's reviewed:
Booklist, March 15, 2000, page 1386
Horn Book Guide, Fall 2000, page 266
Publishers Weekly, March 6, 2000, page 110
School Library Journal, May 2000, page 139

Other books by the same author:
Batwings and the Curtain of Night, 1997
The Paper Dragon, 1997
How Snake Got His Hiss, 1996

Other books you might like:
Harriett Diller, *Big Band Sound*, 1996

When Arlis discovers that Daddy has thrown away her makeshift drum set she searches the trash for appropriate discards and resumes playing.

Alexis O'Neill, *Loud Emily*, 1998

Emily finally finds a positive way to use her very loud voice as a blaring lighthouse warning on foggy days.

Brian Pinkney, *Max Found Two Sticks*, 1994

Max uses two sticks he finds near his urban home to imitate and answer the sounds of the city.

242

ALEXANDRA DAY, Author/Illustrator

Boswell Wide Awake

(New York: Farrar Straus Giroux, 1999)

Subject(s): Animals/Bears; Fantasy; Bedtime
Age range(s): Preschool
Major character(s): Boswell Bear, Bear; Toby, Dog
Time period(s): 1990s (1999)

Locale(s): United States

Summary: Moonlight streaming in his bedroom window keeps Boswell awake so he gets out of bed and tiptoes past his parents' room to explore the house. As he goes he tenderly cares for his pets—closing the curtains to block the moonlight so the fish can sleep, letting the cat out and quieting Toby. Then he goes outside to retrieve the cat, put his tricycle away, and stare at the full moon. Boswell carries the cat inside, says good night to Toby, and kisses his sleeping parents before returning to his bed. (32 pages)

Where it's reviewed:
Children's Book Review Service, December 1999, page37
Children's Bookwatch, October 1999, page 6
Kirkus Reviews, October 15, 1999, page 1642
Publishers Weekly, November 8, 1999, page 66
School Library Journal, December 1999, page 90

Other books by the same author:
Follow Carl!, 1998
Frank and Ernest on the Road, 1994
Carl Goes to Daycare, 1993
Carl's Afternoon in the Park, 1991

Other books you might like:
Kate Banks, *And If the Moon Could Talk*, 1998
    Parents lovingly prepare their child for bed as a brilliant moon shines down on all that it would tell us—if the moon could talk.
Quint Buchholz, *Sleep Well, Little Bear*, 1994
    While a child sleeps, his toy bear climbs atop the bookcase to look out at the moon-covered land and review the play activities of the day.
Helen Cooper, *The Boy Who Wouldn't Go to Bed*, 1997
    A young boy finds that his plan to stay awake all night and play does not work because all his playthings are sleepy.
Jan Ormerod, *Moonlight*, 1982
    Through illustrations alone a young girl's moonlit bedtime ritual is portrayed.

243

ALEXANDRA DAY, Author/Illustrator
COOPER EDENS, Co-Author

Darby: The Special Order Pup

(New York: Dial Books for Young Readers, 2000)

Subject(s): Animals/Dogs; Behavior; Problem Solving
Age range(s): Grades K-2
Major character(s): Darby, Dog (English bull terrier); Mom, Mother; Dad, Father
Time period(s): 2000s (2000)
Locale(s): Pacific Northwest

Summary: The Bell family meet their new pet Darby at the airfreight counter where his unique puppy nature is obvious— he's chewed a hole in the carrier. Mom and Dad have a doghouse, toys and a bed set up for Darby on the patio and by morning Darby has demolished most of it. In the house, Darby eats couch cushions, table legs and picture albums so the children begin obedience training and Darby's behavior improves—until he's left alone in the house. Dad puts Darby back outside with a fenced enclosure around his doghouse knowing he will have shelter from the incessant rain. The family unfortunately ignores Darby's howling as he tries to warn them of an impending mudslide. The Bell home slides down the cliff as the supporting bank, weakened by the rain, gives way. Before rescue crews can arrive, Darby's talent for chewing enables him to tunnel in to the family and they escape from the collapsed house to safety. (32 pages)

Where it's reviewed:
Booklist, November 1, 2000, page 547
Horn Book Guide, Spring 2001, page 34
Publishers Weekly, August 21, 2000, page 72
School Library Journal, October 2000, page 120

Other books you might like:
Marc Brown, *Arthur's New Puppy*, 1993
    Arthur has problems because his new puppy is behaving just like a puppy and making a mess of the house.
Steven Kroll, *Oh, Tucker!*, 1998
    Tucker, a large and enthusiastic dog, leaves a trail of disaster throughout the house.
Rosemary Wells, *Lucy Comes to Stay*, 1994
    Mary Elizabeth tolerates typical puppy mischief as she learns to care for her new pet.

244

C. COCO DE YOUNG

A Letter to Mrs. Roosevelt

(New York: Delacorte Press, 1999)

Subject(s): Depression (Economic); Schools; Family Life
Age range(s): Grades 3-6
Major character(s): Margo Bandini, 11-Year-Old, Daughter (of Italian American immigrants); Rosa Meglio, Friend, 11-Year-Old; Miss Dobson, Teacher, Journalist (part-time)
Time period(s): 1930s (1933)
Locale(s): Johnstown, Pennsylvania

Summary: Miss Dobson explains the impact of the Depression to her students as a series of dominoes falling and Margo learns too soon that the dominoes are dropping on Maple Avenue right to her front porch. First Rosa's dad loses so many hours at the steel mill that he leaves home in search of work and Rosa's family must get meals at the soup kitchen. Margo's family has plenty to eat because farmers often trade food for her father's services at his shoe repair shop. Unfortunately, the barter system does not provide the money to repay a bank loan taken out five years earlier to cover medical expenses for her brother. With the bank threatening foreclosure, Margo completes a school assignment by writing to First Lady Eleanor Roosevelt in response to a request in a newspaper article. Margo's courage is rewarded when the first lady intervenes, Margo's home is spared and Miss Dobson reveals that she is the newspaper reporter who wrote the article to which Margo responded. A concluding author's note gives the family history on which the author's first novel is based. (105 pages)

Where it's reviewed:
Booklist, February 1, 1999, page 972

Bulletin of the Center for Children's Books, March 1999, page 237
Kirkus Reviews, December 15, 1998, page 1796
Publishers Weekly, January 4, 1999, page 90
School Library Journal, March 1999, page 209

Awards the book has won:
Marguerite de Angeli Prize, 1999
Notable Social Studies Trade Books for Young People, 2000

Other books you might like:
Eth Clifford, *The Man Who Sang in the Dark*, 1987
 During the Depression residents of a Philadelphia boarding house befriend a widow with two children.
Cynthia DeFelice, *Nowhere to Call Home*, 1999
 Orphaned by her bankrupt father's suicide, Frances disguises herself as a boy and hops a train heading west to live as a hobo.
Patricia MacLachlan, *Skylark*, 1994
 A drought causes crop failure and forces many families to leave their homes.
Candice F. Ransom, *Jimmy Crack Corn*, 1994
 Jimmy joins his dad in the veteran's march on Washington, D.C. to claim the benefits Congress promised after World War I.
Zilpha Keatley Snyder, *Cat Running*, 1994
 Cat gains insight into the plight of displaced families when her running skill helps an ''Okie'' classmate get medical help for a younger sister.

245

CARMEN AGRA DEEDY
HENRI SORENSEN, Illustrator

The Yellow Star: The Legend of King Christian X of Denmark

(Atlanta: Peachtree Publishers, Ltd, 2000)

Subject(s): Loyalty; Courage; Kings, Queens, Rulers, etc.
Age range(s): Grades 2-4
Major character(s): King Christian, Royalty
Time period(s): 1940s
Locale(s): Copenhagen, Denmark

Summary: King Christian is so beloved by Danes that he daily rides unescorted through the streets of Copenhagen. As war spreads across Europe and Nazi forces occupy his country King Christian courageously resists the oppressive occupation of the Nazi regime. When the Nazi flag is raised atop the palace he has a Danish soldier remove it and responds to the Nazi threat of retaliation by stating that he will remove it himself if it appears again rather than have an innocent soldier shot. When word comes that Jews must sew a yellow star on their clothes King Christian wonders how to protect all his subjects. When Danes see King Christian on his morning ride with a yellow star sewn on his uniform, all Danes follow suit making the Jewish population no more visible with a star than they were without one. A concluding author's note describes the lack of authentication for the legend and gives other information about Danish resistance during the Nazi occupation. (32 pages)

Where it's reviewed:
Booklist, July 2000, page 2024
Five Owls, November 2000, page 45
Publishers Weekly, July 17, 2000, page 194
School Library Journal, September 2000, page 193

Other books by the same author:
The Secret of Old Zeb, 1997
The Library Dragon, 1994
Agatha's Feather Bed: Not Just Another Wild Goose Story, 1991

Other books you might like:
Jane Cutler, *The Cello of Mr. O.*, 1999
 Undeterred by mortar barrages, Mr. O. defiantly plays his cello daily in his war-ravaged city's open square.
Shirley Hughes, *The Lion and the Unicorn*, 1999
 Lenny is evacuated from London for protection during the Blitz; he needs a different kind of fortitude to survive life in the English countryside.
Shulamith Levey Oppenheim, *The Lily Cupboard: A Story of the Holocaust*, 1992
 With no way to escape the Nazis, a little girl depends on the courage of a sympathetic family who hide her behind a wall in their home.
Dorrith M. Sim, *In My Pocket*, 1997
 A young girl bravely bids farewell to her parents and her country before she joins other Jewish children being sent to safety in Great Britain.

246

CYNTHIA DEFELICE
ROBERT ANDREW PARKER, Illustrator

Cold Feet

(New York: DK Ink/Dorling Kindersley Publishing, Inc., 2000)

Subject(s): Trickster Tales; Music and Musicians; Legends
Age range(s): Grades 3-5
Major character(s): Willie McPhee, Musician (bagpiper)
Time period(s): Indeterminate Past
Locale(s): Scotland

Summary: Talent alone does not guarantee a living for bagpiper Willie McPhee during hard times. As he tromps, cold and wet, through a dark winter woods Willie trips over something that he soon realizes is a frozen corpse sporting very nice boots. When Willie tries to take the boots, the feet break off the corpse so he carries the boots with the frozen feet still inside. After spending the night in the barn of an inhospitable farmer, Willie is able to remove the thawed boots from the feet and Willie uses the feet and his old boots to play a trick by making it appear that the farmer's cow has eaten him. Willie, wearing his new boots, plays a second trick on the farmer and his wife who run away leaving Willie to enjoy the shelter of their house. His contentment is short lived when a knock at the door reveals a bootless stranger in search of his cold feet. (32 pages)

Where it's reviewed:
Booklist, September 1, 2000, page 112
Horn Book, September 2000, page 585
Publishers Weekly, September 4, 2000, page 108

School Library Journal, September 2000, page 193

Awards the book has won:
ALA Notable Children's Books, 2001
Horn Book Fanfare, 2001

Other books by the same author:
Clever Crow, 1998
Willy's Silly Grandma, 1997
Casey in the Bath, 1996 (IRA/CBC Children's Choices)
Mule Eggs, 1994

Other books you might like:
Diane Goode, *Diane Goode's Book of Scary Stories and Songs*, 1994
    The not-too-terrifying collection of scary stories also includes songs and poems.
Tony Johnston, *The Ghost of Nicholas Grebe*, 1996
    For 100 years the ghost of Nicholas Grebe haunts the house in which he once lived awaiting the return of his leg bone.
Robert D. San Souci, *Cinderella Skeleton*, 2000
    In a ghoulish retelling of the fairy tale, the prince gets Cinderella's shoe with the foot still inside so he finds her by matching bone to bone.

247

CYNTHIA DEFELICE

Nowhere to Call Home
(New York: Farrar Straus Giroux, 1999)

Subject(s): Depression (Economic); Runaways; Orphans
Age range(s): Grades 4-7
Major character(s): Frances "Frankie" Barrow, 12-Year-Old, Orphan; Stewpot, 15-Year-Old
Time period(s): 1930s (1930)
Locale(s): United States

Summary: Frances Barrow lives a privileged life until the day her father, distraught over his loss of money and his factory in the Great Depression, shoots himself. Suddenly, Frances, orphaned and penniless, is sent to live with her aunt in Chicago. Instead, Frances cashes in her train ticket, dresses as a boy, hops the rails, and becomes a hobo. There she meets Stewpot, a veteran hobo, who renames her Frankie Blue. Riding the rails, though exciting, is also hard and dangerous as the new hobo soon learns when Stewpot succumbs to pneumonia, jolting Frankie back to reality and her life as Frances. (208 pages)

Where it's reviewed:
Booklist, April 1, 1999, page 1425
Horn Book, March 1999, page 207
Kirkus Reviews, February 15, 1999, page 298
Publisher's Weekly, April 26, 1999, page 84
School Library Journal, April 1999, page 133

Awards the book has won:
Notable Social Studies Trade Books for Young People, 2000

Other books by the same author:
Clever Crow, 1998
The Ghost of Fossil Glen, 1998

The Apprenticeship of Lucas Whitaker, 1996 (School Library Journal Best Book of the Year)

Other books you might like:
Christopher Paul Curtis, *Bud, Not Buddy*, 1999
    On the run during the Depression, Bud misses the train west and decides to walk to Grand Rapids to find the father he's never known. Newbery Medal winner.
David K. Fremon, *The Great Depression in American History*, 1997
    This nonfiction book covers important aspects of the Great Depression from the stock market crash to Roosevelt and the New Deal.
Mary Downing Hahn, *The Gentleman Outlaw and Me—Eli*, 1996
    In 1887, 12-year-old Eliza, disguised as a boy, travels to Colorado in search of her father.
Karen Hesse, *Out of the Dust*, 1997
    Billy Jo, trying to escape the dust and her family's troubles during the Oklahoma Dust Bowl, briefly takes to the rails in this Newbery Medal winner.

248

DIANE DEGROAT, Author/Illustrator

Annie Pitts, Burger Kid
(New York: SeaStar Books, 2000)

Subject(s): Food; Contests; Humor
Age range(s): Grades 2-5
Major character(s): Annie Pitts, 9-Year-Old; Mercedes, Cousin (Annie's), Teenager; Matthew McGill, 3rd Grader
Time period(s): 2000s (2000)
Locale(s): New York, New York (Yonkers)

Summary: Aspiring actress Annie Pitts, lover of hamburgers, eagerly anticipates auditioning for (and winning) the Burger Barn poster contest scheduled for the day after Thanksgiving. First, she has to survive the holiday with her fastidious aunt and obnoxious cousin. A severe storm that damages Matthew's home increases the number of dinner guests when Annie's mother invites Matthew and his mother to the meal. When Mercedes arrives with a nose ring and a shaved head, Annie's plans to seat Matthew next to someone boring backfire. Mercedes and Matthew have many shared interests and Annie becomes increasingly annoyed not to be receiving any attention. All will be well after the auditions that Annie still confidently thinks she will win. (76 pages)

Where it's reviewed:
Booklist, October 1, 2000, page 339
Horn Book Guide, Spring 2001, page 60
School Library Journal, October 2000, page 120

Other books by the same author:
Annie Pitts, Swamp Monster, 1994
Annie Pitts, Artichoke, 1992

Other books you might like:
Beverly Cleary, *Ramona Quimby, Age 8*, 1982
    One of several books about energetic Ramona and the ups and downs of life in the Quimby household is a Newbery Honor Book.

Patricia Reilly Giff, *Poopsie Pomerantz, Pick Up Your Feet*, 1089

Poopsie's self esteem drops when she is chosen to play a pig in the class play.

Phyllis Reynolds Naylor, *The Girls' Revenge*, 1998

Caroline's plan seems perfect to the actress wannabe and it does give her attention, but not what she expects.

249

DIANE DEGROAT, Author/Illustrator

Happy Birthday to You, You Belong in a Zoo

(New York: Morrow Junior Books, 1999)

Subject(s): Gifts; Birthdays; Friendship
Age range(s): Grades K-2
Major character(s): Gilbert Possum, Opossum, Son; Mother, Opossum, Mother; Lewis, Beaver, Classmate (Gilbert's)
Time period(s): 1990s
Locale(s): Fictional Country

Summary: Gilbert's excitement with the mail addressed just to him quickly wanes when he opens a birthday party invitation from Lewis, the one classmate Gilbert doesn't want to see on the weekend. Gilbert's Mother assures him that Lewis must consider him a friend or he wouldn't have sent the invitation. However, Gilbert learns otherwise when Lewis rebuffs Gilbert's friendly overtures at school and relates that he was forced to send invitations to all the boys in the class. When Mother takes Gilbert shopping he selects a frying pan as the perfect gift for Lewis. By party day, Gilbert is having second thoughts about his gift and he's relieved when the heavy package Lewis opens from him actually contains a popular toy. (32 pages)

Where it's reviewed:
Booklist, August 1999, page 2063
Children's Bookwatch, October 1999, page 5
Horn Book Guide, Spring 2000, page 33
Publishers Weekly, July 5, 1999, page 70
School Library Journal, October 1999, page 112

Awards the book has won:
IRA/CBC Children's Choices, 2000

Other books by the same author:
Trick or Treat, Smell My Feet, 1998
Roses Are Pink, Your Feet Really Stink, 1996 (IRA/CBC Children's Choices)
Alligator's Toothache, 1977

Other books you might like:
Russell Hoban, *A Birthday for Frances*, 1968
A Chompo bar makes such a delicious birthday gift for a sister that it's no surprise it's nibbled away on the walk home from the store.
Holly Hobbie, *Toot and Puddle: A Present for Toot*, 1998
Puddles has second thoughts about the birthday gift he chooses for Toot, but Toot is pleased to receive an exotic parrot.
Pat Hutchins, *It's MY Birthday!*, 1999
Little monster Billy has difficulty sharing the gifts he receives at his birthday party.

250

DIANE DEGROAT, Author/Illustrator

Jingle Bells, Homework Smells

(New York: HarperCollins Publishers, 2000)

Subject(s): Schools; Responsibility; Christmas
Age range(s): Grades K-2
Major character(s): Gilbert, Opossum, Student—Elementary School; Lewis, Bear, Student—Elementary School; Mrs. Byrd, Bird, Teacher
Time period(s): 2000s
Locale(s): Fictional Country

Summary: Gilbert, usually a responsible student, is having difficulty keeping his mind on his schoolwork with the Christmas holiday approaching. When Mrs. Byrd assigns weekend homework to draw a picture of a favorite book character, Gilbert thinks about what he'll draw but holiday activities are so enticing that he never actually completes the drawing. Monday morning he goes reluctantly to school and meets Lewis, who never does homework, in the schoolyard. As the other students enter the building Lewis and Gilbert work together to create a snow character outside the classroom window. While Mrs. Byrd appreciates their ingenuity, she still expects the assignment completed and gives Gilbert and Lewis one more night to do it. (32 pages)

Where it's reviewed:
Booklist, September 1, 2000, page 131
Horn Book Guide, Spring 2001, page 34
Kirkus Reviews, October 1, 2000, page 1421
Publishers Weekly, September 25, 2000, page 69
School Library Journal, October 2000, page 58

Other books by the same author:
Happy Birthday to You, You Belong in a Zoo, 1999
Trick or Treat, Smell My Feet, 1998
Roses Are Pink, Your Feet Really Stink, 1996 (IRA/CBC Children's Choice)
Alligator's Toothache, 1977

Other books you might like:
Marc Brown, *Arthur in a Pickle*, 1999
Arthur gives an untruthful explanation for his missing homework and then dreams "in a pickle" in this Step into Reading title.
Moira Fain, *Snow Day*, 1996
Snow closes school for the day and Maggie enjoys sledding instead of doing her homework.
Peter O'Donnell, *Carnegie's Excuse*, 1993
Carnegie offers an interesting excuse for being tardy and having incomplete homework—the tiger that jumped in the open window is at fault.

251

MONALISA DEGROSS
FLOYD COOPER, Illustrator

Granddaddy's Street Songs

(New York: Hyperion Books for Children/Jump at the Sun, 1999)

Subject(s): Storytelling; Grandfathers; Work

Age range(s): Grades 1-3
Major character(s): Roddy, Child; Granddaddy, Grandfather; Daybreak, Horse
Time period(s): 1990s (1999); 1950s (1955)
Locale(s): Baltimore, Maryland

Summary: Roddy pleads to hear a story from Granddaddy about his days as an ''arabber.'' With a photo album in their laps, Roddy listens to Granddaddy relive his work as a street vendor. Granddaddy describes a day of waking early to harness Daybreak and get to Camden Market to purchase the fruits and vegetables he'll spend the day peddling from his wagon. Granddaddy enlivens the storytelling with vendor calls and Roddy joins in with some ideas of his own. When they imagine the goods have all been sold Granddaddy's story heads for home. A concluding historical note gives the background for the story. (32 pages)

Where it's reviewed:
Booklist, June 1999, page 1838
Children's Book Review Service, June 1999, page 122
Children's Bookwatch, July 1999, page 2
Horn Book Guide, Fall 1999, page 249
School Library Journal, July 1999, page 68

Awards the book has won:
Notable Social Studies Trade Books for Young People, 2000

Other books by the same author:
Donavan's Word Jar, 1994

Other books you might like:
Angela Johnson, *The Rolling Store*, 1997
 A little girl tells her friend the story of her Grandaddy and his ''rolling store'' that proclaimed, ''We got it all!''
Lynn Joseph, *Jasmine's Parlour Day*, 1994
 Jasmine loves parlour day in Trinidad and the cacophony of cries of the various vendors hawking their wares.
Alan Schroeder, *Carolina Shout!*, 1995
 The songs, calls and cries of many different workers add to the melody of life in Charleston.

252

LULU DELACRE, Author/Illustrator

Salsa Stories

(New York: Scholastic Press, 2000)

Subject(s): Storytelling; Cultures and Customs; Relatives
Age range(s): Grades 4-6
Major character(s): Carmen Teresa, Daughter, Sister (older)
Time period(s): Multiple Time Periods
Locale(s): United States; Earth

Summary: As relatives and friends gather to celebrate the New Year, one special family friend gives Carmen Teresa the gift of a blank book. Carmen Teresa ponders how to use the book during dinner, as the relatives share tales of their early years in their native countries. Aunts, uncles, grandparents and friends share stories from Cuba, Puerto Rico, Guatemala, Mexico, Argentina and Peru. Each thinks their story should be the one to be recorded in Carmen Teresa's book, but Carmen Teresa has a plan of her own. Because food was a central element in each story, Carmen Teresa will gather the recipes pertinent to the tales and each time she cooks she'll remember the person

who shared the story at an important family gathering. An appended glossary defines the Spanish words used in the book. (103 pages)

Where it's reviewed:
Booklist, May 1, 2000, page 1665
Horn Book Guide, Fall 2000, page 302
Publishers Weekly, March 20, 2000, page 94
Riverbank Review, Spring 2000, page 40
School Library Journal, March 2000, page 237

Awards the book has won:
Notable Social Studies Trade Books for Young People, 2001

Other books by the same author:
Golden Tales: Myths and Legends from Latin America, 1996
Vejigante/Masquerader, 1993
Arroz Con Leche: Popular Songs and Rhymes from Latin America, 1989
Nathan's Fishing Trip, 1988

Other books you might like:
Rudolfo Anaya, *My Land Sings: Stories from Rio Grande*, 1999
 Five original folktales and five drawn from Mexican and Native American oral traditions are set in the American Southwest.
Joanne Rocklin, *Strudel Stories*, 1999
 Apple strudel recipes passed down for generations provide the framework for two sisters reminiscing about family history.
Gary Soto, *Neighborhood Odes*, 1992
 A collection of twenty-one poems celebrates life in a Hispanic neighborhood.

253

JUDY DELTON
JILL WEBER, Illustrator

Angel Spreads Her Wings

(Boston: Houghton Mifflin Company, 1999)

Subject(s): Stepfamilies; Vacations; Imagination
Age range(s): Grades 3-6
Major character(s): Angel Poppadopolis, 5th Grader, Sister (oldest); Rudy Poppadopolis, Stepfather; Edna, 5th Grader, Friend (Angel's)
Time period(s): 1990s (1999)
Locale(s): Elm City, Wisconsin; Greece

Summary: Worrywart Angel is anticipating a carefree summer of bike rides with Edna. Not one to adapt well to change, Angel is still adjusting to a stepfather and a new baby sister when she learns that the family is going to Greece to spend the summer with Rudy's parents. Imaginative Angel now has so much to worry about-the plane ride, a foreign country, strangers renting her house—that she is astonished when they actually arrive safely in Greece. Learning that her Greek grandparents live in a house without electricity gives Angel new worries about food poisoning and whether she'll ever see Elm City again. Angel survives the many new experiences, proud that she's learning to spread her wings a little and anticipating a return visit next summer. (143 pages)

Where it's reviewed:
Booklist, May 1, 1999, page 1593
Horn Book, July 1999, page 463
Kirkus Reviews, March 1, 1999, page 374
Publishers Weekly, April 12, 1999, page 78
School Library Journal, April 1999, page 133

Awards the book has won:
Smithsonian's Notable Books for Children, 1999

Other books by the same author:
Angel's Mother's Baby, 1989
Angel's Mother's Wedding, 1987
Angel's Mother's Boyfriend, 1986
Angel in Charge, 1985
Back Yard Angel, 1983

Other books you might like:
C.S. Adler, *Her Blue Straw Hat*, 1997
   Rachel's anticipation of two relaxing months on vacation at the beach changes when she learns her stepfather's daughter will be with them.
Virginia Bernard, *Eliza Down Under*, 2000
   Eliza is unhappy to have to accompany her mother to Sydney, Australia for the Olympics because she will miss a month of school and basketball tryouts.
Paula Danziger, *You Can't Eat Your Chicken Pox, Amber Brown*, 1995
   Amber's plans for a summer vacation in France with her father are interrupted when she breaks out with chicken pox in London.
Johanna Hurwitz, *School's Out*, 1991
   Lucas sees the potential for lots of fun during summer vacation as he takes advantage of the French-speaking au pair his parents hire.

254

CORINNE DEMAS
TED LEWIN, Illustrator

The Disappearing Island

(New York: Simon & Schuster Books for Young Readers, 2000)

Subject(s): Islands; Grandmothers; Birthdays
Age range(s): Grades K-3
Major character(s): Carrie, 9-Year-Old; Grandma, Grandmother
Time period(s): 2000s (2000)
Locale(s): Billingsgate Island, Massachusetts (Wellfleet Harbor)

Summary: As a birthday gift Grandma takes Carrie to an island that only appears at low tide. While they explore and enjoy a picnic lunch Grandma relates the history of the island from its days as a prosperous community to the present as it slowly succumbs to the relentless action of the sea. Hearing the history and seeing the remnants of the structures triggers Carrie's imagination and she ponders life on the island one hundred years ago as the daughter of the lighthouse keeper. Soon the tide begins to reclaim the island so Carrie and Grandma wade to their anchored boat and return to the mainland shore. (32 pages)

Where it's reviewed:
Booklist, June 1, 2000, page 1907
Bulletin of the Center for Children's Books, May 2000, page 313
Kirkus Reviews, June 1, 2000, page 794
Publishers Weekly, June 19, 2000, page 79
School Library Journal, July 2000, page 70

Other books by the same author:
Hurricane!, 2000
Nina's Waltz, 2000
Electra and the Charlotte Russe, 1997
Matthew's Meadow, 1992

Other books you might like:
Karen English, *Neeny Coming, Neeny Going*, 1996
   Growing up on an island off the coast of South Carolina is a unique and cherished experience for Essie.
Kathryn Lasky, *My Island Grandma*, 1993
   Every summer Abbey and Grandma enjoy the time they have together at Grandma's island summer home,
Betsy Lewin, *Booby Hatch*, 1995
   The isolated Galapagos Islands provide a habitat for many unusual animals.
Barbara Mitchell, *Waterman's Child*, 1997
   Despite changes over time, Annie's family has made a living on the water for generations and Annie hopes to continue.

255

CORINNE DEMAS
LENICE U. STROHMEIER, Illustrator

Hurricane!

(New York: Marshall Cavendish, 2000)

Subject(s): Hurricanes; Weather; Family
Age range(s): Grades K-3
Major character(s): Margo, Child, Daughter; Mommy, Mother, Spouse; Daddy, Father, Spouse
Time period(s): 1990s (1991)
Locale(s): Cape Cod, Massachusetts

Summary: The weather forecast gives Margo and her family only a few more hours to prepare before Hurricane Bob hits their coastal town. Each family member, including the dog, helps with a task. Mommy fills containers of water while Daddy brings in lawn furniture and secures their boat. Margo picks the garden's vegetables and flowers and helps Mommy arrange the flowers in the house. Then, the family settles down at a jigsaw puzzle as the wind and rain increases. The old family home withstands the storm's onslaught but the town's electricity is out for five days so they cook outside and "bathe" in the pond until power is restored. A concluding "Author's Note" gives factual information about hurricanes. (32 pages)

Where it's reviewed:
Booklist, March 1, 2000, page 1250
Children's Book Review Service, May 2000, page 114
Horn Book Guide, Fall 2000, page 266
Kirkus Reviews, March 15, 2000, page 380
School Library Journal, April 2000, page 103

Other books by the same author:
If Ever I Return, 2000
Nina's Waltz, 2000
The Disappearing Island, 2000

Other books you might like:
Barbara Bottner, *Hurricane Music*, 1995
Hurricane Gladys blows away Aunt Margaret's clarinet and Hurricane Harold returns it to her.
Lorraine Jean Hopping, *Hurricanes!*, 1995
A nonfiction entry in the ''Hello Reader!'' series gives information about hurricanes, facts on past hurricanes, and safety tips.
Patricia Lakin, *Hurricane!*, 2000
A girl and her father prepare for and safely weather Hurricane Bob when it passes over their vacation community.
Sarah Weeks, *Hurricane City*, 1993
The humorous story in rhyme tells of life in a city where the hurricane season never ends.
David Wiesner, *Hurricane*, 1990
In the aftermath of a hurricane, an uprooted tree becomes a place of imaginative adventure for two brothers.

256

DEMI, Author/Illustrator

The Greatest Treasure

(New York: Scholastic Press, 1998)

Subject(s): Folk Tales; Folklore; Family Life
Age range(s): Grades K-3
Major character(s): Pang, Nobleman, Wealthy; Li, Farmer
Time period(s): Indeterminate Past
Locale(s): China

Summary: Pang spends all of his time counting his money, ignoring his five sons who beg him to play with them. Li, on the other hand, is a very poor man, who spends his time happily playing his flute, while his five daughters sing and dance. After Pang gives Li money, hoping that he will be too busy to play his flute, both Pang and Li realize the importance of peace and happiness—the greatest treasure. (32 pages)

Where it's reviewed:
The Book Report, January 1999, page 76
Booklist, August 19, 1998, page 1998
Kirkus Reviews, July 15, 1998, page 1034
Publishers Weekly, August 17, 1998, page 70
School Library Journal, September 1998, page 190

Other books by the same author:
Happy New Year, Kung-Hsi Fa-Ts'Ai, 1999
Dalai Lama: A Biography of the Tibetan Spiritual and Political Leader, 1998
Liang and the Magic Paintbrush, 1988

Other books you might like:
Margaret Chang, *The Beggar's Magic: A Chinese Tale*, 1997
A greedy, selfish farmer is taught a lesson in sharing.
Laurence Yep, *The Dragon Prince: A Chinese Beauty & the Beast Tale*, 1997
An ancient Chinese tale is reminiscent of the classic Beauty and the Beast story.

Jane Yolen, *The Emperor and the Kite*, 1998
In this Caldecott Medal Honor Book, the emperor's smallest daughter must rescue her father when he is trapped in a tower.

257

DEMI, Author/Illustrator

One Grain of Rice

(New York: Scholastic, 1997)

Subject(s): Folk Tales; Mathematics; Folklore
Age range(s): Grades 2-5
Major character(s): Rani, Young Woman
Time period(s): Indeterminate Past
Locale(s): India

Summary: The raja where Rani lives has collected rice from the people every year in the event of a famine. Now that a famine has arrived, however, the raja refuses to share the rice. Rani, a girl from the local village, does a good deed for the raja and as a reward asks for one grain of rice to be doubled every day for thirty days. The raja agrees to the simple request, not anticipating how quickly the quantity of rice will grow. Through this experience with Rani the raja learns to be wise and fair. (40 pages)

Where it's reviewed:
Booklist, March 1, 1997
Horn Book Guide, Fall 1997, page 332
The New Advocate, Winter 1997, page 84
Reading Teacher, March 1998, page 511
School Library Journal, March 1997, page 172

Awards the book has won:
School Library Journal Best Books, 1997
Notable Social Studies Trade Books for Young People, 1998

Other books by the same author:
The Donkey and the Rock, 1999
Buddha, 1996
The Empty Pot, 1990 (Notable Trade Book in the Field of Social Studies)

Other books you might like:
David Barry, *The Rajah's Rice*, 1994
When Chandra heals the rajah's elephants she requests payment in rice, double for every square on a chessboard.
Marilyn Burns, *Spaghetti and Meatballs for All*, 1997
Fitting all of Mrs. Comfort's dinner guests at one table introduces the concepts of area and perimeter.
Cindy Neuschwander, *Amanda Bean's Amazing Dream*, 1998
Amanda loves to count but remains doubtful of subtraction until she has a truly amazing dream.
Elinor J. Pinczes, *One Hundred Hungry Ants*, 1993
Ants introduce the basic concepts of division when they sample food at a picnic.

258

MARIANNA DENGLER
SIBYL GRABER GERIG, Illustrator

Fiddlin' Sam

(Flagstaff, AZ: Rising Moon, 1999)

Subject(s): Music and Musicians; Mountain Life; Folklore
Age range(s): Grades 1-4
Major character(s): Fiddlin' Sam, Musician (fiddler), Wanderer; Unnamed Character, Son, Wanderer
Time period(s): Indeterminate Past
Locale(s): Ozarks

Summary: Fiddlin' Sam travels the Ozarks entertaining folks in exchange for his meals. Sam's not one to settle down but a rattlesnake bite slows him for a while as he recuperates under the care of a kind young man building a log cabin. Fiddlin' Sam helps when he's able, plays the fiddle and then resumes his nomadic life. As he gets older he worries about passing on his musical knowledge remembering his father's instruction that his talent is a loan not a gift and he's beholden to teach it to another. As Sam rests beside a trail one day, a boy walks past and Fiddlin' Sam recognizes the son of the man who nursed him back to health many years earlier. As the two travel together and Sam plays his fiddle around the campfire each night the boy's gift for the fiddle becomes apparent and Fiddlin' Sam knows he's able to pass on the talent loaned him for his lifetime. (32 pages)

Where it's reviewed:
Booklist, November 15, 1999, page 634
Children's Bookwatch, November 1999, page 7
Horn Book Guide, Spring 2000, page 65
Publishers Weekly, September 27, 1999, page 105
School Library Journal, December 1999, page 90

Other books by the same author:
The Worry Stone, 1996

Other books you might like:
David F. Birchman, *A Green Horn Blowing*, 1997
   A migrant worker introduces a young boy to the joy of music and leaves his trumpet behind for the boy when he leaves the farm.
Hilary Horder Hippely, *A Song for Lena*, 1996
   Grandma relates a childhood memory of sharing the family's strudel with a hungry beggar who expresses his appreciation with a violin serenade.
Natalie Kinsey-Warnock, *The Fiddler of the Northern Lights*, 1996
   While the Northern Lights brighten the sky, a stranger with a fiddle entertains the community at an impromptu dance.

259

SHARON PHILLIPS DENSLOW
CATHIE FELSTEAD, Illustrator

Big Wolf and Little Wolf

(New York: Greenwillow Books/HarperCollins Publishers, 2000)

Subject(s): Animals/Wolves; Bedtime; Parent and Child
Age range(s): Grades K-1
Major character(s): Little Wolf, Wolf; Big Wolf, Wolf, Father; Mama Wolf, Wolf, Mother
Time period(s): Indeterminate
Locale(s): Earth

Summary: Before Little Wolf goes to bed he asks Big Wolf to sing a song and then another. Little Wolf has a song to sing for Big Wolf too, but while singing he hears something moving in the bushes nearby and becomes afraid. When Mama Wolf appears singing her own song Little Wolf is relieved and joins Big Wolf in chasing Mama Wolf. Before he sleeps Little Wolf requests one more song from Mama Wolf and she sings a soothing wolf good night. (32 pages)

Where it's reviewed:
Booklist, May 1, 2000, page 1676
Horn Book Guide, Fall 2000, page 247
Kirkus Reviews, April 15, 2000, page 558
Publishers Weekly, May 15, 2000, page 116
School Library Journal, May 2000, page 140

Other books by the same author:
On the Trail with Miss Pace, 1995
Woollybear Good-bye, 1994
Bus Riders, 1993
At Taylor's Place, 1990
Night Owls, 1990

Other books you might like:
Mem Fox, *Time for Bed*, 1993
   Mothers all over the world are putting their kittens, lambs, fawns and children to sleep.
Mirra Ginsburg, *Asleep, Asleep*, 1992
   Animals are quietly bid good night until only the sleepy child and the wind are awake.
Martin Waddell, *Can't You Sleep, Little Bear?*, 1988
   Big Bear comforts Little Bear when his fear of the dark prevents him from settling down and sleeping.

260

TOMIE DEPAOLA, Author/Illustrator

Jamie O'Rourke and the Pooka

(New York: G.P. Putnam's Sons, 2000)

Subject(s): Conduct of Life; Folklore; Cleanliness
Age range(s): Grades 1-3
Major character(s): Jamie O'Rourke, Spouse; Eileen O'Rourke, Spouse; Pooka, Mythical Creature
Time period(s): Indeterminate Past
Locale(s): Ireland

Summary: While Eileen O'Rourke visits her sister for a week she leaves Jamie to tend the cottage. Jamie's plan for keeping the cottage clean is to stay in bed for the week, but his friends come to visit every evening to share cider and the food Eileen prepared. Looking at the mess, Jamie goes to sleep rather than tackle it, but while he sleeps a Pooka comes in and cleans up the house. Each night the friends return and so does the Pooka until, the night before Eileen returns, kind Jamie expresses his gratitude to the Pooka who is now freed from the punishment that required him to clean for others. Lazy Jamie, however, is faced with a dirty cottage and an angry wife. (32 pages)

Where it's reviewed:
Booklist, January 1, 2000, page 935
Children's Bookwatch, April 2000, page 6
Horn Book, January 2000, page 64
Publishers Weekly, January 17, 2000, page 55
School Library Journal, March 2000, page 194

Other books by the same author:
Bill and Pete to the Rescue, 1998
Days of the Blackbird: A Tale of Northern Italy, 1997
Strega Nona: Her Story, 1996

Other books you might like:
Arnold Lobel, *A Treeful of Pigs*, 1979
   The wife of a lazy farmer resorts to extreme measures to get her husband to change his ways.
Gerald McDermott, *Daniel O'Rourke: An Irish Tale*, 1986
   An encounter with a Pooka causes Daniel to have incredible, unexpected adventures.
Phyllis Root, *Aunt Nancy and Cousin Lazybones*, 1998
   Cousin Lazybones is known as a houseguest who does no work so Aunt Nancy figures out how to shorten his visit in her home.

261

TOMIE DEPAOLA, Author/Illustrator

Strega Nona Takes a Vacation

(New York: G.P. Putnam's Sons, 2000)

Subject(s): Witches and Witchcraft; Vacations; Gifts
Age range(s): Grades 1-3
Major character(s): Strega Nona, Witch, Aged Person; Big Anthony, Assistant; Bambolona, Assistant
Time period(s): Indeterminate Past
Locale(s): Calabria, Italy

Summary: In her dreams Strega Nona recalls childhood vacations with her now deceased grandmother and hears her grandmother encouraging her to once again visit the house by the seashore. Bambolona and Big Anthony agree that Strega Nona needs a vacation and they promise not to touch the pasta pot while she is gone. Kindly, Strega Nona sends gifts to Bambolona and Big Anthony, but Bambolona switches the gifts because she prefers candy to bubble bath. Big Anthony is eager to use his gift and, although he has no experience with bubble bath, he does just what Bambolona tells him and pours it into his bath water. A few bubbles are so much fun that Big Anthony pours in more and more until the village is buried in bubbles. Cleaning up the bubbles, at least, is easier than cleaning the pasta when Big Anthony used the magic pasta pot, but Strega Nona is still angry with both of her assistants when she must end her vacation early. (32 pages)

Where it's reviewed:
Booklist, October 15, 2000, page 444
Horn Book Guide, Spring 2001, page 34
Kirkus Reviews, August 15, 2000, page 1192
Publishers Weekly, August 21, 2000, page 72
School Library Journal, October 2000, page 120

Other books by the same author:
Strega Nona: Her Story, 1996

Strega Nona Meets Her Match, 1993 (Book Links Good Book)
Strega Nona's Magic Lessons, 1982
Strega Nona, 1975 (Caldecott Honor Book)

Other books you might like:
Ida DeLage, *The Old Witch Gets a Surprise*, 1981
   In an Easy Reader, Witch and Wizard's flight on a dragon balloon comes to an unexpected ending.
Janice Lee Smith, *Wizard and Wart*, 1994
   As Wizard begins his new business he finds the many requests for his services so tiring that he needs a vacation.
Viveca Larn Sundvall, *Santa's Winter Vacation*, 1995
   An elderly bearded man and his wife have difficulty enjoying their vacation because of the obnoxious behavior of the Sandworm family.

262

LISA DESIMINI, Author/Illustrator

Sun & Moon: A Giant Love Story

(New York: Scholastic/Blue Sky Press, 1999)

Subject(s): Love; Giants; Romance
Age range(s): Grades K-3
Major character(s): Girl, Child (giant); Boy, Child (giant)
Time period(s): Indeterminate
Locale(s): Earth

Summary: Following the rotation of the moon, Girl hopes to find someone her size with whom to share her love of shooting stars. On the other side of the earth, following the sun, Boy dreams of sharing shadow puppets with someone of his own size. After the Boy and the Girl wish for someone to love at the same exact time, they meet under an eclipse and spend the rest of their days and nights together. (40 pages)

Where it's reviewed:
Booklist, January 1, 1999, page 886
Bulletin of the Center for Children's Books, January 1999, page 165
Kirkus Reviews, December 15, 1998, page 1795
Publishers Weekly, December 21, 1998, page 67
School Library Journal, March 1999, page 173

Other books by the same author:
My House, 1997
Moon Soup, 1993
I Am Running Away Today, 1992

Other books you might like:
Eveline Hasler, *The Giantess*, 1997
   The kindness of a woodsman helps Emmeline, a shy giantess, accept and appreciate her size.
Nicholas Heller, *The Giant*, 1997
   When the giant steps out of the painting in their living room, a boy and his grandmother have to figure out how to get him back in.
Audrey Wood, *The Bunyans*, 1996
   The story of larger-than-life Paul Bunyan, humorously presents the legendary folk hero as a family man.

263

CHRISTEL DESMOINAUX, Author/Illustrator

Mrs. Hen's Big Surprise

(New York: Margaret K. McElderry Books, 2000)

Subject(s): Animals/Chickens; Mothers; Difference
Age range(s): Grades K-1
Major character(s): Mrs. Hen, Hen
Time period(s): Indeterminate
Locale(s): Fictional Country

Summary: In a tale first published in France in 1998 and translated into English, Mrs. Hen's lovely home is lacking one thing—a baby chick to love. So, when Mrs. Hen finds a large spotted egg buried in her vegetable garden she digs it up and carts it home to hatch it. Although the egg is larger than she is, Mrs. Hen perches atop it dreaming of the fun she will have with her own little chick. The other animal mothers think Mrs. Hen (and her egg) are very strange and they whisper derisively about her. After waiting a very long time, Mrs. Hen thinks her egg will never hatch so she tries to return it to the garden, but it rolls down the hill and cracks open. At last! Mrs. Hen's surprise is more surprising than she expects but she loves the large spotted dinosaur that emerges from the egg as much as she would love any chick. (32 pages)

Where it's reviewed:
Booklist, April 1, 2000, page 1468
Children's Book Review Service, April 2000, page 96
Horn Book Guide, Fall 2000, page 247
New York Times Book Review, June 4, 2000, page 49
School Library Journal, April 2000, page 103

Other books you might like:
Molly Bang, *Goose*, 1996
    A woodchuck family accepts the goose that emerges from the egg blown into their nest during a storm and teach her all they know about woodchuck life.
William Joyce, *Bently and Egg*, 1992
    When a shy, singing frog takes on responsibility for a special egg the ensuing events change the frog's life.
Leo Lionni, *An Extraordinary Egg*, 1994
    Free-thinking frog Jessica finds a large "pebble" that hatches into a creature which Jessica and her friends think is a "chicken" that can swim.
Lynn Reiser, *The Surprise Family*, 1994
    A mother hen loves the "chicks" she's hatched from a clutch of abandoned eggs even though they enjoy swimming-just like the ducks that they are.
Dr. Seuss, *Horton Hatches the Egg*, 1940
    A lazy bird leaves loyal elephant Horton to sit on her egg through all kinds of weather and adversity.

264

BABA WAGUE DIAKITE, Author/Illustrator

The Hatseller and the Monkeys

(New York: Scholastic Press, 1999)

Subject(s): Africa; Animals/Monkeys; Folklore
Age range(s): Grades K-3
Major character(s): BaMusa, Merchant
Time period(s): Indeterminate Past
Locale(s): Mali

Summary: BaMusa, the hatseller, is so anxious to sell his hats at a festival in a neighboring village that he does not eat breakfast before beginning his journey. On the way he tires and sits down under a tree for a nap. When he awakens all of his hats are gone, stolen by the monkeys in the tree who pelt BaMusa with the tree's mangoes. BaMusa is so hungry that he can't think clearly so his attempts to get the hats are unsuccessful. Not until BaMusa sits down to eat some of the fruit the monkeys have provided does he conceive a successful plan to reclaim his hats. (32 pages)

Where it's reviewed:
Bulletin of the Center for Children's Books, February 1999, page 199
Horn Book, May 1999, page 342
Kirkus Reviews, December 15, 1998, page 1796
Publisher's Weekly, January 11, 1999, page 71
School Library Journal, February 1999, page 97

Awards the book has won:
ALA Notable Children's Books, 2000

Other books by the same author:
The Hunterman and the Crocodile: A West African Folktale, 1997

Other books you might like:
Verna Aardema, *Why Mosquitoes Buzz in People's Ears: A West African Tale*, 1975
    The illustrated retelling of a folk tale about the consequences of a mosquito's lie won the Caldecott Medal.
T. Obinkaram Echewa, *The Magic Tree: A Folktale from Nigeria*, 1999
    Mbi, a mistreated orphan, plants a magic tree that responds to his wishes.
Mary-Joan Gerson, *Why the Sky Is Far Away: A Nigerian Folktale*, 1992
    Misused by the peasants, the sky responds by moving farther away.
Jane Kurtz, *Fire on the Mountain*, 1994
    In this Ethiopian folktale, a young boy wins a bet with his sister's employer.
Esphyr Slobodkina, *Caps for Sale: A Tale of a Peddler, Some Monkeys and Their Monkey Business*, 1940
    A peddler's hats are stolen by monkeys when he takes a nap under a tree.

265

KATE DICAMILLO

Because of Winn-Dixie

(Cambridge, MA: Candlewick Press, 2000)

Subject(s): Animals/Dogs; Neighbors and Neighborhoods; Single Parent Families
Age range(s): Grades 4-6
Major character(s): India Opal Buloni, 10-Year-Old, Daughter; Winn-Dixie, Dog; Gloria Dump, Aged Person, Neighbor; Franny Block, Aged Person, Librarian
Time period(s): Indeterminate Past

Locale(s): Naomi, Florida

Summary: The summer Opal and her preacher father move to Naomi, Opal is lonely and friendless but because of Winn-Dixie, a stray she finds at the grocery store, Opal's life changes. Winn-Dixie's need for companionship matches Opal's. Soon the dog accompanies Opal to church, the library and the pet store. At the library Opal makes her first friend in Miss Franny, a descendant of one of the town's original inhabitants whose stories about the past entertain Opal and Winn-Dixie. When Winn-Dixie runs off one afternoon Opal follows him into an overgrown yard and makes another friend in Gloria Dump. Almost blind, Gloria Dump sees with her heart and offers Opal insightful comments as she listens to her daily stories. During the summer recorded in the author's first book, Opal grows beyond her loneliness, makes some solid friendships, and learns more about her long-absent mother—all because of Winn-Dixie. (182 pages)

Where it's reviewed:
Booklist, May 1, 2000, page 1665
Five Owls, November 2000, page 45
Horn Book, July 2000, page 455
Riverbank Review, Summer 2000, page 36
School Library Journal, June 2000, page 143

Awards the book has won:
Newbery Honor Book, 2001
Publishers Weekly Best Books, 2000

Other books you might like:
Helen Cresswell, *Posy Bates, Again!*, 1994
  Posy's determination to keep the stray dog she has befriended leads to one hilarious episode after another.
Karen Hesse, *Sable*, 1994
  Tate cares for a stray dog, hoping her parents will allow her to keep the mutt.
Dawn Knight, *Mischief, Mad Mary, and Me*, 1997
  Dog lover Brit wants to find the stray that cantankerous old Mad Mary is feeding and make the large animal her pet.
Hilary McKay, *Dog Friday*, 1995
  Nursing an injured, lost dog back to health helps Robin overcome his fear of dogs.

266

DYANNE DISALVO-RYAN, Author/Illustrator

A Dog Like Jack

(New York: Holiday House, 1999)

Subject(s): Animals/Dogs; Death (of a Pet); Grief
Age range(s): Grades K-3
Major character(s): Jack, Dog; Mike, Child, Son; Mom, Mother
Time period(s): 1990s
Locale(s): United States

Summary: When Mike was still young enough to ride in a stroller his family adopted 8-year-old Jack from an animal shelter. Jack tolerates being a horse for the toddler Mike's cowboy and the sheep for the trick-or-treating shepherd Mike. When Mike is school age, Mom and Jack walk him home from school every day and Mike shares his ice cream cone with Jack. By the time Mike is 8-years-old, Jack is 91 in dog years and no longer able to chase squirrels or walk with Mike on Halloween. One winter day, Jack dies and the grieving family buries his ashes under his favorite tree at their summer beach home. (32 pages)

Where it's reviewed:
Booklist, March 1, 1999, page 1220
Horn Book Guide, Fall 1999, page 250
Publishers Weekly, January 18, 1999, page 337
School Library Journal, April 1999, page 92

Other books by the same author:
City Green, 1994
Uncle Willie and the Soup Kitchen, 1991

Other books you might like:
Amy Ehrlich, *Maggie and Silky and Joe*, 1994
  Joe and his family are saddened by the death of faithful friend and pet Maggie.
Ellen Howard, *Murphy and Kate*, 1995
  After the death of her 14-year-old pet and best friend, Kate fills the void in her life with poignant memories of her activities with Murphy.
Charlotte Zolotow, *The Old Dog*, 1995
  The revised and newly illustrated story relates the memories that flood a young boy's thoughts after finding his pet dog dead.

267

DYANNE DISALVO-RYAN, Author/Illustrator

Grandpa's Corner Store

(New York: HarperCollins Publishers, 2000)

Subject(s): Stores, Retail; Grandfathers; Neighbors and Neighborhoods
Age range(s): Grades K-3
Major character(s): Grandpa, Grandfather, Store Owner (grocer); Lucy, Student—Elementary School, Grocer's Helper
Time period(s): 2000s (2000)
Locale(s): New Jersey

Summary: Everyone's aware of the big, new supermarket being built just a few blocks from Grandpa's corner grocery and it seems to Lucy that many people assume Grandpa will sell or go out of business when the new store opens. Grandpa is concerned enough to put a "For Sale" sign in the store window, but Lucy has a plan that could help to assure that Grandpa's personal service continues for the members of the close-knit community. (40 pages)

Where it's reviewed:
Booklist, May 1, 2000, page 1679
Horn Book Guide, Fall 2000, page 267
Kirkus Reviews, April 15, 2000, page 559
Publishers Weekly, May 15, 2000, page 117
School Library Journal, July 2000, page 70

Awards the book has won:
Notable Social Studies Trade Books for Young People, 2001

Other books by the same author:
A Dog Like Jack, 1999
City Green, 1994

Uncle Willie and the Soup Kitchen, 1991 (Notable Children's Trade Book in the Field of Social Studies)

Other books you might like:

Melrose Cooper, *I Got Community*, 1995
With a catchy rhythm the text describes the important connections that make each person in a community significant.

Angela Johnson, *The Rolling Store*, 1997
Granddaddy recalls the reliance of his childhood community on a well-stocked truck that carries the equivalent of a general store to the neighborhood.

Erika Tamar, *The Garden of Happiness*, 1996
Neighbors cooperate to clean up a litter-strewn lot and plant a community garden.

268

TONY DITERLIZZI, Author/Illustrator

Jimmy Zangwow's Out-of-This World Moon Pie Adventure

(New York: Simon & Schuster Books for Young Readers, 2000)

Subject(s): Space Travel; Food; Fantasy
Age range(s): Grades K-3
Major character(s): Jimmy Zangwow, Child, Space Explorer; Mr. Moon, Celestial Body; Grimble Grinder, Monster
Time period(s): Indeterminate Past
Locale(s): United States; Outer Space; Mars

Summary: No amount of begging will convince Jimmy's mother to let him eat a Moon Pie before dinner so he goes outside to play with his secret project. Seated in his "junk jumbilee jalopy" Jimmy wishes that he could fly to the moon and get a Moon Pie and, unexpectedly, the jalopy takes off! In response to Jimmy's plea, Mr. Moon gives him boxes of Moon Pies and Jimmy heads for the Milky Way to get something to drink with his snack. A loud grumbling sound causes Jimmy to crash land on Mars where 999 little Mars men eagerly offer to share Jimmy's snack. Before any of them can eat, hungry Grimble Grinder appears and devours the one thousand Moon Pies. Now Jimmy is both hungry and late for dinner. The Mars Men and Grimble Grinder help change the jalopy into a hot air balloon and Jimmy floats home in time for dinner with a Moon Pie for dessert in the author's first book. (40 pages)

Where it's reviewed:
Bulletin of the Center for Children's Books, May 2000, page 314
Horn Book Guide, Fall 2000, page 267
Kirkus Reviews, April 1, 2000, page 474
Publishers Weekly, April 17, 2000, page 80
School Library Journal, April 2000, page 103

Other books you might like:

Frank Asch, *Mooncake*, 1978
Believing the moon is made of cake Bear builds a rocket to fly himself there in order to taste it.

Jules Feiffer, *Meanwhile. . .*, 1997
Raymond discovers that with a little imagination and the word "meanwhile" he can travel to the Wild West and outer space.

Catherine Siracusa, *The Banana Split from Outer Space*, 1995
Stanley's ice cream business improves after he meets Zelmo, an alien that has crash-landed on earth.

Audrey Wood, *Sweet Dream Pie*, 1998
The aroma of Ma Brindle's Sweet Dream Pie is so enticing that no one can resist eating some.

269

SEAN DIVINY
JOE ROCCO, Illustrator

Halloween Motel

(New York: Joanna Cotler/Harper Collins Publishers, 2000)

Subject(s): Halloween; Hotels and Motels; Stories in Rhyme
Age range(s): Grades K-2
Major character(s): Unnamed Character, Son, Narrator
Time period(s): Indeterminate
Locale(s): Fictional Country

Summary: In foggy darkness on October 31st a family approaches the Halloween Motel where they have a reservation for the night. The decor certainly fits the theme of the motel; even the snack machine is filled with creepy items. After the boy and his parents don costumes and trick or treat door to door in the motel, the desk clerk, responding to complaints from other guests, confronts them. Only then does the family learn that they have arrived at the wrong motel so they make a hasty exit with real monsters in pursuit. (32 pages)

Where it's reviewed:
Booklist, September 1, 2000, page 131
Horn Book Guide, Spring 2001, page 35
Kirkus Reviews, September 1, 2001, page 1281
Publishers Weekly, September 25, 2000, page 64
School Library Journal, September 2000, page 194

Other books by the same author:
Snow Inside the House, 1998

Other books you might like:

Ken Compton, *Granny Greenteeth and the Noise in the Night*, 1993
Granny asks her unique and somewhat spooky housemates to investigate a noise under her bed, Joanne Compton, co-author.

Judy Sierra, *The House That Drac Built*, 1995
A rhyming cumulative tale introduces such unusual creatures as a manticore and the fiend of Bloodygore living in the house that Darc built.

Erica Silverman, *The Halloween House*, 1997
On Halloween two prison escapees seek refuge in what they think is an unoccupied house but which is actually a haunted one.

270

ANN DIXON
EVON ZERBETZ, Illustrator

Blueberry Shoe

(Portland, OR: Alaska Northwest Books, 1999)

Subject(s): Clothes; Animals; Lost and Found Possessions

Age range(s): Grades K-2
Major character(s): Baby, Child, Brother (younger); Sister, Child, Sister
Time period(s): 1990s
Locale(s): Ptarmigan Mountain, Alaska

Summary: As a family of berry pickers descends the mountain after a day of blueberry picking Baby's red sneaker falls off. The family cannot find the lost shoe but a succession of animals do; each uses it briefly and then loses it too. Through the winter the shoe remains on the mountainside filling with dirt and unpicked berries. When the family returns the following summer to pick blueberries, Sister finds Baby's shoe— with a small blueberry bush growing in it! (32 pages)

Where it's reviewed:
Booklist, October 15, 1999, page 451
ForeWord, October 1999, page 60
Horn Book Guide, Spring 2000, page 33
Publishers Weekly, August 23, 1999, page 57
School Library Journal, December 1999, page 94

Other books by the same author:
Trick-or-Treat!, 1998 (Read with Me)
Merry Birthday, Nora Noel, 1996
The Sleeping Lady, 1994
How Raven Brought Light to the People, 1992

Other books you might like:
Jan Brett, *The Mitten: A Ukranian Folktale*, 1989
    In this retelling of a folktale, a boy's lost mitten provides shelter for an assortment of animals.
Crescent Dragonwagon, *Brass Button*, 1997
    Unbeknownst to Mrs. Moffat a shiny brass button falls off her new coat and begins a long journey about town that leads back to her sidewalk.
Robert McCloskey, *Blueberries for Sal*, 1948
    Sal's blueberry expedition with her mom parallels that of a mother bear and her cub; each youngster loses mom, but the young ones find each other.
Tracey Campbell Pearson, *The Purple Hat*, 1997
    Annie's beloved purple hat is found first by a bird that uses it for a nest.

271

BERLIE DOHERTY
ALISON BARTLETT, Illustrator

Paddiwak and Cozy
(New York: Orchard Books, 1999)

Subject(s): Animals/Cats; Pets; Jealousy
Age range(s): Grades K-1
Major character(s): Sally, Child; Paddiwak, Cat; Cozy, Cat
Time period(s): 1990s
Locale(s): England

Summary: In a revised, newly illustrated edition of a story first published in Britain in 1988, Sally arrives home with a calico cat and her jealous pet, Paddiwak storms out the cat door vowing never, never to return. The shy, frightened new cat hides in the basement while Sally cries that she now has no cat when she thought she would have two cats. After dark, the exhausted new cat climbs into the family's linen cupboard

and sleeps. Rain drives a cold and tired Paddiwak inside to seek shelter in his favorite spot where he finds—Cozy. (32 pages)

Where it's reviewed:
Booklist, August 1999, page 2063
Horn Book Guide, Spring 2000, page 14
Kirkus Reviews, October 1, 1999, page 1578
School Library Journal, October 1999, page 112

Other books by the same author:
The Magic Bicycle, 1995
Snowy, 1993

Other books you might like:
Isabelle Harper, *My Cats Nick and Nora*, 1995
    Two cousins wile away a Sunday afternoon playing dress-up with their patient cats.
Barbara M. Joosse, *Nugget and Darling*, 1997
    Nugget thinks life with Nell is just perfect until they find a stray kitten in the yard that Nell takes in as another pet.
William Mayne, *Pandora*, 1996
    When her owners arrive home with a baby, jealous Pandora, the cat, moves out of the house temporarily.
Charlotte Voake, *Ginger*, 1997
    The intrusion of a kitten into Ginger's contented life drives the cat away until his owner sees her cold, wet pet in the garden and brings him inside.

272

DORIS DORRIE
JULIA KAERGEL, Illustrator

Lottie's Princess Dress
(New York: Dial Books for Young Readers, 1999)

Subject(s): Mothers and Daughters; Clothes; Working Mothers
Age range(s): Grades K-2
Major character(s): Lottie Van Klinkenstopper, Kindergartner, Daughter; Mom, Mother
Time period(s): 1990s (1998)
Locale(s): Germany

Summary: Being awakened for school is no fun for Lottie especially when she's in the middle of a wonderful, glittery, princess dream. Mom is insistent and growing more annoyed every minute so finally Lottie gets out of bed, but refuses to wear the clothes Mom suggests because they are not appropriate for the special day her dream foretells. Rather, Lottie selects her glittery princess dress, beginning an argument when she refuses to change to Mom's idea of something more appropriate. Eventually, Lottie's logic prevails and she convinces her mother that she should change into a more regal outfit. Finally, the princess and the queen are ready for their day. As the author's first book concludes it's obvious to everyone that today is a very special day for Lottie and Mom. Originally published in German in 1998. (32 pages)

Where it's reviewed:
Bulletin of the Center for Children's Books, November 1999, page 90
Horn Book, July 1999, page 453
Kirkus Reviews, June 15, 1999, page 962

Publishers Weekly, July 12, 1999, page 94
School Library Journal, September 1999, page 181

Awards the book has won:
Bulletin of the Center for Children's Books Blue Ribbon, 1999

Other books you might like:
Fred Hiatt, *If I Were Queen of the World*, 1997
    A young girl imagines that as queen she could eat lollipops without sharing and stay up as late as she wants.
Susan L. Roth, *Princess*, 1993
    Despite her mother's repeated attempts to wake her for school a little girl tarries in bed imagining the freedom she would have if she were a princess.
Marisabina Russo, *Time to Wake Up!*, 1994
    Mama tickles the toes of reluctant riser Sam to encourage him to wake up and get out of bed.
Tanja Szekessy, *A Princess in Boxland*, 1996
    Pretending that she is a princess, Marie uses a magical umbrella to transport herself to an enchanted world.

273

ARTHUR DORROS
DAVID CATROW, Illustrator

The Fungus That Ate My School

(New York: Scholastic Press, 2000)

Subject(s): Scientific Experiments; Schools; Problem Solving
Age range(s): Grades 1-3
Major character(s): Mr. Harrison, Teacher; Ms. Moreover, Principal; Ellen, Student
Time period(s): 2000s (2000)
Locale(s): United States

Summary: Ellen and her classmates are a little concerned about leaving their science experiments unattended during spring vacation, but Mr. Harrison assures them, "Fungus can take care of itself." When the rainy vacation ends and Ms. Moreover opens the school doors everyone is astonished to see multicolored fuzz covering the halls. Mr. Harrison is thrilled to see the unique fungi growing everywhere, but no one else is quite as excited. At Ms. Moreover's insistence Mr. Harrison calls in a fungi expert who quickly frees the school of the problem and sends the award-winning growth to the Museum of Fungus and Industry. Mr. Harrison agrees to do no more fungus experiments—this year. (32 pages)

Where it's reviewed:
Booklist, June 1, 2000, page 1907
Horn Book Guide, Fall 2000, page 292
Horn Book, March 2000, page 183
Publishers Weekly, May 15, 2000, page 117
School Library Journal, April 2000, page 104

Other books by the same author:
Ten Go Tango, 2000
Rain Forest Secrets, 1999
A Tree Is Growing, 1997
Isla, 1995

Other books you might like:
Walter Lyon Krudop, *Something Is Growing*, 1995
    A seed planted by a curious boy develops into a plant that threatens to overtake a city.
Reeve Lindbergh, *The Awful Aardvarks Go to School*, 1997
    Four unruly aardvarks are not part of a science experiment, but they do create chaos before they are banished from school.
Elaine Pascoe, *Slime, Molds, and Fungi*, 1999
    A nonfiction title explains the use of science projects to broaden knowledge of fungi.
David Wiesner, *June 29, 1999*, 1992
    Not satisfied with planting seeds in a paper cup, a third grader plans a more ambitious science project with startling results.

274

ERIN DOUGLAS
WONG HERBERT YEE, Illustrator

Get That Pest!

(San Diego: Harcourt, Inc., 2000)

Series: Green Light Readers. Level 2
Subject(s): Farm Life; Stealing; Humor
Age range(s): Grades 1-2
Major character(s): Mom Nash, Farmer, Spouse; Pop Nash, Farmer, Spouse; Unnamed Character, Wolf, Artist
Time period(s): 2000s
Locale(s): Fictional Country

Summary: When Mom and Pop Nash notice their hens' eggs are vanishing before they can collect them each day they devise traps to catch the thief. First Pop catches Mom in a net, then, the next trap entangles both of them rather than the culprit. The third attempt captures a wolf that begs for forgiveness and offers to return the eggs. Rather than eating the eggs he takes, the wolf paints them decoratively giving Mom and Pop a new line of work as sellers of painted eggs. (20 pages)

Where it's reviewed:
Booklist, February 15, 2000, page 1123
Horn Book Guide, Fall 2000, page 288
School Library Journal, July 2000, page 71

Other books you might like:
Kristi T. Butler, *Rip's Secret Spot*, 2000
    When Pat, Mom and Dad notice things missing from their home they follow the dog to his favorite spot and find their belongings buried in Rip's hole.
David McPhail, *A Girl, a Goat, and a Goose*, 2000
    Four brief stories about the activities of a girl, a goat and a goose comprise this entry in the "Hello Reader!" series for beginning readers.
Patti Trimble, *Lost!*, 2000
    In a "Green Light Reader," a lost ant named Gil feels relieved to finally find his way home.

275

MALACHY DOYLE
JUDITH ALLIBONE, Illustrator

Jody's Beans

(Cambridge, MA: Candlewick Press, 1999)

Subject(s): Gardens and Gardening; Food; Grandfathers
Age range(s): Grades K-2
Major character(s): Jody, Child, Daughter; Granda, Grandfather, Gardener
Time period(s): 1990s
Locale(s): Wales

Summary: During a spring visit Granda shows Jody how to plant scarlet runner bean seeds. He tells her what to do to care for them and during his periodic visits they attend to the beans as they grow bigger and bigger. When they pick their first beans Granda shows Jody how to prepare them for cooking so Jody can do it between his visits. While Jody and Granda work, the illustrations show Jody's pregnant mother in the background doing household chores as she grows along with the beans. By the time Granda and Jody harvest the last dried pods to save the seeds for next year's garden, Jody's parents are pictured holding the baby. A brief index refers readers to the pages describing the various steps in the care of beans. (32 pages)

Where it's reviewed:
Booklist, July 1999, page 1950
Horn Book, March 1999, page 187
Kirkus Reviews, March 15, 1999, page 449
Publishers Weekly, May 3, 1999, page 74
School Library Journal, June 1999, page 92

Other books by the same author:
Tales from Old Ireland, 2000
Well, A Crocodile Can!, 2000

Other books you might like:
Judith Caseley, *Grandpa's Garden Lunch*, 1990
Sarah's reward for helping Grandpa in his garden is a delicious lunch made from homegrown vegetables.
Shea Darian, *Grandpa's Garden*, 1996
Grandpa shares special moments in the garden while teaching his grandchild about plants and life.
Lois Ehlert, *Growing Vegetable Soup*, 1987
A father and his child grow the ingredients needed for vegetable soup.
Vivian French, *Oliver's Vegetables*, 1995
While visiting Grandpa, Oliver tries to find the potatoes in Grandpa's garden so he can eat the only vegetable he likes—french fries.
Elaine Moore, *Grandma's Garden*, 1993
Together, Grandma and Kim plant their garden, make a scarecrow and repair the damage of an early season thunderstorm

276

RODDY DOYLE
BRIAN AJHAR, Illustrator

The Giggler Treatment

(New York: Arthur A. Levine Books/Scholastic Press, 2000)

Subject(s): Humor; Fantasy; Family Life
Age range(s): Grades 2-5
Major character(s): Mister Mack, Father; Rover, Dog (talking)
Time period(s): 2000s (2000)
Locale(s): Ireland

Summary: The first children's book for this adult novelist introduces gigglers—small, usually unseen beings whose purpose in life is to punish adults they consider mean to children. The punishment is a pile of dog poop left in the path of the unsuspecting victim. Mister Mack is selected as a victim when the gigglers overhear him punishing his children for breaking a window. Had the gigglers waited to hear the complete story they might have realized in time that Mister Mack is not such a bad fellow, but alas they hurried to set their plan in motion by contracting with Rover for a special pile of his poop. When Mister Mack's children learn of the fate awaiting their father they rush to warn him with Rover, gigglers and their mother all racing to reach the footpath to the train station before Mister Mack's foot lands in Rover's pile. (112 pages)

Where it's reviewed:
Children's Book Review Service, September 2000, page 6
Horn Book Guide, Spring 2001, page 60
Kirkus Reviews, September 15, 2000, page 1355
Publishers Weekly, July 24, 2000, page 94
School Library Journal, November 2000, page 119

Other books you might like:
Allan Ahlberg, *The Better Brown Stories*, 1996
The Brown family visits the writer of their stories to suggest he liven their boring lives with some better adventures.
Dav Pilkey, *Captain Underpants and the Attack of the Talking Toilets*, 1999
Mischief makers Harold and George and their principal's alter ego, Captain Underpants, use cafeteria food to vanquish an invention gone awry.
Jon Scieszka, *The Stinky Cheese Man: And Other Fairly Stupid Tales*, 1992
The Caldecott Honor Book features humorous retellings of well-known fairy tales.

277

ELLEN DREYER

Speechless in New York

(New York: Four Corners Publishing Co., 2000)

Series: Going To. . .
Subject(s): Travel; Singing; Interpersonal Relations
Age range(s): Grades 5-7

Major character(s): Jessie Witt, Singer, Teenager; Mike Ribert, Singer, Teenager; Kendra Roberts, Singer, Teenager
Time period(s): 2000 (2000s)
Locale(s): New York, New York

Summary: Being chosen as one of the members of the Prairie Youth Chorale to compete in a festival in New York gives Jessie the opportunity for an exciting adventure. Jessie's initial experiences, however, seem closer to disaster—her luggage is lost and she develops a sore throat that threatens to keep her from singing. Gamely, Jessie tries to enjoy the group's sightseeing trips around the city while ignoring annoying Kendra and learning to view Mike, a teasing classmate, differently. By the time the chorale is scheduled to perform Jessie's missing luggage has been recovered, her voice is returning to normal and Jessie is beginning to think maybe this trip will be fun after all. Sightseeing information and maps are appended. (96 pages)

Where it's reviewed:
ForeWord, February 2000, page 68
School Library Journal, March 2000, page 233

Other books by the same author:
Wild Animals, 1991
Raggedy Ann and Andy Second Giant Treasury, 1989

Other books you might like:
Betsy Kuhn, *Not Exactly Nashville*, 1998
    Ellen and Valerie practice daily to realize their dream of singing at the Grand Ole Opry.
L.E. Williams, *Rose Faces the Music*, 1997
    An unexpected change of plans threatens Rose's chance of playing saxophone in her school's jazz band at a Presidential inauguration.
Virginia Euwer Wolff, *The Mozart Season*, 1991
    All summer Allegra prepares a Mozart concerto for a competition that becomes secondary to her personal growth.

278

BETSY DUFFEY

Alien for Rent

(New York: Delacorte Press, 1999)

Subject(s): Aliens; Bullies; Schools
Age range(s): Grades 2-4
Major character(s): Bork, Alien; Lexie, 3rd Grader; J.P., 3rd Grader
Time period(s): 1990s (1999)
Locale(s): United States

Summary: Lexie is curious when she sees the green glowing "Alien for Rent, two "gugentocks" an hour" sign on the school bulletin board. While discussing whether to take a chance by renting an alien, Lexie and J.P. inadvertently antagonize the school bully and at recess he comes looking to extract his revenge. Lexie, whose lunch box contains Twinkies ("gugentocks"), is not aware that Bork, considering himself rented by the lunch box owner, complies literally with every statement Lexie makes to the bully. Now J.P. and Lexie have the problem of finding a fifth grader who has been changed into a baby and convincing Bork to change him back when Lexie has run out of "rent." (71 pages)

Where it's reviewed:
Booklist, January 1, 1999, page 876
Bulletin of the Center for Children's Books, February 1999, page 199
Horn Book, January 1999, page 58
Kirkus Reviews, December 15, 1998, page 1796
School Library Journal, March 1999, page 173

Other books by the same author:
Spotlight on Cody, 1998
Virtual Cody, 1997
How to Be Cool in the Third Grade, 1993

Other books you might like:
Daniel Pinkwater, *Mush, a Dog from Space*, 1995
    Kelly's parents are opposed to pets, but when she finds Mush, his gourmet cooking ability convinces them to let her keep the alien dog.
Dyan Sheldon, *Harry and Chicken*, 1992
    Chicken adopts a stray cat that turns out to be an alien from the planet Arcana.
Catherine Siracusa, *The Banana Split from Outer Space*, 1995
    Meeting Zelmo, an alien who has crash-landed on Earth, improves Stanley's ice cream business.

279

BETSY DUFFEY
ELLEN THOMPSON, Illustrator

Cody Unplugged

(New York: Viking, 1999)

Subject(s): Camps and Camping; Parent and Child; Television
Age range(s): Grades 2-5
Major character(s): Cody Michaels, 9-Year-Old, Camper; Arthur Bonner, Camper; Moose, Camper, Bully
Time period(s): 1990s (1999)
Locale(s): Camp Bear

Summary: A summer of non-stop television awaits Cody until his mother pulls the plug and signs him up for camp. Cody is more than a little reluctant to climb on the camp bus; he makes mental lists of camp survival tactics that he constantly revises. Moose, an experienced camper is not happy to share his tent with rookies Cody and Arthur, but the two first-timers are grateful to find each other. Cody's appreciation of Arthur grows when he learns that Arthur is also a TV addict. As Cody becomes involved in the camp activities he finds that real experiences are more interesting than the vicarious ones he has through television shows and video games. Cody measures his progress on his "courage stick" as if he is moving from one level to another of a video game and by week's end he has many reasons to feel proud. (87 pages)

Where it's reviewed:
Booklist, June 1999, page 1828
Horn Book, May 1999, page 328
School Library Journal, July 1999, page 69

Other books by the same author:
Cody's Secret Admirer, 1998
Spotlight on Cody, 1998

Virtual Cody, 1997
Hey, New Kid!, 1996

Other books you might like:
Joanna Cole, *The Gator Girls*, 1995
    Amy and Alice have such extensive summer plans that
    they fear a week at camp will interfere with their activities.
Patricia Reilly Giff, *Ronald Morgan Goes to Camp*, 1995
    A reluctant camper, Ronald is a good friend and helper to
    everyone he meets at Camp Echo Lake.
James Howe, *Pinky and Rex Go to Camp*, 1992
    Pinky and Rex are friends now. Will they still be after
    completing their camp preparations?

280

JOYCE DUNBAR
JANE CABRERA, Illustrator

Eggday

(New York: Holiday House, 1999)

Subject(s): Animals; Contests; Problem Solving
Age range(s): Preschool
Major character(s): Dora Duck, Duck; Hetty Hen, Chicken
Time period(s): Indeterminate
Locale(s): Fictional Country

Summary: Dora Duck announces Eggday and gives the barnyard animals one day to produce the best egg. The pig, horse
and goat try unsuccessfully to comply until Hetty Hen tells
them that laying eggs is not possible for all animals. Hetty
kindly gives each one of her own eggs with suggestions for
decorations. When the animals arrive at Dora's nest on the
morning of the contest she no longer has an entry in the
competition and has changed the name to Duckling Day. (24
pages)

Where it's reviewed:
Booklist, April 1, 1999, page 1420
Horn Book, May 1999, page 313
Publishers Weekly, February 22, 1999, page 93
School Library Journal, July 1999, page 69

Other books by the same author:
Baby Bird, 1998
Indigo and the Whale, 1993
Lollopy, 1992

Other books you might like:
Jeni Bassett, *The Chick's Trick*, 1995
    Two young chicks' find a way to trick their competitive
    mothers so they will stop comparing the two offspring.
Erica Silverman, *Don't Fidget a Feather*, 1994
    Competitive Duck and Gander are so determined to outdo
    one another that they almost end up in Fox's stew pot.
James Stevenson, *The Mud Flat Olympics*, 1994
    Annually a group of animal friends hold their own wacky
    version of the Olympics.

281

JOYCE DUNBAR
MARK EDWARDS, Illustrator

The Sand Children

(New York: Crocodile Books, USA, 1999)

Subject(s): Beaches; Giants; Sandcastles
Age range(s): Grades K-2
Major character(s): Dad, Father; Unnamed Character, Son,
    Child
Time period(s): 1990s

Summary: On a camping trip to the beach with his dad, a
young boy makes a line of sand castles while Dad begins
sculpting a sand giant. Together they add seaweed hair and
shell eyes. As night falls, Dad and son retreat to their tent in
the dunes and watch as children frolicking on the beach
destroy the sand castles, but play gently with the giant. That
night, under a full moon the boy dreams he is playing with the
giant who has built sand children and needs help with the
faces. In the morning, the giant is still above the tide line,
surrounded by the footsteps of the children. (32 pages)

Where it's reviewed:
Horn Book Guide, Fall 1999, page 250
Publishers Weekly, March 15, 1999, page 56
School Library Journal, July 1999, page 69

Other books by the same author:
Baby Bird, 1998
Why Is the Sky Up?, 1991
A Cake for Barney, 1988

Other books you might like:
Jennifer Armstrong, *Sunshine, Moonshine*, 1997
    A boy and his father begin a day of sailing under the sun's
    bright rays and end it by moonlight on the beach path as
    they walk home.
Patricia Lakin, *Dad and Me in the Morning*, 1994
    A young boy and his dad enjoy some special, private time
    together watching the sunrise.
Liz Rosenberg, *Moonbathing*, 1996
    The moon is full and the sky is clear-perfect conditions for
    a moonbathing walk on the beach.

282

JOYCE DUNBAR
HELEN CRAIG, Illustrator

The Secret Friend

(Cambridge, MA: Candlewick Press, 1999)

Series: Read Me: Panda and Gander Stories
Subject(s): Friendship; Letters; Animals
Age range(s): Grades K-1
Major character(s): Panda, Bear, Friend; Gander, Goose,
    Friend
Time period(s): Indeterminate
Locale(s): Fictional Country

Summary: Gander is writing a letter to his secret friend and
Panda is feeling worried. The letter is brief and Panda offers
suggestions to improve the closing so it is a little more

personal than a simple signature. Gander follows Panda's suggestions and then decorates the letter with stickers and original art before depositing it in a shoebox mailbox. While Panda sulks, Gander walks to the mailbox and pulls out the letter, addressed to Panda, of course. (24 pages)

Where it's reviewed:
Bulletin of the Center for Children's Books, June 1999, page 349
Horn Book Guide, Fall 1999, page 273
Kirkus Reviews, March 1, 1999, page 374
Publishers Weekly, March 15, 1999, page 56
School Library Journal, August 1999, page 134

Other books by the same author:
Gander's Pond, 1999
Panda's New Toy, 1999
The Bowl of Fruit, 1999

Other books you might like:
Alma Flor Ada, *Yours Truly, Goldilocks*, 1998
    Goldilocks sends letters to her three little pig friends suggesting a get-together to thank the bears for saving Peter Rabbit from a wolf.
Nancy Jewell, *Two Silly Trolls*, 1992
    In a beginning reader, five brief stories showcase the challenges to a friendship of two trolls.
Arnold Lobel, *Frog and Toad Are Friends*, 1970
    The award-winning celebration of friendship shows the give-and-take necessary to make it successful.

283

JOYCE DUNBAR
DEBI GLIORI, Illustrator

The Very Small

(San Diego: Harcourt, Inc., 2000)

Subject(s): Animals/Bears; Difference; Homesickness
Age range(s): Grades K-2
Major character(s): Giant Baby Bear, Bear, Son; Very Small, Son (lost)
Time period(s): Indeterminate
Locale(s): Fictional Country

Summary: Giant Baby Bear finds a little lost something in the woods crying for his mommy so Giant Baby Bear takes Very Small home to share his mommy. Very Small is frightened of these large creatures and begins crying for his daddy too. Giant Baby Bear makes a little playground in his house for Very Small to use and also shares his dinner. At bedtime, Very Small is unable to sleep because Giant Baby Bear snores too loudly so he tries to pinch his nose but succeeds only in making Giant Baby Bear sneeze. The force of the sneeze propels Very Small out the window and back into the forest where his worried parents are waiting. (26 pages)

Where it's reviewed:
Booklist, December 15, 2000, page 825
Horn Book Guide, Spring 2001, page 14
Kirkus Reviews, September 15, 2000, page 1355
Publishers Weekly, October 2, 2000, page 80
School Library Journal, November 2000, page 119

Other books by the same author:
The Pig Who Wished, 1999
Baby Bird, 1998
Indigo and the Whale, 1996
Lollopy, 1992

Other books you might like:
Anthony Browne, *Willy and Hugh*, 1991
    A chimp and a gorilla find that their differences contribute to the success of their friendship.
Michael Foreman, *The Little Reindeer*, 1997
    When a little reindeer that is accidentally loaded into Santa's sleigh falls out on a rooftop he waits a full year for rescue.
Todd Starr Palmer, *Rhino and Mouse*, 1994
    Although they do not seem to have much in common including their size, Rhino and Mouse enjoy a close friendship.

284

ALICE FAYE DUNCAN
CATHERINE STOCK, Illustrator

Miss Viola and Uncle Ed Lee

(New York: Atheneum Books for Young Readers, 1999)

Subject(s): Friendship; Old Age; African Americans
Age range(s): Grades K-2
Major character(s): Miss Viola, Neighbor, Aged Person; Uncle Ed Lee, Neighbor, Aged Person; Bradley, Child, Neighbor
Time period(s): 1990s
Locale(s): United States

Summary: Bradley lives between very neat Miss Viola's immaculate yard and Uncle Ed Lee's junk strewn one. While playing checkers with Bradley, Uncle Ed Lee mentions that he'd like to make Miss Viola his friend. Bradley finds it humorous to think that the two opposites could hope for a friendship, but he dutifully carries the message to Miss Viola. To satisfy Miss Viola's request, Uncle Ed Lee cleans his yard, mows his grass and repairs his dangling shutters. Then Miss Viola, Bradley and Uncle Ed Lee sit under his shade tree, sipping lemonade and being friends. (40 pages)

Where it's reviewed:
Booklist, February 15, 1999, page 1075
Horn Book Guide, Fall 1999, page 250
Kirkus Reviews, December 15, 1998, page 1797
Publishers Weekly, January 4, 1999, page 89
School Library Journal, February 1999, page 83

Other books by the same author:
Willie Jerome, 1995

Other books you might like:
Crescent Dragonwagon, *Brass Button*, 1997
    A lost brass button from the coat of widowed Mrs. Moffatt is instrumental in facilitating a friendship with her neighbor Mr. Peterson.
Laurie A. Jacobs, *So Much in Common*, 1994
    Philomena the hippo and Horace the goat are very different animals with one important thing in common—their friendship.

Cynthia Rylant, *Mr. Putter and Tabby Series*, 1994-
Elderly Mr. Putter and his cat Tabby share humorous adventures with their neighbor Mrs. Teaberry and her dog Zeke.

285

LOIS DUNCAN
JON McINTOSH, Illustrator

The Longest Hair in the World
(New York: Doubleday, 1999)

Subject(s): Wishes; Hair; Birthdays
Age range(s): Grades K-3
Major character(s): Emily, 6-Year-Old
Time period(s): 1990s (1999)
Locale(s): United States

Summary: On her sixth birthday, Emily wishes for the longest hair in the world so that she can be the princess in her school play. When Emily's wish comes true her hair grows out of control. Although Emily gets the role as the princess, her hair will no longer fit in the family car or in her bedroom. She washes her expanding head of hair in the car wash and combs it with a rake. On her seventh birthday, Emily's family urges her to reverse her wish, but the plan does not turn out as expected. The next school play is about porcupines and Emily ends up with quills. (32 pages)

Where it's reviewed:
Children's Book Review Service, October 1999, page 181
Children's Bookwatch, October 1999, page 6
Horn Book Guide, Spring 2000, page 34
Publisher's Weekly, September 6, 1999, page 102
School Library Journal, December 1999, page 94

Other books by the same author:
The Magic of Spider Woman, 1996
Birthday Moon, 1989
Horses of Dreamland, 1985

Other books you might like:
Nikki Grimes, *Wild, Wild Hair*, 1997
Tisa dreads Monday mornings the day Mommy combs her wild, wild hair and styles it into twenty beautiful braids.
Carolivia Herron, *Nappy Hair*, 1997
At a family reunion, Brenda's uncle notes the uniqueness of her incredibly curly hair and the relatives all chime in their agreement.
James Proimos, *Joe's Wish*, 1998
Joe wishes he could be young again, until he spends the day with his grandson.
Carol Diggory Shields, *I Am Really a Princess*, 1993
A young girl discovers that her imagined life as a princess will have drawbacks which she has not considered previously.
John Warren Stewig, *King Midas*, 1999
In this retelling of the classic Greek myth, everything King Midas touches turns to gold.

286

OLIVIER DUNREA, Author/Illustrator

Bear Noel
(New York: Farrar Straus Giroux, 2000)

Subject(s): Animals/Bears; Animals; Christmas
Age range(s): Grades K-1
Major character(s): Bear Noel, Bear
Time period(s): Indeterminate
Locale(s): Earth

Summary: One by one the clues mount telling the animals of the north woods to gather in anticipation of Bear Noel's arrival. The sound of tramping feet provides the first clue and others such as laughter, singing, and bells jingling confirm the animals' suspicions. Finally, Bear Noel is here. From his heavy sack he takes nuts, seed balls, strands of berries and balls of sugar and salt to decorate a small fir tree. Then he invites the animals to gather and enjoy each other and the gifts with no fear on this one night—Christmas Eve. (32 pages)

Where it's reviewed:
Booklist, September 1, 2000, page 131
Horn Book Guide, Spring 2001, page 35
Kirkus Reviews, July 15, 2000, page 1037
Publishers Weekly, September 25, 2000, page 69
School Library Journal, October 2000, page 59

Other books by the same author:
The Trow-Wife's Treasure, 1998
The Tale of Hilda Louise, 1996
The Painter Who Loved Chickens, 1995

Other books you might like:
Alexandra Day, *The Christmas We Moved to the Barn*, 1997
A family's many pets help with their unexpected move to the barn on Christmas Eve. Cooper Edens, co-author.
Brigitte Weninger, *Merry Christmas, Davy!*, 1998
Animals offer future foraging help in gratitude for Davy's generous gift of most of his family's winter food supply to ease their hunger.
Cliff Wright, *Santa's Ark*, 1997
Each time Santa stops the sleigh a young stowaway reindeer invites baby animals to board until the craft becomes so heavy it can no longer fly.

287

JACQUES DUQUENNOY, Author/Illustrator
ALBIN MICHEL JEUNESSE, Translator

Operation Ghost
(San Diego: Harcourt Brace & Company, 1999)

Subject(s): Ghosts; Hospitals; Illness
Age range(s): Grades K-2
Major character(s): Henry, Spirit (ghost); Doctor Ouch, Doctor, Spirit (ghost)
Time period(s): Indeterminate
Locale(s): France

Summary: Henry has been having some problems lately. First he has the measles, then he becomes jaundiced and finally, Henry falls asleep at night—something ghosts never do.

Henry's friends rush him to the hospital where Doctor Ouch discovers the problem—Henry's internal clock is missing its hands. After a simple procedure Henry is back to normal, except every once in a while, he rings. (48 pages)

Where it's reviewed:
Horn Book Guide, Spring 2000, page 14
Horn Book, November 1999, page 728
Publishers Weekly, August 2, 1999, page 87
School Library Journal, October 1999, page 112

Other books by the same author:
The Ghosts in the Cellar, 1998

The Ghost's Dinner, 1996
The Ghosts' Trip to Loch Ness, 1996

Other books you might like:
Robert Bright, *Georgie*, 1944
    Georgie happily haunts Mr. and Mrs. Whitaker's house, until the step he creaks gets nailed down and he must find another place to stay.
Linda Graham-Barber, *Say Boo!*, 1997
    Little ghost, Ben, must learn to say Boo before Halloween.
Kay Winters, *The Teeny Tiny Ghost*, 1997
    When Halloween arrives the Teeny Tiny Ghost is too scared to spook anyone.

E

288

T. OBINKARAM ECHEWA
E.B. LEWIS, Illustrator

The Magic Tree: A Folktale from Nigeria
(New York: Morrow Junior Books, 1999)

Subject(s): Folklore; Orphans; Behavior
Age range(s): Grades 1-4
Major character(s): Mbi, Orphan, Child
Time period(s): Indeterminate Past
Locale(s): Nigeria

Summary: Mbi lives in a village of unkind, demanding relatives who expect him to respond to their commands. Despite his willingness to comply, no one seems to remember Mbi when food is served so he depends on finding leftovers as he cleans the bowls. One evening while sitting under an udara tree, a piece of ripe fruit drops down to Mbi. Knowing that the tree is not in season, Mbi realizes the magical significance of the gift and, after eating the delicious fruit, he plants the seeds. In a day, Mbi has a fully-grown tree that responds to his commands. The relatives are jealous and try to take the fruit, but only Mbi can control the tree as the villagers soon learn. (32 pages)

Where it's reviewed:
Booklist, June 1999, page 1824
Horn Book Guide, Fall 1999, page 323
Publishers Weekly, June 21, 1999, page 67
School Library Journal, August 1999, page 146

Other books by the same author:
The Ancestor Tree, 1994

Other books you might like:
John Himmelman, *Honest Tulio*, 1997
Although Tulio lacks wealth, family and a home, he is rich in his friends and known for his honesty, a trait that serves him well.
Steven Kellogg, *Jack and the Beanstalk*, 1991
An illustrated retelling of a traditional tale shows what happens when poor Jack plants some magic beans.

Jane Kurtz, *Pulling the Lion's Tale*, 1995
Seeking the love of her stepmother, a girl follows her grandfather's advice and plucks hair from a lion's tail, learning that some things take time.
Emily Arnold McCully, *Little Kit or, the Industrious Flea Circus Girl*, 1995
Mistreated by her dishonest flea circus employer, a young orphan runs away to find a safe home.
John Steptoe, *Mufaro's Beautiful Daughters: An African Tale*, 1987
In an African retelling of the Cinderella story, the kindness of one sister is rewarded, leaving the mean, spiteful sister empty-handed.

289

JULIE ANDREWS EDWARDS
HENRY COLE, Illustrator

Little Bo: The Story of Bonnie Boadicea
(New York: Hyperion Books for Children, 1999)

Subject(s): Animals/Cats; Ships; Pets
Age range(s): Grades 2-4
Major character(s): Boadicea "Bo", Cat; Billy Bates, Sailor
Time period(s): Indeterminate Past
Locale(s): England; *Red Betsy*, At Sea

Summary: Little Bo is one of a litter of six mixed breed kittens born to a purebred champion. The cat's owner orders her butler to deliver five of them to the local pet shop as soon as they are weaned. Unfortunately, the pet shop has more kittens than it needs so the butler makes plans to dispose of the kittens. The kittens escape into the snowy countryside and Bo faces cold and hunger for the first time. Fortunately, she crosses the path of Billy Bates, who gives her shelter for the night with the intention of putting her ashore before his ship sails. By morning Bo vanishes and the *Red Betsy* gets underway with a feline stowaway. The captain, who despises animals on his ship, spots her and the voyage becomes a game of cat and captain as Billy tries to keep Bo safe and out of sight. (88 pages)

Where it's reviewed:
Booklist, February 15, 2000, page 1112
Publishers Weekly, November 1, 1999, page 84
School Library Journal, December 1999, page 94

Other books by the same author:
The Last of the Really Great Whangdoodles, 1974
Mandy, 1971

Other books you might like:
Antonia Barber, *Catkin*, 1994
    A small, but brave cat agrees to enter the land of the little
    people to save a child stolen from her parents.
Pamela D. Greenwood, *I Found Mouse*, 1994
    Tessie finds a kitten in need of a home and convinces her
    dad to let her keep it.
Elke Heidenreich, *Nero Corleone: A Cat's Story*, 1997
    Bold Nero protects his shy sister Rosa by allowing a
    vacationing couple to adopt them as their family pets.
Ursula K. Le Guin, *Wonderful Alexander and the Catwings*,
1994
    When a big, bossy kitten goes exploring, his unexpected
    adventures lead to his introduction to cats with wings.
Joan Sweeney, *Bijou, Bonbon & Beau: The Kittens Who
Danced for Degas*, 1998
    Three kittens born backstage at a Parisian ballet theatre
    endear themselves to everyone but the stage manager who
    tries to evict them.

290

MICHELLE EDWARDS, Author/Illustrator

Pa Lia's First Day

(San Diego: Harcourt Brace and Company, 1999)

Series: Jackson Friends. Book 1
Subject(s): Schools; Friendship; Courage
Age range(s): Grades 1-3
Major character(s): Pa Lia Vang, 2nd Grader; Calliope James,
    2nd Grader, Friend; Howardina "Howie" Smith, 2nd
    Grader, Friend
Time period(s): 1990s (1999)
Locale(s): United States (Jackson Magnet School)

Summary: As Pa Lia dawdles from nervousness on the way to
her new school her brother leaves her in the schoolyard rather
than be late to his own class. Terrified, Pa Lia enters the
building, wondering how to find the second grade classrooms.
After a boy calls her names and knocks her down, Calliope
comes to her rescue and together they go to class. Calliope
introduces Pa Lia to her friend Howie who initially wants
nothing to do with the new student. When Pa Lia demonstrates her courage by admitting to the teacher that her illustrated notes are the reason for Calliope and Howie's giggles
during class, she gains the respect and friendship of both girls.
(50 pages)

Where it's reviewed:
Booklist, November 15, 1999, page 626
The New Advocate, Spring 2000, page 182
Publishers Weekly, September 6, 1999, page 103
School Library Journal, November 1999, page 114

Other books by the same author:
Calliope, 2000
Eve and Smithy: An Iowa Tale, 1994
A Baker's Portrait, 1991
Chicken Man, 1991
Dora's Book, 1990

Other books you might like:
Beverly Cleary, *The Ramona Series*, 1952-1999
    Irrepressible Ramona and her family endure school prob-
    lems and sibling squabbles with love and a sense of humor.
Patricia Reilly Giff, *Today Was a Terrible Day*, 1980
    A kind note from his teacher helps second grader Ronald
    Morgan feel better about his miserable day at school.
Suzanne Williams, *Emily at School*, 1996
    Emily learns that second grade has some unexpected chal-
    lenges, including new student Alex.
Susan Wojciechowski, *Beany (Not Beanhead) and the Magic
Crystal*, 1997
    Beany could use her magic crystal to solve her own prob-
    lems, but instead she unselfishly gives it to an elderly
    neighbor.

291

PAMELA DUNCAN EDWARDS
HENRY COLE, Illustrator

Bravo, Livingstone Mouse!

(New York: Hyperion Books for Children, 2000)

Subject(s): Animals/Mice; Music and Musicians; Animals
Age range(s): Grades K-3
Major character(s): Livingstone Mouse, Mouse, Explorer
Time period(s): Indeterminate
Locale(s): Wild Wood, Fictional Country

Summary: Donning his explorer hat Livingstone Mouse ventures into Wild Wood where he's astonished to find quarrelling, stressed animals preparing for a dance show. None of
the animals are interested in listening to Livingstone's suggestions so he moves on but as he wanders he gathers some
insects that agree with his opinions about the animals need for
rhythm. With the cicada, bee, grasshopper, cricket and katy-
did, Livingstone forms "His Insect Band" and accompanies
each dance number. Thanks to Livingstone the conductor and
his band the show is a success! (32 pages)

Where it's reviewed:
Horn Book Guide, Spring 2001, page 35
Kirkus Reviews, July 15, 2000, page 1037
Publishers Weekly, August 14, 2000, page 357
School Library Journal, October 2000, page 122

Other books by the same author:
Roar!: A Noisy Counting Book, 2000
Honk!, 1998
Livingstone Mouse, 1996
Some Smug Slug, 1996

Other books you might like:
Linda Goss, *The Frog Who Wanted to Be a Singer*, 1996
    Frog overcomes stage fright to realize his desire to sing
    before an audience.

Jonathan London, *Hip Cat*, 1993
    Oobie-do John the Sax Man works hard to achieve his dream of playing jazz.
Ellen Stoll Walsh, *Hop Jump*, 1993
    Betsy is not content to hop and jump as other frogs do so she learns to dance and starts a trend.

292

PAMELA DUNCAN EDWARDS
HENRY COLE, Illustrator

Ed & Fred Flea

(New York: Hyperion Books for Children)

Subject(s): Animals/Insects; Animals/Dogs; Stories in Rhyme
Age range(s): Grades K-2
Major character(s): Ed Flea, Brother, Insect; Fred Flea, Brother, Insect
Time period(s): 1990s
Locale(s): United States

Summary: Ed is content to inhabit the head end of a dog, but Fred is not as happy occupying only the other end. Fred wants the whole canine! When Ed suspects that it is time to move on, Fred fakes illness and refuses to leave. Ed, a fly and a tick bail out leaving a happy Fred to gloat that he now has the entire animal. Alas, greedy Fred's victory dance is cut short by a shower of flea powder. (32 pages)

Where it's reviewed:
Booklist, September 15, 1999, page 266
Children's Bookwatch, November 1999, page 6
Horn Book Guide, Spring 2000, page 34
Publishers Weekly, October 4, 1999, page 74
School Library Journal, September 1999, page 181

Other books by the same author:
Honk!, 1998
Dinorella: A Prehistoric Fairy Tale, 1997
Some Smug Slug, 1996
Four Famished Foxes and Fosdyke, 1995

Other books you might like:
P.D. Eastman, *Go, Dog, Go!*, 1961
    Dogs of varied size, hue and interests cavort in a beginning reader.
Richard Egielski, *Buz*, 1995
    After being swallowed by a child, Buz the bug eludes the medication prescribed by the doctor for the child and saves himself-or so he thinks.
Lisa Westberg Peters, *When the Fly Flew In. . .*, 1994
    When the fly flew into a boy's room it disturbed his sleeping pets with unexpected results.

293

RICHARD EDWARDS
SUSAN WINTER, Illustrator

Copy Me, Copycub

(New York: HarperCollins Publishers, 1999)

Subject(s): Animals/Bears; Behavior; Seasons
Age range(s): Preschool

Major character(s): Copycub, Bear
Time period(s): 1990s (1999)
Locale(s): Earth

Summary: When spring arrives and the bears begin exploring Copycub earns his name by imitating everything his mother does. By following her actions closely through summer and fall, Copycub learns to scratch, to climb trees in search of honey and to wade streams. When his mother tells him they must find a cave, Copycub follows until he becomes disoriented in the falling snow and lies down to sleep. His mother encourages him to keep copying her until they reach the safety of the cave and their long winter's sleep. (32 pages)

Where it's reviewed:
Booklist, September 1999, page 139
Publishers Weekly, July 26, 1999, page 90
School Library Journal, December 1999, page 96

Other books by the same author:
Fly with the Birds, 1996
The Forest Child, 1995
Moon Frog, 1993

Other books you might like:
Dieter Betz, *The Bear Family*, 1992
    A nonfiction title set in the Alaskan wilderness uses photographs to support the story of a grizzly bear and his two cubs.
Ruth Brown, *Copycat*, 1994
    Buddy's tendency to imitate the behaviors of the family's other pets causes a problem when he tries something that is not a good idea for a cat.
Reeve Lindbergh, *North Country Spring*, 1997
    The natural world awakens to the call of spring as bear cubs tumble, geese fly and frogs begin their spring peeping.
Jonathan London, *Honey Paw and Lightfoot*, 1995
    A fictionalized account of a year in the life of a bear includes the birth of Lightfoot and the daily life of a mother and cub.

294

RICHARD EGIELSKI, Author/Illustrator

Three Magic Balls

(New York: Laura Geringer/Harper Collins, 2000)

Subject(s): Magic; Fantasy; Toys
Age range(s): Grades K-2
Major character(s): Rudy, Child, Nephew; Dinkleschmidt, Uncle, Store Owner; Unnamed Character, Aged Person
Time period(s): Indeterminate
Locale(s): Fictional Country

Summary: Two days a week after school Rudy works in Uncle Dinkleschmidt's toy shop which is how he happened to see the strange old lady bring in three balls to sell. Before she vanishes, the woman hands the balls to Uncle Dinkleschmidt and a gold whistle to Rudy, asking him to care for the balls. While Rudy's uncle is away from the shop briefly Rudy hears voices calling to him and he takes the balls out of the cabinet. When he complies with their request and bounces them, the balls change into large rubber men and take off bouncing down the street and into the sky. Although their intentions may be good, the balls create quite a commotion until Rudy blows the gold whistle and the balls magically return to their original shape so Rudy can put them back in the cabinet before Uncle Dinkleschmidt returns. (40 pages)

Where it's reviewed:

Booklist, September 1, 2000, page 121
Bulletin of the Center for Children's Books, September 2000, page 13
Horn Book Guide, Spring 2001, page 14
Publishers Weekly, July 31, 2000, page 93
School Library Journal, September 2000, page 194

Other books by the same author:

Jazper, 1998
The Gingerbread Boy, 1997 (School Library Journal Best Book)
Buz, 1995

Other books you might like:

Lisa Maizlish, *The Ring*, 1996
  After finding a yellow plastic ring in the park, a boy is transported on an imaginary journey over the city.
David McPhail, *The Train*, 1977
  Matthew boards his toy train for a fantastic trip.
Liz Rosenberg, *Eli and Uncle Dawn*, 1997
  The curtain that Uncle Dawn gives Eli becomes a magic flying carpet that takes Eli for a quick ride.

295

LOIS EHLERT, Author/Illustrator

Market Day: A Story Told with Folk Art

(San Diego: Harcourt, Inc., 2000)

Subject(s): Farm Life; Rural Life; Stories in Rhyme
Age range(s): Grades K-3
Time period(s): Indeterminate Past
Locale(s): Fictional Country

Summary: Farm chores are hurriedly completed so carrots can be pulled and loaded in the truck with the other produce. Today is market day in the town square—an opportunity to sell what you have, buy what you need and play when the time allows. When day is done, it's time to load up, return home and get something to eat! (36 pages)

Where it's reviewed:

Bulletin of the Center for Children's Books, July 2000, page 398
Horn Book Guide, Fall 2000, page 248
Kirkus Reviews, May 15, 2000, page 713
Publishers Weekly, May 22, 2000, page 91
School Library Journal, July 2000, page 71

Other books by the same author:

Cuckoo: A Mexican Folktale/Cucu: Un Cuento Folklorico Mexicano, 1997
Hands, 1997
Mole's Hill, 1994

Other books you might like:

Patricia Grossman, *Saturday Market*, 1994
  A Mexican marketplace is busy on Saturday with vendors

selling everything from hand-woven rugs to parrots and sandals.
Paul Brett Johnson, *Farmers' Market*, 1997
  Early on a summer Saturday morning a farm family loads their truck with vegetables to sell at the Farmer's Market.
Katrin Hyman Tchana, *Oh, No, Toto!*, 1997
  When Toto goes to market he's only interested in the food and eating all he can.

296

H.M. EHRLICH
LAURA RADER, Illustrator

Dr. Duck

(New York: Orchard Books, 2000)

Subject(s): Doctors; Illness; Stories in Rhyme
Age range(s): Grades K-1
Major character(s): Dr. Duck, Duck, Doctor
Time period(s): Indeterminate
Locale(s): Fictional Country

Summary: All day Dr. Duck travels in his "Health on Wheels" van. In addition to treating illnesses such as coughs, flu, fevers and measles in his various animal patients Dr. Duck handles accidents for a crow with a broken toe and a mule with a bumped head. By the time Dr. Duck's very busy day ends he's feeling so tired and feverish that he realizes he's become ill. Who will take care of Dr. Duck when he's sick? All the animals that he cares for race to his assistance and soon Dr. Duck is back at work. (36 pages)

Where it's reviewed:

Horn Book Guide, Fall 2000, page 248
Kirkus Reviews, March 1, 2000, page 301
Publishers Weekly, February 28, 2000, page 79
School Library Journal, May 2000, page 140

Other books you might like:

Judy Finchler, *Miss Malarkey Won't Be in Today*, 1998
  When the teacher's sick, a substitute takes over the class and Miss Malarkey sneaks to school to be sure the sub is doing a good job with the students.
Marilyn Hafner, *Mommies Don't Get Sick*, 1995
  Although Daddy tries to care for the children and pets, nothing seems quite right when Mommy is sick.
Vera Rosenberry, *When Vera Was Sick*, 1998
  Mom takes care of Vera when she is sick and her father and sisters try to cheer her too.

297

H.M. EHRLICH
EMILY BOLAM, Illustrator

Louie's Goose

(Boston: Walter Lorraine Books/Houghton Mifflin Company, 2000)

Subject(s): Toys; Animals/Geese; Beaches
Age range(s): Grades K-1
Major character(s): Louie, Child, Son; Rosie, Stuffed Animal, Goose
Time period(s): 2000s (2000)

Locale(s): United States

Summary: Louie enjoys his family's annual beach vacation. This year, time is beginning to catch up with Rosie and she needs repeated mending when first a beak comes loose, then her stuffing begins to ooze out a hole and finally one of her feet breaks off. Patched and mended Rosie is just as lovable as ever to Louie and he drops her on the sand as he builds a sandcastle. Louie doesn't notice a wave carry Rosie away until she's deposited back on shore, very wet and sandy. Louie's parents leave this "fix-it" project to their son so with the help of a towel, a soothing song and a lot of sunshine, Louie dries Rosie. (32 pages)

Where it's reviewed:
Booklist, March 1, 2000, page 1250
Children's Book Review Service, April 2000, page 96
Horn Book Guide, Fall 2000, page 267
Kirkus Reviews, March 15, 2000, page 380
School Library Journal, March 2000, page 196

Other books by the same author:
Dr. Duck, 2000

Other books you might like:
Dorothy Butler, *My Brown Bear Barney*, 1988
　　Life is not complete for one young girl unless Barney is her companion.
Kevin Henkes, *Owen*, 1993
　　Owen carries Fuzzy, a beloved blanket, with him everywhere.
Shulamith Levey Oppenheim, *I Love You, Bunny Rabbit*, 1995
　　Micah's well-worn Bunny Rabbit is soiled with applesauce, chocolate milk and puddle mud, making it irreplaceable.

298

MAX EILENBERG
SUE HEAP, Illustrator

Cowboy Kid

(Cambridge, MA: Candlewick Press, 2000)

Subject(s): Bedtime; Toys; Fathers and Sons
Age range(s): Grades K-1
Major character(s): Cowboy Kid, Child, Son; Sheriff Pa, Father
Time period(s): 2000s (2000)
Locale(s): United States

Summary: In the author's first book, Sheriff Pa tucks Cowboy Kid into bed, but Cowboy Kid has difficulty falling asleep. His stuffed animals are cold and need another hug and a kiss. Then one falls out of bed so Cowboy Kid has to rearrange them and make them cozy in the bed. When he is giving each just one more kiss, Sheriff Pa comes into the bedroom and gives Cowboy Kid and his special friends one last hug and kiss so everyone can get some sleep. (32 pages)

Where it's reviewed:
Booklist, October 15, 2000, page 444
Horn Book Guide, Spring 2001, page 15
Publishers Weekly, May 22, 2000, page 95
School Library Journal, July 2000, page 71

Other books you might like:
Michael Foreman, *Dad! I Can't Sleep*, 1995
　　Dad's going to sleep suggestions for Little Panda fail to produce the desired effect.
Mordicai Gerstein, *Bedtime, Everybody!*, 1996
　　Daisy has difficulty convincing her stuffed animals to settle down for the night.
Sue Heap, *Cowboy Baby*, 1998
　　It takes ingenuity for Sheriff Pa to convince Cowboy Baby and his sidekicks to go to bed.
Christine Loomis, *Cowboy Bunnies*, 1997
　　After playing all day, cowboy bunnies are content to head home at the end of a long day and say good night to their cowboy mamas and papas.

299

DAVID ELLIOTT
PAUL MEISEL, Illustrator

The Cool Crazy Crickets

(Cambridge, MA: Candlewick Press, 2000)

Subject(s): Clubs; Friendship; Summer
Age range(s): Grades 1 3
Major character(s): Leo, Child, Friend; Marcus, Child, Friend; Miranda, Child, Friend; Phoebe, Child, Friend
Time period(s): 2000s (2000)
Locale(s): United States

Summary: A hot summer day is a perfect time for four friends to start a club. After agreeing on a name they try to find a location for their meetings. They visit and reject Phoebe's room (too messy) and Marcus's room that he shares with a younger brother (too loud) and race to Leo's house just as a new refrigerator is being delivered. With an extra box from the truck the Cool Crazy Crickets begin their first project—building their clubhouse. Miranda paints the exterior, Leo makes a secret entrance, and Marcus constructs a booby trap to deter spies. After selecting a mascot the club members are temporarily stymied by deciding on a purpose for the club until they agree to be friends for life. (48 pages)

Where it's reviewed:
Booklist, September 15, 2000, page 240
Horn Book Guide, Fall 2000, page 292
Kirkus Reviews, June 1, 2000, page 795
Publishers Weekly, June 26, 2000, page 75
School Library Journal, August 2000, page 154

Other books by the same author:
The Cool Crazy Crickets to the Rescue, 2001
Transmogrification of Roscoe Wizzle, 2001
An Alphabet of Rotten Kids!, 1991

Other books you might like:
Bill Cosby, *Hooray for the Dandelion Warriors!*, 1999
　　In this beginning reader in the "Little Bill" series a group of friends comprising a coed baseball team argue about the team name.
Johanna Hurwitz, *The Just Desserts Club*, 1999
　　Cricket's club cooks only desserts for school events.
Sara Swan Miller, *Better than TV*, 1998
　　A power outage is no deterrent to two siblings who simply

create their own TV shows to entertain their family during the storm.

Julia Noonan, *Hare and Rabbit: Friends Forever*, 2000
In one of three chapters about Hare and Rabbit the friends share the task of spring-cleaning their home in a Level 3 Hello Reader title.

Suzanne Williams, *Edwin and Emily*, 1995
A beginning chapter book relates both the joys and the challenges faced by friends.

300

SARAH ELLIS
RUTH OHI, Illustrator

Next Stop!

(Toronto: Fitzhenry & Whiteside, 2000)

Subject(s): Transportation; City and Town Life; Parent and Child
Age range(s): Grades K-1
Major character(s): Claire, Child, Daughter; Dad, Father, Driver (bus); Mom, Mother
Time period(s): 2000 (2000)
Locale(s): Canada

Summary: When Claire rides the bus on Saturday she sits near the front and helps the driver. Each time the driver announces a street, Claire adds an attraction for the stop such as museum or shopping mall. Claire observes who gets on and off the bus and when someone's cell phone rings. After many stops a smiling woman boards the bus and kisses Claire who is happy to see Mom. Then Mom kisses the bus driver, Claire's Dad, and the other riders on the bus smile. Next stop—home! (32 pages)

Where it's reviewed:
Booklist, December 1, 2000, page 718
School Library Journal, January 2001, page 93

Other books you might like:
Cari Best, *Red Light, Green Light, Mama and Me*, 1995
Lizzie rides the subway with Mama all the way to her job at the downtown library.
Bruce McMillan, *Grandfather's Trolley*, 1995
A little girl sits in the back seat of the trolley and rides to the end of the line with her grandfather, the conductor.
Mary Quattlebaum, *Underground Train*, 1997
A little girl enjoys a subway ride with her mother.

301

KAREN ENGLISH
ANNA RICH, Illustrator

Just Right Stew

(Honesdale: Boyds Mills Press, 1998)

Subject(s): Family Life; Cooks and Cooking; African Americans
Age range(s): Grades K-3
Major character(s): Victoria, Child; Big Mama, Grandmother
Time period(s): 1990s
Locale(s): United States

Summary: It's Big Mama's birthday and her daughters want to cook her favorite meal—oxtail stew. Each sister has a suggestion about what Big Mama's secret ingredient is, but it's Victoria, Big Mama's granddaughter, who adds the secret ingredient in the end—just in time for a perfect stew. (32 pages)

Where it's reviewed:
Booklist, February 15, 1998, page 1019
Children's Book Review Service, March 1998, page 89
Kirkus Reviews, February 1, 1998, page 196
Publishers Weekly, January 12, 1998, page 59
School Library Journal, March 1998, page 129

Other books by the same author:
Nadia's Hands, 1999
Big Wind Coming!, 1996
Neeny Coming, Neeny Going, 1996

Other books you might like:
Cathryn Falwell, *Feast for 10*, 1993
An African-American family prepares a chicken dinner for ten people.
Maryann MacDonald, *Hedgehog Bakes a Cake*, 1990
Hedgehog's cake preparations are interrupted repeatedly as friends stop and offer advice.
Jerdine Nolen, *In My Momma's Kitchen*, 1999
A young girl describes events that center around her mother's kitchen.
Sylvia Rosa-Casanova, *Mama Provi and the Pot of Rice*, 1997
Mama Provi begins the long walk up to her sick granddaughter's apartment with a pot of arroz con pollo and ends with a multicultural feast.
Leyla Torres, *Saturday Sancocho*, 1995
On Saturday, Maria Lili and Mama Ana barter their eggs at the market for the chicken needed to make the sancocho.

302

KAREN ENGLISH
JONATHAN WEINER, Illustrator

Nadia's Hands

(Honesdale, PA: Boyds Mill Press, 1999)

Subject(s): Weddings; Difference; Cultures and Customs
Age range(s): Grades K-3
Major character(s): Nadia, Child
Time period(s): 1990s (1999)
Locale(s): United States

Summary: Nadia, a Pakistani-American girl, while thrilled to be chosen as the flower girl in her aunt's traditional wedding, is also somewhat apprehensive. For the wedding Nadia's hands will be decorated with mehndi (henna paste) and Nadia worries about the reactions of others. What will the kids at school think when she shows up with intricate designs on her hands? When Nadia sees how happy her entire family is with her willingness to participate in their cultural heritage, Nadia also feels pride, and decides to use her hands as show and tell at school. (32 pages)

Where it's reviewed:
Booklist, March 1, 1999, page 1220
Horn Book Guide, Fall 1999, page 250

Kirkus Reviews, February 1, 1999, page 221
School Library Journal, April 1999, page 92

Other books by the same author:
Just Right Stew, 1998
Big Wind Coming!, 1996
Neeny Coming, Neeny Going, 1996

Other books you might like:
Eleanor Schick, *Navajo Wedding Day: A Dine Marriage Ceremony*, 1999
   A little girl attends a Navajo wedding ceremony with her best friend.
Gary Soto, *Snapshots from the Wedding*, 1997
   Maya, the flower girl, narrates the events of a Mexican-American wedding ceremony.
Jane Breskin Zalben, *Beni's First Wedding*, 1998
   Beni serves as the ring bearer in a traditional Jewish wedding.

303

LOUISE ERDRICH, Author/Illustrator

The Birchbark House
(New York: Hyperion Books for Children, 1999)

Subject(s): Indians of North America; Islands; Seasons
Age range(s): Grades 4-7
Major character(s): Omakayas, 7-Year-Old, Indian (Ojibwa); Old Tallow, Indian (Ojibwa), Aged Person; Andeg, Bird (crow)
Time period(s): 1840s (1847)
Locale(s): La Pointe, Minnesota (an island in Lake Superior)

Summary: Omakayas and her family follow the traditional ways of the Anishinabeg people on Moningwanaykaning, the Island of the Golden-Breasted Woodpecker. In the summer they leave their cabin near the village for another part of the island where they build a birchbark house. Their daily labor includes gathering food, scraping hides and protecting the corn crop from the crows. A natural harmony with nature and animals protects Omakayas from a mother bear and allows her to shelter an injured crow that soon becomes her pet, Andeg. Curmudgeonly Old Tallow, who seems to have a special fondness for Omakayas and her family, shares food from her hunting trips and helps Omakayas care for her family during a winter outbreak of small pox in the village. A concluding glossary defines the Ojibwa terms. (244 pages)

Where it's reviewed:
Booklist, April 1, 1999, page 1427
Horn Book, May 1999, page 329
Publishers Weekly, May 31, 1999, page 94
Riverbank Review, Summer 1999, page 33
School Library Journal, May 1999, page 122

Awards the book has won:
ALA Notable Children's Books, 2000
Publishers Weekly Best Books, 1999

Other books by the same author:
Grandmother's Pigeon, 1996

Other books you might like:
Leigh Casler, *The Boy Who Dreamed of an Acorn*, 1994
   A young Indian boy learns to appreciate the symbolism of his dream about an acorn when he is reminded that it is the source of a mighty tree.
Diane Johnston Hamm, *Daughter of Suqua*, 1997
   As the life of the Suquamish people rapidly changes ten-year-old Ida learns the traditional ways of her people from her grandmother.
Manitonquat, *The Children of the Morning Light: Wampanoag Tales*, 1994
   The traditional stories of the Wampanoag people include those of creation and some that explain life and death.

304

LISA CAMPBELL ERNST, Author/Illustrator

Goldilocks Returns
(New York: Simon & Schuster Books for Young Readers, 2000)

Subject(s): Fairy Tales; Animals/Bears; Humor
Age range(s): Grades K-3
Major character(s): Goldi, Store Owner; Papa Bear, Father, Bear; Mama Bear, Mother, Bear
Time period(s): Indeterminate
Locale(s): Fictional Country

Summary: Fifty years after a naughty little girl with golden curls created problems in the home of three bears she continues to live with the guilt of her actions. She's now known as Goldi, operates a lock and key shop and is determined to right the wrongs of her past. Loading her truck with supplies, Goldi heads back to the house in the woods just after Mama Bear, Papa Bear and their son have left for their morning walk. First Goldi puts multiple locks on the door so others can't break in. Then she replaces the porridge with healthy breakfast bars and celery juice and redecorates the living room. Upstairs Goldi corrects the beds so they'll be just right—according to her standards. When the bears return to find Goldi sleeping she hugs each of them, hands them the keys and takes off in her truck. Mama Bear, Papa Bear and their grown son are so horrified at the changes Goldi has made in their home that when they forget to use the new locks while walking the next morning they hope that the little child they see in the woods will pay them a visit and history will repeat itself. (40 pages)

Where it's reviewed:
Booklist, April 1, 2000, page 1468
Bulletin of the Center for Children's Books, May 2000, page 315
Horn Book Guide, Fall 2000, page 267
Publishers Weekly, June 12, 2000, page 72
School Library Journal, May 2000, page 140

Other books by the same author:
Stella Louella's Runaway Book, 1998
Duke the Dairy Delight Dog, 1996
Little Red Riding Hood: A Newfangled Prairie Tale, 1995
Squirrel Park, 1993

Other books you might like:

Alma Flor Ada, *Yours Truly, Goldilocks*, 1998
  With Peter Rabbit, Goldilocks attends a housewarming for three little pigs.

Jan Brett, *Goldilocks and the Three Bears*, 1987
  This illustrated retelling is true to the original tale of a young girl who seeks shelter in a home, falls asleep and is found by three bears.

James Marshall, *Goldilocks and the Three Bears*, 1988
  In a humorous version of the tale, three bears returning from a walk discover someone sleeping in Baby Bear's bed.

Betty Miles, *Goldilocks and the Three Bears*, 1988
  The traditional tale of the girl in the three bears' home is retold as a beginning reader.

Jane Yolen, *The Three Bears Rhyme Book*, 1987
  Sixteen poems describe the activities of Goldie and the three bears while walking, eating porridge and attending a birthday party.

305

KRISTYN REHLING ESTES
CLAIRE B. COTTS, Illustrator

Manuela's Gift

(San Francisco: Chronicle Books, 1999)

Subject(s): Birthdays; Gifts; Family Life
Age range(s): Grades K-2
Major character(s): Manuela, Child, Daughter; Mama, Mother; Papa, Father, Farmer
Time period(s): 1990s
Locale(s): Mexico

Summary: For her birthday, Manuela asks for a new yellow dress so she is quietly disappointed when her gift is a blue dress made from one of Mama's old ones. When she goes to the barn to feed the chickens, Manuela sees the pinata waiting for her party and imagines it filled with all the things her family needs—chicks and eggs, rain for Papa's crops and a horse to carry tired grandmother. Her reverie helps her feel more appreciative of her gift so she is able to wear the blue dress happily at her party as the author's first book concludes. (32 pages)

Where it's reviewed:

Booklist, June 1999, page 1840
Horn Book Guide, Fall 1999, page 251
School Library Journal, October 1999, page 112

Other books you might like:

Antonio Hernandez Madrigal, *Erandi's Braids*, 1999
  Erandi's selflessness gives the family enough money to repair Mama's fishing net and pay for the yellow dress Erandi wants for her birthday.

Pat Mora, *A Birthday Basket for Tia*, 1992
  Cecilia has an idea for a special birthday gift for her beloved great aunt.

Andrea Spalding, *Sarah May and the New Red Dress*, 1999
  Sarah May's wish for a red dress comes true when a rainstorm washes the blue dye from her new dress and she selects the dye to recolor the garment.

306

DOUGLAS EVANS

The Elevator Family

(New York: Delacorte Press, 2000)

Subject(s): Hotels and Motels; Vacations; Family
Age range(s): Grades 3-5
Major character(s): Walter Wilson, Father; Winona Wilson, Mother; Whitney Wilson, 10-Year-Old, Twin; Winslow Wilson, 10-Year-Old, Twin
Time period(s): 2000s (2000)
Locale(s): San Francisco, California

Summary: The vacationing Wilson family arrives at the San Francisco Hotel to learn that all the rooms are booked. However, they notice a lovely little room just off the lobby with a phone and piped in music that Walter is sure will do nicely for their three-day stay. As they settle into the little room Winona expresses pleasure with the different views on the various floors where the doors open, Winslow's fascinated by the buttons and Whitney is the first to notice that their room doesn't have a number, but a name—Otis. The cheerful family sees nothing odd about their room and during their stay they not only provide a peaceful respite for other guests but also, by observing the activity on the different floors, solve a kidnapping. (87 pages)

Where it's reviewed:

Booklist, May 1, 2000, page 1667
Bulletin of the Center for Children's Books, July 2000, page 398
Horn Book Guide, Fall 2000, page 303
Kirkus Reviews, May 15, 2000, page 713
Publishers Weekly, June 19, 2000, page 80

Other books by the same author:

Apple Island, or, the Truth About Teachers, 1998
So What Do You Do?, 1997
The Classroom at the End of the Hall, 1996

Other books you might like:

David A. Adler, *Cam Jansen and the Catnapping Mystery*, 1998
  Cam passes the time in a hotel lobby observing guests' arrivals and uses her photographic memory of what she sees to recover a guest's stolen cat.

Suzy Kline, *Horrible Harry and the Drop of Doom*, 1998
  Harry would have a horrible time vacationing with the Wilson family—he's afraid of elevators.

Phyllis Reynolds Naylor, *The Bodies in the Bessledorf Hotel*, 1986
  If dead bodies don't stop appearing at the hotel Bernie is afraid his dad might lose his job as manager and thus his family's home.

307

ROBYN EVERSOLE
TIM COFFEY, Illustrator

Red Berry Wool

(Morton Grove, IL: Albert Whitman & Company, 1999)

Subject(s): Animals/Sheep; Farm Life; Clothes
Age range(s): Grades K-2
Major character(s): Lalo, Sheep; Boy, Child, Shepherd
Time period(s): 1990s (1999)
Locale(s): United States

Summary: Lalo is the smartest lamb in the flock so it's no surprise when he notices Boy's new red sweater. When Lalo's mom tells him that the sweater is made from the flock's wool Lalo asks the process and then proceeds to follow each step, using his wool coat, in order to make his own sweater. Unfortunately when Lalo washes the wool he almost drowns and must be rescued by Boy. Then when he ''spins'' the wool by turning himself around repeatedly he becomes so dizzy that he falls off a cliff and Boy rescues him again. While Lalo rolls in the berry bushes to dye his wool, a snake bites him and once more Boy comes to his aid. Finally, as Lalo and Boy sit watching a sunset Lalo decides the knitting process is complete for he and Boy are certainly together. (32 pages)

Where it's reviewed:
Booklist, September 1, 1999, page 139

Children's Bookwatch, November 1999, page 6
Horn Book Guide, Spring 2000, page 34
Kirkus Reviews, July 15, 1999, page 1132
School Library Journal, October 1999, page 112

Other books by the same author:
The Gift Stone, 1998
Flood Fish, 1995
The Magic House, 1992

Other books you might like:
Elsa Beskow, *Pelle's New Suit*, 1929
    Pelle observes the progress of his new suit from the shearing of the fleece to the final tailoring.
Tomie DePaola, *Charlie Needs a Cloak*, 1973
    A shepherd shears the sheep to begin the process of preparing the wool needed to create a cloak.
Satoshi Kitamura, *Sheep in Wolves' Clothing*, 1996
    Wolves with a knit shop steal fleece from three sheep and by the time the sheep recover their coats they are colorful additions to the meadow.
Ragnhild Scamell, *Three Bags Full*, 1993
    Kindly Millie gives away so much of her fleece that Mrs. Farmer must knit a sweater to warm the sheep through the winter.
Barbara Brooks Wallace, *Argyle*, 1987
    Perhaps it's something the sheep ate; the multi-colored fleece that he grows creates great changes on the farm.

F

308

IAN FALCONER, Author/Illustrator

Olivia

(New York: Anne Schwartz Book/Atheneum Books for Young Readers, 2000)

Subject(s): Animals/Pigs; Behavior; Family Life
Age range(s): Grades K-3
Major character(s): Olivia, Pig, Sister (older); Ian, Pig, Brother (younger); Unnamed Character, Mother, Pig
Time period(s): Indeterminate
Locale(s): Fictional Country

Summary: In the author's first book independent Olivia meets life on her terms. She tolerates Ian, up to a point, and then must be firm if he bothers her too much. She can't get dressed without trying on every outfit in the closet. Olivia is always well prepared for every activity, except the time she forgets the sunscreen during a trip to the beach. At naptime when she's not sleepy Olivia simply practices her dancing. After a visit to an art museum with Ian and their mother Olivia returns home and demonstrates (on the wall) her ability to paint just like one of the artists. Olivia gets a time out and a bath instead of an exhibition of her work. At bedtime Olivia is still not tired, but after reading books with her mother she manages to sleep and dream. What's next, Olivia? (40 pages)

Where it's reviewed:
Booklist, August 2000, page 2134
Horn Book Guide, Spring 2001, page 36
Kirkus Reviews, August 1, 2000, page 1116
Publishers Weekly, July 17, 2000, page 193
School Library Journal, September 2000, page 196

Awards the book has won:
Booklist Editors' Choice, 2000
School Library Journal Best Books, 2000

Other books you might like:
Kevin Henkes, *Lilly's Purple Plastic Purse*, 1996
    Self-assured and impatient Lilly makes a bad decision when her teacher tells her to wait until later to show her new purse to the class.
Holly Keller, *Merry Christmas, Geraldine*, 1997
    Geraldine, a pig with a mind of her own, hauls home the biggest tree on the lot, despite the obvious—it won't fit in the house—and makes her plan work.
Susan Meddaugh, *Hog-Eye*, 1995
    A literate, confident pig uses her reading ability to outwit a wolf intent on making her into his next meal.

309

MATT FAULKNER, Author/Illustrator

Black Belt

(New York: Alfred A. Knopf, 2000)

Subject(s): Martial Arts; Bullies; Time Travel
Age range(s): Grades 1-3
Major character(s): Bushi, Student, Bullied Child; Yag-yu, Bully, Student; Mr. Oji, Teacher, Martial Arts Expert
Time period(s): 2000s; Indeterminate Past
Locale(s): Japan

Summary: The older students at Bushi's school make a sport of bullying the younger students. One day when Yag-yu begins to pick on Bushi, the younger child decides he's had enough so he wrestles free of Yag-yu's grasp and runs from the group of boys. To hide from them he takes shelter in a karate studio, tries on a black belt and is magically transported to another time and place. There he observes a great master with his students and learns important lessons before he awakens back in the studio as student's arrive for class. Mr. Oji invites him to stay for class and suggests he begin attending regularly. The next day after school Bushi applies what he learned from his previous day's experiences to his interactions with the bullies at his school and then proceeds safely to Mr. Oji's class. (40 pages)

Where it's reviewed:
Booklist, May 1, 2000, page 1667
Children's Book Review Service, August 2000, page 156
Horn Book Guide, Spring 2001, page 61

Publishers Weekly, June 5, 2000, page 94
School Library Journal, August 2000, page 154

Other books by the same author:
The Amazing Voyage of Jackie Grace, 1987

Other books you might like:
Elizabeth Levy, *The Karate Class Mystery*, 1996
    In the fifth series entry Justin's karate belt is stolen and Invisible Inc. springs into action to solve the mystery and retrieve the belt.
Emily Arnold McCully, *Beautiful Warrior: The Legend of the Nun's Kung Fu*, 1998
    Martial art skill is used in an award-winning title to overpower a gang leader and save a young woman from an unwanted marriage.
Brian Pinkney, *JoJo's Flying Side Kick*, 1995
    JoJo uses advice from Grandaddy, P.J. and her mother to achieve a feared goal in her martial arts class.

310

JAN FEARNLEY, Author/Illustrator

Mr. Wolf's Pancakes

(Waukesha, WI: Little Tiger Press, 1999)

Subject(s): Animals/Wolves; Determination; Cooks and Cooking
Age range(s): Grades 1-2
Major character(s): Mr. Wolf, Wolf
Time period(s): Indeterminate
Locale(s): Fictional Country

Summary: Mr. Wolf has a hankering for pancakes but he's never made them before so he looks for a recipe in a cookbook. Mr. Wolf doesn't read well either, but when his neighbor refuses to help, Mr. Wolf reads the book himself. Each time Mr. Wolf needs help whether to write his list, count his money, borrow a shopping basket or cook the pancakes the neighbor that he asks yells no and slams the door in his face. Sad Mr. Wolf cooks the pancakes without help and is just ready to eat the stack when the hungry neighbors, drawn by the smell, come knocking on his door. At first Mr. Wolf isn't inclined to share, but then he lets the rude, demanding group into his home, closes the door and gobbles up the unruly group—before returning to his stack of delicious pancakes. First published in Great Britain in 1999. (32 pages)

Where it's reviewed:
Bulletin of the Center for Children's Books, February 2000, page 207
Children's Book Review Service, March 2000, page 84
Horn Book, March 2000, page 184
Kirkus Reviews, January 1, 2000, page 58
Publishers Weekly, January 10, 2000, page 67

Other books by the same author:
Just Like You, 2001
A Special Something, 2000
Little Robin's Christmas, 1998

Other books you might like:
Alma Flor Ada, *Yours Truly, Goldilocks*, 1998
    Fer O'Cious and his cousin plan to ambush the guests as they depart the little pigs' housewarming party.

Susan Meddaugh, *Hog-Eye*, 1995
    A literate pig uses her reading ability to outwit a wolf intent on making her into his next meal.
Margie Palatini, *Piggie Pie!*, 1995
    Hungry witch Gritch is so frustrated by her unsuccessful quest for eight piggies to put in a pie that she accepts a wolf's invitation to lunch.

311

JULES FEIFFER, Author/Illustrator

Bark, George

(New York: Michael diCapua Books/HarperCollins Publishers, 1999)

Subject(s): Animals/Dogs; Mothers and Sons; Humor
Age range(s): Grades K-2
Major character(s): George, Dog; Unnamed Character, Mother, Dog; Unnamed Character, Veterinarian
Time period(s): 1990s (1999)
Locale(s): United States

Summary: Each time George's mother asks the pup to bark he emits another animal's sound. After hearing meow, quack, oink and moo from George, his mother gives up and takes him to the vet. Donning his latex gloves, the vet reaches into George's mouth after he barks ''Meow'' and pulls out a cat. Quickly, a duck, pig and cow follow and George leaves the vet's office with his relieved mother. The proud mama wants to show off George's barking skill to the passersby on the street so she tells him to bark and he obligingly responds, ''Hello.'' (32 pages)

Where it's reviewed:
Booklist, August 1999, page 2052
Five Owls, September 1999, page 14
Publishers Weekly, June 21, 1999, page 66
School Library Journal, September 1999, page 182

Awards the book has won:
Booklist Editors' Choice, 1999
School Library Journal Best Books, 1999

Other books by the same author:
I Lost My Bear, 1998
Meanwhile. . ., 1997

Other books you might like:
Robert Bender, *A Most Unusual Lunch*, 1994
    In this food chain hierarchy, no animal adopts another's sound, but each takes on other physical characteristics of the animal just eaten.
David McPhail, *The Glerp*, 1972
    While walking, the Glerp swallows everything in its path until the elephant's tusks get stuck and cause all the swallowed animals to be coughed out.
Simms Taback, *There Was an Old Lady Who Swallowed a Fly*, 1997
    Inventive illustrations in a Caldecott Honor Book tell of the many animals swallowed by the old lady to counteract the tickling fly inside her.

312

EUGENIE FERNANDES, Author/Illustrator

A Difficult Day

(Buffalo, NY: Kids Can Press, 1999)

Subject(s): Mothers and Daughters; Love; Behavior
Age range(s): Grades K-2
Major character(s): Melinda, Student—Elementary School, Daughter; Unnamed Character, Mother
Time period(s): 1980s
Locale(s): Canada

Summary: After a poor night's sleep Melinda hurries unhappily to school where her day goes from bad to worse. When she arrives home she argues with her mother and is sent to her room for her rude behavior. Feeling unloved Melinda crawls under her bed and imagines traveling to the other side of the world where people will love her and console her when she's feeling bad. Melinda's mom realizes her daughter's having a difficult day and brings milk and cookies to her room but she can't find Melinda. She searches frantically for Melinda until she hears a little voice coming from Melinda's hiding place. Melinda's day improves after she shares milk and cookies with her mother under the bed. Originally published in Canada in 1987. (32 pages)

Where it's reviewed:
Booklist, May 15, 1999, page 1702
Candian Book Review Annual 1999, page 454
Horn Book Guide, Fall 1999, page 251
Publishers Weekly, April 26, 1999, page 81

Other books by the same author:
Sleepy Little Mouse, 2000
Baby Dreams, 1999
One Light, One Sun, 1999
Just You and Me, 1993

Other books you might like:
Miranda Hapgood, *Martha's Mad Day*, 1977
   Martha wakes up in a bad mood that stays with her all the long mad day.
Anita Jeram, *Contrary Mary*, 1995
   Mary is having an uncooperative day. She puts her shoes on the wrong feet, refuses to walk under the umbrella and reads books upside down.
Anne F. Rockwell, *No! No! No!*, 1995
   After a little boy has a difficult day, listening to a bedtime story gives him hope that tomorrow will be better.
Alice Schertle, *Down the Road*, 1995
   Hetty is having a good day until she breaks the breakfast eggs. When her parents find her hiding in an apple tree they climb up to join her.
Maurice Sendak, *Where the Wild Things Are*, 1963
   Max is angry to be sent to his room so he sails away to the Land of the Wild Things, but he makes sure he's home in time for dinner.

313

D.H. FIGUEREDO
ENRIQUE O. SANCHEZ, Illustrator

When This World Was New

(New York: Lee & Low Books, 1999)

Subject(s): Emigration and Immigration; Fear; Winter
Age range(s): Grades K-3
Major character(s): Danilito, Son, Immigrant; Papa, Father, Immigrant; Mama, Mother, Immigrant
Time period(s): 1990s (1999)
Locale(s): United States

Summary: In the author's first book, Danilito is overwhelmed to leave his warm Caribbean island for cold, wintry America. Clutching Mama's hand he stands, frightened, in the airport surrounded by people who do not speak Spanish. A relative meets the relieved family and drives them to their new home, already stocked with food and winter clothes. Papa is worried about finding work and medical treatment for his wife while Danilito is frightened to think of attending an English-speaking school. The morning after their arrival, Papa awakens Danilito to prepare him for school, but first the two of them venture outside into their first snowfall. (32 pages)

Where it's reviewed:
Booklist, June 1999, page 1841
Horn Book Guide, Fall 1999, page 251
Publishers Weekly, May 17, 1999, page 77
School Library Journal, June 1999, page 70

Other books you might like:
Arthur Dorros, *Abuela*, 1991
   A glimpse of the Statue of Liberty reminds Rosalba of her arrival in the United States.
Luis Garay, *The Long Road*, 1997
   Political unrest forces Jose and his mother to seek refuge in another country where they must adjust to a different culture and language.
Barbara M. Joosse, *The Morning Chair*, 1995
   Quiet times with mom in the morning chair help Bram adjust to life in a strange, new country.
Ellen Levine, *I Hate English!*, 1989
   The sounds of America are strange to immigrant Mei Mei's ears as she tries to adjust to school and learn a new language.

314

ANNE FINE

Bad Dreams

(New York: Delacorte Press, 2000)

Subject(s): Books and Reading; Friendship; Magic
Age range(s): Grades 4-6
Major character(s): Imogen Tate, Child, Student; Melanie "Mel" Palmer, Student, Friend; Mr. Hooper, Teacher
Time period(s): 2000s (2000)
Locale(s): England

Summary: Retiring Mel is content to go through life with her nose in a book so she's less than pleased when Mr. Hooper assigns the new student to her. It doesn't take long for Mel to notice that Imogen is an unusual person, one that others avoid. While Mel thinks the library and the class book corner are the best places in the school, Imogen appears uneasy when she is near books. As their friendship develops, Mel convinces Imogen to trust her with the story of her ''gift'' to see the reality of the people captured in a book or a photograph. Mel also realizes that this gift is truly a curse and she's determined to use the knowledge gained from years of reading to find the answer and free Imogen. (133 pages)

Where it's reviewed:
Booklist, May 1, 2000, page 1667
Horn Book Guide, Fall 2000, page 303
School Library Journal, June 2000, page 144

Other books by the same author:
The Tulip Touch, 1997 (ALA Notable Book)
Step by Wicked Step, 1996 (School Library Journal Best Book)
The Chicken Gave It to Me, 1993

Other books you might like:
Allan Ahlberg, *The Better Brown Stories*, 1996
    The Brown family visits the Writer to suggest that he liven up their boring lives a little when he writes the next story about them.
Peggy Christian, *The Bookstore Mouse*, 1995
    When the bookstore mouse stumbles into a very old book he finds himself immersed in a story about medieval England.
Edward Eager, *Half Magic*, 1954
    Through trial and error four children learn to double their wishes when they realize the old coin they find is only half magic.
Hazel Hutchins, *The Prince of Tarn*, 1997
    The very spoiled Prince of Tarn, a book character, mysteriously appears in Fred's room, demanding to go home.
Gail Carson Levine, *The Wish*, 2000
    Unpopular Wilma, granted one wish, makes a hasty choice, but learns a great deal about friendship while fulfilling the wish.
Yvonne MacGrory, *The Secret of the Ruby Ring*, 1994
    On her eleventh birthday Lucy receives a magical ruby ring from her grandmother.

315

EDITH HOPE FINE
RENE KING MORENO, Illustrator

Under the Lemon Moon

(New York: Lee & Low Books, Inc., 1999)

Subject(s): Trees; Forgiveness; Stealing
Age range(s): Grades K-3
Major character(s): Rosalinda, Child; Abuela, Grandmother; Anciana, Spirit
Time period(s): 1990s (1999)
Locale(s): Mexico

Summary: During the night a thief strips Rosalinda's prize lemon tree of all its fruit. In the week that follows, the tree's leaves yellow as Rosalinda seeks help from other villagers and Abuela. Only Abuela suggests that Rosalinda search for La Anciana who is known to have the power to make things grow. While searching, Rosalinda sees the thief and his family in the marketplace selling her lemons and she calls again to Anciana. When Anciana appears she gives Rosalinda a tree branch with instructions to use it to heal the tree. Under the light of the full lemon moon Rosalinda complies with Anciana's gesture, healing both the lemon tree and her own heart. (32 pages)

Where it's reviewed:
Booklist, May 15, 1999, page 1702
Horn Book Guide, Fall 1999, page 251
Publishers Weekly, April 19, 1999, page 72
School Library Journal, April 1999, page 94
Smithsonian Magazine, November 1999, page 50

Awards the book has won:
Smithsonian's Notable Books for Children, 1999
Notable Social Studies Trade Books for Young People, 2000

Other books by the same author:
Big on Bugs, 1992
Fantastic Flight, 1992
The Turtle and Tortoise, 1988

Other books you might like:
Alma Flor Ada, *The Gold Coin*, 1991
    When a thief learns an old healer woman has a gold coin he is so intent on stealing it that he travels the countryside searching for her.
Patricia Grossman, *Saturday Market*, 1994
    Artisans display a variety of wares at a weekly Mexican market.
Tony Johnston, *The Magic Maguey*, 1996
    Children in a Mexican village save a large maguey plant from destruction so that it can continue to be used by the community.

316

MARIE-LOUISE FITZPATRICK, Author/Illustrator

Lizzy and Skunk

(New York: DKInk, Dorling Kindersley Publishing, Inc., 2000)

Subject(s): Fear; Toys; Self-Confidence
Age range(s): Grades K-2
Major character(s): Lizzy, Child; Skunk, Puppet
Time period(s): 2000s (2000)
Locale(s): Ireland

Summary: In the author/illustrator's first book Lizzy has many fears that do not seem as frightening when she has Skunk on her hand, leading the way. Skunk doesn't get stage fright or worry about making mistakes. Skunk's not afraid of the dark or of falling either. When Skunk becomes lost, Lizzy has to conquer all her fears in order to find Skunk. Alone Lizzy searches the dark places under the bed and in the attic. When she overhears passersby commenting about a skunk in a tree Lizzy races to the tree and climbs it in order to save Skunk— all by herself. (32 pages)

Where it's reviewed:
Booklist, May 1, 2000, page 1677
Horn Book Guide, Fall 2000, page 248

Publishers Weekly, May 1, 2000, page 69
School Library Journal, July 2000, page 72

Awards the book has won:
School Library Journal Best Books, 2000

Other books you might like:
Kim Lewis, *My Friend Harry*, 1995
James and Harry, a toy elephant, go everywhere together until James begins school.
Clara Vulliamy, *Ellen and Penguin*, 1993
Until they meet a little girl with a toy monkey Ellen and her penguin are too shy to join the children playing at the park.
Martin Waddell, *Small Bear Lost*, 1996
When Small Bear is accidentally left on a train he manages to find his way home to the little girl who lost him.
Ellen Stoll Walsh, *Pip's Magic*, 1994
In the process of searching for magic answers to his fear of the dark, Pip overcomes his problem on his own.
Selina Young, *Ned*, 1993
Emily and Ned, a green cloth donkey, are inseparable until Ned is lost, and then found again, on the first day of school.

317

PAUL FLEISCHMAN
C.B. MORDAN, Illustrator

Lost!: A Story in String

(New York: Henry Holt and Company, 2000)

Subject(s): Survival; Grandmothers; Storytelling
Age range(s): Grades 2-4
Major character(s): Grandmother, Grandmother, Storyteller; Unnamed Character, Child
Time period(s): 2000s (2000); Indeterminate Past
Locale(s): United States (urban area); United States (rural mountains)

Summary: During a storm—caused lack of power a young girl laments her inability to use electrical gadgetry and wonders what she'll do for entertainment. Grandmother tells her a story of a girl so poor that she has only a piece of string for a toy and with it she occupies her time in a small cabin and for days in the woods when she becomes lost while trailing her dog in a snow storm. The granddaughter is impressed to hear this story from Grandmother's childhood and tries to create a string story of her own. The history of string figures and instructions for making the ones used in the story conclude the book. (32 pages)

Where it's reviewed:
Booklist, July 2000, page 2038
Horn Book Guide, Fall 2000, page 292
Publishers Weekly, May 22, 2000, page 93
School Library Journal, June 2000, page 112

Other books by the same author:
Seedfolks, 1997
Time Train, 1991
Shadow Play: Story, 1990
Joyful Noise: Poems for Two Voices, 1988 (Newbery Medal)

Other books you might like:
Anne Akers Johnson, *Cat's Cradle: A Book of String Figures*, 1993

A nonfiction title gives clear directions for making a variety of string figures.
Natalie Kinsey-Warnock, *The Bear that Heard Crying*, 1993
A toddler lost in the woods near her family's colonial homestead is cared for by a bear until found by rescuers.
Una Leavy, *Harry's Stormy Night*, 1995
Coping with a loss of electrical power during a storm, Harry and his family sing and tell stories by candlelight.

318

PAUL FLEISCHMAN
KEVIN HAWKES, Illustrator

Weslandia

(Cambridge: MA: Candlewick Press, 1999)

Subject(s): Gardens and Gardening; Fantasy; Individuality
Age range(s): Grades 1-4
Major character(s): Wesley, Child, Inventor
Time period(s): Indeterminate
Locale(s): United States; Weslandia, Fictional Country

Summary: To his conforming parents, creative Wesley is an embarrassment; to the school bullies, he's a target. With summer's arrival, Wesley undertakes a project using the knowledge he's gained during the school year. Knowing that each civilization has its own staple food crop, Wesley decides to grow his own food and begin a civilization. Although Wesley tills the soil, the planting is done magically at night with help from the west wind. In only five days seedlings sprout and rapidly grow into tall flowering plants that provide Wesley with food, drink, fiber for clothes and oil for suntan lotion and insect repellant. Suddenly, the bullies are interested in learning about Wesley's inventions and by the time school resumes, Wesley is the leader of a crowd conforming to his style. (40 pages)

Where it's reviewed:
Booklist, July 1999, page 1942
Five Owls, November 1999, page 40
Horn Book, March 1999, page 187
Riverbank Review, Fall 1999, page 33
School Library Journal, June 1999, page 94

Awards the book has won:
Publishers Weekly Best Books, 1999
School Library Journal Best Books, 1999

Other books by the same author:
Time Train, 1991
Rondo in C, 1988
The Animal Hedge, 1983

Other books you might like:
Walter Lyon Krudop, *Something Is Growing*, 1995
Unnoticed, Peter plants a seed in an urban neighborhood with results that get everyone's attention.
Jerdine Nolen, *Harvey Potter's Balloon Farm*, 1994
An unusual crop grows on Harvey Potter's farm and his friend is determined to learn the secret of his harvest.
Anne Shelby, *The Someday House*, 1996
Three children imagine the possibilities of living in their red house in a variety of locations.

Mark Teague, *The Lost and Found*, 1998
    While searching for a hat in the school's lost and found box, three children fall into a cavernous, subterranean environment.
Audrey Wood, *The Flying Dragon Room*, 1996
    Using Mrs. Jenkins special tools and his imagination, Patrick creates an amazing underground space.

319

SID FLEISCHMAN
MARYLIN HAFNER, Illustrator

A Carnival of Animals

(New York: Greenwillow Books, 2000)

Subject(s): Tall Tales; Humor; Short Stories
Age range(s): Grades 2-5
Time period(s): Indeterminate Past
Locale(s): Barefoot Mountain

Summary: Six humorous tales describe the aftereffects of a tornado on the residents of Barefoot Mountain. The twister strips the fur off a "Sidehill Clinger" and dumps the poor critter in the flatlands where she's unable to walk because her legs are of uneven length on account of she lives on the mountain. After the tornado hits a caravan of carnival trucks it creates a problem for a cat by leaving behind a vicious dog that chases her and it solves a problem for a non-jumping frog that learns how after dining on a spilled bag of Mexican jumping beans. Unfortunately for the neighbors the tornado gives the local rooster insomnia so he starts crowing at all hours and dining on lightning bugs until he glows in the dark. (48 pages)

Where it's reviewed:
Booklist, September 1, 2000, page 113
Horn Book Guide, Spring 2001, page 61
Kirkus Reviews, September 1, 2000, page 1281
Publishers Weekly, August 28, 2000, page 83
School Library Journal, October 2000, page 124

Other books by the same author:
Here Comes McBroom: Three More Tall Tales, 1992
McBroom's Wonderful One-Acre Farm: Three Tall Tales, 1992
McBroom the Rainmaker, 1982

Other books you might like:
Marguerite W. Davol, *Papa Alonzo Weatherby: A Collection of Tall Tales from the Best Storyteller in Carroll County*, 1995
    During a blizzard Papa's words freeze as he speaks; clever Lulie invents a way to store the words for melting later so the stories come back to life.
Alvin Schwartz, *Whoppers: Tall Tales and Other Lies*, 1975
    Humorous tales from many different authors comprise this collection.
Alex Shearer, *Professor Sniff and the Lost Spring Breezes*, 1998
    When Professor Sniff brings home a baby hurricane as a souvenir he contributes to a shortage of wind in the spring.

320

CANDACE FLEMING
S.D. SCHINDLER, Illustrator

A Big Cheese for the White House: The True Tale of a Tremendous Cheddar

(New York: DK Ink/DK Publishing, Inc., 1999)

Subject(s): Food; Historical; Gifts
Age range(s): Grades 1-4
Major character(s): John Leland, Historical Figure, Leader; Phineas Dobbs, Aged Person; Thomas Jefferson, Political Figure (president)
Time period(s): 1800s (1801)
Locale(s): Cheshire, Massachusetts; Washington, District of Columbia

Summary: The residents of Cheshire are proud of their cheese and want to encourage President Jefferson to serve it at the White House. Elder John suggests that everyone in the community contribute one day's milking and the town will make an enormous wheel of cheddar cheese to present to Jefferson. Phineas Dobbs doubts it can be done and he expresses his opinion at each stage of the process. The townspeople do face challenges because of the huge size of the project, but everyone—except Phineas—contributes ideas, skill and time to move the community project along. When the cheese is completed Phineas doubts that Elder John can deliver the one thousand two hundred and thirty five pounds of cheddar to President Jefferson. Ever optimistic, Elder John believes he can and makes Phineas accompany him on the trip just to prove it can be done. (32 pages)

Where it's reviewed:
Booklist, November 1, 1999, page 538
Bulletin of the Center for Children's Books, September 1999, page 11
Horn Book, September 1999, page 594
Publishers Weekly, September 27, 1999, page 105
School Library Journal, August 1999, page 134

Awards the book has won:
Notable Social Studies Trade Books for Young People, 2000

Other books by the same author:
The Hatmaker's Sign: A Story by Benjamin Franklin, 1998
Gabriella's Song, 1997 (ALA Notable Book)
Madame LaGrande and Her So High, to the Sky, Uproarious Pompadour, 1996

Other books you might like:
David A. Adler, *A Picture Book of Thomas Jefferson*, 1990
    A biography of Thomas Jefferson traces his life and work, but doesn't tell us if he devoured the huge cheese without help.
John Vernon Lord, *The Giant Jam Sandwich*, 1987
    A skilled baker aids the community effort to rid a small town of a wasp invasion. Janet Burroway, co-author.
Emily Arnold McCully, *Popcorn at the Palace*, 1997
    An unconventional farmer plants fields of popcorn and his daughter convinces him to market the crop to the Queen of England.

321

CANDACE FLEMING
GISELLE POTTER, Illustrator

When Agnes Caws

(New York: Atheneum Books for Young Readers, 1999)

Subject(s): Animals/Birds; Humor; Talent
Age range(s): Grades K-3
Major character(s): Agnes Peregrine, Daughter, 8-Year-Old; Octavia Peregrine, Scientist (ornithologist), Mother; Colonel Edwin Pittsnap, Thief, Villain
Time period(s): Indeterminate Past
Locale(s): Earth; Himalayan Mountains, Asia

Summary: By the time Agnes is eight years old her gift for mimicking birdcalls is obvious. With her mother, Agnes travels the globe pursuing Professor Peregrine's work while Agnes learns the birdsongs of each new species she encounters. Impressed with her talent and Professor Peregrine's academic credentials, the World Bird Society sends the pair in search of the rare pink-headed duck. Learning of the mission, the nefarious Colonel Pittsnap realizes this search is his opportunity to add to his collection the one species that is missing. When Agnes succeeds in attracting the pink-headed duck, the Colonel captures it and Agnes must use her wits and her talent to save the rare bird. (40 pages)

Where it's reviewed:
Booklist, February 15, 1999, page 1075
Horn Book, March 1999, page 188
Publishers Weekly, December 21, 1998, page 67
Riverbank Review, Spring 1999, page 28
School Library Journal, February 1999, page 84

Awards the book has won:
School Library Journal Best Books, 1999

Other books by the same author:
The Hatmaker's Sign: A Story by Benjamin Franklin, 1998
Westward Ho, Carlotta!, 1998
Gabriella's Song, 1997
Madame LaGrande and Her So High, to the Sky, Uproarious Pompadour, 1996

Other books you might like:
Louise Erdrich, *Grandmother's Pigeon*, 1996
    When a nest in their eccentric grandmother's room yields three passenger pigeons, the grandchildren set them free to carry messages to Grandmother.
Dr. Seuss, *Mr. Brown Can Moo! Can You?*, 1970
    Mr. Brown can moo and do bird calls as well as a number of other animal sounds.
Diane Stanley, *Rumpelstiltskin's Daughter*, 1997
    Hope outwits the king who kidnaps her thinking she can spin straw into gold as her father does.
Audrey Wood, *Birdsong*, 1997
    From dawn 'til dark the songs of different types of birds accompany the sounds of children playing wherever they live.

322

MIELA FORD
ANITA LOBEL, Illustrator

My Day in the Garden

(New York: Greenwillow Books, 1999)

Subject(s): Playing; Imagination; Games
Age range(s): Preschool
Major character(s): Unnamed Character, Child, Daughter
Time period(s): 1990s (1999)
Locale(s): United States

Summary: It could be dreary for a little girl to be stuck inside on a rainy day, but when three friends come to visit the opportunity for fun begins. The girls dress up as blue morning glories for breakfast before one of them dons a toad costume for a game of hide and seek. As her parents hold the bowls, the girl and her friends, in bird costumes, go berry picking. After a full day of play in a variety of garden-related costumes, the girl waves good-bye to her friends and bids her attentive parents good night. (24 pages)

Where it's reviewed:
Booklist, May 1, 1999, page 1598
Horn Book Guide, Fall 1999, page 232
Publishers Weekly, April 12, 1999, page 74
School Library Journal, May 1999, page 89

Other books by the same author:
Bear Play, 1995
Sunflower, 1995
Little Elephant, 1994

Other books you might like:
Kady MacDonald Denton, *Would They Love a Lion?*, 1995
    Using a reversible bathrobe for a costume, Ann "becomes" many different animals, each of them loved by her family.
Jean Marzollo, *Pretend You're a Cat*, 1990
    Rhyming verse encourages children to imitate various animals' sounds and actions.
Martin Waddell, *The Hollyhock Wall*, 1999
    Mary uses her imagination to embellish the dish garden she grows until it seems to come to life.

323

MEM FOX
MARLA FRAZEE, Illustrator

Harriet, You'll Drive Me Wild!

(San Diego: Harcourt, Inc., 2000)

Subject(s): Mothers and Daughters; Conduct of Life; Anger
Age range(s): Grades K-2
Major character(s): Harriet Harris, Child, Daughter; Unnamed Character, Mother
Time period(s): 2000s (2000)
Locale(s): United States

Summary: Quite unintentionally, or so she says, Harriet is at the center of an escalating series of messes. At breakfast she spills her juice, by snack time she has jam on her pants and when she proudly shows her mother a painting she's just completed she drips paint on the carpet. Harriet's mother doesn't like to yell so she patiently responds to each incident with calm, but growing concern. Even Harriet's mother has limits and her patience is gone by the time Harriet, while not napping, plays tug of war with the dog and rips open a feather pillow. Then Harriet's mother loses her temper and yells. Just as Harriet is apologetic after each mishap so her mother regrets her anger. After a hug and a laugh, the two clean up together. (32 pages)

Where it's reviewed:
Booklist, March 1, 2000, page 1250
Horn Book, March 2000, page 184
Publishers Weekly, March 20, 2000, page 91
Riverbank Review, Spring 2000, page 30
School Library Journal, April 2000, page 104

Other books by the same author:
A Bedtime Story, 1996
Feathers and Fools, 1996
Sophie, 1994
Time for Bed, 1993

Other books you might like:
Quentin Blake, *Simpkin*, 1994
  A rhyming tale uses mischievous Simpkin's unpredictable behavior to explore opposites such as naughty and nice.
Phyllis Reynolds Naylor, *I Can't Take You Anywhere!*, 1997
  Clumsy Amy Audrey seems to unintentionally create disaster wherever she goes.
David Shannon, *No, David!*, 1998
  In a Caldecott Honor Book David hears "No, David!" when he misbehaves. After breaking a vase, the sad, remorseful boy finally hears, "I love you!"

324

MEM FOX
KERRY ARGENT, Illustrator

Sleepy Bears

(San Diego: Harcourt Brace & Company, 1999)

Subject(s): Animals/Bears; Bedtime; Sleep
Age range(s): Grades K-1
Major character(s): Mother Bear, Bear, Mother; Baxter Bear, Bear, Son; Baby Bear, Bear, Son
Time period(s): Indeterminate
Locale(s): Fictional Country

Summary: As winter nears Mother Bear calls her children inside for a bedtime rhyme before they sleep. Baxter, the sleepiest one, is first of the bear children snuggled into the big, soft feather bed to hear the verse Mother Bear creates especially for him. Once Baxter is dozing, Mother Bear recites a poem for her next yawning offspring and then the next until she lulls everyone but Baby Bear to sleep. As the rhyme for Baby Bear concludes, both Mother and Baby join in slumber with the other bears. (32 pages)

Where it's reviewed:
Booklist, November 15, 1999, page 634
Horn Book Guide, Spring 2000, page 15
Kirkus Reviews, August 1, 1999, page 1226
Publishers Weekly, July 19, 1999, page 193

School Library Journal, October 1999, page 114

Other books by the same author:
A Bedtime Story, 1996
Time for Bed, 1993
Koala Lou, 1989

Other books you might like:
Michael Foreman, *Dad! I Can't Sleep*, 1995
  Dad's going to sleep suggestions for Little Panda fail to produce the desired effect.
Don Freeman, *Bearymore*, 1976
  Rather than plan his new circus act, Bearymore settles down for his winter's hibernation.
James Preller, *Wake Me in Spring*, 1994
  A mouse is sad that he will not be able to play with his friend Bear again until Spring.
Martin Waddell, *Can't You Sleep, Little Bear?*, 1988
  Big Bear comforts Little Bear when a fear of the dark keeps him from dozing off.

325

KRISTINE L. FRANKLIN
BARBARA LAVALLEE, Illustrator

The Gift

(San Francisco: Chronicle Books, 1999)

Subject(s): Fishing; Animals/Whales; Old Age
Age range(s): Grades K-3
Major character(s): Jimmy Joe, Child, Fisherman; Fish Woman, Aged Person, Fisherman
Time period(s): 1990s
Locale(s): Pacific Northwest

Summary: Jimmy Joe loves fishing so he's excited when Fish Woman invites him out in her boat for a fishing trip. Bundled against the cold, Jimmy Joe makes plans to catch a bucket of stew fish or maybe a salmon. Fish Woman suggests he can expect something even better. Indeed, after sitting for a very long time, Jimmy Joe hooks a large salmon that he brings in with Fish Woman's help. Seeing the large lifeless fish makes Jimmy Joe feel a little sad, but he's soon distracted by a sound in the fog. Soon nine orca whales visit the boat. Jimmy Joe is so awed by the creatures that he returns his salmon to the sea to provide lunch for one of the whales and then he and Fish Woman go off to catch stew fish. (32 pages)

Where it's reviewed:
Horn Book Guide, Spring 2000, page 35
Kirkus Reviews, November 1, 1999, page 1741
Publishers Weekly, November 15, 1999, page 65
School Library Journal, January 2000, page 96

Other books by the same author:
The Wolfhound, 1996
When the Monkeys Came Back, 1994
The Old, Old Man and the Very Little Boy, 1992

Other books you might like:
Kimberley Smith Brady, *Keeper for the Sea*, 1996
  A young girl helps land a large bluefish that Grandpa decides is a "keeper for the sea" as he slips it back into the water.

Amy Hest, *Rosie's Fishing Trip*, 1994
  After a fishing trip with Grampa, Rosie learns that actually catching fish is not the most important reason for such excursions.

Barbara M. Joosse, *I Love You the Purplest*, 1996
  In the evening Mama and her two sons fish in the lake near their home sharing the gift of their love for each other.

326

DEBRA FRASIER, Author/Illustrator

Miss Alaineus: A Vocabulary Disaster
(San Diego: Harcourt, Inc., 2000)

Subject(s): Language; Schools; Teacher-Student Relationships
Age range(s): Grades 3-5
Major character(s): Sage, 5th Grader; Mrs. Page, Teacher; Starr, 5th Grader, Friend
Time period(s): 2000s (2000)
Locale(s): United States (Webster School)

Summary: Sage manages to make the most of an embarrassing mistake. Because she's absent on the day that Mrs. Page assigns the week's vocabulary words, Sage gets them by phone from Starr who's late for baseball practice and doesn't have time to spell each one. What Sage hears for the fifteenth word is "Miss Alaineus" not miscellaneous. Sage knows the term "Miss Alaineus" in reference to one particular kitchen drawer and she recognizes her as the woman on green spaghetti boxes. Confident that she can define and picture all the words, Sage doesn't use a dictionary for the assignment and happily turns it in when she returns to school on Monday. The error of her ways becomes obvious to Sage when the stunned class bursts out laughing at her definition of the word. Sage is humbled and devastated, but with her mother's help she finds a way to turn tragedy into triumph at the school's tenth annual vocabulary parade. In her Miss Alaineus costume decorated with over 100 miscellaneous objects Sage wins the prize for "Most Original Use of a Word." (32 pages)

Where it's reviewed:
Booklist, September 15, 2000, page 240
Instructor, October 2000, page D21
Kirkus Reviews, July 15, 2000, page 1037
Publishers Weekly, August 21, 2000, page 71
School Library Journal, September 2000, page 197

Other books by the same author:
Out of the Ocean, 1998 (Minnesota Book Award)
On the Day You Were Born, 1991 (Hungry Mind Review Book of Distinction)

Other books you might like:
Monalisa DeGross, *Donavan's Word Jar*, 1994
  Donavan collects words on scraps of paper and when he has a jar full of unusual ones he comes up with a creative idea for what to do with them all.
Marissa Moss, *Amelia Writes Again*, 1996
  In her notebook Amelia records her thoughts and feelings about school using both written comments and humorous illustrations.

Barney Saltzberg, *Phoebe and the Spelling Bee*, 1996
  Phoebe's imagination helps her remember the correct spelling of the words during the class spelling bee.

327

MARTHA FREEMAN

Fourth Grade Weirdo
(New York: Holiday House, 1999)

Subject(s): Schools; Teacher-Student Relationships; Politics
Age range(s): Grades 3-5
Major character(s): Dexter Plum, 4th Grader; Dorian Ditzwinkle, Teacher
Time period(s): 2000s (2000)
Locale(s): Marshall City

Summary: With his mom in a campaign for reelection to her school board seat and an unconventional teacher, Dexter really does feel as if he's the class weirdo. Fourth grade in Mr. Ditzwinkle's room is a little too unpredictable for a student who leads a well-ordered life and carries a briefcase to school. Perfect Dexter likes routine and straightforward assignments while absent-minded Mr. Ditzwinkle likes surprises, innovation and non-traditional learning. When the other students see Dexter's self-portrait (carefully drawn with a ruler) and begin to call him "blockhead" Dexter becomes angry with Mr. Ditzwinkle for giving the assignment and destroys it. Dexter's first disciplinary trip to the principal's office begins his readjustment from perfect to being simply good. Along the way he unintentionally initiates a mud fight at school, attends the forbidden Halloween Carnival in disguise, and helps to capture a school thief thus clearing Mr. Ditzwinkle of suspicion. (147 pages)

Where it's reviewed:
Horn Book Guide, Spring 2000, page 78
Kirkus Reviews, November 15, 1999, page 1808
Publishers Weekly, January 10, 2000, page 68
School Library Journal, January 2000, page 96

Other books by the same author:
The Polyester Grandpa, 1998
The Year My Parents Ruined My Life, 1997
Stink Bomb Mom, 1996

Other books you might like:
Andrew Clements, *Frindle*, 1996
  Frustrated by his teacher's extensive use of the dictionary Nick invents a new word for pen.
Elizabeth Levy, *Keep Ms. Sugarman in the Fourth Grade*, 1992
  A mid-year promotion to principal may be good for Ms. Sugarman but it's devastating to Jackie who's finally having a good year.
Colleen O'Shaughnessy McKenna, *Fourth Grade Is a Jinx*, 1989
  Already the school year is bordering on disastrous for Collette and then it gets worse when her mother is assigned to teach her class!
P.J. Petersen, *Can You Keep a Secret?*, 1997
  With his class trying to plan a surprise birthday party for

teacher Mike, notorious blabbermouth, struggles not to reveal any secrets.

328

MARTHA FREEMAN
CAT BOWMAN SMITH, Illustrator

The Trouble with Cats

(New York: Holiday House, 2000)

Subject(s): Schools; Stepfathers; Animals/Cats
Age range(s): Grades 2-4
Major character(s): Holly Garland, 3rd Grader, Child of Divorced Parents; Mom, Mother, Spouse; William, Stepfather, Spouse
Time period(s): 2000s (2000)
Locale(s): San Francisco, California

Summary: Holly is having a hard time adjusting to life with William and his four cats. Her Mom's marriage not only interferes with the solitary relationship Holly has enjoyed since her parents' divorce when Holly was four but it also necessitates a change of schools when they move into William's apartment. Now, Holly dreads being the new kid in third grade and struggles to coexist with cats that are not accustomed to sharing their space. To Holly, everything is going wrong at home and at school. Mom is patient and Holly's teacher is flexible so eventually Holly's able to look at her situation a little differently and be grateful for the positive aspects of her life. (77 pages)

Where it's reviewed:
Booklist, March 15, 2000, page 1376
Bulletin of the Center for Children's Books, April 2000, page 279
Horn Book Guide, Fall 2000, page 293
Kirkus Reviews, March 15, 2000, page 381
School Library Journal, July 2000, page 72

Other books by the same author:
The Polyester Grandpa, 1998
The Year My Parents Ruined My Life, 1997
Stink Bomb Mom, 1996

Other books you might like:
Lynea Bowdish, *Living with My Stepfather Is Like Living with a Moose*, 1997
After trying (and struggling with) his athletically inept stepfather's hobby, Matt is more appreciative of their different interests and abilities.
Charlotte Watson Sherman, *Eli and the Swamp Man*, 1996
Eli reconsiders his plans to runaway from his stepfather after talking with the Swamp Man.
Eileen Spinelli, *Lizzie Logan, Second Banana*, 1998
Having a stepfather is an adjustment, but when Lizzie learns that her mom is pregnant she knows she'll never be loved as much as the new baby.

329

GINA FRESCHET, Author/Illustrator

Naty's Parade

(New York: Farrar Straus Giroux, 2000)

Subject(s): Carnivals; Fathers and Daughters; Dancing
Age range(s): Grades K-2
Major character(s): Naty, Child, Daughter; Papa, Father
Time period(s): Indeterminate Past
Locale(s): Mexico

Summary: Naty is excited to be old enough to don a costume and dance in the parade this year. Papa helps her get into her mouse costume and she joins the puppet people promising to meet Papa at the end of the parade. Naty spins and spins in her mouse costume making herself so dizzy that she becomes lost. With darkness falling Naty wanders along unfamiliar streets searching for the parade until she finally comes to a familiar street and hears the drums in the distance. Naty finds the other puppets before the parade reaches the square and then searches for Papa in the crowd. Tired from the experience, Naty's still eager to return next year. (32 pages)

Where it's reviewed:
Booklist, May 15, 2000, page 1747
Children's Book Review Service, May 2000, page 108
Kirkus Reviews, March 15, 2000, page 382
Publishers Weekly, February 7, 2000, page 84
School Library Journal, March 2000, page 197

Other books by the same author:
The Lute's Tune, 1992

Other books you might like:
George Ancona, *Carnaval*, 1999
Photographs illustrate the nonfiction text describing the parades, dancing and giant puppets of a five-day Brazilian festival.
Lulu Delacre, *Vejigante/Masquerader*, 1993
By saving carefully Ramon is able to buy the material needed for a Carnival costume so he can participate rather than observe the festival.
Ann Grifalconi, *The Bravest Flute: A Story of Courage in the Mayan Tradition*, 1994
To bring honor to his family a boy leads the exhausting New Year's parade of renewal to the cathedral.

330

CLAUDIA FRIES, Author/Illustrator

A Pig Is Moving In!

(New York: Orchard Books, 2000)

Subject(s): Neighbors and Neighborhoods; Animals; Prejudice
Age range(s): Grades K-2
Major character(s): Theodore, Pig; Henrietta, Hen; Doctor Fox, Fox; Nick Hare, Rabbit
Time period(s): Indeterminate
Locale(s): Fictional Country

Summary: Residents of an apartment building discuss the attributes they hope to see in the new neighbor Doctor Fox hears is arriving that day. Henrietta hopes for someone quiet while Nick thinks a fastidious cat or mole would be good. They are horrified to see that the animal moving in is a pig for they assume pigs are messy and dirty. During the day each one independently observes the pig drop something. Without offering to help or waiting to see what happens next the observer runs off to gossip about the pig and doesn't see how carefully the pig cleans up after each accident. Together Nick, Henrietta, and Doctor Fox ring the pig's doorbell in order to confront him about his messy behavior. What they find is Theodore, a gracious pig with cookies in the oven to share. Theodore welcomes them into his apartment and they quickly see that their uninformed opinion of him was wrong. (28 pages)

Where it's reviewed:
Booklist, December 15, 2000, page 826
Kirkus Reviews, September 1, 2000, page 1282
Publishers Weekly, August 28, 2000, page 82
School Librarian, Autumn 2000, page 130
School Library Journal, September 2000, page 197

Other books you might like:
Janie Bynum, *Otis*, 2000
    Other pigs ostracize fastidious Otis because he doesn't enjoy their muddy games.
Tim Egan, *Metropolitan Cow*, 1996
    When a pig family moves into Bennett's apartment building the calf is happy to have a friend his age though his parents are horrified it's a pig.
Judith Ross Enderle, *Upstairs*, 1998
    When a new tenant moves in above Elbie he hopes for a playmate but instead meets Ethel and her farm animals. Stephanie Gordon Tessler, co-author.
Susanna Gretz, *It's Your Turn, Roger!*, 1985
    Roger, a young pig, studies the dinner chores of all the other families in his apartment building and decides that his job isn't too bad.

331

JONATHAN FROST, Author/Illustrator

Gowanus Dogs
(New York: Farrar Straus Giroux, 1999)

Subject(s): Homeless People; Animals/Dogs; Pets
Age range(s): Grades K-3
Major character(s): Man in the Stocking Cap, Streetperson
Time period(s): 1990s (1999)
Locale(s): New York, New York (Brooklyn)

Summary: A dog living near the Gowanus Canal has puppies, which are watched over by the Man in the Stocking Cap, a man who works on the bridge, and another who works on a boat. When one of the puppies becomes ill, the Man in the Stocking Cap takes her to an animal shelter, and does odd jobs there to pay for her care. When she is better, the workers at the shelter help to find the Man in the Stocking Cap a job, as well as adoptive homes for the other puppies. Author's first book. (48 pages)

Where it's reviewed:
Booklist, April 15, 1999, page 1534
Kirkus Reviews, February 15, 1999, page 299

Publishers Weekly, April 19, 1999, page 73
Riverbank Review, Spring 1999, page 31
School Library Journal, June 1999, page 94

Awards the book has won:
Notable Social Studies Trade Books for Young People, 2000

Other books you might like:
Eve Bunting, *December*, 1997
    A homeless boy and his mother help a needy woman.
Nan Gregory, *How Smudge Came*, 1995
    The stray puppy Cindy finds is not allowed in her group home, so the staff of Hospice House find a way for her to see Smudge every day.
Michael J. Rosen, *Home: A Collaboration of Thirty Distinguished Authors and Illustrators of Children's Books to Aid the Homeless*, 1996
    Thirteen authors and seventeen illustrators celebrate what makes a home.
Deborah Turney-Zagwen, *Long Nellie*, 1993
    Jeremy and his eccentric neighbor take care of a stray cat.

332

CATHERINE MYLER FRUISEN, Author/Illustrator

My Mother's Pearls
(San Rafael, CA: Cedco Publishing Company, 2000)

Subject(s): Mothers and Daughters; Family; Pearls
Age range(s): Grades K-2
Major character(s): Unnamed Character, Daughter, Narrator; Mom, Mother
Time period(s): Multiple Time Periods (18th-21st centuries)
Locale(s): United States

Summary: A little girl enjoys helping Mom get ready for a special event. While there are many wonderful things about preparing for the activity, the moment the little girl most enjoys is helping Mom clasp her pearls. Not only does the little girl appreciate the significance of this heirloom, but she can also recite the family history the strand of pearls holds. From mother to daughter through the generations all the way back to another country in 1788 this little girl imagines the pleasure each ancestor had in using the pearls and in passing them on to the next generation. (32 pages)

Where it's reviewed:
Booklist, August 2000, page 2146
Horn Book Guide, Spring 2001, page 36
Publishers Weekly, May 15, 2000, page 115
School Library Journal, May 2000, page 141

Other books you might like:
Betsy Hearne, *Seven Brave Women*, 1997
    By remembering the peaceful contributions of seven of her female ancestors a young girl views history.
George Shannon, *This Is the Bird*, 1997
    A young girl explains the origins of a simple carved wooden bird that has been in her family for many generations.
Anne Shelby, *Homeplace*, 1995
    A grandmother traces the history of the family from the building of the homestead by the great-great-great-great grandfather to the present.

Joey on the team. Joey has no team experience, but he's expended a lot of energy throwing rocks so Carter places him on the pitcher's mound putting Joey in the position of fulfilling Carter's hopes for success and recognition through his son's achievements. During a night of drinking, Carter declares that he and Joey are man enough to handle their own problems without the crutch of medication and he flushes all Joey's patches down the toilet. Joey now wrestles with multiple fears—the return of the out-of-control kid lurking within him, the desire to please his father, and the need to call his mom to rescue him from an impossible situation. (196 pages)

Where it's reviewed:
Booklist, September 1, 2000, page 114
Horn Book, September 2000, page 567
Publishers Weekly, August 14, 2000, page 356
Riverbank Review, Winter 2000-2001, page 38
School Library Journal, September 2000, page 228

Awards the book has won:
Newbery Honor Book, 2001
School Library Journal Best Books, 2000

Other books by the same author:
Joey Pigza Swallowed the Key, 1998 (ALA Notable Book)
Jack's Black Book, 1997
Heads or Tails: Stories from the Sixth Grade, 1994

Other books you might like:
Caroline Janover, *Zipper, the Kid with ADHD*, 1997
    A dyslexic classmate helps Zipper develop organizational skills to cope with his impulsivity and forgetfulness.
Elizabeth Levy, *My Life as a Fifth Grade Comedian*, 1997
    Bobby finds a positive way to receive attention in school when an understanding teacher has him organize a school-wide comedy contest.
Barbara O'Connor, *Beethoven in Paradise*, 1997
    Music-loving Martin's interest is in conflict with his father's desire that he play baseball because music is for "sissies."
Mark Smith, *Pay Attention, Slosh!*, 1997
    Josh is frustrated by his lack of self-control and inability to concentrate; he copes with support from parents, teachers and doctors.

335

TRICIA GARDELLA
GLO COALSON, Illustrator

Blackberry Booties
(New York: Orchard Books, 2000)

Subject(s): Individuality; Problem Solving; Gifts
Age range(s): Grades K-2
Major character(s): Mikki Jo, Child, Cousin; Samuel, Baby, Cousin
Time period(s): 2000s (2000)
Locale(s): United States

Summary: Mikki Jo wants to give Samuel a gift next week at the family reunion but she has no idea what to make. The only thing Mikki Jo thinks she does well is pick blackberries, so she finds a way to use the blackberries to acquire the perfect present. Using her neighbors' talents Mikki Jo trades one bucket of blackberries for fleece, another for spinning the wool into yarn and a third for knitting the yarn into booties. Finally, to give the gift a personal touch Mikki Jo uses her last bucket of berries to dye the booties a beautiful shade of purple—just like her hands. (32 pages)

Where it's reviewed:
Booklist, March 15, 2000, page 1386
Bulletin of the Center for Children's Books, April 2000, page 279
Horn Book Guide, Fall 2000, page 268
Kirkus Reviews, March 15, 2000, page 382
School Library Journal, May 2000, page 141

Other books by the same author:
Casey's New Hat, 1997
Just Like My Dad, 1993

Other books you might like:
Elsa Beskow, *Pelle's New Suit*, 1929
    Pelle observes the progress of his new suit from the shearing of the fleece to the final tailoring.
Holly Hobbie, *Toot and Puddle: A Present for Toot*, 1998
    Puddle has almost run out of ideas for a present for Toot when the perfect gift finds him.
Shirley Hughes, *Giving*, 1993
    A little girl and her baby brother share the joy of giving—smiles, kisses and presents.
Ragnhild Scamell, *Three Bags Full*, 1993
    Kindly Millie gives away so much of her fleece, that Mrs. Farmer must knit a sweater to warm her through the winter.

336

LINDSEY GARDINER, Author/Illustrator

Here Come Poppy and Max
(New York: Little, Brown and Company, 2000)

Subject(s): Pets; Animals; Imagination
Age range(s): Preschool
Major character(s): Poppy, Child; Max, Dog
Time period(s): 2000s (2000)
Locale(s): Fictional Country

Summary: In the author's first book Poppy imagines being like different animals and she tries stretching tall as a giraffe, splashing like a duck and waddling like a penguin. Max imitates each move as Poppy leaps like a leopard, roars like a tiger and bounces like a kangaroo. Max is Poppy's favorite animal because he loves her as she is and she has no need to pretend to be anything but else. (24 pages)

Where it's reviewed:
Horn Book Guide, Spring 2001, page 16
Publishers Weekly, August 21, 2000, page 71
School Library Journal, September 2000, page 197

Other books you might like:
Kady MacDonald Denton, *Would They Love a Lion?*, 1995
    Using a reversible bathrobe for a costume, Anna "becomes" many different animals, each of them loved by her family.
Jonathan London, *Wiggle Waggle*, 1999
    Humans walk but animals move in different ways; ducks

wiggle waggle, elephants clomp, kangaroos boing and frogs go flop, flop, flop.

Jean Marzollo, *Pretend You're a Cat*, 1990
Rhyming verse encourages children to imitate various animals' sounds and actions.

Caroline Uff, *Hello, Lulu*, 1999
Lulu's favorite things include the color red, a special teddy bear, her best friend, three pets and her family.

337

PATRICIA LEE GAUCH
DAVID CHRISTIANA, Illustrator

Poppy's Puppet

(New York: Henry Holt and Company, Inc., 1999)

Subject(s): Toys; Artists and Art; Identity, Concealed
Age range(s): Grades 1-3
Major character(s): Poppy, Artisan (toymaker); Clarinda, Puppet
Time period(s): Indeterminate Past
Locale(s): Fictional Country

Summary: One reason Poppy has such success as a wood carver, is his willingness to listen to each piece of wood before carving the puppet that the wood is meant to be. By listening patiently, Poppy assembles a troupe of happy marionettes with which he performs shows around the countryside. When Poppy finds a rare piece of teak, he hears nothing from the wood, but impatiently carves it anyway, deciding that it is destined to be a dancer. Clarinda, however, is very clumsy and becomes tangled in her strings onstage. Finally, Poppy stops trying to make her perform and gives her time to find herself. Once Clarinda identifies her true calling, she becomes a marvelous tightrope walker. (32 pages)

Where it's reviewed:
Booklist, September 15, 1999, page 267
Children's Book Review Service, September 1999, page 169
Publishers Weekly, July 19, 1999, page 194
Reading Teacher, April 2000, page 602
School Library Journal, October 1999, page 114

Other books by the same author:
Christina Katerina and Fats: And the Great Neighborhood War, 1997
Tanya and Emily in a Dance for Two, 1994
Uncle Magic, 1992
On to Widecombe Fair, 1978

Other books you might like:
Barbara Helen Berger, *The Jewel Heart*, 1994
In this fantasy of two dolls, injured Gemino is healed by the transforming power of Pavelle's love.

Carlo Collodi, *Pinocchio*, 1996
Kindly Geppetto fashions Pinocchio from a block of wood, but it takes love and the Blue Fairy to transform him into the real boy he's meant to be.

Rachel Isadora, *The Steadfast Tin Soldier*, 1996
The adaptation of Andersen's classic tale maintains the hero, a one-legged tin soldier who is in love with a paper ballerina.

Susan Wojciechowski, *The Christmas Miracle of Jonathan Toomey*, 1995
A gifted woodcarver learns to listen carefully to the suggestions of a young boy as he strives to complete a nativity set.

338

PATRICIA LEE GAUCH
SATOMI ICHIKAWA, Illustrator

Presenting Tanya, the Ugly Duckling

(New York: Philomel Books, 1999)

Subject(s): Ballet; Dancing; Self-Perception
Age range(s): Grades K-3
Major character(s): Tanya, Child, Dancer; Miss Foley, Teacher, Dancer
Time period(s): 1990s (1999)
Locale(s): United States

Summary: Miss Foley selects Tanya to play the lead role in *The Ugly Duckling*. Tanya practices diligently, learns her steps and has no trouble being the awkward ugly duckling, but she has difficulty making the transition to the beautiful swan. To her, despite all the practice, she remains just Tanya. At the dress rehearsal Tanya finally seems to be able to see the swan in herself and to soar as the ugly duckling realizes its transformation to swan. (32 pages)

Where it's reviewed:
Booklist, July 1999, page 1943
Dance Magazine, December 1999, page 57
Horn Book Guide, Fall 1999, page 252
Publishers Weekly, May 24, 1999, page 81
School Library Journal, June 1999, page 95

Awards the book has won:
Booklist Editors' Choice, 1999

Other books by the same author:
Tanya and the Magic Wardrobe, 1997
Tanya and Emily in a Dance for Two, 1994
Bravo, Tanya, 1992

Other books you might like:
Hans Christian Andersen, *The Ugly Duckling*, 1987
The classic story of the misunderstood duckling that, in time, discovers his true worth is retold by Marianna Meyer and illustrated by Thomas Locker.

Lucy Dickens, *Dancing Class*, 1992
Five young aspiring dancers have the opportunity to perform as birds during class.

Rachel Isadora, *Lili at Ballet*, 1993
Four times a week Lili attends ballet classes hoping to achieve her dream of being a ballerina.

Jane O'Connor, *Nina, Nina Ballerina*, 1993
Although she is one of a flock of butterflies, Nina stands out from the crowd during the performance.

339

GAIL GAUTHIER

Club Earth

(New York: G.P. Putnam's Sons, 1999)

Subject(s): Aliens; Humor; Family Life
Age range(s): Grades 4-7
Major character(s): Will Denis, Brother (older), Son; Robby Denis, Brother (younger), Son; Saliva "Sal", Alien
Time period(s): 1990s (1999)
Locale(s): United States

Summary: In the sequel to *My Life Among the Aliens* Will and Robby don't think it's unusual to have an alien visiting their home, but they're surprised to learn that Sal plans to use their house as an interplanetary resort destination and he won't take no for an answer. Although their mother protests about the extra work and their clueless father thinks the plan is a big joke, Will and Robby are initially excited. Each visitor seems to have a particular talent and defines pleasure in terms of his own world—one even enjoys cleaning and yard work—giving Will and Robby some help with burdensome chores. Still, the adventure becomes tiresome and everyone is relieved when Sal terminates the contract. Now, if they could only get that last alien visitor to go home. (152 pages)

Where it's reviewed:
Horn Book Guide, Fall 1999, page 291
Horn Book, May 1999, page 330
Kirkus Reviews, May 15, 1999, page 799
Publishers Weekly, June 7, 1999, page 85
School Library Journal, August 1999, page 155

Other books by the same author:
A Year with Butch and Spike, 1998
My Life Among the Aliens, 1996

Other books you might like:
Bruce Coville, *I Was a Sixth Grade Alien*, 1999
    Tim's dream of meeting an alien comes true when Pleskit, alien son of the new ambassador to Earth enrolls in his class.
Mark Jonathan Harris, *Solay*, 1993
    When the alien Solay drops into Melissa's life about the only thing the two have in common is their desire to be in New York and not California.
Stephen Manes, *It's New! It's Improved! It's Terrible!*, 1989
    He looks like a boy, talks like a television commercial and is really an alien who's driving Arnold and his friends crazy.

340

MARIE-LOUISE GAY, Author/Illustrator

Stella, Queen of the Snow

(Toronto: Groundwood/Douglas & McIntyre, 2000)

Subject(s): Weather; Winter; Brothers and Sisters
Age range(s): Grades K-1
Major character(s): Stella, Child, Sister (older); Sam, Child, Brother
Time period(s): 2000s (2000)
Locale(s): Canada

Summary: Stella introduces Sam to the wonder of a snowy day. Sam has many questions about snow that Stella patiently answers. Together they feel snow as "cold as vanilla ice cream and as soft as baby rabbit fur." Stella helps Sam make a snowman and build a snow fort. She tries to encourage him to ice skate on the frozen pond or join her on a sled ride down the hill, but cautious Sam has his own plans. Stella and Sam conclude their day by making snow angels and listening to their singing. (32 pages)

Where it's reviewed:
Booklist, November 1, 2000, page 548
Horn Book Guide, Spring 2001, page 16
Publishers Weekly, October 23, 2000, page 77
Quill & Quire, September 2000, page 59
School Library Journal, October 2000, page 125

Other books by the same author:
Stella, Star of the Sea, 1999
Fat Charlie's Circus, 1997
Moonbeam on a Cat's Ear, 1996
Rainy Day Magic, 1989

Other books you might like:
Lois Ehlert, *Snowballs*, 1995
    Simple text and clear collages tell of the creation of a snow family and the inevitable result as the weather warms.
Ezra Jack Keats, *The Snowy Day*, 1962
    This Caldecott Medal winner expresses a young boy's joy with the first snowfall.
Steve Sanfield, *Snow*, 1995
    A child marvels at the beauty of the newly fallen snow dotted with the tracks of passing animals.
Nancy Elizabeth Wallace, *Snow*, 1995
    Rabbit brothers hurry outside at the first sign of snow to sled, make snow rabbits and throw snowballs.

341

MARIE-LOUISE GAY, Author/Illustrator

Stella, Star of the Sea

(Toronto: Groundwood/Douglas & McIntyre, 1999)

Subject(s): Brothers and Sisters; Beaches; Summer
Age range(s): Grades K-1
Major character(s): Stella, Child, Sister (older); Sam, Child, Brother (younger)
Time period(s): 1990s
Locale(s): Canada

Summary: Having visited the seashore once before Stella considers herself an expert and cheerfully answers reluctant Sam's many queries. As Sam stands apprehensively on the shore firing off questions Stella imaginatively responds as she swims. Stella's patience is wearing thin by the time Sam finally makes the plunge and the two siblings float happily together. (32 pages)

Where it's reviewed:
Booklist, May 15, 1999, page 1702
Bulletin of the Center for Children's Books, May 1999, page 313
Children's Book Review Service, Spring 1999, page 134

Publishers Weekly, March 29, 1999, page 102
School Library Journal, August 1999, page 134

Awards the book has won:
Bulletin of the Center for Children's Books Blue Ribbon, 1999

Other books by the same author:
Fat Charlie's Circus, 1997
Moonbeam on a Cat's Ear, 1996
Rainy Day Magic, 1989

Other books you might like:
Aliki, *Those Summers*, 1996
 Children frolic in the waves, enjoying a carefree family vacation at the seashore.
Stephanie Calmenson, *Hotter than a Hot Dog!*, 1994
 To escape the summer heat, Granny takes her granddaughter to the beach for the day.
Douglas Florian, *A Beach Day*, 1990
 A family enjoys a relaxing day at the beach looking for sea shells.
Sherry Garland, *Summer Sands*, 1995
 After a storm two children are surprised to see the devastation of the dunes on which they have romped all summer.
Joanne Ryder, *A House by the Sea*, 1994
 A young boy imagines a rollicking life with a variety of marine animals.

342

CAMPBELL GEESLIN
PETRA MATHERS, Illustrator

How Nanita Learned to Make Flan

(New York: Anne Schwartz Book/Atheneum Books for Young Readers, 1999)

Subject(s): Fathers and Daughters; Cooks and Cooking; Work
Age range(s): Grades K-3
Major character(s): Nanita, Child, Daughter; Papa, Father, Artisan (shoemaker); Senor Parrot, Bird
Time period(s): Indeterminate Past
Locale(s): Mexico

Summary: Papa has no time to make shoes for Nanita who is determined not to go to her First Communion without them. While Papa sleeps, Nanita uses leather scraps to make a pair for herself. During the night, as Nanita sleeps in her new shoes, the shoes begin walking and when she awakens she is lost in the dessert near a large house. Nanita goes to the house seeking help and is forced to give up her shoes, become a servant and make flan every night. A captured parrot befriends Nanita and offers stories to cheer her and suggestions for improving the flan. Senor Parrot also has news from other birds of Papa's sadness without his daughter. Nanita and Senor Parrot escape from the house and return to her village. Papa happily makes her a new pair of shoes and Nanita makes delicious flan for everyone to eat after her First Communion. (32 pages)

Where it's reviewed:
Booklist, December 1, 1999, page 710
Bulletin of the Center for Children's Books, November 1999, page 92

Kirkus Reviews, November 1, 1999, page 1741
Publishers Weekly, November 1, 1999, page 82
School Library Journal, December 1999, page 91

Other books by the same author:
On Ramon's Farm, 1998
In Rosa's Mexico, 1996

Other books you might like:
Tony Johnston, *The Magic Maguey*, 1996
 Miguel and his friends save the village maguey plant from destruction by the landowner's plans to build a larger house.
Leyla Torres, *Saturday Sancocho*, 1995
 Maria Lili and Mama Ana visit the market to barter their eggs for the ingredients needed to make a special dinner.
Ana Zamorano, *Let's Eat*, 1997
 Mama has a delicious meal ready to serve her family every day, but each day one family member is busy elsewhere.

343

JEAN CRAIGHEAD GEORGE
WENDELL MINOR, Illustrator

Snow Bear

(New York: Hyperion Books for Children, 1999)

Subject(s): Animals/Bears; Playing; Eskimos
Age range(s): Grades K-2
Major character(s): Bessie Nivyek, Child, Eskimo; Vincent Nivyek, Brother (older), Eskimo; Snow Bear, Bear (polar bear cub)
Time period(s): 1990s (1999)
Locale(s): Arctic

Summary: Bessie walks across the frozen Arctic Ocean to explore a large block of ice. Vincent, hunting for food, crosses Bessie's path and notices bear cub tracks so he follows her trail. Under the watchful eye of Vincent and Snow Bear's mother, Bessie and Snow Bear play happily until a large male polar bear thrusts his head out of the water. Protectively, the mother bear runs to lead Snow Bear away to safety as Vincent and Bessie race in the other direction. (32 pages)

Where it's reviewed:
Booklist, August 1999, page 2063
Publishers Weekly, August 9, 1999, page 351
School Library Journal, September 1999, page 182

Other books by the same author:
Arctic Son, 1997
Look to the North: A Wolf Pup Diary, 1997 (IRA/CBC Children's Choice)
Dear Rebecca, Winter Is Here, 1993

Other books you might like:
Jez Alborough, *It's the Bear!*, 1994
 Remembering the bear he met on his last walk in the woods, Eddie is afraid to return there for a picnic with his mom.
Carolyn Lesser, *Great Crystal Bear*, 1996
 A poetic yet factually accurate description of a year in the life of a polar bear is complemented by illustrations.
Robert McCloskey, *Blueberries for Sal*, 1948
 Sal's blueberry expedition with her mom parallels that of a

bear cub; the two youngsters lose their mothers, but find each other.

344

TWIG C. GEORGE
YONG CHEN, Illustrator

Swimming with Sharks

(New York: HarperCollins Publishers, 1999)

Subject(s): Animals/Sharks; Summer; Grandfathers
Age range(s): Grades 4-6
Major character(s): Sarah Marshall, 10-Year-Old; Joseph Santos, Grandfather, Scientist (marine biologist); Edie Santos, Grandmother
Time period(s): 1990s (1999)
Locale(s): Florida Keys, Florida

Summary: Retiring from his life's work as a marine biologist specializing in sharks has been difficult for Dr. Santos so he welcomes Sarah's summer visit. Sarah had planned to go to camp so she's not happy to be a six-week diversion for her grandparents. Previous visits have enabled her to learn the names of the fish that come to eat Grandma's leftovers each morning and Sarah enjoys snorkeling with them during the day. When a baby lemon shark begins coming to the dock each morning Sarah follows it to its home in the mangroves. Granddad is surprised at Sarah's courage and decides she's ready to travel with him to the deeper waters to see the grown sharks. Neither expects to also find poachers, but when they do Sarah decides to stop them. (121 pages)

Where it's reviewed:
Booklist, July 1999, page 1946
Horn Book Guide, Fall 1999, page 291
School Library Journal, July 1999, page 96

Other books by the same author:
A Dolphin Named Bob, 1996

Other books you might like:
Eric Campbell, *The Shark Callers*, 1994
    A shark hunt in the South Seas presents unexpected challenges when a volcanic eruption causes a tidal wave.
Ann McGovern, *Shark Lady: True Adventures of Eugenie Clark*, 1978
    This biographical title describes the scientist whose life work was inspired by childhood visits to a New York City Aquarium.
Donna Jo Napoli, *Shark Shock*, 1994
    After hearing his friend's school report about sharks, Adam approaches his family's vacation at the beach with fear for his life.
Todd Strasser, *Shark Bite*, 1998
    When their sailing boat sinks in a sudden storm, Ian and his friends are soon afloat in a rubber raft surrounded by sharks.

345

KATRINA GERMEIN
BRONWYN BANCROFT, Illustrator

Big Rain Coming

(New York: Clarion Books, 2000)

Subject(s): Weather; Drought
Age range(s): Grades K-2
Major character(s): Old Stephen, Aged Person; Rosie, Mother
Time period(s): 1990s
Locale(s): Minyerri, Australia

Summary: Old Stephen can see dark clouds off to the south on Sunday afternoon and predicts a big rain coming, but on Monday no rain comes. Even the night air is so hot that Rosie's children sleep outside because so rain comes. By Tuesday dogs are digging holes to try to find some relief from the dry heat and Wednesday the kids go swimming after school, but Thursday comes and still no rain. By Friday the clouds are thicker and rumbling with thunder and Old Stephen repeats his prediction. On Saturday, Old Stephen is proved to be correct when the cool, soothing rain begins. The title was originally published in Australia in 1999. (32 pages)

Where it's reviewed:
Booklist, August 2000, page 2146
Horn Book Guide, Spring 2001, page 36
Kirkus Reviews, July 1, 2000, page 959
Publishers Weekly, July 10, 2000, page 62
School Library Journal, September 2000, page 198

Other books you might like:
Joy Cowley, *Singing Down the Rain*, 1997
    Is it coincidence or does a stranger's rhythmic rain song bring the soothing rain to a dry community?
Karen Hesse, *Come On, Rain!*, 1999
    A heat wave in the city has little Tessie praying for rain when she sees clouds in the distance.
Manya Stojic, *Rain*, 2000
    Using all their senses the animals become aware of the signs of the approaching rain before they actually feel its refreshing showers.

346

PHILLIS GERSHATOR
DAVID SOMAN, Illustrator

Only One Cowry: A Dahomean Tale

(New York: Orchard Books, 2000)

Subject(s): Folklore; Cultures and Customs; Humor
Age range(s): Grades 1-4
Major character(s): Dada Segbo, Royalty; Yo, Trickster; Unnamed Character, Bride, Royalty
Time period(s): Indeterminate Past
Locale(s): Dahomey

Summary: A wealthy, but miserly king announces his intention to marry and proposes paying a bride gift of only one cowry. His people protest, but Yo takes up the challenge of finding a bride for Dada Segbo using only the one cowry he offers. Through a succession of clever trades Yo soon barters the cowry into six sacks of goods and half a jug of oil all of which he offers to a village chief if the chief's daughter will become the king's bride. The daughter is honored until she overhears Yo telling a messenger to the king that she has been found for only one cowry. The clever future queen finds a way to increase the price Dada Segbo will pay for her hand in marriage and foolish, stingy Dada Segbo is so pleased with the bargain that he rewards Yo with a single cowry shell. (32 pages)

Where it's reviewed:
Booklist, October 15, 2000, page 442
Horn Book Guide, Spring 2001, page 100
Horn Book, November 2000, page 764
Kirkus Reviews, September 1, 2000, page 1282
School Library Journal, September 2000, page 216

Awards the book has won:
Notable Social Studies Trade Books for Young People, 2001

Other books by the same author:
Sweet, Sweet Fig Banana, 1996 (CLASP Commended Book)
Rata-Pata-Scata-Fata: A Caribbean Story, 1994
Tukama Tootles the Flute, 1994

Other books you might like:
Baba Wague Diakite, *The Hunterman and the Crocodile: A West African Folktale*, 1997
    An award-winning title retells the story of Donso who learns to appreciate the need for mutual cooperation among all creatures.
Virginia Hamilton, *A Ring of Tricksters: Animal Tales from America, the West Indies and Africa*, 1997
    Eleven read-aloud tales include tricksters from spiders to rabbits and the unwitting animals that bear the brunt of their cleverness.
Eric A. Kimmel, *Bernal & Florinda: A Spanish Tale*, 1994
    Poor, but clever Bernal uses a grasshopper-infested field and skillful trading to convince Florinda's greedy father to allow their marriage.

347

FAYE GIBBONS
TED RAND, Illustrator

Mama and Me and the Model T
(New York: Morrow Junior Books, 1999)

Subject(s): Automobiles; Gender Roles; Mountain Life
Age range(s): Grades K-3
Major character(s): Mandy Searcy, Daughter, Sister; Mama, Mother, Spouse; Mr. Long, Spouse, Stepfather
Time period(s): Indeterminate Past
Locale(s): Georgia

Summary: Before leaving for town on a fine fall morning, Mr. Long tells Mandy he'll be bringing home a surprise, but when Mr. Long returns it's the surprise bringing him as he drives up in a Model T. The large blended family piles into the car with two boys standing on the running boards and holding onto the sides as Mr. Long drives them all over the farm. When the tour concludes Mr. Long scoots the girls out of the way so he can demonstrate to the boys the important steps in starting and operating the car. The more Mr. Long focuses on teaching the boys the closer the girls and Mama huddle. When Mr. Long says, "Any man can do it," Mama leaps into the Model T with Mandy and they take off. Mama is inexperienced but determined and manages to get the car back to its starting point with only minimal damage to the vehicle and the farm. Mama knows she's made her point when Mr. Long acknowledges that the car belongs to everyone in the family. (36 pages)

Where it's reviewed:
Booklist, November 15, 1999, page 634
Horn Book Guide, Spring 2000, page 36
Kirkus Reviews, September 15, 1999, page 1500
Publishers Weekly, December 13, 1999, page 85
School Library Journal, November 1999, page 116

Other books by the same author:
Mountain Wedding, 1996
Night in the Barn, 1995

Other books you might like:
Don Brown, *Alice Ramsey's Grand Adventure*, 1997
    A picture book biography describes the 1909 journey of the first woman to travel by automobile from New York to San Francisco.
Margaret Mahy, *The Rattlebang Picnic*, 1994
    When a wheel falls off the McTavish's old car they use Granny's too-hard-to-eat pizza as a spare.
Lynn Plourde, *Pigs in the Mud in the Middle of the Rud*, 1997
    A Maine farm family is loaded in their Model T with no way to go until Granny convinces the pig to get out of the road.
Peter Spier, *Tin Lizzie*, 1975
    Illustrations depict the "life" of a Model T from its purchase in 1909 to its abandonment and final restoration.

348

JANET GILL
YANGSOOK CHOI, Illustrator

Basket Weaver and Catches Many Mice
(New York: Alfred A. Knopf, 1999)

Subject(s): Animals/Cats; Crafts; Competition
Age range(s): Grades K-3
Major character(s): Basket Weaver, Artisan; Catches Many Mice, Cat; Emperor, Royalty, Father
Time period(s): Indeterminate Past
Locale(s): Asia

Summary: At the Emperor's command Basket Weaver is given one week to produce a basket for the Emperor's newly born daughter. Knowing that this competition will determine his future whether he wins or loses, Basket Weaver searches for the appropriate materials. Alas, winter approaches and he cannot locate all he needs, so he settles for a basket that does not completely satisfy him. After the basket is delivered to the Emperor, Basket Weaver notices that Catches Many Mice is missing. Assuming the wise cat has chosen to move on and avoid his fate, he gloomily goes to the Emperor's competition. There, Catches Many Mice is found in the basket for the newborn—with her own newborn kitten, an auspicious sign that decides the contest in Basket Weaver's favor. (32 pages)

Where it's reviewed:
Booklist, June 1999, page 1841
Horn Book Guide, Fall 1999, page 252
Publishers Weekly, June 21, 1999, page 67
School Library Journal, July 1999, page 70

Other books you might like:
Jennifer Armstrong, *Chin Yu Min and the Ginger Cat*, 1993
 A ginger cat changes the fortunes of a haughty widow and teaches her the value of companionship over wealth.
Andrew Clements, *Temple Cat*, 1996
 Tired of the pampering he receives as a deity in ancient Egypt, a temple cat slips away to experience life as a family cat.
Stefan Czernecki, *The Cricket's Cage: A Chinese Folktale*, 1997
 A lucky cricket helps a lowly carpenter design a model of a tower that is acceptable to the emperor.

349

DON GILLMOR
MARIE-LOUISE GAY, Illustrator

Yuck, a Love Story

(New York: Stoddart Kids, 2000)

Subject(s): Children; Friendship; Fantasy
Age range(s): Grades K-3
Major character(s): Austin Grouper, Child, Neighbor; Sternberg, Friend (Austin's), Child; Amy, Neighbor (Austin's), Child
Time period(s): 2000s
Locale(s): Earth

Summary: Yuck! A girl named Amy moves in next door to Austin and his mother expects him to meet her. Austin doesn't seem to know quite what to do after meeting the freckle-faced girl with bows on her shoes so he appears at her door in his Mr. Impossible costume and builds a life-size Apatosaurus out of Popsicle sticks for her and he tells Sternberg that Amy is yucky. Then an invitation to Amy's birthday arrives. Yuck! The night before the party Austin, in his cowboy gear, and after many attempts lassoes the moon as a gift for Amy. Hauling in the moon is no easy task and Austin has an unexpected ride to foreign lands, but he does return in time for Amy's party. Amy is a bit overwhelmed by the size of Austin's gift and both children think the cheese from which the moon is made tastes yucky so they release the moon and settle for eating some birthday cake. (30 pages)

Where it's reviewed:
Globe & Mail, June 3, 2000, page D21
Publishers Weekly, November 20, 2000, page 67
Resource Links, June 2000, page 2
School Library Journal, November 2000, page 120

Other books by the same author:
The Christmas Orange, 1999
When Vegetables Go Bad!, 1998
The Fabulous Song, 1996

Other books you might like:
Kevin Henkes, *Chester's Way*, 1988
 Chester and Wilson are content with their friendship until

Lilly moves into the neighborhood forcing them to reconsider some ideas.
James Howe, *Pinky and Rex*, 1990
 Pinky and Rex begin their friendship in the first book of the series.
Laura McGee Kvasnosky, *Zelda and Ivy and the Boy Next Door*, 1999
 Eugene moves into Zelda and Ivy's neighborhood and immediately falls in love with Zelda.
Rodney Rigby, *The Night the Moon Fell Asleep*, 1993
 Overtired from too many late nights, the moon falls asleep and crashes to the ground requiring a community effort to restore her to the night sky.
Susan Whitcher, *Moonfall*, 1993
 Sylvie finds the fallen moon in a neighbor's lilac bush and tries to restore its luster.

350

ANDREW GLASS, Author/Illustrator

Bewildered for Three Days: As to Why Daniel Boone Never Wore His Coonskin Cap

(New York: Holiday House, 2000)

Subject(s): Frontier and Pioneer Life; Tall Tales; Legends
Age range(s): Grades 2-3
Major character(s): Daniel Boone, Frontiersman, Quaker; Chester Harding, Artist
Time period(s): 1810s (1818); 1740s (1747)
Locale(s): Pennsylvania, American Colonies; Missouri

Summary: When Chester Harding locates Daniel Boone with the intention of painting his portrait he's surprised that the elder frontiersman sports a wide-brimmed hat with his buckskins rather than a coonskin cap. Daniel Boone then relates a tale from his youth to explain why he promised a mother raccoon that he'd never wear any of her kin on his head again. As the tale unfolds it sounds to the artist as if Daniel Boone was lost in the woods for three days. Daniel denies every being lost but he does recall that he was bewildered for three days after losing his coonskin cap. A lengthy author's note gives historical background to the story and factual information about the life of this famous trailblazer. (32 pages)

Where it's reviewed:
Booklist, September 1, 2000, page 122
Kirkus Reviews, August 15, 2000, page 1193
Publishers Weekly, August 21, 2000, page 75
School Library Journal, October 2000, page 125

Other books by the same author:
A Right Fine Life: Kit Carson on the Santa Fe Trail, 1997
The Sweetwater Run: The Story of Buffalo Bill Cody and the Pony Express, 1996
Folks Call Me Appleseed John, 1995

Other books you might like:
Keith Brandt, *Daniel Boone, Frontier Adventures*, 1983
 A nonfiction title describes Boone's Quaker childhood in Pennsylvania, learning skills that he later put to use making the Wilderness Road.

Catherine E. Chambers, *Daniel Boone and the Wilderness Road*, 1984
In 1827 Grandpa relates the tale of Daniel Boone's role in the settling of Kentucky.

Carl R. Green, *Daniel Boone: Wilderness Pioneer*, 1997
Many of the adventures in the life of this brave, honest, admired American are included in this nonfiction work.

Richard Kozar, *Daniel Boone and the Exploration of the Frontier*, 2000
Photos and maps help to bring the exploits of Daniel Boone to life in this biography.

351

DEBI GLIORI, Author/Illustrator

Mr. Bear to the Rescue
(New York: Orchard Books, 2000)

Subject(s): Animals/Bears; Animals; Weather
Age range(s): Grades K-2
Major character(s): Mr. Bear, Bear, Neighbor; Mrs. Bear, Bear, Spouse; Mr. Rabbit-Bunn, Rabbit, Neighbor
Time period(s): Indeterminate
Locale(s): Fictional Country

Summary: On a stormy night Mr. Bear is just settling into his warm bed when Mrs. Bear hears someone calling for help and she sends Mr. Bear to investigate. On the front steps Mr. Bear finds Mr. Rabbit-Bunn reporting the destruction of the tree that housed three animal families and the disappearance of his baby. Mr. Bear loads a baby carriage with tools and equipment and trudges through the wet, windy night. When he reaches the fallen tree it's obvious that alternate, temporary housing is necessary. First Mr. Bear has to rescue Mr. Rabbit-Bunn's baby from the tree branch to which she's stuck and then he loads everyone in the carriage and wheels them back to his home where Mrs. Bear serves warm soup and makes places for them all to sleep. (32 pages)

Where it's reviewed:
Kirkus Reviews, August 1, 2000, page 1117
Publishers Weekly, September 11, 2000, page 93
School Library Journal, November 2000, page 120

Other books by the same author:
The Snow Lambs, 1996
The Snowchild, 1994
New Big House, 1992

Other books you might like:
Libba Moore Gray, *Is There Room on the Feather Bed?*, 1997
During a storm, the farm animals seek shelter in the teeny tiny house of the wee fat woman and her wee fat husband.

Teddy Slater, *Winnie the Pooh and the Blustery Day*, 1993
Winnie the Pooh tries to save Piglet by grasping a thread from his scarf as the wind carries him away on a blustery day.

Bernard Waber, *Bearsie Bear and the Surprise Sleepover Party*, 1997
On a cold winter night, Bearsie Bear's friends come knocking at the door asking to share his warm bed.

352

DEBI GLIORI, Author/Illustrator

Mr. Bear's New Baby
(New York: Orchard Books, 1999)

Subject(s): Babies; Animals/Bears; Sisters
Age range(s): Grades K-1
Major character(s): Mr. Bear, Father, Bear; Mrs. Bear, Mother, Bear; Small Bear, Sister, Bear
Time period(s): Indeterminate
Locale(s): Fictional Country

Summary: Mr. and Mrs. Bear have tried everything to get their new baby to go to sleep. Even their neighbors have come by to give advice, but the baby just keeps crying. Finally, Small Bear comes down with a suggestion to make her baby sister sleep. The entire bear family snuggles up together, and the baby settles down quietly to rest. (32 pages)

Where it's reviewed:
Booklist, February 1, 1999, page 979
Kirkus Reviews, January 15, 1999, page 144
Publishers Weekly, February 15, 1999, page 106
School Library Journal, March 1999, page 125
Smithsonian Magazine, November 1999, page 44

Awards the book has won:
Smithsonian's Notable Books for Children, 1999

Other books by the same author:
Mr. Bear's Vacation, 2000
Mr. Bear Says Are You There, Baby Bear, 1999
Mr. Bear Says Good Night, 1997

Other books you might like:
Holly Keller, *Geraldine's Baby Brother*, 1994
Gradually, Geraldine becomes more accepting of her noisy baby brother and all the attention he receives.

Clara Vulliamy, *Ellen and Penguin and the New Baby*, 1996
Ellen and Penguin aren't sure they like the new baby, but when the baby won't stop crying, Ellen knows what to do.

Brigitte Weninger, *Will You Mind the Baby, Davy?*, 1997
Davy requests a pet mouse rather than a new baby, but after his sister's birth, he is the one family member who can calm her when she cries.

Martha Weston, *Bad Baby Brother*, 1997
Tess is eager for her infant brother to be old enough to play with her.

Ian Whybrow, *A Baby for Grace*, 1998
Grace adjusts to having a newborn baby in the house.

353

DEBI GLIORI, Author/Illustrator

Mr. Bear's Vacation
(New York: Orchard Books, 2000)

Subject(s): Animals/Bears; Vacations; Camps and Camping
Age range(s): Grades K-1
Major character(s): Small Bear, Bear, Daughter; Mr. Bear, Bear, Father; Mrs. Bear, Bear, Mother
Time period(s): Indeterminate
Locale(s): Fictional Country

Summary: A post card from vacationing friends inspires Small Bear to ask if her family can also go on vacation. Mr. Bear suggests a camping trip so the family gathers tent, sleeping bags and other gear. The backpack is heavy, the hike long and Mr. Bear's patience is wearing thin by the time he selects a camping spot for the night. With some difficulty Mr. Bear erects the moth-eaten tent while Mrs. Bear and Small Bear gather firewood. Too late, they discover that they've forgotten their sleeping bags. Still they are not discouraged, but huddle together in the tent for warmth until a frightening noise sends then scurrying for home. (32 pages)

Where it's reviewed:
Booklist, May 15, 2000, page 1748
Horn Book Guide, Fall 2000, page 249
School Library Journal, March 2000, page 197
Smithsonian, November 2000, page 62

Awards the book has won:
Smithsonian's Notable Books for Children, 2000

Other books by the same author:
Mr. Bear's New Baby, 1999
Mr. Bear Says I Love You, 1997
Mr. Bear Says Good Night, 1995
Mr. Bear's Picnic, 1995

Other books you might like:
Stan Berenstain, *The Berenstain Bears and Too Much Vacation*, 1989
    The Bear family's vacation in the Great Grizzly Mountains turns out to be a succession of unfortunate mishaps. Jan Berenstain, co-author.
Marc Brown, *Arthur's Family Vacation*, 1993
    A week-long family vacation at the beach is spent in the motel room until Arthur's ingenuity finds activities that can be enjoyed despite the rain.
David McPhail, *Emma's Vacation*, 1987
    Emma and her parents have differing opinions about what is a "good" vacation.

354

DEBI GLIORI, Author/Illustrator

No Matter What
(San Diego: Harcourt Brace & Company, 1999)

Subject(s): Parent and Child; Love; Stories in Rhyme
Age range(s): Preschool
Major character(s): Small, Fox, Child; Large, Fox, Parent
Time period(s): 1990s
Locale(s): Fictional Country

Summary: Small feels so unloved that the young fox makes a big, attention-grabbing mess in the living room. When Large notices the problem and asks what is troubling the little one, Small begins a dialogue seeking assurance of Large's love. To each "what if" condition Small proposes—squishy bug, grumpy bear or crocodile—Large assures Small of continuing, unconditional, unbreakable love. (32 pages)

Where it's reviewed:
Booklist, November 15, 1999, page 635
Horn Book Guide, Spring 2000, page 15
Publishers Weekly, November 8, 1999, page 66

School Library Journal, November 1999, page 116
Times Educational Supplement, April 23, 1999, page 11

Other books by the same author:
The Princess and the Pirate King, 1996
The Snow Lambs, 1996
My Little Brother, 1992
New Big Sister, 1991

Other books you might like:
Margaret Wise Brown, *The Runaway Bunny*, 1942
    Mother bunny loves her baby too much to let him run away so she finds him each time he escapes.
Kady MacDonald Denton, *Would They Love a Lion?*, 1995
    Using a reversible bathrobe for a costume, Anna "becomes" many different animals, each of them loved by her family.
Barbara M. Joosse, *Mama, Do You Love Me?*, 1991
    A young Eskimo girl seeks reassurance that her mother will continue to love her if she misbehaves.
Sam McBratney, *Guess How Much I Love You*, 1995
    Little Nutbrown Hare enjoys playing a game with his father in which each professes the magnitude of his love for the other.
Lisa McCourt, *I Love You, Stinky Face*, 1997
    In response to her child's questions, Mama is ready with tender, loving words of reassurance.
Susan L. Roth, *My Love for You*, 1997
    Love is quantified in comparison to animals and their attributes until the pinnacle of being "loftier than ten lovebirds soaring. . ." is reached.

355

PAUL GOBLE, Author/Illustrator

Iktomi Loses His Eyes: A Plains Indian Story
(New York: Orchard Books, 1999)

Subject(s): Legends; Indians of North America; Folklore
Age range(s): Grades 1-3
Major character(s): Iktomi, Indian; Squirrel, Squirrel
Time period(s): Indeterminate Past
Locale(s): United States

Summary: Eager to show off his new trick, Iktomi ignores the important rule to do the trick no more than four times a day. Thus, on the fifth time, Iktomi's eyes do not return to his head and he is unable to see. Squirrel spots Iktomi's eyes in the tree branches and tucks them into an old woodpecker's nest in the tree. Blindly Iktomi searches unsuccessfully for the nest so he borrows one eye from a mouse and another from a buffalo. Now, Iktomi has a strange appearance and he still cannot see well, but he hopes his sight is good enough to find Squirrel and his lost eyes. (32 pages)

Where it's reviewed:
Booklist, August 1999, page 2060
Horn Book Guide, Spring 2000, page 111
Publishers Weekly, September 20, 1999, page 90
School Library Journal, September 1999, page 212

Other books by the same author:
Iktomi and the Coyote, 1998

Iktomi and the Buzzard, 1994
Iktomi and the Buffalo Skull: A Plains Indian Story, 1991
Iktomi and the Berries: A Plains Indian Story, 1989

Other books you might like:

Joseph Bruchac, *The Boy Who Lived with the Bears: And Other Iroquois Stories*, 1995
   The award-winning collection of six stories includes tales of humor and drama written for the primary grades.
Gerald McDermott, *Arrow to the Sun*, 1974
   The Caldecott Medal winner tells of the search a young Indian boy makes for his father, the Sun.
Gayle Ross, *How Rabbit Tricked Otter: And Other Cherokee Trickster Stories*, 1994
   Fifteen stories about trickster Rabbit show him getting the better of many animals and being responsible for some of their physical characteristics too.
Nancy Van Laan, *In a Circle Long Ago: A Treasury of Native Lore from North America*, 1995
   This collection of stories and poems includes source notes and descriptions of the tribes whose folklore is represented.

356

ALEX GODARD, Author/Illustrator
GEORGE WEN, Translator

Mama, Across the Sea

(New York: Henry Holt and Company, 2000)

Subject(s): Grandparents; Mothers and Daughters; Working Mothers
Age range(s): Grades K-3
Major character(s): Cecile, Child, Daughter; Mama, Widow(er), Mother; Grandma, Grandmother, Aged Person
Time period(s): 1990s (1998)
Locale(s): Caribbean

Summary: Daily, since Mama went across the sea to find work, Cecile watches for her return. She tries to stay busy teaching Grandma to read and listening to the island storyteller. Cecile thinks that sending Mama a letter decorated with sand and shells from the beach will inspire her to return home. At first Mama writes to say she's found work and will have no time off for a year, but in a subsequent letter she tells Cecile of the arrangements she's made for Cecile to join her, across the sea, during her school vacation. Originally published in France in 1998. (40 pages)

Where it's reviewed:
Booklist, July 2000, page 2038
Horn Book Guide, Fall 2000, page 268
Publishers Weekly, June 12, 2000, page 72
Riverbank Review, Summer 2000, page 32
School Library Journal, June 2000, page 112

Other books by the same author:
Idora, 1999

Other books you might like:
Regina Hanson, *The Tangerine Tree*, 1995
   Ida is sad that her father must leave his Jamaican home for employment in New York in order to support his family.

Mary Hoffman, *Boundless Grace*, 1995
   Grace travels to Africa to visit the father she knows only from pictures and letters.
Rita Phillips Mitchell, *Hue Boy*, 1993
   Hue Boy is relieved to see his father's ship return to Belize after a long voyage.

357

LAURA GODWIN
JANE CHAPMAN, Illustrator

Happy and Honey

(New York: Margaret K. McElderry Books, 2000)

Series: Happy Honey
Subject(s): Animals/Cats; Animals/Dogs; Playing
Age range(s): Grades K-1
Major character(s): Happy, Dog; Honey, Cat
Time period(s): 2000s
Locale(s): Fictional Country

Summary: Happy is a sleeping dog being pestered by a playful cat. Honey wants to play ball and Honey wants to share a toy. Happy wants Honey to go away. Honey wants to kiss Happy and wash Happy's ears, nose and tail. Happy wakes up with a growl and Honey runs with Happy chasing. Finally, Happy is awake to play with Honey! (32 pages)

Where it's reviewed:
Booklist, December 1, 2000, page 725
Horn Book Guide, Spring 2001, page 56
Publishers Weekly, October 9, 2000, page 86
School Library Journal, December 2000, page 108

Other books by the same author:
Honey Helps, 2000 (Happy Honey)
The Flower Girl, 2000
Forest, 1998
Little White Dog, 1998

Other books you might like:
Ruth Brown, *Copycat*, 1994
   Buddy is a cat that likes to mimic the actions of other animals, including the family dog.
Patricia Casey, *My Cat Jack*, 1994
   A well-loved pet, Jack is a stretching, yawning, playful cat.
Donald Hall, *I Am the Dog, I Am the Cat*, 1994
   Poetically, a dog and cat describe their separate interests.
Isabelle Harper, *My Cats Nick and Nora*, 1994
   Two cousins wile away a Sunday afternoon playing dress-up with the patient cats.
Alex Moran, *Come Here, Tiger!*, 2000
   In a Level 1 Green Light Reader a young girl can find all the household pets, except the cat she's trying to feed.

358

THERESA MARTIN GOLDING

Kat's Surrender

(Honesdale, PA: Boyds Mills Press, 1999)

Subject(s): Friendship; Grief; Schools/Catholic Schools
Age range(s): Grades 5-8

Major character(s): Kathryn "Kat" O'Connor, 13-Year-Old, Friend; Maggie Darcy, 13-Year-Old, Friend (Kat's); Paul, 13-Year-Old, Friend (Kat's)
Time period(s): 1990s
Locale(s): Philadelphia, Pennsylvania

Summary: School and sports hold no interest for Kat in the months after her mother's death from cancer. She grieves silently and alone because no one, including her father, seems willing to talk with her about her loss. Despite Maggie's objections, Kat befriends a mentally ill, homeless man that she passes daily on her walks home from school. Then one evening while Maggie, Paul, and Kat play by the light of the street lamps, Maggie is struck by a car and injured. Visiting Maggie in the hospital awakens feelings Kat has repressed about her mother's illness and death. Although Maggie is sure that the accident is due to the curse of the neighborhood "witch," Kat's homeless friend is arrested and charged with the hit and run accident. Kat's defense of the culprit threatens her friendship with Paul and adds to her sense of disbelief and confused loyalty in Golding's debut novel. (179 pages)

Where it's reviewed:
Booklist, October 15, 1999, page 444
Children's Bookwatch, November 1999, page 4
Horn Book Guide, Spring 2000, page 78
Kirkus Reviews, October 15, 1999, page 1643
School Library Journal, November 1999, page 157

Other books you might like:
Jo Ann Muchmore, *Johnny Rides Again*, 1995
    Slowly Rose comes to accept the recent deaths of both her mother and the family dog and to accept the inevitable changes in her family.
Eileen Walsh Strauch, *Hey You, Sister Rose*, 1993
    Strict Sister Rose encourages Arlene to befriend a classmate whose mother has recently died.
Jane Breskin Zalben, *The Fortuneteller in 5B*, 1991
    Struggling to accept her father's death, Alexandra's life is complicated by a neighbor who may be something more than she seems.

359

CARLA GOLEMBE, Author/Illustrator

Annabelle's Big Move
(Boston: Houghton Mifflin Company, 1999)

Subject(s): Animals/Dogs; Moving, Household; Pets
Age range(s): Grades K-1
Major character(s): Annabelle, Dog; Miranda, Child
Time period(s): 1990s (1999)
Locale(s): North; South

Summary: On a typical snowy winter day Annabelle is aroused from her nap by the fire to see her family putting her bowl and their dishes into boxes. She grows increasingly confused when men enter the home and put the furniture onto a truck. Although she barks for them to stop, they ignore her and drive away. At the airport, Annabelle is put into a crate and separated from her family. Later, she is happy to see Miranda, her parents and their new house. Now Annabelle

sleeps by an open window, enjoying the smell of summer and playing on the beach with new dog friends. (32 pages)

Where it's reviewed:
Booklist, April 15, 1999, page 1535
Horn Book Guide, Fall 1999, page 233
School Library Journal, May 1999, page 89

Other books by the same author:
Dog Magic, 1997

Other books you might like:
Constance W. McGeorge, *Boomer's Big Day*, 1994
    Moving day is confusing for Boomer until he is able to explore his new home and find familiar things.
Cynthia Rylant, *Henry and Mudge and Annie's Good Move*, 1998
    Henry decides to let his pet Mudge help his cousin Annie adjust to her move into the house next door.
Abigail Thomas, *Lily*, 1994
    Eliza's dog, Lily, is apprehensive when the apartment contents vanish into a large truck, but relieved to arrive at the new home and find them again.

360

MERLE GOOD
P. BUCKLEY MOSS, Illustrator

Reuben and the Quilt
(Intercourse, PA: Good Books, 1999)

Subject(s): Quilts; Amish; Values
Age range(s): Grades K-2
Major character(s): Reuben, Brother, Son; Datt, Father
Time period(s): 1990s (1999)
Locale(s): Lancaster County, Pennsylvania

Summary: To raise money for the hospital expenses of an injured elderly neighbor, Reuben's family makes a log cabin quilt for an auction. When the quilt is stolen from the front porch of their home the family knows there is not enough time to make another. Datt suggests "turning the other cheek" and putting the matching pillowcases out by the road with a note for the quilt-taker. The morning after they do so, the quilt and pillowcases are returned to their porch, in plenty of time to be auctioned. (32 pages)

Where it's reviewed:
Booklist, June 1999, page 1842
School Library Journal, June 1999, page 96

Other books by the same author:
Reuben and the Blizzard, 1995
Amos and Susie: An Amish Story, 1993
Reuben and the Fire, 1993

Other books you might like:
Barbara Mitchell, *Down Buttermilk Lane*, 1993
    Mam, Dat and their children travel to town by horse and buggy to shop for supplies and have dinner at the grandparents' home.
Ann Whitford Paul, *The Seasons Sewn: A Year in Patchwork*, 1996
    An award-winning overview presents quilt patterns and their place in 19th century American life.

Patricia Polacco, *Just Plain Fancy*, 1990
When Naomi finds an unusual egg that hatches into a peacock she is concerned that the bird may violate her simple Amish lifestyle.

Jane Yolen, *Raising Yoder's Barn*, 1998
When Matthew's family loses their barn in a fire their Amish neighbors help them build a new one.

361

JANE GOODALL
JULIE LITTY, Illustrator

Dr. White

(New York: Michael Neugebauer/North-South Books, 1999)

Subject(s): Animals/Dogs; Hospitals; Healing
Age range(s): Grades K-3
Major character(s): Dr. White, Dog
Time period(s): Indeterminate Past
Locale(s): London, England

Summary: As Dr. White makes the rounds in a children's hospital he always seems to know which children need a simple tail-wagging greeting and which are so ill they need his full treatment. Then, he leaps onto the bed, curls up beside the child and gently licks a hand to let the sick child know of his presence. In this way Dr. White helps many children recover until a health inspector banishes the unsanitary creature from hospital. Forlornly, Dr. White lies outside the kitchen door for months until a nurse secretly allows him in to work his healing power on the very ill daughter of the health inspector. An author's note explains the true story on which this fictionalized account is based. (32 pages)

Where it's reviewed:
Booklist, May 1, 1999, page 1599
ForeWord Magazine, March 1999, page 54
Horn Book Guide, Fall 1999, page 253
Publishers Weekly, March 1, 1999, page 68
School Library Journal, March 1999, page 175

Other books by the same author:
With Love, 1998
The Chimpanzee Family Book, 1989

Other books you might like:
Robert J. Blake, *Dog*, 1994
A gruff, lonely old man begrudgingly makes room in his life for a dog.
Stephanie Calmenson, *Rosie: A Visiting Dog's Story*, 1994
A nonfiction picture book introduces Rosie who is in training to visit sad or lonely people needing a companion.
Nan Gregory, *How Smudge Came*, 1995
Smudge, a stray puppy, finds a home at Hospice House where she provides comfort to the patients.
Jean Davies Okimoto, *A Place for Grace*, 1993
Too small to realize her ambition to become a guide dog for the blind, Grace is trained to be a companion for a deaf person.

362

DIANE GOODE, Author/Illustrator

Cinderella: The Dog and Her Little Glass Slipper

(New York: The Blue Sky Press/Scholastic Inc., 2000)

Subject(s): Fairy Tales; Animals/Dogs; Princes and Princesses
Age range(s): Grades K-3
Major character(s): Cinderella, Stepsister, Servant
Time period(s): Indeterminate Past
Locale(s): Fictional Country

Summary: The characters in this retelling of the traditional tale are various species of dog. Always kind, Cinderella complies with her cruel stepmother's commands without complaint though she's disappointed not to be able to attend the prince's ball. Cinderella's fairy godmother appears to magically prepare the way for Cinderella to go to the ball in a beautiful gown and carriage. Cinderella catches the prince's eye and obediently leaves fifteen minutes early to return home and ask her fairy godmother to allow her to attend a second ball. At the second ball Cinderella loses track of the time and does not leave until the clock has almost finished striking midnight. In her haste she loses a glass slipper that the prince uses to locate his future bride. (40 pages)

Where it's reviewed:
Booklist, November 1, 2000, page 543
Horn Book Guide, Spring 2001, page 100
Kirkus Reviews, September 1, 2000, page 282
Publishers Weekly, August 7, 2000, page 95
School Library Journal, September 2000, page 216

Other books by the same author:
The Dinosaur's New Clothes, 1999
Mama's Perfect Present, 1996
Where's Our Mama?, 1991

Other books you might like:
Pamela Duncan Edwards, *Dinorella: A Prehistoric Fairy Tale*, 1997
Duke Dudley is delighted to deduce that Dinorella is the daring dancer who defended him from a deionychus.
Janet Perlman, *Cinderella Penguin or, The Little Glass Flipper*, 1992
A spoof of the Cinderella story has penguins in the leading roles.
William Wegman, *Cinderella*, 1993
The classic fairy tale has been recast with dogs playing all the roles, but Cinderella still loses her glass slipper.

363

JOAN ELIZABETH GOODMAN
DOMINIC CATALANO, Illustrator

Bernard's Nap

(Honesdale, PA: Boyds Mill Press, 1999)

Subject(s): Animals/Elephants; Bedtime; Family Life
Age range(s): Grades K-1
Major character(s): Bernard, Elephant, Child
Time period(s): 1990s (1999)

Locale(s): Fictional Country

Summary: It is naptime, but Bernard doesn't want to go to bed. His mother sings him a song, his father tells him a story, his grandmother stays with him, knitting, but only his family falls asleep, not Bernard. Bernard tucks in his parents and grandmother before, finally, singing himself to sleep. (32 pages)

Where it's reviewed:
Booklist, March 15, 1999, page 1333
Horn Book Guide, Fall 1999, page 233
School Library Journal, April 1999, page 94

Other books by the same author:
Hope's Crossing, 1998
Bernard's Bath, 1996
Hush Little Darling: A Christmas Song, 1992

Other books you might like:
Frank Asch, *Good Night, Baby Bear*, 1998
    Mama Bear has a hard time getting Baby Bear to sleep.
Debi Gliori, *Mr. Bear's New Baby*, 1999
    Attempts to put the new baby to bed just make Mr. and Mrs. Bear, as well as all their neighbors, sleepy.
Morag Loh, *Tucking Mommy In*, 1988
    Two sisters tuck their mother in after she falls asleep reading bedtime stories.
Jill Murphy, *A Quiet Night In*, 1994
    A bedtime story has the desired soporific effect. Unfortunately, it is the parents who fall asleep, leaving the kids to put themselves to bed.
Elizabeth Winthrop, *Asleep in a Heap*, 1993
    While waiting for Julia to finish her bath, Daddy falls asleep on the floor where he's soon joined by Mama, Molly, the dog, four cats and—Julia.
Audrey Wood, *The Napping House*, 1984
    Though everyone begins napping in their own spot, they all end up asleep on top of Granny until a wide-awake flea gives a mouse a wake-up bite.

364

VALERI GORBACHEV, Author/Illustrator

Peter's Picture
(New York: North-South Books, 2000)

Subject(s): Schools; Artists and Art; Parent and Child
Age range(s): Grades K-2
Major character(s): Peter, Son, Bear; Father, Bear, Father
Time period(s): Indeterminate Past
Locale(s): Fictional Country

Summary: Peter is so proud of the picture he painted at school today that he shows it to the neighbors on his way home. Unfortunately, the neighbors react to the picture as if it's a real flower and try to smell it, water it, put it in a vase or give it to the bees. Peter is disappointed in these unexpected reactions so he's lost some of his excitement about his artwork by the time he arrives home. His parents, however, know just how to compliment his creation and Father frames the painting and hangs it on the living room wall. Peter is so pleased he hurries to his room to paint another. (32 pages)

Where it's reviewed:
Booklist, April 15, 2000, page 1550

Children's Book Review Service, May 2000, page 108
Children's Bookwatch, April 2000, page 6
Horn Book Guide, Fall 2000, page 249
School Library Journal, June 2000, page 112

Other books by the same author:
Where Is the Apple Pie?, 1999
Nicky and the Big, Bad Wolves, 1998
The Fool of the World and the Flying Ship, 1998
Arnie the Brave, 1997

Other books you might like:
Amy Hest, *Jamaica Louise James*, 1996
    Jamaica Louise uses her love of drawing to create pictures that brighten Grammy's workplace at the 86th Street subway station.
Crockett Johnson, *Harold and the Purple Crayon*, 1958
    Harold has a magic purple crayon, a vivid imagination and a talent for drawing himself into and out of trouble.
Nicola Moon, *Lucy's Picture*, 1995
    While her classmates paint colorful pictures Lucy makes a textured collage for her visiting grandfather to ''see'' with his fingers.

365

CAROL GORMAN

Dork in Disguise
(New York: HarperCollins Publishers, 1999)

Subject(s): Self-Acceptance; Popularity; Schools
Age range(s): Grades 3-6
Major character(s): Jerry Flack, 6th Grader; Brenda McAdams, 6th Grader
Time period(s): 1990s (1999)
Locale(s): Spencer Lake (Nathaniel Hawthorne Middle School)

Summary: Jerry thinks his family's move to Spencer Lake is his opportunity to shed his dork persona and become a cool guy. To achieve that goal, Jerry applies gel to his hair and puts his glasses in his backpack, but Brenda (who also wears glasses) sees through his ruse within minutes of meeting him. Initially, Jerry tells some lies on a class questionnaire because he's sure that his own life is not exciting enough to interest anyone. When he realizes his quest for coolness will mean he has to forsake the science team despite his love of science rather than appear a dork, Jerry begins to reassess his plans. It takes a while, but Jerry finally decides he prefers to be himself and he's grateful that Brenda (who has always considered him cool) is willing to like him as he is, once he discovers who that is. (164 pages)

Where it's reviewed:
Booklist, September 1, 1999, page 133
Horn Book, January 2000, page 75
Kirkus Reviews, September 1, 1999, page 1416
Publishers Weekly, September 27, 1999, page 106
School Library Journal, September 1999, page 225

Other books by the same author:
Lizard Flanagan, Super Model?, 1998
The Miraculous Makeover of Lizard Flanagan, 1994
The Biggest Bully in Brookdale, 1992

Other books you might like:

Elisa Carbone, *Starting School with an Enemy*, 1998
  Sarah is having difficulty adjusting to her family's move and making friends in her new school.
Ralph Fletcher, *Spider Boy*, 1997
  After weeks of watching a new student with an interest in spiders eating alone every day, a self-described nerd reaches out in friendship.
Julie Anne Peters, *How Do You Spell GEEK?*, 1996
  A new student with a natural talent for spelling almost ruins Kim and Ann's plans for the National Spelling Bee.

366

DORIS GOVE
MARILYNN H. MALLORY, Illustrator

My Mother Talks to Trees
(Atlanta: Peachtree Publishers, Ltd., 1999)

Subject(s): Trees; Mothers and Daughters; Nature
Age range(s): Grades 1-3
Major character(s): Mom, Mother; Laura, Daughter
Time period(s): 1990s (1999)
Locale(s): United States

Summary: Laura is embarrassed as she walks home from school with her mother. It's spring, the time of year when Mom stops to view the changes in various trees they pass, congratulating them for their growth and drawing parallels with Laura's achievements. Mom knows a lot about trees and seems to have inspired at least a little interest in her daughter because Laura sneaks back to talk to one of the walnut trees she planted on Arbor Day. Concluding pictures and facts give information to identify trees in the reader's neighborhood. (32 pages)

Where it's reviewed:
Booklist, May 1, 1999, page 1599
Horn Book Guide, Fall 1999, page 253
Publishers Weekly,
School Library Journal, June 1999, page 71

Other books by the same author:
One Rainy Night, 1994
Red-Spotted Newt, 1994
A Water Snake's Year, 1991

Other books you might like:
Jim Arnosky, *Crinkleroot's Guide to Knowing the Trees*, 1991
  A nonfiction introduction to trees describes how to identify trees and how animals use trees.
Eve Bunting, *Someday a Tree*, 1993
  Alice and her family grieve the loss of an ancient oak tree that is killed by illegally dumped chemicals.
Lynne Cherry, *The Great Kapok Tree: A Tale of the Amazon Rain Forest*, 1990
  A man changes his plans to cut down a kapok tree after he dreams about the animals that depend on the tree.
Patricia Lauber, *Be a Friend to Trees*, 1994
  The nonfiction title in the Let's Read and Find Out Science Series explains the importance of trees as sources of food and oxygen.

Gerda Muller, *Around the Oak*, 1994
  When Ben and Caroline visit their uncle, a forest ranger, their adventures provide opportunities for learning more about the forest.
Wendy Pfeffer, *A Log's Life*, 1997
  Although an oak tree is felled by a storm, it continues to be a source of life in the forest as it decays.
Janice May Udry, *A Tree Is Nice*, 1956
  The Caldecott Medal winner celebrates the many simple pleasures that a tree offers.

367

BOB GRAHAM, Author/Illustrator

Benny: An Adventure Story
(Cambridge, MA: Candlewick Press, 1999)

Subject(s): Animals/Dogs; Magicians; Humor
Age range(s): Grades K-2
Major character(s): Benny, Dog, Entertainer; Brillo, Magician; Mary Kelly, Child, Animal Lover
Time period(s): 1990s (1999)
Locale(s): England

Summary: When Benny's stage tricks attract more applause than Brillo's, the magician boots his assistant out of the act and out the door. Lost and forlorn, Benny rides the rails and tries to find work as a tap-dancing sheep dog or a harmonica-playing guard dog but no one seems to appreciate his talents. Finally Benny tires of traveling and stations himself near a city statute where he performs for coins dropped into his cup. He's successful not only at making some money, but also at attracting Mary Kelly and her large, music-loving family. At last, Benny has found a home with people who love him just the way he is. (32 pages)

Where it's reviewed:
Booklist, September 15, 1999, page 267
Publishers Weekly, June 14, 1999, page 69
School Library Journal, July 1999, page 72
Smithsonian Magazine, November 1999, page 46

Awards the book has won:
School Library Journal Best Books, 1999
Smithsonian's Notable Books for Children, 1999

Other books by the same author:
Queenie, One of the Family, 1997
Spirit of Hope, 1996
Rose Meets Mr. Wintergarten, 1992

Other books you might like:
John Burningham, *Courtney*, 1994
  Courtney, an adopted mongrel with many talents, cooks, juggles and rescues the baby from a fire before he mysteriously vanishes.
Peggy Rathmann, *Officer Buckle and Gloria*, 1995
  Behind Officer Buckle's back, police dog Gloria acts out his safety tips, bringing new life to his dull assemblies. Caldecott Medal winner.
Bernard Waber, *Lovable Lyle*, 1977
  Life with the Primm family continues to be appealing for the multi-talented crocodile Lyle.

BOB GRAHAM, Author/Illustrator

Max
(Cambridge, MA: Candlewick Press, 2000)

Subject(s): Heroes and Heroines; Parent and Child; Individuality
Age range(s): Grades K-1
Major character(s): Max, Child, Son; Captain Lightning, Father, Hero; Madam Thunderbolt, Mother, Heroine
Time period(s): 2000s
Locale(s): England

Summary: Max, the superbaby son of superheroes develops normally with one exception—he doesn't learn to fly or appear to have much interest in doing so. Max, despite his superhero garb, is content to stay on the ground. His grandparents, retired from their exciting life as superheroes, fret over Max's inability to fly knowing that he cannot uphold the family tradition without that skill. Madam Thunderbolt gently encourages hovering and swooping while Captain Lightning invites Max up to the ceiling to play with the parakeet. Max prefers being on the floor with the dog. Early one morning while his parents and grandparents sleep, Max sees a bird falling from its nest and, in order to save it he flies into the air, catches the bird and returns it to its nest. Now, Max happily defies gravity at will although he limits his heroics to solving everyday problems. (32 pages)

Where it's reviewed:
Booklist, November 1, 2000, page 548
Publishers Weekly, July 24, 2000, page 93
School Library Journal, September 2000, page 198
Smithsonian, November 2000, page 62

Awards the book has won:
Publishers Weekly Best Books, 2000
School Library Journal Best Books, 2000

Other books by the same author:
Queenie, One of the Family, 1997
Spirit of Hope, 1996 (Smithsonian's Notable Books for Children)
Rose Meets Mr. Wintergarten, 1992

Other books you might like:
Syd Hoff, *Bernard on His Own*, 1993
    Bernard's parents reassure him that one day he'll be able to climb a tree, catch a fish and gather honey on his own.
Robert Kraus, *Leo the Late Bloomer*, 1971
    Father is impatient for Leo to develop ordinary skills; Mother is concerned but confident that, in his own time, Leo will mature.
Mary DeBall Kwitz, *Little Vampire and the Midnight Bear*, 1995
    In order to save his baby sister from danger, Little Vampire forgets his unsuccessful attempts to learn to fly and soars out the window with her.
Jeanne Titherington, *Sophy and Auntie Pearl*, 1995
    Sophy is both surprised and excited to awaken one morning and discover that she has the ability to fly.

JEAN GRALLEY, Author/Illustrator

Hogula: Dread Pig of Night
(New York: Henry Holt, 1999)

Subject(s): Animals/Pigs; Humor; Vampires
Age range(s): Grades K-3
Major character(s): Hogula, Pig; Elvis Ann, Child
Time period(s): 1990s (1999)
Locale(s): Fictional Country

Summary: Hogula has everything in his castle on Grimy Pork Chop Hill, everything that is except friends. Following the suggestion of one of his servants, Hogula goes to the Mall where he meets many new people but does not make new friends. Elvis Ann, Dread Queen of Kissyface, finds a glove dropped by Hogula and goes door to door until she finds the owner and a friend. (32 pages)

Where it's reviewed:
Booklist, November 15, 1999, page 635
Bulletin of the Center for Children's Books, October 1999, page 54
Children's Bookwatch, October 1999, page 6
Horn Book Guide, Spring 2000, page 37
School Library Journal, November 11, 1999, page 116

Other books you might like:
Kim Kennedy, *Frankenfrog*, 1999
    A mad scientist creates Frankenfrog in this humorous spoof.
Deborah Nourse Lattimore, *Cinderhazel: The Cinderella of Halloween*, 1997
    Cinderhazel finds her perfect, dirty match in Prince Alarming.
Dav Pilkey, *Dogzilla*, 1993
    Dogzilla terrorizes Mousopolis.

KES GRAY
NICK SHARRATT, Illustrator

Eat Your Peas
(New York: DK Ink/Dorling Kindersley Publishing, Inc., 2000)

Subject(s): Food; Mothers and Daughters; Family Life
Age range(s): Grades K-1
Major character(s): Daisy, Child, Daughter; Mom, Mother
Time period(s): 2000s
Locale(s): England

Summary: Each time Mom asks Daisy to eat her peas Daisy replies calmly, ''I don't like peas.'' Mom offers ice cream for dessert if Daisy will eat her peas, but Daisy's response does not change. Mom's bribes grow bigger and more absurd—pet elephants and a chocolate factory, but Daisy is unmoved. Finally, Daisy agrees to eat the peas on one condition—Mom must eat her Brussels sprouts. Forlornly Mom replies, ''But I don't like Brussels sprouts.'' It's obvious from the conclusion of the author's first book that both enjoy ice cream. (32 pages)

Where it's reviewed:
Booklist, September 1, 2000, page 122

Horn Book Guide, Spring 2001, page 17
Kirkus Reviews, August 15, 2000, page 1194
Publishers Weekly, September 18, 2000, page 111
School Library Journal, September 2000, page 198

Other books you might like:
Marc Brown, *D.W. the Picky Eater*, 1995
    D.W. learns to be more willing to try new foods in order to join the family when they go out to eat.
Chris L. Demarest, *No Peas for Nellie*, 1988
    Nellie can list many foods she'd be happy to see on her plate other than peas.
Henrik Drescher, *The Boy Who Ate Around*, 1994
    When Mo faces a meal he doesn't enjoy he simply eats around it.
Russell Hoban, *Bread and Jam for Frances*, 1965
    When Frances refuses to eat anything other than bread and jam she is served a steady diet of it until she agrees to try something new.
Mary Ann Hoberman, *The Seven Silly Eaters*, 1997
    The Peters family has seven children with definite food preferences and a tired mother trying to please each one.
Jane Read Martin, *Now I Will Never Leave the Dinner Table*, 1996
    In order to eat the detested spinach on her plate, Patty Jane adds chips, grape juice and ketchup to make it more palatable.
Dan Yaccarino, *If I Had a Robot*, 1996
    As a kid who abhors vegetables, Phil imagines the benefits of having a robot to eat them for him.

371

LIBBA MOORE GRAY
LLOYD BLOOM, Illustrator

When Uncle Took the Fiddle
(New York: Orchard Books, 1999)

Subject(s): Music and Musicians; Aunts and Uncles; Mountain Life
Age range(s): Grades K-2
Major character(s): Uncle, Musician, Uncle; Brown Dog, Dog; Mama, Mother, Musician
Time period(s): Indeterminate Past
Locale(s): Appalachians

Summary: In the evening, family members comment on how tired they feel as they settle into chairs or rockers. Then Uncle picks up his fiddle and Mama gets her guitar. Soon even Brown Dog is howling along with the tune Uncle's fiddle is singing. The neighbors begin to gather from down the hollow and in no time the tired group is dancing, clapping, and tapping to the beat. Under a star-filled sky the neighbors head home and the tired family listens to one last song from Uncle's fiddle. (32 pages)

Where it's reviewed:
Booklist, September 15, 1999, page 267
Horn Book Guide, Spring 2000, page 37
Kirkus Reviews, July 15, 1999, page 1133
Publishers Weekly, August 16, 1999, page 83
School Library Journal, November 1999, page 116

Other books by the same author:
Is There Room on the Feather Bed?, 1997
Little Lil and the Swing-Singing Sax, 1996
My Mama Had a Dancing Heart, 1995 (ALA Notable Book)

Other books you might like:
Natalie Kinsey-Warnock, *The Fiddler of the Northern Lights*, 1996
    The music of a fiddle-playing stranger draws people from their homes and the community dances all night to the glow of the Northern Lights.
George Ella Lyon, *Five Live Bongos*, 1994
    Five lively, noisy, music-making children create the Found Sound Band.
Lloyd Moss, *Zin! Zin! Zin! A Violin*, 1995
    With more formality than Uncle and his fiddle but no less exuberance, the musicians of an orchestra begin playing.

372

CAROL GREENE
LORETTA KRUPINSKI, Illustrator

Where Is That Cat?
(New York: Hyperion Books for Children, 1999)

Subject(s): Animals/Cats; Lost and Found Possessions; Pets
Age range(s): Grades K-1
Major character(s): Fitz, Cat (stray); Miss Perkins, Aged Person
Time period(s): 1990s (1998)
Locale(s): England

Summary: While collecting her mail on a winter day, Miss Perkins spots a cat hiding in a snow drift. Naming him Fitz for the sound he makes when a snowflake lands on his nose, Miss Perkins invites the cat into her home temporarily. She feeds Fitz and places an ad in the newspaper seeking a good home for him. Each day when someone comes in response to the ad Fitz cannot be found and the people leave. Daily, Fitz proves himself more valuable to Miss Perkins so by the time the fifth person responds to the ad, Miss Perkins has decided to keep Fitz as her pet. (32 pages)

Where it's reviewed:
Booklist, September 1, 1999, page 140
Horn Book Guide, Spring 2000, page 38
Kirkus Reviews, July 1, 1999, page 1054
Publishers Weekly, July 26, 1999, page 90
School Library Journal, August 1999, page 136

Other books by the same author:
Cat and Bear, 1998
Red Boots for Christmas, 1995
The Old Ladies Who Liked Cats, 1992
Rain! Rain!, 1982

Other books you might like:
Pamela D. Greenwood, *I Found Mouse*, 1994
    Tessie finds a kitten in need of a home and convinces her dad to let her keep it.
Wolfram Hanel, *Mia the Beach Cat: A Story*, 1994
    On vacation Maggie loses her stuffed tiger but finds a cat that she sneaks into the picnic basket for the trip home.

Ann M. Martin, *Leo the Magnificat*, 1996

A fluffy black and white cat wanders into a churchyard and makes himself at home for the rest of his long life.

Cynthia Rylant, *Mr. Putter and Tabby Pour the Tea*, 1994

At an animal shelter, lonely Mr. Putter finds a lonely old cat with creaking bones and thinning fur—just the match for him!

373

STEPHANIE GREENE
MARTHA WESTON, Illustrator

Owen Foote, Frontiersman
(New York: Clarion Books, 1999)

Subject(s): Bullies; Mothers and Sons; Outdoor Life
Age range(s): Grades 2-4
Major character(s): Owen Foote, 2nd Grader, Friend; Joseph Hobbs, 2nd Grader, Friend; Mrs. Gold, Neighbor, Grandmother
Time period(s): 1990s (1999)
Locale(s): United States

Summary: Owen imagines himself as Daniel Boone in the wilderness each time he puts on his coonskin cap and hikes into the woods behind Mrs. Gold's house to the tree fort he and Joseph have made. Their plans for spring vacation are ruined when they find Mrs. Gold's visiting grandsons in the tree house, threatening to wreck it. Joseph is in favor of seeking help from their mothers, but Owen knows Daniel Boone would never have turned to his mom to solve his problems. Using determination, a little knowledge of the outdoors and ingenuity Owen and squeamish Joseph concoct and carry out a plan that frightens away the bullies. (96 pages)

Where it's reviewed:
Booklist, October 15, 1999, page 444
Horn Book, September 1999, page 610
School Library Journal, October 1999, page 114

Awards the book has won:
School Library Journal Best Books, 1999

Other books by the same author:
Owen Foote, Soccer Star, 1998
Show and Tell, 1998
Owen Foote, Second Grade Strongman, 1996

Other books you might like:
Steven Kroll, *Patrick's Tree House*, 1994

The tree house that Grandad builds as a surprise for visiting Patrick is taken over by the twins who live nearby.

Bonnie Pryor, *The Plum Tree War*, 1989

Robert discovers a different side to bothersome cousin Harriet when the two stop quarrelling long enough to learn that they have a lot in common.

Carol Beach York, *The Key to the Playhouse*, 1994

While visiting Grandmother, two cousins enjoy playing in the playhouse, but lock out a neighborhood child rather than share the space.

374

STEPHANIE GREENE
MARTHA WESTON, Illustrator

Owen Foote, Money Man
(New York: Clarion Books, 2000)

Subject(s): Work; Money; Family Life
Age range(s): Grades 2-4
Major character(s): Owen Foote, 8-Year-Old, Friend; Joseph Hobbs, 8-Year-Old, Friend; Mr. White, Neighbor
Time period(s): 2000s (2000)
Locale(s): United States

Summary: Now that Owen has a catalog of enticing items such as fake vomit he is desperate to make some money so he can acquire these neat products. Unfortunately, his parents think he should work for his allowance and Owen just wants money. With Joseph's help he prepares a list of moneymaking projects and then the two of them try to turn them into profit. Their ideas, unfortunately, generate problems rather than income and Owen is beginning to feel discouraged when Mr. White seeks his advice. Owen feels proud to be the consultant to Mr. White who is planning to create a goldfish pond in his yard. He happily works for hours helping Mr. White dig the hole, line it and fill it with water with no thought of reward. Mr. White's presentation to Owen of twenty dollars as payment for his work helps Owen feel satisfied that his efforts have value in the adult world. Of course, Owen still has to convince his mother that he truly earned the money, but he's sure his sweaty, dirty body is evidence of his labors. (88 pages)

Where it's reviewed:
Booklist, September 1, 2000, page 122
Bulletin of the Center for Children's Books, October 2000, page 63
Horn Book Guide, Spring 2001, page 62
Horn Book, September 2000, page 569
School Library Journal, September 2000, page 198

Other books by the same author:
Owen Foote, Frontiersman, 1999 (School Library Journal Best Book)
Owen Foote, Soccer Star, 1998
Show and Tell, 1998
Owen Foote, Second Grade Strongman, 1996

Other books you might like:
Bill Cosby, *Money Troubles*, 1998

While trying to earn money for a telescope Little Bill learns a lesson about needs greater than his own and the importance of generosity.

Peg Kehret, *The Richest Kids in Town*, 1994

Peter's moneymaking schemes provide a framework for a friendship but do not earn much cash.

Lensey Namioka, *Yang the Eldest and His Odd Jobs*, 2000

With support from his siblings Yang tries to earn enough money for a new violin.

Marilyn Singer, *Josie to the Rescue*, 1999

Realizing that her parents have some financial concerns with a new baby coming Josie decides to earn money to contribute to the family.

Karen Waggoner, *Partners*, 1995

Sensitive Jamie's plan to raise pet mice is complicated by his sister's cat and his brother's plan to sell the animals as snake food.

375

ADELE ARON GREENSPUN, Author/Illustrator
JOANIE SCHWARZ, Illustrator

Bunny and Me

(New York: Cartwheel Books/Scholastic Inc., 2000)

Subject(s): Babies; Animals/Rabbits; Playing
Age range(s): Preschool
Major character(s): Baby, Baby; Bunny, Rabbit
Time period(s): 2000s
Locale(s): United States

Summary: Baby and Bunny imitate each other's behavior—popping bubbles, touching noses and wearing beads. Flop-eared Bunny is more mobile than Baby and hops out of sight while chasing a ball. Poor Baby is sad now. Baby looks everywhere before finding Bunny in a basket—happy playmates once again! (32 pages)

Where it's reviewed:
Booklist, March 15, 2000, page 1386
Horn Book Guide, Fall 2000, page 249
Kirkus Reviews, January 15, 2000, page 120
Publishers Weekly, January 24, 2000, page 310
School Library Journal, April 2000, page 105

Other books by the same author:
Daddies, 1991

Other books you might like:
Jim Arnosky, *Rabbits and Raindrops*, 1997
A mother rabbit watching protectively over her five babies hurries them to shelter as raindrops begin to fall.
Dorothy Kunhardt, *Pat the Bunny*, 1962
In a classic title for the very young, readers can pat the bunny, smell the flowers and play peek-a-boo.
Peter McCarty, *Little Bunny on the Move*, 1999
Little Bunny hops through fields and forests to reach his home.

376

SHEILA GREENWALD

Stucksville

(New York: DK Ink/Dorling Kindersley Publishing, Inc., 2000)

Subject(s): Apartments; Contests; Schools
Age range(s): Grades 3-5
Major character(s): Emerald Costos, 4th Grader, Daughter; Angel Monteros, 4th Grader, Neighbor; Guthry Lauffer, 4th Grader, Friend
Time period(s): 2000s (2000)
Locale(s): New York, New York

Summary: Emerald, only child of aspiring actors, is accustomed to moving often as her parents pursue their careers. The great job opportunities that led to the family's move to New York fell through and the family now lives in "Stucksville"

as they call their tiny partial apartment in an older building. Two of Emerald's classmates also live in the building, but Emerald has learned that frequent moves mean never to get attached to people or places. A school assignment to complete an essay on "My New York" proves difficult for Angel and Guthry because they express themselves through talking and art, but not writing. For Emerald the assignment is difficult because she has no New York to claim as her own. Angel vigorously disagrees with Emerald's opinion and, inspired by a visit to Museum of the City of New York, suggests a team project building display models of their apartments. Through the project and her observation of neighbors across the courtyard, Emerald begins to feel a sense of place and realizes she can claim New York as her home. (152 pages)

Where it's reviewed:
Booklist, November 1, 2000, page 538
Horn Book Guide, Spring 2001, page 73
Kirkus Reviews, October 15, 2000, page 1485
Publishers Weekly, October 16, 2000, page 76
School Library Journal, October 2000, page 125

Other books by the same author:
The Mariah Delaney Lending Library Disaster, 2000
Rosy Cole: She Grows and Graduates, 1997
Rosy Cole: She Walks in Beauty, 1994
My Fabulous New Life, 1993
Rosy's Romance, 1989

Other books you might like:
Amy Goldman Koss, *The Ashwater Experiment*, 1999
Hillary's attended eighteen schools as her parents follow the craft shows, never staying in one place long enough for her to feel at home.
Marissa Moss, *Amelia's Notebook*, 1995
In a journal, Amelia records her thoughts about moving, the friend she's left behind and her apprehensions about beginning a new school.
Vera B. Williams, *Scooter*, 1993
Personable and unpredictable Lanny adjusts easily to a move into a New York apartment, meeting neighbors and making new friends.

377

KRISTIANA GREGORY

The Great Railroad Race: The Diary of Libby West

(New York: Scholastic, 1999)

Series: Dear America
Subject(s): Diaries; Frontier and Pioneer Life; Railroads
Age range(s): Grades 4-7
Major character(s): Libby West, 14-Year-Old, Daughter (of a journalist); Pete, 19-Year-Old, Journalist
Time period(s): 1860s (1868)
Locale(s): West; Utah

Summary: Libby's father is a railroad reporter who decides to follow the story of the great railroad race, in which the Union Pacific and Central Pacific railroads try to meet in the middle of the continent so that the entire country is connected by railroad. Libby's mother refuses to let her father travel alone, so Libby, her mother, her brother, and Pete, her father's friend from the Union Army and newspaper co-worker, all travel along. Riding west is an exciting adventure as are the growing feelings between Libby and Pete. (208 pages)

Where it's reviewed:
Booklist, April 1, 1999, page 1426
Horn Book Guide, Fall 1999, page 292
School Library Journal, August 1999, page 158

Other books by the same author:
Cleopatra VII: Daughter of the Nile, 1999 (Royal Diaries)
Orphan Runaways, 1998
Across the Wide and Lonesome Prairie: The Oregon Trail Diary of Hattie Campbell, 1997 (Dear America)

Other books you might like:
Kathleen Duey, *Willow Chase: Kansas Territory, 1847*, 1997
    Willow Chase must find her way back to her family after being swept away while crossing a flooded river.
Gary Paulsen, *Mr. Tucket*, 1994
    Fourteen-year-old Francis Tucket is captured by Indians while traveling with his family on the Oregon Trail.
Laura Ingalls Wilder, *By the Shores of Silver Lake*, 1939
    Among the many changes to the frontier the Wilder family observes from their prairie homestead is the building of the railroad.
Laura Wilson, *How I Survived the Oregon Trail: The Journal of Jesse Adams*, 1999
    Ten-year-old Jesse Adams describes what it was like to travel west on the Oregon Trail.

378

VALISKA GREGORY
MARSHA WINBORN, Illustrator

A Valentine for Norman Noggs

(New York: HarperCollins Publishers, 1999)

Subject(s): Holidays; Self-Esteem; Schools
Age range(s): Grades K-2
Major character(s): Norman Noggs, Student—Elementary School, Hamster; Wilhelmina Stitch, Hamster, Classmate
Time period(s): 1990s
Locale(s): Fictional Country

Summary: Norman is totally smitten with Wilhelmina and totally intimidated by the attention that two bigger, tougher boys in the class give to her. In fact, the bullies threaten to harm Norman if he dares to give Wilhelmina a valentine. On Valentine's Day morning, they are waiting for Norman as he walks to school and they destroy the two valentines he's prepared for Wilhelmina. Before the bullies can also destroy Norman, Wilhelmina appears and demonstrates her karate skill to free Norman. The two race to school where Wilhelmina gives Norman her valentine and Norman, who has a third one pinned to his sleeve for safekeeping, gives Wilhelmina the real valentine he's made for her. (32 pages)

Where it's reviewed:
Booklist, April 1, 1999, page 1420
Bulletin of the Center for Children's Books, February 1999, page 203
Children's Book Review Service, February 1999, page 74

Publishers Weekly, December 14, 1998, page 75
School Library Journal, January 1999, page 88

Other books by the same author:
Looking for Angels, 1996
When Stories Fell Like Shooting Stars, 1996
Babysitting for Benjamin, 1993

Other books you might like:
Diane DeGroat, *Roses Are Pink, Your Feet Really Stink*, 1996
    Gilbert's plan to use unkind poems on the valentines of two people who tease him backfires and he must apologize to the class or lose his friends.
Jonathan London, *Froggy's First Kiss*, 1998
    Froggy adores Frogilina and her lunch treats until her kiss leads to embarrassing teasing and he gives the valentine he has for Frogilina to his mom.
James Stevenson, *Happy Valentine's Day, Emma!*, 1987
    The receipt of nasty Valentines from two unfriendly witches does not deter kind witch Emma from enjoying the day with her friends.

379

SUSANNA GRETZ, Author/Illustrator

Rabbit Food

(Cambridge, MA: Candlewick Press, 1999)

Subject(s): Food; Animals/Rabbits; Rebellion, Behavioral
Age range(s): Grades K-2
Major character(s): John, Rabbit, Nephew; Uncle Bunny, Rabbit, Uncle
Time period(s): Indeterminate
Locale(s): Fictional Country

Summary: Everyone in John's family enjoys delicious meals of rabbit food—carrots, peas, celery, tomatoes and worst of all mushrooms—everyone except John. He has no interest in growing up big and strong because John can see that big, strong adults all eat vegetables. Hoping to solve John's food problem, his parents plan a trip and call on Uncle Bunny to care for their children. Uncle Bunny keeps the children so active that even John is hungry enough to eat little bits of vegetables. During dinner John notices that Uncle Bunny hides his carrots in the potted plants or under his napkin. No one says anything to Uncle Bunny, but eventually all the food is eaten, except the carrots, and Uncle Bunny is forced to try them. Hmmm, not bad! (24 pages)

Where it's reviewed:
Booklist, May 1, 1999, page 1599
Horn Book Guide, Fall 1999, page 253
Publishers Weekly, March 29, 1999, page 103
School Library Journal, April 1999, page 94

Other books by the same author:
Frog, Duck and Rabbit, 1992
Rabbit Rambles On, 1992
Teddy Bears at the Seaside, 1989

Other books you might like:
Marc Brown, *D.W. the Picky Eater*, 1995
    D.W. learns to be more willing to try new foods in order to join the family when they go out to eat.

Vivian French, *Oliver's Vegetables*, 1995
  Although Oliver says he only eats potatoes Grandpa's idea has him sampling different vegetables from the garden.
Russell Hoban, *Bread and Jam for Frances*, 1965
  When Frances refuses to eat anything other than bread and jam she is served a steady diet of it until she's ready to try something new.

380

ANN GRIFALCONI, Author/Illustrator

Tiny's Hat

(New York: HarperCollins Publishers, 1999)

Subject(s): Music and Musicians; Fathers and Daughters; African Americans
Age range(s): Grades K-3
Major character(s): Tiny, Child, Daughter; Daddy, Father, Musician; Mama, Mother
Time period(s): Indeterminate Past
Locale(s): United States

Summary: The life of a blues musician is one of frequent travel to gigs, sometimes faraway. Tiny misses Daddy so much when he's gone and often Mama cannot console her. Daddy gives Tiny his bowler hat to wear so she'll have something to help her remember him. When she's feeling really sad, Tiny puts on the hat and she can hear Daddy's horn singing to her, taking away her sadness and helping Tiny find a song of her own. (32 pages)

Where it's reviewed:
Horn Book Guide, Fall 1999, page 253
Publishers Weekly, January 4, 1999, page 90
School Library Journal, January 1999, page 90

Other books by the same author:
The Bravest Flute: A Story of Courage in the Mayan Tradition, 1994
Kinda Blue, 1993
The Village of Round and Square Houses, 1986 (Caldecott Honor Book)

Other books you might like:
Alice Faye Duncan, *Willie Jerome*, 1995
  Until Mama takes the time to listen carefully she thinks Willie Jerome can only make "noise" on his trumpet.
Linda England, *The Old Cotton Blues*, 1998
  Dexter longs to acquire an instrument and learn to play well enough to join Johnny Cotton and play the blues with his band.
Libba Moore Gray, *Little Lil and the Swing-Singing Sax*, 1996
  When her uncle pawns his sax to buy medicine for his sick mother, Little Lil knows she must get it back so her mother can hear his healing music.
Mark Karlins, *Music Over Manhattan*, 1998
  With instructions from Uncle Louie, Bernie learns to play the trumpet so well that the music floats over Manhattan.
Andrea Davis Pinkney, *Duke Ellington: The Piano Prince and His Orchestra*, 1998
  A picture book biography describes Ellington's life as a pianist and orchestra leader.

Alan Schroeder, *Satchmo's Blues*, 1996
  The fictionalized biography of Louis Armstrong's childhood in New Orleans portrays his single-minded desire to own and play a cornet.

381

HELEN V. GRIFFITH

Cougar

(New York: Greenwillow Books, 1999)

Subject(s): Animals/Horses; Ghosts; Bullies
Age range(s): Grades 5-7
Major character(s): Nicholas "Nickel", Student, Soccer Player; Cougar, Horse, Spirit; Robbo, Bully, Student
Time period(s): 1990s (1999)
Locale(s): United States

Summary: Nickel is accustomed to starting new schools and letting his soccer skills lead the way to being accepted by classmates. At this school Robbo rules the soccer field using threats and dirty tactics along with athletic ability to stay in the limelight. Nickel's superior skill threatens Robbo and he does all he can to intimidate Nickel into acquiescing as all the other boys have learned to do. Angered by Robbo's actions, Nickel tries not to respond to the harassment and finds he has an ally in Cougar, a horse that was bullied by Robbo during his lifetime and seems to have returned from the dead seeking revenge. What other reason could there be that Nickel can see Cougar, but no one else can? (106 pages)

Where it's reviewed:
Booklist, April 1, 1999, page 1414
Bulletin of the Center for Children's Books, March 1999, page 229
Horn Book, May 1999, page 330
Publishers Weekly, May 17, 1999, page 80
School Library Journal, May 1999, page 125

Other books by the same author:
Dinosaur Habitat, 1998
Doll Trouble, 1993
Caitlin's Holiday, 1990
Foxy, 1984

Other books you might like:
Walter Farley, *The Black Stallion*, 1941
  The first in a series of 19 books for horse lovers features a champion black stallion.
Magdalen Nabb, *The Enchanted Horse*, 1993
  A battered toy horse comes to life and gives a lonely girl nightly rides before leaving her to join a herd of wild horses.
Dyan Sheldon, *My Brother Is a Superhero*, 1996
  When three bullies begin harassing Adam and his friend, Adam realizes having an older brother willing to help you isn't so bad after all.
Susan Shreve, *Joshua T. Bates Takes Charge*, 1993
  Joshua finally finds the courage to stand up to the school bully and stop his abusive treatment of others.

382

EDWARD GRIMM
TED LEWIN, Illustrator

The Doorman

(New York: Orchard Books, 2000)

Subject(s): Apartments; Work; Grief
Age range(s): Grades K-3
Major character(s): John, Worker (doorman), Friend; Bill, Worker (doorman)
Time period(s): 2000s (2000)
Locale(s): New York, New York

Summary: The author's first book is a tribute to John who works the day shift as a doorman in an apartment building. He arrives each morning in time to send the children off to school, inquire about a resident's morning run and assist an elderly tenant with a broken arm into her cab. In the afternoon the children returning from school play tricks on him and share their day's experiences. As John's shift nears its end Bill arrives to take the next shift and John fills him in on the day's events. The next morning the residents find Bill still on duty with the sad news that John has died from a heart attack during the night. The residents are stunned to lose their good friend the doorman. (32 pages)

Where it's reviewed:
Booklist, July 2000, page 2038
Bulletin of the Center for Children's Books, July 2000, page 401
Horn Book Guide, Spring 2001, page 37
Publishers Weekly, September 4, 2000, page 107
School Library Journal, October 2000, page 126

Other books you might like:
Dale Gottlieb, *My Stories by Hildy Calpurnia Rose*, 1991
  In her diary, Brooklynite Hildy records the details of life in her apartment building.
Kevin Henkes, *Good-Bye, Curtis*, 1995
  After 42 years of delivering the mail in the same neighborhood Curtis is treated to a retirement party by the grateful recipients of his service.
Ezra Jack Keats, *Apt. 3*, 1986
  Curiosity leads two brothers to discover who lives in Apt. 3.

383

SALLY GRINDLEY
CAROL THOMPSON, Illustrator

A New Room for William

(Cambridge, MA: Candlewick Press, 2000)

Subject(s): Moving, Household; Divorce; Mothers and Sons
Age range(s): Grades K-3
Major character(s): William, Child of Divorced Parents, Son; Mom, Single Mother; Tom, Child, Neighbor
Time period(s): 2000s (2000)
Locale(s): England

Summary: William's not happy to move into a strange new home with a bedroom that lacks all the comforting features of his old one. Sleeping is hard and William tells Mom he wants to return to his old house. Mom takes William shopping and he picks out dinosaur wallpaper for his new room. He helps Mom hang it until he sees a boy playing next door and runs out to meet Tom. By the time Mom has his room ready William's made a friend. Now William wonders what his room at his father's house will be. (28 pages)

Where it's reviewed:
Booklist, January 1, 2001, page 967
Horn Book Guide, Spring 2001, page 37
Kirkus Reviews, September 15, 2000, page 1356
Publishers Weekly, October 30, 2000, page 74
School Library Journal, November 2000, page 120

Other books by the same author:
Peter's Place, 1996 (IRA/CBC Children's Choices)
Shhh!, 1992
I Don't Want To!, 1990

Other books you might like:
Judith Caseley, *Priscilla Twice*, 1995
  When her parents separate Priscilla must adjust to life in two different households.
Andrea Spalding, *Me and Mr. Mah*, 1999
  His parents' divorce forces a young boy to leave his farm home on the prairie and move to a city far from his father.
Cornelia Maude Spelman, *Mama and Daddy Bear's Divorce*, 1998
  News of her parents' separation leaves Dinah Bear feeling frightened, sad and confused.
Judith Vigna, *I Live with Daddy*, 1997
  After her parents divorce Olivia lives with her father but writes a book about her mother's career in television.

384

SALLY GRINDLEY
PENNY DANN, Illustrator

What Will I Do Without You?

(New York: Kingfisher, 1999)

Subject(s): Animals; Winter; Friendship
Age range(s): Grades K-1
Major character(s): Jefferson Bear, Bear, Friend; Figgy Twosocks, Fox, Friend; Hoptail, Squirrel, Friend (Figgy's)
Time period(s): Indeterminate
Locale(s): Fictional Country

Summary: When Jefferson Bear hibernates Figgy is lonely because she has no friend with whom to share the first snow. Figgy builds a large snow bear to remind her of Jefferson, but when her loneliness changes to anger she begins to pelt the snow bear with snowballs. Hoptail stops her and asks for Figgy's help finding buried nuts. The friendship that develops between Figgy and Hoptail shows the promise of surviving the arrival of spring and Jefferson's return. (32 pages)

Where it's reviewed:
Booklist, December 1, 1999, page 710
Books Magazine, Autumn 1999, page 22
Horn Book Guide, Spring 2000, page 16
School Library Journal, December 1999, page 96

Other books by the same author:
What Are Friends For?, 1998
Peter's Place, 1996
Shhh!, 1992

Other books you might like:
Denise Fleming, *Time to Sleep*, 1997
  The cumulative tale begins with Bear's realization that winter is approaching and it is time to notify the other animals of the need to hibernate.
Anne Hunter, *Possum's Harvest Moon*, 1996
  The sight of the harvest moon inspires Possum to have one last party with his friends before the winter's hibernation begins.
James Preller, *Wake Me in Spring*, 1994
  A mouse is sad that he will not be able to play with his friend Bear again until Spring.
Nancy Willard, *A Starlit Somersault Downhill*, 1993
  A rabbit discovers that hibernating with a bear is not suitable for a creature who wants to be free to somersault down snow-covered banks.

385

WAYNE GROVER
JIM FOWLER, Illustrator

Dolphin Freedom
(New York: Greenwillow Books, 1999)

Subject(s): Animals/Dolphins; Wildlife Rescue; Adventure and Adventurers
Age range(s): Grades 4-6
Major character(s): Baby, Dolphin; Amos, Friend; Wayne Grover, Diver
Time period(s): 1990s (1999)
Locale(s): *Moon Shadow*, At Sea; Dead Man Cay, Bahamas

Summary: When Baby does not greet Wayne's boat he fears that poachers operating out of Dead Man Cay may have captured the dolphin. After finding remnants of Baby's pod including one seriously injured male, Wayne knows the missing dolphins must be captives and he devises a plan to free them. With Amos and another friend, Wayne sets sail for the Bahamas. Along the way members of Baby's pod and other dolphins join them, swimming beside the boat as they all race toward the rescue. (109 pages)

Where it's reviewed:
Appraisal: Science Books for Young People, Winter 2000, page 20
Booklist, May 15, 1999, page 1695
Horn Book Guide, Fall 1999, page 292
Kirkus Reviews, May 15, 1999, page 20
School Library Journal, June 1999, page 129

Other books by the same author:
Dolphin Treasure, 1996
Ali and the Golden Eagle, 1993
Dolphin Adventure, 1990

Other books you might like:
Twig C. George, *Swimming with Sharks*, 1999
  A lazy summer visit to her grandparents in the Florida Keys becomes more exciting when Sarah discovers a shark poacher.
Karen Hesse, *The Music of Dolphins*, 1996
  An award-winning title describes a girl's "rescue" from her dolphin family and eventual return to the sea after being used in a scientific study.
Ginny Rorby, *Dolphin Sky*, 1996
  Concerned about the care dolphins in a show are receiving Buddy plans to rescue them.

386

PAOLO GUARNIERI
BIMBA LANDMANN, Illustrator
JONATHAN GALASSI, Translator

A Boy Named Giotto
(New York: Farrar Straus Giroux, 1999)

Subject(s): Artists and Art; Animals/Sheep; Talent
Age range(s): Grades 2-4
Major character(s): Giotto Bondone, Shepherd, Artist; Cimabue, Artist, Teacher
Time period(s): 13th century
Locale(s): Italy; Florence, Italy

Summary: As a young boy Giotto is responsible for taking the family's sheep to pasture each day and returning them safely to their shelter in the evening. Giotto spends his days drawing in the dirt wishing he had a way to produce something more lasting. When Cimabue visits his town and Giotto sees his painting of *Madonna with Child* he follows the artist to learn more about his work. Cimabue gives Giotto some pigment and tells him how to mix the paint. The next day he sees Giotto's painting and asks Giotto's father to allow his son to become his student. The parents wait to send Giotto to Florence when he is a teen, but quickly he learns and surpasses the teacher in his skill with frescoes. The fictionalized biography of Giotto's youth is the first book for the author. (32 pages)

Where it's reviewed:
Booklist, December 15, 1999, page 789
Kirkus Reviews, September 15, 1999, page 1501
Publishers Weekly, November 29, 1999, page 71
Riverbank Review, Winter 1999-2000, page 37
School Library Journal, October 1999, page 114

Awards the book has won:
Smithsonian's Notable Books for Children, 1999

Other books you might like:
Patricia Maloney Markun, *The Little Painter of Sabana Grande*, 1993
  A shortage of paper does not deter a young Panamanian artist who uses his adobe home as his canvas.
Barbara McClintock, *The Fantastic Drawings of Danielle*, 1996
  As a photographer, Papa thinks Danielle's art lacks realism, but Madame Beton sees Danielle's talent as being similar to her own.
Mike Venezia, *Giotto*, 2000
  A picture book biography covers information about the life and work of Italian artist Giotto.

387

ELISSA HADEN GUEST
CHRISTINE DAVENIER, Illustrator

Iris and Walter

(San Diego: Gulliver Books/Harcourt, Inc.)

Series: Iris and Walter. Book 1
Subject(s): Country Life; City and Town Life; Friendship
Age range(s): Grades 1-3
Major character(s): Iris, Child, Friend; Grandpa, Grandfather; Walter, Child, Friend
Time period(s): 2000s (2000)
Locale(s): United States

Summary: When Iris's family moves to the country, Iris is unhappy. The country is simply too quiet for her and she feels lonely for the noise, activity and people of the city. Although her parents try to cheer her it's Grandpa who has the idea of going for a walk with Iris and listening to her reasons for disliking the country. While walking, Grandpa and Iris come to a large tree. When Iris expresses a desire to climb the tree, a ladder appears. At the top of the ladder Iris finds a small house and in the house she finds Walter. Iris still misses the city life, but she's not lonely now because she and Walter are friends who play hide-and-seek, look at the stars and ride ponies together. (44 pages)

Where it's reviewed:
Booklist, October 15, 2000, page 437
Horn Book Guide, Spring 2001, page 56
Kirkus Reviews, August 15, 2000, page 1194
Publishers Weekly, September 18, 2000, page 112
School Library Journal, November 2000, page 122

Awards the book has won:
Publishers Weekly Best Books, 2000
ALA Notable Children's Books, 2001

Other books by the same author:
Iris and Walter, True Friends, 2001 (Iris and Walter, Book 2)

Other books you might like:
Stephanie Calmenson, *Rockin' Reptiles*, 1997
    Best friends Allie and Amy find their relationship challenged when Gracie moves into the neighborhood. Joanna Cole, co-author
Joyce Champion, *Emily and Alice*, 1993
    As lonely Emily becomes acquainted with the new neighbor Alice, a friendship begins.
James Howe, *Pinky and Rex and the New Neighbors*, 1997
    Good friends Pinky and Rex are not moving but they do worry about who will move into Mrs. Morgan's house when she leaves.
Claudia Mills, *Gus and Grandpa*, 1997
    The first book in a series introduces Gus and the warm, loving relationship he has with Grandpa.

388

BENEDICTE GUETTIER, Author/Illustrator

The Father Who Had 10 Children

(New York: Dial Books for Young Readers, 1999)

Subject(s): Fathers; Parent and Child; Single Parent Families
Age range(s): Preschool
Major character(s): Unnamed Character, Single Father
Time period(s): 1990s (1997)
Locale(s): Belgium

Summary: A father with ten children is a very busy man. Daily he cooks ten breakfasts, finds twenty socks for little feet, puts ten children in the car and drives them to school before going to work. The nighttime routine includes one bedtime story and ten goodnight kisses. Once the children are settled the tired father works on his own secret project. When it is finished, the ten children are impressed with the beautiful boat and they wave to their father as he sets off to sail around the world while grandmother watches the children. After a relaxing evening sleeping solo on the boat, the father realizes he's missing something and he sails the boat back to shore to retrieve what he's forgotten. The author's American debut was first published in Belgium in 1997. (42 pages)

Where it's reviewed:
Horn Book, May 1999, page 313
Kirkus Reviews, May 15, 1999, page 801
Publishers Weekly, May 3, 1999, page 75
Riverbank Review, Winter 1999-2000, page 27
School Library Journal, June 1999, page 96

Other books you might like:
Thierry Courtin, *Daddy and Me*, 1997
    One Daddy plus one child equals lots of fun on Daddy's day off.
Laurence Pringle, *Octopus Hug*, 1993
    Mom is out for the evening and unhappy Jesse and Becky are cheered by Dad's octopus hug.
Tjibbe Veldkamp, *22 Orphans*, 1998
    No parents are around to love these rambunctious orphans who manage to have fun despite the rules of a strict headmistress.

389

DAN GUTMAN

Jackie and Me

(New York: Avon/Camelot, 1999)

Series: Baseball Card Adventure. Book 2
Subject(s): Sports/Baseball; Time Travel; African Americans
Age range(s): Grades 4-7
Major character(s): Joe Stoshack, Student, Baseball Player; Jackie Robinson, Baseball Player, Historical Figure
Time period(s): 1990s (1999); 1940s (1947)
Locale(s): Louisville, Kentucky; New York, New York (Brooklyn)

Summary: Joe combines his love of baseball with a class assignment to research an African American who made an important contribution to the world. Joe borrows a rare 1947

Jackie Robinson baseball card, knowing that, with the card, he can time travel back to Brooklyn and do his research first hand. What Joe does not expect is to arrive in Brooklyn as an African American when he left Louisville as a Polish American. The Polish jokes that set off Joe's temper at home are mild compared to the discrimination he faces as a young black person during the time that Robinson is setting records as the first black baseball player in the major leagues. A concluding author's note gives the historical basis for the story. (145 pages)

Where it's reviewed:
Booklist, February 1, 1999, page 974
Horn Book Guide, Fall 1999, page 292
Kliatt, January 1999, page 7
Publishers Weekly, February 1, 1999, page 87
School Library Journal, March 1999, page 209

Other books by the same author:
Virtually Perfect, 1998
Honus and Me, 1997 (Baseball Card Adventure, Book 1)
The Million Dollar Shot, 1997
The Shortstop Who Knew Too Much, 1997 (Tales from the Sandlot, Number 1)

Other books you might like:
Bill Gutman, *Ken Griffey, Sr. and Ken Griffey, Jr.: Father and Son Teammates*, 1993
  The illustrated biography of two African American baseball players focuses on their professional careers.
W.P. Kinsella, *Shoeless Joe*, 1982
  A mixture of fantasy, time travel and one man's dream combine to produce the ultimate baseball game.
Stephen Manes, *An Almost Perfect Game*, 1995
  As Jake tracks the plays of the Nottingham Shopper's minor league baseball team on his ''lucky'' score card, he seems able to predict every play.
Steven Schnur, *The Koufax Dilemma*, 1997
  When Danny's mother refuses to let him pitch in his first game because it's the first night of Passover, she suggests research on pitcher Sandy Koufax.

H

390

JESSIE HAAS
JOS. A. SMITH, Illustrator

Hurry!

(New York: Greenwillow Books/HarperCollins Publishers, 2000)

Subject(s): Farm Life; Grandparents; Weather
Age range(s): Grades K-3
Major character(s): Nora, Child; Gramp, Grandfather, Farmer; Gram, Grandmother, Farmer
Time period(s): Indeterminate
Locale(s): United States

Summary: Gramp, Gram and Nora anxiously watch the sky as they wait for the freshly cut field to dry. The sunshine gives way to gathering clouds, the sky becomes white, then gray and Gramp sends Nora out to check the grass. Nora feels and smells the grass before announcing that it's ready and then Gramp drives the team of horses pulling the rake. Once the hay is in long windrows Gramp hitches on the hay wagon and hayloader. Now Nora drives while Gramp and Gram use pitchforks to level the hay as it's loaded into the wagon. Racing the clouds they can't get quite all the hay, but they manage to get to the shelter of the barn with a full wagonload before the rain begins to pour. (24 pages)

Where it's reviewed:
Booklist, May 15, 2000, page 1748
Horn Book, July 2000, page 435
Kirkus Reviews, May 15, 2000, page 714
School Library Journal, June 2000, page 114

Awards the book has won:
Notable Social Studies Trade Books for Young People, 2001

Other books by the same author:
Sugaring, 1996
No Foal Yet, 1995
Mowing, 1994

Other books you might like:
Elizabeth Friedrich, *Leah's Pony*, 1996
Leah's quick thinking and personal sacrifice save her family's farm during the dust bowl years of the Great Depression.
Thomas Locker, *Family Farm*, 1988
A family must work together and change with the times to maintain a successful farm.
Cris Peterson, *Century Farm: One Hundred Years on a Family Farm*, 1999
A nonfiction title relates the way of life for five generations of a family on a dairy farm.
Jan Romero Stevens, *Carlos and the Cornfield/Carlos y la Milpa de Maiz*, 1995
Parallel texts in English and Spanish tell how Carlos's father knows his son did not follow instructions carefully when planting the corn crop.

391

JESSIE HAAS

Unbroken

(New York: Greenwillow Books, 1999)

Subject(s): Death; Grief; Orphans
Age range(s): Grades 5-8
Major character(s): Harriet "Harry" Gibson, 13-Year-Old, Orphan; Sarah Hall, Aunt; Clayton Hall, Uncle, Farmer
Time period(s): 1910s (1910)
Locale(s): West Barrett, Vermont; Vinegar Hill, Vermont

Summary: Harry's mother dies following a buggy accident and in accordance with her will, Harry is sent to live with Aunt Sarah, her deceased father's sister. She can't understand why her mother would send her to such a hateful woman on a farm seven miles from her school. Aunt Sarah believes Harry has received enough education and should be content with life on the farm. Determined to find a way to get to school, Harry decides to break her two-year-old colt although Uncle Clayton and the farm hand think the colt is too young. In her grief, anger and desperation, Harry pushes the colt too hard and is seriously injured when the horse bolts. Only then does she understand that she has never recognized the love Aunt Sarah has for her. (185 pages)

Where it's reviewed:
Horn Book, July 1999, page 464
Kirkus Reviews, February 15, 1999, page 299
Publishers Weekly, February 8, 1999, page 215
Riverbank Review, Summer 1999, page 38
School Library Journal, April 1999, page 134

Awards the book has won:
Publishers Weekly Best Books, 1999
School Library Journal Best Books, 1999

Other books by the same author:
Beware and Stogie, 1998
Westminster West, 1997
Be Well, Beware, 1996
Uncle Daney's Way, 1994

Other books you might like:
Alison Hart, *Shadow Horse*, 1999
  Jas attacks the man she thinks is responsible for causing a horse's death and finds her life changes dramatically when she is arrested for assault.
Sally M. Keehn, *The First Horse I See*, 1999
  Willo's alcoholic widowed father thinks she's made a bad choice in horses and gives her three months to train Tess or lose her.
Zilpha Keatley Snyder, *Gib Rides Home*, 1998
  Orphan Gib is ''farmed-out'' to work with the Thornton Family's horses in exchange for room and board.

392

MARY DOWNING HAHN
DIANE DEGROAT, Illustrator

Anna All Year Round
(New York: Clarion Books, 1999)

Subject(s): Family Life; Parent and Child; Historical
Age range(s): Grades 3-5
Major character(s): Anna Elizabeth Sherwood, 3rd Grader, Daughter (only child); Charlie Murphy, 3rd Grader, Friend (Anna's)
Time period(s): 1910s
Locale(s): Baltimore, Maryland

Summary: Times are changing and Anna's not sure whether that is cause for excitement or apprehension. Not one to hold with gender conventions, Anna prefers playing with Charlie rather than the snobby girls in the neighborhood and her willingness to roller skate with him down a steep hill, while winning Charlie's admiration, also earns her a visit from the doctor to suture her chin. Anna listens carefully to her conventional mother's conversations in German so she can learn enough of the language to know the family secrets. Her father supports her curiosity about the new technologies of the day such as motorcars and electricity while understanding her reluctance to see the life she knows change so drastically. As the year goes round, Anna takes the trolley by herself for the first time, rides in a motorcar and, against her mother's wishes, hosts her first birthday party. A concluding glossary defines the German words used in the story. (133 pages)

Where it's reviewed:
Booklist, March 15, 1999, page 1329

Bulletin of the Center for Children's Books, June 1999, page 352
Horn Book, July 1999, page 465
Publishers Weekly, April 19, 1999, page 74
School Library Journal, May 1999, page 90

Other books by the same author:
Following My Own Footsteps, 1996
Stepping on the Cracks, 1991
Tallahassee Higgins, 1987

Other books you might like:
Kimberly Brubaker Bradley, *Ruthie's Gift*, 1998
  As the only girl with six brothers in the family, tomboy Ruthie hopes that playing with the new neighbors will help her become more ladylike.
Maud Hart Lovelace, *Betsy-Tacy and Tib*, 1941
  The warmth of small town neighbors and the activities of close friends make this work a timeless classic.
Barbara Ann Porte, *When Aunt Lucy Rode a Mule and Other Stories*, 1994
  Aunt Lucy's stories of childhood visits to her grandparents' mountain home entertain her two nieces.

393

BRUCE HALE, Author/Illustrator

The Chameleon Wore Chartreuse: From the Tattered Casebook of Chet Gecko, Private Eye
(San Diego: Harcourt, Inc., 2000)

Series: Chet Gecko Mystery. Case #1
Subject(s): Animals/Reptiles; Lost and Found Possessions; Mystery and Detective Stories
Age range(s): Grades 2-4
Major character(s): Chet Gecko, 4th Grader, Reptile; Shirley Chameleon, 4th Grader, Reptile; Natalie Attired, Bird, Student—Elementary School
Time period(s): Indeterminate
Locale(s): Fictional Country (Emerson Hicky School)

Summary: Chet Gecko is the best private eye in the fourth grade and Shirley seeks his help locating her missing younger brother. The case is complicated—Shirley offers few clues to help Chet in his search and Natalie, a private eye wannabe, offers unwanted help, but Chet appreciates a challenge. Although Chet prefers to work alone, Natalie's brains and wings come in handy and they solve the case only moments before a 6th grade gila monster with a grudge (and Shirley's brother) can complete his disastrous plot. (97 pages)

Where it's reviewed:
Booklist, May 15, 2000, page 1744
Horn Book Guide, Spring 2001, page 62
Publishers Weekly, May 1, 2000, page 71
School Library Journal, August 2000, page 155

Other books by the same author:
Farewell, My Lunchbag, 2001 (Chet Gecko Mystery, Case #3)
The Mystery of Mr. Nice, 2000 (Chet Gecko Mystery, Case #2)

Surf Gecko to the Rescue!, 1991

Other books you might like:

Crosby Bonsall, *The Case of the Cat's Meow*, 1965
The four members of the Private Eyes Club solve the mystery of a missing cat.

Ellen Leroe, *Racetrack Robbery*, 1996
Once again, invisible Ghost Dog helps Artie solve a mystery.

Mary Pope Osborne, *Spider Kane and the Mystery at Jumbo Nightcrawler's*, 1993
Spider Kane's case takes him to the seamy underworld of Jumbo Nightcrawler's Supper Club where the good guys are being kidnapped.

Ursel Scheffler, *Rinaldo on the Run*, 1995
Bruno the Duck Detective trails Rinaldo from Italy to Illinois after the fox steals a bag of money from a truck driver.

394

NANCY CHRISTENSEN HALL
BUKET ERDOGAN, Illustrator

Mouse at Night

(New York: Orchard Books, 2000)

Subject(s): Animals/Mice; Behavior
Age range(s): Preschool
Major character(s): Unnamed Character, Mouse
Time period(s): Indeterminate
Locale(s): Fictional Country

Summary: Late at night if the moon is full, a little blue mouse comes out of his hole for a night of fun. While the homeowner sleeps the mouse watches TV and, inspired by a television program, cooks breakfast. Amazingly, the mouse even cleans up and retires to his hole leaving breakfast on the table. (24 pages)

Where it's reviewed:
Booklist, May 1, 2000, page 1678
Horn Book Guide, Fall 2000, page 249
Kirkus Reviews, March 1, 2000, page 302
School Library Journal, April 2000, page 106

Other books you might like:

Alan Durant, *Mouse Party*, 1995
A mouse invites friends to a party at the vacant home he's located.

Laura Joffe Numeroff, *If You Give a Mouse a Cookie*, 1985
Be careful! Giving a cookie to a mouse can lead to many more requests from the mouse for milk and a napkin and. . .

Linnea Riley, *Mouse Mess*, 1997
The nighttime forays of this mouse leave a mess in the kitchen for the family to find in the morning.

395

GEORG HALLENSLEBEN, Author/Illustrator

Pauline

(New York: Frances Foster Books/Farrar, Straus and Giroux, 1999)

Subject(s): Animals/Weasels; Animals/Elephants; Friendship
Age range(s): Grades K-3
Major character(s): Pauline, Weasel (young), Friend; Rasbusius, Elephant (young), Friend
Time period(s): Indeterminate
Locale(s): Earth (jungle)

Summary: The first book written by illustrator Hallensleben introduces Pauline, who lives in the jungle's treetops and Rabusius who lives on the ground. The friends are inseparable so when Rabusius is captured and put into a truck, Pauline is determined to save him. With her parents' help she disguises herself as a monster and then travels through the treetops to a position along the road ahead of the hunter's truck. When Pauline the monster leaps onto the truck's windshield, the driver loses control, crashes into a ditch and the hunters leap out in terror. Quickly Pauline releases Rabusius and they hurry home to celebrate with all the other animals who come to a party dressed as monsters. (32 pages)

Where it's reviewed:
Booklist, November 15, 1999, page 635
Bulletin of the Center for Children's Books, November 1999, page 94
Kirkus Reviews, September 15, 1999, page 1508
Publishers Weekly, October 4, 1999, page 73
School Library Journal, September 1999, page 183

Other books you might like:

Kate Banks, *The Bird, the Monkey, and the Snake in the Jungle*, 1999
While searching for a new tree home, three friends protect each other from dangerous elements in the jungle.

Jean De Brunhoff, *Babar and Zephir*, 1937
One of the classic stories about the elephant Babar includes his adventures with his mischievous monkey friend.

H.A. Rey, *Curious George*, 1941
Curiosity leads a little monkey into captivity and a life of adventure with the man with the yellow hat.

396

SHEILA HAMANAKA, Author/Illustrator

I Look Like a Girl

(New York: Morrow Junior Books, 1999)

Subject(s): Imagination; Animals; Stories in Rhyme
Age range(s): Grades K-2
Time period(s): 1990s
Locale(s): United States

Summary: Looks are deceiving as young girls engaged in typical play activities creatively imagine themselves as roaring tigers, leaping dolphins or racing mustangs. The girls in this book are not waiting to be rescued by fairy godmothers or princes; they believe they are capable of controlling their destiny and they seek only the freedom to be. (32 pages)

Where it's reviewed:
Booklist, October 1, 1999, page 362
Bulletin of the Center for Children's Books, November 1999, page 94
Children's Book Review Service, Winter 2000, page 63
Horn Book Guide, Spring 2000, page 38
School Library Journal, June 2000, page 114

Awards the book has won:
Notable Social Studies Trade Books for Young People, 2000

Other books by the same author:
Peace Crane, 1995
All the Colors of the Earth, 1994
Screen of Frogs, 1993

Other books you might like:
Thylias Moss, *I Want to Be*, 1993
   A young girl considers her future in terms of qualities of being rather than career choices.
Keiko Narahashi, *Two Girls Can!*, 2000
   An energetic tribute to the power of friendship celebrates all that girls can do together.
Sarah Perry, *If. . .*, 1995
   A fanciful book explores a range of seemingly implausible ideas.

397

VIRGINIA HAMILTON

Bluish

(New York: The Blue Sky Press/Scholastic Inc., 1999)

Subject(s): Friendship; Cancer; School Life
Age range(s): Grades 4-7
Major character(s): Natalie "Bluish" Winburn, 5th Grader, Cancer Patient; Dreanne "Dreenie", 5th Grader, Friend; Tulithia "Tuli", 5th Grader, Friend
Time period(s): 1990s (1999)
Locale(s): New York, New York

Summary: Dreenie is fascinated by the new student in the class who comes to school in a wheelchair with a puppy in her lap. She seems so fragile and pale, the color of moonlight, bluish. Natalie, in her cap with her cold hands, is obviously sick and the students aren't sure how to treat her. Dreenie is new to the school too and seeking friendship. Tuli seeks to befriend Dreenie, but Tuli's needy exuberance, though interesting, is tiring. It takes Natalie to point out to Dreenie that she and Tuli have similar traits yet Dreenie is more tolerant of them in Natalie that she is Tuli. Slowly the friendship grows large enough to hold all three together, best friends forever. (127 pages)

Where it's reviewed:
The Book Report, November 1999, page 61
Booklist, September 15, 1999, page 257
Horn Book, January 2000, page 75
Publishers Weekly, October 25, 1999, page 81
School Library Journal, November 1999, page 158

Other books by the same author:
Second Cousins, 1998
Plain City, 1993
Cousins, 1990

Other books you might like:
Cherie Bennett, *Zink*, 1999
   As Becky battles leukemia she is visited by comforting zebras that take her to the Serengeti where she sees Zink, a zebra with polka dots.
Lurlene McDaniel, *Too Young to Die*, 1991
   Melissa accepts the fact that she has leukemia.
Sally Warner, *Sort of Forever*, 1998
   Nana's diagnosis of leukemia makes Cady wonder how long the best friends will be together.

398

VIRGINIA HAMILTON
LEO DILLON, Illustrator
DIANE DILLON, Illustrator

The Girl Who Spun Gold

(New York: Blue Sky Press/Scholastic Inc., 2000)

Subject(s): Folklore; Gold; Greed
Age range(s): Grades 1-4
Major character(s): Lit'mahn, Trickster, Mythical Creature; Quashiba, Daughter, Artisan; Big King, Royalty, Spouse
Time period(s): Indeterminate Past
Locale(s): West Indies

Summary: Lit'mahn hiding in the shade hears Quashiba's mother tell Big King that her daughter is planning to spin a field of gold cloth for the handsome king. Big King vows to marry the girl who is none to happy with her mother. After the wedding Big King announces that Quashiba has a year and a day to enjoy the luxury of her position and then she must spin three rooms full of fleece into golden things. Quashiba expects Big King to forget, but he does not and Quashiba is bereft when she is locked into the first room a year later. An ugly little man appears to make a bargain with her. He will produce the golden cloth and Quashiba has three nights to guess his real, complete name or he will make her small also to live in the shade with him. For two nights the ugly little man produces gold and Quashiba fails to guess his name, but Big King is so happy he invites his wife to dine with him. While eating, Big King relates a story of a funny little man he happened to see in the woods, dancing and singing a song. From the song, Quashiba learns the answer to the little man's question. After he completes the transformation of the final room into gold, Quashiba guesses his real name correctly and Lit'mahn Bittyun is so angry that he explodes and is never seen again—except when his tale is told. A concluding author's note gives background information for this West Indian variant of a tale also found in English and German folklore. (40 pages)

Where it's reviewed:
Booklist, August 2000, page 2134
Five Owls, September 2000, page 17
Horn Book, September 2000, page 586
Publishers Weekly, July 31, 2000, page 95
School Library Journal, September 2000, page 217

Awards the book has won:
Booklist Editors' Choice, 2000

Other books by the same author:

A Ring of Tricksters: Animals Tales from America, the West Indies, and Africa, 1997 (Publishers Weekly Best Children's Book)

When Birds Could Talk & Bats Could Sing: The Adventures of Bruh Sparrow, Sis Wren, and Their Friends, 1996 (ALA Notable Book for Children)

In the Beginning: Creation Stories from Around the World, 1988 (Newbery Honor Book)

Other books you might like:

Felix Pitre, *Paco and the Witch: A Puerto Rican Folktale*, 1995

> Tricked by a witch, Paco falls under her spell and must guess her name in order to free himself.

Robert D. San Souci, *Cendrillon: A Caribbean Cinderella*, 1998

> The traditional story of Cinderella is set in Martinique in this retelling.

Paul O. Zelinsky, *Rumpelstiltskin*, 1986

> This illustrated retelling of the Grimm Brother's tale is true to the original version.

399

WOLFRAM HANEL
KIRSTEN HOCKER, Illustrator
J. ALISON JAMES, Translator

Mary and the Mystery Dog

(New York: North-South Books, 1999)

Subject(s): Beaches; Animals/Dogs; Parent and Child
Age range(s): Grades 1-3
Major character(s): Mary, Child, Daughter; Mother, Mother; Father, Father
Time period(s): 1990s
Locale(s): Ireland

Summary: During a wet, windy, March vacation at the beach, Mother wants to stay inside and read and Father is content in front of the fire, but Mary goes exploring. Bundled up against the cold, Mary finds shells, feathers and empty bottles washed up on the beach. She chases seagulls and is surprised to be joined by a shaggy dog. Mary is sure this is the legendary mystery dog who lives somewhere in dunes. She plays with him all morning, but the dog vanishes when Father appears to call her for lunch. To convince her parents that the dog is real, Mary makes them walk back to the beach with her after lunch. Not only do they discover the dog, but they also begin to appreciate the fun of playing on the beach, even when the weather is cold. (45 pages)

Where it's reviewed:
ForeWord Magazine, May 1999, page 54
Horn Book Guide, Fall 1999, page 278
School Library Journal, May 1999, page 90

Other books by the same author:
Abby, 1996
Lila's Little Dinosaur, 1994
Mia the Beach Cat: A Story, 1994

Other books you might like:

Claudia Mills, *Gus and Grandpa*, 1997

> The first book in a series for beginning readers introduces Gus, Grandpa and his dog Skipper.

Charlotte Pomerantz, *The Outside Dog*, 1993

> When a stray dog "adopts" Marisol her grandfather begrudgingly concedes to Marisol's wish for a pet.

Cynthia Rylant, *Henry and Mudge*, 1987

> Finally, Henry's parents agree to have a pet in the family and the fun with slobbery Mudge begins.

400

WOLFRAM HANEL
ULRIKE HEYNE, Illustrator
ROSEMARY LANNING, Translator

Rescue at Sea!

(New York: North-South Books, 1999)

Subject(s): Rescue Work; Weather; Animals/Dogs
Age range(s): Grades 1-3
Major character(s): Paul, 8-Year-Old, Son; Johnny, Dog; Dad, Father, Fisherman
Time period(s): Indeterminate Past
Locale(s): Ireland

Summary: A severe storm keeps Paul's father in port, but another fishing boat is foundering near and Paul's father joins the rescue effort. Paul watches from shore as the fisherman leap from the sinking boat into the lifeboat. When all hands are safely aboard the lifeboat, it comes to shore, but Paul has spotted a dog on the bridge and decides to save it. He walks onto the rocks knowing that as the waves force the boat closer he may be able to retrieve the dog from the surf. At Paul's urging the dog jumps, but the slippery rocks and the weight of the dog almost combine to pull Paul into the surf until Dad arrives to haul them both to safety. The crew of the boat is grateful for the rescue and give Johnny, the dog he's always wanted, to Paul. (59 pages)

Where it's reviewed:
Booklist, June 1999, page 1829
ForeWord Magazine, May 1999, page 55
Horn Book Guide, Fall 1999, page 278
School Library Journal, July 1999, page 72

Other books by the same author:
Mary and the Mystery Dog, 1999
Abby, 1996
The Old Man and the Bear, 1994

Other books you might like:

Una Leavy, *Harry's Stormy Night*, 1994

> Coping with a loss of electric power during a storm, Harry and his family sing and tell stories by candlelight.

Gloria Rand, *Aloha, Salty!*, 1996

> A sudden storm dumps Zack and Salty into the surf before they can reach a sheltered port and Salty pulls his unconscious master to safety on the beach.

Frances Ward Weller, *Madaket Millie*, 1997

> Voluntarily Madaket Millie rescues ships and sailors in trouble either on her own or by calling the Coast Guard.

401

JOY HARJO
PAUL LEE, Illustrator

The Good Luck Cat

(San Diego: Harcourt. Inc., 2000)

Subject(s): Animals/Cats; Indians of North America; Pets
Age range(s): Grades K-3
Major character(s): Woogie, Cat; Unnamed Character, Child, Narrator; Shelly, Aunt
Time period(s): 2000s
Locale(s): United States

Summary: In the author's first book, Woogie's reputation as a cat that brings luck to anyone who pats her is well established in the family. Aunt Shelly says such a good luck cat is one in a million and she's sure to pat Woogie before she goes to bingo. Like all cats though, Woogie has only nine lives and her owner can relate how Woogie loses each one. After eight of Woogie's lives are gone she vanishes and her owner, her cousins and Aunt Shelly look everywhere for her. Not wanting to believe that Woogie could have lost her ninth and final life, her owner puts Woogie's food dish and favorite toys on the porch before she goes to sleep on the fourth night. In the morning Woogie is sleeping on the porch looking as if she should have lost that last life. Aunt Shelly says Woogie has so much good luck she must have more than nine lives. (32 pages)

Where it's reviewed:
Bulletin of the Center for Children's Books, April 2000, page 281
Children's Book Review Service, May 2000, page 109
Kirkus Reviews, April 1, 2000, page 476
Publishers Weekly, May 22, 2000, page 92
School Library Journal, April 2000, page 106

Awards the book has won:
Charlotte Zolotow Highly Commended Book, 2001

Other books you might like:
Jan Brett, *Comet's Nine Lives*, 1996
　　After losing the first of his nine lives, Comet searches for a home in which to live out the remaining eight but loses seven more while looking.
Minna Jung, *William's Ninth Life*, 1993
　　When William is asked to choose the next and final of his nine lives, the cat chooses to return to his elderly mistress.
Gina Wilson, *Prowlpuss*, 1995
　　A rough, tough one-eyed, one-eared alley cat returns home after a night of carousing to become a pampered pussy.

402

BEATRICE ORCUTT HARRELL
TONY MEERS, Illustrator

Longwalker's Journey: A Novel of the Choctaw Trail of Tears

(New York: Dial Books for Young Readers, 1999)

Subject(s): Indians of North America; Frontier and Pioneer Life; Indian Removal

Age range(s): Grades 3-6
Major character(s): Minko Ushi, 10-Year-Old, Indian (Choctaw); Itilakna, Father, Indian (Choctaw); Black Spot, Pony
Time period(s): 1830s (1831-1832)
Locale(s): Mississippi (USA); Indian Territory

Summary: To the sorrow felt by the Choctaw forced from their homes in Mississippi the U.S. Government's poor planning and the winter's harsh weather, add hardship, illness and death. Although the terms of the relocation force the Choctaw to leave most of their possessions behind, Black Spot secretly trails the slowly moving group. By the time they are bogged down on the banks of the Mississippi awaiting boats, Black Spot reappears and Itilakna decides to take Minko Ushi with his pony ahead of the group and establish a home for the rest of the family. Though they receive official approval, they are given few supplies and poor directions because there is no clear trail to show the way. Itilakna uses his skill to head west, provide food and shelter and instruction for his son in survival strategies of the trail. A concluding author's note gives the family history on which the story is based. (128 pages)

Where it's reviewed:
Booklist, March 1, 1999, page 1213
Children's Book Review Service, May 1999, page 117
Horn Book Guide, Fall 1999, page 293
Publishers Weekly, March 8, 1999, page 69
School Library Journal, April 1999, page 136

Other books by the same author:
How Thunder and Lightning Came to Be: A Choctaw Legend, 1995

Other books you might like:
Sara Harrell Banks, *Remember My Name*, 1993
　　Annie Rising Fawn Stuart and Righteous Cry escape from Georgia and flee to the Cherokee mountain homeland rather than be forced onto a reservation.
Patricia C. McKissack, *Run Away Home*, 1997
　　When Sarah finds an escaped, feverish Apache in her family's barn she hides him despite the danger to her family in post-Civil War Alabama.
Elisabeth Jane Stewart, *On the Long Trail Home*, 1994
　　Separated from her family, 9-year-old Meli finds her brother and the two run from the Trail of Tears to their home in North Carolina.
Gloria Whelan, *Night of the Full Moon*, 1993
　　Libby is visiting her Indian friend Fawn when soldiers arrive, forcing the Indians farther west.

403

LEE HARRIS
DEBBIE TILLEY, Illustrator

Never Let Your Cat Make Lunch for You

(Berkeley, CA: Tricycle Press, 1999)

Subject(s): Cooks and Cooking; Animals/Cats; Food
Age range(s): Grades K-2
Major character(s): Pebbles, Cat; Unnamed Character, Child, Student—Elementary School
Time period(s): 1990s (1999)
Locale(s): United States

Summary: Pebbles is quite a cook and her owner enjoys the cat's culinary feats at breakfast even if they are garnished with an occasional cat hair. When Pebbles insists on expanding her repertoire to include lunch, the cat's efforts are less successful. After taking the first gigantic bite of the peanut butter and jelly sandwich Pebbles makes for her, the young girl can eat no more. No one at the lunch table is willing to trade their lunch for a PB & J with anchovy so, Pebbles' owner goes hungry, but she learns not to let her cat pack her school lunch again in the author's first children's book. (24 pages)

Where it's reviewed:
Booklist, October 15, 1999, page 452
Children's Bookwatch, October 1999, page 6
Horn Book Guide, Spring 2000, page 39
Publishers Weekly, October 25, 1999, page 79
School Library Journal, December 1999, page 98

Other books you might like:
Henrik Drescher, *The Boy Who Ate Around*, 1994
   Mo decides to eat around his unappetizing dinner until he's consumed the world and is left with his plate, heartburn and the inevitable burp.
Bill Grossman, *My Little Sister Ate One Hare*, 1996
   One hare is only the beginning of the items a young girl devours in the course of her magic act.
Cynthia Rylant, *Mr. Putter and Tabby Bake the Cake*, 1994
   Elderly Mr. Putter and his pet cat must learn how to bake a cake before they can give one as a present to a neighbor.
John Stadler, *The Cats of Mrs. Calamari*, 1997
   Mrs. Calamari's many cats may not cook but they are masters of disguise.
Rosemary Wells, *Bunny Cakes*, 1997
   Max considers the earthworm cake he bakes for Grandma's birthday a masterpiece needing "Red Hot Marshmallow Squirters" to complete the decorations.

404

TROON HARRISON
ALAN DANIEL, Illustrator
LEA DANIEL, Illustrator

The Dream Collector
(Buffalo, NY: Kids Can Press, 1999)

Subject(s): Dreams and Nightmares; Fantasy; Animals/Dogs
Age range(s): Grades K-2
Major character(s): Zachary, Child; Dream Collector, Worker
Time period(s): 1990s (1999)
Locale(s): Canada

Summary: Zachary hurries outside early one morning in pursuit of two zebras and a dog that he sees drinking from the birdbath. The animals vanish, but then Zachary spots a truck in the street and races to learn more about the stranger under the truck's hood. He meets the official Dream Collector who has a problem. Because it is almost dawn, the Dream Collector must repair the truck quickly or the dreams will not be off the streets before sunrise. If he fails to clean the streets of dreams, those that are touched by sunlight become real. With Zachary's help all the dreams but one are herded into the truck. The repairs are completed just as sunlight touches the one loose dream and Zachary now has the dog he's always wanted. (32 pages)

Where it's reviewed:
Booklist, March 1, 1999, page 1220
Children's Bookwatch, July 1999, page 3
ForeWord Magazine, April 1999, page 60
Horn Book Guide, Fall 1999, page 254
School Library Journal, July 1999, page 72

Other books by the same author:
Don't Dig So Deep, Nicholas!, 1997
Lavender Moon, 1997
Aaron's Awful Allergies, 1996
The Long Weekend, 1994

Other books you might like:
Takamodo No Miya Hisako, *Katie and the Dream Eater: Her Imperial Highness Princess Takamodo*, 1997
   A baby Baku, a creature that eats nightmares, finds his way to the "awake" world where Katie befriends him until his parents retrieve him.
Naomi Shihab Nye, *Benito's Dream Bottle*, 1995
   Benito believes that the source of dreams is a bottle within each person that must periodically be refilled.
Audrey Wood, *Sweet Dream Pie*, 1998
   After the neighbors eat her sweet dream pie, Ma stands ready with a broom to sweep away the inevitable dreams before they fill the neighborhood.

405

MARC HARSHMAN
FELIPE DAVALOS, Illustrator

All the Way to Morning
(New York: Marshall Cavendish, 1999)

Subject(s): Bedtime; Sleep; Fathers and Sons
Age range(s): Grades K-1
Major character(s): Dad, Father, Camper; Unnamed Character, Son, Camper
Time period(s): 1990s
Locale(s): Earth

Summary: While camping under a starlit sky, Dad tells his son that all over the world, as the earth turns and night begins children listen and prepare for sleep. The boy is listening to katydids and he wonders what children in other countries hear. Dad suggests possibilities ranging from rain in the bamboo groves of Kampuchea to blowing sand in the Egyptian desert to foghorns in the misty fjords of Norway. Contentedly the boy snuggles into his sleeping bag imagining children around the world listening for sleep, all the way to morning. (32 pages)

Where it's reviewed:
Booklist, September 15, 1999, page 268
Children's Book Review Service, January 2000, page 51
Horn Book Guide, Spring 2000, page 16
School Library Journal, November 1999, page 118

Other books by the same author:
The Storm, 1995
Moving Days, 1994
Only One, 1993

Uncle James, 1993
Snow Company, 1990
A Little Excitement, 1989

Other books you might like:
Margaret Wise Brown, *Little Donkey Close Your Eyes*, 1995
Animals throughout the world are falling asleep in this newly illustrated reissue of a gentle poem.
Mem Fox, *Time for Bed*, 1993
Through appealing illustrations and comforting verse, the whole wide world goes to sleep.
Megan McDonald, *My House Has Stars*, 1996
All over the world youngsters from their many different homes can see the stars shining overhead and enjoy the shared experience.

406

ALISON HART

Shadow Horse

(New York: Random House, 1999)

Subject(s): Animals/Horses; Animals, Treatment of; Mystery and Detective Stories
Age range(s): Grades 5-8
Major character(s): Jasmine "Jas" Schuler, 13-Year-Old, Equestrian; Chase, Teenager, Animal Lover; Diane Hahn, Foster Parent, Animal Lover
Time period(s): 1990s (1999)
Locale(s): Stanford, Virginia

Summary: Charged with assault and sentenced to 45 days of electronic monitoring in a foster home for assaulting the man she suspects killed a horse and caused her grandfather's stroke, Jas finds herself in the care of Miss Hahn, owner of Second Chance Farm. The animals at the farm have been rescued from abusive situations and, as Chase introduces Jas to the feeding routine, she discovers some in pitiful condition. Although Jas is experienced in caring for horses, she's never seen any in such poor health. More important to Jas than the animals' care is catching the man who caused the death of at least one horse and possibly more. She suspects Miss Hahn might be in cahoots with the horse murderer when he discovers the location of her foster home. Afraid to trust anyone, Jas endures her probation in isolation, reading, working and sleuthing for answers. (230 pages)

Where it's reviewed:
Booklist, July 1999, page 1946
Horn Book Guide, Fall 1999, page 293
School Library Journal, October 1999, page 152

Other books by the same author:
Haunted Horseback Holiday, 1996
Lessons for Lauren, 1994
Mary Beth's Haunted Ride, 1994

Other books you might like:
Jessie Haas, *Beware the Mare*, 1993
Gram and Gramps don't share Lily's excitement about the new mare that Lily hopes will be hers.
Sally M. Keehn, *The First Horse I See*, 1999
Against Granddad's advice, Willo buys the first horse she sees, a beautiful but abused former racehorse.

Anna Sewell, *Black Beauty*, 1877
The classic story of a beautiful black horse with a succession of owners, some of them abusive, has been reissued many times.

407

JUANITA HAVILL
ANNE SIBLEY O'BRIEN, Illustrator

Jamaica and the Substitute Teacher

(Boston: Houghton Mifflin Company, 1999)

Subject(s): Teachers; Schools; Cheating
Age range(s): Grades K-2
Major character(s): Jamaica, Student—Elementary School, Friend; Brianna, Student—Elementary School, Friend; Mrs. Duval, Teacher (substitute)
Time period(s): 1990s (1999)
Locale(s): United States

Summary: Mrs. Duval is the substitute teacher in Jamaica's class for one week. From the first day, Jamaica and Brianna are sure they will like this substitute. Jamaica beams as she is complimented for her reading and her perfect paper in math class. Then, it's time for a spelling test and Jamaica realizes she forgot to study. During the test, she becomes stuck on one word and copies the answer from Brianna's paper rather than have a less than perfect score. Immediately feeling guilty, Jamaica puts the paper in her desk rather than turn it in to Mrs. Duval. Later, Jamaica admits her error and apologizes to Mrs. Duval. She is relieved to be forgiven and looks forward to the rest of the week. (32 pages)

Where it's reviewed:
Booklist, February 15, 1999, page 1075
Horn Book, May 1999, page 314
The New Advocate, Fall 1999, page 387
School Library Journal, May 1999, page 90

Other books by the same author:
Jamaica's Blue Marker, 1995
Jamaica and Brianna, 1993
Jamaica Tag-Along, 1989
Jamaica's Find, 1986

Other books you might like:
Harry Allard, *Miss Nelson Is Back*, 1985
When the students learn that their teacher will be away for one week, they make plans to enjoy their time during her absence.
Judy Finchler, *Miss Malarkey Won't Be in Today*, 1998
Although she has a fever, Miss Malarkey has a hard time staying home and letting the substitute teach her class.
Kevin Henkes, *Lilly's Purple Plastic Purse*, 1996
Lilly thinks better of her actions toward her teacher when she discovers a kind letter from him and apologizes on the next school day.
Peggy Parish, *Teach Us, Amelia Bedelia*, 1977
Amelia Bedelia follows the instructions for the substitute teacher in her customary literal way.

408

BETSY HEARNE
CHRISTY HALE, Illustrator

Who's in the Hall: A Mystery in Four Chapters

(New York: Greenwillow Books/HarperCollins Publishers, 2000)

Subject(s): Apartments; Babysitters; Mystery
Age range(s): Grades 2-5
Major character(s): Lizzy, Child; Rowan, Child, Sister; Ryan, Child, Brother
Time period(s): 2000s (2000)
Locale(s): United States

Summary: New tenants, a new janitor, a new baby-sitter and a stopped up sink lead to mysterious knocks on the doors of two apartments. Lizzy lives on the top floor of the apartment building that Rowan and Ryan move into on the first floor. While Lizzy's babysitter takes a load of laundry to the basement washers, Lizzy refuses to open her apartment door to a person claiming to be the janitor. As Ryan and Rowan's babysitter goes searching for the building janitor, someone claiming to be the same knocks on their door. The identity of the mystery knocker becomes apparent when the knocking starts again at Lizzy's apartment while Ryan, Rowan and their babysitter are inside meeting some potential friends. Now that the identity of the mysterious knocker and the location of the stopped up sink have been confirmed, Ryan, Rowan, Lizzy and the baby-sitters head for the park while the janitor goes to work. (32 pages)

Where it's reviewed:
Booklist, September 15, 2000, page 240
Horn Book, November 2000, page 746
Kirkus Reviews, July 15, 2000, page 1039
Publishers Weekly, July 3, 2000, page 70
School Library Journal, August 2000, page 156

Other books by the same author:
Seven Brave Women, 1997 (Boston Globe/Horn Book Honor Book)
Eliza's Dog, 1996
Beauties and Beasties, 1993

Other books you might like:
Judi Barrett, *Old MacDonald Had an Apartment House*, 1998
  The super of a city apartment building turns the vacant apartments into a farm.
Ursel Scheffler, *The Spy in the Attic*, 1997
  Martin, amateur detective, investigates the stranger with the coffin who moves into his apartment building; the true story surprises him.
John Stadler, *The Cats of Mrs. Calamari*, 1997
  Mrs. Calamari devises ingenious ways to hide her many cats from the new cat-hating manager of her apartment building.

409

ROBERT HEIDBREDER
KADY MACDONALD DENTON, Illustrator

I Wished for a Unicorn

(Niagara Falls, NY: Kids Can Press Ltd., 2000)

Subject(s): Imagination; Unicorns; Stories in Rhyme
Age range(s): Grades K-2
Major character(s): Unnamed Character, Child; Unnamed Character, Dog
Time period(s): 2000s; Indeterminate Past
Locale(s): Canada; Fictional Country

Summary: A wish comes true for a child who finds a unicorn peeking from behind the oak tree in the back yard. Although the unicorn has lost its horn, gnaws on a bone and barks rather than neighs the child's faith that the animal is a unicorn is sufficient to carry the two onto a day of imaginative play in a land of dragons, castles, wizards and buried treasure. Exhausted, the adventurers fall asleep, but the child awakes, the unicorn is gone and only the family dog remains sleeping in the yard. Ah well, tomorrow is another day for making wishes come true. (32 pages)

Where it's reviewed:
Booklist, April 15, 2000, page 1545
Bulletin of the Center for Children's Books, May 2000, page 320
Children's Book Review Service, April 2000, page 97
Five Owls, May 2000, page 120
School Library Journal, August 2000, page 156

Other books by the same author:
Python Play and Other Recipes for Fun, 2000
Don't Eat Spiders, 1997

Other books you might like:
Tomie DePaola, *The Unicorn and the Moon*, 1994
  When a unicorn sees the moon stuck between two mountains, the mythical creature tries to rescue it.
Rafe Martin, *Will's Mammoth*, 1989
  Will is convinced he will meet a mammoth on a snowy day despite his parents' assurance that the animal is extinct.
Dyan Sheldon, *Unicorn Dreams*, 1997
  A unicorn follows Dan into his apartment to eat snacks and spend the night.
Carol Diggory Shields, *I Wish My Brother Was a Dog*, 1997
  A young boy imagines how much better life would be if only his baby brother was a dog.

410

FLORENCE PARRY HEIDE
JUDITH HEIDE GILLILAND, Co-Author
MARY GRANDPRE, Illustrator

The House of Wisdom

(New York: Melanie Kroupa/DK Ink, 1999)

Subject(s): Books and Reading; Libraries; Historical
Age range(s): Grades 3-6
Major character(s): Ishaq, Son, Explorer; Hunayn, Father, Linguist; Caliph al-Ma'mun, Ruler, Scholar

Time period(s): 9th century
Locale(s): Baghdad, Persia

Summary: As the son of Hunayn, the Caliph's best translator, Ishaq lives in the House of Wisdom with his family and observes the dedicated work of the scholars from many lands. Ishaq is both curious about and overwhelmed by the peoples from other countries who flock to Baghdad to study from the Caliph's extensive book collection, but he does not completely understand their motivation. Although Ishaq wants to be a man of learning like Hunayn he also wants to travel and experience these other cultures that he knows only from books. The Caliph provides the opportunity when he sends Ishaq on an extensive expedition to find more books. It is this three-year search yielding thousands of books from many different cultures that finally kindles the fire for knowledge in Ishaq and determines his life's work. (40 pages)

Where it's reviewed:
Booklist, September 15, 1999, page 261
Bulletin of the Center for Children's Books, September 1999, page 14
Kirkus Reviews, September 1, 1999, page 1417
Publishers Weekly, August 23, 1999, page 58
School Library Journal, January 2000, page 132

Awards the book has won:
Notable Social Studies Trade Books for Young People, 2000

Other books by the same author:
Timothy Twinge, 1993
Sami and the Time of the Troubles, 1992
The Day of Ahmed's Secret, 1990

Other books you might like:
Jack Knowlton, *Books and Libraries*, 1991
   A nonfiction title explores the history of libraries beginning with cave paintings.
Susan L. Roth, *Marco Polo: His Notebook*, 1991
   A picture book presents a fictionalized diary telling of the journeys and discoveries of Marco Polo.
Peter Sis, *Starry Messenger*, 1996
   A picture book biography for older readers portrays Galileo and his views of the universe, considered radical in his time.

411

M.C. HELLDORFER
S.D. SCHINDLER, Illustrator

Hog Music

(New York: Viking, 2000)

Subject(s): Frontier and Pioneer Life; Voyages and Travels; Gifts
Age range(s): Grades 1-4
Major character(s): Lucy Owen, Child, Niece; Aunt Liza, Aunt, Aged Person
Time period(s): 1840s
Locale(s): Maryland; Vandalia, Illinois

Summary: When Lucy's parents load the family's belongings into a Conestoga wagon and leave their home for opportunities farther west, Aunt Liza refuses to accompany them to a place that offers nothing but "hog music." Months later, still

grumbling, Aunt Liza ships a straw hat to Lucy for her birthday by giving it to a friend heading west on a mail coach. The wooden box containing the hat bounces off the coach on the rutted National Road and begins a circuitous route to Lucy. Each person who finds it along the way adds a little something to the box to make up for the slight damage that's been done to the hat in transit. When the hat finally arrives weeks later Lucy and her parents are astonished by the collection in the hatbox. Lucy's letter thanking Aunt Liza for each item is such a mystery to the old woman that she boards a stagecoach in hopes of having some of the same adventures that the hat had on the way to Illinois. (32 pages)

Where it's reviewed:
Horn Book Guide, Fall 2000, page 270
Kirkus Reviews, February 15, 2000, page 242
Publishers Weekly, May 22, 2000, page 92
School Library Journal, May 2000, page 142

Other books by the same author:
Phoebe and the River Flute, 2000
Carnival, 1996
Jack, Skinny Bones and the Golden Pancakes, 1996
Gather Up, Gather In, 1994 (School Library Journal Best Book)
Cabbage Rose, 1993

Other books you might like:
Pat Brisson, *Magic Carpet*, 1991
   Aunt Agatha and Elizabeth imagine the many places their rug traveled on its journey from China to their home in America.
Dick Gackenbach, *With Love from Gran*, 1989
   Grandmother travels around the world sending gifts to her grandson from each place she visits.
Donald Hall, *The Ox-Cart Man*, 1979
   A Caldecott Medal winner depicts the cycle of production of goods and their eventual sale or barter for a New England family in the 19th century.
Scott Russell Sanders, *Here Comes the Mystery Man*, 1993
   Twice a year, Merchant Meeks peddles his wares to homes along the frontier.

412

M.C. HELLDORFER
YVONNE GILBERT, Illustrator

Night of the White Stag

(New York: Doubleday Book for Young Readers, 1999)

Subject(s): Fairy Tales; Folklore; Winter
Age range(s): Grades 2-4
Major character(s): Finder, Son; Unnamed Character, Aged Person, Hunter
Time period(s): Indeterminate Past
Locale(s): Fictional Country

Summary: At the conclusion of the king's war Finder's father does not return and his family now suffers during the cold winter. To plea for help from the king, Finder's mother sends her son out into a snowstorm to find his castle. Finder ignores his mother's warning to remain on the road and ventures into the forest where he hopes to find rabbits in the royal hunters' traps. Instead he is found by an old, blind man hunting the white stag and bemoaning the loss of his son during the recent wars. The old man takes Finder as his guide and eventually they find the legendary white stag. To Finder's dismay, the hunter wounds the stag with his spear, but then is healed by the droplets of blood on the snow as the stag disappears. Now the old man, his sight restored, leads the boy to the king's castle. Once inside, Finder realizes that the old man is the king, healthy again with Finder's help. Finder returns home with food, gifts and the king's promise that his family will not be forgotten. Source notes give the background for the author's tale. (32 pages)

Where it's reviewed:
Booklist, December 1, 1999, page 711
Children's Book Review Service, December 1999, page 38
Children's Bookwatch, December 1999, page 6
Horn Book Guide, Spring 2000, page 66
School Library Journal, November 1999, page 119

Other books by the same author:
Jack, Skinny Bones and the Golden Pancakes, 1996
Cabbage Rose, 1993
The Mapmaker's Daughter, 1991

Other books you might like:
Carol Carrick, *Melanie*, 1996
   Blind Melanie searches for her grandfather, lost in the Dark Forest; her love and courage free him from the spell in which she finds him trapped.
Katherine Paterson, *Celia and the Sweet, Sweet Water*, 1998
   When Celia's mother falls ill, Celia sets off with her dog to find the sweet water of her mother's childhood believing it will cure her.
Paul O. Zelinsky, *Rapunzel*, 1997
   Blinded by his fall from her tower, a prince wanders in the wilderness until he finds Rapunzel and her tears restore his sight.

`413`

M.C. HELLDORFER
PAUL HESS, Illustrator

Phoebe and the River Flute
(New York: Doubleday Book for Young Readers, 2000)

Subject(s): Freedom; Animals/Birds; Fairy Tales
Age range(s): Grades 2-5
Major character(s): Phoebe, Orphan, Captive; Unnamed Character, Royalty (prince), Hunter; Unnamed Character, Uncle (prince's), Aged Person
Time period(s): Indeterminate Past
Locale(s): Fictional Country

Summary: Phoebe and a young prince grow up together playing in the walled garden that holds the king's collection of birds. Both wonder what exists beyond the garden walls and when the king dies, the prince leaves the kingdom under his uncle's care and goes to learn about the lands beyond the river. For the next three years Phoebe cares for the birds under the cruel watchfulness of the prince's uncle. When a bird accidentally escapes from the garden, the uncle imprisons Phoebe. Sightings of the rare river flute bird give Phoebe one

month of freedom to search for and capture the bird. As she searches she finds an injured hunter in a pit and frees him. He joins her search which is finally successful. After holding the rare bird, Phoebe lets it fly free although she knows it means the end of her freedom. The hunter returns with Phoebe to the castle and, when the uncle angrily denounces her failure, reveals that he is the prince, returned to reclaim his kingdom. The prince proposes to Phoebe, but respects her desire for freedom, trusting that, like the released birds, she is now free to return. (32 pages)

Where it's reviewed:
Booklist, March 1, 2000, page 1250
Horn Book Guide, Fall 2000, page 270
Publishers Weekly, February 21, 2000, page 87
School Library Journal, March 2000, page 204

Other books by the same author:
Night of the White Stag, 1999
Jack, Skinny Bones and the Golden Pancakes, 1996
Gather Up, Gather In, 1994 (School Library Journal Best Book)
Cabbage Rose, 1993

Other books you might like:
Alma Flor Ada, *The Malachite Palace*, 1998
   Shut away in the palace for protection a lonely princess lacks the one thing she truly wants—a friend—so she frees herself.
Byrd Baylor, *Hawk, I'm Your Brother*, 1976
   When a young boy frees a captured hawk, he finally begins to realize his own dream of flying. Caldecott Honor Book.
Emma Bull, *The Princess and the Lord of the Night*, 1994
   Through her own initiative an overprotected princess frees herself from a lifelong curse by defeating the Lord of the Night.
Tomie DePaola, *Days of the Blackbird: A Tale of Northern Italy*, 1997
   Throughout a harsh winter a white bird stays to sing for a gravely ill Duke, sacrificing its beauty to repay the Duke's kindness.
Vivian French, *The Thistle Princess*, 1998
   The wall that a king and queen build to protect their beloved child actually stifles her and deprives her of happiness.
Rafe Martin, *The Language of Birds*, 2000
   In a retelling of a Russian folktale a mother bird repays Ivan's kindness by teaching him the language of birds.

`414`

M.C. HELLDORFER
TERESA FLAVIN, Illustrator

Silver Rain Brown
(Boston: Houghton Mifflin Company, 1999)

Subject(s): Summer; Mothers and Sons; Babies
Age range(s): Grades K-2
Major character(s): Unnamed Character, Child, Son; Momma, Mother; Silver Rain Brown, Baby, Sister (younger)
Time period(s): 1990s (1999)
Locale(s): Baltimore, Maryland

Summary: A heat wave makes life uncomfortable for everyone in the city and no rain comes to provide relief. A little boy is concerned for his pregnant mother, but Momma seems to be worrying more about her wilting flowers and the grass turning brown. Finally, the rain and the baby arrive on the same night. Momma wants to call the baby Rain while her son prefers Silver to remind him of the rain's color and so the baby is named Silver Rain Brown. (32 pages)

Where it's reviewed:
Booklist, February 15, 1999, page 1075
Children's Book Review Service, June 1999, page 123
Horn Book Guide, Fall 1999, page 254
Kirkus Reviews, March 1, 1999, page 376
School Library Journal, May 1999, page 90

Other books by the same author:
Jack, Skinny Bones and the Golden Pancakes, 1996
Gather Up, Gather In, 1994 (School Library Journal Best Book)
Cabbage Rose, 1993

Other books you might like:
Stephanie Calmenson, *Hotter than a Hot Dog!*, 1994
   On a hot, hot day Granny and granddaughter escape their steamy city stoop and find relief at the beach.
Dorothy Carter, *Wilhe'mina Miles After the Stork Night*, 1999
   Wilhe'mina's pregnant mother sends her daughter out into the night to fetch the midwife Mis' Hattie.
Nancy Poydar, *Cool Ali*, 1996
   Ali uses her artistic talents to cool the neighbors until the rain begins to fall.
James Stevenson, *Heat Wave at Mud Flat*, 1997
   The residents of Mud Flat are suffering from an extended spell of hot dry weather.

415

NICHOLAS HELLER
JOS. A. SMITH, Illustrator

Elwood and the Witch

(New York: Greenwillow Books/HarperCollins Publishers, 2000)

Subject(s): Animals/Pigs; Witches and Witchcraft; Magic
Age range(s): Grades K-2
Major character(s): Elwood, Pig; Unnamed Character, Witch
Time period(s): Indeterminate
Locale(s): Fictional Country

Summary: Elwood, while walking in the woods on a moonlit night, finds a broom that is perfect for sweeping. As he grasps it to carry it home, however, the broom trembles and shoots into the sky. Too late, Elwood realizes he must be astride a witch's broom and down below the angry witch appears hurling threats and spells into the night sky. Apparently she can't hear Elwood over her screams so she's not aware that he'd gladly return the broom if he only knew how to land it. None of the witch's spells connect with Elwood though they do change other innocent objects, including the moon. When the moon becomes a huge bee it buzzes angrily to earth and demands to be returned to its previous state. The moon relays Elwood's need for instructions, the witch yells them to Elwood and he gradually brings the broom under control and

back to the ground. The witch turns the bee back into a moon and flies away leaving a relieved Elwood to continue his walk. (32 pages)

Where it's reviewed:
Booklist, August 2000, page 2146
Children's Bookwatch, September 2000, page 4
Horn Book Guide, Spring 2001, page 38
Kirkus Reviews, August 1, 2000, page 1117
School Library Journal, September 2000, page 199

Other books by the same author:
Ogres! Ogres! Ogres!: A Feasting Frenzy from A to Z, 1999
This Little Piggy, 1997
A Book for Woody, 1995
Goblins in Green, 1995
A Troll Story, 1990

Other books you might like:
Caralyn Buehner, *A Job for Wittilda*, 1993
   Thanks to her trusty broom Wittilda is one of the fastest pizza delivery drivers in town.
Margie Palatini, *Zoom Broom*, 1998
   Gritch's broom seems to be beyond repair, even with magic, so she's shopping for a new one.
James Stevenson, *Emma*, 1985
   Not a typical witch, Emma even needs flying lessons.

416

MARILYN HELMER
PAUL MOMBOURQUETTE, Illustrator

Fog Cat

(Buffalo, NY: Kids Can Press, 1999)

Subject(s): Animals/Cats; Grandfathers; Pets
Age range(s): Grades K-3
Major character(s): Hannah, Child; Grandpa, Grandfather; Fog Cat, Cat (stray)
Time period(s): 1990s
Locale(s): Falls Harbor, Canada

Summary: Not long after Hannah comes to live with Grandpa she spots the elusive gray cat on the rocks near the shore and names her Fog Cat. With great patience she tames the cat with food, each plate set nearer and nearer the house. Fog Cat lives with Grandpa and Hannah each winter night and heads outside every morning until three kittens are born. Two are stillborn, but Fog Cat stays with the third for a month before she goes out the door for the last time, leaving Hannah with the kitten. (32 pages)

Where it's reviewed:
Booklist, March 15, 1999, page 1333
Horn Book Guide, Fall 1999, page 278
Kirkus Reviews, February 1, 1999, page 222
Publishers Weekly, March 15, 1999, page 58
School Library Journal, May 1999, page 90

Other books by the same author:
The Boy, the Dollar and the Wonderful Hat, 1996

Other books you might like:
Lady Borton, *Fat Chance!*, 1993
   Marty's patience tames a blind, sickly stray cat in her yard;

now if she can only convince her mother, she'll finally have a pet.

Mary Calhoun, *Tonio's Cat*, 1996

New to his neighborhood, Tonio recognizes some of his own loneliness in the stray cat he feeds and protects.

Wolfram Hanel, *Mia the Beach Cat: A Story*, 1994

A friendly cat enlivens lonely Maggie's vacation at the beach so much she doesn't want to part with Mia.

417

KATHY HENDERSON
TONY KERINS, Illustrator

The Baby Dances
(Cambridge, MA: Candlewick Press, 1999)

Subject(s): Babies; Growing Up; Family Life
Age range(s): Grades K-1
Major character(s): Unnamed Character, Baby, Sister (younger)
Time period(s): 1990s (1999)
Locale(s): United States

Summary: The baby is born in winter. As the seasons change, the baby grows. At first she sleeps, then she smiles and one warm day she learns to roll over by herself. By the time the leaves are falling, the baby is crawling and when winter comes again she takes her first steps. (32 pages)

Where it's reviewed:
Booklist, July 1999, page 1943
Horn Book Guide, Fall 1999, page 234
New York Times Book Review, November 21, 1999, page 54
Publishers Weekly, June 14, 1999, page 68
School Library Journal, July 1999, page 72

Awards the book has won:
Booklist Editors' Choice, 1999

Other books by the same author:
Cars, Cars, Cars!, 1999
The Little Boat, 1998
Bounce Bounce Bounce, 1996

Other books you might like:
Catherine Anholt, *When I Was a Baby*, 1989
A mother talks with her daughter about the girl's life as an infant.
Peter McCarty, *Baby Steps*, 2000
Month by month baby Suki grows and changes until she takes her first steps.
Norma Simon, *The Baby House*, 1995
First her cat, then her dog and finally her mother deliver the babies a little girl has eagerly awaited.
Susan Winter, *A Baby Just Like Me*, 1994
Martha is disappointed that her baby sister is not able to be her playmate immediately.

418

KATHY HENDERSON
CAROLINE BINCH, Illustrator

Newborn
(New York: Dial Books, 1999)

Subject(s): Babies; Family Life; Brothers and Sisters
Age range(s): Grades K-1
Major character(s): Unnamed Character, Baby
Time period(s): 1990s (1999)
Locale(s): United States

Summary: A newborn baby meets older siblings, listens to new sounds and experiences home for the first time. Loving parents and other relatives embrace the tiny babe, hover watchfully near, change a diaper and cuddle the sleepy new addition to the family. (32 pages)

Where it's reviewed:
Booklist, May 1, 1999, page 1599
Horn Book Guide, Fall 1999, page 234
Publishers Weekly, May 17, 1999, page 78
School Library Journal, June 1999, page 96

Other books by the same author:
The Baby Dances, 1999
In the Middle of the Night, 1992
The Baby's Book of Babies, 1989

Other books you might like:
Tony Bradman, *This Little Baby*, 1990
The routine activities of an infant's life are portrayed.
Trish Cooke, *So Much*, 1994
In this happy family there's no doubt that everyone loves the baby. . .so much!
Robie H. Harris, *Happy Birth Day!*, 1996
Eloquent pictures and simple text capture the joy and wonder of a baby's birth and the love of her parents from the very first day.
Amy Schwartz, *A Teeny Tiny Baby*, 1994
This baby's eye view of the world is one of simple needs that receive immediate, loving attention from a doting family.

419

KATHY HENDERSON, Author/Illustrator

The Storm
(Cambridge, MA: Candlewick Press, 1999)

Subject(s): Weather; Nature; Beaches
Age range(s): Grades K-1
Major character(s): Jim, Child, Son; Mom, Mother; Grandma, Grandmother
Time period(s): 1990s
Locale(s): Earth

Summary: As winter nears its end Jim stands atop a sand dune anticipating the summer day when all he sees will be his to enjoy. During the night storm winds stir the ocean waves and flood sirens call a warning to residents. Jim looks out the window and sees the sea breaking over the dune line. Mom sandbags the door and takes Jim up the hill to Grandma's house until the wind dies down and the tide turns. With the storm past, a humbled Jim again climbs the dune line to acknowledge the power of wind and water over his beach. (24 pages)

Where it's reviewed:
Horn Book, November 1999, page 728
Kirkus Reviews, November 15, 1999, page 1809
Publishers Weekly, December 6, 1999, page 77
Riverbank Review, Spring 2000, page 33
School Library Journal, December 1999, page 98

Other books by the same author:
Cars, Cars, Cars!, 1999
The Baby Dances, 1999
The Little Boat, 1995
Bounce Bounce Bounce, 1994
Bumpety Bump, 1994

Other books you might like:
Marie Hall Ets, *Gilberto and the Wind*, 1963
  Through his play, a young boy learns to understand and appreciate the wind.
G. Brian Karas, *The Windy Day*, 1998
  Most townspeople don't appreciate the havoc caused by a strong wind but one boy finds pleasure imagining all the places the wind has already traveled.
Mary Stolz, *Storm in the Night*, 1998
  During a storm-caused power outage Grandfather tells Thomas a story from his childhood when a similar experience frightened him.
Charlotte Zolotow, *The Storm Book*, 1952
  This depiction of people's varied reactions to a summer storm is a Caldecott Honor Book.

420

DIANA HENDRY
JANE CHAPMAN, Illustrator

The Very Noisy Night

(New York: Dutton Children's Books, 1999)

Subject(s): Animals/Mice; Bedtime; Sleep
Age range(s): Grades K-2
Major character(s): Little Mouse, Mouse; Big Mouse, Mouse
Time period(s): 1990s
Locale(s): Fictional Country

Summary: Little Mouse encounters one problem after another as he tries to fall asleep. Each time he hears a sound he wakes Big Mouse who has a simple explanation for the noise—the huffing is the wind, the tapping is a branch, and the who-who comes from an owl. Little Mouse would feel better if he were in Big Mouse's bed, but Big Mouse knows that Little Mouse wriggles and has cold paws so he says no to Little Mouse's suggestion. Finally, Big Mouse's snoring is the problem noise and Little Mouse complains of being lonely so Big Mouse lets him into the bed and they both sleep peacefully right through the sound of the alarm clock. First published in the United Kingdom in 1999. (32 pages)

Where it's reviewed:
Booklist, December 1, 1999, page 711
Horn Book Guide, Spring 2000, page 16

Kirkus Reviews, November 1, 1999, page 1742
Publishers Weekly, November 15, 1999, page 64
School Library Journal, November 1999, page 119

Other books by the same author:
Happy Old Birthday, Owl, 1996
Dog Donovan, 1995
Back Soon, 1994
Not Anywhere House, 1991

Other books you might like:
Russell Hoban, *Bedtime for Frances*, 1960
  Frances imagines so many scary things in her room that she is unable to sleep.
Tony Johnston, *Little Rabbit Goes to Sleep*, 1994
  Grandpa comforts Little Rabbit when his fear of the dark and night noises keep him awake long after bedtime.
Bethany Roberts, *A Mouse Told His Mother*, 1997
  A young mouse's plans do not include sleep but his mother is ready with a creative response to each idea so he completes the bedtime ritual happily.
Martin Waddell, *Can't You Sleep, Little Bear?*, 1992
  Big Bear comforts Little Bear when his fear of the dark prevents him from settling down and sleeping.

421

KEVIN HENKES

The Birthday Room

(New York: Greenwillow Books, 1999)

Subject(s): Family Life; Aunts and Uncles; Self-Acceptance
Age range(s): Grades 5-7
Major character(s): Ben Hunter, 12-Year-Old, Nephew; Ian, Uncle, Artisan
Time period(s): 1990s (1999)
Locale(s): Madison, Wisconsin; Eugene, Oregon

Summary: Along with the usual gift of two-dollar bills from his grandmother, Ben receives two unusual gifts for his twelfth birthday—a room and a letter. Ben's parents give him a room in their home to use as an art studio and in doing so also present him with the burden of their expectations. Uncle Ian gives Ben a letter of invitation to visit him in Oregon and in doing so provides the opportunity to heal the past. Ben is eager to visit his uncle and meet the man responsible for the accident that left Ben with only nine fingers. Ben's mother is opposed to the trip, but reluctantly agrees because it means so much to Ben. After the visit with Uncle Ian, Ben feels grateful for the birthday room, not because he wants an art studio, but because his family needs a guest room for the Oregon relatives. (152 pages)

Where it's reviewed:
Booklist, July 1999, page 1946
Five Owls, September 1999, page 18
Horn Book, September 1999, page 611
Riverbank Review, Fall 1999, page 34
School Library Journal, October 1999, page 152

Other books by the same author:
Sun & Spoon, 1997 (School Library Journal Best Book)
Protecting Marie, 1995 (School Library Journal Best Book)
Words of Stone, 1992 (Horn Book Fanfare Honor Book)

Other books you might like:
Claudia Mills, *You're a Brave Man, Julius Zimmerman*, 1999
    Julius struggles to satisfy his mother's expectations and, in the process, finds he has talents neither one of them suspected.
Barbara O'Connor, *Beethoven in Paradise*, 1997
    Martin, a natural musician, has no interest in trying to meet his father's expectation that he play baseball.
Anne Quirk, *Dancing with Great-Aunt Cornelia*, 1997
    The trip from Queens to Manhattan to visit Aunt Cornelia is a short one for Connie yet it introduces her to a life that is far removed from her own.

422

KEVIN HENKES
LAURA DRONZEK, Illustrator

Oh!

(New York: Greenwillow Books, 1999)

Subject(s): Animals; Playing; Winter
Age range(s): Preschool
Time period(s): 1990s
Locale(s): United States

Summary: All night the snow falls coloring everything white. Oh what fun for animals and children to run, jump and play in the bright snow all day long! As darkness falls, playtime must end for rabbits, cats, dog, squirrels and children—until tomorrow. (24 pages)

Where it's reviewed:
Booklist, October 1, 1999, page 354
Children's Book Review Service, November 1999, page 26
New York Times Book Review, November 21, 1999, page 41
Publishers Weekly, October 11, 1999, page 74
School Library Journal, October 1999, page 114

Other books by the same author:
Lilly's Purple Plastic Purse, 1996 (School Library Journal Best Book)
Good-Bye, Curtis, 1995
Owen, 1993 (Caldecott Honor Book)

Other books you might like:
Nancy White Carlstrom, *The Snow Speaks*, 1992
    Two children enjoy the sights and sounds of the season's first snow.
Cheryl Chapman, *Snow on Snow on Snow*, 1994
    Colorful pictures and playful text celebrate the joy of snow.
Lois Ehlert, *Snowballs*, 1995
    Simple text and clear collages tell of the creation of a snow family and the inevitable result as the weather warms.
Mick Inkpen, *Kipper's Snowy Day*, 1996
    Kipper is a dog that dearly loves the snow and is happy to play in it all day.
Ezra Jack Keats, *The Snowy Day*, 1962
    The Caldecott Medal winner expresses a young boy's joy with the first snowfall.

423

KEVIN HENKES, Author/Illustrator

Wemberly Worried

(New York: Greenwillow Books, 2000)

Subject(s): Animals/Mice; Schools; Conduct of Life
Age range(s): Grades K-1
Major character(s): Wemberly, Mouse, Daughter; Petal, Doll; Jewel, Mouse, Preschool
Time period(s): 2000s (2000)
Locale(s): Fictional Country

Summary: Wemberly is an expert in the art of worrying because she always worries about everything. When she is really worried she rubs Petal's floppy ears and then she worries that she might rub the ears right off her doll. As the first day of nursery school approaches Wemberly's worrying increases to levels never seen before and her mind is filled with "What if. . .?" questions as she considers all the things that could go wrong. Her parents walk her to the classroom the first day where her understanding teacher introduces her to a student standing alone in the room clutching a doll. Wemberly and Jewel were made for each other! After a day of playing together, they go home cheerfully with parting assurances to the teacher that she need not worry—they'll be back. (32 pages)

Where it's reviewed:
Booklist, August 2000, page 214
Five Owls, September 2000, page 15
Horn Book, September 2000, page 550
Riverbank Review, Winter 2000-2001, page 33
School Library Journal, August 2000, page 156

Awards the book has won:
Publishers Weekly Best Books, 2000
School Library Journal Best Books, 2000

Other books by the same author:
Lilly's Purple Plastic Purse, 19996 (School Library Journal Best Book)
Owen, 1993 (Caldecott Honor Book)
Chrysanthemum, 1991

Other books you might like:
Jonathan London, *Froggy Goes to School*, 1996
    Froggy's feeling nervous about his first day of school, but he survives and enjoys the day.
Mary Serfozo, *Benjamin Bigfoot*, 1993
    Benjamin's reservations about beginning kindergarten vanish after a visit to the teacher.
Jean Van Leeuwen, *Emma Bean*, 1993
    Molly and her beloved Emma Bean, a stuffed rabbit, anxiously begin school where they meet a little girl with a special teddy bear.

424

YUMI HEO, Author/Illustrator

One Sunday Morning

(New York: Orchard Books, 1999)

Subject(s): Fathers and Sons; Asian Americans; Dreams and Nightmares

Age range(s): Grades K-1

Major character(s): Minho, Son, Child; Unnamed Character, Father

Time period(s): 1990s (1999)

Locale(s): New York, New York (Central Park)

Summary: Early one morning, Minho rides the subway to the park with his father. Together they enjoy the sounds of passing bikers, the animals in the zoo, and the music of the carousel. The perfect day ends, when Minho's father awakens him, and Minho realizes that he has been dreaming. (32 pages)

Where it's reviewed:
Booklist, April 1, 1999, page 1420
Horn Book, March 1999, page 190
Kirkus Reviews, February 15, 1999, page 300
Publishers Weekly, February 8, 1999, page 212
School Library Journal, April 1999, page 97

Other books by the same author:
The Green Frogs: A Korean Folktale, 1996
Father's Rubber Shoes, 1995
One Afternoon, 1994

Other books you might like:
Craig McFarland Brown, *City Sounds*, 1992
    Farmer Brown discovers the sounds of a city.
Margaret Wise Brown, *The Noisy Book*, 1939
    A participatory celebration of noise explores environmental sounds.
Sheila Hamanaka, *Bebop-a-Do-Walk!*, 1995
    Emi's walk to Central Park with her father is no dream.
Elaine Moore, *Good Morning, City*, 1995
    Early in the morning, people of a city begin the varied activities that contribute to the bustle of an urban community.
Paul Showers, *The Listening Walk*, 1991
    A young girl and her father go for a quiet walk and try to identify the environmental sounds around them.
Chris K. Soentpiet, *Around Town*, 1994
    On a summer day, a girl and her mother share a day in New York City, enjoying all that a vibrant city has to offer.

425

CHARLOTTE HERMAN
KATYA KRENINA, Illustrator

How Yussel Caught the Gefilte Fish: A Shabbos Story

(New York: Dutton Children's Books, 1999)

Subject(s): Jews; Religious Traditions; Fishing
Age range(s): Grades K-3

Major character(s): Yussel, Child, Son; Papa, Father, Fisherman; Mama, Mother, Cook

Time period(s): Indeterminate Past

Locale(s): Vasser Lake (USA)

Summary: Yussel is pleased when Papa finally considers him old enough to help catch the gefilte fish for the Shabbos dinner. As Papa teaches Yussel about the different baits (challah dough, cheese and worms) that are effective, Yussel catches a carp, a trout and a pike. Papa keeps them all and Mama seems pleased when they arrive home, but Yussel is disappointed because he did not catch any gefilte fish. Papa assures Yussel that Mama can work miracles in the kitchen and, as Yussel watches, she transforms his three fish into his favorite meal. A glossary defines Yiddish words used in the text and a recipe for gefilte fish is included. (32 pages)

Where it's reviewed:
Booklist, February 1, 1999, page 979
Horn Book Guide, Fall 1999, page 279
Kirkus Reviews, January 1, 1999, page 66
School Library Journal, July 1999, page 72

Other books by the same author:
Millie Cooper and Friends, 1995
Max Malone, Superstar, 1992
My Mother Didn't Kiss Me Good Night, 1980

Other books you might like:
Kathryn Lasky, *Marven of the Great North Woods*, 1997
    While living and working temporarily at a logging camp young Marven gives the non-kosher portions of his daily meals to a friendly lumberjack.
Fran Manushkin, *Starlight and Candles: The Joys of the Sabbath*, 1995
    Together, a family prepares for and celebrates the simple, but never-ending joys of the Sabbath.
Joan Rothenberg, *Inside-Out Grandma*, 1995
    As a reminder to purchase the oil needed for making potato latkes, Rosie's grandma wears her clothes inside out.

426

GAIL HERMAN
MERYL TREATNER, Illustrator

Just Like Mike

(New York: Delacorte Press, 2000)

Subject(s): Remarriage; Names, Personal; Stepfathers
Age range(s): Grades 2-4

Major character(s): Michael "Mike" Jordan, 3rd Grader, Stepson; Tim, 3rd Grader, Friend; Mr. Jordan, Stepfather

Time period(s): 2000s (2000)

Locale(s): United States

Summary: Michael Jordan is no athlete and he knows it. In fact, he'd like to go back to being Mike Brown but his widowed mother married Mr. Jordan. She insisted they become one family with one name so Mike receives a famous moniker and kids in his new school expect him to live up to it. Tim includes him in basketball and baseball games, but this Michael Jordan finds excuses to avoid playing. When Mike notices try-outs for a play at his new school he auditions, wins the part and finally hears the applause that the real Michael Jordan is accustomed to receiving. (56 pages)

Where it's reviewed:
Booklist, February 15, 2000, page 1112
Bulletin of the Center for Children's Books, March 2000, page 244
Horn Book Guide, Fall 2000, page 293
School Library Journal, March 2000, page 204

Other books by the same author:
Fairy Cloud Parade, 1999
Tooth Fairy Travels, 1999 (Fairy School)
No Business Like Show Business, 1998

Other books you might like:
Betsy Duffey, *Virtual Cody*, 1997
   Proud to be named after Buffalo Bill, Cody's looking forward to reporting to the class on the origin of his name—then he learns he's named for a dog.
Bonnie Graves, *No Copycats Allowed!*, 1998
   The spelling of Gabrielle's long name gives her one more problem as she adjusts to a new school.
Johanna Hurwitz, *The Adventures of Ali Baba Bernstein*, 1985
   Eight-year-old David Bernstein changes his name to something more exciting.
Suzy Kline, *ORP*, 1989
   Michael Jordan would probably like to join the "I Hate My Name" club formed by Orville Rudmeyer Pygenski Jr.
Candice F. Ransom, *More than a Name*, 1995
   When Cammie's mother remarries Cammie wishes she could have gotten a new last name, too, instead of a teasing cousin.
Mildred Pitts Walter, *Suitcase*, 1999
   Because of Xander's height and big hands he's nicknamed Suitcase and expected to be good at basketball when his real love is art.

427

PATRICIA HERMES

Calling Me Home

(New York: Avon/Camelot, 1998)

Subject(s): Frontier and Pioneer Life; Fathers and Daughters; Christian Life
Age range(s): Grades 4-6
Major character(s): Abbie Chrisman, 12-Year-Old, Sister (older); Mamma, Mother, Settler; Papa, Father, Settler
Time period(s): 1850s
Locale(s): Nebraska (prairie homestead); Grand Island, Nebraska

Summary: Abbie has dreams of living in a real house and having a piano just like she did in St. Joseph before Mamma and Papa made the decision to homestead in order to own land that can be passed on to her brothers. Giving up her piano when she can't even own land seems simply unfair to Abbie. Mamma urges her to accept her life and be happy with what she has while Papa admires her spirit and encourages her dreams. When her baby brother dies of cholera, Abbie knows her daydreaming is responsible for delaying the doctor. Abbie doesn't have time to mourn because she too falls ill and by the

time she recovers she has a better appreciation for her life on the prairie. (140 pages)

Where it's reviewed:
Booklist, January 1, 1999, page 876
Horn Book Guide, Spring 1999, page 67
Kirkus Reviews, November 15, 1998, page 1669
Publishers Weekly, December 14, 1998, page 76
School Library Journal, December 1998, page 124

Other books by the same author:
Cheat the Moon, 1998
On Winter's Wind, 1995
Nothing but Trouble, Trouble, Trouble, 1994

Other books you might like:
Jennifer Armstrong, *Black-Eyed Susan*, 1995
   Susan uses the awe-inspiring prairie sunrise to draw her depressed mother out of the dugout home and into life.
Pam Conrad, *Prairie Songs*, 1985
   As a lifelong resident, Louisa understands the lonely beauty of the Nebraska prairie and tries to help a new neighbor as she struggles to adapt.
Laurie Lawlor, *Addie Across the Prairie*, 1986
   As the oldest child of a family homesteading in a sod house on the prairie, Addie dutifully helps her mother
Laura Ingalls Wilder, *Little House on the Prairie*, 1935
   Seeking a better life, the Wilder family settles on a prairie homestead.

428

KAREN HESSE
JON J. MUTH, Illustrator

Come On, Rain!

(New York: Scholastic Press, 1999)

Subject(s): Weather; Mothers and Daughters; Summer
Age range(s): Grades K-2
Major character(s): Tessie, Child, Daughter; Mamma, Mother, Gardener; Jackie-Joyce, Child, Friend
Time period(s): Indeterminate
Locale(s): United States

Summary: After three weeks of dry heat, Mamma feels as parched and wilted as her tomato plants. Tessie notices the distant signs of an approaching rainstorm and alerts Jackie-Joyce to come over in her suit, knowing that will convince Mamma to let her change to her bathing suit also. Tessie and Jackie-Joyce gather two other friends and they all race outside to await the rain. The girls' mothers watch from apartment windows until the cooling shower and the dancing daughters tempt them out of doors to join in the happy moment. (32 pages)

Where it's reviewed:
Booklist, February 1, 1999, page 982
Horn Book, July 1999, page 454
The New Advocate, Fall 1999, page 389
Riverbank Review, Spring 1999, page 30
School Library Journal, March 1999, page 176

Awards the book has won:
Bulletin of the Center for Children's Books Blue Ribbon, 1999

Other books by the same author:
Lester's Dog, 1993
Poppy's Chair, 1993

Other books you might like:
Stephanie Calmenson, *Hotter than a Hot Dog!*, 1994
  On a hot, hot day Granny and granddaughter escape their steamy city stoop and find relief at the beach.
Joy Cowley, *Singing Down the Rain*, 1997
  The children are first to join a stranger who comes to sing down the much needed rain in a rural community.
Nancy Poydar, *Cool Ali*, 1996
  On a hot summer day, Ali brings relief to her neighbors by drawing pictures of cool breezes, shade trees and snow until rain washes her art away.

429

KAREN HESSE

A Light in the Storm: The Civil War Diary of Amelia Martin

(New York: Scholastic, Inc., 1999)

Series: Dear America
Subject(s): Historical; Civil War; Lighthouses
Age range(s): Grades 4-7
Major character(s): Amelia Martin, Daughter; Father, Lighthouse Keeper (assistant), Father; Napoleon, Cat
Time period(s): 1860s (1860-1861)
Locale(s): Fenwick Island, Delaware

Summary: Amelia enjoys helping Father and the lighthouse keeper tend the light, but her mother abhors such work and their life on the windswept island. Amelia strives to please both parents and hold together a marriage that is fractured by opposing views on slavery, the turmoil confronting the country and differing opinions about island life. When rats eat her mother's garden, Amelia acquires Napoleon to ease her mother's life on the island. Napoleon also eases Amelia's loneliness during her five-hour watch, but he has no opinion on the threat of war. Amelia shares Father's abolitionist sentiments while her mother sides with the slavery supporters. Life in Amelia's home and small community mirrors the nationwide struggle as friends depart for war and neighbors shun neighbors because of contrary viewpoints. Concluding historical notes give the factual background on which the story is based. (167 pages)

Where it's reviewed:
Booklist, October 15, 1999, page 444
Horn Book Guide, Spring 2000, page 79
Kliatt, September 1999, page 8
School Library Journal, November 1999, page 158

Other books by the same author:
Just Juice, 1998
Out of the Dust, 1997 (Newbery Medal)
The Music of Dolphins, 1996 (School Library Journal Best Book)

Other books you might like:
Barry Denenberg, *When Will This Cruel War Be Over? The Civil War Diary of Emma Simpson*, 1996

This entry in the Dear America series presents the perspective of a Virginian during the last year of the Civil War.
Dorothy Hoobler, *Sally Bradford: The Story of a Rebel Girl*, 1997
  Although Sally's family owns no slaves, as Virginians they feel obligated to support the Confederacy.
Janet Lunn, *The Root Cellar*, 1983
  Orphan Rose travels back in time to the Civil War where she finds friendship, danger and an opportunity for leadership.

430

AMY HEST
CHRISTINE DAVENIER, Illustrator

Mabel Dancing

(Cambridge, MA: Candlewick Press, 2000)

Subject(s): Bedtime; Dancing
Age range(s): Grades K-1
Major character(s): Mabel, Child, Daughter; Curly Dog, Dog
Time period(s): Indeterminate Past
Locale(s): United States

Summary: On the night of the dancing party Mabel's parents tuck her into bed before the guests arrive, but the music drifts upstairs to lonely Mabel. With Curly Dog for company Mabel and her yellow blanket sit at the top of the stairs watching the dancers below. The mesmerizing music drifts up to Mabel who begins dancing with her yellow blanket down the stairs past the guests and around the room. Mabel bows as the guests applaud and her parents dance with her up the stairs and back to bed where Mabel drifts off to sleep to the soothing sound of the music. (40 pages)

Where it's reviewed:
Booklist, April 15, 2000, page 1552
Horn Book Guide, Fall 2000, page 250
Kirkus Reviews, June 1, 2000, page 797
Publishers Weekly, June 12, 2000, page 73
School Library Journal, June 2000, page 114

Other books by the same author:
Gabby Growing Up, 1998
You're the Boss, Baby Duck, 1997
Baby Duck and the Bad Eyeglasses, 1996 (Booklist Editors' Choice)
Jamaica Louise James, 1996
Nana's Birthday Party, 1993 (Booklist Editors' Choice)

Other books you might like:
Patricia Lee Gauch, *Bravo, Tanya*, 1992
  Tanya's dancing improves after she learns to move to the feel of the music in her head.
Libba Moore Gray, *My Mama Had a Dancing Heart*, 1995
  Memories of her mother's love for movement inspire a dancer's performance.
Bill Harley, *Nothing Happened*, 1995
  Jack is so sure that his family has a party after he goes to bed every night that he stays awake and discovers the truth—nothing happens.

431

AMY HEST
JILL BARTON, Illustrator

Off to School, Baby Duck!

(Cambridge, Massachusetts: Candlewick Press, 1999)

Subject(s): Schools; Fear; Grandfathers
Age range(s): Grades K-1
Major character(s): Baby Duck, Duck, Student—Elementary School; Grampa, Duck, Grandfather; Miss Posy, Duck, Teacher
Time period(s): Indeterminate
Locale(s): Fictional Country

Summary: It's the first day of school and Baby Duck is much too nervous to eat the toast or drink the juice that her parents offer for breakfast. Slowly Baby puts on her school sweater, buckles her new school shoes and picks up her new blue backpack. While her parents and baby sister waddle happily along, Baby lingers and frets all the way to the schoolyard where she finds Grampa waiting. Grampa understands Baby's fears, admires the contents of her backpack and asks Miss Posy all the right questions. By the time Miss Posy rings the school bell, Baby has found a friend and the confidence to have a good first day at school. (26 pages)

Where it's reviewed:
Booklist, September 15, 1999, page 259
School Library Journal, September 1999, page 183

Awards the book has won:
Booklist Editors' Choice, 1999
School Library Journal Best Books, 1999

Other books by the same author:
You're the Boss, Baby Duck, 1997
Baby Duck and the Bad Eyeglasses, 1996 (Booklist Editors' Choice)
In the Rain with Baby Duck, 1995 (Boston Globe/Horn Book Fanfare Award)

Other books you might like:
Laurence Anholt, *Billy and the Big New School*, 1999
    Watching a baby sparrow helps Billy overcome his fear of starting school.
Paulette Bourgeois, *Franklin Goes to School*, 1995
    Friends help Franklin overcome his fears of entering school for the first time.
Nancy Carlson, *Look Out Kindergarten, Here I Come!*, 1999
    Henry's enthusiasm for school wanes as he approaches the building.
Jonathan London, *Froggy Goes to School*, 1996
    Although he feels nervous about the first day of school, Froggy not only survives, but also enjoys the day.

432

FRED HIATT
MARK GRAHAM, Illustrator

Baby Talk

(New York: Margaret K. McElderry Books, 1999)

Subject(s): Babies; Brothers; Family Life

Age range(s): Grades K-2
Major character(s): Joey, Brother, Child; Baby, Baby, Brother
Time period(s): 1990s (1999)
Locale(s): United States

Summary: Joey is not interested in responding to Baby's cries signaling hunger, a wet diaper or a need to sleep. Gradually Baby begins babbling and Joey's grandmother reminds Joey that since he spoke baby talk not long ago, he should understand what Baby is saying. Joey begins responding to Baby's sounds and soon he is translating his brother's needs for the other family members. (32 pages)

Where it's reviewed:
Booklist, July 1999, page 1951
Children's Book Review Service, Spring 1999, page 135
Horn Book Guide, Fall 1999, page 234
Publishers Weekly, June 7, 1999, page 81
School Library Journal, August 1999, page 136

Other books by the same author:
If I Were Queen of the World, 1997

Other books you might like:
Bruce Coville, *The Lapsnatcher*, 1997
    Jacob is disillusioned by the arrival of his time-consuming, loud baby sister; she is no fun, but his parents assure him she will be.
Holly Keller, *Geraldine's Baby Brother*, 1994
    Gradually, Geraldine becomes more accepting of her noisy baby brother and all the attention he receives.
Phyllis Root, *What Baby Wants*, 1998
    While Mama naps everyone in the family tries to determine what will soothe the crying baby.

433

ELIZABETH STARR HILL
LESLEY LIU, Illustrator

Bird Boy

(New York: Farrar Straus Giroux, 1999)

Subject(s): Animals/Birds; Bullies; Mutism
Age range(s): Grades 2-5
Major character(s): Chang, Bullied Child (mute); Jinan, Bully, Child; Mei Mei, Child, Sister (of Jinan), of bully
Time period(s): Indeterminate Past
Locale(s): China (Li River)

Summary: From the family houseboat, Chang helps his father care for the cormorants used in the family fishing business. After Chang proves himself capable of fishing with his father, he is allowed to help raise the next cormorant chick. Because Chang, though mute, makes noises like the birds, Jinan makes fun of him, but Jinan's sister, Mei Mei, befriends Chang. After Jinan steals Chang's baby cormorant, Chang rescues the bird and, with Mei Mei's help, nurses the chick back to health. (64 pages)

Where it's reviewed:
Horn Book Guide, Fall 1999, page 279
Publishers Weekly, March 29, 1999, page 105
Riverbank Review, Summer 1999, page 34
School Library Journal, June 1999, page 96

Other books by the same author:
Evan's Corner, 1991

Other books you might like:
Eleanor Frances Lattimore, *Little Pear and His Friends*, 1991
   Six-year-old Little Pear and his friend Big Head find their
   fun sometimes leads to trouble in their Chinese village.
Elizabeth Foreman Lewis, *Young Fu of the Upper Yangtze*, 1932
   In this Newbery Medal winner, a young boy and his
   mother move from a rural Chinese village to Chungking
   where the boy's apprenticeship to a coppersmith brings
   good luck.
Ching Yeung Russell, *First Apple*, 1994
   Ying wishes to buy her Ah Pau an apple for her birthday,
   since she has never tasted one.

434

KIRKPATRICK HILL

The Year of Miss Agnes

(New York: Margaret K. McElderry Books/Simon & Schuster, 2000)

Subject(s): Schools; Teachers; Indians of North America
Age range(s): Grades 3-5
Major character(s): Agnes Sutterfield, Teacher; Frederika
"Fred", 10-Year-Old, Sister (Bokko's); Bokko, 12-Year-
Old, Deaf Person
Time period(s): 1940s (1948)
Locale(s): Koyukuk, Alaska

Summary: During the four years Fred has attended the one
room school house in her village teachers have come and
gone, some more quickly than others, but no teacher ever
returned for a second year. No teacher ever arranged the desks
in a circle or began her instruction by having the students pack
up all the books as unorthodox Miss Agnes does either. Miss
Agnes reads aloud to the students, plays records on a battery-
operated turntable and individualizes her instruction to the
interests and abilities of each student. When Bokko arrives at
school carrying Fred's forgotten lunch one day, Miss Agnes
takes her on as a pupil too. While respecting the culture and
way of life of her students Miss Agnes also introduces the
world to them and makes them aware of the potential each has
within. Fred wishes that the year with Miss Agnes would
never end, but her experience is that when all the students
leave for summer fish camp the teacher departs too and is not
seen again. (113 pages)

Where it's reviewed:
Booklist, October 15, 2000, page 438
Horn Book, November 2000, page 755
Riverbank Review, Winter 2000-2001, page 45
School Library Journal, September 2000, page 199
Smithsonian, November 2000, page 66

Awards the book has won:
School Library Journal Best Books, 2000
Smithsonian's Notable Books for Children, 2000

Other books by the same author:
Winter Camp, 1993
Toughboy and Sister, 1990

Other books you might like:
Patricia Reilly Giff, *Shark in School*, 1994
   With help from an understanding teacher and a compas-
   sionate classmate Matthew begins to overcome his reading
   problem.
Susie Morgenstern, *Secret Letters from 0 to 10*, 1998
   Enthusiastic, talkative Victoria joins Ernest's class and
   transforms the quiet boy's monotonous life.
Jerry Spinelli, *Maniac Magee*, 1990
   In a Newbery Medal winner Maniac Magee runs into
   town; his presence changes people for the better.
Eileen Walsh Strauch, *Hey You, Sister Rose*, 1993
   Arlene is not happy to have strict Sister Rose as her
   teacher, but she learns to appreciate her during their year
   together.

435

LILLIAN HOBAN, Author/Illustrator

Arthur's Birthday Party

(New York: HarperCollins Publishers, 1999)

Series: I Can Read Book
Subject(s): Birthdays; Animals/Chimpanzees; Competition
Age range(s): Grades K-2
Major character(s): Arthur, Chimpanzee, Brother; Violet,
Chimpanzee, Sister (younger); Norman, Chimpanzee,
Friend (Arthur's)
Time period(s): Indeterminate
Locale(s): Fictional Country

Summary: Arthur doesn't like any of Violet's "baby" suggestions for birthday party activities. He plans to use the backyard playset and Norman's trampoline for a gymnastics party
with medals awarded to the winners. All week the party
guests practice and on the big day, each wins an individual
event medal and Arthur's birthday wish comes true when he
receives the "best all-around gymnast" prize. What a great
party! (64 pages)

Where it's reviewed:
Booklist, March 15, 1999, page 1337
Horn Book, January 1999, page 63
School Library Journal, February 1999, page 84

Other books by the same author:
Arthur's Back to School Day, 1996
Arthur's Camp-Out, 1993
Arthur's Loose Tooth, 1985

Other books you might like:
Russell Hoban, *A Birthday for Frances*, 1968
   A Chompo bar makes such a delicious birthday gift for a
   sister that it's no surprise it's nibbled away on the walk
   home from the store.
Syd Hoff, *Happy Birthday, Danny and the Dinosaur!*, 1995
   The friendly dinosaur from the museum joins Danny and
   his friends for a lively birthday celebration in this begin-
   ning reader.
Suzy Kline, *Herbie Jones and the Birthday Showdown*, 1993
   Herbie tries to help his friend Ray thinks of a great, but
   inexpensive, idea for a birthday party.

Cynthia Rylant, *Henry and Mudge and the Best Day of All*, 1995

In a series entry Henry and his dog Mudge enjoy Henry's birthday party so much they declare May 1st to be the best day ever.

436

RUSSELL HOBAN
QUENTIN BLAKE, Illustrator

Trouble on Thunder Mountain

(New York: Orchard Books, 2000)

Subject(s): Dinosaurs; Amusement Parks; Conservation
Age range(s): Grades 2-3
Major character(s): Mom O'Saurus, Mother, Dinosaur; Dad O'Saurus, Father, Dinosaur; J.M. Flatbrain, Businessman (Megafright International)
Time period(s): Indeterminate
Locale(s): Thunder Mountain, Fictional Country

Summary: The O'Saurus family lives a contented life on Thunder Mountain until a notice arrives from Mr. Flatbrain that they've been evicted to make way for the leveling of the mountain and the creation of an all-plastic theme park. With no time to mount a protest before the bulldozers begin, Mom and Dad load the family's belongings and move to the designated relocation area—a garbage dump—with other displaced former residents of Thunder Mountain. Mom has an idea and with everyone's help—and a lot of Monsta-Gloo-the former residents reclaim their mountain home and send Mr. Flatbrain's creation, piece by piece, down the Tunnel of Terror to Endsville. Originally published in Great Britain in 1999. (40 pages)

Where it's reviewed:
Booklist, June 2000, page 1892
Horn Book Guide, Fall 2000, page 293
School Library Journal, July 2000, page 80
Smithsonian, November 2000, page 66

Awards the book has won:
Smithsonian's Notable Books for Children, 2000

Other books by the same author:
Ace Dragon, 1980
A Bargain for Frances, 1970
Best Friends for Frances, 1969
Tom and the Two Handles, 1965

Other books you might like:
Stan Berenstain, *The Berenstain Bears and the G. Rex Bones*, 1999

An unscrupulous group tries to swindle Professor Actual Factual by offering to sell dinosaur bones (that are fake) to his museum.

Laurie Krasny Brown, *Rex and Lilly Family Time*, 1995

The dinosaur family in this "Dino Easy Reader" plans a birthday surprise, experiments with a robot housecleaner and searches for the perfect pet.

Arnold Lobel, *Ming Lo Moves the Mountain*, 1982

Using advice from a wise man Ming Lo moves a mountain that he thinks is too near his house.

James Skofield, *Detective Dinosaur: Lost and Found*, 1998

In a beginning reader Detective Dinosaur and Officer Pterodactyl solve mysteries involving lost (and later found) items, including each other.

437

HOLLY HOBBIE, Author/Illustrator

Toot & Puddle: You Are My Sunshine

(Boston: Little, Brown and Company, 1999)

Subject(s): Animals/Pigs; Friendship; Problem Solving
Age range(s): Grades K-2
Major character(s): Toot, Pig, Friend; Puddle, Pig, Friend; Tulip, Bird, Friend
Time period(s): Indeterminate
Locale(s): Woodstock Pocket, Fictional Country

Summary: Puddle revels in the beauty of the day, but Toot sits inside moping. Puddle and Tulip understand that sometimes everyone feels a little blue; still they make plans to cheer Toot. Puddle bakes Toot's favorite five-berry cobbler with whipped cream and gets a smile from Toot, but the next morning he's still moping. Puddle and Tulip plan an exciting adventure with Toot who remains blase. Finally, they invite all their friends to a party and everyone has a good time except Toot. Then, the weather changes, bringing a storm. Puddle and Tulip huddle inside but Toot can be seen outside walking in the rain. The next morning the sun is shining and Toot is once again the cheerful friend they know. (32 pages)

Where it's reviewed:
Bulletin of the Center for Children's Books, September 1999, page 16
Horn Book Guide, Spring 2000, page 17
Kirkus Reviews, July 15, 1999, page 1133
Publishers Weekly, September 20, 1999, page 90
School Library Journal, August 1999, page 136

Other books by the same author:
Toot and Puddle: Puddle's ABC, 2000
Toot and Puddle: A Present for Toot, 1998
Toot and Puddle, 1997

Other books you might like:
Amy Hest, *In the Rain with Baby Duck*, 1995

Grampa knows how to soothe Baby Duck when a rainy day puts her out of sorts. In no time, she's ready for a stroll with Grampa.

Arnold Lobel, *Frog and Toad Are Friends*, 1970

In an award-winning title Frog and Toad share some of the difficulties as well as the pleasures of friendship.

Hiawyn Oram, *Badger's Bad Mood*, 1998

To help lift Badger's spirits Mole plans a surprise so Badger will realize how much his friends appreciate him.

438

VALERIE HOBBS

Carolina Crow Girl

(New York: Farrar Straus Giroux, 1999)

Subject(s): Freedom; Identity; Mothers and Daughters

Age range(s): Grades 4-7
Major character(s): Carolina Lewis, 11-Year-Old, Friend; Stefan Crouch III, Handicapped, Friend
Time period(s): 1990s (1999)
Locale(s): California

Summary: Carolina lives with her mother and baby sister in a big yellow school bus, making it convenient for them to relocate each time Carolina's mother gets the urge to move on. While her home is parked in a field near a mansion, Carolina finds a baby crow that has fallen from its nest and tries to take care of it. She also befriends wheelchair-bound Stefan who lives in the mansion. When her mother decides it's time to move, Carolina accepts an invitation to stay behind with the Crouch family. Stefan and his mother help Carolina understand her unique life and decide where she, and her crow, belong. (144 pages)

Where it's reviewed:
Booklist, February 15, 1999, page 1070
Kirkus Reviews, February 1, 1999, page 222
Publishers Weekly, February 15, 1999, page 60
Riverbank Review, Summer 1999, page 35
School Library Journal, April 1999, page 136

Other books by the same author:
Charlie's Run, 2000
Get It While It's Hot or Not, 1996
How Far Would You Have Gotten If I Hadn't Called You Back?, 1995

Other books you might like:
Avi, *Blue Heron*, 1992
    Maggie befriends a blue heron while visiting her father and his new wife and baby.
Frances Hodgson Burnett, *The Secret Garden*, 1911
    Orphaned Mary is sent to live on the Yorkshire Moors where she unlocks the secret to an overgrown garden and an invalid cousin's health.
Jean Craighead George, *There's an Owl in the Shower*, 1995
    A family of loggers makes a place in their home for an owl.
Dick King-Smith, *The Cuckoo Child*, 1993
    Jack raises a pet ostrich, but eventually realizes he must let it go.

439

MARY ANN HOBERMAN
LYNNE CRAVATH, Illustrator

The Two Sillies

(San Diego: Gulliver Books/Harcourt, Inc., 2000)

Subject(s): Problem Solving; Humor; Stories in Rhyme
Age range(s): Grades K-2
Major character(s): Lilly, Friend; Sammy, Milkman
Time period(s): Indeterminate Past
Locale(s): United States

Summary: Two silly people use complicated methods to solve simple problems. Sammy's answer to Lilly's inquiry about acquiring a cat seems odd but Lilly does what he says. She cuts down trees, builds a shed and buys a cow to put in it. Lilly doesn't understand how her efforts will get her a cow but Sammy assures her if she'll milk the cow she'll get a cat and

sure enough a cat appears while Lilly is milking. Lilly is sure she didn't need to do all the work that Sammy instructed her to do in order to get the cat but before she can raise the issue Sammy sees mice and shrieks in fear. Now it's Lilly's turn to tell Sammy what to do in order to get rid of the mice. Sammy sees no sense in Lilly's instructions, but he does what she orders and sure enough the shed is soon free of mice (Lilly's new cat is also well fed). (32 pages)

Where it's reviewed:
Booklist, December 1, 2000, page 721
Horn Book, November 2000, page 747
Publishers Weekly, October 9, 2000, page 86
School Library Journal, December 2000, page 110

Other books by the same author:
One of Each, 1997 (School Library Journal Best Book)
The Seven Silly Eaters, 1997
The Cozy Book, 1995

Other books you might like:
Sue Denim, *Make Way for Dumb Bunnies*, 1996
    In the third book about a family of bunnies who happily do everything in a way contrary to reason, a stormy day is perfect for a trip to the beach.
Peggy Parish, *Come Back, Amelia Bedelia*, 1971
    As usual, Amelia Bedelia interprets instructions literally, causing her to lose a series of jobs.
Ann Whitford Paul, *Silly Sadie, Silly Samuel*, 2000
    A chapter book for beginning readers describes the lifestyle of a foolish farm couple who enjoy their unconventional relationship.

440

MARY HOFFMAN
CAROLINE BINCH, Illustrator

Starring Grace

(New York: Phyllis Fogelman Books, 2000)

Subject(s): Playing; Friendship; Imagination
Age range(s): Grades 2-5
Major character(s): Grace, Child of Divorced Parents, Friend; Nana, Grandmother; Gerda Myerson, Neighbor, Recluse
Time period(s): 2000s (2000)
Locale(s): United States

Summary: School vacation and hot summer days provide the perfect time for Grace and her friends to indulge their penchant for imaginative play. Grace's apartment is the gathering spot since Grace has no siblings to interfere and Nana is home to supervise the activity. The changing activities Grace and friends plan include pretending to be circus performers, detectives, time travelers and ghost busters. Their exploration of a "haunted" house in the neighborhood leads them to help Mrs. Myerson, a fearful, reclusive neighbor by cleaning up her overgrown yard. Through interaction with the children, Mrs. Myerson comes out of her home more often and sometimes has tea with Nana. As summer draws to an end Nana notices an audition for a play and Grace and her friends land non-speaking roles in *Annie*. Grace is sure that she and her friends have had a much better summer than the kids who traveled or went to camp. (95 pages)

Where it's reviewed:
Booklist, February 15, 2000, page 1112
Horn Book, March 2000, page 196
Kirkus Reviews, May 15, 2000, page 715
Publishers Weekly, May 15, 2000, page 119
School Library Journal, July 2000, page 80

Other books by the same author:
Clever Katya: A Fairy Tale from Old Russia, 1998
Sun, Moon, and Stars, 1998
Boundless Grace, 1995
The Four-Legged Ghosts, 1993 (Book Links Good Book)
Amazing Grace, 1991

Other books you might like:
Patricia Reilly Giff, *Dance with Rosie*, 1996
    Rosie's summer is not beginning as she expects, but she hopes it will improve.
Johanna Hurwitz, *Spring Break*, 1997
    Cricket's plans for a vacation trip change when she breaks her ankle and has to stay home, but she makes a new friend during the week of inactivity.
Maud Hart Lovelace, *Betsy-Tacy and Tib*, 1941
    When Tib moves to town, best friends Betsy and Tacy invite her join them in play.
Sally Warner, *Totally Confidential*, 2000
    Quinney decides to turn her talent for listening and mediation into a summer job and earn some money.

441

JENNIFER L. HOLM

Our Only May Amelia
(New York: HarperCollins Publishers, 1999)

Subject(s): Frontier and Pioneer Life; Brothers and Sisters; Gender Roles
Age range(s): Grades 5-7
Major character(s): May Amelia Jackson, 12-Year-Old, Sister; Wilbert Jackson, 13-Year-Old, Brother
Time period(s): 1890s (1899)
Locale(s): Nasel River Valley, Washington; Astoria, Oregon

Summary: May Amelia bemoans the fact that she is the only May Amelia in a large family of boys and the only girl in the Nasel River settlement of Finnish Americans. With her mother pregnant, May Amelia must help with many of the "women's" chores, such as cooking that she dislikes. Wilbert, May Amelia's favorite brother, seems to understand her tomboy spirit and is a source of comfort and adventure for his sister. May Amelia is constantly admonished to be a "proper" young lady, something she has no intention of being even if she knew how. She's doesn't understand why she is constantly in trouble for doing the very same things that her brothers do. Whether she's accidentally stepped into one of her brother's traps or gotten treed by an angry mother bear, trouble has a way of finding May Amelia. When May Amelia escapes a family tragedy by running away to the home of relatives in Astoria, she learns about city life, meets a girl her age and makes friends with a young Chinese immigrant. Months later, she returns home, still not a proper lady, but with a different perspective of her life on the Nasel. A con-

cluding author's note gives the family history on which this first novel is based. (251 pages)

Where it's reviewed:
Booklist, September 1, 1999, page 133
Bulletin of the Center for Children's Books, September 1999, page 16
Horn Book Guide, Fall 1999, page 293
Publishers Weekly, June 14, 1999, page 71
School Library Journal, June 1999, page 129

Awards the book has won:
Newbery Honor Book, 2000
Publishers Weekly Best Books, 1999

Other books you might like:
Carol Ryrie Brink, *Caddie Woodlawn*, 1935
    The Newbery Medal winner describes the life of an adventurous young girl and her loving family on the frontier in Wisconsin.
Celia Barker Lottridge, *Wings to Fly*, 1999
    As her family settles into their homestead on the Canadian prairie, 11-year-old Josie begins to wonder about what the future holds for a girl.
Rhea Beth Ross, *The Bet's On, Lizzie Bingham!*, 1988
    To prove a point, Lizzie bets her older brother that she can fend for herself all summer without asking for his help.
Laura Ingalls Wilder, *On the Banks of Plum Creek*, 1937
    A Newbery Honor book in the Little House series relates the daily activities of the Wilder family in their home on the frontier.

442

BELL HOOKS
CHRIS RASCHKA, Illustrator

Happy to Be Nappy
(New York: Jump at the Sun/Hyperion Books for Children, 1999)

Subject(s): Hair; African Americans; Self-Acceptance
Age range(s): Grades K-3
Time period(s): 1990s (1999)
Locale(s): United States

Summary: Girls have many options for hairstyles and the author's first book for children celebrates them all. Brushing and braids require some quiet sitting, but when the work is complete the hair brings joy and satisfaction. Girls of all sizes enjoy their hair in different ways—curly, straight, long or short. Hair makes one feel happy! (32 pages)

Where it's reviewed:
Booklist, August 1999, page 2064
Horn Book Guide, Spring 2000, page 40
Publishers Weekly, July 19, 1999, page 194
Riverbank Review, Winter 1999, page 28
School Library Journal, November 1999, page 120

Other books you might like:
Nancy Cote, *Palm Trees*, 1993
    A bad hair day threatens a friendship until Renne and Millie creatively turn the problem into a fashion statement.
Nikki Grimes, *Wild, Wild Hair*, 1997
    Tisa dreads Monday mornings when Mommy combs her

wild, wild hair but she loves the twenty beautiful braids that Mommy plaits.

Carolivia Herron, *Nappy Hair*, 1997

At a family reunion, Brenda's uncle notes the uniqueness of her incredibly curly hair and the relatives all chime in their agreement.

Natasha Anastasia Tarpley, *I Love My Hair!*, 1998

Kenyana endures the combing of tangles from her hair because she enjoys the many different ways her mother can style her curly locks.

443

WILLIAM H. HOOKS
KATE DUKE, Illustrator

Mr. Big Brother

(New York: Byron Preiss/Bantam Books, 1999)

Series: Bank Street Ready-to-Read. Level 1
Subject(s): Babies; Brothers and Sisters; Sibling Rivalry
Age range(s): Grades 1-2
Major character(s): Eli, Son, Brother; Jon, Son, Brother (oldest); Unnamed Character, Baby, Sister
Time period(s): 1990s (1999)
Locale(s): United States

Summary: Eli is excited that his baby brother is almost ready to be born and he will finally be in Jon's role as the big brother. Eli's looking forward to teaching the baby many things so when he visits his mother and the baby at the hospital he's very disappointed to learn that the baby is a girl. It doesn't take long before Eli realizes he's still a big brother and the baby is kind of cute so as long as Jon remembers to call him "Mr. Big Brother" Eli thinks having a "Mr. Sister" will work out. (32 pages)

Where it's reviewed:
Booklist, February 15, 2000, page 1124
Horn Book Guide, Fall 2000, page 288
School Library Journal, September 1999, page 184

Other books by the same author:
Freedom's Fruit, 1996
How Do You Make a Bubble?, 1992 (Bank Street Ready-to-Read)
Mr. Baseball, 1991 (Bank Street Ready-to-Read)

Other books you might like:
Amy Hest, *Nannies for Hire*, 1994
Jenny and her friends discover how difficult baby care can be when they offer to be "nannies" for Jenny's new sibling.

James Howe, *Pinky and Rex and the New Baby*, 1993
Concerned they she will be displaced by the new baby, Rex becomes such a "perfect" big sister that she neglects her friend Pinky.

Brigitte Weninger, *Will You Mind the Baby, Davy?*, 1997
Davy is not sure he's ready to be a big brother but after his sister's birth he realizes she will need his protection and experience as she grows.

444

JACKIE MIMS HOPKINS
MICHAEL AUSTIN, Illustrator

The Horned Toad Prince

(Atlanta: Peachtree Publishers Ltd., 2000)

Subject(s): Animals/Frogs and Toads; American West; Folklore
Age range(s): Grades K-3
Major character(s): Reba Jo, Daughter, Cowgirl
Time period(s): Indeterminate Past
Locale(s): Southwest

Summary: As Reba Jo rides near a dry riverbed, a dangerous place she's forbidden to visit, the wind blows her new hat into a dry well and Reba Jo has a problem. If she doesn't retrieve the hat she has to explain to her father where it is, but she also has no way of getting into the well. A bilingual horned toad proposes a bargain. In exchange for a bowl of chili, a song and a nap in her hat, the toad will go into the well and recover the hat. Reba Jo lowers the toad into the well in a bucket, grabs the hat when it reaches the surface and rides off without the toad. True to the original tale on which this one is based, the horned toad appears at Reba Jo's door and her father insists she fulfill her part of the bargain. Rather than let the toad sleep in her hat, Reba Jo kisses the varmint and releases the prince, long trapped by a spell. As promised, the toad/prince leaves, but Reba Jo may have other ideas for the now handsome visitor. A pronunciation guide and glossary for the Spanish words used in the text are included. (32 pages)

Where it's reviewed:
Booklist, May 15, 2000, page 1756
ForeWord, April 2000, page 52
Horn Book Guide, Fall 2000, page 340
Publishers Weekly, March 6, 2000, page 110
School Library Journal, April 2000, page 106

Other books by the same author:
Tumbleweed Tom on the Texas Trail, 1994

Other books you might like:
Alix Berenzy, *A Frog Prince*, 1989
The enchanted frog is the narrator in a retelling of the traditional folktale from the amphibian's point of view.

J. Patrick Lewis, *The Frog Princess: A Russian Folktale*, 1994
A prince falls in love with and marries a frog before learning that she is the beautiful Vasilisa transformed by a spell.

Jon Scieszka, *The Frog Prince Continued*, 1991
An award-winning title takes a satirical and rather different view of the fate of the frog transformed into a prince by the kiss of a princess.

445

DEBORAH HOPKINSON
RAUL COLON, Illustrator

A Band of Angels: A Story Inspired by the Jubilee Singers

(New York: Anne Schwartz Book/Atheneum Books for Young Readers, 1999)

Subject(s): African Americans; Singing; Education
Age range(s): Grades 2-4
Major character(s): Beth, Aunt, Storyteller; Ella Sheppard, Grandmother (great-great grandmother), Singer; George White, Teacher (music)
Time period(s): 1990s; 1870s
Locale(s): Nashville, Tennessee

Summary: Aunt Beth tells the story of Grandma Ella, a former slave whose desire for an education propels her to Fisk School. Although she works many odd jobs to earn the fees, Ella still may lose her chance for an education if the lack of funding to maintain the school forces it to close. At the suggestion of Professor White, a group of nine students forms a traveling chorus in hopes of raising money for Fisk. Initially they meet with little success but when Ella begins one performance with a spiritual or jubilee song, the audience is so appreciative that the Jubilee Singers know they have found their identity. The successful group travels all over the United States and Europe for seven years, assuring the school's success. (40 pages)

Where it's reviewed:
Booklist, April 15, 1999, page 1529
Horn Book, March 1999, page 190
Publishers Weekly, January 4, 1999, page 90
Riverbank Review, Summer 1999, page 29
School Library Journal, February 1999, page 84

Other books by the same author:
Birdie's Lighthouse, 1997
Sweet Clara and the Freedom Quilt, 1993
Pearl Harbor, 1991

Other books you might like:
Sandra Belton, *From Miss Ida's Front Porch*, 1993
    The stories told on Miss Ida's porch teach the children about past discriminations against black people and encourage pride in their heritage.
Elizabeth Fitzgerald Howard, *Papa Tells Chita a Story*, 1995
    Although she knows the story by heart, Chita loves to hear Papa tell of his bravery during the Spanish-American War.
William Miller, *Richard Wright and the Library Card*, 1997
    In the segregated South of the 1920s, it is illegal for 17-year-old Richard to check out a library book, but he finds a way to satisfy his desire to read.
Margaree King Mitchell, *Uncle Jed's Barbershop*, 1993
    In an award-winning story, Sarah Jean recalls the determination of her Uncle Jed to save enough money to open his own barbershop.
Michael J. Rosen, *A School for Pompey Walker*, 1995
    With help from a white friend, Pompey Walker uses the system of slavery to get the income needed to achieve his goal of educating black children.

Carole Boston Weatherford, *Juneteenth Jamboree*, 1995
    Soon after moving to her parent's hometown in Texas, Cassandra learns about the history behind the Juneteenth holiday.

446

DEBORAH HOPKINSON
DEBORAH LANINO, Illustrator

Maria's Comet

(New York: Atheneum Books for Young Readers, 1999)

Subject(s): Biography; Astronomy; Discovery and Exploration
Age range(s): Grades 1-3
Major character(s): Papa, Scientist, Father; Andrew Mitchell, Son, Brother (older); Maria Mitchell, Daughter, Sister
Time period(s): 1820s
Locale(s): Nantucket Island, Massachusetts

Summary: The fictionalized account of Maria's childhood as one of nine children shows her interest in Papa's nightly forays to the roof to "sweep the sky" with his telescope. While playing in the attic with Andrew he tells tales of sailors while Maria shares stories of early astronomers. When Andrew invites her to join him as he runs away to explore the world aboard a sailing ship, Maria realizes that her dream is to explore the stars and hopefully find a comet. Given courage by Andrew's bold move, Maria approaches Papa and her astronomy lessons begin. A concluding author's note gives the factual basis for the story and information about the astronomy terms used. (32 pages)

Where it's reviewed:
Booklist, September 15, 1999, page 268
Children's Book Review Service, September 1999, page 174
Kirkus Reviews, September 1, 1999, page 1418
Publishers Weekly, October 11, 1999, page 75
School Library Journal, October 1999, page 114

Other books by the same author:
A Band of Angels: A Story Inspired by the Jubilee Singers, 1999 (ALA Notable Book)
Birdie's Lighthouse, 1997 (Bulletin of the Center for Children's Books Blue Ribbon)
Sweet Clara and the Freedom Quilt, 1993 (IRA Children's Choice)

Other books you might like:
Gary Crew, *Bright Star*, 1997
    When John Tebbutt, an astronomer, speaks to Alicia's school he is impressed by her scientific curiosity and invites her to visit his observatory.
Beatrice Gormley, *Maria Mitchell: The Soul of an Astronomer*, 1995
    The life of the first woman astronomer in the United States and discoverer of a telescopic comet is presented in a biography.
Stephanie McPherson, *Rooftop Astronomer: A Story about Maria Mitchell*, 1990
    A biography describes the life of the American woman who became the first professional astronomer in her country.

447

RUTH HOROWITZ
KATE KIESLER, Illustrator

Crab Moon

(Cambridge, MA: Candlewick Press, 2000)

Subject(s): Animals, Treatment of; Animals/Marine; Beaches
Age range(s): Grades 1-3
Major character(s): Daniel, 7-Year-Old, Son; Unnamed Character, Mother
Time period(s): 2000s (2000)
Locale(s): East Coast

Summary: Daniel and his family arrive at their rental beach cottage the weekend of a full moon in June when the horseshoe crabs come ashore to lay their eggs on the beach. In the middle of night, with his mother's guidance, Daniel walks to the beach and observes the amazing sight and sound of thousands of the ancient creatures coming ashore at high tide, depositing their eggs and then returning to the sea. As the tide recedes the number of crabs dwindles and Daniel returns to the cottage. The next morning he hurries to the beach and discovers one crab, on her back, stranded on shore. Gingerly, Daniel turns the crab over and watches her scurry to the ocean. Factual information about horseshoe crabs concludes the story. (32 pages)

Where it's reviewed:
Booklist, August 2000, page 2147
Horn Book Guide, Fall 2000, page 270
Publishers Weekly, June 12, 2000, page 73
Riverbank Review, Summer 2000, page 30
School Library Journal, May 2000, page 144

Other books by the same author:
Mommy's Lap, 1993
Bat Time, 1991

Other books you might like:
Liz Rosenberg, *Moonbathing*, 1996
    Michael and his young cousin walk the beach on a clear night under a full moon.
Mark Shasha, *The Night of the Moonjellies*, 1992
    Seven-year-old Mark and his family explore the beach on the night of the moonjellies.
Suzanne Tate, *Harry Horseshoe Crab: A Tale of Crawly Creatures*, 1991
    Two horseshoe crabs live in a touch tank.
Martin Waddell, *The Big, Big Sea*, 1994
    Mother and daughter walk along the shore of a big, big sea on a moonlit night savoring a moment that will live in their memories.

448

POLLY HORVATH
WENDY ANDERSON HALPERIN, Illustrator

The Trolls

(New York: Farrar Straus Giroux, 1999)

Subject(s): Aunts and Uncles; Storytelling; Family Life
Age range(s): Grades 3-6
Major character(s): Sally, Aunt, Storyteller
Time period(s): 1990s
Locale(s): Ohio

Summary: When the Anderson children's parents go on a week-long trip to Paris, Aunt Sally comes to stay with her two nieces and nephew as a substitute for the family baby-sitter who is taken ill at the last moment. Although the children are meeting their aunt for the first time, they soon learn that she is a wonderful storyteller who shares stories they've never heard about their father's childhood in Canada. The tales tell of many family members, but the one about the Trolls has the deepest meaning for the children as it explains why the children's father and Aunt Sally don't get along to this day. (144 pages)

Where it's reviewed:
Booklist, March 1, 1999, page 1206
Horn Book, July 1999, page 466
Publishers Weekly, February 8, 1999, page 214
Riverbank Review, Fall 1999, page 39
School Library Journal, April 1999, page 97

Awards the book has won:
Boston Globe/Horn Book Honor Book, 1999
Booklist Editors' Choice, 1999

Other books by the same author:
When the Circus Came to Town, 1996
No More Cornflakes, 1990
An Occasional Cow, 1989

Other books you might like:
Kevin Henkes, *The Zebra Wall*, 1988
    Aunt Irene comes to stay when Adine's mother has her sixth baby.
Patricia MacLauchlan, *Seven Kisses in a Row*, 1983
    Life changes for Emma and Zach when their aunt and uncle care for them while their parents are away.
Bonnie Pryor, *Toenails, Tonsils, and Tornadoes*, 1997
    Life gets exciting for Martin when great-aunt Henrietta comes to visit.

449

ARTHUR HOWARD, Author/Illustrator

Cosmo Zooms

(San Diego: Harcourt Brace & Company, 1999)

Subject(s): Animals/Dogs; Talent; Sports/Skateboarding
Age range(s): Grades K-1
Major character(s): Cosmo, Dog; Pearl, Cat
Time period(s): 1990s
Locale(s): United States

Summary: Cosmo is the only dog on Pumpkin Lane without a specialty. The other dogs on the block have skills ranging from howling to drooling to herding, but Cosmo has no talent. Pearl suggests climbing trees or catching mice, but Cosmo doesn't see a future in either of those areas. Feeling discouraged, Cosmo lies down for a nap and soon notices inanimate objects moving past his droopy eyes. When Cosmo sits up he notices that he is on a skateboard, gathering speed as it rolls down Pumpkin Lane. The ride comes to an end in a hydrangea bush to the congratulations of the other dogs, impressed by Cosmo's new talent. (32 pages)

Where it's reviewed:
Booklist, November 1, 1999, page 538
Horn Book Guide, Spring 2000, page 41
Kirkus Reviews, August 1, 1999, page 1227
Publishers Weekly, July 12, 1999, page 93
School Library Journal, September 1999, page 184

Awards the book has won:
IRA/CBC Children's Choices, 2000

Other books by the same author:
When I Was Five, 1996 (IRA/CBC Children's Choice)

Other books you might like:
Margaret Wise Brown, *The Little Scarecrow Boy*, 1998
   Little Scarecrow must master six scary faces before he can join his father in the cornfields.
Syd Hoff, *Bernard on His Own*, 1993
   Bernard's parents reassure him that one day he'll be able to climb a tree, catch a fish and gather honey on his own.
Robert Kraus, *Leo the Late Bloomer*, 1971
   While Father frets, Mother patiently waits until the day when son Leo is finally ready to "bloom."
John Prater, *The Greatest Show on Earth*, 1995
   Harry's talented family performs with the circus, but Harry can't seem to do anything right.
Ellen Stoll Walsh, *Hop Jump*, 1993
   Bored with hopping and jumping like all the other frogs, Betsy dances instead, starting a trend in frog movement.

450

ELIZABETH FITZGERALD HOWARD
E.B. LEWIS, Illustrator

Virgie Goes to School with Us Boys

(New York: Simon & Schuster Books for Young Readers, 2000)

Subject(s): African Americans; Gender Roles; Schools
Age range(s): Grades 1-4
Major character(s): Virgie Fitzgerald, Sister, Child; Cornelius "C.C." Fitzgerald, Brother (older), Student
Time period(s): 19th century (post Civil War)
Locale(s): May Day, Tennessee; Jonesborough, Tennessee

Summary: All summer long Virgie pesters her brothers and her parents about school. Her brothers offer excuses why Virgie should stay home—she's too little to go, girls have no need for reading and arithmetic, the seven-mile walk is too long and the weeklong stay away from home will make her cry. Only C.C. speaks up on Virgie's behalf and he questions why girls can't also be educated. Determined, Virgie persists until her parents, recognizing the need for free people to have an education, give permission for her to go to the Quaker school seven miles away in Jonesborough. With their pails packed for the week with clean underwear and food the six siblings set off on their long walk to school. Upon arrival, Virgie, amazed by all the books in the school, declares her intention to read them all and to share the knowledge with her parents every weekend so they can also learn to be free. A concluding author's note gives the family history upon which the story is based. (32 pages)

Where it's reviewed:
Black Issues Book Review, May 2000, page 75
Booklist, November 1, 1999, page 525
Children's Book Review Service, March 2000, page 88
Horn Book Guide, Fall 2000, page 270
School Library Journal, March 2000, page 208

Awards the book has won:
ALA Notable Children's Books, 2001
Coretta Scott King Honor Book for Illustration, 2001

Other books by the same author:
What's in Aunt Mary's Room?, 1996
Papa Tells Chita a Story, 1995
Mac and Marie and the Train Toss Surprise, 1993
Chita's Christmas Tree, 1989 (ALA Notable Book)

Other books you might like:
Marie Bradby, *More than Anything Else*, 1995
   This fictionalized account describes the 9-year-old Booker T. Washington learning to read his name.
Robert Coles, *The Story of Ruby Bridges*, 1995
   Courageously, six-year-old Ruby daily faces angry white protesters as the first black child to attend a formerly all-white elementary school.
Michael J. Rosen, *A School for Pompey Walker*, 1995
   With help from a white friend, Pompey Walker manipulates the slavery system to finance the education of black children.

451

ELIZABETH FITZGERALD HOWARD
NINA CREWS, Illustrator

When Will Sarah Come?

(New York: Greenwillow Books, 1999)

Subject(s): Brothers and Sisters; Playing; School Buses
Age range(s): Preschool
Major character(s): Jonathan, Child, Brother (younger); Sarah, Student—Elementary School, Sister (older)
Time period(s): 1990s (1999)
Locale(s): United States

Summary: Sarah goes to school and Jonathan waits. All day as he plays with blocks or his fire truck or play dough he listens for the sounds of the school bus signaling Sarah's arrival. He hears many sounds that he hopes are signs of Sarah's return but are actually the mail being delivered and the noise of the garbage truck until finally the school bus arrives and Sarah runs to play with him. (24 pages)

Where it's reviewed:
Booklist, October 15, 1999, page 454
Bulletin of the Center for Children's Books, October 1999, page 55
Children's Book Review Service, December 1999, page 39
Horn Book Guide, Spring 2000, page 17
School Library Journal, September 1999, page 184

Other books by the same author:
What's in Aunt Mary's Room?, 1996
Papa Tells Chita a Story, 1995
Mac and Marie and the Train Toss Surprise, 1993

Other books you might like:

Penny Dale, *Big Brother, Little Brother*, 1997
  Little Brother shows that he's learned sensitivity to others from the example set by Big Brother.
Jonathan London, *Puddles*, 1997
  After a heavy rain, a brother and sister enjoy a day of outdoor play jumping over puddles and slogging through mud.
Ashley Wolff, *Stella and Roy*, 1993
  Overly confident, big sister Stella challenges younger brother Roy to a race and learns that age and size are not guarantees of success.

452

ELLEN HOWARD

The Gate in the Wall

(New York: Jean Karl Book/Atheneum Books for Young Readers, 1999)

Subject(s): Orphans; Labor Conditions; Canals
Age range(s): Grades 4-7
Major character(s): Emma Deane, 10-Year-Old, Orphan; Aggie Minshull, Aged Person, Businesswoman (canal boat owner); Rosie, Horse
Time period(s): 19th century
Locale(s): Macclesfield, England; *Cygnet*, England

Summary: Emma's heart is heavy at the thought of going home to a beating from her sister's husband when she's shut out of a day's work at the mill for arriving a minute late. In hopes of finding some fresh greens to bring home by way of a peace offering she wanders through a gate in the wall across from the mill and finds a narrow body of water and a long boat smelling of potatoes. Starving, Emma eats a raw potato and plans to take some home to her sister when Mrs. Minshull finds her hiding on the *Cygnet*. Since Mrs. Minshull's huffler (helper) has run off, she puts Emma to work walking with Rosie as payment for the potato. While Emma worries about getting back to her sister she also enjoys the freedom, outdoor life, kindness and good food that life with Mrs. Minshull offers. After being away from her sister's home more days than she imagined it could take to deliver the potatoes, Emma must decide just where is her home? (148 pages)

Where it's reviewed:
Booklist, February 15, 1999, page 1070
Horn Book, March 1999, page 208
Kirkus Reviews, February 15, 1999, page 300
Publishers Weekly, March 15, 1999, page 59
School Library Journal, March 1999, page 210

Other books by the same author:
A Different Kind of Courage, 1996
The Cellar, 1991
Sister, 1990

Other books you might like:
Karen Cushman, *Catherine, Called Birdy*, 1994
  Birdy, daughter of an English country knight strives to break away from the traditional expectations for women in medieval times.

Barry Denenberg, *So Far from Home: The Diary of Mary Driscoll, an Irish Mill Girl*, 1997
  During the Industrial Age working conditions in the textile mills are harsh, but Mary can find no other means of support.
Charles Dickens, *Oliver Twist*, 1996
  An abridgement by Lesley Baxter makes the classic tale of life in 19th-century England accessible to young readers.

453

JAMES HOWE
ALAN DANIEL, Illustrator

Bunnicula Strikes Again!

(New York: Atheneum Books for Young Readers, 1999)

Subject(s): Animals; Pets; Vampires
Age range(s): Grades 3-5
Major character(s): Harold, Dog, Narrator; Bunnicula, Rabbit, Vampire (vegetarian); Chester, Cat; Howie, Dog
Time period(s): 1990s (1999)
Locale(s): Centerville

Summary: Harold is very concerned about Bunnicula when he sees the lively pet lying listlessly in its cage day after day. Chester, vigilant defender against vampire bunnies, seems to be up to something and gradually Harold suspects the worst about his dear friend. Could Chester really be trying to rid the world of Bunnicula? When Bunnicula escapes from the vet's office Harold and Howie hurry to the old and soon to be demolished theater where Bunnicula was first found. The dogs find Bunnicula just as Chester leaps at the bunny and the wrecking ball demolishes the first wall of the building. Harold wonders if he'll ever see his dear friends again. (116 pages)

Where it's reviewed:
Booklist, October 1, 1999, page 356
Horn Book Guide, Spring 2000, page 80
Kirkus Reviews, September 1, 1999, page 1418
Publishers Weekly, August 30, 1999, page 84
School Library Journal, December 1999, page 100

Other books by the same author:
Return to Howliday Inn, 1992
Nighty-Nightmare, 1987
The Celery Stalks at Midnight, 1983
Howliday Inn, 1982
Bunnicula: A Rabbit-Tale of Mystery, 1979

Other books you might like:
Dan Greenburg, *Don't Count on Dracula*, 2000
  The prize Zack wins in a contest is to meet horror film star Mella Bugosi whose odd habits make Zack wonder if the actor actually is a vampire.
Eric Sanvoisin, *The Ink Drinker*, 1998
  Bunnicula drains the juice from vegetables and the vampire in this tale survives by slurping the ink right off the pages of books.
G.E. Stanley, *The Vampire Kittens of Count Dracula*, 1997
  After Jonathan observes his new kitten biting the necks of dolls he discovers that the animal was intended for someone else—Count Dracula.

454

JAMES HOWE
AMY WALROD, Illustrator

Horace and Morris but Mostly Dolores

(New York: Atheneum Books for Young Readers, 1999)

Subject(s): Animals/Mice; Friendship; Gender Roles
Age range(s): Grades K-3
Major character(s): Horace, Mouse, Friend; Morris, Mouse, Friend; Dolores, Mouse, Friend
Time period(s): Indeterminate
Locale(s): Fictional Country

Summary: Three adventure-loving pals fearlessly engage in activities that they probably shouldn't be doing, but feel compelled to try. At least, they do until the day that Horace and Morris without Dolores join the Mega-Mice, a boys only club. Dejected, lonely Dolores reluctantly enters the Cheese Puffs clubhouse where no boys are allowed. Day after dreary day passes until utterly bored Dolores tries to interest the club members in building a fort or going exploring. When no one appears interested, Dolores quits the club and one other mouse leaves with her. They head over to the Mega Mice looking for fellow explorers. Horace and Morris and one other mouse from their club join them. The five friends build a new clubhouse where any gender is welcome as long as they are interested in fun and adventure. (32 pages)

Where it's reviewed:
Booklist, February 15, 1999, page 1063
Horn Book Guide, Fall 1999, page 254
Kirkus Reviews, January 15, 1999, page 145
Publishers Weekly, February 15, 1999, page 107
School Library Journal, March 1999, page 176

Awards the book has won:
Booklist Editors' Choice, 1999
School Library Journal Best Books, 1999

Other books by the same author:
Pinky and Rex and the New Neighbors, 1997
There's a Dragon in My Sleeping Bag, 1994
Rabbit-Cadabra!, 1993
Hot Fudge, 1990

Other books you might like:
Patricia Lee Gauch, *Christina Katerina and Fats: And the Great Neighborhood War*, 1997
    A neighborhood "war" brews when a new neighbor threatens the friendship of Fats and Christina Katerina.
Kevin Henkes, *Chester's Way*, 1988
    Chester and Wilson are content with their friendship until Lilly moves into the neighborhood forcing them to reconsider some ideas.
Russell Hoban, *Best Friends for Frances*, 1969
    Being excluded from Albert's "no girls" baseball game gives Frances the idea that her little sister, Gloria, might be worthy of some attention.

455

NAOMI HOWLAND, Author/Illustrator

Latkes, Latkes Good to Eat: A Chanukah Story

(New York: Clarion Books, 1999)

Subject(s): Fairy Tales; Magic; Holidays, Jewish
Age range(s): Grades K-2
Major character(s): Sadie, Sister (older); Herschel, Brother
Time period(s): Indeterminate Past
Locale(s): Russia

Summary: While collecting firewood to cook her poor family's meager Chanukah dinner, Sadie meets an elderly woman shivering from the cold and kindly gives the woman all the firewood she's gathered. In return, the woman gives Sadie a magic frying pan with instructions to use it for cooking Chanukah latkes. Sadie happily prepares a delicious meal for her curious brothers each night, ignoring their pleas to be allowed to try the magic pan. On the last day of Chanukah, as Sadie searches the woods for the old woman to invite her to dinner, Herschel uses the magic pan. When the brothers are full of latkes, Herschel tries to stop the cooking, but he has not correctly overheard Sadie's magic words and the pan continues to cook. When Sadie arrives home, she stops the pan with the magic words and invites the entire village to a Chanukah feast. A recipe for latkes and a background note about the holiday conclude the book. (32 pages)

Where it's reviewed:
Booklist, September 1, 1999, page 149
Horn Book Guide, Spring 2000, page 41
School Library Journal, October 1999, 71

Other books by the same author:
ABCDrive!: A Car Trip Alphabet, 1994

Other books you might like:
Tomie DePaola, *Strega Nona*, 1975
    Oh no! Big Anthony is alone with Strega Nona's magic pot and he's trying to cook pasta in it!
Paul Galdone, *The Magic Porridge Pot*, 1976
    A magic porridge pot cooks porridge and more porridge and more porridge because the words that tell the pot to stop are forgotten.
Barbara Diamond Goldin, *Just Enough Is Plenty: A Hanukkah Tale*, 1988
    A poor family includes a stranger at their holiday table confident that Mama can cook enough to be plenty for all.
Malka Penn, *The Miracle of the Potato Latkes: A Hanukkah Story*, 1994
    During a drought-caused potato shortage, Tante Golda's faith is rewarded with more than enough potatoes to make the latkes for Hanukkah.

456

DEAN HUGHES

Home Run Hero

(New York: Atheneum Books for Young Readers, 1999)

Series: Scrappers. Number 2

Subject(s): Sports/Baseball; Conduct of Life; Competition
Age range(s): Grades 3-6
Major character(s): Wilson Love, Baseball Player (catcher); Adam Pfitzer, Baseball Player (pitcher); Thurlow Coates, Baseball Player
Time period(s): 1990s (1999)
Locale(s): Wasatch, Utah

Summary: The Scrappers are a hodge-podge of players and abilities trying to make it as a team. Wilson knows they could do better if they would start working together rather than criticizing each other. Thurlow has talent, but no apparent desire to play; Adam is developing into a pretty good pitcher, but he's inconsistent and easily rattled. From behind the plate Wilson sees it all and wonders what he can do to help his team improve and get himself out of a hitting slump. (119 pages)

Where it's reviewed:
Booklist, June 1999, page 1829
Horn Book Guide, Fall 1999, page 293
School Library Journal, June 1999, page 97

Other books by the same author:
Bases Loaded, 1999 (Scrappers, Number 5)
Team Player, 1999 (Scrappers, Number 3)
Now We're Talking, 1999 (Scrappers, Number 4)

Other books you might like:
Fred Bowen, *Playoff Dreams*, 1997
  When Josh's hitting slump finally ends Brendan's team has a chance to make the playoffs.
Matt Christopher, *Pressure Play*, 1993
  New to town, Travis's baseball skill wins acceptance from peers but also leads to pressure to help his team win the championship.
David Halecroft, *Championship Summer*, 1991
  Rivalry between players effects performance on the field and threatens a team's chance to make the playoffs.

457

DEAN HUGHES

Play Ball!

(New York: Atheneum Books for Young Readers, 1999)

Series: Scrappers. Number 1
Subject(s): Sports/Baseball; Summer; Problem Solving
Age range(s): Grades 3-6
Major character(s): Robbie Marquez, Baseball Player, Friend (Trent's); Trent Lubak, Baseball Player, Friend (Robbie's); Gloria Gibbs, Student—Middle School, Baseball Player
Time period(s): 1990s (1999)
Locale(s): Wasatch, Utah

Summary: Robbie's plans to play shortstop in the city's summer recreation league fall victim to Trent's poor memory—he forgot to turn in their applications. The boys are given four hours to find enough players for a team. When they come up one short, Robbie submits an application for a nonexistent cousin and his dishonesty almost costs him the chance to play. Gloria talks her dad into sponsoring the team and Jack's Scrapper's begins practice with a retired minor league player

as coach. The rag-tag team has more desire than skill, but the players give it their best effort. (121 pages)

Where it's reviewed:
Booklist, June 1999, page 1829
Horn Book Guide, Fall 1999, page 293
Publishers Weekly, January 4, 1999, page 90
School Library Journal, April 1999, page 99

Other books by the same author:
Home Run Hero, 1999 (Scrappers Number 2)
Team Picture, 1996
Back Up Goalie, 1992

Other books you might like:
Fred Bowen, *Playoff Dreams*, 1997
  Facing the prospect of another losing season, Brendan learns to appreciate that playing the game is more important than winning playoffs.
Matt Christopher, *Baseball Turnaround*, 1997
  After an arrest for shoplifting, Sandy must regain his confidence and his focus on playing the game he loves.
Matt Christopher, *Prime-Time Pitcher*, 1998
  Although Koby's pitching propels the Cardinals from last place into contention his teammates seem unappreciative of the attention he receives.
Elizabeth Levy, *Cheater, Cheater*, 1993
  One incident of lying labels Lucy as a cheater and she learns how hard it is to overcome such a mistake.

458

SHIRLEY HUGHES, Author/Illustrator

The Lion and the Unicorn

(New York: A DK Ink Book/DK Publishing, Inc., 1999)

Subject(s): World War II; Courage; Jews
Age range(s): Grades 2-5
Major character(s): Lenny Levi, Child, Refugee; Mick De Vass, Veteran, Amputee; Nelly, Servant
Time period(s): 1930s; 1940s (1939-1945)
Locale(s): London, England; England

Summary: During the blitz of London, Lenny's mother puts him on a train with other children being evacuated to the safety of the countryside. In a large home, Lenny faces many fears: separation from his mother, teasing in the new school, the isolation of being a Jew, and the shame of bed-wetting. Nelly sympathetically sneaks extra linens to his space in the attic and willingly takes care of the extra laundry. Finding solace in a walled garden, Lenny meets Mick who is recovering from injuries and awaiting an artificial leg. Through all his experiences, Lenny clutches a lion and unicorn medal given by his father before he left to fight in the war. Finally, in the garden, Lenny also finds the courage to overcome his fears. (64 pages)

Where it's reviewed:
Booklist, April 1, 1999, page 1428
Horn Book Guide, Fall 1999, page 279
Publishers Weekly, May 3, 1999, page 76
School Library Journal, April 1999, page 99

Other books by the same author:
Enchantment in the Garden, 1997

Here Comes Charlie Moon, 1990
Alfie Gives a Hand, 1984

Other books you might like:

Frances Hodgson Burnett, *The Secret Garden*, 1911
Orphaned Mary is sent to live on the Yorkshire Moors where she unlocks the secret to an overgrown garden and an invalid cousin's health.

Donald Hall, *The Farm Summer 1942*, 1994
During World War II Peter's parents send him to his grandparent's farm while they serve their country.

Dorrith M. Sim, *In My Pocket*, 1997
Along with other Jewish children, a young girl is evacuated from Holland to England and finally settled in the lonely safety of Scotland.

459

TED HUGHES
JACKIE MORRIS, Illustrator

How the Whale Became: And Other Stories

(New York: Orchard Books, 2000)

Subject(s): Short Stories; Fables; Animals
Age range(s): Grades 2-5
Time period(s): Indeterminate Past
Locale(s): Earth

Summary: Eleven fables originally published in Great Britain in 1963 are illustrated for this first American edition. Owl's daytime behavior results from a trick he plays on other birds so he will have a ready supply of them to eat; he still pays the price by having to hide each morning from the angry flocks of awakening birds. Foursquare and Slylooking both want the job of guarding Man's farm, but for different reasons; Slylooking wants ready access to the cabbages while Foursquare wants to lie near the hearth on cold nights. Devious Slylooking outfoxes himself and earns a new name. Other tales describe the origin of animals such as whales, bees, cats and donkeys. (94 pages)

Where it's reviewed:

Booklist, December 1, 2000, page 709
Books for Keeps, July 2000, page 23
Publishers Weekly, September 25, 2000, page 120
School Librarian, Autumn 2000, page 145
School Library Journal, November 2000, page 123

Other books by the same author:
Tales of the Early World, 1988
The Iron Giant: A Story in Five Nights, 1988
Meet My Folks, 1973

Other books you might like:

Martin H. Greenberg, *A Newbery Zoo: A Dozen Animal Stories by Newbery Award-Winning Authors*, 1995
A collection of animal stories and one poem includes realism, fantasy, fable and adventure.

Dick King-Smith, *Dick King-Smith's Animal Friends*, 1996
Thirty-one stories tell the true tales of the many different animals in the author's life.

Rudyard Kipling, *Just So Stories*, 1912
The classic book includes a dozen animal stories and has been reissued many times with different illustrations.

460

STEPHEN HUNECK, Author/Illustrator

Sally Goes to the Beach

(New York: Harry N. Abrams, Inc., 2000)

Subject(s): Animals/Dogs; Vacations; Beaches
Age range(s): Grades K-2
Major character(s): Sally, Dog (black lab), Narrator
Time period(s): 2000s
Locale(s): East Coast

Summary: One glimpse of a suitcase and Sally knows a beach vacation is coming. Sally loves to ride the ferry to the island where she mingles with the other dog passengers. As soon as the suitcase is unpacked Sally and her human companions go to the beach. Sally loves the scent of the air at the beach because it reminds her of cat food. She chases balls thrown into the ocean, rides in a boat, digs a big hole and explores the beach. Then it's early to bed so she'll be ready for another day of play. (36 pages)

Where it's reviewed:

Booklist, May 15, 2000, page 1748
Horn Book Guide, Fall 2000, page 271
Publishers Weekly, May 29, 2000, page 82
School Library Journal, June 2000, page 115

Other books by the same author:
Sally Goes to the Mountains, 2001
My Dog's Brain, 1997

Other books you might like:

Sylvia Francia, *Roberta's Vacation*, 1998
While Roberta walks to the beach a larger dog frightens her, but later she sees Jerome struggling in the ocean and leaps in to save him.

Karla Kuskin, *City Dog*, 1994
A city dog on a trip to the country bounds excitedly across the vast expanse of open space and chases waves on the beach.

Janet McLean, *Dog Tales*, 1995
A rhyming text describes the varied activities in the daily lives of five dogs.

Betty Paraskevas, *Hoppy & Joe*, 1999
On the beach a lonely dog finds and helps an injured seagull.

461

JOHANNA HURWITZ
KAREN DUGAN, Illustrator

The Just Desserts Club

(New York: Morrow Junior Books, 1999)

Subject(s): Cooks and Cooking; Clubs; Schools
Age range(s): Grades 3-5

Major character(s): Cricket Kaufman, 6th Grader, Friend; Lucas Cott, 6th Grader, Friend; Sara Jane Cushman, 6th Grader, Friend
Time period(s): 1990s (1999)
Locale(s): United States

Summary: August boredom and an overabundance of zucchini prompts Cricket to find new ways to cook the vegetable. Her initial efforts attract Lucas and other friends into a cooking project that becomes a club when school starts. First they expand the class food drive to include a fund-raising bake sale. With Sara Jane and another friend Cricket bakes items while Lucas and his friends collect cans. Throughout the year the Just Desserts Club finds any opportunity to put their baking abilities to work. Each chapter concludes with four recipes. (95 pages)

Where it's reviewed:
Booklist, August 1999, page 2056
Children's Bookwatch, November 1999, page 1
Horn Book Guide, Spring 2000, page 80
Publishers Weekly, August 2, 1999, page 87
School Library Journal, October 1999, page 116

Other books by the same author:
Starting School, 1998
Spring Break, 1997
School Spirit, 1994
Class President, 1990

Other books you might like:
Paula Danziger, *Amber Brown Is Feeling Blue*, 1998
    Amber's life is becoming more complicated and she doesn't know what to do about it.
Suzy Kline, *Mary Marony and the Chocolate Surprise*, 1995
    Eager to win a special pizza lunch with the teacher, Mary manipulates the contest outcome and is stuck with a guilty conscience.
E.L. Konigsburg, *T-Backs, T-Shirts, Coat and Suit*, 1993
    Chloe spends the summer in Florida with her aunt, helping her with "meals-on-wheels" deliveries.

462

JOHANNA HURWITZ
MARK GRAHAM, Illustrator

Llama in the Library
(New York: Morrow Junior Books, 1999)

Subject(s): Animals/Llamas; Ghosts; Babies
Age range(s): Grades 3-6
Major character(s): Adam Fine, 5th Grader, Brother (older); Alana Brown, 5th Grader, Friend (Adam's); Justin Rice, 5th Grader, Friend (Adam's)
Time period(s): 1990s (1999)
Locale(s): Wilmington, Vermont

Summary: When Adam learns that his mother is pregnant he wonders how she'll be able to continue her llama excursion business and how he'll face his teasing friends. Justin's suggestion that they go ghost hunting in an old hotel in town provides the diversion Adam needs from the news. After a little snooping and some research at the local library, Justin and Adam learn that the ghost seems to appear to people named Brown. Fortunately, the school has a new student that Adam is interested in knowing better whose last name is Brown. Now, the boys have to figure out how to interest Alana in their ghost hunt. (113 pages)

Where it's reviewed:
Booklist, May 1, 1999, page 1594
Horn Book Guide, Fall 1999, page 294
School Library Journal, June 1999, page 98

Other books by the same author:
Faraway Summer, 1998
A Llama in the Family, 1994
Class President, 1990

Other books you might like:
Judy Blume, *Superfudge*, 1980
    When Peter learns that his mother is pregnant he cannot understand why anyone with a child like his brother Fudge would want to have another kid.
Amy Hest, *The Great Green Notebook of Katie Roberts: Who Just Turned 12 on Monday*, 1998
    Although Katie loves her twin brothers she also misses the time she once had alone with her mother.
Margie Palatini, *The Wonder Worm Wars*, 1997
    A broken arm and the responsibility of babysitting for his older sister's toddler while she has another baby changes Elliot's summer plans.

463

PAT HUTCHINS, Author/Illustrator

It's MY Birthday!
(New York: Greenwillow Books, 1999)

Subject(s): Birthdays; Gifts; Monsters
Age range(s): Preschool
Major character(s): Billy, Monster; Hazel, Monster
Time period(s): Indeterminate
Locale(s): Fictional Country

Summary: On Billy's special day, the birthday boy enjoys all his gifts without involving any of his family or party guests in his play. The guests don't seem to mind because they are using the balloons, ribbons and gift boxes to have a great time. When Hazel gives Billy a box of board games she refuses his invitation to play with him and Billy begins to realize what he's done. Billy's friends are willing to play board games with him, but first Billy shares his ball, jump rope, toy car and cake with the guests he's been ignoring. (32 pages)

Where it's reviewed:
Booklist, June 1999, page 1842
Horn Book Guide, Fall 1999, page 235
School Library Journal, March 1999, page 176

Other books by the same author:
Shrinking Mouse, 1997
Titch and Daisy, 1996
Three-Star Billy, 1994
Silly Billy!, 1992
The Very Worst Monster, 1985

Other books you might like:

Nancy White Carlstrom, *Happy Birthday, Jesse Bear!*, 1994
  From the first preparations, through the party fun, to the last good night kiss, Jesse Bear excitedly describes his fourth birthday.

Lee Davis, *P.B. Bear's Birthday Party*, 1994
  Stuffed-animal friends gather to help P.B. Bear celebrate his birthday.

Helen Oxenbury, *It's My Birthday*, 1993
  Animal friends bring the ingredients needed for a young child to make a birthday cake, assist with the cooking and help to eat the finished product.

I

464

EVA IBBOTSON
ANNABEL LARGE, Illustrator

Which Witch?

(New York: Dutton Children's Books, 1999)

Subject(s): Witches and Witchcraft; Wizards; Magic
Age range(s): Grades 5-8
Major character(s): Arriman Canker, Wizard; Belladona, Witch; Terence Mugg, Orphan, Child
Time period(s): Indeterminate
Locale(s): Todcaster, England; England (Darkington Hall)

Summary: After years of practicing the black arts, wizard Arriman the Awful looks forward to retiring. When the expected replacement wizard fails to appear, Arriman's secretary suggests that he marry a witch with the hopes that their son could carry on the tradition. Thus, a competition is announced to all the witches of Todcaster with the prize to the witch who performs the blackest magic to be Arriman's bride. Belladonna, a beautiful and kind white witch, knows she has no chance to succeed, but vows to try—for she is in love with Arriman. Inadvertently, she meets Terence Mugg and kindly agrees to rescue the crying child from the miserable orphanage and take him with her. Surprisingly, when Belladonna is with Terence and his pet worm she succeeds with black magic tricks. Both assume that the worm is serving as Belladonna's ''familiar'' or animal that helps witches with their magic. Only later, do they realize that Terence is not only the source of the power but also the replacement wizard for whom Arriman has been waiting. Originally published in England in 1979, this is the first American edition of the title. (231 pages)

Where it's reviewed:
Booklist, August 1999, page 2056
Bulletin of the Center for Children's Books, September 1999, page 18
Horn Book Guide, Spring 2000, page 80
Publishers Weekly, August 23, 1999, page 61
School Library Journal, August 1999, page 158

Other books by the same author:
The Secret of Platform 13, 1998
The Great Ghost Rescue, 1994
Not Just a Witch, 1992

Other books you might like:
Roald Dahl, *Witches*, 1983
    A boy and his grandmother team up to prevent witches from changing children into mice.
Patricia MacLachlan, *Tomorrow's Wizard*, 1996
    A wizard's apprentice learns more about the role of a wizard.
Anne Mazer, *The Accidental Witch*, 1995
    When clumsy Bee tumbles into a circle of witches she absorbs some of their power but none of their experience and the results are disastrous.
J.K. Rowling, *Harry Potter and the Sorcerer's Stone*, 1997
    Orphan Harry Potter is surprised to learn that he is a wizard with a powerful destiny to fulfill.

465

BRUCE INGMAN, Author/Illustrator

A Night on the Tiles

(New York: Houghton Mifflin, 1999)

Subject(s): Animals/Cats; Pets; Conduct of Life
Age range(s): Grades K-2
Major character(s): Lionel, Cat, Student; Audrey, Cat, Friend
Time period(s): 1990s
Locale(s): England

Summary: Each night while his owner sleeps, Lionel attends the Cat Academy, taking classes in sewing, mechanics and woodworking. He meets up with Audrey for a movie and gives her a ride home on his scooter. Then he hurries home and awakens his unsuspecting owner by leaping on her bed. The book was first published in Great Britain in 1998. (32 pages)

Where it's reviewed:
Booklist, April 1, 1999, page 1420
Horn Book Guide, Fall 1999, page 255

Kirkus Reviews, February 15, 1999, page 300
Publishers Weekly, February 15, 1999, page 107
School Library Journal, March 1999, page 176

Other books by the same author:
Lost Property, 1998
When Martha's Away, 1995

Other books you might like:
Garrison Keillor, *Cat, You Better Come Home*, 1995
  Jack's pet, Puff, runs away from home and becomes a celebrity doing commercials for cat food before returning home, disillusioned.
Nina Laden, *The Night I Followed the Dog*, 1994
  While a family sleeps, their pet dog secretly leads an exciting nightlife.
Jonathan London, *Hip Cat*, 1993
  Oobie-Do John, a sax-playing cat hops the night train for San Francisco so he'll be free to play the jazz he loves.

466

MICK INKPEN, Author/Illustrator

The Great Pet Sale
(New York: Orchard Books, 1999)

Subject(s): Animals; Animals/Rats; Pets
Age range(s): Grades K-1
Major character(s): Unnamed Character, Narrator, Child
Time period(s): 1990s (1998)
Locale(s): England

Summary: In this lift-the-flaps book, a young boy goes to a pet store that is having an "Everything Must Go" sale. The reasonable prices offer a rat for one cent, a terrapin for two, a turtle for three, a tortoise for four, and a Komodo dragon for only twenty-five cents. The rat tries to convince the boy to pick him, pointing out his many positive features and bargain price. The boy quietly takes out a dollar, and buys the entire shop, including the rat. (16 pages)

Where it's reviewed:
Booklist, April 15, 1999, page 1535
Horn Book Guide, Fall 1999, page 235
Kirkus Reviews, January 15, 1999, page 146
Publishers Weekly, December 21, 1998, page 66
School Library Journal, July 1999, page 74

Other books by the same author:
Nothing, 1998
Kipper, 1992
The Blue Balloon, 1990

Other books you might like:
Marc Brown, *Arthur's Pet Business*, 1990
  To show that he is able to handle the responsibility of his pet, Arthur opens a pet-care business which is far more popular than he anticipated.
Rod Campbell, *Dear Zoo*, 1999
  In this lift-the-flaps book, a child asks the zoo for a pet, and receives one inappropriate pet after another.
Heather Maisner, *Find Mouse in the Yard*, 1994
  By lifting the flaps and following the clues, readers can locate the missing mouse.

467

WASHINGTON IRVING
WILL MOSES, Co-Author

Rip Van Winkle
(New York: Philomel Books, 1999)

Subject(s): Folklore; Folk Tales; Sleep
Age range(s): Grades 3-5
Major character(s): Rip Van Winkle, Spouse, Unemployed; Dame Van Winkle, Spouse, Mother; Wolf, Dog
Time period(s): Indeterminate Past
Locale(s): Catskill Mountains, American Colonies

Summary: A friendly soul, Rip is always willing to help a child or a stranger, but otherwise resists any and all useful work. To avoid the nagging of Dame Van Winkle, Rip and Wolf go squirrel hunting high in the Catskills. There, Rip meets a strange man who seeks Rip's assistance carrying a keg into one of the hollows where Rip faces a strange assortment of men to whom he's expected to serve the drink in the keg. Feeling a little thirsty himself, Rip too drinks from the keg and soon slips into a deep slumber. When Rip awakens he is alarmed that he slept on the mountain all night and annoyed that he cannot find Wolf, but as he approaches the village he meets only strangers in the streets. Rip learns that he's been asleep for twenty years, his children are grown and his wife and friends have died. The experience does not change Rip; he moves in with his daughter and spends his days fishing and talking. Moses also illustrated this title. (48 pages)

Where it's reviewed:
Booklist, November 1, 1999, page 530
Bulletin of the Center for Children's Books, December 1999, page 134
Horn Book Guide, Spring 2000, page 67
Publishers Weekly, June 28, 1999, page 78
School Library Journal, October 1999, page 121

Other books by the same author:
Silent Night, 1997
The Legend of Sleepy Hollow, 1995

Other books you might like:
Washington Irving, *Rip Van Winkle*, 1999
  N.C. Wyeth illustrates this adaptation of Irving's classic tale.
Neil Philip, *American Fairy Tales: From Rip Van Winkle to the Rootabaga Stories*, 1996
  A collection of fairy tales includes the work of American authors from Washington Irving to Carl Sandburg with comments by the compiler, Philip.
Carl Sandburg, *Rootabaga Stories: Part Two*, 1923
  A companion volume to *Rootabaga Stories*, the humorous collection of nonsense tales was reissued in 1989.

468

RACHEL ISADORA, Author/Illustrator

Sophie Skates
(New York: G.P. Putnam's Sons, 1999)

Subject(s): Sports/Ice Skating; Determination; Competition

Age range(s): Grades K-3
Major character(s): Sophie, 8-Year-Old, Skater
Time period(s): 1990s (1994-1999)
Locale(s): United States

Summary: At the age of three Sophie begins ice-skating with her family on the pond near their home. To achieve her dream of being a professional skater she now has classes five mornings and three afternoons a week on the ice as well as ballet lessons two afternoons a week. To prepare for competitions Sophie meets with a choreographer to plan her music, programs and costumes. Now, when her brother invites her to skate on the pond with him, he finds the tired Sophie already asleep after a long day. (32 pages)

Where it's reviewed:
Booklist, December 1, 1999, page 711
Horn Book, January 2000, page 66
Publishers Weekly, October 11, 1999, page 74

School Library Journal, November 1999, page 143

Other books by the same author:
Lili Backstage, 1997
The Steadfast Tin Soldier, 1996
Lili on Stage, 1995
Lili at Ballet, 1993

Other books you might like:
Patty Cranston, *Magic on Ice: Figure Skating Stars, Tips and Facts*, 1998
   A nonfiction title gives basic information about the training of a figure skater.
Amy Hest, *Party on Ice*, 1995
   Casey celebrates her ninth birthday with an ice skating party.
Ruth Yaffe Radin, *A Winter Place*, 1982
   A family skates together on a frozen mountain lake.

J

469

JENNIFER RICHARD JACOBSON
BENREI HUANG, Illustrator

Moon Sandwich Mom

(Morton Grove, IL: Albert Whitman & Company, 1999)

Subject(s): Mothers and Sons; Animals/Foxes; Animals
Age range(s): Grades K-1
Major character(s): Mrs. Fox, Mother, Artist; Rafferty Fox, Son, Fox
Time period(s): Indeterminate
Locale(s): Fictional Country

Summary: Rafferty becomes so frustrated when his mother is too busy painting to play with him that he packs his bags and leaves home in search of a mother who is more fun. Several friends offer their homes and mothers as fun alternatives and Rafferty gives each a try. At the porcupine's home the sandwiches are boring rectangles not exciting stars and moons like Mrs. Fox makes. The beaver children are put down for a rest with no story and the raccoons must all crowd into the bathtub with no bubbles or toys. Realizing what a fun mom he actually has, Rafferty returns home to find Mrs. Fox waiting with an art project and moon sandwiches for dinner. (24 pages)

Where it's reviewed:
Booklist, July 1999, page 1951
Children's Book Review Service, August 1999, page 160
Horn Book Guide, Fall 1999, page 235
School Library Journal, June 1999, page 98

Other books by the same author:
A Net of Stars, 1998

Other books you might like:
Lynne Jonell, *Mommy Go Away!*, 1997
  For just a little while, Christopher wishes he could be big and give orders; when his wish comes true, Mommy learns to see her son's perspective.
Barbara M. Joosse, *I Love You the Purplest*, 1996
  Mama's responses to her sons' many questions affirm her love for each of them.

Marisabina Russo, *Trade-In Mother*, 1993
  At the end of difficult day, Max announces his intention to trade in his mother for someone who can prevent misfortune.
Maurice Sendak, *Where the Wild Things Are*, 1963
  When angry Max is sent to his room, he imagines traveling to the Land of the Wild Things and returning home to find that Mom has his supper waiting.

470

LISA JAHN-CLOUGH

Missing Molly

(Boston: Houghton Mifflin Company, 2000)

Subject(s): Playing; Neighbors and Neighborhoods; Friendship
Age range(s): Grades K-1
Major character(s): Simon, Friend, Child; Molly, Child, Friend
Time period(s): 2000s (2000)
Locale(s): United States

Summary: Best friends Simon and Molly play their favorite game, hide-and-seek, every day. When Simon complains that Molly is too easy to find, she tries hiding in different places, but still Simon finds her quickly. One day Simon arrives to play and Molly doesn't appear so Simon thinks she's already started the game and he begins searching in all Molly's favorite hiding places. No Molly! Now Simon's feeling worried and accepts the help of an unfamiliar girl who comes to the house also looking for Molly. They search all the possible hiding places outside and when Molly can't be found the new girl suggests that Simon play with her. Simon would rather have Molly because she's his best friend so he's happy to discover that he's had Molly all along—in disguise. (32 pages)

Where it's reviewed:
Booklist, February 1, 2000, page 1029
Children's Book Review Service, May 2000, page 109
Kirkus Reviews, March 15, 2000, page 384

Publishers Weekly, March 27, 2000, page 80
School Library Journal, April 2000, page 107

Other books by the same author:
My Friend and I, 1999
ABC Yummy, 1997
My Happy Birthday Book, 1996
Alicia Has a Bad Day, 1994

Other books you might like:
Joyce Champion, *Emily and Alice*, 1993
    When Alice moves in next door to Emily, the two become
    friends.
Pat Hutchins, *Titch and Daisy*, 1996
    Shy Titch can't find his friend Daisy at a party so he hides
    under the table and discovers Daisy hiding too.
Simon James, *Leon and Bob*, 1997
    Leon plays with an imaginary playmate until a real friend
    moves into the house next door.

471

BETSY JAMES, Author/Illustrator

Tadpoles
(New York: Dutton Children's Books, 1999)

Subject(s): Brothers and Sisters; Animals/Frogs and Toads;
    Growing Up
Age range(s): Grades K-2
Major character(s): Molly, Child, Sister (older); Davey, Baby,
    Brother; Ma, Mother
Time period(s): 1990s (1999)
Locale(s): United States

Summary: Molly grumbles because she has to walk everywhere while Ma carries Davey who is too little to walk. When
they walk to the pond on a spring day, Molly wades into the
water and finds frog eggs floating in the pond. Ma gives her a
plastic bag so she can carry some home. Ma also compares the
tiny dot visible in the egg that will grow into a frog to the tiny
dot that Molly and Davey once were before they developed
into babies. All spring and summer as Molly watches the eggs
develop into tadpoles and then begin to grow legs, she also
observes the changes in Davey. By the time the tadpoles have
developed four legs and Molly returns the frogs to the pond,
Davey has developed the ability to walk—right into the
water. (32 pages)

Where it's reviewed:
Booklist, July 1999, page 1950
School Library Journal, August 1999, page 137

Other books by the same author:
Flashlight, 1997
Blow Away Soon, 1995
Mary Ann, 1994

Other books you might like:
Christine Back, *Tadpole and Frog*, 1984
    In a nonfiction title, photos show a frog's life cycle from
    egg to tadpole to frog.
Vivian French, *Growing Frogs*, 2000
    With Mom's help a little girl collects frog spawn from a
    pond and watches the frog's development in her home
    aquarium.

Steven Kellogg, *The Mysterious Tadpole*, 1977
    The rapid growth of his pet tadpole makes Louis wonder
    just what it will become.
Barbara Ann Porte, *Tale of a Tadpole*, 1997
    By carefully following the instructions from the Nature
    Center, Francine raises a tadpole that develops into a toad
    rather than a frog.

472

J. ALISON JAMES
TSUKUSHI, Illustrator

The Drums of Noto Hanto
(New York: DK Ink/DK Publishing, Inc., 1999)

Subject(s): Samurai; Courage; Historical
Age range(s): Grades 2-5
Major character(s): Kenshin, Warlord; Unnamed Character,
    Aged Person
Time period(s): 1570s (1576)
Locale(s): Nabune, Japan (on the peninsula of Noto Hanto)

Summary: When Kenshin decides to take from Nabune by
force what he cannot get any other way, he sends samurai
warriors by ship to attack the village. A messenger warns the
villagers who fearfully recognize that the samurai have the
superior weapons and skill. Unwilling to accept defeat, an old
man in the village suggests to the villagers a plan to defeat the
samurai by cunning rather than force. Gathering the drums
that have traditionally signaled the change of season, the
villagers hurry to the beach where they build many fires. As
the samurai ships draw close enough to launch a barrage of
arrows onto the shore, villagers disguised as monsters dance,
the fires blaze and the drums of Noto Hanto beat all night. As
the sun rises, the ships pull away, assuring the village's safety.
(32 pages)

Where it's reviewed:
Booklist, September 1, 1999, page 140
Horn Book Guide, Spring 2000, page 42
Kirkus Reviews, September 1, 1999, page 1418
Publishers Weekly, July 12, 1999, page 94
School Library Journal, August 1999, page 137

Awards the book has won:
Notable Social Studies Trade Books for Young People, 2000

Other books by the same author:
Eucalyptus Wings, 1995

Other books you might like:
Eric A. Kimmel, *Sword of the Samurai: Adventure Stories
    from Japan*, 1999
    In eleven stories, samurai fight their battles with skill, wit
    and cunning.
Rafe Martin, *Mysterious Tales of Japan*, 1996
    Ten traditional tales are gathered and retold by the author
    in an illustrated collection that includes general informa-
    tion and a bibliography.
Alan Schroeder, *Lily and the Wooden Bowl*, 1994
    By faithfully fulfilling a promise made to her dying grand-
    mother, Lily is protected from the evil Matsu and rewarded
    with true love and riches.

473

HARLEY JESSUP, Author/Illustrator

Grandma Summer

(New York: Viking, 1999)

Subject(s): Beaches; Grandmothers; Summer
Age range(s): Grades K-2
Major character(s): Ben, Child; Grandma, Grandmother
Time period(s): 1990s (1999)
Locale(s): Twin Rocks, Oregon

Summary: Ben sees the ocean for the first time when Grandma takes him with her to the family's old beach cottage. The shuttered, old, dark house is scary to Ben, but to Grandma it holds the memories of summers past. When Ben finds a glass fishing float in the garage Grandma explains how his father found it years ago. A picnic on the beach and wading in the cold surf introduce Ben to the shore. The morning after a storm, Grandma wakes Ben early and hurries him to the beach to see the changes wrought by the storm. Ben's search yields another fishing float so Grandma celebrates with Ben by buying ice cream for breakfast. (32 pages)

Where it's reviewed:
Booklist, August 1999, page 2064
Children's Book Review Service, August 1999, page 160
Horn Book Guide, Fall 1999, page 255
Publishers Weekly, June 21, 1999, page 66
School Library Journal, July 1999, page 74

Other books by the same author:
What's Alice Up To?, 1997

Other books you might like:
Aliki, *Those Summers*, 1996
    Children frolic in the waves, enjoying a carefree family vacation at the seashore.
Stephanie Calmenson, *Hotter than a Hot Dog!*, 1994
    Granny takes her granddaughter to the beach to find relief from the heat of the city.
Maryann Cocca-Leffler, *Clams All Year*, 1996
    The morning after a storm Grandpa leads the family to the beach to collect enough clams to last all year.
Douglas Florian, *A Beach Day*, 1990
    A family enjoys a relaxing day at the beach looking for sea shells.
Troon Harrison, *The Long Weekend*, 1994
    For his birthday, Michael chooses to spend three days playing at the beach with his mom.

474

FRANCISCO JIMENEZ
CLAIRE B. COTTS, Illustrator

The Christmas Gift/El Regalo de Navidad

(Boston: Houghton Mifflin Company, 2000)

Subject(s): Migrant Labor; Mexican Americans; Christmas
Age range(s): Grades 2-5
Major character(s): Panchito, Child, Son; Papa, Father, Migrant Worker; Mama, Mother, Migrant Worker
Time period(s): Indeterminate Past
Locale(s): Corcoran, California

Summary: A bilingual short story from the author's award-winning collection *The Circuit* tells how weeks of rain prevent Papa and Mama from picking cotton thus increasing the hardship for already impoverished migrant workers. Mama scrounges for discarded food behind stores to make soup and Panchito worries that he will not receive the ball he wants for Christmas. Indeed, on Christmas morning Panchito and his brothers each receive a small bag of candy. Seeing Mama's tear streaked face, Panchito hides his disappointment and shares his candy with his parents as he offers thanks for the gift. (32 pages)

Where it's reviewed:
Booklist, September 1, 2000, page 132
Horn Book Guide, Spring 2001, page 40
Publishers Weekly, September 25, 2000, page 72
School Library Journal, October 2000, page 60

Awards the book has won:
ALA Notable Children's Books, 2001
Americas Award for Children's and Young Adult Literature, 2000

Other books by the same author:
La Mariposa, 1998
The Circuit: Stories from the Life of a Migrant Child, 1997

Other books you might like:
Eve Bunting, *Going Home*, 1996
    Carlos and his family leave the farm work of California to return to their Mexican village for a joyful Christmas reunion.
Arthur Dorros, *Radio Man/Don Radio*, 1993
    Diego uses his ever-present radio to keep up with friends as he and his family follow the crops.
Douglas Keister, *Fernando's Gift/El Regalo de Fernando*, 1995
    When someone chops down Carmina's favorite climbing tree, Fernando gives her a new one to plant as a birthday gift.
Jane Resh Thomas, *Lights on the River*, 1994
    At the end of each day's labor in the fields Mami lights a candle from abuela to remind the family of the link to their Mexican homeland.

475

MARTHE JOCELYN, Author/Illustrator

Hannah's Collections

(New York: Dutton Children's Books, 2000)

Subject(s): Collectors and Collecting; Problem Solving; Mathematics
Age range(s): Grades K-2
Major character(s): Hannah, Child, Collector
Time period(s): 2000s (2000)
Locale(s): United States

Summary: Hannah is stymied. Her teacher expects the students to bring a collection to school next week and Hannah collects so many things that she can't decide on just one collection. Within each of her collections Hannah sees so much variety because she can sort by shape or color or arrange the items in different patterns. After reviewing her collections, Hannah thinks of just what she'll do to complete the school assignment—use something from each collection to create the first sculpture for her newest collection. (24 pages)

Where it's reviewed:
Booklist, September 15, 2000, page 236
Horn Book Guide, Spring 2001, page 18
Kirkus Reviews, August 15, 2000, page 1198
Publishers Weekly, August 7, 2000, page 97
School Library Journal, October 2000, page 128

Awards the book has won:
Booklist Editors' Choice, 2000

Other books by the same author:
Hannah and the Seven Dresses, 1999

Other books you might like:
Margery Cuyler, *100th Day Worries*, 2000
    Other first graders have assembled their collections for the 100th day of school but Jessica is still worrying about what to bring.
Barbara DeRubertis, *A Collection for Kate*, 1999
    For a school assignment Kate has to think of a collection that includes a specific number of items.
Bonnie Dobkin, *Collecting*, 1993
    In a rhyming story a collector describes various collections of different objects.
Elisa Kleven, *The Puddle Pail*, 1997
    Brothers take different approaches to collecting items. Sol finds shells, rocks and feathers while Ernst collects puddles, clouds and stars.
Wendy Pfeffer, *Marta's Magnets*, 1995
    Her sister Rosa thinks Marta's magnet collection is worthless but Marta finds it very useful.

476

ANGELA JOHNSON
SHANE W. EVANS, Illustrator

Down the Winding Road

(New York: DK Ink/Dorling Kindersley Publishing, Inc., 2000)

Subject(s): Country Life; Family Life; African Americans
Age range(s): Grades K-3
Major character(s): Unnamed Character, Sister, Narrator; Jesse, Brother, Son; Daddy, Father, Nephew
Time period(s): 2000s (2000)
Locale(s): United States

Summary: Down the winding road live the Old Ones, the aunts and uncles who raised Daddy and whom the family visits each summer on the last day of vacation. The seven elderly relatives embrace Jesse and his sister, feed them traditional favorites, tell family stories, and walk them through the woods along the winding road. They watch the children swim in the pond that they remember swimming in years ago before turning back to their home so the children can climb in the car with their parents and go down the winding road again, back to the city. (32 pages)

Where it's reviewed:
Booklist, February 15, 2000, page 1118

Kirkus Reviews, April 1, 2000, page 478
Publishers Weekly, March 6, 2000, page 109
Riverbank Review, Spring 2000, page 29
School Library Journal, May 2000, page 146

Other books by the same author:
The Rolling Store, 1997
The Aunt in Our House, 1996
Julius, 1993

Other books you might like:
Sandra Belton, *May'naise Sandwiches & Sunshine Tea*, 1994
    Big Mama shares with her granddaughter the story of a childhood friendship.
Valerie Flournoy, *Tanya's Reunion*, 1995
    While helping Grandma prepare for a family reunion Tanya visits and learns about the Virginia farm where Grandma lived as a child.
Elizabeth Fitzgerald Howard, *What's in Aunt Mary's Room?*, 1996
    Sarah and Susan discover that Aunt Mary's room is a treasure trove of family history.

477

ANGELA JOHNSON
DAVID SOMAN, Illustrator

The Wedding

(New York: Orchard Books, 1999)

Subject(s): Weddings; Sisters; African Americans
Age range(s): Grades K-2
Major character(s): Daisy, Sister, Child
Time period(s): 1990s (1999)
Locale(s): United States

Summary: Daisy's sister is getting married and she happily helps her sister pick a dress, taste the food, and select a place for the wedding. When the wedding day arrives, Daisy cheerfully serves as the flower girl, while trying to ignore her worries about her sister leaving the family. (32 pages)

Where it's reviewed:
Horn Book Guide, Fall 1999, page 250
Kirkus Reviews, January 1, 1999, page 66
Publisher's Weekly, March 22, 1999, page 91
School Library Journal, March 1999, page 176

Other books by the same author:
One of Three, 1991
When I Am Old with You, 1990
Tell Me a Story, Mama, 1989

Other books you might like:
Marc Brown, *D.W. Thinks Big*, 1993
    D.W. finds a way to participate in her cousin's wedding.
Judy Cox, *Now We Can Have a Wedding!*, 1998
    A young girl helps her neighbors prepare delicacies for her sister's wedding.
Karen English, *Nadia's Hands*, 1999
    Nadia serves as the flower girl in her cousin's wedding.

478

D.B. JOHNSON, Author/Illustrator

Henry Hikes to Fitchburg

(Boston: Houghton Mifflin Company, 2000)

Subject(s): Nature; Hiking; Travel
Age range(s): Grades K-3
Major character(s): Henry, Bear, Traveler; Unnamed Character, Bear, Friend
Time period(s): Indeterminate Past
Locale(s): Concord, Massachusetts; Fitchburg, Massachusetts

Summary: Henry and a friend plan to go to Fitchburg, thirty miles away, but they choose different means to reach the town with the goal of learning which method is fastest. Henry simply walks to Fitchburg, enjoying the sights, sounds and tastes of nature along the way. Henry's friend frantically works a succession of odd jobs to earn the ninety cents he needs to purchase a train ticket. As Henry's friend adds to his money supply, Henry's hike reduces the number of miles remaining in his walk to Fitchburg. Finally Henry's friend has enough money to purchase the train ticket and reaches Fitchburg just at sundown. Henry strolls in later by moonlight, unconcerned that the train was faster because Henry has a pail of blackberries picked along the way. The first picture book written by this illustrator concludes with background information about Henry David Thoreau and the story in *Walden* that inspired this book. (32 pages)

Where it's reviewed:
Booklist, April 15, 2000, page 1548
Horn Book, May 2000, page 296
Publishers Weekly, April 10, 2000, page 98
Riverbank Review, Summer 2000, page 31
School Library Journal, June 2000, page 116

Awards the book has won:
Boston Globe/Horn Book Award, 2000
School Library Journal Best Books, 2000

Other books you might like:
Bonny Becker, *The Quiet Way Home*, 1995
    With her grandfather a little girl chooses a quiet walk past grasshoppers chirping, sprinklers splashing and hoes chopping.
Ann Jonas, *Watch William Walk*, 1997
    William wanders along the shore with his dog Wally while watching friend Wilma and her waddling duck.
Jane Yolen, *Miz Berlin Walks*, 1997
    While walking with elderly Miz Berlin every evening Mary Louise hears stories of Miz Berlin's childhood and local history.

479

DINAH JOHNSON
JAMES RANSOME, Illustrator

Quinnie Blue

(New York: Henry Holt and Company, 2000)

Subject(s): Grandmothers; African Americans; Family Life
Age range(s): Grades K-2

Major character(s): Hattie Lottie Annie Quinnie Blue, Child; Quinnie Blue, Grandmother
Time period(s): 2000s
Locale(s): United States

Summary: While Hattie Lottie Annie Quinnie Blue loves the rhythm of her grandmother and namesake's name she prefers to call her simply Quinnie Blue. As the granddaughter goes about the simple pleasures of her day, she ponders what life was like for her grandmother. Did Quinnie Blue have braids too and like to swing high where the wind could sing her name? She loves the way the rain on the tin roof repeats the rhythm of their shared name and Hattie Lottie Annie Quinnie Blue is grateful to be named after her loving grandma. (32 pages)

Where it's reviewed:
Booklist, April 15, 2000, page 1552
Horn Book Guide, Fall 2000, page 271
Kirkus Reviews, May 15, 2000, page 715
Publishers Weekly, May 29, 2000, page 82
School Library Journal, June 2000, page 116

Other books by the same author:
Sitting Pretty, 2000
Sunday Week, 1999
All Around Town: The Photographs of Richard Samuel Roberts, 1998

Other books you might like:
Valerie Flournoy, *Tanya's Reunion*, 1995
    While helping Grandma prepare for a family reunion Tanya visits and learns about the Virginia farm where Grandma lived as a child.
Jan Spivey Gilchrist, *Indigo and Moonlight Gold*, 1993
    Secure in her mother's love, Autrie imagines the changes that will inevitably come with time.
Angela Shelf Medearis, *Our People*, 1994
    Father and daughter playfully share a history lesson and a hope for the future in a nonfiction picture book.
Gloria Jean Pinkney, *The Sunday Outing*, 1994
    Ernestine and Great-Aunt Odessa share stories of their family history and their dreams for the future.

480

DINAH JOHNSON
TYRONE GETER, Illustrator

Sunday Week

(New York: Henry Holt and Company, 1999)

Subject(s): African Americans; City and Town Life; Christian Life
Age range(s): Grades 1-3
Major character(s): Unnamed Character, Child, Narrator
Time period(s): 1990s
Locale(s): South

Summary: ''Blue Monday'' begins the week slowly but soon Tuesday's double Dutch practice puts some life into a young girl's activities. Wednesday is a time for midweek services and choir practice while Thursday brings a trip to the library for story time. On Friday different kinds of fish are cooked and shared with everyone on the block and on Saturday everyone pitches in to complete the week's work. Finally, Sunday comes again, a day for worship, family dinners, fancy clothes, and an afternoon drive to visit friends. (32 pages)

Where it's reviewed:
Booklist, February 15, 1999, page 1075
Horn Book, March 1999, page 191
Kirkus Reviews, February 1, 1999, page 223
Publishers Weekly, February 22, 1999, page 94
School Library Journal, June 1999, page 98

Other books by the same author:
Belindy's Girls, 2000
Quinnie Blue, 2000
All Around Town: The Photographs of Richard Samuel Roberts, 1998

Other books you might like:
Eloise Greenfield, *Night on Neighborhood Street*, 1991
    The joys of an inner city neighborhood come to life through poems depicting the feelings of the people and the sights and sounds of the environment.
Patricia C. McKissack, *Ma Dear's Aprons*, 1997
    David Earl knows the days of the week and the work of the day by the apron his mother dons each morning; Sunday is a no-apron day, a day of rest.
Jeanne Whitehouse Peterson, *My Mama Sings*, 1994
    Mama has a song for every occasion, adding a feeling of constancy to a young boy's life experiences.

481

DOLORES JOHNSON, Author/Illustrator

My Mom Is My Show-and-Tell

(New York: Marshall Cavendish, 1999)

Subject(s): Mothers and Sons; Schools; African Americans
Age range(s): Grades K-3
Major character(s): Allie Spencer, Mother, Teacher; David Spencer, Son, Student—Elementary School
Time period(s): 1990s (1999)
Locale(s): United States

Summary: As David escorts his mother to school on Parent Show-and-Tell Day he offers advice and suggestions for her presentation. According to David, Mrs. Spencer is not allowed to call him by his nickname, bore the class, tell jokes, or embarrass him in any way. Allie Spencer takes his directions in stride and demonstrates that she plans to be herself. By the time David introduces his mother, a teacher, he is willing to allow her that opportunity. (32 pages)

Where it's reviewed:
Booklist, April 15, 1999, page 1536
Horn Book Guide, Fall 1999, page 255
School Library Journal, May 1999, page 91

Other books by the same author:
Papa's Stories, 1994
Your Dad Was Just Like You, 1993
The Best Bug to Be, 1992
What Will Mommy Do When I'm at School, 1990

Other books you might like:
Grace Maccarone, *Sharing Time Troubles*, 1997
    Sam is in a quandary wondering what to bring for the weekly sharing time that could compare with his classmates' selections.
Joanne Oppenheim, *The Show-and-Tell Frog*, 1992
    A beginning reader tells of some unusual adventures for a small, green frog.
Barney Saltzberg, *Show and Tell*, 1994
    Phoebe's parents make extravagant plans for show and tell when Phoebe simply wants to share her own ideas.
Elvira Woodruff, *Show and Tell*, 1991
    The day Andy finds a magic bottle of bubbles, his kindergarten class has a most unexpected show-and-tell experience.

482

GILLIAN JOHNSON, Author/Illustrator

My Sister Gracie

(Plattsburgh, NY: Tundra Books, 2000)

Subject(s): Animals/Dogs; Pets; Stories in Rhyme
Age range(s): Grades K-2
Major character(s): Fabio, Dog; Gracie, Dog
Time period(s): 2000s (2000)
Locale(s): England

Summary: Fabio has a lovely life with his family but still he's not completely happy because he'd like a playful brother. When his family announces that they're getting another dog Fabio tells all the other neighborhood dogs about the new brother that Fabio imagines will be a miniature copy of him. The new dog is as opposite from Fabio's dreams as possible. Gracie is not only female but she's also an old, overweight dog from the pound, content to do nothing—on the couch with the family adoring her. Fabio invites Gracie for a walk with the intention of ditching her, but then he hears the neighborhood dogs insulting her and he comes to the defense of his sister. After all she's not such a bad companion, if you pick the right activity. (32 pages)

Where it's reviewed:
Horn Book Guide, Spring 2001, page 40
School Library Journal, December 2000, page 111

Other books by the same author:
Saranohair, 1992

Other books you might like:
Paul Fehlner, *Dog and Cat*, 1990
    An elderly dog and an overweight cat coexist peacefully because such a life is all they are capable of physically.
Isabelle Harper, *Our New Puppy*, 1996
    It takes the established family dog a little while to adjust to the arrival of a puppy that steals his toys, chews on his ears and eats his snacks.
Kevin Henkes, *Julius, the Baby of the World*, 1990
    Although Lilly is jealous of the attention given her baby brother she comes to his defense when a cousin makes an insulting remark about him.

483

PAUL BRETT JOHNSON, Author/Illustrator

Bearhide and Crow

(New York: Holiday House, 2000)

Subject(s): Folklore; Mountain Life; Trickster Tales
Age range(s): Grades 1-4
Major character(s): Amos Dyer, Spouse, Trickster; Sam Hankins, Neighbor
Time period(s): Indeterminate Past
Locale(s): Appalachians

Summary: Amos Dyer's wife is none too happy that he traded a prize-winning gourd to that swindler Sam Hankins for a smelly old bearhide. While Amos is hiding out in the woods waiting for her to calm down he overhears two robbers talking about where they've buried some money. In the morning Amos awakens to find a crow snacking on the flies attracted to the bearhide and decides to tell Sam that the crow told him where to find money on Sam's property. By convincing Sam that the crow can talk (once Sam uses the bearhide to learn ''crow'' talk) Amos is able to swap the crow and the hide for the bag of buried money and buy his wife some things in town to ease her anger. (32 pages)

Where it's reviewed:
Booklist, April 1, 2000, page 1469
Bulletin of the Center for Children's Books, May 2000, page 322
Kirkus Reviews, February 15, 2000, page 243
Publishers Weekly, February 28, 2000, page 79
School Library Journal, May 2000, page 146

Other books by the same author:
A Perfect Pork Stew, 1998
Farmers' Market, 1997 (Smithsonian's Notable Books for Children)
The Cow Who Wouldn't Come Down, 1993

Other books you might like:
Eric A. Kimmel, *Anansi and the Talking Melon*, 1994
    Anansi tricks the other animals into thinking that the melon in which he's hiding is actually speaking.
Gerald McDermott, *Coyote: A Trickster Tale from the American Southwest*, 1994
    Coyote's desire to fly with the crows is fulfilled for only a short time due to his boastful behavior.
Phyllis Root, *Aunt Nancy and Old Man Trouble*, 1996
    Aunt Nancy turns her troubles into triumphs, confounding Old Man Trouble and sending him on his way to bother someone less clever.
Kathleen Stevens, *Aunt Skilly and the Stranger*, 1994
    Aunt Skilly uses mountain hospitality to outsmart a stranger and would-be thief who comes calling from the ''wrong'' side of Which-Way Mountain.

484

PAUL BRETT JOHNSON, Author/Illustrator

Mr. Persnickety and the Cat Lady

(New York: Orchard Books, 2000)

Subject(s): Animals/Cats; Neighbors and Neighborhoods; Humor
Age range(s): Grades K-2
Major character(s): Albert Persnickety, Neighbor; Lucille ''Cat Lady'', Neighbor
Time period(s): 2000s (2000)
Locale(s): United States

Summary: Mr. Persnickety pays no attention to his next-door neighbor until she acquires a cat. Cat Lady not only refuses to get rid of the cat, she likes the cat so much that she begins taking in strays until she has 37 cats. Mr. Persnickety tries everything from squirting the cats (and the Cat Lady) with a garden hose to reporting her to the Humane Society. Nothing works. Cat Lady grows weary of the discord so she sneaks next door and releases mice into Mr. Persnickety's house. Every device that Mr. Persnickety tries to get rid of the mice fails and he's finally forced to borrow the Cat Lady's cats. In no time he's mouse-free and makes an appreciated truce with the Cat Lady whom he now knows as Lucille. (32 pages)

Where it's reviewed:
Bulletin of the Center for Children's Books, July 2000, page 407
Horn Book Guide, Spring 2001, page 40
Kirkus Reviews, July 15, 2000, page 1039
School Library Journal, May 2000, page 125

Other books by the same author:
A Perfect Pork Stew, 1998
Farmers' Market, 1997 (Smithsonian's Notable Books for Children)
Lost, 1996 (Celeste Lewis, co-author)

Other books you might like:
Judy Hindley, *Mrs. Mary Malarky's Seven Cats*, 1990
    Each one of Mrs. Malarky's cats has its own special story to tell.
Carol Purdy, *Mrs. Merriwether's Musical Cat*, 1994
    A stray cat inspires changes in Mrs. Merriwether's outlook on life and improves the playing of her piano students.
John Stadler, *The Cats of Mrs. Calamari*, 1997
    A new, cat-hating manager takes over Mrs. Calamari's apartment building, forcing her to devise ingenious ways to hide her many cats.

485

PAUL BRETT JOHNSON, Author/Illustrator

Old Dry Frye: A Deliciously Funny Tall Tale

(New York: Scholastic Press, 1999)

Subject(s): Folklore; Problem Solving; Humor
Age range(s): Grades 2-4
Major character(s): Old Dry Frye, Religious (preacher)
Time period(s): Indeterminate Past

Locale(s): Troublesome Creek, Appalachians

Summary: Old Dry Frye is a preacher who so loves fried chicken that he can follow his nose to the table of any house where the delicacy is being cooked. One Sunday while dining with a family Old Dry Frye chokes on a bone and dies. The farmer and his wife, fearful of being accused of murder, carry Old Dry Frye to a neighbor's hen house. There, he's thought to be a chicken thief and bopped on the head with a skillet. Each family suspects they'll be accused of murdering Old Dry Frye and everyone who comes to be in possession of him tries to quickly send the well-known preacher on his way. It's said he's traveling still. (32 pages)

Where it's reviewed:
Booklist, December 1, 1999, page 707
Horn Book Guide, Spring 2000, page 112
Kirkus Reviews, August 1, 1999, page 1228
Publishers Weekly, October 11, 1999, page 76
School Library Journal, September 1999, page 214

Other books by the same author:
A Perfect Pork Stew, 1998
Farmers' Market, 1997 (Smithsonian's Notable Book for Children)
The Cow Who Wouldn't Come Down, 1993 (School Library Journal Best Book)

Other books you might like:
Tom Birdseye, *Soap! Soap! Don't Forget the Soap! An Appalachian Folktale*, 1993
Plug Honeycutt tries to overcome his poor memory and remember the soap he is fetching from town for his mother.
Richard Chase, *Grandfather Tales*, 1948
The collection of classic folktales from the South includes the tale upon which Johnson's story is based.
Vivian French, *Lazy Jack*, 1995
In a retelling of the traditional tale about Jack, who prefers sleeping to any other activity, Jack can't seem to make it home with his wages.
Tres Seymour, *Hunting the White Cow*, 1993
A wayward cow becomes a legend in a mountain community as attempts to capture her fail.

486

PAUL BRETT JOHNSON, Author/Illustrator

The Pig Who Ran a Red Light
(New York: Orchard Books, 1999)

Subject(s): Animals/Pigs; Animals/Cows; Humor
Age range(s): Grades K-2
Major character(s): George, Pig; Gertrude, Cow; Miss Rosemary, Farmer
Time period(s): Indeterminate Past
Locale(s): United States

Summary: Since Gertrude learned to fly in *The Cow Who Wouldn't Come Down*, George has tried to accomplish the same feat. In fact, George tries to copy everything Gertrude does so when Gertrude gets behind the wheel of the tractor, George climbs into Miss Rosemary's pickup truck and heads down the road. Not only does he run a red light, but he also causes an accident. Miss Rosemary realizes that George will not listen to her so she has a long talk with Gertrude. The next day, Gertrude begins rooting in the soil and wallowing in the mud and sure enough, George joins in. Soon he's acting just like a pig—and so is Miss Rosemary's duck. (32 pages)

Where it's reviewed:
Booklist, May 1, 1999, page 1599
Horn Book Guide, Spring 1999, page 256
Kirkus Reviews, January 15, 1999, page 146
Publishers Weekly, March 29, 1999, page 103
School Library Journal, March 1999, page 177

Awards the book has won:
IRA/CBC Children's Choices, 2000

Other books by the same author:
A Perfect Pork Stew, 1998
Farmers' Market, 1997 (Smithsonian's Notable Book for Children)
The Cow Who Wouldn't Come Down, 1993 (School Library Journal Best Book)

Other books you might like:
Amy Ehrlich, *Parents in the Pigpen, Pigs in the Tub*, 1993
The farm animals move into the house and the family heads for the barn in a humorous reversal of roles.
Lynn Plourde, *Pigs in the Mud in the Middle of the Rud*, 1997
Grandma needs to get down the road, but first the pigs and other animals have to move out of the muddy way.
Phyllis Root, *Mrs. Potter's Pig*, 1996
When Mrs. Potter finds a pig in her dirty daughter Ermajean's baby carriage she thinks her worst fears have come true.

487

TONY JOHNSTON
JAMES WARHOLA, Illustrator

Bigfoot Cinderrrrrella
(New York: G.P. Putnam's Sons, 1999)

Subject(s): Fairy Tales; Folklore; Humor
Age range(s): Grades K-3
Major character(s): Rrrrrella, Stepsister; Unnamed Character, Royalty (prince)
Time period(s): Indeterminate Past
Locale(s): Fictional Country

Summary: Deep in an old growth forest live a band of Bigfoots who prize nature, dirt, and odor. Rrrrrella is the stepsister of two small, clean, flower-loving Bigfoots who torment Rrrrrella by bathing her and putting flowers in her matted fur. When the day comes for the annual Bigfoot funfest, Rrrrrella wants to attend the logrolling contest in hopes of dunking the prince and being his bride. Of course, Rrrrrella's wicked stepmother and stepsisters leave her behind where she is found by her beary godfather who grants her wish, mats her fur and gives her a pair of wooden clogs for the logrolling contest. And the winner is. . . (32 pages)

Where it's reviewed:
Booklist, December 1, 1998, page 668
Children's Book Review Service, February 1999, page 75
Horn Book Guide, Spring 1999, page 96

Publishers Weekly, November 2, 1998, page 81
School Library Journal, November 1998, page 106

Other books by the same author:
Fishing Sunday, 1996
The Magic Maguey, 1996
The Tale of Rabbit and Coyote, 1994

Other books you might like:
Pamela Duncan Edwards, *Dinorella: A Prehistoric Fairy Tale*, 1997
  In this spoof of the Cinderella story, diligent Dinorella dances with Duke Dudley and saves him from a hungry deionychus.
Deborah Nourse Lattimore, *Cinderhazel: The Cinderella of Halloween*, 1997
  Hazel is a witch whose ability to make a dirty mess of anything, including the Witches' Halloween Ball, impresses Prince Alarming.
William Wegman, *Cinderella*, 1993
  The classic fairy tale has been recast with dogs playing all the roles, but Cinderella still loses her glass slipper.

488

LYNNE JONELL
PETRA MATHERS, Illustrator

I Need a Snake
(New York: G.P. Putnam's Sons, 1998)

Subject(s): Animals/Reptiles; Mothers and Sons; Pets
Age range(s): Grades K-2
Major character(s): Robbie, Son, Child; Mommy, Mother
Time period(s): 1990s (1998)
Locale(s): United States

Summary: Robbie is sure that he needs a snake and Mommy is just as sure that he can have one when he grows up and has his own home. Mommy reads Robbie a book about snakes and then visits a museum with him and finally they go to a pet store. Robbie still wants his own snake and creatively finds three in his house. The white one is in his mother's closet, the green one is under his sister's bed and the black one with the gold head is found wrapped around his father's pants. When Mommy comes looking for the shoelace, jump rope, and belt, Robbie shows her how nice a well-behaved snake can be as a pet. (24 pages)

Where it's reviewed:
Booklist, May 15, 1998, page 1632
Horn Book Guide, Fall 1998, page 273
Kirkus Reviews, April 15, 1998, page 583
Publishers Weekly, May 11, 1998, page 66
School Library Journal, June 1998, page 111

Awards the book has won:
School Library Journal Best Books, 1998

Other books by the same author:
It's My Birthday, Too!, 1999
Mommy Go Away!, 1997

Other books you might like:
Lois G. Grambling, *Can I Have a Stegosaurus, Mom? Can I? Please?*, 1995

To convince his mom to accept a stegosaurus as a family pet, a child lists the dinosaur's positive attributes.
Libba Moore Gray, *Small Green Snake*, 1994
  A sassy, flashy garter snake does not heed his mother's warning and wanders into unexpected danger.
Faith McNulty, *A Snake in the House*, 1994
  A snake that a young boy brings home escapes and hides in the house for days before finally finding a way to freedom.
Holly Meade, *John Willy and Freddy McGee*, 1998
  An open cage door leads to adventure and excitement in the otherwise boring lives of pet guinea pigs John Willy and Freddy McGee.

489

LYNNE JONELL
PETRA MATHERS, Illustrator

It's My Birthday, Too!
(New York: G.P. Putnam's Sons, 1999)

Subject(s): Brothers; Birthdays; Sibling Rivalry
Age range(s): Grades K-2
Major character(s): Christopher, Brother (older), 6-Year-Old; Robbie, Brother (younger)
Time period(s): 1990s (1999)
Locale(s): United States

Summary: Christopher has no patience for Robbie who keeps insisting that while it may be Christopher's birthday, it is also Robbie's. Christopher tells Robbie that not only is it not his birthday, but also he is not allowing Robbie to attend the party because of the problems he caused last year. When Robbie learns he's not even a guest, he tells Christopher that he is no longer his brother. That is good news to Christopher who has always preferred a puppy. So, guess who joins the party—a ''puppy'' that has a remarkable resemblance to a younger brother. (32 pages)

Where it's reviewed:
Booklist, March 1, 1999, page 1207
Horn Book, May 1999, page 316
Kirkus Reviews, February 15, 1999, page 301
Publishers Weekly, March 1, 1999, page 68
School Library Journal, May 1999, page 91

Awards the book has won:
Booklist Editors' Choice, 1999
IRA/CBC Children's Choices, 2000

Other books by the same author:
I Need a Snake, 1998
Mommy Go Away!, 1997

Other books you might like:
Betsy Byars, *Ant Plays Bear*, 1997
  Ant's big brother is patiently understanding of his little brother's need for attention.
Jane Cutler, *No Dogs Allowed*, 1992
  Allergies prevent two brothers from having pets so 5-year-old Edward decides to ''become'' a dog.
Carol Diggory Shields, *I Wish My Brother Was a Dog*, 1997
  A young boy imagines how much better life would be if only Andy was a pet dog and not his little brother.

490

JENNIFER B. JONES

Dear Mrs. Ryan, You're Ruining My Life

(New York: Walker & Company, 2000)

Subject(s): Mothers and Sons; School Life; Authors and Writers

Age range(s): Grades 3-6

Major character(s): Harvey Ryan, 5th Grader, Child of Divorced Parents; Cecelia ''Seal'' Spicer, 5th Grader, Friend; Mr. Stevens, Principal, Widow(er)

Time period(s): 2000s (2000)

Locale(s): New York

Summary: It's bad enough, Harvey thinks, having a mother who writes humorous children's books but when she comes to your school and admits to using her son's experiences as inspiration for her work it's truly humiliating. Seal suggests playing matchmaker so Harvey's mom will have something else to occupy her time and the nearest available single man is Mr. Stevens. What Harvey and Seal have not considered is how successful their plan will be and how much additional teasing Harvey receives when the budding relationship becomes obvious to the students. Although Seal and Harvey plot to undo their plan, Harvey realizes it's too late and he begrudgingly admits that Mr. Stevens is a nice guy, his mom seems happy and Mr. Steven's love of history has given his mom some other writing ideas in the author's first novel. (122 pages)

Where it's reviewed:
Booklist, April 1, 2000, page 1461
Bulletin of the Center for Children's Books, April 2000, page 284
Kirkus Reviews, April 1, 2000, page 478
Publishers Weekly, April 24, 2000, page 92
School Library Journal, May 2000, page 172

Other books you might like:
Mary Jane Auch, *Mom Is Dating Weird Wayne*, 1988
    How embarrassing! Jenna's mother is dating the TV weatherman known for his outlandish costumes.
Andrew Clements, *The Janitor's Boy*, 2000
    Fifth grader Jack futilely hopes that no one will discover the embarrassing fact that his father is the head custodian of the school.
Sarah Weeks, *Regular Guy*, 1999
    Guy's weird parents are so embarrassing that he's sure he must have been switched at birth and he has a plan to learn the truth.

491

BARBARA M. JOOSSE
SUE TRUESDELL, Illustrator

Alien Brain Fryout

(New York: Clarion Books)

Series: Wild Willie Mystery. Number 4

Subject(s): Bullies; Mystery and Detective Stories; Aliens

Age range(s): Grades 2-5

Major character(s): Kyle Krane, Detective—Amateur, Friend; Willie, Detective—Amateur, Friend; Lucy, Detective—Amateur, Friend; Scarface, Parrot; Chuckie Herman, Bully, 10-Year-Old

Time period(s): 2000s (2000)

Locale(s): Grafton

Summary: Chuckie, known for conning kids out of their money (or worse) follows Lucy and Willie as they walk home from Kyle's house. The next day Willie sees him staring at Lucy's house and when the detectives observe and interrogate him, Chuckie behaves strangely. In fact, Chuckie seems nice, but Willie suspects he's missing something—like part of his brain. The amateur detectives also notice a change in Scarface and convince themselves that there is only one explanation for these changes—aliens. Sure that aliens have abducted and transformed both Scarface and Chuckie to achieve some nefarious goal, Kyle, Willie and Lucy take on the responsibility of solving the case and keeping Grafton safe. (96 pages)

Where it's reviewed:
Booklist, September 15, 2000, page 241
Horn Book Guide, Spring 2001,, page 63
Kirkus Reviews, July 15, 2000, page 1040
School Library Journal, September 2000, page 200

Other books by the same author:
Ghost Trap, 1998 (Wild Willie Mystery, Number 3)
The Losers Fight Back, 1994 (Wild Willie Mystery, Number 2)
Wild Willie and King Kyle Detectives, 1993 (Wild Willie Mystery, Number 1)

Other books you might like:
Mary Blount Christian, *The Sebastian (Super Sleuth) Series*, 1982-
    Although his owner considers himself the detective, the sheepdog Sebastian knows who really solves the mysteries.
Donald J. Sobol, *Encyclopedia Brown, Boy Detective*, 1979
    Confident and affordable, Encyclopedia Brown opens a detective agency, charging 25 cents per case.
Gertrude Chandler Warner, *The Boxcar Children Mystery Series*, 1953-
    Four children are involved in a variety of mysteries in this timeless series.

K

492

KIMIKO KAJIKAWA, Adaptor
YUMI HEO, Illustrator

Yoshi's Feast

(New York: DK Ink/Dorling Kindersley Publishing, Inc., 2000)

Subject(s): Neighbors and Neighborhoods; Food; Folklore
Age range(s): Grades 1-4
Major character(s): Yoshi, Artisan (fanmaker), Neighbor; Sabu, Cook, Neighbor
Time period(s): Indeterminate Past
Locale(s): Yedo, Japan

Summary: Yoshi watches Sabu catch and cook eels every day but he's not willing to part with any income from the sale of his fans to purchase Sabu's broiled eels. Yoshi thinks Sabu should share the leftovers each day, but Sabu thinks Yoshi should buy what he wants to eat and then Sabu would make some money and no eels would be leftover. The friction between the neighbors increases until Sabu presents Yoshi with a bill charging him for the scent of the broiled eels. Yoshi responds in kind by counting the money into a box and then dancing in the street while jingling the coins so Sabu can hear the sound of money. Sabu is angry and begins to broil a smelly fish that drives Yoshi inside. The desire to get rid of the awful smell inspires Yoshi to offer a plan that will benefit both neighbors. Once Yoshi and Sabu begin working together cooperatively they each benefit. (32 pages)

Where it's reviewed:
Booklist, March 1, 2000, page 1242
Horn Book, May 2000, page 325
Kirkus Reviews, March 15, 2000, page 385
Publishers Weekly, February 28, 2000, page 80
School Library Journal, May 2000, page 146

Awards the book has won:
Booklist Editors' Choice, 2000
Riverbank Review Children's Books of Distinction, 2001

Other books by the same author:
Sweet Dreams: How Animals Sleep, 1999

Other books you might like:
Dick Gackenbach, *Barker's Crime*, 1996
   Greedy Mr. Gobble gets his comeuppance when he accuses a stray dog of stealing the aroma from his food.
Francoise Richard, *On Cat Mountain*, 1994
   The kindness of Sho, a mistreated servant who strives to protect her cat from a cruel mistress is remembered and rewarded.
Ann Tompert, *Bamboo Hats and a Rice Cake: A Tale Adapted from Japanese Folklore*, 1993
   A poor, but kind old man is granted the gift of prosperity for the New Year.
Yoshiko Uchida, *The Sea of Gold and Other Tales from Japan*, 1965
   The collection of Japanese folktales includes a retelling of a story in which kindness is generously rewarded.

493

MAIRA KALMAN, Author/Illustrator

Next Stop Grand Central

(New York: G.P. Putnam's Sons, 1999)

Subject(s): City and Town Life; Trains; Work
Age range(s): Grades 1-4
Time period(s): 1990s
Locale(s): New York, New York (Grand Central Station)

Summary: Grand Central Station is a bustling place. Workers perform a myriad of tasks from changing light bulbs to delivering mail to overseeing all the work. In addition to the workers the station is filled with people coming and going from jobs, shopping, school field trips or the museum. This big, busy station operates all day and all night serving passengers. (32 pages)

Where it's reviewed:
Booklist, December 15, 1998, page 749
Horn Book, May 1999, page 317
Kirkus Reviews, December 1, 1998, page 1734
Publishers Weekly, November 30, 1998, page 71
School Library Journal, February 1999, page 85

Awards the book has won:
Notable Social Studies Trade Books for Young People, 2000

Other books by the same author:
Swami on Rye (Max in India), 1995
Chicken Soup, Boots, 1993
Max Makes a Million, 1990
Sayonara, Mrs. Kackleman, 1989
Hey Willy, See the Pyramids!, 1988

Other books you might like:
Patricia Grossman, *The Night Ones*, 1991
   On the night bus people who work while others sleep travel to their various jobs and return home on the morning bus.
Amy Hest, *Jamaica Louise James*, 1996
   To brighten her grandmother's workplace, Jamaica Louise James decorates the 86th Street subway station with her paintings.
Christine Loomis, *Rush Hour*, 1996
   Subway trains are one of the many means of transportation workers use to rush to their jobs and home again.

494

JEF KAMINSKY, Author/Illustrator

Poppy & Ella: 3 Stories about 2 Friends
(New York: Hyperion Books for Children, 2000)

Subject(s): Friendship; Animals/Birds
Age range(s): Grades K-1
Major character(s): Poppy, Bird, Friend; Ella, Bird, Friend
Time period(s): Indeterminate
Locale(s): Fictional Country

Summary: Good friends Poppy and Ella do not always agree, but they know just when to help each other. In the first story, Ella helps Poppy overcome his self-consciousness about his appearance. A trip to the beach in the second story seems to be an exercise in disagreement—if Ella is swimming, Poppy is reading, if Ella's in the sun, Poppy's in the shade. Finally, a power failure forces Ella to admit to Poppy that she's afraid of the dark. Poppy's ingenious solution helps her overcome her fear, almost, as the author/illustrator's first book concludes. (48 pages)

Where it's reviewed:
Bulletin of the Center for Children's Books, September 2000, page 24
Horn Book Guide, Fall 2000, page 271
Publishers Weekly, April 10, 2000, page 97
School Library Journal, July 2000, page 80

Other books you might like:
Laurie A. Jacobs, *So Much in Common*, 1994
   Although Philomena and Horace seem to have little in common, it is enough to build a friendship.
Arnold Lobel, *Frog and Toad Together*, 1972
   The Newbery Honor book is one of four titles describing the adventures and misadventures of loyal friends Frog and Toad.
James Marshall, *George and Martha*, 1972
   The first book in a series about George and Martha uses several brief, humorous stories to describe the antics of two hippo buddies.

Jean Van Leeuwen, *Amanda Pig and Her Best Friend Lollipop*, 1998
   Classmates Amanda and Lollipop schedule after school play times and a sleepover in a beginning reader about new friends.

495

G. BRIAN KARAS, Author/Illustrator

The Windy Day
(New York: Simon & Schuster Books for Young Readers, 1998)

Subject(s): Weather; Imagination; Childhood
Age range(s): Grades K-3
Major character(s): Bernard, Child, Student—Elementary School
Time period(s): Indeterminate Past
Locale(s): United States

Summary: When the wind whooshes through a small town most people think it ruins a beautiful day by blowing flowers, papers, and leftover food all over. Bernard, however, breathes deeply of the wind and imagines the people, places and things that have been touched by this wind. As the wind continues its journey, Bernard calls out his name and the wind carries it along. (32 pages)

Where it's reviewed:
Children's Book Review Service, August 1998, page 160
Horn Book, March 1998, page 214
Kirkus Reviews, May 1, 1999, page 660
Publishers Weekly, May 11, 1998, page 67
School Library Journal, June 1998, page 111

Other books by the same author:
Home on the Bayou: A Cowboy's Story, 1996 (Boston Globe/Horn Book Honor Book)

Other books you might like:
Marie Hall Ets, *Gilberto and the Wind*, 1963
   Through his play a young boy learns to understand and appreciate the wind.
Pat Hutchins, *The Wind Blew*, 1974
   A rhyming story describes the cumulative effect of a wind that blows away many objects.
Betsy James, *Blow Away Soon*, 1995
   Nana teaches Sophie how to make a ''blow-away-soon'' so she can appreciate the wind rather than be frustrated by it.

496

ROBERTA KARIM
BETHANNE ANDERSEN, Illustrator

Kindle Me a Riddle: A Pioneer Story
(New York: Greenwillow Books, 1999)

Subject(s): Frontier and Pioneer Life; Family Life; American West
Age range(s): Grades 1-4
Major character(s): Constance, Daughter, Sister; Papa, Father, Settler; Jack, Brother (Younger), Son
Time period(s): 1850s

Locale(s): Utah

Summary: Constance cries as she and Papa carry embers from the neighbor's fire to rekindle the fire that Constance did not bank properly the night before. To cheer her, Papa asks a riddle. The game is such fun that Constance keeps it up all day, involving Jack and even the schoolteacher in the game. The riddles are not jokes but questions about the origins of commonly used implements in their pioneer home and everyone has fun playing the game right up until bedtime. Facts about the various items in each riddle are appended. (40 pages)

Where it's reviewed:
Booklist, September 1, 1999, page 140
Children's Book Review Service, September 1999, page 174
Kirkus Reviews, August 1, 1999, page 1228
Publishers Weekly, August 16, 1999, page 84
School Library Journal, January 2000, page 105

Awards the book has won:
Notable Social Studies Trade Books for Young People, 2000

Other books by the same author:
This Is a Hospital, Not a Zoo!, 1998
Mandy Sue Day, 1994

Other books you might like:
Raymond Bial, *Frontier Home*, 1993
 Diary excerpts enliven descriptions of the homes and tools used by pioneer families in this non-fiction view of life long ago.
Glen Rounds, *Sod Houses on the Great Plains*, 1995
 A non-fiction picture book describes the sod houses built by the early settlers in the treeless plains.
Jean Van Leeuwen, *A Fourth of July on the Plains*, 1997
 On the journey to Oregon a wagon train stops to rest and celebrate the Fourth of July.

497

GAIL LANGER KARWOSKI
JAMES WATLING, Illustrator

Seaman: The Dog Who Explored the West with Lewis & Clark

(Atlanta: Peachtree, 1999)

Subject(s): Discovery and Exploration; American History; Animals/Dogs
Age range(s): Grades 5-7
Major character(s): Seaman, Dog (Newfoundland); Meriwether Lewis, Explorer; John Colter, Explorer
Time period(s): 1800s (1803-1806)
Locale(s): Pittsburg, Pennsylvania; West (unexplored territory)

Summary: When Meriwether Lewis arrives in Pittsburg to pick up the keelboat for the journey to explore the lands of the Lousiana Purchase and find a route to the Pacific he also purchases a dog for the trip. Seaman quickly proves to Lewis that he has correctly assessed his courage and hunting skill. Throughout the long dangerous journey, Seaman proves a valiant companion to all members of the Corps of Discovery. As the expedition concludes and members prepare to return to the United States, John Colter asks to be discharged from his membership to return to the Yellowstone River area to live as a hunter and trapper. Lewis gives Seaman to Colter knowing that the dog is better suited to a life in the wild than to one of city living. A concluding author's note gives factual information about the history on which the book is based. (183 pages)

Where it's reviewed:
Book Report, September 1999, page 60
Booklist, August 1999, page 2058
School Library Journal, October 1999, page 152

Awards the book has won:
ABA Children's Pick of the Lists, 1999

Other books by the same author:
The Tree That Owns Itself: And Other Adventure Tales from Out of the Past, 1996 (Loretta Johnson Hammer, co-author)

Other books you might like:
Scott O'Dell, *Streams to the River, River to the Sea: A Novel of Sacagawea*, 1986
 This fictionalized account portrays the contributions of Sacagawea who traveled with the Lewis and Clark expedition.
Peter Roop, *Girl of the Shining Mountains: Sacagawea's Story*, 1999
 The adventures of Seaman and the Corps of Discovery are presented through the eyes of their Indian guide and interpreter. Connie Roop, co-author.
Roland Smith, *The Captain's Dog: My Journey with the Lewis and Clark Tribe*, 1999
 Seaman tells the story of his travels with the Lewis and Clark expedition.

498

SUSAN KATZ

Snowdrops for Cousin Ruth

(New York: Simon & Schuster Books for Young Readers, 1998)

Subject(s): Death; Grief; Family Problems
Age range(s): Grades 4-6
Major character(s): Johanna "Josie" Rush, 4th Grader, Sister (older); Susie Rush, Sister (younger), Twin (mute); Cousin Ruth, Aged Person, Widow(er)
Time period(s): 1990s
Locale(s): Thornton, Pennsylvania

Summary: In a tragic accident two days after Christmas, Susie's twin brother loses his life. While Susie is physically unharmed by the accident, she stops speaking. In the months following her brother's death, Josie often hears her brother's voice and talks to him, but other family members do not mention him at all. Josie grieves for her brother and for the loss of her mother's laugh, the sparkle in her father's eye and Susie's playfulness. When exuberant Cousin Ruth moves to town she brings the hope for happiness with her. Gradually, as she shares her memories of her deceased husband and her feelings about his unexpected death, Cousin Ruth enables the family to understand how to work through their grief in a healthy way and move on with life in the author's debut novel. (183 pages)

Where it's reviewed:
Booklist, July 1998, page 192
Horn Book, May 1998, page 345
Kirkus Reviews, May 15, 1998, page 739
Publishers Weekly, June 1, 1998, page 63
School Library Journal, June 1998, page 147

Awards the book has won:
Paterson Prize for Books for Young People, 1999

Other books you might like:
Carol Fenner, *Yolanda's Genius*, 1995
 Yolanda is protective of her younger brother who chooses to communicate through the music of the harmonica given him by their deceased father.
Katherine Paterson, *Flip-Flop Girl*, 1994
 After their father's death, Vinnie's brother stops talking and her mother is so busy working that Vinnie must find her own solutions to problems.
Nancy Hope Wilson, *Flapjack Waltzes*, 1998
 An elderly neighbor helps Natalie as she grieves for her brother following his death in an automobile accident.

499

VERLA KAY
S.D. SCHINDLER, Illustrator

Gold Fever

(New York: G.P. Putnam's Sons, 1999)

Subject(s): Gold; American West; Stories in Rhyme
Age range(s): Grades 1-3
Major character(s): Jasper, Farmer, Prospector
Time period(s): 1840s (1849)
Locale(s): Midwest; California

Summary: The lure of gold draws Jasper from his fields and family to follow his dreams across the desert to the mountain streams of California. While miners are plentiful, gold is scarce and in time Jasper returns to his home, satisfied to wave at the other forty-niners as they pass the farm. First book. (32 pages)

Where it's reviewed:
Booklist, January 1, 1999, page 888
Horn Book, March 1999, page 192
Kirkus Reviews, December 15, 1998, page 1798
Publishers Weekly, January 11, 1999, page 71
School Library Journal, March 1999, page 177

Other books by the same author:
Iron Horses, 1999

Other books you might like:
Marian Harris, *Tuesday in Arizona*, 1998
 A down on his luck prospector being pestered by a pack rat finally locates the pack rat's home and the treasure he seeks.
Sonia Levitin, *Boom Town*, 1998
 While Pa mines for gold, Amanda bakes pies that Pa sells to the miners. Soon the family makes more money selling pies than mining gold.
Catherine McMorrow, *Gold Fever*, 1996
 A beginning reader traces the history of the California

Gold Rush beginning with the first discovery of gold at Sutter's Mill.
Rosalyn Schanzer, *Gold Fever! Tales from the California Gold Rush*, 1999
 A nonfiction overview describes the frenzied rush to California in hopes of finding wealth in the gold fields.

500

VERLA KAY
MICHAEL MCCURDY, Illustrator

Iron Horses

(New York: G.P. Putnam's Sons, 1999)

Subject(s): Railroads; Stories in Rhyme; Historical
Age range(s): Grades 1-4
Time period(s): 1860s
Locale(s): West

Summary: Succinct text combined with scratchboard illustrations describes the creation of the nation's first transcontinental railroad from Congressional approval to final spike. The harsh living conditions and dangerous work make the task formidable and exciting. A concluding author's note and map gives background information for the story. (32 pages)

Where it's reviewed:
Booklist, June 1999, page 1842
Horn Book, July 1999, page 456
Kirkus Reviews, May 15, 1999, page 802
Publishers Weekly, June 21, 1999, page 67
School Library Journal, July 1999, page 74

Awards the book has won:
Notable Social Studies Trade Books for Young People, 2000

Other books by the same author:
Covered Wagons, Bumpy Trails, 2000
Gold Fever, 1999

Other books you might like:
Darice Bailer, *The Last Rail*, 1996
 A picture book for older readers describes the building of the transcontinental railroad through the eyes of a young observer.
Eve Bunting, *Train to Somewhere*, 1996
 Train transportation provided a way for city orphans to meet potential adoptive families in the Midwest.
David Galef, *Tracks*, 1996
 After breaking his glasses, Albert has difficulty seeing the terrain on which railroad tracks are being built but he still meets the deadline.

501

SALLY M. KEEHN

The First Horse I See

(New York: Philomel Books, 1999)

Subject(s): Animals/Horses; Death; Grief
Age range(s): Grades 5-8
Major character(s): Willojean "Willo", Child of an Alcoholic, Animal Lover; Granddad, Grandfather; Tess, Horse
Time period(s): 1990s (1999)

Locale(s): Mas-Que, Maryland

Summary: Before she dies, Willo's mother elicits a promise from her father that Willo will be allowed to have a horse. Because Willo's dad travels a lot with his work, Willo lives with Granddad who takes her horse shopping. Tess is the first horse that Willo sees and in that abused, frightened former racehorse, Willo sees an animal that needs her as much as Willo needs the horse to fill the emptiness in her life. Willo's dad does not approve of her choice and gives her a limited amount of time to show that she can manage Tess. (215 pages)

Where it's reviewed:
Booklist, September 1, 1999, page 133
Horn Book Guide, Fall 1999, page 294
Kirkus Reviews, June 1, 1999, page 884
Publishers Weekly, July 5, 1999, page 71
School Library Journal, July 1999, page 96

Other books by the same author:
Moon of Two Dark Horses, 1995
I Am Regina, 1991

Other books you might like:
Jessie Haas, *Beware the Mare*, 1993
    Gram and Gramps do not share Lily's excitement about the new mare that Lily hopes will be hers.
Chris Platt, *Willow King*, 1998
    Katie convinces the owner not to destroy a colt born with twisted legs; with Katie's help Willow King develops into a worthy racehorse.
Chris St. John, *A Horse of Her Own*, 1989
    Saving gift money and earnings, Jessie is able to buy her favorite horse, Time-Out.

502

PEG KEHRET

My Brother Made Me Do It
(New York: Minstrel Hardcover/Pocket Books, 2000)

Subject(s): Physically Handicapped; Brothers and Sisters; Letters
Age range(s): Grades 4-6
Major character(s): Frankie Welsh, 9-Year-Old, Brother; Julie Welsh, 5th Grader, Sister; Mrs. Kaplan, Aged Person
Time period(s): 2000s (2000)
Locale(s): United States

Summary: Julie's fifth grade teacher assigns Mrs. Kaplan to be Julie's 89-year-old pen pal. Through their correspondence Mrs. Kaplan becomes Julie's confidant when she's in time-out for participating in one of Frankie's wacky ideas or suffering the pain and embarrassment of newly diagnosed juvenile rheumatoid arthritis (JRA). In her responses to the question-of-the-week posed by Julie's teacher Mrs. Kaplan reveals interesting facts that inspire the class to further study. Mrs. Kaplan also encourages Julie to keep trying despite the pain and fatigue from JRA and gives Julie the confidence to run for a student government office, enter a talent contest, and participate in a fund-raising fun run at her school. (130 pages)

Where it's reviewed:
Booklist, June 2000, page 1892
Children's Bookwatch, May 2000, page 2

Horn Book Guide, Fall 2000, page 305
School Library Journal, September 2000, page 232

Other books by the same author:
The Flood Disaster, 1999
The Blizzard Disaster, 1998
Searching for Candlestick Park, 1997
The Richest Kids in Town, 1994

Other books you might like:
Beverly Cleary, *Dear Mr. Henshaw*, 1983
    In a Newbery Award winning book, Leigh Botts writes letters about the problems of his life to an admired author.
Rebecca C. Jones, *Angie and Me*, 1981
    While hospitalized for treatment of juvenile rheumatoid arthritis 12-year-old Jenna begins to accept her illness.
Colin Thiele, *Jodie's Journey*, 1988
    Twelve-year-old Jodie can no longer ride her horse due to the disabling effects of juvenile rheumatoid arthritis.

503

HOLLY KELLER, Author/Illustrator

Angela's Top-Secret Computer Club
(New York: Greenwillow Books, 1998)

Subject(s): Computers; Schools; Mystery and Detective Stories
Age range(s): Grades 2-4
Major character(s): Angela Spiegelhoff, Student—Elementary School; Mrs. Grover, Librarian; Albert, Student—Elementary School
Time period(s): 1990s (1998)
Locale(s): United States

Summary: The last day of school becomes one of unexpected chaos when it's discovered that someone has hacked into the computer system and changed everyone's report cards. Curious Angela inadvertently lands the school's computer club in the middle of the investigation by promising that they can solve the mystery during summer vacation. Mrs. Grover, sponsor of the club, allows the students to continue meeting in the library where they have access to computers and their e-mail accounts. Using e-mail messages sent accidentally to Albert by "Black Cat" the sleuths have no other clues, but manage to deduce the answer before school reopens. (60 pages)

Where it's reviewed:
Booklist, August 1998, page 2006
Bulletin of the Center for Children's Books, March 1998, page 247
Horn Book Guide, Fall 1998, page 320
School Library Journal, June 1998, page 111

Other books by the same author:
A Bed Full of Cats, 1999
I Am Angela, 1997
Geraldine First, 1996

Other books you might like:
David A. Adler, *The Many Troubles of Andy Russell*, 1998
    Try as he might, Andy's plans seem to go awry and problems crop up everywhere for him.

Elizabeth Levy, *Parent's Night Fright*, 1998
> In the sixth title of the Invisible Inc. series, a group of amateur sleuths track a prize-winning story that appears to be as invisible as Chip.

Marjorie Weinman Sharmat, *The Nate the Great Series*, 1972-
> Nate follows one clue after another emulating the style of Sherlock Holmes in this series for beginning readers.

504

HOLLY KELLER, Author/Illustrator

A Bed Full of Cats

(San Diego: Harcourt Brace & Company, 1999)

Series: Green Light Readers. Level 2
Subject(s): Animals/Cats; Lost and Found Possessions; Pets
Age range(s): Grades 1-2
Major character(s): Lee, Child; Flora, Cat
Time period(s): 1990s (1999)
Locale(s): United States

Summary: Lee is accustomed to sleeping with Flora at the foot of his bed, purring when he pets her and playing when he wiggles his fingers. When Flora is not in his bed one night, Lee is worried. The next day he searches the house for Flora; his parents and grandmother help to search the neighborhood. Days and week pass and then, one night, Lee finds himself sleeping in a bed full of cats. Flora has come home—with her four kittens. (20 pages)

Where it's reviewed:
Booklist, October 1, 1999, page 365
Horn Book Guide, Spring 2000, page 61
School Library Journal, November 1999, page 112

Other books by the same author:
Angela's Top-Secret Computer Club, 1998
I Am Angela, 1997
Geraldine First, 1996
Grandfather's Dream, 1994

Other books you might like:
Patricia Casey, *My Cat Jack*, 1994
> Jack is a stretching, yawning, scratching cat and a child's beloved pet.
Tad Hardy, *Lost Cat*, 1996
> The rhyming story describes a man's attempts to find his lost pet.
Gina Wilson, *Prowlpuss*, 1995
> A rough, tough one-eyed, one-eared alley cat returns home after a night of carousing to become a pampered pussy.

505

HOLLY KELLER, Author/Illustrator

Brave Horace

(New York: Greenwillow Books, 1998)

Subject(s): Animals; Fear; Courage
Age range(s): Grades K-2
Major character(s): Horace, Leopard, Friend; George, Tiger, Friend; Marvin, Tiger, Brother (George's older)
Time period(s): Indeterminate
Locale(s): Fictional Country

Summary: An invitation to George's monster-movie party causes timid Horace to approach the event apprehensively. All week he practices being brave by wearing scary costumes and making loud noises. On the day of the party, when Marvin complains to the arriving party guests that the plans have been changed to make the party less scary, Horace feels relieved. Horace and his friends have fun until Marvin turns out the lights and tries to frighten everyone by making them touch the monster brains and livers that he carries in a box. When Marvin taunts the party guests, Horace becomes so angry that he bravely agrees to be first to touch the contents of the box and reveal their true identity. (32 pages)

Where it's reviewed:
Booklist, March 1, 1998, page 1140
Horn Book, July 1998, page 475
Kirkus Reviews, February 15, 1998, page 269
Publishers Weekly, March 23, 1998, page 102
School Library Journal, April 1998, page 102

Other books by the same author:
Merry Christmas, Geraldine, 1997
Harry and Tuck, 1993
Horace, 1991

Other books you might like:
Valiska Gregory, *Kate's Giants*, 1995
> When Kate imagines scary things behind the attic door, her parents help her find the courage to confront her fears.
Kevin Henkes, *Sheila Rae, the Brave*, 1987
> When brave Sheila Rae and her timid sister Louise become lost it is Louise who courageously finds the way home.
Libuse Palacek, *Brave as a Tiger*, 1995
> The other tigers take timid Fang's stripes until he displays the courage expected of his breed.
Ellen Stoll Walsh, *Pip's Magic*, 1994
> While searching for a way to overcome his fear of the dark, Pip unwittingly solves his problem.

506

HOLLY KELLER, Author/Illustrator

Geraldine and Mrs. Duffy

(New York: Greenwillow Books/HarperCollins Publishers, 2000)

Subject(s): Animals/Pigs; Babysitters; Brothers and Sisters
Age range(s): Grades K-2
Major character(s): Geraldine, Pig, Sister (older); Willy, Pig, Brother; Mrs. Duffy, Pig, Babysitter
Time period(s): 2000s (2000)
Locale(s): Fictional Country

Summary: With a new babysitter in charge for the evening Geraldine plans a little trick at bath time by hiding the pet iguana in the tub. When Mrs. Duffy insists that they take the iguana out of the tub, the pet scampers out of the bathroom with two dripping, naked siblings and their babysitter in pursuit. By the time Geraldine and Willy spot the iguana and Mrs. Duffy retrieves it Geraldine and Willy are dressed in their pajamas and ready to enjoy milk and cookies before going to bed. (32 pages)

Where it's reviewed:
Booklist, October 1, 2000, page 348
Publishers Weekly, September 11, 2000, page 92
School Library Journal, August 2000, page 158

Other books by the same author:
Merry Christmas, Geraldine, 1997
Geraldine First, 1996
Geraldine's Baby Brother, 1994

Other books you might like:
Timothy Bush, *Benjamin McFadden and the Robot Babysitter*, 1998
    Benjamin regrets programming his robot babysitter to be more fun when it delivers more than Benjamin anticipated.
Valiska Gregory, *Babysitting for Benjamin*, 1993
    Frances and Ralph, elderly mice, learn that babysitting for Benjamin, an active young rabbit, is quite a challenge.
John Himmelman, *J.J. Versus the Babysitter*, 1996
    The speed with which J.J. moves about amazes babysitter Stephanie until she realizes it's a twin thing and then she plans her own trick.
Rosemary Wells, *Max's Dragon Shirt*, 1991
    Ruby is responsible for her younger brother Max while shopping but she loses him just long enough for Max to select a new shirt.

507

HOLLY KELLER, Author/Illustrator

Jacob's Tree

(New York: Greenwillow Books, 1999)

Subject(s): Growing Up; Parent and Child; Family Life
Age range(s): Grades K-1
Major character(s): Jacob, Bear, Brother (youngest); Mama, Bear, Mother; Papa, Bear, Father
Time period(s): Indeterminate
Locale(s): Fictional Country

Summary: Jacob is too small—too small to reach the cookie jar, too small to see in the mirror and too small to climb the jungle gym—and Jacob hates being too small. Mama cautions him to wait and assures him that he will grow bigger. Papa paints a line on the elm tree to show how tall Jacob is. Jacob eats his vegetables, drinks his milk and checks his height on the tree, but there is no change. During the long winter months the snow is so deep around the tree that Jacob has no choice but to wait for spring before he can check his growth again. This time when Papa marks his son's height on Jacob's tree the evidence clearly shows that Jacob is growing taller! (24 pages)

Where it's reviewed:
Booklist, July 1999, page 1952
Horn Book, March 1999, page 193
Kirkus Reviews, March 15, 1999, page 452
Publishers Weekly, April 5, 1999, page 240
School Library Journal, May 1999, page 91

Other books by the same author:
Brave Horace, 1998
Geraldine First, 1996
Harry and Tuck, 1993

A Bear for Christmas, 1986

Other books you might like:
Syd Hoff, *Bernard on His Own*, 1993
    Bernard's parents assure the young bear that one day he'll be able to accomplish, on his own, the many tasks that frustrate him now.
Robert Kraus, *Leo the Late Bloomer*, 1971
    Father is impatient for Leo to learn to do things for himself, but Mother knows that Leo will bloom in his own time.
Joan Lowery Nixon, *When I Am Eight*, 1994
    Herbie's big brother tells him he's too little to do things so Herbie imagines life as an 8-year-old when all things will be possible.

508

HOLLY KELLER, Author/Illustrator

That's Mine, Horace

(New York: Greenwillow Books/HarperCollins Publishers, 2000)

Subject(s): Animals; Honesty; Conduct of Life
Age range(s): Grades K-2
Major character(s): Horace, Leopard, Student; Walter, Tiger, Student; Mrs. Pepper, Teacher
Time period(s): 2000s
Locale(s): Fictional Country

Summary: Horace finds a terrific truck on the playground that no one retrieves when Mrs. Pepper rings the bell for recess to end so Horace puts the truck in his pocket. Later he's playing with the truck in the classroom when Walter recognizes it as his truck. Horace disputes Walter's claim and lies to Mrs. Pepper when she asks him about it. At home he tells his mother that Walter has given him the truck. The guilt from his dishonesty weighs upon his conscience. Bad dreams disrupt his sleep and the next day he feels too sick to go to school. When his class sends get well messages, including one from Walter, Horace feels even worse. Fortunately, Walter phrases his letter in such a way that Horace has a face-saving way to return the truck to its rightful owner and that's just what he does when he returns to school. (24 pages)

Where it's reviewed:
Booklist, August 2000, page 2147
Horn Book Guide, Spring 2001, page 251
Horn Book, July 2000, page 437
School Library Journal, June 2000, page 116

Other books by the same author:
Brave Horace, 1998
Geraldine First, 1996
Horace, 1991

Other books you might like:
Marc Brown, *Arthur in a Pickle*, 1999
    Bad dreams disrupt Arthur's sleep after he lies about his homework in this "Step into Reading" title.
Bill Cosby, *My Big Lie*, 1999
    When Little Bill gives an untruthful explanation for his late arrival at dinner he creates a bigger problem than his tardiness does.

Sam McBratney, *I'm Sorry*, 2000

After a quarrel two friends feel sad and each hopes the other will be first to apologize.

Marissa Moss, *Who Was It?*, 1989

Rather than admit the truth, Isabelle and Jerome offer Mom several incredible stories to explain the broken cookie jar.

Joanne Oppenheim, *Rooter Remembers: A Bank Street Book about Values*, 1991

The stories Rooter Rabbit tells to explain his mother's missing carrot pie eventually lead to the truth—Rooter ate it.

509

HEATHER KELLERHALS-STEWART
WERNER ZIMMERMAN, Illustrator

Brave Highland Heart
(New York: Stoddart Kids, 1999)

Subject(s): Music and Musicians; Traditions; Family
Age range(s): Grades K-2
Major character(s): Mom, Mother; Unnamed Character, Father, Musician; Little One, Daughter, Sister (younger)
Time period(s): 1990s (1999)
Locale(s): Canada

Summary: After spending the day preparing for the ceilidh by sweeping the hayloft, stringing the lights, and cooking with Mom, Little One's excitement about the evening is dampened when her brothers tell her she's too young to stay up all night. Little One can't see much use in having a brave Highland heart if she isn't even allowed to stay up and enjoy the fun. Stuck in the house welcoming the guests while her brothers go to the barn, the pouting little girl refuses to go to sleep. The house is empty, the barn is full and Little One and her dog sit wide-awake on her bed until the sounds of her father's bagpipes begin. Then she quietly sneaks into the barn to listen and her father finds her hiding in the hay. (32 pages)

Where it's reviewed:
Booklist, August 1999, page 2064
Children's Book Review Service, April 1999, page 101
Children's Bookwatch, April 1999, page 4
Quill & Quire, April 1999, page 36
School Library Journal, June 1999, page 98

Other books by the same author:
My Brother's Train, 1997

Other books you might like:
Thomas Locker, *Family Farm*, 1988

A family must work together and change with the times to maintain a successful family farm.

Jonathan London, *The Sugaring-Off Party*, 1995

Paul looks forward to participating for the first time in the family's traditional celebration of the maple syrup harvest.

Maryann N. Weidt, *Daddy Played Music for the Cows*, 1995

A young girl reflects on life on a dairy farm and the music her father plays while he milks the cows.

Laura Ingalls Wilder, *Dance at Grandpa's*, 1994

Adapted from the Little House series, the story tells of the family's preparations for a night of dancing at Grandpa's home.

510

STEVEN KELLOGG, Author/Illustrator

The Missing Mitten Mystery
(New York: Dial Books for Young Readers, 2000)

Subject(s): Lost and Found Possessions; Clothes; Winter
Age range(s): Grades K-3
Major character(s): Annie, Child; Oscar, Dog
Time period(s): 1970s
Locale(s): United States

Summary: Uh Oh! Annie's just discovered that she's lost her fifth mitten of the winter and she's destined for trouble. With Oscar's help Annie retraces her steps and searches all the places she's played today, hoping to find the mitten. Annie finds many lost articles of clothing belonging to her friends, but no red mitten. Annie imagines her mitten being carried off by an eagle to keep a chick's head warm or used by a mouse for a sleeping bag. When rain begins Annie reluctantly goes inside. From the window she sadly watches the rain melting the snowman in the yard. As the snowman melts a red ''heart'' patch begins to appear and Annie finds her mitten! (32 pages)

Where it's reviewed:
Booklist, October 15, 2000, page 435
Horn Book Guide, Spring 2001, page 18
Kirkus Reviews, September 1, 2000, page 1284
Publishers Weekly, July 24, 2000, page 95

Other books by the same author:
The Three Little Pigs, 1997
I Was Born about 10,000 Years Ago, 1996
Mike Fink: A Tall Tale, 1992
Prehistoric Pinkerton, 1987
The Mysterious Tadpole, 1977

Other books you might like:
Jan Brett, *The Mitten: A Ukranian Folktale*, 1990

Nicki's lost mitten becomes a temporary shelter to a large group of animals seeking warmth on a snowy day.

Lisa Campbell Ernst, *Stella Louella's Runaway Book*, 1998

Stella frantically searches for the library book that is due by five o'clock today.

Jules Feiffer, *I Lost My Bear*, 1998

A young girl searches everywhere for her favorite bear, finding many other lost items while the bear turns up in an obvious, but overlooked place.

Joan L. Nodeset, *Who Took the Farmer's Hat?*, 1963

A farmer searches for his lost hat, not taken, but carried away by the wind, and put to good use.

511

STEVEN KELLOGG, Author/Illustrator

The Three Sillies
(Cambridge, MA: Candlewick Press, 1999)

Subject(s): Folklore; Humor; Folk Tales

Age range(s): Grades K-3
Major character(s): Unnamed Character, Young Woman, Daughter; Unnamed Character, Gentleman
Time period(s): Indeterminate Past
Locale(s): Fictional Country

Summary: A gentleman courts a farmer's daughter who goes to the cellar to draw a mug of cider to serve after dinner. While there, the daughter imagines an implausible series of events with such a sad ending that could unfold if she were to marry the gentleman that she begins to cry. When the daughter does not return with cider first her mother and then her father go looking for her and each begins to cry upon hearing the daughter's story. The gentleman finds them awash in tears in the cellar and laughs at the silly sight. Then he resumes his travels seeking three silly people who are sillier than the three in the cellar. It doesn't take long for the gentleman to achieve his goal and fulfill his promise to return and wed the farmer's daughter. Soon enough there is a new family of three sillies destined for adventure. (36 pages)

Where it's reviewed:
Booklist, November 1, 1999, page 531
Horn Book, January 2000, page 87
Kirkus Reviews, November 15, 1999, page 1811
Publishers Weekly, December 13, 1999, page 82
School Library Journal, November 1999, page 143

Other books by the same author:
The Three Little Pigs, 1997
I Was Born about 10,000 Years Ago, 1996
Mike Fink: A Tall Tale, 1992

Other books you might like:
Brock Cole, *Buttons*, 2000
    What could be sillier than three sisters searching for buttons to replace those that popped off pudgy Papa's pants?
Mary Ann Hoberman, *The Two Sillies*, 2000
    Lilly and Sammy have nonsensical strategies for solving problems that are silly, but effective.
Uri Shulevitz, *The Golden Goose*, 1995
    A kind but simple man inadvertently causes an unhappy princess to laugh and wins her hand in marriage.

512

KIM KENNEDY
DOUG KENNEDY, Illustrator

Frankenfrog
(New York: Hyperion, 1999)

Subject(s): Animals/Frogs and Toads; Animals/Insects; Monsters
Age range(s): Grades K-2
Major character(s): Dr. Franken, Scientist; Frankenfrog, Frog; Hyperfly, Fly
Time period(s): Indeterminate
Locale(s): Fictional Country

Summary: Dr. Franken is a brilliant scientist whose most famous invention is hyper-sizing tonic, which does a great job making huge lollypops. One day, an ordinary fly flies into this tonic and becomes—Hyperfly. Now Dr. Franken, realizing the need to combat Hyperfly, turns a regular frog into Frank-enfrog. With Frankenfrog's help, everyone is saved from Hyperfly. (32 pages)

Where it's reviewed:
Bulletin of the Center for Children's Books, October 1999, page 57
Children's Book Review Service, August 1999, page 160
Children's Bookwatch, November 1999, page 6
Publisher's Weekly, August 2, 1999, page 83
School Library Journal, August 1999, page 138

Other books by the same author:
Mr. Bumble Buzzes through the Year, 1998
Mr. Bumble, 1997
Napoleon, 1995

Other books you might like:
Dav Pilkey, *Dogzilla*, 1993
    The residents of Mousopolis must rid themselves of Dogzilla.
Jennifer Rae, *Gilbert de la Frogponde: A Swamp Story*, 1997
    Gilbert must convince two gourmet chefs that bugs, not frogs are all the rage.
Jon Sciezka, *The Frog Prince Continued*, 1991
    An award-winning, satirical and rather different view of the fate of the frog who is transformed into a prince by the kiss of a princess.

513

GABRIELA KESELMAN
PEP MONTSERRAT, Illustrator
LAURA MCKENNA, Translator

The Gift
(Brooklyn, NY: Cranky Nell Book/Kane/Miller Book Publishers, 1999)

Subject(s): Gifts; Birthdays; Parent and Child
Age range(s): Grades K-2
Major character(s): Mikie, Child, Son; Mr. Goodparents, Father, Spouse; Mrs. Goodparents, Mother, Spouse
Time period(s): 1990s (1996)
Locale(s): Spain

Summary: Mr. and Mrs. Goodparents are stuck. Unable to think of an idea for Mikie's birthday present they ask him what he wants and his answer truly stymies them. Mikie describes the perfect gift and with each adjective his parents become more overwhelmed. Mikie says "big" and his parents think elephant, but he wants the gift to "rock from side to side" so maybe he really wants a sailboat. For days Mr. and Mrs. Goodparents think about the nine clues Mikie gives to describe his gift and finally, when his birthday arrives, they apologetically offer a hug in place of the gift they haven't thought of yet. Mikie smiles because the big, strong, soft, sweet, warm hug is just what he wants so his parents rock him from side to side, toss him flying into the air and make him laugh for a long time. The book was originally published in Spain in 1996. (34 pages)

Where it's reviewed:
Children's Book Review Service, February 2000, page 75
Horn Book Guide, Spring 2000, page 43
Kirkus Reviews, November 1, 1999, page 1744
Publishers Weekly, October 1, 1999, page 74

School Library Journal, December 1999, page 100

Other books you might like:

Jez Alborough, *Hug*, 2000
    Bobo searches the jungle for just one thing—a hug from his mother.
Natalie Babbitt, *Bub: Or the Very Best Thing*, 1994
    The King and Queen seek the ''very best thing'' to give their child, but no one understands that, to Prince, ''bub'' means love.
Diane Goode, *Mama's Perfect Present*, 1996
    Two children search the shops of Paris to find just the right gift for Mama's birthday.
Barbara M. Joosse, *I Love You the Purplest*, 1996
    Mama's responses to her sons' many questions affirm her love for each of them.

514

CRISTINA KESSLER
WALTER LYON KRUDOP, Illustrator

My Great-Grandmother's Gourd

(New York: Orchard Books, 2000)

Subject(s): Grandmothers; Change; Deserts
Age range(s): Grades 2-4
Major character(s): Fatima, Child; Grandmother, Grandmother, Aged Person
Time period(s): Indeterminate Past
Locale(s): Sudan

Summary: When Fatima's village installs a pump she is selected to be the first to operate the hand pump to demonstrate the ease with which the villagers can now draw water. No longer will camels be used to draw water from the well nor will the villagers need to laboriously store water in the baobab tree during the rainy season. Grandmother is not ready to completely let go of the old ways. Her family's baobab tree is known as great-grandmother's gourd—for it has stored the family's water for many generations. While villagers mock her, Grandmother prepares her tree for the rain and Fatima joins in the effort as she makes the deep ditch around the tree to trap rainwater. Each time the rains fill the ditch Fatima and Grandmother haul the water by buckets up to the top of the tree and pour it into the hollow cavity. Thus, when the pump breaks from overuse, Grandmother has water to share with her neighbors while they wait for the part needed to fix it. (32 pages)

Where it's reviewed:
Booklist, January 1, 2001, page 970
Horn Book Guide, Spring 2001, page 40
Kirkus Reviews, September 1, 2000, page 1284
School Library Journal, December 2000, page 112

Other books by the same author:
Konte Chameleon Fine, Fine, Fine! A West African Folktale, 1997
All the King's Animals, 1995
One Night: A Story from the Desert, 1995 (Book Links Good Book)

Other books you might like:

Richard E. Albert, *Alejandro's Gift*, 1994
    In the desert of the American Southwest Alejandro digs a water hole as a gift to the animals for easing his loneliness with their presence.
Robin Bernard, *Juma and the Honey Guide: An African Story*, 1996
    Bakari teaches Juma how to follow the honey guide bird a bee's nest, extract the honey and leave a piece of honeycomb as thanks to the bird.
Pete Watson, *The Market Lady and the Mango Tree*, 1994
    The greedy Market Lady learns the importance of the tradition of sharing the fruit that falls from the mango tree.

515

SALLIE KETCHAM
TIMOTHY BUSH, Illustrator

Bach's Big Adventure

(New York: Orchard Books, 1999)

Subject(s): Music and Musicians; Historical
Age range(s): Grades K-3
Major character(s): Johann Sebastian Bach, 10-Year-Old, Musician (organist); Jan Adam Reincken, Historical Figure, Musician
Time period(s): 17th century (1690s)
Locale(s): Ohrdruf, Germany; Hamburg, Germany

Summary: In the author's first book, young Bach is convinced that he is the best organist in all of Germany and the world. His brother disagrees, telling Bach that Adam Reincken of Hamburg is the greatest. Interested in learning more about Reincken, Bach walks to Hamburg to hear Reincken play and is impressed and humbled by his talent. Reincken's willingness to play with Bach gives the young organist the confidence to continue his studies and fulfill his dream of being the best organist in all of Germany and the world. (32 pages)

Where it's reviewed:
Booklist, April 1, 1999, page 1429
Horn Book Guide, Fall 1999, page 257
Publishers Weekly, April 5, 1999, page 241
School Library Journal, June 1999, page 99

Other books you might like:

Barbara Nichol, *Beethoven Lives Upstairs*, 1994
    Through letters to his uncle, Christoph complains about his family's intolerable renter and gains some understanding of the musician's eccentricities.
Andrea Davis Pinkney, *Duke Ellington: The Piano Prince and His Orchestra*, 1998
    An award-winning picture book biography tells of the early life and eventual success of a renowned musician, pianist and composer.
Anne Rachlin, *Bach*, 1992
    A biography of Bach concentrates on his childhood.
Alan Schroeder, *Satchmo's Blues*, 1999
    The story of Louie Armstrong's impoverished childhood expresses his determination to play the cornet.
Jeanette Winter, *Sebastian*, 1999
    A picture book biography describes Bach's later years as a respected composer and organist.

516

HELEN KETTEMAN
KEITH GRAVES, Illustrator

Armadillo Tattletale

(New York: Scholastic Press)

Subject(s): Animals/Armadillos; Animals; Conduct of Life
Age range(s): Grades K-3
Major character(s): Armadillo, Armadillo, Outcast; Alligator, Alligator
Time period(s): Indeterminate Past
Locale(s): Southwest

Summary: Armadillo's very large ears enhance his hearing but make it difficult for him to move quickly. Since Armadillo tends to repeat what he hears to others (and not always accurately) he's not popular with other animals. Armadillo's ears cause him to trip so he never makes it to the water hole first and subsists on murky, muddy water because the other animals refuse to share with him. Armadillo finally angers the wrong animal when he repeats Alligator's conversation incorrectly. Alligator gives Armadillo a piece of her mind and takes from him large pieces of his ears. Seeing his reflection, Armadillo cries at the sight of his tiny ears, but he quickly realizes that, though his eavesdropping days are over, he can now move quickly enough to enjoy all the fresh water he can find—and he does. (32 pages)

Where it's reviewed:
Booklist, December 15, 2000, page 827
Horn Book Guide, Spring 2001, page 40
Kirkus Reviews, August 15, 2000, page 1198
Publishers Weekly, September 25, 2000, page 117
School Library Journal, September 2000, page 201

Other books by the same author:
Bubba, the Cowboy Prince, 1997
Grandma's Cat, 1996
The Christmas Blizzard, 1995
The Year of No More Corn, 1993

Other books you might like:
Verna Aardema, *How the Ostrich Got Its Long Neck*, 1995
    When Ostrich agrees to help Crocodile by pulling out a bothersome tooth he escapes with his life but ends up with a very long neck.
Barbara Knutson, *How the Guinea Fowl Got Her Spots: A Swahili Tale of Friendship*, 1990
    Cow rewards Guinea Fowl with spots to help her hide from predators.
Judy Sierra, *The Mean Hyena: A Folktale from Malawi*, 1997
    This folktale explains why hyenas have rough fur with blotchy coloration and a laughing bark.

517

HELEN KETTEMAN
SCOTT GOTO, Illustrator

Shoeshine Whittaker

(New York: Walker & Company, 1999)

Subject(s): Cleanliness; American West; Tall Tales
Age range(s): Grades K-3
Major character(s): Shoeshine Whittaker, Businessman, Traveler; Clara, Horse; Sheriff Blackstone, Lawman
Time period(s): Indeterminate Past
Locale(s): Mudville

Summary: When Shoeshine Whittaker rolls into Mudville he remarks to Miss Clara that, in the muddy boots of the citizens, they have hit paydirt. The first boots Shoeshine polishes belong to Sheriff Blackstone who is so amazed by the shine that he inspires everyone in the town to pay for one of Shoeshine's guaranteed shines. By nightfall Shoeshine has enough money to move on to the next town after a good night's sleep. Unfortunately, Sheriff Blackstone awakens Shoeshine in the morning complaining that his guaranteed shine is dull and Shoeshine will hang or stand behind his work. Each solution Shoeshine tries creates another problem that Sheriff Blackstone considers to be Shoeshine's responsibility. Finally Shoeshine devises a plan that makes the citizens happy and fills his strongbox with cash. Before Sheriff Blackstone can think of something else Shoeshine and Miss Clara mosey on out of town. (32 pages)

Where it's reviewed:
Booklist, October 15, 1999, page 454
Horn Book Guide, Spring 2000, page 43
Kirkus Reviews, September 15, 1999, page 1502
Publishers Weekly, November 15, 1999, page 66
School Library Journal, October 1999, page 117

Other books by the same author:
Grandma's Cat, 1996
Luck with Potatoes, 1995
The Christmas Blizzard, 1995
The Year of No More Corn, 1993

Other books you might like:
Cynthia DeFelice, *Mule Eggs*, 1994
    Patrick, new to the world of farming, outsmarts a neighbor who has tricked him into buying mule eggs.
Roy Gerrard, *Rosie and the Rustlers*, 1989
    A story in rhyme describes how Rosie catches the rustlers who have stolen her cattle.
Eric A. Kimmel, *Four Dollars and Fifty Cents*, 1990
    When a ne'er-do-well cowboy tries to avoid paying a debt by faking his own death he almost finds himself buried alive.

518

ERIC A. KIMMEL
JON J. MUTH, Illustrator

Gershon's Monster

(New York: Scholastic Press, 2000)

Subject(s): Folklore; Jews; Holidays, Jewish
Age range(s): Grades 2-4
Major character(s): Gershon, Spouse, Baker; Fayga, Spouse, Mother
Time period(s): Indeterminate Past
Locale(s): Constanta, Europe (shores of Black Sea)

Summary: Gershon is an imperfect man known to be impolite, to lose his temper or to tell a small untruth from time to time.

Unfortunately, Gershon never atones for these sins. Rather, he sweeps his mistakes into the cellar once a week and annually bundles them up and tosses them into the sea on Rosh Hashanah. For years Gershon gets away with these unrepentant actions, but when he seeks a rabbi's help to end the childless state of his marriage, the rabbi helps him only because Fayga is a good woman. The charm the rabbi prepares for Fayga comes with a dire prophesy to Gershon, one that forces him to eventually face and atone for his many sins in order to save his children. A concluding author's note gives the background for the story and the steps for repentance. (32 pages)

Where it's reviewed:
Booklist, October 1, 2000, page 362
Bulletin of the Center for Children's Books, October 2000, page 68
Horn Book, September 2000, page 587
Kirkus Reviews, October 1, 2000, page 1425
School Library Journal, September 2000, page 219

Awards the book has won:
Bulletin of the Center for Children's Books Blue Ribbon, 2000
ALA Notable Children's Books, 2001

Other books by the same author:
The Bird's Gift: A Ukranian Easter Story, 1999
A Hanukkah Treasury, 1998
The Magic Dreidels: A Hanukkah Story, 1996
Asher and the Capmakers, 1993
Days of Awe: Stories for Rosh Hashanah and Yom Kippur, 1991

Other books you might like:
Malka Drucker, *The Family Treasury of Jewish Holidays*, 1994
    With stories, games, songs and recipes, a nonfiction title explains ten Jewish holidays and their traditions.
Barbara Diamond Goldin, *The World's Birthday: A Rosh Hashanah Story*, 1990
    Daniel thinks that the way to celebrate this holiday is to invite the world over for a birthday party.
Howard Schwartz, *The Day the Rabbi Disappeared: Jewish Holiday Tales of Magic*, 2000
    Each retold folktale in the illustrated collection links to one of twelve Jewish holidays.
Jane Breskin Zalben, *Happy New Year, Beni*, 1993
    The traditions observed for the Rosh Hashanah celebration help Beni and cousin Max begin to appreciate their differences.

519

ERIC A. KIMMEL
MORDICAI GERSTEIN, Illustrator

The Jar of Fools: Eight Hanukkah Stories from Chelm

(New York: Holiday House, 2000)

Subject(s): Holidays, Jewish; Short Stories; Jews
Age range(s): Grades 1-4
Time period(s): Indeterminate Past

Locale(s): Chelm, Poland

Summary: The collection of eight stories includes some original tales and others based on folklore. All depend on the logic of the citizens of Chelm whose foolishness is explained in the first story. ''How They Play Dreidel in Chelm'' with no letters on the dreidel seems logical after hearing why the citizens of Chelm originally decided to remove the letters. The reasoning of a young boy with no cooking skill but a desire to please his mother when sent to the market for chicken fat to cook the latkes leads him to bring home water knowing it is ''Sweeter than Honey, Purer than Oil'' and save his mother's money. A concluding author's note explains the origins of the stories based on folklore. (56 pages)

Where it's reviewed:
Booklist, September 1, 2000, page 133
Horn Book, September 2000, page 587
Publishers Weekly, September 25, 2000, page 66
School Library Journal, October 2000, page 64

Other books by the same author:
The Magic Dreidels: A Hanukkah Story, 1996
The Chanukkah Guest, 1990
Hershel and the Hanukkah Goblins, 1989 (Caldecott Honor Book)

Other books you might like:
Malka Drucker, *The Family Treasury of Jewish Holidays*, 1994
    Traditions, songs, stories and recipes associated with nine holidays of the Jewish year are included in an award-winning collection.
Barbara Diamond Goldin, *While the Candles Burn: Eight Stories for Hanukkah*, 1996
    Themes of each of eight stories support the lesson of why Hanukkah is celebrated.
Steve Sanfield, *The Feather Merchants and Other Tales of the Fools of Chelm*, 1991
    Thirteen tales drawn from Jewish folklore offer humor and heritage.

520

ERIC A. KIMMEL

Sword of the Samurai: Adventure Stories from Japan

(San Diego: Browndeer Press/Harcourt Brace & Company, 1999)

Subject(s): Samurai; Cultures and Customs; Short Stories
Age range(s): Grades 4-7
Time period(s): Indeterminate Past
Locale(s): Japan

Summary: Eleven stories tell of the service, courage and honor of the samurai. The first tale in the collection, ''Dohaku's Head,'' is one of a samurai who is ambushed and beheaded yet still becomes the victor rather than the vanquished. Hido, an unlucky samurai, has a change of fortune in the nick of time in ''The Samurai and the Dragon.'' ''The Ronin and the Tea Master'' demonstrates that skill does not need to be in the martial arts in order to win a sword fight. The book concludes with a glossary of Samurai terms and source notes for the stories. (114 pages)

Where it's reviewed:
The Book Report, November 1999, page 70
Booklist, March 15, 1999, page 1329
Publishers Weekly, April 5, 1999, page 242
Riverbank Review, Fall 1999, page 40
School Library Journal, June 1999, page 132

Other books by the same author:
Billy Lazroe and the King of the Sea, 1996
Onions and Garlic, 1996
Three Sacks of Truth: A Story from France, 1993

Other books you might like:
Jan Freeman Long, *The Bee and the Dream: A Japanese Tale*, 1996
   A traditional tale explains that wealth is sometimes found where we least expect it.
Rafe Martin, *Mysterious Tales of Japan*, 1996
   Each of ten illustrated traditional tales begins with a haiku while the collection concludes with source notes and a bibliography.
Eric Quayle, *The Shining Princess and Other Japanese Legends*, 1989
   An illustrated collection includes ten Japanese folktales.

521

LESLIE KIMMELMAN
PAUL YALOWITZ, Illustrator

The Runaway Latkes

(Morton Grove, IL: Albert Whitman & Company, 2000)

Subject(s): Holidays, Jewish; Cooks and Cooking; Cultures and Customs
Age range(s): Grades K-2
Major character(s): Rebecca Bloom, Cook
Time period(s): 2000s
Locale(s): United States

Summary: Known as the best latke cook in the synagogue, Rebecca arrives early to begin cooking enough for the evening Hanukkah celebration. Her plans take a detour when three latkes leap out of the frying pan and begin rolling away while singing a taunting little ditty. Rebecca races after the latkes, calling for them to stop. The latkes keep rolling as more and more people join the chase. By the time the latkes are captured (and eaten by the pursuers) quite a crowd has gathered. Rebecca invites them all to return to the synagogue later after she cooks more latkes. A recipe is included. (32 pages)

Where it's reviewed:
Booklist, September 1, 2000, page 133
Horn Book Guide, Spring 2001, page 41
Kirkus Reviews, August 15, 2000, page 1199
Publishers Weekly, September 25, 2000, page 66
School Library Journal, October 2000, page 65

Other books by the same author:
Hooray! It's Passover!, 1996
Hanukkah Lights, Hanukkah Nights, 1992
Me and Nana, 1990

Other books you might like:
Jim Aylesworth, *The Gingerbread Man*, 1998
   An impertinent gingerbread man runs away from his creators, a butcher, a cow and a sow and into the mouth of a clever fox.
Richard Egielski, *The Gingerbread Boy*, 1997
   A rat, street musicians and a construction crew chase the Gingerbread Boy through the streets of New York until he meets the fox.
Joan Rothenberg, *Inside-Out Grandma*, 1995
   As Rosie learns to latkes she also learns that her grandma wears her clothes inside out as a reminder to purchase the needed oil.

522

STEPHEN MICHAEL KING, Author/Illustrator

Henry and Amy (Right-Way-Round and Upside Down)

(New York: Walker and Company, 1999)

Subject(s): Friendship; Individuality; Self-Acceptance
Age range(s): Grades K-1
Major character(s): Henry, Child, Friend; Amy, Child, Friend
Time period(s): 1990s (1998)
Locale(s): Australia

Summary: Although Henry is a happy little boy he always seems to end up doing the opposite of what he intends to do—his straight lines become wiggly and rain spoils his picnic plans. So, one day while Henry walks backward although he really wants to walk forward, he accidentally bumps into perfect Amy. Nothing ever goes wrong for Amy—she can write her name, she remembers her umbrella and she knows right from left. Henry is impressed and pleased that Amy is willing to teach him front from back and to work together with him to plan and build a tree house. Then, Henry learns that Amy isn't really happy being perfect so he teaches her how to be topsy-turvy and right-way-round and upside down. (32 pages)

Where it's reviewed:
Booklist, June 1999, page 1842
Horn Book Guide, Fall 1999, page 236
Kirkus Reviews, April 15, 1999, page 631
Magpies, November 1998, page 5
School Library Journal, June 1999, page 99

Other books by the same author:
A Special Kind of Love, 1996

Other books you might like:
Anthony Browne, *Willy and Hugh*, 1991
   The chimp and the gorilla find that their differences contribute to the success of their friendship.
Laurie A. Jacobs, *So Much in Common*, 1994
   Neighbors Philomena and Horace discover that, despite their obvious differences, they have just enough in common for a friendship.
Arnold Lobel, *Frog and Toad Are Friends*, 1970
   In several brief stories, Frog and Toad share some of the difficulties as well as the pleasures of friendship.

Ellen Stoll Walsh, *Hop Jump*, 1993

A blue frog decides she is tired of hopping and learns to dance, starting a new trend for other frogs as well.

523

DICK KING-SMITH
LINA CHESAK, Illustrator

Charlie Muffin's Miracle Mouse

(New York: Crown Publishers, Inc., 1999)

Subject(s): Animals/Mice; Inventions; Contests
Age range(s): Grades 3-5
Major character(s): Charlie Muffin, Taxidermist, Inventor; Merry Day, Animal Lover; Adam Muffin, Mouse
Time period(s): 1990s (1999)
Locale(s): England

Summary: Among his many talents, Charlie Muffin is an extraordinary mouse farmer, breeding them in all colors, selling them as pets and stuffing the deceased ones as household decorations. When Merry Day purchases two mice as pets she also inspires Charlie Muffin to take up her challenge to breed a green mouse. His first attempts are futile, but Merry keeps making suggestions and finally, Adam Muffin, a pea green mouse, is born. During his short life he is named Supreme Champion at a mouse show and after his death takes his place of honor on the mantel. (105 pages)

Where it's reviewed:
Booklist, April 15, 1999, page 1528
Horn Book Guide, Fall 1999, page 279
Kirkus Reviews, March 15, 1999, page 459
Publishers Weekly, February 22, 1999, page 96
School Library Journal, June 1999, page 132

Other books by the same author:
Mr. Ape, 1998
The Water Horse, 1998
A Mouse Called Wolf, 1997
Mr. Potter's Pet, 1996
The School Mouse, 1995 (School Library Journal Best Book)

Other books you might like:
David A. Adler, *The Many Troubles of Andy Russell*, 1998
One of Andy's troubles is the escaped pet gerbils that he frantically tries to return to their cages before his parents discover they're loose.
Mary Hoffman, *The Four-Legged Ghosts*, 1993
The normal-looking white mouse Alex receives as a pet soon demonstrates the unusual power to call up the ghosts of the home's previous pets.
Karen Waggoner, *Partners*, 1995
His sister's hungry cat and his brother's plans to sell the animals as snake food make Jamie question the wisdom of his plans to raise pet mice.

524

DICK KING-SMITH
ANN KRONHEIMER, Illustrator

Mysterious Miss Slade

(New York: Crown Publishers, 2000)

Subject(s): Conduct of Life; Neighbors and Neighborhoods; Animals
Age range(s): Grades 2-4
Major character(s): Miss Slade, Recluse, Aged Person; Patsy Reader, 8-Year-Old, Sister; Jim Reader, 6-Year-Old, Brother
Time period(s): 1990s
Locale(s): Blackberry Bottom, England

Summary: When Patsy and Jim move into the cottage on the hill above Blackberry Bottom Miss Slade's wish for young companionship seems to be coming true. Since they are new to the neighborhood, Patsy and Jim are unaware of the rumors that disheveled reclusive Miss Slade is a witch. After their experience with the very gracious old woman, Patsy and Jim don't believe the rumors when they are told them. For the first time in many years, Miss Slade has friends. The entire Reader family takes an interest in Miss Slade and she, in turn, responds to the gestures of friendship by modifying her life slightly, cleaning up her living quarters and using some modern conveniences. Originally published in Great Britain in 1999 and titled *The Witch of Blackberry Bottom*. (123 pages)

Where it's reviewed:
Booklist, August 2000, page 2140
Horn Book, July 2000, page 458
Publishers Weekly, June 26, 2000, page 75
School Library Journal, July 2000, page 81

Other books by the same author:
The Water Horse, 1998
A Mouse Called Wolf, 1997
Mr. Potter's Pet, 1996
The School Mouse, 1995 (School Library Journal Best Book)

Other books you might like:
Marianna Dengler, *The Worry Stone*, 1996
Elderly Amanda befriends a sad young boy she sees daily at the park easing the loneliness felt by both.
Berlie Doherty, *Willa and Old Miss Annie*, 1994
Willa, lonely after moving away from her best friend, develops a friendship with an elderly neighbor and helps her care for animals in need.
Carolyn J. Gold, *Dragonfly Secret*, 1997
Although Gramps is growing older, Nathan and Jessie do not agree with Aunt Louise's plan to put him in a nursing home.
Marilyn Singer, *Josie to the Rescue*, 1999
Second grader Josie's many ideas to assist her family are more inspired than helpful.

525

DICK KING-SMITH
PETER BAILEY, Illustrator

Spider Sparrow

(New York: Crown Publishers Inc., 2000)

Subject(s): Farm Life; Parent and Child; Mentally Handicapped
Age range(s): Grades 4-6
Major character(s): John Joseph ''Spider'' Sparrow, Abandoned Child, Mentally Challenged Person; Tom Sparrow, Father, Shepherd; Percy Pound, Foreman, Farmer
Time period(s): 20th century (1926-1942)
Locale(s): Wylye Valley, England (Outoverdown Farm)

Summary: Tom and his wife willingly raise an infant abandoned in one of the lambing pens. As the boy grows it becomes obvious to everyone that his development is not normal. As a toddler he neither crawls nor walks but moves about with such an odd motion that he's soon known as Spider. Spider's parents love him unconditionally, protect him as best they can from the taunts of the village bullies and nurture his gifts. Though his speech is delayed, Spider can mimic the sound of any bird or animal and communicates more easily with animals both wild and domestic than with humans. When the outset of World War II takes the young farm hands to military service, Percy turns to the teen-aged Spider for help on the farm with work such as scaring the crows out of newly sown fields and polishing tack. Though Spider is neither bright nor agile, he does his simple jobs with dedication and diligence and without complaint in all kinds of weather. Unschooled and unaware of threatening world events, the kind, happy, loved young man lives his life to the fullest. Originally published in Great Britain in 1998 as *The Crowstarver*. (163 pages)

Where it's reviewed:
Booklist, January 1, 2000, page 924
Horn Book Guide, Fall 2000, page 306
Publishers Weekly, December 6, 1999, page 77
Riverbank Review, Summer 2000, page 40
School Library Journal, March 2000, page 239

Other books by the same author:
Mr. Ape, 1998
The Water Horse, 1998
Mr. Potter's Pet, 1996
The School Mouse, 1995 (School Library Journal Best Book)
Babe: The Gallant Pig, 1991 (Boston Globe-Horn Book Honor Book)

Other books you might like:
Sara Harrell Banks, *Under the Shadow of Wings*, 1997
    In 1940s Alabama, as Tatnall grows into a mature teenager her cousin Obie, whom she's spent a lifetime protecting, remains childlike.
Betsy Byars, *Summer of the Swans*, 1970
    Sarah's handicapped brother runs away and is later found visiting the swans.
Paula Fox, *Radiance Descending*, 1997
    Paul's parents love Jacob and accept his limitations but Paul is embarrassed by his brother's loud clumsy behavior.

Harry Mazer, *The Wild Kid*, 1998
    When Sammy becomes lost in the woods the handicapped boy stumbles onto a runaway's hideout.

526

DANIEL KIRK, Author/Illustrator

Humpty Dumpty

(New York: G.P. Putnam's Sons)

Subject(s): Kings, Queens, Rulers, etc.; Birthdays; Stories in Rhyme
Age range(s): Grades K-1
Major character(s): Humpty Dumpty, Son; King Moe, Child, Son
Time period(s): Indeterminate Past
Locale(s): Fictional Country

Summary: Bored Humpty Dumpty begs his mom to allow him to attend the parade celebrating King Moe's birthday and she reluctantly agrees. As eager as Humpty is to get out of the house, King Moe is to stay inside. A timid child, he hates the parade, the clowns and his high coach with no seat belts. His mother insists he participate and so it happens that when Humpty tumbles from the brick wall serving as his vantage point for viewing the parade the egg crashes through the roof of King Moe's carriage. King Moe uses his skill with jigsaw puzzles and a few band-aids to put Humpty together again and then the two new friends head to Humpty's house to play. (32 pages)

Where it's reviewed:
Booklist, May 15, 2000, page 1757
Horn Book Guide, Fall 2000, page 272
Kirkus Reviews, May 1, 2000, page 634
New York Times Book Review, May 14, 2000, page 22
School Library Journal, June 2000, page 118

Other books by the same author:
Hush, Little Alien, 1999
Trash Trucks!, 1997
Lucky's 24-Hour Garage, 1996

Other books you might like:
David Martin, *Five Little Piggies*, 1998
    The story behind the nursery rhyme about the activities of young pigs explains, in five brief episodes, the meaning of each piggy's adventure.
Ann McGovern, *Eggs on Your Nose*, 1987
    In this rhyming tale a child makes a huge mess just eating eggs.
Anne Miranda, *To Market, to Market*, 1997
    After the fat pig is purchased this story in rhyme diverges from the traditional nursery rhyme.
John O'Brien, *Mother Hubbard's Christmas*, 1996
    Ignoring her bare cupboard Mother Hubbard tries to prepare for the holidays in this rhyming tale but her big blue dog has plans of his own.

527

DANIEL KIRK, Author/Illustrator

Moondogs

(New York: G.P. Putnam's Sons, 1999)

Subject(s): Animals/Dogs; Pets; Stories in Rhyme
Age range(s): Grades K-2
Major character(s): Willy Joe Jehosephat, Child, Space Explorer; Scrappy, Dog (stray)
Time period(s): 1990s (1999)
Locale(s): United States; Moon (Earth's)

Summary: When Will's parents decide he needs a pet to provide companionship to the boy who is content to gaze at stars, not just any pet will satisfy Will. He admires moondogs and builds a rocket in the garage that he launches for the moon intent on selecting a special pet. While traveling, Will takes a snack break and finds a stowaway that has eaten the food. Will names the thin dog Scrappy and plans to trade him for a moondog, but reconsiders after Scrappy saves him from the monstrous man in the moon. Together the boy and his dog return to Earth and become companion stargazers. (32 pages)

Where it's reviewed:
Booklist, March 15, 1999, page 1333
Horn Book, March 1999, page 193
Kirkus Reviews, January 1, 1999, page 67
Publishers Weekly, March 15, 1999, page 59
School Library Journal, March 1999, page 177

Other books by the same author:
Bigger, 1998
Trash Trucks!, 1997
Lucky's 24-Hour Garage, 1996

Other books you might like:
Martha Alexander, *You're a Genius, Blackboard Bear*, 1995
    With help from Blackboard Bear, Anthony builds a spaceship to the moon.
David Milgrim, *Here in Space*, 1997
    With his dog and his bike a young boy explores the uniqueness of the planet earth, suspended in outer space.
Dan Yaccarino, *Zoom! Zoom! Zoom! I'm Off to the Moon!*, 1997
    In a bright red rocket a young boy travels to the moon, collects some rocks and returns safely to Earth in time for a good night's sleep.

528

DANIEL KIRK, Author/Illustrator

Snow Family

(New York: Hyperion Books for Children, 2000)

Subject(s): Fantasy; Parent and Child; Stories in Rhyme
Age range(s): Grades K-2
Major character(s): Jacob, Child, Son
Time period(s): Indeterminate Past
Locale(s): United States

Summary: Jacob leaves his chores in the barn to scurry after a group of snow children. He straightens their scarves, looks for their lost carrot noses and worries that they have no one to care for them. The snow children play recklessly and waken a bear in his den. The snow children scamper away safely, but Jacob seeks refuge in a tree. Fortunately his parents come and scare the bear away. Jacob knows just what the snow children need—a family—so the next day he makes snow parents to take care of them. (32 pages)

Where it's reviewed:
Booklist, September 1, 2000, page 130
Horn Book Guide, Spring 2001, page 18
Publishers Weekly, September 11, 2000, page 90
School Library Journal, September 2000, page 201

Other books by the same author:
Humpty Dumpty, 2000
Hush, Little Alien, 1999
Lucky's 24-Hour Garage, 1996

Other books you might like:
Lois Ehlert, *Snowballs*, 1995
    Simple text and clear collages tell of the creation of a snow family and the inevitable result as the weather warms.
Ezra Jack Keats, *The Snowy Day*, 1962
    The Caldecott Medal winner portrays a young child's enjoyment of the season's first snowfall.
Steve Sanfield, *Snow*, 1995
    A young boy marvels at the beauty of the newly fallen snow dotted with the tracks of passing animals.

529

DAVID KIRK, Author/Illustrator

Little Miss Spider

(New York: Scholastic Press, 1999)

Subject(s): Mothers; Animals/Spiders; Mothers and Daughters
Age range(s): Grades K-1
Major character(s): Little Miss Spider, Spider, Child; Betty, Insect (beetle)
Time period(s): Indeterminate
Locale(s): United States

Summary: When Little Miss Spider is born, she looks around for her mother, but can't find her. Betty kindly offers to help her search. Eventually a bigger spider advises Little Miss Spider to look up in a nest, but instead of finding her own mother she finds a mother bird intent on feeding Little Miss Spider to her young. After Betty rescues Little Miss Spider, she invites the babe to live with her and Little Miss Spider learns that a mother is "the one who loves you best." (32 pages)

Where it's reviewed:
Booklist, December 1, 1999, page 712
Children's Bookwatch, January 2000, page 7
Horn Book Guide, Spring 2000, page 18
Publishers Weekly, September 20, 1999, page 87
School Library Journal, November 1999, page 121

Other books by the same author:
Miss Spider's ABC, 1998
Miss Spider's New Car, 1997
Miss Spider's Tea Party, 1994

Other books you might like:

Molly Bang, *Goose*, 1996

After a storm blows a goose egg out of its nest and into a woodchuck's den, the goose is raised by the woodchucks.

Janell Cannon, *Stellaluna*, 1993

Separated from her mother, Stellaluna, the fruit bat, falls into a bird's nest where she is treated like one of the family.

P.D. Eastman, *Are You My Mother?*, 1960

After falling from the nest, a baby bird tries to find its mother.

Keiko Kasza, *A Mother for Choco*, 1992

While searching for its mother, a young bird is adopted by a bear.

530

KATHERINE KIRKPATRICK
RONALD HIMLER, Illustrator

Redcoats and Petticoats

(New York: Holiday House, 1999)

Subject(s): Revolutionary War; American History; Spies
Age range(s): Grades 3-5
Major character(s): Thomas Strong, Son, Patriot; Mother, Patriot, Spy; Father, Patriot, Father
Time period(s): 1770s; 1780s (1778-1784)
Locale(s): Setauket, New York (Long Island)

Summary: After British soldiers imprison Father and move into Thomas's home, Mother moves the family to a cottage on the water. There, Mother's changed behavior puzzles and concerns Thomas. Daily, Mother hangs red petticoats on the clothesline and sends Thomas out in the rowboat to fish or clam, always to a distant bay with instructions to look for a whaleboat. Thomas is fearful because British soldiers sometimes accost him and steal his catch. When Mother learns where Father is imprisoned she and Thomas barter for his freedom with the last of the season's vegetable harvest. Not until the war ends does Thomas realize that Mother has been an important part of a spy ring sending messages to the Patriot army. (32 pages)

Where it's reviewed:

Booklist, March 1, 1999, page 1213
Horn Book Guide, Fall 1999, page 279
Kirkus Reviews, February 15, 1999, page 301
School Library Journal, April 1999, page 100

Other books by the same author:

Trouble's Daughter: The Story of Susanna Hutchinson, Indian Captive, 1998

Other books you might like:

Lisa Banim, *A Spy in the King's Colony*, 1994

Emily and Maggie try to continue their routine activities despite the occupation of Boston by the British and worry about who might be a Loyalist spy.

Sarah Garland, *Seeing Red*, 1996

A display of bright red petticoats along the cliff tops fools the French forces into thinking the British are defending the cliffs.

Karen B. Winnick, *Sybil's Night Ride*, 2000

Sybil, teenage daughter of a Patriot colonel, courageously rides through the night to warn her father that the British are burning Danbury, New York.

531

SATOSHI KITAMURA, Author/Illustrator

Me and My Cat?

(New York: Farrar Straus Giroux, 2000)

Subject(s): Animals/Cats; Magic; Witches and Witchcraft
Age range(s): Grades K-3
Major character(s): Nicholas, Child, Student—Elementary School; Leonardo, Cat
Time period(s): 1990s (1999)
Locale(s): England

Summary: There's something strange about the night-time visit Nicholas receives from a witch who comes in through his bedroom window, mumbles something and leaves without saying good-bye. In the morning Nicholas realizes just how strange when he discovers that he's at home in the body of his cat while Leonardo's psyche embodied in his form has just been put on the school bus. Quickly Nicholas learns of the challenges of Leonardo's life—being put outside for misbehaving and having three neighborhood cats pick a fight with him. At the end of the school day Nicholas can see that the day has not been easy for Leonardo either as he sits on the stoop wondering how to get a boy's body through the cat door. Nicholas and his pet are sent to bed early where the witch visits them again, apologizes for getting the wrong address, mumbles a few words and leaves without saying good-bye. The title was first published in Great Britain in 1999. (40 pages)

Where it's reviewed:

Booklist, March 1, 2000, page 1250
Horn Book, March 2000, page 187
Publishers Weekly, March 20, 2000, page 91
Riverbank Review, Summer 2000, page 32
School Library Journal, March 2000, page 209

Other books by the same author:

Goldfish Hide-and-Seek, 1997
Sheep in Wolves' Clothing, 1996
A Boy Wants a Dinosaur, 1990
Captain Toby, 1988
When Sheep Cannot Sleep, 1986

Other books you might like:

William Joyce, *George Shrinks*, 1985

When George awakens shrunk to the size of a mouse he wonders how he'll care for his cat and his baby brother.

John O'Brien, *Poof!*, 1999

A couple of wizards complete their household chores by transforming them and each other into something else.

David Small, *Imogene's Antlers*, 2000

In a reissue of a 1985 title Imogene grows antlers while sleeping, a condition she accepts more easily than her parents do.

532

ELISA KLEVEN, Author/Illustrator

A Monster in the House

(New York: Dutton Children's Books, 1998)

Subject(s): Brothers and Sisters; Babies; Monsters
Age range(s): Grades K-2
Major character(s): Unnamed Character, Child, Neighbor; Unnamed Character, Child, Sister (older); Unnamed Character, Baby, Brother
Time period(s): 1990s (1998)
Locale(s): United States

Summary: As new neighbors unload their belongings from a truck, a child dressed as a monster roars about, complaining about the new house. Spotting the girl next door, he asks if she's interested in playing monster. The girl declines because a "real" monster is sleeping in her house. Fascinated, the boy asks many questions about the monster, imagining from the girl's description a huge grotesque hair-pulling creature that spits food on everyone and sucks his toes. Gradually, the responses cause the boy to revise his image into something smaller and softer and soon he meets the monster—the girl's baby brother! (32 pages)

Where it's reviewed:
Booklist, October 1, 1998, page 335
Children's Book Review Service, January 1999, page 51
Kirkus Reviews, September 1, 1998, page 1287
Publishers Weekly, October 5, 1998
School Library Journal, January 1999, page 96

Other books by the same author:
The Puddle Pail, 1997 (School Library Journal Best Book)
Hooray, a Pinata!, 1996 (Booklist Editors' Choice)
The Paper Princess, 1994

Other books you might like:
Mary Jane Auch, *Monster Brother*, 1994
    Rodney gains relief from his nightly fear of monsters when his crying baby brother Sidney turns out to be the ultimate monster-chaser.
John Hassett, *We Got My Brother at the Zoo*, 1993
    Mary Margaret has some unusual stories to tell about the origins of the new baby at her house. Ann Hassett, co-author.
Salvatore Murdocca, *Baby Wants the Moon*, 1995
    Fear of displacement by the new baby is expressed in Sonny's dreams that his new sister is growing into a giant.

533

SUZY KLINE
FRANK REMKIEWICZ, Illustrator

Horrible Harry at Halloween

(New York: Viking, 2000)

Subject(s): Schools; Halloween; Students
Age range(s): Grades 2-3
Major character(s): Doug, 3rd Grader, Friend; Harry Spooger, 3rd Grader, Detective—Amateur; Miss Mackle, Teacher
Time period(s): 2000s (2000)
Locale(s): Connecticut

Summary: Harry's reputation for scary costumes has everyone wondering what he will wear this year. On Halloween morning Doug is the first to arrive wearing his centaur costume. He willingly assists Miss Mackle, dressed as a witch, with preparations for class. Just as the bell rings Harry arrives. The students are disappointed to see Harry dressed in a coat and tie as if he's coming from church. In fact, for Halloween this year Harry is adopting the costume and persona of Sergeant Joe Friday and from his dialogue it's obvious that he's watched a lot of reruns in order to perfect his imitation. After lunch Harry's detecting skills are used to solve the case of a classmate dressed as Tinker Bell who has lost her box of pixie dust. (64 pages)

Where it's reviewed:
Booklist, September 15, 2000, page 241
Horn Book Guide, Spring 2001, page 63
Kirkus Reviews, August 1, 2000, page 1118
Publishers Weekly, September 25, 2000, page 65
School Library Journal, September 2000, page 202

Other books by the same author:
Horrible Harry Goes to the Moon, 2000
Horrible Harry Moves Up to Third Grade, 1998
Horrible Harry and the Drop of Doom, 1998
Horrible Harry and the Purple People, 1997
Horrible Harry's Secret, 1992

Other books you might like:
Marion Dane Bauer, *Alison's Fierce and Ugly Halloween*, 1997
    Forsaking the ballerina and fairy costumes of her past, Alison's seeks to be scary this year but she's not succeeding despite her pirate costume.
Patricia Reilly Giff, *Beast and the Halloween Horror*, 1990
    When an author unexpectedly accepts Beast's offer to be in his school's Halloween parade Beast realizes he's facing a horror of his own making.
Kate McMullan, *Fluffy's Happy Halloween*, 1998
    Fluffy, the class pet, participates in the school's Halloween activities in the "Hello Reader" story.

534

SUZY KLINE
FRANK REMKIEWICZ, Illustrator

Song Lee and the "I Hate You" Notes

(New York: Viking, 1999)

Subject(s): Schools; Behavior; Korean Americans
Age range(s): Grades 2-4
Major character(s): Doug, 3rd Grader; Song Lee Park, 3rd Grader; Mary, 3rd Grader
Time period(s): 1990s (1999)
Locale(s): United States

Summary: Doug cannot understand why anyone would send "I hate you" notes to Song Lee, the nicest girl in class. After Song Lee receives two such notes, Doug, with help from a classmate, figures out that their classmate, Mary, is the anonymous sender. When their teacher reads a story about someone receiving hate notes and encourages class discussion about such notes, Song Lee finds a way to respond. Mary is initially angry to receive Song Lee's note, but she finally admits to her wrongdoing and tries to be friendly. (51 pages)

Where it's reviewed:
Booklist, May 1, 1999, page 1594
Horn Book Guide, Fall 1999, page 279
School Library Journal, June 1999, page 99

Other books by the same author:
Horrible Harry Moves Up to Third Grade, 1998
Horrible Harry and the Drop of Doom, 1998
Marvin and the Mean Words, 1997
Song Lee and the Leech Man, 1995
Song Lee in Room 2B, 1993

Other books you might like:
Beverly Cleary, *Ramona Quimby, Age 8*, 1982
    A Newbery Honor book continues the story of energetic Ramona and the humorous trials and tribulations of life at school and at home.
Paula Danziger, *Amber Brown Is Not a Crayon*, 1994
    Third grader Amber Brown learns the importance of communication to the success of a friendship.
Betsy Duffey, *How to Be Cool in the Third Grade*, 1993
    Robbie views third grade as an opportunity to grow and change.
Patricia Reilly Giff, *Today Was a Terrible Day*, 1980
    A kind note from his teacher helps 2nd-grader Ronald Morgan feel better about his miserable day at school.

535

JACKIE FRENCH KOLLER
LYNN MUNSINGER, Illustrator

One Monkey Too Many

(San Diego: Harcourt Brace & Company, 1999)

Subject(s): Animals/Monkeys; Stories in Rhyme; Behavior
Age range(s): Grades K-1
Time period(s): 1990s
Locale(s): Fictional Country

Summary: One monkey over the recommended limit for a bike, golf cart and a canoe cause calamity for all the monkeys aboard. The silly monkeys do not learn their lesson and crowd one too many monkeys at a restaurant table causing a disastrous meal and one too many into a hotel bed leads to a mini war. The monkeys even crowd one too many into the pages of the book while the author is at lunch. What a mess, what fun, one too many for everyone! (32 pages)

Where it's reviewed:
Booklist, April 15, 1999, page 1536
Horn Book, March 1999, page 194
Publishers Weekly, April 19, 1999, page 72
School Library Journal, May 1999, page 92

Other books by the same author:
Bouncing on the Bed, 1999
No Such Thing, 1997 (Bulletin of the Center for Children's Books Blue Ribbon)
Fish Fry Tonight, 1992
Mole and Shrew, 1991

Other books you might like:
Eileen Christelow, *Five Little Monkeys with Nothing to Do*, 1996
    Mama has plenty for these bored monkeys to do in preparation for Grandma Bessie's visit.
Nancy Jewell, *Silly Times with Two Silly Trolls*, 1996
    Three brief stories in an award-winning beginning reader continue the escapades of silly trolls Nip and Tuck.
H.A. Rey, *Curious George*, 1941
    George is introduced in the first of many tales about the young primate whose curiosity leads to unexpected adventure.

536

JACKIE FRENCH KOLLER
JACQUELINE ROGERS, Illustrator

The Promise

(New York: Alfred A. Knopf, 1999)

Subject(s): Animals/Dogs; Grief; Christmas
Age range(s): Grades 3-5
Major character(s): Pa, Father, Widow(er); Matt, 10-Year-Old, Brother (older); Sara, Dog
Time period(s): Indeterminate Past
Locale(s): United States

Summary: Still grieving over his mother's recent death, Matt is determined to follow the Christmas traditions that she established. On Christmas Eve, while Matt ties suet balls for the birds on a tree near the barn, he and Sara spot a bear between them and the cabin. Not realizing the bear is following the scent of the suet in the bag he carries, Matt takes off running trying to get away so he can circle back to the house. Instead he becomes lost and Sara, while trying to protect him, is seriously injured. Matt stays with Sara until a voice—an angel's or Sara's—tells him to find Pa and gives him directions home. Pa helps Matt carry Sara to the doctor who is not hopeful of her recovery, but on Christmas morning she is still alive. Matt is sure his deceased mother is responsible for the miracle. (71 pages)

Where it's reviewed:
Booklist, September 1, 1999, page 145
Horn Book Guide, Spring 2000, page 67
School Library Journal, October 1999, page 67

Other books by the same author:
Dragon Trouble, 1997 (Dragonling, Number 5)
The Dragonling, 1995 (Dragonling, Number 1)
The Last Voyage of the Misty Day, 1992
Nothing to Fear, 1991

Other books you might like:
Eth Clifford, *The Remembering Box*, 1985
    Grandma's gift to Joshua of a ''remembering'' box helps to console him after her death.
Kevin Henkes, *Sun & Spoon*, 1997
    Struggling to understand his grief, Spoon believes that possessing something that was once Grandma's will assure that he'll never forget her.

Susan Hart Lundquist, *Wander*, 1998
James and Sary find a stray dog that provides needed love and comfort following their mother's death.

537

LISA KOPPER, Author/Illustrator

Daisy Knows Best

(New York: Dutton Children's Books, 1999)

Subject(s): Animals/Dogs; Babies; Behavior
Age range(s): Preschool
Major character(s): Daisy, Dog, Mother; Baby, Baby; Mommy, Mother
Time period(s): 1990s (1998)
Locale(s): England

Summary: Daisy is a diligent instructor to her three puppies, teaching them how to open the mail, set the table and go to the bathroom. Baby watches carefully and mimics the puppy's behavior. When Daisy leads her pups outside to teach them how to clean up the garbage and dig in the garden, Baby follows and teaches Daisy how to fold laundry. Baby also tries to teach Mommy when she appears, aghast at the mess before her. Mommy is more interested in teaching Baby and the dogs about the necessity of a bath at the end of a busy day. The title was first published in Great Britain in 1998. (28 pages)

Where it's reviewed:
Booklist, January 1, 1999, page 888
Horn Book Guide, Fall 1999, page 236
Kirkus Reviews, December 15, 1998, page 1799
Publishers Weekly, January 4, 1999, page 88
School Library Journal, April 1999, page 101

Other books by the same author:
Daisy Is a Mommy, 1998
I'm a Baby, You're a Baby, 1995
Daisy Thinks She's a Baby, 1994
Ten Little Babies, 1990

Other books you might like:
Alexandra Day, *Follow Carl!*, 1998
When the neighborhood children play follow the leader, Carl, a gentle lab, positions himself right at the front of the line.
Charlotte Voake, *Mr. Davies and the Baby*, 1996
Mr. Davies, a curious dog, invites himself along for the neighbor's daily stroll with her baby.
Rosemary Wells, *The McDuff Series*, 1997-
A West Highland terrier finds a home, adjusts to a baby's arrival and saves Santa Claus from the chimney in an award-winning series.

538

GORDON KORMAN
VICTOR VACCARO, Illustrator

Nose Pickers from Outer Space

(New York: Hyperion Books for Children, 1999)

Series: L.A.F.

Subject(s): Aliens; Schools; Humor
Age range(s): Grades 3-5
Major character(s): Devin Hunter, 4th Grader; Stan Mflxnys, Student—Exchange, Alien
Time period(s): 1990s (1999)
Locale(s): United States

Summary: Most of the kids in Devin's class are buddies to cool exchange students through the National Student Exchange Program. So, Devin wonders why he got a dweeb like Stan who not only wears a tie, sports a crewcut, has glasses as thick as soda bottles, but who also sticks his finger up his nose in class! Devin soon figures out that there is more to Stan than anyone suspects. In fact, Devin discovers that Stan is an alien with a computer up his nose. He's been sent from the planet Pan to scout the earth as a tourist location for fellow "Pants." Having alien tourists might not be bad, but if earth doesn't win the competition, the Pants plan to move it to an orbit farther away for the sun so it won't disturb the view. (137 pages)

Where it's reviewed:
Booklist, August 1999, page 2058
Publishers Weekly, August 2, 1999, page 85
School Library Journal, January 2000, page 106

Other books by the same author:
The 6th Grade Nickname Game, 1998
Liar, Liar, Pants on Fire, 1997
The Chicken Doesn't Skate, 1996
Toilet Paper Tigers, 1993

Other books you might like:
Bruce Coville, *I Was a Sixth Grade Alien*, 1999
Science fiction fan Tim is eager to befriend the new student, Pleskit, son of the alien ambassador to Earth.
Stephen Manes, *It's New! It's Improved! It's Terrible!*, 1989
He looks like a boy and talks like a television commercial, but he's really an alien.
Daniel Pinkwater, *Ned Feldman, Space Pirate*, 1994
Under the sink, Ned discovers Captain Bugbeard, an alien pirate who takes Ned for a ride through outer space.
Jeanne Willis, *The Long Blue Blazer*, 1987
The new kid at school is a puzzle to everyone. Why won't he remove that blazer?

539

AMY GOLDMAN KOSS

The Ashwater Experiment

(New York: Dial Books for Young Readers, 1999)

Subject(s): Moving, Household; Friendship; Parent and Child
Age range(s): Grades 4-7
Major character(s): Hillary Siegel, 12-Year-Old; Serena Montgomery, Student—Middle School, Friend (Hillary's); Cass Davis, Student—Middle School, Friend (Hillary's)
Time period(s): 1990s (1999)
Locale(s): Ashwater, California

Summary: After twelve years and eighteen different schools Hillary has become so accustomed to her parents' nomadic life, traveling to craft shows in different states, that she is alarmed when her father announces plans to house-sit for nine months in a small town. Hillary dreads being in one place for that length of time and decides that the entire experience must be an experiment created by the "Watchers" as a test for her. Recording her thoughts in a journal addressed to this imaginary group, Hillary enters school and meets the same stereotypes of people that she's found in previous schools—the popular girl, the class clown and the sleepwalkers. The difference in Ashwater is that Hillary learns to see beyond the stereotypes and to appreciate the value of friendship. Serena, the popular girl, surprises Hillary when she shows an interest in knowing Hillary better. Weeks later, in English class while listening to unpopular Cass read a paper, Hillary knows instantly that she and Cass have common interests and a basis for friendship. Gradually Hillary begins to see the reality of her experiences and to dismiss her idea about the "Watchers" as illusory. When the Ashwater experiment ends prematurely, she is sad to leave the first place where she has put down roots. (153 pages)

Where it's reviewed:
Booklist, June 1999, page 1829
Bulletin of the Center for Children's Books, June 1999, page 356
Horn Book, July 1999, page 468
Publishers Weekly, June 14, 1999, page 71
School Library Journal, August 1999, page 158

Awards the book has won:
Bulletin of the Center for Children's Books Blue Ribbon, 1999
School Library Journal Best Books, 1999

Other books by the same author:
The Girls, 2000
How I Saved Hanukkah, 1998
The Trouble with Zinny Weston, 1998

Other books you might like:
Nina Bawden, *Granny the Pag*, 1996
　Cat lives most of her life with an unconventional, motorcycle-riding grandmother while her parents travel to pursue acting careers.
Polly Horvath, *When the Circus Came to Town*, 1996
　As Ivy learns more about the ex-circus family next door she becomes convinced that they are characters in a book she is writing.
Susie Morgenstern, *Secret Letters from 0 to 10*, 1998
　Ernest's sheltered, monotonous life with Grandmother changes dramatically when outgoing Victoria joins his class and becomes his friend.
Susan Shreve, *Amy Dunn Quits School*, 1993
　The pressure of her mother's expectations becomes too much for Amy and she plays hooky from school

---

540

ROBERT KRAUS
JOHN HIMMELMAN, Illustrator

Mort the Sport
(New York: Orchard Books, 2000)

Subject(s): Sports/Baseball; Music and Musicians; Parent and Child
Age range(s): Grades K-2
Major character(s): Mort, Elephant, Son
Time period(s): Indeterminate
Locale(s): Fictional Country

Summary: Mort loves sports and he's good at everything he tries, but his favorite sport is baseball. Mort's dad is a big baseball fan who encourages his son to do well. To please his mother, Mort also takes violin lessons. Juggling the two activities soon becomes overwhelming for Mort and he ends up carrying his bat to violin lessons and swinging at a pitch with his violin. His parents, realizing that Mort is under too much pressure, ask him what he wants to do. Mort's ready with a reply since he's chosen an activity that allows him to sit down—chess. (32 pages)

Where it's reviewed:
Booklist, February 15, 2000, page 1118
Horn Book Guide, Fall 2000, page 272
Kirkus Reviews, February 15, 2000, page 244
School Library Journal, April 2000, page 107

Other books by the same author:
Big Squeak, Little Squeak, 1996
Strudwick: A Sheep in Wolf's Clothing, 1995
Another Mouse to Feed, 1987

Other books you might like:
Barbara Bottner, *Nana Hannah's Piano*, 1996
　Sonny prefers baseball practice to piano lessons; with Nana Hannah's help he learns to appreciate both.
Gavin Curtis, *The Bat Boy & His Violin*, 1998
　A baseball team's manager who does not understand his son's love for the violin expects him to serve as the team's bat boy.
Emily Arnold McCully, *Mouse Practice*, 1999
　From his musician parents Monk learns the importance of practice and with lots of it he becomes a capable baseball player.

541

ROBERT KRAUS
JOSE ARUEGO, Illustrator
ARIANE DEWEY, Illustrator

Mouse in Love
(New York: Orchard Books, 2000)

Subject(s): Animals/Mice; Neighbors and Neighborhoods; Stories in Rhyme
Age range(s): Grades K-2
Major character(s): Unnamed Character, Mouse
Time period(s): Indeterminate
Locale(s): Fictional Country

Summary: As he plucks daisy petals a romantic young mouse discovers that ''she'' loves him. He doesn't know the identity of this true love foretold by the daisy but he sets off to find her. After traveling by land, sea and air the mouse admits to feeling tired and hungry so he returns to his home. Only then does the little mouse realize that the one he loves lives right next door. (32 pages)

Where it's reviewed:
Booklist, September 15, 2000, page 249
Horn Book Guide, Spring 2001, page 41
Kirkus Reviews, June 15, 2000, page 886
Publishers Weekly, July 24, 2000, page 93
School Library Journal, August 2000, page 158

Other books by the same author:
Little Louie the Baby Bloomer, 1998
Big Squeak, Little Squeak, 1996
Come Out and Play, Little Mouse, 1991
Another Mouse to Feed, 1989
Leo the Late Bloomer, 1987

Other books you might like:
Eric Carle, *Do You Want to Be My Friend?*, 1971
    In a wordless book a mouse searches for a friend.
Petra Mathers, *Victor and Christabel*, 1993
    Victor, a museum guard, falls in love with the painting of Christabel.
Ed Young, *Mouse Match: A Chinese Folktale*, 1997
    Papa mouse, seeking an appropriate mate for his daughter, realizes that the right match is obvious.

542

STEPHEN KRENSKY
SUSANNA NATTI, Illustrator

Louise Goes Wild

(New York: Dial Books for Young Readers, 1999)

Subject(s): Self-Perception; Conduct of Life; Change
Age range(s): Grades 2-4
Major character(s): Louise Page, Sister (older), Student—Elementary School; Megan, Friend, Student—Elementary School; Emily, Friend, Student—Elementary School
Time period(s): 1990s (1999)
Locale(s): United States

Summary: Reliable, dependable Louise decides that such traits smack of boring predictability and she begins a campaign to change her image. Using her mom's curling iron, Louise creates a new look that astonishes everyone. When her hair experiment flops, Louise fashions a colorful new outfit that is a real eye-popper at breakfast. Louise is feeling a little discouraged that her plan to change her image is not going as expected. Her parents caution that Louise should work on changing one thing at a time and should begin with inner change not outer appearances. Louise finally heeds the pleas from Megan and Emily for the return of the old, familiar Louise to help them with their talent show act. Louise is out of her rut! (80 pages)

Where it's reviewed:
Booklist, July 1999, page 1946
Horn Book Guide, Fall 1999, page 280

School Library Journal, July 1999, page 75

Other books by the same author:
Louise Takes Charge, 1998
Lionel and His Friends, 1996
Lionel and Louise, 1992

Other books you might like:
Marc Brown, *Arthur and the Popularity Test*, 1998
    The results of a magazine's popularity test cause some of Arthur's friends to change in hopes of being more likeable.
Ann Cameron, *Gloria's Way*, 2000
    Gloria learns some important lessons about promises, friendship and the importance of being herself.
Betsy Duffey, *How to Be Cool in the Third Grade*, 1993
    Robbie has a plan to change his image this year, but he needs some cooperation from his mother before it can work.
Beverly Lewis, *Tree House Trouble*, 1998
    In the sixteenth entry in the Cul-de-Sac Kids series, Abby and Stacy create big trouble when they decide not to share the new tree house with boys.

543

WALTER LYON KRUDOP, Author/Illustrator

The Man Who Caught Fish

(New York: Farrar Straus Giroux, 2000)

Subject(s): Fairy Tales; Kings, Queens, Rulers, etc.; Greed
Age range(s): Grades 1-3
Major character(s): Unnamed Character, Fisherman; Unnamed Character, Royalty (king)
Time period(s): Indeterminate Past
Locale(s): Thailand

Summary: Unobtrusively a stranger carrying a fishing pole enters a village, drops his line in the water and pulls out a fish that he hands to the first person he sees saying, ''One person, one fish.'' The stranger repeats this ritual over and over again until most of the village is supplied with fish. Word quickly travels to the king who considers himself worthy of a basket full of fish, however, the stranger does not change his chant. The king is furious and tries both trickery and imprisonment to force the stranger to produce a basket of fish as befits royalty. Finally the king, after receiving one fish, dons a peasant's clothes and goes forward in disguise for another fish. The king, victim of his own arrogance, receives far more from the stranger than the basket of fish he seeks. (32 pages)

Where it's reviewed:
Booklist, February 15, 2000, page 1118
Horn Book, March 2000, page 188
School Library Journal, April 2000, page 107

Other books by the same author:
Something Is Growing, 1995
Blue Claws, 1993

Other books you might like:
Alma Flor Ada, *The Three Golden Oranges*, 1999
    Two selfish brothers who ignore the advice of an old woman to work with their younger brother to achieve a goal suffer the consequences.

Jeff Brumbeau, *The Quiltmaker's Gift*, 1999
  A greedy king must change his mercenary ways in order to acquire a quilt from a quiltmaker who gives them away only to those in need.
Margaret Read MacDonald, *The Girl Who Wore Too Much: A Folktale from Thailand*, 1998
  Indecisive Aree wears all her fine dresses to a dance but doesn't achieve her goal of impressing (or keeping) her friends.

544

JANE KURTZ
E.B. LEWIS, Illustrator

Faraway Home

(San Diego: Gulliver Books/Harcourt, Inc., 2000)

Subject(s): Fathers and Daughters; African Americans; Family
Age range(s): Grades 1-4
Major character(s): Desta, Child, Daughter; Daddy, Father
Time period(s): 2000s (2000); Indeterminate Past
Locale(s): Portland, Oregon; Ethiopia

Summary: Desta's sad to think of Daddy traveling to Ethiopia to visit his elderly, sick mother. Desta has never been to Daddy's native country and the stories he tells of his life as a child sound wild, strange and foreign to her. She tries to imagine cooking over an open fire, sleeping on the floor and walking to school barefoot. Desta offers Daddy her nightlight for the trip, but learns his mother's home has no electricity. Gradually, Desta accepts the upcoming trip, believes in her father's eventual return and knows his stories will be her link to him during his trip to his faraway home. (32 pages)

Where it's reviewed:
Booklist, February 15, 2000, page 1105
Bulletin of the Center for Children's Books, May 2000, page 323
Kirkus Reviews, March 15, 2000, page 385
Publishers Weekly, February 28, 2000, page 80
School Library Journal, April 2000, page 107

Awards the book has won:
Notable Social Studies Trade Books for Young People, 2001

Other books by the same author:
Only a Pigeon, 1997
Miro in the Kingdom of the Sun, 1996
Fire on the Mountain, 1994

Other books you might like:
Marie Bradby, *Momma, Where Are You From?*, 2000
  Momma comes not from another country, but from another time in America when life was very different than it is now for her daughter.
Mary Hoffman, *Boundless Grace*, 1995
  Grace travels to Gambia to visit the father and the country she knows only from pictures and letters.
Marissa Moss, *In America*, 1994
  Grandpa recalls his Lithuanian childhood and his decision to emigrate to America as a 10-year-old seeking religious freedom.

Allen Say, *Grandfather's Journey*, 1993
  A grandson completes his grandfather's journey between home land and adopted land, memory and desire in a Caldecott Medal winner.

545

JANE KURTZ
SUSAN HAVICE, Illustrator

I'm Sorry, Almira Ann

(New York: Henry Holt and Company, 1999)

Subject(s): Frontier and Pioneer Life; Friendship; Voyages and Travels
Age range(s): Grades 2-4
Major character(s): Sarah Eliza Benton, 8-Year-Old, Friend; Almira Ann Hastings, 8-Year-Old, Friend; Grandmother, Grandmother, Pioneer
Time period(s): Indeterminate Past
Locale(s): Missouri; West

Summary: Grandmother describes Sarah as having a "hasty spirit" and Sarah has to admit that her impetuous nature seems to be the cause of problems for her and others. Although Sarah is eager to begin the overland journey by wagon train to Oregon and grateful that her best friend Almira Ann's family is also making the trip, the tedium of the experience soon begins to test her patience. After her "hasty spirit" leads to an accident in which Almira Ann breaks her leg, Sarah worries about how she can ever right the wrong she's done. By the time the wagon train reaches Soda Springs for the 4th of July and the friends' shared birthday, Sarah has the opportunity to show Almira Ann what a good and truly remorseful friend she is. (119 pages)

Where it's reviewed:
Booklist, November 15, 1999, page 626
Horn Book, March 2000, page 196
Kirkus Reviews, October 15, 1999, page 1645
Publishers Weekly, November 22, 1999, page 56
School Library Journal, November 1999, page 121

Other books by the same author:
The Storyteller's Beads, 1998
Only a Pigeon, 1997
The Oregon Trail: Dangers and Dreams, 1990

Other books you might like:
Marissa Moss, *Rachel's Journal: The Story of a Pioneer Girl*, 1998
  A fictionalized diary gives an account of daily life for a family traveling to California in 1850.
Jean Van Leeuwen, *A Fourth of July on the Plains*, 1997
  After eight weeks of travel on the Oregon Trail, a wagon train stops to celebrate the Fourth of July.
Elvira Woodruff, *Dear Levi: Letters from the Overland Trail*, 1994
  In letters to his younger brother, 12-year-old Austin Ives describes his journey from Pennsylvania to Oregon.

546

KARLA KUSKIN
DYANNA WOLCOTT, Illustrator

I Am Me

(New York: Simon & Schuster Books for Young Readers, 2000)

Subject(s): Individuality; Family Life; Relatives
Age range(s): Grades K-1
Major character(s): Unnamed Character, Child; Dad, Father; Mom, Mother
Time period(s): 2000s
Locale(s): United States

Summary: A little girl is surrounded by family members noting how her features remind them of one family member or another. She's thin like Dad and has Mom's hands and chin. The little girl listens to everyone's opinion about whose voice, smile, eyebrows, feet and hair she has before she expresses her own opinion. Emphatically the girl lets everyone know that she is exclusively herself and no one else. (32 pages)

Where it's reviewed:
Booklist, June 1, 2000, page 1909
Horn Book Guide, Fall 2000, page 251
Kirkus Reviews, May 15, 2000, page 716
School Library Journal, July 2000, page 81

Other books by the same author:
The Upstairs Cat, 1997
James and the Rain, 1995
City Dog, 1994

Other books you might like:
David Shannon, *A Bad Case of Stripes*, 1998
  Too late Camilla recognizes the importance of being herself and not succumbing to peer pressure.
Lisa Thiesing, *Me & You: A Mother-Daughter Album*, 1998
  A mom tells her daughter the ways in which the daughter reminds the mother of herself as a young girl.
Martha M. Vertreace, *Kelly in the Mirror*, 1993
  Seeing herself in an outfit from her mother's childhood strengthens Kelly's awareness of family ties.

547

LAURA MCGEE KVASNOSKY, Author/Illustrator

Zelda and Ivy One Christmas

(Cambridge, MA: Candlewick Press, 2000)

Subject(s): Animals/Foxes; Sisters; Christmas

Age range(s): Grades 1-3
Major character(s): Mrs. Brownlie, Neighbor, Fox; Zelda, Fox, Sister (older); Ivy, Fox, Sister
Time period(s): Indeterminate
Locale(s): Fictional Country

Summary: In the first of three brief chapters Zelda and Ivy help Mrs. Brownlie, a recently widowed neighbor, bake gingerbread cookies. When the sisters return home they make a Christmas present for Mrs. Brownlie and hide it under the tree. In the next chapter Zelda pretends to see into the future using an ornament for her crystal ball until the smell of apple pie propels her to Mrs. Brownlie's house. Finally the anticipation of Christmas morning makes if difficult for Zelda and Ivy to fall asleep so they pretend and finally are successful. The next morning they open packages with matching bathrobes from Santa rather than the gifts they were hoping to find. However, packages from the "Christmas Elf" contain Ivy's doll and Zelda's velvet gown—just what they each wanted! (48 pages)

Where it's reviewed:
Booklist, November 15, 2000, page 648
Horn Book, November 2000, page 747
Publishers Weekly, September 25, 2000, page 76
School Library Journal, October 2000, page 60

Other books by the same author:
Zelda and Ivy and the Boy Next Door, 1999
Zelda and Ivy, 1998 (School Library Journal Best Book)
Mr. Chips!, 1996
See You Later, Alligator!, 1995

Other books you might like:
Holly Keller, *Merry Christmas, Geraldine*, 1997
  Geraldine is confident that she has selected the perfect Christmas tree and ignores her brother's objections to its size.
Mariana, *Miss Flora McFlimsey's Christmas Eve*, 1949
  With help from Timothy Mouse, an angel, and her own belief Miss Flora has a joyful Christmas that proves wishes do come true.
Claudia Mills, *Gus and Grandpa and the Christmas Cookies*, 1997
  Grandpa and Gus have so many Christmas cookies they devise a plan for the excess in keeping with the spirit of the season.
Jan L. Waldron, *Angel Pig and the Hidden Christmas*, 1997
  A visit from Angel Pig convinces seven shoppers that Christmas can be celebrated without lots of money.

L

548

MARY LABATT
TROY HILL-JACKSON, Illustrator

Strange Neighbors

(Niagara Falls, NY: Kids Can Press, 2000)

Series: Sam, Dog Detective
Subject(s): Animals/Dogs; Mystery and Detective Stories; Communication
Age range(s): Grades 3-5
Major character(s): Jennie Levinsky, 10-Year-Old; Sam, Dog; Beth Morrison, Friend (Jennie's)
Time period(s): 1990s (1999)
Locale(s): Woodford

Summary: Sam is the first to notice that there is something odd about the new neighbors and she communicates her observations to Jennie who can understand the dog's thoughts. In fact, Sam concludes that strange neighbors with a box of toads capable of walking in a straight line are definitely witches and she decides that Jennie and Beth should help her spy on them. Jennie and Beth also do some research at the library and the more they read the more sure they are that the three women are witches who are responsible for the freakish stormy weather the town is having. Now, with Sam's help Jennie and Beth try to develop a plan to protect themselves and the town. (110 pages)

Where it's reviewed:
Booklist, May 1, 2000, page 1668
Horn Book Guide, Fall 2000, page 306
Quill & Quire, March 2000, page 66
School Library Journal, September 2000, page 202

Other books by the same author:
A Weekend at the Grand Hotel, 2001 (Sam, Dog Detective)
Aliens in Woodford, 2000 (Sam, Dog Detective)
Spying on Dracula, 1999 (Sam, Dog Detective)
The Ghost of Captain Briggs, 1999 (Sam, Dog Detective)

Other books you might like:
Mary Blount Christian, *The Sebastian (Super Sleuth) Series*, 1982-
   Sebastian, an English sheepdog, is the case-solving sidekick of his master John Jones.
Debbie Dadey, *Witches Don't Do Backflips*, 1994
   When the Bailey School Kids see the gym decorations they suspect that the new gymnastics teacher is a witch, Marcia Thornton-Jones, co-author.
Ellen Leroe, *Ghost Dog*, 1993
   Only Artie can see a ghost dog that helps him solve a mystery.

549

JULIE LACOME, Author/Illustrator

Ruthie's Big Old Coat

(Cambridge, MA: Candlewick Press, 2000)

Subject(s): Clothes; Playing; Animals/Rabbits
Age range(s): Preschool
Major character(s): Ruthie, Rabbit, Friend; Fiona, Rabbit, Friend
Time period(s): Indeterminate
Locale(s): Fictional Country

Summary: The coat handed down to Ruthie from a cousin is too big, but Ruthie's mother assures her daughter that she will grow into it. Ruthie doesn't seem to grow fast enough and when she wears it outside Fiona agrees that the coat is large. In Fiona's eyes the size makes the coat just perfect for two friends to wear together so Fiona climbs into the coat, zips it up and begins dancing with Ruthie. They move on to other creative activities until they get a case of the giggles and Ruthie realizes she needs to get to the bathroom quickly. Unfortunately, the zipper on Ruthie's big, old coat is stuck and the friends haven't much time to solve the problem. (26 pages)

Where it's reviewed:
Booklist, April 1, 2000, page 1469

Bulletin of the Center for Children's Books, June 2000, page 363

Horn Book, May 2000, page 297

Kirkus Reviews, April 1, 2000, page 479

School Library Journal, May 2000, page 146

Other books by the same author:

I'm a Jolly Farmer, 1994

Funny Business, 1991

Hocus Pocus, 1991

Other books you might like:

May Garelick, *Just My Size*, 1990

As this little girl grows her coat is remade into smaller, useful garments until it becomes a coat for her doll.

Mordicai Gerstein, *Stop Those Pants!*, 1998

Murray's pants are too lively for him to catch so he's having difficulty getting dressed for school.

Amy Hest, *The Purple Coat*, 1986

Gabby pleads with her grandfather, the tailor, to make her a purple coat.

Laura F. Nielsen, *Jeremy's Muffler*, 1995

Jeremy tries unsuccessfully to lose the overly long muffler knit for his birthday, but is grateful for its length when he uses it to rescue someone.

550

NINA LADEN, Author/Illustrator

Bad Dog

(New York: Walker & Company, 2000)

Subject(s): Animals/Dogs; Behavior; Humor

Age range(s): Grades 1-4

Major character(s): Bad Dog, Dog; Butch, Dog

Time period(s): 2000s (2000)

Locale(s): United States

Summary: Bad Dog doesn't consider himself a bad dog and it hardly seems fair to be in trouble just for responding to junk mail advertising "free-range chickens." Bad Dog can't imagine anything better than free chickens and his friend Butch agrees. Together they borrow a car (a real dog) from the garage where Butch works and head for the country. When they reach the farm they discover that the chickens aren't eager to be caught and their squawking arouses the farmer and the police. Bad Dog tries to get away in a stolen police car, but he crashes it into a barn and gets hauled off to jail. After Bad Dog's owners free him from jail he spots an unattended bucket of fried chicken and gets what he wanted all along—finger-licking good chicken—and it's all free. (32 pages)

Where it's reviewed:

Bulletin of the Center for Children's Books, October 2000, page 69

Horn Book Guide, Spring 2001, page 41

Publishers Weekly, September 11, 2000, page 90

School Library Journal, September 2000, page 202

Other books by the same author:

Roberto, the Insect Architect, 2000

When Pigasso Met Mootisse, 1998

Private I. Guana: The Case of the Missing Chameleon, 1995

The Night I Followed the Dog, 1994

Other books you might like:

Thacher Hurd, *Art Dog*, 1996

Art Dog uses his painting skill to foil thieves trying to steal the Mona Woofa from the Dogopolis Museum of Art.

Dav Pilkey, *Dog Breath: The Horrible Trouble with Hally Tosis*, 1994

The Tosis family considers giving away their beloved pet Hally until her bad breath becomes a security feature deserving of reward.

Danny Shanahan, *Buckledown the Workhound*, 1993

After working himself to the bone, a dog-tired Buckledown retires to become a full-time family dog.

Alan Snow, *How Dogs Really Work!*, 1993

A winner of the New York Times Best Illustrated Children's Book Award is a humorous instruction manual for dog owners.

551

JIM LAMARCHE, Author/Illustrator

The Raft

(New York: HarperCollins Publishers, 2000)

Subject(s): Grandmothers; Rafting; Rivers

Age range(s): Grades 3-5

Major character(s): Nicky, Child, Son; Grandma, Grandmother; Dad, Father

Time period(s): 2000s (2000)

Locale(s): Wisconsin

Summary: As Dad drives Nicky to Grandma's house on the river Nicky complains about being stuck in such an isolated location for the summer, but stuck he is. Grandma is an artist and self-proclaimed "river rat" who's capable of doing just what Dad predicts—keeping Nicky busy. While Nicky fishes from the dock one afternoon a raft floats into the morose boy's life and changes his summer. Grandma teaches him how to pole the raft upstream and float down to the dock and gives him drawing supplies so he can sketch the many birds and animals that seem to be attracted to the raft. The evening before Nicky's summer stay ends Grandma helps him trace his raft sketches with oil paints to preserve them. An introductory author's note explains the childhood memories on which this illustrator's picture book is based. (40 pages)

Where it's reviewed:

Booklist, May 1, 2000, page 1679

Horn Book Guide, Fall 2000, page 273

Publishers Weekly, April 3, 2000, page 81

Riverbank Review, Winter 2000-2001, page 32

School Library Journal, May 2000, page 146

Awards the book has won:

School Library Journal Best Books, 2000

Other books you might like:

Marion Dane Bauer, *When I Go Camping with Grandma*, 1995

A young girl enjoys a wilderness camping adventure with Grandma.

Meredith Hooper, *River Story*, 2000

Beginning as a mountain stream fed by melting snow a river grows as it rushes to the sea.

Thomas Locker, *Where the River Begins*, 1984
Grandfather's camping trip with two grandsons takes them upstream to locate the source of the river that flows past their home.

Jane B. Mason, *River Day*, 1994
A serene day in a canoe on the river with her grandfather seems incomplete until Alex spots a bald eagle.

Lynn Reiser, *Tomorrow on Rocky Pond*, 1993
As a young girl settles into her family's vacation cabin her thoughts turn to the activities planned for the next day on Rocky Pond.

552

C. DREW LAMM
BARBARA MCCLINTOCK, Illustrator

The Prog Frince: A Mixed-Up Tale
(New York: Orchard Books, 1999)

Subject(s): Fairy Tales; Animals/Frogs and Toads; Love
Age range(s): Grades 1-4
Major character(s): Jaylee, Servant (stable girl); Jane, Sorceress, Child (unimaginative); Frog Prince, Royalty, Frog (enchanted)
Time period(s): Indeterminate Past
Locale(s): Fictional Country

Summary: Jane is an ordinary, practical girl, who has what seems to her an ordinary wish—to buy muffins—until she encounters a talking frog who runs away with her muffin money. Then, in order to retrieve her money, she listens to the frog's story about a prince and the girl he loved who become enchanted by a magic potion. Now, the Frog Prince is trying to undo the spell. Although Jane is annoyed by the theft of her money, she has such an enjoyable afternoon with the frog that, when he disappears, the unimaginative girl realizes she misses him. By that imaginative act, the spell is finally broken, Jane again becomes Jaylee and the frog returns to being a prince. (32 pages)

Where it's reviewed:
Booklist, February 1, 1999, page 974
Bulletin of the Center for Children's Books, February 1999, page 206
Horn Book, March 1999, page 194
Publishers Weekly, January 11, 1999, page 71
School Library Journal, March 1999, page 177

Other books by the same author:
Sea Lion Roars, 1997
Screech Owl at Midnight Hollow, 1996
Cottontail at Clover Crescent, 1995

Other books you might like:
Natalie Babbitt, *Ouch!*, 1998
After a common boy is predicted to marry a princess, the king tries to prevent a royal wedding.
Lisa Campbell Ernst, *Little Red Riding Hood: A Newfangled Prairie Tale*, 1995
Both Little Red Riding Hood and the big, bad wolf learn a lesson in this fractured fairy tale.

Jon Sciezka, *The Frog Prince Continued*, 1991
Life for the frog prince isn't all it's cracked up to be after he marries his princess.

553

SARAH MARWIL LAMSTEIN
NANCY COTE, Illustrator

I Like Your Buttons!
(Morton Grove, IL: Albert Whitman & Company, 1999)

Subject(s): Behavior; Conduct of Life; Fathers and Daughters
Age range(s): Grades K-2
Major character(s): Cassandra, Student—Elementary School, Daughter; Julian, Father, Worker (restaurant); Buttons, Cat
Time period(s): 1990s (1999)
Locale(s): United States

Summary: As the school day begins Cassandra compliments her teacher on her attractive buttons inspiring the teacher to offer kind words to the custodian who then says something positive to the class down the hall. Each kind gesture produces another until a compliment to the cook in a local restaurant leads to a brief break for his helper, Julian. As Julian rests outside he shares some ribs with a stray cat and at the end of his workday brings the animal home as a surprise for his daughter, Cassandra, who happily names him Buttons because of his big, bright eyes. (32 pages)

Where it's reviewed:
Booklist, August 1999, page 2064
Horn Book Guide, Fall 1999, page 257
School Library Journal, December 1999, page 102

Other books by the same author:
Annie's Shabbat, 1997

Other books you might like:
Addie Adam, *Hilda and the Mad Scientist*, 1995
Helpful Hilda's do-good housekeeping plans unintentionally foil Dr. Weinerstein's monster-making experiments.
Dorothea Lachner, *Andrew's Angry Words*, 1995
Andrew's angry words start a behavioral chain reaction just as Cassandra's kind words do but with a less positive result.
David L. Rice, *Because Brian Hugged His Mother*, 1999
Brian begins everyone's day on a happy note when he hugs his mother and compliments her.

554

OLOF LANDSTROM, Author/Illustrator
LENA LANDSTROM, Co-Author
JOAN SANDIN, Translator

Boo and Baa Get Wet
(New York: R & S Books, 2000)

Subject(s): Animals/Sheep; Weather; Fear
Age range(s): Grades K-1
Major character(s): Boo, Sheep, Brother; Baa, Sheep, Sister
Time period(s): 2000s (2000)

Locale(s): Fictional Country

Summary: After an active day of play in their yard Boo and Baa are sitting in their bunk beds reading when the lights go out. Looking out their window they see lightning and realize they've left their croquet set outside. Bundling up against the storm they race outside using a flashlight to light the way. When the light shines on two ''ghosts'' Boo races to Baa for help and both fall into the wading pool. Baa can see that the flashlight is actually illuminating their bathrobes so they finish carrying everything inside and then hang up their very wet clothes in the bathroom. Just as they're settling back into bed, the power comes on again so they turn off the lights and go to sleep. Originally published in Sweden in 1999. (28 pages)

Where it's reviewed:
Booklist, November 15, 2000, page 648
Horn Book Guide, Spring 2001, page 18
Publishers Weekly, September 11, 2000, page 92
Riverbank Review, Winter 2000-2001, page 30
School Library Journal, September 2000, page 203

Other books by the same author:
Boo and Baa in the Woods, 2000
Boo and Baa at Sea, 1997
Boo and Baa on a Cleaning Spree, 1997
Boo and Baa in Windy Weather, 1996
Boo and Baa in a Party Mood, 1996

Other books you might like:
Russell Hoban, *Bedtime for Frances*, 1960
    Frances imagines so many scary things in her room that she is unable to sleep.
Nancy Shaw, *Sheep Trick or Treat*, 1997
    The scary Halloween costumes on six unsuspecting sheep save them from hungry wolves searching from them in the dark woods.
Mary Wormell, *Hilda Hen's Scary Night*, 1996
    Fearfully, Hilda Hen crosses the dark farmyard, scurrying past snakes (garden hose) and monsters (toy) as she seeks the refuge of the henhouse.

555

JONATHAN LANGLEY, Author/Illustrator

Missing!

(New York: Marshall Cavendish, 2000)

Subject(s): Animals/Cats; Pets; Lost and Found Possessions
Age range(s): Grades K-1
Major character(s): Daisy, Child; Lupin, Cat
Time period(s): 2000s (2000)
Locale(s): England

Summary: Lupin and Daisy have a routine. Daisy goes to school and Lupin stays home and meets Daisy at the corner after school. The system works well until the holidays begin and no one tells Lupin not to meet Daisy at the corner. All day each is busy with their familiar activities and in the afternoon Lupin waits in vain for Daisy at the corner while Daisy searches for her missing pet. Each imagines the worst as they search for the other. Finally, in despair, Daisy comes home to find Lupin sleeping in the cat basket and happy to see her pet

again. Originally published in Great Britain in 2000. (32 pages)

Where it's reviewed:
Booklist, September 1, 2000, page 124
Horn Book Guide, Spring 2001, page 18
Kirkus Reviews, July 15, 2000, page 1040
School Library Journal, September 2000, page 203

Other books by the same author:
Hansel and Gretel, 1997
Three Little Pigs: Nursery Pop-Up Book, 1996
Rain, Rain Go Away!, 1991

Other books you might like:
Leslie Baker, *Paris Cat*, 1999
    Annie's cat becomes lost while chasing a mouse and tours Paris while looking for the way home.
Tad Hardy, *Lost Cat*, 1996
    A rhyming tale describes the efforts of a worried pet owner to find his cat.
Holly Keller, *A Bed Full of Cats*, 1999
    Lee worries when he can't find his pet Flora but she reappears leading the reason for her absence.

556

ANA MARTIN LARRANAGA, Author/Illustrator

Woo! The Not-So-Scary Ghost

(New York: Arthur A. Levine Books/Scholastic Press, 2000)

Subject(s): Ghosts; Runaways; Fear
Age range(s): Preschool
Major character(s): Woo, Spirit, Son
Time period(s): Indeterminate
Locale(s): Fictional Country

Summary: Woo is tired of being told to clean his room, do his homework and brush his teeth so early one morning, when good little ghosts should be asleep, he runs away from home. At first Woo enjoys practicing his scaring although the animals don't seem to be frightened of him, but as the day brightens Woo begins to feel a little worried. Searching for a hiding place he's chased by a playful farmer's dog. When the farmer sees the dog she thinks it's playing with one of her clean sheets so she throws Woo in the washing machine. When he's dry, only a ringing telephone saves Woo from being squashed by a hot iron and he escapes. Home looks mighty good tonight! This is the author's first book published in English. (32 pages)

Where it's reviewed:
Booklist, December 1, 2000, page 722
Horn Book Guide, Spring 2001, page 19
School Library Journal, September 2000, page 203

Other books you might like:
Robert Bright, *Georgie and the Runaway Balloon*, 1983
    A helium-filled balloon runs away with a mouse that little ghost Georgie wants to rescue.
Jacques Duquennoy, *The Ghosts' Trip to Loch Ness*, 1996
    The travels of four ghosts take them to Loch Ness where they hope to see the famous monster.

Kay Winters, *The Teeny Tiny Ghost*, 1997
  The teeny, tiny, timid ghost has difficulty doing his haunting homework because he scares himself so easily.

557

KIRBY LARSON
ROSANNE LITZINGER, Illustrator

The Magic Kerchief
(New York: Holiday House, 2000)

Subject(s): Fairy Tales; Magic; Conduct of Life
Age range(s): Grades K-3
Major character(s): Griselda, Aged Person; Unnamed Character, Traveler
Time period(s): Indeterminate Past
Locale(s): Fictional Country

Summary: Villagers avoid Griselda because of her sharp tongue and insulting comments so a knock at her door surprises her. Griselda finds a stranger wearing a beautifully embroidered kerchief asking for shelter. Begrudgingly Griselda allows the woman into the cottage for food and a bed for the night. In the morning the woman pays Griselda by giving her the kerchief, with the warning that it is magic. Gridselda doesn't believe the kerchief is any such thing, but she dons it for its beauty and begins her day's shopping. At each stop Griselda thinks of a biting comment, but the words that actually come out of her mouth are positive and kind. Both Griselda and the villagers are astonished by her gentle words and soon Griselda is no longer lonely. (32 pages)

Where it's reviewed:
Booklist, August 2000, page 2148
Horn Book, September 2000, page 551
Publishers Weekly, September 18, 2000, page 111
School Library Journal, October 2000, page 128

Other books by the same author:
Cody and Quinn, Sitting in a Tree, 1996
Second-Grade Pig Pals, 1994

Other books you might like:
Jeff Brumbeau, *The Quiltmaker's Gift*, 1999
  For a greedy king possessions do not bring happiness; when he learns to give, then he receives the happiness he seeks.
Joan Rothenberg, *Yettele's Feathers*, 1995
  Lonely Yettele learns that the conversations she finds so entertaining actually spread hurtful gossip and make her more isolated when people avoid her.
Chris Van Allsburg, *The Sweetest Fig*, 1993
  Annoyed to be paid for his services with two figs, pompous Bibot learns to appreciate the figs' magic, but never achieves his dreams.

558

KATHRYN LASKY
DAVID CATROW, Illustrator

The Emperor's Old Clothes
(San Diego: Harcourt Brace & Company, 1999)

Subject(s): Clothes; Humor; Lost and Found Possessions
Age range(s): Grades 1-4
Major character(s): Henry, Farmer
Time period(s): Indeterminate Past
Locale(s): Fictional Country

Summary: As Henry walks home from market on the day of the emperor's birthday celebration a fast-moving carriage hurtles past him and something floats out of the window and lands on Henry's face. Henry peels off the silk stockings, puts them on and proceeds toward home. Around every corner of the road Henry finds another item of clothing from fancy, feathered high-heeled shoes to golden pantaloons, an embroidered doublet and a wig. Feeling mighty fine, Henry is sure his animals will be impressed with his new attire—it's certainly better than what the emperor's wearing in the parade. Soon enough, Henry realizes that these fine clothes are not practical for farm work and when he lands in the mud with the animals laughing at him simple Henry has sense enough to know what to do. (32 pages)

Where it's reviewed:
Booklist, March 1, 1999, page 1221
Horn Book Guide, Fall 1999, page 257
Publishers Weekly, March 8, 1999, page 67
Reading Teacher, October 1999, page 150
School Library Journal, May 1999, page 92

Other books by the same author:
Sophie and Rose, 1998
Marven of the Great North Woods, 1997 (ALA Notable Book for Children)
Lunch Bunnies, 1996 (Publishers Weekly Best Book)
The Gates of the Wind, 1995

Other books you might like:
Anthea Bell, *The Emperor's New Clothes*, 1986
  This traditional retelling of Andersen's classic tale has the same well-known outcome for the vain emperor but no clues about the discarded clothes.
Jon Scieszka, *The Stinky Cheese Man: And Other Fairly Stupid Tales*, 1992
  Classic fairy tales are humorously retold in this Caldecott Honor book.
David Small, *Fenwick's Suit*, 1996
  Fenwick quickly realizes that his new suit is not his style but the suit has plans of its own to avoid being returned to the tailor.
Eugene Trivizas, *The Three Little Wolves and the Big Bad Pig*, 1993
  A familiar tale takes a new turn when the big, bad pig tries to outmaneuver the three little wolves and ends up surprising himself.

559

KATHRYN LASKY
MARYLIN HAFNER, Illustrator

Lucille's Snowsuit

(New York: Crown Publishers, 2000)

Subject(s): Animals/Pigs; Clothes; Brothers and Sisters
Age range(s): Grades K-2
Major character(s): Lucille, Pig, Sister (younger); Franklin, Pig, Brother (older); Frances, Pig, Sister (older)
Time period(s): Indeterminate
Locale(s): Fictional Country

Summary: As a preschooler Lucille doesn't appreciate the significance of a snow day as Franklin and Frances do, but she quickly assesses the value of being big enough to have a parka and ski pants rather than a snowsuit. Franklin and Frances are outside having fun in the snow while Lucille is inside trying to pull the snowsuit on over her boots. When she finally gets out of the boots and gets the snowsuit on the zipper becomes stuck. Lucille is so hot and sweaty she no longer wants to go outside because she's too tired to play. Franklin and Frances come in and drag her out for a variety of snow activities. By the time Lucille plays all day she appreciates her warm snowsuit. (32 pages)

Where it's reviewed:
Booklist, September 15, 2000, page 249
Bulletin of the Center for Children's Books, October 2000, page 69
Kirkus Reviews, August 1, 2000, page 1119
Publishers Weekly, August 21, 2000, page 73
School Library Journal, September 2000, page 203

Other books by the same author:
Sophie and Rose, 1998
Lunch Bunnies, 1996 (Publishers Weekly Best Children's Books)
Pond Year, 1995

Other books you might like:
Barbara M. Joosse, *Snow Day!*, 1995
    When Snow forces the cancellation of school, Robby and his family have a day to play outside.
Ezra Jack Keats, *The Snowy Day*, 1962
    The Caldecott Medal winner portrays a young child's enjoyment of the season's first snowfall.
Jean Van Leeuwen, *Oliver and Amanda and the Big Snow*, 1995
    Siblings Oliver and Amanda enjoy the day romping in the snow with their parents.

560

KATHRYN LASKY
MARYLIN HAFNER, Illustrator

Science Fair Bunnies

(Cambridge, MA: Candlewick Press, 2000)

Subject(s): Animals/Rabbits; Science; Schools
Age range(s): Grades K-2
Major character(s): Clyde, Rabbit, Student—Elementary School; Rosemary, Rabbit, Student—Elementary School
Time period(s): 2000s (2000)
Locale(s): Fictional Country

Summary: A week before the Science Fair Clyde and Rosemary are faced with a dilemma when the bean plants they were growing for their project die. Fortunately, each of them has a loose tooth to provide the materials needed for an alternate experiment. By soaking their teeth (and one additional donation) in different liquids, Clyde and Rosemary demonstrate the staining properties of common foods and beverages. Although they are simply grateful to have a last-minute project successfully completed, they also are fortunate to be awarded a blue ribbon for "most original and independent work." They'll be completely happy if the tooth fairy accepts discolored teeth. (32 pages)

Where it's reviewed:
Booklist, July 2000, page 2040
Horn Book Guide, Fall 2000, page 273
Publishers Weekly, May 1, 2000, page 70
School Library Journal, July 2000, page 81

Other books by the same author:
Show and Tell Bunnies, 1998
Sophie and Rose, 1998
Lunch Bunnies, 1996 (Publishers Weekly Best Children's Books)
Pond Year, 1995

Other books you might like:
Janice Lee Smith, *Serious Science: An Adam Joshua Story*, 1993
    At first Adam Joshua is upset to discover his destroyed science project but he uses the incident as inspiration for a last-minute replacement.
Rosemary Wells, *Fritz and the Mess Fairy*, 1991
    Something unexpected happens to Fritz's science project causing the Mess Fairy to appear.
Jim Wiese, *Head to Toe Science: Over 40 Eye-Popping, Spine-Tingling, Heart-Pounding Activities that Teach Kids about the Human Body*, 2000
    A non-fiction title includes many ideas for experiments suitable for science projects.

561

LAURIE LAWLOR

Adventure on the Wilderness Road, 1775

(New York: Pocket Books/Minstrel, 1999)

Series: American Sisters. Number 4
Subject(s): Frontier and Pioneer Life; Sisters; Historical
Age range(s): Grades 4-6
Major character(s): Elizabeth Poage, 11-Year-Old, Sister; Martha Poage, Sister (younger), Pioneer
Time period(s): 1770s (1775)
Locale(s): Holston River, Tennessee, American Colonies; Boonesborough, Kentucky, American Colonies

Summary: While the Holston settlement could hardly seem overdeveloped, Elizabeth's father decides his family needs to relocate to a land of greater opportunities. The family packs all they can onto horses, Elizabeth drives the cow and pig and Martha shepherds the younger brothers as they travel across the mountains to Boonesborough. Encounters with Indians and Elizabeth's reading of *Gulliver's Travels* to her fellow travelers moderate the monotony of hunger and hardship on the trail. Elizabeth's annoyance with Martha and her free-spirited ways changes during the journey to appreciation, especially after Martha vanishes in the woods and the family fears she's been captured by Indians. After the arduous trip, they all arrive safely at their destination only to find their home incompletely built and the first snows of winter approaching. An "Afterword" and bibliography give the historical background for the story. (185 pages)

Where it's reviewed:
Booklist, April 1, 1999, page 1426
Horn Book Guide, Spring 2000, page 81
School Library Journal, November 1999, page 160

Other books by the same author:
Crossing the Colorado Rockies, 1999 (American Sisters, Number 5)
Voyage to a Free Land, 1999 (American Sisters, Number 3)
West Along the Wagon Road, 1998 (American Sisters, Number 1)

Other books you might like:
Joseph Bruchac, *The Arrow Over the Door*, 1998
    The Abenaki arrow over the Quaker Meeting House door denotes the peacefulness of Quakers and their neutrality in America's fight for independence.
Lynda Durrant, *The Beaded Moccasins: The Story of Mary Campbell*, 1998
    Delaware Indians capture Mary to replace the granddaughter of their chief and take her from Pennsylvania to their campsite in Ohio.
Laura Ingalls Wilder, *Little House on the Prairie*, 1935
    The Wilder family travels by covered wagon from the Wisconsin woods to the prairie braving dangerous river crossings and fearing Indian attack.
Patricia Willis, *Danger Along the Ohio*, 1997
    Three children, separated from their father by an Indian attack, make their way along banks of the Ohio hoping to find their father safe in Marietta.

562

NEAL LAYTON, Author/Illustrator

Smile If You're Human

(New York: Dial Books for Young Readers, 1999)

Subject(s): Aliens; Animals; Zoos
Age range(s): Grades K-1
Major character(s): Unnamed Character, Alien
Time period(s): 1990s
Locale(s): Earth

Summary: An alien family lands in a zoo when they visit Earth to photograph a human. The alien child suspects each animal of being a human but the parents consult the "Alien's Guide to Earth" and assure their child that humans do not hop like a kangaroo or have a tail and four legs like a tiger. Based on that description, the alien child is sure that penguins are humans,

but soon learns that the wings and webbed feet make that impossible. When they reach the last house on their tour of the "planet" (as they consider the zoo) they finally see the animal that they think matches the description of the human, snap a picture and hurry to the spaceship for the trip home. (24 pages)

Where it's reviewed:
Booklist, April 1, 1999, page 1421
Horn Book, March 1999, page 195
Kirkus Reviews, February 15, 1999, page 301
Publishers Weekly, March 29, 1999, page 102
School Library Journal, April 1999, page 101

Awards the book has won:
IRA/CBC Children's Choices, 2000

Other books you might like:
Colin McNaughton, *Here Come the Aliens!*, 1995
    A rhyming tale humorously tells of a group of aliens intent on invading earth until they are frightened by an earthly object floating in space.
Michael Rosen, *Mission Ziffoid*, 1999
    In this picture book a young boy visits the planet Ziffoid and meets the inhabitants.
Martha Weston, *Space Guys!*, 2000
    In simple verse this easy reader describes a night visit from "space guys" to a young boy's home.
Jeanne Willis, *Earthlets, as Explained by Professor Xargle*, 1989
    Wise alien Professor Xargle teaches his class about the unusual behavior of the earthlet—or—baby as humans call the smallest of their species.

563

URSULA K. LE GUIN
S.D. SCHINDLER, Illustrator

Jane on Her Own: A Catwings Tale

(New York: Orchard Books, 1999)

Subject(s): Animals/Cats; Fantasy; Freedom
Age range(s): Grades 1-4
Major character(s): Jane, Cat (winged), Adventurer; Jane Tabby, Cat, Mother (Jane's); Sarah Wolf, Aged Person
Time period(s): 1990s
Locale(s): United States (Overhill Farm)

Summary: Life at Overhill Farm is too dull for Jane who wants to put her wings to good use by going somewhere. Ignoring her siblings' advice, she strikes out on an adventure that quickly becomes a lonely trail to nowhere. Finally she enters the city where she was born and flies into an open window. The man in the apartment treats her kindly, feeds her well, but controls her every move. Jane longs to be free of the confinement of the apartment, cat carriers and hot television studios. She manages to escape and searches the city until she finds her mother's home. Sarah Wolf is surprised to awaken with Mrs. Jane Tabby on one side of her bed and an unfamiliar black cat on the other, but she welcomes Jane, accepts her as a pet and does not try to make her a television star. This is the life for Jane! (42 pages)

Where it's reviewed:
Booklist, February 1, 1999, page 974
Horn Book Guide, Fall 1999, page 280
Kirkus Reviews, January 15, 1999, page 147
Publishers Weekly, February 8, 1999, page 216
School Library Journal, April 1999, page 101

Other books by the same author:
Wonderful Alexander and the Catwings, 1994
Catwings Return, 1989 (IRA/CBC Children's Choice)
Catwings, 1988 (IRA/CBC Children's Choice)

Other books you might like:
Lloyd Alexander, *Time Cat: The Remarkable Journeys of Jason and Gareth*, 1996
    With his talking cat Gareth as companion and facilitator, Jason travels through time and space visiting other lands and peoples.
Adele Geras, *Fabulous Fantoras: Book Two: Family Photographs*, 1999
    In the second book of the series Ozzie, the family cat, narrates events in the strange lives of a peculiar multi-talented family,
John Peterson, *The Littles*, 1967
    The Tiny family lives a relativity safe life in the walls of the Bigg family's home, but must take special precautions to avoid the house cat.

564

LAURIE LEARS
KAREN RITZ, Illustrator

Waiting for Mr. Goose

(Morton Grove, IL: Albert Whitman & Company, 1999)

Subject(s): Behavior; Animals/Geese; Wildlife Rescue
Age range(s): Grades K-3
Major character(s): Stephen, Child; Mr. Goose, Goose
Time period(s): 1990s (1999)
Locale(s): United States

Summary: Stephen likes to be outside where he's free to move without parents or teachers telling him to pay attention or sit still so it's not surprising that he spots a goose near the pond trailing a chain from a trap clamped on one leg. Stephen wants to catch Mr. Goose, as he calls the injured bird, but he's not able to do so and neither is the wildlife rescuer his mom calls. Unlike the adult rescuer, Stephen has the determination to find an effective plan. He's not sure he has the patience, but his desire to free Mr. Goose from the trap is so great that he successfully waits for days until Mr. Goose trusts him enough to come within reach. An introductory author's note describes attention deficit hyperactivity disorder suggesting that Stephen may be representative of ADHD children. (32 pages)

Where it's reviewed:
Booklist, December 1, 1999, page 712
Horn Book Guide, Spring 2000, page 44
Kirkus Reviews, October 15, 1999, page 1645
School Library Journal, January 2000, page 106

Other books by the same author:
Ben Has Something to Say, 2000
Ian's Walk: A Story about Autism, 1998

Other books you might like:
Nancy Carlson, *Sit Still!*, 1996
    The mother of a hyperactive little boy comes up with an innovative idea to help him sit still.
Phyllis Carpenter, *Sparky's Excellent Misadventures: My A.D.D. Journal*, 2000
    Sparky keeps a journal reflecting the challenges of home and school for a child with attention deficit disorder.
Sally Grindley, *Peter's Place*, 1996
    Following an oil spill near his coastal home, Peter helps with the rescue effort and patiently saves one of his favorite eider ducks.

565

NORMA LEHR

Dance of the Crystal Skull

(Flagstaff, AZ: Rising Moon, 1999)

Subject(s): Supernatural; Indians of North America; Cultures and Customs
Age range(s): Grades 4-7
Major character(s): Kathy Wicklow, 11-Year-Old; Willow, 12-Year-Old; Concha, Friend, Store Owner
Time period(s): 1990s (1999)
Locale(s): Santa Tierra, New Mexico

Summary: A crystal skull that others cannot see appears to Californian Kathy while she tries to enjoy her visit with Concha, a friend of Kathy's aunt. Unfamiliar with local legend and considered an outsider in the small town, Kathy isn't sure in whom to confide. Willow's aunt, a local healer, wears a small skull just like the apparition that appears to Kathy, but she seems unwilling to enlighten Kathy about the meaning of the skull. Concha becomes ill and Kathy uses Willow's horse to ride for help, but soon she is also in need of rescue. Answers to the mystery of the skull and Kathy's role in the resolution of centuries' old conflict are given to her while she awaits rescue. Will the townspeople believe that an outsider is the chosen one? (149 pages)

Where it's reviewed:
Booklist, June 1999, page 1829
Horn Book Guide, Fall 1999, page 295
School Library Journal, August 1999, page 158

Other books by the same author:
The Secret of the Floating Phantom, 1994
The Shimmering Ghost of Riversend, 1991

Other books you might like:
Will Hobbs, *Kokopelli's Flute*, 1995
    Thirteen-year-old Tep retrieves a bone flute dropped by fleeing artifact thieves, unaware that he now holds an object of unusual power.
Kimberley Griffiths Little, *Enchanted Runner*, 1999
    Seen as an outsider and a half-breed, Kendall must prove worthy of his Acoma heritage when he visits his deceased mother's village for the first time.
Kenneth Thomasma, *Amee-Nah: Zuni Boy Runs the Race of His Life*, 1995
    Surgery to correct a clubfoot enables Amee-Zah "Lazy"

to disprove his name in an entry in the Amazing Indian Children series .

566

ALISON LESTER, Author/Illustrator

Celeste Sails to Spain

(New York: Walter Lorraine/Houghton Mifflin Co., 1999)

Subject(s): Individuality; Children; Playing
Age range(s): Grades K-2
Major character(s): Celeste, Child; Clive, Child; Rosie, Child
Time period(s): 1990s (1997)
Locale(s): Australia

Summary: Seven children engage in varied activities. On Saturday Rosie bounces on a pogo stick while Celeste twirls around an ice-skating rink and Clive participates in football. At a museum Clive looks at dinosaurs, Celeste experiments with light and prisms and Rosie views a horse. The children enjoy different adventures such as water-skiing, wild water rafting and downhill skiing. In their dreams they travel far: Rosie rides horseback into the Grand Canyon, Clive visits the alligator-infested waters of Kakadu but Celeste sails to Spain in a title originally published in Australia in 1997. (32 pages)

Where it's reviewed:
Booklist, October 1, 1999, page 362
Horn Book Guide, Spring 2000, page 44
School Library Journal, October 1999, page 118
Smithsonian, November 1999, page 46

Awards the book has won:
Smithsonian's Notable Books for Children, 1999

Other books by the same author:
When Frank Was Four, 1996
Isabella's Bed, 1993
Tessa Snaps Snakes, 1991
Clive Eats Alligators, 1989
Rosie Sips Spiders, 1989

Other books you might like:
Catherine Anholt, *What I Like*, 1991
  Rhyming text describes the varied interests of six children.
Sally Derby, *My Steps*, 1996
  The five steps and stoop leading to an urban home are a place for games, coloring, snacks and imaginative play for a young girl and her friends.
P.K. Hallinan, *A Rainbow of Friends*, 1994
  A diverse group of children respect their individuality and enjoy the contributions each makes to the others.
Stephen Michael King, *Henry and Amy (Right-Way-Round and Upside Down)*, 1999
  Henry and Amy's different interests and talents contribute to the success of their friendship.
Joanne Ryder, *A House by the Sea*, 1994
  Imaginative children describe their fantasy life in a house by the sea and their daily adventures with a variety of marine animals.

567

HELEN LESTER
LYNN MUNSINGER, Illustrator

Hooway for Wodney Wat

(Boston: Houghton Mifflin Company, 1999)

Subject(s): Schools; Bullies; Animals/Rats
Age range(s): Grades K-3
Major character(s): Rodney ''Wodney'' Rat ''Wat'', Rodent, Student—Elementary School; Camilla Capybara, Rodent, Bully; Miss Fuzzleworth, Teacher, Rodent
Time period(s): 1990s
Locale(s): Fictional Country (P.S. 142 Elementary School)

Summary: Poor Rodney Rat! Other students tease him because a speech impediment causes him to mispronounce words with the letter R, including his name. When new student Camilla Capybara storms into the classroom loudly announcing her arrival, her ability, her size and her meanness all the students cower in her path, especially shy Rodney. After Miss Fuzzleworth pulls Wodney's name from the hat as the leader for Simon Says, Wodney can hide no longer. Bravely he gives the commands and the students familiar with his speech comply with what they know he meant to say while Camilla follows the directions literally. As Wodney watches her response, he becomes more confident with his commands until he shouts out the final direction, ''Go west!'' Everyone falls down to rest except Camilla who marches west and is never seen again. (32 pages)

Where it's reviewed:
Booklist, May 1, 1999, page 1600
Horn Book, July 1999, page 457
Publishers Weekly, April 19, 1999, page 72
School Library Journal, May 1999, page 92

Awards the book has won:
ALA Notable Children's Books, 2000
School Library Journal Best Books, 1999

Other books by the same author:
Tacky in Trouble, 1998
Princess Penelope's Parrot, 1996
Listen, Buddy, 1995

Other books you might like:
Barbara Bottner, *Bootsie Barker Bites*, 1992
  Rather than allow obnoxious Bootsie to terrorize her one more time, a young girl carefully plans the activities for Bootsie's visit.
Jim McMullan, *Hey, Pipsqueak!*, 1995
  In order to cross the bridge to go to a party, Jack must outwit the troll blocking his way and demanding the gift. Kate McMullan, co-author.
Susan Meddaugh, *Martha Walks the Dog*, 1998
  Martha the talking dog learns from a parrot's example that kind words have a more positive impact on Bad Dog Bob than insults.
John Nickle, *The Ant Bully*, 1999
  When Sid squirts Lucas the frustrated victim turns his squirt gun on some ants and suffers the consequences when he shrinks to ant size.

568

HELEN LESTER
LYNN MUNSINGER, Illustrator

Tacky and the Emperor

(Boston: Walter Lorraine/Houghton Mifflin Company, 2000)

Subject(s): Animals/Penguins; Humor; Kings, Queens, Rulers, etc.
Age range(s): Grades K-3
Major character(s): Tacky, Penguin; Unnamed Character, Penguin (emperor), Ruler
Time period(s): Indeterminate
Locale(s): Fictional Country

Summary: Tacky's companions are in a tizzy of preparation for the visit of the emperor. One decorates a throne, one practices a dance, and two create fish-flavored punch, cupcakes and ice cream. Tacky blows up balloons. As usual, unconventional Tacky gets everything wrong and in so doing makes the day turn out exactly right. The emperor is bored with the monotonous visits to his subjects, but the visit to Tacky and his friends is out of the ordinary and very enjoyable despite the fact that nothing went the way it was planned. (32 pages)

Where it's reviewed:
Booklist, August 2000, page 2148
Horn Book, November 2000, page 748
Publishers Weekly, September 11, 2000, page 92
School Library Journal, November 2000, page 126

Other books by the same author:
Tacky in Trouble, 1998
Three Cheers for Tacky, 1994
Tacky the Penguin, 1988

Other books you might like:
Sonia W. Black, *Plenty of Penguins*, 1999
This "Hello Reader!" science title gives factual information about several varieties of penguins.
Pat Hutchins, *Rosie's Walk*, 1968
Rosie enjoys her walk, oblivious to the fact that she is leading a hungry fox from one accident to another as he tries to catch her.
Janet Perlman, *The Emperor Penguin's New Clothes*, 1995
Hans Christian Andersen's classic tale about a vain emperor who is tricked into buying a new (invisible) outfit is retold with penguins in the lead.
Mary Wormell, *Hilda Hen's Happy Birthday*, 1995
Self-absorbed Hilda awakens on the morning of her birthday confident that the horse's oats and the farmer's cookies are gifts for her to enjoy.

569

JULIUS LESTER
JOE CEPEDA, Illustrator

What a Truly Cool World

(New York: Scholastic Press, 1999)

Subject(s): Creation; God; Heaven
Age range(s): Grades K-2

Major character(s): God, Deity; Shaniqua, Angel; Bruce, Angel, Secretary (God's)
Time period(s): Indeterminate
Locale(s): Earth; Heaven

Summary: God thinks he can call it quits after creating Earth, but bossy Shaniqua proclaims his creation boring and God reluctantly admits she is right. With a lot of thinking and planning and some assistance from efficient Bruce, God adds bushes and grass to the landscape. Still, Shaniqua is not satisfied so God tries one more thing. He invents music and the music becomes colors and shapes as it floats through space to become flowers on Earth. Even Shaniqua is impressed, but the flowers complain of being lonely so God knows his creation is not complete. The final gesture that makes the world truly cool comes from the universe's reaction to Shaniqua and her beautiful voice. (32 pages)

Where it's reviewed:
Booklist, February 15, 1999, page 1076
Bulletin of the Center for Children's Books, February 1999, page 207
Horn Book, March 1999, page 196
Publishers Weekly, January 4, 1999, page 89
School Library Journal, April 1999, page 102

Awards the book has won:
Bulletin of the Center for Children's Books Blue Ribbon, 1999

Other books by the same author:
Sam and the Tigers: A New Telling of Little Black Sambo, 1996
John Henry, 1994
The Last Tales of Uncle Remus, 1994

Other books you might like:
John Burningham, *Whaddayamean*, 1999
When God awakens from his nap he is disappointed to see that his creation has been mistreated and enlists two children to help change things.
Carolyn Forche, *Colors Came from God Just Like Me*, 1996
An African American girl talks about God's creations including the many variations of skin color.
Kim Henry, *Seeds of Heaven*, 2000
While walking with his son, a father points out the simple signs in nature that reveal heaven's glory
Douglas Wood, *Making the World*, 1998
Children observe how the natural world is being remade daily.
Harriet Ziefert, *First He Made the Sun*, 2000
A simple rhyming text describes the seven days in which God creates the world and its many creatures.

570

BETTY LEVIN
JOS. A. SMITH, Illustrator

Creature Crossing

(New York: Greenwillow Books, 1999)

Subject(s): Animals/Salamanders; Friendship; Wildlife Conservation
Age range(s): Grades 3-5

Major character(s): Ben Addario, Child, Friend; Kate, Child, Friend; Foster Baring, Child, Friend

Time period(s): 1990s (1999)

Locale(s): United States (Flint Farm Road)

Summary: Ben thinks that the strange creature he finds in a muddy roadside ditch is a dinosaur embryo that will make him famous. He tells only Foster and Kate about his secret "liz-thing" and enlists their help in researching the animal's identity. Kate agrees to keep the creature at her house, but then fears that her new kitten may have eaten it. When Kate seeks help from an elderly neighbor, she discovers that the "liz-thing" is actually a salamander, endangered by its need to migrate from its winter hibernation to the pond on the other side of Flint Farm Road. Ben, Foster and Kate rally the neighbors to stage a nighttime closing of the road and to carry the migrating animals to the pond so they are not killed by road traffic. (92 pages)

Where it's reviewed:
Booklist, March 1, 1999, page 1214
Horn Book, May 1999, page 331
School Library Journal, June 1999, page 100

Other books by the same author:
Island Bound, 1997
Fire in the Wind, 1995
Starshine and Sunglow, 1994
Brother Moose, 1990

Other books you might like:
Nina Alexander, *Megan and the Borealis Butterfly*, 1999
   In this episode of the Magic Attic Club series, the magic mirror lands Megan in the midst of a rain forest search for an endangered butterfly.
Jean Craighead George, *The Fire Bug Connection: An Ecological Mystery*, 1993
   When Maggie's unusual birthday gift fails to develop she uses her ability to reason scientifically to determine the cause of the fire bugs' death.
Linda Glaser, *Tanya's Big Green Dream*, 1994
   Tanya plans an Earth Day project that requires the cooperative efforts of her classmates to be successful.
Sara St. Antoine, *The Green Musketeers and the Fabulous Frogs*, 1994
   Two friends learn that encroaching development threatens an unusual tree frog and organize their classmates to save the frogs' habitat.

571

ABBY LEVINE
PAIGE BILLIN-FRYE, Illustrator

This Is the Turkey

(Morton Grove, IL: Albert Whitman & Company, 2000)

Subject(s): Holidays; Family Life; Stories in Rhyme

Age range(s): Grades K-2

Major character(s): Max, Son; Dad, Father

Time period(s): 2000s (2000)

Locale(s): United States

Summary: Max picks out the turkey for the big dinner at his house. Dad stirs the cranberries for the sauce and relatives and neighbors arrive with pies, salads, and vegetables. The table laden with food is ready for the turkey that accidentally sails through the air and into the fish tank. Max feels responsible for his mother's loss of balance that leads to the turkey-less Thanksgiving feast, but everyone enjoys the meal, feeling full, satisfied and thankful. (32 pages)

Where it's reviewed:
Booklist, September 1, 2000, page 133
Horn Book Guide, Spring 2001, page 42
Publishers Weekly, September 25, 2000, page 65
School Library Journal, September 2000, page 204

Other books by the same author:
Gretchen Groundhog, It's Your Day!, 1998
This Is the Pumpkin, 1997
Ollie Knows Everything, 1994
Too Much Mush!, 1989

Other books you might like:
Eve Bunting, *A Turkey for Thanksgiving*, 1991
   Mr. and Mrs. Moose change to a vegetarian menu after their live turkey causes them to have second thoughts about the Thanksgiving meal.
Joy Cowley, *Gracias, the Thanksgiving Turkey*, 1996
   Miguel becomes so attached to the turkey his father gives him to fatten for Thanksgiving that the family eats chicken with their meal.
Alison Jackson, *I Know an Old Lady Who Swallowed a Pie*, 1997
   Beginning with the pie, an invited guest downs the entire Thanksgiving dinner, including the turkey.
Kimberly Weinberger, *Our Thanksgiving*, 1999
   A simple rhyming tale describes a family's Thanksgiving Day in a "My First Hello Reader."

572

GAIL CARSON LEVINE

Dave at Night

(New York: HarperCollins Publishers, 1999)

Subject(s): Orphans; Jews; African Americans

Age range(s): Grades 5-8

Major character(s): Dave Caros, 11-Year-Old, Orphan; Solly Gruber, Aged Person, Friend; Irma Lee, Child, Friend

Time period(s): 1920s (1926)

Locale(s): New York, New York

Summary: After their father's accidental death an uncle takes Dave's quiet, studious older brother to Chicago, but none of the relatives want Dave. Even Dave's stepmother won't keep him and promptly delivers him to the Hebrew Home for Boys. Angered by the HHB's theft of his few positions and appalled by the harsh conditions, Dave sneaks out at night to enjoy a different life. On his first foray he meets Solly who uses him in his work as a fortuneteller and proves to be a true friend. Through Solly he also meets Irma Lee, a beautiful, wealthy, lonely orphan about his age who seeks and returns Dave's friendship. Before Dave can fulfill his plan to run away from the HHB, he develops such an appreciation for the other "elevens" with whom he lives that he changes his goal to making life in the home better for all of them. An "Afterword'' gives the historical background on which the story is based. (281 pages)

Where it's reviewed:
Booklist, June 1999, page 1829
Five Owls November 1999, page 44
Horn Book, January 2000, page 78
Publishers Weekly, August 30, 1999, page 84
School Library Journal, September 1999, page 226

Awards the book has won:
Publishers Weekly Best Books, 1999
School Library Journal Best Books, 1999

Other books by the same author:
Cinderellis and the Glass Hill, 2000 (Princess Tales)
The Wish, 2000
The Fairy's Mistake, 1999 (Princess Tales)
Ella Enchanted, 1997 (Newbery Honor Book)

Other books you might like:
Christopher Paul Curtis, *Bud, Not Buddy*, 1999
   In a Newbery Award winning title, Bud runs away from an abusive foster home in search of his father, using his deceased mother's belongings as clues.
Charles Dickens, *Oliver Twist*, 1996
   An abridgement by Lesley Baxter makes the classic tale of orphans, street urchins, and the criminals who prey on them accessible to young readers.
Joan Lowery Nixon, *The Orphan Train Quartet*, 1987-1989
   In the 1850s, children abandoned or orphaned in New York City were sent on orphan trains to the West to be adopted.
Zilpha Keatley Snyder, *Gib Rides Home*, 1998
   A job opportunity at Mr. Thornton's ranch enables Gib to leave his orphanage home after four years.
Barbara Brooks Wallace, *Sparrows in the Scullery*, 1997
   Kidnappers deliver Colley, a wealthy but sickly orphan, to the Broggin Home for Boys where other boys befriend him until all are rescued.

573

GAIL CARSON LEVINE
MARK ELLIOTT, Illustrator

The Princess Test
(New York: HarperCollins Publishers, 1999)

Series: Princess Tales
Subject(s): Fairy Tales; Princes and Princesses; Conduct of Life
Age range(s): Grades 3-6
Major character(s): Lorelei, Daughter (of blacksmith), Maiden; Nicholas, Royalty (prince); Trudy, Housekeeper
Time period(s): Indeterminate Past
Locale(s): Snettering-on-Snoakes, Fictional Country

Summary: Lorelei is a fragile, highly sensitive child who is coddled and pampered by her father and mother. When Lorelei is fourteen her mother dies and her father hires Trudy to keep house and care for his daughter. Eager to please, Lorelei offers to help Trudy with chores that her mother never allowed her to do, but each attempt results in more work for Trudy. Finally, hopelessly frustrated, Trudy decides to do

away with Lorelei. Her first attempts do not work so Trudy ''loses'' Lorelei in the forest while her father is away on a trip. Kind Lorelei feels responsible for Trudy and, thinking Trudy is the one lost, goes in search of her. What Lorelei does not find is Trudy, but she does stumble upon a castle holding a contest to determine the princess who will marry Prince Nicholas. With her sensitive nature and fragile constitution, Lorelei easily passes all the tests and, of course, lives happily ever after with Prince Nicholas. (90 pages)

Where it's reviewed:
Booklist, April 15, 1999, page 1531
Bulletin of the Center for Children's Books, May 1999, page 320
Horn Book, May 1999, page 332
Publishers Weekly, February 15, 1999, page 108
School Library Journal, May 1999, page 92

Other books by the same author:
Princess Sonora and the Long Sleep, 1999 (Princess Tales)
The Fairy's Mistake, 1999 (Princess Tales)
Ella Enchanted, 1997 (Newbery Honor Book)

Other books you might like:
Hans Christian Andersen, *Twelve Tales*, 1994
   Translated and illustrated by Eric Blegvad, the collection includes familiar as well as less well-known fairy tales by Andersen.
Ellen Conford, *The Frog Princess of Pelham*, 1997
   In a twist on a fairy tale, a kiss from a popular boy changes Chandler into a frog.
Bruce Lansky, *Newfangled Fairy Tales*, 1997
   A collection of fractured fairy tales edited by Lansky includes one entitled ''The Prince and the Pea.''

574

SONIA LEVITIN
CAT BOWMAN SMITH, Illustrator

Taking Charge
(New York: Orchard Books, 1999)

Subject(s): Babies; Frontier and Pioneer Life; American West
Age range(s): Grades K-3
Major character(s): Amanda, Child, Sister (oldest); Nathan, Baby, Brother (youngest); Mama, Mother
Time period(s): Indeterminate Past
Locale(s): California

Summary: When Mama must travel back to Missouri to care for her own mother who is recovering from an accident Amanda is in charge of the household duties and baby Nathan. The minute Mama leaves, Nathan begins walking and becomes a challenge for Amanda every second until she remembers Mama advice to ask for help if she needs it. Once Amanda does that and makes some toys to occupy Nathan, she is able to complete the chores and cook dinner. Everyone is happy to see Mama step off the stagecoach when her journey is complete. (32 pages)

Where it's reviewed:
Booklist, April 15, 1999, page 1536
Horn Book, March 1999, page 196
Kirkus Reviews, February 1, 1999, page 223

Publishers Weekly, April 5, 1999, page 241
School Library Journal, April 1999, page 102

Other books by the same author:
Boom Town, 1998
Nine for California, 1997 (School Library Journal Best Book)
The Golem and the Dragon Girl, 1993

Other books you might like:
Raymond Bial, *Frontier Home*, 1993
   A nonfiction look at the life of pioneer families uses excerpts from diaries to enliven descriptions of the homes and tools of the time.
Betsy Byars, *The Golly Sisters Go West*, 1986
   Six stories trace the amusing travels of two comical sisters on the frontier.
Steven Kellogg, *Sally Ann Thunder Ann Whirlwind Crockett: A Tall Tale*, 1995
   Sally Ann departs for the frontier on her eighth birthday where she continues her larger than life exploits and eventually marries Davy Crockett.

575

TED LEWIN, Author/Illustrator

Nilo and the Tortoise

(New York: Scholastic, 1999)

Subject(s): Animals; Adventure and Adventurers; Animals/Turtles
Age range(s): Grades K-3
Major character(s): Nilo, Child
Time period(s): Indeterminate
Locale(s): Galapagos Islands, Pacific Islands

Summary: Briefly stranded on an island, Nilo is chased by an angry sea lion, sees a beautifully colored bird, and climbs to the top of a volcano. There he discovers an old giant tortoise that lets Nilo ride on his back. That evening Nilo sleeps near the tortoise, and in the morning, he heads down to the beach where he finds that his father has returned for him in the repaired boat. (40 pages)

Where it's reviewed:
Booklist, August 1999, page 2065
Children's Book Review Service, Spring 1999, page 136
Horn Book Guide, Fall 1999, page 258
Publishers Weekly, May 31, 1999, page 93
School Library Journal, April 1999, page 102

Awards the book has won:
Notable Social Studies Trade Books for Young People, 2000

Other books by the same author:
Gorilla Walk, 1999
Fair, 1997
Market, 1996

Other books you might like:
Lynn Joseph, *Coconut Kind of Day: Island Poems*, 1990
   This collection of poems depicts a day in the life of a girl from Trinidad.
Deirdre Langeland, *Kangaroo Island: An Australian Mallee Forest*, 1998

A kangaroo goes through a day in the Australian Mallee Forest.
Betsy Lewin, *Booby Hatch*, 1995
   A blue-footed booby grows up on the Galapagos Islands.
Nicholas Millhouse, *Blue-Footed Booby: Bird of the Galapagos*, 1986
   A non-fiction account describes the life cycle of the blue-footed booby of the Galapagos Islands.

576

J. PATRICK LEWIS, Adaptor
KATYA KRENINA, Illustrator

At the Wish of the Fish: A Russian Folktale

(New York: Atheneum Books for Young Children, 1999)

Subject(s): Folklore; Fairy Tales; Wishes
Age range(s): Grades 1-3
Major character(s): Emelya, Brother (youngest); Marya, Daughter (of Tsar)
Time period(s): Indeterminate Past
Locale(s): Russia

Summary: Emelya proves himself to be more than the lazy simpleton his family and village expects. While his two older brothers travel, Emelya is responsible for doing their wives' bidding in order to receive the reward promised by his brothers. As Emelya hauls water from the icy lake a talking pike offers to grant all his wishes if Emelya will agree to put the pike back into the water rather than eating it. Emelya accepts the bargain, chooses his wishes thoughtfully and ends up with Marya as his bride, a beautiful home and more wits than he had at the beginning of the tale. (32 pages)

Where it's reviewed:
Booklist, June 1999, page 1833
Horn Book Guide, Fall 1999, page 325
Publishers Weekly, May 31, 1999, page 93
School Library Journal, May 1999, page 109
Teacher Librarian, October 1999, page 57

Awards the book has won:
Notable Social Studies Trade Books for Young People, 2000

Other books by the same author:
Night of the Goat Children, 1999
The House of Boo, 1998
The Christmas of the Reddle Moon, 1994

Other books you might like:
Eric A. Kimmel, *Onions and Garlic*, 1996
   Though Getzel's older brothers consider him a fool he proves his worth to his merchant father by making a wise trade.
Arthur Ransome, *The Fool of the World and the Flying Ship*, 1968
   In a Caldecott Medal winning folktale a peasant reveals himself to be no fool as his attention to good advice enables him to marry the princess.
Uri Shulevitz, *The Golden Goose*, 1995
   A retelling of a Grimm tale explains how a kind, but simple woodsman unwittingly wins the hand of a princess in marriage.

577

J. PATRICK LEWIS
ALEXI NATCHEV, Illustrator

Night of the Goat Children

(New York: Dial Books for Young Readers, 1999)

Subject(s): Princes and Princesses; Animals/Goats; Courage
Age range(s): Grades 1-4
Major character(s): Birgitta, Royalty (princess); Ubo Skald, Outlaw, Leader
Time period(s): Indeterminate Past
Locale(s): Beda, Germany (Black Forest)

Summary: With the walled town of Beda under seige by Ubo Skald and his outlaw band, Princess Birgitta knows that her people face starvation if a solution is not found quickly. The brave princess devises a plan that requires courageous action from five small children to support her dangerous mission. After disguising herself, Princess Birgitta enters the forest and is quickly captured by Ubo Skald's men. The captured ''hag'' tells the outlaws the ''secrets'' she knows about the princess of Beda and the superstitious men begin to doubt their mission. When goats (the children, wearing goatskins stuffed with fleece) appear on the ramparts and survive a flurry of arrows, the outlaws are sure the hag speaks the truth and soon flee in terror. An author's note gives the historical basis for the story. (32 pages)

Where it's reviewed:
Booklist, May 15, 1999, page 1703
Horn Book Guide, Fall 1999, page 258
Kirkus Reviews, February 15, 1999, page 302
Publishers Weekly, April 5, 1999, page 240
School Library Journal, March 1999, page 178

Other books by the same author:
At the Wish of the Fish: A Russian Folktale, 1999
Black Swan White Crow, 1995
The Christmas of the Reddle Moon, 1994

Other books you might like:
Emily Arnold McCully, *Starring Mirette & Bellini*, 1997
    Bravely, Mirette walks the high wire across a canal in order to free Bellini from a Russian prison cell.
Susan L. Roth, *Brave Martha and the Dragon*, 1996
    Martha courageously saves a village from the terrifying nightly visits of a wicked fire-breathing dragon.
Audrey Wood, *Rude Giants*, 1993
    Persuasive Beatrix convinces two rude giants to clean up their act and become good neighbors.

578

KEVIN LEWIS
DANIEL KIRK, Illustrator

Chugga-Chugga Choo-Choo

(New York: Hyperion Books for Children, 1999)

Subject(s): Trains; Toys; Stories in Rhyme
Age range(s): Preschool
Time period(s): 1990s
Locale(s): United States

Summary: With the rising of the sun a toy train begins its daily run, chugging along the track as its whistle blows. Around and about the room the train goes, into tunnels (under the bed) and over the river (the aquarium) until the train reaches the city. When the day's work is done, the train, the toys and a little boy settle down for a night of sleep as the author's first picture book concludes. (32 pages)

Where it's reviewed:
Booklist, October 15, 1999, page 455
Children's Book Review Service, July 1999, page 148
Publishers Weekly, May 17, 1999, page 77
School Library Journal, September 1999, page 193
Teacher Librarian, December 1999, page 46

Other books you might like:
Donald Crews, *Freight Train*, 1978
    Simple text and illustrations of this Caldecott Honor Book introduce color concepts through the gathering speed of a moving train.
Mary Murphy, *My Puffer Train*, 1999
    Penguin invites the animals he meets along the way to board the train as he drives it to the seashore.
Watty Piper, *The Little Engine That Could*, 1930
    The Little Engine proves that gumption is more important than size if there is a job to be done.

579

MAGGIE LEWIS
MICHAEL CHESWORTH, Illustrator

Morgy Makes His Move

(Boston: Houghton Mifflin Company, 1999)

Subject(s): Moving, Household; Schools; Family Life
Age range(s): Grades 2-5
Major character(s): Morgan ''Morgy'' MacDougal-MacDuff, 3rd Grader; Byron Noonan, 3rd Grader, Friend (Morgy's); Savanna MacDuff, Aunt, Teacher (art)
Time period(s): 1990s (1999)
Locale(s): Puckett Corner, Massachusetts

Summary: His family's move from California to Massachusetts puts Morgy into a new school that might as well be in another country—the kids play ice hockey not soccer, the school has no playground and Morgy cannot understand what anyone is saying. What a lot of changes! A visit from Aunt Savanna coincides with a Thanksgiving blizzard and the forced time together gives out-going Aunt Savanna plenty of time to encourage Morgy in the art of making friends and overlooking bullies. In the author's first book, Morgy gradually adjusts, begins to understand Byron's dialect, tries to learn ice hockey and prepares for the birth of twin siblings. (74 pages)

Where it's reviewed:
Booklist, December 15, 1999, page 784
Bulletin of the Center for Children's Books, October 1999, page 59
Horn Book, January 2000, page 79
Kirkus Reviews, October 1, 1999, page 1581
School Library Journal, November 1999, page 122

Awards the book has won:
Horn Book Fanfare, 2000

Other books you might like:
Betsy Duffey, *Hey, New Kid!*, 1996
    Cody is so unhappy to be entering a new school that he makes up a new identity rather than tell people the truthful, boring story of his life.
Johanna Hurwitz, *Roz and Ozzie*, 1992
    Ozzie, Roz's younger neighbor complicates her adjustment to a new school.
Suzy Kline, *Herbie Jones*, 1985
    Herbie doesn't have to move to experience the challenges of third grade including losing his group on a field trip and improving his reading.
Louis Sachar, *Marvin Redpost: Is He a Girl?*, 1993
    Third grader Marvin hears a classmate's claim that kissing his elbow will change him into a girl and he worries that it is true.

580

ROSE LEWIS
JANE DYER, Illustrator

I Love You Like Crazy Cakes

(Boston: Little, Brown and Company, 2000)

Subject(s): Adoption; Babies; Single Parent Families
Age range(s): Grades K-2
Major character(s): Unnamed Character, Single Mother, Narrator; Unnamed Character, Baby, Adoptee
Time period(s): 2000s (2000)
Locale(s): China; United States

Summary: A woman describes her efforts to adopt a Chinese infant and her travel to that country for the baby that becomes her daughter. Quickly, she falls in love with the sweet baby before they ever board the plane for home. Upon arrival in America many relatives greet them with hugs and kisses. The baby's room is outfitted with a crib and full of toys and stuffed animals just waiting for a little girl to play. Many people come to visit bringing gifts, but it's the new mother who rocks the baby to sleep at the end of her first day in a new country. (32 pages)

Where it's reviewed:
Booklist, September 1, 2000, page 124
Children's Book Review Service, September 2000, page 3
Kirkus Reviews, August 1, 2000, page 1120
Publishers Weekly, July 31. 2000, page 94
School Library Journal, October 2000, page 129

Other books you might like:
Jamie Lee Curtis, *Tell Me Again about the Night I Was Born*, 1996
    A little girl knows the story of her adoption so well that she can fill in all the details of the story herself.
Karen Katz, *Over the Moon: An Adoption Tale*, 1997
    Receiving news of a baby's birth, a couple travels to another country to complete the process of adopting the child.
Allen Say, *Allison*, 1997
    Allison, wondering why she looks more like her doll than

her parents, struggles to understand the story of her adoption from another country.

581

DEE LILLEGARD
REX BARRON, Illustrator

The Big Bug Ball

(New York: G.P. Putnam's Sons, 1999)

Subject(s): Animals/Insects; Dancing; Stories in Rhyme
Age range(s): Grades K-1
Major character(s): Unnamed Character, Insect
Time period(s): Indeterminate
Locale(s): Fictional Country

Summary: Insects of all kinds gather for the Big Bug Ball, but a hesitant little sow bug repeats that she doesn't know how to dance. The little sow bog lingers on the sidelines observing the action until a handsome sow bug in a top hat pulls her onto the dance floor and the shy bug learns that she can dance. By the time the Big Bug Ball ends the sow bug has an evening of memories and a budding romance. (32 pages)

Where it's reviewed:
Horn Book Guide, Fall 1999, page 258
Kirkus Reviews, April 15, 1999, page 632
Publishers Weekly, May 17, 1999, page 78
School Library Journal, July 1999, page 75

Awards the book has won:
IRA/CBC Children's Choices, 2000

Other books by the same author:
Tortoise Brings the Mail, 1997
The Day the Daisies Danced, 1996
My Yellow Ball, 1993

Other books you might like:
Frank Asch, *Insects from Outer Space*, 1995
    Alien spaceships loaded with friendly bugs arrive to attend the annual Bug Ball. Vladimir Vagin, co-author.
Richard Egielski, *Jazper*, 1998
    While house sitting for some moths in Bugtown Jazper learns magic tricks.
David Kirk, *Miss Spider's Tea Party*, 1994
    Bugs don't accept lonely Miss Spider's invitation to tea because they don't realize she's interested in eating the floral centerpiece and not them.

582

GRACE LIN, Author/Illustrator

The Ugly Vegetables

(Watertown, MA: Talewinds/Charlesbridge, 1999)

Subject(s): Gardens and Gardening; Neighbors and Neighborhoods; Chinese Americans
Age range(s): Grades K-3
Major character(s): Mommy, Mother, Gardener; Unnamed Character, Child, Daughter
Time period(s): 1990s (1999)
Locale(s): United States

Summary: Up and down the street neighbors are digging their gardens. As a little girl helps her mother she questions why Mommy is using different tools and marking the rows with Chinese characters instead of pretty seed packets. Mommy explains that their family's garden will grow Chinese vegetables, not flowers. As the seeds sprout and the neighbors' gardens begin blooming, the little girl is disappointed that her garden holds only ugly vegetables and no colorful, sweet-smelling floral displays. After Mommy harvests the vegetables to make soup, the fragrance wafting from the kitchen attracts all the neighbors to see the colorful soup she creates. Everyone shares in the ''Ugly Vegetable'' soup and the next year all the gardeners make space for some ugly vegetables beside their flowers. The author's first book is based on childhood memories. (32 pages)

Where it's reviewed:
Booklist, September 15, 1999, page 268
Horn Book, September 1999, page 595
Kirkus Reviews, June 15, 1999, page 966
Publishers Weekly, July 5, 1999, page 69
School Library Journal, September 1999, page 193

Awards the book has won:
Notable Social Studies Trade Books for Young People, 2000

Other books you might like:
Betty G. Birney, *Pie's in the Oven*, 1996
    The fragrant odor of Grandma's apple pie attracts neighbors, friends and relatives eager for a taste.
Jane Cutler, *Mr. Carey's Garden*, 1996
    While comparing gardening tips with his neighbors Mr. Carey explains the reason for his tolerance of the snails in his garden.
Lois Ehlert, *Planting a Rainbow*, 1988
    A mother and her child plant a family garden, carefully planning the placement of the flowers to create a rainbow of colors.
Anna Grossnickle Hines, *Miss Emma's Wild Garden*, 1997
    While visiting Miss Emma, Chloe notices the contrast between neat rows in her father's garden and a wild profusion of plants in Miss Emma's garden.
Lynne Rae Perkins, *Home Lovely*, 1995
    Tiffany's beginning efforts at gardening are noticed and nurtured by a friendly letter carrier.
George Shannon, *Seeds*, 1994
    A package of seeds from a former neighbor enables Warren to create a garden reminiscent of the one he enjoyed with Bill.

583

TANYA LINCH, Author/Illustrator

My Duck

(New York: Scholastic Inc., 2000)

Age range(s): Grades K-2
Major character(s): Unnamed Character, Teacher; Unnamed Character, Student—Elementary School, Narrator; Unnamed Character, Duck
Time period(s): 2000s (2000)
Locale(s): England

Summary: A little girl's imaginative attempts to complete a writing assignment are continually thwarted by her teacher. When she begins by drawing a duck with shoes the teacher rejects the whimsy of her idea and instructs her to start a new story. The student willingly attempts another story, but the duck won't leave and sits beneath the tree in the new picture eating his lunch. The teacher rejects the girl's second and third creative attempts too and now she has two characters wandering through her stories. Finally, on the fourth try the girl simply retells a trip to the zoo, but her imaginary characters insist on being a part of the picture despite the frustrated student's attempts to banish them. Fortunately, the teacher doesn't notice the duo walking up the hill to visit the penguins. This is the first book also written by the children's book illustrator. (32 pages)

Where it's reviewed:
Books Magazine, Autumn 2000, page 17
Horn Book Guide, Spring 2001, page 43
Kirkus Reviews, September 15, 2000, page 1357
Publishers Weekly, October 23, 2000, page 75
School Library Journal, October 2000, page 129

Other books you might like:
Katherine Hook Berlan, *Andrew's Amazing Monsters*, 1993
    Andrew's artwork comes to life, steps out of his drawings and prepares a surprise party for him.
Marc Brown, *Arthur Writes a Story*, 1996
    A class assignment to write a story challenges Arthur to select a topic and be willing to revise the story again and again.
June Crebbin, *Danny's Duck*, 1995
    Danny's artwork chronicles the changes in a duck's nest. When he sadly shows his teacher a picture of an empty nest she leads him to the pond.
Amy Hest, *Jamaica Louise James*, 1996
    Jamaica's artistic masterpieces find acceptance by all as they brighten the subway station where her grandmother works.
Ellen Stoll Walsh, *Jack's Tale*, 1997
    Reluctantly, Jack agrees to an author's request to walk through the story he's writing from beginning to end.

584

REEVE LINDBERGH
TRACEY CAMPBELL PEARSON, Illustrator

The Awful Aardvarks Shop for School

(New York: Viking, 2000)

Subject(s): Stores, Retail; Animals/Aardvarks; Stories in Rhyme
Age range(s): Grades K-2
Time period(s): Indeterminate
Locale(s): Fictional Country

Summary: Clutching mom's list four aardvark siblings arrive at the mall to do their back-to-school shopping. Although they are sent for sneakers, they try on sunglasses, clothes and roller blades instead. In each store the aardvarks create chaos while shopping for everything except what's written on the list. Totally unaware of the mess they leave behind them they venture from store to store before concluding the day with the required haircut and then they're out of the mall until next year. (32 pages)

Where it's reviewed:
Booklist, June 1, 2000, page 1910
Horn Book Guide, Spring 2001, page 43
Kirkus Reviews, June 1, 2000, page 800
Publishers Weekly, June 12, 2000, page 74
School Library Journal, July 2000, page 81

Other books by the same author:
The Circle of Days, 1998
North Country Spring, 1997
The Awful Aardvarks Go to School, 1997
If I'd Known Then What I Know Now, 1994
The Day the Goose Got Loose, 1990

Other books you might like:
Cooper Edens, *The Animal Mall*, 2000
    A rhyming tale describes a family's shopping trip to choose a birthday gift for Mom at the frenetic, crowded Animal Mall.
Ann Jonas, *Aardvarks, Disembark!*, 1994
    In an award-winning title, when the flood subsides, Noah calls the role from A to Z so the animals can leave the ark.
Lisa Lawston, *A Pair of Red Sneakers*, 1998
    A story in rhyme lists the many features Miles requires in a new shoe with the most important being the color.

585

BARBRO LINDGREN
OLOF LANDSTROM, Illustrator
ELISABETH KALLICK DYSSEGAARD, Translator

Benny's Had Enough!

(New York: R&S Books, 1999)

Subject(s): Animals/Pigs; Cleanliness; Mothers and Sons
Age range(s): Grades K-1
Major character(s): Benny, Pig, Son; Little Piggy, Toy
Time period(s): 1990s (1999)
Locale(s): Fictional Country

Summary: When Benny's mother tries to put Little Piggy in the washing machine Benny decides he's had enough of her cleanliness and marches out the door. Then Benny faces the dilemma of finding a home. No one wants to share a home with Benny and Little Piggy so Benny finds a field and digs a hole. He is happily wallowing in the hole when an old man chases him away. Frightened, Benny runs off and then realizes he has forgotten Little Piggy. He gathers his courage to enter the angry man's field and with a little luck finds Little Piggy and hurries home to his mother. (28 pages)

Where it's reviewed:
Booklist, October 15, 1999, page 456
Horn Book, November 1999, page 729
Kirkus Reviews, November 1, 1999, page 1746
Publishers Weekly, November 15, 1999, page 64
School Library Journal, December 1999, page 102

Awards the book has won:
Horn Book Fanfare, 2000
Riverbank Review Children's Books of Distinction, 2000

Other books by the same author:
Shorty Takes Off, 1990
Sam's Wagon, 1986
Sam's Teddy Bear, 1982
The Wild Baby, 1981

Other books you might like:
Janice Boland, *Annabel Again*, 1995
    Annabel seeks a residence more exciting than her mud puddle but discovers that there is no place like home.
Phyllis Root, *Mrs. Potter's Pig*, 1996
    Ermajean's habits are in such stark contrast to those of her neat mother that Mrs. Potter is only mildly surprised to find a pig in her baby carriage.
Mark Teague, *Pigsty*, 1994
    Wendell's room becomes so cluttered that pigs move in and then the mess really begins!

586

SUSAN HART LINDQUIST

Summer Soldiers

(New York: Delacorte Press, 1999)

Subject(s): Fathers and Sons; World War I; Bullies
Age range(s): Grades 4-7
Major character(s): Joseph Michael ''Joey'' Farrington, 11-Year-Old, Brother (older); Luther Thornton, Friend, Brother (of three bullies); Jim Morgan, Friend
Time period(s): 1910s (1917-1918)
Locale(s): California (near Maxwell)

Summary: The escalation of the war changes the relationships of Joe and his friends when three of the fathers enlist leaving their sons to care for the sheep and their families. When Jim's father does not enlist the entire Morgan family is subjected to taunts of cowardice, especially from Luther's older brothers. Always willing to bully the younger boys, the behavior of Luther's brothers worsens after their father leaves. As the summer's events unfold, Joe begins to learn a deeper appreciation of the meaning of courage when his father is reported missing and Jim's father's efforts to save some shipwrecked horses results in his death. (178 pages)

Where it's reviewed:
Booklist, May 15, 1999, page 1695
Bulletin of the Center for Children's Books, July 1999, page 393
Horn Book Guide, Fall 1999, page 296
Publishers Weekly, June 21, 1999, page 68
School Library Journal, June 1999, page 134

Other books by the same author:
Wander, 1998
Walking the Rim, 1992

Other books you might like:
Kimberly Brubaker Bradley, *One-of-a-Kind Mallie*, 1999
    Life in a small midwestern town during World War I revolves around Red Cross knitting meetings, victory gardens and rationing.
Mary Downing Hahn, *Stepping on the Cracks*, 1991
    This award-winning novel explores a young girl's

thoughts about her brother fighting in Europe and the town bully who hides his pacifist brother.

Gregory Maguire, *The Good Liar*, 1999

Although they live in occupied France during World War II, three brothers try to enjoy their usual summer activities.

587

SUSAN HART LINDQUIST

Wander

(New York: Delacorte Press, 1998)

Subject(s): Animals/Dogs; Parent and Child; Death
Age range(s): Grades 3-6
Major character(s): James Christie, 12-Year-Old, Brother; Sary Christie, Sister, 7-Year-Old; Wander, Dog
Time period(s): 1990s
Locale(s): California

Summary: A year after James and Sary's mother is killed in an car accident and their father moves them to his sister's home, the distance between the father, his children and the memories of their mother is still as great as the distance from their home in town to this outlying homestead. James notices that his father, though physically present, is just as "gone" as his mother. Perhaps James and Sary have as much need to nurture the stray dog they find as the dog has need of a family to love and care for him. Keeping their relationship with the dog a secret from everyone leads to a potentially dangerous situation when a local sheep rancher accuses the stray of killing his sheep. With the danger comes the potential for the family to face their grief and move forward with their lives. (133 pages)

Where it's reviewed:
Booklist, September 15, 1998, page 230
Bulletin of the Center for Children's Books, November 1998, page 105
Children's Book Review Service, Winter 1999, page 69
Horn Book Guide, Spring 1999, page 70
School Library Journal, September 1998, page 204

Other books by the same author:
Summer Soldiers, 1999
Walking the Rim, 1992

Other books you might like:
Kristine L. Franklin, *Lone Wolf*, 1997
   After a traffic accident kills his sister, leading to his parent's divorce, Perry moves with his father to a remote area of Minnesota.
Kevin Henkes, *Sun & Spoon*, 1997
   As Spoon struggles to understand his grief he decides that possessing something that once belonged to Grandma will assure that he never forgets her.
Karen Hesse, *Sable*, 1994
   Tate wants desperately to keep the stray dog that appears in the yard of her mountain home, but first she must prove she can care for it responsibly.
Colby Rodowsky, *The Turnabout Shop*, 1998
   When Livvy's only relative, her mother, dies, Livvy moves to Baltimore to live with her mother's college friend and adjusts to a very different life.

588

JANET TAYLOR LISLE
SATOMI ICHIKAWA, Illustrator

The Lost Flower Children

(New York: Philomel Books, 1999)

Subject(s): Sisters; Aunts and Uncles; Gardens and Gardening
Age range(s): Grades 3-6
Major character(s): Olivia, 9-Year-Old, Sister; Nellie, 5-Year-Old, Sister; Minty, Aunt (great aunt), Aged Person
Time period(s): 1990s (1999)
Locale(s): United States

Summary: Still grieving over their mother's recent death, Olivia and Nellie are aghast when their father packs them off to Aunt Minty's for the summer. Aunt Minty is no more excited than the sisters are about their arrival, but she tries to make them welcome. Her efforts frequently backfire because of Nellie's obsessive "rules" that Olivia understands better than anyone except their deceased mother. Aunt Minty's overgrown garden provides a distraction, then a purpose for the summer and finally an avenue for healing. When a storybook found in Aunt Minty's house suggests that long ago angry fairies planted teacups in the garden and changed the children using them into flowers, the search unites the sisters with their great aunt. By finding the complete tea set, Olivia and Nellie expect to free the flower children from the spell, but without planning to do so, they free themselves. (122 pages)

Where it's reviewed:
Booklist, May 15, 1999, page 1690
Horn Book, May 1999, page 333
Publishers Weekly, April 12, 1999, page 75
Riverbank Review, Winter 1999-2000, page 30
School Library Journal, June 1999, page 100

Awards the book has won:
ALA Notable Children's Books, 2000
School Library Journal Best Books, 1999

Other books by the same author:
Angela's Aliens, 1996
The Lampfish of Twill, 1991
Afternoon of the Elves, 1989 (Newbery Honor Book)

Other books you might like:
Frances Hodgson Burnett, *The Secret Garden*, 1911
   Orphaned Mary is sent to live on the Yorkshire Moors where she unlocks the secret to an overgrown garden and an invalid cousin's health.
Paul Fleischman, *Seedfolks*, 1997
   Kim's simple act of planting bean seeds in a vacant lot inspires others in her diverse community to notice and care about each other.
Jean Van Leeuwen, *Blue Sky, Butterfly*, 1996
   Tending a garden helps Twig's mother come out of her depression and helps the family recover from the parents' separation.

589

JEAN LITTLE
JENNIFER PLECAS, Illustrator

Emma's Magic Winter
(New York: HarperCollins Publishers, 1998)

Series: I Can Read
Subject(s): Shyness; Friendship; Self-Confidence
Age range(s): Grades 1-2
Major character(s): Emma, Student—Elementary School, Friend; Sally Gray, Neighbor (Emma's), Friend; Josh Gray, Brother (Sally's)
Time period(s): 1990s (1998)
Locale(s): Canada

Summary: Shy Emma is unable to read above a whisper when the teacher calls on her to read aloud in class. Emma feels so shy that when her mother sends her with a pie to meet the new neighbors she imagines that she has magic boots in order to give her the confidence to greet Sally. Noticing that Sally has the same boots, Emma teaches her the "magic boots" game and they hurry out to play in the snow. When reading time comes the next day in school, Emma confesses to her new friend how difficult it is to read in class. Sally reminds Emma of the good job that she did reading to Josh and suggests she use the "magic boots" to help her in class. Sally's idea works and by the time spring arrives and the boots are put away, Emma has more confidence and a solid friendship. (64 pages)

Where it's reviewed:
Booklist, November 1, 1998, page 507
Bulletin of the Center for Children's Books, October 1998, page 65
Horn Book, September 1998, page 610
Kirkus Reviews, August 15, 1998, page 1191
School Library Journal, October 1998, page 106

Other books by the same author:
Bats about Baseball, 1995
Jess Was the Brave One, 1992
Revenge of the Small Small, 1992
From Anna, 1972

Other books you might like:
James Howe, *Pinky and Rex and the New Neighbors*, 1997
   When their long-time neighbor sells her house, Pinky and Rex worry about who will buy it and become their new neighbors.
Tony Johnston, *Sparky and Eddie: The First Day of School*, 1997
   Neighbors Sparky and Eddie are eager to begin school until they learn they've been assigned to different classrooms.
Stephen Krensky, *Lionel in the Winter*, 1994
   In four brief easy-to-read stories Lionel makes the most of the winter weather that others in his family dislike.
Megan McDonald, *Beezy Magic*, 1998
   Three stories in an easy reader tell of humorous events in Beezy's life.
Suzanne Williams, *Emily at School*, 1996
   Emily learns that second grade has some unexpected challenges, including new student Alex.

590

KIMBERLEY GRIFFITHS LITTLE

Enchanted Runner
(New York: Avon/Camelot, 1999)

Subject(s): Indians of North America; Racially Mixed People; Grandfathers
Age range(s): Grades 5-7
Major character(s): Kendall Drennan, 12-Year-Old, Runner; Trina Ramirez, Indian (Acoma), Artisan; Armando Abeyta, Indian (Acoma), Grandfather (Kendall's)
Time period(s): 1990s (1999)
Locale(s): New Mexico; Sky City, New Mexico

Summary: A year after Kendall's mother's death, an unfulfilled promise to Armando Abeyta, Kendall's great grandfather, unexpectedly changes his plans to spend summer vacation traveling with his older brother and father as they haul freight across the country. In her annual letter to Armando Abeyta prior to her death, Kendall's mother promised that when he was 12 years old, she would return to her native home with him and Armando requests by letter that the promise be kept. Bearing a resemblance to his Acoma mother Kendall recalls suffering taunts because of his mixed heritage yet, when he arrives at Sky City, he doesn't feel as if he fits in there either. After touring the mesa with Trina he realizes that he wants to belong, to learn about his heritage and to find the answers to his inner need to run. Evenings of listening to his great grandfather's stories fill in some of the pieces of the puzzle as Kendall comes to know himself, his urge to run and the "magic strings" that bind him to this land. (147 pages)

Where it's reviewed:
Booklist, September 1, 1999, page 133
Bulletin of the Center for Children's Books, September 1999, page 20
Horn Book Guide, Spring 2000, page 82
Kirkus Reviews, July 1, 1999, page 1056
School Library Journal, December 1999, page 137

Other books by the same author:
Breakaway, 1997

Other books you might like:
Joseph Bruchac, *Eagle Song*, 1997
   When unemployment on their Iroquois reservation forces Danny's family to move to Brooklyn he depends on his cultural heritage to overcome prejudice.
Michael Dorris, *Sees Behind Trees*, 1996
   A visually impaired Native American boy learns how to use other senses in order to be a contributing member of his tribe.
Craig Kee Strete, *The World in Grandfather's Hands*, 1995
   After his father's death, Jimmy's family moves to a noisy, confining city and Jimmy misses the quiet of his desert pueblo home.

591

AMY LITTLESUGAR
FLOYD COOPER, Illustrator

Tree of Hope

(New York: Philomel Books, 1999)

Subject(s): African Americans; Actors and Actresses; Depression (Economic)
Age range(s): Grades 1-3
Major character(s): Florrie, Child, Daughter; Daddy, Father, Actor; Mama, Mother
Time period(s): 1930s
Locale(s): New York, New York (Harlem)

Summary: Before the Depression closed the Lafayette Theatre Daddy was an actor there and met Mama after a performance. Now, Daddy makes doughnuts at an all-night bakery, but he hasn't stopped dreaming of returning to the stage. Florrie wishes right along with him each time they visit the ''Tree of Hope'' in front of the theatre and one day their wishes come true. Daddy successfully auditions for a small role in *Macbeth*. By the time opening night arrives and Mama comes to see the show, Florrie knows Mama has found the ability to hope again after years of hardship. A concluding author's note gives background for the story. (40 pages)

Where it's reviewed:
Booklist, December 15, 1999, page 790
Horn Book Guide, Spring 2000, page 68
Kirkus Reviews, October 15, 1999, page 1646
Publishers Weekly, November 29, 1999, page 70
School Library Journal, November 1999, page 123

Awards the book has won:
Notable Social Studies Trade Books for Young People, 2000

Other books by the same author:
Shake Rag: From the Life of Elvis Presley, 1998
A Portrait of Spotted Deer's Grandfather, 1997
The Spinner's Daughter, 1994

Other books you might like:
Sandra Belton, *From Miss Ida's Front Porch*, 1993
    The older residents of the Miss Ida's neighborhood share their memories of the challenges faced by African American performers.
Debbi Chocolate, *The Piano Man*, 1998
    With the advent of sound in movies the piano man loses his job playing during silent films and becomes a piano tuner.
Belinda Rochelle, *When Jo Louis Won the Title*, 1994
    Sitting on the steps of her Harlem home, Jo Louis listens as her grandfather explains how she came to have her name.

592

JONATHAN LONDON
FRANK REMKIEWICZ, Illustrator

Froggy Goes to Bed

(New York: Viking, 2000)

Subject(s): Bedtime; Sleep; Animals/Frogs and Toads
Age range(s): Grades K-1
Major character(s): Froggy, Frog, Son

Time period(s): Indeterminate
Locale(s): Fictional Country

Summary: Froggy feels exhausted from a busy day of play until he hears bedtime announced. Suddenly, he has to search for the right toy for the bathtub, locate his pajamas and dig his toothbrush out of the cookie jar. Then, before Froggy can fall asleep he needs a snack, a drink, the nightlight and another glass of water to replace the one he spills. At last he's ready for his mother to read a story and just before he falls asleep he gives his dozing mom one last kiss. (32 pages)

Where it's reviewed:
Booklist, March 1, 2000, page 1250
Horn Book Guide, Fall 2000, page 252
Kirkus Reviews, May 15, 2000, page 716
School Library Journal, June 2000, page 119

Other books by the same author:
The Waterfall, 1999
At the Edge of the Forest, 1998
Froggy Goes to School, 1996
Froggy Gets Dressed, 1992

Other books you might like:
Peggy Perry Anderson, *To the Tub*, 1996
    Although Joe understands it's bath time his father has quite a challenge actually getting him ready and into the tub.
Michael Foreman, *Dad! I Can't Sleep*, 1995
    Dad's going-to-sleep suggestions fail to produce the desired effect.
Jill Murphy, *A Quiet Night In*, 1994
    When parents read a bedtime story to their children so they can enjoy a quiet evening alone, they put themselves, not the children, to sleep.
Elizabeth Winthrop, *Asleep in a Heap*, 1993
    While waiting for Julia to finish her bubble bath, first Daddy then Mama, sister Molly, the dog, and four cats fall asleep on the bathroom floor.

593

JONATHAN LONDON
FRANK REMKIEWICZ, Illustrator

Froggy Plays Soccer

(New York: Viking, 1999)

Subject(s): Sports/Soccer; Animals/Frogs and Toads; Competition
Age range(s): Grades K-1
Major character(s): Froggy, Frog, Soccer Player
Time period(s): Indeterminate
Locale(s): Fictional Country

Summary: On the day of the big soccer game to determine the city champion Froggy's dad reminds him that he is not the goalie and cannot let his hands touch the ball. The fact that Froggy spends most of his time on the field picking daisies, turning cartwheels and tying his shoes could explain why he makes a great save—by catching the ball. Froggy is embarrassed because his error enables the other team to tie the score, but he redeems himself later in the game and uses his hands for high fives after his team wins. (32 pages)

Where it's reviewed:
Booklist, March 1, 1999, page 1221
Horn Book Guide, Fall 1999, page 258
Kirkus Reviews, January 1, 1999, page 68
Publishers Weekly, February 8, 1999, page 216
School Library Journal, March 1999, page 180

Awards the book has won:
IRA/CBC Children's Choices, 2000

Other books by the same author:
Froggy's First Kiss, 1998
Froggy Learns to Swim, 1995
Froggy Gets Dressed, 1992

Other books you might like:
Anthony Browne, *Willy the Wizard*, 1996
    Willy the chimpanzee gains the confidence to play on team of gorillas when he's given a special pair of soccer boots.
Peter Catalanotto, *Dylan's Day Out*, 1089
    When dalmatian Dylan runs off for the day he joins a soccer game between the skunks and the penguins.
Colin McNaughton, *Preston's Goal!*, 1998
    As usual, Preston is oblivious to the consequences of his actions as he kicks his soccer ball along the street.

594

JONATHAN LONDON
FRANK REMKIEWICZ, Illustrator

Froggy's Best Christmas
(New York: Viking, 2000)

Subject(s): Christmas; Animals/Frogs and Toads; Animals
Age range(s): Grades K-1
Major character(s): Froggy, Frog, Friend; Max, Beaver, Friend
Time period(s): Indeterminate
Locale(s): Fictional Country

Summary: Hibernating Froggy dreams of snow when a real snowball hits his window. Max is outside inviting Froggy to wake up and enjoy Christmas. Froggy has never celebrated Christmas because he sleeps through it every year. Max's gift to Froggy is a Christmas holiday and they wake up two other hibernating friends to help select the tree. Once they've found the perfect one Max cuts it down and they carry it back to Froggy's house to decorate. Everyone agrees this is the best (and only) Christmas they've ever had. (32 pages)

Where it's reviewed:
Booklist, October 2000, page 61
Horn Book Guide, Spring 2001, page 19
Kirkus Reviews, August 15, 2000, page 1199
Publishers Weekly, September 25, 2000, page 75

Other books by the same author:
The Waterfall, 1999
Froggy Goes to School, 1996 (IRA/CBC Children's Choice)
Froggy Learns to Swim, 1995
Let's Go, Froggy!, 1994 (IRA/CBC Children's Choice)
Froggy Gets Dressed, 1992

Other books you might like:
Mariana, *Miss Flora McFlimsey's Christmas Eve*, 1949
    With help from Timothy Mouse, an angel, and her own belief, Miss Flora has a joyful Christmas that proves wishes do come true.
John O'Brien, *Mother Hubbard's Christmas*, 1996
    A rhyming story describes Mother Hubbard's efforts to prepare a simple holiday celebration despite her empty cupboards.
Brigitte Weninger, *Merry Christmas, Davy!*, 1998
    Davy's family is initially concerned to learn he's given most of the family's winter food supply to hungry animals, but his kindness is rewarded.

595

JONATHAN LONDON
FRANK REMKIEWICZ, Illustrator

Froggy's Halloween
(New York: Viking, 1999)

Subject(s): Halloween; Animals/Frogs and Toads; Imagination
Age range(s): Grades K-2
Major character(s): Froggy, Frog
Time period(s): Indeterminate
Locale(s): Fictional Country

Summary: During the week prior to Halloween Froggy's homework goes undone and his attention wanders in class because he spends all his time worrying about his Halloween identity. Finally, the night before Halloween Froggy decides that he will trick-or-treat as the Frog Prince. Proudly he dons a cape, crown, and sword to begin his door-to-door quest for candy. When his bag is full he heads home, unaware that his sword has torn the bag and he's leaving a trail of candy behind. When Froggy arrives home with an empty sack, his mother cheerfully gives him the leftover candy which the trick-or-treaters didn't seem to want—chocolate covered flies—Froggy's favorite! (32 pages)

Where it's reviewed:
Booklist, September 1, 1999, page 149
Horn Book Guide, Spring 2000, page 45
School Library Journal, September 1999, page 193

Other books by the same author:
Froggy Goes to School, 1996
Let's Go, Froggy!, 1994
Froggy Gets Dressed, 1992

Other books you might like:
Diane DeGroat, *Trick or Treat, Smell My Feet*, 1998
    Gilbert's carefully made Halloween costume plans go awry when he grabs the wrong bag as he hurries to the school costume parade.
Judith Ross Enderle, *Six Creepy Sheep*, 1992
    Wearing their ghost costumes, six sheep set off for a night of Halloween fun. Stephanie G. Tessler, co-author.
Dav Pilkey, *The Hallo-Weiner*, 1995
    Oscar is embarrassed to wear the Halloween costume his mother makes for him.

596

JONATHAN LONDON
RENEE WILLIAMS-ANDRIANI, Illustrator

Shawn and Keeper and the Birthday Party

(New York: Dutton Children's Books, 1999)

Series: Dutton Easy Reader
Subject(s): Birthdays; Animals/Dogs; Pets
Age range(s): Grades 1-2
Major character(s): Shawn, 6-Year-Old; Keeper, Dog; Dad, Father
Time period(s): 1990s (1999)
Locale(s): United States

Summary: Shawn and Keeper were born on the same day and are growing up together, celebrating their shared birthday every year. Shawn seeks Keeper's advice with plans for the party and they eagerly prepare for the day. The party is great fun until Shawn's cake vanishes. When the search for it is unsuccessful everyone suspects Keeper of secretly eating the cake until Dad appears bearing the cake to which he has secretly added Keeper's name. (32 pages)

Where it's reviewed:
Booklist, October 1, 1999, page 365
Horn Book Guide, Spring 2000, page 62
School Library Journal, November 1999, page 124

Other books by the same author:
Puddles, 1997
The Village Basket Weaver, 1996
A Koala for Katie: An Adoption Story, 1993

Other books you might like:
Marion Dane Bauer, *Alison's Puppy*, 1997
    When Alison receives a kitten rather than the puppy she wanted for her birthday she names the feline "Puppy."
Syd Hoff, *Happy Birthday, Danny and the Dinosaur!*, 1995
    A beginning reader features 6-year-old Danny's birthday party to which he invites his pal dinosaur.
Cynthia Rylant, *Henry and Mudge and the Best Day of All*, 1995
    Both Henry and his pet dog Mudge enjoy Henry's birthday party so much that they declare May 1st to be the best day ever.

597

MELINDA LONG
HOLLY MEADE, Illustrator

When Papa Snores

(New York: Simon & Schuster Books for Young Readers, 2000)

Subject(s): Grandparents; Sleep
Age range(s): Grades K-3
Major character(s): Papa, Grandfather; Nana, Grandmother; Unnamed Character, Child, Narrator
Time period(s): 2000s (2000)
Locale(s): United States

Summary: In the author's first book a little girl tries to decide which of her grandparents snores the loudest. When Papa snores the bedside lamp shakes, the dresser drawers open and the mops in the closet dance about. Nana's snores, on the other hand, clank the window blinds, shake the dishes dry and cause shoes to tumble down the stairs. Although the neighbors complain when both of them snore at the same time, the little girl thinks it's a comforting sound and drifts off to sleep—though not too quietly. (32 pages)

Where it's reviewed:
Horn Book Guide, Spring 2001, page 43
Horn Book, September 2000, page 552
Kirkus Reviews, August 1, 2000, page 1120
School Library Journal, October 2000, page 129
Tribune Books, October 8, 2000, page 5

Other books you might like:
Charles C. Black, *The Royal Nap*, 1995
    King Gordo needs absolute silence throughout his kingdom in order to complete his daily nap.
M.L. Miller, *The Enormous Snore*, 1995
    The sounds of snoring keep the residents of a castle from sleeping until Letty solves the problem.
Audrey Wood, *The Napping House*, 1984
    Everyone in the napping house ends up sleeping on top of Granny.

598

LENORE LOOK
STEPHEN T. JOHNSON, Illustrator

Love as Strong as Ginger

(New York: Atheneum Books for Young Readers, 1999)

Subject(s): Chinese Americans; Grandmothers; Work
Age range(s): Grades 1-4
Major character(s): Katie, Child; GninGnin, Grandmother, Worker (crab picker)
Time period(s): 1970s
Locale(s): Seattle, Washington

Summary: During her Saturday visits to GninGnin's Chinatown apartment, Katie grows curious about her grandmother's work and the thick, stinky rubber gloves she is required to wear. GninGnin patiently answers Katie's questions about her job at a crab factory and the small wages from which she tries to save a little money so Katie can have a better life than an immigrant who knows no English. Finally, Katie is allowed to accompany GninGnin to work. In the noisy, smelly crab "chong" Katie is amazed at the speed with which GninGnin and her coworkers crack the crabs and shake out the meat. Katie comes away tired, but with a better appreciation for her grandmother's effort and the "love as strong as ginger" that GninGnin has for Katie. The author's first book is based on family memories. (32 pages)

Where it's reviewed:
Booklist, October 15, 1999, page 443
Horn Book Guide, Fall 1999, page 259
Horn Book, May 1999, page 318
Publishers Weekly, May 24, 1999, page 79
School Library Journal, July 1999, page 76

Awards the book has won:
Booklist Editors' Choice, 1999
Notable Social Studies Trade Books for Young People, 2000

Other books you might like:

Sook Nyul Choi, *Yunmi and Halmoni's Trip*, 1997
With her grandmother, Yunmi travels to Seoul to meet her cousins and celebrate her deceased grandfather's birthday.

Georgia Guback, *Luka's Quilt*, 1994
The traditional Hawaiian quilt Luka's grandmother makes for her granddaughter teaches a lesson in compromise and understanding.

William Low, *Chinatown*, 1997
A young boy accompanies his grandmother as she conducts her daily errands along crowded streets of Chinatown.

599

ALICE LOW
JANE MANNING, Illustrator

The Witch Who Was Afraid of Witches

(New York: HarperCollins Publishers, 1999)

Series: I Can Read Chapter Book
Subject(s): Witches and Witchcraft; Sisters; Halloween
Age range(s): Grades 2-3
Major character(s): Wendy, Witch, Sister (youngest); Roger, Child, Neighbor
Time period(s): 1990s
Locale(s): United States

Summary: Poor little Wendy has two obnoxious older sisters who are quick to remind her of her lack of witch power. When Wendy loses her broom, her sisters leave her home on Halloween night. Against their instructions Wendy answers a knock at the door and discovers a trick-or-treater dressed as a ghost. Roger invites Wendy to come with him as he makes the rounds. At Roger's house, Wendy gains some confidence in her witch power when she takes flight on the kitchen broom and turns Roger's costume black so he can be a witch too. With Roger's positive feedback Wendy's witch power grows along with her confidence and she gains respect from her sisters. This easy reader adaptation of Low's original story published in 1978 is newly illustrated. (48 pages)

Where it's reviewed:
Booklist, September 1, 1999, page 146
Horn Book Guide, Spring 2000, page 68
School Library Journal, December 1999, page 103

Other books by the same author:
Witches' Holiday, 1997 (Read with Me)
Spooky Stories for a Dark and Stormy Night, 1994
The Popcorn Shop, 1994 (Hello Reader!)

Other books you might like:

Lorna Balian, *Humbug Witch*, 1987
Despite her efforts, becoming a witch does not come easily to an apprentice.

James Stevenson, *Emma*, 1985
Not your typical witch, Emma even needs flying lessons!

Jane Yolen, *Best Witches: Poems for Halloween*, 1989
This collection of witch poems includes some surprising observations on the real activities of witches.

600

SUSAN LOWELL
JANE MANNING, Illustrator

Cindy Ellen: A Wild Western Cinderella

(New York: Joanna Cotler Books/HarperCollins Publishers, 2000)

Subject(s): Fairy Tales; Folklore; American West
Age range(s): Grades K-3
Major character(s): Cindy Ellen, Cowgirl, Stepdaughter; Joe Prince, Cowboy
Time period(s): Indeterminate Past
Locale(s): West

Summary: This western Cinderella tale has the requisite cruel stepmother and stepsisters and, of course, a fairy godmother. Cindy Ellen's fairy godmother fires pistols that shoot the fairy dust to give timid Cindy Ellen some gumption so she can use the magic coming her way. Then she gets a new outfit and a fancier horse for the rodeo. Cindy Ellen wows Joe Prince at the rodeo, but dashes away before midnight leaving him in the dust. They meet again at a square dance that the fairy godmother has helped Cindy Ellen prepare for with a new dress, fancy spurs for her boots and a stagecoach for transportation. When Cindy Ellen hears the clock strike midnight, she races away, leaving Joe Prince with a spur and a determination to find the boot that it fits. (40 pages)

Where it's reviewed:
Booklist, May 15, 2000, page 1757
Horn Book Guide, Fall 2000, page 341
Kirkus Reviews, May 1, 2000, page 636
Publishers Weekly, June 19, 2000, page 78
School Library Journal, June 2000, page 134

Other books by the same author:
Little Red Cowboy Hat, 1997
The Bootmaker and the Elves, 1997 (IRA/CBC Children's Choices)
The Tortoise and the Jackrabbit, 1994
The Three Little Javelinas, 1992

Other books you might like:

Ellen Jackson, *Cinder Edna*, 1994
In a Cinderella tale with a feminist twist Cinder Edna doesn't wait for a fairy godmother; she takes charge of her life and gets the prince herself.

Charles Perrault, *Cinderella*, 1954
Cinderella overcomes mistreatment by her stepfamily to win a Prince's hand in marriage in this retelling of a classic tale of love and inner beauty.

Alan Schroeder, *Smoky Mountain Rose: An Appalachian Cinderella*, 1997
Rose, an orphan in the Smoky Mountains, marries the ''rich feller'' in the neighborhood.

601

LOIS LOWRY
DIANE DEGROAT, Illustrator

Zooman Sam

(Boston: Houghton Mifflin Company, 1999)

Subject(s): Careers; Schools/Preschool; Literacy
Age range(s): Grades 3-5
Major character(s): Sam Krupnik, 4-Year-Old, Student; Mrs. Bennett, Teacher; Anastasia Krupnik, Sister (older)
Time period(s): 1990s (1999)
Locale(s): Massachusetts

Summary: Sam uses Mrs. Bennett's note about Future Job Day as a paper airplane so his parents have no advance warning of the important day. The night before the big day Sam realizes he has nothing to wear for his chosen career of zookeeper. His sympathetic family comes to the rescue with a way to make Sam's idea a reality. His mom fashions coveralls out of pajamas and embroiders Zooman Sam on them. Anastasia borrows hats from a neighbor to complete Sam's costume and Sam considers his contribution to the class activity a complete success. (155 pages)

Where it's reviewed:
Booklist, July 1999, page 1947
Bulletin of the Center for Children's Books, September 1999, page 21
Horn Book, September 1999, page 613
Publishers Weekly, September 13, 1999, page 85
School Library Journal, September 1999, page 193

Other books by the same author:
See You Around, Sam!, 1996 (School Library Journal Best Book)
Attaboy Sam!, 1992
All About Sam, 1988

Other books you might like:
Beverly Cleary, *The Ramona Series*, 1952-1999
    Irrepressible Ramona and her family endure school problems and sibling squabbles with love and a sense of humor.
Johanna Hurwitz, *Starting School*, 1998
    Twins Marcus and Marius switch places on the same day that the teachers change classrooms so each can experience the other twin.
Philippa Pearce, *Here Comes Tod!*, 1994
    The episodic beginning chapter book features a lively 6-year-old and his loving family.

602

BRIGITTE LUCIANI
EVE THARLET, Illustrator
ROSEMARY LANNING, Translator

How Will We Get to the Beach?

(New York: A Michael Neugebauer Book/North-South Books, 2000)

Subject(s): Parent and Child; Transportation; Beaches
Age range(s): Grades K-1
Major character(s): Roxanne, Mother; Unnamed Character, Baby
Time period(s): 2000s (2000)
Locale(s): Europe

Summary: Roxanne loads a turtle, an umbrella, ball, book and her baby into the car for a day at the beach, but the car will not start. Each of the alternate modes of transportation Roxanne considers has a problem because it will require that one item be left behind. Roxanne won't go unless everything goes so it looks is if they might not make it to the beach. Then a farmer in a horse-drawn cart happens by and gives Roxanne, the baby, the book, the umbrella, the ball and the turtle a ride to the beach where they all have a great time. (34 pages)

Where it's reviewed:
Booklist, May 15, 2000, page 1748
Horn Book Guide, Fall 2000, page 252
School Library Journal, June 2000, page 119

Other books you might like:
Stella Blackstone, *Bear on a Bike*, 1998
    A bike is only one of the vehicles a bear and a little boy use for traveling.
John Burningham, *Harvey Slumfenburger's Christmas Present*, 1993
    In order to deliver a forgotten present Santa is forced to make alternate travel arrangements.
Rebecca Kai Dotlich, *Away We Go!*, 2000
    No matter where you want to go this rhyming story offers ideas for a way to get there.
Margaret Mahy, *A Busy Day for a Good Grandmother*, 1993
    Mrs. Oberon needs a variety of unique modes of transportation to overcome the obstacles between her and a teething grandson.

603

KATE LUM
ADRIAN JOHNSON, Illustrator

What! Cried Granny: An Almost Bedtime Story

(New York: Dial Books for Young Readers, 1999)

Subject(s): Grandmothers; Bedtime; Humor
Age range(s): Grades K-3
Major character(s): Patrick, Child; Granny, Grandmother
Time period(s): 1990s (1998)
Locale(s): England

Summary: As the sun sets during Patrick's first sleepover at Granny's house, his grandmother tells him to get ready for bed. Calmly, Patrick points out that he does not have a bed at Granny's house and quickly Granny races to the yard to chop down a tree that she uses to build a bed for Patrick. Still, he's unable to go to bed because he has no pillow, no blanket and no teddy bear. Granny is able to solve each problem Patrick presents except the last one. It's taken so long to make each item that morning has come. This first book by the author and illustrator was first published in Great Britain in 1998. (32 pages)

Where it's reviewed:
Booklist, May 1, 1999, page 1600
Horn Book, March 1999, page 197
Kirkus Reviews, February 1, 1999, page 224

Publishers Weekly, April 19, 1999, page 72
School Library Journal, March 1999, page 180

Awards the book has won:
ALA Notable Children's Books, 2000
School Library Journal Best Books, 1999

Other books you might like:
Joan Blos, *Bedtime!*, 1998
    The clock, the dark sky and Grandma say it's time for bed, but a little boy refuses to accept the obvious.
Berkeley Breathed, *Goodnight Opus*, 1993
    Grandma falls asleep while reading Opus's favorite bedtime story for the 210th time so Opus carries on with his own imaginative version of the tale.
Margaret Mahy, *A Busy Day for a Good Grandmother*, 1993
    A resourceful grandmother overcomes unusual obstacles to reach and soothe her teething grandson.

604

JILLIAN LUND, Author/Illustrator

Two Cool Coyotes
(New York: Dutton Children's Books, 1999)

Subject(s): Animals/Coyotes; Friendship; Deserts
Age range(s): Grades K-2
Major character(s): Frank, Coyote, Friend; Angelina, Coyote, Friend; Larry, Coyote, Friend (Frank's)
Time period(s): Indeterminate
Locale(s): Southwest

Summary: Frank and Angelina live in neighboring dens and have been friends for a long time. They play and learn together every day, appreciating each other's talents. Frank is the faster runner but Angelina can howl at the moon louder than anyone. When Angelina's family moves away Frank is sad and lonely. The activities they enjoyed together are simply no fun when he does them by himself. Then a family with a pup Frank's age moves into the den next door. Frank invites Larry to play and learns that, though Larry can't replace Angelina, he has his own attributes and Frank is happy to have a friend again. (32 pages)

Where it's reviewed:
Booklist, September 15, 1999, page 268
Horn Book Guide, Spring 2000, page 45
Publishers Weekly, September 20, 1999, page 89
School Library Journal, October 1999, page 119

Other books by the same author:
Way Out West Lives a Coyote Named Frank, 1993 (IRA/CBC Children's Choice)

Other books you might like:
Aliki, *We Are Best Friends*, 1987
    Peter's sad to move away and leave his best friend Robert feeling lonely. Both boys learn they can make new friends without forgetting each other.
Paulette Bourgeois, *Franklin's New Friend*, 1997
    Franklin feels a little uneasy about meeting the new family in his neighborhood, but once he does he makes a new friend.

Kevin Henkes, *Chester's Way*, 1988
    Best friends, Chester and Wilson, have no use for the new kid, Lily, until she helps them out of a jam.
Nette Hilton, *Andrew Jessup*, 1993
    Andrew Jessup remains a little girl's best "faraway friend" even after Madeline's family moves into his old house.

605

LISE LUNGE-LARSEN
BETSY BOWEN, Illustrator

The Troll with No Heart in His Body: And Other Tales of Trolls from Norway
(Boston: Houghton Mifflin Company, 1999)

Subject(s): Folklore; Folk Tales; Short Stories
Age range(s): Grades 2-5
Time period(s): Indeterminate Past
Locale(s): Norway

Summary: Retold by this Norwegian storyteller from an 1841 collection of Norwegian folktales by Asbjornsen and Moe, the most familiar of these nine troll tales is "The Three Billy Goats Gruff." While trolls are big, ugly and dangerous they are also dim witted and prone to bragging so their captives are able to outsmart them and gain their freedom. "The Boy Who Became a Lion, a Falcon, and an Ant" includes trolls with multiple heads and an orphaned boy whose kindness results in the freeing of trapped princesses, one of whom becomes his wife. In the title story the compassion and generosity of the youngest prince is rewarded when he finds his older brothers and their brides turned to stone by a troll. Because this troll does not carry his heart in his body, he is impossible to kill. Trickery, courage and help from the animals the prince has befriended during his travel are needed to locate the heart and rescue the captives. Each tale ends with the traditional expression "Snipp, snapp, snout, this tale's told out!" Source notes, a bibliography, and background information about trolls contribute to the book. (96 pages)

Where it's reviewed:
Booklist, September 1, 1999, page 128
Horn Book, November 1999, page 748
Kirkus Reviews, July 15, 1999, page 1135
Riverbank Review, Fall 1999, page 41
School Library Journal, November 1999, page 144

Awards the book has won:
ALA Notable Children's Books, 2000
Horn Book Fanfare, 2000

Other books by the same author:
The Legend of the Lady Slipper: An Ojibwe Tale, 1999

Other books you might like:
Peter Christen Asbjornsen, *East O' the Sun and West O' the Moon: Fifty-Nine Norwegian Folk Tales from the Collection of Peter Christen Asbjornsen and Jorgen Moe*, 1970
    The illustrated reissue of the original translation by George Webbe Dasent published in 1888 includes popular Norwegian folktales.
Peter Christen Asbjornsen, *Norwegian Folktales: From the Collection of Peter Christen Asbjornsen and Jorgen Moe*,

1982
This reprint of a translation by Pat Shaw and Carl Norman originally published in the 1960s contains many stories of trolls.

Virginia Haviland, *Favorite Fairy Tales Told in Norway*, 1961
This illustrated collection includes the familiar "Three Billy Goats Gruff," "Boots and the Troll" and other stories.

606

ALISON LURIE
JESSICA SOUHAMI, Illustrator

The Black Geese: A Baba Yaga Story from Russia

(New York: DK Inc/DK Publishing, Inc., 1999)

Subject(s): Folklore; Fairy Tales; Brothers and Sisters
Age range(s): Grades 1-3
Major character(s): Elena, Daughter, Sister (older); Baba Yaga, Witch
Time period(s): Indeterminate Past
Locale(s): Russia

Summary: Elena's parents expect her to watch her brother while they go to the market. While playing, Elena momentarily forgets about her brother and Baba Yaga's black geese carry him away with Elena in pursuit through the forest. As she runs she passes three different animals in need of help and Elena kindly helps each one. In turn, each animal gives her an object to use should she ever be in danger. Elena can't see much value in a shell, a walnut or a pebble but she puts the items in her pocket anyway. Baba Yaga is sleeping when Elena reaches her hut so she grabs her brother and hurries away into the forest. The squawking of the black geese awakens Baba Yaga who pursues Elena. One by one, Elena throws out the items she received from the animals and each time she and her brother are saved so they reach the safety of home before Elena's parents return from market. (32 pages)

Where it's reviewed:
Booklist, June 1999, page 1833
Horn Book, May 1999, page 343
Publishers Weekly, April 12, 1999, page 75
Reading Teacher, December 1999, page 345
School Library Journal, June 1999, page 118

Other books by the same author:
The Heavenly Zoo: Legends and Tales of the Stars, 1996
Fabulous Beasts, 1981
Clever Gretchen and Other Forgotten Folktales, 1980

Other books you might like:
Joanna Cole, *Bony-Legs*, 1983
A girl's kindness to mistreated animals gives her the magical items she needs to escaped from a wicked witch who wants to eat her.
Eric A. Kimmel, *Baba Yaga: A Russian Folktale*, 1991
In this retelling of a traditional tale Marina's cruel stepmother sends her to the forest witch, but Marina's compassionate nature saves her.

Maida Silverman, *Anna and the Seven Swans*, 1984
In this retelling of the Russian folktale seven swans carry Anna's little brother to Baba Yaga as Anna searches the forest for him.

607

GEORGE ELLA LYON
IRENE TRIVAS, Illustrator

One Lucky Girl

(New York: DK Ink/Dorling Kindersley Publishing, Inc., 2000)

Subject(s): Weather; Family Life; Dwellings
Age range(s): Grades K-3
Major character(s): Becky, Baby, Sister; Nick "Hawkeye", Brother (older), Son; Dad, Father, Jockey
Time period(s): 1990s
Locale(s): United States

Summary: In a field across from the racetrack, Nick plays baseball and his skill in the outfield earns him the nickname Hawkeye from Dad. One summer afternoon as the family relaxes while Becky naps in the trailer, the sky suddenly darkens and a tornado approaches. With no time to do anything but "hit the dirt" Nick and his parents survive the tornado's onslaught with minimal injuries. After the storm passes and they survey the damaged trailers the family quickly realizes that their trailer and Becky are gone. Nick and his parents run in the direction of the debris, searching for Becky. Nick's keen eye spots something in a distant field toward which he races—Becky's crib with his uninjured sister still asleep in it. (32 pages)

Where it's reviewed:
Booklist, March 1, 2000, page 1250
Bulletin of the Center for Children's Books, March 2000, page 235
Horn Book, May 2000, page 297
Publishers Weekly, March 13, 2000, page 84
School Library Journal, March 2000, page 210

Other books by the same author:
A Day at Damp Camp, 1996
Ada's Pal, 1996
Mama Is a Miner, 1994
Dreamplace, 1993 (Carolyn W. Field Award)
Who Came Down That Road?, 1992

Other books you might like:
Darleen Bailey Beard, *Twister*, 1999
Natt and Lucille huddle in the storm cellar wondering if their mother has reached safety before a tornado rushes over their home.
Georgia Graham, *The Strongest Man This Side of Cremona*, 1998
Matthew and his father are working in the fields when an approaching tornado forces them to race to safety in a culvert.
Gloria Rand, *Baby in a Basket*, 1997
A baby, securely bundled in a basket, is lost in an accident on a narrow bridge in Alaska when the sleigh tips; hours later trappers find her.

M

608

ANTONIO HERNANDEZ MADRIGAL
GERARDO SUZAN, Illustrator

Blanca's Feather

(Flagstaff, AZ: Rising Moon, 2000)

Subject(s): Animals/Chickens; Pets; Cultures and Customs
Age range(s): Grades K-3
Major character(s): Rosalia, Child, Sister; Blanca, Chicken; Padre Santiago, Religious
Time period(s): Indeterminate Past
Locale(s): Mexico

Summary: Tomorrow is October 4th, the day of Saint Francis of Assisi and Rosalia feels so excited about carrying Blanca to the church for the blessing that she can hardly sleep. In the morning Rosalia helps her mother prepare flower garlands for the animals and watches her brothers bathe and brush their pets. When it's time to depart, Rosalia cannot locate Blanca. Despite a frantic search, the only sign of her pet that Rosalia can find is a white feather. Sadly, she carries the feather to the blessing, enduring laughter from her brothers and fearing a similar reaction from Padre Santiago. As Rosalia explains her predicament to Padre Santiago he commends her good idea, blesses the feather and tells her to rub it on Blanca's head when she goes home. (32 pages)

Where it's reviewed:
Children's Book Review Service, May 2000, page 110
Horn Book Guide, Fall 2000, page 275
Publishers Weekly, May 15, 2000, page 117
School Library Journal, July 2000, page 83
Smithsonian, November 2000, page 66

Awards the book has won:
Smithsonian's Notable Books for Children, 2000

Other books by the same author:
Erandi's Braids, 1999
The Eagle and the Rainbow: Timeless Tales from Mexico, 1997

Other books you might like:
Bob Graham, *Queenie, One of the Family*, 1997
  Queenie, a hen who wanders, has her own ideas about where to lay her daily egg.
Tololwa M. Mollel, *Kele's Secret*, 1997
  Yoanes follows Kele all day long trying to find her nest so he can gather the eggs for market.
Martin Waddell, *John Joe and the Big Hen*, 1995
  During a visit to a neighbor's farm John Joe is confronted by a very large, but friendly hen.
Mary Wormell, *Hilda Hen's Search*, 1994
  Hilda Hen confidently searches until she finds a perfectly original spot for her nest.

609

ANTONIO HERNANDEZ MADRIGAL
TOMIE DEPAOLA, Illustrator

Erandi's Braids

(New York: G.P. Putnam's Sons, 1999)

Subject(s): Hair; Mothers and Daughters; Mexicans
Age range(s): Grades K-3
Major character(s): Erandi, 7-Year-Old, Daughter; Mama, Mother
Time period(s): Indeterminate Past
Locale(s): Patzcuaro, Mexico

Summary: On the morning of Erandi's 7th birthday, Mama takes her shopping. Although Erandi really wants a new doll, she knows she needs a new dress and Mama cannot afford both because Mama's old fishing net must be replaced. After selecting a pretty yellow dress, Erandi accompanies Mama to the barbershop where women are waiting in line to sell their long braids. Mama's braids are rejected because they are too short and she prepares to leave the shop when Erandi volunteers to sell her long, beautiful hair. Although Mama is sad and Erandi is surprised to see herself with short hair, they can now afford both a new fishing net and the doll that Erandi wants. (32 pages)

Where it's reviewed:
Booklist, January 1, 1999, page 861
Children's Book Review Service, April 1999, page 101
Horn Book Guide, Fall 1999, page 260
Publishers Weekly, February 15, 1999, page 106
School Library Journal, February 1999, page 87

Awards the book has won:
Americas Award for Children's and Young Adult Literature, 2000

Other books by the same author:
Blanca's Feather, 2000
The Eagle and the Rainbow: Timeless Tales from Mexico, 1997

Other books you might like:
Amelia Lau Carling, *Mama & Papa Have a Store*, 1998
   A young immigrant describes a day in Guatemala City as she watches her parents wait on customers in their store.
Sandra Cisneros, *Hairs Pelitos*, 1997
   A bilingual story celebrates the diversity of hair within a family.
Campbell Geeslin, *On Ramon's Farm*, 1998
   A glossary defines the Spanish terms used in this tale of Ramon and the animals on his farm.
Jan Romero Stevens, *Carlos and the Cornfield/Carlos y la Milpa de Maiz*, 1995
   Parallel texts in English and Spanish tell how Carlos's father knows his son did not follow instructions carefully when planting the corn crop.

610

THIERRY MAGNIER
GEORG HALLENSLEBEN, Illustrator

Isabelle and the Angel

(San Francisco: Chronicle Books, 2000)

Subject(s): Animals/Pigs; Food; Museums
Age range(s): Grades K-2
Major character(s): Isabelle, Pig, Friend; Angel, Angel, Friend
Time period(s): Indeterminate
Locale(s): Fictional Country

Summary: Isabelle lives alone in a messy apartment. Other than food, a substance she enjoys both for eating and for painting, Isabelle's only pleasure is visiting the art museum and staring at the little Angel in the corner of her favorite picture. When the figure comes to life and gives Isabelle a tour of the museum Isabelle knows she cannot return to her lonely apartment so she gets a job as a museum guard and keeps watch over her little Angel all the time. The author's first book was originally published in French as *Solange et L'Ange* in 1997. (40 pages)

Where it's reviewed:
Booklist, December 1, 2000, page 722
Children's Book Review Service, August 2000, page 158
Horn Book Guide, Spring 2001, page 44
School Library Journal, December 2000, page 116

Other books you might like:
Jon Agee, *The Incredible Painting of Felix Clousseau*, 1988
   An artist is unaware that his unusual paintings come to life.

Mary Jane Auch, *Eggs Mark the Spot*, 1996
   Pauline's unique talent for laying eggs that are reproductions of what she observes helps to nab a burglar stealing from an art museum.
Thacher Hurd, *Art Dog*, 1996
   Arthur Dog leads a quiet life by day as a guard in an art museum but, when the moon is full, he becomes Art Dog, talented painter.
Petra Mathers, *Victor and Christabel*, 1993
   The loving attention of Victor, a museum guard, frees Christabel from the painting in which her evil cousin has imprisoned her.
Diane Stanley, *The Gentleman and the Kitchen Maid*, 1994
   Nightly, the portraits in an art museum converse about the feelings a gentleman in one portrait has for a kitchen maid in another.

611

GREGORY MAGUIRE
ELAINE CLAYTON, Illustrator

Four Stupid Cupids

(New York: Clarion Books, 2000)

Series: Hamlet Chronicles. Volume 4
Subject(s): Love; Teachers; Humor
Age range(s): Grades 3-6
Major character(s): Germaine Earth, Teacher; Fawn Petros, Student—Elementary School
Time period(s): 2000s (2000)
Locale(s): Hamlet, Vermont (Josiah Fawcett Elementary School)

Summary: Valentine's Day is a sad holiday for Miss Earth because it brings back memories of her deceased fiance. As an elementary school teacher, the excitement of the day is a fact of life and one that Miss Earth tries to deal with professionally. Her students, desiring her happiness, decide to play matchmaker and find unexpected assistance in the Greek vase Fawn brings to school to show the class. When the vase is accidentally broken, four little cupids materialize from the dust and the students think their matchmaking problem is solved. In some ways the problems are just beginning because the cupids have poor aim and their arrows cause Miss Earth to fall in love, but not with the man they've selected as her future mate. That relationship develops the old fashioned way. (183 pages)

Where it's reviewed:
Booklist, December 1, 2000, page 706
Horn Book Guide, Spring 2001, page 76
Kirkus Reviews, October 15, 2000, page 1487
School Library Journal, October 2000, page 164

Other books by the same author:
Five Alien Elves, 1998
Six Haunted Hairdos, 1997
Seven Spiders Spinning, 1994

Other books you might like:
Laura Hawkins, *Valentine to a Flying Mouse*, 1993
   A local bookstore owner helps Tammy prepare for the

class Valentine's Day party and deal with a personal problem.

Elaine Moore, *The Trouble with Valentines*, 1998
    Lexi wants to make Valentine's Day special for her teacher.

Phyllis Reynolds Naylor, *A Spy Among the Girls*, 2000
    Nine-year-old Caroline decides to experience love on Valentine's Day in order to promote her acting career.

Robert Newton Peck, *Soup in Love*, 1992
    In anticipation of Valentine's Day in their small Vermont town, Soup and Rob experience love in several forms.

Maggie Twohill, *Valentine Frankenstein*, 1991
    Amanda wonders if she's doing the right thing by stuffing the class box with Valentines for Walter in order to make him appear more popular.

612

GREGORY MAGUIRE

The Good Liar

(New York: Clarion Books, 1999)

Subject(s): World War II; Brothers; Behavior
Age range(s): Grades 4-6
Major character(s): Marcel Delarue, Artist, Brother (youngest); Maman, Mother
Time period(s): 1990s (1995); 1940s
Locale(s): Mont-Saint-Martin, France; Florida

Summary: For a class assignment, three girls send a letter to M. Delarue asking him to tell them about his life during World War II. Marcel responds to the students' request with a series of recollections of his childhood activities in a small town in occupied France. To enliven their sometime dreary days and to avoid punishment Marcel and his older brothers become accomplished liars or at least great embellishers of the truth. Maman preaches truth and is swift to discipline if she learns her sons are lying, but after years of war Marcel learns that Maman has been the best liar of the family. (129 pages)

Where it's reviewed:
Booklist, April 15, 1999, page 1530
Five Owls, September 1999, page 17
Horn Book, July 1999, page 471
Kirkus Reviews, September 1, 1999, page 1335
Publishers Weekly, March 22, 1999, page 93

Awards the book has won:
Booklist Editors' Choice, 1999
Notable Social Studies Trade Books for Young People, 2000

Other books by the same author:
Confessions of an Ugly Stepsister, 1999
Five Alien Elves, 1998
Oasis, 1996
Lucas Fishbone, 1990

Other books you might like:
Patricia Reilly Giff, *Lily's Crossing*, 1997
    Lily could be Marcel's American soul mate in lying as she copes with life without her father during World War II.

Ellen Howard, *A Different Kind of Courage*, 1996
    Refugee children, fearing the loss of their parents, still struggle to escape from war-torn France.

Carol Matas, *Greater than Angels*, 1998
    During the German occupation of their country, French citizens of one community shelter Jewish refugee children.

613

MARGARET MAHY
PATRICIA MACCARTHY, Illustrator

Down the Dragon's Tongue

(New York: Orchard Books, 2000)

Subject(s): Playing; Fathers; Parent and Child
Age range(s): Grades K-2
Major character(s): Mr. Prospero, Businessman, Father; Harry, Twin, Son; Miranda, Twin, Daughter
Time period(s): 2000s (2000)
Locale(s): Earth

Summary: When staid Mr. Prospero arrives home from work Harry and Miranda are waiting, begging to be taken to the park so they can slide down the Dragon's Tongue slide. Without waiting for their father to change out of his business suit they rush him out the door. At first Mr. Prospero is reluctant to tackle the very high slide, but after a few trips he's having so much fun that he continues sliding long after Harry and Miranda have grown tired of climbing the stairs to the top of the slide. By the time they return home Mr. Prospero, known for neatness, is looking rather disheveled, but happy. (28 pages)

Where it's reviewed:
Booklist, July 2000, page 2041
Horn Book Guide, Spring 2001, page 45
Kirkus Reviews, July 15, 2000, page 1042
Publishers Weekly, July 17, 2000, page 192
School Library Journal, December 2000, page 116

Other books by the same author:
The Horrendous Hullabaloo, 1992
Making Friends, 1990
17 Kings and 42 Elephants, 1987

Other books you might like:
James Howe, *Pinky and Rex and the Double-Dad Weekend*, 1995
    Rain doesn't dampen plans for a weekend camping trip; it simply relocates the tent as flexible fathers enjoy the weekend with their children.

Reeve Lindbergh, *If I'd Known Then What I Know Now*, 1994
    Although Dad is far from perfect and certainly not neat the family loves him just as he is.

Laurence Pringle, *Octopus Hug*, 1993
    In this family it's the babysitting father who livens up the children by teaching them an octopus hug and playing games.

614

MARGARET MAHY
JONATHAN ALLEN, Illustrator

Simply Delicious!

(New York: Orchard Books, 1999)

Subject(s): Food; Animals; Problem Solving
Age range(s): Grades K-3
Major character(s): Mr. Minky, Father; Finnegan Minky, Son
Time period(s): 1990s
Locale(s): Fictional Country

Summary: After Mr. Minky buys a ''double-dip-chocolate-chip-and-cherry ice cream with rainbow twinkles and chopped-nut sprinkles'' for Finnegan he's faced with the problem of getting the cone home before it melts. He points his bicycle in the direction of the shortcut through the jungle to his back yard and rides off with ice cream held safely aloft. As Mr. Minky rides along the bumpy path he strategically maneuvers the cone and the bike past the growing collection of animals attracted to the cone and delivers the ''simply delicious'' concoction safely to Finnegan. The disappointed animals look at each other hungrily and race back into the jungle to pursue alternate plans for nourishment. (32 pages)

Where it's reviewed:
Booklist, September 1, 1999, page 141
Horn Book, September 1999, page 596
School Library Journal, September 1999, page 195

Other books by the same author:
The Rattlebang Picnic, 1994 (School Library Journal Best Books)
A Busy Day for a Good Grandmother, 1993
The Horrendous Hullabaloo, 1992
The Great White Man-Eating Shark, 1990

Other books you might like:
Jim Aylesworth, *My Sister's Rusty Bike*, 1996
    Astride his sister's rusty bike, an older brother tours America seeing some mighty strange sights.
Bill Grossman, *My Little Sister Ate One Hare*, 1996
    Eating one hare is only the first of the items consumed during a magic act.
David Macauley, *Shortcut*, 1995
    As Albert and his horse make their weekly trip to market, their simple acts create havoc for those who come after them.
Mark Teague, *The Secret Shortcut*, 1996
    Floyd and Wendell take a shortcut to school that leads them into a jungle filled with snakes, birds, monkeys and crocodiles.

615

BARBARA MAITLAND
ANDREW KULMAN, Illustrator

Moo in the Morning

(New York: Farrar Straus Giroux, 2000)

Subject(s): City and Town Life; Country Life; Animals
Age range(s): Grades K-1
Major character(s): Mom, Mother; Jack, Uncle; Unnamed Character, Child
Time period(s): 2000s (2000)
Locale(s): United States

Summary: Mom loves the hustle bustle of city life, but not the noise in the morning so she packs her suitcase, puts her child in the car and heads for Uncle Jack's farm in the quiet, peaceful country. Fun by day and quiet by night the farm is lively in the morning. The sounds begin with a single cow mooing then the rooster crows and all the cows, ducks, sheep, hens and birds join in to add to the noise. Mom's heard enough! She's ready to return to the quiet, peaceful city. (32 pages)

Where it's reviewed:
Bulletin of the Center for Children's Books, July 2000, page 411
Horn Book Guide, Spring 2001, page 20
Kirkus Reviews, June 15, 2000, page 888
Publishers Weekly, July 10, 2000, page 62
School Library Journal, August 2000, page 159

Other books by the same author:
My Bear and Me, 1999
The Bookstore Ghost, 1998
The Bear Who Didn't Like Honey, 1997

Other books you might like:
Arlene Alda, *Pig, Horse, or Cow, Don't Wake Me Now*, 1994
    A peacock's call is the first sound a little boy hears in the morning.
Christine Loomis, *Rush Hour*, 1996
    The busy city springs to life with the sound of alarms, buses and taxis as workers awaken and hurry to their jobs.
Ann McGovern, *Too Much Noise*, 1967
    A noisy house keeps an old man awake. After following the advice of the village wise man, he finally finds the quiet he seeks.
Alan Schroeder, *Carolina Shout!*, 1995
    To Bettina the streets of Charleston are noisy, but to Delia the songs, calls and cries of the workers are a melody of life in the city.

616

KATHY MALLAT, Author/Illustrator

Brave Bear

(New York: Walker and Company, 1999)

Subject(s): Animals/Bears; Animals/Birds; Courage
Age range(s): Preschool
Major character(s): Unnamed Character, Bear; Unnamed Character, Bird
Time period(s): 1990s
Locale(s): Fictional Country

Summary: When a young bear comes upon a little bird on the ground, he expresses concern for the bird and offers to help. What the bird wants is to be returned to its tree. The bear is not sure he can climb that high, but he's willing to try and with the bird clinging to his t-shirt he begins. When the bear feels scared, the bird encourages him. When the bear needs help, the bird tugs on the t-shirt to free it from a branch. Together they reach the bird's nest and share a moment of satisfaction for completing a difficult task. (24 pages)

Where it's reviewed:
Booklist, December 1, 1999, page 712
Children's Book Review Service, September 1999, page 171
Horn Book, September 1999, page 597
Publishers Weekly, August 2, 1999, page 82
School Library Journal, September 1999, page 195

Other books by the same author:
Seven Stars More!, 1998
The Picture that Mom Drew, 1997

Other books you might like:
Hans De Beer, *Little Polar Bear, Take Me Home!*, 1996
    When Lars finds Sasha, a lonely young tiger, lost and far from home, he travels with him until they find Sasha's homeland.
Syd Hoff, *Bernard on His Own*, 1993
    Bernard's parents assure him that one day he will be able to climb a tree without their help.
Martin Waddell, *Let's Go Home, Little Bear*, 1993
    While walking in the snowy woods, Big Bear comforts a frightened Little Bear.

617

PETER MALONEY, Author/Illustrator
FELICIA ZEKAUSKAS, Co-Author

The Magic Hockey Stick
(New York: Dial Books for Young Readers, 1999)

Subject(s): Sports/Hockey; Stories in Rhyme; Competition
Age range(s): Grades K-2
Major character(s): Tracy, Hockey Player (amateur), Child; Wayne Gretzky, Hockey Player (professional)
Time period(s): 1990s
Locale(s): New York, New York

Summary: When Tracy's parents unintentionally place the winning bid at a charity auction, Tracy becomes the proud owner of an autographed hockey stick. Her parents are unaware of Wayne Gretzky's fame, but the renowned player is Tracy's hero. Despite her father's admonitions, Tracy sneaks the hockey stick out of the house and into the skating rink to use in her games. While Tracy's scoring ability soars, her hero is in a slump. Once again using her stuffed giraffe to hide the hockey stick, Tracy sneaks into Madison Square Garden to return the stick to Wayne Gretzky who is so pleased that he has Tracy autograph the magic hockey stick. (40 pages)

Where it's reviewed:
Booklist, December 1, 1999, page 712
Globe and Mail, January 8, 2000, page D13
School Library Journal, October 1999, page 120

Other books by the same author:
Redbird at Rockefeller Center, 1997

Other books you might like:
Anthony Browne, *Willy the Wizard*, 1996
    In his new soccer shoes that Willy thinks must be magic he finally shows that he has the skill to make the team.

Ellen Stoll Walsh, *Pip's Magic*, 1994
    Searching for a magical way to overcome his fear of the dart, Pip learns that the solution was within him all along.
Willy Welch, *Playing Right Field*, 1995
    Willy, a ballplayer with little skill, spends his time in right field daydreaming about famous players making game-saving plays.

618

AINSLIE MANSON
DEAN GRIFFITHS, Illustrator

Ballerinas Don't Wear Glasses
(Custer, WA: Orca Book Publishers, 2000)

Subject(s): Brothers and Sisters; Ballet; Humor
Age range(s): Grades 1-3
Major character(s): Ben, Brother (older); Allison, Sister (younger), Dancer; Mom, Mother
Time period(s): 2000s (2000)
Locale(s): Canada

Summary: Today is absolutely the worst day for Ben's mother to work late and expect him to care for Allison after school. For one thing there is a fresh snowfall that'll be perfect for a snowball fight and Ben will have to miss it. As if missing that isn't bad enough Allison's dance recital is tonight and Ben's stuck altering her costume, fixing her hair, boosting her confidence and soothing her nervousness about performing. Allison believes Ben's comment about how lucky she is to be able to take off her glasses—she'll never see the audience. Now Allison understands the remarks of the kids at school who told her ballerinas don't wear glasses. Ben skips hockey practice to watch his sister and Mom arrives as the curtain goes up. (32 pages)

Where it's reviewed:
Booklist, December 1, 2000, page 722
Globe and Mail, June 24, 2000, page D14
Horn Book Guide, Spring 2001, page 64
Resource Links, June 2000, page 4
School Library Journal, August 2000, page 159

Other books by the same author:
Just Like New, 1995 (Resource Links Best Picture Book)
A Dog Came, Too: A True Story, 1993

Other books you might like:
Patricia Lee Gauch, *Bravo, Tanya*, 1992
    After Tanya learns to move to the feel of the music in her head, her dancing improves.
Kate McMullan, *Nutcracker Noel*, 1993
    Noel is initially disappointed to be cast as a tree in the upcoming ballet, but the elegant costume helps her feel better about her role.
Jane O'Connor, *Nina, Nina, Star Ballerina*, 1997
    In her recital, Nina is one of the stars dancing around Eric in the role of the moon.

619

FRED MARCELLINO, Author/Illustrator

I, Crocodile

(New York: Michael diCapua Books/Harper Collins, 1999)

Subject(s): Animals/Crocodiles; Humor; Food
Age range(s): Grades 1-4
Major character(s): Unnamed Character, Crocodile; Napoleon, Ruler
Time period(s): 1790s (1799)
Locale(s): Egypt; Paris, France

Summary: A self-assured crocodile lives a life of ease in Egypt dining on the delicacies that wander across his path and sleeping in the warm sun. This idyllic life comes to an end when Napoleon decides to add the crocodile to his shipload of plunder. A fountain becomes the humiliated crocodile's public home and his diet suffers greatly although he does bask in the attention. Too soon the crocodile's popularity ends and plans are made to turn him into a pie. The crocodile manages to escape into the sewers of Paris where he thinks he'll live quite comfortably as soon as he locates a food source. This is the first book also written by this illustrator. (32 pages)

Where it's reviewed:
Booklist, October 15, 1999, page 456
Five Owls, November 1999, page 41
Horn Book, January 2000, page 66
Publishers Weekly, September 27, 1999, page 103
School Library Journal, November 1999, page 125

Awards the book has won:
Publishers Weekly Best Books, 1999
New York Times Best Illustrated Children's Books, 1999

Other books you might like:
Mary Jo Collier, *The King's Giraffe*, 1996
    In 1826 the giraffe that the pasha of Egypt sends the king of France as a gift generates excitement and creates new fashion trends.
Tomie DePaola, *Bill and Pete to the Rescue*, 1998
    Crocodile Bill is captured while attempting to rescue his cousin, but with the help of his bird friend Pete all are soon freed.
Gilles Eduar, *Jooka Saves the Day*, 1997
    Jooka is an odd-looking crocodile feared by others who learns to accept and use his flying and fire-breathing talents when he discovers he's a dragon.
Roy Gerrard, *Croco'nile*, 1994
    When Hamut and Nekatu are kidnapped on the Nile their crocodile friend comes to their rescue just in time.

620

HEIDI STETSON MARIO, Author/Illustrator

I'd Rather Have an Iguana

(Watertown, MA: A Talewinds Book/Charlesbridge Publishing, 1999)

Subject(s): Babies; Sibling Rivalry; Brothers and Sisters
Age range(s): Grades K-1
Major character(s): Unnamed Character, Daughter, Sister (older); Charles, Baby, Brother
Time period(s): 1990s (1999)
Locale(s): United States

Summary: A big sister does not agree that she should be happy to have a baby brother. She didn't ask her parents to bring home any baby and they completely ignored her great ideas for names and selected Charles instead of "Cornflake" or "Spot." In fact they ignored her preference for an iguana and give her a hamster instead. The hamster is cute, but not as cute as Charles when he smiles—right at her. (32 pages)

Where it's reviewed:
Booklist, January 1, 1999, page 888
Horn Book Guide, Fall 1999, page 260
Kirkus Reviews, January 1, 1999, page 69
Publishers Weekly, January 25, 1999, page 94
School Library Journal, April 1999, page 104

Other books you might like:
Martha Alexander, *Nobody Asked Me If I Wanted a Baby Sister*, 1977
    Despite the fact that too much attention is paid to his baby sister, a little boy begrudgingly admits to feeling some affection for her.
Jane Cutler, *Darcy and Gran Don't Like Babies*, 1993
    Big sister Darcy is relieved when Gran professes to share her lack of interest in the new baby and spends time alone with Darcy.
Amy Hest, *You're the Boss, Baby Duck*, 1997
    Fortunately Grampa lives nearby to provide the attention Baby Duck needs now that her little sister commands all of her parents' time.
Holly Keller, *Geraldine's Baby Brother*, 1994
    An annoyed, awakened, yet ever-resourceful Geraldine has a heart-to-heart talk with the screaming baby to help him understand his place in the family.
Clara Vulliamy, *Ellen and Penguin and the New Baby*, 1996
    Ellen agrees with her stuffed Penguin's observation that having a new baby in the house is not such a good idea.

621

MERRILL MARKOE
ERIC BRACE, Illustrator

The Day My Dogs Became Guys

(New York: Viking, 1999)

Subject(s): Animals/Dogs; Pets; Humor
Age range(s): Grades 1-4
Major character(s): Carey, Student, Son
Time period(s): 1990s (1999)
Locale(s): United States

Summary: In the author's first children's book, Carey is frustrated by the lack of understanding of instructions exhibited by his three dogs and thinks wistfully that if they were human their comprehension would improve. The afternoon following a school lesson about a solar eclipse and ancient peoples' belief that eclipses cause magic, Carey discovers that his wishful thinking comes true. During the period of the eclipse Carey's dogs become people or at least creatures that look like people but who have the interests and behaviors of his pets. They cause no end of trouble in the neighborhood and his home before the abruptly reverting to being dogs. Carey learns that while his pets' behavior may be annoying at times it is even worse when the dogs look like people. (32 pages)

Where it's reviewed:
Booklist, February 15, 1999, page 1076
Bulletin of the Center for Children's Books, March 1999, page 248
Horn Book Guide, Fall 1999, page 281
Publishers Weekly, January 18, 1999, page 337
School Library Journal, April 1999, page 104

Other books you might like:
Nina Laden, *The Night I Followed the Dog*, 1994
    While a family sleeps, their pet dog secretly leads an exciting nightlife.
Susan Meddaugh, *Martha Calling*, 1994
    Martha the talking dog makes the most of the vacation she wins in a radio call-in contest despite the resort's ''No Dogs Allowed'' policy.
David Milgrim, *Dog Brain*, 1996
    A young boy thinks his pet is smart enough to fake stupidity while his parents think Sneakers is too dumb to understand the house rules.
Carol Diggory Shields, *I Wish My Brother Was a Dog*, 1997
    A young boy imagines how much better life would be if only Andy was his pet dog and not his little brother.
Alan Snow, *How Dogs Really Work!*, 1993
    A winner of the New York Time Best Illustrated Children's Book Award is a humorous instruction manual for dog owners.

622

SAMUEL MARSHAK
RICHARD PEVEAR, Translator
MARC ROSENTHAL, Illustrator

The Absentminded Fellow

(New York: Farrar Straus Giroux, 1999)

Subject(s): Humor; Folk Tales; Memory
Age range(s): Grades K-3
Major character(s): Unnamed Character, Eccentric
Time period(s): Indeterminate
Locale(s): London, England

Summary: In this classic Russian folktale, originally published in 1928 and now translated for the first time into English, the absentminded fellow from Portobello Road doesn't do anything quite right. He puts his pants on his arms, his shirt on his legs and uses his landlady's cat as a hat. When he tries to take a trip to Birmingham, he falls asleep in an empty car and never leaves the station, but, upon awakening, assumes that he's been to Birmingham and back. (32 pages)

Where it's reviewed:
Booklist, July 1999, page 1952
Horn Book, March 1999, page 198
Kirkus Reviews, February 15, 1999, page 302
Publishers Weekly, May 3, 1999, page 75
School Library Journal, March 1999, page 180

Other books by the same author:
Hail to Mail, 1991

The Month-Brothers: A Slavic Tale, 1983

Other books you might like:
Harry Allard, *The Stupids Step Out*, 1974
    With their dog, Kitty, the Stupid family enjoys a silly, fun-filled day.
Matt S. Cibula, *What's Up with you, Taquandra Fu?*, 1997
    Taquandra Fu behaves in a unique manner at school.
Alvin Alexsi Currier, *Alyosha's Apple: A Tale of Old Russia*, 1997
    A poor orphan girl braves the dangers of the forest to help her crippled brother.
J. Patrick Lewis, *At the Wish of the Fish: A Russian Folktale*, 1999
    A fool catches a magic fish, who promises to fulfill all his wishes.
Chad Stuart, *The Ballymara Flood*, 1996
    In this rhyming story, a young boy floods the whole town when he leaves his bath water running.

623

JAMES MARSHALL
MAURICE SENDAK, Illustrator

Swine Lake

(New York: Harper Collins Publishers/Michael de Capua Books, 1999)

Subject(s): Animals/Pigs; Animals/Wolves; Ballet
Age range(s): Grades 1-4
Major character(s): Unnamed Character, Wolf
Time period(s): Indeterminate
Locale(s): Fictional Country

Summary: An aging, hungry wolf follows the unmistakable scent of pork and happens upon the New Hamsterdam Theater where the Boarshoi Ballet is presenting Swine Lake. Too broke to purchase a ticket, the wolf lucks into box seats when a wealthy sow patron gives hers away to him. The wolf intends to leap from his seat to the stage and devour the dancers, but he becomes so entranced in the story that he forgets his hunger. The next night, he spends his savings to purchase a ticket. During the second show, he does jump onto the stage, but only to join the ballet and not to dine on the performers. (40 pages)

Where it's reviewed:
Booklist, May 1, 1999, page 1590
Horn Book Guide, Fall 1999, page 282
Horn Book, July 1999, page 457
Publishers Weekly, May 3, 1999, page 74
School Library Journal, July 1999, page 77

Other books by the same author:
Fox Be Nimble, 1994
Fox on Stage, 1993
George and Martha Round and Round, 1988

Other books you might like:
Mary Jane Auch, *Hen Lake*, 1995
    Poulette, the determined hen ballerina, challenges a conceited barnyard peacock to a talent contest.
Sara Fanelli, *Wolf*, 1997
    Lonely Wolf's quest for friends is unsuccessful due to people's fear and misunderstanding of his motives.

Jon Scieszka, *The True Story of the Three Little Pigs*, 1989
At last, A. Wolf is able to set the record straight about just what happened between him and those three pigs.

624

ANN M. MARTIN
LAURA GODWIN, Co-Author
BRIAN SELZNICK, Illustrator

The Doll People

(New York: Hyperion Books for Children, 2000)

Subject(s): Dolls and Dollhouses; Fantasy; Family Life
Age range(s): Grades 3-5
Major character(s): Annabelle Doll, Doll, Sister (older); Tiffany Funcraft, Doll, Friend; Kate Palmer, 8-Year-Old, Sister (older)
Time period(s): 2000s (2000)
Locale(s): United States

Summary: Despite the wear and tear of a century of little girls' play, the china Doll family and their wooden home have changed little since they arrived from England as a gift for one of Kate's ancestors. Forever eight years old, Annabelle remembers Kate's grandmother and mother as the little girls playing with the dollhouse and she recalls that when Kate's grandmother was a child the Doll family included an aunt. After forty-five years Annabelle decides to search for her missing aunt and convinces her family to help her. On their first night of exploring they discover the Funcraft family boxed and in a closet waiting for the birthday of Kate's younger sister. As soon as the Funcraft's home is set up they visit the Doll family and plastic Tiffany becomes Annabelle's first friend. Inexperienced in the rules of doll life, adventurous Tiffany eagerly becomes Annabelle's partner in the search for her missing aunt. Together they sneak through the house trying to avoid the family cat and always returning to the places they were last left by Kate before anyone in the Palmer family wakens. After one hundred years, Annabelle's grateful to have a friend. (256 pages)

Where it's reviewed:
Booklist, August 2000, page 2140
Children's Book Review Service, September 2000, page 10
Kirkus Reviews, August 15, 2000, page 1200
Publishers Weekly, July 3, 2000, page 71
School Library Journal, November 2000, page 128

Awards the book has won:
ALA Notable Children's Books, 2001
School Library Journal Best Books, 2000

Other books you might like:
Rumer Godden, *The Doll's House*, 1976
Two little girls enjoy adventures with their dollhouse.
Peni R. Griffin, *Margo's House*, 1996
Two dolls being made by Margo's father are incomplete when he has a heart attack but they become an important factor in his recovery.
Margaret Mahy, *The Five Sisters*, 1997
A chain of paper dolls blows away on the wind to be found by different people as they travel.

Ann Turner, *Finding Walter*, 1997
Dolls that Emily and Rose find in their aunt's old dollhouse try to persuade the sisters to find a missing doll.
Sylvia Waugh, *The Mennyms*, 1994
When their creator dies, a family of life-size rag dolls comes alive and lives happily in her home.

625

BILL MARTIN JR.
STEVEN KELLOGG, Co-Author

A Beasty Story

(San Diego: Silver Whistle/Harcourt Brace & Company, 1999)

Subject(s): Animals/Mice; Surprises; Stories in Rhyme
Age range(s): Grades K-1
Major character(s): Nick, Mouse; Hank, Mouse; Silly, Mouse
Time period(s): Indeterminate
Locale(s): Fictional Country

Summary: A group of mice with rhyming names on their numbered t-shirts ventures through a dark, dark wood to a dark, dark house with a dark, dark interior. Silly records the adventure and the changes in color as they proceed. At the bottom of the dark, dark red stairs the foursome finds a dark, dark purple cupboard containing a dark, dark green bottle out of which floats—a beast! Over the heads of the startled mice flies the beast with the yellow eyes retracing their steps up the stairs then up the chimney, out of the house and into another dark, dark house where an even bigger beast grabs it. The bedside light reveals a sheet-shrouded boy awakening to pull the cover off the beast that is revealed to be mischievous Nick and Hank, masters of tricks and pranks. Steven Kellogg also illustrates this story.(40 pages)

Where it's reviewed:
Booklist, September 15, 1999, page 268
Horn Book Guide, Spring 2000, page 20
The New Advocate, Spring 2000, page 188
Publishers Weekly, July 19, 1999, page 193
School Library Journal, September 1999, page 195

Awards the book has won:
IRA/CBC Children's Choices, 2000

Other books by the same author:
The Wizard, 1994
Old Devil Wind, 1993
Polar Bear, Polar Bear, What Do You Hear?, 1991

Other books you might like:
Jez Alborough, *Watch Out! Big Bro's Coming!*, 1997
A little mouse warns all the other animals that rough, tough Big Bro is coming! When he arrives it's obvious that size is relative.
Anita Jeram, *Daisy Dare*, 1995
Daisy, a fearless mouse, may have accepted her last dare when she's challenged to take the bell off the cat.
Sam McBratney, *The Dark at the Top of the Stairs*, 1996
Rejecting the suggestions of a wise, old mouse, three young mice insist on climbing the stairs to see what lurks in the dark at the top.

Michael Rosen, *We're Going on a Bear Hunt*, 1989
Bravely a group sets off in search of a bear until, arriving at their goal, they hurriedly retreat.

626

BILL MARTIN JR.
STEVEN SALERNO, Illustrator

Chicken Chuck

(Delray Beach, FL: Winslow Press, 2000)

Subject(s): Animals; Individuality; Circus
Age range(s): Grades K-2
Major character(s): Chicken Chuck, Rooster; Unnamed Character, Monkey
Time period(s): Indeterminate Past
Locale(s): United States

Summary: Ever hungry Chicken Chuck eats an odd blue seed in the barnyard and changes his perspective on life. After eating the blue seed, a sparkly blue feather grows from the middle of Chicken Chuck's forehead. Seeing the other animals' desire for such a feather, Chicken Chuck develops a haughty bossiness. His sense of self-importance is shattered when a circus poster picturing a prancing white horse with not one, but two blue feathers on his head is pasted on the barn. Chicken Chuck leads the animals to the circus in search of the horse but instead finds a monkey so allergic to blue feathers that he rips Chicken Chuck's feather right out of his head. Then the monkey gives the animals an entire box of blue feathers just like the ones tied to the horse's head. After returning to the barnyard all the animals proudly strut about each with a blue feather tied to its head—all except Chicken Chuck who has two blue feathers, of course. (32 pages)

Where it's reviewed:
ForeWord, April 2000, page 51
Horn Book Guide, Fall 2000, page 276
Kirkus Reviews, April 15, 2000, page 563
Publishers Weekly, April 17, 2000, page 80
School Library Journal, June 2000, page 120

Other books by the same author:
A Beautiful Feast for a Big King Cat, 1994
Old Devil Wind, 1993
Polar Bear, Polar Bear, What Do You Hear?, 1991
Brown Bear, Brown Bear, What Do You See?, 1983

Other books you might like:
Marcus Pfister, *Rainbow Fish*, 1992
A unique but lonely fish learns a lesson in sharing and friendship.
Janet Morgan Stoeke, *A Hat for Minerva Louise*, 1994
Minerva Louise is a chicken with a mind of her own and creative problem-solving ability.
Hans Wilhelm, *The Royal Raven*, 1996
In his desire to be special, Crawford acquires elegant plumage and loses his freedom because of it.

627

FRANCESCA MARTIN, Author/Illustrator

Clever Tortoise: A Traditional African Tale

(Cambridge, MA: Candlewick Press, 2000)

Subject(s): Folklore; Animals; Africa
Age range(s): Grades K-2
Major character(s): Clever Tortoise, Turtle
Time period(s): Indeterminate Past
Locale(s): Lake Nyasa, Tanzania

Summary: The animals living on the shores of Lake Nyasa are happy until the elephant and hippopotamus become boastful of their strength. The smaller animals call a meeting and Clever Tortoise suggests a plan to restore harmony. Clever Tortoise challenges both the elephant and the hippopotamus to a tug-of-war and then enlists the help of the smaller animals to make a long rope. On the morning of the contest Clever Tortoise gives one end of the rope to the elephant and the other to the hippopotamus. Neither of the large animals can see each other so they are unaware as they struggle with the surprisingly strong Clever Tortoise that they are actually competing with a much larger animal. When the contest is well under way Clever Tortoise chops the rope in two and the big animals fall with a crash. Clever Tortoise must have knocked some sense into those boastful animals because all the animals feel happy again. (32 pages)

Where it's reviewed:
Booklist, May 15, 2000, page 1757
School Library Journal, September 2000, page 221

Other books by the same author:
The Honey Hunters, 1992

Other books you might like:
Verna Aardema, *Rabbit Makes a Monkey of Lion*, 1989
With the help of her friends Turtle and Bush-rat, Rabbit outsmarts Lion and devours his honey.
Virginia Hamilton, *A Ring of Tricksters: Animal Tales from America, the West Indies and Africa*, 1997
Eleven read-aloud tales include tricksters from spiders to rabbits and the unwitting animals who bear the brunt of their cleverness.
Betsy Lewin, *Chubbo's Pool*, 1996
Claiming ownership of a pool, Chubbo the hippo refuses to share the water with the other animals

628

RAFE MARTIN
SUSAN GABER, Illustrator

The Language of Birds

(New York: G.P. Putnam's Sons, 2000)

Subject(s): Folklore; Brothers; Conduct of Life
Age range(s): Grades 1-5
Major character(s): Unnamed Character, Father, Merchant; Vasilii, Son (older); Ivan, Son (younger)
Time period(s): Indeterminate Past
Locale(s): Russia

Summary: A merchant sends his two sons off into the world with ten gold coins each and instructions to report back in a week on the profit they have made. Although Vasilii squanders his money on himself he tells his father a different tale that suggests future profits. Ivan returns the ten gold coins to his father saying that he spent the week learning the language of birds for which there was no charge. Furious with Ivan and proud of Vasilii, the merchant does not believe Ivan's ability to interpret the song of the wren at the window yet life proves him wrong. Indeed, the wren's prophecy becomes true due to Ivan's ability to understand the language of birds that respond to his kind nature and offer help whenever he needs it. A concluding author's note gives background for the folktale. (32 pages)

Where it's reviewed:
Booklist, May 15, 2000, page 1758
Horn Book, July 2000, page 470
Publishers Weekly, June 19, 2000, page 79
School Library Journal, July 2000, page 96

Other books by the same author:
The Eagle's Gift, 1997
Mysterious Tales of Japan, 1996 (ALA Notable Books for Children)
The Boy Who Lived with the Seals, 1993 (Booklist Editors' Choice)

Other books you might like:
Demi, *The Firebird*, 1994
    In one of many retellings of a classic Russian tale, Dimitri searches for the beautiful but elusive firebird.
M.C. Helldorfer, *Phoebe and the River Flute*, 2000
    Phoebe understands the language of the birds in her care and their desire for freedom.
Eric A. Kimmel, *Onions and Garlic*, 1996
    Although his older brothers consider Getzel a fool he is able to trade onions for diamonds while his brothers receive only garlic in exchange.

629

CLAIRE MASUREL
HANAKO WAKIYAMA, Illustrator

Too Big!

(San Francisco: Chronicle Books, 1999)

Subject(s): Dinosaurs; Toys; Parent and Child
Age range(s): Grades K-1
Major character(s): Charlie, Child, Son; Tex, Toy, Dinosaur
Time period(s): Indeterminate Past
Locale(s): United States

Summary: When Charlie wins a game at the carnival he selects a large toy dinosaur as his prize. Charlie's parents think the stuffed animal is much too big to go the store or the park, but Charlie knows Tex is just right. Poor, lonely Tex is stuck at home while Charlie brings other special toys along on outings until the day that Charlie is sick and the only special friend that can be found when it's time to go to the doctor is Tex. Together the pals bravely face the doctor who declares them both in need of bed rest. That is just what they get and when

they are well Charlie's mom promises a trip to the movies. (36 pages)

Where it's reviewed:
Booklist, August 1999, page 2065
Horn Book Guide, Fall 1999, page 237
Kirkus Reviews, May 15, 1999, page 804
Publishers Weekly, April 26, 1999, page 80
School Library Journal, June 1999, page 102

Other books by the same author:
Christmas Is Coming!, 1998
No, No Titus!, 1997
Good Night!, 1994

Other books you might like:
Catherine Anholt, *Bear and Baby*, 1993
    In any kind of weather, a girl and her special teddy bear will be found going places together.
Nancy White Carlstrom, *Barney Is Best*, 1994
    A young boy, anxious about a hospital visit, selects his toy elephant Barney as his companion.
Martin Waddell, *Small Bear Lost*, 1996
    When Small Bear is left on a train he manages to find his way home to the little girl who lost him.

630

PETRA MATHERS, Author/Illustrator

A Cake for Herbie

(New York: Anne Schwartz Book/Atheneum Books for Young Readers, 2000)

Subject(s): Animals; Poetry; Contests
Age range(s): Grades K-2
Major character(s): Herbie, Duck, Friend; Lottie, Hen, Friend
Time period(s): 2000s (2000)
Locale(s): Fictional Country

Summary: While grocery shopping with Lottie, Herbie spots a poster advertising a poetry contest with a cake for a grand prize. Herbie's love of food convinces him to enter the contest by writing an alphabet poem about food. Thinking about Lottie's presence in the audience helps quell Herbie's nervousness until she calls to tell him that she is sick and unable to attend. The quaking quacker begins his monologue but quickly exits the stage when he overhears unkind remarks from the audience. As the dejected duck huddles near a restaurant's dumpster he's found by a worker and led into a kitchen filled with pundits who appreciate Herbie's poetic bent so much that they feed him and reward him with a cake. (32 pages)

Where it's reviewed:
Booklist, May 1, 2000, page 1666
Horn Book, May 2000, page 298
Publishers Weekly, May 15, 2000, page 116
Riverbank Review, Summer 2000, page 29
School Library Journal, June 2000, page 122

Awards the book has won:
Horn Book Fanfare, 2001

Other books by the same author:

Lottie's New Friend, 1999 (New York Times Best Illustrated
Children's Book)
Lottie's New Beach Towel, 1998
Victor and Christabel, 1993

Other books you might like:

Diane DeGroat, *Roses Are Pink, Your Feet Really Stink*, 1996
The poems Gilbert creates for two of his classmates Valentine cards lead to problems at school.
Syd Hoff, *Duncan the Dancing Duck*, 1994
Duncan enjoys a moment of fame on stage, but finds life on
Broadway so tiring that he's grateful to return to the farm,
his mom and his pond.
James Stevenson, *The Mud Flat Olympics*, 1994
Friendly rivalry between the animals of Mud Flat during
their various competitions contributes to the community.

631

PETRA MATHERS, Author/Illustrator

Lottie's New Friend

(New York: Anne Schwartz/Atheneum Books for Young Readers, 1999)

Subject(s): Friendship; Animals/Birds; Jealousy
Age range(s): Grades K-3
Major character(s): Lottie, Chicken, Friend; Herbie, Duck;
Dorothea ''Dodo'' Kugelhopf, Bird, Neighbor
Time period(s): 1990s (1999)
Locale(s): Oysterville, Fictional Country

Summary: Herbie looks forward to his daily visits with Lottie
so he feels displaced when he discovers her enjoying cookies
with the new neighbor, Dodo. Lottie seems so impressed with
Dodo and her movie career that Herbie is sure Lottie no
longer cares about their friendship. When Lottie must go out
of town to care for a sick relative, lonely Herbie mopes for
days until he decides to visit Dodo and see how she's doing
with her home repairs. Herbie arrives just in time to rescue
Dodo from the roof of the house. As Dodo thanks Herbie she
refers to Lottie's admiration for his friendship. Herbie feels so
much better that he's able to include Dodo in his welcome
home plans for Lottie. (32 pages)

Where it's reviewed:

Booklist, July 1999, page 1952
Horn Book Guide, Fall 1999, page 260
Kirkus Reviews, January 15, 1999, page 147
New York Times Book Review, August 15, 1999, page 25
School Library Journal, March 1999, page 181

Other books by the same author:

A Cake for Herbie, 2000
Lottie's New Beach Towel, 1998
Kisses from Rosa, 1995
Victor and Christabel, 1993

Other books you might like:

Kevin Henkes, *Chester's Way*, 1988
Chester and Wilson are content with their friendship until
Lilly moves into the neighborhood forcing them to reconsider some ideas.
Arnold Lobel, *Frog and Toad Together*, 1972
The Newbery Honor book is one of four titles describing

the adventures and misadventures of loyal friends Frog and
Toad.
Chris Raschka, *Ring! Yo?*, 2000
A one-sided phone conversation has one boy momentarily
worried about his friendship.

632

NANCY MATSON
MICHAEL CHESWORTH, Illustrator

The Boy Trap

(Chicago: Front Street/Cricket Books, 1999)

Subject(s): Scientific Experiments; Schools; Gender Roles
Age range(s): Grades 4-6
Major character(s): Emma, 5th Grader, Scientist (aspiring);
Louise Zarotsky, 5th Grader, Friend (Emma's)
Time period(s): 1990s (1999)
Locale(s): United States

Summary: Emma is eager to participate in the school's Science Fair as she considers the project an opportunity to further
her goal of becoming a scientist. Emma's topic of choice is
based on emotional factors—her annoyance with boys—
rather than scientific consideration. Along with her partner
Louise she sets out to prove that girls are better than boys
while a pair of boys in the class tries to prove that boys are
better than girls. What they all learn is the difficulty of applying scientific principles to a subjective hypothesis. By the end
of the author's first book Emma's also decided to switch
partners and begin planning ahead for next year's project.
(108 pages)

Where it's reviewed:

Booklist, January 1, 2000, page 926
Children's Book Review Service, Winter 2000, page 72
Children's Bookwatch, May 2000, page 2
Publishers Weekly, November 29, 1999, page 71
School Library Journal, November 1999, page 161

Other books you might like:

Gordon Korman, *The Chicken Doesn't Skate*, 1996
A chicken brought to school for a science project escapes
and becomes the mascot of a hockey team.
Beverly Lewis, *The Stinky Sneakers Mystery*, 1996
Jason doubts that his science project will win a prize after
he sees the entries planned by the other students.
Janice Lee Smith, *Serious Science: An Adam Joshua Story*,
1993
Two days before the science fair, Adam Joshua discovers
that his younger sister and his dog have eaten his science
project.

633

CAITLIN MATTHEWS
JUDITH CHRISTINE MILLS, Illustrator

While the Bear Sleeps: Winter Tales and
Traditions

(New York: Barefoot Books, 1999)

Subject(s): Winter; Folk Tales; Traditions

Age range(s): Grades 3-6
Major character(s): Unnamed Character, Child; Unnamed Character, Bear
Time period(s): Indeterminate Past
Locale(s): Earth

Summary: On a cold day during the season's first snow, a young girl seeks shelter in a cave not knowing it is a bear's den. Fortunately, the den belongs to a magical bear that kindly invites her to stay. While they sleep, the bear visits the girl's dreams and takes her on a tour of customs related to the winter season. In addition to general tales about snow or the return of spring, the bear takes the girl to the lands where the traditions surrounding Hanukkah, Christmas, Kwanzaa, the New Year, and Twelfth Night originate. Brief source notes and bibliography give the basis for the text. (80 pages)

Where it's reviewed:
Booklist, November 15, 1999, page 627
Hungry Mind Review, Winter 1999, page 53
School Librarian, Winter 1999, page 222
School Library Journal, October 1999, page 69
Times Educational Supplement, December 24, 1999, page 26

Other books by the same author:
The Blessing Seed, 1998
The Little Book of Celtic Lore, 1998
The Barefoot Book of Princesses, 1997

Other books you might like:
David Christiana, *The First Snow*, 1996
   Mother Nature hates winter and tries to keep him away so Aunt Arctica suggests that Winter try a gentle entry and he does so with the first snow.
Jean Craighead George, *Dear Rebecca, Winter Is Here*, 1993
   On the day of the winter solstice, a grandmother writes to her granddaughter describing the changes that indicate winter's arrival.
Margaret Mayo, *Magical Tales from Many Lands*, 1993
   An international collection presents fairy tales and folklore from different countries.
Barbara Rogasky, *Winter Poems*, 1994
   A collection of poems focus simply yet eloquently on the season of winter.

634

MARIANNA MAYER, Adaptor
GARY A. LIPPINCOTT, Illustrator

The Prince and the Pauper
(New York: Dial Books for Young Readers, 1999)

Subject(s): Kings, Queens, Rulers, etc.; Identity; Adventure and Adventurers
Age range(s): Grades 2-4
Major character(s): Tom Canty, Child (poor); Edward, Royalty (Prince of Wales), Child; Miles Hendon, Nobleman
Time period(s): 16th century
Locale(s): London, England

Summary: The picture book adaptation of Mark Twain's novel describes the unintentional mix-up of identities when a prince and a pauper change outfits. Edward, Prince of Wales finds himself thrown out onto the streets with no one believing his true identity. Tom has the same problem, but he now lives a regal life and is soon to be crowned king! Tom's wicked father beats Edward and tries to force him into a life of stealing, but Edward is rescued by kind Miles Hendon. With Miles' help, Edward makes his way to London and the case of mistaken identities is discovered just in time to assure the crowning of Edward rather than Tom as the next King of England. (48 pages)

Where it's reviewed:
Booklist, November 1, 1999, page 529
Publishers Weekly, November 15, 1999, page 66
School Library Journal, November 1999, page 125

Other books by the same author:
Pegasus, 1998
Noble-Hearted Kate: A Celtic Tale, 1990
The Twelve Dancing Princesses, 1989
The Unicorn and the Lake, 1982
Carlo Collodi's: The Adventures of Pinocchio, 1981

Other books you might like:
Debbie Dadey, *Cherokee Sister*, 2000
   Mistaken for a Cherokee, 12-year-old Allie is forced to join the Trail of Tears with no idea how to reach her family again.
Caroline Leavitt, *The Prince and the Pooch*, 1997
   Joe's first coaching experience reminds Wishbone of the poor boy who trades places with the crown prince in an *Adventures of Wishbone* series entry.
Mark Twain, *The Prince and the Pauper: A Tale for Young People of All Ages*, 1909
   The original novel describes conditions in England in the early 16th century through the eyes of two boys who inadvertently change identities.

635

MERCER MAYER, Author/Illustrator

Shibumi and the Kitemaker
(Tarrytown, NY: Marshall Cavendish, 1999)

Subject(s): Fathers and Daughters; Kings, Queens, Rulers, etc.; Change
Age range(s): Grades 2-4
Major character(s): Shibumi, Royalty (princess); Unnamed Character, Artisan (kitemaker), Aged Person; Unnamed Character, Warrior (samurai)
Time period(s): Indeterminate Past
Locale(s): Japan

Summary: The emperor and empress protect their cherished daughter Princess Shibumi by confining her to the palace grounds. As she plays she hears the sounds of the city and assumes it is as beautiful as her world until she climbs a tree and peers over the wall to speak to some children in the street. Shibumi is shocked to see the deplorable conditions beyond the palace grounds and decides to do something to improve life for the city's residents. Commanding the royal kitemaker to make her a large kite, Shibumi sails into the air where she intends to stay until her father has fulfilled her wishes. Palace intrigue threatens to end her plans and her life, but the faithful kitemaker soars away with Shibumi to safety. Years later a young samurai seeks out Shibumi to tell her that her father has fulfilled her wish and to encourage her to honor the emperor's desire to see his daughter again. Although the elderly kitemaker has died, Shibumi uses the skills she learned from him to return with the samurai to the palace grounds and her father. (48 pages)

Where it's reviewed:
Booklist, October 15, 1999, page 444
ForeWord, August 1999, page 77
Kirkus Reviews, August 15, 1999, page 1313
Publishers Weekly, July 19, 1999, page 193
School Library Journal, September 1999, page 196

Other books by the same author:
There's a Nightmare in My Closet, 1985
East of the Sun and West of the Moon, 1980
Appelard & Liverwurst, 1978
Liza Lou and the Yeller Belly Swamp, 1976
A Boy, a Dog, and a Frog, 1967

Other books you might like:
Alma Flor Ada, *The Malachite Palace*, 1998
   Shut away in the palace for protection, a lonely princess cannot be given what she truly wants—a friend—so she frees herself.
Vivian French, *The Thistle Princess*, 1998
   The wall that a king and queen build to protect their beloved child actually stifles her and deprives her of happiness.
Eric Quayle, *The Shining Princess and Other Japanese Legends*, 1989
   An illustrated collection includes ten traditional folktales from Japan.
Paul O. Zelinsky, *Rapunzel*, 1997
   This retelling of the classic story of the pain and power of love captured the Caldecott Medal.

636

JAMES MAYHEW, Author/Illustrator

Katie and the Mona Lisa
(New York: Orchard Books, 1999)

Subject(s): Artists and Art; Museums; Grandmothers
Age range(s): Grades K-3
Major character(s): Katie, Child; Mona Lisa, Historical Figure
Time period(s): 1990s (1999)
Locale(s): England

Summary: When Katie visits the art museum with her grandmother she declares that her favorite painting is of the Mona Lisa, because the portrait smiles at her. While Katie tries to figure out why Mona Lisa smiles, she is invited into the picture where she learns Mona Lisa is none too happy. Katie and Mona Lisa go visiting other paintings trying to find friends or something to do. Adventure after adventure ends in mishap and eventually Mona Lisa returns to her frame with happy memories to keep her smiling. (32 pages)

Where it's reviewed:
Booklist, September 1, 1999, page 140

Bulletin of Center for Children's Books, September 1999, page 21
Children's Bookwatch, September 1999, page 6
Kirkus Reviews, July 15, 1999, page 1136
School Library Journal, December 1999, page 104

Other books by the same author:
Katie and the Impressionists, 1999
Koschka's Tales: Stories from Russia, 1993
Katie and the Dinosaurs, 1992

Other books you might like:
Elaine Clayton, *Ella's Trip to the Museum*, 1996
   While in an art museum, Ella pretends to be part of the paintings.
Tony Parillo, *Michaelangelo's Surprise*, 1998
   Sandro, a page in the Medici household, searches the palace on the day of a snowstorm for Michaelangelo and finds him making a snow sculpture.
Bjorn Sortland, *Anna's Art Adventure*, 1999
   While on a trip to an art museum, Anna finds herself inside several paintings.
Neil Waldman, *The Starry Night*, 1999
   Bernard, a young boy, finds Vincent van Gogh in Central Park and shows him around town.

637

BILL MAYNARD
FRANK REMKIEWICZ, Illustrator

Quiet, Wyatt!
(New York: G.P. Putnam's Sons, 1999)

Subject(s): Growing Up; Communication; Self-Confidence
Age range(s): Grades K-2
Major character(s): Wyatt, Child, Brother (younger)
Time period(s): 1990s (1999)
Locale(s): United States

Summary: Wyatt wants to be included, to be allowed to help fly a model airplane, wash the family car, buy a puppy or fry an egg, but each time he communicates his interest to the older person involved with the activity he's told, "Quiet, Wyatt," because he's not old enough to help. He tries shouting his name and proclaiming his destiny in a variety of venues, but still no one really listens; they just yell at Wyatt to be quiet. So, Wyatt becomes quiet. When he observes a problem he says nothing and lets events happen until he sees a puppy run away from the pet store. Wyatt tries to remain quiet, but the puppy appears to be in danger he speaks up loud and clear to save the puppy's life. Wyatt's family and neighbors now realize they may have misjudged his abilities. (32 pages)

Where it's reviewed:
Booklist, June 1999, page 1842
Horn Book Guide, Fall 1999, page 260
Kirkus Reviews, June 1, 1999, page 886
Publishers Weekly, June 14, 1999, page 69
School Library Journal, July 1999, page 77

Other books by the same author:
Incredible Ned, 1997
Santa's Time Off: Poems, 1997

Other books you might like:

Margaret Wise Brown, *The Little Scarecrow Boy*, 1998
  Little Scarecrow Boy wants to join his father in the corn-fields but first he must master six scary faces that will chase the crows away.

Syd Hoff, *Bernard on His Own*, 1993
  Bernard's parents reassure him that one day the young bear will be able to climb a tree, catch a fish and gather honey without their help.

Stephen Kroninger, *If I Crossed the Road*, 1997
  A little boy is too young to cross the road alone, but not too young to plan what he'll do when his mother gives him the go ahead.

Alexis O'Neill, *Loud Emily*, 1998
  Emily is born loud and unappreciated until she finds work where her voice is needed as a foghorn.

638

ANNE MAZER
PAUL MEISEL, Illustrator

The Fixits

(New York: Hyperion Books for Children, 1999)

Subject(s): Accidents; Brothers and Sisters; Humor
Age range(s): Grades K-2
Major character(s): Augusta, Child, Sister (younger); Ed Fixit, Repairman; Tom Fixit, Repairman
Time period(s): 1990s (1999)
Locale(s): United States

Summary: When Augusta and her brother crack a plate while their mother is out, they expect Ed and Tom to fix it quickly. Instead, Tom drops the plate so it is completely broken. Ed pours a huge puddle of glue on the pieces to repair it while Augusta dances with glee and her brother cowers behind a chair fretting about mom's reaction. The Fixits are as confident as they are clueless and each of the actions they take to correct their accidents creates an even bigger problem. Augusta sees the positive side of everything while her brother tries to clean up some of the mess. The Fixits never lose their confidence that they "can fix anything" even after the house collapses due to their incompetent repair strategy. (24 pages)

Where it's reviewed:
Booklist, April 1, 1999, page 1421
Horn Book Guide, Fall 1999, page 261
Publishers Weekly, March 8, 1999, page 67
School Library Journal, June 1999, page 102
Teacher Librarian, October 1999, page 53

Other books by the same author:
The Oxboy, 1993 (ALA Notable Book)
The Salamander Room, 1993
Moose Street, 1992

Other books you might like:
Eileen Browne, *Tick-Tock*, 1994
  When Skip becomes so excited playing with Brainy that they break a cuckoo clock, the squirrels must get it repaired before Mom comes home.
David Galef, *Tracks*, 1996
  While supervising the laying of railroad tracks Albert

breaks his glasses but continues directing in a blur with predictable results.

Richard McGuire, *What Goes Around Comes Around*, 1995
  One event causes another that causes another and so it continues until we're back to the beginning.

Linnea Riley, *Mouse Mess*, 1997
  A mouse's nighttime visit to a kitchen is fun for the mouse, but leaves a mess by morning.

Dr. Seuss, *The Cat in the Hat*, 1957
  One rainy afternoon while Mom is away an unexpected visitor creates havoc for two siblings before Mom returns.

639

NORMA FOX MAZER

Good Night, Maman

(San Diego: Harcourt Brace & Company, 1999)

Subject(s): Holocaust; World War II; Jews
Age range(s): Grades 4-7
Major character(s): Karin Levi, Daughter, Refugee; Marc Levi, Brother (older), Refugee; Maman, Mother
Time period(s): 1940s (1940-1945)
Locale(s): France; Italy; Oswego, New York (Fort Ontario)

Summary: After a year of cramped, but relatively safe existence in an attic closet, Maman, Marc and Karin are evicted because the widow sheltering them decides it is no longer safe for her to harbor them. Traveling by night, the family walks south, finding refuge for a time in a home in southern France where Marc and Karin are forced to leave their ailing mother when she is unable to travel. The siblings finally reach southern Italy and board an American ship carrying wounded soldiers and refugees to America. Initially, their life in America defies their concept of freedom because, with other refugees, Marc and Karin are quarantined behind a barbed wire fence guarded by soldiers. They make friends with other refuges, practice their English, try to establish some routine in their life and wait the day they can return to France. A concluding historical note gives the background on which the story is based. (185 pages)

Where it's reviewed:
Booklist, August 1999, page 2053
Horn Book, November 1999, page 743
Kirkus Reviews, October 15, 1999, page 1647
Publishers Weekly, November 8, 1999, page 68
School Library Journal, December 1999, page 137

Awards the book has won:
Notable Social Studies Trade Books for Young People, 2000

Other books by the same author:
When She Was Good, 1997
Missing Pieces, 1995
Out of Control, 1993

Other books you might like:
Karen Ackerman, *The Night Crossing*, 1994
  In 1938, fearing persecution, Clara and her family leave their Austrian home and flee to the safety of Switzerland.
Anne Frank, *The Diary of a Young Girl*, 1947
  Anne Frank's diary relates the true story of the years her family hides from the Nazis in an Amsterdam warehouse.

Lois Lowry, *Number the Stars*, 1989

> While sheltering her Jewish friend Ellen from the Nazis, Annemarie learns about herself and the meaning of courage. Newbery Medal winner.

Ida Vos, *Anna Is Still Here*, 1993

> The Nazi threat has ended, but the impact of being hidden in an attic, alone, for three years has not left Anna.

Laura E. Williams, *Behind the Bedroom Wall*, 1996

> The danger to Jews and those who hide them becomes real to Korinna when she's warned of the Nazi plan to raid her house.

640

SAM MCBRATNEY
JENNIFER EACHUS, Illustrator

I'm Sorry

(New York: HarperCollins Publishers, 2000)

Subject(s): Friendship; Playing; Anger
Age range(s): Preschool
Major character(s): Unnamed Character, Child, Friend; Unnamed Character, Child, Friend
Time period(s): 2000s (2000)
Locale(s): Ireland

Summary: A young boy describes the easy-going friendship he has with a little girl. They play with each other daily at one house or the other, enjoying simple activities and sharing according to an established routine—he's the teacher and she's the doctor. One day the little boy shouts at his friend in anger and she shouts back. Now each is alone and feeling sad. They no longer speak or play together until the simple words, "I'm sorry," bring smiles back to their faces. (40 pages)

Where it's reviewed:
Booklist, August 2000, page 2148
Horn Book Guide, Fall 2000, page 252
Publishers Weekly, June 12, 2000, page 71
School Library Journal, June 2000, page 120

Other books by the same author:
Just You and Me, 1998
The Dark at the Top of the Stairs, 1996 (Booklist Editors' Choice)
Guess How Much I Love You, 1995 (Booklist Editors' Choice)

Other books you might like:
Holly Hobbie, *Toot & Puddle: You Are My Sunshine*, 1999

> The sun shines, but Toot mopes so Puddle and Tulip try to cheer their friend.

Dorothea Lachner, *Andrew's Angry Words*, 1995

> When Andrew shouts angry words at this older sister he learns how far ranging the impact of such an outburst can be.

Kim Lewis, *Friends*, 1997

> Friends Sam and Alice squabble briefly over a dropped egg, but put their differences aside when they hear the hen clucking again.

Mercer Mayer, *I Was So Mad*, 1983

> A child tries different techniques to dissipate angry feelings.

641

PETER MCCARTY, Author/Illustrator

Little Bunny on the Move

(New York: Henry Holt and Company, 1999)

Subject(s): Animals/Rabbits; Self-Confidence; Determination
Age range(s): Grades 1-2
Major character(s): Little Bunny, Rabbit
Time period(s): Indeterminate
Locale(s): United States

Summary: Little Bunny, determined to reach his destination, ignores the cow and sheep in his path. Resolutely, he clambers over the train tracks and through a fence. Despite the growing darkness and a little girl's offer to give him a place to stay, Little Bunny keeps moving toward his goal—home. (32 pages)

Where it's reviewed:
Booklist, December 15, 1999, page 790
New York Times Book Review, November 21, 1999, page 57
School Library Journal, December 1999, page 103

Awards the book has won:
New York Times Best Illustrated Children's Books, 1999

Other books you might like:
Jim Arnosky, *Rabbits and Raindrops*, 1997

> A mother rabbit watches over her five babies as they hop out of the nest to munch grass for the first time.

Margaret Wise Brown, *Goodnight Moon*, 1947

> A bunny says goodnight to all the objects in the great green room before bidding the moon goodnight.

Christine Loomis, *Cowboy Bunnies*, 1997

> After playing all day on their rocking horses, cowboy bunnies are tired at day's end.

Beatrix Potter, *The Tale of Peter Rabbit*, 1902

> Peter Rabbit is grateful for the sanctuary of home after his ill-advised visit to Mr. McGregor's garden.

642

GERALDINE MCCAUGHREAN
MOIRA KEMP, Illustrator

Grandma Chickenlegs

(Minneapolis: Carolrhoda Books, 2000)

Subject(s): Folklore; Stepmothers; Courage
Age range(s): Grades K-3
Major character(s): Tatia, Child, Stepdaughter; Drooga, Doll; Grandma Chickenlegs, Witch, Aged Person
Time period(s): Indeterminate Past
Locale(s): Russia

Summary: Before Tatia's mother dies she advises Tatia to be "giving and forgiving" and to "beware of Grandma Chickenlegs." Tatia has no difficulty following her mother's advice until her cruel stepmother sends her on an errand to Grandma Chickenlegs' home to borrow a needle. The stepmother thinks this will be the last she sees of Tatia, but she hasn't counted on the wisdom of Drooga or the kindness of Tatia. Together Tatia and Drooga approach Grandma Chickenlegs and explain the reason for their visit. Though the witch invites Tatia in for supper, her motive soon becomes clear when she orders her dog and cat to fill the tub so her food can be washed before she eats it. Kindly, Tatia shares the supper with the dog and cat and uses her butter to quiet the door's squeaky hinges. Those actions enable her to escape from Grandma Chickenlegs and to stop the witch's pursuit before she is captured. As luck would have it Tatia also runs into her father, tells her story and the two of them return home to live happily ever after without the stepmother and her daughters. (32 pages)

Where it's reviewed:
Booklist, October 15, 1999, page 449
ForeWord, December 1999, page 53
Horn Book, January 2000, page 88
Publishers Weekly, October 25, 1999, page 80
School Library Journal, January 2000, page 124

Other books by the same author:
Unicorns! Unicorns!, 1997
The Cherry Tree, 1992
Saint George and the Dragon, 1989

Other books you might like:
Katya Arnold, *Baba Yaga: A Russian Folktale*, 1993
  Witch Baba Yaga is no match for a clever child in this retelling of the Russian folktale.
Joanna Cole, *Bony-Legs*, 1983
  A young girl's kindness to a witch's dog and cat helps her escape in this beginning reader version of a Russian folktale
Eric A. Kimmel, *Baba Yaga: A Russian Folktale*, 1991
  In a retelling of the traditional tale, Marina's stepmother sends her into the forest to the wicked witch.

643

GILLIAN MCCLURE, Author/Illustrator

Selkie

(New York: Farrar Straus and Giroux)

Subject(s): Animals/Seals and Sea Lions; Islands; Legends
Age range(s): Grades K-3
Major character(s): Peter, Child; Selkie, Shape-Changer, Seal; Mr. Oysterman, Fisherman
Time period(s): Indeterminate Past
Locale(s): Seal Island, Scotland

Summary: Peter's not allowed near Mr. Oysterman or Seal Island but the island that can be reached from his coastal village only at low tide seems to call to him. Mr. Oysterman refuses to teach him the path he uses when he goes to gather oysters, but Peter watches and remembers. He hears Mr. Oysterman planning to capture a selkie and the first time Peter sneaks over to the island he finds a seal trapped in a net. When Peter frees the seal she takes off her skin, becoming a girl. In appreciation, Selkie teaches Peter the language of the sea, but both children are inattentive to the time and the tide. When low tide comes again Mr. Oysterman returns and nabs Selkie. The next day while Mr. Oysterman is in town selling his oysters, Peter frees Selkie so she can return to Seal Island. (32 pages)

Where it's reviewed:
Booklist, December 15, 1999, page 791
Books for Keeps, May 1999, page 6
Horn Book Guide, Spring 2000, page 45
School Library Journal, November 1999, page 124

Other books by the same author:
The Christmas Donkey, 1993
What's the Time Rory Wolf?, 1982
Prickly Pig, 1980

Other books you might like:
Susan Cooper, *The Selkie Girl*, 1986
  The illustrated retelling of a Scottish tale introduces the selkie—a seal that can shed its skin and take on human form.
Sheila MacGill-Callahan, *The Seal Prince*, 1995
  As a child, Princess Grainne rescues a seal that returns years later in human form to ask the princess to join his kingdom beneath the sea.
Jill Paton Walsh, *Matthew and the Sea Singer*, 1993
  When the seal-queen steals Matthew, Birdy must strike a bargain to get him back.

644

WENDY MCCORMICK
JENNIFER EACHUS, Illustrator

Daddy, Will You Miss Me?

(New York: Simon & Schuster Books for Young Readers, 1999)

Subject(s): Fathers and Sons; Africa; Work
Age range(s): Grades K-3
Major character(s): Unnamed Character, Child, Son; Daddy, Father
Time period(s): 1990s (1999)
Locale(s): United States

Summary: The author's first book opens as Daddy prepares to leave on a 4-week trip to Africa. After helping his father pack, his son runs to his own room, overwhelmed with feelings. Daddy follows to say just how much he will miss his family and to describe how he will stay in touch with his son from afar by whispering his name on the wind and blowing kisses that will travel to him. The son replies that he will mark the days on the calendar and collect one special thing for each day to share with Daddy when he returns. Finally, when the last day is crossed off the boy, his baby sister and their mother meet Daddy at the airport when he comes home from Africa. (32 pages)

Where it's reviewed:
Children's Book Review Service, July 1999, page 148
Horn Book Guide, Fall 1999, page 259
Publishers Weekly, June 7, 1999, page 81
School Librarian, Autumn 1999, page 131
School Library Journal, June 1999, page 100

Other books by the same author:
The Night You Were Born, 2000

Other books you might like:
Caroline Feller Bauer, *My Mom Travels a Lot*, 1985
  Although it's difficult to have a traveling parent, anticipating her return helps the time pass quickly.

Susi Gregg Fowler, *I'll See You When the Moon Is Full*, 1994
While packing for a business trip, Daddy reassures Abe that he will return, "When the moon is full."

Pamela D. Greenwood, *I Found Mouse*, 1994
To pass the time during her mother's 3-week business trip, Tessie focuses on a stray kitten she finds.

Rita Phillips Mitchell, *Hue Boy*, 1993
After a long absence the ship carrying Hue Boy's father appears in the harbor.

645

LISA MCCOURT
CYD MOORE, Illustrator

It's Time for School, Stinky Face

(Mahwah, NJ: Troll/BridgeWater Books, 2000)

Subject(s): Imagination; Schools; Mothers and Sons
Age range(s): Grades K-1
Major character(s): Mama, Mother; Stinky Face, Son, Student—Elementary School
Time period(s): 2000s (2000)
Locale(s): United States

Summary: It's time to go to school, but Stinky Face is full of questions about imaginative disasters that could befall him. Mama is ready with a solution to everything he can suggest. If the bus gets flat tires Mama will call the circus to drive the kids in clown cars and if that makes Stinky Face dizzy and he ends up in the principal's office then the principal will help him find his class. Of course, Stinky Face imagines that the principal could be a witch or his classroom door could be glued shut or his teacher could forget all her stories and expect him to tell one at circle time. Mama is certain that Stinky Face would have no difficulty thinking of a story to tell. (32 pages)

Where it's reviewed:
Booklist, October 15, 2000, page 446
Horn Book Guide, Spring 2001, page 44
Kirkus Reviews, August 1, 2000, page 1121
Publishers Weekly, August 14, 2000, page 357
School Library Journal, October 2000, page 130

Other books by the same author:
I Miss You, Stinky Face, 1999
I Love You, Stinky Face, 1997
The Rain Forest Counts!, 1997

Other books you might like:
Doug Johnson, *Never Ride Your Elephant to School*, 1995
It's not a good idea to use your elephant to transport you to school because it can lead to problems.

Stephen Krensky, *My Teacher's Secret Life*, 1996
A student imagines what the teachers and principal do at school after the students leave.

Jonathan London, *Froggy Goes to School*, 1996
First-day-of-school jitters have Froggy dreaming that he's gone to school in his underwear.

646

EMILY ARNOLD MCCULLY, Author/Illustrator

Hurry!

(San Diego: Browndeer Press/Harcourt, Inc., 2000)

Subject(s): Wildlife Conservation; Animals; Animals, Treatment of
Age range(s): Grades 1-3
Major character(s): Tom Elson, 10-Year-Old; Murray Bayliss, Traveler; Mr. Krebs, Blacksmith
Time period(s): 1910s (1916)
Locale(s): Vosburgh, Iowa

Summary: While strolling past Mr. Kreb's shop on a hot summer afternoon, Tom notices yellow eyes peering from a crate in the back of a wagon awaiting service. Inside the crate is the oddest animal Tom has ever seen. Murray Bayliss announces that the talking creature is a farivox. When Tom learns that he can buy the animal for ten dollars he prepares to run home and get his life's savings. As Tom passes the crate he hears the farivox say "Hurry!" Although Tom runs faster than he's ever run in his life, by the time he counts his money and races back to the blacksmith's shop, Murray Bayliss, his wagon and the farivox are gone in this adaptation of *Farewell to the Farivox* by Harry Hartwick. (32 pages)

Where it's reviewed:
Booklist, March 15, 2000, page 1388
Horn Book, November 2000, page 748
Publishers Weekly, March 13, 2000, page 84
School Library Journal, April 2000, page 108

Other books by the same author:
Beautiful Warrior: The Legend of the Nun's Kung Fu, 1998
(ALA Notable Book)
Popcorn at the Palace, 1997
The Bobbin Girl, 1996

Other books you might like:
David Dobson, *Can We Save Them?: Endangered Species of North America*, 1997
Descriptions of the habitats and characteristics of twelve species facing extinction are illustrated in this title.

Louise Erdrich, *Grandmother's Pigeon*, 1996
Surprisingly, eggs in a decorative nest near a stuffed pigeon hatch and are identified as passenger pigeons, thought to be extinct.

Margery Facklam, *And Then There Was One: The Mysteries of Extinction*, 1990
A nonfiction title discusses how humans contribute to the vanishing of native species.

Cristina Kessler, *All the King's Animals*, 1995
A conservationist tries to save endangered species by starting a wildlife preserve in Swaziland that is described in this nonfiction title.

Alexandra Wright, *Will We Miss Them?*, 1992
After endangered species vanish forever, will we regret not working to save them?

647

EMILY ARNOLD MCCULLY, Author/Illustrator

Mirette & Bellini Cross Niagara Falls

(New York: G.P. Putnam's Sons, 2000)

Subject(s): Emigration and Immigration; Adventure and Adventurers; Friendship
Age range(s): Grades 1-4
Major character(s): Mirette, Child, Entertainer (tightrope walker); Bellini, Entertainer (tightrope walker); Jakob, Immigrant, Orphan
Time period(s): Indeterminate Past
Locale(s): *SS Magnifique*, At Sea; Ellis Island, New York; Niagara Falls, New York

Summary: While traveling to America to perform at Niagara Falls Mirette befriends Jakob who sneaks up from steerage to watch her practice. When the ship docks, Mirette and Bellini notice that Jakob's uncle has not come to meet him at Ellis Island. Knowing that this will mean Jakob's return to Poland, Bellini claims that Jakob is his assistant and takes him to Niagara Falls until they have time to locate the uncle. An American aerialist challenges Bellini, claiming that he will perform an even greater feat during his crossing of the falls. Bellini plans carefully to compensate for the effect of the wind on the wire, but he does not plan for sabotage. Jakob observes the trickery of the other aerialist and tries to warn Bellini, but already he and Mirette are over the roaring water. The stabilizing wires begin to break threatening to plunge Mirette and Bellini into the water, but they successfully maintain their balance and race to the other side. Jakob reports what he has seen and the challenger is arrested. The newspaper reports attract the attention of Jakob's uncle who is grateful to know where to find him at last. (32 pages)

Where it's reviewed:
Booklist, November 15, 2000, page 638
Kirkus Reviews, October 1, 2000, page 1429
Publishers Weekly, August 14, 2000, page 357
School Library Journal, November 2000, page 126

Other books by the same author:
Starring Mirette & Bellini, 1997
Little Kit or, the Industrious Flea Circus Girl, 1995
Mirette on the High Wire, 1992 (Caldecott Medal)

Other books you might like:
Mary Calhoun, *High-Wire Henry*, 1991
To reclaim some of the family's attention after they acquire a puppy feline Henry learns to walk a tightrope.
Esther Kalman, *Tchaikovsky Discovers America*, 1995
A week after attending a concert by guest conductor Tchaikovsky, Jenny sees him on a train traveling alone to Niagara Falls and meets him in person.
Ian Wallace, *Morgan the Magnificent*, 1987
Visiting a circus with a tightrope-walking act enables Morgan to view professionals doing the tricks she's taught herself.

648

EMILY ARNOLD MCCULLY, Author/Illustrator

Monk Camps Out

(New York: Arthur A. Levine Books/Scholastic Press, 2000)

Subject(s): Animals/Mice; Camps and Camping; Parent and Child
Age range(s): Grades K-2
Major character(s): Monk, Mouse, Son; Mom, Mouse, Mother; Dad, Mouse, Father
Time period(s): 2000s (2000)
Locale(s): Fictional Country

Summary: Mom and Dad try to keep their distance as Monk ventures out to the backyard for his first overnight camping experience. Monk's foray into independence is only partially successful as his parents watch his every move from the house so they'll be ready to offer assistance—but only a little. After dark they tiptoe out to give him one last hug and then settle into their chairs to read, expecting Monk to give up and come inside. Monk and his parents fall asleep, but awaken suddenly during the night—Monk to race inside to find his baseball mitt and his parents to race outside to check on Monk. Mom and Dad lie down in the grass beside the tent and Monk snuggles into Mom's warm chair. In the morning, the family meets at the breakfast table where they all quickly fall asleep. (32 pages)

Where it's reviewed:
Booklist, May 15, 2000, page 1748
Horn Book, March 2000, page 189
Publishers Weekly, May 1, 2000, page 69
School Library Journal, April 2000, page 108
Smithsonian, November 2000, page 64

Awards the book has won:
Smithsonian's Notable Books for Children, 2000

Other books by the same author:
Mouse Practice, 1999
Popcorn at the Palace, 1997
Mirette on the High Wire, 1992 (Caldecott Medal)

Other books you might like:
Lillian Hoban, *Arthur's Camp-Out*, 1993
Arthur embarks on a solo camping trip in the woods near his home where he encounters unanticipated problems.
Hiawyn Oram, *Reckless Ruby*, 1992
To convince her overprotective parents to change their ways, Ruby adopts some reckless behavior.
Cynthia Rylant, *Henry and Mudge and the Starry Night*, 1998
A family camping trip includes hiking, singing around the campfire and quiet times with Henry's dog Mudge.
Bernard Waber, *Ira Sleeps Over*, 1973
An invitation to spend the night at Reggie's house creates a dilemma for Ira—should he bring his teddy?

649

EMILY ARNOLD MCCULLY, Author/Illustrator

Mouse Practice

(New York: Arthur Levine/Scholastic Press, 1999)

Subject(s): Animals/Mice; Sports/Baseball; Music and Musicians
Age range(s): Grades K-2
Major character(s): Monk, Mouse, Baseball Player (aspiring); Dad, Musician, Mouse; Mom, Musician, Mouse
Time period(s): 1990s
Locale(s): Fictional Country

Summary: Monk's debut baseball game is disastrous and the big kids suggest he come back when he grows up a little. Although Mom and Dad are sympathetic and try to help Monk, they know nothing about sports. They do know the importance of practice, however, and as their band practices every day, Monk devises his own system to improve his baseball skills. Several weeks later, Monk returns to the baseball diamond, no bigger, but with a surprisingly accurate throwing arm and musical accompaniment as he pitches. (32 pages)

Where it's reviewed:
Booklist, April 15, 1999, page 1537
Bulletin of the Center for Children's Books, February 1999, page 208
Horn Book, March 1999, page 198
Publishers Weekly, March 29, 1999, page 102
School Library Journal, March 1999, page 180

Other books by the same author:
Crossing the New Bridge, 1994
My Real Family, 1994 (School Library Journal Best Book)
Grandmas at Bat, 1993
Mirette on the High Wire, 1992 (Caldecott Medal)
Speak Up, Blanche!, 1991

Other books you might like:
Barbara Bottner, *Nana Hannah's Piano*, 1996
   Sonny prefers baseball practice to piano lessons.
Gloria Rand, *Willie Takes a Hike*, 1996
   While on a "pretend" hike, Willie ventures so far from his new home that the mouse becomes lost and must use the safety rules he's learned to survive.
Linnea Riley, *Mouse Mess*, 1997
   A self-sufficient, hungry mouse searches the kitchen for a nighttime snack, leaving a mess behind him when he heads off to bed.
James Stevenson, *All Aboard!*, 1995
   On a trip to the World's Fair, Hubie gets aboard the wrong train after a brief stop and heads for California while his family goes to New York.

650

GERALD MCDERMOTT, Author/Illustrator

The Fox and the Stork

(San Diego: Harcourt Brace & Company, 1999)

Series: Green Light Reader. Level 2

Subject(s): Fables; Animals/Foxes; Animals/Birds
Age range(s): Grades 1-2
Major character(s): Fox, Fox, Trickster; Stork, Bird
Time period(s): Indeterminate Past
Locale(s): Fictional Country

Summary: Fox enjoys playing tricks on others so when he invites Stork to dinner he serves soup in a dish so shallow Stork cannot eat it with her long beak. Fox gobbles all the food and Stork goes home hungry, but not before she issues a dinner invitation to Fox. When Fox arrives at Stork's home for dinner the next night Stork serves soup made with fresh greens from her garden. It smells delicious to Fox, but he'll never know the taste because Stork serves it in a tall jar just right for her beak, but inaccessible to Fox. When Fox goes home hungry he learns his lesson to treat friends kindly. (20 pages)

Where it's reviewed:
Booklist, October 1, 1999, page 366
Horn Book Guide, Spring 2000, page 62

Other books by the same author:
The Golden Goose, 2000
Musicians of the Sun, 1997
Arrow to the Sun, 1974 (Caldecott Medal)

Other books you might like:
Doug Cushman, *Possum Stew*, 1990
   Bear and Gator are tired of being tricked by Possum so they invite him to dinner, yum.
Lois Ehlert, *Mole's Hill*, 1994
   A mole with a mind of her own ignores Fox's demand that she move her hill; instead she beautifies it and tunnels a path through it.
Alex Moran, *Six Silly Foxes*, 2000
   Six foxes romp through a rhyming beginning reader.

651

MEGAN MCDONALD
PAUL BRETT JOHNSON, Illustrator

Bedbugs

(New York: Orchard Books, 1999)

Subject(s): Bedtime; Imagination; Stories in Rhyme
Age range(s): Grades K-2
Major character(s): Susan, Daughter, Child; Daddy, Father
Time period(s): 1990s (1999)
Locale(s): United States

Summary: At the first call for bath time Susan's imagination begins to turn bugs, mops and slippers into fantastic and ferocious creatures. Daddy continues with his evening routine calling out gentle reassurance each time Susan exclaims about another animal that she sees. Finally, once Susan has gotten herself snuggled into bed Daddy agrees to come get the porcupine out. He removes the pinecone while playing along with Susan's game and soon Susan is fast asleep. As Daddy tiptoes out of the room all the animals Susan has imagined are visible sleeping on her bed and floor. (32 pages)

Where it's reviewed:
Horn Book Guide, Spring 2000, page 19
Kirkus Reviews, July 15, 1999, page 1141

School Library Journal, September 1999, page 194

Other books by the same author:
Beezy at Bat, 1998
My House Has Stars, 1996
Insects Are My Life, 1995

Other books you might like:
Katherine Hook Berlan, *Andrew's Amazing Monsters*, 1993
During the night Andrew's artwork comes to life and prepares a surprise party for him.
Russell Hoban, *Bedtime for Frances*, 1960
Fear of one imagined thing after another keeps Frances from settling down to sleep.
Penelope Lively, *Good Night, Sleep Tight*, 1995
Although Mary Ann is tired after a day of play her stuffed animals are not and they make plans for a bedtime adventure.
Kate McMullan, *Good Night, Stella*, 1994
An overly active imagination keeps Stella from falling asleep.

652

MEGAN MCDONALD
NANCY POYDAR, Illustrator

Beezy and Funnybone

(New York: Orchard Books, 2000)

Series: Orchard Chapters
Subject(s): Animals/Dogs; Humor; Pets
Age range(s): Grades 1-2
Major character(s): Beezy, Child; Funnybone, Dog; Gran, Grandmother
Time period(s): 2000s (2000)
Locale(s): Florida

Summary: In the first of three stories Beezy teaches Funnybone how to "fetch" a ball. Funnybone takes to the game so well that he fetches items from neighbors, from other pets and from Beezy and Gran. Sometimes he buries what he fetches so Beezy has a hard time finding a birthday invitation that arrives in the mail until Funnybone digs it up for her. For a homework assignment Beezy and her friends learn multiple meanings of the word "spat" but none fit the context of the story until Gran identifies the immature snail on the flower Funnybone digs up for her. One activity at a birthday party Beezy attends is a ride in a hot air balloon. The preparations for take-off are so unsettling to Beezy that she and her friend jump out of the balloon's basket before lift-off leaving Funnybone to have a great ride! (48 pages)

Where it's reviewed:
Booklist, July 2000, page 2045
Horn Book Guide, Fall 2000, page 295
School Library Journal, September 2000, page 204

Other books by the same author:
Beezy Magic, 1998
Beezy at Bat, 1998
Beezy, 1997

Other books you might like:
James Howe, *Pinky and Rex*, 1990
Pinky and Rex begin their friendship in the first book of the series.
Claudia Mills, *Gus and Grandpa*, 1997
The first book in a series introduces Gus and the warm, loving relationship he has with Grandpa.
Cynthia Rylant, *The Henry and Mudge Series*, 1987-
Adventures of Henry and his lovable, slobbery dog Mudge entertain beginning readers.

653

MEGAN MCDONALD
PETER REYNOLDS, Illustrator

Judy Moody

(Cambridge, MA: Candlewick Press, 2000)

Subject(s): Schools; Friendship; Brothers and Sisters
Age range(s): Grades 2-4
Major character(s): Judy Moody, 3rd Grader, Sister; Rocky, Friend, 3rd Grader; Stink Moody, 2nd Grader, Brother
Time period(s): 2000s (2000)
Locale(s): Virginia

Summary: Judy Moody lives up to her name as she alternates between bad moods and good ones. The first day of school is a particularly grouchy day for Judy—she has no exciting summer travel to report via a souvenir t-shirt, Rocky is assigned a seat too far away for note passing, and she's in the front row next to a boy she doesn't like. A month-long assignment to create a "Me Collage" gives some framework to Judy's moods depending on whether she's acquiring a Venus fly trap as her "favorite pet" or struggling to identify the "funniest thing" that ever happened to her. Stink is often the reason for Judy's bad moods especially when his class goes on a field trip to the nation's capital and Judy's stuck in the role of a cavity at a "Mr. Tooth" assembly. Tricking Stink and sharing his reaction with Rocky finally enables Judy to have a "funniest thing" to complete her collage. Stink is also the reason her collage is almost ruined on the way to school, but Judy shows she knows how to make the best of a bad situation and uses the spilled juice stain to her advantage. (160 pages)

Where it's reviewed:
Booklist, July 2000, page 2028
Bulletin of the Center for Children's Books, May 2000, page 324
Kirkus Reviews, April 15, 2000, page 564
Publishers Weekly, April 17, 2000, page 81
School Library Journal, July 2000, page 83

Awards the book has won:
Publishers Weekly Best Books, 2000
ALA Notable Children's Books, 2001

Other books by the same author:
Shadows in the Glasshouse, 2000 (History Mysteries #7)
The Bridge to Nowhere, 1993
The Great Pumpkin Switch, 1992 (Carolyn W. Field Award)

Other books you might like:
Beverly Cleary, *Ramona Quimby, Age 8*, 1981
Spirited Ramona continues to keep her family guessing

about her next adventure as she enters third grade in this Newbery Honor book.

Holly Keller, *I Am Angela*, 1997

Angela is a contented child who seems to quite naturally make the routine events of life exciting.

Susan Wojciechowski, *Beany (Not Beanhead) and the Magic Crystal*, 1997

Beany considers and rejects several ideas for use of her new crystal (that just might have the power to grant a wish) before deciding on the best one.

654

MEGAN MCDONALD
PONDER GOEMBEL, Illustrator

The Night Iguana Left Home

(New York: Richard Jackson Book/DK Ink, 1999)

Subject(s): Animals/Reptiles; Friendship; Pets
Age range(s): Grades 1-3
Major character(s): Alison Frogley, Child, Friend; Iguana, Friend, Iguana
Time period(s): 1990s (1999)
Locale(s): Schenectady, New York; Key West, Florida

Summary: Iguana has a pleasant life with her friend Alison, eating anchovy pizza and being sprayed daily with salt water. Still, something is not right and Iguana longs to be someplace warm with lots of seaweed to eat. After deliberating on the locales pictured in travel posters in Alison's room Iguana decides to pack her things and get on a bus for Key West. Initially all goes well for Iguana. She enjoys the beach, the food and sending post cards to Alison, but when her money runs out Iguana is forced to take a job doing what she hates the most—washing dishes. When the restaurant's cook wants to make Iguana the main course, she quickly escapes and devises a plan to return to Alison—for a little while. (32 pages)

Where it's reviewed:
Booklist, November 1, 1999, page 540
Horn Book, September 1999, page 596
Kirkus Reviews, August 1, 1999, page 1229
Publishers Weekly, October 4, 1999, page 74
School Library Journal, September 1999, page 195

Awards the book has won:
IRA/CBC Children's Choices, 2000

Other books by the same author:
Bedbugs, 1999
Insects Are My Life, 1995
Is This a House for a Hermit Crab?, 1990

Other books you might like:
Judith Caseley, *Mr. Green Peas*, 1995
Norman, a child with no pets, is excited to become the temporary caretaker of an iguana.
Tony Johnston, *The Iguana Brothers: A Tale of Two Lizards*, 1995
Two iguana brothers reflect on the meaning of life, friendship, their diet and their identity.
Susan Tews, *Lizard Sees the World*, 1997
Lizard is not content to sit around catching flies; he wants to climb to the top of the world and take in the view.

655

JILL MCELMURRY, Author/Illustrator

Mad about Plaid

(New York: HarperCollins Publishers, 2000)

Subject(s): Magic; Lost and Found Possessions; Problem Solving
Age range(s): Grades K-2
Major character(s): Madison Pratt, Child, Daughter
Time period(s): Indeterminate
Locale(s): Fictional Country

Summary: The purse Madison finds while skipping through the park has a most unusual effect on her. As Madison swings the purse and sings a silly song she becomes covered in plaid. Infuriated, she flings the purse away and walks home crying plaid tears. Her mother consults a book on curing plaid curses and learns that the curse will end in a week. Unfortunately, everything Madison touches becomes plaid and soon Madison's home and the town are plaid. Madison retrieves the purse from the park and turns it inside out thus making everything blue to match the purse's lining. However, as everyone knows, it's much easier to cure the blues than the plaids and by the time the author's first book concludes Madison has the town back to normal. (32 pages)

Where it's reviewed:
Booklist, April 1, 2000, page 1469
Horn Book Guide, Fall 2000, page 274
Kirkus Reviews, April 15, 2000, page 564
Publishers Weekly, April 10, 2000, page 99
School Library Journal, May 2000, page 148

Other books you might like:
Dr. Seuss, *My Many Colored Days*, 1996
A rhyming story links colors with moods.
David Shannon, *A Bad Case of Stripes*, 1998
Stress causes Camilla to break out in a bad case of stripes and that's just the beginning of her troubles.
David Small, *Fenwick's Suit*, 1996
Fenwick's new suit does more than brighten his life; the suit takes over his life and Fenwick wants to be himself again.

656

LYN ROSSITER MCFARLAND
JIM MCFARLAND, Illustrator

The Pirate's Parrot

(Berkeley, CA: Tricycle Press, 2000)

Subject(s): Pirates; Humor; Animals/Bears
Age range(s): Grades K-2
Major character(s): Cur, Pirate, Sea Captain; Barr, Stuffed Animal, Bear; Mr. Bellows, Sailor, Pirate
Time period(s): Indeterminate Past
Locale(s): *Mongrel*, At Sea

Summary: Cur, grieving over the death of his parrot, accidentally stomps on his monocle. The near-sighted captain orders Mr. Bellows to send men ashore to shoplift a monocle and a parrot. When the box they return with yields a teddy bear rather than a parrot the crew have to come up with a scheme for fooling Cur. It helps that the stuffed toy bear talks so they name her Barr, teach her to squawk, and dress her as a pirate. From her perch on Cur's shoulder Barr does her job so capably that when he finally receives a monocle and can see the true identity of the new parrot, Cur decides to keep Barr. (40 pages)

Where it's reviewed:
Booklist, May 15, 2000, page 1744
Children's Book Review Service, May 2000, page 112
Kirkus Reviews, March 1, 2000, page 303
Publishers Weekly, May 8, 2000, page 221
School Library Journal, May 2000, page 148

Other books you might like:
Tony Bradman, *A Treasury of Pirate Stories*, 1999
　　An illustrated collection includes excerpts from novels about pirates as well as texts of picture books on the subject.
Mem Fox, *Tough Boris*, 1994
　　When his pet parrot dies, Tough Boris cries right along with the crew.
Kathy Tucker, *Do Pirates Take Baths?*, 1994
　　A story in rhyme provides details of the daily life of pirates.

657

CONSTANCE W. MCGEORGE
MARY WHYTE, Illustrator

Boomer's Big Surprise

(San Francisco: Chronicle Books, 1999)

Subject(s): Animals/Dogs; Pets; Jealousy
Age range(s): Grades K-1
Major character(s): Boomer, Dog; Baby, Dog (puppy)
Time period(s): 1990s (1999)
Locale(s): United States

Summary: Newspapers cover the kitchen floor when Boomer comes in from playing and he sees a new bowl beside his own. Then his family arrives carrying a bundle that holds everyone's attention. No one notices Boomer, but Boomer notices the puppy that peers out of the blanket. Although the puppy looks just like a miniature Boomer, Baby's behavior is very different. The family allows Baby to eat when it isn't dinnertime and plays with him on the living room sofa, a place that is off limits to Boomer. When the pets and the family go outside, Boomer is sad and feels ignored until Baby runs up to play with him. Then, Boomer thinks that maybe this new pet won't be so bad after all. (32 pages)

Where it's reviewed:
Booklist, May 1, 1999, page 1600
Horn Book Guide, Fall 1999, page 237
Kirkus Reviews, April 15, 1999, page 633
Publishers Weekly, April 5, 1999, page 243
School Library Journal, June 1999, page 101

Other books by the same author:
Boomer Goes to School, 1996
Snow Riders, 1995
Boomer's Big Day, 1994

Other books you might like:
Alexandra Day, *Carl's Afternoon in the Park*, 1991
　　Carl, the family's pet rottweiler, "babysits" a puppy and a toddler while Mom visits with a friend.
Isabelle Harper, *Our New Puppy*, 1996
　　It takes the established family dog a little while to adjust to the arrival of a puppy that steals his toys, chews on his ears and eats his snacks.
Charlotte Voake, *Ginger*, 1997
　　Lucky Ginger lives a contented life until her young owner introduces a playful young kitten to be the older cat's friend.

658

ALICE MCGILL
CHRIS K. SOENTPIET, Illustrator

Molly Bannaky

(Boston: Houghton Mifflin Company, 1999)

Subject(s): Historical; Literacy; Farm Life
Age range(s): Grades 2-4
Major character(s): Molly Walsh, Teenager, Servant (indentured); Molly Bannaky, Spouse, Farmer; Bannaky, Slave (freed), Farmer
Time period(s): 17th century (1683); 18th century
Locale(s): England; Maryland, American Colonies

Summary: Molly Walsh's ability to read the Bible spares her a death sentence when the dairymaid is convicted of "stealing" her lord's milk after the cow kicks over the milk bucket. Instead of death, she is sent to the New World as an indentured servant. Seven years of labor in the tobacco fields earns Molly her freedom and the opportunity to establish a homestead and make a new life for herself. With help from neighbors this single woman builds a cabin and grows a tobacco crop. To get the help she needs with the farm, Molly purchases a slave at auction. Soon she frees Bannaky and breaks colonial law by marrying him. The small farm grows to over 100 acres and four daughters are borne before Bannaky dies. When their oldest daughter marries and has a son named Benjamin Banneker, Molly teaches her grandson to read and write and tells him stories of his grandfather, a prince from Africa. A concluding historical note gives the basis for the story. (32 pages)

Where it's reviewed:
Booklist, September 15, 1999, page 269
Bulletin of the Center for Children's Books, October 1999, page 61
Kirkus Reviews, July 15, 1999, page 1135
Publishers Weekly, August 2, 1999, page 84
School Library Journal, October 1999, page 119

Awards the book has won:
ALA Notable Children's Books, 2000

Other books by the same author:
In the Hollow of Your Hand, 2000
Miles' Song, 2000

Other books you might like:

Betsy Hearne, *Seven Brave Women*, 1997
Seven generations of courageous women in one family make a difference in the lives of those around them.

Andrea Davis Pinkney, *Dear Benjamin Banneker*, 1994
A picture book biography describes the contributions of Benjamin Banneker to the development of our national capital.

Kate Waters, *Sarah Morton's Day: A Day in the Life of a Pilgrim Girl*, 1989
Photographs compliment the essay about one day in Plymouth Colony as experienced by a young pilgrim.

659

ANIK McGRORY, Author/Illustrator

Mouton's Impossible Dream

(San Diego: Gulliver Books/Harcourt, Inc., 2000)

Subject(s): Animals/Sheep; Balloons; Air Travel
Age range(s): Grades K-3
Major character(s): Mouton, Sheep; Canard, Duck; Cocorico, Rooster
Time period(s): 1780s (1783)
Locale(s): France

Summary: Mouton stares at the drawings of flying machines on the barn wall and Canard's wings and feathers and tries to teach herself to fly, but she only succeeds in her dreams. When the drawings and Cocorico are packed into a wagon and leave the farm Canard and Mouton follow. Eventually they reach a large city and on the palace grounds they find the wagon and the flying machine. The animals hide in a nearby empty basket and inadvertently become the guinea pigs for the first test flight of the hot-air balloon. As a reward for their bravery Cocorico, Mouton and Canard live at the palace as pets of the royal family for their remaining days though they never fly again. Historical notes give the factual basis for the author's first story. (32 pages)

Where it's reviewed:
Booklist, June 1, 2000, page 1910
Bulletin of the Center for Children's Books, April 2000, page 287
Horn Book, May 2000, page 297
Publishers Weekly, May 8, 2000, page 220
School Library Journal, April 2000, page 108

Other books you might like:

Janie Bynum, *Altoona Baboona*, 1999
A silly rhyming story describes the travels of Altoona Baboona in his hot air balloona.

Mary Calhoun, *Hot-Air Henry*, 1981
Henry's hiding place takes flight giving the surprised Siamese cat an unexpected hot air balloon ride across the mountains.

Neil Johnson, *Fire & Silk: Flying in a Hot Air Balloon*, 1991
Photographic illustrations support the history of this invention and the mechanics of a hot air balloon flight described in a nonfiction title

James Marshall, *Wings: A Tale of Two Chickens*, 1986
Adventurous Winnie accepts a ride in a fox's hot air balloon while her friend Harriet tries to rescue her and keep both chickens from the stew pot.

Sarah Wilson, *Three in a Balloon*, 1990
Three farm animals gain celebrity as the first passengers to travel in a hot-air balloon.

660

LESLIE McGUIRK, Author/Illustrator

Tucker Flips!

(New York: Dutton Children's Books, 1999)

Subject(s): Animals/Dogs; Behavior; Winter
Age range(s): Preschool
Major character(s): Tucker, Dog (puppy), Brother
Time period(s): 1990s (1999)
Locale(s): United States

Summary: One of three puppies born on a snowy night as dog angels hover above, Tucker enjoys eating, napping, playing and watching television with his brothers. Tucker is more adventurous than his brothers so he also likes to ride a skateboard and dive from the couch to a cushion of the floor. When the puppies are old enough their mother takes them outside to learn how to dig tunnels and make yellow snow. Watching children on sleds gives Tucker dreams of sledding while his brothers continue dreaming about food. One snowy day when Tucker spots an unattended sled he leaps on and takes off down the hill until he hits a bump and flips through the air, landing in the snow. (32 pages)

Where it's reviewed:
Booklist, January 1, 2000, page 936
Horn Book Guide, Spring 2000, page 19
Kirkus Reviews, September 15, 1999, page 1502
Publishers Weekly, October 25, 1999, page 79
School Library Journal, December 1999, page 104

Other books by the same author:
Tucker Off His Rocker, 2000
Tucker Over the Top, 2000

Other books you might like:

Mick Inkpen, *Kipper's Snowy Day*, 1996
Kipper is a dog that loves to play in the snow either alone or with his friend Tiger.

Jean Van Leeuwen, *Oliver and Amanda and the Big Snow*, 1995
Oliver and his younger sister enjoy sledding, tossing snowballs and making a snow pig.

Nancy Elizabeth Wallace, *Snow*, 1995
Rabbit brothers hurry outside at the first sign of snow to sled, make snow rabbits and throw snowballs.

661

HILARY MCKAY

Dolphin Luck

(New York: Margaret K. McElderry Books/Simon and Schuster, 1999)

Subject(s): Brothers and Sisters; Pets; Humor
Age range(s): Grades 4-7

Major character(s): Beany Robinson, 8-Year-Old, Sister; Sun Dance Robinson, 10-Year-Old, Brother; Mrs. Brogan, Neighbor
Time period(s): 1990s (1998)
Locale(s): Eastcliffe, England (Porridge Hall); Hemingford North, England

Summary: The four Robinson children are farmed out in different directions while their parents travel to Barbados so their mother can convalesce from pneumonia. With very little notice and in a raging snowstorm, the twins are put on a train to their great aunt and godmother whom they know only by family stories. Beany and Sun Dance are staying with the neighbor who shares the other half of Porridge Hall. Sun Dance takes so seriously his father's instruction to look after things that he sets up elaborate burglar traps to protect their home. When no burglars appear promptly, Sun Dance tries to entice one into their home with a trail of valuables. Beany takes to heart a story Mrs. Brogan tells to wile the hours during the storm and begins searching the old house for a lucky sword on which to make wishes. When the twins return home unexpectedly with two dogs, four cats and a parrot it seems to Beany that her wish for a replacement for their recently deceased dog has come true. In fact, by story's end, all of Beany's wishes come true, or so she thinks. (153 pages)

Where it's reviewed:
Booklist, July 1999, page 1943
Horn Book, July 1999, page 470
Publishers Weekly, May 3, 1999, page 77
School Library Journal, July 1999, page 96

Awards the book has won:
Booklist Editors' Choice, 1999
School Library Journal Best Books, 1999

Other books by the same author:
The Exiles in Love, 1998 (Horn Book Fanfare)
The Amber Cat, 1997 (School Library Journal Best Book)
Dog Friday, 1995 (Booklist Editors' Choice)

Other books you might like:
Eth Clifford, *Harvey's Wacky Parrot Adventure*, 1990
    Begrudgingly Harvey accepts the help of his disliked cousin Nora in a search for hidden treasure.
Helen Cresswell, *The Bagthorpes Series*, 1978-
    The Bagthorpe family encounters one adventure after another, whether they're at home or on vacation.
Jane Louise Curry, *The Great Smith House Hustle*, 1993
    The many children in the Smith family are just settling in for a visit with Grandma when a ''Sold'' sign unexpectedly appears in the yard.
Adele Geras, *The Fabulous Fantoras: Book One: Family Files*, 1998
    Each member of the Fantora Family has an unusual trait or gift. Mother flies, Marco becomes invisible and Bianca animates objects.
Margaret Mahy, *Tangled Fortunes*, 1994
    In the final book of The Cousins Quartet, siblings Jackson and Tracey begin to explore different interests, but as usual, all paths lead to mystery and adventure.

662

DAVID MCKEE, Author/Illustrator

Elmer and the Lost Teddy

(New York: Lothrop, Lee & Shepard Books)

Subject(s): Animals/Elephants; Toys; Lost and Found Possessions
Age range(s): Grades K-2
Major character(s): Elmer, Elephant (patchwork), Cousin (Wilbur's); Wilbur, Elephant (checked), Cousin; Baby Elephant, Elephant
Time period(s): Indeterminate
Locale(s): Fictional Country

Summary: Losing a teddy bear right before bedtime has Baby Elephant crying and Elmer coming to the rescue with the loan of his teddy and the promise to search for the missing one. Wilbur offers to call Elmer if he should see Baby Elephant's teddy bear and he does, using his ventriloquist skill so Elmer briefly thinks the teddy bear is talking. Wilbur and Elmer carry the lost teddy back to a very happy Baby Elephant and his relieved mother. (32 pages)

Where it's reviewed:
Booklist, June 1999, page 1842
Horn Book Guide, Fall 1999, page 237
Kirkus Reviews, April 15, 1999, page 633
Publishers Weekly, April 5, 1999, page 243
School Library Journal, July 1999, page 76

Other books by the same author:
Elmer and the Kangaroo, 2000
Elmer Takes Off, 1998
Elmer and Wilbur, 1996

Other books you might like:
Jez Alborough, *Where's My Teddy?*, 1992
    As Eddie searches the dark woods for his lost teddy bear he encounters a large bear with a similar problem.
Camilla Ashforth, *Humphrey Thud*, 1995
    Humphrey tries to copy Horatio's trick but no amount of magic can make a big toy elephant like Humphrey disappear into a sock.
Martin Waddell, *Small Bear Lost*, 1996
    When Small Bear is left on a train he manages to find his way home to the little girl who lost him.

663

PATRICIA C. MCKISSACK
GISELLE POTTER, Illustrator

The Honest-to-Goodness Truth

(New York: Anne Schwartz Book/Atheneum Books for Young Readers, 2000)

Subject(s): Honesty; Conduct of Life; Interpersonal Relations
Age range(s): Grades K-3
Major character(s): Libby Louise Sullivan, Daughter, Friend (Ruthie Mae's); Mama, Mother; Ruthie Mae, Child, Friend
Time period(s): Indeterminate Past
Locale(s): Briarsville

Summary: When Mama catches Libby in a lie, Libby is punished twice—for the chore she didn't do and for lying about it. From now on, Libby vows to always tell the truth no matter how much it hurts. What Libby doesn't realize is that the truth told thoughtlessly can hurt others. The first person Libby meets after her decision is Ruthie Mae and she boldly notes that her friend has a hole in her sock. Libby is confused by the reactions of Ruthie Mae and others because what she says is always truthful. When Libby becomes the recipient of someone else's thoughtless, though truthful remark she begins to see the error of her ways and carefully apologizes to each person she has hurt. (32 pages)

Where it's reviewed:
Booklist, December 15, 1999, page 791
Bulletin of the Center for Children's Books, February 2000, page 215
Five Owls, May 2000, page 119
Publishers Weekly, January 10, 2000, page 67
School Library Journal, January 2000, page 108

Awards the book has won:
School Library Journal Best Books, 2000

Other books by the same author:
Ma Dear's Aprons, 1997
A Million Fish. . .More or Less, 1992
Mirandy and Brother Wind, 1988

Other books you might like:
Pat Brisson, *The Summer My Father Was Ten*, 1998
    A thoughtless act of destruction teaches a ten-year-old a lesson that produces a gardener for life.
Eve Bunting, *A Day's Work*, 1994
    A young boy learns the value of honesty when his efforts to help his immigrant grandfather backfire.
Holly Keller, *That's Mine, Horace*, 2000
    When Horace claims a classmate's truck is his own, he feels so guilty about lying that he feels too sick to go to school
Jan Romero Stevens, *Carlos and the Cornfield/Carlos y la Milpa de Maiz*, 1995
    The truth of Carlos's failure to follow his father's planting directions becomes obvious as the plants grow.

664

CLEMENCE MCLAREN

Dance for the Land

(New York: Atheneum Books for Young Readers, 1999)

Subject(s): Moving, Household; Prejudice; Family Life
Age range(s): Grades 4-7
Major character(s): Kathryn Maluhia ''Kate'' Kahele, 12-Year-Old, Dancer; David Kaleo Kahele, Brother (older), Student—High School
Time period(s): 1990s (1993)
Locale(s): Honolulu, Hawaii

Summary: When Kate's father returns to his native Hawaii with Kate and David to offer his legal services in the fight for native sovereignty, Kate has the greatest difficulty adjusting to the change. David inherited his father's Hawaiian appearance, but Kate has the fair skin and light hair of her deceased mother so she faces discrimination as a *haole* or white person. Missing her dog, her California home, ballet and her friends, Kate struggles to survive, feeling embarrassed at school and with her relatives because she frequently misunderstands the native language. A class hula performance for a school talent show gives Kate the opportunity to dance again, to appreciate the native culture, to find a way to be a part of it and to bring peace to her squabbling relatives. (153 pages)

Where it's reviewed:
Booklist, February 15, 1999, page 1070
Bulletin of the Center for Children's Books, March 1999, page 247
Horn Book Guide, Fall 1999, page 297
Publishers Weekly, February 1, 1999, page 86
School Library Journal, June 1999, page 134

Other books by the same author:
Waiting for Odysseus: A Novel, 2000
Inside the Walls of Troy, 1996

Other books you might like:
Joseph Bruchac, *Eagle Song*, 1997
    A lack of employment on the reservation forces Danny's family to move to Brooklyn where prejudiced classmates make Danny's life miserable.
Mildred D. Taylor, *The Gold Cadillac*, 1987
    When an African-American family from Ohio visits relatives in the South they face the racism that is part of 1950s life in the South.
Laurence Yep, *The Star Fisher*, 1991
    In 1927 a Chinese family faces discrimination when they move from Ohio to West Virginia to open a laundry.

665

KRISTINA THERMAENIUS MCLAREY
MYRA MCLAREY, Co-Author
MARJORY WUNSCH, Illustrator

When You Take a Pig to a Party

(New York: Orchard Books, 2000)

Subject(s): Animals/Pigs; Birthdays; Humor
Age range(s): Grades K-2
Major character(s): Adelaide, Child, Friend; Sherman, Pig; Ethan, 8-Year-Old, Friend
Time period(s): 2000s (2000)
Locale(s): United States

Summary: Adelaide's pet pig Sherman is so sweet and well mannered that she's sure he'll be no trouble at Ethan's birthday party. She bathes him and makes sure he's well dressed for the event and all seems fine until Adelaide becomes so fascinated by the entertaining magician that she forgets Sherman. Ethan's father shouts when he spots Sherman munching on the peonies and the startled pig starts running with all the party guests in pursuit. Sherman runs through a pool, a parlor, some paint and into some pastries before coming full circle through the neighborhood and back to Ethan's house where he finally stops right in Ethan's birthday cake. This is the first picture book for the mother/daughter authors. (32 pages)

Where it's reviewed:
Booklist, April 15, 2000, page 1553

Children's Bookwatch, May 2000, page 5
Horn Book Guide, Fall 2000, page 275
Publishers Weekly, February 14, 2000, page 200
School Library Journal, April 2000, page 110

Other books you might like:
Amy Ehrlich, *Parents in the Pigpen, Pigs in the Tub*, 1993
The farm animals move into the house and the family heads for the barn in a humorous reversal of roles.
Satomi Ichikawa, *Nora's Surprise*, 1994
Nora is not expecting to attend a party with a sheep that devours the floral centerpiece she brings and eats most of the food.
Angela Johnson, *Julius*, 1993
Even Maya is surprised when the gift Granddaddy brings to her from his trip is a pet pig.
Laura Joffe Numeroff, *If You Give a Pig a Pancake*, 1998
If an uninvited pig shows up at breakfast to share your pancakes, be prepared for a busy day.

666

KATE MCMULLAN
JIM MCMULLAN, Illustrator

Papa's Song

(New York: Farrar Straus Giroux, 2000)

Subject(s): Animals/Bears; Babies; Sleep
Age range(s): Preschool
Major character(s): Baby Bear, Bear, Baby; Mama Bear, Bear, Mother; Papa Bear, Father, Bear
Time period(s): Indeterminate
Locale(s): Fictional Country

Summary: It's bedtime, but no one can get Baby Bear to sleep. The grandparents each sing a special song to the little cub, but the little one is still wide-awake. Mama Bear's lullabies cause her eyes to close but not Baby Bear's. Papa Bear tries a new kind of music. He carries Baby Bear to the family boat and poles down the river so the sounds of fish, frogs, owls and crickets can lull the baby to sleep. (32 pages)

Where it's reviewed:
Booklist, February 15, 2000, page 1118
Horn Book, March 2000, page 189
Publishers Weekly, April 10, 2000, page 97
School Library Journal, May 2000, page 149

Other books by the same author:
Noel the First, 1996
Hey, Pipsqueak!, 1995
Good Night, Stella, 1994

Other books you might like:
Kathi Appelt, *Bayou Lullaby*, 1995
A parent soothes a child with a bedtime lullaby about the animals of the bayou as they also settle down for the night.
Kate Banks, *And If the Moon Could Talk*, 1998
Inside, as parent and child begin the nightly bedtime ritual the moon observes what is happening outside all over the world.
Quint Buchholz, *Sleep Well, Little Bear*, 1994
While a child sleeps, his toy bear climbs atop the bookcase

to look out at the moon-covered land and review the play activities of the day.
Mem Fox, *Time for Bed*, 1993
All over the world mothers are putting their kittens, lambs, fawns and children to sleep.
Martin Waddell, *Can't You Sleep, Little Bear?*, 1988
Little Bear is comforted by Big Bear when a fear of the dark interferes with his ability to fall asleep.

667

GRAHAM MCNAMEE

Nothing Wrong with a Three-Legged Dog

(New York: Delacorte Press, 2000)

Subject(s): Animals/Dogs; Bullies; Racism
Age range(s): Grades 4-6
Major character(s): Keath Fraser, 4th Grader, Friend; Lynda Brook, 4th Grader, Friend; Leftovers, Dog
Time period(s): 2000s (2000)
Locale(s): New York, New York

Summary: As the only white fourth grader at Frederick Douglass Elementary Keath is accustomed to being called Whitey and a host of other racial nicknames. The names he can handle; it's the physical bullying and resultant bruises that he'd like to stop. As a bi-racial child, Lynda deals with name calling too and sympathizes with Keath's plight. The real bond to their friendship is Leftovers, Lynda's one-eared, three-legged beagle. Keath is such a dog lover that he wants to be a golden retriever when he grows up. For now he's content to help Lynda's mother at her veterinary practice and scoop the poop when Lynda's father, a dog walker, takes nine dogs for a stroll after school. (134 pages)

Where it's reviewed:
Booklist, August 2000, page 2141
Bulletin of the Center for Children's Books, September 2000, page 31
Kirkus Reviews, July 1, 2000, page 962
Publishers Weekly, July 31, 2000, page 95
School Library Journal, September 2000, page 234

Other books by the same author:
Hate You, 1999

Other books you might like:
Beverly Cleary, *Strider*, 1991
Leigh and his friend Barry share joint custody of an abandoned dog they find on the beach.
Betsy Duffey, *Throw-Away Pets*, 1993
Evie and Megan have 24 hours to find homes for abandoned pets at the animal shelter or the animals will be destroyed.
Vivian Sathre, *J.B. Wigglebottom and the Parade of Pets*, 1993
Daily, J.B. Higgenbottom endures the insults and pranks of a classmate who's sure he'll win first prize in the school's annual parade of pets.
Bill Wallace, *A Dog Called Kitty*, 1980
Ricky overcomes his fear of dogs and the taunts of a bully to save a starving stray pup found in his barn.

668

COLIN MCNAUGHTON, Author/Illustrator

Yum!: A Preston Pig Story

(San Diego: Harcourt Brace & Company, 1999)

Subject(s): Animals/Pigs; Animals/Wolves; Work
Age range(s): Grades K-3
Major character(s): Preston, Pig; Mr. Wolf, Wolf
Time period(s): Indeterminate
Locale(s): Fictional Country

Summary: When Preston notices Mr. Wolf dozing beneath his window, waiting to capture and eat him the clever pig tries to interest Mr. Wolf in finding a job to earn the money to purchase his food. Mr. Wolf envisions every occupation that Preston suggests from soccer player to astronaut to teacher as a direct means to his ultimate goal-eating pigs. Finally, Preston is called to dinner leaving Mr. Wolf to sulk outside. (32 pages)

Where it's reviewed:
Booklist, September 1, 1999, page 141
Bulletin of the Center for Children's Books, November 1999, page 101
Horn Book Guide, Fall 2000, page 275
Kirkus Reviews, August 1, 1999, page 1229
School Library Journal, October 1999, page 120

Awards the book has won:
IRA/CBC Children's Choices, 2000

Other books by the same author:
Preston's Goal!, 1998
Oops!, 1997
Boo!, 1996
Suddenly!, 1995

Other books you might like:
Susan Meddaugh, *Hog-Eye*, 1995
  According to the story she tells her family, only quick wits and reading ability keep a little pig from becoming a wolf's dinner.
Margie Palatini, *Piggie Pie!*, 1995
  Hungry witch Gritch is so frustrated by her unsuccessful quest for eight piggies to put in a pie that she accepts and invitation to lunch from a wolf.
Tony Ross, *Stone Soup*, 1987
  A hen cleverly avoids becoming a wolf's dinner by offering him a taste of her stone soup.

669

DAVID MCPHAIL, Author/Illustrator

Big Brown Bear

(San Diego: Harcourt Brace & Company, 1999)

Series: Green Light Readers. Level 1
Subject(s): Animals/Bears; Dwellings; Accidents
Age range(s): Grades K-2
Major character(s): Bear, Bear; Little Bear, Bear
Time period(s): Indeterminate
Locale(s): Fictional Country

Summary: With a ladder and a bucket of blue paint, Bear prepares to paint a tree house. Little Bear bats a big ball bumping Bear and causing him to fall off the ladder and land on the ground covered with blue paint. After washing off, Bear tries again with green paint. Little Bear is now riding a tricycle and not watching where she's going. . . . (20 pages)

Where it's reviewed:
Booklist, May 15, 1999, page 1705
Christian Science Monitor, June 17, 1999, page 18
Kirkus Reviews, March 1, 1999, page 378
Publishers Weekly, March 15, 1999, page 61
School Library Journal, April 1999, page 101

Other books by the same author:
Tinker and Tom and the Star Baby, 1998
Edward and the Pirates, 1997
Pigs Ahoy!, 1995

Other books you might like:
Barbara Baker, *One Saturday Morning*, 1994
  Six members of the bear family are featured in an easy reader about their Saturday experience.
Nanette Newman, *There's a Bear in the Bath!*, 1994
  Liza's day is enlivened when she finds Jam, a friendly bear, in her garden.
Kay Winters, *Where Are the Bears?*, 1998
  In a beginning reader, two bear cubs have fun creating mischief for a family on a camping trip.

670

DAVID MCPHAIL, Author/Illustrator

Drawing Lessons from a Bear

(Boston: Little Brown and Company, 2000)

Subject(s): Animals/Bears; Growing Up; Talent
Age range(s): Grades K-2
Major character(s): Unnamed Character, Bear, Artist
Time period(s): Indeterminate
Locale(s): Fictional Country

Summary: A bear tells of his youthful days when his mother would try to teach him proper bear behavior as he drew pictures in the dirt floor of the den or on scraps of paper at the dump. In school his teacher encourages his artistic talents and the bear practices all the time, sometimes he even wakes up from his winter's nap to sketch. After many years, the now-famous bear is content to draw and help other budding young artists recognize their talents and pursue their dream. (32 pages)

Where it's reviewed:
Booklist, February 15, 2000, page 1118
Kirkus Reviews, April 15, 2000, page 564
Publishers Weekly, March 6, 2000, page 110
School Library Journal, May 2000, page 149
Smithsonian, November 2000, page 64

Awards the book has won:
Smithsonian's Notable Books for Children, 2000

Other books by the same author:
Tinker and Tom and the Star Baby, 1998
Edward and the Pirates, 1997

Moony B. Finch, the Fastest Draw in the West, 1994

Other books you might like:

Allison Barrows, *The Artist's Model*, 1996
After serving as a model for her artist-father, a young girl is able to watch the drawing proceed from first sketch to printed illustration.

Barbara Brenner, *The Boy Who Loved to Draw: Benjamin West*, 1999
A picture book biography introduces a colonial artist who used his father's forbidden quill pen for his first portrait.

Ed Emberley, *Three: An Emberley Family Scrapbook*, 1998
Each member of a talented family, Ed, Rebecca and Michael, contributes one third of a book showing their distinctive styles based on the number three.

Kathy Mallat, *The Picture that Mom Drew*, 1997
A cumulative story describes an artist mother's creation of a drawing from blank paper to completed picture.

Abigail Thomas, *Pearl Paints*, 1994
A birthday gift of a set of paints, brushes and paper is the catalyst for Pearl's discovery of artistic talent.

671

DAVID MCPHAIL, Author/Illustrator

Mole Music

(New York: Henry Holt and Company, 1999)

Subject(s): Animals/Moles; Music and Musicians; Peace
Age range(s): Grades K-2
Major character(s): Mole, Mole, Musician (violinist)
Time period(s): Indeterminate
Locale(s): Fictional Country

Summary: Mole lives a solitary underground life digging tunnels by day and watching television at night. When he hears a violinist on television he realizes that he needs to learn to make music too in order to feel fulfilled. Mole orders a violin by mail and teaches himself to play. Although his initial efforts are not melodious, he improves with practice until he eventually considers himself better than the person he'd once heard on TV. He wonders what it would be like to play for others, unaware that his music drifts upwards and attracts audiences each night. Mole imagines the power of his music and the illustrations show the wonders that his music works although Mole has no knowledge of his impact on the above ground world. (32 pages)

Where it's reviewed:
Booklist, February 15, 1999, page 1076
Bulletin of the Center for Children's Books, May 1999, page 321
Horn Book Guide, Fall 1999, page 260
Publishers Weekly, March 1, 1999, page 68
School Library Journal, April 1999, page 104

Awards the book has won:
Publishers Weekly Best Books, 1999

Other books by the same author:
The Puddle, 1998
Tinker and Tom and the Star Baby, 1998
Edward and the Pirates, 1997
The Train, 1977

Other books you might like:

Richard Edwards, *Moles Can Dance*, 1994
Despite admonitions to the contrary, a young mole decides to dance, not dig.

Lois Ehlert, *Mole's Hill*, 1994
A mole with a mind of her own ignores the demands of other animals to move her hill. Instead she beautifies it and tunnels a path through it.

Jane Yolen, *Eeny, Meeny, Miney Mole*, 1992
Meeny and Miney are content in the safety of their home, but Eeny wants to know what's "Up Above" and bravely ventures up to find out.

672

ALICE MEAD

Soldier Mom

(New York: Farrar Straus Giroux, 1999)

Subject(s): Gulf War; Mothers and Daughters; Single Parent Families
Age range(s): Grades 5-7
Major character(s): Jasmyn "Jas" Williams, 11-Year-Old, Child of Divorced Parents; Jake, Single Father (Andrew's), Worker (factory); Andrew, Baby, Brother (Jas's half-brother)
Time period(s): 1990s (1990-1991)
Locale(s): Stroudwater, Maine

Summary: The repercussions of Iraq's invasion of Kuwait reach all the way into Jasmyn's small town when her mother, an Army reservist, is called up for duty in Saudi Arabia. Jas is stunned and hurt, but no more so than her mother who has no alternative for her children except to ask Jake, Andrew's father, to move in and care for them. Jake, inexperienced with parenting, is as resentful at being responsible for Jas as she is of having him in her life. Angrily they try to adjust to their situation, the worries about the war, the demands of caring for Andrew, the responsibility of serving as captain of the summer basketball team, and the difficulty of being a working single parent. (152 pages)

Where it's reviewed:
The Book Report, January 2000, page 67
Booklist, September 1, 1999, page 127
Horn Book, September 1999, page 614
School Library Journal, September 1999, page 227

Other books by the same author:
Junebug and the Reverend, 1998
Junebug, 1995

Other books you might like:

Patricia Reilly Giff, *Lily's Crossing*, 1997
The Newbery Honor Book about life in the states during World War II describes Lily's struggle to adjust while her father is in Europe.

Patricia Hermes, *Someone to Count On*, 1993
Sam's mother leaves her temporarily with a cantankerous grandfather who didn't know of her existence until she arrived at his ranch.

Cynthia Stowe, *Dear Mom, in Ohio for a Year*, 1992
Mom sends her sixth-grader to Vermont to live with relatives so she is free to attend college.

673

SUSAN MEDDAUGH, Author/Illustrator

The Best Place

(Boston: Houghton Mifflin Company, 1999)

Subject(s): Animals/Wolves; Animals; Dwellings
Age range(s): Grades K-2
Major character(s): Unnamed Character, Wolf
Time period(s): Indeterminate
Locale(s): Fictional Country; Earth

Summary: An old wolf is content in his home with the screened porch until a well-traveled bird suggests that he needs to broaden his experiences before he can be sure that his porch is the best place. Just in case the bird is right, the wolf sells his house and begins traveling. It doesn't take long for the wolf to appreciate the advantages of his screened porch—protection from mosquitoes, nice breezes and no rain. When the wolf returns home, the rabbit family that purchased the house is not interested in selling it back to the wolf. Wolf's frustration boils over into a temper tantrum that reminds everyone that he has very sharp teeth. Embarrassed, the wolf runs away and inadvertently finds the place that truly is the best. (32 pages)

Where it's reviewed:
Booklist, November 1, 1999, page 540
Horn Book Guide, Spring 2000, page 46
IRA/CBC Children's Choices, 2000
Kirkus Reviews, September 15, 1999, page 1503
School Library Journal, September 1999, page 197

Other books by the same author:
Cinderella's Rat, 1997
Martha Blah Blah, 1996
Hog-Eye, 1995

Other books you might like:
Penny Carter, *A New House for the Morrisons*, 1993
After a day of fruitless searching for a new house, the Morrisons return to the one they like best—their own home.
Emma Chichester Clark, *Across the Blue Mountains*, 1993
Although she's content in her home, Miss Bilberry wants to see the other side of the mountain so she packs her pets and starts off.
Kevin Kiser, *Sherman the Sheep*, 1994
Sherman is chosen to lead the flock to "the best field in the whole valley" and he does—right back where they started.
Carol P. Saul, *Someplace Else*, 1995
After a lifetime in the white house, Mrs. Tillby is ready to live someplace else, but has a hard time deciding just where.

674

SUSAN MEDDAUGH, Author/Illustrator

Martha and Skits

(Boston: Houghton Mifflin Company, 2000)

Subject(s): Animals/Dogs; Pets; Individuality
Age range(s): Grades K-3
Major character(s): Martha, Dog; Skits, Dog
Time period(s): 2000s (2000)
Locale(s): United States

Summary: Martha's family surprises her by bringing home a new puppy that behaves just like a puppy. Soon the house is a shambles, shoes are missing, socks are chewed and everyone is saying "Bad dog!" Martha, watching from her chair, thinks the puppy is adorable until Skits accidentally spills her alphabet soup. Now, Martha asserts her position as the alpha dog and lets Skits know not to touch her alphabet soup. When Skits is big enough the family gives him a bowl of alphabet soup, expecting him to talk as Martha does. Although Skits devours two bowls full of letters, the words he speaks are "Woof" and "Arf." Obviously Skits's talent is something other than talking and soon Martha and her family learn just what it is. (32 pages)

Where it's reviewed:
Booklist, June 1, 2000, page 1910
Horn Book Guide, Spring 2001, page 45
Kirkus Reviews, June 15, 2000, page 890
Publishers Weekly, August 7, 2000, page 94
School Library Journal, August 2000, page 159

Other books by the same author:
Martha Walks the Dog, 1998
Martha Blah Blah, 1996 (Horn Book Fanfare)
Martha Calling, 1994 (School Library Journal Best Book)
Martha Speaks, 1992 (ALA Notable Book)

Other books you might like:
Isabelle Harper, *Our New Puppy*, 1996
The other family pets, including dog Rosie, are slow to adjust to the new puppy that intrudes on their peaceful life.
Gail Herman, *My Dog Talks*, 1995
A beginning reader describes the pleasure a young boy has playing with his "talking" dog.
Alan Snow, *How Dogs Really Work!*, 1993
A winner of the New York Times Best Illustrated Children's Book Award is a humorous instruction manual for dog owners.

675

ANGELA SHELF MEDEARIS
DANIEL MINTER, Illustrator

Seven Spools of Thread

(Morton Grove, IL: Albert Whitman & Company, 2000)

Subject(s): Cultures and Customs; Brothers; Conduct of Life
Age range(s): Grades 1-4
Major character(s): Chief, Ruler
Time period(s): Indeterminate Past
Locale(s): Ghana

Summary: Seven brothers, to the despair of the widowed father, do nothing but quarrel all day about the weather, the crops, the food and the time. After the father's death, the Chief of their village advises the brothers of the father's inheritance and the conditions they must meet in order to each receive an equal share. Each brother is given a spool of thread with the instructions to turn the seven different colored spools into gold by moonrise. Realizing the need to work cooperatively, the brothers agree to make peace in honor of their father's memory. In their mutual task the brothers also succeed in turning the seven spools of thread into gold and begin a new tradition for the Ashanti by creating the first kente cloth. An introductory author's note gives information about the Kwanzaa festival and weaving instructions conclude the title. (40 pages)

Where it's reviewed:
Booklist, September 15, 2000, page 249
Horn Book Guide, Spring 2001, page 4
Kirkus Reviews, October 15, 2000, page 1488
Publishers Weekly, September 25, 2000, page 66
School Library Journal, October 2000, page 65

Awards the book has won:
ALA Notable Children's Books, 2001
Notable Social Studies Trade Books for Young People, 2001

Other books by the same author:
The Ghost of Sifty Sifty Sam, 1997
Tailypo: A Newfangled Tall Tale, 1996
Poppa's New Pants, 1995
Too Much Talk, 1995
The Singing Man: Adapted from a West African Folktale, 1994

Other books you might like:
Debbi Chocolate, *Kente Colors*, 1996
    Rhyming text and vivid illustrations explain the history, making and use of kente cloth.
Andrea Davis Pinkney, *Seven Candles for Kwanzaa*, 1993
    During a seven-day festival people of African descent learn about and celebrate their heritage.
Pete Watson, *The Market Lady and the Mango Tree*, 1994
    The greedy Market Lady learns the importance of sharing the fruit that falls from the mango tree.

676

MICHAEL MEDEARIS
ANGELA SHELF MEDEARIS, Co-Author
LARRY JOHNSON, Illustrator

Daisy and the Doll

(Middlebury, VT: The Vermont Folklife Center, 2000)

Series: Family Heritage
Subject(s): African Americans; Self-Esteem; Prejudice
Age range(s): Grades 1-3
Major character(s): Jessie Daisy Turner, 8-Year-Old, Daughter; Papu, Father, Farmer; Miss Clark, Teacher
Time period(s): 1890s (1891)
Locale(s): Grafton, Vermont

Summary: To each girl in the integrated class Miss Clark distributes dolls from different countries and a poem appro-priate to the doll's nationality for the end of school program. Each girl is to memorize the teacher's poem and present it from the stage. Daisy is filled with anger when she reads the poem assigned to the black doll given to her and for the first time she notices that her skin is a different color from others in her class. Papu encourages her to be proud and to memorize the poem, but the words seem to stick in Daisy's throat. On the night of the program Daisy listens forlornly as the other students perform their recitations. Daisy tries to recite the poem written by Miss Clark, but instead she gives an extemporaneous poem urging the black doll to stand proudly and claim her rightful place. Papu and Miss Clark are initially shocked, but everyone is proud of Daisy when the judges declare her original and honest presentation the winner. (32 pages)

Where it's reviewed:
Booklist, September 15, 2000, page 242
Publishers Weekly, August 28, 2000, page 83
School Library Journal, September 2000, page 205

Awards the book has won:
Notable Social Studies Trade Books for Young People, 2001

Other books by the same author:
Cooking, 1997 (African-American Arts)
Music, 1997 (African-American Arts)
Dance, 1997 (African-American Arts)

Other books you might like:
Robert Coles, *The Story of Ruby Bridges*, 1995
    Daily in 1960, 6-year-old Ruby bravely faces angry mobs in order to exercise her right to attend an elementary school in the segregated South.
Elizabeth Fitzgerald Howard, *Virgie Goes to School with Us Boys*, 2000
    Strong-willed Virgie is sure she deserves the same chance for an education as her brothers and her parents agree.
William Miller, *Night Golf*, 1999
    The only time James can play on the town's "whites only" golf course is at night after the course is closed.
Alan Schroeder, *Minty: A Story of Young Harriet Tubman*, 1996
    An award-winning picture-book biography introduces 8-year-old Minty, a rebellious slave who dreams of freedom and plots her escape.

677

CARI MEISTER
RICH DAVIS, Illustrator

Tiny Goes to the Library

(New York: Viking, 2000)

Series: Viking Easy-to-Read. Level 1
Subject(s): Animals/Dogs; Books and Reading; Libraries
Age range(s): Grades K-1
Major character(s): Tiny, Dog; Unnamed Character, Child
Time period(s): 2000s (2000)
Locale(s): United States

Summary: Tiny goes everywhere with his young owner, but when they go to the library only the little boy can go inside. Tiny waits outside, peering in the window as his owner selects books, many books. In fact, when the boy carries his books out to the wagon, the books fill it and make it so heavy that only Tiny is strong enough to pull the wagon home. (32 pages)

Where it's reviewed:
Booklist, April 15, 2000, page 1555
Bulletin of the Center for Children's Books, July 2000, page 412
Horn Book Guide, Fall 2000, page 29
School Library Journal, July 2000, page 83

Other books by the same author:
Catch That Cat!, 1999 (Rookie Reader, Level A)
When Tiny Was Tiny, 1999 (Viking Easy-to-Read, Level 1)
Tiny's Bath, 1999 (Viking Easy-to-Read, Level 1)

Other books you might like:
Norman Bridwell, *Clifford and the Big Parade*, 1998
    While enjoying the town's birthday with Emily Elizabeth, Clifford, the big red dog, helps to assure the parade's success.
William Cole, *Have I Got Dogs!*, 1996
    A rhyming story introduces different types of dogs.
Cynthia Rylant, *Henry and Mudge*, 1987
    The first book of a now classic series introduces Henry and his slobbery pet Mudge.

678

CARI MEISTER
RICH DAVIS, Illustrator

When Tiny Was Tiny
(New York: Viking, 1999)

Series: Viking Easy-to-Read. Level 1
Subject(s): Animals/Dogs; Pets; Growing Up
Age range(s): Grades K-1
Major character(s): Tiny, Dog; Unnamed Character, Child
Time period(s): 1990s (1999)
Locale(s): United States

Summary: As a puppy a child's pet is so small that he fits in a shoe, the child's pocket and even his own dog house. Tiny has grown and he is no longer lives up to his name, but he still enjoys digging in the dirt and licking his owner. Now that he is bigger he can run fast and do tricks. Tiny is a good dog! (32 pages)

Where it's reviewed:
Booklist, October 1, 1999, page 366
Horn Book Guide, Spring 2000, page 62
Kirkus Reviews, August 1, 1999, page 1229
School Library Journal, December 1999, page 104

Other books by the same author:
Tiny Goes to the Library, 2000 (Viking Easy-to-Read, Level 1)
Catch That Cat!, 1999 (Rookie Readers, Level A)
Tiny's Bath, 1999 (Viking Easy-to-Read, Level 1)

Other books you might like:
Norman Bridwell, *Clifford the Small Red Puppy*, 1972
    Clifford was the smallest puppy in the litter, but with Emily Elizabeth's care, he's grown and grown.

Alyssa Satin Capucilli, *Biscuit*, 1996
    New puppy Biscuit has difficulty sleeping until his owner brings him just one more thing.
Cynthia Rylant, *Henry and Mudge*, 1987
    In the first book of a now classic series, Henry convinces his parents to allow him to have a dog.

679

LAURA KRAUSS MELMED
DAVID SLONIM, Illustrator

Moishe's Miracle: A Hanukkah Story
(New York: HarperCollins Publishers, 2000)

Subject(s): Fairy Tales; Holidays, Jewish; Magic
Age range(s): Grades K-3
Major character(s): Baila, Spouse, Housewife; Moishe, Milkman, Spouse
Time period(s): Indeterminate Past
Locale(s): Wishniak, Fictional Country

Summary: Baila criticizes her kind husband when he gives away milk to villagers, but her scolding does not deter Moishe's generosity. With only two cows Moishe has not a lot of milk to sell and even less to give away, but he cannot pass by a cottage in need. On the eve of Hanukkah Baila complains so vigorously that Moishe's habits have made them too poor to buy the ingredients for potato latkes that Moishe flees to the cowshed and falls asleep in the hay. When he awakens his cows tell him of a magic gift left in the straw—an old frying pan that can only be used by Moishe. Later, Moishe puts the pan on the fire and instantly it produces plump, light latkes. The next day Moishe invites all the villagers to his home for latkes, singing and games. Baila is not happy with the mess and in the morning she sends Moishe on an errand while she, ignoring the pan's warning, uses the pan for a greedy scheme. As soon as Baila sets the pan on the fire she regrets her actions. Though the pan never cooks again for anyone, its lasting miracle is the effect on Baila who becomes more cooperative and less critical and on the town that prospers as visitors come to see the magic pan on display. (32 pages)

Where it's reviewed:
Booklist, September 1, 2000, page 134
Five Owls, November 2000, page 44
Horn Book, September 2000, page 588
Publishers Weekly, September 25, 2000, page 66
School Library Journal, October 2000, page 65

Other books by the same author:
Little Oh, 1997 (ALA Notable Book)
The Marvelous Market on Mermaid, 1996 (IRA/CBC Children's Choices)
Prince Nautilus, 1994

Other books you might like:
Barbara Diamond Goldin, *Just Enough Is Plenty: A Hanukkah Tale*, 1988
    A poor family is willing to include a stranger at their holiday table because they believe Mama can cook enough for everyone.

Naomi Howland, *Latkes, Latkes Good to Eat: A Chanukah Story*, 1999

Poor Sadie's kindness to an old woman is rewarded with a magic frying pan that produces latkes for Sadie and chaos for her greedy brothers.

Nina Jaffe, *In the Month of Kislev: A Story for Hanukkah*, 1992

When a rich merchant files a court action against a poor peddler and his family the outcome teaches a lesson about the meaning of Hanukkah.

Malka Penn, *The Miracle of the Potato Latkes: A Hanukkah Story*, 1994

During a drought-caused potato shortage, Tante Golda's faith is rewarded with more than enough potatoes to make latkes for Hanukkah.

680

JONATHAN MERES
JACQUELINE EAST, Illustrator

The Big Bad Rumor

(New York: Orchard Books, 2000)

Subject(s): Communication; Animals; Humor
Age range(s): Grades K-2
Major character(s): Goose, Goose; Unnamed Character, Wolf
Time period(s): Indeterminate
Locale(s): Fictional Country

Summary: An excited goose sounds the alarm by yelling to the other animals about a big, bad, mad wolf on the way. Each animal mishears what Goose is saying slightly so the description of the wolf changes from ferocious to funny to preposterous. Goose tries to get all the animals to stop talking at once and listen to what he's saying. Just as Goose repeats the original warning there's a knock at the door... (40 pages)

Where it's reviewed:
Horn Book Guide, Spring 2001, page 20
Kirkus Reviews, June 15, 2000, page 890
Publishers Weekly, July 31, 2000, page 93
School Library Journal, November 2000, page 128

Other books by the same author:
Somewhere Out There, 1998

Other books you might like:
Jez Alborough, *Watch Out! Big Bro's Coming!*, 1997
Though the animals hear the message about Big Bro's arrival correctly the scary (to a little mouse) creature that appears is not what they expect.
Helen Lester, *Listen, Buddy*, 1995
Little rabbit Buddy's inattentiveness to parental directions puts him in the wrong part of town face to face with Scruffy Varmint.
Nancy Elizabeth Wallace, *Tell-a-Bunny*, 2000
A phone call to plan a surprise party begins a series of distorted messages changing the party plans in a way that surprises the hostess.

681

RICHARD MICHELSON
BARRY MOSER, Illustrator

Grandpa's Gamble

(Tarrytown, NY: Marshall Cavendish, 1999)

Subject(s): Grandfathers; Jews; Prayer
Age range(s): Grades 1-4
Major character(s): Grandpa Sam, Grandfather, Immigrant; Unnamed Character, Sister (older); Unnamed Character, Brother
Time period(s): 20th century; 1990s (1999)
Locale(s): Poland; United States

Summary: Grandpa Sam prays all morning and all afternoon complain a brother and sister, disappointed that they don't have an exciting grandfather like their friends do. Boredom brought on by the enforced silence during Grandpa Sam's prayers leads to horseplay and the accidental spilling of old photographs, including one of Grandpa Sam as a young man. The photograph prompts Grandpa Sam to tell his grandchildren the story of his lonely emigration from Poland without his family to a land where many more arriving immigrants found poverty than the riches they had expected. In order to survive, Grandpa Sam learned to play cards and supported himself by gambling for many years. The illness of his daughter (the children's mother) led Grandpa Sam to forsake gambling and turn to prayer and he continues to give thanks daily for her recovery. (32 pages)

Where it's reviewed:
Booklist, March 15, 1999, page 1333
Bulletin of the Center for Children's Books, April 1999, page 288
Kirkus Reviews, March 1, 1999, page 379
Publishers Weekly, March 22, 1999, page 90
School Library Journal, June 1999, page 102

Other books by the same author:
Ten Times Better, 2000
A Book of Flies Real or Otherwise, 1999
Did You Say Ghosts, 1993

Other books you might like:
Riki Levinson, *Watch the Stars Come Out*, 1985
Grandma relates the story of her voyage to America as a child.
Marissa Moss, *In America*, 1994
Grandpa explains to his grandson Walter why he chose to leave his homeland and family as a child and come to America.
Sheldon Oberman, *The Always Prayer Shawl*, 1994
Adam cherishes the prayer shawl, a parting gift from his grandfather, as a constant in a life of change and a connection to his heritage.
Patricia Polacco, *The Keeping Quilt*, 1988
The lives, love and faith of four generations of an immigrant Jewish family are symbolically bound in a homemade quilt.

682

C.M. MILLEN
CHRISTINE DAVENIER, Illustrator

The Low-Down Laundry Line Blues

(Boston: Houghton Mifflin Company, 1999)

Subject(s): Sisters; Change; Stories in Rhyme
Age range(s): Grades K-2
Major character(s): Unnamed Character, Sister (older); Unnamed Character, Sister (younger)
Time period(s): Indeterminate Past
Locale(s): United States

Summary: A young girl is having a down-in-the-dumps day and wants to be left alone with her "laundry line blues," but her cheerful little sister persistently tries to cheer her. At first none of her ideas work, but when she ties one end of the laundry line to a garbage can and starts jumping rope to a perky rhyme, her older sister can't resist. Soon, both girls are smiling and jumping. (32 pages)

Where it's reviewed:
Booklist, April 15, 1999, page 1537
Horn Book, March 1999, page 199
Kirkus Reviews, March 1, 1999, page 379
Publishers Weekly, February 1, 1999, page 83
School Library Journal, May 1999, page 93

Other books you might like:
Jan Carr, *Dark Day, Light Night*, 1996
    Aunt Ruby helps 'Manda overcome her grumpiness by encouraging her to look for something positive.
Miranda Hapgood, *Martha's Mad Day*, 1977
    Martha wakes up in a bad mood that stays with her all the long mad day.
William Steig, *Pete's a Pizza*, 1998
    Pete's parent put the giggles back in his disappointing day by pretending to transform him into a pizza.
Tynia Thomassie, *Feliciana Meets d'Loup Garou: A Cajun Tall Tale*, 1998
    Feliciana is having such a bad day that she even yells at d'Loup Garou who teaches her to howl at the moon as an antidote for a bad mood.
Judith Viorst, *Alexander and the Terrible, Horrible, No Good, Very Bad Day*, 1972
    Alexander is having a day in which everything that can possibly go wrong does.

683

WILLIAM MILLER
CEDRIC LUCAS, Illustrator

Night Golf

(New York: Lee and Low Inc., 1999)

Subject(s): African Americans; Sports/Golf; Prejudice
Age range(s): Grades 1-3
Major character(s): James, Child, Golfer (amateur); Charlie, Golfer (amateur), Teacher
Time period(s): 1950s
Locale(s): United States

Summary: Too small for football and too short for the basketball court, James discovers the sport at which he can be successful when he finds a golf club and some old balls in the trash. Although James practices until he has control of the ball, his father does not encourage him to pursue this white man's game. Still James visits the town's only golf course watching through the fence until he's allowed to be a caddy. Charlie, who has twenty years experience as a caddy, acts as a mentor and golf instructor to the youngster. In James, Charlie sees the desire that he had twenty years earlier to play this game and knows the frustration of serving as caddy to those less skilled. Charlie gets around the "whites only" rule of the golf club by playing the course at night and he invites James to join him. (32 pages)

Where it's reviewed:
Children's Book Review Service, August 1999, page 162
Horn Book Guide, Fall 1999, page 282
Kirkus Reviews, April 15, 1999, page 634
Publishers Weekly, May 24, 1999, page 79
School Library Journal, June 1999, page 103

Awards the book has won:
Parents' Choice Gold Award, 1999

Other books by the same author:
A House by the River, 1997
Richard Wright and the Library Card, 1997 (Smithsonian's Notable Books for Children)
Zora Hurston and the Chinaberry Tree, 1994

Other books you might like:
Barbara E. Barber, *Allie's Basketball Dream*, 1996
    Allie faces ridicule from guys at the basketball court and discouragement from friends who think basketball is not for girls.
Evelyn Coleman, *White Socks Only*, 1996
    In 1950s Mississippi a young black child stands in her white socks to drink from a "whites only" water fountain with unexpected consequences.
Robert Coles, *The Story of Ruby Bridges*, 1995
    Courageously, six-year-old Ruby daily faces angry white protesters as the first black child to attend a formerly all-white elementary school.
Lauren M. Smith, *My First Golf Book*, 1999
    A diverse group of four children learn the basics of golf without having to overcome prejudice. Co-author James Smith.

684

WILLIAM MILLER
SUSAN KEETER, Illustrator

The Piano

(New York: Lee & Low Books Inc., 2000)

Subject(s): Music and Musicians; Old Age; African Americans
Age range(s): Grades 2-5
Major character(s): Miss Hartwell, Aged Person, Employer; Tia, Child, Student (piano); Johnny, Servant, Child
Time period(s): Indeterminate Past
Locale(s): South

Summary: While her mother and brothers work in the cotton mill, Tia is free during the summer to wander in search of the music that she loves. One morning, Tia roams all the way over to the white part of town where she's listening to a beautiful melody drifting from a large home when Johnny spots her and assumes she's come to apply for the maid's position. Tia's not interested in that kind of work but she's willing to do anything to get closer to the music. In Miss Hartwell's home Tia discovers a record player making the music and a piano that arthritis prevents Miss Hartwell from playing. Daily, while Miss Hartwell naps, Tia tries to teach herself to copy the music that she hears on the record player with the piano. Finally, Tia asks Miss Hartwell to teach her. Tia soothes Miss Harwell's swollen hands with warm water and salt just as she does her mother's after a day in the cotton mill. When Johnny takes a job at another home, Tia does his work and her own, causing her hands to be so sore by the time the piano lesson begins that Miss Hartwell gets warm water for them—a trick she learned from a friend. (32 pages)

Where it's reviewed:
Booklist, July 2000, page 2042
Horn Book Guide, Fall 2000, page 276
Kirkus Reviews, May 15, 2000, page 718
Publishers Weekly, June 12, 2000, page 73
School Library Journal, July 2000, page 84

Other books by the same author:
Night Golf, 1999
A House by the River, 1997
Richard Wright and the Library Card, 1997 (Book Links Lasting Connections)
The Conjure Woman, 1996

Other books you might like:
Barbara Bottner, *Nana Hannah's Piano*, 1996
    Sonny hates piano lessons, but still he secretly practices on Nana's piano in hopes that the music he learns will cheer her after she injures her ankle.
Debbi Chocolate, *The Piano Man*, 1998
    An old man's daughter buys the piano he once played for silent movies and presents it to her father as a gift.
Mary Lyn Ray, *Pianna*, 1994
    Anna, an 80-year-old widow, reflects back on her life and the pleasure she's derived from playing the piano.
Jane Yolen, *Miz Berlin Walks*, 1997
    Nightly young Mary Louise walks with Miz Berlin and listens to the elderly woman's stories.

685

ISAAC MILLMAN

Moses Goes to School

(New York: Frances Foster Books/Farrar, Straus and Giroux, 2000)

Subject(s): Deafness; Language; Schools
Age range(s): Grades 1-3
Major character(s): Moses, Student—Elementary School, Deaf Person; John, Student—Elementary School, Deaf Person; Mr. Samuels, Teacher, Deaf Person
Time period(s): 2000s (2000)
Locale(s): New York, New York

Summary: Eagerly, Moses returns to school after vacation and shares the news of summer activities with his friends. Moses has new glasses, John's excited about new hearing aids and others have tales of summer travels. After a morning devoted to language arts and computer activities, Mr. Samuels teaches the class the words to "Take Me Out to the Ball Game" with the music coming from a boom box as the students sign the lyrics. In no time it seems, Moses, John and other classmates board the bus for the ride home. Moses hugs his dog and tells his mother the exciting news about his first day of school. An introductory author's note gives background information about American Sign Language (ASL) and the education of children who are deaf and hard of hearing. Portions of the text are presented in ASL. (32 pages)

Where it's reviewed:
Booklist, August 2000, page 2148
Horn Book Guide, Spring 2001, page 45
Kirkus Reviews, July 1, 2000, page 962
Publishers Weekly, June 19, 2000, page 82
School Library Journal, August 2000, page 160

Other books by the same author:
Moses Goes to a Concert, 1998 (Bank Street Best Children's Book of 1998)

Other books you might like:
Claire H. Blatchford, *Going with the Flow*, 1998
    A family move to a new state puts Mark in a school where he is the only deaf student.
Dorothy Hoffman Levi, *A Very Special Friend*, 1989
    When Frannie learns that her new neighbor Laura is deaf she tries to learn enough sign language to make communication easier.
Jean Davies Okimoto, *A Place for Grace*, 1993
    Although Grace is too small to be a guide dog for the blind Charlie thinks she would be the perfect companion for him as a hearing ear dog.

686

CLAUDIA MILLS
CATHERINE STOCK, Illustrator

Gus and Grandpa and Show-and-Tell

(New York: Farrar Straus Giroux, 2000)

Subject(s): Schools; Grandfathers; Problem Solving
Age range(s): Grades 1-2
Major character(s): Gus, 2nd Grader; Grandpa, Grandfather; Mrs. Hall, Teacher
Time period(s): 2000s (2000)
Locale(s): Colorado

Summary: In first grade Gus enjoyed show-and-tell day because he could bring in anything he wanted to share. In Mrs. Hall's class the students are expected to select an item that matches a designated theme such as natural habitats or Colorado history. Since Grandpa's lived in Colorado for 70 years Gus goes to ask him about an idea for show-and-tell. As Grandpa shares stories of his grandparents coming to Colorado and shows pictures from his youth Gus suddenly has an idea for the perfect show-and-tell presentation. Now he's eager for the day to arrive! (48 pages)

Where it's reviewed:
Booklist, October 1, 2000, page 352
Horn Book Guide, Spring 2001, page 64
Kirkus Reviews, June 15, 2000, page 890
School Library Journal, August 2000, page 160

Other books by the same author:
Gus and Grandpa and the Two-Wheeled Bike, 1999
Gus and Grandpa Ride the Train, 1998
Gus and Grandpa at the Hospital, 1998
Gus and Grandpa, 1997 (IRA/CBC Children's Choices)

Other books you might like:
Laurie Krasny Brown, *Rex and Lilly School Time*, 1997
  At school, siblings Rex and Lilly read, trade lunches and take part in show and tell.
Stephanie Greene, *Show and Tell*, 1998
  Second grader Woody is dismayed when the student teacher does not appreciate the dead fish he brings to school for show-and-tell.
Kathryn Lasky, *Show and Tell Bunnies*, 1998
  Clyde overcomes the jitters to share a great surprise with his class.
Grace Maccarone, *Sharing Time Troubles*, 1997
  Sam struggles to think of something to share that compares favorably with the presentations of his classmates.
Barney Saltzberg, *Show and Tell*, 1994
  Phoebe's parents are far too helpful with plans for show and tell, complicating Phoebe's desire to bring something simple of her own choosing.

687

CLAUDIA MILLS
CATHERINE STOCK, Illustrator

Gus and Grandpa and the Two-Wheeled Bike

(New York: Farrar, Strauss and Giroux, 1999)

Subject(s): Bicycles and Bicycling; Grandfathers; Growing Up
Age range(s): Grades 1-3
Major character(s): Gus, Child; Grandpa, Grandfather, Aged Person; Ryan Mason, Neighbor, Child
Time period(s): 1990s (1999)
Locale(s): United States

Summary: Gus cannot understand why Ryan seems so happy with his new bike—it has no training wheels! True, the water bottle looks pretty nifty and Ryan's bike has hand brakes and gears, but without training wheels Gus is sure that bike must wobble a lot. Gus is content with security. His father surprises him with a new bike, but all Gus gets (other than a drink from the water bottle) is band-aids on both knees from all his falls. Gus is content to use his old stand-by with the training wheels, but Grandpa cleans up the old bike on which Gus's father learned to ride and patiently works with Gus until he masters a two-wheeler. Once Gus experiences the sensation of riding a bike, he knows he's ready to give up the training wheels. (48 pages)

Where it's reviewed:
Booklist, February 1, 1999, page 975

Horn Book, March 1999, page 211
Kirkus Reviews, January 1, 1999, page 70
School Library Journal, April 1999, page 105

Other books by the same author:
Gus and Grandpa Ride the Train, 1998
Gus and Grandpa at the Hospital, 1998
Gus and Grandpa and the Christmas Cookies, 1997

Other books you might like:
Marc Brown, *D.W. Rides Again!*, 1993
  With help from her brother Arthur, D.W. learns to ride her two-wheeler and proves to her father that she no longer needs training wheels.
Crescent Dragonwagon, *Annie Flies the Birthday Bike*, 1993
  Annie's excitement with her birthday gift turns to frustration and finally elation as she masters the art of riding a two-wheeled bicycle.
Donna Jakob, *My Bike*, 1994
  First-time author Jakob portrays the determination and excitement of a new bike rider.

688

CLAUDIA MILLS

You're a Brave Man, Julius Zimmerman

(New York: Farrar, Straus and Giroux, 1999)

Subject(s): Identity; Self-Acceptance; Mothers and Sons
Age range(s): Grades 4-7
Major character(s): Julius Zimmerman, 12-Year-Old, Baby-sitter; Edison Blue, 3-Year-Old; Octavia Aldridge, Neighbor (Edison's)
Time period(s): 1990s (1999)
Locale(s): West Creek, Colorado

Summary: Julius has many relaxing ideas for his summer vacation, but his mother has other plans for his time. She signs him up for French classes, a job babysitting Edison and requires him to read and keep a weekly journal of goals and accomplishments. Julius, ever eager to please his mom, agrees to everything. It comes as no surprise to Julius that he's a disaster at French, but discovering the 3-year-old he's in charge of every afternoon is still in diapers is close to a catastrophe. Rather than learn to change a diaper, Julius decides to teach Edison to use the potty. Edison's new neighbor Octavia is sympathetic to the travails of babysitting and a friendship begins that could prove to be the one bright spot of the summer. As summer nears its end, Julius's mom is, as usual, disappointed that Julius has not accomplished enough. Compliments from the French teacher and Edison's mom help her to see that Julius has achievements and talents that are as valuable as some of the goals she has created for him. (152 pages)

Where it's reviewed:
Booklist, October 15, 1999, page 446
Horn Book, September 1999, page 614
Publishers Weekly, July 26, 1999, page 91
Riverbank Review, Winter 1999/2000, page 34
School Library Journal, September 1999, page 227

Other books by the same author:
Standing Up to Mr. O., 1998

Losers, Inc., 1997
Dinah Forever, 1995
Dinah for President, 1992

Other books you might like:

Betsy Byars, *Bingo Brown and the Language of Love*, 1989
   Bingo's venture into romance teaches him that speaking the "language of love" is like learning a foreign language.
Lynn Cullen, *The Three Lives of Harris Harper*, 1996
   Harris takes a summer baby-sitting job that doesn't turn out to be as easy as he expected it to be.
James Howe, *The New Nick Kramer, or My Life as a Babysitter*, 1995
   Determined to impress Jennifer with his sensitivity, Nick enrolls in a babysitting class, only to be stuck watching a 7-year-old terror.
Peg Kehret, *The Richest Kids in Town*, 1994
   Peter Dodge's get-rich-quick schemes backfire, jeopardizing his friendship with Wishbone who is losing money.
Lois Lowry, *Rabble Starkey*, 1987
   Friends Rabble and Veronica share many adventures during their year as sixth graders.
Lois Lowry, *Taking Care of Terrific*, 1983
   Enid's life turns upside-down following a baby-sitting job.

689

ADRIAN MITCHELL
STEPHEN LAMBERT, Illustrator

Nobody Rides the Unicorn

(New York: Arthur A. Levine Books/Scholastic Press, 2000)

Subject(s): Unicorns; Good and Evil; Conduct of Life
Age range(s): Grades 1-4
Major character(s): Zoe, Orphan, Child; Unnamed Character, Royalty; Doctor Slythe, Villain
Time period(s): Indeterminate
Locale(s): Joppardy, Fictional Country

Summary: At the advice of Doctor Slythe a king seeks a unicorn's horn to make a goblet and eating utensils as protection against food poisoning. Knowing that only a quiet young girl with a gentle voice can attract a unicorn, Doctor Slythe sends for Zoe and convinces her to go on a mission for the king. As predicted, Zoe's quiet singing brings a unicorn out of hiding and the king's hunters capture it. Zoe is sad and angry to be tricked and she tends the unicorn's wounds, then, frees the animal. The angry king banishes Zoe from the kingdom so she finds her way to the secret valley of the unicorns. (32 pages)

Where it's reviewed:
Booklist, April 15, 2000, page 1546
Children's Bookwatch, July 2000, page 5
Kirkus Reviews, April 15, 2000, page 565
Publishers Weekly, April 24, 2000, page 90
School Librarian, Spring 2000, page 19

Other books by the same author:
The Steadfast Tin Soldier, 1996
The Ugly Duckling: Hans Christian Andersen, 1994
Our Mammoth, 1987

Other books you might like:

Lynne Cherry, *The Dragon and the Unicorn*, 1995
   From a unicorn the king's daughter learns of the importance of conserving the remaining forest habitat and convinces her father to do so.
Tomie DePaola, *The Unicorn and the Moon*, 1994
   When a unicorn sees the moon stuck between two mountains the mythical creature tries to rescue it.
Geraldine McCaughrean, *Unicorns! Unicorns!*, 1997
   The kind unicorns are so busy helping the other animals climb aboard the ark that they are unable to save themselves.
Dyan Sheldon, *Unicorn Dreams*, 1997
   Dan's teacher thinks he's daydreaming but he's actually watching a unicorn.

690

LORI MITCHELL, Author/Illustrator

Different Just Like Me

(Watertown, MA: Talewinds/Charlesbridge, 1999)

Subject(s): Individuality; Grandmothers; Difference
Age range(s): Grades K-3
Major character(s): April, Child, Daughter; Mom, Mother; Grammie, Grandmother
Time period(s): 1990s (1999)
Locale(s): United States

Summary: While waiting for the week to pass so they can visit Grammie, April and Mom take care of many errands. On the bus they see two children about April's age communicating in sign language. At the farmer's market people of many different ages and ethnicities shop for fruits and vegetables, some unfamiliar to April. While waiting for the elevator in her father's office building, April sees a woman with a guide dog using the Braille numbers to locate her floor. April notices the variety in her community yet recognizes the sameness of people too. At Grammie's house she admires the many flowers in the garden and cannot pick just one favorite. At the end of April's visit Grammie gives her a huge bouquet of different flowers to take home. This is the first picture book also written by this illustrator. (32 pages)

Where it's reviewed:
Booklist, March 1, 1999, page 1221
Horn Book Guide, February 1999, page 261
Kirkus Reviews, January 1, 1999, page 70
Publishers Weekly, January 4, 1999, page 88
School Library Journal, March 1999, page 181

Other books you might like:

Jane Cowan-Fletcher, *Mama Zooms*, 1993
   A little boy uses his imagination, a willing Mom and her wheelchair to try out different roles.
Juanita Havill, *Jamaica and Brianna*, 1993
   Jamaica and Brianna learn not to let appearances get in the way of their friendship.
Isaac Millman, *Moses Goes to a Concert*, 1998
   When Moses and his class go to a concert they use inflated balloons to sense the vibrations of the music they cannot hear.

Chris Raschka, *Yo! Yes?*, 1993
   An award-winning celebration of friendship shows two boys of different races becoming acquainted.

691

MITRA MODARESSI, Author/Illustrator

Yard Sale!

(New York: DK Ink, 2000)

Subject(s): Neighbors and Neighborhoods; Magic; Change
Age range(s): Grades K-3
Major character(s): Mr. Flotsam, Neighbor
Time period(s): Indeterminate
Locale(s): Spudville, Fictional Country

Summary: No one in Spudville can remember anyone having a yard sale so when Mr. Flotsam advertises one, the town's residents hurry to his house to buy something. The day after the sale strange things begin happening with the purchases. A small rug flies out the window with a child, a typewriter spews out neatly typed pages, a pasta maker never stops, seeds grow into a jungle, a phone rings mysteriously with callers from the past and a family's music box will not stop playing. When the angry neighbors meet at Mr. Flotsam's house they begin comparing problems and quickly discover that what is a nuisance to one is a delight to the other. The pasta is tasty, the jungle is great for climbing, the book being written by the typewriter is pretty good and when the rug returns the boy, other children clamor for a ride. The neighbors decide that their purchases are worth keeping and look forward to Mr. Flotsam's next sale. (32 pages)

Where it's reviewed:
Booklist, March 1, 2000, page 1251
Horn Book Guide, Fall 2000, page 277
Publishers Weekly, February 14, 2000, page 197
School Library Journal, July 2000, page 84
Smithsonian, Novemeber 2000, page 64

Awards the book has won:
Smithsonian's Notable Books for Children, 2000

Other books by the same author:
Monster Stew, 1998
The Beastly Visits, 1996
The Parent Thief, 1995

Other books you might like:
Carol Purdy, *Mrs. Merriwether's Musical Cat*, 1994
   Somehow a stray cat transforms both Mrs. Merriwether's outlook on life and her piano students' playing ability.
Roni Schotter, *Nothing Ever Happens on 90th Street*, 1997
   On Eva's boring street the simple act of scattering crumbs for the pigeons sets off a chain of events that transforms the neighborhood.
James Stevenson, *Yard Sale*, 1996
   The residents of Mud Flat have a community yard sale culminating in a party at which they share their purchases with the former owners.

692

JEANNE MODESITT
ROBIN SPOWART, Illustrator

Little Bunny's Easter Surprise

(New York: Simon & Schuster Books for Young Readers, 1999)

Subject(s): Animals/Rabbits; Surprises; Family
Age range(s): Grades K-1
Major character(s): Little Bunny, Rabbit, Sister; Baby Brother, Rabbit, Brother
Time period(s): Indeterminate
Locale(s): Fictional Country

Summary: Little Bunny feels extra excited when she wakes up on Easter morning. She knows she and Baby Brother will have Easter baskets hidden in the house, but this year for the first time she has planned a surprise for her family. After Little Bunny and Baby Brother find their beautiful baskets, Little Bunny tells her brother and parents that they have another surprise to find. Little Bunny has hidden her surprise so well that she needs to offer a few clues, but finally the baskets are located. Baby Brother expresses his appreciation by leaving a surprise under Little Bunny's pillow. The book concludes with directions for making an egg-filled Easter basket. (32 pages)

Where it's reviewed:
Booklist, February 1, 1999, page 982
Horn Book Guide, Fall 1999, page 238
Kirkus Reviews, December 15, 1998, page 1801
Publishers Weekly, January 11, 1999, page 70
School Library Journal, February 1999, page 87

Other books by the same author:
It's Hanukkah!, 1999
Lunch with Milly, 1995
Mama, If You Had a Wish, 1993

Other books you might like:
Adrienne Adams, *The Easter Egg Artists*, 1991
   Guided by their creative son a family of rabbits paints many dozen eggs in time for Easter.
DuBose Heyward, *The Country Bunny and the Little Gold Shoes*, 1939
   To prove her worth as one of the chosen Easter Bunnies, kind but tired Cottontail makes a concerted effort to deliver each of her assigned eggs.
Susan Hood, *Little Bunny's Easter Egg Surprise*, 1996
   After much searching Little Bunny finds an egg at the Easter Egg hunt that surprises everyone when it hatches into a turtle!
Rosemary Wells, *Max's Chocolate Chicken*, 1989
   Rabbit siblings Max and Ruby both want the chocolate chicken left by the Easter Bunny.

693

TOLOLWA M. MOLLEL
E.B. LEWIS, Illustrator

My Rows and Piles of Coins

(New York: Clarion Books, 1999)

Subject(s): Money; Bicycles and Bicycling; Parent and Child
Age range(s): Grades K-3
Major character(s): Saruni, Child, Son; Yeyo, Mother; Murete, Father
Time period(s): 1960s
Locale(s): Tanzania

Summary: Each time Saruni helps Yeyo with market day she rewards him with a few coins so he can buy something for himself. Secretly, Saruni saves the coins to buy a new bicycle to help transport Yeyo's goods to market. As part of his plan Saruni learns to ride Murete's big bicycle and to balance while carrying a load. After repeatedly arranging his coins in piles and the piles in rows to count them, Saruni is sure he must have saved enough and he approaches the bike dealer at the market. Saruni is disappointed when the bike dealer scoffs at the money and Saruni's belief that it would be sufficient. Apparently Murete has been saving too because he comes home on a motorbike and "sells" his bicycle to Saruni. Now, Saruni thinks, if he only had a cart to pull behind it... A concluding author's note gives background for the story and a brief glossary of Maasai and Swahili terms. (32 pages)

Where it's reviewed:
Booklist, August 1999, page 2066
Five Owls, January 2000, page 67
Horn Book Guide, Spring 2000, page 47
Publishers Weekly, August 16, 1999, page 83
School Library Journal, August 1999, page 140

Awards the book has won:
ALA Notable Children's Books, 2000
Coretta Scott King Honor Book for Illustration, 2000

Other books by the same author:
Song Bird, 1999
Ananse's Feast: An Ashanti Tale, 1997
Kele's Secret, 1997
Big Boy, 1995

Other books you might like:
Luis Garay, *Pedrito's Day*, 1997
    Pedrito saves his shoeshine money to buy a bicycle, but when he loses his aunt's money he must repay her from his savings.
Jane Kurtz, *Only a Pigeon*, 1997
    After school Ondu-ahlem shines shoes to earn money to buy feed for his homing pigeon.
Karen Lynn Williams, *Tap-Tap*, 1994
    Sasifi is proud to assist her mother on market day and uses some of her earnings to pay for their ride home on the tap-tap.

694

TOLOLWA M. MOLLEL
SYNTHIA SAINT JAMES, Illustrator

To Dinner, for Dinner

(New York: Holiday House, 2000)

Subject(s): Animals/Rabbits; Animals/Leopards; Problem Solving
Age range(s): Grades 1-3
Major character(s): Juhudi, Rabbit; Fuko, Mole, Friend; Leopard, Leopard
Time period(s): Indeterminate Past
Locale(s): Africa

Summary: Leopard is interested in having Juhudi to dinner in order to eat her for dinner, but the clever rabbit convinces him to wait until she grows larger. Her plan works twice as she tries to think of a way to avoid being eaten. Fuko has an idea to save his friend and enlists the help of hippos in a nearby lake. Bravely Juhudi meets Leopard and tricks the vain animal into the trap that Fuko sets. A concluding author's note explains the folktale elements of the original story and a pronunciation guide for the Swahili words in the text. (32 pages)

Where it's reviewed:
Booklist, September 1, 2000, page 124
School Library Journal, August 2000, page 162

Awards the book has won:
Notable Social Studies Trade Books for Young People, 2001

Other books by the same author:
Ananse's Feast: An Ashanti Tale, 1997
Kele's Secret, 1997
Big Boy, 1995 (Writer's Guild of Alberta Award for Children's Literature)
Orphan Boy, 1991 (Governor's General Award)

Other books you might like:
Baba Wague Diakite, *The Hunterman and the Crocodile: A West African Folktale*, 1997
    Rabbit cleverly solves a problem between Donso the Hunterman and a hungry crocodile.
Suzanne Crowder Han, *The Rabbit's Escape*, 1995
    In a retelling of a Korean folktale, wily rabbit tricks a turtle in order to keep his liver and his life.
Gerald McDermott, *Zomo the Rabbit: A Trickster Tale from West Africa*, 1992
    Seeking wisdom in exchange for his labor, Zomo completes tasks for the Sky God that require courage and cunning.

695

LYDIA MONKS, Author/Illustrator

The Cat Barked?

(New York: Dial Books for Young Readers, 1999)

Subject(s): Animals/Cats; Animals/Dogs; Stories in Rhyme
Age range(s): Grades K-1
Major character(s): Unnamed Character, Cat; Unnamed Character, Dog

Time period(s): 1990s (1998)
Locale(s): England

Summary: When a cat lists the many reasons that dogs have the best life and expresses a desire to be a dog, the pet's owner disagrees. While the cat thinks that walks to the park, howling at the moon and protecting the house must be lots of fun the owner points out all the things that dogs must do that the cat might not appreciate. Would the cat like to be on a leash all the time or have to eat bones and fetch sticks? Probably not, because cats are free to wander at will and nap in sunny spots. Why, a cat's life sounds so good that now the eavesdropping dog has a wish. The author's first book was originally published in England in 1998. (32 pages)

Where it's reviewed:
Booklist, March 1, 1999, page 1207
Children's Book Review Service, June 1999, page 127
Horn Book Guide, Fall 1999, page 261
Publishers Weekly, April 19, 1999, page 71
School Library Journal, April 1999, page 105

Other books you might like:
Ruth Brown, *Copycat*, 1994
    Buddy, the family cat, tries to imitate the behaviors of the other family pets and hurts himself when he gnaws the dog's bone.
Patricia Casey, *My Cat Jack*, 1994
    Jack is a stretching, yawning, scratching cat and a child's beloved pet.
Paul Fehlner, *Dog and Cat*, 1990
    An elderly dog and an overweight cat have learned to coexist peacefully.
Donald Hall, *I Am the Dog, I Am the Cat*, 1994
    Poetically, a dog and a cat describe their separate interests.

696

PAT MORA
ELIZABETH SAYLES, Illustrator

The Rainbow Tulip

(New York: Viking, 1999)

Subject(s): Mexican Americans; Mothers and Daughters; Individuality
Age range(s): Grades K-3
Major character(s): Estelita "Stella", Daughter, Student—Elementary School; Mama, Mother; Mrs. Douglas, Teacher
Time period(s): Indeterminate Past
Locale(s): El Paso, Texas

Summary: Estelita leads two lives. At home she speaks Spanish and is known by her Spanish name. At school she and her brothers speak English and Mrs. Douglas calls her Stella. Mama speaks only Spanish; she talks quietly and wears somber colors. When Mrs. Douglas announces a May Day celebration to the class, Estelita knows immediately what color she will choose for her tulip costume—she wants them all! On May Day, Mrs. Douglas compliments Stella, but still she feels a little self-conscience being the only multi-colored tulip in the class. Stella wonders if Mama's inability to understand the others makes her feel the same way. A con-

cluding author's note gives the background to the story. The Spanish words in the story are defined in context. (32 pages)

Where it's reviewed:
Booklist, November 1, 1999, page 540
Bulletin of the Center for Children's Books, December 1999, page 143
Horn Book Guide, Spring 2000, page 47
Kirkus Reviews, September 1, 1999, page 1419
School Library Journal, November 1999, page 126

Other books by the same author:
Tomas and the Library Lady, 1997
Confetti, 1996
Pablo's Tree, 1994

Other books you might like:
Mary Hoffman, *Amazing Grace*, 1991
    With her family's support Grace learns that she can realize her dream of acting in the school play.
Loretta Lopez, *The Birthday Swap*, 1997
    A Mexican American family travels to the home of Mexican relatives for a birthday celebration.
Gary Soto, *Too Many Tamales*, 1993
    Maria's attempt to help her mother prepare for a large family meal leads to a dilemma with a humorous solution.

697

MICHAEL MORPURGO
CHRISTIAN BIRMINGHAM, Illustrator

Wombat Goes Walkabout

(Cambridge, MA: Candlewick Press, 2000)

Subject(s): Animals; Mothers and Sons; Problem Solving
Age range(s): Grades K-3
Major character(s): Wombat, Son
Time period(s): 2000s
Locale(s): Australia

Summary: Young Wombat enjoys digging deep holes in which he sits and thinks. Unfortunately, one day when he crawls out of the hole he's made he can't find his mother. As he searches various animals greet him and ask what he can do. Wombat's reply is the same to each—his skills are digging and thinking. When Wombat climbs to the top of a hill to try and find his mother he spots a fire heading in his direction. The other animals are trying to fly, hop and run away from it, but Wombat begins digging since he thinks the fire can't be outrun. Wombat makes a hole so big that all the animals he's met can find shelter until the fire is past. Then they help him find his very relieved mother. (32 pages)

Where it's reviewed:
Booklist, August 2000, page 2148
Horn Book Guide, Fall 2000, page 277
Publishers Weekly, May 15, 2000, page 116
School Library Journal, May 2000, page 150
Smithsonian, November 2000, page 62

Awards the book has won:
Smithsonian's Notable Books for Children, 2000

Other books by the same author:
The Silver Swan, 2000

Red Eyes at Night, 1999
Jo-Jo the Melon Donkey, 1987

Other books you might like:

Kerry Argent, *Wombat and Bandicoot: Best of Friends: Three Stories*, 1990
    Friends Wombat and Bandicoot share a picnic and go to the beach together.
Mem Fox, *Wombat Divine*, 1996
    After auditioning for a Nativity play Wombat is not sure which is the right part.
Rod Trinca, *One Wooly Wombat*, 1985
    A humorous rhyming tale introduces fourteen Australian animals.

698

MARISSA MOSS, Author/Illustrator

The All-New Amelia

(Middleton, WI: Pleasant Company Publications, 1999)

Subject(s): Self-Perception; Archaeology; Schools
Age range(s): Grades 3-5
Major character(s): Amelia, Student—Elementary School, Friend (Carly's); Charisse, Classmate (Amelia's); Carly, Friend (Amelia's)
Time period(s): 1990s (1999)
Locale(s): United States

Summary: Amelia considers school more exciting this year for two reasons. Perfect Charisse is a new student in Amelia's class and the class will participate in an archaeological dig. In hopes of winning Charisse's friendship Amelia tries to emulate her speech and appearance. While recreating herself, Amelia neglects her writing and her good friend Carly. The teacher assigns Charisse as Amelia's partner for the archaeological dig and Amelia soon learns that Charisse does not share her excitement for the project or the work required. When Amelia decides she prefers the original Amelia to the all-new one she's been trying to be, her friendship with Carly is soon restored. (40 pages)

Where it's reviewed:
Booklist, November 1, 1999, page 530
Horn Book Guide, Spring 2000, page 80
Publishers Weekly, September 27, 1999, page 107
School Library Journal, October 1999, page 121

Other books by the same author:
Amelia Hits the Road, 1997
Amelia Writes Again, 1996
Amelia's Notebook, 1995

Other books you might like:
Judith Caseley, *Jorah's Journal*, 1997
    In her journal, Jorah records her unhappy thoughts about her new home, school and difficulty making friends.
Sheila Greenwald, *Rosy Cole: She Walks in Beauty*, 1994
    Rosy tries to remake herself into one of the ''beautiful'' people, unintentionally sacrificing her friendships.
Sharon Bell Mathis, *Running Girl: The Diary of Ebonee Rose*, 1997
    Prior to an important track meet, Ebonee records her hopes, dreams and fears in a diary.

Phyllis Reynolds Naylor, *Outrageously Alice*, 1997
    Now that Alice is in the eighth grade she thinks it's time for a new image—something extraordinary.

699

MARISSA MOSS, Author/Illustrator

Amelia Works It Out

(Middleton, WI: Pleasant Company Publications, 2000)

Subject(s): Artists and Art; Money; Clothes
Age range(s): Grades 3-5
Major character(s): Amelia, Daughter, Sister (younger); Carly Darrow, Friend (Amelia's); Cleo, Sister (older)
Time period(s): 2000s (2000)
Locale(s): Oopa, Oregon

Summary: Amelia simply must have the latest shoes that everyone is wearing including her best friend Carly and her creepy sister Cleo. Amelia's mother thinks the shoes are too expensive so Amelia tries to earn the money on her own. Although she has many ideas, most are not profitable and walking dogs is downright expensive when Amelia has to pay for the damage caused by one of the dogs in her care. For each idea, Amelia creates a unique business card and before long she realizes that what she enjoys the most is using her artistic ability to design cards. By the time Amelia finally earns enough to buy the shoes she realizes that she wants to spend her hard-earned money on something more important than her feet and she buys an art kit. (44 pages)

Where it's reviewed:
Booklist, September 1, 2000, page 115
Horn Book Guide, Spring 2001, page 65
School Library Journal, September 2000, page 206

Other books by the same author:
Amelia's Family Ties, 2000
The All-New Amelia, 1999
Amelia Hits the Road, 1997
Amelia Writes Again, 1996
Amelia's Notebook, 1995

Other books you might like:
Tom Birdseye, *Tarantula Shoes*, 1995
    Ryan uses his pet tarantula as a moneymaking attraction so he can afford new basketball shoes.
Stephanie Greene, *Owen Foote, Money Man*, 2000
    When Owen thinks he's in trouble with the IRS he desperately tries a series of unsuccessful moneymaking schemes.
Marilyn Singer, *Josie to the Rescue*, 1999
    Trying to help her family by earning some extra money, most of Josie's plans inadvertently create problems and earn little.

700

MARISSA MOSS, Author/Illustrator

Amelia's Family Ties

(Middleton, WI: Pleasant Company Publications, 2000)

Subject(s): Fathers and Daughters; Divorce; Stepfamilies
Age range(s): Grades 3-5

Major character(s): Amelia, 10-Year-Old, Child of Divorced Parents; Dad, Father, Journalist; Clara, Stepmother
Time period(s): 2000s (2000)
Locale(s): Oopa, Oregon; Chicago, Illinois

Summary: Although Amelia is curious enough about the father she's never met to write to him she's unsure what to do with his reply. Bravely, she accepts his invitation to fly to Chicago to meet him and his new family. Clara, Dad and Amelia are all nervous so it takes some time to get to know one another. Amelia's baby half-brother is the only family member acting naturally. Then, Clara compliments Amelia's writing and Amelia realizes she's read her private notebook. In anger she goes to her room, packs her suitcase and calls her best friend who encourages her to stay until she knows her dad better. The incident strains Amelia's relationship with Clara, but helps to build a bridge to her dad who also kept a notebook when he was young. Finally, Amelia asks the questions she's wanted to ask for ten years and her dad answers honestly. Amelia knows the connections have begun and in time she hopes to like Clara and understand what it means to have a father in her life. (40 pages)

Where it's reviewed:
Booklist, February 15, 2000, page 1113
Horn Book Guide, Fall 2000, page 309
Publishers Weekly, February 14, 2000, page 203
School Library Journal, June 2000, page 122

Other books by the same author:
Amelia Hits the Road, 1997
Amelia Writes Again, 1996
Amelia's Notebook, 1995

Other books you might like:
Paula Danziger, *Amber Brown Is Feeling Blue*, 1998
   Amber's adjustment to life without a father is complicated when her mother becomes engaged and her father moves back to town.
Amy Hest, *The Private Notebook of Katie Roberts, Age 11*, 1995
   Katie records her thoughts and feelings when her widowed mother remarries, moving them from New York to Texas.
P.J. Petersen, *I Want Answers and a Parachute*, 1993
   Matt and his younger brother are flying to California to visit their dad and meet his new wife and her daughter.

701

MARISSA MOSS, Author/Illustrator

Emma's Journal: The Story of a Colonial Girl

(San Diego: Silver Whistle/Harcourt Brace & Company, 1999)

Series: Young American Voices
Subject(s): Historical; Spies; Diaries
Age range(s): Grades 3-5
Major character(s): Emma Millar, 10-Year-Old, Patriot; Harmony, Aunt (Emma's), Aged Person; Thankful Bliss, 14-Year-Old, Boarder
Time period(s): 1770s (1774-1776)
Locale(s): Boston, Massachusetts, American Colonies

Summary: After Emma is sent from her farm home near Boston to the city to assist Aunt Harmony with her boarding house, she records her thoughts and experiences in a journal. Emma's annoyance with the British presence is compounded by proper, insufferable Thankful, the only boarder remaining at Aunt Harmony's and a definite sympathizer of the King's army. Emma wants to be helpful to the cause of liberty, but all she seems to do is spin, weave, churn and scrub for Aunt Harmony. When the house is taken as headquarters for a British general, Emma is able to use her position to spy on British officers and secretly relay the information to American forces. (56 pages)

Where it's reviewed:
Booklist, September 15, 1999, page 261
Horn Book Guide, Spring 2000, page 84
Publishers Weekly, September 27, 1999, page 107
School Library Journal, December 1999, page 108

Other books by the same author:
Rachel's Journal: The Story of a Pioneer Girl, 1998
Amelia Hits the Road, 1997
In America, 1994

Other books you might like:
Lisa Banim, *A Spy in the King's Colony*, 1994
   Emily chafes under the British occupation of her city and wonders whom she can trust as a true Patriot to deliver an important message.
John A. Minahan, *Abigail's Drum*, 1995
   When British forces take their father hostage, Rebecca and Abigail play their fife and drum in the lighthouse; the amplified sound convinces the British to retreat.
Doreen Rappaport, *The Boston Coffee Party*, 1988
   Based on an actual incident during the Revolutionary War, a group of women forces a greedy merchant to relinquish the coffee he's been hiding.

702

MARISSA MOSS, Author/Illustrator

Hannah's Journal: The Story of an Immigrant Girl

(San Diego: Silver Whistle/Harcourt, Inc. 2000)

Series: Young American Voices
Subject(s): Emigration and Immigration; Jews; Diaries
Age range(s): Grades 3-5
Major character(s): Hannah, 10-Year-Old, Immigrant; Esther, 14-Year-Old, Cousin; Samuel, Orphan, Immigrant
Time period(s): 1900s (1901)
Locale(s): Lithuania; *Atlanta*, At Sea; New York, New York

Summary: Hannah has the unexpected fortune to receive one of two tickets to America sent to Esther's family. The other ticket was intended for Esther's older sister who died before she could make the journey and Hannah is the nearest relative who can use the passport. Both girls travel as someone else—Hannah as Esther and Esther as her deceased sister. At the end of a long train ride from their home they meet Samuel, young but resourceful and with a reason for going to America much sadder than their own. The three youth travel together, look out for each other during this strange, new experience, and endure a nerve-wracking month's delay on Ellis Island while the authorities search for their sponsor. Once settled, Hannah and Esther begin work by day and school in the evenings so they can send for other family members. A concluding glossary and author's note contribute to the understanding of the historical and cultural background of the tale. (56 pages)

Where it's reviewed:
Booklist, October 1, 2000, page 340
Horn Book Guide, Spring 2001, page 65
Kirkus Reviews, September 15, 2000, page 1360
Publishers Weekly, September 11, 2000, page 93
School Library Journal, November 2000, page 129

Awards the book has won:
Notable Social Studies Trade Books for Young People, 2001

Other books by the same author:
Emma's Journal: The Story of a Colonial Girl, 1999 (Young American Voices)
Amelia Hits the Road, 1997
The Ugly Menorah, 1996
Amelia's Notebook, 1995
In America, 1994

Other books you might like:
Amy Hest, *When Jessie Came Across the Sea*, 1997
    Thirteen-year-old Jessie receives the gift of a ticket to America. For three years she saves to buy a ticket for her grandmother to join her.
Joan Lowery Nixon, *Land of Hope*, 1992
    Fleeing the Russian pogroms, Rebekah and her family find life hard in New York City though Rebekah is happy for the opportunity to attend school.
Lillian Hammer Ross, *Sarah, Also Known as Hannah*, 1994
    After her father's death, Sarah is sent, in place of her sister Hannah, to live with her aunt and uncle in America.

703

MARISSA MOSS
C.F. PAYNE, Illustrator

True Heart

(San Diego: Harcourt Brace & Company, 1999)

Subject(s): Railroads; Gender Roles; American West
Age range(s): Grades 1-4
Major character(s): Bee, Orphan, 16-Year-Old; Ole Pete, Engineer (locomotive)
Time period(s): 1890s (1893)
Locale(s): Cheyenne, Wyoming

Summary: With eight younger brothers and sisters to support, Bee takes the only job in town that pays a living wage—loading freight for the Union Pacific railroad. Her goal though is to drive a train. Bee hitches rides when she can, watching the engineers closely. Ole Pete will let her take over the train to hitch and unhitch cars in the yard and to drive to the next town. When bandits wound Ole Pete just outside Cheyenne and he is unable to continue his run, Bee volunteers to take over. Reluctantly, the station manager agrees and Bee realizes her dream when she's allowed to take over the controls on the *True Heart*. (32 pages)

Where it's reviewed:
Booklist, April 1, 1999, page 1424
Bulletin of the Center for Children's Books, April 1999, page 289
Horn Book Guide, Fall 1999, page 282
Publishers Weekly, March 1, 1999, page 68
School Library Journal, April 1999, page 106

Awards the book has won:
Notable Social Studies Trade Books for Young People, 2000

Other books by the same author:
Rachel's Journal: The Story of a Pioneer Girl, 1998
Amelia Hits the Road, 1997
Amelia's Notebook, 1995

Other books you might like:
Avi, *Abigail Takes the Wheel*, 1999
    When the first mate falls ill, Abigail takes command of her father's ship and brings it safely to the pier.
Betsy Hearne, *Seven Brave Women*, 1997
    A young girl views history through the peaceful contributions of seven female ancestors.
Deborah Hopkinson, *Birdie's Lighthouse*, 1997
    When her father is too ill to tend the lamps Birdie keeps the lighthouse operating during a storm, ensuring the safety of mariners.
Verla Kay, *Iron Horses*, 1999
    An illustrated story in rhyme describes the building of the transcontinental railroad.
Emily Arnold McCully, *The Ballot Box Battle*, 1996
    By fighting for women's suffrage, Elizabeth Cady Stanton makes a difference in the lives of women.
Michael O. Tunnell, *Mailing May*, 1997
    Creative thinking and new postal regulations allow May to travel by train at an affordable rate to visit her grandmother in Idaho.

704

BERNARD MOST, Author/Illustrator

The Very Boastful Kangaroo

(San Diego: Harcourt Brace & Company, 1999)

Series: Green Light Readers. Level 2
Subject(s): Animals/Kangaroos; Competition; Humor
Age range(s): Grades 1-2
Major character(s): Unnamed Character, Kangaroo (big and boastful); Unnamed Character, Kangaroo (tiny)
Time period(s): Indeterminate
Locale(s): Fictional Country

Summary: A very boastful kangaroo proudly claims to be able to jump higher than any other. A jumping contest is held to determine the best jumper and the boastful kangaroo appears to be winning until a very tiny kangaroo challenges the boastful kangaroo to jump higher than a nearby tree. The boastful kangaroo admits the tree is higher than his jumping ability. The tiny kangaroo then wins the contest with a tiny jump because, as everyone knows, trees cannot jump. (20 pages)

Where it's reviewed:
Booklist, October 1, 1999, page 366

Horn Book Guide, Spring 2000, page 62
School Library Journal, November 1999, page 112

Other books by the same author:
A Pair of Protoceratops, 1998
Catbirds and Dogfish, 1995
Zoodles, 1992

Other books you might like:
Erica Silverman, *Don't Fidget a Feather*, 1994
 Two competitive friends learn that some things are more important than winning.
Janet Stevens, *The Tortoise and the Hare: An Aesop Fable*, 1984
 An illustrated retelling of the classic story of the race between the underdog tortoise and the overly confident hare.
James Stevenson, *The Mud Flat Olympics*, 1994
 Annually a competitive group of animal friends hold their own wacky version of the Olympics.

705

BERNARD MOST, Author/Illustrator

Z-Z-Zoink!

(San Diego: Harcourt Brace & Company, 1999)

Subject(s): Animals/Pigs; Farm Life; Sleep
Age range(s): Grades K-1
Major character(s): Unnamed Character, Pig; Unnamed Character, Farmer
Time period(s): 1990s (1999)
Locale(s): United States

Summary: A little pig sleeps soundly but the other pigs cannot because she snores too loudly. After being oinked away by the pigs, the little pig tries to sleep with the cows, the sheep, the ducks, the chickens, the goats, and the frogs. With each group of animals the little pig is the only one sleeping because as soon as she falls asleep and begins to snore, the others wake up and kick her out. The little pig even ventures into the farmhouse, but she wakes up everyone there too and the farmer shoos her away. By now the little pig feels sad, but when she returns to the barn she hears one group of animals still awake and she knows she's found the perfect place to sleep. To the wide-awake barn owls the pig is no bother at all. (32 pages)

Where it's reviewed:
Horn Book Guide, Fall 1999, page 238
Publishers Weekly, May 17, 1999, page 77
School Library Journal, July 1999, page 78

Other books by the same author:
Cock-a-Doodle-Moo!, 1996
Catbirds and Dogfish, 1995
The Cow That Went Oink, 1990
My Very Own Octopus, 1980

Other books you might like:
Alyssa Capucilli, *Inside a Barn in the Country: A Rebus Read-Along Story*, 1997
 In a barn a mouse's squeak begins a chain of increasingly noisy reactions until all the animals are awake.

Teri Sloat, *The Thing That Bothered Farmer Brown*, 1995
 It's not a snoring pig but a buzzing mosquito that keeps Farmer Brown from sleeping.
Martin Waddell, *The Pig in the Pond*, 1992
 An impulsive pig creates a commotion on the farm when he jumps into the pond to cool off.

706

SHIRLEY MOZELLE
JENNIFER PLECAS, Illustrator

The Pig Is in the Pantry, the Cat Is on the Shelf

(New York: Clarion Books, 2000)

Subject(s): Animals; Farm Life; Humor
Age range(s): Grades K-2
Major character(s): Mr. McDuffel, Farmer
Time period(s): 2000s (2000)
Locale(s): United States

Summary: Mr. McDuffel drives to town for supplies leaving the farmhouse unlocked. His eight farm animals seize the opportunity to soak in the tub, raid the pantry, relax on the sofa, read on the rug and make faces in the mirror. A flat tire on Mr. McDuffel's truck delays him and the animals dress up in his clothes and dance to music on the radio. At noon they make lunch and clean up before watching television. Then they all fall asleep in the living room where Mr. McDuffel finds them when he arrives home. (32 pages)

Where it's reviewed:
Booklist, August 2000, page 2149
Horn Book Guide, Fall 2000, page 253
Kirkus Reviews, March 15, 2000, page 387
Publishers Weekly, March 27, 2000, page 79
School Library Journal, May 2000, page 150

Other books by the same author:
Zack's Alligator Goes to School, 1994 (I Can Read Book)
Zack's Alligator, 1989 (I Can Read Book)

Other books you might like:
Amy Ehrlich, *Parents in the Pigpen, Pigs in the Tub*, 1993
 The farm animals move into the house and the family heads for the barn in a humorous reversal of roles.
Libba Moore Gray, *Is There Room on the Feather Bed?*, 1997
 During a storm, the farm animals seek shelter in the teeny, tiny house of the wee fat woman and her wee fat husband.
David McPhail, *Pigs Aplenty, Pigs Galore*, 1993
 A quiet evening becomes a noisy free-for-all when a man's home is invaded by pigs intent on enjoying pizza.
Mark Teague, *Pigsty*, 1994
 Wendell's room becomes so cluttered that pigs move in and then the mess really begins!

707

ROBERT MUNSCH
EUGENIE FERNANDES, Illustrator

Ribbon Rescue

(New York: Cartwheel Books/Scholastic Press, 1999)

Subject(s): Weddings; Native Americans; Problem Solving
Age range(s): Grades K-2
Major character(s): Jillian, Indian (Mohawk), Child
Time period(s): Indeterminate
Locale(s): United States

Summary: Soon after Jillian's grandmother completes her traditional Mohawk ribbon dress, the kind child uses the ribbons to solve the problems of several passersby and inadvertently damages the dress. First, the groom in a wedding comes rushing by and Jillian gives him two ribbons to tie his shoes. Then, her ribbons help to fix the bride's hair, wrap a family's present, and tie the ring to the best man's finger. Jillian saves the wedding, but her ruined dress keeps her from being admitted to the church. When the bride and groom arrive, they express their gratitude by making Jillian the flower girl. (32 pages)

Where it's reviewed:
Booklist, July 1999, page 1952
Horn Book Guide, Fall 1999, page 262
School Library Journal, June 1999, page 104

Other books by the same author:
Get Out of Bed!, 1998
Moira's Birthday, 1989
Angela's Airplane, 1988

Other books you might like:
Faye Gibbons, *Mountain Wedding*, 1996
    A simple mountain wedding is delayed when the mules run away with the wagon of household items.
Gail Herman, *Flower Girl*, 1996
    At her sister's wedding, the flower girl depends on her lucky ring to make the day perfect.
Wendy Cheyette Lewison, *I Am A Flower Girl*, 1999
    Katie helps her aunt and uncle with their wedding.
Phyllis Reynolds Naylor, *I Can't Take You Anywhere!*, 1997
    The relatives fear disaster when klutzy Amy Audrey attends Aunt Linda's wedding; though accidents do happen, Amy is not responsible this time.
Eleanor Schick, *Navajo Wedding Day: A Dine Marriage Ceremony*, 1999
    A young girl attends a traditional Navajo wedding ceremony.

708

ROBERT MUNSCH
MICHAEL MARTCHENKO, Illustrator

We Share Everything!

(New York: Cartwheel Books/Scholastic Inc., 1999)

Subject(s): Schools; Behavior; Teachers
Age range(s): Grades K-1

Major character(s): Jeremiah, Kindergartner; Amanda, Kindergartner; Unnamed Character, Teacher
Time period(s): 1990s (1999)
Locale(s): United States

Summary: Amanda and Jeremiah seem to be only momentarily intimidated on the first day of school. Once they make their way to the kindergarten classroom they immediately use previously learned problem-solving strategies. Amanda refuses to share a book so Jeremiah screams just as he does at home when his little brother won't cooperate. In class, that behavior elicits a response from the teacher who reminds them that, in kindergarten, "We share everything." Amanda and Jeremiah don't come to a complete understanding of the kindergarten plan until the teacher has repeated her mantra after two other altercations. Then Jeremiah and Amanda get with the program so completely that they literally share everything and swap their shoes, shirts and pants, much to the teacher's surprise. (32 pages)

Where it's reviewed:
Booklist, September 1, 1999, page 142
Bulletin of the Center for Children's Books, November 1999, page 101
Horn Book Guide, Spring 2000, page 20
Publishers Weekly, August 23, 1999, page 57
School Library Journal, September 1999, page 198

Awards the book has won:
IRA/CBC Children's Choices, 2000

Other books by the same author:
Aaron's Hair, 2000
Andrew's Loose Tooth, 1998
Alligator Baby, 1997
Angela's Airplane, 1988

Other books you might like:
Nancy Carlson, *Look Out Kindergarten, Here I Come!*, 1999
    Henry's eager to go to kindergarten but, after he arrives, he's not sure he wants to stay.
Jack Gantos, *Back to School for Rotten Ralph*, 1998
    Sarah's jealous cat Ralph follows her to school and tries to interfere with her efforts to make friends.
Reeve Lindbergh, *The Awful Aardvarks Go to School*, 1997
    Four jolly aardvarks forget every rule, anger the anteater and cause chaos in school—all in one day!

709

SHIRLEY ROUSSEAU MURPHY
DIANE DILLON, Illustrator
LEO DILLON, Illustrator

Wind Child

(New York: HarperCollins Publishers, 1999)

Subject(s): Fairy Tales; Loneliness; Talent
Age range(s): Grades 2-5
Major character(s): Resshie, Daughter, Artisan (weaver); Unnamed Character, Spirit, Immortal
Time period(s): Indeterminate Past
Locale(s): Fictional Country

Summary: Child of the wind and a mortal woman who dies at her birth, Resshie is raised by an old woman who expects her to find her own way in the world when she is grown. After her childhood ends, Resshie lives alone with her loom and longs for a husband. Her skill at weaving draws people to her cottage from near and far, but no suitable men appear. At first Resshie tries to weave a suitable mate, but none last long. Then she weaves a net and traps a handsome hunter, but he longs for freedom and Resshie lets him go. The winds swirl around her cottage looking at her beautiful weavings, but none answer her call. Finally a young prince comes to see her fabrics and Resshie strikes a bargain with him that she expects will yield a husband. When the prince returns he agrees that Resshie's fabric captures his spirit and he weaves the air into a soft breeze that carries the couple home to the sky where Resshie is finally happy. (40 pages)

Where it's reviewed:
Booklist, June 1999, page 1843
Children's Book Review Service, July 1999, page 149
Five Owls, May 1999, page 106
Publishers Weekly, May 17, 1999, page 79
School Library Journal, April 1999, page 106

Other books by the same author:
The Song of the Church Mouse, 1990
Valentine for a Dragon, 1984
Tattie's River Journey, 1983
The Pig Who Could Conjure the Wind, 1978

Other books you might like:
Valerie Scho Carey, *Tsugele's Broom*, 1993
    The ALA Notable Book tells of hard-working Tsugele's discovery that her broom is not only reliable, but also somewhat magical.
Sarah Hayes, *The Candlewick Book of Fairy Tales*, 1993
    This illustrated collection includes abridged retellings of ten traditional fairy tales.
Sheila MacGill-Callahan, *To Capture the Wind*, 1997
    To free her betrothed Conal, a weaver kidnapped by pirates, Oonagh correctly answers four riddles.
Pat Pflieger, *The Fog's Net*, 1994
    Although Devora weaves a new net for the fog, it still takes her brother, but Devora has cleverly woven a way to save him into the net.
Jane Yolen, *Sleeping Ugly*, 1981
    In this twist on a classic fairy tale, beauty of spirit wins out over physical beauty and all live happily ever after.

710

SUSAN MUSGRAVE
MARIE-LOUISE GAY, Illustrator

Dreams Are More Real than Bathtubs

(Custer, WA: Orca Book Publishers, 1999)

Subject(s): Dreams and Nightmares; Bedtime; Imagination
Age range(s): Grades K-3
Major character(s): Girl, 1st Grader, Sister
Time period(s): 1990s (1998)
Locale(s): Canada

Summary: The young heroine of this story, likes to "stay up early" because she often has nightmares, including one where a giant hotdog tries to devour her head. On the day before she starts Grade One, the girl has a good dream involving her dog and her stuffed lion. School turns out to be the same way, a little scary at first, but eventually enjoyable and familiar. (32 pages)

Where it's reviewed:
Booklist, July 1999, page 1952
Horn Book Guide, Fall 1999, page 262
Kirkus Reviews, January 15, 1999, page 148
Publishers Weekly, February 1, 1999, page 84
School Library Journal, August 1999, page 140

Other books by the same author:
Hag Head, 1980

Other books you might like:
Robert Burleigh, *It's Funny Where Ben's Train Takes Him*, 1999
    At bedtime, Ben draws a train which takes him through his room to "In My Bed" station.
Mercer Mayer, *There's a Nightmare in My Closet*, 1968
    A young boy comes to terms with the "nightmares in his closet."
Francesca Simon, *Spider School*, 1996
    Kate's first day of school is a nightmare—literally.
Chris Van Allsburg, *Ben's Dream*, 1998
    Ben dreams of traveling past the monuments of the world after falling asleep studying for a geography test.

711

ANNA MYERS

Captain's Command

(New York: Walker & Company, 1999)

Subject(s): World War II; Family Life; Christmas
Age range(s): Grades 5-7
Major character(s): Gail Harmon, 6th Grader, Sister (older); Captain, Dog (golden retriever); Ned Harmon, Uncle, Blind Person
Time period(s): 1940s (1943-1944)
Locale(s): Stonewall, Oklahoma; Europe

Summary: As Gail's family begins making preparations to celebrate Christmas while her father fights in Europe, a telegram arrives announcing that his plane has been shot down and he is missing. Gail's mother refuses to accept his death and Gail tries to believe that he is missing and alive for the sake of her brother and sister. Uncle Ned, seriously wounded in the war, is further hurt by the news of his brother and drowns his anger in a neighbor's moonshine. Gail seeks reassurance from her great-grandmother and comfort from Captain, a gift from her father before he departed. On Christmas Eve the family learns that her father has died of injuries in the crash, but a late night visit from Santa helps restore Gail's belief in the goodness of people. Eventually she is also able to honor her father's memory and his request that she help Uncle Ned when she gives Captain to him for training as a guide dog. (134 pages)

Where it's reviewed:
Book Report, November 1999, page 63
Booklist, December 15, 1999, page 784
Children's Book Review Service, November 1999, page 34

Publishers Weekly, November 29, 1999, page 72
School Library Journal, October 1999, page 156

Other books by the same author:
Ethan Between Us, 1998
The Keeping Room, 1997
Rosie's Tiger, 1994
Red-Dirt Jessie, 1992

Other books you might like:
Janet Carey, *Molly's Fire*, 2000
  News that her father's plane has been shot down over Holland during World War II does not convince Molly that he is dead.
Jane Cutler, *My Wartime Summers*, 1994
  Uncle Bob's service during World War II changes him so much that Ellen and her family are unsure how to relate to him.
Patricia Reilly Giff, *Lily's Crossing*, 1997
  Lily is tired of this war that has taken her father across the ocean that she once enjoyed, but now sees as a barrier between her and her father.
Sollace Hotze, *Summer Endings*, 1991
  Christine worries when the end of World War II does not bring her imprisoned father home from Poland.

712

CHRISTOPHER MYERS, Author/Illustrator

Black Cat

(New York: Scholastic Press, 1999)

Subject(s): Animals/Cats; City and Town Life
Age range(s): Grades 3-6
Major character(s): Black Cat, Cat
Time period(s): 1990s (1999)
Locale(s): New York, New York

Summary: Black Cat saunters through an urban landscape as an unseen narrator asks the whereabouts of the cat's home. Past flashing lights on police cars, hearing music and city sounds, creeping along subway platforms, chasing mice or rats and sipping water from fire hydrants Black Cat stays on the move because home is wherever the cat roams. (40 pages)

Where it's reviewed:
Booklist, April 15, 1999, page 1531
Horn Book, March 1999, page 199
The New Advocate, Fall 1999, page 389
Publishers Weekly, March 29, 1999, page 104
School Library Journal, March 1999, page 181

Awards the book has won:
Coretta Scott King Honor Book for Illustration, 2000
School Library Journal Best Books, 1999

Other books by the same author:
Wings, 2000

Other books you might like:
Eve Bunting, *Secret Place*, 1996
  Unseen by many, a polluted river flows through a city, past warehouses, under freeways providing a home for wildlife.
William Low, *Chinatown*, 1997
  As a boy walks the crowded streets of Chinatown he passes

street vendors, delivery trucks and an early morning tai chi class.
Walter Dean Myers, *Harlem*, 1997
  This poetic celebration of Harlem was recognized as a Caldecott Honor Book.
Gina Wilson, *Prowlpuss*, 1995
  A rough, tough, one-eyed, one-eared alley cat returns home after a night of carousing to become a pampered pussy.

713

CHRISTOPHER MYERS, Author/Illustrator

Wings

(New York: Scholastic Press, 2000)

Subject(s): Mythology; Individuality
Age range(s): Grades 1-4
Major character(s): Ikarus Jackson, Outcast, Student; Unnamed Character, Narrator, Outcast
Time period(s): 2000s (2000)
Locale(s): United States

Summary: A shy girl understands the feelings of the new student as he faces stares, giggles and teasing about his appearance—for she endures teasing simply because she's quiet. For Ikarus, his wings make him a topic of conversation that is so distracting one teacher sends him away to learn to keep his wings out of the way in the classroom. Ikarus tries to play with the other children, but they consider him a show-off because of his flying ability. Finally, the shy, silent girl finds the courage to speak up for Ikarus, to tell the others to stop teasing and to compliment Ikarus for his beautiful flying. A friendship begins to soar. (40 pages)

Where it's reviewed:
Booklist, May 15, 2000, page 1754
Horn Book Guide, Spring 2001, page 65
Kirkus Reviews, September 15, 2000, page 1360
Publishers Weekly, September 11, 2000, page 90
School Library Journal, October 2000, page 130

Awards the book has won:
Publishers Weekly Best Books, 2000
ALA Notable Children's Books, 2001

Other books by the same author:
Black Cat, 1999 (Coretta Scott King Honor Book)
McCrephy's Field, 1991 (Lynne Myers, co-author)

Other books you might like:
Debbie Allen, *Dancing in the Wings*, 2000
  Teased because of her height and large feet, Sassy perseveres and gains confidence when she's selected for an elite summer dance program.
Eric Jon Nones, *Angela's Wings*, 1995
  When wings sprout from Angela's back she endures teasing until she accepts the change and chooses to enjoy the pleasure of flying.
Faith Ringgold, *Tar Beach*, 1991
  Cassie dreams of flying over the city, imagining her future.
David Shannon, *A Bad Case of Stripes*, 1998
  Camilla's denial of her individual interests in her quest for

popularity causes a bad case of stripes and that's just the beginning of her troubles.

714

LAURIE MYERS
DAN YACCARINO, Illustrator

Surviving Brick Johnson

(New York: Clarion Books, 2000)

Subject(s): Schools; Brothers; Conduct of Life
Age range(s): Grades 3-5
Major character(s): Brick Johnson, 5th Grader, Bully; Alex Wilson, 5th Grader, Brother; Bob Wilson, 1st Grader, Brother
Time period(s): 2000s (2000)
Locale(s): United States

Summary: Appearances can be deceiving as Alex learns when he expects Brick Johnson to maim him for doing an imitation of the very large classmate at lunch. Alex tries avoiding Brick until he takes enough karate lessons to defend himself. Bob is astonished to learn Alex's opinion of the student that the first grade knows as an entertaining reader who peppers his readings to Bob's class with sound effects. Alex has difficulty reconciling Bob's view with that of his friends who agree that Alex is in serious trouble. Alex is sure the karate lessons will solve his problem until Brick shows up at the second class to refresh his skills. If Alex can master an important karate rule, "respect," he may be able to not only survive Brick Johnson but also make an unlikely new friend. (74 pages)

Where it's reviewed:
Booklist, September 15, 2000, page 242
Children's Book Review Service, September 2000, page 7
Horn Book Guide, Spring 2001, page 65
Kirkus Reviews, July 15, 2000, page 1044
School Library Journal, October 2000, page 131

Awards the book has won:
ALA Notable Children's Books, 2001

Other books by the same author:
Guinea Pigs Don't Talk, 1994
Earthquake in the Third Grade, 1993
Garage Sale Fever, 1993

Other books you might like:
Betsy Duffey, *How to Be Cool in the Third Grade*, 1993
Robbie's determination to be cool faces the challenge of being assigned as a reading buddy to the class bully.
Barbara Robinson, *The Best School Year Ever*, 1994
Students learn to look beneath the facade of the incorrigible Herdmans to find the real person.
Dona Schenker, *Fearsome's Hero*, 1994
In fifth grade Honey was a bully but this year she's turned over a new leaf which could be even worse for Tully because now Honey likes him.

715

TIM MYERS
OKI S. HAN, Illustrator

Basho and the Fox

(Tarrytown, NY: Marshall Cavendish, 2000)

Subject(s): Animals/Foxes; Poetry; Fables
Age range(s): Grades 1-3
Major character(s): Basho, Writer (poet); Unnamed Character, Fox
Time period(s): 17th century
Locale(s): Fukagawa, Japan

Summary: Basho lives a simple, secluded life writing the haiku for which he is famous. In late summer he enjoys cherries from a tree near his hut so he is not happy to notice a fox dining on the cherries. The fox refuses to stop eating the cherries and explains that he has a right to the cherries because foxes are actually the greatest poets and whisper their leftovers into the ears of sleeping humans. However, the fox proposes a contest. Basho can have all the cherries next year if he can create a great poem by the time the tree blossoms again. The fox gives Basho three trics but shakes Basho's confidence by dismissing the first two haiku as inadequate. Basho approaches the fox the third time with nothing prepared and offers him a haiku that he creates spontaneously when he sees the fox in the moonlight. Finally fox thinks the haiku is outstanding because the poem has a fox in it—teaching Basho the importance of writing poetry for its own sake and not to please another. (32 pages)

Where it's reviewed:
Booklist, September 15, 2000, page 249
Horn Book, September 2000, page 553
Riverbank Review, Winter 2000-2001, page 30
School Library Journal, October 2000, page 131
Smithsonian, November 2000, page 64

Awards the book has won:
Smithsonian's Notable Books for Children, 2000

Other books by the same author:
Let's Call Him Lau-Wili-Wili-Humu-Humu-Nukuauku-Nukunukai-Apuaa-Oioi, 1993

Other books you might like:
Matthew Gollub, *Cool Melons—Turn to Frogs!: The Life and Poems of Issa*, 1998
A picture book biography of a Japanese haiku poet includes thirty of his poems.
George Shannon, *Spring: A Haiku Story*, 1996
Fourteen haiku describe a spring walk.
Dawnine Spivak, *Grass Sandals: The Travels of Basho*, 1997
Haiku inspired by Basho's journey across Japan enhance this picture book biography.

716

WALTER DEAN MYERS
NINA LADEN, Illustrator

The Blues of Flats Brown

(New York: Holiday House, 2000)

Subject(s): Animals/Dogs; Music and Musicians; Animals, Treatment of

Age range(s): Grades 1-4

Major character(s): A.J. Grubbs, Businessman (junkyard owner); Flats Brown, Dog, Musician; Caleb, Dog, Friend

Locale(s): Mound Bayou, Mississippi; Memphis, Tennessee; New York, New York

Summary: Born in a junkyard, Flats is content to strum his guitar and sing the blues but A.J. intends to use his dogs for fighting. When Flats hears A.J.'s plan, he runs away with his guitar and Caleb. The dogs begin as street musicians until they get a gig in a nightclub where A.J. finds them. Flats and Caleb escape and make their way to Memphis where Flats is hired by a recording studio. Again A.J. tracks them down and, after the dogs get away from him, Caleb leaves the partnership while Flats continues on to New York. Each experience is written into a blues number that becomes part of Flats'

repertoire; by the time A.J. finds him in New York, Flats has a song that touches A.J.'s lonely, mean heart. (32 pages)

Where it's reviewed:
Booklist, March 1, 2000, page 1242
Bulletin of the Center for Children's Books, February 2000, page 217
Kirkus Reviews, January 15, 2000, page 121
Publishers Weekly, January 24, 2000, page 311
School Library Journal, March 2000, page 210

Other books by the same author:
Harlem, 1997 (Caldecott Honor Book)
The Story of the Three Kingdoms, 1995
The Dragon Takes a Wife, 1994

Other books you might like:
Linda England, *The Old Cotton Blues*, 1998
   Dexter learns to make the music that he feels within him come to life on a used harmonica as he plays the "Old Cotton Blues."
Nina Laden, *The Night I Followed the Dog*, 1994
   While a family sleeps, their pet dog secretly leads an exciting nightlife.
Jonathan London, *Hip Cat*, 1993
   Oobie-do John, a sax-playing cat, hops the night train to San Francisco where he feels free to play the jazz that he loves.

N

717

ANN WHITEHEAD NAGDA
STEPHANIE ROTH, Illustrator

Dear Whiskers

(New York: Holiday House, 2000)

Subject(s): Schools; Letters; Emigration and Immigration
Age range(s): Grades 2-4
Major character(s): Jenny, 4th Grader; Sameera, 2nd Grader, Immigrant; Mrs. Steele, Teacher
Time period(s): 2000s (2000)
Locale(s): United States

Summary: In the author's first book, Jenny struggles with a class assignment to write a letter to an assigned 2nd grade pen pal as if she is a mouse living in the child's desk. When a brief, poorly written response to Whiskers (Jenny's mouse persona) comes from Sameera, Jenny is embarrassed to read the letter in front of the class. Of course, when no other letters come Jenny feels even worse so she asks Mrs. Steele for a different pen pal. Instead, Mrs. Steele sends her to the second grade teacher with a note suggesting the two students meet. Then, Jenny learns that Sameera knows only a little English, having recently emigrated from Saudi Arabia. Sameera does not respond to Jenny's letters because of language and cultural differences—even writing the date is hard because Sameera is accustomed to a different calendar. Jenny tries several ideas before making mouse-shaped cookies to act out the content of her letters to Sameera and finally some understanding (and a friendship) begins. More importantly, the other students begin to accept Sameera and when Jenny's classmates learn about her idea, their positive response boosts her self-esteem. (76 pages)

Where it's reviewed:
Booklist, November 15, 2000, page 642
Horn Book, March 2001, page 210
School Library Journal, January 2001, page 104

Other books you might like:
Aliki, *Marianthe's Story: Painted Words/Spoken Memories*, 1998

Two stories in one book describe the introduction of a non-English speaking child to an American school.
Patricia Reilly Giff, *The War Began at Supper: Letters to Miss Loria*, 1991
Mrs. Clark's class writes letters to their former student teacher about events during the Persian Gulf crisis.
Peg Kehret, *My Brother Made Me Do It*, 2000
A class pen pal assignment pairs Julie with elderly Mrs. Kaplan who responds compassionately to Julie's questions and concerns.
Ellen Levine, *I Hate English!*, 1989
A picture book explains Mei Mei's frustrating experiences adjusting to a new school and a new language.
Doris Orgel, *Don't Call Me Slob-O*, 1996
Shrimp decides to befriend the new student from Croatia because he knows what it's like to be teased for being different.

718

LENSEY NAMIOKA
KEES DE KIEFTE, Illustrator

Yang the Eldest and His Odd Jobs

(Boston: Little, Brown and Company, 2000)

Subject(s): Chinese Americans; Music and Musicians; Brothers and Sisters
Age range(s): Grades 3-6
Major character(s): Yingwu "Eldest Brother" Yang, Musician (violinist), Immigrant; Yingmei "Mary" Yang, Sister (third), Immigrant
Time period(s): 2000s (2000)
Locale(s): Seattle, Washington

Summary: Eldest Brother, the most gifted of the musical Yang children needs a new violin. In China this would not have been a problem because the government provides for people with talent, but in America, Eldest Brother must earn the money to purchase a new instrument. Friends and family offer suggestions to help Eldest Brother make some money and he tries a variety of odd jobs—babysitter, street musician, telemarketer, busboy, waiter and carpenter. Eldest Brother is now so busy working and so tired from his efforts he has no time for his music. When he seriously injures his hand on the construction job, Mary fears he may lose the ability to use his musical gift. (121 pages)

Where it's reviewed:
Booklist, February 15, 2000, page 1114
Kirkus Reviews, March 1, 2000, page 304
Publishers Weekly, April 24, 2000, page 93
Riverbank Review, Summer 2000, page 42
School Library Journal, April 2000, page 140

Other books by the same author:
Yang the Second and Her Secret Admirers, 1998
Yang the Third and Her Impossible Family, 1996
Yang the Youngest and His Terrible Ear, 1994

Other books you might like:
Peg Kehret, *The Richest Kids in Town*, 1994
  Peter's moneymaking schemes are not financially successful but they do provide a framework for his friendship with Wishbone.
Barbara O'Connor, *Beethoven in Paradise*, 1997
  Martin's father does not support his love of music and desire to play the violin; he wants his son to play baseball.
Laurence Yep, *Ribbons*, 1996
  Chinese American Robin, a gifted ballet student, must give up her expensive lessons when the family's money is needed to bring Grandmother to America.

719

KEIKO NARAHASHI, Author/Illustrator

Two Girls Can!

(New York: Margaret K. McElderry Books, 2000)

Subject(s): Friendship; Playing; Childhood
Age range(s): Grades K-1
Time period(s): 2000s (2000)
Locale(s): United States

Summary: Pairs of girls of different ethnicities joyfully play leapfrog, dig holes, fly kites and hold hands. Sometimes even best friends become angry but they can get over it and go on to play tug-of-war or ride a seesaw. Together two girls can climb trees, share treats and sing songs. If two girls decide to dance more will join in until everybody's dancing. (32 pages)

Where it's reviewed:
Booklist, March 15, 2000, page 1388
Bulletin of the Center for Children's Books, June 2000, page 368
Horn Book Guide, Fall 2000, page 253
Publishers Weekly, May 22, 2000, page 92
School Library Journal, June 2000, page 122

Other books by the same author:
Is That Josie?, 1994
I Have a Friend, 1987

Other books you might like:
Virginia Kroll, *New Friends, True Friends, Stuck-Like-Glue Friends*, 1994

Rhythmic lyrical text describes the many different kinds of friends one can have.
W. Nikola-Lisa, *Bein' with You This Way*, 1994
  A rap poem describes the ways in which children of different races can interact positively.
Sherley Anne Williams, *Girls Together*, 1999
  Although one friend can't join their planned activity four other girls play together all day.

720

PHYLLIS REYNOLDS NAYLOR
ALAN DANIEL, Illustrator

Carlotta's Kittens and the Club of Mysteries

(New York: Atheneum Books for Young Readers, 2000)

Subject(s): Animals/Cats; Adventure and Adventurers; Humor
Age range(s): Grades 3-5
Major character(s): Carlotta, Cat, Mother; Marco, Cat, Brother (Polo's); Polo, Cat, Brother
Time period(s): 2000s (2000)
Locale(s): United States

Summary: Carlotta is on the mind of each member of the Club of Mysteries. Marco and Polo leave the comfort of home on a snowy day to search for her and end up at the clubhouse where a meeting is underway. None of the club members has seen her since she left to have her kittens so the club leader assigns different members to search for her. When Carlotta reappears in her own time, the club members feel responsible for protecting the kittens, teaching them survival skills, keeping them out of the pound and locating the right home for them. It's an awesome task, but together they succeed. (131 pages)

Where it's reviewed:
Booklist, November 15, 2000, page 642
Horn Book Guide, Spring 2001, page 76
School Library Journal, January 2001, page 106

Other books by the same author:
The Healing of Texas Jake, 1997
The Grand Escape, 1993
Shiloh, 1991 (Newbery Medal)

Other books you might like:
Avi, *Poppy and Rye*, 1998
  Courageous mouse Poppy saves Rye and his family from the flooding created by a beaver dam.
Elke Heidenreich, *Nero Corleone: A Cat's Story*, 1997
  To better care for his shy sister, Rosa, Nero gives up his life as a farm cat for the greater comforts of being a house cat.
Dick King-Smith, *The School Mouse*, 1995
  In the school building that is her family's home Flora takes advantage of the daily lessons and uses her literacy to save her family.
Ursula K. Le Guin, *Wonderful Alexander and the Catwings*, 1994
  When a big, bossy kitten goes exploring, his unexpected adventures lead to his introduction to cats with wings.

721

PHYLLIS REYNOLDS NAYLOR

Peril in the Bessledorf Parachute Factory

(New York: Jean Karl/Atheneum Books for Young Readers, 2000)

Subject(s): Family Life; Humor; Brothers and Sisters
Age range(s): Grades 4-6
Major character(s): Bernie Magruder, 11-Year-Old, Brother; Delores Magruder, Sister (older), Worker; Dwayne Hopper, Worker
Time period(s): 1990s
Locale(s): Middleburg, Indiana

Summary: In the sixth episode about the Magruder family, Bernie makes plans to get a room of his own at the Bessledorf Hotel—as soon as he gets Delores out of hers. To achieve his goal Bernie plays matchmaker for he's sure if he can marry off Delores, he'll be given her room. Dwayne Hopper becomes the unwitting marriage partner in the scheme when he rents a room at the Bessledorf Hotel. Bernie and his friends create fake love letters between Dwayne and Delores that seem to be successful until the love-struck Delores's job performance at the Bessledorf Parachute Factory falters and she is required to demonstrate her parachute-packing ability by jumping from a plane. Realizing that Delores could die, Bernie begins to rethink his plans and suspects the mysterious Dwayne Hopper may have something to do with Delores's dilemma. Can he prove his suspicions right in time to save his sister? (148 pages)

Where it's reviewed:
Booklist, January 1, 2000, page 926
Horn Book Guide, Spring 2001, page 76
School Library Journal, February 2000, page 124

Other books by the same author:
The Treasure of Bessledorf Hill, 1998
The Bomb in the Bessledorf Bus Depot, 1996
The Face in the Bessledorf Funeral Parlor, 1993
Bernie and the Bessledorf Ghost, 1990
The Bodies in the Bessledorf Hotel, 1986

Other books you might like:
Betsy Byars, *Wanted. . .Mud Blossom*, 1991
    In one of several stories about an unusual family, Junior accuses the family dog of causing the disappearance of a hamster.
Sid Hite, *Those Darn Dithers*, 1996
    In the sequel to *Dither Farm* the Dither family enjoys a summer that is far from the quiet that might be expected in a small rural community.
Gordon Korman, *The Chicken Doesn't Skate*, 1996
    It's Henrietta the chicken who needs saving from her destiny as the culmination of a food cycle experiment in this humorous novel.

722

PHYLLIS REYNOLDS NAYLOR

A Spy Among the Girls

(New York: Delacorte Press, 2000)

Subject(s): Brothers; Sisters; Behavior
Age range(s): Grades 4-6
Major character(s): Beth Malloy, 10-Year-Old, Sister; Caroline Malloy, 9-Year-Old, Sister (youngest); Eddie Malloy, 11-Year-Old, Sister; Josh Hatford, Twin, Neighbor
Time period(s): 1990s
Locale(s): Buckman, West Virginia

Summary: Aspiring actress Caroline is jealous that Beth's budding romance with Josh is depriving Caroline of her position as the center of the family's attention so she concocts a plan to make Josh's younger brother fall in love with her by Valentine's Day. Beth insists she's only spying on the Hatfords and of course Josh gives the same excuse to his brothers for his interest in Beth. Eddie is disgusted with the behavior of both her sisters and desperate for a science project idea. When Eddie decides to measure gender differences and gullibility by using purported sightings of the "abaguchie," a monster in local folklore, she arouses the interest of the Hatford brothers who threaten the project's secrecy unless they are included. Caroline secretly dresses as the "abaguchie" and leaps right back into the spotlight for one afternoon. Her plan to woo a Hatford is less successful and the stress of deception and sibling pressure brings an end to Beth and Josh's relationship. What's next in the ongoing feud between the Hatfords and the Malloys? (134 pages)

Where it's reviewed:
Booklist, September 1, 2000, page 115
Horn Book Guide, Spring 2001, page 76
Kirkus Reviews, August 15, 2000, page 1202
School Library Journal, September 2000, page 234

Other books by the same author:
A Traitor Among the Boys, 1999
The Girls' Revenge, 1998
Boys Against Girls, 1994
The Boys Start the War, 1993
The Girls Get Even, 1993

Other books you might like:
Eleanor Estes, *The Middle Moffat*, 1942
    A Newbery Honor book describes the plans of plain, boring Jane Moffat to become the intriguing "Middle Moffat" and add excitement to her life.
Colleen O'Shaughnessy McKenna, *Valentine's Day Can Be Murder*, 1996
    Roger likes to play tricks on Marsha but when a Valentine's poem he writes is accidentally put in Marsha's mailbox, it is no laughing matter!
Stephen Roos, *Never Trust a Sister Over Twelve*, 1993
    As sisters grow up their relationship adjusts to accommodate their changing interests.

723

PHYLLIS REYNOLDS NAYLOR

A Traitor Among the Boys

(New York: Delacorte Press, 1999)

Subject(s): Brothers and Sisters; Humor; Teasing
Age range(s): Grades 4-6
Major character(s): Beth Malloy, 10-Year-Old, Sister (middle); Peter Hatford, 7-Year-Old, Brother (youngest); Mrs. Hatford, Mother
Time period(s): 1990s
Locale(s): Buckman, West Virginia

Summary: As the four Hatford brothers try to devise a joint New Year's Resolution to satisfy their mother, she becomes aware of the way they have treated the three Malloy sisters since the Malloy family began renting the former home of the Hatford's best friends. Mrs. Hatford demands that the boys treat the girls nicely-as if they were sisters. Now, the Hatfords have no sisters, but they assume that brothers and sisters would not always get along any more than brothers and brothers do so they happily agree to their mother's plan knowing that it allows them to continue their mischief making against the girls. Peter, a sucker for the delicious cookies that Beth bakes, takes his mother's instructions to heart and informs the sisters of his brothers plans' in exchange for freshly baked treats-until his brothers discover he's the traitor in their midst. (118 pages)

Where it's reviewed:
Booklist, September 1, 1999, page 133
Children's Bookwatch, October 1999, page 4
Horn Book Guide, Spring 2000, page 84
Publishers Weekly, September 13, 1999, page 86
School Library Journal, September 1999, page 228

Other books by the same author:
The Girls' Revenge, 1998
Boys Against Girls, 1994
The Boys Start the War, 1993
The Girls Get Even, 1993

Other books you might like:
Gery Greer, *This Island Isn't Big Enough for the Four of Us*, 1987
   A "war" begins when the island Pete and Scott consider their private place becomes a campsite for Sunny and Jill. Co-author Bob Ruddick.
Elizabeth Levy, *Gorgonzola Zombies in the Park*, 1993
   The Bamford brothers must learn to work with obnoxious cousin Mabel in order to stop the vandalism in Central Park.
Gregory Maguire, *Six Haunted Hairdos*, 1997
   The sequel to *Seven Spiders Spinning* pits the boys against the girls to determine who can successfully scare the other with ghost stories.
Margaret Mahy, *The Good Fortunes Gang*, 1993
   Tracey, leader of the cousins, considers Pete an outsider and expects him to prove that he is a "real" Fortune.
Hilary McKay, *Dog Friday*, 1995
   The ingenuous efforts of four irrepressible children who

become neighbors to Robin and his widowed mother add unexpected humor to their lives.

724

SHIRLEY NEITZEL
NANCY WINSLOW PARKER, Illustrator

I'm Taking a Trip on My Train

(New York: Greenwillow Books, 1999)

Subject(s): Railroads; Imagination; Stories in Rhyme
Age range(s): Grades K-1
Major character(s): Unnamed Character, Child, Son
Time period(s): 1990s (1999)
Locale(s): United States

Summary: A young boy pretends to be the engineer of the train and he's taking a trip. As the cumulative tale develops each pictured item becomes a rebus in the ever-lengthening text. The train has a black engine, red caboose, gondolas, tanker and boxcars that click along the track over a trestle and through a tunnel from one end of the little boy's house to the other. His mother's impressed with his work, but still wants the tracks cleaned up before he goes to bed. (32 pages)

Where it's reviewed:
Booklist, April 15, 1999, page 1537
Horn Book Guide, Fall 1999, page 262
School Library Journal, March 1999, page 182

Other books by the same author:
The House I'll Build for the Wrens, 1997
We're Making Breakfast for Mother, 1997
The Bag I'm Taking to Grandma's, 1995

Other books you might like:
Alyssa Satin Capucilli, *Inside a Barn in the Country: A Rebus Read-Along Story*, 1995
   A cumulative rebus tale starts with the squeak of a mouse and ends with the animals wide awake and noisy.
Jane Cowan-Fletcher, *Mama Zooms*, 1993
   Inspired by his mom and her wheelchair, a young boy imagines himself in many roles.
David McPhail, *The Train*, 1977
   After his father puts him to bed Matthew boards his toy train for an imaginary trip.

725

MARY NETHERY
PAUL YALOWITZ, Illustrator

Mary Veronica's Egg

(New York: Orchard Books, 1999)

Subject(s): Animals/Ducks; Contests; Determination
Age range(s): Grades K-2
Major character(s): Mary Veronica, Student—Elementary School, Sister; Mary Louise, Sister (older); Mary Margaret, Sister (younger)
Time period(s): 1990s
Locale(s): United States

Summary: When Mary Veronica finds an egg near a pond she's sure that it contains a creature so unique that it will win the gold ribbon for "Most Unusual Pet" in the school's pet competition. Mary Louise looks disdainfully upon the egg, sure that it is rotten and will simply stink when it inevitably breaks. Mary Margaret, however, is sure that Mary Veronica holds a dinosaur egg and she begs for it. Mary Veronica perseveres with her plan, but the egg does not cooperate by hatching in time for the contest. Finally, the egg yields a baby duck that looks prize-winning to Mary Veronica. (32 pages)

Where it's reviewed:
Booklist, July 1999, page 1953
Bulletin of the Center for Children's Books, February 1999, page 211
Horn Book Guide, Fall 1999, page 262
Publishers Weekly, January 25, 1999, page 95
School Library Journal, March 1999, page 182

Other books by the same author:
Hannah and Jack, 1996

Other books you might like:
Joyce Dunbar, *Eggday*, 1999
   The barnyard animals are unsure how to enter Dora the duck's competition on "eggday," but all are eager to win the prize for best egg.
William Joyce, *Bently and Egg*, 1992
   When a shy, singing frog takes on responsibility for a special egg the ensuing events change the frog's life. ALA Notable Book.
Leo Lionni, *An Extraordinary Egg*, 1994
   Three frogs disagree about a pebble that one declares is a chicken egg. When the egg hatches, all agree that the "chicken" swims quite well for a bird.
Lynn Reiser, *The Surprise Family*, 1994
   Much to the surprise of a mother hen, the "chicks" she's hatched from a clutch of abandoned eggs enjoy swimming—just like ducks.

726

JOHN NICKLE, Author/Illustrator

The Ant Bully

(New York: Scholastic Press, 1999)

Subject(s): Animals/Ants; Bullies; Fantasy
Age range(s): Grades K-3
Major character(s): Lucas, Bullied Child; Sid, Bully
Time period(s): 1990s
Locale(s): United States

Summary: Lucas often gets picked on by Sid, who likes to attack him with his water hose. Lucas in turn picks on the ants, drenching them with his squirt gun. Pretty soon the ants have had enough however, and they take Lucas hostage, forcing him to work with the other ants until he develops sympathy for them. Finally, the ants release Lucas because of his good behavior and the next time Sid tries to bully Lucas, the ants are waiting with appropriate punishment. (32 pages)

Where it's reviewed:
Booklist, February 1, 1999, page 982
Bulletin of the Center for Children's Books, February 1999, page 212
Horn Book, January 1999, page 54

Publishers Weekly, January 1, 1999, page 94
School Library Journal, March 1999, page 182

Awards the book has won:
IRA/CBC Children's Choices, 2000

Other books you might like:
Nancy Carlson, *Loudmouth George and the Sixth-Grade Bully*, 1987
   After a bully steals his lunch, Loudmouth George decide to pay him back.
Phyllis Reynolds Naylor, *King of the Playground*, 1991
   With the help of his father, Kevin confronts the neighborhood bully.
Scott Taylor, *Dinosaur James*, 1990
   James' obsession with dinosaurs becomes an asset when the schoolyard bully singles out James for attention.
Hans Wilhelm, *Tyrone and the Swamp Gang*, 1995
   Tyrone, the neighborhood bully, tries to make everyone join his gang.

727

VIRGINIA NIELSEN

Batty Hattie

(New York: Marshall Cavendish, 1999)

Subject(s): Animals/Bats; Schools; Mothers and Daughters
Age range(s): Grades 4-6
Major character(s): Harriet, Niece, 6th Grader; Mike Henry, Uncle, Scientist; Brady Howell, 6th Grader, Friend
Time period(s): 1990s (1999)
Locale(s): Nugget, California

Summary: Harriet feels as abandoned as one of Uncle Mike's orphaned bats when her widowed mother seizes an opportunity to go on tour for a year with a band and leaves Harriet in a dinky little town with an uncle known to everyone as the batman. Uncle Mike happily shares his knowledge of bats with Harriet, but insists that she must never pick up one. As her interest in bats grows, lonely Harriet is teased by classmates and called "Batty Hattie." When she finds a young bat on the ground she sees the bat as a potential friend and carefully brings it home. Now she has to find a way to hide and feed the creature without Uncle Mike becoming suspicious. Harriet succeeds for three weeks with help from new friend Brady, but eventually her disobedience is discovered and she must accept her responsibility to return the bat to the wild. Harriet's experience helps her understand her mother's difficult choice between love for her daughter and her passion for music. (142 pages)

Where it's reviewed:
Booklist, March 1, 1999, page 1214
Bulletin of the Center for Children's Books, April 1999, page 290
Horn Book Guide, Fall 1999, page 297
Kirkus Reviews, April 1, 1999, page 536
School Library Journal, April 1999, page 140

Other books by the same author:
The House of Three Sisters, 1982

Other books you might like:
Luli Gray, *Falcon's Egg*, 1995
  As the dragon that hatches from the odd egg Falcon finds rapidly grows, she realizes she cannot hide it forever and reluctantly sets it free.
Patricia Hermes, *Someone to Count On*, 1993
  Sam's widowed mother leaves her with a cantankerous grandfather who didn't know of her existence while her mother pursues other interests.
Cynthia Stowe, *Dear Mom, in Ohio for a Year*, 1992
  Mom sends her sixth-grader to Vermont to live with relatives so she is free to attend college.
Jacqueline Wilson, *The Lottie Project*, 1999
  A school project gives Charlie the opportunity to create a life she can control through the imagined diaries of Lottie, a Victorian maid.

728

MICHELLE NIKLY
JEAN CLAVERIE, Illustrator

The Perfume of Memory

(New York: Arthur A. Levine Books/Scholastic, 1999)

Subject(s): Memory; Fairy Tales; Fathers and Daughters
Age range(s): Grades 2-4
Major character(s): Yasmin, Daughter
Time period(s): Indeterminate Past
Locale(s): Middle East

Summary: In a long-ago, far-away kingdom, lives a perfume-maker and his daughter, Yasmin. After Yasmin's mother dies, her father keeps the mother's memory alive through the scents selected for his various perfumes. Although perfume making is a trade open only to males, Yasmin learns her father's craft and soon makes a perfume so delightful that Yasmin and her father decide to enter it in a national contest. Before the queen smells Yasmin's perfume, her memory is erased by another entry, the perfume of Forgetfulness. Remembering the way in which her father maintained the memory of her deceased mother with scents, Yasmin tries to use the same technique to restore the queen's memory. (40 pages)

Where it's reviewed:
Children's Book Review Service, February 2000, page 76
Horn Book Guide, Spring 2000, page 69
Kirkus Reviews, October 1, 1999, page 1583
Publishers Weekly, November 22, 1999, page 55
School Library Journal, November 1999, page 162

Other books by the same author:
The Emperor's Plum Tree, 1982
The Princess on the Nut, 1981

Other books you might like:
Rebecca Hickox, *The Golden Sandal: A Middle Eastern Cinderella Story*, 1998
  Maha is helped by a magic fish after being mistreated by her stepmother.
Robert Ingpen, *Folk Tales and Fables of the Middle East and Africa*, 1998
  Ten classic stories reflect the cultures of the Middle East and Africa.

Eric A. Kimmel, *The Three Princes: A Tale from the Middle East*, 1994
  Three princes, vying for a beautiful princess, must prove their worth on a quest to find rare gifts.

729

JOAN LOWERY NIXON

Caesar's Story: 1759

(New York: Delacorte Press, 2000)

Series: Young Americans. Number 2
Subject(s): Slavery; Historical; Growing Up
Age range(s): Grades 4-6
Major character(s): Caesar, Slave, 9-Year-Old; Nathaniel "Nat" Burwell, 9-Year-Old, Heir
Time period(s): 1750s (1759)
Locale(s): Carter's Grove, Virginia, American Colonies; Williamsburg, Virginia, American Colonies

Summary: Caesar longs for the carefree days of childhood when he and Nat played together on the plantation grounds. Now each struggles to adjust to their respective roles. At his father's death three years earlier, Nat became the heir to the extensive holdings of the Burwell family and he is trying to carry out his responsibilities in a manner worthy of his father's memory. Caesar loses the limited freedom of the field slave to at least live with his family when he is called by Nat to become his personal servant. While living in the "Big House" is considered a privilege by many slaves it also means doing whatever the master requires, whenever he requests help and wherever he happens to be. Caesar misses his parents and sisters, but gradually learns to recognize the unquenchable spirit within him, to adapt, to accept what he cannot change and to make the most of what he has. Like Nat, Caesar wants his family to feel proud of him. Extensive background material including a map, pictures and a recipe concludes the story that is presented as a narrative program by a costumed interpreter at Colonial Williamsburg. (167 pages)

Where it's reviewed:
Booklist, June 1, 2000, page 1894
Children's Book Review Service, June 2000, page 126
Horn Book Guide, Fall 2000, page 309
School Library Journal, August 2000, page 186

Other books by the same author:
Maria's Story: 1773, 2001 (Young Americans, Number 5)
Will's Story: 1771, 2001 (Young Americans, Number 4)
Ann's Story: 1747, 2000 (Young Americans, Number 1)
Aggie's Home, 1998 (Orphan Train Children, Number 3)
Will's Choice, 1998 (Orphan Train Children, Number 2)

Other books you might like:
Kathleen Duey, *Summer MacCleary: Virginia, 1749*, 1998
  In the tenth book of the "American Diaries" series the plantation master's daughter accuses Summer, an indentured servant, of stealing.
Patricia C. McKissack, *A Picture of Freedom: The Diary of Clotee, a Slave Girl*, 1997
  Clotee, a twelve-year-old house slave considers escaping to freedom in this "Dear America" series entry set in 1859.

Connie Porter, *Meet Addy: An American Girl*, 1993
When the master sells her father and brother, Addy and her mother escape from the North Carolina plantation to freedom in the North.

730

JOAN LOWERY NIXON
DIANE DEGROAT, Illustrator

Gus & Gertie and the Missing Pearl
(New York: SeaStar Books, 2000)

Subject(s): Animals; Vacations; Humor
Age range(s): Grades 2-4
Major character(s): Gertie, Penguin, Vacationer; Gus, Penguin, Vacationer
Time period(s): Indeterminate
Locale(s): Holiday Island, Fictional Country

Summary: After the ferry delivers Gus and Gertie to Holiday Island for a week's vacation at the Hotel de View, Gus is certain they have been unloaded at the wrong place. A driverless taxi sits at the dock, but the only shelter as the rain begins is a decrepit hotel filled with noisy scallywags. Gus is certain these are the notorious "bad guys" that they've been warned to avoid, but when the unruly group notices Gertie's pearl necklace they insist on having a party for the guests. Unsure what to make of events, Gus takes many Polaroid pictures which are useful in solving the mystery of the disappearance of Gertie's necklace. Once Gertie retrieves her necklace she decides to enjoy the vacation from the comforts of home. (48 pages)

Where it's reviewed:
Booklist, November 1, 2000, page 540
Children's Book Review Service, September 2000, page 7
Kirkus Reviews, September 1, 2000, page 1288
Publishers Weekly, August 21, 2000, page 73
School Library Journal, October 2000, page 132

Other books by the same author:
Aggie's Home, 1998 (Orphan Train Children, Book 3)
Will's Choice, 1998 (Orphan Train Children, Book 2)
Lucy's Wish, 1998 (Orphan Train Children, Book 1)

Other books you might like:
David A. Adler, *The Cam Jansen Series*, 1980-
Cam needs no camera to solve mysteries; she has a photographic memory.
Doug Cushman, *Aunt Eater's Mystery Vacation*, 1992
Aunt Eater's plans to relax on her vacation change when she spots a diamond ring thief, a missing ferryboat captain, and a suspicious-looking woman.
Howard Goldsmith, *The Twiddle Twins' Music Box Mystery*, 1997
The Twiddle family's music box is stolen; amateur detectives solve the case by using the clues left behind by the thief.
Richard Scarry, *Richard Scarry's Great Steamboat Mystery*, 1975
Two detectives on the trail of jewel thieves add to the excitement of a wedding party on a steamboat.

Marjorie Weinman Sharmat, *The Nate the Great Series*, 1972-
In a series for beginning readers Nate methodically follows clues to solve mysteries.

731

LUCY NOLAN
JILL KASTNER, Illustrator

The Lizard Man of Crabtree County
(New York: Marshall Cavendish, 1999)

Subject(s): Monsters; Country Life; Imagination
Age range(s): Grades 1-3
Major character(s): James Arthur, Child, Son; Miss Bunch, Aged Person
Time period(s): Indeterminate Past
Locale(s): Crabtree County

Summary: James Arthur lives in such a dull place that one summer day he covers himself with branches so he appears to be a bush in hopes of generating some excitement. Little does he know how successfully his plan works. James Arthur fools no birds or animals, but some bugs take up residence in his underwear and the itchy boy makes a mad dash for Miss Bunch's pond to wash them away. In the late afternoon sun, the shadow James Arthur in bush disguise casts on Miss Bunch's barn is large and terrifying. Miss Bunch calls the neighbors and town officials to report a lizard man running toward her pond. When James Arthur learns of the report he is disappointed to miss the excitement and makes plans to investigate further. The sightings continue, each time after James Arthur has just left the spot and the youngster never makes the connection between his actions and the purported sightings. After a few days Miss Bunch reports seeing the lizard man board a truck headed for Alabama and the summer excitement ends. (32 pages)

Where it's reviewed:
Booklist, November 15, 1999, page 636
Bulletin of the Center for Children's Books, October 1999, page 63
Children's Book Review Service, September 1999, page 171
Kirkus Reviews, September 1, 1999, page 1420
School Library Journal, October 1999, page 121

Other books by the same author:
Jack Quack, 2001

Other books you might like:
Karen Ackerman, *Bingleman's Midway*, 1995
A flat tire on a carnival truck brings excitement right to Nathaniel's farm during an otherwise boring summer.
Jackie French Koller, *No Such Thing*, 1997
Howard's mother doesn't believe his claim that a monster is under his bed just as Monster's mother refuses to accept that a boy is in the bed.
Mary Wormell, *Hilda Hen's Scary Night*, 1996
James Arthur cannot see monsters although he looks while Hilda Hen sees them in each everyday item of the darkened yard.

732

JERDINE NOLEN
KADIR NELSON, Illustrator

Big Jabe

(New York: Lothrop, Lee & Shepard Books, 1999)

Subject(s): Slavery; African Americans; Tall Tales
Age range(s): Grades 2-5
Major character(s): Addy, Slave; Jabe, Foundling, Hero; Momma Mary, Storyteller
Time period(s): 2000s (2000); Indeterminate Past
Locale(s): South (Plenty Plantation)

Summary: A pear tree too old to bear fruit is the focus for one of Momma Mary's most popular stories. Years ago when the land was part of a plantation worked by slaves, Addy, a house slave, was sent to catch some fish for her master's dinner. At the river, Addy fishes a boy in a basket out of the water. Jabe offers Addy a pear and plants the seed that quickly grows into a mature tree. Before leaving the riverbank, Jabe calls so many fish from the water that the people in the Big House and those in the slave quarters have plenty to eat. Jabe grows rapidly into a larger-than-life man with strength, speed and amazing powers. Each time a slave is disciplined, within a day the slave and all his or her family vanish. The slaves know that somehow that pear tree with the North Star shining through its branches and Jabe's magic are setting them free. (32 pages)

Where it's reviewed:
Booklist, April 1, 2000
Horn Book, July 2000, page 440
Publishers Weekly, April 17, 2000, page 79
Riverbank Review, Fall 2000, page 26
School Library Journal, June 2000, page 122

Awards the book has won:
Publishers Weekly Best Books, 2000
Bulletin of the Center for Children's Books Blue Ribbon, 2000

Other books by the same author:
In My Momma's Kitchen, 1999
Raising Dragons, 1998
Harvey Potter's Balloon Farm, 1994 (ALA Notable Book)

Other books you might like:
Evelyn Coleman, *The Foot Warmer and the Crow*, 1994
    Enslaved Hezekiah uses his ability to communicate with crows to outwit his master and gain his release from bondage.
Virginia Hamilton, *The People Could Fly: American Black Folktales*, 1985
    A collection of African-American folktales relates stories of slavery and people's escape from bondage.
William H. Hooks, *Freedom's Fruit*, 1996
    Mama Marina, an enslaved conjure woman, gains freedom for her daughter by using a powerful spell to trick the master.
Julius Lester, *John Henry*, 1994
    The Caldecott Honor Book retells the traditional tale of John Henry, a legendary steel-driving man.

Angela Shelf Medearis, *The Freedom Riddle*, 1995
    With determination and ingenuity a young slave wins freedom by besting his master in a riddle contest.

733

JERDINE NOLEN
COLIN BOOTMAN, Illustrator

In My Momma's Kitchen

(New York: Lothrop, Lee & Shepard Books, 1999)

Subject(s): Cooks and Cooking; Family Life; African Americans
Age range(s): Grades K-3
Major character(s): Unnamed Character, Child, Daughter; Nadene Jefferies, Sister (older); Momma, Mother
Time period(s): Indeterminate Past
Locale(s): United States

Summary: A little girl knows for sure that the good things in life happen right in Momma's kitchen. Nadene stood in the kitchen to announce her music scholarship to college while the family cheered. Dolls and cats participate in pretend wedding ceremonies in the kitchen. Even cooking takes place in the kitchen—pots of soup, crab apple jelly, fried chicken dinners and her father's famous corn pudding. On nights when the family can't sleep they gather around the table for snacks and serenades in Momma's kitchen. (32 pages)

Where it's reviewed:
Booklist, February 15, 1999, page 1077
Bulletin of the Center for Children's Books, June 1999, page 360
Kirkus Reviews, March 15, 1999, page 454
Publishers Weekly, April 12, 1999, page 75
School Library Journal, May 1999, page 94

Other books by the same author:
Big Jabe, 2000
Raising Dragons, 1998
Harvey Potter's Balloon Farm, 1994 (ALA Notable Book)

Other books you might like:
Valerie Flournoy, *Tanya's Reunion*, 1995
    Tanya visits the Virginia farm where Grandma lived as a child and learns about her heritage.
Jan Spivey Gilchrist, *Indigo and Moonlight Gold*, 1993
    Autrie and her mother share quiet times in the evening when the rest of the family has gone to bed.
Jeanne Whitehouse Peterson, *My Mama Sings*, 1994
    Mama has a song for every occasion, adding a feeling of constancy to a young boy's life experiences.

734

CARL NORAC
CLAUDE K. DUBOIS, Illustrator

Hello, Sweetie Pie

(New York: Doubleday Book for Young Readers, 2000)

Series: Lola Book
Subject(s): Names, Personal; Animals/Hamsters; Teasing
Age range(s): Preschool

Major character(s): Lulu, Hamster, Friend; Lola, Hamster, Student
Time period(s): Indeterminate
Locale(s): Fictional Country

Summary: Lola's first day of school has been so successful that she sings cheerfully as she walk home. Then, she meets Lulu who wants to know what Lola's parents call her and Lola happily lists several endearing nicknames. The laughing response from Lulu and the other students takes the joy out of Lola's day. As she continues walking home she asks everyone she sees if they had a nickname as a child and she learns that most parents use nicknames for their children. At home Lola responds grumpily to ''babycake'' or ''fairy princess'' but she still falls for ''sweetie pie.'' The next day at school Lulu apologizes and admits to feeling jealous of Lola because her parents never use little nicknames. Lulu taught them the ones that Lola told her and now it's Lola's turn to overcome the jealousy she feels over having sharing ''her'' nicknames. First published in French in 1999. (32 pages)

Where it's reviewed:
Booklist, April 1, 2000, page 1470
Children's Bookwatch, August 2000, page 5
Kirkus Reviews, June 15, 2000, page 890
Publishers Weekly, July 31, 2000, page 97
School Library Journal, August 2000, page 162

Other books by the same author:
I Love to Cuddle, 1999 (Lola Book)
I Love You So Much, 1998 (Lola Book)

Other books you might like:
Diana Engel, *Josephina Hates Her Name*, 1989
    After Grandma tells Josephina about the relative for whom she is named Josephina begins to appreciate her name.
Kevin Henkes, *Chrysanthemum*, 1991
    Unhappy Chrysanthemum arrives home from her first day of school feeling humiliated by teasing from classmates about her name.
Bernard Waber, *But Names Will Never Hurt Me*, 1976
    When Alison Wonderland learns how she came by her unusual name she also begins to learn how to live with it.

735

HOWARD NORMAN
TOM POHRT, Illustrator

Trickster and the Fainting Birds

(San Diego: Gulliver Books/Harcourt Brace & Company, 1999)

Subject(s): Trickster Tales; Indians of North America; Folklore
Age range(s): Grades 4-7
Major character(s): Trickster, Trickster, Shape-Changer
Time period(s): Indeterminate Past
Locale(s): United States

Summary: From the oral tradition of the Algonquian peoples Norman fashions seven tales featuring shape-changing Trickster. In the first story ''Trickster and the Best Hermit,'' Trickster is not able to live up to the boast he makes to a crow that he is the best at being alone. In ''Trickster and the Shut-Eye Dancers'' Trickster offers to teach a fox how to capture ducks that Trickster then eats, leaving the unwitting fox with only duck feet. The concluding story, ''Trickster and the Fainting Birds,'' features a sleepwalking contest with the winner marrying a beautiful young woman. Jealous Trickster tries to marry the woman by cheating and changes the legitimate winner into a kingfisher. The woman is resolute and Trickster finally admits defeat, but he never does restore the winner to his human form. An introduction by the author and concluding source notes give background information about the stories. (82 pages)

Where it's reviewed:
Booklist, January 1, 2000, page 916
Horn Book, November 1999, page 749
Publishers Weekly, October 25, 1999, page 81
Riverbank Review, Winter 1999/2000, page 35
School Library Journal, December 1999, page 114

Awards the book has won:
Aesop Prize, 1999

Other books by the same author:
The Girl Who Dreamed Only Geese and Other Tales of the Far North, 1997 (School Library Journal Best Books)

Other books you might like:
James E. Connolly, *Why the Possum's Tail Is Bare: And Other North American Indian Nature Tales*, 1992
    Thirteen Native American folktales explain the legendary reason for certain animals' behavior.
Virginia Hamilton, *A Ring of Tricksters: Animal Tales from America, the West Indies and Africa*, 1997
    Eleven read-aloud tales include tricksters from spiders to rabbits and the unwitting animals who bear the brunt of their cleverness.
Tom Pohrt, *Coyote Goes Walking*, 1995
    Four legends present coyote as a mythical creator, a trickster, and a victim of his own cockiness.
Gayle Ross, *How Rabbit Tricked Otter: And Other Cherokee Trickster Stories*, 1994
    Fifteen stories about Rabbit show him to be a trickster, outsmarting many animals and being responsible for some of their physical characteristics.
Nancy Van Laan, *In a Circle Long Ago: A Treasury of Native Lore from North America*, 1995
    A collection of stories and poems includes source notes and descriptions of the tribes whose folklore is represented.

736

LESLIE NORRIS
MORDICAI GERSTEIN, Illustrator

Albert and the Angels

(New York: Farrar, Strauss and Giroux, 2000)

Subject(s): Christmas; Lost and Found Possessions; Animals/Dogs
Age range(s): Grades 2-5
Major character(s): Albert O'Keefe, Child, Son; Lucille, Dog; A.N. Angel, Aged Person
Time period(s): Indeterminate Past
Locale(s): Fictional Country

Summary: Years ago Albert's mother received a gold medallion necklace for Christmas but lost it and Albert buys a replacement for her that, unfortunately, he loses on the way home. After his parents are in bed on Christmas Eve Albert and Lucille sneak out into a snowstorm to search for the lost gift. They're taken (by someone claiming to be an angel) to a warehouse of found possessions operated by A.N. Angel. In the jewelry section Mr. Angel locates Albert's found gift with which he happily returns home. On Christmas morning Albert's mother opens the box and finds the very necklace she lost many years ago. (48 pages)

Where it's reviewed:
Booklist, September 15, 2000, page 243
Horn Book Guide, Spring 2001, page 65
Horn Book, November 2000, page 761
Publishers Weekly, September 25, 2000, page 72
School Library Journal, October 2000, page 62

Other books by the same author:
Norris's Ark, 1988

Other books you might like:
Claudia Mills, *Gus and Grandpa and the Christmas Cookies*, 1997
   While baking Christmas cookies, Gus and Grandpa decide that sharing them with people less fortunate is the best thing to do.
Katherine Paterson, *Angels and Other Strangers*, 1979
   A collection of original short stories reflects on some of the mysteries of the Christmas season.
Robert Westall, *Christmas Spirit: Two Stories*, 1994
   On Christmas Eve a boy's faith and courage avert a tragedy. A young girl secretly shelters a pregnant cat and befriends a boy.

737

MATT NOVAK, Author/Illustrator

Jazzbo and Googy
(New York: Hyperion Books for Children, 2000)

Subject(s): Friendship; Animals/Bears; Toys
Age range(s): Preschool
Major character(s): Jazzbo, Bear; Googy, Pig; Big Bear, Bear, Stuffed Animal
Time period(s): Indeterminate
Locale(s): Fictional Country (Super School)

Summary: Although Big Bear isn't good at some games, he's still Jazzbo's best friend and goes everywhere with him including school. Some of the other students have classmates as friends, but not Googy who tries to make friends, but ends up making messes. When Googy tries to play with Jazzbo on the playground he accidentally gets sand in Jazzbo's eyes and causes Big Bear to be dropped in the mud when he pushes Jazzbo too high on the swings. Quickly, Googy, the expert at messes, snatches Big Bear out of the puddle and cleans him in the sink. Jazzbo appreciates Googy's gesture and, with Big Bear's approval invites Goody to play. (32 pages)

Where it's reviewed:
Bulletin of the Center for Children's Books, September 2000, page 32

Horn Book Guide, Fall 2000, page 254
Publishers Weekly, April 24, 2000, page 93
School Library Journal, June 2000, page 123

Other books by the same author:
Jazzbo Goes to School, 1999
The Pillow War, 1998
Elmer Blunt's Open House, 1996
Gertie and Gumbo, 1995
Mouse TV, 1994 (School Library Journal Best Book)

Other books you might like:
John Burningham, *The Friend*, 1975
   A young boy enjoys playing with his good friend Arthur.
Barbro Lindgren, *Sam's Teddy Bear*, 1982
   Sam's faithful doggie helps recover his lost teddy bear.
John Wallace, *Little Bean's Friend*, 1997
   When Bouncer flies over the garden wall Little Bean makes a friend when Paul returns her favorite bear.

738

MATT NOVAK, Author/Illustrator

The Robobots
(New York: DK Ink/DK Publishing, Inc., 1999)

Subject(s): Robots; Neighbors and Neighborhoods; Difference
Age range(s): Grades K-3
Major character(s): D.A.D. Robobot, Father, Robot; M.O.M. Robobot, Mother, Robot; Mr. Peebles, Neighbor
Time period(s): Indeterminate
Locale(s): Littlewood Lane, Fictional Country

Summary: Mr. Peebles is astonished to see the strange vehicle stopping in front of the vacant house across the street. When the Robobot family emerges and introduces themselves to him, Mr. Peebles races into his house. D.A.D and M.O.M. assume he's just shy as are all the other neighbors they speak to—the lamppost, mailbox and fire hydrant. They move into their new home, complete some renovations and then search for jobs, stores and a school for the two children. Everywhere they go the buildings are closed and the Robobots begin to sense they are not welcome in the community. A gathering of neighbors at Mr. Peebles's home decides to confront the new, strange family and tell them to go, but when they reach the Robobot's home they are graciously invited inside. Everyone is so fascinated by the house that they quickly see the ways in which this strange family is similar rather than different from their own and they change their minds about asking them to leave the neighborhood. (32 pages)

Where it's reviewed:
Booklist, June 1999, page 1844
Bulletin of the Center for Children's Books, May 1999, page 324
Horn Book Guide, Fall 1999, page 263
Kirkus Reviews, April 1, 1999, page 537
School Library Journal, June 1999, page 104

Awards the book has won:
IRA/CBC Children's Choices, 2000

Other books by the same author:
Newt, 1996
Gertie and Gumbo, 1995

Mouse TV, 1994 (School Library Journal Best Books)
Elmer Blunt's Open House, 1993

Other books you might like:

Michael Garland, *Dinner at Magritte's*, 1995
Pierre enjoys joining his unusual neighbors for dinner because the surroundings are not exactly what they seem at first glance.

Peter Glassman, *The Wizard Next Door*, 1993
A young boy doesn't know what to make of the strange things that happen after Mr. Myers moves into the neighborhood.

Ingrid Slyder, *The Fabulous Flying Fandinis!*, 1996
Shy Bobby's mother encourages him to visit the new family next door although other neighbors consider them strange.

739

LAURA JOFFE NUMEROFF
FELICIA BOND, Illustrator

If You Take a Mouse to the Movies

(New York: Laura Geringer/HarperCollins Publishers, 2000)

Subject(s): Animals/Mice; Christmas; Movies
Age range(s): Grades K-1
Major character(s): Unnamed Character, Mouse; Unnamed Character, Child
Time period(s): 2000s (2000)
Locale(s): United States

Summary: Taking a mouse to the movies is the start of unexpected holiday preparations. The young boy hosting the event buys popcorn to eat during the movie, but the mouse puts the popcorn on a string and then wants to hang it on a Christmas tree so the boy has to buy one on the way home from the movies. Building a snowman and a snow fort distracts the mouse briefly but when he comes inside feeling cold and snuggles up for a nap and the radio plays Christmas carols he gets up to sing along. By the time the mouse has made the ornaments and decorated the tree he realizes he needs a popcorn string and working with the popcorn makes the mouse think of. . .the movies again. (40 pages)

Where it's reviewed:
Booklist, December 1, 2000, page 722
Publishers Weekly, September 25, 2000, page 69
School Library Journal, October 2000, page 62

Other books by the same author:
If You Give a Pig a Pancake, 1998
If You Give a Moose a Muffin, 1991
If You Give a Mouse a Cookie, 1985

Other books you might like:

Patricia Baehr, *Mouse in the House*, 1994
There's a mouse loose in the house and Mrs. Teapot's pets are trying to catch it.

Becky Bloom, *Mice Make Trouble*, 2000
Using his sister's magic pencil to draw the first mouse is what starts all the trouble for Henry.

Bethany Roberts, *A Mouse Told His Mother*, 1997
A mouse tells his mother his plans to go to the moon and she counters each idea with a suggestion that quickly has the mouse ready for bed.

Wong Herbert Yee, *Eek! There's a Mouse in the House*, 1992
Each animal pursuing a mouse is larger than the previous one sent to catch it; the chaos increases proportionately.

O

740

JOHN O'BRIEN, Author/Illustrator

Poof!

(Honesdale, PA: Boyds Mills Press, 1999)

Subject(s): Wizards; Humor; Problem Solving
Age range(s): Grades K-2
Major character(s): Unnamed Character, Wizard, Father; Unnamed Character, Wizard, Spouse
Time period(s): Indeterminate
Locale(s): Fictional Country

Summary: The crying baby is the impetus to a competition between wizard parents who use their magic wands to avoid their daily chores. When the wizard's wife reminds him that it is his turn to ''change the baby'' he obliges with a wave of his wand by changing the baby into a cat. The wizard's wife agrees that it is her turn to feed the cat and with a wave of her wand, she transforms the cat into a dog waiting to be walked by the wizard. The afternoon continues with each ''poof!'' of magic solving one problem and creating a new one until the family of three is together outside, happily quacking in the rain. (40 pages)

Where it's reviewed:
Children's Book Review Service, September 1999, page 171
Horn Book Guide, Spring 2000, page 48
Publishers Weekly, August 30, 1999
School Library Journal, November 1999, page 126

Other books by the same author:
Mother Hubbard's Christmas, 1996 (IRA/CBC Children's Choice)
Sam and Spot: A Silly Story, 1995
Twelve Days of Christmas, 1993

Other books you might like:
Peter Glassman, *The Wizard Next Door*, 1993
    Strange things have been happening in the neighborhood since Mr. Myers moved in next door.
Helen Lester, *The Wizard, the Fairy and the Magic Chicken*, 1983

Three magicians trying to outdo one another create a problem that they must work together to solve.
Bill Martin Jr., *The Wizard*, 1994
A wizard's clumsiness while conjuring leads to an unexpected result.

741

BARBARA O'CONNOR

Me and Rupert Goody

(New York: Frances Foster Books/Farrar Straus Giroux, 1999)

Subject(s): Fathers and Sons; Stores, Retail; Mentally Handicapped
Age range(s): Grades 4-7
Major character(s): Jennalee Helton, 11-Year-Old; Beauregard ''Uncle Beau'' Goody, Businessman, Friend; Rupert B. Goody, Mentally Challenged Person, Son (Uncle Beau's)
Time period(s): 1990s
Locale(s): Claytonville, North Carolina (Smoky Mountains)

Summary: Jennalee's refuge from her helter skelter home is Uncle Beau's General Store so she doesn't take kindly to Rupert waltzing in the door and claiming to be Uncle Beau's son. Although Uncle Beau isn't really her uncle he's the closest thing to a caring family Jennalee has and she appreciates the routine they have established at the store. When Jennalee learns that Rupert, a black man, is the son of white Uncle Beau, her secure world begins to change and Jennalee has to find a way to adjust. (106 pages)

Where it's reviewed:
The Book Report, January 2000, page 68
Booklist, November 1, 1999, page 530
Five Owls, March 2000, page 100
Horn Book, September 1999, page 615
School Library Journal, October 1999, page 156

Awards the book has won:
School Library Journal Best Books, 1999
ALA Notable Children's Books, 2001

Other books by the same author:
Beethoven in Paradise, 1997

Other books you might like:
Sara Harrell Banks, *Under the Shadow of Wings*, 1997
 Tatnall defends her slow cousin Obie from bullies but she cannot protect him from his own inner turmoil and ultimately, he determines his fate.
Betsy Byars, *Summer of the Swans*, 1970
 Sarah's handicapped brother runs away and is found visiting the swans.
Paula Fox, *Radiance Descending*, 1997
 As Paul begins to see the acceptance of others for his younger brother with Down syndrome he becomes able to love Jacob unconditionally.
Colby Rodowsky, *What About Me?*, 1989
 Dorris resents the attention her younger brother receives just because he has Down syndrome.

742

ISAAC O. OLALEYE
ANN GRIFALCONI, Illustrator

In the Rainfield: Who Is the Greatest?

(New York: Blue Sky Press/Scholastic, Inc., 2000)

Subject(s): Folk Tales; Contests; Africa
Age range(s): Grades 1-4
Major character(s): Wind, Mythical Creature; Fire, Mythical Creature; Rain, Mythical Creature
Time period(s): Indeterminate Past
Locale(s): Africa

Summary: Many years ago, according to a Nigerian folktale, in the Rainfield, Rain, Fire, and Wind argue with each claiming to be the greatest. Wind cannot be seen or caught, Fire is too hot for anyone to stand near yet Rain claims her gentleness makes her the greatest. To prove their power they hold a contest. First Wind blows and blows from a gentle breeze to a howling storm only stopping when Rain and Fire call time. Next Fire rages devouring everything in its path and refusing to stop when Wind and Rain call time. Wind tries to blow out Fire but only makes it bigger. Quietly, but quickly the sky darkens, thunder rumbles and Rain begins to fall gently on everything, including Fire. Finally, Fire agrees to stop, but both Rain and Wind recognize it is too late. Rain proves to be the greatest and to this day defeated Fire hisses when water touches it and Wind travels with Rain. (32 pages)

Where it's reviewed:
Booklist, February 15, 2000, page 1118
Children's Book Review Service, March 2000, page 86
Horn Book Guide, Fall 2000, page 342
Los Angeles Times Book Review, February 13, 2000, page 12
Publishers Weekly, January 10, 2000, page 67

Awards the book has won:
Notable Social Studies Trade Books for Young People, 2001

Other books by the same author:
Bikes for Rent, 2001
Lake of the Big Snake: An African Rain Forest Adventure, 1998

The Distant Talking Drum: Poems from Nigeria, 1995 (ALA Notable Book)
Bitter Bananas, 1994 (Parents Council Outstanding Read-Aloud)

Other books you might like:
Verna Aardema, *Misoso: Once Upon a Time Tales from Africa*, 1994
 Each story in this collection by an award-winning author includes a map to locate its origin and a glossary of terms.
Ashley Bryan, *Beat the Story-Drum, Pum-Pum*, 1987
 An illustrated collection retells five Nigerian folktales.
Mary-Joan Gerson, *Why the Sky Is Far Away: A Nigerian Folktale*, 1992
 Considering itself misused by the peasants, the sky responds by moving farther away.
Walter Dean Myers, *The Story of the Three Kingdoms*, 1995
 The wisdom in the People's stories gives them the strength to share the kingdoms of earth, sky and water with the creatures living there.

743

EFFIN OLDER
NANCY HAYASHI, Illustrator

My Two Grandmothers

(San Diego: Harcourt, Inc., 2000)

Subject(s): Grandmothers; Traditions; Holidays
Age range(s): Grades K-2
Major character(s): Lily, Child; Bubbe Silver, Grandmother; Grammy Lane, Grandmother
Time period(s): 2000s (2000)
Locale(s): United States

Summary: During visits with each of her grandmothers Lily learns about different family traditions. With Bubbe Silver, Lily enjoys Hanukkah, lunches after a golf game and her first gefilte fish with horseradish. Grammy Lane teaches Lily the family tradition of red flannel hash after a day of hiking in snowshoes and singing Christmas carols with the family after eating a big turkey dinner. Wanting to share the traditions she loves from each of them, Lily plans her own tradition for her beloved grandmothers-the "First Traditional Grandmothers' Party." (32 pages)

Where it's reviewed:
Booklist, October 15, 2000, page 446
Horn Book Guide, Spring 2001, page 47
Kirkus Reviews, September 1, 2000, page 1289
School Library Journal, October 2000, page 133

Other books by the same author:
Ice Dreams, 1996 (Silver Blades, Number 1)

Other books you might like:
Joan C. Hawxhurst, *Bubbe and Gram: My Two Grandmothers*, 1997
 A grandchild learns more about holiday traditions of different faiths by sharing them with her Jewish and Christian grandmothers.
Toyomi Igus, *Two Mrs. Gibsons*, 1996
 Toyomi's loving descriptions compare and contrast the

two Mrs. Gibsons—her mother and grandmother—in her young life.

Emily Arnold McCully, *Grandmas at Bat*, 1993
  Two competitive grandmothers with good intentions complicate things for Pip's baseball team in this easy reader.

744

KEVIN O'MALLEY, Author/Illustrator

Bud
(New York: Walker & Company, 2000)

Subject(s): Parent and Child; Gardens and Gardening; Individuality

Age range(s): Grades K-3

Major character(s): Bud Sweet-William, Rhinoceros, Son; Grandfather Sweet-William, Grandfather, Rhinoceros; Mr. Sweet-William, Father, Rhinoceros

Time period(s): 2000s

Locale(s): Fictional Country

Summary: Bud's parents cannot understand where he acquired his love of dirt and interest in gardening for such tastes are contrary to the clean, orderly way of life to which they are accustomed. As Bud grows and learns more about plants and compost his room becomes a jungle and soon he's taken over the backyard with a disorderly assortment of flowering plants. Mr. Sweet-William has to admit that Bud's a pleasant boy, but with his father coming to visit the parents must be sure to hide any evidence of Bud's interests. Grandfather uses his visits to teach Bud how to organize his crayons in the box and to alphabetize the canned goods. All goes well until an intense storm strikes one night. In the morning Bud hurries to his garden to survey the damage and Grandfather finds him there crying. Bud tells his impressed Grandfather about flowers, bugs and compost. By the time Bud's parents awaken Bud and Grandfather are both covered with dirt and having a great time. (32 pages)

Where it's reviewed:
Booklist, April 1, 2000, page 1470
Bulletin of the Center for Children's Books, June 2000, page 368
Kirkus Reviews, April 1, 2000, page 482
Publishers Weekly, April 3, 2000, page 80
School Library Journal, June 2000, page 123

Other books by the same author:
Leo Cockroach. . .Toy Tester, 1999
Velcome, 1997
Carl Caught a Flying Fish, 1996
Roller Coaster, 1995

Other books you might like:
Pat Brisson, *Wanda's Roses*, 1994
  While others see only weeds in a vacant lot, Wanda sees potential beauty and works to improve the space.
Jane Cutler, *Mr. Carey's Garden*, 1996
  Mr. Carey's neighbors cannot understand his tolerance for snails in his garden until they view the unconventional garden on a moonlit night.
Paul Fleischman, *Weslandia*, 1999
  Contented nonconformist Wesley plants a garden and

transforms his backyard into a new civilization based on the crop he produces.

Sarah Stewart, *The Gardener*, 1997
  Lydia Grace uses her gift for gardening to transform her temporary home and her dour uncle.

745

KEVIN O'MALLEY, Author/Illustrator

Leo Cockroach. . .Toy Tester
(New York: Walker and Company, 1999)

Subject(s): Animals/Insects; Toys; Business Enterprises

Age range(s): Grades K-2

Major character(s): Leo, Cockroach; Mildred Splatt, Businesswoman; Magnus Worm, Businessman

Time period(s): Indeterminate

Locale(s): Fictional Country

Summary: Leo Cockroach enjoys his self-appointed role as a toy tester for Waddatoy Toys. Nightly, after selecting the toy he considers the best, Leo leaves it on the desk of Mildred Splatt, president and CEO of the company. Ms. Splatt quickly learns that these particular toys sell well, but she doesn't know how they arrive on her desk. Mildred does notice a cockroach in her office and she tries diligently to kill it. Finally Leo grows tired of having shoes thrown at him and being sprayed with bug killer so he seeks employment at Notsogouda Toys across the street. Unfortunately, Mr. Worm keeps Leo in a cage and brings poorly conceived and executed toys to him for approval. As Leo fails to recommend anything, Magnus Worm grows annoyed and Leo devises a plan to escape and return to Mildred Splatt's company. After Leo writes her a letter explaining his role, she puts away the bug spray and Leo becomes a faithful and visible employee. (32 pages)

Where it's reviewed:
Booklist, April 15, 1999, page 1537
Bulletin of the Center for Children's Books, June 1999, page 360
Children's Book Review Service, April 1999, page 101
Publishers Weekly, March 29, 1999, page 104
School Library Journal, April 1999, page 106

Other books by the same author:
Bud, 2000
My Lucky Hat, 1999
Velcome, 1997
The Bear Hunt, 1996

Other books you might like:
Richard Egielski, *Jazper*, 1998
  Jazper, an enterprising insect, finds work to support the family when his father is injured at the tomato plant.
David Kirk, *Miss Spider's New Car*, 1997
  While shopping for a new car, Miss Spider and her husband try out several models.
J. Otto Seibold, *Free Lunch*, 1996
  Mr. Lunch runs afoul of the new, evil and greedy owner of a seed company who has him arrested for spying. Vivian Walsh, co-author.

746

KENNETH OPPEL
TERRY WIDENER, Illustrator

Peg and the Whale

(New York: Simon & Schuster Books for Young Readers, 2000)

Subject(s): Animals/Whales; Fishing; Tall Tales
Age range(s): Grades K-3
Major character(s): Peg, Child, Fisherman
Time period(s): Indeterminate Past
Locale(s): At Sea

Summary: Born aboard her parents' fishing boat, Peg is an award-winning fisherman by the time she's seven years old. In fact, in her quest to catch the biggest fish she conquers everything but a whale. Her father's explanation that a whale is a mammal not a fish does not deter Peg who signs aboard a whaler in hopes of achieving her goal. Using her rod and reel Peg hooks the first whale that comes in sight. Although Peg soon finds herself in the whale's belly she simply builds a ladder from driftwood and climbs in and out the blowhole as needed. Although she lives comfortable in the belly of the whale, she becomes bored with the adventure and is happy the whale swims past her parents' fishing boat so she can move on to bigger adventures. (32 pages)

Where it's reviewed:
Booklist, November 15, 2000, page 639
Bulletin of the Center for Children's Books, July 2000, page 413
Horn Book, July 2000, page 442
Kirkus Reviews, August 15, 2000, page 1203
School Library Journal, November 2000, page 129

Awards the book has won:
Booklist Editors' Choice, 2000

Other books by the same author:
Emma's Emu, 1999
Follow That Star, 1997
Colin's Fantastic Video Adventure, 1985

Other books you might like:
Anne Isaacs, *Swamp Angel*, 1994
    When Angelica sees a problem she takes the initiative to solve it; she earns her nickname by rescuing a wagon train stuck in Dejection Swamp.
Steven Kellogg, *Sally Ann Thunder Ann Whirlwind Crockett: A Tall Tale*, 1995
    Sally Ann departs for the frontier on her eighth birthday where she continues her larger than life exploits and eventually marries Davy Crockett.
Alexis O'Neill, *Loud Emily*, 1998
    Emily's voice is so loud it can be heard over the sounds of a storm at sea thus attracting whales that help to save the ship.

747

SHULAMITH LEVEY OPPENHEIM
DOUG CHAYKA, Illustrator

Yanni Rubbish

(Honesdale, PA: Boyds Mills Press, 1999)

Subject(s): Animals/Donkeys; Mothers and Sons; Problem Solving
Age range(s): Grades K-3
Major character(s): Yanni Stavros, Child, Maintenance Worker (garbage collector); Lamia, Donkey
Time period(s): Indeterminate Past
Locale(s): Greece

Summary: After Yanni's father finds work in Germany, it becomes Yanni's responsibility to continue the family's garbage collection business. All day Yanni drives the cart pulled by Lamia through the village, hauling the smelly garbage, while enduring taunts and teasing from the village boys. With a little help from his mother, Yanni manages to turn the tables so the boys are asking for rides with him. (32 pages)

Where it's reviewed:
Booklist, March 1, 1999, page 1222
Horn Book Guide, Fall 1999, page 282
Kirkus Reviews, January 15, 1999, page 149
Publishers Weekly, March 8, 1999, page 68
School Library Journal, August 1999, page 141

Other books by the same author:
What Is the Moon Full Of?, 1997
I Love You, Bunny Rabbit, 1995
The Lily Cupboard: A Story of the Holocaust, 1995

Other books you might like:
Elisa Bartone, *Peppe the Lamplighter*, 1993
    This Caldecott Honor book tells of hard-working Peppe who labors to support his large immigrant family and win his father's repect.
Lady Borton, *Junk Pile!*, 1997
    Daily Jamie endures the taunts of a new neighbor as his school bus passes her junkyard home, but quietly and creatively she reaches out in friendship.
Eve Bunting, *I Have an Olive Tree*, 1999
    When her grandfather dies, Sophia travels to Greece to discover her roots.
Daniel Kirk, *Trash Trucks!*, 1997
    Each morning, trash trucks make their way through the city streets cleaning the town.
Andrea Zimmerman, *Trashy Town*, 1999
    Mr. Gilly goes through his day as a trash collector.

748

HIAWYN ORAM
SUSAN VARLEY, Illustrator

Princess Chamomile Gets Her Way

(New York: Dutton Children's Books, 1999)

Subject(s): Animals/Mice; Princes and Princesses; Problem Solving
Age range(s): Grades K-2

Major character(s): Chamomile, Royalty (princess), Mouse; Nanny Nettle, Child-Care Giver, Mouse; Bags-Eye, Cat, Store Owner
Time period(s): Indeterminate
Locale(s): Fictional Country

Summary: Nanny Nettle has so many rules against doing anything fun that Princess Chamomile is not even allowed to eat candy at her own birthday party. Deciding that she has had enough of being "not-allowed" to do anything Princess Chamomile dons old clothes, sneaks past still-sleeping Nanny Nettle and escapes the castle grounds in search of a candy store. In no time, Chamomile finds Bags-Eye the Bad Cat's Candy Store and hurries inside. When Bags-Eye expects her to pay for the candy Princess Chamomile announces that princesses are not allowed to handle money. With plans for easy riches, Bags-Eye seizes the opportunity to capture the princess and forces her to write a ransom note to her parents. Since Bags-Eye is illiterate, Chamomile revises the note to reveal her whereabouts and negotiates a piece of candy for every word. While Bags-Eye delivers the note, Chamomile devours all the candy making herself rather sick by the time her parents and Nanny Nettle arrive to rescue her in a title originally published in Great Britain in 1998. (32 pages)

Where it's reviewed:
Booklist, July 1999, page 1953
Horn Book Guide, Fall 1999, page 263
Kirkus Reviews, May 15, 1999, page 805
Publishers Weekly, May 17, 1999, page 77
School Library Journal, June 1999, page 104

Other books by the same author:
Princess Chamomile's Garden, 2000
Badger's Bad Mood, 1998
Badger's Bring Something Party, 1995
The Second Princess, 1994

Other books you might like:
Arnold Lobel, *Mouse Soup*, 1977
   Mouse has a plan that he hopes will keep him out of Weasel's soup pot.
Susan Meddaugh, *Hog-Eye*, 1995
   Quick wits and the ability to read keep a little pig from becoming a wolf's dinner.
Gary Soto, *Chato's Kitchen*, 1995
   Cool cat Chato thinks he's in for a delicious meal when he invites his new neighbors to dinner, but the family of mice has other ideas.

749

WENDY ORR
KERRY MILLARD, Illustrator

Ark in the Park

(New York: Henry Holt and Company, 2000)

Subject(s): Pets; Grandparents; Wishes
Age range(s): Grades 2-3
Major character(s): Sophie, 7-Year-Old; Mrs. Noah, Store Owner, Spouse; Mr. Noah, Store Owner, Spouse
Time period(s): 1990s (1994)
Locale(s): Australia

Summary: For Mr. and Mrs. Noah owning a pet store shaped like a large ship is a logical occupation with a name such as theirs. Though they enjoy their work, they've always wished to have children or grandchildren. For Sophie owning a pet, having cousins or grandparents would be a welcome relief from her dreary life in a high-rise apartment building overlooking a park. Her parents are usually too busy with work or her twin siblings to do things with Sophie, but for her birthday they agree to walk through the park with her to visit the big pet store they can see from their window. That visit is the beginning of the fulfillment of Sophie's and Mr. and Mrs. Noah's complimentary wishes as Sophie is invited to return and help at the store. Originally published in Australia in 1994. (78 pages)

Where it's reviewed:
Booklist, September 15, 2000, page 243
Bulletin of the Center for Children's Books, September 2000, page 33
Horn Book Guide, Fall 2000, page 296
School Library Journal, June 2000, page 123

Other books by the same author:
A Light in Space, 1994
Pegasus & Ooloo-Moo-loo, 1993
Aa-Choo!, 1992

Other books you might like:
Maggie Harrison, *Lizzie's List*, 1993
   Lizzie doesn't depend on wishes to find relatives "missing" from her single-parent family; she makes a list and goes out looking for some to "adopt."
Dick King-Smith, *The Invisible Dog*, 1993
   For Janie imagining a new pet (with help from a neighborhood widow) results in the acquisition of a new dog matching the imaginary one.
Amy Lawson, *Star Baby*, 1992
   Allie's wish on a falling star is fulfilled, but not with the baby sister for which she wished.

750

MARY POPE OSBORNE
GISELLE POTTER, Illustrator

Kate and the Beanstalk

(New York: Anne Schwartz/Atheneum Books for Young Readers, 2000)

Subject(s): Fairy Tales; Folklore; Giants
Age range(s): Grades K-3
Major character(s): Kate, Daughter, Heroine; Mother, Mother, Widow(er); Unnamed Character, Mythical Creature (fairy)
Time period(s): Indeterminate Past
Locale(s): Fictional Country

Summary: In this retelling of a tale that traditionally has a hero it is Kate who tries to help save her poor family from starvation by setting off to sell their cow but instead trading it for magic beans. Mother angrily throws the beans out the window and a remorseful Kate, while seeking refuge in the garden that night, discovers the enormous beanstalk that springs from the magic beans. Ambitiously Kate climbs the beanstalk into the unknown and arrives at a castle that she learns from an old woman has been stolen from a knight along with his treasures.

The old woman (who is actually a fairy in disguise) suggests that Kate is the one to right these past wrongs and restore the castle and its treasures to the knight's widow and daughter. Never suspecting that she is personally linked to this sad history Kate makes three trips into the castle to retrieve the objects and restore them to their rightful owner. Only after she completes her quest and the giant dies in the fall from the toppled beanstalk does Kate learn that the knight killed by the giant was her father and the fairy has tested her worthiness to claim the family treasure. (40 pages)

Where it's reviewed:
Booklist, November 15, 2000, page 639
Children's Bookwatch, September 2000, page 4
Kirkus Reviews, September 1, 2000, page 1289
Publishers Weekly, September 4, 2000, page 106
School Library Journal, October 2000, page 151

Awards the book has won:
Booklist Editors' Choice, 2000
School Library Journal Best Books, 2000

Other books by the same author:
Rocking Horse Christmas, 1997
Molly and the Prince, 1994
American Tall Tales, 1991

Other books you might like:
Ann Keay Beneduce, *Jack and the Beanstalk*, 1999
    A fairy encourages Jack to avenge his father's death at the hands of a giant and magically makes a beanstalk grow to aid him.
Virginia Haviland, *Favorite Fairy Tales Told in England*, 1994
    A folklore collection includes ''Jack and the Beanstalk'' and other well-known tales.
Steven Kellogg, *Jack and the Beanstalk*, 1991
    In one of many retellings of the English tale, Jack outsmarts the giant and his wife in order to save himself and provide for his mother.
Audrey Wood, *Rude Giants*, 1993
    Persuasive Beatrix convinces two rude giants to clean up their act and become good neighbors.

751

MARY POPE OSBORNE

My Brother's Keeper: Virginia's Diary
(New York: Scholastic Inc., 2000)

Series: My America
Subject(s): Diaries; Family; War
Age range(s): Grades 3-5
Major character(s): Virginia B. Dickens, 9-Year-Old, Sister; Jedidiah ''Jed'' Dickens, Teenager, Brother; Pa, Father, Musician
Time period(s): 1860s (1863)
Locale(s): Gettysburg, Pennsylvania

Summary: When Pa and Jed head out of town to hide their horses at a relative's farm Virginia is angry to be left behind with the reverend's family and Jed's diary. Jed instructs her to honestly record all she hears, sees and feels during his absence. Those critical few days stretch into weeks as first

Confederate and then Union troops march through town and gather in the fields to the west and south. Virginia now has far more to record than she would like as she faces the build-up and the aftermath of battle, the theft of her family's belongings from their empty home, and the fear when Pa and Jed do not return. Finally, Pa comes, expecting to find Jed caring for Virginia. When he learns Jed has not been seen he and Virginia tour the many hospitals set up in churches and schools across the countryside until they find Jed, wounded during his escape from Rebel forces, but alive. The historical note concluding the book includes Lincoln's Gettysburg Address. (109 pages)

Where it's reviewed:
Booklist, October 1, 2000, page 341
Horn Book Guide, Fall 2000, page 304
School Library Journal, August 2000, page 156

Awards the book has won:
Notable Social Studies Trade Books for Young People, 2001

Other books by the same author:
Adaline Falling Star, 2000
Standing in the Light: The Captive Diary of Catharine Carey Logan, 1998 (Dear America)
Pirates Past Noon, 1994 (Magic Tree House, Number 4)

Other books you might like:
Sara Harrell Banks, *Abraham's Battle: A Novel of Gettysburg*, 1999
    Abraham, a former slave, serves as an ambulance driver delivering those wounded during the Battle of Gettysburg to makeshift hospitals.
Patricia Lee Gauch, *Thunder at Gettysburg*, 1975
    The story of 14-year-old Tillie, inadvertently caught up in the Battle at Gettysburg was reissued in 1990.
Nancy Johnson, *My Brother's Keeper: A Civil War Story*, 1997
    Orphaned Josh joins the 20th Maine regiment as a drummer boy just before the Battle for Little Round Top.

752

CAROLYN OTTO
MEGAN LLOYD, Illustrator

Pioneer Church
(New York: Henry Holt and Company, 1999)

Subject(s): American History; Christian Life; Pioneers
Age range(s): Grades 2-5
Major character(s): Elisabeth Lapp, Settler; Zachary Lapp, Settler
Time period(s): Indeterminate Past; 1990s
Locale(s): Elisabethville, Pennsylvania

Summary: Elisabeth and Zachary Lapp are one of the first four German families to settle in a remote Pennsylvania valley early in the 18th century. The men build a log cabin church atop a hill that serves the growing community for many years as school, social hall, meeting place, and hospital during the Revolutionary War. After the church burns a new larger church is built in the same location. By the end of World War II it too closes as people begin to worship in more modern facilities in the valley. Eventually, the old church is restored and continues to be used on special occasions such as Easter sunrise services. An author's note gives the historical background of a church in Brickerville, Pennsylvania, on which the story is based. (32 pages)

Where it's reviewed:
Booklist, October 1, 1999, page 374
Bulletin of the Center for Children's Books, December 1999, page 145
Kirkus Reviews, September 15, 1999, page 1504
Publishers Weekly, January 3, 2000, page 78
School Library Journal, December 1999, page 109

Awards the book has won:
Notable Social Studies Trade Books for Young People, 2000

Other books by the same author:
Our Puppies Are Growing, 1998
What Color Is Camouflage?, 1996

Raccoon at Clear Creek Road, 1995

Other books you might like:
Debbie Atwell, *Barn*, 1996
    Changes in the use of a barn over two centuries provide an overview of American life.
Virginia Lee Burton, *The Little House*, 1942
    A Caldecott Medal winner reveals the passage of time and family connectedness over generations through the experiences of a house.
Donald Hall, *Old Home Day*, 1996
    The cycle of growth, decline and renewal of a New England town is described through the history of its settlers.
Anne Shelby, *Homeplace*, 1995
    While rocking a grandchild, a grandmother tells the history of the family from the original building of the family homestead to the present.

P

| 753 |

V.J. PACILIO
SCOTT COOK, Illustrator

Ling Cho and His Three Friends
(New York: Farrar Straus Giroux, 2000)

Subject(s): Friendship; Conduct of Life; Stories in Rhyme
Age range(s): Grades 2-4
Major character(s): Ling Cho, Farmer
Time period(s): Indeterminate Past
Locale(s): China

Summary: Annually, three of Ling Cho's friends and their families come from their farms to the north, east and west to assist Ling Cho's family with the harvest. When the work is complete the four families celebrate another successful year. Ling Cho realizes that his farm is the most prosperous of the four because his friends have inherited land with poor soil and he struggles to find a way to help them without hurting their pride. The year that Ling Cho's wheat crop is so bountiful he cannot store it all he realizes he has a way to assist his friends. To each he gives a wagon full of wheat with instructions to sell it in their city, returning half the payment to him and keeping the other half as payment for their services. When the friends return, each has a tale of woe as to why they have no coins for Ling Cho. Each friend learns an important lesson from the experience but only one will be invited to help Ling Cho with future harvests. The original tale written in rhymed couplets is the author's first book. (32 pages)

Where it's reviewed:
Booklist, March 1, 2000, page 1252
Children's Book Review Service, April 2000, page 98
Horn Book Guide, Fall 2000, page 278
Publishers Weekly, March 20, 2000, page 92
School Library Journal, May 2000, page 151

Other books you might like:
Dominique Falda, *The Treasure Chest*, 1999
  Other forest animals imagine the riches that could be in the chest Squirrel digs up in the forest but Squirrel knows true wealth is his friends.

Linda Fang, *The Ch'i-lin Purse: A Collection of Ancient Chinese Stories*, 1995
  This collection includes illustrated retellings of nine folktales.
Ai-Ling Louie, *Yeh-Shen: A Cinderella Story from China*, 1982
  Kindness of heart gathers riches for poor Yeh-Shen while her cruel, devious stepmother and stepsister receive their just reward.

| 754 |

SOYUNG PAK
SUSAN HARTUNG, Illustrator

Dear Juno
(New York: Viking, 1999)

Subject(s): Grandmothers; Letters; Korean Americans
Age range(s): Grades K-2
Major character(s): Juno, Child, Student—Elementary School; Grandma, Grandmother
Time period(s): 1990s (1999)
Locale(s): United States; Korea, South (near Seoul)

Summary: In the author's first book, Juno recognizes the stamp on the letter that he holds and knows it is from Grandma. He's not able to read the Korean characters, but from the picture and the dried flower Grandma encloses Juno "reads" her message. At school, Juno proudly shows the letter to his teacher who pins it to the board. Right after school, Juno begins his response by picking a leaf from his swinging tree. Then he draws three pictures to show his parents next to their house, his dog playing under his swinging tree and himself looking up at an airplane in a starry sky. When Grandma replies, Juno understands from items included with her letter exactly what she's saying and he looks forward to her visit. (32 pages)

Where it's reviewed:
Booklist, November 15, 1999, page 636
Horn Book Guide, Spring 2000, page 48
Kirkus Reviews, October 15, 1999, page 1650

Publishers Weekly, October 25, 1999, page 79
School Library Journal, December 1999, page 109

Other books you might like:
Frank Asch, *Dear Brother*, 1992
  As two mice brothers read the letters of their ancestors they realize the importance of their relationship and letter writing.
Judith Caseley, *Dear Annie*, 1992
  A story unfolds in the correspondence between Annie and her grandfather.
Sook Nyul Choi, *Yunmi and Halmoni's Trip*, 1997
  Yunmi travels with her grandmother to Seoul to visit relatives.

755

MARGIE PALATINI
JACK E. DAVIS, Illustrator

Bedhead
(New York: Simon & Schuster Books for Young Readers, 2000)

Subject(s): Hair; Humor; Problem Solving
Age range(s): Grades K-3
Major character(s): Oliver, Son, Student—Elementary School; Mary Margaret, Student—Elementary School; Mrs. Oppenheimer, Teacher
Time period(s): 2000s (2000)
Locale(s): United States

Summary: When Oliver looks in the bathroom mirror and sees a serious case of ''bedhead'' his screams bring his family running. They all try to help Oliver conquer the problem but no amount of water, spray or gel controls the unruly locks. Brushing is no help because the brush becomes stuck in the gel so finally Oliver slaps a cap on his head and goes to school. The perfect solution will not work as Mary Margaret quickly points out because it is class picture day and, as Mrs. Oppenheimer reminds everyone, no hats allowed. Oliver leaves the hat on until the very last second, but as soon as it is removed his hair bounces back into ''bedhead'' with such force that Mary Margaret and Mrs. Oppenheimer are hit by the brush as it is flung loose. Oliver's class has a memorable school picture. (34 pages)

Where it's reviewed:
Bulletin of the Center for Children's Books, October 2000, page 78
Children's Book Review Service, August 2000, page 159
Horn Book Guide, Spring 2001, page 47
Kirkus Reviews, May 15, 2000, page 718
School Library Journal, July 2000, page 84

Other books by the same author:
Zak's Lunch, 1998
Zoom Broom, 1998
Moosetache, 1997
Piggie Pie!, 1995 (ALA Notable Book)

Other books you might like:
Pat Brisson, *Bertie's Picture Day*, 2000
  Thanks to his sister Bertie has a terrifically interesting haircut to go with his shiner and missing teeth for his noteworthy school picture.

Nancy Cote, *Palm Trees*, 1993
  A bad hair day threatens a friendship when Renne makes fun of Millie's appearance.
Nikki Grimes, *Wild, Wild Hair*, 1997
  Tisa dreads Monday mornings when Mommy combs her wild, wild hair and styles it into twenty beautiful braids.
Linda Breiner Milstein, *Amanda's Perfect Hair*, 1993
  Amanda gives herself a haircut in hopes that people will notice her for something other than her hair.

756

MARGIE PALATINI
HOWARD FINE, Illustrator

Ding Dong Ding Dong
(New York: Hyperion Books for Children, 1999)

Subject(s): Animals/Monkeys; Work; Humor
Age range(s): Grades K-3
Major character(s): Big Guy, Ape, Salesman
Time period(s): Indeterminate Past
Locale(s): New York, New York; Hollywood, California

Summary: Big Guy graduates at the top of his class with a degree in Monkey Business but still he can't make a sale as he goes door-to-door with his sample case of Ape-On Cosmetics. He decides he's in the wrong location and goes to the Big Apple hoping for better luck. Instead he's mistaken for a window washer, a job he takes on while peddling his wares as he climbs the building, one floor of dirty windows at a time. Just as the Big Guy thinks he has a customer, he loses his footing and falls to the street where he's discovered and signed to a Hollywood contract. (32 pages)

Where it's reviewed:
Bulletin of the Center for Children's Books, December 1999, page 145
Children's Book Review Service, December 1999, page 40
Kirkus Reviews, July 15, 1999, page 1137
Publishers Weekly, September 13, 1999, page 83
School Library Journal, September 1999, page 199

Other books by the same author:
Zoom Broom, 1998
Moosetache, 1997
Piggie Pie!, 1995

Other books you might like:
Cynthia DeFelice, *Casey in the Bath*, 1996
  After Casey's mother buys bath soap from a door-to-door salesman reluctant Casey not only enjoys his bath but also comes out of the tub clean.
Esphyr Slobodkina, *Caps for Sale: A Tale of a Peddler, Some Monkeys and Their Moneky Business*, 1947
  In an award-winning classic, a group of mischievous monkeys interferes with a peddler's ability to sell his caps.
James Stevenson, *Heat Wave at Mud Flat*, 1997
  Raymond the Rainmaker sells the parched residents of Mud Flat umbrellas and then charges an additional fee for the rain.

757

MARGIE PALATINI
HENRY COLE, Illustrator

Mooseltoe

(New York: Hyperion Books for Children, 2000)

Subject(s): Christmas; Animals/Moose; Trees
Age range(s): Grades K-3
Major character(s): Moose, Moose, Father
Time period(s): Indeterminate
Locale(s): Fictional Country

Summary: Highly organized Moose completes all the items on his long checklist of Christmas preparations. Feeling quite proud for completing the shopping, cooking and decorating for the holiday, Moose is chagrined when the family notices on Christmas Eve that there is no tree to decorate. After tromping through the snow past one empty tree lot after another Moose returns home knowing there's only one solution to the problem. With the glue pot in hand, his family arranges Moose's spectacular mustache into a tree shape and decorates Moose with lights and ornaments. It's not perfect, but it fits the spirit of the season. (32 pages)

Where it's reviewed:
Booklist, September 1, 2000, page 134
Horn Book Guide, Spring 2001, page 47
Publishers Weekly, September 25, 2000, page 76
School Library Journal, October 2000, page 62

Other books by the same author:
Zak's Lunch, 1998
Zoom Broom, 1998
Elf Help: http://www.falala.com, 1997
Moosetache, 1997
Piggie Pie!, 1995 (ALA Notable Book)

Other books you might like:
Laura Joffe Numeroff, *If You Give a Moose a Muffin*, 1991
    There's no telling what can happen if you give a moose that first muffin; he may just ask for something more.
Daniel Pinkwater, *Blue Moose*, 1975
    A restaurant owner hires a talking blue moose to serve as the head waiter for the winter.
Bernard Wiseman, *Morris and Boris at the Circus*, 1988
    Morris and Boris are looking forward to seeing the circus and are surprised when they become participants.

758

JERRY PALLOTTA
DAVID BIEDRZYCKI, Illustrator

Dory Story

(Watertown, MA: Talewinds/Charlesbridge Publishing, 2000)

Subject(s): Boats and Boating; Animals/Marine; Imagination
Age range(s): Grades K-2
Major character(s): Danny, Child
Time period(s): 2000s (2000)
Locale(s): United States

Summary: Fascinated by plankton, Danny wants to learn more about what happens to them during the day when they are not visible. Taking a forbidden solo trip in the family dory, Danny observes shrimp eating plankton and in turn being eaten by sand eels. A school of mackerel devours the sand eels and then bluefish come in pursuit of the mackerel. As Danny stands to get a better look at the bluefish, five tuna appear chasing the bluefish and then an even larger predator—the killer whale—comes after the tuna. Danny's almost caught in this food web when his dory capsizes—in the bathtub where he's been playing and imagining the events. (32 pages)

Where it's reviewed:
Booklist, February 1, 2000, page 1019
Children's Book Review Service, May 2000, page 111
Horn Book Guide, Fall 2000, page 278
School Library Journal, March 2000, page 210

Other books by the same author:
The Freshwater Alphabet Book, 1996
Going Lobstering, 1990
The Frog Alphabet Book. . .and Other Awesome Amphibians, 1990

Other books you might like:
Kimberley Smith Brady, *Keeper for the Sea*, 1996
    Grandpa releases the large bluefish that he and his granddaughter catch on an early morning fishing trip.
Brenda Z. Guiberson, *Lobster Boat*, 1993
    Tommy spends a day on his uncle's lobster boat, helping to check pots and replace bait.
Jonathan London, *Old Salt, Young Salt*, 1996
    When Dad becomes seasick his inexperienced son catches the salmon without help and guides the boat back to the harbor.
April Pulley Sayres, *Turtle, Turtle, Watch Out!*, 2000
    From hatching to maturity sea turtles face the risk of being part of the food chain for some animals.

759

SUSAN PARADIS, Author/Illustrator

My Daddy

(Asheville, NC: Front Street, 1998)

Subject(s): Fathers and Sons; Family; Imagination
Age range(s): Preschool
Major character(s): Unnamed Character, Child, Son; Unnamed Character, Father
Time period(s): 1990s (1998)
Locale(s): United States

Summary: A young boy admires the many things that his father can do such as crossing the street alone, riding a two-wheeler, and reading a bedtime story with him. With his father, the boy feels safe and secure as well and he enjoys playing with his father and receiving his father's hugs. (30 pages)

Where it's reviewed:
Booklist, July 1998, page 1878
Horn Book Guide, Fall 1998, page 277
Kirkus Reviews, June 1, 1998, page 815
Publishers Weekly, June 1, 1998, page 60
School Library Journal, January 1999, page 100

Other books you might like:

Frank Asch, *Just Like Daddy*, 1984
  A young bear describes all the activities he does which are just like daddy.
Mercer Mayer, *Just Me and My Dad*, 1982
  When father and son go camping together it becomes unclear who is taking care of whom.
Laura Joffe Numeroff, *What Mommies Do Best, What Daddies Do Best*, 1998
  These two back to back texts feature the different things which mothers and fathers do well.

760

HERMAN PARISH
LYNN SWEAT, Illustrator

Amelia Bedelia 4 Mayor

(New York: Greenwillow Books, 1999)

Subject(s): Elections; Humor; Government
Age range(s): Grades 1-3
Major character(s): Amelia Bedelia, Housekeeper, Candidate; Mayor Thomas, Political Figure; Mr. Rogers, Employer (Amelia's)
Time period(s): 1990s (1999)
Locale(s): United States

Summary: Amelia Bedelia takes Mr. Rogers at his word when he suggests she should run for mayor and runs all the way to Mayor Thomas's office in City Hall. Amelia interrupts a press conference and with her literal interpretation of what she hears, she creates quite a clamor. In frustration, Mayor Thomas suggests that Amelia could not even be the town dogcatcher so Amelia, offended, challenges the mayor by entering the upcoming election. The lively campaign leads to a debate between the two candidates that is interrupted by a dog chasing a cat. When Amelia catches the barking dog she proves her point that she is capable of being dogcatcher and withdraws from the mayoral contest. (48 pages)

Where it's reviewed:
Booklist, August 1999, page 2058
Horn Book Guide, Spring 2000, page 62
Publishers Weekly, August 2, 1999, page 87
School Library Journal, September 1999, page 1999

Other books by the same author:
Bravo, Amelia Bedelia, 1997
Good Driving, Amelia Bedelia, 1995

Other books you might like:
Betsy Byars, *The Golly Sisters Ride Again*, 1994
  Rose and May-May tackle the American frontier with the same enthusiasm and naivete that Amelia brings to the American electoral system.
Judy Delton, *Molly for Mayor*, 1999
  In an entry in the *Pee Wee Scouts* series Molly searches for a campaign idea that tops competitor Roger's offer of candy in exchange for votes.
Elinor Batezat Sisulu, *The Day Gogo Went to Vote*, 1996
  Although she is in poor health, elderly Gogo insists on exercising her right to vote for the first time in a South African election.

761

FRANCES PARK
GINGER PARK, Co-Author
CHRISTOPHER ZHONG-YUAN ZHANG, Illustrator

The Royal Bee

(Honesdale, PA: Boyds Mills Press, 2000)

Subject(s): Poverty; Schools; Literacy
Age range(s): Grades K-3
Major character(s): Song-ho, Child, Son; Master Min, Teacher
Time period(s): 19th century (late)
Locale(s): Republic of Korea

Summary: In the late nineteenth century, education in Korea is only for the wealthy, but Master Min appreciates the courage and determination of the poor boy secretly eavesdropping at the classroom door. When cold weather arrives, Master Min invites Song-ho inside, asks the students to quiz him on the material they have studied and, when Song-ho answers every question correctly, welcomes him to the class. In the spring, Song-ho's classmates choose him to represent the school in The Royal Bee and present him with a gift of a ceremonial costume to wear to the event. Song-ho hopes to bring home a surprise for his widowed mother in a story based on the authors' family history. (32 pages)

Where it's reviewed:
Horn Book Guide, Fall 2000, page 278
Kirkus Reviews, March 1, 2000, page 305
Publishers Weekly, January 31, 2000, page 106
School Library Journal, April 2000, page 111

Other books by the same author:
My Freedom Trip: A Child's Escape from North Korea, 1998
  (IRA Children's Book Award)

Other books you might like:
Marie Bradby, *More than Anything Else*, 1995
  Booker T. Washington yearns for the freedom literacy will give him.
Elizabeth Fitzgerald Howard, *Virgie Goes to School with Us Boys*, 2000
  In post Civil War Tennessee Virgie convinces her family that she too is capable of benefiting from an education.
Tony Johnston, *Amber on the Mountain*, 1994
  Isolated in her family's mountain home, a new world opens to Amber when she is taught to read and write.

762

LINDA SUE PARK
JEAN TSENG, Illustrator
MOU-SIEN TSENG, Illustrator

Seesaw Girl

(New York: Clarion Books, 1999)

Subject(s): Gender Roles; Historical; Cultures and Customs
Age range(s): Grades 4-6
Major character(s): Jade, 12-Year-Old, Noblewoman; Willow, Cousin (Jade's), Noblewoman; Tiger Heart, Brother (older), Nobleman
Time period(s): 1650s

Locale(s): Republic of Korea (near Seoul)

Summary: To relieve the monotony of a girl's life of washing, serving food and sewing Jade delights in planning pranks with the help of Willow. After Willow's marriage, Jade misses her companion for, according to custom, Willow now belongs to her husband's household and noblewomen rarely leave their homes. Jade tries unsuccessfully to sneak out to see Willow, but only brings dishonor to her family. Tiger Heart is patient with his sister's many questions and offers what insights he can to life beyond the Inner Court of their home. As the eldest son Tiger is being groomed to take over his father's role as advisor to the king and frequently accompanies his father to the palace. Tiger Heart brings Jade sweets from the market and information about the life she will never know. Ever curious, Jade devises a primitive seesaw and enlists the help of a younger cousin to jump on one end and propel her into the air so she can get a brief glimpse of what is outside the wall surrounding her home. A concluding author's note gives historical background for the story and a bibliography offers options for further reading. (90 pages)

Where it's reviewed:
Booklist, September 1, 1999, page 134
Horn Book Guide, Spring 2000, page 69
Publishers Weekly, August 9, 1999, page 352
School Library Journal, September 1999, page 228

Other books by the same author:
The Kite Fighters, 2000

Other books you might like:
Debra Fritsch, *A Part of the Ribbon: A Time Travel Adventure through the History of Korea*, 1997
   Six-year-old Charlotte and her 13-year-old brother Jeffrey travel through 3000 years of Korean history.
Patricia McMahon, *Chi-Hoon: A Korean Girl*, 1998
   Photographs illustrate one week in the life of Chi-Hoon, an eight-year-old Korean girl living in Seoul.
Anne E. Neuberger, *The Girl-Son*, 1994
   In the late 19th century Induk Pahk's widowed mother disguises her daughter as a boy so she can attend school and better her station in life.

763

JOANNE PARTIS, Author/Illustrator

Stripe

(Minneapolis: Carolrhoda Books, Inc., 2000)

Subject(s): Animals/Tigers; Parent and Child; Adventure and Adventurers
Age range(s): Grades K-1
Major character(s): Stripe, Tiger (young), Son
Time period(s): Indeterminate
Locale(s): Fictional Country

Summary: In the author's first book, Stripe's parents warn him never to venture into the dangerous jungle alone, but while the parents nap on a hot day Stripe seeks a cooler environ in the shady jungle. Fascinated, Stripe wanders farther and farther from home when he spots a beehive and tries to reach the honey. The angry bees chase Stripe who leaps into the river where he's safe from bees, but not from hungry crocodiles.

Floating on a log, Stripe hurries downstream ahead of the crocodiles and into a large cave that turns out to be a whale's open mouth. Frightened, but still resourceful, Stripe tickles the whale with his tail, the whale sneezes and Stripe flies out the blowhole and back to his home before his parents awaken from their nap. (32 pages)

Where it's reviewed:
Booklist, April 15, 2000, page 1553
Horn Book Guide, Fall 2000, page 254
Kirkus Reviews, March 1, 2000, page 306
Publishers Weekly, May 1, 2000, page 69
School Library Journal, July 2000, page 85

Other books you might like:
Marsha Diane Arnold, *Heart of a Tiger*, 1995
   A young tiger saves Beautiful Bengal from a hunter's trick and earns the name Heart of a Tiger.
Libuse Palecek, *Brave as a Tiger*, 1995
   Other tigers take timid Fang's stripes until he displays the courage expected of his breed.
Jane Simmons, *Come Along, Daisy!*, 1998
   Daisy doesn't intend to lose sight of Mama Duck but she has and now she's alone, lost and surrounded by scary sounds.

764

KATHERINE PATERSON

Preacher's Boy

(New York: Clarion Books, 1999)

Subject(s): Family Life; Fathers and Sons; Christian Life
Age range(s): Grades 5-7
Major character(s): Robert Burns ''Robbie'' Hewitt, 10-Year-Old, Son; Reverend Hewitt, Religious, Father
Time period(s): 1890s (1899)
Locale(s): Leonardstown, Vermont

Summary: The strain of living up to the town's expectations of proper behavior and cleanliness for the son of the Reverend Hewitt, congregational minister, proves to be more than Robbie can handle in the summer of 1899. By declaring himself an ''apeist'' he thinks he can avoid the Ten Commandments, the end of the world as the new century begins, and the consequences of his well-known temper. However, his ten years as a preacher's boy have molded his character more than Robbie wants to admit and eventually he has to face himself and his responsibilities or an innocent man could go to the gallows. (168 pages)

Where it's reviewed:
The Book Report, January 2000, page 69
Booklist, August 1999, page 2044
Horn Book, September 1999, page 615
Publishers Weekly, June 21, 1999, page 69
School Library Journal, August 1999, page 160

Awards the book has won:
Booklist Editors' Choice, 1999
Jefferson Cup, 2000

Other books by the same author:
Jip: His Story, 1996
Flip-Flop Girl, 1994

Lyddie, 1991
Bridge to Terebithia, 1977 (Newbery Medal)

Other books you might like:
Patricia Beatty, *Behave Yourself, Bethany Brant!*, 1986
 Bethany, a circuit preacher's daughter struggles to adjust
 to unexpected changes in her life.
Eve Bunting, *Blackwater*, 1999
 Guilt weighs heavily on Brodie who feels responsible for
 the accidental deaths of two people for whom his pastor
 father conducts funerals.
Robert Newton Peck, *Soup*, 1974
 Although Soup is no preacher's boy his well-intentioned,
 though misguided, ideas are sometimes enough to prick
 even his conscience.
Stephanie Tolan, *Save Halloween!*, 1993
 As a fundamentalist preacher's daughter, Johnna's participation in the class Halloween play is in defiance of her
 family's beliefs.

765

KATHERINE PATERSON
VLADIMIR VAGIN, Illustrator

The Wide-Awake Princess
(New York: Clarion Books, 2000)

Subject(s): Kings, Queens, Rulers, etc.; Gifts; Conduct of Life
Age range(s): Grades 2-4
Major character(s): Miranda, Royalty, Daughter; Gwen, Arti-
san (weaver), Widow(er); Amonth, Grandfather, Worker
Time period(s): Indeterminate Past
Locale(s): Fictional Country

Summary: As an infant, Miranda receives the gift of being
wide-awake and alert, a trait that makes her more observant
than most royalty. Although her parents die when she is only
twelve, Miranda is not designated queen because of her age
and because the three nobles squabbling over the role of king
do not think her capable of the job. Miranda wanders the
countryside getting to know the kingdom and the people
living in it. She meets Amonth and brings medicinal herbs he
cannot afford to his ailing granddaughter. Miranda admires
the tapestry Amonth's daughter Gwen is weaving to tell the
history of the country. The injustice of the life of the peasants
disturbs Miranda and for five years she prepares them and
herself to change the kingdom. When finally the peasants are
ready to revolt, Miranda's plan peacefully removes the power
from the nobles and makes Miranda queen of her people. (48
pages)

Where it's reviewed:
Booklist, March 15, 2000, page 1378
Horn Book Guide, Fall 2000, page 296
Kirkus Reviews, March 15, 2000, page 388
Publishers Weekly, March 13, 2000, page 84

Other books by the same author:
Celia and the Sweet, Sweet Water, 1998
Marvin's Best Christmas Present Ever, 1997
The King's Equal, 1992

Other books you might like:
M.M. Kaye, *The Ordinary Princess*, 1984
 Princess Amethyst enjoys the fairy's pronouncement that
 she will be ordinary as she has a happy, unconventional
 royal life.
Howard Pyle, *Bearskin*, 1997
 An abandoned infant raised by a bear with magical powers
 grows up to fulfill his destiny and marry the king's daugh-
 ter.
Jane Yolen, *Not One Damsel in Distress: World Folktales for
Strong Girls*, 2000
 Thirteen folktales feature strong and resourceful women
 from different countries.

766

ANN WHITFORD PAUL
MAGGIE SMITH, Illustrator

Everything to Spend the Night from A to Z
(New York: Melanie Kroupa/DK Publishing Inc., 1999)

Subject(s): Grandfathers; Bedtime; Stories in Rhyme
Age range(s): Grades K-2
Major character(s): Grandpa, Grandfather; Unnamed Charac-
ter, Child
Time period(s): 1990s (1999)
Locale(s): United States

Summary: Confident that she has packed everything she could
possible need for a visit to Grandpa's house, a little girl
excitedly shows him apples to share and elephant earmuffs for
him to wear if she becomes too loud. Jigsaw puzzles and a
music box keep her entertained while Grandpa drinks tea and
naps in his chair. Although she's not tired she plugs in her
nightlight and brushes her teeth with her carefully packed
toothbrush. Then, she pulls the last few items from her bag,
zips the zipper and realizes that she packed a pillow, but not
pajamas. Fortunately, Grandpa's fit just fine. (32 pages)

Where it's reviewed:
Booklist, April 1, 1999, page 1422
Horn Book, March 1999, page 200
Kirkus Reviews, March 1, 1999, page 379
Publishers Weekly, February 22, 1999, page 93
School Library Journal, June 1999, page 104

Other books by the same author:
Silly Sadie, Silly Samuel, 2000
Hello Toes! Hello Feet!, 1998
The Seasons Sewn: A Year in Patchwork, 1996
Eight Hands Round: A Patchwork Alphabet, 1991

Other books you might like:
Shirley Neitzel, *The Bag I'm Taking to Grandma's*, 1995
 A young boy and his mother disagree about just which
 items are essential to pack into his bag for a trip to
 Grandma's house.
Joseph Slate, *Miss Bindergarten Stays Home from Kindergar-
ten*, 2000
 A rhythmic tale alphabetically describes what happens in
 class on the day that Miss Bindergarten is too sick to go to
 school.

Jan Slepian, *Emily Just in Time*, 1998

Although Emily's growing she's still not ready to pack her bags for an overnight stay at Grandma's house.

767

TRACEY CAMPBELL PEARSON, Author/Illustrator

Where Does Joe Go?

(New York: Farrar Straus Giroux, 1999)

Subject(s): Restaurants; Winter; Santa Claus
Age range(s): Grades K-1
Major character(s): Joe, Store Owner, Aged Person
Time period(s): 1990s
Locale(s): United States

Summary: Every Spring Joe returns to town to reopen his snack bar from which he sells hot dogs and ice cream cones during the summer. Each fall, after Joe boards up the snack bar, he vanishes for the winter. The townspeople speculate about just where Joe goes when he's not operating the snack bar. Maybe he's at the beach, or flying to the moon or having tea with the queen. Joe tells no one where he goes in the winter, but the concluding picture gives a big clue to alert readers. (32 pages)

Where it's reviewed:
Booklist, November 1, 1999, page 525
Horn Book Guide, Spring 2000, page 49
Kirkus Reviews, October 15, 1999, page 1650
School Library Journal, October 1999, page 122

Other books by the same author:
The Purple Hat, 1997
The Howling Dog, 1991
Sing a Song of Sixpence, 1985

Other books you might like:
Stephen Krensky, *How Santa Got His Job*, 1998
Santa tries a variety of different jobs before meeting some toy-making elves and conceiving an idea to use his skills for the benefit of children.
Tom Paxton, *The Story of Santa Claus*, 1995
When an overworked woodcarver moves to the North Pole for assistance from elves with his toy production, he must initiate a delivery system.
Viveca Larn Sundvall, *Santa's Winter Vacation*, 1994
On a family vacation, three brothers meet an elderly, bearded man and his wife who just might be—guess who?

768

JUDY PEDERSEN, Author/Illustrator

When Night Time Comes Near

(New York: Viking, 2000)

Subject(s): Bedtime; Neighbors and Neighborhoods; Family Life
Age range(s): Preschool
Major character(s): Unnamed Character, Child, Son; Mr. Mann, Aged Person, Neighbor
Time period(s): 2000s
Locale(s): United States

Summary: When night time comes near in one little boy's neighborhood and the setting sun turns the house to gold, he knows it's time to ride his bike home, past Mr. Mann folding the flag and the neighbors putting away their croquet set. The boy also notices the lights come on in the houses, sees the flowers closing their petals for the night and watches the squirrels hurrying to their nests to sleep. The cat comes into the house, the boy bids good night to the neighbors and greets the rising moon before entering his warm home and hugging his parents. After getting ready for bed, bidding his parents and cat good night the boy is ready to sleep. (40 pages)

Where it's reviewed:
Children's Book Review Service, May 2000, page 111
Horn Book Guide, Fall 2000, page 254
Publishers Weekly, January 10, 2000, page 66
School Library Journal, February 2000, page 96
Smithsonian, November 2000, page 64

Awards the book has won:
Smithsonian's Notable Books for Children, 2000

Other books by the same author:
Out in the Country, 1991
The Tiny Patient, 1989

Other books you might like:
Kate Banks, *And If the Moon Could Talk*, 1998
As parent and child begin their nightly bedtime ritual inside the house the moon observes what is happening outside all over the world.
Margaret Wise Brown, *Goodnight Moon*, 1947
In a classic of bedtime stories, a little rabbit's bedtime ritual is to say goodnight to everything in sight, including the moon.
Jan Ormerod, *Moonlight*, 1982
Through illustrations alone a young girl's moonlit bedtime ritual is portrayed.
Jane Yolen, *Nocturne*, 1997
With mom and a flashlight a young boy wanders through the "velvet night" before snuggling into bed to join the animals in rest.

769

LYNNE RAE PERKINS, Author/Illustrator

All Alone in the Universe

(New York: Greenwillow Books, 1999)

Subject(s): Friendship; Neighbors and Neighborhoods; Family Relations
Age range(s): Grades 5-8
Major character(s): Debbie Pelbry, Student—Junior High, Friend (Maureen's); Maureen Berck, Friend (Debbie's), Classmate; Glenna Flaiber, Friend (Maureen's), Neighbor (Maureen's)
Time period(s): 1960s (1969)
Locale(s): Seldem

Summary: In the picture book author's first novel, Debbie learns, in a few months' time, that a solid friendship can slowly dissolve and leave one feeling "all alone in the universe." Maureen has been Debbie's absolute best friend since third grade so at first Debbie is unconcerned when Maureen neither returns nor initiates phone calls. Gradually, Debbie becomes aware that Glenna Flaiber is intruding in their relationship and she notes that three is a number that simply doesn't work on carnival rides, walks to school or friendship. For much of the summer Debbie is miserable, but with help from supportive adults she gains insight into her situation and, as the new school year begins, is cheered by the promise of a new friendship. (140 pages)

Where it's reviewed:
Booklist, September 1, 1999, page 127
Horn Book, September 1999, page 616
Publishers Weekly, October 18, 1999, page 84
Riverbank Review, Winter 1999-2000, page 29
School Library Journal, November 1999, page 162

Awards the book has won:
Booklist Editors' Choice, 1999
Horn Book Fanfare, 2000

Other books by the same author:
Clouds for Dinner, 1997 (Riverbank Review Children's Books of Distinction)
Home Lovely, 1995 (Boston Globe-Horn Book Honor Book)

Other books you might like:
Judy Blume, *Just as Long as We're Together*, 1987
When a new student arrives in town, two young teens face the challenge of trying to include a third person in their friendship.
Phyllis Reynolds Naylor, *All but Alice*, 1992
In one of many titles about Alice growing up, she decides to give up her goal to be popular if it means she must forsake her good friend Patrick.
Rachel Vail, *The Friendship Ring*, 1998
Each title in this series focuses on one friend's life and interactions with the others in their ring of seventh grade friends.

770

JULIE ANNE PETERS

Romance of the Snob Squad

(Boston: Little, Brown, and Company, 1999)

Subject(s): Family Problems; Schools; Scientific Experiments
Age range(s): Grades 4-6
Major character(s): Jenny Solano, 6th Grader (overweight); Prairie Cactus, 6th Grader, Handicapped; Hugh Torkerson, 6th Grader
Time period(s): 1990s (1999)
Locale(s): United States

Summary: When the Snob Squad learns that one of their members has a crush on Hugh Torkerson, a.k.a. Tork the Dork, they decide to concoct a plan to make sure that Hugh asks Prairie to the school dance. Of course, in the meantime, the group also has to plan and execute a science project, and Jenny has to deal with her family conflicts. Eventually the Snob Squad's project of training a pet rat attracts Hugh's interest, and gradually Jenny's family starts to work out their problems. (166 pages)

Where it's reviewed:
Booklist, April 1, 1999, page 1414

Bulletin of the Center for Children's Books, March 1999, page 253
Kirkus Reviews, March 1, 1999, page 380
Publishers Weekly, April 12, 1999, page 78
School Library Journal, June 1999, page 136

Other books by the same author:
Revenge of the Snob Squad, 1998
How Do You Spell GEEK?, 1996
The Stinky Sneakers Contest, 1993

Other books you might like:
Eve Bunting, *Our Sixth-Grade Sugar Babies*, 1991
Vicki and her friends worry that their sixth-grade project will make the wrong impression with the seventh-grade boys they like.
Barthe DeClements, *Sixth Grade Can Really Kill You*, 1985
Helen is sure she'll be in sixth grade forever, until her reading teacher recognizes her learning disability.
Richard Mosher, *The Taxi Navigator*, 1996
Kyle prefers to ride around with his taxi-driving uncle rather than spend time with his parents who are constantly fighting.

771

LISA WESTBERG PETERS
SAM WILLIAMS, Illustrator

Cold Little Duck, Duck, Duck

(New York: Greenwillow Books/HarperCollins Publishers, 2000)

Subject(s): Animals/Ducks; Spring; Stories in Rhyme
Age range(s): Grades K-1
Major character(s): Duck, Duck
Time period(s): 1990s
Locale(s): United States

Summary: When a young duck arrives at the pond too soon, soon, soon she finds her feet stuck on the pond's still frozen surface. The helpful bear cub suggests she hurry away, but Duck uses the power of positive thinking to solve her problem. As Duck concentrates on all she loves about the pond from worms and beetles to grass and apple buds, changes begin. By the time little Duck opens her eyes spring, spring, spring has arrived. (32 pages)

Where it's reviewed:
Booklist, May 15, 2000, page 1749
Horn Book, July 2000, page 443
Publishers Weekly, March 20, 2000, page 92
Riverbank Review, Summer 2000, page 30
School Library Journal, May 2000, page 151

Awards the book has won:
ALA Notable Children's Books, 2001

Other books by the same author:
When the Fly Flew In..., 1994
Purple Delicious Blackberry Jam, 1992
Good Morning, River!, 1990

Other books you might like:
June Crebbin, *Danny's Duck*, 1995
Through his artwork, Danny shows his teacher the progression of events in a duck's nest.

Reeve Lindbergh, *North Country Spring*, 1997
Bear cubs tumble, frogs peep and geese fly as the natural world awakens to spring's call.
Phyllis Root, *One Duck Stuck*, 1998
Large groups of animals try to get a stuck duck out of the marsh.
Nancy Tafuri, *Have You Seen My Duckling?*, 1984
With her other ducklings following, a mother duck searches the pond for her one missing offspring in a Caldecott Honor Book.

772

P.J. PETERSEN
LYNNE CRAVATH, Illustrator

I Hate Weddings

(New York: Dutton Children's Books, 2000)

Subject(s): Weddings; Remarriage; Stepfamilies
Age range(s): Grades 3-5
Major character(s): Dan, Child of Divorced Parents, Stepbrother; Riley, Stepbrother (younger); Hannah, Stepsister (older)
Time period(s): 2000s (2000)
Locale(s): Los Angeles, California

Summary: Dan didn't enjoy the wedding he had to go to two weeks ago in his itchy blue suit and the one he's flying to now will be even worse. His father is getting married to a woman with two children that he's never met and Dan is sure he's losing his dad to the new family. At the airport, Riley greets him eagerly as his "big brother" and is excited to be sharing his room (and his pet tarantula) with Dan for the weekend. Hannah doesn't look any happier about the weekend than Dan feels and does her best to make Dan look bad. Dan wants to make a good impression so he'll be invited back, but his nervousness contributes to many unintended mishaps. By the time the wedding and reception are behind him, Dan's feeling a little better because he's been assured that he's welcome to return to visit his new family. (104 pages)

Where it's reviewed:
Booklist, March 1, 2000, page 1245
Bulletin of the Center for Children's Books, March 2000, page 252
Horn Book Guide, Fall 2000, page 310
Kirkus Reviews, February 15, 2000, page 245
School Library Journal, June 2000, page 124

Other books by the same author:
Can You Keep a Secret?, 1997
I Hate Company, 1994
I Hate Camping, 1991

Other books you might like:
Paula Danziger, *Forever Amber Brown*, 1996
Amber's friend helps her understand that even if her mother marries Max, she will forever be Amber Brown.
Candice F. Ransom, *More than a Name*, 1995
After her mother's remarriage, Cammie must adjust to a stepfather and a large extended family.
Susan Wojciechowski, *Beany and the Dreaded Wedding*, 2000

Worrywart Beany is sure something will go wrong with her cousin's wedding because she is both the flower girl and the ring bearer.
Elvira Woodruff, *The Magnificent Mummy Maker*, 1994
Underachieving Andy feels overshadowed by his gifted, boastful stepbrother.

773

NEIL PHILIP, Editor
JACQUELINE MAIR, Illustrator

Stockings of Buttermilk: American Folktales

(New York: Clarion Books, 1999)

Subject(s): Folk Tales; Traditional Stories; Folklore
Age range(s): Grades 4-6
Time period(s): Indeterminate Past
Locale(s): United States

Summary: Sixteen tales originating from the European tradition are retold as they evolved after reaching America's shores. Several tales come from the storytelling lore of Kentucky including "Jack and the Beanstalk" and a version of "Snow White" entitled "A Stepchild That Was Treated Mighty Bad." Other stories such as "King Peacock" from Louisiana and "The Enchanted Prince" from New Mexico are less well known although the concluding notes trace their origins in European lore. A bibliography of suggestions for further reading concludes the book. (124 pages)

Where it's reviewed:
Booklist, September 1, 1999, page 130
Horn Book, November 1999, page 751
Publishers Weekly, August 23, 1999, page 61
Riverbank Review, Fall 1999, page 40
School Library Journal, October 1999, page 174

Other books by the same author:
Celtic Fairy Tales, 1999
The Illustrated Book of Myths: Tales and Legends of the Word, 1995
The Arabian Nights, 1994

Other books you might like:
Virginia Hamilton, *A Ring of Tricksters: Animal Tales from America, the West Indies, and Africa*, 1997
Eleven tales grouped by geographic area of origin and united by the trickster theme include the familiar Anansi and the less well-known Cunnie Rabbit.
Margaret Mayo, *Tortoise's Flying Lesson*, 1995
A collection of retold and adapted folk stories tells of animals supporting, tricking and learning from one another.
Howard Norman, *The Girl Who Dreamed Only Geese and Other Tales of the Far North*, 1997
The award-winning collection of folktales from the Inuit culture ranges from serious and meaningful to light and humorous.
Robert D. San Souci, *Cut from the Same Cloth: American Women of Myth, Legend and Tall Tale*, 1993
The illustrated collection of twenty tales is drawn from folk tales, ballads and popular stories.

774

TAMORA PIERCE

Briar's Book

(New York: Scholastic Press, 1999)

Series: Circle of Magic. Book 4
Subject(s): Magic; Diseases; Friendship
Age range(s): Grades 5-8
Major character(s): Briar, Magician, Student; Dedicate Rosethorn, Magician, Teacher; Flick, Streetperson, Child
Time period(s): Indeterminate Past
Locale(s): Summersea, Fictional Country

Summary: Briar is an apprentice to Rosethorn, a powerful plant mage. Briar hasn't forgotten his roots among those of the street, and when his friend, Flick, gets sick, he tries to help. Soon everyone in Summersea is sick and it will take all of Briar's power, and that of his friends to combat the illness—both in Summersea, and in their own teacher, Rosethorn. (272 pages)

Where it's reviewed:
Booklist, May 15, 1999, page 1691
Bulletin of the Center for Children's Books, March 1999, page 253
Horn Book Guide, Fall 1999, page 306
Locus, June 1999, page 29
School Library Journal, March 1999, page 210

Other books by the same author:
Daja's Book, 1998 (Circle of Magic, Book 3)
Tris' Book, 1998 (Circle of Magic, Book 2)
Sandry's Book, 1997 (Circle of Magic, Book 1)

Other books you might like:
Diane Duane, *A Wizard Abroad*, 1997
   Nita, a wizard, has to fight evil when her parents send her to Ireland.
Vivian Vande Velde, *Curses, Inc. and Other Stories*, 1997
   Ten short stories with characters who discover the wonder of spells and curses.
Patricia C. Wrede, *Book of Enchantments*, 1996
   Ten short stories comprise this collection by a noted author.

775

TAMORA PIERCE

First Test

(New York: Random House, 1999)

Series: Protector of the Small. Book 1
Subject(s): Knights and Knighthood; Gender Roles; Fantasy
Age range(s): Grades 4-7
Major character(s): Keladry of Mindelan "Kel", 10-Year-Old, Knight (in training); Nealan of Queenscove "Neal", Knight (in training), 15-Year-Old; Lord Wyldon, Nobleman, Knight
Time period(s): Indeterminate Past
Locale(s): Kingdom of Tortall, Fictional Country

Summary: In the ten years since the approval was given for girls to enter the training school for knights, no girl has applied until Keladry's father requests the same training for her that his sons received. Lord Wyldon has taken on the role of training master and opposes the inclusion of girls, considering them a risk to the warriors with whom they serve. At the king's insistence Lord Wyldon agrees to accept Keladry for a one-year probationary period. Angered by the discriminatory probation, Kel enters the school determined to show her ability and to earn a place beside the boy pages. Fortunately, Neal offers to be her sponsor and spares her some of the inevitable torment accorded a first-year page. Despised by many of the pages because of her sex, Kel must work harder and perform better to prove herself to Lord Wyldon's satisfaction. While she adopts the stoic facade of the Yamani with whom she lived for five years, she quietly displays kindness to animals, compassion to underdogs and a will to survive. (216 pages)

Where it's reviewed:
Book Report, November 1999, page 65
Booklist, June 1999, page 1832
Horn Book Guide, Fall 1999, page 298
Publishers Weekly, May 24, 1999, page 80
School Library Journal, July 1999, page 99

Other books by the same author:
Magic Steps, 2000 (Circle Opens, Book 1)
Page, 2000 (Protector of the Small, Book 2)
Daja's Book, 1998 (Circle of Magic, Book 3)
Alanna: The First Adventure, 1983 (Song of the Lioness Quartet, Book 1)

Other books you might like:
Bruce Coville, *The Dragonslayers*, 1994
   To free herself from her father's pledge to marry her to anyone who can kill a dragon, Princess Wilhelmina in disguise plans to slay the beast.
Brian Jacques, *Mariel of Redwall*, 1992
   Mariel, a young mouse with the heart of a warrior, seeks to rid the land of a cruel pirate.
Patricia C. Wrede, *Dealing with Dragons*, 1990
   Strong-willed Cimorene prefers the excitement of combat and politics to an arranged marriage to a boring prince so she becomes a dragon's princess.
Jane Yolen, *Not One Damsel in Distress: World Folktales for Strong Girls*, 2000
   Thirteen folktales from twelve countries feature warriors, goddesses, pirates, princesses and ordinary courageous heroes who just happen to be female.

776

DAV PILKEY, Author/Illustrator

Captain Underpants and the Attack of the Talking Toilets

(New York: Blue Sky Press/Scholastic Inc., 1999)

Subject(s): Schools; Behavior; Humor
Age range(s): Grades 3-5
Major character(s): George Beard, Student—Elementary School, Friend; Harold Hutchins, Student—Elementary School, Friend; Mr. Krupp, Principal
Time period(s): 1990s (1999)

Locale(s): Piqua, Ohio (Jerome Horwitz Elementary School)

Summary: George and Harold are sure they can win first prize in the school's Invention Convention this year. However, after the problems with their entry last year Mr. Krupp has no plans to allow them to even enter the contest. In fact, he will not allow them to attend the program and sends the eager inventors to a study hall for two days. Not to be outdone, George and Harold simply sneak into the school after the displays are set up and make some adjustments to the inventions. When the invention convention again becomes a messy disaster, Mr. Krupp assigns George and Harold to permanent detention. To pass the time, the two artists create a comic book about talking toilets and copy it on one of the student inventions that transforms a one-dimensional picture into a three-dimensional object. Thus, vicious toilets invade the school. Can the principal's alter ego, Captain Underpants, save the day? (139 pages)

Where it's reviewed:
Booklist, May 1, 1999, page 1594
Horn Book Guide, Fall 1999, page 298
Publishers Weekly, February 1, 1999, page 85
School Library Journal, June 1999, page 136

Other books by the same author:
Captain Underpants and the Perilous Plot of Professor Poopypants, 2000
Captain Underpants and the Invasion of the Incredibly Naughty Cafeteria Ladies from Outer Space, 1999
The Adventures of Captain Underpants, 1997 (IRA/CBC Children's Choice)

Other books you might like:
Robb Armstrong, *Drew and the Bub Daddy Showdown*, 1996
 Drew uses his artistic talents to create a comic book featuring his daredevil older brother.
Daniel Pinkwater, *The Hoboken Chicken Emergency*, 1999
 The illustrated reissue of a 1977 novel features Arthur and a 266-pound chicken that does things her own way.
Meredith Sue Willis, *The Secret Super Powers of Marco*, 1994
 Marco convinces himself that he has super powers that help him befriend and survive bully Tyrone.

777

DAV PILKEY, Author/Illustrator

Captain Underpants and the Perilous Plot of Professor Poopypants

(New York: The Blue Sky Press/Scholastic, Inc., 2000)

Series: Captain Underpants. 4th Epic Novel
Subject(s): Schools; Behavior; Humor
Age range(s): Grades 2-4
Major character(s): George Beard, 4th Grader; Harold Hutchins, 4th Grader; Pippy P. Poopypants, Teacher, Scientist
Time period(s): 2000s
Locale(s): Piqua, Ohio (Jerome Horwitz Elementary School)

Summary: The latest antics of George and Harold convince the science teacher that he's losing his mind so he submits his resignation. As a replacement the principal hires Professor Poopypants, but his name sends the class into such hysterics

that they're unable to learn. The unique name inspires George and Harold to create a new comic book that the students find hilarious but that enrages Professor Poopypants who is quite sensitive about his name. Vowing revenge, Professor Poopypants uses his inventions to force everyone in town to change their names according to his plans and soon everyone has ridiculous names. George and Harold know just the superhero to tackle the job of saving the planet from Professor Poopypants and his evil plans. (153 pages)

Where it's reviewed:
Booklist, February 15, 2000, page 1114
Horn Book Guide, Fall 2000, page 310
Parents Magazine, March 2000, page 46
Publishers Weekly, January 17, 2000, page 58
School Library Journal, May 2000, page 151

Other books by the same author:
Captain Underpants and the Attack of the Talking Toilets, 1999 (Captain Underpants, 2nd Epic Novel)
Captain Underpants and the Invasion of the Incredibly Naughty Cafeteria Ladies from Outer Space, 1999 (Captain Underpants, 3nd Epic Novel)
The Adventures of Captain Underpants, 1997 (Captain Underpants, 1st Epic Novel)

Other books you might like:
Duncan Ball, *Selby: The Secret Adventures of a Talking Dog*, 1997
 Excessive television viewing gives Selby the ability to speak, a fact that he keeps from his owner, an inventor who might have other plans for his pet.
Daniel Manus Pinkwater, *The Hoboken Chicken Emergency*, 1977
 In lieu of turkey for Thanksgiving dinner, a mad inventor sells Arthur a 6-foot, 266 pound chicken that gets loose in town and causes a panic.
William Steig, *The Toy Brother*, 1996
 Ignoring the warnings of his scientist father to stay out of his lab, Yorick accidentally shrinks himself.

778

DAV PILKEY
MARTIN ONTIVEROS, Illustrator

Ricky Ricotta's Giant Robot: An Adventure Novel

(New York: The Blue Sky Press/Scholastic, Inc., 2000)

Series: Ricky Ricotta. Number 1
Subject(s): Animals/Mice; Bullies; Robots
Age range(s): Grades 2-4
Major character(s): Ricky Ricotta, Mouse, Bullied Child; Robot, Robot; Stinky McNasty, Scientist, Inventor
Time period(s): Indeterminate
Locale(s): Squeakyville, Fictional Country

Summary: Ricky Ricotta longs for a friend so he does not have to face the bullies alone every morning as he walks to school. Dr. Stinky McNasty creates Robot to destroy Squeakyville, but apparently he neglected to program the robot to be mean and nasty. When Ricky saves Robot from Dr. Stinky's angry attempt to destroy his creation, he wins the friend for which he's hoped. Ricky adopts Robot as his pet and his daily problem with bullies ends. Frustrated, evil Dr. Stinky seeks revenge by changing Ricky's classroom lizard into a huge, mean monster. Robot battles the monster to save the school and the town before returning to a quiet life as Ricky's pet. (109 pages)

Where it's reviewed:
Horn Book Guide, Fall 2000, page 296
Kirkus Reviews, December 15, 1999, page 1961
Publishers Weekly, January 3, 2000, page 76
School Library Journal, April 2000, page 112

Other books by the same author:
Ricky Ricotta's Giant Robot vs. the Voodoo from Venus, 2001 (Ricky Ricotta, Number 3)
Captain Underpants and the Perilous Plot of Professor Poopypants, 2000
Ricky Ricotta's Giant Robot vs. the Mutant Mosquitoes from Mercury, 2000 (Ricky Ricotta, Number 2)
The Adventures of Captain Underpants, 1997
The Paperboy, 1996 (Caldecott Honor Book)

Other books you might like:
Stan Berenstain, *The Berenstain Bear Scouts and the Run-Amuck Robot*, 1997
    Professor Actual Factual has no control over his latest invention—a supercharged robot destroying Bear Country if the scouts don't stop it.
Burny Bos, *Alexander the Great*, 2000
    Taking a lesson from his superhero Mighty Bruno, Mouse Alexander faces a vicious cat and finds food for his family.
Margaret Mahy, *Raging Robots and Unruly Uncles*, 1993
    Twin brothers reconsider their opinion of their children after two out-of-control robots visit them.
Marianne Meyer, *Metal Heads: The Case of the Rival Robots*, 1997
    The Kinetic City all-girl engineering club competes against rival Blizzard Creek's club in the National "Robot Round-Up."

779

ANDREA DAVIS PINKNEY

Silent Thunder: A Civil War Story

(New York: Jump at the Sun/Hyperion Books for Children, 1999)

Subject(s): Civil War; Slavery; African Americans
Age range(s): Grades 5-8
Major character(s): Summer Parnell, Slave, 11-Year-Old; Roscoe Parnell, 13-Year-Old, Slave; Thea, Slave
Time period(s): 1860s (1862)
Locale(s): Hobbs Hollow, Virginia (Parnell Plantation)

Summary: Being the personal servant to the master's sickly son provides Roscoe the opportunity to attend the boy's classes and surreptitiously learn to read. With a book taken from the classroom, he secretly begins to teach his sister Summer the skill despite their mother's fears. Thea with her gift for knowing what a person is thinking often before the person does understands the silent thunder or longing within Summer and Roscoe and tries to caution them to quiet their desires if they are to survive as slaves. A concluding author's note and bibliography give the historical background for the story. (218 pages)

Where it's reviewed:
Booklist, September 1, 1999, page 134
Children's Book Review Service, November 1999, page 35
Horn Book Guide, Spring 2000, page 86
Publishers Weekly, October 4, 1999, page 76
School Library Journal, December 1999, page 138

Awards the book has won:
Notable Social Studies Trade Books for Young People, 2000

Other books by the same author:
Solo Girl, 1997
Hold Fast to Dreams, 1995

Other books you might like:
Kathleen Duey, *Evie Peach: St. Louis, 1857*, 1997
    Evie and Pa, freed slaves, save their meager earnings until they are able to purchase Mama's freedom.
Patricia C. McKissack, *A Picture of Freedom: The Diary of Clotee, a Slave Girl*, 1997
    In 1859, Clotee ponders her life as a slave and wonders whether to risk an escape.
Connie Porter, *Addy Learns a Lesson, A School Story*, 1993
    With her mother, Addy escapes to freedom in Philadelphia where she begins attending school for the first time.

780

BRIAN PINKNEY, Author/Illustrator

Cosmo and the Robot

(New York: Greenwillow Books, 2000)

Subject(s): Science Fiction; Robots; Mars
Age range(s): Grades K-2
Major character(s): Cosmo, Child, Brother (younger); Rex, Robot, Friend; Jewel, Sister (older)
Time period(s): Indeterminate Future
Locale(s): Mars

Summary: When a bump on the head changes gentle Rex into a monster, Cosmo's father hauls the damaged robot to the asteroid dump. To console Cosmo his parents give him a Super Solar System Utility Belt and Cosmo uses one of the ten supersonic attachments to take apart Jewel's toy oven. The squabbling that ensues earns both children the opportunity to collect rocks for their parents from another part of the planet. Cosmo buckles on his new utility belt for the trek and soon puts it to good use dismantling an abandoned terrain rover. Impatiently, Jewel goes off to collect rocks alone and when she doesn't return Cosmo becomes concerned. With the binoculars from his belt Cosmo sees Jewel being chased by Rex and devises a plan to save her. Fortunately, Rex is still afraid of shadows and Cosmo uses the belt's flashlight to create one that causes startled Rex to fall and break. Pulling out more tools from his trusty utility belt Cosmo repairs Rex to his former gentle condition. Jewel's so impressed she asks Cosmo to fix her oven after they return home with the rocks. (32 pages)

Where it's reviewed:
Booklist, July 2000, page 2042
Horn Book, July 2000, page 444

Kirkus Reviews, April 1, 2000, page 483
Publishers Weekly, May 1, 2000, page 70
School Library Journal, June 2000, page 124

Other books by the same author:
The Adventures of Sparrow Boy, 1997 (Boston Globe/Horn
  Book Award)
JoJo's Flying Side Kick, 1995
Max Found Two Sticks, 1994

Other books you might like:
Timothy Bush, *Benjamin McFadden and the Robot Babysitter*, 1998
  Benjamin's plan to reprogram the family robot to party
  mode backfires on him.
Nicole Jussek, *Seymour and Opal*, 1996
  Earthbound siblings disagree when Seymour is too bossy
  but younger Opal's stubborn patience proves to be the
  winner.
Dan Yaccarino, *If I Had a Robot*, 1996
  Phil imagines the many advantages of a family robot that
  he could send to piano lessons in his place and that could
  eat his vegetables too.

`781`

JERRY PINKNEY, Author/Illustrator

Aesop's Fables

(New York: SeaStar Books/North-South, 2000)

Subject(s): Fables; Conduct of Life; Traditional Stories
Age range(s): Grades 1-4
Time period(s): Indeterminate Past
Locale(s): Earth

Summary: An introduction by the collector, reteller and illustrator of these sixty-one fables gives information about the
Greek slave Aesop to whom these tales are attributed. The
collection includes familiar fables such as ''The Shepherd
Boy and the Wolf,'' ''The Town Mouse and the City
Mouse,'' and ''The Tortoise and the Hare,'' as well as lesser
known ones such as ''The Astrologer,'' ''The Miser,'' and
''The Boy and the Almonds.'' Each fable states the moral at
the story's conclusion. (87 pages)

Where it's reviewed:
Booklist, December 15, 2000, page 814
Horn Book, January 2001, page 100
Publishers Weekly, August 14, 2000, page 354
Riverbank Review, Winter 2000-2001, page 46
School Library Journal, October 2000, page 151

Awards the book has won:
Booklist Editors' Choice, 2000
Publishers Weekly Best Books, 2000

Other books by the same author:
The Little Match Girl, 1999 (Notable Social Studies Trade
  Books for Young People)
The Ugly Duckling, 1999 (Caldecott Honor Book)
Rikki-Tikki-Tavi, 1997 (Booklist Editors' Choice)

Other books you might like:
Leslie Ann Hayashi, *Fables from the Sea*, 2000
  A companion to *Fables from the Garden* uses sea creatures

as the characters of original fables, each with a concluding
moral.
Robert Kraus, *Fables Aesop Never Wrote: But Robert Kraus
Did*, 1994
  Fifteen original fables are written as spoofs of Aesop's
  traditional ones.
Arnold Lobel, *Fables*, 1980
  The illustrated collection of twenty original American fa-
  bles won the Caldecott Medal.
Doris Orgel, *The Lion and the Mouse: And Other Aesop's
Fables*, 2000
  Twelve fables are retold in an illustrated collection that
  allows readers to draw their own conclusions as to the
  moral of the story.
Paul Rosenthal, *Yo, Aesop!: Get a Load of These Fables*, 1998
  Nine modern, humorous fables conclude, not with a moral,
  but with a ''comment'' by Aesop.

`782`

JERRY PINKNEY, Adaptor

The Little Match Girl

(New York: Phyllis Fogelman Books, 1999)

Subject(s): Fairy Tales; Poverty; Winter
Age range(s): Grades 2-4
Major character(s): Unnamed Character, Child, Immigrant
Time period(s): 1920s
Locale(s): United States

Summary: On New Year's Eve a young girl is sent from her
cold, crowded tenement home to peddle matches and the
flowers that she and her siblings have made. Though she
wanders the crowded streets all afternoon, no one buys her
wares or takes much notice of her. As evening comes, the girl
seeks shelter from the cold wind, knowing she dare not go
home or face a beating. To ward off the cold, she strikes a
match and then another and another. With each burst of flame,
a vision of warmth, comfort, food, or happiness comes to her.
Finally, she sees her deceased grandmother and strikes all the
remaining matches in order to keep the vision with her. In the
morning, the girl's body is discovered huddled in the sheltered corner, her matches burned and her flowers scattered in
the wind. (32 pages)

Where it's reviewed:
Booklist, October 15, 1999, page 443
Five Owls, November 1999, page 42
Horn Book Guide, Spring 2000, page 26
Publishers Weekly, September 13, 1999, page 84
School Library Journal, October 1999, page 102

Awards the book has won:
Notable Social Studies Trade Books for Young People, 2000

Other books by the same author:
The Ugly Duckling, 1999 (Caldecott Honor Book)
Rikki-Tikki-Tavi, 1997 (Booklist Editors' Choice)

Other books you might like:
Hans Christian Andersen, *The Fairy Tales of Hans Christian
Andersen*, 1995
  Collected and retold by Neil Philip, the title includes
  twelve classic tales.

Tomie DePaola, *Days of the Blackbird: A Tale of Northern Italy*, 1997
Throughout the harsh winter, a white bird stays to sing for a gravely ill Duke, sacrificing its beauty to repay the Duke's kindness.

Walter Wangerin Jr., *Branta and the Golden Stone*, 1993
Rather than watch a flock of geese perish during an early winter storm, orphaned Branta does what she must to save them and is changed forever.

Brigitte Weninger, *Lumina: A Story for the Dark Time of the Year*, 1997
Lumina wanders the countryside alone with only a small lantern for warmth and light until she meets a kind boy who invites her to his farm for dinner.

Oscar Wilde, *The Happy Prince*, 1995
An illustrated adaptation by Jane Ray retells Wilde's 1888 tale of sacrifice by the sparrow to bring happiness to the little prince statue.

783

JERRY PINKNEY, Adaptor

The Ugly Duckling

(New York: Morrow Junior Books, 1999)

Subject(s): Fairy Tales; Folklore; Self-Acceptance
Age range(s): Grades K-3
Major character(s): Unnamed Character, Bird, Orphan
Time period(s): Indeterminate Past
Locale(s): Europe

Summary: In Pinkney's adaptation of Andersen's original tale, a huge, awkward duckling hatches from one large, odd egg in a mother duck's nest. Scorned by the other animals, including his nest mates, the ugly duckling leaves the farm and seeks refuge in a nearby pond. There, duck hunters and their dogs terrify him and once again the ugly duckling sets off to find a haven. Unable to fly to warmer climates, he suffers during the winter and almost dies when he becomes frozen in the pond. In the spring, the ugly duckling joins a group of beautiful swans he notices in the water and is astonished to see by his reflection in the pool that he looks just like them. At last the ugly duckling has found peace. (40 pages)

Where it's reviewed:
Booklist, March 1, 1999, page 1207
Horn Book, May 1999, page 310
Publishers Weekly, February 22, 1999, page 93
Riverbank Review, Summer 1999, page 32
School Library Journal, May 1999, page 79

Awards the book has won:
Caldecott Honor Book, 2000
Booklist Editors' Choice, 1999

Other books by the same author:
The Little Match Girl, 1999 (adapted and illustrated by Jerry Pinkney)

Other books you might like:
Hans Christian Andersen, *The Ugly Duckling*, 1987
Marianna Meyer's retelling of the classic story of the misunderstood duckling who, in time, discovers his true worth is illustrated by Thomas Locker.

Molly Bang, *Goose*, 1996
A gosling feels out of place with her adoptive woodchuck family until, after falling from a cliff, she discovers how unique she is—she can fly!

John Schoenherr, *Rebel*, 1995
One of a clutch of five Canadian geese eggs hatches into a gosling with a mind of his own.

784

DANIEL PINKWATER
JILL PINKWATER, Illustrator

Ice Cream Larry

(Tarrytown, NY: Marshall Cavendish, 1999)

Subject(s): Animals/Bears; Food; Business Enterprises
Age range(s): Grades 1-3
Major character(s): Larry, Bear; I. Berg, Businessman; Mildred Frobisher, Friend (Larry's)
Time period(s): 1990s
Locale(s): United States

Summary: A friendly ice cream store proprietor allows Larry to cool off in her large walk-in freezer until she discovers how much ice cream he's devouring. Mildred retrieves the polar bear and the two quickly leave the store. The newspaper report of Larry's ability to eat an eighth of a ton of ice cream with no ill effects impresses Mr. Berg who invites Larry to visit his ice cream factory. Larry and Mr. Berg get together several times before Mildred and her parents learn the surprise that Larry and Mr. Berg are plotting. (32 pages)

Where it's reviewed:
Booklist, April 1, 1999, page 1422
Bulletin of the Center for Children's Books, June 1999, page 361
Horn Book Guide, Fall 1999, page 282
Publishers Weekly, February 8, 1999, page 216
School Library Journal, May 1999, page 94

Awards the book has won:
IRA/CBC Children's Choices, 2000

Other books by the same author:
At the Hotel Larry, 1997
Young Larry, 1997
Wallpaper from Space, 1996

Other books you might like:
Barbara Baker, *One Saturday Morning*, 1994
A family of bears enjoys an active Saturday morning together.

Lisa Campbell Ernst, *Duke the Dairy Delight Dog*, 1996
Darla doesn't want a stray dog near her ice cream parlor until Duke becomes a symbol for the Dairy Delight's famous Chocolate-Vanilla Swirl.

Nanette Newman, *There's a Bear in the Bath!*, 1994
Liza's discovery of Jam, a friendly bear, in her garden enlivens her day.

785

DANIEL PINKWATER
JILL PINKWATER, Illustrator

The Magic Pretzel

(New York: Atheneum Books for Young Readers, 2000)

Series: Werewolf Club. Number 1
Subject(s): Werewolves; Clubs; Humor
Age range(s): Grades 3-5
Major character(s): Norman Gnormal, 4th Grader; Mr. Talbot, Teacher, Monster (wolf-man); Lance Von Sweeney, Brother (half-brother), Monster (giant)
Time period(s): 2000s (2000)
Locale(s): United States

Summary: Mr. Talbot, sponsor of the Werewolf Club at Norman's school is an odd looking individual in his long coat, scarf and sunglasses. Some might say the same about Norman whose father really wanted a dog and sent Norman to obedience school so he could learn to be a well-trained substitute. With his early training, Norman is tolerated by the other three members of the Werewolf Club who actually do have the ability to change form when the moon is full. Poor Mr. Talbot is stuck halfway between wolf and man shape due to a curse put on him by his evil half-brother Lance Von Sweeney and the club members decide to acquire the magic pretzel used in the curse and free Mr. Talbot. (78 pages)

Where it's reviewed:
Booklist, July 2000, page 2030
Bulletin of the Center for Children's Books, September 2000, page 35
Horn Book Guide, Spring 2001, page 66
School Library Journal, November 2000, page 129

Other books by the same author:
Fat Camp Commandos, 2001
The Werewolf Club meets Dorkula, 2001 (Werewolf Club, Number 3)
The Lunchroom of Doom, 2000 (Werewolf Club, Number 2)
Mush, a Dog from Space, 1995
Jolly Roger, a Dog of Hoboken, 1985
Lizard Music, 1976 (ALA Notable Book)

Other books you might like:
David Lubar, *The Wavering Werewolf*, 1997
    In the third entry of The Accidental Monsters series, Norman's walk in the woods transforms him into one hairy kid who likes to howl at the moon.
Dav Pilkey, *Captain Underpants and the Attack of the Talking Toilets*, 1999
    Mischief-makers Harold and George and their principal's alter ego, Captain Underpants, use cafeteria food to vanquish an invention gone awry.
Mordecai Richler, *Jacob Two-Two's First Spy Case*, 1997
    With help from his neighbor Jacob investigates Mr. Greedyguts, the new headmaster at his school, and the suspicious changes in the school lunches.

786

DANIEL PINKWATER
JILL PINKWATER, Illustrator

Rainy Morning

(New York: Atheneum Books for Young Readers, 1999)

Subject(s): Food; Animals; Humor
Age range(s): Grades K-3
Major character(s): Mr. Submarine, Spouse; Mrs. Submarine, Spouse; Ludwig Van Beethoven, Musician
Time period(s): Indeterminate
Locale(s): United States

Summary: As Mr. and Mrs. Submarine look out the window on a rainy morning they notice the cat and dog in the wet yard and invite them in for a corn muffin. The horse comes in dripping wet next, then a coyote, crows and some chickens. As Mrs. Submarine makes batch after batch of corn muffins, Mr. Submarine opens the door to Ludwig Van Beethoven, the U.S. Marine Band and a traveling circus. Mrs. Submarine isn't sure about extending hospitality to a circus but when she learns it has no elephants she relents. This is the first picture book collaboration for these authors. (32 pages)

Where it's reviewed:
Booklist, March 1, 1999, page 1223
Bulletin of the Center for Children's Books, March 1999, page 254
New York Times Book Review, August 15, 1999, page 25
Publishers Weekly, February 22, 1999, page 94
School Library Journal, March 1999, page 184

Other books you might like:
Mirra Ginsburg, *Mushroom in the Rain*, 1974
    In an adaptation of a Russian tale an ant seeking refuge from the rain is joined under a mushroom by many other animals with the same idea.
Libba Moore Gray, *Is There Room on the Feather Bed?*, 1997
    During a storm, the farm animals seek shelter in the teeny, tiny house of the wee fat woman and her wee fat husband.
Laura Joffe Numeroff, *If You Give a Moose a Muffin*, 1991
    There's no telling what can happen if you give a moose that first muffin; he may just ask for something more.
Bernard Waber, *Bearsie Bear and the Surprise Sleepover Party*, 1997
    On a cold winter night Bearsie Bear's friends come knocking at the door asking to share his warm bed.

787

LYNN PLOURDE
GREG COUCH, Illustrator

Wild Child

(New York: Simon & Schuster Books for Young Readers, 1999)

Subject(s): Seasons; Nature; Bedtime
Age range(s): Grades K-3
Major character(s): Mother Earth, Spirit; Autumn, Child, Spirit
Time period(s): Indeterminate
Locale(s): Earth

Summary: Mother Nature is ready for her wild child to settle down for a nap but her offspring has other plans—a song, a snack, a kiss and more. Patiently, Mother Nature complies with the crackle of leaves, the flitter of birds, the crunch of chestnuts and the snap of cider apples. Mother Nature's kiss is frosty, blustery, whirly and successful at getting little Autumn to drift off to sleep as Mother Nature tries to get some rest, knowing that another child will soon awaken. (32 pages)

Where it's reviewed:
Booklist, December 15, 1999, page 791
Five Owls, November 1999, page 40
Horn Book Guide, Spring 2000, page 49
Publishers Weekly, August 16, 1999, page 82
School Library Journal, December 1999, page 110

Other books by the same author:
Moose, Of Course!, 1999
Pigs in the Mud in the Middle of the Rud, 1997 (School Library Journal Best Book)

Other books you might like:
David Christiana, *The First Snow*, 1996
 Mother Nature tries to scare Winter away by painting the leaves bright colors, but she comes to appreciate Winter when he learns to make snow.
Anne Hunter, *Possum's Harvest Moon*, 1996
 The sight of a huge harvest moon inspires Possum to have one last party before the winter's hibernation begins.
Marty Kelley, *Fall Is Not Easy*, 1998
 In a humorous story in rhyme a tree describes how difficult the task of changing one's leaf color can be.
Bill Martin Jr., *The Turning of the Year*, 1998
 A rhyming picture book illustrates the unique characteristics of each month of the year.

788

PATRICIA POLACCO, Author/Illustrator

The Butterfly

(New York: Philomel Books, 2000)

Subject(s): Jews; World War II; Courage
Age range(s): Grades 1-5
Major character(s): Marcel ''Maman'' Solliliage, Mother, Resistance Fighter; Monique, Daughter; Sevrine, Child (Jew), Refugee
Time period(s): 1940s
Locale(s): France

Summary: The ghost child that visits Monique's room at night is but a dream says Maman, but when Monique has the courage to speak to the ghost she learns it is a child named Sevrine who lives in Monique's home. Monique is astonished to learn that her home has a secret basement in which Sevrine and her parents hide silently from the Nazi troops who occupy the town. Unbeknownst to the adults, Monique and Sevrine secretly meet to play at night in Monique's room and Monique brings daytime treasures for Sevrine. The night a neighbor sees the two children release a butterfly from Monique's window they know they must awaken Marcel. Quickly, Marcel alerts the resistance to implement a plan of escape for Sevrine and her parents. A concluding author's

note relates the family history on which the story is based. (48 pages)

Where it's reviewed:
Booklist, April 1, 2000, page 1478
Bulletin of the Center for Children's Books, June 2000, page 371
Kirkus Reviews, June 1, 2000, page 802
Publishers Weekly, June 12, 2000, page 72
School Library Journal, May 2000, page 151

Awards the book has won:
Notable Social Studies Trade Books for Young People, 2001

Other books by the same author:
Mrs. Mack, 1998
In Enzo's Splendid Garden, 1997
The Trees of the Dancing Goats, 1996
Pink and Say, 1994 (ALA Notable Book)

Other books you might like:
Karen Ackerman, *The Night Crossing*, 1994
 In 1938, fearing persecution because they are Jews, Clara and her family leave their Austrian home and flee to the safety of Switzerland.
Jo Hoestland, *Star of Fear, Star of Hope*, 1995
 Helen's childhood friendship with Lydia ends abruptly when Lydia and her family vanish during the Nazi occupation of France.
Claire A. Nivola, *Elisabeth*, 1997
 When Ruth's Jewish family flees Nazi Germany she is forced to leave everything including her doll Elisabeth.
Shulamith Levey Oppenheim, *The Lily Cupboard: A Story of the Holocaust*, 1992
 With no way to escape the Nazis, a little girl finds protection behind the wall of a house in the Netherlands.
Dorrith M. Sim, *In My Pocket*, 1997
 With other Jewish children, a young girl flees Germany for England where the refuges will live and await the end of Nazi rule.

789

PATRICIA POLACCO, Author/Illustrator

Welcome Comfort

(New York: Philomel Books, 1999)

Subject(s): Santa Claus; Christmas; Foster Children
Age range(s): Grades K-3
Major character(s): Welcome Comfort, Foster Child; Quintin Hamp, Maintenance Worker, Friend
Time period(s): 20th century
Locale(s): Union City, Michigan

Summary: Teased by classmates because of his size and his name, Welcome Comfort finds a friend in Mr. Hamp, the jolly and rather rotund custodian at his new school. Mr. Hamp also takes an interest in Welcome that extends beyond the school day. As Welcome visits Mr. Hamp and his wife he comes to know a sense of family for the first time in a life of constant moving from one foster home to another. With Mr. Hamp's help, Welcome even learns to believe in Christmas and Santa Claus. As the years pass, Welcome follows in Quintin's footsteps at the school and is promoted to head custodian when Quintin retires. For the first time, Quintin invites Welcome to his vacation cabin on Christmas Eve where Welcome learns that he must also take over another important job for the retiring Mr. Hamp. (32 pages)

Where it's reviewed:
Bulletin of the Center for Children's Books, November 1999, page 103
New York Times Book Review, December 19, 1999, page 31
Publishers Weekly, September 27, 1999, page 56
School Library Journal, October 1999, page 70
Smithsonian, November 1999, page 50

Awards the book has won:
Smithsonian's Notable Books for Children, 1999

Other books by the same author:
Mrs. Mack, 1998 (Smithsonian's Notable Books for Children)
Thank You, Mr. Falker, 1998 (Notable Social Studies Trade Books for Young People)
The Trees of the Dancing Goats, 1996

Other books you might like:
David McPhail, *Santa's Book of Names*, 1993
    Poor reader Edward helps Santa with his list of names and receives a fitting gift in return.
Tom Paxton, *The Story of Santa Claus*, 1995
    When an overworked woodcarver moves to the North Pole to get assistance from elves with his toy production he also develops a delivery system.
Viveca Larn Sundvall, *Santa's Winter Vacation*, 1994
    On a family vacation, three brothers meet an elderly, bearded man and his wife whom they suspect may be— guess who?
Chris Van Allsburg, *The Polar Express*, 1985
    The Caldecott Medal winner relates the memory of a magical Christmas Eve train ride to the North Pole.

790

AMY LOWRY POOLE, Author/Illustrator

The Ant and the Grasshopper

(New York: Holiday House, 2000)

Subject(s): Fables; Folklore; Animals/Insects
Age range(s): Grades K-3
Major character(s): Unnamed Character, Insect (grasshopper)
Time period(s): Indeterminate Past
Locale(s): China (summer palace)

Summary: In this retelling of Aesop's fable a colony of ants and a grasshopper live near the courtyard of the emperor's Summer Palace. The industrious ants spend their days preparing for the approaching winter, while the grasshopper sleeps late and entertains the members of the royal family. The grasshopper ignores the ants' admonitions to set aside food and make a winter home. After celebrating the harvest the royal family departs and leaves the Summer Palace empty except for a cold, hungry grasshopper wishing he'd followed the ants' advice. A concluding author's note gives background information about the tale and unusual setting for this retelling. (32 pages)

Where it's reviewed:
Booklist, August 2000, page 2144

Horn Book Guide, Spring 2001, page 102
Kirkus Reviews, July 1, 2000, page 964
Publishers Weekly, August 7, 2000, page 94
School Library Journal, September 2000, page 221

Other books by the same author:
How the Rooster Got His Crown, 1999

Other books you might like:
Robert Kraus, *Fables Aesop Never Wrote: But Robert Kraus Did*, 1994
    Fifteen original fables are written as spoofs of Aesop's original ones.
Lynn Reiser, *Two Mice in Three Fables*, 1995
    An indoor mouse and an outdoor mouse meet for three adventures.
Janet Stevens, *The Town Mouse and the Country Mouse: An Aesop Fable*, 1987
    One of many retellings of the classic tale describes two mice attempting to adapt to different life styles.

791

BARBARA ANN PORTE
NANCY CARPENTER, Illustrator

If You Ever Get Lost: The Adventures of Julia and Evan

(New York: Greenwillow Books/HarperCollins Publishers, 2000)

Subject(s): Brothers and Sisters; Family Life; Parent and Child
Age range(s): Grades 1-4
Major character(s): Julia, Sister (older), Student—Elementary School; Evan, Brother (younger), Kindergartner
Time period(s): 2000s (2000)
Locale(s): United States

Summary: Nine stories describe the adventures that Julia, Evan and family members have in the course of daily life. In the crowds of people watching a marathon in which their father is running Julia and Evan become separated from their mother and grandmother, but they head for the finish line on their own, collecting other children whose parents are lost along the way. While shopping Julia and Evan help their mother by filling a cart with pet supplies so they'll be ready for the puppy they hope to get some day. Evan learns to ride Julia's two-wheeler at the park and takes off down a hill leading to a pond before he learns how to stop. Julia makes up a story about furry creatures living in the attic and ends up scaring herself instead of Evan. Finally, while visiting an exotic pet store Evan sees two customers grab their purchases and run out without paying and is able to give a description that helps the police apprehend them. (80 pages)

Where it's reviewed:
Booklist, June 1, 2000, page 1897
Horn Book Guide, Fall 2000, page 297
School Library Journal, July 2000, page 86

Other books by the same author:
Harry's Pony, 1997
When Aunt Lucy Rode a Mule and Other Stories, 1994
A Turkey Drive and Other Tales, 1993

Other books you might like:

Pat Brisson, *Hot Fudge Hero*, 1997
    In each of three stories Bertie manages to be treated to his favorite—hot-fudge sundaes—three times for his various accomplishments.
Ann Cameron, *The Stories Julian Tells*, 1981
    Six episodes of happy family interaction are told from the perspective of Julian in the first award-winning book about his family.
Lisa Westberg Peters, *The Hayloft*, 1995
    Three episodes in a beginning chapter book relate the summer activities of two sisters living on a farm
Cynthia Rylant, *The Blue Hill Meadows*, 1997
    For Willie, each season of the year holds a special memory of his family and their rural home near the small community of Blue Hill.
Marilyn Sachs, *JoJo & Winnie Again: More Sister Stories*, 2000
    The rivalry between JoJo and Winnie is obvious in eight episodic chapters but so is the support the sisters offer one another.

792

BARBARA ANN PORTE
ANNIE CANNON, Illustrator

Ma Jiang and the Orange Ants

(New York: Orchard Books, 2000)

Subject(s): Animals/Insects; Family; Work
Age range(s): Grades 1-3
Major character(s): Ma Jiang, Child, Daughter; Bao, Baby
Time period(s): Indeterminate Past
Locale(s): China

Summary: When her father and two older brothers are taken away to become soldiers in the emperor's army, Ma Jiang and her mother don't not know how they can carry on the family livelihood of retrieving orange ant nests from trees and selling them in the market. Jiang and her mother weave mats, bags, slippers and baskets to sell at the market, but still the family grows poorer. After Jiang's mother trades some woven items to a beekeeper for honey and Bao spills some, Jiang sees the way the honey attracts ants and devises a way to use the honey and her mother's tightly woven bags to attract and trap orange ants. Once again food is plentiful. When Jiang's father and brothers finally return, the family is complete, prosperous and happy once again. A concluding author's note gives information about citrus ants. (32 pages)

Where it's reviewed:
Booklist, October 15, 2000, page 446
Horn Book Guide, Spring 2001, page 48
Kirkus Reviews, September 15, 2000, page 1362
School Library Journal, December 2000, page 123

Other books by the same author:
Tale of a Tadpole, 1997
Chickens! Chickens!, 1995
Taxicab Tales, 1992

Other books you might like:

Janell Cannon, *Crickwing*, 2000
    Crickwing, a lonely cockroach, helps a colony of leaf-cutter ants solve the problem of invading army ants.
Lily Toy Hong, *The Empress and the Silkworm*, 1995
    Long ago the curiosity of an empress leads to the discovery of a method for unwinding the long silken thread of a cocoon to produce a valuable cloth.
Jeanne M. Lee, *The Song of Mu Lan*, 1995
    The Chinese folk poem tells the tale of a young girl who, in disguise, takes her father's place in battle.

793

LEE POSEY
MICHAEL G. MONTGOMERY, Illustrator

Night Rabbits

(Atlanta: Peachtree Publishers, Ltd., 1999)

Subject(s): Animals/Rabbits; Summer; Fathers and Daughters
Age range(s): Grades K-2
Major character(s): Elizabeth, Daughter, Animal Lover; Unnamed Character, Father
Time period(s): 1990s (1999)
Locale(s): United States

Summary: In the author's first book, Elizabeth sympathizes with her father's consternation when he sees evidence that rabbits are dining on his carefully tended lawn at the summer cabin. Elizabeth loves the rabbits and often watches them while drifting off to sleep in the porch hammock. To try to solve the problem, Elizabeth sprinkles lettuce leaves over the lawn hoping the rabbits will choose it over the grass. Her father, noticing her kind gesture, decides that perhaps the lawn can be shared. In appreciation, Elizabeth begins helping with the yard work. (32 pages)

Where it's reviewed:
Booklist, May 1, 1999, page 1600
Horn Book Guide, Fall 1999, page 264
Publishers Weekly, March 1, 1999, page 68
School Library Journal, May 1999, page 94

Other books you might like:

Jim Arnosky, *Rabbits and Raindrops*, 1997
    Five baby rabbits munch clover and frolic with butterflies until a rain shower forces them to seek shelter.
Bill Easterling, *Prize in the Snow*, 1994
    Trying to emulate his older brother, a young boy sets a box trap and catches a rabbit, but chooses to let the frightened creature go free.
Jessie Haas, *Mowing*, 1994
    When Nora and Gramp mow the hayfield, they are careful to avoid the habitats of the animals living there.
Jonathan London, *Jackrabbit*, 1996
    Separated from her littermates by a bulldozer's destruction of their home, a baby jackrabbit is cared for until old enough to return to the wild.

794

CONSIE POWELL, Author/Illustrator

Old Dog Cora and the Christmas Tree

(Morton Grove, IL: Albert Whitman & Company, 1999)

Subject(s): Animals/Dogs; Christmas; Old Age
Age range(s): Grades K-1
Major character(s): Cora, Dog (Newfoundland); Susan, Child, Daughter; Mom, Mother
Time period(s): 1990s (1999)
Locale(s): North

Summary: Just as old Cora's settling down for a nap, she hears her family readying to go out. Instantly alert, Cora notes Susan putting harnesses on her daughter and granddaughter and looks plaintively at her harness, thinking of all the hauling she's done with it over the years. Mom wants to leave Cora home, saying she's too old to haul the Christmas tree anymore. Susan insists that Cora come along and Cora is happy to be a part of the annual event that proceeds as Cora expects until the felled tree is loaded and only the two younger dogs are hitched to the toboggan and Cora is left out. Her attempts to be a part of the team cause problems when she becomes tangled in the traces. Cora knows her way around the woods though so she races ahead, meeting the team just as they near the road where she falls into her customary place in the lead, proudly bringing home the tree just as she always has whether she's in harness or not. (32 pages)

Where it's reviewed:
Booklist, September 1, 1999, page 150
Horn Book Guide, Spring 2000, page 69
Kirkus Reviews, July 15, 1999, page 1138
Publishers Weekly, September 27, 1999, page 56
School Library Journal, October 1999, page 70

Other books by the same author:
A Bold Carnivore: An Alphabet of Predators, 1995

Other books you might like:
Robert J. Blake, *Akiak: A Tale from the Iditarod*, 1997
    Injury forces lead-dog Akiak from the race, but she tracks her team for days knowing her experience can help them get on the path to victory.
Louise Borden, *Just in Time for Christmas*, 1994
    After disappearing for five days, Will's dog Luke arrives along with the relatives just in time for Christmas.
Marc McCutcheon, *Grandfather's Christmas Camp*, 1995
    Grandfather's dog vanishes into the snowy woods, but reappears on Christmas morning.

795

NANCY POYDAR, Author/Illustrator

First Day, Hooray!

(New York: Holiday House, Inc., 1999)

Subject(s): School Life; Dreams and Nightmares; Parent and Child
Age range(s): Grades K-2

Major character(s): Ivy Green, Student—Elementary School, Daughter; Miss Wheeler, Driver (school bus); Ms. Bell, Teacher
Time period(s): 1990s (1999)
Locale(s): United States

Summary: As Ivy shops for new shoes and a lunch box she worries. Maybe Miss Wheeler will miss her bus stop, maybe she won't find her classroom or maybe she'll forget her lunch. At the school teachers and custodians are completing last-minute preparations and feeling concerns about overlooking something. The night before school opens, Ivy's parents are reassuring as they say good night, but still her dreams are crowded with worries. Miss Wheeler and Ms. Bell also have concerns popping up in their dreams but by the time school begins it's obvious that no one's dreams will come true and the school day will be terrific. (32 pages)

Where it's reviewed:
Booklist, October 15, 1999, page 456
Children's Book Review Service, December 1999, page 40
Horn Book Guide, Spring 2000, page 49
School Library Journal, August 1999, page 141

Other books by the same author:
Snip, Snip. . .Snow!, 1997
Cool Ali, 1996
Busy Bea, 1994

Other books you might like:
Maribeth Boelts, *Summer's End*, 1995
    Jill is not sure she really wants to return to school now that summer is over.
Miriam Cohen, *Will I Have a Friend?*, 1967
    First day of school jitters are put to rest when Paul makes friends with Jim.
Amy Hest, *Off to School, Baby Duck!*, 1999
    Grampa soothes Baby Duck's fears about entering school for the first time.
Marisabina Russo, *I Don't Want to Go Back to School*, 1994
    With his older sister's dire warnings ringing in his ears, Ben dreads the beginning of the new school year, but finds he's worried needlessly.

796

NANCY POYDAR, Author/Illustrator

Mailbox Magic

(New York: Holiday House, 2000)

Subject(s): Perseverance; Magic; Parent and Child
Age range(s): Grades K-1
Major character(s): Will Post, Son; Jennifer, Child, Friend
Time period(s): 2000s (2000)
Locale(s): Alphabet, New York

Summary: Will feels discouraged that his magical mailbox never produces any mail addressed to him. Writing letters and sending them to himself is not satisfying so Will takes advantage of an offer to send away for a personalized cereal bowl. His parents, Jennifer and even the mailman help eat three boxes of cereal so Will can mail in the offer before the deadline. Then, Will begins waiting by the mailbox night and day, rain or shine. By the time Will's terrific bowl arrives he has a plan for the next item he will try to get by mail. (32 pages)

Where it's reviewed:
Booklist, June 1, 2000, page 1911
Kirkus Reviews, August 1, 2000, page 1122
School Library Journal, September 2000, page 207

Other books by the same author:
Snip, Snip. . .Snow!, 1997
Cool Ali, 1996
Busy Bea, 1994

Other books you might like:
Janet Ahlberg, *The Jolly Postman, or Other People's Letters*, 1986
   The letters he will deliver tell the story of a postman's route. Allan Ahlberg, co-author.
Maribeth Boelts, *Grace and Joe*, 1994
   Preschooler Grace walks through her neighborhood with Joe as he delivers the mail.
Judith Caseley, *Dear Annie*, 1991
   A story unfolds in the correspondence between Annie and her grandfather.
Elizabeth Spurr, *The Long, Long Letter*, 1996
   Aunt Hetta sits by her mailbox waiting for a letter that comes page by page due to a tornado that rips open the box in which it's mailed.

797

MARJORIE PRICEMAN, Author/Illustrator

Emeline at the Circus
(New York: Alfred A. Knopf, 1999)

Subject(s): Circus; School Life; Teachers
Age range(s): Grades K-3
Major character(s): Emeline, Student—Elementary School, 2nd Grader; Ms. Splinter, Teacher
Time period(s): 1990s (1999)
Locale(s): United States

Summary: Ms. Splinter seats her class of second graders at the circus and proceeds to regale them with facts from the books piled in her lap. As the illustrations show Emeline buying a bag of peanuts the text has Ms. Splinter reading facts about elephants and their long trunks. The circus elephant uses its long trunk to lift Emeline and her peanuts into the ring where she becomes part of the show. Oblivious to Emeline's plight (or delight), Ms. Splinter continues reading about llamas, clowns, giraffes, horses, monkeys and tigers. The students follow their classmate's progress while listening to the origins of the word acrobat and the definition of a trapeze, an apparatus from which Emeline flies and flips back to her seat right beside her astonished teacher. (40 pages)

Where it's reviewed:
Booklist, April 1, 1999, page 1408
Five Owls, September 1999, page 14
Horn Book, May 1999, page 320
Publishers Weekly, March 8, 1999, page 68
School Library Journal, May 1999, page 94

Awards the book has won:
Bulletin of the Center for Children's Books Blue Ribbon, 1999
New York Times Best Illustrated Children's Books, 1999

Other books by the same author:
Froggie Went A-Courting, 2000
My Nine Lives by Clio, 1998
How to Make an Apple Pie and See the World, 1994 (ALA Notable Book)
Friend or Frog, 1989

Other books you might like:
Ludwig Bemelmans, *Madeleine and the Gypsies*, 1959
   A trip to the Carnival becomes an unexpected adventure for Madeleine and Pepito who tire of the travel and long to return to Miss Clavell.
Lois Ehlert, *Circus*, 1992
   A unique picture book illustrates the colorful excitement of the circus.
Rebecca Emberley, *My Mother's Secret Life*, 1998
   A little girl dreams that her mother leads a secret life as a circus performer.
Ingrid Slyder, *The Fabulous Flying Fandinis!*, 1996
   When Bobby visits the new neighbors he is overwhelmed to enter a house that is a non-stop circus.

798

MARY SKILLINGS PRIGGER
BETSY LEWIN, Illustrator

Aunt Minnie McGranahan
(New York: Clarion Books, 1999)

Subject(s): Aunts and Uncles; Orphans; Conduct of Life
Age range(s): Grades K-3
Major character(s): Minnie McGranahan, Aunt
Time period(s): 1920s
Locale(s): St. Clere, Kansas; North Dakota

Summary: Neat Minnie McGranahan lives in a systematic way with no children to disturb her sense of order. When a telegram arrives requesting that Minnie hurry to North Dakota to claim the nine, orphaned offspring of her recently deceased brother and his wife, Minnie dons her white gloves and hurries off. The people of St. Clere assume Minnie cannot manage children, but they underestimate Aunt Minnie's systems. Indeed, Aunt Minnie has no problem raising nine children because the oldest ones care for the youngest, the middle ones care for each other and Aunt Minnie takes care of everyone. Aunt Minnie assigns the chores, the hugs, the grocery shopping and the waiting system for the outhouse. Everyone survives, everyone has fun, and everyone feels loved. The author's first book is based on her family history. (32 pages)

Where it's reviewed:
Booklist, May 1, 1999, page 1600
Bulletin of the Center for Children's Books, May 1999, page 325
Kirkus Reviews, March 1, 1999, page 380
Publishers Weekly, February 8, 1999, page 213
School Library Journal, May 1999, page 95

Other books you might like:

Mary Ann Hoberman, *The Seven Silly Eaters*, 1997
Lessons from Aunt Minnie might help patient Mrs. Peters cope with her children's peculiar eating habits.

Eileen Kurtis-Kleinman, *When Aunt Lena Did the Rhumba*, 1997
Aunt Lena's system of attending a Broadway matinee every Wednesday afternoon fails when she sprains her ankle.

Jama Kim Rattigan, *Truman's Aunt Farm*, 1994
Truman's eccentric Aunt Fran sends him an ant farm for his birthday that actually yields an abundance of aunts.

799

ELISE PRIMAVERA, Author/Illustrator

Auntie Claus

(San Diego: Harcourt Brace & Company, 1999)

Subject(s): Christmas; Aunts and Uncles; Santa Claus
Age range(s): Grades K-2
Major character(s): Auntie Claus, Aunt; Sophie Kringle, Niece, Sister
Time period(s): Indeterminate
Locale(s): New York, New York; North Pole, Antarctica

Summary: Sophie Kringle lives with her family in the Bing Cherry Hotel in New York City. Her entire family loves Christmas, especially Sophie's Auntie Claus. Sophie and her brother always receive everything they want for Christmas, although Auntie Claus reminds Sophie that it is actually better to give than receive. Every year Auntie Claus goes away on business from Halloween to Valentine's Day and Sophie wants to know where she goes so she goes along as a stowaway. Sophie finds herself in the North Pole, where, mistaken for an elf, she is put to work. When Sophie sees her brother's name on the list of bad boys and girls she erases his name and substitutes her own, thus learning Auntie Claus's lesson— and earning a trip home for Christmas. (40 pages)

Where it's reviewed:

Booklist, September 1, 1999, page 150.
Bulletin of the Center for Children's Books, December 1999, page 147
Kirkus Reviews, September 1, 1999, page 1420
Publishers Weekly, September 27, 1999, page 56
School Library Journal, October 1999, page 70

Other books by the same author:

Plantpet, 1995
The Three Dots, 1994

Other books you might like:

Ludwig Bemelmans, *Madeline's Christmas*, 1985
Santa Claus visits Madeline in Paris.
William Joyce, *Santa Calls*, 1993
Art Atchinson Aimesworth, boy inventor, goes to visit Santa Claus at the North Pole accompanied by his sister and best friend.
Kay Thompson, *Eloise at Christmastime*, 1958
Eloise brings Christmas cheer to the Plaza Hotel.

800

JAMES PROIMOS, Author/Illustrator

The Loudness of Sam

(San Diego: Harcourt Brace & Company, 1999)

Subject(s): Individuality; Aunts and Uncles; Parent and Child
Age range(s): Grades K-2
Major character(s): Sam, Child, Nephew; Tillie, Aunt
Time period(s): 1990s
Locale(s): United States

Summary: Sam and his loud voice are adored from the moment of his birth and first loud cry. As he grows, his parents dote on each sound and never suggest he use a lower decibel range or in any way inhibit his expression of his feelings through laughter or crying. Sam has no idea that his loud exhibitions are not pleasing to everyone until he visits Aunt Tillie in a large city. Neither Aunt Tillie nor other residents of the city seem to notice funny shaped clouds or react to sad stories with tears. During Sam's visit with Aunt Tillie he hears "shush" for the first time in his life, but before he departs Aunt Tillie has discovered the joy of Sam's approach to life. (32 pages)

Where it's reviewed:

Booklist, July 1999, page 1953
Horn Book Guide, Fall 1999, page 264
Kirkus Reviews, March 1, 1999, page 380
Publishers Weekly, March 1, 1999, page 68
School Library Journal, May 1999, page 95

Awards the book has won:

IRA/CBC Children's Choices, 2000

Other books by the same author:

Joe's Wish, 1998

Other books you might like:

Rebecca C. Jones, *Great Aunt Martha*, 1995
A family plans quiet activities during Great Aunt Martha's visit only to learn that she prefers a livelier life style.
Alexis O'Neill, *Loud Emily*, 1998
Emily's parents are not accepting of her loud voice until she finds success working as a foghorn.
Alan Schroeder, *Carolina Shout!*, 1995
To some the street vendors are a noisy bunch, but to Delia they make music as they ply their wares on the Charleston streets.

801

VERA W. PROPP

When the Soldiers Were Gone

(New York: G.P. Putnam's Sons, 1999)

Subject(s): Jews; Holocaust; Parent and Child
Age range(s): Grades 4-6
Major character(s): Benjamin "Henk" Van Sorg, 8-Year-Old, Son; David Van Sorg, Father; Elsbeth Van Sorg, Mother
Time period(s): 1940s (1945)
Locale(s): Hengelo, Netherlands; Apelhem, Netherlands

Summary: A true story of postwar readjustment from a child's perspective is the basis for Propp's first novel. In a brief moment life as Henk knows it changes. Two strangers who call him Benjamin and insist they are his real parents take him from what he thinks is his home and family. When he arrives in Apelhem, Henk meets a baby brother, enrolls in school for the first time and learns that he and his parents are Jews who were forced into hiding during the Nazi occupation of Holland. A farm family took in Benjamin and gave him a Christian name for protection while David and Elsbeth, his parents, hid wherever they could find refuge waiting for the day when the soldiers were really gone so they could reclaim their son. (101 pages)

Where it's reviewed:
Booklist, January 1, 1999, page 861
Horn Book, July 1999, page 472
Kirkus Reviews, December 15, 1998, page 1803
Publishers Weekly, January 11, 1999, page 73
School Library Journal, February 1999, page 111

Awards the book has won:
Booklist Editors' Choice, 1999
Notable Social Studies Trade Books for Young People, 2000

Other books you might like:
Karen Ackerman, *The Night Crossing*, 1994
   In 1938, fearing persecution, Clara and her family leave their Austrian home and flee to the safety of Switzerland.
David A. Adler, *Hilde & Eli: Children of the Holocaust*, 1994
   The lives of two children, victims of the Holocaust, are described through the recollections of surviving siblings.
Lois Lowry, *Number the Stars*, 1989
   While sheltering her Jewish friend Ellen from the Nazis, Annemarie learns about herself and the meaning of courage. Newbery Medal winner.
Shulamith Levey Oppenheim, *The Lily Cupboard: A Story of the Holocaust*, 1992
   With no way to escape the Nazis, a little girl finds protection behind the wall of a house in the Netherlands.
Dorrith M. Sim, *In My Pocket*, 1997
   A young German child lives as a refugee in Scotland during World War II longing to be reunited with her parents.
Ida Vos, *Anna Is Still Here*, 1993
   The Nazi threat is over, but the effect of being hidden, alone, for three years in an attic is still with Anna.

802

BONNIE PRYOR
BERT DODSON, Illustrator

Luke: 1849-On the Golden Trail

(New York: Morrow Junior Books, 1999)

Series: American Adventures
Subject(s): Frontier and Pioneer Life; Voyages and Travels; Aunts and Uncles
Age range(s): Grades 3-6
Major character(s): Luke Reed, 11-Year-Old, Nephew; Eli Reed, Uncle, Adventurer
Time period(s): 1840s (1849)
Locale(s): Iowa; Boston, Massachusetts

Summary: Since moving from Ohio to settle on the Iowa prairie Luke has helped his father break the sod and put in crops to establish a farm. The family hopes to move out of the crowded sod house into a frame dwelling as soon as they can grow enough crops to sell as well as sustain themselves. After a prairie fire burns the fields there is no crop for Luke to tend and his parents allow him to accompany Uncle Eli back to Boston where he will receive some education before returning to the farm for the spring planting season. The trip by horseback, stagecoach, ferry and train amazes Luke who was unaware of the vastness of the country. He records all his new experiences in drawings to mail his family. In time he'll learn to read and write, but until he goes home there is no one to read the letters so he communicates with his art. Appended historical notes give background information for the time period. (163 pages)

Where it's reviewed:
Booklist, August 1999, page 2059
Horn Book Guide, Fall 1999, page 298
School Library Journal, August 1999, page 163

Other books by the same author:
Luke on the High Seas, 2000 (American Adventures)
Joseph: 1861—A Rumble of War, 1999 (American Adventures)
Thomas in Danger, 1999 (American Adventure)

Other books you might like:
Patricia MacLachlan, *Skylark*, 1994
   A drought causes crop failure and forces many families to leave their prairie homes.
Laura Ingalls Wilder, *Farmer Boy*, 1953
   Almanzo and his siblings live on an established farm rather than the prairie but still have farm chores to complete.
Elvira Woodruff, *Dear Levi: Letters from the Overland Trail*, 1994
   Letters from Austin to his young brother describe the journey from Pennsylvania to Oregon as Austin seeks to reach their deceased father's land claim.

803

PHILIP PULLMAN
S. SAELIG GALLAGHER, Illustrator

The Firework-Maker's Daughter

(New York: Arthur A. Levine Books/Scholastic Press, 1999)

Subject(s): Magic; Animals/Elephants; Adventure and Adventurers
Age range(s): Grades 3-6
Major character(s): Lila, Daughter, Apprentice; Chulak, Friend (Lila's), Servant; Hamlet, Elephant
Time period(s): Indeterminate Past
Locale(s): Asia

Summary: Raised by her widowed father, a firework-maker, Lila grows up surrounded by the sounds and sights of the materials and the finished product. Although Lila's father is willing to teach her some of his art, he has a more traditional future in mind for her. Lila, however, is determined to be a firework-maker. Chulak offers to help her, but the knowledge he weasels out of Lila's father is incomplete. When Chulak realizes that he has sent Lila on a dangerous mission, he sneaks away with Hamlet, the king's elephant, to rescue Lila from certain death. Although Chulak and Hamlet are able to save Lila, their actions may cost her father's life for he is imprisoned and condemned to death for assisting with Hamlet's escape. Courage, wit, skill and luck combine to save Lila's father and to ensure Lila's future as a firework-maker. (97 pages)

Where it's reviewed:
Book Report, September 1999, page 62
Booklist, September 15, 1999, page 260
Horn Book Guide, Spring 2000, page 86
Publishers Weekly, October 4, 1999, page 75
School Library Journal, November 1999, page 163

Awards the book has won:
Booklist Editors' Choice, 1999

Other books by the same author:
I Was a Rat!, 2000
Clockwork, or, All Wound Up, 1998
Count Karlstein, 1998

Other books you might like:
Lloyd Alexander, *The Iron Ring*, 1997
    On a journey from Sundhari to Jaya's palace Tamar faces danger, battles enemies and acquires some unusual traveling companions.
Roald Dahl, *George's Marvelous Medicine*, 1982
    George's idea to concoct a potion and transform his crabby grandmother does not go exactly according to plan.
Ruth Stiles Gannett, *Three Tales of My Father's Dragon*, 1997
    A collection of three previously issued books about a flying baby dragon includes the Newbery Honor Book, *My Father's Dragon*.

804

PHILIP PULLMAN
KEVIN HAWKES, Illustrator

I Was a Rat!

(New York: Borzoi/Alfred A. Knopf, 2000)

Subject(s): Newspapers; Fairy Tales; Humor
Age range(s): Grades 4-6
Major character(s): Roger, Child; Bob Jones, Artisan (cobbler), Spouse; Joan Jones, Spouse, Worker (laundrywoman)
Time period(s): Indeterminate Past
Locale(s): England

Summary: Older and childless, Bob and Joan willingly offer shelter to a dirty boy dressed as a page who knocks at their door claiming to have been a rat. When their diligent efforts to locate the parents of the boy they name Roger are futile they simply take him into their lives, try to teach him polite "boy" behavior, and discourage some of his instinctive behavior such as eating pencils and shredding the bed linens to make his nest. New to the ways of humans, Roger falls prey to unscrupulous people trying to use him for their own gain and is almost executed for being a monster. By following the tabloid stories Bob and Joan think the new princess (whom

Roger refers to her by another name) may be able to help them save Roger. Roger learns from his former friend and current princess that his memory is correct. He was a rat that was changed into a boy who was happily sliding down the palace banisters and missed the midnight deadline to return to the pumpkin coach. Now Roger is stuck being a boy forever just as the once wishful scullery maid is trapped in her role as princess. (165 pages)

Where it's reviewed:
Booklist, February 1, 2000, page 1023
Children's Book Review Service, April 2000, page 102
Horn Book, January 2000, page 82
School Library Journal, March 2000, page 241
Voice of Youth Advocates, April 2000, page 49

Awards the book has won:
School Library Journal Best Books, 2000

Other books by the same author:
The Firework-Maker's Daughter, 1999
Clockwork, or, All Wound Up, 1998
Count Karlstein, 1998

Other books you might like:
Franny Billingsley, *Well Wished*, 1997
    The magical, but somewhat diabolical wishing well in the town of Bishop Mayne grants one wish per lifetime, but using it is a risk.
Carlo Collodi, *Pinocchio*, 1996
    An illustrated adaptation of the 1892 translation tells of the transforming power of love and kindness for a wooden puppet that becomes a real boy.
Dick King-Smith, *Spider Sparrow*, 2000
    A childless couple adopts an abandoned infant and loves the boy unconditionally despite his odd appearance and slow achievement.
Gail Carson Levine, *Ella Enchanted*, 1997
    The Cinderella theme weaves through this fantasy of an orphaned girl, her quest to remove a fairy's curse and her eventual happiness.
David Henry Wilson, *The Coachman Rat*, 1989
    Robert, the rat who drove the coach for Cinderella, wants to return to his human state.

805

ROBIN PULVER
TEDD ARNOLD, Illustrator

Axle Annie

(New York: Dial Books for Young Readers, 1999)

Subject(s): School Buses; Winter; Perseverance
Age range(s): Grades K-3
Major character(s): Axle Annie, Driver (school bus); Shifty Rhodes, Driver (school bus)
Time period(s): 1990s
Locale(s): Burskyville, Fictional Country (Tiger Hill)

Summary: Almost everyone in town loves Axle Annie, a bus driver famous for magic tricks, a cheerful attitude and the ability to conquer Tiger Hill in a snowstorm. Shifty Rhodes dislikes Axle Annie because she is the reason Burskyville schools never close for snow. The superintendent bases his decision on Axle Annie's confidence that she can drive her bus up Tiger Hill. So far, she's been successful on every attempt, but when Shifty Rhodes brings in a snow machine to help the snowstorm pile it up on Tiger Hill it looks as if Axle Annie might go down in defeat with a busload of children. Thanks to the kindness of all the motorists Axle Annie has helped over the years, Shifty Rhodes' plan fails and the school district keeps its record for zero snow days. (32 pages)

Where it's reviewed:
Booklist, February 15, 2000, page 1120
Horn Book Guide, Spring 2000, page 50
Kirkus Reviews, August 1, 1999, page 1230
Publishers Weekly, August 23, 1999, page 58
School Library Journal, October 1999, page 123

Awards the book has won:
Smithsonian's Notable Books for Children, 1999

Other books by the same author:
Way to Go, Alex!, 1999
Alicia's Tutu, 1997
Nobody's Mother Is in Second Grade, 1992

Other books you might like:
Virginia Lee Burton, *Katy and the Big Snow*, 1971
    A blizzard halts all transportation in Geoppolis except for faithful snowplow Katy—happily doing her job.
Donald Crews, *School Bus*, 1984
    School buses deliver children to school and carry them safely home again in all kinds of weather.
Judy Hindley, *The Big Red Bus*, 1995
    When a wheel on the big red bus gets stuck in a pothole none of the traffic can get past.

Q

806

MARY QUATTLEBAUM
MICHAEL CHESWORTH, Illustrator

Aunt CeeCee, Aunt Belle, and Mama's Surprise

(New York: A Doubleday Book for Young Readers, 1999)

Subject(s): Mothers and Daughters; Birthdays; Aunts and Uncles
Age range(s): Grades 1-4
Major character(s): Mama, Mother; CeeCee, Aunt, Sister (youngest); Belle, Aunt, Sister (oldest); Unnamed Character, Daughter, Niece
Time period(s): 1920s
Locale(s): United States

Summary: Mama says she doesn't want a birthday party, but her daughter doesn't believe her. She knows that Mama loves birthdays so she gets together with Aunt CeeCee, the procrastinator, and picky Aunt Belle to plan a surprise party for Mama's June birthday. The plans seem to be progressing with only a few problems until the party planner arrives at Aunt Belle's house and discovers the preparations are incomplete and the guests are soon to arrive. Mama's daughter takes charge, puts her aunts, cousins and the party guests to work and by the time Mama arrives, all is perfectly in order for a terrific surprise party. (32 pages)

Where it's reviewed:
Bulletin of the Center for Children's Books, June 1999, page 361
Children's Book Review Service, August 1999, page 165
Horn Book Guide, Fall 1999, page 264
Publishers Weekly, June 7, 1999, page 82
School Library Journal, July 1999, page 78

Other books by the same author:
Underground Train, 1997
A Year on My Street, 1996
Jazz, Pizazz and the Silver Threads, 1996
In the Beginning, 1995

Other books you might like:
Cari Best, *Three Cheers for Catherine the Great!*, 1999
    When Grandma insists on ''no presents'' for her birthday Sara thinks of a ''no present'' surprise for her special grandmother.
Eve Bunting, *Flower Garden*, 1994
    With her father's help a little girl shops for and secretly plants a window box garden as a birthday surprise for her mother.
Diane Goode, *Mama's Perfect Present*, 1996
    Two sisters search the shops of Paris trying to find the perfect gift for Mama's birthday.

R

807

LINDA THERESA RACZEK
GARY BENNETT, Illustrator

Rainy's Powwow

(Flagstaff, AZ: Rising Moon, 1999)

Subject(s): Indians of North America; Dancing; Cultures and Customs
Age range(s): Grades 2-4
Major character(s): Lorraine "Rainy", Sister (older), Dancer (beginner); Raymond, Brother (younger); Grandmother White Hair, Grandmother, Dancer (retired)
Time period(s): 1990s
Locale(s): United States

Summary: As Rainy and Raymond stand with Grandmother White Hair to watch the grand entry of the many different dancers at the Thunderbird powwow Rainy wonders when she'll know which dance style is hers. She questions Grandmother White Hair about traditional dancing, her friend about jingle dancing and the Powwow Princess about shawl dancing. When the music begins again, Rainy has the courage to join Raymond in the arena where she senses such harmony with Mother Earth that she continues moving after the drums stop. Rainy's initial embarrassment soon changes to pleasure when she receives an eagle's feather and her dancing name, White Plume Dancing. A concluding glossary defines the terms and dances mentioned in the text. (32 pages)

Where it's reviewed:
Booklist, April 1, 1999, page 1414
ForeWord, May 1999, page 54
Publishers Weekly, April 19, 1999, page 73
School Library Journal, June 1999, page 105

Other books by the same author:
Stories from Native North America, 2000
The Night the Grandfathers Danced, 1995

Other books you might like:
George Ancona, *Powwow*, 1993
   A nonfiction title uses photographs to complement the informational text about the brightly costumed dancers at the annual Crow Fair in Montana.
Bobbie Kalman, *Celebrating the Powwow*, 1997
   From preparation to final performance, a powwow requires work and cooperation.
Barbara Mitchell, *Red Bird*, 1996
   As Katie travels to the annual powwow of the Nanticoke people she readies herself to take on her Red Bird persona and become a shawl dancer for the weekend.
Marcie R. Rendon, *Powwow Summer: A Family Celebrates the Circle of Life*, 1996
   A Native American family attends powwows each weekend to maintain their connection with their culture.

808

JENNIFER RAE
ROSE COWLES, Illustrator

Dog Tales

(Berkeley, CA: Tricycle Press, 1999)

Subject(s): Humor; Fairy Tales; Short Stories
Age range(s): Grades 1-3
Time period(s): Indeterminate Past
Locale(s): Fictional Country

Summary: Dogs play the leading roles in each of six fractured fairy tales. In "Cindersmelly" the Prince finds the hound of his dreams, Cindersmelly, at the Pet Show. The treasure stolen in "Jack Russell and the Beanstalk" is a Great Dane's big bag of bones that Jack takes home to his happy mother. The two cats that offer commentary from the margins of the stories actually have a role in the final one, "The Doberman's New Clothes." Cast as the tailors, the cats sell King Doberman on the value of wearing invisible clothes. Soon the entire kingdom is duped and King Doberman prepares for a parade through the kingdom. Rather than appearing to be too dumb to see the clothes, the citizens all order clothing from the feline tailors explaining why, to this day, dogs prefer not to wear clothes. (28 pages)

Where it's reviewed:
Kirkus Reviews, September 15, 1999, page 1505
MacLean's, November 30, 1998, page 90
Publishers Weekly, August 23, 1999, page 58
Quill & Quire, January 1999, page 45
School Library Journal, December 1999, page 111

Other books by the same author:
Gilbert de la Frogponde: A Swamp Story, 1997

Other books you might like:
Lisa Campbell Ernst, *Little Red Riding Hood: A Newfangled Prairie Tale*, 1995
  Grandma proves to be more than the wolf bargained for in this updated retelling of a fairy tale.
Sara Swan Miller, *Three Stories You Can Read to Your Dog*, 1995
  Simple activities such as digging holes or barking are so tiring for dogs that they must have many naps
Janet Perlman, *The Emperor Penguin's New Clothes*, 1995
  Andersen's classic fairy tale is retold using penguins as the characters.
Jon Scieszka, *The Stinky Cheese Man: And Other Fairly Stupid Tales*, 1991
  Classic fairy tales are humorously retold in this Caldecott Honor Book.
Jeanne Steig, *A Handful of Beans: Six Fairy Tales*, 1998
  These six retellings of familiar tales remain true to the originals while adding touches of humor to the lyrical narratives.
William Wegman, *Cinderella*, 1993
  The classic fairy tale has been recast with dogs playing all the roles, but Cinderella still loses her glass slipper.

809

CANDICE F. RANSOM
ELLEN BEIER, Illustrator

The Promise Quilt

(New York: Walker & Company, 1999)

Subject(s): Civil War; Family Life; Mountain Life
Age range(s): Grades 2-4
Major character(s): Addie, Daughter, Sister (younger); Aldine, Son, Brother (older); Mama, Mother, Widow(er)
Time period(s): 1860s (1861-1865)
Locale(s): Lost Mountain, Virginia

Summary: When "the Cause" takes Addie's father from his mountain farm, it threatens to also take his promise that she will one day walk to the other side of Lost Mountain to attend school. After the war ends Aldine and Addie wait in vain for their father's return, but the only thing that comes home is his red flannel shirt sent by a woman in Pennsylvania with word of his death in a hospital up North. Addie fears the promise of an education is lost now because the soldiers burned the schoolhouse, but Mama writes to the Pennsylvania lady who agrees to raffle a quilt to pay for replacement books. Mama uses all the scraps of fabric in the cabin and still lacks enough material for a border so Addie gives up her father's red flannel shirt to complete the quilt. The quilt brings enough money to buy the books and Addie knows that father's promise has

finally been kept. A concluding author's note gives historical background for the story. (32 pages)

Where it's reviewed:
Booklist, November 1, 1999, page 540
Children's Book Review Service, January 2000, page 52
Horn Book Guide, Spring 2000, page 50
School Library Journal, November 1999, page 128

Other books by the same author:
The Christmas Dolls, 1998
One Christmas Dawn, 1996 (Smithsonian's Notable Books for Children)
When the Whippoorwill Calls, 1995

Other books you might like:
Deborah Hopkinson, *Sweet Clara and the Freedom Quilt*, 1993
  The quilt Clara stitches is a road map to freedom and an escape from the bitter memories of slavery.
Patricia Polacco, *Pink and Say*, 1994
  An award-winning account of the accidental meeting of two Union soldiers, separated by skin color but united by fear of war and a quest for freedom.
Barbara Smucker, *Selina and the Bear Paw Quilt*, 1996
  Forced to move to a safer area during the Civil War Selina finds comfort in the quilt made by her grandmother from scraps of the family's clothes.

810

CHRIS RASCHKA, Author/Illustrator

Like Likes Like

(New York: DK Publishing, Inc., 1999)

Subject(s): Animals/Cats; Love; Loneliness
Age range(s): Preschool
Major character(s): Unnamed Character, Cat (white); Unnamed Character, Cat (brown)
Time period(s): Indeterminate
Locale(s): Fictional Country

Summary: One lonely cat watches other animals pair off and walk away. Feeling unlucky and forlorn, the white cat meanders through roses, past ocean waters, under blue skies and into the path of a brown cat. It's "like" at first sight and the lucky two return to frolic in the roses, together. (30 pages)

Where it's reviewed:
Booklist, April 1, 1999, page 1409
Horn Book Guide, Fall 1999, page 265
Kirkus Reviews, February 15, 1999, page 304
Publishers Weekly, January 4, 1999, page 88
School Library Journal, March 1999, page 184

Other books by the same author:
Simple Gifts: A Shaker Hymn, 1998
The Blushful Hippopotamus, 1996
Yo! Yes?, 1993 (Caldecott Honor Book)

Other books you might like:
Tomek Bogacki, *Cat and Mouse*, 1996
  Naively unaware that their species do not socialize, a little mouse and a young cat enjoy playing together.

Patricia Casey, *My Cat Jack*, 1994

A well-loved pet, Jack is a stretching, yawning, playful cat.

Isabelle Harper, *My Cats Nick and Nora*, 1994

Two cousins wile away a Sunday afternoon playing dress-up with two patient cats.

Laurie A. Jacobs, *So Much in Common*, 1994

Although Philomena and Horace seem to have little in common, it is enough to build a friendship.

Vivian Sathre, *Mouse Chase*, 1995

Brief rhyming sentences describe the actions of a mouse and the responses from a cat.

811

CHRIS RASCHKA, Author/Illustrator

Ring! Yo?

(New York: DK Ink/A Richard Jackson Book, 2000)

Subject(s): Friendship; Communication
Age range(s): Grades 1-3
Major character(s): Unnamed Character, Friend, Child
Time period(s): 2000s (2000)
Locale(s): United States

Summary: A ringing phone begins a conversation between two friends, with one side of the conversation revealed by the simple text. The young boy's face shows the range of emotions from the initial excitement of hearing his friend's voice to a puzzled expression to alarm, anger and chagrin. Before the conversation ends the boy is happy again. The book concludes with one possibility for a complete conversation and the suggestion that other dialogues are up to the imagination. (40 pages)

Where it's reviewed:
Booklist, March 15, 2000, page 1375
Horn Book, March 2000, page 190
Publishers Weekly, January 31, 2000, page 105
School Library Journal, May 2000, page 152

Other books by the same author:
The Blushful Hippopotamus, 1996
Yo! Yes?, 1993 (Caldecott Honor Book)
Charlie Parker Played Be Bop, 1992

Other books you might like:
Juanita Havill, *Jamaica and Brianna*, 1993

Insults temporarily sidetrack the friendship of two girls who face their feelings and find a way to work together cooperatively.

James Howe, *Pinky and Rex*, 1990

Pinky and Rex begin their friendship in the first book of a series about two good friends.

Charlotte Pomerantz, *You're Not My Best Friend Anymore*, 1998

An argument between best friends and neighbors Molly and Ben takes a few days to resolve.

Lynn Reiser, *Best Friends Think Alike*, 1997

A disagreement threatens to end the fun two friends are having, but after playing alone they realize they prefer each others company.

812

MARY LYN RAY
BARBARA COONEY, Illustrator

Basket Moon

(Boston: Little, Brown and Company, 1999)

Subject(s): Fathers and Sons; Mountain Life; Self-Acceptance
Age range(s): Grades 1-3
Major character(s): Pa, Father, Artisan (basket weaver); Unnamed Character, 9-Year-Old, Son; Big Joe, Artisan (basket weaver), Aged Person
Time period(s): Indeterminate Past
Locale(s): Columbia County, New York; Hudson, New York

Summary: Pa's monthly trips into town to trade baskets for goods always happens at a full moon or "basket moon" as the boy knows it so Pa will have enough light for his return trip. The eager boy waits and waits to be considered ready to accompany Pa. Finally, after his son's ninth birthday, Pa decides he's ready and they leave their mountain home for Hudson. The boy's excitement at being in a city for the first time vanishes when he and Pa are taunted by some townspeople who call them "bushwhackers." The hurt festers in the boy and he angrily knocks down the stack of baskets Pa and Big Joe have made. Big Joe quietly sets the baskets to rights and tells the boy of the gift that is given only to a few to hear the language of the wind and trees. The boy realizes he doesn't want to forsake his heritage so he goes into the woods and listens until he too can hear what Pa and Big Joe hear. (32 pages)

Where it's reviewed:
Booklist, June 1999, page 1844
Five Owls, January 2000, page 66
Horn Book, November 1999, page 731
Riverbank Review, Fall 1999, page 31
School Library Journal, September 1999, page 200

Awards the book has won:
Publishers Weekly Best Books, 1999
Smithsonian's Notable Books for Children, 1999

Other books by the same author:
Mud, 1996
Pianna, 1994
Shaker Boy, 1994

Other books you might like:
Jonathan London, *The Village Basket Weaver*, 1996

Tavio studies the art of basket weaving so he can take over this important responsibility when his grandfather, the village basket weaver, dies.

Miska Miles, *Annie and the Old One*, 1972

Realizing that her beloved grandmother, a skilled weaver, will soon die, Annie tries to control the inevitable.

Candice F. Ransom, *When the Whippoorwill Calls*, 1995

After her family is forced to move from their mountain home to the flatlands, Polly and Pap find some solace in a springtime hike to the old homestead.

Cynthia Rylant, *When I Was Young in the Mountains*, 1982

The book celebrates the needed support of family to survive the often harsh, yet always beautiful simplicity of mountain life.

813

MARY LYN RAY
LAUREN STRINGER, Illustrator

Red Rubber Boot Day

(San Diego: Harcourt, Inc., 2000)

Subject(s): Weather; Playing; Imagination
Age range(s): Grades K-2
Major character(s): Unnamed Character, Child; Mr. Humphrey, Neighbor
Time period(s): 2000s (2000)
Locale(s): United States

Summary: The smell of rain appeals to a young child who stands with nose pressed against the screen door before turning to indoor activities such as coloring, playing with blocks and reading. As the rain continues, the child dons a yellow raincoat and red rubber boats before heading outside. Pretending to be a fish the child "swims" through puddles past Mr. Humphrey who stands barefoot in his yard enjoying the feel of wet grass on his feet. Splashing in puddles with boot-covered feet is more to this young one's liking on a red rubber boot day. (32 pages)

Where it's reviewed:
Booklist, March 15, 2000, page 1389
Horn Book Guide, Fall 2000, page 255
Kirkus Reviews, April 15, 2000, page 566
Riverbank Review, Spring 2000, page 32
School Library Journal, April 2000, page 112

Other books by the same author:
Mud, 1996
Pianna, 1994
Shaker Boy, 1994
Pumpkins, 1992

Other books you might like:
Karla Kuskin, *James and the Rain*, 1995
    Wearing his yellow slicker, James goes outside to play rainy day games.
Jonathan London, *Puddles*, 1997
    A brother and sister delight in the puddles and mud created by a storm.
Jack Prelutsky, *Rainy Rainy Saturday*, 1980
    Fourteen poems celebrate the fun to be had on a rainy day, even if you're stuck inside.
Taro Yashima, *Umbrella*, 1958
    After receiving red boots and an umbrella for her birthday, Momo eagerly awaits a rainy day.

814

HELEN RECORVITS
LLOYD BLOOM, Illustrator

Goodbye, Walter Malinski

(New York: Farrar, Straus and Giroux, 1999)

Subject(s): Depression (Economic); Brothers and Sisters; Family
Age range(s): Grades 4-7
Major character(s): Wanda Malinski, 5th Grader, Sister; Walter Malinski, 15-Year-Old, Brother
Time period(s): 1930s (1934)
Locale(s): United States

Summary: In the author's debut novel, Wanda lives with her family in a dying mill town. Her father has been laid off from his job at the cloth mill, and the pressure falls on Wanda's older brother and sister to support the family. Her father threatens to send Walter off to the Civilian Conservation Corps, even though he is not yet old enough. The conflict between father and son continues, until a horrible accident brings the family and the Polish-American community to which they belong back together. (85 pages)

Where it's reviewed:
Booklist, May 1, 1999, page 1596
Horn Book, May 1999, page 338
Publishers Weekly, March 1, 1999, page 68
Riverbank Review, Summer 1999, page 37
School Library Journal, June 1999, page 106

Awards the book has won:
Notable Social Studies Trade Books for Young People, 2000

Other books you might like:
C. Coco De Young, *A Letter to Mrs. Roosevelt*, 1999
    Based on a true story, Margo writes to Mrs. Roosevelt asking for help when her family is about to lose their home during the Depression.
Karen Hesse, *Out of the Dust*, 1997
    The Newbery Medal winning novel in verse describes the harsh life of Billie Jo and her family on their Oklahoma panhandle farm during the 1930s.
Polly Horvath, *The Happy Yellow Car*, 1994
    During the Depression, Betty tries to solve her family's financial difficulties by locating a treasure hidden on her deceased grandmother's farm.
Candice F. Ransom, *Jimmy Crack Corn*, 1994
    When Jimmy's family falls on hard times during the Great Depression, he and his father join the veteran's march on Washington.
Arvella Whitmore, *The Bread Winner*, 1990
    Sarah starts a small bread-making project when her parents are unable to find work during the Great Depression.

815

CAROLYN REEDER

Captain Kate

(New York: Avon Books, Inc., 1999)

Subject(s): Determination; Brothers and Sisters; Historical
Age range(s): Grades 4-7
Major character(s): Kate Betts, 12-Year-Old, Stepsister; Seth Hillerman, 12-Year-Old, Stepbrother
Time period(s): 1860s
Locale(s): Cumberland, Maryland (C & O Canal); *The Mary Ann*, At Sea

Summary: Kate faces more life changes in a short time than she can graciously handle. Still mourning her father's death, Kate is angry that her mother remarries so soon bringing Seth and his younger sister into their home. With her stepfather fighting in the Union Army and her mother bedridden with a difficult pregnancy, Kate decides to ignore her mother's plans to rent out their canal boat and takes a load of coal from Cumberland to Georgetown. Although Kate is stubborn she's knowledgeable enough of canal life to realize she can't do the job alone. Begrudgingly Kate enlists inexperienced Seth's help and the pair embark without telling Kate's mother of their plans. The journey is difficult and made more dangerous by the threat of Rebel troops, but as *The Mary Ann* moves slowly along the canal, Kate makes a journey of self-discovery that leads to acceptance of her life situation and appreciation for Seth. (210 pages)

Where it's reviewed:
Booklist, January 1, 1999, page 857
Bulletin of the Center for Children's Books, February 1999, page 214
Horn Book Guide, Fall 1999, page 298
Publishers Weekly, January 4, 1999, page 90
School Library Journal, January 1999, page 132

Other books by the same author:
Foster's War, 1998
Across the Lines, 1997
Moonshiner's Son, 1993
Grandpa's Mountain, 1991
Shades of Gray, 1989

Other books you might like:
Sara Harrell Banks, *Abraham's Battle: A Novel of Gettysburg*, 1999
 The Battle of Gettysburg is seen through the eyes of a former slave and the wounded Confederate soldier he helps.
Richard Berleth, *Mary Patten's Voyage*, 1994
 With her husband bed-ridden with tuberculosis and the first mate in the brig, Mary Patten takes the helm and brings the *Neptune* safely to port.
Carol Ryrie Brink, *Caddie Woodlawn*, 1935
 A Newbery Medal winner details the adventures and resourcefulness of unconventional Caddie and her brothers.
Patricia Calvert, *Sooner*, 1998
 After the Civil War determined Tyler travels from Missouri to Texas to try to convince his father to return home.

816

BARBARA REID, Author/Illustrator

The Party

(New York: Scholastic Press, 1999)

Subject(s): Family Life; Relatives; Stories in Rhyme
Age range(s): Grades K-3
Major character(s): Unnamed Character, Sister (older), Cousin; Unnamed Character, Sister (younger), Cousin
Time period(s): 1990s
Locale(s): Canada

Summary: Two sisters sit forlornly in the back seat of the car that propels them to an annual family picnic. Arrival is the worst part of the day because all the older relatives eagerly greet them with hugs and kisses. Once the sisters get past that gauntlet they tentatively approach the group of cousins wait-

ing to share the family news and organize some games. Family, food and a birthday celebration for their grandmother add up to a day of fun for the tired, but satisfied sisters who reluctantly depart when the party ends. The book was originally published in Canada in 1997. (32 pages)

Where it's reviewed:
Booklist, May 1, 1999, page 1600
Horn Book Guide, Fall 1999, page 265
Publishers Weekly, May 3, 1999, page 75
Reading Teacher, October 1999, page 151
School Library Journal, May 1999, page 95

Awards the book has won:
Governor-General's Award for Children's Literature Illustration, 1997

Other books by the same author:
Acorn to Oak Tree, 1999
Caterpillar to Butterfly, 1999
Fun with Modeling Clay, 1998 (Kids Can Crafts)
Two by Two, 1993

Other books you might like:
Eve Bunting, *Going Home*, 1996
 Carlos and his siblings feel confused when his parents speak of "going home" to Mexico for Christmas; they think America is home.
Cynthia Rylant, *The Relatives Came*, 1985
 A Caldecott Honor Book celebrates childhood memories of the joyful confusion of a houseful of relatives.
Gary Soto, *Snapshots from the Wedding*, 1997
 After a family wedding, Maya, the flower girl, falls asleep in the car with her memories of the day framed in her mind like snapshots.
Jane Resh Thomas, *Celebration!*, 1997
 Carloads of relatives arrive at Maggie's house for the food, fun and games at the Fourth of July picnic.

817

H.A. REY, Author/Illustrator
MARGRET REY, Co-Author

Whiteblack the Penguin Sees the World

(Boston: Houghton Mifflin Company, 2000)

Subject(s): Animals/Penguins; Adventure and Adventurers; Transportation
Age range(s): Grades K-3
Major character(s): Whiteblack, Penguin, Adventurer; Seal, Seal, Friend; Polar Bear, Bear, Friend
Time period(s): 1930s
Locale(s): Penguinland, Earth

Summary: To gather new material for his radio show Whiteblack decides he needs to travel. Seal gives him part of an old sealskin, Polar Bear gives him a rope and with help from other penguins Whiteblack makes a small boat and sails away promising to return with stories and presents. After losing the boat in a collision with an iceberg Whiteblack (who's always wanted to be in an accident) uses the salvaged rope to climb aboard a passing cruiser. He's accidentally blasted from the gun barrel (he's always wanted to fly) onto a desert island where he meets an ostrich family and rides a camel, but not for long because he's never wanted to be seasick while on land. Whiteblack hitches a ride aboard a plane bound for Penguinland in a carrier strapped to the plane. Naturally, the curious penguin steps out of his carrier for a better view and falls into the ocean where he's caught in a net and hauled aboard a fishing boat. Now he's near enough to home to swim, pulling a net and bringing all his friends presents of fish and lots of adventure stories. A concluding note explains the discovery of this previously unpublished work. (32 pages)

Where it's reviewed:
Booklist, November 1, 2000, page 548
Christian Science Monitor, September 7, 2000, page 21
Horn Book Guide, Spring 2001, page 48
Publishers Weekly, July 31, 2000, page 94
School Library Journal, November 2000, page 130

Awards the book has won:
Publishers Weekly Best Books, 2000

Other books by the same author:
Curious George Rides a Bike, 1952
Curious George Takes a Job, 1947
Cecily G. and the Nine Monkeys, 1942
Curious George, 1941

Other books you might like:
Sonia W. Black, *Plenty of Penguins*, 1999
This "Hello Reader!" science title gives factual information about several varieties of penguins.
Helen Lester, *Tacky in Trouble*, 1998
Tacky has an unexpected trip when the wind catches the penguin's flowered shirt and he sails away to a rocky island.
Holly Meade, *John Willy and Freddy McGee*, 1998
Two guinea pigs with comfortable, but boring lives escape from their cage for a rollicking adventure in the house.

818

ADRIAN REYNOLDS, Author/Illustrator

Pete and Polo's Big School Adventure
(New York: Orchard Books, 2000)

Subject(s): Schools; Animals/Bears; Toys
Age range(s): Grades K-1
Major character(s): Pete, Child, Son; Polo, Stuffed Animal, Bear; Henry, Child, Student
Time period(s): 1990s (1999)
Locale(s): England

Summary: Polo is not sure he agrees with Pete's opinion that their first day of school will be their best adventure yet. In fact, Polo is not sure that polar bears go to school, but Pete's already got Polo in his bag. At school Pete meets Henry who's carrying his brown teddy bear. In fact, all the students are carrying teddy bears and Polo is the only white one in the room. The day is a little scary for Polo, but he copes reasonably well. When the students go outside for recess, Polo and all the other bears must stay in the room. When the children come back in, only one child does not have a problem finding his bear. Polo, the only white bear in the bunch stands out from all the brown ones so he and Pete are quickly reunited.

This best adventure for two good friends was originally published in Great Britain in 1999 as *Pete and Polo's Nursery School Adventure*. (32 pages)

Where it's reviewed:
Booklist, September 1, 2000, page 125
Kirkus Reviews, September 1, 2000, page 1290
School Library Journal, December 2000, page 123

Other books you might like:
Amy Hest, *Off to School, Baby Duck!*, 1999
With Grampa Duck's support Baby Duck overcomes her fears, enters school for the first time and makes a friend before the first day is over.
Jean Van Leeuwen, *Emma Bean*, 1993
Molly's stuffed rabbit, Emma Bean goes with her to kindergarten where they meet a little girl with a special teddy bear.
Selina Young, *Ned*, 1993
Emily and Ned, her green cloth donkey, are inseparable until Ned is lost, and then found again, on the first day of school.

819

MARILYNN REYNOLDS
DON KILBY, Illustrator

The Prairie Fire
(Custer, WA: Orca Book Publishers, 1999)

Subject(s): Fires; Frontier and Pioneer Life; Fear
Age range(s): Grades 2-3
Major character(s): Percy, Son, Settler; Father, Settler, Farmer; Maud, Horse
Time period(s): Indeterminate Past
Locale(s): Prairie Provinces, Canada

Summary: The dry October weather means that fire is an ever present danger for homesteaders. Percy begs to help plow the fireguard around the sod house and barn but Father thinks he's still too young. It's Percy though who first spots the signs of an approaching prairie fire and alerts his parents. Fathers hitches Maud to a sled, puts the barrel of rain water on it and gives frightened Percy the job of dousing any sparks on the house, yard, barn or hay stacks. With his parents in the fireguard beating out sparks with gunny sacks, Percy is left alone to prove that he can do the job. In time the fire passes, Percy and his parents are safe as is the sod house and Father knows Percy is ready to do a man's job on the farm. (32 pages)

Where it's reviewed:
Booklist, January 1, 2000, page 937
Children's Book News, Spring 1999, page 25
Horn Book Guide, Spring 2000, page 51
Quill & Quire, May 1999, page 36
School Library Journal, January 2000, page 110

Other books by the same author:
The New Land: A First Year on the Prairie, 1997
A Dog for a Friend, 1994
Belle's Journey, 1994

Other books you might like:

Marc Harshman, *The Storm*, 1995

When Jonathan faces a tornado alone he finds the courage to save himself and the family animals.

Teddy Jam, *The Year of Fire*, 1993

Grandfather tells his granddaughter the story of a forest fire that swept through the area when Grandfather was a young boy.

Patricia MacLachlan, *Skylark*, 1994

A drought causes crop failure and prairie fires, forcing many families to leave their homes.

Ann Turner, *Grasshopper Summer*, 1989

Sam soon realizes the approaching storm cloud is grasshoppers not rain or fire, but the threat to the family's prairie survival is just as great.

820

SHARON A. RILEY, Adaptor
DAVID MCPHAIL, Illustrator

A Friend for Growl Bear

(New York: HarperCollins Publishers, 1999)

Subject(s): Animals/Bears; Friendship; Communication
Age range(s): Grades K-2
Major character(s): Growl Bear, Bear (young); Old Owl, Owl
Time period(s): Indeterminate
Locale(s): Fictional Country

Summary: In a newly illustrated adaptation of a work originally published in 1951, Growl Bear tries unsuccessfully to make friends with the other forest creatures. His attempts to communicate are misunderstood as bullying and the forest animals are unkind to him. Growl Bear seeks help from Old Owl who also fails to comprehend his message until Growl Bear begins to cry. Then Old Owl realizes that Growl Bear is simply too young to talk. (32 pages)

Where it's reviewed:
Booklist, May 15, 1999, page 1701
Horn Book, March 1999, page 184
Publishers Weekly, February 22, 1999, page 97
School Library Journal, February 1999, page 77

Other books by the same author:
Barney's Adventure, 1941

Other books you might like:
Jez Alborough, *It's the Bear!*, 1994

When Eddie and him mom plan a picnic in the woods, he is afraid that he may meet the bear again.

Diane Marcial Fuchs, *A Bear for All Seasons*, 1995

For Bear, any time of year is great if it's shared with a friend.

Kim Lewis, *Friends*, 1997

Sam becomes angry with his visiting friend Alice, but not for long.

821

ANN RINALDI

My Heart Is on the Ground: The Diary of Nannie Little Rose, a Sioux Girl

(New York: Scholastic, 1999)

Series: Dear America
Subject(s): Native Americans; Diaries; Schools/Boarding Schools
Age range(s): Grades 4-7
Major character(s): Nannie Little Rose, 12-Year-Old, Indian (Lakota Sioux)
Time period(s): 1880s (1880)
Locale(s): Carlisle, Pennsylvania

Summary: Nannie Little Rose is sent by her father to the Carlisle Indian School to learn the ways of the white man, and to perform one brave act. Without her family, friends, and culture, how can Nannie be brave? Nannie discovers her brave act, when a sickly friend joins her at school. She must care for her friend, and bring honor to her family. (208 pages)

Where it's reviewed:
Booklist, April 1, 1999, page 1428
Bulletin of the Center for Children's Books, February 1999, page 215
Horn Book Guide, Fall 1999, page 298
Kirkus Reviews, February 1, 1999, page 228
School Library Journal, April 1999, page 141

Other books by the same author:
An Acquaintance with Darkness, 1999 (Great Episode)
Mine Eyes Have Seen, 1998
Broken Days, 1997 (Quilt Trilogy, Book 2)

Other books you might like:
Cornelia Cornelissa, *Soft Rain: A Story of the Cherokee Trail of Tears*, 1998

Nine-year-old Soft Rain and her mother are forced to travel west on the Trail of Tears.

Shirley Sterling, *My Name Is Seepeetza*, 1997

Seepeetza, a Canadian Indian girl, is forced by the government to attend a Catholic boarding school.

Ann Turner, *The Girl Who Chased Away Sorrow: The Diary of Sarah Nita, a Navajo Girl*, 1999

Part of the Dear America series, this book tells the story of Sarah Nita on the Long Walk of 1863-64.

822

FAITH RINGGOLD, Author/Illustrator

The Invisible Princess

(New York: Crown Publishers, Inc., 1999)

Subject(s): Slavery; African Americans; Freedom
Age range(s): Grades 2-5
Major character(s): Mama Love, Mother, Slave; Patience Pepper, Blind Person, Daughter; Captain Pepper, Plantation Owner, Father (Patience's)
Time period(s): Indeterminate Past
Locale(s): Village of Visible, South

Summary: In an original tale, Mama Love and her husband, despite their love for children, refuse to begin a family of their own for fear that cruel Captain Pepper will sell their child to another plantation. Thus, when Mama Love learns she will have a baby, she begs the forces of nature to protect the infant's freedom. Magically, her wish is granted and the baby becomes an invisible princess who is "seen" one day by Patience. When Captain Pepper learns of her existence, the Love family is threatened. A combination of myth and magic saves the family, frees the slaves and leads Captain Pepper to repent his ways. (32 pages)

Where it's reviewed:
Booklist, December 1, 1998, page 672
Horn Book, March 1999, page 200
The New Advocate, Summer 1999, page 289
Publishers Weekly, November 23, 1998, page 67
School Library Journal, December 1998, page 89

Other books by the same author:
If a Bus Could Talk: The Story of Rosa Parks, 1999
Bonjour, Lonnie, 1996
Aunt Harriet's Underground Railroad in the Sky, 1993
Dinner at Aunt Connie's House, 1993
Tar Beach, 1991 (Caldecott Honor Book)

Other books you might like:
Evelyn Coleman, *The Foot Warmer and the Crow*, 1994
  Enslaved Hezekiah uses his ability to communicate with crows to outwit his master and gain his release from bondage.
Virginia Hamilton, *The People Could Fly: American Black Folktales*, 1985
  A collection of African folk tales includes those describing ways in which slaves achieved freedom.
William H. Hooks, *Freedom's Fruit*, 1996
  An enslaved conjure woman gains freedom for her daughter and her beloved by using a powerful spell to trick the master.
Angela Shelf Medearis, *The Freedom Riddle*, 1995
  With determination and ingenuity, a young slave wins freedom by besting his master in a riddle contest.

823

JOANNE ROCKLIN

Strudel Stories

(New York: Delacorte Press, 1999)

Subject(s): Jews; Cooks and Cooking; Storytelling
Age range(s): Grades 3-5
Major character(s): Lori, 8-Year-Old, Sister; Jessica, 12-Year-Old, Sister; Willy, Grandfather, Storyteller
Time period(s): 19th century; 20th century
Locale(s): Russia; United States

Summary: Jessica and Lori mourn for recently deceased Grandpa Willy while keeping his memory alive by baking apple strudel. The sisters remember that the most important ingredient in strudel, according to Grandpa Willy, is the stories. As they peel apples and prepare the strudel for baking, Jessica and Lori repeat the stories that Grandpa Willy told for many years. The stories begin while the family's ancestors still live in Russia and continue through the generations, the immigration to America and into Grandpa Willy's kitchen where Jessica and Lori learn the stories. The book includes two recipes for apple strudel and an author's note gives the historical background for the fictionalized account. (130 pages)

Where it's reviewed:
Booklist, January 1, 1999, page 879
Bulletin of the Center for Children's Books, May 1999, page 326
Five Owls, May 1999, page 109
Publishers Weekly, February 1, 1999, page 86
School Library Journal, January 1999, page 100

Awards the book has won:
ALA Notable Children's Books, 2000
School Library Journal Best Books, 1999

Other books by the same author:
The Very Best Hanukkah Gift, 1999
For Your Eyes Only, 1997
Discovering Martha, 1991
Dear Baby, 1988

Other books you might like:
Malka Drucker, *The Family Treasury of Jewish Holidays*, 1994
  The traditions, songs, stories and recipes associated with nine holidays of the Jewish year are in an award-winning collection.
Kathryn Lasky, *Dreams in the Golden Country: The Diary of Zipporah Feldman, a Jewish Immigrant Girl*, 1998
  Leaving Russia for the Lower East Side of New York is hard for immigrants, but Zipporah holds onto her dreams to become an actress.
Howard Schwartz, *Next Year in Jerusalem: 3000 years of Jewish Stories*, 1996
  The illustrated volume compiles stories from the legends and folklore of many countries.

824

JOANNE ROCKLIN
CATHARINE O'NEILL, Illustrator

The Very Best Hanukkah Gift

(New York: Delacorte Press, 1999)

Subject(s): Family Life; Holidays, Jewish; Animals/Dogs
Age range(s): Grades 2-4
Major character(s): Daniel Bloom, 8-Year-Old, Brother; Jonah Bloom, 10-Year-Old, Brother (oldest); Amy Bloom, 5-Year-Old, Sister (youngest)
Time period(s): 1990s (1999)
Locale(s): United States

Summary: A family's celebration of Hanukkah provides the framework for a retelling of the Jewish history that provides the basis for the holiday. As Daniel awaits the lighting of the first candle he tries to ignore cynical Jonah's claims of skepticism about a miracle with no scientific explanation. The green latkes his mother is cooking are a little harder to overlook, but the Bloom children soon discover that zucchini latkes are tasty and they know potato latkes will appear later in the week. Amy is now old enough for her own menorah and to Daniel seems older than he because she is not afraid of dogs. Daniel, after being bitten by a dog, has developed a fear that he thinks only another miracle can melt. A week of family stories, daily gift sharing, and traditional games culminates during an ice storm that causes a power outage and prevents the relatives from traveling to the Bloom home for the last night of Hanukkah. The celebration becomes an ecumenical one as the residents of the Bloom's apartment building bring turkeys and latkes to Daniel's apartment for a miraculous candle-lit feast. Recipes for both potato and zucchini latkes are included. (114 pages)

Where it's reviewed:
Booklist, September 1, 1999, page 146
Horn Book Guide, Spring 2000, page 86
Publishers Weekly, September 27, 1999, page 52
School Library Journal, October 1999, page 72

Other books by the same author:
Strudel Stories, 1999
Jake and the Copycats, 1998
For Your Eyes Only, 1997
Three Smart Pals, 1994 (Hello Reader! Level 4)

Other books you might like:
Eric A. Kimmel, *A Hanukkah Treasury*, 1998
    The collection of material relating to Hanukkah ranges from games to recipes and history to contemporary stories.
Amy Golman Koss, *How I Saved Hanukkah*, 1998
    Marla's curiosity about Hanukkah helps change her mom's half-hearted interest in the holiday into a full-scale celebration.
Roni Schotter, *Hanukkah!*, 1990
    As five families celebrate the holiday the traditions behind the activities are described.

825

LIZZY ROCKWELL, Author/Illustrator

Hello Baby!
(New York: Crown Publishers, Inc., 1999)

Subject(s): Babies; Brothers and Sisters; Parent and Child
Age range(s): Grades K-1
Major character(s): Mommy, Mother; Dr. Marin, Doctor; Unnamed Character, Child, Son, Brother (older)
Time period(s): 1990s (1999)
Locale(s): United States

Summary: A little boy accompanies Mommy to Dr. Marin's office where he delights to hear the heartbeat of the baby growing in his mother's womb. The boy is eager for "our" baby to be born and he knows when his grandmother comes to care for him that the baby's birth will be soon. When Mommy brings his little sister home from the hospital the youngster is able to help his father bathe her and to soothe her when she cries by winding up a musical ball that he remembers enjoying as a baby. (32 pages)

Where it's reviewed:
Booklist, March 15, 1999, page 1334
Horn Book Guide, Fall 1999, page 358
Kirkus Reviews, April 1, 1999, page 537

Publishers Weekly, May 10, 1999, page 67
School Library Journal, June 1999, page 106

Other books by the same author:
Good Enough to Eat: A Kid's Guide to Food and Nutrition, 1999

Other books you might like:
Joanna Cole, *I'm a Big Brother*, 1997
    A big brother proudly explains all about new babies and how he can help care for the one at his house.
Fred Rogers, *The New Baby: A Mister Rogers First Experience Book*, 1996
    A realistic presentation of the impact of a new baby on a household lets an older sibling know that parents have love enough for two children.
Harriet Ziefert, *Waiting for Baby*, 1998
    Max is eager for his new sibling to be born but no amount of encouragement from him seems to hurry the birth.

826

COLBY RODOWSKY
THOMAS F. YEZERSKI, Illustrator

Not My Dog
(New York: Farrar Strauss Giroux, 1999)

Subject(s): Animals/Dogs; Aunts and Uncles; Pets
Age range(s): Grades 2-4
Major character(s): Ellie Martin, 8-Year-Old, Niece; Margaret, Aunt (great aunt); Preston, Dog
Time period(s): 1990s (1999)
Locale(s): Baltimore, Maryland; Hagerstown, Maryland

Summary: For years Ellie make plans for the puppy she's been promised when she is nine so she is more than a little disappointed when her parents surprise her with the news that they are adopting great-aunt Margaret's dog for her. Ellie's parents see no difference in a grown dog and a puppy, but to Ellie the two are simply not the same. First, she has to accept a pet named Preston, definitely not a dog's name, and then he turns out to be a boring brown dog with a skinny tail just as she predicts. Preston is obviously homesick when he first arrives in Ellie's home and Ellie is not very welcoming, but gradually, as Preston comforts her when she's sick and leads the way home when she becomes lost, Ellie is able to accept that "Preston is my dog." (69 pages)

Where it's reviewed:
Booklist, February 1, 1999, page 975
Horn Book, March 1999, page 212
Kirkus Reviews, January 15, 1999, page 150
Publishers Weekly, January 18, 1999, page 339
School Library Journal, April 1999, 107

Awards the book has won:
ALA Notable Children's Books, 2000
Horn Book Fanfare, 2000

Other books by the same author:
The Turnabout Shop, 1998
Dog Days, 1990
Gathering Room, 1985

Other books you might like:

Beverly Cleary, *Strider*, 1991

Leigh and his friend Barry share joint custody of an abandoned dog they find on the beach.

Betsy Hearne, *Eliza's Dog*, 1996

Finally, 9-year-old Eliza's parents agree to her request for a dog.

Karen Hesse, *Sable*, 1994

Tate is excited to find a stray dog in the yard and works to keep her new pet despite parental objections and neighbor's complaints.

Dick King-Smith, *The Invisible Dog*, 1993

Janie is so eager for a pet that she invents an invisible dog named Henry.

Barbara Moe, *Dog Days for Dudley*, 1994

Dudley is overjoyed when his parents finally agree to allow him to have a pet dog.

827

SUSAN ROLLINGS, Author/Illustrator

New Shoes, Red Shoes

(New York: Orchard Books, 2000)

Subject(s): Growing Up; Shopping; Mothers and Daughters
Age range(s): Preschool
Major character(s): Unnamed Character, Child, Daughter
Time period(s): 2000s (2000)
Locale(s): United States

Summary: A little girl outgrows her shoes and goes shopping with her mother to buy new ones. On the way to the store she notices the many different styles of shoes, even tiny baby shoes. The store has shoes in many colors, but the red, shiny ones are the new shoes for this happy little girl. (32 pages)

Where it's reviewed:

Booklist, February 1, 2000, page 1030
Horn Book Guide, Fall 2000, page 255
Kirkus Reviews, January 15, 2000, page 123
Publishers Weekly, January 31, 2000, page 105
School Library Journal, May 2000, page 153

Other books you might like:

Marilee Robin Burton, *My Best Shoes*, 1994

Illustrations of joyous children and their activities complement a rhyming celebration of shoes.

Johanna Hurwitz, *New Shoes for Silvia*, 1993

Silvia finds many uses for her new red shoes while she waits to grow into them.

Denise Lewis Patrick, *Red Dancing Shoes*, 1993

Grandma's gift of red shoes has her granddaughter's feet dancing around the neighborhood.

828

PETER ROOP
CONNIE ROOP, Co-Author
THOMAS B. ALLEN, Illustrator

Good-bye for Today: The Diary of a Young Girl at Sea

(New York: Atheneum Books for Young Readers, 2000)

Subject(s): Sea Stories; Diaries; Animals/Whales
Age range(s): Grades 2-5
Major character(s): Laura, 9-Year-Old, Daughter (of sea captain); William, 7-Year-Old, Brother (Laura's); Papa, Father, Sea Captain
Time period(s): 1870s (1871)
Locale(s): *Monticello*, At Sea

Summary: Required by her mother to keep a journal of her first voyage, Laura is initially impatient and reluctant to do so. Daily, she records the details of life aboard ship, the schooling she and William receive from their mother and the plans to return to the New England home she and William have never seen as soon as all the ship's barrels are filled with whale oil. The trip to the whaling grounds is fraught with danger, storms, and the loss of life. When time permits, Papa teaches Laura to sail a small boat, the crew has the day off to celebrate Fourth of July and on the cold summer nights they see the aurora borealis. A cold and early winter in the Arctic adds to the danger the ship and crew experience as they attempt to fulfill their mission. A concluding authors' note gives the basis for this fictionalized story in the actual experiences of two whaling families. (42 pages)

Where it's reviewed:

Booklist, June 1, 2000, page 1897
Bulletin of the Center for Children's Books, April 2000, page 292
Publishers Weekly, June 19, 2000, page 80
Riverbank Review, Fall 2000, page 34
School Library Journal, December 2000, page 124

Other books by the same author:

Walk on the Wild Side!, 1997
Pilgrim Voices: Our First Year in the New World, 1995
Keep the Lights Burning, Abbie, 1985

Other books you might like:

Richard Berleth, *Mary Patten's Voyage*, 1994

With her husband bed-ridden with tuberculosis and the first mate in the brig, Mary Patten takes the helm and brings the *Neptune Car* safely to port.

Loretta Krupinski, *Bluewater Journal: The Voyage of the Sea Tiger*, 1995

Benjamin Slocum records the daily events of his voyage on his father's clipper ship from Boston to the Sandwich Islands.

Armstrong Sperry, *All Sail Set: A Romance of the Flying Cloud*, 1935

The fictitious diary of a boy sailing on the maiden voyage of the clipper ship *Flying Cloud* was reissued in 1984.

829

PHYLLIS ROOT
BETH KROMMES, Illustrator

Grandmother Winter

(Boston: Houghton Mifflin Company, 1999)

Subject(s): Winter; Weather; Animals
Age range(s): Grades K-2
Major character(s): Grandmother Winter, Aged Person
Time period(s): Indeterminate Past
Locale(s): Fictional Country

Summary: Grandmother Winter lives alone tending her flock of white geese. During the summer she gathers their feathers to use in the fall for the quilt she carefully stitches and stuffs with the fluffy white down. When the quilt is complete, Grandmother Winter shakes it and the first flakes of snow begin to fall. Everywhere people and animals make preparations for the change in season as Grandmother Winter continues to shake her quilt and the flakes of snow gradually cover the ground. After one last shake, Grandmother Winter climbs into bed to sleep until spring. (32 pages)

Where it's reviewed:
Booklist, November 15, 1999, page 637
Five Owls, September 1999, page 15
Horn Book, September 1999, page 599
Publishers Weekly, August 30, 1999, page 82
School Library Journal, September 1999, page 201

Other books by the same author:
What Baby Wants, 1998
Rosie's Fiddle, 1997
Aunt Nancy and Old Man Trouble, 1996

Other books you might like:
David Christiana, *The First Snow*, 1996
  In order to convince Mother Nature to accept the winter season Aunt Arctica suggests a gentle approach so Winter invents snow.
Stephen Gammell, *Is That You, Winter?*, 1997
  Feeling unappreciated, Old Man Winter is reluctant to climb into his old truck to fling about the snow and ice of a blizzard.
Jean Craighead George, *Dear Rebecca, Winter Is Here*, 1993
  On the day of the winter solstice, a grandmother writes to her granddaughter describing the changes that indicate winter's arrival.
Leo Yerxa, *Last Leaf First Snowflake to Fall*, 1994
  Collage illustrations illuminate a poetic story giving the origin of snow from a Native American perspective.

830

PHYLLIS ROOT
WILL HILLENBRAND, Illustrator

Kiss the Cow!

(Cambridge, MA: Candlewick Press, 2000)

Subject(s): Animals/Cows; Magic; Rituals
Age range(s): Grades K-2
Major character(s): Mama May, Mother; Annalisa, Child, Daughter; Luella, Cow
Time period(s): Indeterminate Past
Locale(s): Fictional Country

Summary: Mama May feeds her many, many children by milking Luella and giving the children milk in the morning and cheese with their supper. It takes a magic cow to give enough milk for so many children and Mama May has a ritual that produces the magic effect on Luella. Annalisa, the most curious of Mama May's children, observes her mother daily, memorizes the little song, and tries to satisfy her curiosity by milking Luella. Unfortunately, Annalisa does not complete the ritual properly because she doesn't kiss Luella after she gives milk. Luella is so sad that the next day she'll give no milk to Mama May. Mama May and all Annalisa's hungry siblings beg her to kiss the cow, but she refuses. Finally Annalisa's curiosity does what hunger and pleading could not and she kisses Luella to the cheers of her siblings. (32 pages)

Where it's reviewed:
Booklist, November 15, 2000, page 650
Horn Book, January 2001, page 85
Publishers Weekly, November 27, 2000, page 76
School Library Journal, December 2000, page 124

Other books by the same author:
What Baby Wants, 1998 (School Library Journal Best Book)
Rosie's Fiddle, 1997
Mrs. Potter's Pig, 1996 (IRA/CBC Children's Choices)

Other books you might like:
Chris Babcock, *No Moon, No Milk!*, 1993
  Martha refuses to give her owner any milk until she fulfills her dream to be a "cowsmonaut" and walk on the moon.
Paul Brett Johnson, *The Cow Who Wouldn't Come Down*, 1993
  Gertrude, a cow with a mind of her own, has a mind to fly. When she succeeds, she has no interest in returning to the barn.
Nancy Van Laan, *The Tiny, Tiny Boy and the Big, Big Cow*, 1993
  None of Ma's suggestions help tiny, tiny boy convince the cow to stand still and be milked until the cow decides for herself to cooperate.

831

Leola and the Honeybears: An African-American Retelling of Goldilocks and the Three Bears

(New York: Cartwheel Books/Scholastic, Inc., 1999)

Subject(s): Fairy Tales; Grandmothers; African Americans
Age range(s): Grades K-3
Major character(s): Leola, Child; Lil' Honey Honeybear, Child, Bear
Time period(s): Indeterminate
Locale(s): United States

Summary: When Leola gets bored watching her grandmother do laundry she wanders off and is soon lost. Leola feels relieved when she happens upon the Honeybear's Inn where she helps herself to a taste of the Honeybear's food and eats Lil' Honey's huckleberry tart. Next, she tries out all the Honeybears' chairs to find the one that is just right and finally, exhausted, she falls asleep in Lil' Honey's bed. When the Honeybears discover Leola, they help her to find her way safely home to her grandmother. (38 pages)

Where it's reviewed:
Booklist, November 1, 1999, page 536
Publishers Weekly, November 15, 1999, page 65
School Library Journal, November 1999, page 147

Other books by the same author:
'Twas the Night b'fore Christmas: An African American Version, 1996
Double Dutch and the Voodoo Shoes, 1992

Other books you might like:
Cindy Meyers, *Rolling Along with Goldilocks and the Three Bears*, 1999
  In her surprise visit to his house, Goldilocks is fascinated by Baby Bear's wheelchair and mechanized bed.
Alan Osmond, *Just Right*, 1998
  This story tells what happens to Goldilocks and the Three Bears when they are grown up.
Heidi Petach, *Goldilocks and the Three Hares*, 1995
  After Mama Hare burns the oatmeal, the Hares go out to breakfast, while at the same time Goldilocks drops by.

832

MICHAEL ROSEN
NEAL LAYTON, Illustrator

Rover

(New York: A Doubleday Book for Young Readers, 1999)

Subject(s): Animals/Dogs; Pets; Family Life
Age range(s): Grades K-2
Major character(s): Rover, Child, Daughter; Rex, Father, Spouse; Cindy, Mother, Spouse
Time period(s): 1990s (1999)
Locale(s): England

Summary: In this view of family life through the eyes of the household pet, a dog thinks of Rover as his pet human. While the dog is disappointed that Rover has weak claws, a squeaky bark, poor hearing and an inadequate coat that covers only her head he still enjoys her companionship. The dog enjoys trips to the park where he helps Rover find the ball that she keeps throwing away. It's also fun to travel by car to the beach with Rover, Rex and Cindy although the dog can't understand humans' fascination with the huge sand pit. When the dog tires of the beach he goes to find Rover to bring her home with him and unwittingly locates the lost child for her appreciative parents. (28 pages)

Where it's reviewed:
Booklist, July 1999, page 1953
Children's Book Review Service, July 1999, page 151
Horn Book Guide, Fall 1999, page 266
Publishers Weekly, June 7, 1999, page 83
School Library Journal, June 1999, page 106

Other books by the same author:
Mission Ziffoid, 1999

This Is Our House, 1996
Little Rabbit Foo Foo, 1990

Other books you might like:
Nina Laden, *The Night I Followed the Dog*, 1994
  While a family sleeps, their pet dog secretly leads an exciting nightlife.
Merrill Markoe, *The Day My Dogs Became Guys*, 1999
  During a solar eclipse Carey's three pets transform into humans with the same annoying behaviors they had as dogs.
David Milgrim, *Dog Brain*, 1996
  A young boy is sure that his pet is smarter than his parents give him credit for being.
Alan Snow, *How Dogs Really Work!*, 1993
  A winner of the New York Times Best Illustrated Children's Book Award is a humorous instruction manual for dog owners.

833

MICHAEL J. ROSEN
DYANNE DISALVO-RYAN, Illustrator

Our Eight Nights of Hanukkah

(New York: Holiday House, 2000)

Subject(s): Holidays, Jewish; Family; Cultures and Customs
Age range(s): Grades K-3
Major character(s): Unnamed Character, Child, Narrator; Dad, Father; Grandma, Grandmother, Cook
Time period(s): 2000s (2000)
Locale(s): United States

Summary: One of three siblings describes the family's annual celebration of Hanukkah. Each night blends Jewish custom and family traditions so that, by the end of the eight days, they have eaten Grandma's latkes, sung songs, attended synagogue, shopped for gifts and decorated a friend's Christmas tree. Finally, on the last night of Hanukkah, they open their gifts and Dad expresses appreciation for the miracle of their family. (32 pages)

Where it's reviewed:
Booklist, September 1, 2000, page 135
Horn Book Guide, Spring 2001, page 91
Kirkus Reviews, September 1, 2000, page 1291
Publishers Weekly, September 25, 2000, page 66
School Library Journal, October 2000, page 65

Other books by the same author:
A School for Pompey Walker, 1995
Bonesy and Isabel, 1995
All Eyes on the Pond, 1994
Elijah's Angel: A Story for Chanukah and Christmas, 1992

Other books you might like:
Linda Glaser, *The Borrowed Hanukkah Latkes*, 1997
  Rachel could be starting a new tradition when she finds a way to seat a crowd of relatives and include a lonely neighbor in the Hanukkah celebration.
Marissa Moss, *The Ugly Menorah*, 1996
  When Rachel learns the history of Grandma's ugly menorah she understands why it is so important to her recently widowed grandmother.

Stephen Schnur, *The Tie-Man's Miracle: A Chanukah Tale*, 1995

On a night of remembering, elderly, lonely Mr. Hoffman shares memories of a family lost and a childhood belief that may bring about a miracle for him.

834

MICHAEL J. ROSEN
JOHN THOMPSON, Illustrator

A Thanksgiving Wish

(New York: Blue Sky Press/Scholastic, Inc., 1999)

Subject(s): Holidays; Grandmothers; Jews
Age range(s): Grades 1-4
Major character(s): Amanda, Child; Bubbe, Grandmother (deceased); Mrs. Yee, Neighbor
Time period(s): 1990s (1999)
Locale(s): United States

Summary: Amanda and her family know that their beloved Thanksgiving holiday will not be the same now that Bubbe has died. Who will cook all the delicious dishes, and break wishbones with the children? Amanda's family tries to cook all the same foods that they remember Bubbe making, but in doing so they blow out all the fuses in their house. Mrs. Yee comes over to help and soon the family's dinner is cooking all over the neighborhood. Mrs. Yee is invited to stay for dinner and she takes Bubbe's place in breaking a wishbone with Amanda. (32 pages)

Where it's reviewed:
Booklist, September 1, 1999, page 150
Bulletin of the Center for Children's Books, October 1999, page 67
Children's Book Review Service, November 1999, page 32
Publishers Weekly, September 27, 1999, page 50
School Library Journal, October 1999, page 124

Awards the book has won:
Notable Social Studies Trade Books for Young People, 2000

Other books by the same author:
Elijah's Angel: A Story for Chanukah and Christmas, 1997
A School for Pompey Walker, 1995
Bonesy and Isabel, 1995
The Greatest Table: A Banquet to Fight Against Hunger, 1994

Other books you might like:
Laurie Halse Anderson, *Turkey Pox*, 1996
Charity's family fails to notice that she has developed chicken pox, until they arrive at Nana's house for dinner.
Barbara Cohen, *Molly's Pilgrim*, 1990
Molly, a Russian Jewish immigrant, celebrates Thanksgiving for the first time.
Joy Cowley, *Gracias, the Thanksgiving Turkey*, 1996
Miguel convinces his family to eat chicken on Thanksgiving, rather than eat his pet turkey, Gracias.

835

LIZ ROSENBERG
CHRIS K. SOENTPIET, Illustrator

The Silence in the Mountains

(New York: Orchard Books, 1999)

Subject(s): Refugees; Emigration and Immigration; Grandparents
Age range(s): Grades 1-4
Major character(s): Iskander, Refugee, Child
Time period(s): 1990s (1999)
Locale(s): United States

Summary: Iskander and his family are forced to flee their war-torn home country. Upon arriving in America, Iskander's family hopes the good features of their new farm home will reassure Iskander, but something is still missing for him. Only his grandfather knows what is making Iskander unhappy, and they walk up the mountains near their new home to listen, once again, to the silence. (32 pages)

Where it's reviewed:
Booklist, February 1, 1999, page 982
Horn Book Guide, Fall 1999, page 266
Kirkus Reviews, January 1, 1999, page 70
Publishers Weekly, March 22, 1999, page 92
School Library Journal, July 1999, page 79

Other books by the same author:
Eli and Uncle Dawn, 1997
Grandmother and the Runaway Shadow, 1996
Monster Mama, 1993

Other books you might like:
Aliki, *Marianthe's Story: Painted Words/Spoken Memories*, 1998
Through painted pictures, immigrant Marianthe communicates her feelings until she learns enough English to speak of her past.
Luis Garay, *The Long Road*, 1997
When a civil war breaks out in Jose's village, he must flee to America with his mother.
Florence Parry Heide, *Sami and the Time of the Troubles*, 1992
Ten-year-old Sami describes daily life in war-torn Beirut.
Robert Munsch, *From Far Away*, 1995
Saoussan and her family move to Canada from war-torn Lebanon.

836

VERA ROSENBERRY, Author/Illustrator

Vera Runs Away

(New York: Henry Holt and Company, 2000)

Subject(s): Family Life; Runaways; Sisters
Age range(s): Grades K-2
Major character(s): Vera, 1st Grader, Daughter; Norman, Neighbor, Student—Elementary School; Mother, Mother
Time period(s): Indeterminate Past
Locale(s): United States

Summary: When Norman sees that Vera has a straight "A" report card he excitedly relates what his mother's reaction would be if he brought home such grades. Anticipating a similar reaction at her house, Vera races home eager for recognition but Mother is coping with a flooded bathroom due to a baby-caused toilet problem. Vera's older sisters think nothing of her report card because, to them, all first graders get A's. Vera's father has no time for her news because he's trying to fix the toilet. Frustrated and disappointed, Vera runs away to find a family that appreciates her. Vera makes a little home in the woods near her house and feels content to live alone until hunger leads her to pack her things again and return to her house only to find it empty. Everyone is searching for Vera and everyone is hungry but Mother hasn't been able to cook dinner because she's been looking for Vera. Norman was right about one thing—a straight "A" report card will get you a pizza dinner. (32 pages)

Where it's reviewed:
Booklist, October 15, 2000, page 446
Horn Book Guide, Spring 2001, page 22
Kirkus Reviews, October 15, 2000, page 1490
Publishers Weekly, November 20, 2000, page 70
School Library Journal, November 2000, page 131

Other books by the same author:
Run, Jump, Whiz, Splash, 1999
Vera's First Day of School, 1999 (Riverbank Review Children's Books of Distinction)
When Vera Was Sick, 1998

Other books you might like:
Martha Alexander, *And My Mean Old Mother Will Be Sorry, Blackboard Bear*, 2000
New illustrations enhance the story first published in 1969 of a little boy who briefly runs away when his mom becomes angry about his messy behavior.
SuAnn Kiser, *The Catspring Somersault Flying One-Handed Flip-Flop*, 1993
Willy's large family has no time to watch her latest gymnastic trick so she runs away sure that no one will notice her absence.
Emily Arnold McCully, *My Real Family*, 1994
An evening of disappointments convinces Sarah that she must be in the wrong family and she runs away to find her real one.
Erik Jon Slangerup, *Dirt Boy*, 2000
Fister gets entirely too much attention from his mother who has expectations of cleanliness that exceed Fister's style.

837

VERA ROSENBERRY, Author/Illustrator

Vera's First Day of School

(New York: Henry Holt and Company, 1999)

Subject(s): Schools; Sisters; Fear
Age range(s): Grades K-1
Major character(s): Vera, Student—Elementary School, Sister; Elaine, Student—Elementary School, Sister (older); June, Student—Elementary School, Sister (older)
Time period(s): Indeterminate Past

Locale(s): United States
Summary: Vera is awake and dressed before sunrise, eager to be ready on time for the first day of school. She walks to school with Elaine and June who leave her at the playground while they hurry off to meet their friends. Vera is so overwhelmed by the many children she sees that she seeks shelter under a large tree and watches a caterpillar. Thus, Vera does not notice the children entering the building and when she hears a bell ring she looks at an empty playground. Afraid to enter the school late, Vera sadly walks home and quietly goes up to her room where her mother finds her under the bed. Vera's mother washes her tear-stained face, brushes her hair again and walks her back to school all the way to the classroom where she introduces Vera to the teacher and Vera's first day of school begins only a little late. (32 pages)

Where it's reviewed:
Booklist, September 15, 1999, page 269
Horn Book, September 1999, page 599
Riverbank Review, Spring 2000, page 35
School Library Journal, September 1999, page 201

Awards the book has won:
Riverbank Review Children's Books of Distinction, 2000

Other books by the same author:
When Vera Was Sick, 1998

Other books you might like:
Miriam Cohen, *Will I Have a Friend?*, 1967
First-day-of-school fears are put to rest when Paul makes friends with Jim.
Kevin Henkes, *Chrysanthemum*, 1991
Unhappy Chrysanthemum arrives home from her first day of school feeling humiliated by teasing from classmates about her unusual name.
Tony Johnston, *Sparky and Eddie: The First Day of School*, 1997
A beginning chapter book introduces two friends who learn to accept some changes in their plans when they enter school for the first time.
Amy Schwartz, *Annabelle Swift, Kindergartner*, 1988
Listening to her big sister's experiences helps Annabelle have a successful first day of kindergarten.

838

ALICE ROSS
KENT ROSS, Co-Author
TED RAND, Illustrator

Jezebel's Spooky Spot

(New York: Dutton Children's Books, 1999)

Subject(s): Fear; Fathers and Daughters; Courage
Age range(s): Grades 1-4
Major character(s): Jezebel, Child, Daughter; Little Brother, Child, Brother (younger); Papa, Father, Widow(er)
Time period(s): Indeterminate Past
Locale(s): South

Summary: As Papa prepares to leave for war he cautions Jezebel to look fear in the eye while he's gone just as he'll be doing whenever he feels fearful. As Papa walks from sight, Jezebel races into the woods and runs until she trips and falls on the ground in an awful scary part of the swampy woods. She remembers Papa's words and faces her fear claiming the spot in the woods as her own. During Papa's absence, Jezebel returns to the same spot when she feels lonely, each time confronting something frightening—spiders, fog, "pixie" lights. When Jezebel returns home after each confrontation she tells Little Brother how she faced the scary things and overcame them. Jezebel is in her special place when she hears something coming through the woods. At first she's too frightened to realize it's Papa, heading home from the war with only a slight wound. Only then does Jezebel learn that her "spooky" spot is Papa's special quiet place in the woods too. (32 pages)

Where it's reviewed:
Booklist, February 15, 1999, page 1076
Children's Book Review Service, April 1999, page 105
Horn Book Guide, Fall 1999, page 283
Publishers Weekly, December 14, 1998, page 75
School Library Journal, April 1999, page 107

Other books by the same author:
The Copper Lady, 1997
Cemetery Quilt, 1995
Whistle Punk, 1994

Other books you might like:
Mercer Mayer, *Liza Lou and the Yeller Belly Swamp*, 1976
    Liza Lou outwits all the witches, haunts and spooks in the Yeller Belly Swamp.
Melissa Milich, *Can't Scare Me!*, 1995
    Eugenia loves the stories Papa tells, but they frighten Mr. Munroe so brave Eugenia has to walk the neighbor home after a night of storytelling.
Tynia Thomassie, *Feliciana Meets d'Loup Garou: A Cajun Tall Tale*, 1998
    When courageous Feliciana meets the dreaded swamp monster, Loup Garou teaches her how to howl at the moon as a remedy for a bad day.
Marcia Vaughan, *Whistling Dixie*, 1995
    Dixie Lee feels no fear of the swamp creatures she brings home as pets; rather she things they have important protective purposes—and she's right.

839

NAN PARSON ROSSITER, Author/Illustrator

The Way Home
(New York: Dutton Children's Books, 1999)

Subject(s): Animals/Geese; Farm Life; Animals, Treatment of
Age range(s): Grades K-3
Major character(s): Samuel, Child, Son; Dad, Father, Farmer; Chicory, Goose
Time period(s): Indeterminate Past
Locale(s): North

Summary: While Dad and Samuel enjoy a late-afternoon walk around the pond, their dog comes upon an injured goose hiding in the grass. With the goose's mate following, Dad carries the goose home and cuts off the fishing line wrapped around one wing and foot. Samuel cares for Chicory, as he names her, feeding both the geese and giving them shelter in

the barn every night. While Samuel is grateful to see Chicory's wing healing, he is saddened when she and her mate resume their flight south for the winter. Warmer weather brings many signs of spring including the return of Chicory and her mate who nest near the pond. (32 pages)

Where it's reviewed:
Booklist, September 15, 1999, page 270
Horn Book Guide, Spring 2000, page 52
Kirkus Reviews, August 1, 1999, page 230
School Library Journal, November 1999, page 128
Smithsonian Magazine, November 1999, page 48

Awards the book has won:
Smithsonian's Notable Books for Children, 1999

Other books by the same author:
Rugby and Rosie, 1997

Other books you might like:
Sheryl McFarlane, *Eagle Dreams*, 1994
    Robin rescues an injured eagle and cares for it until it can fly again and return to its mate.
John Schoenherr, *Rebel*, 1995
    One independent gosling is almost left behind at the pond when the family answers nature's call to fly away.
Pirko Vaino, *The Snow Goose*, 1993
    A little girl raises a gosling hatched from the egg of a dying goose only to watch it join a flock and fly away as the summer ends.
Jane Yolen, *Honkers*, 1993
    A lonely young girl and three abandoned geese share a summer of activity before being separated by the approach of winter.

840

CAROL ROTH
VALERI GORBACHEV, Illustrator

Little Bunny's Sleepless Night
(New York: North-South Books, 1999)

Subject(s): Animals/Rabbits; Sleep; Loneliness
Age range(s): Grades K-1
Major character(s): Little Bunny, Rabbit; Squirrel, Squirrel, Friend; Owl, Owl, Neighbor
Time period(s): Indeterminate
Locale(s): Fictional Country

Summary: Little Bunny feels lonely at night alone in his bed in his own room and sometimes has difficulty sleeping so he decides to visit his neighbor. Squirrel is happy to share his bed with Little Bunny who is sleeping soundly when loud crunching sounds awaken him. Squirrel is having a snack and Little Bunny can't sleep with the noise of cracking acorns so he seeks a different bed. Little Bunny tries a succession of other friendly neighbors who welcome him, but whom Little Bunny quickly leaves because their beds are too smelly, full of prickly quills, noisy from snoring or filled with the light of a reading lamp. Finally, wise Owl advises Little Bunny to go home and try his own bed and Little Bunny does. The peace and quiet is just what Little Bunny needs to sleep. (32 pages)

Where it's reviewed:
Booklist, June 1999, page 1844

Horn Book Guide, Fall 1999, page 266
Kirkus Reviews, March 1, 1999, page 381
Publishers Weekly, February 22, 1999, page 93
School Library Journal, July 1999, page 79

Awards the book has won:
IRA/CBC Children's Choices, 2000

Other books by the same author:
Ten Dirty Pigs, Ten Clean Pigs: An Upside-Down, Turn-Around Bathtime Counting Book, 1999
Quiet as a Mouse, 1991

Other books you might like:
Maryann MacDonald, *Sam's Worries*, 1991
   Anxious Sam is unable to sleep until he shares his many worries with his toy bear who promises to do the worrying at night while Sam sleeps.
Ann McGovern, *Too Much Noise*, 1967
   Unable to sleep because his house is too noisy, an old man follows the advice of the village wise man and finally finds the quiet he seeks.
Kate McMullan, *Papa's Song*, 2000
   Papa Bear has just the right song to sooth Baby Bear into sleep.

841

JOAN ROTHENBERG, Author/Illustrator

Matzah Ball Soup

(New York: Hyperion Books for Children, 1999)

Subject(s): Holidays, Jewish; Food; Traditions
Age range(s): Grades K-3
Major character(s): Rosie, Child, Cook; Grandma, Grandmother, Cook
Time period(s): 1990s (1999); Indeterminate Past
Locale(s): United States

Summary: While helping Grandma make the matzah balls for the family's Seder, Rosie learns the family tradition behind the four matzah balls in each bowl of chicken soup. When Grandma was just Rosie's age, her mother and sisters argued over who made the best matzah balls so to keep the peace, every year each of the four sisters made her own recipe and the family members diplomatically selected one of each. Although Grandma uses only her mother's recipe, she continues the tradition of placing four matzah balls in each bowl. (32 pages)

Where it's reviewed:
Booklist, October 1, 1999, page 374
Horn Book Guide, Spring 2000, page 52
School Library Journal, September 1999, page 201

Other books by the same author:
Inside-Out Grandma, 1995
Yettele's Feathers, 1995

Other books you might like:
Malka Drucker, *The Family Treasury of Jewish Holidays*, 1994
   The nonfiction collection of stories, games, songs and recipes explains the traditions of ten Jewish holidays.

Fran Manushkin, *The Matzah that Papa Brought Home*, 1995
   The award-winning cumulative tale begins with the matzah Papa brings home and continues through the family Seder.
Miriam Nerlove, *Passover*, 1989
   A rhyming text describes the Jewish holiday.
Roni Schotter, *Passover Magic*, 1995
   Molly and Ben eagerly welcome the relatives arriving for the special Passover dinner.
Lauren Wohl, *Matzoh Mouse*, 1991
   Sarah finds some of the Passover offerings so tempting that she has difficulty waiting for the Seder.

842

J.K. ROWLING
MARY GRANDPRE, Illustrator

Harry Potter and the Chamber of Secrets

(New York: Scholastic Press, 1999)

Subject(s): Wizards; Magic; Schools/Boarding Schools
Age range(s): Grades 3-6
Major character(s): Harry Potter, 12-Year-Old, Wizard (in training); Ron Weasley, Friend (Harry's), Wizard (in training); Dobby, Mythical Creature
Time period(s): Indeterminate
Locale(s): England (Hogwarts School of Witchcraft)

Summary: Harry Potter gratefully returns to Hogwarts School of Witchcraft and Wizardry, after a depressing summer with his disagreeable ''Muggle'' family. However life at Hogwarts presents its own set of challenges. Dobby, who first visited Harry during the summer, follows him to Hogwarts and seems to be connected in some way to the strange happenings at school. Someone is threatening the Hogwarts' residents and students start turning into stone. Harry's presence at the school is suspected of causing the problems. With help from Ron and second-year magic skills, Harry works hard to prove the rumor wrong, and save the school from He-Who-Cannot-Be-Named. (352 pages)

Where it's reviewed:
Booklist, May 15, 1999, page 1690
Horn Book, July 1999, page 472
Publishers Weekly, May 31, 1999, page 94
School Library Journal, July 1999, page 1999
Times Literary Supplement, September 18, 1998, page 28

Awards the book has won:
Publishers Weekly Best Books, 1999
School Library Journal Best Books, 1999

Other books by the same author:
Harry Potter and the Prisoner of Azkaban, 1999 (Smithsonian Notable Books for Children)
Harry Potter and the Sorcerer's Stone, 1998 (Booklist Editor's Choice)

Other books you might like:
Eva Ibbotson, *Which Witch?*, 1979
   Arriman the Awful wants to marry a beautiful witch, hoping their baby will inherit his magic skills. However, not all witches are what they seem.

Diana Wynne Jones, *Witch Week*, 1997
When someone in a class at an English boarding school is accused of being a witch, magical things happen.

Jill Murphy, *A Bad Spell for the Worst Witch*, 1991
Mildred attempts to save her boarding school for witches, with disastrous results

Gillian Rubinstein, *Under the Cat's Eye: A Tale of Morph and Mystery*, 1998
Jai befriends shapeshifters at his boarding school.

843

J.K. ROWLING
MARY GRANDPRE, Illustrator

Harry Potter and the Prisoner of Azkaban
(New York: Arthur A. Levine Books/Scholastic Press, 1999)

Subject(s): Wizards; Magic; Schools/Boarding Schools
Age range(s): Grades 4-8
Major character(s): Harry Potter, Wizard (in training), Student—Boarding School; Ron Weasley, Friend (Harry's), Wizard (in training); Hermione Granger, Friend, Witch (in training)
Time period(s): Indeterminate
Locale(s): England (Hogwarts School of Witchcraft)

Summary: Who is trying to kill Harry? Is it the prisoner who's escaped from Azkaban? Hogwarts is taking no chances with the students' safety and has dementors posted around the periphery to guard the school. As a third year student Harry should have the privilege to leave campus and visit the nearby village, but his "Muggle" family will not fill out the permission form so Harry must find a way to do it without being noticed. Events soon make Harry believe that danger also lies within the security of the school grounds. Hermione is acting strangely tired from her course load and her new cat seems to hate Ron's pet rat so Harry wonders just who or what will be killed first. As Harry and his friends work together to unravel the mystery, Harry also gains more knowledge about his parents, the legacy they left him and their hopes for his future. (435 pages)

Where it's reviewed:
The Book Report, November 1999, page 65
Booklist, September 1, 1999, page 127
Horn Book, November 1999, page 744
School Library Journal, October 1999, page 158
Smithsonian Magazine, November 1999, page 52

Awards the book has won:
Publishers Weekly Best Books, 1999
Smithsonian's Notable Books for Children, 1999

Other books by the same author:
Harry Potter and the Chamber of Secrets, 1999 (School Library Journal Best Book)
Harry Potter and the Sorcerer's Stone, 1997 (ALA Best Book for Young Adults)

Other books you might like:
Diane Duane, *A Wizard Abroad*, 1997
In the fourth book of the Wizardry series, Nita travels to Ireland, only to discover she must use her magic there as well.

Brian Jacques, *Redwall*, 1986
The evil rat Cluny destroys the peace of ancient Redwall Abbey as he and his hordes of villains attempt to seize control.

Ursula K. Le Guin, *A Wizard of Earthsea*, 1991
A young wizard must combat the evil that he unwittingly released as an apprentice.

Tamora Pierce, *Sandry's Book*, 1997
This entry in the Circle of Magic series features Sandry, a young magician in training at the Winding Circle Temple.

844

RON ROY
JOHN STEVEN GURNEY, Illustrator

The Goose's Gold
(New York: Random House, 1999)

Series: A to Z Mysteries
Subject(s): Treasure, Buried; Mystery and Detective Stories; Vacations
Age range(s): Grades 2-4
Major character(s): Donald David "Dink" Duncan, Child, Friend; Josh, Child, Friend; Ruth Rose, Child, Friend
Time period(s): 1990s (1999)
Locale(s): Key West, Florida

Summary: While visiting Ruth Rose's grandmother during winter vacation, three friends stumble onto a scam. At the airport, when Dink calls home to report his safe arrival, he overhears a conversation in the next phone booth that sounds suspicious. Josh and Ruth Rose think Dink misunderstood what he heard, but when they learn that two men have plans to get Ruth Rose's grandmother and her friends to invest in their search for sunken treasure, the friends begin investigating. They locate the boat belonging to the men who visited the house soliciting investors. Dink, Josh and Ruth Rose become trapped on the boat when the men return but they do overhear the plans from their hiding place—plans that jeopardize their lives as well as the senior citizens' savings. (86 pages)

Where it's reviewed:
Booklist, October 15, 1999, page 446
Horn Book Guide, Fall 1999, page 283
School Library Journal, July 1999, page 79

Other books by the same author:
The Canary Caper, 1998
The Deadly Dungeon, 1998
The Bald Bandit, 1997

Other books you might like:
David A. Adler, *The Cam Jansen Series*, 1980-
Using her photographic memory, Cam Jansen solves a variety of mysteries with her friend Eric.

Patricia Reilly Giff, *Kidnap at the Catfish Cafe*, 1998
While Minnie's fledgling detective business searches for the owner of a ring, her cat vanishes and she has a bigger case to solve.

Marjorie Weinman Sharmat, *The Nate the Great Series*, 1972-
Nate follows one clue after another copying the style of Sherlock Holmes in this series for beginning readers.

845

KAREN GRAY RUELLE, Author/Illustrator

Snow Valentines

(New York: Holiday House, 2000)

Series: Holiday House Readers. Level 2
Subject(s): Parent and Child; Gifts; Brothers and Sisters
Age range(s): Grades 1-2
Major character(s): Harry, Cat, Brother (older); Emily, Cat, Sister
Time period(s): Indeterminate
Locale(s): Fictional Country

Summary: Harry and Emily are trying to think of a unique valentine for their parents. They can't give hugs because their mother is the best hugger and they can't draw a picture because their father is the best at drawing pictures. They consider and discard several unique ideas as being unsuitable for one reason or another. When Harry awakens on Valentine's Day morning and sees newly fallen snow, he wakes Emily and the siblings hurry outside to create a snow valentine surprise for their appreciative parents. (32 pages)

Where it's reviewed:
Booklist, July 2000, page 2045
Kirkus Reviews, September 15, 2000, page 1362
School Library Journal, September 2000, page 207

Other books by the same author:
Trick or Treat Surprise, 2001 (Holiday House Reader, Level 2)
The Monster in Harry's Backyard, 1999 (Holiday House Reader, Level 2)
The Thanksgiving Beast Feast, 1999 (Holiday House Reader, Level 2)

Other books you might like:
Bill Cosby, *Super-Fine Valentine*, 1998
Little Bill feels too shy to give a valentine to a girl he secretly likes, but he gains the necessary confidence when other students exchange cards.
Liza Donnelly, *Dinosaur Valentine*, 1994
In a ''Read with Me'' series entry a romance between a dog and a small dog-like dinosaur begins with an invitation to a Valentine's Day party.
Lillian Hoban, *Silly Tilly's Valentine*, 1998
Forgetful Silly Tilly is so busy with the snow that she misses Mr. Bunny's hint about the special day in an ''I Can Read'' beginning reader.
Marjorie Weinman Sharmat, *Nate the Great and the Mushy Valentine*, 1995
Nate the Great solves two Valentine's Day mysteries.

846

KAREN GRAY RUELLE, Author/Illustrator

The Thanksgiving Beast Feast

(New York: Holiday House, 1999)

Series: Holiday House Reader. Level 2
Subject(s): Holidays; Brothers and Sisters; Animals
Age range(s): Grades 1-2
Major character(s): Harry, Cat, Brother (older); Emily, Cat, Sister (younger); Unnamed Character, Mother, Cook
Time period(s): 1990s
Locale(s): Fictional Country

Summary: Harry and Emily's mother may think that Thanksgiving is about more than food, but after hearing her explanation of the pilgrims and the first Thanksgiving, Harry and Emily can think of nothing else. When they notice squirrels without nuts, birds at the empty bird feeder and chipmunks scurrying about the yard searching for food, Harry and Emily decide the animals are just like the pilgrims with no stores of food. The siblings decide to be like the Indians and plan a Thanksgiving beast feast. While their parents get the family feast ready, Harry and Emily prepare a feast for the animals that live in their yard. (32 pages)

Where it's reviewed:
Booklist, September 1, 1999, page 150
Horn Book, September 1999, page 617
Publishers Weekly, September 27, 1999, page 51
School Library Journal, September 1999, page 202

Other books by the same author:
Snow Valentines, 2000
The Monster in Harry's Backyard, 1999 (Holiday House Reader, Level 2)

Other books you might like:
Alyssa Satin Capucilli, *Happy Thanksgiving, Biscuit!*, 1999
Energetic puppy Biscuit enjoys his first Thanksgiving holiday.
Gail Gibbons, *Thanksgiving Day*, 1983
Simple text explains both the first Thanksgiving and the way we now celebrate the holiday.
Robert Kraus, *How Spider Saved Thanksgiving*, 1991
How can the class have their Thanksgiving play without a turkey? Spider has a plan.
Marion Hess Pomeranc, *The Can-Do Thanksgiving*, 1998
Thanksgiving is especially meaningful for Dee this year when she helps a church feed the needy.
Leslie Tryon, *Albert's Thanksgiving*, 1994
Students at Pleasant Valley School plan a Thanksgiving feast with help from Albert the duck.

847

CHING YEUNG RUSSELL
JONATHAN T. RUSSELL, Illustrator

Child Bride

(Honesdale, PA: Boyd's Mill Press, 1999)

Subject(s): Marriage; Grandparents; Cultures and Customs
Age range(s): Grades 4-7
Major character(s): Ying Yeung, 11-Year-Old; Ah Pau Chan, Grandmother (maternal); Ah Mah Yeung, Grandmother (paternal)
Time period(s): 1940s (1948)
Locale(s): Tai Kong, China

Summary: Ying, who lives with Ah Pau in a small village, is sent to visit Ah Mah, who is reported to be ill. Upon arriving at Ah Mah's, Ying discovers that she has been deceived,for Ah Mah is healthy, but wanted Ying for an arranged marriage.

Refusing to accept Ah Mah's plan, Ying runs away, but is captured. The future bridegroom is sensitive enough to recognize Ying's concern for Ah Pau's poor health and allows Ying to return to the village to care for her. (133 pages)

Where it's reviewed:
The Book Report, November 1999, page 66
Booklist, March 1, 1999, page 1214
Horn Book Guide, Fall 1999, page 299
Kirkus Reviews, February 1, 1999, page 228
School Library Journal, April 1999, page 141

Other books by the same author:
Lichee Tree, 1997
Water Ghost, 1995
First Apple, 1994

Other books you might like:
Carol Kendall, *Sweet and Sour: Tales from China*, 1990
   Twenty-four tales from various periods in Chinese history reveal the customs and culture of the country.
Elizabeth Foreman Lewis, *Young Fu of the Upper Yangtze*, 1932
   A young boy and his mother move from their rural village to Chungking where the boy's apprenticeship to a coppersmith brings good luck. Newbery Medal winner.
Amy Tan, *The Moon Lady*, 1992
   On a rainy day, Nai-nai entertains her three granddaughters with stories of her childhood in China.

848

PAM MUNOZ RYAN
BRIAN SELZNICK, Illustrator

Amelia and Eleanor Go for a Ride

(New York: Scholastic Press, 1999)

Subject(s): American History; Airplanes; Independence
Age range(s): Grades 1-4
Major character(s): Amelia Earhart, Pilot, Historical Figure; Eleanor Roosevelt, Historical Figure, Friend (Amelia's)
Time period(s): 1930s (1933)
Locale(s): Washington, District of Columbia

Summary: Amelia Earhart and her husband are guests at a small dinner party at the White House when the conversation inevitably turns to flying. As one of the few people to have flown at night, Amelia describes so eloquently the experience that she and Eleanor, a student pilot, leave the table before dessert to take a quick flight over the city just to see the lights of the nation's capital at night. The view is breathtaking and Eleanor tries to think of something comparable. Before the friends return to the White House for dessert, Eleanor and Amelia go for a ride in Eleanor's new car. A concluding author's note gives the factual basis for the story. (40 pages)

Where it's reviewed:
Booklist, October 15, 1999, page 447
Kirkus Reviews, October 1, 1999, page 1583
Publishers Weekly, September 27, 1999, page 105
Riverbank Review, Winter 1999-2000, page 26
School Library Journal, September 1999, page 202

Awards the book has won:
ALA Notable Children's Books, 2000

Other books by the same author:
Armadillos Sleep in Dugouts: And Other Places Animals Live, 1997
California Here We Come!, 1997
One Hundred Is a Family, 1994

Other books you might like:
Shana Corey, *You Forgot Your Skirt, Amelia Bloomer!*, 2000
   Women's rights activist Amelia Bloomer is a trendsetter not a proper lady in corsets and hoop skirts, but a practical one in pants.
Betsy Hearne, *Seven Brave Women*, 1997
   Seven generations of women in one family make a difference in the lives of those around them.
Kathryn Lasky, *She's Wearing a Dead Bird on Her Head!*, 1995
   Founders of the Audobon Society work to stop the killing of birds for fashion.
Emily Arnold McCully, *The Ballot Box Battle*, 1996
   Elizabeth Cady Stanton's fight for women's suffrage affects the lives of women in her generation and for the future.

849

CYNTHIA RYLANT
NANCY HAYASHI, Illustrator

Bunny Bungalow

(San Diego: Harcourt Brace & Company, 1999)

Subject(s): Animals/Rabbits; Housing; Family
Age range(s): Preschool
Major character(s): Mother Bunny, Mother, Rabbit; Father Bunny, Father, Rabbit
Time period(s): Indeterminate
Locale(s): United States

Summary: Using a little green paint and a lot of love, Mother and Father Bunny turn a ramshackle bungalow into a home. Mother Bunny makes quilts for the five Bunny children's beds and Father Bunny makes a carrot weather vane for the roof. After fixing the old house into a cozy home, the family lives there happily. (32 pages)

Where it's reviewed:
Booklist, April 15, 1999, page 1537
Publisher's Weekly, March 15, 1999, page 56
School Library Journal, June 1999, page 106

Other books by the same author:
The Heavenly Village, 1999
In Aunt Lucy's Kitchen, 1998 (Cobble Street Cousins, Book 1)
The Old Woman Who Named Things, 1998
Dog Heaven, 1995

Other books you might like:
Annie Ingle, *The Bunnies Ball*, 1994
   Cottontails, jackrabbits, and lop-ears gather together for a ball.
Peter McCarty, *Little Bunny on the Move*, 1999
   Little Bunny knows what he's doing and where he's going as he keeps moving, ignoring all distractions.

Brigitte Weniger, *What Have You Done, Davy?*, 1996
Davy, an energetic young bunny, gets into lots of mischief and must learn to apologize to his family.

850

CYNTHIA RYLANT
G. BRIAN KARAS, Illustrator

The Case of the Missing Monkeys
(New York: Greenwillow Books, 2000)

Series: The High-Rise Private Eyes. Case #001
Subject(s): Animals; Mystery and Detective Stories; Lost and Found Possessions
Age range(s): Grades 1-2
Major character(s): Bunny Brown, Rabbit, Detective—Private; Jack Jones, Raccoon, Detective—Private; Mac, Restaurateur, Businessman
Time period(s): 2000s (2000)
Locale(s): Fictional Country

Summary: Rather than stay in the office arguing over what to eat for breakfast, Bunny and Jack go to the diner next door for pancakes. Mac is happy to see them so he can report a stolen glass monkey. He hires Jack and Bunny to solve the case and locate his monkey. The next morning the private eyes return to the diner to study the patrons. Bunny takes notes and then deduces that an absent-minded father borrowed the monkey to calm his baby while he ate breakfast the previous morning. Bunny correctly guesses that he will quietly return the monkey by placing it on the table when he leaves. Jack is pleased to see that not only does the culprit return the monkey but he also leaves a powdered donut on his plate. (48 pages)

Where it's reviewed:
Booklist, October 1, 2000, page 352
Horn Book, September 2000, page 582
Publishers Weekly, August 7, 2000, page 95
School Library Journal, August 2000, page 164

Other books by the same author:
The Case of the Puzzling Possum, 2001 (High Rise Private Eyes, Case #003)
Mr. Putter and Tabby Paint the Porch, 2000
The Case of the Climbing Cat, 2000 (High Rise Private Eyes, Case #002)
Henry and Mudge and Annie's Good Move, 1998

Other books you might like:
David A. Adler, *Young Cam Jansen and the Missing Cookie*, 1996
When Jason discovers his chocolate chip cookie is missing from his lunch box Cam Jansen solves the mystery of its disappearance.
Eth Clifford, *Flatfoot Fox and the Case of the Missing Schoolhouse*, 1997
Flatfoot Fox feels confident that he can recover the new schoolhouse and identify the culprit responsible.
Elizabeth Levy, *The Snack Attack Mystery*, 1996
The third entry in the Invisible, Inc. series investigates a classroom's vanishing snacks.
Marjorie Weinman Sharmat, *Nate the Great and the Missing Key*, 1981

Annie turns to Nate for help when her friend hides Annie's key in a safe place and gives her a poem full of clues to its location.

851

CYNTHIA RYLANT, Author/Illustrator

The Cookie-Store Cat
(New York: Scholastic, 1999)

Subject(s): Animals/Cats; Cooks and Cooking; Food
Age range(s): Grades K-2
Major character(s): Cookie-Store Cat, Cat
Time period(s): Indeterminate
Locale(s): United States

Summary: When the Cookie-Store Cat was just a kitten she wasn't a cookie store cat at all—she was a stray. One day, one of the bakers in the cookie store finds her, and takes her to live in the store. Now the Cookie-Store Cat lives full, happy days, being cared for by the bakers, visiting the neighbors, and playing with the children who come by. (40 pages)

Where it's reviewed:
Booklist, May 15, 1999, page 1703
Horn Book Guide, Fall 1999, page 266
Publishers Weekly, May 24, 1999, page 77
School Library Journal, April 1999, page 108

Other books by the same author:
The Bird House, 1998
Tulip Sees America, 1998
Cat Heaven, 1997
The Bookshop Dog, 1996
Dog Heaven, 1995

Other books you might like:
Yangsook Choi, *New Cat*, 1999
New Cat helps his owner, Mr. Kim, at his tofu factory.
Pamela D. Greenwood, *I Found Mouse*, 1994
Tessie finds a kitten in need of a home and convinces her dad to let her keep it.
Mauro Magellan, *Max the Apartment Cat*, 1989
Max escapes his apartment and goes exploring.
Ann M. Martin, *Leo the Magnificat*, 1996
A fluffy black and white cat wanders into a churchyard and makes himself at home for the rest of his long life.
Christopher Myers, *Black Cat*, 1999
A black cat explores his urban landscape in an award-winning picture book for older readers.

852

CYNTHIA RYLANT
SUCIE STEVENSON, Illustrator

Henry and Mudge and the Snowman Plan
(New York: Simon & Schuster Books for Young Readers, 1999)

Series: Henry and Mudge. Number 19
Subject(s): Animals/Dogs; Fathers and Sons; Contests
Age range(s): Grades 1-2
Major character(s): Henry, Child, Son; Mudge, Dog; Dad, Father

Time period(s): 1990s
Locale(s): United States

Summary: Three brief chapters describe the Snowman Contest at the park in Henry's hometown. Inspired by Dad's chair-painting technique, Henry and his dad arrive at the park with a plan for their snowman. Mudge spends the day socializing with other pets whose owners are in the contest. When the deadline for judging begins Henry and Dad look at the field of angels, animals and aliens all carefully crafted from snow. The judges study each entry carefully, especially the one made by Henry and Dad. Finally, they ask what the green covered snowman represents and Henry explains it's a sculpture of his dad painting a chair. The entry wins third place for "Most Original Snowman." (40 pages)

Where it's reviewed:
Booklist, October 1, 1999, page 366
Horn Book Guide, Spring 2000, page 62
School Library Journal, March 2000, page 212

Other books by the same author:
Henry and Mudge and Annie's Perfect Pet, 2000 (Henry and Mudge, Number 20)
Henry and Mudge and the Starry Night, 1998 (Henry and Mudge, Number 17)
Henry and Mudge and the Best Day of All, 1995 (Henry and Mudger, Number 14)

Other books you might like:
Lois Ehlert, *Snowballs*, 1995
Simple text and clear collages tell of the creation of a snow family and the inevitable result as the weather warms.
Barbara M. Joosse, *Snow Day!*, 1995
When snow forces the cancellation of school, Robby and his family have a day to play outside.
Stephen Krensky, *Lionel in the Winter*, 1994
In four brief easy-to-read stories Lionel makes the most of the winter weather that others in his family dislike.
Jean Van Leeuwen, *Oliver and Amanda and the Big Snow*, 1995
Oliver and his younger sister enjoy sledding, tossing snowballs and making a snow pig.

853

CYNTHIA RYLANT
ARTHUR HOWARD, Illustrator

Mr. Putter and Tabby Paint the Porch

(San Diego: Harcourt, Inc., 2000)

Subject(s): Animals/Cats; Animals/Dogs; Humor
Age range(s): Grades 2-3
Major character(s): Mr. Putter, Aged Person, Neighbor; Tabby, Cat; Mrs. Teaberry, Aged Person, Neighbor
Time period(s): 2000s (2000)
Locale(s): United States

Summary: As Mr. Putter settles down on the porch to read to Tabby he notices that the railings need painting. Patient Tabby is willing to wait for the story because Mr. Putter sings and yodels as he paints and that's really entertaining! When a squirrel hops onto the porch, Tabby gives chase, spilling the paint and making a splattered pink mess of Mr. Putter's work.

Undaunted, Mr. Putter selects blue paint to cover the mess when Mrs. Teaberry and her dog stop by to see what Mr. Putter is doing. The dog chases a chipmunk off the porch and recreates the paint problem in a new color. Finally, Mrs. Teaberry keeps both pets in her house while Mr. Putter single-handedly paints the porch yellow. Now, the only paint-splattered objects in sight are the animals. (44 pages)

Where it's reviewed:
Booklist, April 15, 2000, page 1542
Horn Book Guide, Fall 2000, page 290
Kirkus Reviews, March 15, 2000, page 389
Publishers Weekly, February 14, 2000, page 203
School Library Journal, July 2000, page 86

Other books by the same author:
Mr. Putter and Tabby Toot the Horn, 1998
Mr. Putter and Tabby Row the Boat, 1997
Mr. Putter and Tabby Pick the Pears, 1995

Other books you might like:
Lloyd Alexander, *How the Cat Swallowed Thunder*, 2000
Mother Holly's cat makes a mess when she's not home and swallows some of the evidence while cleaning up hurriedly.
Larry L. Hench, *Boing-Boing the Bionic Cat*, 2000
Professor George builds Daniel a bionic cat since he's allergic to the live kind.
Phyllis Root, *Here Comes Tabby Cat*, 2000
Four stories in a beginning reader describe the activities of Tabby Cat.
Ellen Stoll Walsh, *Mouse Paint*, 1898
Three white mice fall in and out of jars of primary colored paint, confusing a cat as they change colors.

854

CYNTHIA RYLANT
MARK TEAGUE, Illustrator

Poppleton Has Fun

(New York: The Blue Sky Press/Scholastic Inc., 2000)

Series: Poppleton Pig. Book 7
Subject(s): Animals/Pigs; Animals; Friendship
Age range(s): Grades 1-2
Major character(s): Poppleton, Pig, Friend; Cherry Sue, Llama, Friend
Time period(s): Indeterminate
Locale(s): Fictional Country

Summary: In the first of three stories Cherry Sue is not able to go to the movies with Poppleton so he goes alone. At first he thinks a solo trip to the movies will be fun because he will not have to share his snacks. During the movie, Poppleton realizes he also has no one with whom to share the funny, scary or sad parts of the movie and he vows never again to attend a movie without a friend. Inspired by a quilt show at the Fair Cherry Sue and Poppleton invite two other friends to join them in making a quilt. While they stitch each one tells a story about an event in their life that they're stitching into their section of the quilt. When the beautiful quilt is complete they assign a season to each friend and agree to pass the quilt along so each of them can sleep under stories for three months. In the final story Poppleton runs out of bath soaks. He tries to borrow some from Cherry Sue, but she showers so she offers various spices as substitutes and makes Poppleton so hungry he forgets the bath and goes out with Cherry Sue to eat banana splits. (52 pages)

Where it's reviewed:
Booklist, November 15, 2000, page 650
Horn Book Guide, Spring 2001, page 57
Kirkus Reviews, September 1, 2000, page 1291
School Library Journal, December 2000, page 124

Other books by the same author:
Poppleton in Fall, 1999 (Poppleton Pig, Book 6)
Poppleton in Spring, 1999 (Poppleton Pig, Book 5)
Poppleton Forever, 1998 (Poppleton Pig, Book 4)
Poppleton and Friends, 1997 (Poppleton Pig, Book 2)

Other books you might like:
Mary Ann Hoberman, *One of Each*, 1997
   Oliver Tolliver learns that just one of something, if shared, is much better that the whole enjoyed alone.
Betsy Lewin, *Chubbo's Pool*, 1996
   Chubbo, a selfish young hippo, quickly grows lonely when he refuses to share his pool.
James Marshall, *George and Martha Back in Town*, 1984
   A sense of humor helps two hippos survive the ups and downs of friendship.

855

CYNTHIA RYLANT
MARK TEAGUE, Illustrator

Poppleton in Fall

(New York: The Blue Sky Press/Scholastic, Inc., 1999)

Series: Poppleton. Number 6
Subject(s): Animals/Pigs; Seasons; Friendship
Age range(s): Grades 1-3
Major character(s): Poppleton, Pig, Friend; Cherry Sue, Llama, Friend; Zacko, Ferret, Store Owner
Time period(s): 1990s
Locale(s): Fictional Country

Summary: Three brief stories for beginning readers tell of the contented life of Poppleton. Friendly Poppleton feeds cookies to the geese that stop to rest in his yard on their journey south. As the weather cools off Poppleton goes shopping for a coat, but is insulted when Zacko tells him that the store has no coats to fit Poppleton because he is too big. Cherry Sue consoles Poppleton and gives him a coat catalog for big and tall pigs and soon Poppleton is sporting a new, warm coat. In the last story, Poppleton invites Cherry Sue to the Lion's Club annual Pancake Breakfast where Poppleton acknowledges that Cherry Sue is the perfect friend. (48 pages)

Where it's reviewed:
Booklist, October 15, 1999, page 456
Children's Bookwatch, January 2000, page 7
Horn Book Guide, Spring 2000, page 62
Kirkus Reviews, July 15, 1999, page 1139
School Library Journal, September 1999, page 203

Other books by the same author:
Poppleton in Spring, 1999 (Poppleton, Number 5)

Poppleton Everyday, 1998 (Poppleton, Number 3)
Poppleton, 1997 (Poppleton, Number 1)

Other books you might like:
Nancy Jewell, *Two Silly Trolls*, 1992
   In a beginning reader, five brief stories showcase the challenges to a friendship of two trolls.
Jef Kaminsky, *Poppy & Ella: 3 Stories about 2 Friends*, 2000
   Poppy and Ella are great friends who agree about everything and even when they disagree they are still friends.
Arnold Lobel, *Frog and Toad All Year*, 1976
   Through all the seasons of the year, Frog and Toad's friendship endures.
Hiawyn Oram, *Badger's Bad Mood*, 1998
   Mole secretly makes plans to lift the spirits of his friend Badger.

856

CYNTHIA RYLANT
WENDY ANDERSON HALPERIN, Illustrator

Some Good News

(New York: Simon & Schuster Books for Young Readers, 1999)

Series: Cobble Street Cousins. Book 4
Subject(s): Newspapers; Cousins; Neighbors and Neighborhoods
Age range(s): Grades 2-4
Major character(s): Lily, 9-Year-Old, Sister (Rosie's), Cousin; Rosie, 9-Year-Old, Sister (Lily's), Cousin; Tess, 9-Year-Old, Cousin, Niece
Time period(s): 1990s (1999)
Locale(s): United States

Summary: While their parents are on a world tour with the ballet, Tess, Rosie and Lily are living with their aunt on Cobble Street. Lily has the idea to produce a neighborhood newspaper and the "Cobble Street Courier" is born. Rosie handles recipes, Tess includes jokes and Lily writes a poem for the first issue. As they deliver the newspaper to the neighbors, the girls quickly find ideas for the next issue. It'll be a busy year! (55 pages)

Where it's reviewed:
Booklist, June 1999, page 1832
Horn Book Guide, Fall 1999, page 283
Publishers Weekly, June 7, 1999, page 85
School Library Journal, June 1999, page 106

Other books by the same author:
Special Gifts, 1999 (Cobble Street Cousins, Book 3)
A Little Shopping, 1998 (Cobble Street Cousins, Book 2)
In Aunt Lucy's Kitchen, 1998 (Cobble Street Cousins, Book 1)

Other books you might like:
Charlotte Herman, *Millie Cooper and Friends*, 1995
   The arrival of a new student threatens Millie's friendship with Sandy.
Kathleen Leverich, *Best Enemies Forever*, 1995
   Priscilla's nemesis, Felicity, fails to undermine the respect Priscilla's classmates have for her ideas to provide service to others.

Maud Hart Lovelace, *Betsy-Tacy and Tib*, 1941

The warmth of small town neighbors and the shared activities of close friends make this work a timeless classic.

857

CYNTHIA RYLANT
MAGGIE KNEEN, Illustrator

Thimbleberry Stories

(San Diego: Harcourt, Inc., 2000)

Subject(s): Animals; Friendship; Neighbors and Neighborhoods
Age range(s): Grades 1-3
Major character(s): Nigel Chipmunk, Chipmunk, Friend
Time period(s): Indeterminate
Locale(s): Fictional Country

Summary: Nigel enjoys adventures with his different neighbors on Thimbleberry Lane. In the first of four stories he meets a new neighbor, a hummingbird living in a round house with round windows and doors. Helping a fussy owl neighbor with some decorating occupies Nigel's time in the second story and in the third Nigel convinces a snake to plant strawberries in his garden. Finally, a hot day prompts Nigel to suggest a boating trip with a neighboring salamander that has skill on the water that naturally exceeds Nigel's ability. (56 pages)

Where it's reviewed:
Booklist, May 1, 2000, page 1680
Horn Book Guide, Fall 2000, page 297
Publishers Weekly, April 17, 2000, page 81
School Library Journal, May 2000, page 154

Other books by the same author:
Poppleton in Spring, 1999
The Bird House, 1998
Mr. Putter and Tabby Row the Boat, 1997
The Old Woman Who Named Things, 1996

Other books you might like:
Kenneth Grahame, *The Wind in the Willows*, 1908
The classic tale of four animal friends set in the English countryside has been revised, re-illustrated and retold many times.
Paul Peabody, *Blackberry Hollow*, 1993
In an animal fantasy, kindly Parnassus expects his latest invention to put an end to Tom McPaddy's homesickness.
Beatrix Potter, *The Tale of Jeremy Fisher*, 1906
A frog fishing contentedly from his lily pad boat "catches" a frightening and exciting tale, but no fish.
James Stevenson, *Mud Flat April Fool*, 1998
The friendly residents of Mud Flat have fun trying to trick one another with April Fool's Day jokes in ten brief chapters.

S

858

ROBERT SABUDA, Author/Illustrator

The Blizzard's Robe

(New York: Atheneum Books for Young Readers, 1999)

Subject(s): Winter; Weather; Fear
Age range(s): Grades 1-4
Major character(s): Teune, Artisan, Child; Blizzard, Spirit
Time period(s): Indeterminate Past
Locale(s): Arctic

Summary: In an original tale, a clan of people living near the Arctic Sea learn to fear the winter when the sun's warming rays cannot reach them and Blizzard's icy winds and snow swirl over the village. Teune's responsibilities as the village robe maker keep her from joining the other children at play during the sunny summer months but her talent gives her the opportunity to create a wondrous icy robe when Blizzard's original one is damaged by fire. The villagers are initially angry when they realize what Teune has made, but when Blizzard soars away into the dark sky and fills it with all the colors Teune has worked into the robe the people lose their fear of the winter nights. (32 pages)

Where it's reviewed:
Booklist, November 15, 1999, page 637
Horn Book Guide, Spring 2000, page 52
Kirkus Reviews, September 15, 1999, page 1506
Publishers Weekly, November 29, 1999, page 70
School Library Journal, October 1999, page 125

Other books by the same author:
The 12 Days of Christmas: A Pop-Up Celebration, 1996
Arthur and the Sword, 1995
The Christmas Alphabet, 1994

Other books you might like:
Mindy Dwyer, *Aurora: A Tale of the Northern Lights*, 1997
　　Lost on the Arctic tundra, a young girl gathers the colors of the sky thus creating the Aurora Borealis as she seeks a path home.

Natalie Kinsey-Warnock, *The Fiddler of the Northern Lights*, 1996
　　Henry believes Grandpa Pepin's tale about the fiddler whose music brings the Northern Lights to blaze in the winter sky.
Gerald McDermott, *Raven: A Trickster Tale from the Pacific Northwest*, 1993
　　Raven steals light from its hiding place and shares it with everyone in a Caldecott Honor Book.
Elinor J. Pinczes, *Arctic Fives Arrive*, 1996
　　Arctic animals watch the Northern Lights from a hilltop.

859

LOUIS SACHAR
AMY WUMMER, Illustrator

Marvin Redpost: Class President

(New York: Stepping Stone/Random House, 1999)

Series: Marvin Redpost. Number 5
Subject(s): Schools; Presidents; Humor
Age range(s): Grades 2-4
Major character(s): Marvin Redpost, 3rd Grader; Mrs. North, Teacher
Time period(s): 1990s (1999)
Locale(s): Maryland

Summary: The students at Dogwood Elementary are excited to be celebrating "hole" day. Everyone—from the principal to Mrs. North to Marvin and his classmates—is wearing holey, old clothes. Not a way to make a good impression on the President of the United States, but that's exactly what they do when he makes an unexpected visit to the school and selects Marvin's 3rd grade classroom for a question and answer session. At the end of the day Marvin is still so overcome by the opportunity to meet such a famous person that he forgets his mother is waiting to take him shoe shopping after school. Instead, he plays with friends and arrives home to angry parents who refuse to listen to the story of his day. When Marvin appears on the evening news the family reconsiders their reaction to his forgetfulness about shoes. (67 pages)

Where it's reviewed:
Booklist, April 15, 1999, page 1531
Bulletin of the Center for Children's Books, April 1999, page 293
Horn Book Guide, Fall 1999, page 284
Kirkus Reviews, March 15, 1999, page 456
School Library Journal, July 1999, page 79

Other books by the same author:
Marvin Redpost: Alone in His Teacher's House, 1994 (Marvin Redpost, Number 4)
Marvin Redpost: Is He a Girl?, 1993 (Marvin Redpost, Number 3)
Marvin Redpost: Kidnapped at Birth?, 1992 (Marvin Redpost, Number 1)

Other books you might like:
Judy Blume, *Superfudge*, 1980
Peter's life is filled with the unexpected as the family tries to stay one step ahead of little brother Fudge.
Patricia Reilly Giff, *The Secret at the Polk Street School*, 1987
One title in a series about the many adventures of students at Polk Street School.
Suzy Kline, *Herbie Jones and the Class Gift*, 1987
Herbie's adventures continue as he and Raymond are chosen to select the class gift for the teacher.

860

MARILYN SACHS
MEREDITH JOHNSON, Illustrator

JoJo & Winnie: Sister Stories
(New York: Dutton Children's Books, 1999)

Subject(s): Sisters; Family Life; Sibling Rivalry
Age range(s): Grades 2-4
Major character(s): Josephine ''JoJo'', Sister (older); Winifred ''Winnie'', Sister (younger)
Time period(s): 1990s
Locale(s): Seattle, Washington

Summary: For six years JoJo has contended with Winnie's sometimes embarrassing, always annoying behavior. Having a sister means sharing when neither wants to share and feeling as if the other receives more of the parents' attention. Shortly after Winnie's sixth birthday she is not included in the birthday party of a neighbor and friend. JoJo, realizing how hurt Winnie must feel, kindly spends the entire afternoon playing with her. (70 pages)

Where it's reviewed:
Booklist, September 15, 1999, page 261
Horn Book Guide, Fall 1999, page 284
Kirkus Reviews, June 1, 1999, page 888
Publishers Weekly, June 14, 1999, page 70
School Library Journal, July 1999, page 80

Other books by the same author:
Fran Ellen's House, 1987
Call Me Ruth, 1982
Amy and Laura, 1966

Other books you might like:
Judy Blume, *The Pain and the Great One*, 1974
A brother and sister each resent the other for being the best-loved in the family.
Judith Ross Enderle, *What's the Matter Kelly Beans?*, 1996
A family move forces Kelly to share a room with messy sister Erin.
Jean Van Leeuwen, *Two Girls in Sister Dresses*, 1994
As the older sister, Jennifer is alternately protective of Molly and jealous of the attention others give her.

861

BENJAMIN ALIRE SAENZ
GERONIMO GARCIA, Illustrator
PILAR HERRERA, Translator

Grandma Fina and Her Wonderful Umbrellas
(El Paso, TX: Cinco Puntos Press, 1999)

Subject(s): Grandmothers; Birthdays; Neighbors and Neighborhoods
Age range(s): Grades K-2
Major character(s): Grandma Fina, Grandmother, Neighbor
Time period(s): 1990s
Locale(s): United States

Summary: Parallel blocks of English and Spanish text tell the story of Grandma Fina who thinks her familiar yellow umbrella is a wonderful, if somewhat tattered, way to shade herself from the sun as she strolls her neighborhood. Her neighbors must think differently. When Grandma Fina's birthday arrives, each gives her an umbrella in a color reminiscent of the giver. Grandma Fina graciously accepts the gifts and then visits her elderly friends at a local nursing home. When the friends go out for a walk each carries one of Grandma Fina's new umbrellas while Grandma carries her wonderful yellow one. (40 pages)

Where it's reviewed:
Bloomsbury Review, November 1999, page 26
Children's Bookwatch, October 1999, page 5
ForeWord Magazine, October 1999, page 61
Horn Book Guide, Spring 2000, page 52
School Library Journal, October 1999, page 125

Other books you might like:
Nancy Evans Cooney, *The Umbrella Day*, 1989
After some initial reluctance to carry her umbrella, Missy is grateful that she has it and appreciates the adventures that it brings her way.
Lucia Gonzalez, *The Bossy Gallito*, 1994
The bilingual rendition of a Cuban folktale tells of a bossy rooster and the difficulty he has en route to his uncle's wedding.
Janet Lunn, *The Umbrella Party*, 1998
A little rain does not bother this birthday girl's plans—she has umbrellas!
Taro Yashima, *Umbrella*, 1958
After receiving red boots and an umbrella for her birthday, Momo eagerly awaits a rainy day.

862

BARNEY SALTZBERG, Author/Illustrator

The Soccer Mom from Outer Space

(New York: Crown Publishers, 2000)

Subject(s): Sports/Soccer; Parent and Child; Storytelling
Age range(s): Grades K-2
Major character(s): Lena Drinkwater, Daughter, Soccer Player; Ruben Drinkwater, Father
Time period(s): 2000s (2000); Indeterminate Past
Locale(s): United States

Summary: The night before Lena's first soccer game her father tells her a story about a young soccer player named Ruben and the soccer mom from outer space. Ruben had a normal mom except at soccer games when she cheered louder than anyone and embarrassed him with her weird costumes. When Ruben asked his mom to be just like the other parents she arrives in normal dress and the coach and other players are upset because they depend on her cheering to play well. Fortunately, the soccer mom has inspired other parents who all arrive, by blimp, dressed in costumes. The story perhaps is intended as a forewarning to Lena whose parents arrive at her first game dressed as the Galactic Grapes and ready to cheer. (32 pages)

Where it's reviewed:
Children's Bookwatch, September 2000, page 5
Horn Book Guide, Spring 2001, page 49
New York Times Book Review, August 13, 2000, page 16
Publishers Weekly, June 19, 2000, page 79
School Library Journal, August 2000, page 164

Other books by the same author:
The Flying Garbanzos, 1998
Phoebe and the Spelling Bee, 1996
This Is a Great Place for a Hot Dog Stand, 1995
Show and Tell, 1994
Mrs. Morgan's Lawn, 1993

Other books you might like:
Jonathan London, *Froggy Plays Soccer*, 1999
  Despite the instructions his dad shouts from the sidelines Froggy makes an unintentional error in his first championship soccer game.
Grace Maccarone, *Soccer Game!*, 1994
  The rhyming text of a "Hello Reader!" describes the exciting action of a soccer game.
Colin McNaughton, *Preston's Goal!*, 1998
  A walk to the store to buy bread gives Preston a chance to practice the shots he imagines he'll use to win a soccer game.

863

BARBARA SAMUELS, Author/Illustrator

Aloha, Dolores

(New York: DK Ink/Dorling Kindersley Publishing, Inc., 2000)

Subject(s): Contests; Animals/Cats; Humor
Age range(s): Grades 1-3
Major character(s): Duncan, Cat; Dolores, Child, Sister; Faye, Sister (older)

Time period(s): 2000s (2000)
Locale(s): United States

Summary: Dolores is so confident that Duncan will win the Meow Munchies contest and a trip to Hawaii that she wears a grass skirt to show and tell, practices snorkeling in the bathtub and drapes a lei around Duncan's neck. On the day the contest winner is to be announced Dolores sits by the phone awaiting the call confirming her overly confident belief. However, Faye hears the contest winner announced on the radio and it's not Duncan. Dolores retreats to her room, but Faye has a plan to give her a taste of Hawaii and some pictures for her scrapbook. By the next day Dolores packs away her grass skirt because she's come up with a new idea for travel. (32 pages)

Where it's reviewed:
Booklist, March 1, 2000, page 1252
Horn Book Guide, Fall 2000, page 280
Kirkus Reviews, March 15, 2000, page 390
School Library Journal, April 2000, page 113

Other books by the same author:
Happy Birthday, Dolores, 1989
Duncan and Dolores, 1986
Faye and Dolores, 1985

Other books you might like:
Debra Barracca, *Maxi, the Star*, 1993
  Maxi's successful audition wins the dog an opportunity to travel to Hollywood to make a dog food commercial.
Susan Meddaugh, *Martha Calling*, 1994
  Talking dog Martha makes the most of the prize she wins in a radio contest despite the vacation resort's "No Dogs" policy.
Barbara Ann Porte, *Harry's Pony*, 1997
  After winning a pony in a contest Harry needs to find a creative way to keep it as a pet.
Peggy Rathmann, *Officer Buckle and Gloria*, 1995
  With a mind of her own, police dog Gloria enlivens Officer Buckle's safety presentations in a humorous Caldecott Medal winner.

864

DANIEL SAN SOUCI
EUJIN KIM NEILAN, Illustrator

In the Moonlight Mist: A Korean Tale

(Honesdale, PA: Boyds Mills Press, 1999)

Subject(s): Folklore; Koreans; Folk Tales
Age range(s): Grades 1-3
Major character(s): Woodcutter, Worker
Time period(s): Indeterminate Past
Locale(s): Republic of Korea

Summary: For helping a deer escape from a hunter, kindly Woodcutter is rewarded by the deer with directions to travel to a lake in which celestial maidens bathe. While they are bathing, Woodcutter follows the deer's suggestion and takes the clothes of one of the maidens so she will have to remain on earth. Soon, he and the maiden are married. After their first child is born, Woodcutter's wife longs for her celestial clothing. Ignoring the deer's warning, Woodcutter complies with his wife's request. Upon receiving the clothing, the maiden returns to heaven with their child, and Woodcutter must find a way to join her. (32 pages)

Where it's reviewed:
Booklist, March 1, 1999, page 1218
Horn Book Guide, Fall 1999, page 327
Publishers Weekly, February 15, 1999, page 106
School Library Journal, April 1999, page 123

Other books by the same author:
North Country Night, 1994

Other books you might like:
Odds Bodkin, *The Crane Wife*, 1998
A poor sail maker's kind treatment of an injured crane brings him a wife.
Barbara Diamond Goldin, *The Girl Who Lived With the Bears*, 1997
The daughter of an Indian chief insults a bear in human form and is then forced to live with the bears.
Zong Insob, *Folk Tales from Korea*, 1982
This collection of traditional Korean folk tales, includes the original story of "The Maiden and the Woodcutter."

865

ROBERT D. SAN SOUCI
DON DAILY, Illustrator

Callie Ann and Mistah Bear

(New York: Dial Books for Young Readers, 2000)

Subject(s): Folklore; African Americans; Animals
Age range(s): Grades 1-4
Major character(s): Callie Ann, Child, Daughter; Mose, Neighbor, Farmer; Mistah Bear, Bear
Time period(s): Indeterminate Past
Locale(s): South

Summary: Callie Ann tries to encourage her widowed mother's interest in Mose as a potential second husband but her mother is seeking a "quality" gentleman for her next mate. When just such a gentleman comes calling Callie Ann watches carefully as the guest gobbles cookies and biscuits with honey and then notices the brown fur peeping out from around his spats. When he departs Callie Ann follows him and sure enough, the caller is Mistah Bear in disguise. Callie Ann has a hard time convincing her mother of the ruse, but eventually Callie Ann gets the last laugh when she outsmarts Mistah Bear and her mother finally admits that appearances can be deceiving. As Callie Ann suspects, Mose makes a fine husband and stepfather. (32 pages)

Where it's reviewed:
Booklist, December 1, 2000, page 716
Five Owls, November 2000, page 44
Horn Book Guide, Spring 2001, page 102
Kirkus Reviews, July 15, 2000, page 1045
School Library Journal, October 2000, page 152

Awards the book has won:
Notable Social Studies Trade Books for Young People, 2001

Other books by the same author:
A Weave of Words, 1998

Fa Mulan: The Story of a Woman Warrior, 1998
The Hired Hand, 1997 (Aesop Prize)
The Red Heels, 1996 (Smithsonian's Notable Books for Children)
The Faithful Friend, 1995 (Caldecott Honor Book)

Other books you might like:
Virginia Hamilton, *When Birds Could Talk & Bats Could Sing: The Adventures of Bruh Sparrow, Sis Wren, and Their Friends*, 1996
A collection of eight stories based on African American folklore is set in the time long ago when animals could talk and sported fancy clothes too.
Julius Lester, *More Tales of Uncle Remus: Further Adventures of Brer Rabbit, His Friends, Enemies, and Others*, 1988
Thirty-seven stories feature the activities of famous trickster Brer Rabbit.
Janet Stevens, *Tops and Bottoms*, 1995
Industrious Hare is a gardening partner to slumbering Bear in a contemporary interpretation of a trickster tale.

866

ROBERT D. SAN SOUCI
DAVID CATROW, Illustrator

Cinderella Skeleton

(San Diego: Silver Whistle/Harcourt, Inc., 2000)

Subject(s): Fairy Tales; Folklore; Stories in Rhyme
Age range(s): Grades 3-5
Major character(s): Cinderella Skeleton, Stepsister, Stepdaughter; Charnel, Royalty (prince); Skreech, Stepmother
Time period(s): Indeterminate Past
Locale(s): Boneyard Acres, Fictional Country

Summary: Cinderella Skeleton tends to the needs of cruel Stepmother Skreech and two stepsisters. She obliges them by hanging cobwebs, arranging dead flowers and feeding the bats, but still she receives only cast-off tattered gowns and scorn from Stepmother Skreech. When the invitation to Prince Charnel's annual Halloween Ball arrives, Cinderella Skeleton begs to go but Stepmother Skreech forces her to stay home and work. A kind and good witch assists Cinderella and soon she is off to the ball in a funeral wagon pulled by creatures that are part horse and part dragon. Prince Charnel is dazzled by this wraith in gossamer with a dandelion headdress and the two dance the night away. When Cinderella Skeleton realizes the time for the spell to end is nearing she tries to race away. Prince Charnel grabs her foot and is left holding a shoe complete with foot and partial leg bone. A search for the matching shin eventually reunites Prince Charnel and Cinderella Skeleton who live happily ever after, leaving Skreech and her daughters in their own dust. (32 pages)

Where it's reviewed:
Booklist, September 1, 2000, page 128
Horn Book, September 2000, page 589
Publishers Weekly, September 25, 2000, page 62
School Library Journal, September 2000, page 256

Other books by the same author:
Cendrillon: A Caribbean Cinderella, 1998 (Booklist Editors' Choice)
The Hired Hand, 1997 (Aesop Prize)
The Red Heels, 1996 (Smithsonian's Notable Books for Children)
The Faithful Friend, 1995 (Caldecott Honor Book)
Sootface: An Ojibwa Cinderella Story, 1994

Other books you might like:
Robert Kraus, *Fables Aesop Never Wrote: But Robert Kraus Did*, 1994
Fifteen original fables are written as spoofs of the traditional Aesop tales.
Deborah Nourse Lattimore, *Cinderhazel: The Cinderella of Halloween*, 1997
Hazel impresses Prince Alarming with her talent for making a dirty mess of anything, including the witches' Halloween Ball.
Susan Meddaugh, *Cinderella's Rat*, 1997
The Cinderella story is viewed through the eyes of the rat chosen to be a coach-boy for the pumpkin carriage.
Frances Minters, *Sleepless Beauty*, 1996
A rhyming take-off on *Sleeping Beauty* places the action in a contemporary, urban setting.
Jon Scieszka, *The Stinky Cheese Man: And Other Fairly Stupid Tales*, 1992
Classic fairy tales take on a new look in these humorous retellings comprising a Caldecott Honor book.
Diane Stanley, *Rumpelstiltskin's Daughter*, 1997
The similarity between this fractured fairy tale and the original ends when the straw is spun into gold.
Vivian Vande Velde, *Tales From the Brothers Grimm and the Sisters Weird*, 1995
Thirteen traditional stories are humorously rewritten with a new twist in this collection of "fractured" fairy tales.

867

ROBERT D. SAN SOUCI
SERGIO MARTINEZ, Illustrator

Little Gold Star: A Spanish American Cinderella Tale

(New York: HarperCollins Publishers, 2000)

Subject(s): Fairy Tales; Folklore; Conduct of Life
Age range(s): Grades 2-4
Major character(s): Teresa, Daughter, Stepdaughter; Miguel, Gentleman, Landowner; Tomas, Father, Shepherd
Time period(s): Indeterminate Past
Locale(s): New Mexico

Summary: Tomas feels content with his simple life as a sheepherder with kind Teresa to care for their home when he is away and soon regrets agreeing to marry a nearby widow with two daughters. Tomas copes by staying on the hills with the sheep while leaving Teresa behind to do the chores and deal with her cruel stepmother. Teresa's kind nature serves her well when a woman in blue asks for her help. As a reward the woman places a gold star on her forehead. The stepmother attempts to achieve the same end for her daughters and sends

them on the same errand but the woman in blue does not reward their cruel behavior in the same way. Teresa's star and gentle nature attract Miguel who seeks to marry her. Teresa's stepmother puts three seemingly impossible tasks for Teresa to accomplish in order to receive permission to wed. The magic in the gold star enables Teresa to complete the stepmother's demands and achieve her dreams for a life of happiness. (32 pages)

Where it's reviewed:
Booklist, October 1, 2000, page 343
Horn Book Guide, Spring 2001, page 102
Horn Book, January 2001, page 102
Kirkus Reviews, October 15, 2000, page 1491
School Library Journal, October 2000, page 153

Other books by the same author:
Cinderella Skeleton, 2000
Brave Margaret: An Irish Adventure, 1999
Cendrillon: A Caribbean Cinderella, 1998
Fa Mulan: The Story of a Woman Warrior, 1998
Sootface: An Ojibwa Cinderella Story, 1994

Other books you might like:
Joe Hayes, *Little Gold Star/Estrellita de Oro*, 2000
A bilingual version of the story is drawn from the same folklore sources as San Souci's retelling.
Charlotte Huck, *Toads and Diamonds*, 1996
A kind stepdaughter receives a reward of diamonds and flowers each time she speaks; her bitter stepsister receives toads and snakes instead.
Susan Lowell, *Cindy Ellen: A Wild Western Cinderella*, 2000
Magic from her fairy godmother gives Cindy Ellen some gumption and new cowboy boots just perfect for Joe Prince's rodeo and square dance.

868

ROBERT D. SAN SOUCI
ALEXI NATCHEV, Illustrator

Peter and the Blue Witch Baby

(New York: Doubleday Book for Young Readers, 2000)

Subject(s): Fairy Tales; Folklore; Kings, Queens, Rulers, etc.
Age range(s): Grades 1-4
Major character(s): Peter, Royalty; Molnya, Witch; Little Sister of the Sun, Maiden
Time period(s): Indeterminate Past
Locale(s): Russia

Summary: A beautiful young woman, rejected by Tsar Peter, angrily reveals that she is the wicked Molnya. She puts a curse on Peter that will begin when he finds the woman he hopes to take for his bride. When that day comes, as Peter rides off in search of Little Sister of the Sun, the ruler accepts a foundling child and leaves it in the care of his servants. Peter expects to woo Little Sister of the Sun with his three most prized magical possessions. However, as Peter rides he meets three forlorn giants and each one receives one of Peter's magical items to solve his problems. Thus, Peter arrives at the cloud castle empty-handed, but still welcome by Little Sister. Through a magical window in the cloud castle Peter sees that his own castle is in ruin and he hurries home to attend to the problem.

He learns that the foundling infant is actually Molnya in disguise. The witch baby has now grown to gigantic, destructive proportions and she chases Peter when he tries to return to the cloud castle. Each of the giants repays Peter's kindness by slowing the witch baby enough for him to finally reach the cloud castle. Then Little Sister calls to her brother sun to help end the wickedness and Peter and Little Sister of the Sun live happily ever after. (32 pages)

Where it's reviewed:
Booklist, November 1, 2000, page 544
School Library Journal, November 2000, page 148

Other books by the same author:
Six Foolish Fisherman, 2000
Brave Margaret: An Irish Adventure, 1999
A Weave of Words, 1998
Fa Mulan: The Story of a Woman Warrior, 1998
Nicholas Pipe, 1997
Young Arthur, 1997

Other books you might like:
Andrej Dugin, *Dragon Feathers*, 1993
    To win his true love, a young man plucks three feathers from a dragon in this retelling of a German folktale. Olga Dugina, co-author.
Mirra Ginsburg, *Clay Boy*, 1997
    In the retelling of a Russian folktale a lonely couple faces the greed of a child fashioned from a lump of clay.
Eric A. Kimmel, *Bearhead: A Russian Folktale*, 1991
    Unlike the blue witch baby, this foundling with the head of a bear and body of a human grows up to be kind and outsmarts a witch.

869

CARL SANDBURG
DAVID SMALL, Illustrator

The Huckabuck Family and How They Raised Popcorn in Nebraska and Quit and Came Back

(New York: Farrar Straus Giroux, 1999)

Subject(s): Humor; Farm Life; Family Life
Age range(s): Grades 1-4
Major character(s): Jonas Jonas Huckabuck, Farmer, Father; Mama Mama Huckabuck, Mother, Spouse; Pony Pony Huckabuck, Daughter
Time period(s): 1930s (1935-1938)
Locale(s): Nebraska; United States

Summary: One of the Rootabaga Stories originally published in 1923, the tale of the Huckabuck family is reproduced as a picture book. Jonas Jonas, Mama Mama and Pony Pony settle in Nebraska to raise popcorn. One year their harvest is so great that it fills every corner of the farm. Then Pony Pony finds a Chinese silver slipper buckle in a squash. Jonas Jonas and Mama Mama know that finding such a buckle is a sign that their luck will change one way or another and that very night it does. A fire starts in the barn and all the popcorn on the farm pops and pops and pops. Jonas Jonas decides that the family has raised too much popcorn so they leave the state and travel, following the work opportunities. Pony Pony keeps looking for the sign that will send them back to Nebraska and three years later she finds it in another squash. When Pony Pony returns to the farm with her parents she's sporting black slippers with matching silver buckles. (40 pages)

Where it's reviewed:
Booklist, September 15, 1999, page 270
Bulletin of the Center for Children's Books, September 1999, page 29
Horn Book, September 1999, page 600
Publishers Weekly, July 26, 1999, page 89
School Library Journal, August 1999, page 141

Awards the book has won:
Bulletin of the Center for Children's Books Blue Ribbon, 1999
School Library Journal Best Books, 1999

Other books by the same author:
More Rootabagas, 1993
Potato Face, 1930
Rootabaga Pigeons, 1923
Rootabaga Stories, 1922

Other books you might like:
Tomie DePaola, *The Popcorn Book*, 1978
    Tony devours popcorn while Tiny shares factual information about the appealing snack.
Sid Fleischman, *Here Comes McBroom: Three More Tall Tales*, 1992
    The collection of three previously published stories include tales of Farmer McBroom's zoo, a rainmaking scheme and a visit from a ghost.
Helen Ketteman, *The Year of No More Corn*, 1993
    A tall tale explains how Grampa saved the 1928 corn crop by planting whittled corn kernels that grew into corn trees.
Kate Lied, *Potato: A Tale from the Great Depression*, 1997
    After a two-week job in Idaho a family returns to their farm with a car full of potatoes that they barter for food, clothes and a pig.

870

RUTH SANDERSON, Author/Illustrator

The Crystal Mountain

(Boston: Little, Brown and Company, 1999)

Subject(s): Fairy Tales; Folklore; Mothers and Sons
Age range(s): Grades 2-4
Major character(s): Anna, Mother, Artisan (weaver); Perrin, Son (youngest), Musician; Eve, Mythical Creature (fairy)
Time period(s): Indeterminate Past
Locale(s): Europe

Summary: With her skillful weaving of brocades Anna supports herself and her three sons. A dream inspires the creation of a tapestry that Anna feels compelled to complete although the project requires years of work and removes the source of the family income. When the tapestry is finally complete and hanging on the wall of their home, Anna and her sons are astonished to see it carried out the window by the wind. Anna's two oldest sons go in search of the tapestry, but each is dissuaded by easy wealth along the way and abandons the quest. Perrin, the youngest, endures the trials of fire and ice to reach the Crystal Mountain and successfully locates the tapestry in the fairies' palace. Before the fairies will release Anna's creation they want to finish weaving a copy of it. The last fairy at the loom embroiders her image into the tapestry before rolling it up for transport. Perrin hurries home to show his mother and, as he unrolls the tapestry, it comes to life. The fairy pictured in the tapestry also emerges from the weaving to become Perrin's wife, Eve, in this folktale combining elements of Chinese and Norwegian folklore. (32 pages)

Where it's reviewed:
Booklist, September 1, 1999, page 129
Horn Book Guide, Spring 2000, page 114
Kirkus Reviews, July 1, 1999, page 1058
Publishers Weekly, September 13, 1999, page 84
School Library Journal, October 1999, page 142

Awards the book has won:
Notable Social Studies Trade Books for Young People, 2000

Other books by the same author:
Tapestries: Stories of Women in the Bible, 1998
Rose Red & Snow White, 1997
Papa Gatto: An Italian Fairy Tale, 1995

Other books you might like:
Tanya Robyn Batt, *The Fabrics of Fairytale: Stories Spun from Far and Wide*, 2000
 The common thread in a collection of folktales is the use of textiles, brocade and tapestry from many cultures as an element of each story.
Marilee Heyer, *The Weaving of a Dream: A Chinese Folktale*, 1986
 In a retelling of a Chinese folktale, fairies steal a poor woman's tapestry and her three sons undertake a magical journey to reclaim it.
Claire Martin, *Boots and the Glass Mountain*, 1992
 Boots, the youngest of three brothers, wins the hand of a princess in this retelling of a Norwegian folktale.
Robert D. San Souci, *A Weave of Words*, 1998
 Vachagan and Anait use multiple skills—literacy, weaving and swordsmanship to defeat a three-headed ogre that imprisons Vachagan.
Grace Tseng, *White Tiger, Blue Serpent*, 1999
 When a greedy goddess steals his mother's brocade a young Chinese boy embarks on a perilous journey to retrieve it.

871

ADELE SANSONE
ALAN MARKS, Illustrator
J. ALISON JAMES, Translator

The Little Green Goose

(New York: Michael Neugebauer Book/North-South Books, 1999)

Subject(s): Animals; Love; Parenthood
Age range(s): Grades K-3
Major character(s): Mr. Goose, Goose, Father; Daisy, Dog; Unnamed Character, Baby, Dinosaur
Time period(s): Indeterminate
Locale(s): Fictional Country

Summary: Playing with the many chicks on the farm is fun for Mr. Goose but doesn't satisfy his longing to be father with a baby goose calling him Daddy. Although Mr. Goose politely asks all the hens to give him just one egg, they each refuse. Poor Mr. Goose is out of ideas when Daisy comes running up with news of a large egg that she's found while digging in the woods. The egg's a bit smelly, but Mr. Goose ignores that fact and quickly builds a nest. When the egg finally begins to crack, the goose that emerges is green with a long tail and no feathers. The hatchling recognizes Mr. Goose as "Mama" and begs to be fed. Caring for a baby is hard work, but Mr. Goose loves his little green goose. When the barnyard chicks rudely point out the difference in appearance between Mr. Goose and the little green goose, the very large baby sadly goes searching for his real mother. Neither a frog, a fish nor a lizard is willing to claim motherhood and the sad little green goose realizes that appearances do not determine a loving parent. (32 pages)

Where it's reviewed:
Booklist, April 15, 1999, page 1538
Bulletin of the Center for Children's Books, July 1999, page 399
Horn Book Guide, Fall 1999, page 266
Publishers Weekly, April 26, 1999, page 82
School Library Journal, September 1999, page 203

Other books you might like:
Molly Bang, *Goose*, 1996
 A gosling feels out of place with her adoptive woodchuck family until she learns to fly—right back to the comfort of her woodchuck home.
Keiko Kasza, *A Mother for Choco*, 1992
 While searching for its mother a young bird is adopted by a bear.
Holly Keller, *Horace*, 1991
 Horace, sensitive to the difference between his spots and his parents' stripes, learns that belonging to a family is based on feeling, not appearance.
Lynn Reiser, *The Surprise Family*, 1994
 Much to the surprise of a mother hen, the "chicks" she's hatched from a clutch of abandoned eggs enjoy swimming—just like ducks.

872

SCOTT SANTORO, Author/Illustrator

Isaac the Ice Cream Truck

(New York: Henry Holt and Company, 1999)

Subject(s): Transportation; Work; Self-Acceptance
Age range(s): Grades K-1
Major character(s): Isaac, Truck
Time period(s): Indeterminate Past
Locale(s): United States

Summary: In the author's first book Isaac knows the preferred ice cream flavors of all the customers on his route, but still he feels inferior compared to the other trucks he sees on the road. Somehow selling ice cream does not seem as important to Isaac as delivering cars, building highways, or even collecting garbage. When Isaac sees fire trucks hurrying to a burning building he's sure that being a fire truck is the best job for a truck. However, when the firemen complete their work, their joy at seeing an ice cream truck full of cool, refreshing treats convinces Isaac that making others happy is a special job after all. (32 pages)

Where it's reviewed:
Booklist, July 1999, page 1954
Horn Book, May 1999, page 321
Kirkus Reviews, May 1, 1999, page 727
Publishers Weekly, May 17, 1999, page 77
School Library Journal, June 1999, page 107

Other books you might like:
Lydia Monks, *The Cat Barked?*, 1998
  A cat considers the far better life that a dog appears to have but decides she still prefers being a feline.
Libba Gray Moore, *The Little Black Truck*, 1994
  After years of hard but mundane work a little black truck is abandoned in the woods when it is too old to keep going.
Watty Piper, *The Little Engine That Could*, 1930
  The Little Engine proves that gumption is more important than size if there is a job to be done.

873

ERIC SANVOISIN
MARTIN MATJE, Illustrator
GEORGES MOROZ, Translator

A Straw for Two
(New York: Delacorte Press, 1999)

Subject(s): Vampires; Books and Reading; Friendship
Age range(s): Grades 2-4
Major character(s): Odilon, Student, Vampire; Carmilla, Student, Vampire; Draculink, Vampire, Uncle (Carmilla's)
Time period(s): Indeterminate Past
Locale(s): France

Summary: In the sequel to *The Ink Drinker* Odilon feels lonely because he has no friends with whom to share his thirst for slurping the ink from books. Then a new student appears in his class and the teacher assigns her the seat next to Odilon. Soon he notices that his homework has vanished from the pages of his notebook—almost as if someone sucked the ink off the page. Following Carmilla after school, Odilon learns that she is the niece of Draculink and is happy to share a straw and a book with him. (40 pages)

Where it's reviewed:
Booklist, December 21, 1999, page 707
Children's Bookwatch, November 1999, page 4
Horn Book Guide, Spring 2000, page 70
New York Times Book Review, November 21, 1999, page 49
Publishers Weekly, August 16, 1999, page 85

Awards the book has won:
New York Times Best Illustrated Children's Books, 1999

Other books by the same author:
The Ink Drinker, 1998

Other books you might like:
Jayne Harvey, *Great-Uncle Dracula*, 1992
  An easy-reader features Emily Normal's adjustment to a new school populated by witches, ghosts and werewolves.

James Howe, *Bunnicula: A Rabbit-Tale of Mystery*, 1979
  Harold, the family dog, suspects that Bunnicula is a vampire rabbit and not an ordinary family pet.
Mary DeBall Kwitz, *Little Vampire and the Midnight Bear*, 1995
  Little vampire learns to fly in order to save his baby sister from the ferocious Midnight Bear.

874

VIVIAN SATHRE
SALLY ANNE LAMBERT, Illustrator

Slender Ella and Her Fairy Hogfather
(New York: Delacorte Press, 1999)

Series: Yearling First Choice Chapter Book
Subject(s): Animals/Pigs; Humor; Fairy Tales
Age range(s): Grades 1-3
Major character(s): Slender Ella, Pig, Stepsister; Harley Joe Goldsnoot, Pig, Bachelor; Fairy Hogfather, Pig, Mythical Creature
Time period(s): Indeterminate Past
Locale(s): Fictional Country

Summary: Ella, daughter of a traveling salesman, does all the housework for her cruel stepmother and stepsisters who call the skinny pig Slender Ella. Her one pleasure is to plow the fields—for no one can bother her when she's on the tractor. When an invitation arrives to a fancy hoedown at Harley Joe's ranch the stepsister's mock Slender Ella's desire to attend and hurry off without her. Magically, Slender Ella's Fairy Hogfather appears to change her old clothes into a fancy party dress and to give her jewel encrusted cowboy boots for her feet. Her tractor becomes a car, a firefly a driver, and she's off. One look at stout Harley Joe and Slender Ella is swept off her feet. They dance the night away until Slender Ella races from the ranch when she hears the clock striking midnight. She loses a boot on the way and the next day Harley Joe shows up at her home searching for the boot's owner. Of course, they live happily ever after and Slender Ella plows the fields with the new tractor Harley Joe gives her as a wedding present. (47 pages)

Where it's reviewed:
Booklist, March 15, 1999, page 1338
Bulletin of the Center for Children's Books, April 1999, page 294
Horn Book Guide, Fall 1999, page 284
Kirkus Reviews, January 1, 1999, page 71
School Library Journal, June 1999, page 107

Other books by the same author:
Hansel & Gretel, 1999 (Wishbone Early Years)
Leroy Potts Meets the McCrooks, 1999
On Granpa's Farm, 1997

Other books you might like:
Pamela Duncan Edwards, *Dinorella: A Prehistoric Fairy Tale*, 1997
  A Fairydactyl works the magic that brings Dinorella and Duke Dudley together.
Deborah Nourse Lattimore, *Cinderhazel: The Cinderella of Halloween*, 1997

Hazel impresses Prince Alarming with her ability to make a dirty mess of anything including the Witches' Halloween Ball.

Susan Lowell, *Cindy Ellen: A Wild Western Cinderella*, 2000
Magic from her fairy godmother gives Cindy Ellen some gumption and new cowboy boots just perfect for Joe Prince's rodeo and square dance.

Janet Perlman, *Cinderella Penguin or, The Little Glass Flipper*, 1992
A spoof of the Cinderella story has penguins in the leading roles.

875

ALLEN SAY, Author/Illustrator

The Sign Painter

(Boston: Walter Lorraine Books/Houghton Mifflin Company, 2000)

Subject(s): Artists and Art; Work; Asian Americans
Age range(s): Grades 4-6
Major character(s): Unnamed Character, Artist; Unnamed Character, Businessman
Time period(s): Indeterminate Past
Locale(s): California

Summary: A young man steps off the early bus in a small town and heads for the only lit storefront he sees—a sign shop. When the aspiring painter demonstrates his ability to paint a woman's face on a large billboard he is hired to paint the same image and the word "ArrowStar" on twelve billboards strung out across the desert. With the shop owner driving his truck and providing the tent and food they drive to the first billboard, complete their work in three days and move on to the next billboard. The painting becomes monotonous and the young man would like to add clouds or a landscape to the large signs, but the limits of the commission prevent that bit of creativity. Finally they reach the location of the last sign and discover that the previous night's dust storm has damaged it. As they stare at it a strange construction (or apparition) in the distance—a convertible—driven by the woman pictured on the billboards, races past them. (32 pages)

Where it's reviewed:
Booklist, October 1, 2000, page 341
Horn Book, September 2000, page 555
Publishers Weekly, September 18, 2000, page 110
School Library Journal, September 2000, page 208

Awards the book has won:
Publishers Weekly Best Books, 2000

Other books by the same author:
Allison, 1997
Emma's Rug, 1996
Stranger in the Mirror, 1995
Grandfather's Journey, 1993

Other books you might like:
Anthony Browne, *Willy the Dreamer*, 1998
Willy's dreams take shape in the form of the works of famous artists, with modifications of course for Willy's bananas.

Michael Garland, *Dinner at Magritte's*, 1995
Pierre visits his artist neighbors for dinner where illusion and reality meet.

Arthur Geisert, *The Etcher's Studio*, 1997
As a young boy helps his grandfather, an etcher, prepare for a show he imagines himself in each of the scenes.

Barbara McClintock, *The Fantastic Drawings of Danielle*, 1996
As a photographer, Papa thinks Danielle's drawings lack realism, but Danielle finds a market for her fantasies.

Roger Roth, *The Sign Painter's Dream*, 1993
Inspired by a dream and a request a sign painter creates the most spectacular sign of his career—to give away.

876

ALLEN SAY, Author/Illustrator

Tea with Milk

(Boston: Walter Lorraine Books/Houghton Mifflin Company, 1999)

Subject(s): Homesickness; Cultures and Customs; Loneliness
Age range(s): Grades 2-5
Major character(s): Masako "May" Moriwaki, Daughter (Japanese American), Friend; Joseph Say, Businessman, Friend
Time period(s): Indeterminate Past
Locale(s): California (San Francisco Bay Area); Osaka, Japan

Summary: Following May's graduation from an American high school her hopes of attending college are ruined when her homesick parents decide to return to their native country. Now, May must use her given name of Masako, dress in kimonos, learn the proper behavior of a Japanese lady and return to high school to learn Japanese. Her parents' attempt to arrange her marriage is the final straw for the homesick, independent Masako. She boards a train for Osaka and finds a job at a department store in this city that reminds her of San Francisco. Finally, May is able to speak English while giving tours of the store to foreign businessmen. After touring with her for three consecutive days Joseph invites her to tea, with milk, just as he learned to drink it at an English boarding school in Shanghai. The two "foreigners" in their native lands have much in common including a search for a place to call home. When Joseph learns he will be transferred to Yokohama he and May decide to create their own home where they speak English to each other, Japanese to their child and drink their tea with milk and sugar. (32 pages)

Where it's reviewed:
Booklist, March 15, 1999, page 1327
Horn Book, July 1999, page 458
Publishers Weekly, March 8, 1999, page 67
Riverbank Review, Fall 1999, page 32
School Library Journal, May 1999, page 96

Awards the book has won:
Publishers Weekly Best Books, 1999
School Library Journal Best Books, 1999

Other books by the same author:
Allison, 1997
Stranger in the Mirror, 1995
Grandfather's Journey, 1993 (Caldecott Medal)

Tree of Cranes, 1991

Other books you might like:

Elaine Hosozawa-Nagana, *Chopsticks from America*, 1994
Japanese-American siblings learn about their cultural heritage when a job change moves the family from America to Japan.

Toyomi Igus, *Two Mrs. Gibsons*, 1996
A young girl describes the two loving Mrs. Gibsons in her life—the African American grandmother and the Japanese American mother.

Mimi Otey Little, *Yoshiko and the Foreigner*, 1996
Secretly, Yoshiko befriends a lost soldier and begins a relationship that she knows is contrary to her culture and her parents' wishes.

877

MARTINE SCHAAP
ALEX DE WOLF, Illustrator

Mop to the Rescue

(Peru, IL: Front Street/Cricket Books, 1999)

Subject(s): Animals/Dogs; Twins; Pets
Age range(s): Preschool
Major character(s): Mop, Dog; Julie, Sister, Twin; Justin, Brother, Twin
Time period(s): 1990s
Locale(s): United States

Summary: Seven vignettes portray life with a new dog in this Netherlands' author's first American picture book. When Justin and Julie receive a puppy as their birthday present, the dog's name becomes obvious when the fluffy pet laps up Julie's spilled milk. Creatively, Julie and Justin involve Mop in their play, adopting the "if you can't lick them, join them" attitude toward cooperative interaction. Although Mop's curiosity causes some problems, the pet also earns everyone's admiration for coming to the rescue at important times. (33 pages)

Where it's reviewed:

Booklist, May 1, 1999, page 1601
Horn Book Guide, Fall 1999, page 267
Publishers Weekly, May 10, 1999, page 66
School Library Journal, November 1999, page 129

Other books you might like:

Marc Brown, *Arthur's New Puppy*, 1993
Arthur's initial enthusiasm about a new puppy quickly wanes as he discovers the amount of work required to care for a pet.

Alyssa Satin Capucilli, *Biscuit*, 1996
New puppy Biscuit has difficulty sleeping until his owner brings him just one more thing.

Isabelle Harper, *Our New Puppy*, 1996
The family pet, Rosie, learns to tolerate the antics of the new puppy.

Steven Kroll, *Oh, Tucker!*, 1998
Despite the chaos he creates in their home, a dog's owners find it difficult to scold a dog as nice as Tucker.

Rosemary Wells, *The McDuff Series*, 1997-
A West Highland terrier finds a home, adjusts to a baby's

arrival, and saves Santa Claus from the chimney in a new award-winning series.

878

JUDITH BYRON SCHACHNER, Author/Illustrator

The Grannyman

(New York: Dutton Children's Books, 1999)

Subject(s): Animals/Cats; Old Age; Pets
Age range(s): Grades K-2
Major character(s): Simon, Cat
Time period(s): 1990s
Locale(s): United States

Summary: Although Simon is so old that most of his body parts have stopped working well he can still remember the joy of being a kitten. He also reflects appreciatively on the quality of life that he has with his human family. Just when Simon decides that he's completely useless and prepares to leave this world he feels something soft on his stomach. Using his last working sense, Simon sniffs and sniffs until he identifies the softness as a kitten. Now Simon's life has value again—for he is needed. His attentiveness to this kitten earns him the nickname "Grannyman." (32 pages)

Where it's reviewed:

Booklist, March 15, 2000, page 1389
Five Owls, November 1999, page 41
Publishers Weekly, October 18, 1999, page 81
Riverbank Review, Winter 1999-2000, page 28
School Library Journal, November 1999, page 129

Other books by the same author:

Mr. Emerson's Cook, 1998
Willy and May, 1995

Other books you might like:

Connie Heckert, *Dribbles*, 1993
Friendship, aging and grief are presented from the perspective of three cats saying good-bye to their peer, elderly Dribbles.

Minna Jung, *William's Ninth Life*, 1993
For his ninth life William is offered many choices but he remains with his elderly companion Elizabeth.

Ruth Wallace-Brodeur, *Goodbye, Mitch*, 1995
Michael's mom tries to prepare him for the inevitable death of his old cat.

879

CAROLE LEXA SCHAEFER
VANESSA CABBAN, Illustrator

Down in the Woods at Sleepytime

(Cambridge, MA: Candlewick Press, 2000)

Subject(s): Bedtime; Animals; Storytelling
Age range(s): Preschool
Major character(s): Grandma Owl, Owl, Storyteller
Time period(s): Indeterminate
Locale(s): Fictional Country

Summary: Various animal mothers try to encourage their babies to settle down for "sleepytime" but each species thinks they have an important play activity to complete. From high in her tree Grandma Owl calls for story time and the cubs, bunnies, toadlets and baby hedgehogs snuggle close to each other to listen to her story as they drift off to sleep. (32 pages)

Where it's reviewed:
Booklist, November 15, 2000, page 650
Kirkus Reviews, September 15, 2000, page 1363
Publishers Weekly, October 2, 2000, page 80
School Library Journal, November 2000, page 131

Other books by the same author:
The Copper Tin Cup, 2000
The Squiggle, 1996 (ALA Notable Book for Children)
Under the Midsummer Sky, 1994

Other books you might like:
Kathi Appelt, *Bayou Lullaby*, 1995
    A rhyming lullaby about the animals of the bayou soothes a little girl at bedtime.
Margaret Wise Brown, *Little Donkey Close Your Eyes*, 1995
    Animals throughout the world are bid good night in this gentle poem.
Mem Fox, *Time for Bed*, 1993
    Mothers all over the world are putting their kittens, lambs, fawns and children to sleep.

880

CAROLE LEXA SCHAEFER
PIERR MORGAN, Illustrator

Snow Pumpkin

(New York: Crown Publishers, 2000)

Subject(s): Winter; Weather; Pumpkins
Age range(s): Grades K-2
Major character(s): Gram, Grandmother; Lily, Child, Friend; Jesse, Child, Friend
Time period(s): Indeterminate Past
Locale(s): United States

Summary: An early snowfall gives Lily and Jesse a chance to build a snowman. When they can't get enough snow to make a head they wander over to the Lily and Gram's vegetable garden and find a pumpkin that appears to have a face to use. The pumpkin-headed snowman attracts a lot of attention at the park, but Gram is too busy sewing Halloween costumes to see it until the following morning. By then, the early snow has melted and the only thing that remains of Lily and Jesse's creation is the snow pumpkin head. (36 pages)

Where it's reviewed:
Booklist, September 15, 2000, page 237
Bulletin of the Center for Children's Books, October 2000, page 81
Horn Book Guide, Spring 2001, page 49
Publishers Weekly, September 18, 2000, page 111
School Library Journal, September 2000, page 208

Other books by the same author:
Sometimes Moon, 1999
The Squiggle, 1996 (ALA Notable Books for Children)
Under the Midsummer Sky, 1994

Other books you might like:
Nancy White Carlstrom, *The Snow Speaks*, 1992
    Two children enjoy the sights and sounds of the season's first snow.
Lois Ehlert, *Snowballs*, 1995
    Simple text and clear collages tell of the creation of a snow family and the inevitable result as the weather warms.
Zoe Hall, *It's Pumpkin Time!*, 1994
    Siblings plant and tend their own pumpkin patch eager for the day the big pumpkins are ready for picking and carving.
Huy Voun Lee, *In the Snow*, 1995
    Xiao Ming's mother uses the fresh snow as a canvas for a lesson in Chinese characters.
Uri Shulevitz, *Snow*, 1998
    A boy and his dog have faith that the falling snowflakes will continue until the town is covered in white.

881

CAROLE LEXA SCHAEFER
PIERR MORGAN, Illustrator

Sometimes Moon

(New York: Crown Publishers, Inc., 1999)

Subject(s): Family; Nature; Imagination
Age range(s): Grades K-2
Major character(s): Selene, Child, Sister (older); Grandpapa, Grandfather
Time period(s): Indeterminate
Locale(s): Mediterranean

Summary: On an unnamed Mediterranean beach Selene waits with her family for the rise of the moon so they can enjoy their "full moon" picnic. Selene and Grandpapa talk about the phases of the moon and Selene shares the imaginative ways in which she views the moon's changing shape. The crescent moon reminds her of Grandpapa's dory boat and the half moon is her mother's knitting basket. When the moon is rounded and almost full it looks like her baby brother's chubby cheeks. Tonight the moon rises as full and shiny as a queen's treasure on the family enjoying a ride in Grandpapa's rowboat. (32 pages)

Where it's reviewed:
Booklist, August 1999, page 2066
Horn Book Guide, Spring 2000, page 53
Kirkus Reviews, June 15, 1999, page 969
Publishers Weekly, July 5, 1999, page 70
School Library Journal, September 1999, page 204

Other books by the same author:
Snow Pumpkin, 2000
The Copper Tin Cup, 2000
The Squiggle, 1996 (Booklist Editors' Choice)

Other books you might like:
Tim Chadwick, *Cabbage Moon*, 1994
    Bunny Albert discovers that the moon is a giant cabbage that must be nibbled by hungry rabbits in order to achieve its crescent shape.
Lois Ehlert, *Moon Rope: A Peruvian Folktale/Un Lazo a La Luna: Una Leyenda Peruana*, 1992

The bilingual text explains why fox's face is seen in a full moon and mole's is seen only on a dark night.

May Garelick, *Look at the Moon*, 1996
A newly illustrated reissue of a 1969 title follows the moon around the world observing that the same moon shines down on each of us.

Anne Hunter, *Possum's Harvest Moon*, 1996
The sight of a huge harvest moon inspires Possum to gather his friends for one last party before the annual hibernation begins.

882

RAFIK SCHAMI
ELS COOLS, Illustrator
OLIVER STREICH, Illustrator
ANTHEA BELL, Translator

Albert & Lila
(New York: North-South Books, 1999)

Subject(s): Animals/Pigs; Animals/Chickens; Friendship
Age range(s): Grades K-2
Major character(s): Albert, Pig, Outcast; Lila, Hen, Outcast
Time period(s): Indeterminate
Locale(s): Fictional Country

Summary: The chickens and pigs on a farm do not interact as a group and also scorn those of their own group who are different. Albert, having been born white rather than pink, is mocked by the pink pigs and forced to play alone. Lila, now too old to lay eggs, is destined for the stew pot without help from her peers, but instead the rooster banishes her from the henhouse. Albert notices Lila crying and offers his friendship. The two hide in the hay and sleep all day while the other animals are about then sit atop the dung heap all night enjoying the view and each other. Thus, they are the first to spot the fox creeping into the farm and quickly devise a plan to outwit the predator. Their brave and kind action helps the other animals to reconsider their treatment of Albert and Lila and they now have many friends, but none better than each other. (32 pages)

Where it's reviewed:
Bloomsbury Review, November 1999, page 27
Booklist, October 1, 1999, page 363
Horn Book Guide, Spring 2000, page 53
Publishers Weekly, September 13, 1999, page 84
School Library Journal, November 1999, page 129

Other books by the same author:
Fatima and the Dream Thief, 1996 (Child Magazine Best Children's Book)
The Crow Who Stood on His Beak, 1996
A Hand Full of Stars, 1992

Other books you might like:
Janie Bynum, *Otis*, 2000
A clean pig is a lonely pig as fastidious Otis discovers until he meets a frog who also dislikes mud and a friendship begins.

Todd Starr Palmer, *Rhino and Mouse*, 1994
Despite their obvious differences, Rhino and Mouse enjoy a close friendship.

Sheila White Samton, *Tilly and the Rhinoceros*, 1993
Kind Tilly teaches Rhinoceros a lesson in friendship and cooperation.

Ellen Stoll Walsh, *For Pete's Sake*, 1998
Pete's flamingo friends accept him as the flamingo he thinks he is although others would say the green four-legged creature resembles an alligator.

883

URSEL SCHEFFLER
CHRISTA UNZNER, Illustrator
ROSEMARY LANNING, Translator

The Man with the Black Glove
(New York: North-South Books, 1999)

Subject(s): Mystery and Detective Stories; Lost and Found Possessions; Problem Solving
Age range(s): Grades 2-4
Major character(s): Martin Pittman, Detective—Amateur, Child; Pauline Conner, Child, Friend; Sgt. Paterson, Police Officer
Time period(s): 1990s (1999)
Locale(s): Germany

Summary: From the top of a cherry tree Martin and Pauline watch a man put a suitcase in a shed and then drive away in a van. Suspicious of the actions, Martin notes the license number and picks up a black glove dropped by the man. Then, on the way home Martin finds an old wallet with a lot of money in it that his mother tells him to take to the police. Sgt. Paterson seems surprised by Martin and Pauline's clever ideas for tracing the owner, but he's busy with a series of attacks on security guards and doesn't have time to follow-up. Martin and Pauline continue to sleuth and enlist the help of two friends. Together they are able to give Sgt. Paterson the information needed to apprehend the man with the black glove. (62 pages)

Where it's reviewed:
Booklist, November 15, 1999, page 628
Horn Book Guide, Spring 2000, page 70
School Library Journal, December 1999, page 112

Other books by the same author:
The Spy in the Attic, 1997
Rinaldo on the Run, 1995
The Return of Rinaldo, the Sly Fox, 1993

Other books you might like:
David A. Adler, *The Cam Jansen Series*, 1980-
Using her photographic memory, Cam Jansen helps solve mysteries.

Elizabeth Levy, *Parent's Night Fright*, 1998
In the sixth title in the Invisible Inc. series, a group of amateur sleuths track a prize-winning story that appears to be as invisible as Chip.

Marjorie Weinman Sharmat, *The Nate the Great Series*, 1972-
Nate follows one clue after another in the style of Sherlock Holmes in this series for beginning readers.

884

ELEANOR SCHICK, Author/Illustrator

Mama

(New York: Marshall Cavendish, 2000)

Subject(s): Grief; Death; Mothers and Daughters
Age range(s): Grades K-3
Major character(s): Unnamed Character, Daughter, Child; Mama, Mother (deceased); Louise, Housekeeper, Child-Care Giver
Time period(s): 1990s
Locale(s): United States

Summary: For a little girl left with only memories her mother's death seems a long time ago. The girl remembers hearing Mama tell of her illness, watching Mama become weaker, and seeing Louise come to help Mama with cooking and housework. Now, with her bereaved father lost in his work, Louise is a constant source of comfort to the motherless girl, holding her as she cries, reminding her of Mama's love and taking her to the park. Gradually, the girl accepts the truth of Louise's statement that Mama will always be in her heart. (32 pages)

Where it's reviewed:
Booklist, February 15, 2000, page 1122
Children's Book Review Service, April 2000, page 99
Horn Book Guide, Fall 2000, page 281
Kirkus Reviews, March 1, 2000, page 307
School Library Journal, May 2000, page 154

Other books by the same author:
Navaho Wedding Day: A Dine Marriage Ceremony, 1999
My Navaho Sister, 1996
Art Lessons, 1987
A Piano for Julie, 1984

Other books you might like:
Eve Bunting, *The Memory String*, 2000
    Laura, grieving for her deceased mother, finds comfort in a string of buttons representing important events in her mother's life.
Nancy White Carlstrom, *Blow Me a Kiss, Miss Lilly*, 1990
    When Sara's friend, the elderly Miss Lilly dies, Sara learns that friends live on in one's memory.
Jane Yolen, *Grandad Bill's Song*, 1994
    Jon finds support from family members as he struggles to cope with his feelings about his grandfather's death.

885

ALAN SCHROEDER
ANDREW GLASS, Illustrator

The Tale of Willie Monroe

(New York: Clarion Books, 1999)

Subject(s): Tall Tales; Folklore; Contests
Age range(s): Grades 1-4
Major character(s): Willie Monroe, Wrestler, Young Man; Delilah, Mountain Woman; Granny, Grandmother, Aged Person
Time period(s): Indeterminate Past

Locale(s): Tennessee

Summary: In a retelling of a Japanese folktale adapted to a setting in rural America, Willie Monroe reckons to take advantage of his huge biceps and mosey down to Carolina to enter a contest and win a bag of money and ten acres of free land. Along the way he encounters Delilah who is not only quick, but also strong, and soon she's got a grip on Willie and is leading him home to Granny. Both women are former winners of the "Arm-wrestlin', log-stackin', cow-milkin', field-plowin', barn-raisin' contest" and they know "weak as water" Willie hasn't a chance of winning. Seems they've taken a liking to Willie so they feed and exercise him until he's fit to win. The training is more work than Willie's done in his life, but when Granny declares him ready for the contest he resumes his journey with the hope of winning not only the money and the land, but also the heart of Delilah. (32 pages)

Where it's reviewed:
Booklist, April 15, 1999, page 1534
Bulletin of the Center for Children's Books, June 1999, page 365
Horn Book, March 1999, page 214
Publishers Weekly, April 12, 1999, page 75
School Library Journal, June 1999, page 122

Other books by the same author:
Smoky Mountain Rose: An Appalachian Cinderella, 1997
Minty: A Story of Young Harriet Tubman, 1996 (Coretta Scott King Award for Illustration)
Lily and the Wooden Bowl, 1994 (Marion Vannett Ridgway Honor Award)
The Stone Lion, 1994

Other books you might like:
Irene Hedlund, *Mighty Mountain and the Three Strong Women*, 1990
    In a retelling of the Japanese folktale inspiration for Willie Monroe, a sumo wrestler going to a contest meets three women with greater strength.
Anne Isaacs, *Swamp Angel*, 1994
    An original tall tale that is also a Caldecott Honor Book describes the achievements of Angelica and how she earns her nickname.
Steven Kellogg, *Paul Bunyan, a Tall Tale*, 1984
    Paul Bunyan, a lumberjack of extraordinary size and strength, leads a life of unusual adventures.
Claus Stamm, *Three Strong Women: A Tall Tale from Japan*, 1990
    In another version of the Japanese folktale, Forever-Mountain, a sumo wrestler, seeks to win the Emperor's Wrestling Match.

886

STEVE SCHUCH
PETER SYLVADA, Illustrator

A Symphony of Whales

(San Diego: Harcourt Brace & Company, 1999)

Subject(s): Animals/Whales; Wildlife Rescue; Music and Musicians
Age range(s): Grades 2-5

Major character(s): Glashka, Eskimo, Daughter
Time period(s): 1980s (1984-1985)
Locale(s): Senyavina Strait, Russia (Siberia)

Summary: From her earliest memories, Glashka hears music in her head that seems to call to her and the old people tell her she is the first of her people to hear the song of the whales in many years. Coupled with the sound that appears unexpectedly, Glashka also dreams prophetically. Following such a dream Glashka finds many beluga whales trapped by the rapidly forming ice on the strait. Glashka and her parents gather all the villagers to feed the whales and keep the ice broken until an icebreaker can clear the way for the whales escape to the open sea. After the ship opens the path, the whales are too frightened to follow even when tapes of whale sounds are played. Worried, Glashka sleeps and dreams again of music, different music. Following her suggestion the captain of the ship tries many types of music and finally, a classical piece attracts the whales' attention. They respond by singing and following the ship to safety. A concluding historical note gives the factual basis for the story. (32 pages)

Where it's reviewed:
Booklist, January 1, 2000, page 937
New York Times Book Review, November 21, 1999, page 52
School Library Journal, November 1999, page 129
Smithsonian Magazine, November 1999, page 50

Awards the book has won:
New York Times Best Illustrated Children's Books, 1999
Smithsonian's Notable Books for Children, 1999

Other books you might like:
Maggie S. Davis, *A Garden of Whales*, 1993
    Concerned that whales are diminishing in number, an imaginative young boy dreams of a way to save them.
Arnika Esterl, *Okino and the Whales*, 1995
    Awaiting the return of the whales, Takumi sits quietly with his mother listening to her tales of family and the sea.
Cynthia Rylant, *The Whales*, 1996
    The wonder of whales in the world's oceans and their profound impact on those who see them are sensitively portrayed.
Dyan Sheldon, *The Whales' Song*, 1990
    Learning from her grandmother about the whales' song, Lilly dreams of hearing it herself.

887

MAXINE ROSE SCHUR
KIMBERLY BULCKEN ROOT, Illustrator

The Peddler's Gift

(New York: Dial Books for Young Readers, 1999)

Subject(s): Jews; Rural Life; Conduct of Life
Age range(s): Grades 1-4
Major character(s): Shimon "Shnook", Peddler; Leibush, Student, Son
Time period(s): Indeterminate Past
Locale(s): Korovenko, Russia

Summary: Most peddlers that visit Leibush's village regale the families with tales of their travels and dramatically present their wares to potential buyers. Shimon is not like other peddlers. He is so quiet, self-effacing and apparently forgetful that the village boys think he is a simpleton and call him Shnook. Leibush learns when he steals one of Shimon's dreidels that, beneath the bumbling exterior, the peddler may be more astute and is definitely more compassionate than Leibush realizes. (32 pages)

Where it's reviewed:
Booklist, October 1, 1999, page 375
Horn Book Guide, Spring 2000, page 71
Publishers Weekly, September 27, 1999, page 52
School Library Journal, October 1999, page 72
Smithsonian Magazine, November 1999, page 48

Awards the book has won:
Smithsonian's Notable Books for Children, 1999
Sidney Taylor Award for Younger Readers, 1999

Other books by the same author:
When I Left My Village, 1996
Day of Delight: A Jewish Sabbath in Ethopia, 1994
Samantha's Surprise, 1986

Other books you might like:
Frances Harber, *The Brothers' Promise*, 1998
    Two brothers discover that their mutual kindness, secretly expressed, fulfills the promise made to their dying father and the angels do "weep tears of joy."
Isaac Bashevis Singer, *Stories for Children*, 1984
    Yiddish tradition inspires this collection of tales.
Esphyr Slobodkina, *Caps for Sale: A Tale of a Peddler, Some Monkeys and Their Monkey Business*, 1947
    A peddler of caps needs an ingenious solution to reclaim his misappropriated wares from a group of monkeys.

888

AMY SCHWARTZ, Author/Illustrator

How to Catch an Elephant

(New York: A Richard Jackson Book/DK Publishing, Inc., 1999)

Subject(s): Humor; Animals/Elephants; Problem Solving
Age range(s): Grades K-1
Major character(s): Jack, Uncle; Unnamed Character, Child, Niece
Time period(s): Indeterminate
Locale(s): Fictional Country

Summary: Uncle Jack has specific instructions for catching an elephant. His niece assembles the required materials: three cakes, two raisins, one telescope and a pair of tweezers before following Uncle Jack to a spot where she's apt find an elephant. Uncle Jack leaves her with a final word of caution—remember to use the telescope. Carefully adhering to the directions, the young girl puts out a cake with one raisin on top. An elephant comes and devours the raisin (something elephants like) then stomps the hated cake. By the time the girl has repeated this bait with each cake the elephant is in a rage so she uses the telescope (aimed the wrong way) to shrink the elephant down to a manageable size that she then picks up with the tweezers. (40 pages)

Where it's reviewed:
Booklist, November 15, 1999, page 639
Horn Book Guide, Spring 2000, page 53

Kirkus Reviews, July 1, 1999, page 1059
Publishers Weekly, July 26, 1999, page 90
School Library Journal, February 2000, page 103

Other books by the same author:
Some Babies, 2000
A Teeny Tiny Baby, 1994
Annabelle Swift, Kindergartner, 1988
Her Majesty, Aunt Essie, 1984

Other books you might like:
Alyssa Satin Capucilli, *Inside a Zoo in the City: A Rebus Read-Along Story*, 2000
    The alarm wakes the parrot who begins waking all the other animals from the tiger to the elephant so they can report to the zoo on time.
Doug Johnson, *Never Ride Your Elephant to School*, 1995
    Even if you can catch the elephant, it's not a good idea to ride it to school.
Helen Lester, *Tacky in Trouble*, 1998
    The large ''rock'' on which Tacky the penguin dances is actually an elephant angered by Tacky's presence.

889

AMY SCHWARTZ, Author/Illustrator

Some Babies

(New York: Orchard Books, 2000)

Subject(s): Babies; Bedtime; Parent and Child
Age range(s): Preschool
Major character(s): Baby, Son; Mommy, Mother
Time period(s): 2000s
Locale(s): United States

Summary: Mommy tucks Baby in his crib, but Baby is not ready to sleep. Baby wants to hear about some babies so Mommy describes the antics of some babies in the park, what they wear and how they play. Each time tired Mommy stops talking, Baby calls out ''More.'' Mommy talks until her mouth is ''fuzzy'' and she simply can't talk any more. Baby, still wide-awake, simply calls for ''Daddy!'' when Mommy drifts off to sleep. (32 pages)

Where it's reviewed:
Booklist, December 15, 2000, page 829
Horn Book, September 2000, page 555
Publishers Weekly, July 31, 2000, page 93
Riverbank Review, Fall 2000, page 31
School Library Journal, October 2000, page 136

Other books by the same author:
A Teeny Tiny Baby, 1994
Annabelle Swift, Kindergartner, 1988
Begin at the Beginning, 1983

Other books you might like:
Russell Hoban, *Bedtime for Frances*, 1960
    Frances is a master at avoiding sleep, but her patient parents have a response for every problem.
Jill Murphy, *A Quiet Night In*, 1994
    When two parents, seeking a quiet night at home, read a bedtime story to their children, they put themselves, not the children to sleep.

Charles R. Smith Jr., *Brown Sugar Babies*, 2000
    The babies in this photographic essay come in all shades of brown—some peanut butter creamy, some cinnamon spice and some swee as honey.

890

ELLEN SCHWARTZ
KRISTI, Illustrator

Jesse's Star

(Custer, WA: Orca Book Publishers, 2000)

Series: Orca Young Reader
Subject(s): Jews; Superstition; Time Travel
Age range(s): Grades 2-5
Major character(s): Jesse, Student—Elementary School; Yossi Mendelsohn, Immigrant
Time period(s): 2000s (2000); 1890s (1890)
Locale(s): Canada; Braslav, Russia

Summary: To complete a school assignment Jesse needs to learn how and why his ancestors originally came to Canada. His mother sends him to the attic to look in an old traveling case where he finds a group picture dated 1890 and a Star of David on a chain. When Jesse slips the chain around his neck he is magically transported back to Russia and becomes his great-great-grandfather Yossi. As Yossi, Jesse experiences the persecution of the Jews in their small village by Russian soldiers and learns of Yossi's heroic role in the villagers' dangerous nighttime escape to freedom. As Yossi reaches the shores of Canada, Jesse returns to the present with a new appreciation for his ancestors and eager to write the report. The book concludes with a brief historical background to the events depicted in the story. (108 pages)

Where it's reviewed:
Booklist, July 2000, page 2026
Quill & Quire, May 2000, page 37
Resource Links, June 2000, page 9
School Library Journal, November 2000, page 132
Voice of Youth Advocates, October 2000, page 278

Other books by the same author:
Mr. Belinsky's Bagels, 1998

Other books you might like:
Lillian Hammer Ross, *Sarah, Also Known as Hannah*, 1994
    After her father's death, Sarah is sent, in place of her sister Hannah, to live with her aunt and uncle in America
Jon Scieszka, *Summer Reading Is Killing Me!*, 1998
    Book characters have the Time Warp Trio trapped in their summer reading list.
Elvira Woodruff, *The Orphan of Ellis Island: A Time-Travel Adventure*, 1997
    Dominic, a lonely foster child, learns about his family history when he travels back in time to Italy and sails with his ancestors to America.

JON SCIESZKA
LANE SMITH, Illustrator

It's All Greek to Me
(New York: Viking, 1999)

Series: Time Warp Trio
Subject(s): Time Travel; Mythology; Humor
Age range(s): Grades 3-5
Major character(s): Joe, Time Traveler, Student—Elementary School; Fred, Time Traveler, Student—Elementary School; Sam, Time Traveler, Student—Elementary School
Time period(s): 1990s (1999); Indeterminate Past
Locale(s): United States; Mount Olympus, Greece

Summary: The intrepid Time Warp Trio have parts in a class play based on Greek mythology, but have accidentally been transported in time back to Mount Olympus where they face actual monsters, beasts, gods and goddesses armed only with their stage props. Joe intended to return *The Book* that causes the time travel to his uncle but somehow the play's script and *The Book* got mixed up in Joe's backpack and now Joe, Fred and Sam are face to face with a snarling three-headed dog. Fred tames the beast with a Ding Dong and the trio escapes to search for a way to travel home. As in their previous adventures the three pals find their way home with help from a goddess who looks a lot like Joe's mother. The book concludes with a glossary identifying the mythological characters, instructions for making the stage props and a website for accessing the complete script. (73 pages)

Where it's reviewed:
Booklist, November 15, 1999, page 628
Horn Book Guide, Spring 2000, page 87
Kirkus Reviews, October 15, 1999, page 1651
Publishers Weekly, October 18, 1999, page 85
School Library Journal, October 1999, page 126

Other books by the same author:
Summer Reading Is Killing Me!, 1998 (Time Warp Trio)
Tut, Tut, 1996 (Time Warp Trio)
2095, 1995 (Time Warp Trio)

Other books you might like:
Leonard Everett Fisher, *The Olympians: Great Gods and Goddesses of Ancient Greece*, 1984
Biographical sketches describe twelve gods and goddesses of Greek mythology.
Dan Greenburg, *The Boy Who Cried Bigfoot*, 2000
While attending summer camp Zack and Spencer go looking for a legendary creature in this latest entry in the Zack files series.
Hazel Hutchins, *The Prince of Tarn*, 1997
A character in one of Fred's deceased mother's books comes to life and expects Fred to return him to his homeland.
Robert Kraus, *Near Myths: Dug Up and Dusted Off*, 1996
Five stories combining tidbits of myths with characters from Greek, Roman and Biblical accounts humorously parody the traditional tales.

Mary Pope Osborne, *Favorite Greek Myths*, 1989
The collection retells thirteen classic Greek myths.

JON SCIESZKA
ADAM MCCAULEY, Illustrator

See You Later, Gladiator
(New York: Viking, 2000)

Series: Time Warp Trio
Subject(s): Time Travel; Sports/Wrestling; Humor
Age range(s): Grades 3-5
Major character(s): Joe, Time Traveler, Friend; Fred, Time Traveler, Friend; Sam, Time Traveler, Friend
Time period(s): Indeterminate Past; 2000s (2000)
Locale(s): Rome, Italy; United States

Summary: If only Joe, Fred and Sam had not knocked *The Book* off the bookcase during their innocent horseplay in Joe's bedroom they might still be in an imaginary wrestling ring instead of facing a gladiator in ancient Rome. Certain that they will die, the Time Warp Trio feels relief to know they've landed in a school for gladiators and the weapons are fake. Still, they are stuck with the problem of locating *The Book* that can transport them home while avoiding certain death at the next tournament. (87 pages)

Where it's reviewed:
Booklist, January 1, 2001, page 961
Horn Book Guide, Spring 2001, page 79
Kirkus Reviews, August 15, 2000, page 1203
School Library Journal, November 2000, page 133

Other books by the same author:
It's All Greek to Me, 1999 (Time Warp Trio)
Summer Reading Is Killing Me!, 1998 (Time Warp Trio)
Tut, Tut, 1996 (Time Warp Trio)
2095, 1995 (Time Warp Trio)
Your Mother Was a Neanderthal, 1993 (Time Warp Trio)

Other books you might like:
Edward Eager, *Seven-Day Magic*, 1962
Susan checks out a library book that unexpectedly brings magic into her life.
H.G. Wells, *The Time Machine*, 1964
A classic time travel story tells of a young scientist who develops a machine in which he travels through time to another civilization.
Henry Winterfield, *Detectives in Togas*, 1990
Students of a Roman school try to solve the mystery of a defaced temple and a manacled teacher.

C. ANNE SCOTT
STEPHANIE ROTH, Illustrator

Lizard Meets Ivana the Terrible
(New York: Henry Holt, 1999)

Subject(s): Schools; Friendship; Grandmothers
Age range(s): Grades 2-5

Major character(s): Lizzie Gardner, 3rd Grader, 8-Year-Old; Ivana the Terrible, 3rd Grader, 8-Year-Old
Time period(s): 1990s (1999)
Locale(s): Texas

Summary: When Lizzie moves to Texas to live with her grandmother, she is sure that she will never make a friend in her new school. To make matters worse, Lizzie is assigned Ivana the Terrible as her journal buddy. Lizzie learns that she and Ivana have a lot in common, but Lizzie is afraid the other kids will make fun of her as they do Ivana. With a little work and a little courage however, Lizzie and Ivana become friends. (115 pages)

Where it's reviewed:
Booklist, November 1, 1999, page 531
Publishers Weekly, November 15, 1999, page 67
School Library Journal, November 1999, page 129

Other books by the same author:
Old Jake's Skirts, 1998

Other books you might like:
Beverly Cleary, *Ellen Tebbits*, 1951
  Eight-year-old Ellen Tebbits finds a friend in Austine Allen.
Paula Danziger, *Amber Brown Is Not a Crayon*, 1995
  Amber's third grade year is made more difficult when she learns that her best friend Justin is moving.
Betsy Duffey, *How to Be Cool in the Third Grade*, 1993
  When the teacher assigns Robbie to be the class bully's "Book Buddy," Robbie is sure his life is over, but the experience teaches him a lot.
Gina Willner-Pardo, *Daphne Eloise Slater, Who's Tall for Her Age*, 1997
  Daphne is assigned to be Leonard's lab partner, after he has tormented her about her height for weeks.

894

RICHARD SCRIMGER
LINDA HENDRY, Illustrator

The Way to Schenectady

(Plattsburgh, NY: Tundra Books, 1999)

Subject(s): Family; Travel; Homeless People
Age range(s): Grades 4-6
Major character(s): Jane Peeler, 12-Year-Old, Sister (older); Helen "Grandma" Collins, Grandmother, Widow(er); Marty Oberdorf, Aged Person, Streetperson
Time period(s): 1990s (1998)
Locale(s): Toronto, Ontario, Canada; Schenectady, New York; Pittsfield, Massachusetts

Summary: A simple family trip to join their mother at a relative's home begins auspiciously when the chicken legs being fried for the picnic lunch ignite and a last minute phone call adds grouchy Grandma to the entourage. During a routine stop for gas and a change of her younger brother's diaper, Jane spots Marty sleeping next to the dumpster and listens to his tale of woe. Estranged for many years from his family, Marty has seen an obituary for his brother and is trying to walk to Schenectady for the memorial service. Jane smuggles Marty into the van, makes excuses for the odors and sounds that emanate from the cargo space and manages to keep his existence a secret until they stop for the night. The next morning Grandma discovers Jane's plans and, surprisingly, is willing to participate in the deception. When the van breaks down, Marty's skill as a mechanic comes in handy and he earns a seat in the passenger compartment. By the time the family reaches Schenectady, Grandma and Marty have visited a used clothing store and a barber so he's presentable and Jane has developed a new appreciation for her grandmother. Eventually, they actually reach Pittsfield, too. The book was originally published in Canada in 1998. (162 pages)

Where it's reviewed:
Booklist, May 1, 1999, page 1596
Canadian Book Review Annual, 1998, page 520
Children's Bookwatch, April 1999, page 1
Quill & Quire, December 1998, page 38
School Library Journal, June 1999, page 137

Other books by the same author:
A Nose for Adventure, 2001
The Nose from Jupiter, 1998
Still Life with Children: Tales of Family Life, 1997

Other books you might like:
Judy Delton, *Angel Spreads Her Wings*, 1999
  A family vacation in Greece to meet her stepfather's family ruins Angel's summer plans but gives her new insights into her relatives.
Carolyn J. Gold, *Dragonfly Secret*, 1997
  At the conclusion of a family trip, Gramps, Nathan and Jessie discover a "hitchhiker" that is actually an injured fairy stuck to the car.
Marissa Moss, *Amelia Hits the Road*, 1997
  In her diary Amelia describes the long car trip with her family, her fear that her sister will become carsick and the sights they see along the way.

895

AFI SCRUGGS
DAVID DIAZ, Illustrator

Jump Rope Magic

(New York: The Blue Sky Press/Scholastic, Inc., 2000)

Subject(s): Fantasy; Playing; Stories in Rhyme
Age range(s): Grades K-3
Major character(s): Shameka, Child; Miss Minnie, Aged Person
Time period(s): 2000s
Locale(s): United States

Summary: The author's first picture book celebrates the rhythm of jump roping. Shameka, Shameka see her go. She can jump high; she can jump low. Friends call out as Shameka jumps about. Their noise gets so loud that Miss Minnie sees the crowd. Happy children, why so glad when Miss Minnie feels sad? Out her door goes Miss Minnie; she's mad. Children run away but Shameka's here to stay. Asks Miss Minnie to jump and play. Miss Minnie does and she sails away—all the way to heaven where she plans to stay. (40 pages)

Where it's reviewed:
Booklist, February 1, 2000, page 1030

Horn Book Guide, Fall 2000, page 281
Kirkus Reviews, March 15, 2000, page 390
Publishers Weekly, February 21, 2000, page 87
School Library Journal, April 2000, page 113

Other books you might like:
Jim Aylesworth, *My Sister's Rusty Bike*, 1996
     Rhyming text describes a brother's tour of America on his sister's rusty bike.
Joanna Cole, *Anna Banana: 101 Jump Rope Rhymes*, 1989
     This nonfiction title categorizes the rhymes by the type of jumping done with each.
Angela Shelf Medearis, *Rum-a-Tum-Tum*, 1997
     The rhythmic cry of street vendors awakens a young girl who hurries out to watch the activity.
Andrea Davis Pinkney, *Solo Girl*, 1997
     Cass gets help from Pearl to improve her ability to jump double dutch.

896

BRENDA SEABROOKE

The Vampire in My Bathtub

(New York: Holiday House, 1999)

Subject(s): Vampires; Moving, Household; Divorce
Age range(s): Grades 4-7
Major character(s): Jeffrey "Jeff" Martin, 13-Year-Old, Child of Divorced Parents; Eugene Carondelet, Vampire; Alison Gennero, Neighbor
Time period(s): 1990s (1999)
Locale(s): Wicklow, West Virginia

Summary: Jeff thinks nothing could be worse than his parents' divorce until his mother accepts a teaching position in a tiny West Virginia town. Now Jeff faces a miserable summer with only nosy neighbor Allison for companionship. The challenge of opening a locked closet in the bedroom of the old house gives Jeff some initial focus. Inside the closet Jeff finds a locked trunk and when that is open, Jeff is face to face with Eugene, a "good" vampire who's been locked up for over a hundred years. Now Jeff really has a problem—hiding a curious vampire with no knowledge of modern technology from his mother. The humor of the situation gives way to terror when Eugene's evil cousin travels through time to finish off the job he started long ago. (150 pages)

Where it's reviewed:
Booklist, January 1, 2000, page 927
Horn Book, January 2000, page 84
Publishers Weekly, January 3, 2000, page 76
School Library Journal, December 1999, page 140

Other books by the same author:
The Care and Feeding of Dragons, 1998
The Haunting of Holroyd Hill, 1995
Jerry on the Line, 1990

Other books you might like:
Susan Cooper, *The Boggart*, 1993
     No vampires but lots of mischief when the Volniks accidentally import an ancient, fun-loving shape-changer from a Scottish castle to their Canadian home.

Lila Sprague McGinnis, *The Ghost Upstairs*, 1982
     After losing his home of 75 years a ghost moves into a nearby house, creating havoc as he experiences modern conveniences.
Eric Sanvoisin, *The Ink Drinker*, 1998
     The unusual vampire in this story survives by slurping the print from the pages of books.
S.P. Somtow, *The Vampire's Beautiful Daughter*, 1997
     Fifteen-year-old Rebecca has until her birthday to decide if she will remain a mortal or become a vampire like her father.

897

J. OTTO SEIBOLD, Author/Illustrator
V.L. WALSH, Co-Author

Penguin Dreams

(San Francisco: Chronicle Books, 1999)

Subject(s): Animals/Penguins; Dreams and Nightmares; Stories in Rhyme
Age range(s): Grades K-3
Major character(s): Chongo Chingi, Penguin
Time period(s): Indeterminate
Locale(s): Fictional Country

Summary: In his dreams Chongo Chingi takes flight and soars out of his zoo home and into the sky with ducks, jets, and bats. About the time Chongo Chingi reaches a barren icy landscape filled with penguins the ringing of his alarm brings his dream to an end. Sigh, flying is fun—even in dreams. (32 pages)

Where it's reviewed:
Booklist, September 15, 1999, page 270
Horn Book Guide, Spring 2000, page 54
New York Times Book Review, November 221, 1999, page 51
Publishers Weekly, September 20, 1999, page 86
School Library Journal, January 2000, page 110

Awards the book has won:
New York Times Best Illustrated Children's Books, 1999

Other books by the same author:
Free Lunch, 1996
Monkey Business, 1995
Mr. Lunch Borrows a Canoe, 1994

Other books you might like:
Nancy Kapp Chapman, *Doggie Dreams*, 2000
     Silly, colorful illustrations enliven a rhyming text about bones, phones, planes and other dreams of dogs
Lynda R. Rymill, *Good Knight*, 1998
     An imaginative little boy uses every tactic he can think of to delay his mother's attempts to get him ready for bed.
Dan Yaccarino, *Good Night, Mr. Night*, 1997
     A young boy views the dark night sky as Mr. Night, quietly putting the world to bed and giving the boy sleep-inducing dreams.

898

BARBARA SEULING
PAUL BREWER, Illustrator

Oh No, It's Robert
(Chicago: Front Street/Cricket Books, 1999)

Subject(s): School Life; Friendship; Competition
Age range(s): Grades 2-4
Major character(s): Robert Dorfman, Student—Elementary School, Friend; Paul Felcher, Student—Elementary School, Friend; Mrs. Bernthal, Teacher
Time period(s): 1990s (1999)
Locale(s): United States

Summary: Just once, Robert would like to be the student who receives some positive recognition in class so his parents maybe would stop noticing that he's not a very good reader or a neat worker. When Mrs. Bernthal announces a class contest with five different ways to earn points toward the goal Robert is determined to win. He knows it's unlikely that he can be successful with some of the options, but he thinks he can do well with the teacher's helper category. Paul helps Robert prepare fliers that he distributes to all the teachers in the school and soon he's arriving early to help the music teacher and assisting the art teacher during class. Mrs. Bernthal puts him in charge of the class library and Robert begins to see some hope of achieving his goal. (117 pages)

Where it's reviewed:
Booklist, July 1999, page 1947
Horn Book Guide, Fall 1999, page 284
The New Advocate, Spring 2000, page 182
Publishers Weekly, June 14, 1999, page 70
School Library Journal, July 1999, page 80

Other books by the same author:
Winter Lullaby, 1998
Elephants Can't Jump and Other Freaky Facts about Animals, 1985
The Teeny Tiny Woman: An Old English Folk Tale, 1978

Other books you might like:
David A. Adler, *The Many Troubles of Andy Russell*, 1998
    Try as he might, Andy's plans seem to go awry and unexpected problems crop up everywhere for him.
Betsy Duffey, *How to Be Cool in the Third Grade*, 1993
    Third grade begins with one mishap after another, but eventually Robbie learns what it really means to be cool.
Becky Thoman Lindberg, *Thomas Tuttle, Just in Time*, 1994
    Thomas, a procrastinator at heart, tries to improve his school performance by completing his work by the due date.
Susan Shreve, *Joshua T. Bates in Trouble Again*, 1997
    When faced with the choice of peer acceptance or fulfilling his new classroom responsibility Joshua makes an important decision to do the right thing.

899

TRES SEYMOUR
MARSHA GRAY CARRINGTON, Illustrator

Jake Johnson: The Story of a Mule
(New York. DK Ink/DK Publishing, Inc., 1999)

Subject(s): Animals/Mules; Obstinacy; Holidays
Age range(s): Grades K-3
Major character(s): Jake Johnson, Mule; Farmer Puckett, Farmer; Mrs. Puckett, Spouse
Time period(s): Indeterminate Past
Locale(s): United States

Summary: To haul his wagon loaded with fireworks to the town's Fourth of July celebration Farmer Puckett buys a very large mule. Unfortunately, Jake Johnson is so content in Farmer Puckett's yard that he sits down and refuses to move despite all Farmer Puckett's efforts to make the stubborn mule budge. Skeptical Mrs. Puckett's advice is ignored until Independence Day arrives and still Jake Johnson sits. Farmer Puckett loads the wagon with fireworks, hitches Jake Johnson to it and Mrs. Puckett lights a fire under Jake Johnson. The ornery mule stands and moves just far enough to be out of the flames before sitting down again with the wagon now directly over the fire. When the sparklers and Roman candles begin exploding Jake Johnson races away with Mrs. Puckett clinging to the wagon as the mule runs to the County Courthouse where he's probably sitting still. (32 pages)

Where it's reviewed:
Booklist, July 1999, page 1955
Bulletin of the Center for Children's Books, April 1999, page 294
Horn Book Guide, Fall 1999, page 267
Publishers Weekly, March 22, 1999, page 91
School Library Journal, April 1999, page 108

Awards the book has won:
IRA/CBC Children's Choices, 2000

Other books by the same author:
Our Neighbor Is a Strange, Strange Man, 1999
We Played Marbles, 1998
Too Quiet for These Old Bones, 1997
Black Sky River, 1996
Hunting the White Cow, 1993 (ALA Notable Book)

Other books you might like:
David F. Birchman, *Jigsaw Jackson*, 1996
    A farmer spends his winters playing checkers with his plow horse until an interest in jigsaw puzzles temporarily takes him from the farm.
Cynthia DeFelice, *Mule Eggs*, 1994
    Patrick, new to the world of farming, outsmarts a neighbor who has tricked him into buying mule eggs.
Sid Fleischman, *McBroom's Wonderful One-Acre Farm: Three Tall Tales*, 1992
    A collection of humorous tall tales about Farmer McBroom and his family was originally published in 1967.

PHYLLIS SHALANT
ANNA VOJTECH, Illustrator

Bartleby of the Mighty Mississippi

(New York: Dutton Children's Books, 2000)

Subject(s): Animals/Turtles; Pets; Fantasy
Age range(s): Grades 4-6
Major character(s): Bartleby, Turtle; Seezer, Alligator
Time period(s): 2000s (2000)
Locale(s): United States

Summary: Bartleby's life as a pampered family pet comes to an abrupt end when one of his owners tosses him into a pond for a swim. With no experience fending for himself for food, shelter, or protection from predators, Bartleby uses his glib tongue to save himself and win the friendship of Seezer, another abandoned pet that wants to reach his home in the mighty Mississippi. To avoid being eaten by the alligator, Bartleby pretends to know the way to the "traveling water" and eventually he proves to himself and to Seezer that he really does. (164 pages)

Where it's reviewed:
Booklist, May 15, 2000, page 1744
Horn Book, February 2000, page 312
Horn Book Guide, Fall 2000, page 312
Kirkus Reviews, June 1, 2000, page 803
School Library Journal, August 2000, page 189

Other books by the same author:
The Great Eye, 1996
Beware of Kissing Lizard Lips, 1995
Shalom, Geneva Peace, 1992

Other books you might like:
Avi, *Poppy*, 1995
    With help from other animals, a young mouse seeking to improve her community's life courageously journeys into the unknown and defeats an evil owl.
Brooks Hansen, *Caesar's Antlers*, 1997
    Kindly Caesar uses his antlers to transport a sparrow with her nest of babies as she searches for her lost mate.
Cynthia Rylant, *Gooseberry Park*, 1995
    A dog, a bat and a hermit crab are stuck babysitting for young squirrels whose mother is lost after an ice storm destroys their tree home.

DAVID SHANNON, Author/Illustrator

David Goes to School

(New York: The Blue Sky Press/Scholastic Inc., 1999)

Subject(s): Schools; Behavior; Teacher-Student Relationships
Age range(s): Grades K-1
Major character(s): David, Student—Elementary School; Unnamed Character, Teacher
Time period(s): 1990s
Locale(s): United States

Summary: Irrepressible David enters school, tardy of course, and discovers rules, rules and more rules. The unseen teacher dominates the dialogue, but David's out-of-bounds behavior is a greater force in the classroom. He speaks out without raising his hand, chews a huge mouthful of gum, breaks in the lunch line and pays close attention to the clouds out the window, but not to the teacher's instruction. Recess ends and David is still outside playing ball; other children try to read while David uses his pencils to drum on his book. The final straw is when David uses his desktop for a coloring project and he must stay after school to clean all the desks. When finished, David beams at the teacher as she bestows a gold star and permission to go home. (32 pages)

Where it's reviewed:
Booklist, August 1999, page 2053
Horn Book Guide, Spring 2000, page 23
Kirkus Reviews, July 1, 1999, page 1059
Publishers Weekly, July 5, 1999, page 69
School Library Journal, September 1999, page 205

Awards the book has won:
Booklist Editors' Choice, 1999
Publishers Weekly Best Books, 1999

Other books by the same author:
A Bad Case of Stripes, 1998
No, David!, 1998 (Caldecott Honor Book)
The Amazing Christmas Extravaganza, 1995
How Georgie Radbourn Saved Baseball, 1994 (New York Times Best Illustrated Book)

Other books you might like:
Quentin Blake, *Simpkin*, 1994
    A rhyming tale uses mischievous Simpkin's unpredictable behavior to explore opposites such as naughty and nice.
Phyllis Reynolds Naylor, *I Can't Take You Anywhere!*, 1997
    Amy Audrey is so prone to clumsiness that her parents stay home rather than take her out in public.
Judith Viorst, *Alexander and the Terrible, Horrible, No Good, Very Bad Day*, 1972
    Alexander is having a day in which everything that can possibly go wrong does.

DAVID SHANNON, Author/Illustrator

The Rain Came Down

(New York: The Blue Sky Press/Scholastic, Inc., 2000)

Subject(s): Behavior; Weather; Humor
Age range(s): Grades K-3
Major character(s): Unnamed Character, Police Officer
Time period(s): Indeterminate Past
Locale(s): United States

Summary: The rain comes down on a family, pets, storekeepers, travelers and shoppers who are feeling cranky on a gloomy day. A policeman stops to investigate a commotion at one house, blocking the street with his car, causing traffic to back up and leading to more noise and more frayed nerves. The arguments, tears and general ruckus abruptly stop along with the rain and the people on the street gaze at the beautiful rainbow. The sunshine changes everyone's mood and brings a cooperative friendly spirit to the previously argumentative group. When it's obvious to the policeman that all is well he calmly gets in his car and drives away. (32 pages)

Where it's reviewed:
Booklist, October 15, 2000, page 447
Five Owls, September 2000, page 16
Horn Book, September 2000, page 556
Publishers Weekly, October 16, 2000, page 75
School Library Journal, October 2000, page 136

Other books by the same author:
David Goes to School, 1999 (School Library Journal Best Book)
A Bad Case of Stripes, 1998
No, David!, 1998 (Caldecott Honor Book)
The Amazing Christmas Extravaganza, 1995

Other books you might like:
Karen Hesse, *Come On, Rain!*, 1999
    Everyone in Tessie's neighborhood welcomes the cooling rain when it finally comes to soothe their heat-induced irritability.
Jack Prelutsky, *Rainy Rainy Saturday*, 1980
    Fourteen poems celebrate the fun one can have on a rainy day, even when stuck inside.
Mary Lyn Ray, *Red Rubber Boot Day*, 2000
    A little boy would argue that with the right boots a rainy day can be delightful.
Manya Stojic, *Rain*, 2000
    A dry African plain is transformed by a rainstorm.
Charlotte Zolotow, *The Quarreling Book*, 1963
    A misinterpreted event leads to family quarrels until the dog saves the day.

903

GEORGE SHANNON
JOSE ARUEGO, Illustrator
ARIANE DEWEY, Illustrator

Lizard's Home

(New York: Greenwillow Books, 1999)

Subject(s): Animals/Reptiles; Honesty; Problem Solving
Age range(s): Grades K-2
Major character(s): Lizard, Lizard, Friend (Toad's); Toad, Toad, Friend (Lizard's); Snake, Snake, Bully
Time period(s): Indeterminate
Locale(s): Fictional Country

Summary: After a day of play with Toad, Lizard looks forward to returning to his rock home. One day Lizard finds his rock occupied by Snake who insists he has not mistakenly settled on Lizard's rock, but has chosen it because it suits him and he plans to keep it. Lizard doesn't want to find a new home so he tries several strategies both diplomatic and wishful to try to convince Snake to give up the rock. Nothing works. Finally Lizard challenges Snake to a contest. Snake tries to fix the outcome, but Lizard outsmarts him and wins back his rock—or at least the top of it. (32 pages)

Where it's reviewed:
Booklist, October 1, 1999, page 363
Horn Book Guide, Spring 2000, page 54
Publishers Weekly, September 13, 1999, page 83

School Library Journal, September 1999, page 206

Other books by the same author:
This Is the Bird, 1997
Heart to Heart, 1995
Climbing Kansas Mountains, 1993 (School Library Journal Best Book)
Lizard's Song, 1981

Other books you might like:
Kate Banks, *The Bird, the Monkey, and the Snake in the Jungle*, 1999
    When their tree home topples over in a storm, a bird, a monkey and a snake search for another dwelling place.
Linda Hayward, *Hello, House!*, 1988
    Cunning Brer Rabbit uses his wits to get the best of Brer Wolf.
Ellen Stoll Walsh, *Pip's Magic*, 1994
    Pip, a salamander, discovers that he already possesses the ''magic'' he seeks to overcome his fear of the dark.

904

MARJORIE WEINMAN SHARMAT
MARTHA WESTON, Illustrator

Nate the Great and the Monster Mess

(New York: Delacorte Press, 1999)

Subject(s): Food; Lost and Found Possessions; Mystery and Detective Stories
Age range(s): Grades 2-3
Major character(s): Nate, Detective—Amateur, Son; Sludge, Dog; Oliver, Child, Neighbor
Time period(s): 1990s (1999)
Locale(s): United States

Summary: When Nate's mother cannot find the recipe for his favorite monster cookies Nate begins to search the house and the neighborhood for it. Although Sludge is not particularly interested in cookies he accompanies Nate as the amateur sleuth questions friends and develops clues. Observing Oliver make notations on a card gives Nate an idea that turns out to be incorrect. His next theory leads him to the discovery of the recipe. When his mother discovers the mess Nate creates while looking, he has a new challenge—cleaning! (48 pages)

Where it's reviewed:
Horn Book Guide, Spring 2000, page 62
School Library Journal, December 1999, page 112

Other books by the same author:
Nate the Great and Me, 1998
Nate the Great Saves the King of Sweden, 1997
Nate the Great and the Stolen Base, 1992

Other books you might like:
David A. Adler, *Young Cam Jansen and the Missing Cookie*, 1996
    Jason depends on Cam's photographic memory to solve the mystery of the cookie missing from his lunch box.
Patricia Reilly Giff, *Mary Moon Is Missing*, 1998
    Amateur detective Minnie tries to locate a missing homing pigeon before the big race on Saturday.
Howard Goldsmith, *The Twiddle Twins' Music Box Mystery*, 1997

Timothy and Tabitha discover the identity of the thief who takes a family's music box.

Elizabeth Levy, *The Something Queer Series*, 1971-
Gwen, Jill and basset hound Fletcher enjoy adventures as they solve mysteries.

905

MARJORIE WEINMAN SHARMAT
MITCHELL SHARMAT, Co-Author
MARTHA WESTON, Illustrator

Nate the Great: San Francisco Detective

(New York: Delacorte Press, 2000)

Series: Nate the Great
Subject(s): Lost and Found Possessions; Mystery and Detective Stories; Problem Solving
Age range(s): Grades 1-3
Major character(s): Nate the Great, Child, Detective—Amateur; Sludge, Dog; Olivia Sharp, Cousin, Detective—Amateur
Time period(s): 2000s (2000)
Locale(s): San Francisco, California

Summary: Nate the Great and Sludge fly to San Francisco to visit Olivia but are met at the airport by her chauffeur. Olivia is busy with a case in which Nate quickly becomes involved simply by answering Olivia's phone. One of Olivia's clients lost a new joke book and needs to find it by two o'clock. Nate doesn't have much time, but he puts his mind, his powers of observation and the services of Olivia's limo to good use to locate the book with time to spare. (48 pages)

Where it's reviewed:
Booklist, July 2000, page 2045
Kirkus Reviews, June 15, 2000, page 893
School Library Journal, November 2000, page 133

Other books by the same author:
The Green Toenails Gang, 1991 (Olivia Sharp, Agent for Secrets)
The Sly Spy, 1990 (Olivia Sharp, Agent for Secrets)
The Pizza Monster, 1989 (Olivia Sharp, Agent for Secrets)

Other books you might like:
David A. Adler, *The Cam Jansen Series*, 1980-
Using her photographic memory, Cam Jansen helps solve a variety of mysteries.
Eth Clifford, *Flatfoot Fox and the Case of the Bashful Beaver*, 1995
Flatfoot Fox, an overly confident detective, solves the mystery of Beaver's stolen button bag with assistance from Secretary bird.
Elizabeth Levy, *Parent's Night Fright*, 1998
Charlene's leadership, Chip's invisibility and deaf Justin's lip-reading are used to solve the mystery of a missing short story.

906

CAROL DIGGORY SHIELDS
HIROE NAKATA, Illustrator

Lucky Pennies and Hot Chocolate

(New York: Dutton Children's Books, 2000)

Subject(s): Grandfathers; Humor
Age range(s): Grades K-2
Major character(s): Unnamed Character, Grandfather; Unnamed Character, Child
Time period(s): 2000s (2000)
Locale(s): United States

Summary: A grandson and his grandfather have many shared interests so visiting each other is an opportunity for mutual enjoyment of knock-knock jokes, watching construction machinery and riding with the top down on the convertible. A visit is also a time to pick up lucky pennies on walks, drink hot chocolate on a cold day, and play dominoes repeatedly because neither likes to lose. They both adore peanut butter and share the task of washing dishes after a meal. These two just love to be together! (32 pages)

Where it's reviewed:
Booklist, August 2000, page 2149
Horn Book Guide, Spring 2001, page 23
Publishers Weekly, August 14, 2000, page 354
Riverbank Review, Fall 2000, page 30
School Library Journal, September 2000, page 209

Other books by the same author:
Martian Rock, 1999
Month by Month a Year Goes Round, 1998
I Wish My Brother Was a Dog, 1997
Saturday Night at the Dinosaur Stomp, 1997
I Am Really a Princess, 1993

Other books you might like:
Vivian French, *Oliver's Fruit Salad*, 1998
Oliver enjoys his visits with his grandfather because there's always a new food to sample from his garden.
Helen V. Griffith, *Grandaddy's Place*, 1987
Janetta visits Grandaddy on his farm, getting to know the mule, the cat and a simple way of life.
Jessie Haas, *Sugaring*, 1996
Nora and Gramps tramp the snowy woods gathering the sap of maple trees during the annual sugaring ritual.
Amy Hest, *In the Rain with Baby Duck*, 1995
Baby Duck can count on a visit with her understanding Grampa to cheer her on a bad day.

907

CAROL DIGGORY SHIELDS
SCOTT NASH, Illustrator

Martian Rock

(Cambridge, MA: Candlewick Press, 1999)

Subject(s): Discovery and Exploration; Space Exploration; Stories in Rhyme
Age range(s): Grades K-2
Time period(s): Indeterminate

Locale(s): Spaceship; Earth

Summary: Martian explorers blast off in search of other forms of life in the solar system. Beginning with the outermost planet, "Orb Number Nine" in Martian lore, they systematically visit Orb Nine through Orb Five, and then head for Orbs One and Two. By the time they reach their final planet, Orb Number Three, the explorers are weary and ready to go home. They fly over the snow and ice-covered South Pole convinced that the planet holds no life when they spot a small black and white creature. Landing the spacecraft, the Martians are initially frightened when many of the winged creatures surround them. Soon they realize the "life forms" are friendly so they phone home to report their discovery. Then the Martians leave their friends with a souvenir and blast off for their own planet. Factual information about the numbered orbs, including their Earth name concludes the text. (40 pages)

Where it's reviewed:
Booklist, January 1, 2000, page 938
Horn Book Guide, Spring 2000, page 54
Kirkus Reviews, November 15, 1999, page 1816
Publishers Weekly, December 20, 1999, page 79
School Library Journal, January 2000, page 111

Other books by the same author:
I Wish My Brother Was a Dog, 1997
Lunch Money and Other Poems about School, 1995
I Am Really a Princess, 1993

Other books you might like:
Nancy Coffelt, *Dogs in Space*, 1993
    Dogs in astronaut gear travel through the solar system searching for playmates.
Loreen Leedy, *Postcards from Pluto: A Tour of the Solar System*, 1993
    Dr. Quasar, robot tour guide, leads a group of children on a spaceship tour requiring that they send home informative post cards from each stop.
Lynn Wilson, *What's Out There?: A Book About Space*, 1993
    An "All Aboard Book" gives factual information about planets, stars and comets.
Dan Yaccarino, *Zoom! Zoom! Zoom! I'm Off to the Moon!*, 1997
    Rhyming text and bright pictures describe a young boy's flight to the moon and return home.

908

SUSAN SHREVE

Ghost Cats

(New York: Arthur A. Levine Books/Scholastic Press, 1999)

Subject(s): Ghosts; Animals/Cats; Brothers and Sisters
Age range(s): Grades 5-8
Major character(s): Peter Hall, 11-Year-Old, Brother; Jonathan Hall, Doctor (pediatric neurologist), Father
Time period(s): 1990s (1999)
Locale(s): Boston, Massachusetts

Summary: Peter, the oldest of four children, is having the most difficulty adjusting to his family's new settled life in Boston. Dr. Hall has moved his family all over the globe as he teaches at different hospitals. Peter loves the constant change, relying on his siblings for friendships and feeling important because his parents depend on his help with the younger ones. His mother, however, has dreams of attending law school and owning a home. So, the family is now settled in Boston and nothing is the same. Peter's younger siblings have many friends and after school activities and his mother has her studies so there is never any of family time that Peter cherishes. Then, three of the family's six cats die or vanish and Peter thinks he is seeing their ghosts. (162 pages)

Where it's reviewed:
The Book Report, November 1999, page 66
Booklist, September 1, 1999, page 134
Five Owls, November 1999, page 45
Publishers Weekly, August 16, 1999, page 86
School Library Journal, November 1999, page 164

Other books by the same author:
Jonah the Whale, 1998
Joshua T. Bates in Trouble Again, 1997
The Formerly Great Alexander Family, 1995
The Gift of the Girl Who Couldn't Hear, 1991

Other books you might like:
C.S. Adler, *Courtyard Cat*, 1995
    After her family moves, Lindsay adjusts to the change with help from neighbors and a cat that frequents the apartment's courtyard.
Mary Hoffman, *The Four-Legged Ghosts*, 1993
    Alex and Carrie discover that their new pet mouse has unexpected talents as he fills their home with animals that only they can see.
Margaret Mahy, *The Good Fortunes Gang*, 1993
    When Pete's parents end their nomadic life by settling in his father's childhood home Pete must prove to his cousins that he's a "real" Fortune.
Phyllis Reynolds Naylor, *Danny's Desert Rats*, 1998
    Danny and his brother T.R. help their new friend Paul hide his pet cat from the apartment manager.

909

URI SHULEVITZ, Author/Illustrator

What Is a Wise Bird Like You Doing in a Silly Tale Like This?

(New York: Farrar Straus Giroux, 2000)

Subject(s): Animals/Birds; Kings, Queens, Rulers, etc.; Humor
Age range(s): Grades K-3
Major character(s): Lou, Bird; Aunt Millie, Bird; Emperor of Pickleberry, Royalty, Twin
Time period(s): Indeterminate
Locale(s): Pickleberry, Fictional Country

Summary: Wise Lou, an advisor to the Emperor of Pickleberry, lives more grandly than the Emperor's twin brother but, alas, the bird is not free. When the Emperor's twin is sent on an ambassadorial mission Lou asks him to convey a message to Aunt Millie. Upon hearing the message, Aunt Millie faints and appears to be dead, but in moments she flies away. When Lou hears the story of Aunt Millie's reaction to the news that he is a caged bird he knows just how to gain his freedom. Once he does, Lou flies to Aunt Millie and tells her the story of the twin brothers and how one came to be a greedy Emperor and the other a compassionate janitor. (40 pages)

Where it's reviewed:
Booklist, August 2000, page 2135
Horn Book, September 2000, page 557
Publishers Weekly, July 17, 2000, page 193
School Library Journal, August 2000, page 164

Other books by the same author:
Snow, 1998 (Caldecott Honor Book)
The Golden Goose, 1995
The Treasure, 1978 (Caldecott Honor Book)

Other books you might like:
Allan Ahlberg, *It Was a Dark and Stormy Night*, 1994
    Kidnapped Antonio's ability to spin a tale enables him to sneak away from his captors.
Helen Lester, *Princess Penelope's Parrot*, 1996
    Spoiled Princess Penelope gets her comeuppance from a parrot.
Hans Wilhelm, *The Royal Raven*, 1996
    In his desire to be special, Crawford trades freedom for a unique appearance and learns which is more important.

910

KIM L. SIEGELSON
BRIAN PINKNEY, Illustrator

In the Time of the Drums

(New York: Jump at the Sun/Hyperion Books for Children, 1999)

Subject(s): Slavery; African Americans; Grandmothers
Age range(s): Grades 2-5
Major character(s): Mentu, Child, Slave; Twi, Grandmother, Slave
Time period(s): Indeterminate Past
Locale(s): Georgia

Summary: Islanders, free and slave alike fear Twi, a powerful conjure woman who remembers her African roots. Island-born Mentu knows only kindness and love from his grandmother and depends on her to teach him the language, music and culture of Africa. While learning, Mentu longs to show off his strength but Twi cautions that his time to be ''strong-strong'' will come. When a slave ship carrying an entire village of Ibo docks near Mentu's home the captives hear the islander's drums communicating the message of the ship's arrival and think they have returned to their home. One glimpse from above decks shows them the reality of their situation and the group refuses to leave the ship. The heartfelt message of their song reaches Twi who cautions Mentu to remember all she has taught him and then runs to the ship. As Twi leads the captives into the water their chains dissolve and Mentu knows they will walk across the ocean floor all the way to Africa. An Author's Note explains the story's historical basis in the oral traditions of the Gullah. (32 pages)

Where it's reviewed:
Booklist, April 1, 1999, page 1428
Five Owls, March 2000, page 98
Horn Book, Mary 1999, page 345

Publishers Weekly, April 26, 1999, page 82
School Library Journal, May 1999, page 96

Awards the book has won:
Coretta Scott King Illustrator Award, 2000
Notable Social Studies Trade Books for Young People, 2000

Other books by the same author:
Escape South, 2000 (Road to Reading)
The Terrible, Wonderful Tellin' at Hog Hammock, 1996

Other books you might like:
Virginia Hamilton, *The People Could Fly: American Black Folktales*, 1985
    A collection of African folktales includes those describing ways in which slaves achieved freedom.
William H. Hooks, *Freedom's Fruit*, 1996
    Mama Marina, an enslaved conjure woman, gains freedom for her daughter and her beloved by using a powerful spell to trick the master.
William Miller, *The Conjure Woman*, 1996
    To treat Toby's illness Madame Zina flies with him across the ocean to their African homeland and the village healers.

911

JUDY SIERRA
VICTORIA CHESS, Illustrator

The Beautiful Butterfly: A Folktale from Spain

(New York: Clarion Books, 2000)

Subject(s): Folklore; Animals/Insects; Grief
Age range(s): Grades K-3
Major character(s): Unnamed Character, Butterfly; Unnamed Character, Mouse
Time period(s): Indeterminate Past
Locale(s): Spain

Summary: Soon after a butterfly sets up residence in a hollow tree potential suitors begin to visit. She rejects several because their singing is not acceptable as a lullaby for babies. Finally a mouse's song sounds soothing and the two are wed. When the newlywed mouse goes to the pond to fetch water for his bride he falls in and a fish swallows him. Hearing the news, the butterfly goes into mourning and sits crying beside the pond. A dove, the tree and the pond join in mourning so that when the queen arrives for water, the pond is almost dry. When the queen learns the reason she breaks her water jars in support of the butterfly's grief and then the king takes off his robes and parades about the pond in his underwear. The sight of the king is so funny that the fish laughs and expels the mouse. Now the newlyweds truly can live happily ever after. A concluding note gives information about the many variations of the tale. (32 pages)

Where it's reviewed:
Booklist, March 15, 2000, page 1384
Bulletin of the Center for Children's Books, May 2000, page 332
Children's Book Review Service, May 2000, page 112
Kirkus Reviews, March 1, 2000, page 307
Publishers Weekly, March 27, 2000, page 80

Other books by the same author:
Counting Crocodiles, 1997 (IRA/CBC Children's Choice)
The Mean Hyena: A Folktale from Malawi, 1997
Good Night Dinosaurs, 1996

Other books you might like:
Eric A. Kimmel, *Bernal & Florinda: A Spanish Tale*, 1994
 Through a series of clever trades Bernal begins with a bag of grasshoppers and ends with a trick on Don Garcilaso and marriage to Florinda.
Uri Shulevitz, *The Golden Goose*, 1995
 Inadvertently, a simple young man causes a sad princess to laugh and thus wins her hand in marriage.
Harriet Peck Taylor, *Coyote and the Laughing Butterflies*, 1995
 Butterflies enjoy tricking Coyote so much that to this day the memory brings them laughter that prevents them from flying in a straight line.

912

JUDY SIERRA
JESSE SWEETWATER, Illustrator

The Dancing Pig

(San Diego: Gulliver Books/Harcourt Brace & Company, 1999)

Subject(s): Folklore; Folk Tales; Twins
Age range(s): Grades K-3
Major character(s): Klonching, Sister, Twin; Klodan, Sister, Twin; Rangsasa, Witch (ogress), Kidnapper
Time period(s): Indeterminate Past
Locale(s): Bali Island, Indonesia

Summary: In a retelling of a Balinese folk tale, the kindness that Klodan and Klonching show to the family pig, a small mouse and the frogs in their compound is repaid when the animals save them from the evil Rangsasa. While the twins' mother goes to market to sell seeds she locks her daughters in the house with instructions to open the door only in response to her voice. Rangsasa watches the mother's return every afternoon until she learns the secret signal and she uses it to trick the girls into opening the door. Gleefully Rangsasa snatches Klodan and Klonching, races to her house and locks the twins in a chest while readying the fire to prepare her meal. When the mother arrives home to an empty house she is surprised to hear the pig explain a plan for rescuing the girls. With the frogs providing the music, the pig performs a traditional dance enticing Rangsasa to join in and the mouse sneaks into the house to free Klodan and Klonching. (32 pages)

Where it's reviewed:
Booklist, September 15, 1999, page 264
Bulletin of the Center for Children's Books, November 1999, page 107
Horn Book Guide, Spring 2000, page 114
Kirkus Reviews, August 15, 1999, page 1315
School Library Journal, October 1999, page 142

Other books by the same author:
Antarctic Antics: A Book of Penguin Poems, 1998
Counting Crocodiles, 1997
The House That Drac Built, 1995

The Elephant's Wrestling Match, 1992

Other books you might like:
Eric A. Kimmel, *Baba Yaga: A Russian Folktale*, 1991
 In a retelling of the traditional tale, Marina's stepmother sends her into the forest to the wicked witch.
Jane Ray, *Hansel & Gretel*, 1997
 The siblings free themselves from the wicked witch's house in this retelling of the Grimm tale.
Ruth Sanderson, *Rose Red & Snow White*, 1997
 One of many retellings of the story explains the rewards for kindness freely offered by the sisters.

913

JUDY SIERRA
REYNOLD RUFFINS, Illustrator

The Gift of the Crocodile: A Cinderella Story

(New York: Simon & Schuster Books for Young Readers, 2000)

Subject(s): Fairy Tales; Folklore; Stepmothers
Age range(s): Grades 1-4
Major character(s): Damura, Stepdaughter, Servant; Unnamed Character, Stepsister; Grandmother Crocodile, Crocodile
Time period(s): Indeterminate Past
Locale(s): Spice Islands, Indonesia

Summary: Damura remembers the words of her dying mother to be kind to animals and uses that kindness when the cruelty of her stepmother and stepsister become overbearing. Grandmother Crocodile is the fairy godmother in this tale that shows Damura kindness and provides her with finery to attend the prince's ball. After the prince and Damura are wed, the stepmother and stepsister trick Damura again and throw her into the river where she is swallowed by a crocodile. This time the prince pleads for help and Grandmother Crocodile rescues Damura and commands the other crocodiles to eat the stepmother and stepsister if they come near the river. An author's note gives background information about the folktale. (40 pages)

Where it's reviewed:
Booklist, January 1, 2001, page 962
Horn Book, January 2001, page 104
Publishers Weekly, November 13, 2000, page 104
School Library Journal, November 2000, page 148

Awards the book has won:
School Library Journal Best Books, 2000

Other books by the same author:
Counting Crocodiles, 1997
The Mean Hyena: A Folktale from Malawi, 1997
Good Night Dinosaurs, 1996

Other books you might like:
Jose Aruego, *Rockabye Crocodile*, 1988
 Two boars with different dispositions care for a baby crocodile and are repaid in kind.
Oki S. Han, *Kongi and Potgi: A Cinderella Story from Korea*, 1996
 Kongi's ability to treat others kindly despite her mistreat-

ment by her stepmother and stepsister is eventually rewarded.

Charles Perrault, *Cinderella*, 1954

In one of many retellings of a classic tale of love and inner beauty, Cinderella survives years of torment to win a prince's hand in marriage.

Robert D. San Souci, *Cendrillon: A Caribbean Cinderella*, 1998

Cendrillon seeks assistance from the washerwoman with the magic wand when she needs help getting to a fancy ball in proper attire.

914

JUDY SIERRA
MEILO SO, Illustrator

Tasty Baby Belly Buttons

(New York: Alfred A. Knopf, 1999)

Subject(s): Folk Tales; Folklore; Monsters
Age range(s): Grades 1-3
Major character(s): Uriko, Child, Daughter
Time period(s): Indeterminate Past
Locale(s): Japan (small village); Onigashima, Japan

Summary: An elderly couple with no children is blessed with a daughter found within a melon floating in the river. More quickly than other children Uriko grows large and strong. By the time she is five her father is teaching her sword fighting and her mother is cooking millet dumplings with her. Uriko's skills serve her well when a group of monstrous oni storm into town grabbing babies in order to enjoy the delicacy of tasty baby belly buttons. Because Uriko comes from a melon, she has no belly button so the oni leave her behind. Infuriated with the actions of the oni, Uriko pursues the monsters armed only with a sword and millet dumplings. Along the way she befriends a pheasant, a monkey and a dog and together they free the babies and return them to their parents. An ''Author's Note'' gives the legend on which the story is based. (40 pages)

Where it's reviewed:
Booklist, May 1, 1999, page 1596
Five Owls, September 1999, page 16
Publishers Weekly, May 17, 1999, page 78
Riverbank Review, Summer 1999, page 31
School Library Journal, May 1999, page 112

Awards the book has won:
ALA Notable Children's Books, 2000
Bulletin of the Center for Children's Books Blue Ribbon, 1999

Other books by the same author:
Counting Crocodiles, 1997
The Mean Hyena: A Folktale from Malawi, 1997
Wiley and the Hairy Man, 1996

Other books you might like:
William H. Hooks, *Peach Boy*, 1992
In an easy-to-read adaptation of a Japanese folktale, a childless couple is blessed with a boy born from a peach.

Rafe Martin, *Mysterious Tales of Japan*, 1996
Ten traditional tales are retold in an illustrated, award-winning collection.

Linda Shute, *Momotaro the Peach Boy: A Traditional Japanese Tale*, 1986
From a large peach a childless couple receives a son who grows up to conquer oni in a more traditional telling of the tale.

915

ERICA SILVERMAN
G. BRIAN KARAS, Illustrator

Follow the Leader

(New York: Farrar Straus and Giroux, 2000)

Subject(s): Games; Playing; Stories in Rhyme
Age range(s): Grades K-1
Major character(s): Unnamed Character, Brother (older); Unnamed Character, Brother (younger)
Time period(s): 2000s (2000)
Locale(s): United States

Summary: Two brothers, tucked into bed, don't stay there long when the older brother (on the top bunk, of course) suggests a game of follow the leader. The imaginative movements give big brother satisfaction as he directs his younger brother's activity. The little brother tires of the game and goes off to do his own thing. Rather than play alone, big brother consents to give him a turn and agrees to follow his lead. Neither brother plans a path that leads back to the bed. (32 pages)

Where it's reviewed:
Booklist, October 15, 2000, page 447
Horn Book, September 2000, page 558
Riverbank Review, Fall 2000, page 28
School Library Journal, October 2000, page 137

Other books by the same author:
The Halloween House, 1997 (IRA/CBC Children's Choices)
Don't Fidget a Feather, 1994
Big Pumpkin, 1992

Other books you might like:
Nicole Jussek, *Seymour and Opal*, 1996
Big brother Seymour's smug wielding of power backfires when Opal contentedly plays alone and shuts out a very bored Seymour.

Holly Keller, *Geraldine First*, 1996
Geraldine finds a way to use little brother Willie's aggravating copycat behavior to her advantage.

Laura McGee Kvasnosky, *Zelda and Ivy*, 1998
Zelda, the older sister, dominates the play activities with her ideas, but Ivy's learning to fend for herself.

Rosemary Wells, *Max's Dragon Shirt*, 1991
While shopping, Max becomes separated (accidentally?) from bossy big sister Ruby and her control.

916

ERICA SILVERMAN
SUSAN GABER, Illustrator

Raisel's Riddle

(New York: Farrar Straus Giroux, 1999)

Subject(s): Jews; Fairy Tales; Folklore
Age range(s): Grades K-3
Major character(s): Raisel, Servant
Time period(s): Indeterminate Past
Locale(s): Poland

Summary: After her grandfather's death, Raisel is forced to find work as a servant girl in the house of a Rabbi where she is mistreated by the cook. During the Purim feast, Raisel gives her food to a beggar woman who then grants Raisel three wishes. Raisel uses one wish to go to the Purim feast where she catches the eye of the Rabbi's son. She tells him a riddle, but leaves at midnight before he can answer. The Rabbi's son searches the next day for the girl who told him the riddle, and upon finding Raisel, seeks to marry her. Raisel insists on hearing his answer to the riddle first. (40 pages)

Where it's reviewed:
Booklist, May 1, 1999, page 1590
Bulletin of the Center for Children's Books, February 1999, page 217
Horn Book, March 1999, page 215
Publishers Weekly, February 22, 1999, page 94
School Library Journal, March 1999, page 200

Other books by the same author:
Gittel's Hands, 1996
Don't Fidget a Feather, 1994
Big Pumpkin, 1992

Other books you might like:
Valerie Scho Carey, *Tsugele's Broom*, 1993
In an award-winning book set in Poland, industrious, but independent Tsugele discovers that her trusty broom is also somewhat magical.
Rebecca Hickox, *The Golden Sandal: A Middle Eastern Cinderella Story*, 1999
Maha receives assistance from a magical fish in this Cinderella story from Iraq.
Ai-Ling Louie, *Yeh-Shen: A Cinderella Story from China*, 1996
Yeh-Shen is able to attend the party of a rich neighbor thanks to a fish with magical powers.
Robert D. San Souci, *Cendrillon: A Caribbean Cinderella*, 1998
In a Cinderella story from Martinique, Cendrillion is helped by a washerwoman, who knew her mother.

917

JANE SIMMONS, Author/Illustrator

Daisy and the Beastie

(Boston: Little, Brown and Company, 2000)

Subject(s): Animals/Ducks; Brothers and Sisters; Farm Life
Age range(s): Preschool

Major character(s): Daisy, Duck, Sister (older); Pip, Duck, Brother (younger); Grandpa, Duck, Storyteller
Time period(s): 2000s
Locale(s): England

Summary: When Grandpa concludes Daisy's favorite story with the words ''. . .no one found the Beastie!'' Daisy and Pip hurry off to find the Beastie while Grandpa naps. They search the barnyard, the chicken house, the pigsty and the meadow with no sign of a Beastie. Finally, in the dark shed, glowing eyes frighten Daisy and Pip and they race back to Grandpa with the Beastie close behind. Grandpa laughs to see the kittens that have followed Daisy and Pip and the ducks play happily with the kittens all afternoon. (32 pages)

Where it's reviewed:
Booklist, March 1, 2000, page 1252
Horn Book Guide, Fall 2000, page 256
Kirkus Reviews, January 15, 2000, page 124
Publishers Weekly, January 10, 2000, page 66
School Library Journal, May 2000, page 155

Other books by the same author:
Daisy Says Coo!, 2000
Go to Sleep Daisy, 1999
Come Along, Daisy!, 1998 (Booklist Editors' Choice)
Daisy and the Egg, 1998

Other books you might like:
Pat Hutchins, *Little Pink Pig*, 1994
A mother pig asks the other farm animals for help locating her wandering child.
Anita Jeram, *All Together Now*, 1999
A family of rabbits provide a home and playmates for Little Duckling and Miss Mouse.
Nancy Tafuri, *Have You Seen My Duckling?*, 1984
A mother duck followed by her ducklings searches around a pond for one lost duckling in a Caldecott Honor Book.

918

JANE SIMMONS, Author/Illustrator

Daisy and the Egg

(Boston: Little, Brown and Company, 1999)

Subject(s): Animals/Ducks; Babies; Brothers and Sisters
Age range(s): Grades K-1
Major character(s): Daisy, Duck, Daughter; Mama, Duck, Mother; Buttercup, Duck, Aunt
Time period(s): 1990s
Locale(s): England

Summary: Daisy is curious about the eggs—three of her own and one of Mama's—in Aunt Buttercup's nest and wants to help by sitting on one. Quickly, Daisy discovers it's not an easy task for a small duck to sit atop an egg. Instead, Daisy helps by bringing food to Aunt Buttercup daily so she's the first to be informed that the hatching is underway. While Daisy's three wet bedraggled cousins struggle out of their shells, Mama's egg shows no signs of life. Rather than abandon the egg, Daisy creates a hole in the nest's feather lining, rolls the egg into it and then is able to sit atop it until her little brother hatches the following day. The title was first published in Great Britain in 1998. (32 pages)

Where it's reviewed:
Booklist, February 15, 1999, page 1076
Horn Book, May 1999, page 321
Kirkus Reviews, February 1, 1999, page 229
Publishers Weekly, January 25, 1999, page 94
School Library Journal, July 1999, page 80

Other books by the same author:
Daisy and the Beastie, 2000
Daisy's Favorite Things, 1999
Go to Sleep Daisy, 1999
Ebb and Flo and the New Friend, 1999
Come Along, Daisy!, 1998 (Booklist Editors' Choice)

Other books you might like:
June Crebbin, *Danny's Duck*, 1995
  Danny's teacher shows him what has become of the nine eggs he's observed in a nest near his school.
Amy Hest, *You're the Boss, Baby Duck*, 1997
  Baby Duck does not greet her new sister with the same eagerness that Daisy shows toward her baby brother.
Nancy Tafuri, *Have You Seen My Duckling?*, 1984
  With her other ducklings following, a mother duck searches the pond for her one missing offspring in a Caldecott Honor Book.

919

JANE SIMMONS, Author/Illustrator

Ebb and Flo and the New Friend

(New York: Margaret K. McElderry Books, 1999)

Subject(s): Animals/Dogs; Animals/Birds; Jealousy
Age range(s): Preschool
Major character(s): Ebb, Dog; Flo, Child; Bird, Goose
Time period(s): 1990s (1998)
Locale(s): England

Summary: Ebb's sitting in her favorite spot in the bow of the boat when an uninvited guest swoops in to share the space. In fact, Bird quickly shares everything—Ebb's bed, Ebb's food and Ebb's attention from Flo. Ebb is jealous that Flo seems happy to have Bird and wishes Bird gone. The next morning when Ebb's wish comes true and Bird cannot be found, Ebb's favorite spot in the boat seems a little lonely. Although Ebb is grateful not to have Bird bothering her, she notices that she's not sleeping well without Bird's companionship. One day Bird returns. This time when Bird settles into Ebb's favorite spot the space feels just right for sharing. Originally published in Great Britain in 1998. (32 pages)

Where it's reviewed:
Booklist, December 1, 1999, page 714
Bulletin of the Center for Children's Books, November 1999, page 107
Kirkus Reviews, August 15, 1999, page 1316
Publishers Weekly, September 6, 1999, page 106
School Library Journal, October 1999, page 127

Other books by the same author:
Daisy's Hide and Seek, 2001
Ebb & Flo and the Greedy Gulls, 2000
Come Along, Daisy!, 1998 (School Library Journal Best Books)

Daisy and the Egg, 1998

Other books you might like:
Marjorie Flack, *Angus and the Ducks*, 1930
  Curious Angus investigates the unusual quacking sounds coming from the other side of the hedge.
Amy Hest, *You're the Boss, Baby Duck*, 1997
  Grampa provides the attention Baby Duck needs when a new sibling takes too much of her parents' time.
Charlotte Voake, *Ginger*, 1997
  Ginger has a difficult time adjusting the young kitten her owner brings into the home.
Rosemary Wells, *The McDuff Series*, 1997-
  A West Highland terrier finds a home, adjusts to a baby's arrival and saves Santa Claus from the chimney in a new award-winning series.

920

MARILYN SINGER
S.D. SALINGER, Illustrator

Josie to the Rescue

(New York: Scholastic Press, 1999)

Subject(s): Babies; Brothers and Sisters; Money
Age range(s): Grades 2-4
Major character(s): Josie Jellico, 2nd Grader, Sister (older)
Time period(s): 1990s
Locale(s): United States

Summary: With her mom expecting a baby, helpful Josie wants to do her part for the family. In improve her mother's diet and to save the family money, Josie plants a garden. However, Josie can only afford dandelion and radish seeds, and, in the process of planting them, digs up her mother's tulips. Josie then tries to get free diapers and a stroller for the baby with similarly disastrous results. In the end, it is obvious to all that Josie is the asset to her family and her well-intentioned schemes are not. (96 pages)

Where it's reviewed:
Booklist, May 1, 1999, page 1596
Horn Book Guide, Fall 1999, page 284
Publishers Weekly, January 25, 1999, page 96
School Library Journal, June 1999, page 108

Other books by the same author:
Good Day, Good Night, 1998
Chester the Out-of-Work Dog, 1997
Family Reunion, 1994

Other books you might like:
Malorie Blackman, *Girl Wonder and the Terrific Twins*, 1991
  With her twin brothers, Maxine tries to be helpful around the house, but most of her good intentions backfire and create more, not less, work less for her mom.
Beverly Cleary, *Ramona Quimby, Age 8*, 1981
  Ramona copes with her family, friends, and turning eight.
Paula Danziger, *Amber Brown Is Not a Crayon*, 1994
  Amber is upset when she learns that her best friend is moving away.
Karen Ray, *The T.F. Letters*, 1998
  Alex tries to find her place and help out when her family moves across the country.

921

PETER SIS, Author/Illustrator

Madlenka
(New York: Frances Foster Books/Farrar Straus Giroux, 2000)

Subject(s): Neighbors and Neighborhoods; City and Town Life; Growing Up
Age range(s): Grades 1-4
Major character(s): Madlenka, Child, Neighbor; Cleopatra, Friend, Student
Time period(s): 2000s (2000)
Locale(s): New York, New York

Summary: The sensation of a wiggly tooth sends Madlenka racing from her apartment to share the news with friends and neighbors on her block. While it appears that Madlenka only walks around the block telling each shopkeeper about her tooth, she also journeys around the world. Knowing the nationality of each neighbor inspires Madlenka's imagination to propel her to France, Italy and Germany. Meeting Cleopatra, who is eager to lose a tooth, gives both girls a chance to visit Egypt while playing. Asia, Latin America and India are also part of Madlenka's imaginary trip. Unfortunately, Madlenka's literal journey returns her home a little late to worried parents, but with the good news that, along the way, she lost her tooth! (48 pages)

Where it's reviewed:
Booklist, September 1, 2000, page 126
Horn Book, September 2000, page 558
Publishers Weekly, August 7, 2000, page 94
School Library Journal, October 2000, page 137
Smithsonian, November 2000, page 64

Awards the book has won:
Horn Book Fanfare, 2001
Publishers Weekly Best Books, 2000

Other books by the same author:
Tibet through the Red Box, 1998 (Caldecott Honor Book)
Starry Messenger, 1996 (Caldecott Honor Book)
The Three Golden Keys, 1994
Komodo!, 1993 (Booklist Editors' Choice)

Other books you might like:
Norah Dooley, *Everybody Bakes Bread*, 1996
    As Carrie visits the neighbors on a rainy day errand she is treated to a different kind of bread at each house in her multiethnic neighborhood.
Marjorie Priceman, *How to Make an Apple Pie and See the World*, 1994
    A young girl imagines traveling around the world, gathering the ingredients for an apple pie from the country of origin for each.
Sylvia Rosa-Casanova, *Mama Provi and the Pot of Rice*, 1997
    Mama Provi begins the walk up to her sick grandchild's apartment with a pot of arroz con pollo and ends with a multicultural feast.

922

PETER SIS, Author/Illustrator

Trucks Trucks Trucks
(New York: Greenwillow Books, 1999)

Subject(s): Imagination; Transportation; Toys
Age range(s): Preschool
Major character(s): Matt, Child, Son
Time period(s): 1990s (1999)
Locale(s): United States

Summary: Responding to a request that he put his trucks away Matt imagines the work each vehicle does as he playfully cleans. As Matt becomes more engrossed in his activity the illustrations show him shrinking, as the trucks and the text describing the action grow larger. When Matt's task is complete he's ready to go out and view real trucks in action. (24 pages)

Where it's reviewed:
Booklist, June 1999, page 1844
Bulletin of the Center for Children's Books, May 1999, page 328
Horn Book, May 1999, page 322
Publishers Weekly, April 26, 1999, page 81
School Library Journal, May 1999, page 97

Awards the book has won:
ALA Notable Children's Books, 2000
Horn Book Fanfare, 2000

Other books by the same author:
Ship Ahoy!, 1999
Fire Truck, 1998
Beach Ball, 1990

Other books you might like:
Donald Crews, *Truck*, 1980
    A wordless Caldecott Honor Book follows a truck from the loading of its cargo to delivery destination.
Kirsten Hall, *My Trucks*, 1995
    While playing with his toy trucks, a little boy imagines that he is driving real ones.
Stephen Schlossberg, *Big Red Truck*, 1994
    Ray rides his tricycle about the yard pretending that he is at the wheel of a big red truck.

923

MINDY WARSHAW SKOLSKY
DIANE PALMISCIANO, Illustrator

Hannah and the Whistling Teakettle
(New York: DK Ink/Dorling Kindersley Publishing, Inc., 2000)

Subject(s): Grandparents; Gifts; Travel
Age range(s): Grades K-3
Major character(s): Hannah, Child, Daughter; Grandma, Grandmother, Store Owner; Grandpa, Grandfather, Store Owner
Time period(s): 1930s
Locale(s): New York, New York (the Bronx)

Summary: On Hannah's first solo trip to visit Grandma and Grandpa in the Bronx she brings a teakettle with a whistling bird on its spout as a gift to Grandma. Hannah enjoys her visits to her grandparents' home tucked behind their candy and ice cream store. Just before the store's closing time Hannah puts the kettle on to boil water for tea and then goes out to help Grandma with the last customers who turn out to be thieves stealing from the pay phone in the store. When the crooks hear the shrill sound of a police whistle they run away. The persistent whistle is still shrieking when Grandpa arrives home moments later and Hannah explains that the sound is not a whistle—the bird atop the teakettle scared the crooks away. (36 pages)

Where it's reviewed:
Booklist, March 1, 2000, page 1252
Horn Book, May 2000, page 299
Kirkus Reviews, March 15, 2000, page 390
Publishers Weekly, February 14, 2000, page 197
School Library Journal, April 2000, page 114

Other books by the same author:
Welcome to the Grand View, Hannah!, 2000
You're the Best, Hannah!, 2000
Love from Your Friend, Hannah, 1998

Other books you might like:
Betty G. Birney, *Pie's in the Oven*, 1996
   When this little boy visits his grandparents he helps Grandpa pick apples that Grandma makes into delicious pies.
Jessie Haas, *Hurry!*, 2000
   Nora helps her grandparents bring in the hay before the rain begins.
Amy Hest, *Nana's Birthday Party*, 1993
   On a visit to Nana's New York apartment, two cousins collaborate to make her a memorable birthday present.

924

LIESEL MOAK SKORPEN
JOE CEPEDA, Illustrator

We Were Tired of Living in a House
(New York: G.P. Putnam's Sons, 1999)

Subject(s): Dwellings; Brothers and Sisters; Housing
Age range(s): Grades K-1
Major character(s): Unnamed Character, Child, Sister; Unnamed Character, Child, Brother; Unnamed Character, Child, Brother
Time period(s): Indeterminate Past
Locale(s): United States

Summary: A newly illustrated edition of a story originally published in 1969 portrays three siblings as they scamper away from their house. Perhaps they're tired of living in it while it's being painted so they pack a bag with important belongings and move to a tree. Although they like the tree they eventually tumble out and take up residence on a raft in a pond—until it sinks. Each time they move they add a memento from their most recent, unsuccessful home to their bag of belongings. Over time they live also in a cave and by the sea, but each dwelling place has a drawback that brings their

residence to an abrupt end. Finally they head home to live, once again, in a house—a newly painted one, too. (32 pages)

Where it's reviewed:
Booklist, March 15, 1999, page 1334
Horn Book Guide, Fall 1999, page 240
New York Times Book Review, June 20, 1999, page 20
Publishers Weekly, April 12, 1999, page 73
School Library Journal, April 1999, page 109

Other books by the same author:
His Mother's Dog, 1978
All the Lassies, 1970
Outside My Window, 1968

Other books you might like:
Penny Carter, *A New House for the Morrisons*, 1993
   After a day of futile searching for a new house, the Morrisons return to the one they like best—their own home.
Megan McDonald, *My House Has Stars*, 1996
   Children in all kinds of houses all over the world can see stars from their residences.
Anne Shelby, *The Someday House*, 1996
   While they never leave their red house, three children imagine moving it to different locations—on a mountaintop, underground or in space.

925

GLORIA SKURZYNSKI
ALANE FERGUSON, Co-Author

Deadly Waters
(Washington, D.C.: National Geographic Society, 1999)

Series: National Parks Mystery. Number 4
Subject(s): National Parks; Mystery and Detective Stories; Animals/Marine
Age range(s): Grades 4-7
Major character(s): Ashley Landon, 10-Year-Old, Sister; Jack Landon, 12-Year-Old, Brother; Bridger Conley, 14-Year-Old, Foster Child
Time period(s): 1990s (1999)
Locale(s): Everglades National Park, Florida

Summary: While their parents investigate the deaths of manatees, Ashley, Jack and Bridger get to know the Everglades. Jack's opportunity to use the trip to pursue his photography hobby ends unexpectedly when his camera is stolen. As the youths search for the camera, they discover the clues needed to solve the mystery of the dying manatees and learn of the danger pollution presents to the fragile ecology of the Everglades. (145 pages)

Where it's reviewed:
Booklist, October 15, 1999, page 446
Children's Bookwatch, September 1999, page 3
Horn Book Guide, Spring 2000, page 98
School Library Journal, October 1999, page 158

Other books by the same author:
The Hunted, 2000 (National Parks Mystery, Number 5)
Cliff-Hanger, 1999 (National Parks Mystery, Number 3)
Rage of Fire, 1998 (National Parks Mystery, Number 2)
Wolf Stalker, 1997 (National Parks Mystery, Number 1)

Other books you might like:

Jean Craighead George, *The Missing 'Gator of Gumbo Limbo: An Ecological Mystery*, 1992
   Pollution from condos threatens the Everglades but an alligator's habits keeps the water around a spring clean for homeless residents in a tent city.

John Vigor, *Danger, Dolphins and Ginger Beer*, 1993
   A camping trip in the British Virgin Islands becomes dangerous for Sally and her brothers when they rescue an injured dolphin.

Gertrude Chandler Warner, *The Panther Mystery*, 1998
   In Boxcar Children #66, the Aldens wonder if Ranger Belden's disappearance is connected to his interest in the endangered Florida panther.

926

ERIK JON SLANGERUP
JOHN MANDERS, Illustrator

Dirt Boy

(Morton Grove, IL: Albert Whitman & Company, 2000)

Subject(s): Cleanliness; Giants; Runaways
Age range(s): Grades K-2
Major character(s): Fister ''Dirt Boy'' Farnello, Child, Runaway; Mom, Mother; Dirt Man, Monster (giant)
Time period(s): 2000s (2000)
Locale(s): United States

Summary: Fister Farnello revels in dirt while Mom appreciates cleanliness. When Fister cannot face another bath he runs away and falls asleep in the woods. In the morning he discovers he's been sleeping in Dirt Man's belly button. Fister proclaims himself Dirt Boy and seeks to emulate this giant who has not bathed in a thousand years. As Dirt Boy becomes smellier and dirtier he begins to be repulsed by his appearance and smell but to Dirt Man he finally appears to be simply delicious. Realizing he's destined to be Dirt Man's next meal, Fister races for home where Mom, with some help from the garden hose, finally recognizes her son and tosses him into the bath. In the author's first book Fister learns to appreciate a balance between cleanliness and filth. (32 pages)

Where it's reviewed:

Booklist, March 1, 2000, page 1252
Bulletin of the Center for Children's Books, May 2000, page 332
Horn Book Guide, Fall 2000, page 281
School Library Journal, April 2000, page 114

Other books you might like:

Cynthia DeFelice, *Casey in the Bath*, 1996
   To make baths more appealing to Casey his mother buys soap from a traveling salesman; only Casey knows the magical power it has.

Phyllis Root, *Mrs. Potter's Pig*, 1996
   Neat Mrs. Potter's daughter Ermajean is a stark contrast to her compulsively clean mother.

Mark Teague, *Pigsty*, 1994
   Wendell's room becomes so cluttered that pigs move in and then the mess really begins!

927

TERI SLOAT
NADINE BERNARD WESTCOTT, Illustrator

Farmer Brown Goes Round and Round

(New York: DK Ink/DK Publishing, Inc., 1999)

Subject(s): Farm Life; Animals; Stories in Rhyme
Age range(s): Grades K-3
Major character(s): Farmer Brown, Farmer
Time period(s): Indeterminate Past
Locale(s): United States

Summary: With his chores complete, Farmer Brown settles down to rest in the porch rocker as the sounds of animals in the barnyard lull him to sleep. The noise of an approaching tornado disturbs his reverie. The twister lifts Farmer Brown and all his animals into the air, whirling them round and round. When the wind stops Farmer Brown and his animals are on the ground again, but each animal is making the sounds of another. Farmer Brown crows like the rooster while his cows oink and the sheep cluck. Fortunately, a second twister swirls all the sounds back to their right place—except when the weather is windy. (32 pages)

Where it's reviewed:

Booklist, March 1, 1999, page 1223
Horn Book, March 1999, page 202
Kirkus Reviews, February 15, 1999, page 306
Publishers Weekly, January 4, 1999, page 89
School Library Journal, April 1999, page 109

Awards the book has won:
IRA/CBC Children's Choices, 2000

Other books by the same author:
Sody Sallyratus, 1997
The Thing That Bothered Farmer Brown, 1995
From One to One Hundred, 1991

Other books you might like:

Charles Causely, *''Quack!'' Said the Billy Goat*, 1986
   In a humorous rhyming story the noisy animals mix up their sounds.

Bernard Most, *Cock-a-Doodle-Moo!*, 1996
   When rooster loses his voice and is unable to awaken the farmer and the barnyard animals a helpful cow almost masters the art of crowing.

Bernard Most, *The Cow That Went Oink*, 1990
   When an oinking cow meets a mooing pig the two animals share their knowledge of sounds and become the only bilingual animals on the farm.

Dr. Seuss, *Mr. Brown Can Moo! Can You?*, 1970
   In a rhyming beginning reader Mr. Brown mimics sounds as loud as thunder and as soft as a butterfly whisper.

928

TERI SLOAT
NADINE BERNARD WESTCOTT, Illustrator

Farmer Brown Shears His Sheep: A Yarn about Wool

(New York: DK Ink/Dorling Kindersley Publishing, Inc., 2000)

Subject(s): Animals/Sheep; Farm Life; Stories in Rhyme
Age range(s): Grades K-2
Major character(s): Farmer Brown, Farmer
Time period(s): 2000s (2000)
Locale(s): United States

Summary: Farmer Brown's spring calendar directs him to shear the sheep and so he does. As he takes the fleece to be carded, spun and dyed the shivery sheep follow him crying to have their wool returned. Farmer Brown gets the message and quickly knits sweaters for each of the sheep. Now they look forward to spring and the brightly colored coats they receive to cover their fuzz. (32 pages)

Where it's reviewed:
Booklist, October 15, 2000, page 447
Horn Book, September 2000, page 561
Publishers Weekly, September 25, 2000, page 120
School Library Journal, October 2000, page 137

Other books by the same author:
Farmer Brown Goes Round and Round, 1999
Sody Sallyratus, 1997
The Thing That Bothered Farmer Brown, 1995
From One to One Hundred, 1991

Other books you might like:
Tomie DePaola, *Haircuts for the Woolseys*, 1989
    Spring means haircuts for the sheep on Fiddle-Dee-Dee Farm, but when a cold wind returns, Granny helps the chilly sheep stay warm.
Satoshi Kitamura, *Sheep in Wolves' Clothing*, 1996
    Wolves steal the fleecy coats of three sheep as they swim; by the time the sheep retrieve them the coats have become a colorful addition to the meadow.
Ragnhild Scamell, *Three Bags Full*, 1993
    Kindly Millie gives away so much of her fleece that her owner must knit a sweater to warm her through the winter.
Barbara Brooks Wallace, *Argyle*, 1987
    Perhaps it's something the sheep ate; the multi-colored fleece that he grows creates great changes on the farm.

929

TERI SLOAT, Author/Illustrator

Patty's Pumpkin Patch

(New York: G.P. Putnam's Sons, 1999)

Subject(s): Gardens and Gardening; Pumpkins; Stories in Rhyme
Age range(s): Grades K-2
Major character(s): Patty, Gardener
Time period(s): 1990s
Locale(s): United States

Summary: From the spring plowing of the field to the final harvest Patty demonstrates how to grow pumpkins. Letters of the alphabet parade across the bottom of the page with each one illustrated by an insect or animal that can be found in Patty's pumpkin patch. Patty enjoys the labor of planting seeds, pulling weeds, selling pumpkins and carving some for Halloween. From the last big pumpkin Patty scoops out seeds—some to save for next year's crop and some to roast and enjoy as a winter snack. (32 pages)

Where it's reviewed:
Booklist, September 1, 1999, page 143
Bulletin of the Center for Children's Books, October 1999, page 68
Kirkus Reviews, August 15, 1999, page 1316
Publishers Weekly, September 27, 1999, page 107
School Library Journal, October 1999, page 127

Other books by the same author:
The Thing That Bothered Farmer Brown, 1995
From One to One Hundred, 1991
The Eye of the Needle, 1990

Other books you might like:
Eve Bunting, *The Pumpkin Fair*, 1997
    A little girl enjoys all the activities of the Pumpkin Fair while protectively clutching her home-grown pumpkin.
Zoe Hall, *It's Pumpkin Time!*, 1994
    Siblings describe the growth of the pumpkins in their specially planted jack-o'-lantern patch. Booklist Editors' Choice award winner.
Jeanne Titherington, *Pumpkin, Pumpkin*, 1986
    Carefully Jamie plants a seed, tends the plant, carves the pumpkin and saves some seeds to plant in the spring.
Tasha Tudor, *Pumpkin Moonshine*, 1938
    Seeking the very best pumpkin in her grandparents' patch, a little girl selects a big one that rolls down the hill and arrives home ahead of her.

930

MAGGIE SMITH, Author/Illustrator

Dear Daisy, Get Well Soon

(New York: Crown Publishers Inc., 2000)

Subject(s): Illness; Friendship; Gifts
Age range(s): Preschool
Major character(s): Daisy, Child, Friend; Peter, Child, Friend
Time period(s): 2000s (2000)
Locale(s): United States

Summary: Peter's friend Daisy can't play on Sunday because she's just broken out in chicken pox. In sympathy, Peter sends a gift to Daisy every day beginning with one get-well card on Monday and concluding on Friday with five balloons. On Saturday, Daisy sends a note to Peter inviting him to come over and play—so he does. (36 pages)

Where it's reviewed:
Booklist, July 2000, page 2043
Horn Book Guide, Fall 2000, page 256
Kirkus Reviews, April 15, 2000, page 568
Publishers Weekly, May 1, 2000, page 69
School Library Journal, April 2000, page 114

Other books by the same author:

Counting Our Way to Maine, 1995
My Grandma's Chair, 1992
There's a Witch Under the Stairs, 1991
Noly Poly Rabbit Tail and Me, 1990

Other books you might like:

Marc Brown, *Arthur's Chicken Pox*, 1994
    D.W. is jealous of the attention that chicken pox brings to her brother Arthur.
True Kelley, *I've Got Chicken Pox*, 1994
    Initially euphoric about missing school because of the chicken pox, Jess soon tires of ice cream, ginger ale and itching!
Vera Rosenberry, *When Vera Was Sick*, 1998
    Vera is miserable when she's sick, but as soon as she's better she's eager to play outside.

931

LEMONY SNICKET (Pseudonym of Daniel Handler)
BRETT HELQUIST, Illustrator

The Bad Beginning

(New York: HarperCollins Publishers, 1999)

Series: Series of Unfortunate Events. Book the First
Subject(s): Orphans; Brothers and Sisters; Inheritance
Age range(s): Grades 4-7
Major character(s): Violet Baudelaire, 14-Year-Old, Sister; Klaus Baudelaire, 12-Year-Old, Brother; Sunny Baudelaire, Baby, Sister
Time period(s): Indeterminate Past
Locale(s): England

Summary: Orphaned by a fire that destroys their home and kills their parents, Violet, Klaus and Sunny are placed in the home of an unknown relative who is appointed guardian according to the obscure terms of the parents' will. The evil actor has no interest in the children or their welfare, but plots nefarious schemes to take control of their inheritance in which he has an obsessive interest. The siblings use their various talents—Violet's for mechanical inventions, Klaus's for research and Sunny's for biting to protect themselves and escape from their despicable guardian—for now. (162 pages)

Where it's reviewed:

Booklist, December 1, 1999, page 707
Bulletin of the Center for Children's Books, September 1999, page 32
Kirkus Reviews, July 15, 1999, page 1139
Publishers Weekly, September 6, 1999, page 104
School Library Journal, November 1999, page 165

Other books by the same author:

The Austere Academy, 2000 (Series of Unfortunate Events, Book the Fifth)
The Miserable Mill, 2000 (Series of Unfortunate Events, Book the Fourth)
The Wide Window, 2000 (Series of Unfortunate Events, Book the Third)
The Reptile Room, 1999 (Series of Unfortunate Events: Book the Second)

Other books you might like:

Charles Dickens, *Oliver Twist*, 1996
    An abridgement by Lesley Baxter makes the classic tale of orphans, street urchins and the criminals who prey on them accessible to young readers.
J.K. Rowling, *Harry Potter and the Sorcerer's Stone*, 1997
    Harry Potter, an orphan, leaves a miserable life with his muggle relatives when he enters Hogwarts School.
Barbara Brooks Wallace, *Sparrows in the Scullery*, 1997
    Colley is kidnapped and held for ransom in deplorable conditions by evil individuals determined to profit from his parents' estate.

932

ZILPHA KEATLEY SNYDER

The Runaways

(New York: Delacorte Press, 1999)

Subject(s): Runaways; Parent and Child; Deserts
Age range(s): Grades 4-7
Major character(s): Danielle "Dani" O'Donnell, 12-Year-Old, Runaway; Stormy Arigotti, 9-Year-Old, Abuse Victim; Portia "Pixie" Smithson, 5th Grader, Runaway
Time period(s): 1950s (1951)
Locale(s): Rattler Springs, Nevada

Summary: Dani is desperate to get away from Rattler Springs and return to the coastal California community from which she and her mother moved four years earlier when her mother inherited a ranch. The ranch and its ramshackle house are so worthless that no one will purchase them and Dani and her mom are stuck in a dying desert town. Nonreader Stormy pesters Dani to read to him and she obliges rather than suffer through his temper tantrums. When Stormy learns of Dani's plans to run away from Rattler Springs he wants to be included and helps her earn money for bus fare. Then imaginative Pixie's geologist parents rent the ranch house and Pixie decides to join the runaway plans so she can return to her grandmother's home in San Francisco. Although Dani reconsiders her plans, Stormy's beating by his abusive mother convinces her that she must follow through in order to save Stormy. Pixie's birthday money arrives just in time to purchase the bus tickets, but the runaways' plans still fail. Life improves though for each of the children as they face their problems. In time, they may all get out of Rattler Springs, though not as runaways. (245 pages)

Where it's reviewed:

Booklist, January 1999, page 879
Horn Book Guide, Fall 1999, page 299
Kirkus Reviews, January 1, 1999, page 71
Publishers Weekly, January 18, 1999, page 340
School Library Journal, March 1999, page 215

Other books by the same author:

Gib Rides Home, 1998
The Gypsy Game, 1997
Cat Running, 1994
The Egypt Game, 1967 (Newbery Honor Book)

Other books you might like:

Peg Kehret, *Searching for Candlestick Park*, 1997
Rather than give up his cat when he and his mom move into his aunt's house, Spencer leaves in search of his father, hoping to find a home with him.

Harry Mazer, *The Wild Kid*, 1998
Fearing punishment, Sammy runs away, becomes lost in the forest and stumbles upon the hideout of an escapee from a juvenile detention facility.

Rodman Philbrick, *Max the Mighty*, 1998
After Max kidnaps ''Worm'' from her abusive stepfather the duo travels to a ghost town in Montana searching for her father.

June Rae Wood, *A Share of Freedom*, 1994
Freedom runs away with her younger brother to prevent the siblings from being separated and placed in foster care.

933

DONALD J. SOBOL
WARREN CHANG, Illustrator

Encyclopedia Brown and the Case of the Slippery Salamander

(New York: Delacorte Press, 1999)

Series: Encyclopedia Brown. Volume 22
Subject(s): Mystery and Detective Stories; Short Stories; Fathers and Sons
Age range(s): Grades 4-6
Major character(s): Leroy ''Encyclopedia'' Brown, 10-Year-Old, Detective—Amateur; Chief Brown, Police Officer, Father
Time period(s): 1990s (1999)
Locale(s): Idaville

Summary: Leroy's brain is so crammed with facts that most people know him as Encyclopedia. Once again he uses his extensive knowledge and deductive reasoning skills to keep Idaville free of crime. At times he assists Chief Brown when a case such as the Slippery Salamander one has his father stymied, but during the summer months, he operates his own private detective agency. Most clients are his friends and he sees justice done by identifying the real banana thief or helping a friend locate a stolen surfboard. The solutions to each case are included in the back of the book. (87 pages)

Where it's reviewed:
Booklist, September 1, 1999, page 134
Children's Bookwatch, October 1999, page 4
Horn Book Guide, Spring 2000, page 88
School Library Journal, November 1999, page 166

Other books by the same author:
Encyclopedia Brown and the Case of the Sleeping Dog, 1998 (Encyclopedia Brown, Volume 21)
Encyclopedia Brown and the Case of the Two Spies, 1994 (Encyclopedia Brown, Volume 19)
Encyclopedia Brown Lends a Hand, 1979 (Encyclopedia Brown, Volume 11)
Encyclopedia Brown, Boy Detective, 1963 (Encyclopedia Brown, Volume 1)

Other books you might like:

Duncan Ball, *Emily Eyefinger and the Lost Treasure*, 1994
Emily solves one mystery after another with the assistance of a third eye on the end of her finger.

Franklin W. Dixon, *Footprints under the Window*, 1965
The amateur detectives take on their eighth case in the popular Hardy Boys Mystery series.

Caroline Levine, *The Detective Stars and the Case of the Super Soccer Team*, 1994
The mystery behind the sudden good fortune of a losing soccer team is solved by the detective skills of Veronica and Ernest.

934

AKI SOGABE, Author/Illustrator

Aesop's Fox

(San Diego: Browndeer Press/Harcourt Brace & Company, 1999)

Subject(s): Fables; Folklore; Animals
Age range(s): Grades K-3
Major character(s): Fox, Fox
Time period(s): Indeterminate Past
Locale(s): Fictional Country

Summary: Fox's day has one event after another, each summarizing one of Aesop's fables. First, he hopes to dine on a rooster for breakfast. Though Fox succeeds in using flattery to catch the rooster, he follows rooster's suggestion without thinking first, thus freeing the rooster. The hungry Fox tries to eat grapes that are out of reach and decides they wouldn't be tasty anyway so he gives up. Fox finally does get something to eat when he flatters a crow into singing, causing a piece of cheese to drop right into Fox's mouth. And so the day proceeds, Fox learns some lessons and teaches some too. (32 pages)

Where it's reviewed:
Bulletin of the Center for Children's Books, November 1999, page 108
Horn Book Guide, Spring 2000, page 114
Kirkus Reviews, August 15, 1999, page 1316
Publishers Weekly, August 16, 1999, page 84
School Library Journal, December 1999, page 127

Other books you might like:

Mitsumasa Anno, *Anno's Aesop: A Book of Fables*, 1989
Father Fox interprets the stories in these retellings translated from Japanese.

Paul Galdone, *Three Aesop Fox Fables*, 1971
These three retellings include ''The Fox and the Rooster'' and ''The Fox and the Grapes.''

Jerry Pinkncy, *Aesop's Fables*, 2000
An award-winning illustrated collection of Aesop's work gathers some of the less well-known fables with the frequently retold ones.

Charles Santore, *The Fox and the Rooster*, 1998
A simple version of Aesop's fable tells how the fox catches the rooster and then loses him again.

935

EDWARD SOREL, Author/Illustrator
CHERYL CARLESIMO, Co-Author

The Saturday Kid

(New York: Margaret K. McElderry Books, 2000)

Subject(s): Bullies; Movies; Music and Musicians
Age range(s): Grades 1-4
Major character(s): Leo, Bullied Child, Musician; Morty, Bully, Student—Elementary School; Mr. Kleinberg, Teacher, Musician
Time period(s): 1930s
Locale(s): New York, New York

Summary: Other than his mother, Leo has two loves in life—Saturday matinees and playing the violin. Morty seems to have one love—picking on Leo—after school or at the matinee. Each time Leo has an encounter with Morty he imagines (using scenes from a movie to set the stage) how he will deal with Morty. In reality, it is Leo's musical talent that finally puts Morty in his place. As his school's representative to the Mayor's Young Musicians Concert Leo goes to City Hall to play for and meet the mayor as the newsreel cameras roll. He misses a lesson with Mr. Kleinberg while at the concert and makes up the time on a Saturday. Leo's disappointed to miss the Saturday matinee, but his mother surprises him with an evening trip to Loew's Paradise. Leo fears the evening is ruined when he and his mother are seated next to Morty and his parents, but Leo's musical concert saves the day. As the pre-show newsreels begin to run Leo's image appears on the big screen playing the violin and shaking hands with the mayor. Morty is, at last, speechless and Leo's confident he'll stay that way for quite some time. (32 pages)

Where it's reviewed:
Booklist, December 15, 2000, page 829
Horn Book Guide, Spring 2001, page 67
Los Angeles Times Book Review, September 24, 2000, page 6
Publishers Weekly, August 28, 2000, page 83
School Library Journal, September 2000, page 209

Awards the book has won:
Parents' Choice Gold Award, 2000

Other books by the same author:
Johnny on the Spot, 1998
The Zillionaire's Daughter, 1989

Other books you might like:
Jules Feiffer, *Meanwhile. . .*, 1997
  Raymond discovers that with imagination and the word ''meanwhile'' he can zip from one exciting adventure to another just like a comic book hero.
Rachel Isadora, *The Pirates of Bedford Street*, 1988
  After Joey watches a pirate movie with his sisters he continues to imagine the action.
David McPhail, *Edward and the Pirates*, 1997
  While Edward reads the stories come alive for him so vividly that he's kidnapped by the pirates in his book and must be saved by other literary heroes.
Carol Snyder, *Ike & Mama and the Once-in-a-Lifetime Movie*, 1981

Ike's family is surprised that he and his friends are extras in a movie.

936

GARY SOTO
SUSAN GUEVARA, Illustrator

Chato and the Party Animals

(New York: G.P. Putnam's Sons, 2000)

Subject(s): Animals/Cats; Birthdays; Friendship
Age range(s): Grades K-3
Major character(s): Chato, Cat, Friend; Novio Boy, Cat, Friend
Time period(s): 2000s
Locale(s): Los Angeles, California

Summary: Chato learns that his best friend Novio Boy, a former pound kitty, has never had a birthday party and he decides to change that. Secretly, he plans a big birthday party and invites all Novio Boy's friends and neighbors. Unfortunately, he forgets to tell Novio Boy to come so the party guests search the town for the guest of honor. When he can't be found in any of his usual haunts, the guests return to Chato's and mourn the loss of their friend. Novio Boy arrives, looking for food and the delayed party begins. A glossary defines the Spanish terms used in the text. (32 pages)

Where it's reviewed:
Booklist, August 2000, page 2150
Horn Book Guide, Spring 2001, page 51
Kirkus Reviews, June 15, 2000, page 893
Publishers Weekly, July 3, 2000, page 73
School Library Journal, July 2000, page 88

Awards the book has won:
ALA Notable Children's Books, 2001

Other books by the same author:
Snapshots from the Wedding, 1997 (Booklist Editors' Choice)
Chato's Kitchen, 1995 (ALA Notable Book)
Too Many Tamales, 1993 (Booklist Editors' Choice)

Other books you might like:
George Ancona, *The Pinata Maker*, 1994
  The bilingual text and bright photographic illustrations of this nonfiction title explain the craft of a Mexican pinata maker.
Mary Calhoun, *Tonio's Cat*, 1996
  Bilingual text describes the growing relationship between a young Mexican immigrant and a stray cat that he befriends.
Elisa Kleven, *Hooray, a Pinata!*, 1996
  Samson anticipates that his friend Clara will be unable to smash the cute dog pinata at her party and gives her a monster one to use instead.
Vivian Sathre, *Three Kind Mice*, 1997
  Three mice bake a cake as a birthday surprise for a cat.

937

ANDREA SPALDING
JANET WILSON, Illustrator

Me and Mr. Mah

(Custer, WA: Orca Book Publishers, 2000)

Subject(s): Divorce; Moving, Household; Friendship
Age range(s): Grades 1-3
Major character(s): Ian, Child of Divorced Parents; Mr. Mah, Aged Person, Neighbor
Time period(s): 1990s (1999)
Locale(s): Canada

Summary: His parents' separation forces Ian to leave his father and his prairie home and move to a city many miles from all he knows. Through the fence slats of the tiny back yard Ian watches an elderly man work in his garden. One morning when Ian finds a gift of sunflower seeds stuck in the fence and lonely Ian develops a friendship with Mr. Mah. They share stories of their lives in distant places. Each has a memory box, Ian's with hay, cow bones and postcards from his father; Mr. Mah's with red silk, incense and a photograph of his deceased wife. The summer friendship ends along with Ian's parents' marriage. As soon as the divorce is final Ian's mother buys a house in another part of town and they move again. School and new friends take Ian's time and he loses touch with Mr. Mah until, on a shopping trip to secondhand store, Ian sees Mr. Mah's black lacquer memory box. Diligently Ian tracks down his friend and when he finds him in a nursing home recovering from a broken hip, Ian returns the box and resumes the friendship. Originally published in Canada in 1999. (32 pages)

Where it's reviewed:
Booklist, March 15, 2000, page 1390
Books in Canada, February 2000, page 34
Horn Book Guide, Fall 2000, page 282
Kirkus Reviews, December 1, 1999, page 1891
School Library Journal, March 2000, page 217

Other books by the same author:
Phoebe and the Gypsy, 1999 (Orca Young Reader)
Sarah May and the New Red Dress, 1999

Other books you might like:
DyAnne DiSalvo-Ryan, *City Green*, 1994
    A young girl and an elderly neighbor transform an empty lot into a community garden.
George Shannon, *Seeds*, 1994
    A move to another town interrupts Warren's friendship with a neighbor who sends seeds so Warren can begin a garden at his new home.
Bettye Stroud, *Down Home at Miss Dessa's*, 1996
    When Miss Dessa injures her ankle, two sisters provide her with companionship while she recovers.

938

ANDREA SPALDING
JANET WILSON, Illustrator

Sarah May and the New Red Dress

(Custer: Orca Book, 1999)

Subject(s): Clothes; Grandparents; Childhood
Age range(s): Grades K-3
Major character(s): Sarah May, Child; Grandma, Grandmother
Time period(s): 1990s; Indeterminate Past
Locale(s): United States

Summary: Sarah May wasn't always called Grandma. She was once a young girl who wanted nothing more than a pretty red dress. Sarah May whispers her wish to the wind, but when her mother buys the fabric for a new dress it is a sensible, but dismal blue. While Sarah May hates the color of the dress, she believes the wind's message as it whispers "Waaaiit and seeeee." Soon, Sarah May is caught outside during a rainstorm and all the blue dye washes out of the dress. After that, as Grandma remembers, Sarah May is allowed to choose the color dye to buy for the dress and finally she has the bright red dress she always wanted. (32 pages)

Where it's reviewed:
Booklist, February 1, 1999, page 983
ForeWord Magazine, March 1999, page 55
Publishers Weekly, February 8, 1999, page 213
Resource Links, December 1998, page 5
School Library Journal, July 1999, page 80

Other books by the same author:
Phoebe and the Gypsy, 1999
Finders Keepers, 1997
The Most Beautiful Kite in the World, 1996

Other books you might like:
Niki Daly, *Jamela's Dress*, 1999
    Jamela so loves the newly purchased material that she can't resist wearing the fabric around town and it is ruined before her dress can be sewn.
Doris Dorrie, *Lottie's Princess Dress*, 1999
    Lottie tries to convince her mother to let her wear her sparkly, gold princess dress to school.
Kathy Stinson, *Red Is Best*, 1982
    A little girl loves all her red clothes best.
Christine Widman, *The Lemon Drop Jar*, 1992
    After a young girl finds a glass lemon-drop jar her great-aunt explains how she got it.

939

TOBY SPEED
BARRY ROOT, Illustrator

Brave Potatoes

(New York: G.P. Putnam's Sons, 2000)

Subject(s): Food; Fairs; Stories in Rhyme
Age range(s): Grades K-3
Major character(s): Hackemup, Cook
Time period(s): Indeterminate Past

Locale(s): United States

Summary: Most of the vegetables at the county fair are sleeping, but the potatoes are wide-awake and planning to visit the rides and enjoy the night. While the potatoes are flipping through the air on a ride Chef Hackemup spots them—the missing ingredient for his chowder. Hackemup stuffs the scurrying potatoes into a large sack and carries them back to his kitchen. There the other vegetables, already resigned to their fate, suggest surrender but the brave potatoes have other plans. Before Hackemup can chop another veggie the potatoes dump Hackemup in the chowder pot and lead the remaining vegetables to freedom. Just to be on the safe side they carry the chef's knife away too. (32 pages)

Where it's reviewed:
Booklist, September 15, 2000, page 250
Bulletin of the Center for Children's Books, June 2000, page 374
Horn Book, May 2000, page 300
Publishers Weekly, May 22, 2000, page 92
School Library Journal, July 2000, page 88

Awards the book has won:
Bulletin of the Center for Children's Books Blue Ribbon, 2000

Other books by the same author:
Two Cool Cows, 1995
Hattie Baked a Wedding Cake, 1994

Other books you might like:
Aubrey Davis, *The Enormous Potato*, 1998
    A tiny potato eye grows into a potato so large that a farmer needs a lot of help to harvest and eat it.
Christopher L. King, *The Vegetables Go to Bed*, 1994
    Each vegetable in a garden has a particular way of preparing for a good night's sleep.
Kate Lied, *Potato: A Tale from the Great Depression*, 1997
    Harvesting potatoes provides livelihood for an unemployed family during the Depression.
David Wiesner, *June 29, 1999*, 1992
    A third grader's science project has some unexpected results when enormous vegetables begin falling from the sky.

940

ROB SPENCE
AMY SPENCE, Co-Author
MARGARET SPENGLER, Illustrator

Clickety Clack

(New York: Viking, 1999)

Subject(s): Trains; Animals; Stories in Rhyme
Age range(s): Grades K-1
Major character(s): Driver Zach, Engineer
Time period(s): Indeterminate Past
Locale(s): Fictional Country

Summary: In the authors' first book for children an unusual assortment of boisterous passengers board a little black train with a red caboose in the back. As the train goes clickety clack down the track the yaks talk, the tumbling acrobats sing and the quacking ducks dance. Driver Zach tolerates the growing noise level, including the stomping elephants, but when two little mice set off firecrackers, he's had enough. After Driver Zach yells for quiet the passengers continue the journey silently with the only sound coming from the train's wheels on the track—clickety clack. (32 pages)

Where it's reviewed:
Booklist, July 1999, page 1955
Horn Book Guide, Fall 1999, page 240
Kirkus Reviews, May 1, 1999, page 728
Publishers Weekly, May 17, 1999, page 78
School Library Journal, August 1999, page 142

Other books you might like:
Donald Crews, *Freight Train*, 1978
    Colorful train cars gather speed as they're pulled along the tracks in this Caldecott Honor Book.
Kevin Lewis, *Chugga-Chugga Choo-Choo*, 1999
    A rhyming picture book follows a train through a busy day of work until both the train and the tired engineer are ready to sleep.
Watty Piper, *The Little Engine That Could*, 1930
    The Little Engine proves that gumption is more important than size if there is a job to be done.

941

JUNG-HEE SPETTER, Author/Illustrator

Lily and Trooper's Spring

(Asheville, NC: Front Street, 1999)

Subject(s): Animals/Dogs; Pets; Spring
Age range(s): Preschool
Major character(s): Lily, Child; Trooper, Dog
Time period(s): 1990s
Locale(s): Earth

Summary: Lily awakens to the sound of birds declaring spring and immediately plans a picnic with Trooper. Just as they settle on their blanket with their tea, a cow yanks the blanket, spilling everything. Lily and Trooper run home to clean up and go outside to swing. A swing mishap tumbles the twosome onto some sheep and into a mud puddle filled with pigs. After washing up again, Lily puts Trooper in a doll's carriage for a stroll past a flock of ducks that are given a ride in the carriage to the pond. Now, it's time to head home for a bedtime bath. (24 pages)

Where it's reviewed:
Booklist, May 1, 1999, page 1601
ForeWord, April 1999, page 60
Publishers Weekly, April 19, 1999, page 71
School Library Journal, July 1999, page 81

Other books by the same author:
Lily and Trooper's Fall, 1999
Lily and Trooper's Winter, 1999
Lily and Trooper's Summer, 1999

Other books you might like:
Ruth Lercher Bornstein, *Rabbit's Good News*, 1995
    An early rising rabbit eagerly tells her family the news that spring has arrived.

Alyssa Satin Capucilli, *Biscuit*, 1996

    A young girl prepares her puppy to sleep in his own bed, but Biscuit wanders upstairs to sleep in her room.

Kay Chorao, *Little Farm by the Sea*, 1998

    Each season has different activities for Farmer Brown and his family on their farm by the sea.

Cynthia Rylant, *The Henry and Mudge Series*, 1987-

    The adventures of Henry and his lovable, slobbery dog Mudge entertain beginning readers.

942

EILEEN SPINELLI
MELISSA IWAI, Illustrator

Night Shift Daddy

(New York: Hyperion Books for Children,)

Subject(s): Fathers and Daughters; Bedtime; Stories in Rhyme
Age range(s): Grades K-1
Major character(s): Daddy, Father; Unnamed Character, Child, Daughter
Time period(s): 2000s (2000)
Locale(s): United States

Summary: Every evening after dinner Daddy plays with his daughter, reads to her in the rocking chair and tucks her into bed with a good night kiss. Then he leaves for work. Without his knowledge, the little girl watches from her window as Daddy waits for the bus and, once he's safely on his way, she climbs into bed again. In the morning Daddy arrives home in time to share his daughter's breakfast. Then she reads to him in the rocking chair and tucks him into bed with a kiss before going out to play. (32 pages)

Where it's reviewed:
Booklist, August 2000, page 2150
Bulletin of the Center for Children's Books, June 2000, page 375
Kirkus Reviews, April 15, 2000, page 568
Publishers Weekly, May 8, 2000, page 221
School Library Journal, October 2000, page 138

Other books by the same author:
Six Hogs on a Scooter, 2000
When Mama Comes Home Tonight, 1998
Where Is the Night Train Going?: Bedtime Poems, 1996

Other books you might like:
Karen Ackerman, *By the Dawn's Early Light*, 1994
    Mom works the graveyard shift at a box factory, arriving home to her children "by the dawn's early light."
Kate Banks, *And If the Moon Could Talk*, 1998
    Papa and child begin their nightly bedtime ritual by reading a book together.
Patricia Grossman, *The Night Ones*, 1991
    The night bus carries the people who work all night to their various jobs.

943

EILEEN SPINELLI
SCOTT NASH, Illustrator

Six Hogs on a Scooter

(New York: Orchard Books, 2000)

Subject(s): Animals/Pigs; Transportation; Humor
Age range(s): Grades K-1
Major character(s): Horace Hog, Pig, Son; Penelope Hog, Pig, Daughter; Grandma Hog, Pig, Grandmother
Time period(s): Indeterminate
Locale(s): Fictional Country

Summary: The Hog family is gussied up, loaded in the car and ready to drive to the opera but the car won't start. Horace offers his scooter as transportation but six hogs on a scooter flattens the tires before they leave the driveway. Penelope suggests roller-skating to the opera but six hogs on roller skates when only two have experience is a formula that doesn't add up to forward progress. Several other transportation options fail for one reason or another and Grandma finally suggests they take the bus. The bus does a great job of getting the family to the opera house, but the opera is over, the building is locked and the buses have stopped running for the night. Six hogs sleep on a bench at the bus stop ready to catch the first bus home in the morning. (40 pages)

Where it's reviewed:
Booklist, March 1, 2000, page 1253
Horn Book Guide, Fall 2000, page 282
Kirkus Reviews, January 15, 2000, page 124
Publishers Weekly, January 24, 2000, page 311
School Library Journal, April 2000, page 115

Other books by the same author:
Where Is the Night Train Going?: Bedtime Poems, 1996
Somebody Loves You, Mr. Hatch, 1994
Thanksgiving at Tappletons', 1982

Other books you might like:
John Burningham, *Harvey Slumfenburger's Christmas Present*, 1993
    Circumstances force Santa to use a variety of alternate means of transportation in order to deliver one last gift.
Lynne Cherry, *The Armadillo from Amarillo*, 1994
    Trying to get a sense of his place in space an armadillo hitches rides on an eagle and the space shuttle.
Marjorie Priceman, *How to Make an Apple Pie and See the World*, 1994
    With the market closed, a young girl considers traveling by various modes of transportation to the countries in which apple pie ingredients originate.
Nancy Shaw, *Sheep in a Jeep*, 1986
    A group of exuberant sheep take off in a jeep and, as usual, find themselves in a bit of a predicament.

944

STEPHANIE SPINNER
TERRY BISSON, Co-Author

Be First in the Universe
(New York: Delacorte Press, 2000)

Subject(s): Twins; Aliens; Science Fiction
Age range(s): Grades 3-5
Major character(s): Tessa Gibson, 9-Year-Old, Twin; Tod Gibson, 9-Year-Old, Twin; Jack, Twin, Alien
Time period(s): 2000s (2000)
Locale(s): United States

Summary: On a trip to the mall to buy baking pans for their grandmother Tod and Tessa happen upon Gemini Jack's rental store where they rent the pans for a day. Jack also loans them an electronic pet that gobbles up fibs with a cheery ''beep.'' Tessa is so taken with it she breaks the rules by bringing it to school where its beeping during a politician's presentation to her civics class leads to its confiscation. When Tod and Tessa return the pans to Jack and explain about the problem, he loans them another gadget to help locate the e-pet. Jack's helpfulness is a cover for his mission to locate a nasty set of twins; his planet needs their DNA to reduce the ''nice'' factor in its own population. Jack recognizes that the remorseful Tod and Tessa couldn't possibly be the type of twins he's been sent to get. Fortunately, the e-pet was stolen by the only other set of twins in town whose disposition suits Jack's purposes. (133 pages)

Where it's reviewed:
Booklist, January 1, 2000, page 927
Bulletin of the Center for Children's Books, February 2000, page 223
Horn Book Guide, Fall 2000, page 312
Publishers Weekly, January 31, 2000, page 107
School Library Journal, February 2000, page 104

Other books by the same author:
Gerbilitis, 1996 (Ellen Weiss, co-author)
Aliens for Breakfast, 1988 (Jonathan Etra, co author)
The Mummy's Tomb, 1985

Other books you might like:
Bruce Coville, *The Skull of Truth*, 1997
    After compulsive liar Charlie steals an enchanted skull he is forced to speak the truth and no one believes him.
Jostein Gaarder, *Hello? Is Anybody There?*, 1998
    After Joe searches for the object he sees falling from the sky he finds a baby alien named Mika.
Stephen Manes, *It's New! It's Improved! It's Terrible!*, 1989
    He looks like a boy, talks like a television commercial and is really an alien who's driving Arnold and his friends crazy.

945

ELIZABETH SPIRES
CLAIRE NIVOLA, Illustrator

The Mouse of Amherst
(New York: Farrar, Straus and Giroux, 1999)

Subject(s): Animals/Mice; Poetry; Biography
Age range(s): Grades 2-5
Major character(s): Emmaline, Writer, Mouse; Emily Dickinson, Historical Figure, Writer
Time period(s): 1860s
Locale(s): Amherst, Massachusetts

Summary: Emmaline has no idea what an adventure she has in store when she moves into the Dickinson household. Living in Emily's room, Emmaline discovers Emily's poetry, as well as a desire to write poetry herself. In a symbiotic relationship, the two trade poems for mutual enjoyment and benefit. Although Emmaline must eventually move on, she does so knowing that her interlude with Emily has been her artistic awakening. (64 pages)

Where it's reviewed:
Booklist, March 15, 1999, page 1330
Kirkus Reviews, February 15, 1999, page 306
Publishers Weekly, January 25, 1999, page 96
School Library Journal, May 1999, page 98

Awards the book has won:
Publishers Weekly Best Books, 1999

Other books by the same author:
Riddle Road: Puzzles in Poems and Pictures, 1999
With One White Wing: Puzzles in Poems and Pictures, 1995

Other books you might like:
Michael Bedard, *Emily*, 1992
    A young girl befriends her neighbor, Emily Dickinson.
Emily Dickinson, *A Brighter Garden*, 1990
    A selection of Dickinson's poems is written especially for children.
Dick King-Smith, *A Mouse Called Wolf*, 1997
    Wolf uses his beautiful singing voice to call for help when Mrs. Honeybee falls and injures herself.
E.B. White, *Stuart Little*, 1945
    A dapper young mouse leaves his human family and sets off in search of his beloved sparrow.

946

KATE SPOHN, Author/Illustrator

Turtle and Snake at Work
(New York: Viking, 1999)

Series: Viking Easy-to-Read. Level 1
Subject(s): Animals/Turtles; Animals/Reptiles; Work
Age range(s): Grades K-1
Major character(s): Turtle, Turtle, Worker; Snake, Snake, Cook
Time period(s): 1990s
Locale(s): Fictional Country

Summary: Neighbors Turtle and Snake awaken early to prepare for their workday. Turtle stops the cars so students can safely cross the street to school. Snake mixes pizza dough and shows off his talent to customers as he twirls the dough. Oops! He tosses it too high and it lands on his head. At the end of the workday Turtle comes to Snake's pizza place and they all sit down to eat pizza with their friends. (32 pages)

Where it's reviewed:
Booklist, March 15, 1999, page 1338
Horn Book Guide, Spring 2000, page 62
School Library Journal, May 1999, page 98

Other books by the same author:
Turtle and Snake Go Camping, 2000
Dog and Cat Make a Splash, 1997
Dog and Cat Shake a Leg, 1996

Other books you might like:
Lucy Floyd, *Rabbit and Turtle Go to School*, 2000
    While Turtle rides the bus, Rabbit races along the route sure that he will arrive at school first in a Level 1 Green Light Reader.
Lars Klinting, *Bruno the Carpenter*, 1996
    Bruno works diligently to construct a toolbox in which to store all his tools.
Cynthia Rylant, *Poppleton Has Fun*, 2000
    In the seventh book about the kindly pig, Poppleton enjoys activities more when he shares them with his friends.
Hans Wilhelm, *It's Too Windy!*, 2000
    The Hello Reader! Level 1 title reveals how a small dog, reluctant to be outside on a windy day, saves the baby when the stroller rolls away.

947

DIANE STANLEY
G. BRIAN KARAS, Illustrator

Raising Sweetness

(New York: G.P. Putnam's Sons, 1999)

Subject(s): Orphans; Literacy; Humor
Age range(s): Grades K-3
Major character(s): Sweetness, Adoptee, Child; Pa, Father, Lawman; Lucy Locket, Teacher, Spouse
Time period(s): Indeterminate Past
Locale(s): Possum Trot, West

Summary: The sequel to *Saving Sweetness* finds the eight orphans living with Pa, an illiterate sheriff with a big heart, no cooking skills and unconventional ideas about housekeeping. The children continually suggest that he marry, but his heart was broken when Lucy Locket moved back east. When a letter arrives that no one can read, Sweetness volunteers to sit outside the schoolhouse and eavesdrop on the lessons so she can learn to read and teach the others in the evening. The plan works well enough—for Sweetness is finally able to decipher the letter and write a response on the only paper in the house—a wrapper from a bar of soap. The letter brings Lucy Locket to the door to announce that she has decided to accept the marriage proposal Pa made several years earlier on the condition that she can also return to her position as the town's school teacher. (32 pages)

Where it's reviewed:
Booklist, February 15, 1999, page 1077
Horn Book, March 1999, page 202
Publishers Weekly, February 1, 1999, page 84
School Library Journal, January 1999, page 102
Smithsonian, November 1999, page 52

Awards the book has won:
ALA Notable Children's Books, 2000
School Library Journal Best Books, 1999

Other books by the same author:
Rumpelstiltskin's Daughter, 1997
Saving Sweetness, 1996
The True Adventures of Daniel Hall, 1995
The Gentleman and the Kitchen Maid, 1994

Other books you might like:
Becky Bloom, *Wolf!*, 1999
    Noting that his intended victims are too busy reading to see him as a threat, Wolf learns to read, establishing a basis for friendship with the animals.
Patricia Polacco, *Aunt Chip and the Great Triple Creek Dam Affair*, 1996
    Aunt Chip, a retired librarian, teaches the children of Triple Creek how to read and inspires an interest in books.
Suzanne Williams, *Library Lil*, 1997
    Lil is such an enthusiastic librarian that she is able to get a motorcycle gang interested in reading.

948

DIANE STANLEY
HOLLY BERRY, Illustrator

Roughing It on the Oregon Trail

(New York: Joanna Cotler Books/HarperCollins, 2000)

Series: Time Traveling Twins. Book 1
Subject(s): Relatives; Frontier and Pioneer Life; Time Travel
Age range(s): Grades 2-4
Major character(s): Grandma, Grandmother; Lenny, Brother, Twin; Liz, Sister, Twin
Time period(s): 2000s (2000); 1840s (1843)
Locale(s): Oregon Trail

Summary: Liz and Lenny have no idea what's in store for them during their visit with Grandma. Not only is Grandma interested in family history, but she also has a magic hat that enables them to travel back in time to visit their ancestors. On this trip they join relatives that traveled the Oregon Trail. Although the months of dirt, danger and hardship last only moments in real time, they give Liz and Lenny a first-hand history lesson of life as a pioneer. An author's note gives historical background and a source for additional information. Maps on the endpapers follow the route and identify landmarks mentioned in the text. (44 pages)

Where it's reviewed:
Booklist, April 1, 2000, page 1479
Horn Book Guide, Fall 2000, page 282
Publishers Weekly, May 22, 2000, page 93
School Library Journal, June 2000, page 126

Other books by the same author:
Rumpelstiltskin's Daughter, 1997

Leonardo da Vinci, 1996
Saving Sweetness, 1996

Other books you might like:

Verla Kay, *Covered Wagons, Bumpy Trails*, 2000
　Life in a covered wagon is described in a rhyming tale of
　parents with an infant son trekking west to California.
Marissa Moss, *Rachel's Journal: The Story of a Pioneer Girl*,
　1998
　A fictionalized diary gives an account of daily life for a
　family traveling to California in 1850.
Jean Van Leeuwen, *A Fourth of July on the Plains*, 1997
　Jesse and his family are halfway to Oregon when the
　wagon train stops so everyone can celebrate the Fourth of
　July.
David Williams, *Grandma Essie's Covered Wagon*, 1993
　As a child Essie traveled by covered wagon across the vast
　prairies.
Laura Wilson, *How I Survived the Oregon Trail: The Journal
　of Jesse Adams*, 1999
　Ten-year-old Jesse's diary relates events on his family's
　harrowing journey westward.

949

WILLIAM STEIG
QUENTIN BLAKE, Illustrator

Wizzil

(New York: Farrar Straus Giroux, 2000)

Subject(s): Witches and Witchcraft; Behavior; Change
Age range(s): Grades 1-4
Major character(s): Wizzil, Witch; DeWitt Frimp, Farmer,
　Aged Person; Beatrice, Bird (parrot)
Time period(s): Indeterminate
Locale(s): Fictional Country (Frimp Farm)

Summary: Beatrice has a suggestion to ease Wizzil's boredom—buzz over to the Frimp Farm and bug them. Wizzil
likes the idea, changes into a housefly and zips over to explore
the territory. When she lands on DeWitt Frimp's face she
awakens a man who hates flies and who tries his hardest to
swat her. Taking the attack personally, Wizzil angrily plots
revenge that Beatrice agrees is fitting. Wizzil becomes a left-
handed work glove that DeWitt takes such a liking to he rarely
takes it off even though his fly-swatting ability deteriorates
considerably. When his children suggest that the glove is
responsible for his problems, DeWitt slowly comes to see the
truth and he throws the glove into the river. Well, Wizzil
never has liked water so, as she transforms into witch shape,
she begins struggling to stay afloat and DeWitt leaps in to
save her. His selfless action and the cleansing water transform
Wizzil into a "sweet old lady" who is never bored again,
although Beatrice might be at times. (32 pages)

Where it's reviewed:

Booklist, October 1, 2000, page 337
Bulletin of the Center for Children's Books, October 2000,
　page 82
Horn Book, July 2000, page 446
Publishers Weekly, July 3, 2000, page 70
School Library Journal, August 2000, page 165

Other books by the same author:

Pete's a Pizza, 1998 (Booklist Editors' Choice)
The Toy Brother, 1996 (School Library Journal Best Book)
Zeke Pippin, 1994 (School Library Journal Best Book)
The Amazing Bone, 1977 (Caldecott Honor Book)
Sylvester and the Magic Pebble, 1969 (Caldecott Medal)

Other books you might like:

Peter Glassman, *My Working Mom*, 1994
　Hilarious illustrations communicate the unique advantage
　of having a mom who really is a witch.
John O'Brien, *Poof!*, 1999
　Two wizards tackle their chores by waving their magic
　wands and transforming each job into the other's responsi-
　bility.
Margie Palatini, *Zoom Broom*, 1998
　Gritch's broom seems to be broken beyond repair so she
　shops for a new one.
James Stevenson, *Emma*, 1985
　Not your typical witch, Emma even needs flying lessons.

950

MAGGIE STERN
BLANCHE SIMS, Illustrator

George

(New York: Orchard Books, 1999)

Series: Orchard Chapters
Subject(s): Schools; Behavior; Humor
Age range(s): Grades 1-3
Major character(s): George, Student—Elementary School;
　Mrs. Elton, Teacher; Pumpkin, Rabbit
Time period(s): 1990s (1999)
Locale(s): United States

Summary: Three brief stories tell of eager-to-please, but impetuous George. Because George forgets to raise his hand and
wait his turn when class jobs are assigned, Mrs. Elton does not
choose him to feed Pumpkin. However, when Pumpkin runs
away, George is the one with the patience to track down the
class pet and coax him from his hiding place with a piece of
lettuce. George is reluctant to go to school on cooking day,
but eagerly agrees to mix the "secret agent" with the flour
when the class makes bread. Finally, George attends the
school fair with his brother and sister using all his tickets to
enter the raffle five times in hopes of winning tickets to a
baseball game. (48 pages)

Where it's reviewed:

Horn Book Guide, Spring 2000, page 63
Publishers Weekly, November 22, 1999, page 56
School Library Journal, October 1999, page 128

Other books by the same author:

George and Diggety, 2000 (Orchard Chapters)
Acorn Magic, 1998
The Missing Sunflowers, 1997

Other books you might like:

Patricia Reilly Giff, *Today Was a Terrible Day*, 1980
　A kind note from his teacher helps 2nd-grader Ronald
　Morgan feel better about his miserable day at school.

Tony Johnston, *Sparky and Eddie: The First Day of School*, 1997

A beginning chapter book introduces two friends who learn that some changes are acceptable when they enter school for the first time.

Stephen Krensky, *Lionel and His Friends*, 1996

Four stories in a beginning reader tell of the daily adventures of Lionel and his friends at home and at school.

Megan McDonald, *Beezy Magic*, 1998

Three brief stories tell of the events in Beezy's life with friends, family and her dog.

Suzanne Williams, *Emily at School*, 1996

Emily learns that second grade has some unexpected challenges, including new student Alex.

951

MAGGIE STERN
BLANCHE SIMS, Illustrator

George and Diggety

(New York: Orchard Books, 2000)

Subject(s): Animals/Dogs; Pets; Brothers and Sisters
Age range(s): Grades 2-3
Major character(s): Diggety, Dog; George, Brother (younger); Lulu, Sister; Henry, Brother (older)
Time period(s): 2000s (2000)
Locale(s): United States

Summary: In the sequel to *George*, Lulu and Henry help George administer a doggie IQ test to Diggety. Although the test results are disappointing to George, when snow falls, Diggety demonstrates other admirable traits. He's willing to pull the sibling's sleds up the hill for them and even hops aboard and enjoys a ride down the hill. For Diggety's birthday George plans a special dinner—hamburgers for the family and homemade dog biscuits for Diggety. The hot dog biscuits smell so good that George samples one and then offers them to other family members. By the time the taste test is complete the unhappy birthday dog is the only one who hasn't had a biscuit. Diggety is smart enough to find an alternate source of food and the family soon knows how it feels to face an empty plate. A recipe for dog biscuits concludes the book. (48 pages)

Where it's reviewed:
Booklist, September 1, 2000, page 119
Horn Book, September 2000, page 582
School Library Journal, September 2000, page 210

Other books by the same author:
George, 1999
Acorn Magic, 1998
The Missing Sunflowers, 1997

Other books you might like:
Stephen Krensky, *Lionel and His Friends*, 1996

Four brief stories continue the adventures of Lionel and his friends in this beginning reader.

Megan McDonald, *Beezy Magic*, 1998

In one of three brief stories about Beezy her dog breaks his collar in order to join her on a field trip.

Cynthia Rylant, *The Henry and Mudge Series*, 1987

The satisfying friendship between a boy and his dog is portrayed in many books about Henry and his lovable, slobbery dog Mudge.

952

JANET STEVENS, Author/Illustrator
SUSAN STEVENS CRUMMEL, Co-Author

Cook-a-Doodle-Doo!

(San Diego: Harcourt Brace & Company, 1999)

Subject(s): Animals; Cooks and Cooking; Humor
Age range(s): Grades K-3
Major character(s): Big Brown Rooster, Rooster, Cook; Iguana, Iguana; Pig, Pig (potbellied)
Time period(s): Indeterminate
Locale(s): Fictional Country

Summary: Bored, bored, bored with a steady diet of chicken feed, Big Brown Rooster remembers a tale told by his mother about his famous great-grandmother and her cooking ability. He finds her cookbook, *The Joy of Cooking Alone* by L.R. Hen and decides to make strawberry shortcake. The first three animals Rooster meets refuse to help him but Iguana, Pig and a literate turtle are willing to assist. As the turtle reads the recipe, literally minded Iguana leaps to conclusions and Pig hovers near the ingredients, eager to offer his skill at tasting. Rooster coordinates the teamwork, gently correcting Iguana with instructions about cooking with wheat flour and not a petunia, using a measuring cup rather than a ruler for the flour or an eggbeater and not a bat to beat the eggs. He also guides the kitchen chaos and restrains Pig's appetite until the completed shortcake is ready to serve. (48 pages)

Where it's reviewed:
Booklist, April 15, 1999, page 1530
Horn Book, May 1999, page 324
Publishers Weekly, April 5, 1999, page 240
School Library Journal, April 1999, page 110

Other books by the same author:
My Big Dog, 1999
Shoe Town, 1999

Other books you might like:
Mary Ann Hoberman, *The Seven Silly Eaters*, 1997

A mother's seven children, each one a picky eater, surprise her by creating a cake for her birthday that all of the family enjoys.

Maryann MacDonald, *Hedgehog Bakes a Cake*, 1990

In an easy reader, Hedgehog's cake preparations are interrupted repeatedly as friends stop and offer advice.

Peggy Parish, *Amelia Bedelia Helps Out*, 1979

Amelia doesn't confuse words intentionally, but her misunderstandings lead to some humorous events.

Cynthia Rylant, *Mr. Putter and Tabby Bake the Cake*, 1994

The fact that he knows nothing about baking does not deter Mr. Putter from his intention to bake a light, airy cake for his neighbor.

Harriet Ziefert, *Little Red Hen*, 1995

A beginning reader retells the folktale of the Little Red Hen who bakes bread alone when none of the other animals will help her.

953

JANET STEVENS, Author/Illustrator
SUSAN STEVENS CRUMMEL, Co-Author

Shoe Town

(San Diego: Harcort Brace & Company, 1999)

Series: Green Light Readers. Level 2
Subject(s): Animals/Mice; Dwellings; Stories in Rhyme
Age range(s): Grades 1-2
Major character(s): Unnamed Character, Mouse, Mother
Time period(s): Indeterminate
Locale(s): Shoe Town, Fictional Country

Summary: With her children grown and out of the nest a mother mouse looks forward to relaxing in a nice hot bath in her purple shoe home. As she stands with the water hose, ready to fill the tub she is visited by a succession of fairy tale characters, each wanting to share her shoe. To each the mouse replies that her shoe is too small and she recommends that instead the character find a shoe to place near hers. Thus, Shoe Town grows and grows, but the little mouse may still be waiting for her bath. (20 pages)

Where it's reviewed:
Booklist, May 15, 1999, page 1705
School Library Journal, May 1999, page 85

Other books by the same author:
Cook-a-Doodle-Doo!, 1999
My Big Dog, 1999

Other books you might like:
Alma Flor Ada, *Dear Peter Rabbit*, 1994
    Through letters, Peter Rabbit makes plans to attend the pigs' housewarming while Goldilocks plans to visit Baby Bear to see his repaired chair.
Janet Ahlberg, *The Jolly Christmas Postman*, 1991
    Cards and letters from one nursery-rhyme character to another expand the story of the postman's rounds in a book. Allen Ahlberg, co-author.
Joanne Oppenheim, *Eency Weency Spider*, 1991
    In an expanded tale of the spider washed down the waterspout, Eency Weency meets other nursery rhyme characters.

954

JAMES STEVENSON, Author/Illustrator

Christmas at Mud Flat

(New York: Greenwillow Books/HarperCollins, 2000)

Subject(s): Animals; Christmas; Humor
Age range(s): Grades 1-3
Major character(s): Freddie, Repairman, Duck
Time period(s): Indeterminate
Locale(s): Mud Flat, Fictional Country

Summary: Everyone in Mud Flat is busy the week before Christmas taking care of last-minute preparations for the holiday. Much of the activity involves delivering broken items to Freddie's repair shop with the expectation that he can have them fixed by Christmas Eve when he departs for his annual journey south. Not only does Freddie deliver the repaired drum and bass in time for the Christmas Eve party, but he also "fixes" a melodious surprise for his neighbors before he departs. (48 pages)

Where it's reviewed:
Booklist, September 1, 2000, page 128
Horn Book, November 2000, page 750
Publishers Weekly, September 25, 2000, page 76
School Library Journal, October 2000, page 63

Other books by the same author:
Heat Wave at Mud Flat, 1997 (School Library Journal Best Book)
The Mud Flat Mystery, 1997
Yard Sale, 1996
The Mud Flat Olympics, 1994 (Booklist Editors' Choice)

Other books you might like:
Larry Dane Brimner, *Merry Christmas, Old Armadillo*, 1995
    While lonely Old Armadillo naps on Christmas Eve his friends prepare a surprise just for him.
Doug Cushman, *Aunt Eater's Mystery Christmas*, 1995
    Aunt Eater's holiday preparations are sidetracked repeatedly by suspicious events that require curious Aunt Eater's attention.
Wende Devlin, *Cranberry Christmas*, 1976
    Maggie and her grandmother kindly help Mr. Whiskers solve some problems so he can have a pleasant Christmas.
Brigitte Weninger, *Merry Christmas, Davy!*, 1998
    Trying to show Santa that he is kind, good and generous, Davy shares his family's winter food supply with hungry animals.

955

JAMES STEVENSON, Author/Illustrator

Don't Make Me Laugh

(New York: Frances Foster Books/Farrar, Straus and Giroux, 1999)

Subject(s): Humor; Behavior; Animals
Age range(s): Grades K-1
Major character(s): Mr. Frimdimpny, Narrator, Reptile
Time period(s): Indeterminate
Locale(s): Fictional Country

Summary: Mr. Frimdimpny narrates three stories by bossily stating rules such as "Do not laugh," "Do not even smile." Mr. Frimdimpny never laughs and suggests that readers practice not smiling in front of a mirror before beginning the book. Anyone who does not follow the rules must return to the front of the book. After establishing the rules, Mr. Frimdimpny tells stories about a ticklish waiter, an elephant with a cold and a hippo in a fancy glass store. Additional rules are stated for each story ("Don't touch the X!" "No humming! No Singing!") and Mr. Frimdimpny checks in periodically to enforce them. By the book's conclusion even Mr. Frimdimpny succumbs to the story's humor and is sent to the front of the book. (32 pages)

Where it's reviewed:
Booklist, June 1999, page 1844
Publishers Weekly, September 6, 1999, page 101
School Library Journal, September 1999, page 206

Other books by the same author:
Mud Flat Spring, 1999
Mud Flat April Fool, 1998
Sam the Zamboni Man, 1998
Fun, No Fun, 1994

Other books you might like:
Jules Feiffer, *Meanwhile. . .*, 1997
When his mom calls, Raymond writes "meanwhile. . ." on his wall hoping it will be a "pause" button for his entertaining comic book, but instead. . ..
Mordicai Gerstein, *Stop Those Pants!*, 1998
Murray's pants must be bribed with the promise of a yo-yo in the pocket before they will come down from the ceiling fixture to be worn.
Peggy Rathmann, *10 Minutes till Bedtime*, 1998
A hamster tour guide leads hamster tourists on the "10-Minute Bedtime Tour" of a child's nightly routine from first announcement to good night kiss.
David Small, *Fenwick's Suit*, 1996
Fenwick tries to change his image with a new suit, but the suit dumps Fenwick and goes to work in his place.
William Steig, *Pete's a Pizza*, 1998
When rain forces the cancellation of Pete's plans to play ball, his parents try to cheer him by pretending to make him into a cheese pizza.

956

JAMES STEVENSON, Author/Illustrator

The Most Amazing Dinosaur

(New York: Greenwillow Books/HarperCollins Publishers, 2000)

Subject(s): Animals; Museums; Animals/Rats
Age range(s): Grades K-3
Major character(s): Wilfred, Rat, Traveler; Harry, Snail; Mr. Thrawl, Reptile, Director (museum)
Time period(s): Indeterminate
Locale(s): Fictional Country

Summary: Cold and tired from a long journey by bike, Wilfred seeks shelter in a large, imposing building. Initially he finds only large, frightening skeletons; as he tries to get away from them he bumps into an owl. Soon he's introduced to all the animals that call the museum home and learns the importance of avoiding Mr. Thrawl. One night, while hiding, the animals accidentally break a large dinosaur skeleton and Mr. Thrawl angrily throws them out into the snow. The museum inspectors are due in the morning and Mr. Thrawl is sure the broken skeleton will end his career. The animals do what they can to fix the problem they've caused and the inspectors declare the repaired skeleton to be the best they've seen. Mr. Thrawl hires the animals as assistants so they're assured a warm place for the winter. In the spring Wilfred climbs back on his bike, with Harry in his pocket, to resume his adventures. (32 pages)

Where it's reviewed:
Booklist, July 2000, page 2043
Horn Book Guide, Fall 2000, page 282
Kirkus Reviews, May 1, 2000, page 640
Publishers Weekly, May 8, 2000, page 221
School Library Journal, June 2000, page 126

Other books by the same author:
Sam the Zamboni Man, 1998
The Mud Flat Mystery, 1997
All Aboard!, 1995

Other books you might like:
Rod Clement, *Frank's Great Museum Adventure*, 1999
A visit to a museum takes dog Frank and his owner on an unexpected trip through time.
Steven Kellogg, *Prehistoric Pinkerton*, 1987
Pinkerton's natural desire to chew creates chaos when the large dog visits a museum filled with dinosaur bones.
James Mayhew, *Katie and the Dinosaurs*, 1992
When Katie visits a natural history museum she finds herself in a land of living dinosaurs and helps one that is lost find the way home.
Eric Rohmann, *Time Flies*, 1994
In a wordless picture book a bird flying inside a natural history museum appears to be prey for a dinosaur that seems to come to life.

957

JAMES STEVENSON, Author/Illustrator

Mud Flat Spring

(New York: Greenwillow Books, 1999)

Subject(s): Animals; Spring; Humor
Age range(s): Grades 1-2
Major character(s): Morgan, Bear; Fergus, Snail; Watson, Mouse
Time period(s): Indeterminate
Locale(s): Mud Flat, Fictional Country

Summary: Each of the many animals of Mud Flat enjoys a particular feature of spring and has a unique way to celebrate it. Morgan continues sleeping, not ready for his winter's hibernation to end. Fergus begins dancing and inspires many other residents to express themselves with their own dance of spring. Watson views the sunset and goes to sleep content that he's experiencing the best spring ever. The next morning Watson and the other animals of Mud Flat awaken to a world blanketed with snow. Rather than let the late season storm ruin the coming of spring the animals rush out to enjoy the last taste of winter knowing that this year they will be able to enjoy the arrival of spring for a second time. (40 pages)

Where it's reviewed:
Booklist, May 1, 1999, page 1601
Horn Book Guide, Fall 1999, page 285
Publishers Weekly, April 5, 1999, page 243
School Library Journal, March 1999, page 185

Other books by the same author:
Christmas at Mud Flat, 2000
Mud Flat April Fool, 1998
Heat Wave at Mud Flat, 1997 (School Library Journal Best Book)
The Mud Flat Mystery, 1997
Yard Sale, 1996
The Mud Flat Olympics, 1994 (Booklist Editors' Choice)

Other books you might like:

Ruth Lercher Bornstein, *Rabbit's Good News*, 1995
   Rabbit hops outside early one morning and then hurries home to tell her family that, "Spring is here!"

Anne Hunter, *Possum and the Peeper*, 1998
   A loud and persistent "Peep!" awakens Possum and other animals that go in search of the source—a small frog celebrating a glorious spring day.

Cynthia Rylant, *Poppleton in Spring*, 1999
   In the spring Poppleton cleans, thinks about exercising and spends the night outside in a tent—wide-awake enjoying the sights and sounds of the season.

958

JENNIFER J. STEWART

If That Breathes Fire, We're Toast!

(New York: Holiday House, 1999)

Subject(s): Moving, Household; Time Travel; Dragons
Age range(s): Grades 4-6
Major character(s): Rick Morales, 11-Year-Old; Natalie Randall, 6th Grader, Neighbor; Madam Yang, Dragon
Time period(s): 1990s (1999)
Locale(s): Tucson, Arizona

Summary: Not long after Rick and his mom move to Tucson they must replace the ancient furnace in their home, a converted bunkhouse. Perhaps the name of the furnace company, Dragonwerks, should have been a clue—for when Rick opens the crate containing the replacement, he's surprised to find a real dragon inside. Rick and Natalie try to keep Madam Yang happy with peanut butter sandwiches and marshmallows while hiding her from Rick's mom. Magical Madam Yang dispenses her own brand of wisdom while whisking the children on time travel adventures. With her purpose for coming—helping Rick adjust to the move complete—Madam Yang flies away and in a few days the actual replacement furnace arrives. Natalie and Rick discover that Madam Yang has entrusted something to Rick's care suggesting that the author's first book may have a sequel. (118 pages)

Where it's reviewed:
Booklist, August 1999, page 2059
Bulletin of the Center for Children's Books, September 1999, page 32
Horn Book Guide, Fall 1999, page 300
Publishers Weekly, May 3, 1999, page 77
School Library Journal, December 1999, page 142

Other books you might like:

Bruce Coville, *Jeremy Thatcher, Dragon Hatcher*, 1991
   Jeremy buys a small, unusual ball that is actually a dragon's egg.

Ruth Stiles Gannett, *Three Tales of My Father's Dragon*, 1998
   A collection of three previously issued books about a baby flying dragon includes the Newbery Honor book, *My Fathers' Dragon*.

Luli Gray, *Falcon's Egg*, 1995
   The strange egg that Falcon finds in the park hatches into a rapidly growing dragon that must be set free.

Dick King-Smith, *The Water Horse*, 1998
   A kelpie or Water Horse hatches from an unusual egg and quickly outgrows the backyard pond so the family puts it into nearby Loch Ness.

959

MARTHA BENNETT STILES
DANIEL SAN SOUCI, Illustrator

Island Magic

(New York: Atheneum Books for Young Readers, 1999)

Subject(s): Nature; Islands; Grandfathers
Age range(s): Grades K-3
Major character(s): Grandad, Grandfather, Farmer (retired); David, Child, Son; Mom, Mother
Time period(s): 1990s (1999)
Locale(s): Grosse Ile, Michigan

Summary: After Grandad sells his dairy farm and moves to David's island home, David and his parents notice how quiet Grandad seems. David wants Grandad to be happy, but he thinks Grandad misses his cows and feels sad. Using his memories of visits to Grandad's dairy farm for ideas, David gently introduces Grandad to the features of the island that he enjoys. Each morning they feed the geese and give them silly names; they watch the ships go past and the fog roll over the land. As the seasons change Grandad gradually adjusts enough to express his pleasure at living on David's island and to finally enjoy Mom's pancakes for breakfast. (32 pages)

Where it's reviewed:
Booklist, February 1, 2000, page 1030
Horn Book Guide, Spring 2000, page 55
Kirkus Reviews, November 1, 1999, page 1748
School Library Journal, January 2000, page 111

Other books by the same author:
James the Vine Puller: A Brazilian Folktale, 1992

Other books you might like:

Lena Anderson, *Stina's Visit*, 1991
   In a sequel to *Stina* a young girl returns to her grandfather's island for another memorable summer visit.

Marion Dane Bauer, *When I Go Camping with Grandma*, 1995
   A granddaughter's description of her camping trip with grandma reflects the beauty of nature and of a special relationship.

Helen V. Griffith, *Grandaddy's Stars*, 1995
   Grandaddy leaves his Georgia farm to visit Janetta in Baltimore.

Kathryn Lasky, *My Island Grandma*, 1993
   Abbey and Grandma share a special relationship during their time together each summer on Grandma's island.

Claudia Mills, *Gus and Grandpa*, 1997
   In the first book of a series Gus and Grandpa's warm, loving relationship contributes to the pleasure they find in shared activities.

960

JANET MORGAN STOEKE, Author/Illustrator

Minerva Louise at the Fair

(New York: Dutton Children's Books, 2000)

Subject(s): Animals/Chickens; Fairs; Humor
Age range(s): Grades K-2
Major character(s): Minerva Louise, Chicken
Time period(s): 2000s (2000)
Locale(s): United States

Summary: While gazing contentedly at the stars, after the other chickens have drifted off to sleep, Minerva Louise hears noises that are definitely not the nightly crickets chirping. Ever curious, she marches off to learn what's happening and discovers fireworks at the county fair that she mistakes for stars falling from the sky. As Minerva Louise continues her exploration of the fair she rides in a moving bulldozer, admires the circular horse barn, and eventually finds a henhouse with an empty space for her to sleep. In the morning she's discovered by her own farmer who gives her a ride home in the truck and prepares a new nesting box in celebration of her trip to the fair. (32 pages)

Where it's reviewed:
Booklist, September 1, 2000, page 125
Horn Book Guide, Spring 2001, page 24
Kirkus Reviews, July 1, 2000, page 967
Publishers Weekly, July 3, 2000, page 73
School Library Journal, August 2000, page 165

Other books by the same author:
A Friend for Minerva Louise, 1997 (School Library Journal Best Book)
Minerva Louise at School, 1996 (IRA/CBC Children's Choices)
A Hat for Minerva Louise, 1994 (Horn Book Fanfare)
Minerva Louise, 1988

Other books you might like:
Donald Crews, *Night at the Fair*, 1998
    The excitement of a trip to the fair is displayed in bright illustrations and simple text.
David Martin, *Little Chicken Chicken*, 1996
    Imaginative Little Chicken Chicken entertains the other birds in the henhouse with her juggling and tightrope walking.
Tasha Tudor, *The County Fair*, 1940
    The events of a typical county fair of long ago are beautifully illustrated and simply related.

961

MANYA STOJIC, Author/Illustrator

Rain

(New York: Crown Publishers, Inc. 2000)

Subject(s): Animals; Weather; Africa
Age range(s): Grades K-1
Time period(s): 2000s (2000)
Locale(s): Africa

Summary: In the author's first book a sniffing porcupine is the first animal to sense that rain is coming to the hot parched African plain. A herd of zebras see flashes of lightning and baboons hear the thunder rumble. Feeling a raindrop, a rhino tells a lion of the rain's arrival, but the lion is already reveling in the sight, smell, feel, sound and taste of the falling drops. After the rain stops the animals enjoy its benefits in foliage, grass, fruit and a full water hole. Gradually the heat changes the green land back to a hot parched place as the animals await the rain again. (32 pages)

Where it's reviewed:
Booklist, July 2000, page 2044
Horn Book, July 2000, page 447
Kirkus Reviews, May 1, 2000, page 640
Publishers Weekly, May 15, 2000, page 115
School Library Journal, May 2000, page 155

Awards the book has won:
School Library Journal Best Books, 2000

Other books you might like:
Verna Aardema, *Bringing the Rain to Kapiti Plain: A Nandi Tale*, 1981
    A rhyming retelling of an African folktale explains how Ki-pat brings the rain to the dry Kapiti Plain and its wildlife.
Daniel Adlerman, *Africa Calling: Nighttime Falling*, 1996
    A young girl imagines each of her stuffed animals in their native African habitat as she settles into bed at night.
Betsy Lewin, *Chubbo's Pool*, 1996
    When Chubbo's water hole dries up the hippo regrets not being more generous with his animal neighbors who still have water.

962

B.J. STONE

Ola's Wake

(New York: Henry Holt and Company, 2000)

Subject(s): Mothers and Daughters; Mountain Life; Death
Age range(s): Grades 3-6
Major character(s): Josephine ''Josie'', 10-Year-Old, Daughter; Ginny, Single Mother; Granny Ola, Grandmother (Ginny's)
Time period(s): 1960s
Locale(s): Fort Worth, Texas; Ozarks, Missouri

Summary: Josie is not happy with Ginny's plan to leave their little trailer park in Texas and drive to the Ozarks for the funeral of a relative she doesn't know. For Ginny the trip is an important one back to happy memories from her past when she lived with Granny Ola. At the wake Josie first meets Granny Ola lying in her casket and she learns about her great grandmother by listening to the stories mourners tell about this independent, feisty woman. Josie begins to wish she had known this interesting person and she's jealous of a neighbor child who relates experiences she's had with Granny Ola. Before the funeral Josie develops a fever and Ginny makes her stay in bed, but in her feverish delirium Josie ''travels'' with Ola to the funeral and then through the nearby woods doing all the things they never did as Josie grew up. By the time her fever breaks Josie has a greater understanding and appreciation for her heritage. (100 pages)

Where it's reviewed:
Bulletin of the Center for Children's Books, June 2000, page 375
Horn Book, July 2000, page 466
Publishers Weekly, July 10, 2000, page 64
School Library Journal, July 2000, page 110

Other books by the same author:
Girl on the Bluff, 1999

Other books you might like:
Sharon Creech, *Chasing Redbird*, 1997
　　Grieving for Aunt Jessie and worried by Uncle Nate's increasingly bizarre behavior, Zinny looks for solace and finds answers to family mysteries.
Kevin Henkes, *Sun & Spoon*, 1997
　　Spoon knew his deceased grandmother well but still he worries that time will erase his memories.
Cynthia Rylant, *Missing May*, 1992
　　A Newbery Award winner looks at the impact of May's death on her husband of many years and their orphaned niece.

963

PHOEBE STONE, Author/Illustrator

Go Away, Shelley Boo!

(Boston: Little, Brown and Company, 1999)

Subject(s): Imagination; Neighbors and Neighborhoods; Behavior
Age range(s): Grades 1-3
Major character(s): Emily Louise, Child, Friend (Henry's); Henry, Child, Friend; Shelley Boo, Child, Neighbor
Time period(s): 1990s (1999)
Locale(s): United States

Summary: Imaginative Emily Louise sees the moving van in front of the house next door and immediately imagines that the little girl she sees is a misbehaving child named Shelley Boo. In Emily Louise's mind Shelley Boo will steal her friend Henry, dance on the desks, swipe swings at recess and hog the back seat of the bus. Emily Louise is unable to sleep just imagining all the horrid things that will happen with Shelley Boo in the neighborhood. In the morning Emily Louise's mother tells her she's been invited to a teddy bear tea party to meet the new neighbor. Emily Louise is very reluctant to go and very surprised to learn, when she arrives, that the sweet little girl's name is not Shelley Boo. What a relief! (32 pages)

Where it's reviewed:
Children's Book Review Service, December 1999, page 41
Horn Book Guide, Spring 2000, page 56
Kirkus Reviews, July 15, 1999, page 1140
School Library Journal, November 1999, page 131

Other books by the same author:
What Night Do the Angels Wander?, 1998
When the Wind Bears Go Dancing, 1997

Other books you might like:
Joyce Champion, *Emily and Alice*, 1993
　　As lonely Emily becomes acquainted with the new neighbor Alice, a friendship begins.
Don Gillmor, *Yuck, a Love Story*, 2000
　　Austin has no interest in meeting the new neighbor, but when he does it's love at first sight for the shy boy.
Kevin Henkes, *Wemberly Worried*, 2000
　　Wemberly worries about everything, imagining the worst for every situation although in reality the anticipated problems do not materialize.
James Howe, *Pinky and Rex and the New Neighbors*, 1997
　　Pinky and Rex worry about who will buy Mrs. Morgan's house and be their new neighbors.

964

KEITH STRAND
THOMAS LOCKER, Illustrator

Grandfather's Christmas Tree

(San Diego: Silver Whistle/Harcourt Brace & Company, 1999)

Subject(s): Christmas; Animals/Geese; Frontier and Pioneer Life
Age range(s): Grades 1-3
Major character(s): Unnamed Character, Settler, Spouse; Unnamed Character, Settler, Spouse
Time period(s): 1880s (1886-1887)
Locale(s): Colorado

Summary: A young couple leaves the crowded cities of the east and settles in a Colorado valley, building a home in a grove of spruce trees. Although they try to prepare for their first winter and the birth of their first child they are overwhelmed by the fury of the winter storms. The supply of wood quickly dwindles and the husband is forced to chop down the spruce trees for firewood. Under the last tree, the couple find a pair of geese, one with an injured wing and unable to fly south to safety. They refuse to doom the geese to death by cutting down their shelter and their faith is rewarded when the storms stop on Christmas morning. A year later by Christmas time the father carves a nest with two geese and five goslings that he and his son place in the spruce tree, beginning a family tradition as the author's first children's book concludes. (32 pages)

Where it's reviewed:
Booklist, September 1, 1999, page 151
Horn Book Guide, Spring 2000, page 56
New York Times Book Review, December 19, 1999, page 30
Publishers Weekly, September 27, 1999, page 61
School Library Journal, October 1999, page 71

Other books you might like:
Eve Bunting, *Night Tree*, 1991
　　By the light of a Christmas Eve moon, a family decorates a tree in the woods with seeds, apples and popcorn for the animals.
Gloria Houston, *The Year of the Perfect Christmas Tree*, 1988
　　In 1918, with Papa away at war, Mama and Ruthie must honor his promise to provide the town's Christmas tree.
Barbara M. Lucas, *Snowed In*, 1993
　　In 1915 a frontier family in Wyoming knows that winter

snows will confine them to their homestead until the spring thaw.

Candice F. Ransom, *One Christmas Dawn*, 1996
Severe weather during the winter of 1917 forces Daddy to seek work in a distant town, but he finds his way home for Christmas.

965

TODD STRASSER

Close Call

(New York: G.P. Putnam's Sons, 1999)

Subject(s): Friendship; Sports/Baseball; Family Problems
Age range(s): Grades 4-6
Major character(s): Ian Piccolo, 11-Year-Old, Baseball Player; Jenny Long, Baseball Player, Friend; Krishnan, Baseball Player, 5th Grader
Time period(s): 1990s (1999)
Locale(s): United States

Summary: With increasing frequency the friendly after-school baseball games are halted by rock-throwing from nearby teenagers or arguing by Jenny. At first Krishnan and Ian don't understand what's troubling Jenny, but gradually they learn that Jenny's mom has gone to work while her stepfather is in drug treatment. Jenny must care for her younger brother weekends and after school so she's often unable to play. With sensitivity, the other players try to reach out to her and maintain their friendship. When they try to stop the rock throwers by challenging them to a game, the older guys accept and apply their throwing skills to baseballs. After Jenny acknowledges her added responsibilities to her friends they suggest she bring her little brother to the games and everyone takes turns watching him. Now their baseball games are only called for rain. (118 pages)

Where it's reviewed:
Horn Book Guide, Fall 1999, page 300
Kirkus Reviews, February 1, 1999, page 230
Publishers Weekly, February 15, 1999, page 108
School Library Journal, April 1999, page 142

Other books by the same author:
Kidnap Kids, 1998
Shark Bite, 1998
Hey Dad, Get a Life!, 1996
Friends Til the End, 1991

Other books you might like:
Matt Christopher, *Pressure Play*, 1993
Travis, a talented baseball player, sees his initial acceptance by new teammates vanish when the team's chance to win the championship is in jeopardy.
Dean Hughes, *All Together Now*, 1991
Teamwork pays off for this baseball team on its way to the regional championship.
Steven Schnur, *The Koufax Dilemma*, 1997
Danny's the starting pitcher in the opening game but his mom won't let him play because the game conflicts with the first night of Passover.

966

LINDA LEOPOLD STRAUSS
SUE TRUESDELL, Illustrator

A Fairy Called Hilary

(New York: Holiday House, 1999)

Subject(s): Fairies; Magic; Friendship
Age range(s): Grades 2-4
Major character(s): Caroline, Daughter, Student—Elementary School; Hilary, Mythical Creature (fairy), Friend
Time period(s): 1990s (1999)
Locale(s): United States

Summary: As Caroline muses about the possible existence of fairies one appears in the car right beside her and politely asks to accompany the family to the museum. Caroline's startled father is skeptical of Hilary's existence, but Caroline and her mother are happy believers—although a bit disappointed that Hilary does not have wings. Hilary moves in with Caroline's family pretending to be a distant cousin and tries to control her magic so as not to give away her identity. If anyone outside the family discovers the truth about Hilary, then her visit is over and she must return to fairyland. (113 pages)

Where it's reviewed:
Booklist, March 1, 1999, page 1215
Children's Book Review Service, June 1999, page 127
Horn Book Guide, Fall 1999, page 285
Publishers Weekly, January 25, 1999, page 96
School Library Journal, March 1999, page 185

Other books by the same author:
Alice Elizabeth Loved Surprises, 1993

Other books you might like:
Lynne Reid Banks, *The Fairy Rebel*, 1985
Tiki's willingness to respond to a human's request for help is definitely against the Fairy Queen's rules for proper fairy behavior.
Kimberly Burke-Weiner, *The Maybe Garden*, 1992
In her imagination, a little girl changes her mother's garden into one filled with fairies.
Carolyn J. Gold, *Dragonfly Secret*, 1997
The dragonfly Jesse and Nathan find on the car after a trip is actually an injured fairy that needs to be secretly nursed back to health.
Cassie Kendall, *Laurel the Woodfairy*, 1998
Laurel bravely enters the Great Forest to retrieve an item stolen from the fairies.
Jahnna N. Malcolm, *The Emerald Princess Finds a Fairy*, 1998
A fairy princess runs away from Fairy Land in the seventh title in the Jewel Kingdom series.
Gerda Marie Scheidl, *Loretta and the Little Fairy*, 1993
As Loretta helps a young fairy with the task of ''growing up'' she does some growing up herself.
Jane Yolen, *Child of Faerie, Child of Earth*, 1997
When the faerie magic allows visits between their two worlds, a girl and a faerie boy meet and marvel, temporarily, at each other's world.

967

CRAIG KEE STRETE
STEVE JOHNSON, Illustrator
LOU FANCHER, Illustrator

The Lost Boy and the Monster

(New York: G.P. Putnam's Sons, 1999)

Subject(s): Monsters; Animals; Conduct of Life
Age range(s): Grades 1-3
Major character(s): Old Foot Eater, Monster; Unnamed Character, Child (lost boy), Indian
Time period(s): Indeterminate Past
Locale(s): Southwest

Summary: A young boy has been lost for so long that he's forgotten the name he once had. Near the tree in which Old Foot Eater lives he encounters first a rattlesnake and then a scorpion. Since he treats each with kindness and a willingness to share the world with them they each consider him a brother and give him a name in appreciation. Unfortunately, the boy walks into the trap set by Old Foot Eater and is hauled up into the monster's tree so his feet can become lunch. When Old Foot Eater goes for water, the rattlesnake helps the lost boy get out of the monster's huge pot. As the lost boy climbs down from the tree to run away, the scorpion gives him a bag of poison to use in case of danger. Old Foot Eater soon provides the danger by chasing the lost boy who throws out scorpion's bag and Old Foot Eater is caught in the cactus that spring up from the poison. (32 pages)

Where it's reviewed:
Booklist, July 1999, page 1955
Horn Book, May 1999, page 324
Publishers Weekly, May 24, 1999, page 78
Reading Teacher, April 2000, page 601
School Library Journal, July 1999, page 81

Other books by the same author:
How the Indians Bought the Farm, 1996
They Thought They Saw Him, 1996
Big Thunder Magic, 1990

Other books you might like:
Joanna Cole, *Bony-Legs*, 1983
    A young girl's compassion toward mistreated animals gives her the magic she needs to escape from Baba Yaga.
M.C. Helldorfer, *Jack, Skinny Bones and the Golden Pancakes*, 1996
    Skinny Bones saves Jack from the desert and, in time, Jack returns the dog's favor by saving them both from Granny Trick and the devil.
David Kudler, *The Seven Gods of Luck*, 1997
    For showing kindness to the Seven Gods of Luck a poor, but generous brother and sister are rewarded.

968

PHILEMON STURGES
AMY WALROD, Illustrator

The Little Red Hen (Makes a Pizza)

(New York: Dutton Children's Books, 1999)

Subject(s): Animals; Folk Tales; Cooks and Cooking
Age range(s): Grades K-3
Major character(s): Little Red Hen, Chicken, Cook
Time period(s): Indeterminate
Locale(s): Fictional Country (urban setting)

Summary: In this retelling of the folktale a can of tomato sauce inspires Little Red Hen to make a pizza. While she has the sauce, Little Red Hen is lacking many other ingredients as she discovers each time she returns from a trip to the store. Her animal friends are busy playing outside and are not willing to go to the store to get a pizza pan, or flour or mozzarella cheese. Little Red Hen does her own shopping and always comes home with much more than she plans to buy. At last she has all the ingredients and completes the pizza—still with no help from her friends. When the delicious smell of the very large pizza wafts outside the friends are finally willing to respond to Little Red Hen's call for help. Everyone enjoys eating the pizza and the three friends do the dishes too while Little Red Hen relaxes. (32 pages)

Where it's reviewed:
Booklist, November 15, 1999, page 639
Horn Book Guide, Spring 2000, page 114
The New Advocate, Spring 2000, page 184
Publishers Weekly, August 16, 1999, page 83
School Library Journal, December 1999, page 113

Awards the book has won:
School Library Journal Best Books, 1999

Other books by the same author:
I Love Trucks, 1999
What's That Sound, Wooly Bear?, 1996
Ten Flashing Fireflies, 1995

Other books you might like:
Byron Barton, *The Little Red Hen*, 1993
    The story of the busy little hen is reinterpreted in this illustrated version of the folktale.
Alan Garner, *The Little Red Hen*, 1997
    An illustrated retelling follows the traditional tale.
Jon Scieszka, *The True Story of the Three Little Pigs*, 1989
    A humorous retelling of a classic tale gives a different idea of just what happened with those three pigs.
Janet Stevens, *Cook-a-Doodle-Doo!*, 1999
    While using his great-grandmother Little Red Hen's cookbook patient Big Brown Rooster has some "help" in the kitchen. Susan Stevens Crummel, co-author.
Jane Yolen, *Sleeping Ugly*, 1981
    A classic fairy tale is modified to reward a poor, kind, but ugly maiden. Conventionally, they all live happily ever after.

969

STEPHANIE STUVE-BODEEN
CHRISTY HALE, Illustrator

Mama Elizabeti

(New York: Lee & Low Books, Inc., 2000)

Subject(s): Brothers and Sisters; Babies; Responsibility
Age range(s): Grades K-2
Major character(s): Elizabeti, Sister (older); Obedi, Brother (younger); Eva, Doll
Time period(s): 2000s
Locale(s): Tanzania

Summary: After her mother has her third child Elizabeti wants to demonstrate her responsibility by caring for Obedi. Elizabeti's had so much practice taking care of Eva she's sure she'll be able to do it with no difficulty. Soon Elizabeti learns that a doll does not squirm, pull hair, spill rice or throw the clean laundry in the dirt as Obedi does from his position in the kanga tied to Elizabeth's back. After Obedi causes the water jug to spill on the walk home from the well, Elizabeti spreads the kanga on the ground and settles Obedi on it while she refills the jug. When she turns to get Obedi, he's vanished. Frightened, Elizabeti sits down to cry when she hears the sound of Obedi's voice and he comes toddling toward her. Elizabeti has to admit that Eva's never given her a big, wet kiss. Now that Obedi can walk, Elizabeti uses the kanga in a different way to assure that both Obedi and the water jug arrive home in time for dinner. (32 pages)

Where it's reviewed:
Booklist, August 2000, page 2150
Horn Book, July 2000, page 448
Kirkus Reviews, May 15, 2000, page 722
Publishers Weekly, May 1, 2000, page 73
School Library Journal, July 2000, page 88

Other books by the same author:
Elizabeti's Doll, 1998 (ALA Notable Book)
We'll Paint the Octopus Red, 1998

Other books you might like:
Tololwa M. Mollel, *Big Boy*, 1995
A young African boy looks forward to the day when he is big enough to take on more responsibility.
Katrin Hyman Tchana, *Oh, No, Toto!*, 1997
As Toto's grandmother tries to shop in the Cameroon market the hungry two-year-old helps himself to any food within reach.
Brigitte Weninger, *Will You Mind the Baby, Davy?*, 1997
Only Davy seems to be able to comfort his crying baby sister.

970

SAM SWOPE
SUE RIDDLE, Illustrator

Gotta Go! Gotta Go!

(New York: Farrar, Straus Giroux, 2000)

Subject(s): Animals/Insects; Migration; Nature
Age range(s): Grades K-2
Major character(s): Unnamed Character, Insect
Time period(s): Indeterminate
Locale(s): United States; Mexico

Summary: A small striped caterpillar feels an urgent need to go to Mexico although the bug doesn't know where it's going or why. None of the insects it meets in the meadow know either, but the caterpillar keeps moving slowly in what it hopes is the right direction. The effort tires the caterpillar so it settles on a branch to sleep and is enveloped in a chrysalis. When it awakens it has beautiful orange and black wings attached to its body. Traveling is much faster now and the insect successfully reaches Mexico where it sleeps through the winter with thousands of other butterflies. In spring the butterfly returns to America to lay eggs and begin the cycle again. (32 pages)

Where it's reviewed:
Booklist, March 1, 2000, page 1243
Horn Book, May 2000, page 300
Publishers Weekly, January 31, 2000, page 105
School Library Journal, May 2000, page 156

Other books by the same author:
The Krazees, 1997
The Araboolies of Liberty Street, 1989

Other books you might like:
Eric Carle, *The Very Hungry Caterpillar*, 1969
A caterpillar feels compelled to eat everything in its path with surprising results.
Gail Gibbons, *Monarch Butterfly*, 1989
A nonfiction title depicts the life cycle of the monarch butterfly.
Deborah Heligman, *From Caterpillar to Butterfly*, 1996
In a classroom portrayed in this "Let's-Read-and-Find-Out Science" series entry, students observe the process of metamorphosis.
Virginia Kroll, *Butterfly Boy*, 1997
Red admiral butterflies return to Emilio's yard annually with the arrival of warm weather.
Mary Ling, *Butterfly*, 1992
This title in the nonfiction "See How They Grow" series uses color photographs to explain the life of butterflies.

T

SIMMS TABACK, Author/Illustrator

Joseph Had a Little Overcoat

(New York: Viking, 1999)

Subject(s): Clothes; Resourcefulness; Problem Solving
Age range(s): Grades K-3
Major character(s): Joseph Kohn, Tailor
Time period(s): Indeterminate Past
Locale(s): Yehupetz, Poland

Summary: This reillustrated version of Taback's 1977 story inspired by a Yiddish folksong creatively explores many ways to recycle a garment. When thrifty Joseph's overcoat becomes old he patches the holes and continues to wear it until his animals show disdain for his appearance. So, Joseph converts the coat to a jacket and then the patched jacket becomes a vest. The coat experiences several other reincarnations before it functions as a button—a button that pops off Joseph's pants and is lost on the floor, leaving Joseph with nothing. Just to prove that you can make something from nothing Joseph trades needle and thread for paper and pencil and creates a book about his overcoat. (40 pages)

Where it's reviewed:
Booklist, January 1, 2000, page 936
Five Owls, March 2000, page 97
Horn Book, January 2000, page 68
Riverbank Review, Spring 2000, page 30
School Library Journal, January 2000, page 112

Awards the book has won:
Caldecott Medal, 2000
ALA Notable Children's Books, 2000

Other books by the same author:
This Is the House That Jack Built, 2001
There Was an Old Lady Who Swallowed a Fly, 1997

Other books you might like:
May Garelick, *Just My Size*, 1990
 As a young girl grows, her beautiful coat is made into a jacket, vest, cap, knapsack and finally a new coat for her doll.
Phoebe Gilman, *Something from Nothing*, 1993
 A tailor presents his grandson with a beautiful blanket that he remakes into smaller and smaller items as use and age leave less and less usable fabric.
Steve Sanfield, *Bit by Bit*, 1995
 As Zundel's beautiful coat shows signs of wear he remakes it into smaller clothing items until nothing is left but the threads of a story.

NANCY TAFURI, Author/Illustrator

Will You Be My Friend?

(New York: Scholastic Press, 2000)

Subject(s): Animals/Rabbits; Animals/Birds; Friendship
Age range(s): Grades K-1
Major character(s): Bird, Bird; Bunny, Rabbit
Time period(s): Indeterminate
Locale(s): Fictional Country

Summary: Bunny, who lives in a hole at the base of the old apple tree, tries to befriend Bird who lives in a hole higher up the tree, but Bird is too shy. When Bird becomes wet and cold during a rainstorm Bunny hears her crying and invites her to seek shelter in his warm, dry hole. The experience helps Bird overcome her shyness and accept Bunny's offer to help her rebuild her nest with dry materials. Bunny asks a squirrel and a chipmunk to help also and when the task is complete Bird has a new, soft nest and three friends. (32 pages)

Where it's reviewed:
Booklist, January 1, 2000, page 938
Children's Book Review Service, April 2000, page 100
Kirkus Reviews, December 15, 1999, page 1964
Publishers Weekly, January 10, 2000, page 67
School Library Journal, March 2000, page 217

Other books by the same author:
Silly Little Goose!, 2001
Snowy Flowy Blowy: A Twelve Months Rhyme, 1999

Counting to Christmas, 1998
I Love You, Little One, 1998

Other books you might like:
Holly Hobbie, *Toot and Puddle*, 1997
  Toot and Puddle have different interests but share a friendship.
Matt Novak, *Jazzbo and Googy*, 2000
  Jazzbo and his teddy bear look beyond Googy's messiness to see a good friend.
Paul Stewart, *A Little Bit of Winter*, 1998
  Rabbit complies with friend Hedgehog's request and saves a bit of winter for him to experience in the spring when he completes his hibernation.

973

HUDSON TALBOTT, Author/Illustrator

O'Sullivan Stew: A Tale Cooked Up in Ireland

(New York: G.P. Putnam's Sons, 1999)

Subject(s): Witches and Witchcraft; Animals/Horses; Storytelling
Age range(s): Grades 2-5
Major character(s): Kate O'Sullivan, Daughter, Storyteller
Time period(s): Indeterminate Past
Locale(s): Crookhaven, Ireland

Summary: The king's men take the local witch's horse as a tax payment for the village of Crookhaven and Kate seeks help for the witch from the villagers. When no one answers Kate's plea, the witch storms home in anger and disaster befalls the village. Kate decides that the solution to the misery is for her family to retrieve the witch's horse from the king's palace, return it to the witch so she'll be happy and Crookhaven can return to normal. Unfortunately, the king's guards capture the O'Sullivan's and haul them before the king who intends to hang them for horse stealing. Kate bargains for their freedom by telling tales of situations they've each been in before that were surely even worse than the spot they're in now. After successfully bargaining for their freedom and that of the horse, Kate returns the horse to the witch who promptly gives it to her as a gift. Although the king is so taken with Kate's stories that he proposes, Kate embarks on a real adventure, promising to return in five years to see if his offer stands. (32 pages)

Where it's reviewed:
Booklist, February 1, 1999, page 983
Horn Book Guide, Fall 1999, page 285
Kirkus Reviews, December 15, 1998, page 1804
Publishers Weekly, January 11, 1999, page 72
School Library Journal, January 1999, page 102

Awards the book has won:
Notable Social Studies Trade Books for Young People, 2000

Other books by the same author:
Excalibur, 1996
King Arthur and the Round Table, 1995
King Arthur: The Sword in the Stone, 1991

Other books you might like:
Teresa Bateman, *The Ring of Truth*, 1997
  When the king of the leprechauns gives Patrick a ring of truth he loses his gift for blarney but still wins a storytelling contest.
Robert Byrd, *Finn MacCoul and His Fearless Wife: A Giant Tale from Ireland*, 1999
  Finn MacCoul, a hero of Celtic lore, depends on his wife's magic harp and clever wits to defeat the giant Cucullin.
Una Leavy, *Irish Fairy Tales and Legends*, 1997
  Ten Irish legends comprise this collection.
Sheila MacGill-Callahan, *To Capture the Wind*, 1997
  To free her betrothed from a pirate, Oonagh must correctly answer four riddles.
Robert D. San Souci, *Brave Margaret: An Irish Adventure*, 1999
  In a retelling of a traditional tale, Margaret bravely faces adventure and danger to achieve her goal.

974

CLIFTON L. TAULBERT
E.B. LEWIS, Illustrator

Little Cliff and the Porch People

(New York: Dial Books for Young Readers, 1999)

Subject(s): Food; Neighbors and Neighborhoods; African Americans
Age range(s): Grades K-3
Major character(s): Little Cliff, Child; Poppa Joe, Grandfather (great-grandfather); Mama Pearl, Grandmother (great-grandmother), Cook
Time period(s): 1950s
Locale(s): Mississippi Delta, Mississippi

Summary: Little Cliff is home with Mama Pearl who is preparing Poppa Joe's favorite food—sweet potatoes cooked in her magic skillet. Mama Pearl gives Little Cliff some money and asks him to walk down the road and buy some special butter. Little Cliff feels proud to be sent on his first errand. He tries to hurry as Mama Pearl instructs but the neighbors all call from their porches wanting to talk to him. Little Cliff also wants to obey Poppa Joe's admonition to be polite so he carefully explains to each about his job for Mama Pearl. When each of the "porch people" learns of his errand they contribute their own ingredient to help make the magic in the sweet potatoes. Finally Little Cliff completes the task and returns home not only with the butter but also with whole nutmegs, vanilla and fresh grease. Mama Pearl knows just what to do and soon the smells from her skillet suggest to Little Cliff that the magic is working. As Little Cliff, Mama Pearl and Poppa Joe sit down to eat the neighbors appear to help devour the creation from the magic skillet. (32 pages)

Where it's reviewed:
Booklist, February 15, 1999, page 1077
Horn Book Guide, Fall 1999, page 285
Publishers Weekly, January 11, 1999, page 71
Riverbank Review, Spring 1999, page 32
School Library Journal, March 1999, page 186

Awards the book has won:
Notable Social Studies Trade Books for Young People, 2000

Other books you might like:

Sandra Belton, *From Miss Ida's Front Porch*, 1993
> On a warm summer evening Miss Ida's front porch is the gathering spot as older neighbors share their memories with the children.

Angela Johnson, *The Rolling Store*, 1997
> When Granddaddy was growing up in a rural area with no stores the community depended on the arrival of the "Rolling Store" for supplies and news.

Alice Schertle, *Down the Road*, 1995
> Mama sends Hetty down the road on her first solo errand to buy eggs from the general store for Papa's breakfast.

Alan Schroeder, *Carolina Shout!*, 1995
> The songs, calls and cries of many different workers add to the melody of life in Charleston.

975

MATT TAVARES, Author/Illustrator

Zachary's Ball

(Cambridge, MA: Candlewick Press, 2000)

Subject(s): Sports/Baseball; Fathers and Sons; Fantasy
Age range(s): Grades 2-4
Major character(s): Zachary, Child, Son
Time period(s): Multiple Time Periods
Locale(s): Boston, Massachusetts

Summary: In the author/illustrator's first book Zachary's father catches a foul ball and hands it to his son who is attending his first major league baseball game. Magically, Zachary is transported to the mound where he throws the winning pitch. Over the years holding the ball enables Zachary to have other imaginary baseball adventures until the ball simply disappears. As an adult Zachary is walking past Fenway Park when a ball is hit out of the stands and he catches it. Thinking of the ball he had years before he passes this one to a girl entering the stadium with her father. She, too, declares that the ball is magic. (32 pages)

Where it's reviewed:
Booklist, April 15, 2000, page 1546
Horn Book Guide, Fall 2000, page 283
Kirkus Reviews, March 15, 2000, page 391
Publishers Weekly, March 27, 2000, page 80
School Library Journal, August 2000, page 165

Other books you might like:

David A. Adler, *The Babe & I*, 1999
> During the Depression a young boy sells a newspaper to Babe Ruth who gives him a tip big enough to buy tickets for the game.

Ron Cohen, *My Dad's Baseball*, 1994
> Max's discovery of an autographed baseball in his grandparents' attic prompts his dad to tell the story behind the ball.

Mindy Avra Portnoy, *Matzah Ball: A Passover Story*, 1994
> Aaron attends a baseball game during Passover and is lucky enough to catch a ball hit into the stands while his friends are at the concession stand.

976

HARRIET PECK TAYLOR, Author/Illustrator

Secrets of the Stone

(New York: Farrar Straus Giroux, 2000)

Subject(s): Cave Paintings; Indians of North America; Animals
Age range(s): Grades K-3
Major character(s): Coyote, Coyote; Badger, Badger; Jackrabbit, Rabbit
Time period(s): Indeterminate Past
Locale(s): Southwest

Summary: Coyote and Badger pursue a Jackrabbit that escapes through a small opening between a boulder and a cliff wall. Badger digs under the boulder to loosen it and with Coyote's help the two hunters roll the boulder away from the entrance to a cave. Once inside they forget about pursuing Jackrabbit because they are awestruck by the images on the cave wall. Coyote's excited howling attracts other desert animals that enter the cave and stare at pictures of what must be their ancestors. A storm traps them in the cave and Coyote falls asleep by the fire, dreaming of the life of the Ancient Ones. Awakened by his friends, Coyote spots Jackrabbit race past and resumes the chase with Badger. A concluding Author's Note gives background information for the tale and source notes. (32 pages)

Where it's reviewed:
Booklist, November 15, 2000, page 650
Horn Book Guide, Spring 2001, page 51
Kirkus Reviews, August 1, 2000, page 1125
Publishers Weekly, October 16, 2000, page 75
School Library Journal, October 2000, page 140

Other books by the same author:
Two Days in May, 1999
Ulaq and the Northern Lights, 1998
When Bear Stole the Chinook: A Siksika Tale, 1997
Brother Wolf: A Seneca Tale, 1996
Coyote and the Laughing Butterflies, 1995

Other books you might like:

Gerald McDermott, *Coyote: A Trickster Tale from the American Southwest*, 1994
> Pompous, blue-furred coyote's rude, boastful behavior undermines his attempt to fly with the crows and contributes to the change in his coloration.

Tom Pohrt, *Coyote Goes Walking*, 1995
> Four legends present coyote as a mythical creator, a trickster, and a victim of his own cockiness.

Janet Stevens, *Coyote Steals the Blanket: A Ute Tale*, 1993
> Coyote refuses to accept advice from anyone and suffers the consequences.

977

HARRIET PECK TAYLOR, Author/Illustrator

Ulaq and the Northern Lights

(New York: Farrar Straus Giroux, 1998)

Subject(s): Animals/Foxes; Astronomy; Folk Tales

Age range(s): Grades K-3
Major character(s): Ulaq, Fox
Time period(s): Indeterminate
Locale(s): North America

Summary: When Ulaq sees the Northern Lights for the first time he decides to find out exactly what they are. Each animal he asks has a different opinion—the seal says they are fish, caribou says they are ghosts, while wolf says they are the flames of a hunter's fire. In the end Ulaq decides for himself, that the Northern Lights are simply there for people to enjoy the beauty. (32 pages)

Where it's reviewed:
Booklist, December 1, 1998, page 673
Horn Book Guide, Spring 1999, page 46
Kirkus Reviews, October 1, 1998, page 1465
School Library Journal, January 1999, page 104

Other books by the same author:
Two Days in May, 1999
Brother Wolf: A Seneca Tale, 1996
Coyote Places the Stars, 1993

Other books you might like:
Natalie Kinsey-Warnock, *The Fiddler of the Northern Lights*, 1996
  Henry goes in search of the fiddler who causes the Northern Lights to dance.
Elinor J. Pinczes, *Arctic Fives Arrive*, 1996
  In this counting book, groups of arctic animals gather to view the Northern Lights.
D.M. Souza, *Northern Lights*, 1994
  This nonfiction book explains the Northern and Southern lights known as auroras.

978

KATRIN HYMAN TCHANA
TRINA SCHART HYMAN, Illustrator

The Serpent Slayer

(Boston: Little, Brown and Company, 2000)

Subject(s): Folklore; Fairy Tales; Women
Age range(s): Grades 3-5
Time period(s): Indeterminate Past
Locale(s): Earth

Summary: Eighteen folktales celebrate the strength and cleverness of heroines of all ages. Many of the tales are found in different cultures with the heroines having different names depending on the country in which the story is being told. In "Kate Crackernuts" a kind, patient and attentive young girl saves her stepsister from a curse while learning how to cure a prince of a mysterious illness and thus gains his hand in marriage. Maria learns that she has the courage to restore her husband's soul when he returns from the war in "Three Whiskers from a Lion's Chin." A daughter, in "Tokoyo," while seeking her banished father saves him and frees the emperor of a curse when she willingly sacrifices herself to do battle with a sea god. Source notes for each story are appended. (113 pages)

Where it's reviewed:
Booklist, December 15, 2000, page 818

Children's Bookwatch, September 2000, page 3
Horn Book, November 2000, page 765
Publishers Weekly, August 7, 2000, page 95
School Library Journal, November 2000, page 148

Other books by the same author:
Oh, No, Toto!, 1997 (Louise Tchana Pami, co-author)

Other books you might like:
Virginia Hamilton, *Her Stories: African American Folktales, Fairy Tales, and True Tales*, 1995
  An award-winning collection of women's tales is retold without losing the qualities of the oral traditions on which they are based.
Robert D. San Souci, *Cut from the Same Cloth: American Women of Myth, Legend and Tall Tale*, 1993
  This illustrated collection of twenty stories, each with a female protagonist, is drawn from folktales, ballads and popular stories.
Jane Yolen, *Not One Damsel in Distress: World Folktales for Strong Girls*, 2000
  Thirteen folktales relate the bravery of women known through the traditional literature of many countries.

979

MARK TEAGUE

One Halloween Night

(New York: Scholastic Press, 1999)

Subject(s): Halloween; Fantasy; Teasing
Age range(s): Grades K-3
Major character(s): Floyd, Child, Friend; Wendell, Child, Friend; Mona, Child, Friend
Time period(s): 1990s (1999)
Locale(s): United States

Summary: As Wendell, Floyd and Mona walk home from school on Halloween afternoon, a black cat crosses their path. A few hours later, the friends begin to realize the truth of Wendell's observation that "Anything can happen on Halloween." The treats they receive have weird names such as "Broccoli Chews" or "Eggplant Fizzlers" and some houses have tricks and no treats at all. Then, they run into a bully from school with her friends all dressed as witches and eager to chase and tease them. They each use a feature of their costumed character to magically save themselves from the witches and finally end up back where they started with bags full of normal candy. For a little while Wendell, Floyd and Mona had one Halloween night to remember! (32 pages)

Where it's reviewed:
Booklist, September 1, 1999, page 151
Bulletin of the Center for Children's Books, September 1999, page 33
Kirkus Reviews, July 15, 1999, page 1140
Publishers Weekly, September 27, 1999, page 47
School Library Journal, September 1999, page 207

Other books by the same author:
The Lost and Found, 1998
Baby Tamer, 1997
The Secret Shortcut, 1996

Other books you might like:

Brian J. Heinz, *The Monster's Test*, 1996
  The fierce monsters become the frightened ones when they meet a group of trick-or-treaters.
Dav Pilkey, *The Hallo-Weiner*, 1995
  Oscar's bravery on Halloween night wins him some respect despite the embarrassing costume his mother has made.
Judy Sierra, *The House That Drac Built*, 1995
  A rhyming cumulative tale introduces such unusual creatures as a manticore and the fiend of Bloodygore living in the house that Drac built.
Jean Van Leeuwen, *Oliver and Amanda's Halloween*, 1992
  In a beginning reader, siblings Oliver and Amanda Pig disagree on appropriate costumes for Halloween.

980

PHYLLIS THEROUX
MARJORIE PRICEMAN, Illustrator

Serefina under the Circumstances

(New York: Greenwillow Books, 1999)

Subject(s): Imagination; Grandmothers; Storytelling
Age range(s): Grades K-3
Major character(s): Serefina, 7-Year-Old; Grandma, Grandmother, Storyteller; Buster, Brother
Time period(s): 1990s
Locale(s): United States

Summary: Grandma thinks Serefina's active imagination is one sign that she is destined for greatness, but her more immediate concern is Serefina's ability to keep a secret. Although Serefina doesn't have a reputation for skill with keeping secrets, Grandma depends on her to distract Buster after school while his friends arrive for a birthday party. Serefina is determined to do it, but that secret grows and grows in her mind until she can scarcely see or think. When she finds Buster crying after school the only way Serefina can think of to soothe him is by whispering the secret in his ear. Grandma is disappointed, but enthralled with the imaginative story Serefina tells to explain why she thought it was critical to divulge the secret. The visual imagery of accomplished illustrator Priceman literally interprets Grandma's colloquialisms in the author's first book for children. (32 pages)

Where it's reviewed:

Booklist, September 1, 1999, page 144
Children's Book Review Service, January 2000, page 55
Kirkus Reviews, September 1, 1999, page 1422
Publishers Weekly, July 5, 1999, page 70
School Library Journal, September 1999, page 207

Other books you might like:

Anthony Browne, *Changes*, 1990
  A boy ponders what his father means by the statement, "Things are going to change around here."
Rebecca Emberley, *My Mother's Secret Life*, 1998
  A dream convinces a little girl that her mother is keeping a big secret.
Dr. Seuss, *And to Think That I Saw It on Mulberry Street*, 1937

An imaginative boy reports to his father the incredible sights he's seen while walking home from school.

981

FRANCES THOMAS
ROSS COLLINS, Illustrator

What If?

(New York: Hyperion Books for Children, 1999)

Subject(s): Monsters; Imagination; Parent and Child
Age range(s): Grades K-2
Major character(s): Little Monster, Monster, Child; Mother Monster, Monster, Mother
Time period(s): Indeterminate
Locale(s): Fictional Country

Summary: To his mom Little Monster proposes a terrifying imaginary disaster that could happen if he woke up in the morning with a big black hole in the floor and big spiders and the house on fire. Mother Monster agrees that it would be scary to wake up to such a sequence of events but she proposes her own imaginary day. What if Little Monster woke up to find pancakes for breakfast and a walk with mom and balloons and ice cream and a bedtime story. Little Monster agrees that his mom's imaginary day sounds very nice. Originally published in Great Britain in 1998. (32 pages)

Where it's reviewed:

Booklist, July 1999, page 1955
Bulletin of the Center for Children's Books, September 1999, page 3
Children's Book Review Service, August 1999, page 163
Horn Book Guide, Spring 2000, page 24
Kirkus Reviews, June 1, 1999, page 890

Awards the book has won:

Bulletin of the Center for Children's Books Blue Ribbon, 1999

Other books by the same author:

One Day, Daddy, 2001
The Bear and Mr. Bear, 1995
The Prince and the Cave, 1992

Other books you might like:

Mercer Mayer, *There's a Monster in My Closet*, 1968
  Sometimes inviting monsters out of the closet helps them seem less scary.
Lisa McCourt, *I Love You, Stinky Face*, 1997
  A child imagines becoming a succession of horrid creatures and her mother assures her that she could love and care for her child in any guise.
Michael Rosen, *We're Going on a Bear Hunt*, 1989
  Bravely a group sets off in search of a bear until, arriving at their goal, fear propels them into a hurried retreat.
Ann Tompert, *Little Fox Goes to the End of the World*, 1984
  In conversation with her mother Little Fox imagines how she will travel through danger to the end of the world and return safely to her home.

982

JOYCE CAROL THOMAS
HOLLY BERRY, Illustrator

The Bowlegged Rooster and Other Tales That Signify

(New York: Joanna Cotler/HarperCollins Publishers, 2000)

Subject(s): Animals/Birds; Animals; Short Stories
Age range(s): Grades 2-5
Major character(s): Papa Rooster, Father, Rooster; Mama Hen, Mother, Hen; Baby Rooster, Chicken
Time period(s): Indeterminate Past
Locale(s): Possum Neck, Mississippi

Summary: In the first of five brief stories Papa Rooster and Mama Hen proudly welcome Baby Rooster into the world. Before the egg opens Mama Hen can tell that Baby Rooster will be just like his bowlegged father and indeed he is. By participating in funerals and weddings that take place in or near their barnyard home Baby Rooster learns how to live life according to Papa Rooster with some side advice from the experiences of buzzards, crows and lizards. In the final story Baby Rooster celebrates his first Christmas by making a snow goose and accompanying Papa Rooster as he visits the neighbors. With each family Baby Rooster participates in one Christmas tradition until all the animals gather for a Christmas feast and gift exchange. (104 pages)

Where it's reviewed:
Booklist, October 1, 2000, page 342
Horn Book Guide, Spring 2001, page 67
Kirkus Reviews, August 15, 2000, page 1204
School Library Journal, November 2000, page 135

Other books by the same author:
I Have Heard of a Land, 1998 (ALA Notable Book for Children)
Gingerbread Days, 1995
Brown Honey in Broomwheat Tea, 1993

Other books you might like:
Benedict Blathwayt, *Stories from Firefly Island*, 1993
   Tortoise is the resident storyteller for the animals living on Firefly Island.
Virginia Hamilton, *When Birds Could Talk & Bats Could Sing: The Adventures of Bruh Sparrow, Sis Wren, and Their Friends*, 1996
   A collection of eight stories based on African American folklore explains the impact of past behaviors on the current appearance of birds and bats.
Margaret Mayo, *Tortoise's Flying Lesson*, 1995
   A collection of retold and adapted folktales tells of animals supporting, tricking and learning from one another.
Paul Peabody, *Blackberry Hollow*, 1993
   Parnussus, a kindly bear, tries to ease the homesickness of Tom, a Scottish frog, in hopes he'll stop playing his bagpipes.
Cynthia Rylant, *Thimbleberry Stories*, 2000
   Four stories chronicle the peaceful life of the animal residents of Thimbleberry Lane.

983

SHELLEY MOORE THOMAS
JENNIFER PLECAS, Illustrator

Good Night, Good Knight

(New York: Dutton Children's Books, 2000)

Series: Dutton Easy Reader
Subject(s): Bedtime; Dragons; Knights and Knighthood
Age range(s): Grades 2-3
Major character(s): Good Knight, Knight
Time period(s): Indeterminate Past
Locale(s): Fictional Country

Summary: As Good Knight stands watch from his solitary post atop a crumbly tower atop a high wall he hears an enormous roar in the distance. Valiantly he climbs down the tower, mounts his horse and rides through the forest to dispatch whatever creature threatens the kingdom. When Good Knight reaches a dark cave, he finds a small dragon, dressed in pajamas, that requests a glass of water. Being a good knight, he complies, returns to his post and again hears a roar so he repeats his journey and finds a second dragon. This one requests a story, but still the Good Knight's mission of mercy is not complete. The third time he responds a different dragon asks for a song and on the fourth trip all three want a kiss. After clambering up and down the wall and riding through the forest most of the night, Good Knight flops into bed (still in his armor) for a good night's sleep. (48 pages)

Where it's reviewed:
Booklist, February 15, 2000, page 1124
Bulletin of the Center for Children's Books, February 2000, page 255
Horn Book, January 2000, page 84
Publishers Weekly, December 13, 1999, page 81
School Library Journal, March 2000, page 218

Awards the book has won:
Horn Book Fanfare, 2000
School Library Journal Best Books, 2000

Other books by the same author:
A Baby's Coming to Your House, 2001
Somewhere Today: A Book of Peace, 1998
Putting the World to Sleep, 1995

Other books you might like:
Tomie DePaola, *The Knight and the Dragon*, 1980
   A knight with little experience fighting dragons prepares to face an equally inexperienced dragon.
Barbara Shook Hazen, *The Knight Who Was Afraid of the Dark*, 1989
   The castle bully tries to take advantage of Sir Fred's fear of the dark by arranging a midnight meeting with Lady Wendylyn, but the plan backfires.
Penelope Lively, *Good Night, Sleep Tight*, 1995
   Although Mary Ann is tired after a day of play her stuffed animals are not so they make plans for a bedtime adventure.

984

VALERIE THOMAS
KORKY PAUL, Illustrator

Winnie Flies Again

(Brooklyn, NY: Kane/Miller Book Publishers, 2000)

Subject(s): Witches and Witchcraft; Humor; Accidents
Age range(s): Grades K-3
Major character(s): Winnie, Witch; Wilbur, Cat
Time period(s): Indeterminate
Locale(s): Fictional Country

Summary: When Winnie first begins to have accidents she thinks the problems are with her broom so she tries other means of transportation with equally disastrous results. Gamely, Wilbur continues to ride with Winnie despite his mounting injuries. Changing to a bicycle doesn't help Winnie as she rides it into a pond and using a skateboard is really a problem. Winnie learns that even walking has hazards when she tumbles into an open manhole. Seeking a cup of tea to steady her nerves Winnie stumbles into just the shop she needs although it offers, not tea, but eyeglasses. Wilbur's relieved by the solution to Winnie's problems and the return to broomstick travel. Originally published in England in 1999. (28 pages)

Where it's reviewed:
Horn Book Guide, Fall 2000, page 283
Publishers Weekly, March 27, 2000, page 79
School Librarian, Summer 2000, page 90
School Library Journal, July 2000, page 88

Other books by the same author:
Winnie in Winter, 1998
Winnie the Witch, 1987

Other books you might like:
Patricia Reilly Giff, *Watch Out, Ronald Morgan!*, 1985
    One little accident after another happens to Ronald Morgan until he receives a pair a glasses that improve his vision.
Libba Moore Gray, *Fenton's Leap*, 1994
    Fenton, the near-sighted frog, sees more clearly after a catfish gives him a pair of glasses found on the bottom of the pond.
Amy Hest, *Baby Duck and the Bad Eyeglasses*, 1996
    Grampa Duck is the one to help Baby Duck realize the advantage of having glasses that enable her to see.
Paul Brett Johnson, *A Perfect Pork Stew*, 1998
    Having broken her glasses, Baba Yaga's blurred vision leads to an interesting pot of stew and a pork dinner for Ivan.

985

TYNIA THOMASSIE
ANDREW GLASS, Illustrator

Cajun Through and Through

(Boston: Little, Brown and Company, 2000)

Subject(s): Cousins; Humor; Family
Age range(s): Grades 1-3
Major character(s): Remington Terrebonne Toups, Cousin; Ti-Boy, Brother, Cousin; Baptiste, Brother, Cousin
Time period(s): Indeterminate Past
Locale(s): Louisiana

Summary: News that cousin Remington is coming from the big city to visit their family is met with memories of his last disastrous visit. Ti-boy and Baptiste cannot imagine that anyone who thinks jambalaya is too spicy and raw oysters don't look fit to eat can be a Cajun relative, but their mother insists he's family and they need to show him a good time. Remington tries to fit in but he's been raised not to spit so the watermelon seed-spitting contest isn't successful and the brown bayou water discourages swimming in Remington's opinion. Finally, Ti-boy and Baptiste try taking him fishing for dinner. Remington likes the idea, but he's not a successful fisherman either. When Baptiste cons Ti-boy into letting Remington use his new rod, Remington hooks a fish but is unable to land it and the rod goes into the dark water. One look at Ti-boy's expression and Remington goes in after it and proves himself Cajun through and through. (32 pages)

Where it's reviewed:
Booklist, March 15, 2000, page 1390
Horn Book Guide, Fall 2000, page 283
School Library Journal, May 2000, page 156

Other books by the same author:
Feliciana Meets d'Loup Garou: A Cajun Tall Tale, 1998 (Notable Children's Trade Books in the Field of Social Studies)
Mimi's Tutu, 1996
Feliciana Feydra LeRoux: A Cajun Tall Tale, 1995

Other books you might like:
Caroline Binch, *Gregory Cool*, 1994
    On his first visit to his grandparent's home in Tobago, all-American Gregory is initially overwhelmed by the cultural differences.
Karen English, *Neeny Coming, Neeny Going*, 1996
    Essie loves the simple rhythm of life on an island and feels sad that cousin Neeny loses this appreciation after moving to the mainland.
Irene Smalls, *Because You're Lucky*, 1997
    Jonathan doesn't like sharing his room and his things with his homeless cousin Kevin until he begins to appreciate just how lucky he is.

986

COLIN THOMPSON, Author/Illustrator

The Last Alchemist

(New York: Alfred A. Knopf, 1999)

Subject(s): Alchemy; Gold; Kings, Queens, Rulers, etc.
Age range(s): Grades 2-4
Major character(s): Spinifex, Scientist (alchemist); Arthur, Apprentice
Time period(s): Indeterminate
Locale(s): Fictional Country

Summary: Spinifex is the nineteenth alchemist to serve a kingdom that, for centuries, has had one goal—making gold. Despite the resources of a vast library filled with the writings and experiments of the previous alchemists, Spinifex is unsuccessful and his quest is beginning to make him mad. Arthur is able to find gold everywhere—in sunflowers, egg yolks, sunlight and carp—and he does not understand the obsession that Spinifex has with the metallic substance. The final experiment that Spinifex creates covers the land and the dark library and inner reaches of the castle with golden light, but leaves only a small pool of gold metal that Arthur fashions into a sunflower for the king. Originally published in Great Britain in 1999. (32 pages)

Where it's reviewed:
Booklist, July 1999, page 1947
Kirkus Reviews, June 15, 1999, page 970
Magpies, May 1999, page 31
Publishers Weekly, June 14, 1999, page 70
School Library Journal, September 1999, page 207

Other books by the same author:
Looking for Atlantis, 1997
The Tower to the Sun, 1997

Other books you might like:
Jan Mark, *The Midas Touch*, 1999
  Too late a king learns the foolishness of his wish to have the power to turn everything he touches to gold in this illustrated retelling of a classic.
Diane Stanley, *Rumpelstiltskin's Daughter*, 1997
  In a take-off on the original tale, greedy kings still expect straw to be spun into gold.
William Steig, *The Toy Brother*, 1996
  Preoccupied with his efforts to turn donkey dung into gold, Yorick ignores his father's warning to stay out of lab and suffers the consequences.

987

COLIN THOMPSON
ANNA PIGNATARO, Illustrator

Unknown

(New York: Walker & Company, 2000)

Subject(s): Animals/Dogs; Animals, Treatment of; Courage
Age range(s): Grades 1-3
Major character(s): Unknown, Dog; Grown-too-Large, Dog
Time period(s): 2000s (2000)
Locale(s): Australia

Summary: Shelter dogs break into a cacophony of cries pleading for the visiting humans to give them a home. Some of the dogs are chosen but others wait to take their place in the cages. Grown-too-Large barks too much and scares people away. The big dog also scares timid little Unknown who shivers in the corner of her cage and is simply overlooked by the human visitors. During a violent storm, lightning ignites the trees beside the shelter and no one can hear the dogs' pleas for help over the noise of the storm. Grown-too-Large quivers in his cage, feeling too frightened to move. Unknown leaps into action, making a hole in her cage just big enough to wiggle through so she can race to the caretaker's cottage for help. Now Unknown is well known as a hero and soon has a home while Grown-too-Large simply drops his ferocious attitude and moves in with the caretaker's family. (32 pages)

Where it's reviewed:
Booklist, May 1, 2000, page 1680
Bulletin of the Center for Children's Books, May 2000, page 335
Horn Book Guide, Fall 2000, page 283
New York Times Book Review, May 14, 2000, page 29
School Library Journal, July 2000, page 88

Other books by the same author:
The Paradise Garden, 1998
How to Live Forever, 1996
Looking for Atlantis, 1993

Other books you might like:
Gloria Rand, *A Home for Spooky*, 1998
  Annie tries to secretly care for a starving stray dog, but realizes she needs her parent's help with Spooky's weak condition.
Tres Seymour, *Pole Dog*, 1993
  An abandoned dog sits forlornly near a telephone pole until rescued by a sympathetic family.
Jane Resh Thomas, *Scaredy Dog*, 1996
  Patiently a little girl helps her timid shelter puppy grow into a contented pet.

988

PATTI TRIMBLE
DANIEL MORETON, Illustrator

What Day Is It?

(San Diego: Harcourt, Inc., 2000)

Series: Green Light Readers. Level 1
Subject(s): Animals; Birthdays; Surprises
Age range(s): Grades K-1
Major character(s): Gil, Insect (ant); Ann, Insect (ladybug), Friend; Todd, Insect, Friend
Time period(s): Indeterminate
Locale(s): Fictional Country

Summary: What a great day! Gil looks forward to a special day, knowing that it is his birthday. When he meets Ann and asks her what day it is, Ann replies, ''Monday.'' The same thing happens when he runs into Todd. Gil feels dejected because his friends have forgotten him. He can't see what his friends try to hide whenever he appears, but finally the surprise is ready—a birthday party for Gil! (20 pages)

Where it's reviewed:
Booklist, April 15, 2000, page 1556
Horn Book Guide, Fall 2000, page 290
Publishers Weekly, March 27, 2000, page 83
School Library Journal, August 2000, page 154

Other books by the same author:
Lost!, 2000

Other books you might like:
Judy Katschke, *Flik's Perfect Gift*, 1998
  After considering many possible birthday gifts for Queen Atta, Flik settles on something simple that he makes himself.
David Kirk, *Miss Spider's ABC*, 1998
  Insects of every letter of the alphabet surprise Miss Spider with a wonderful birthday party.

Leslie Tryon, *Albert's Birthday*, 1999

Patsy Pig plans to surprise Albert with a birthday party but she forgets to include one detail—Albert!

989

VALERIE TRIPP
WALTER RANE, Illustrator

Meet Kit: An American Girl

(Middleton, WI: Pleasant Company Publications, 2000)

Series: American Girls, Kit Kittredge. Book 1
Subject(s): Depression (Economic); Resourcefulness; Change
Age range(s): Grades 2-4
Major character(s): Kit Kittredge, Daughter, 9-Year-Old; Ruthie Smithens, Friend (Kit's), 9-Year-Old; Stirling Howard, Child, Invalid
Time period(s): 1930s (1934)
Locale(s): Cincinnati, Ohio

Summary: The reality of the Depression comes to Kit's home first when Stirling and his mother move into the guest room. Stirling's father has been without a job for two years, the family loses its house and his father leaves town to look for work. Not long after Stirling's arrival Kit's father closes his car dealership for lack of business. Although Kit's willing to help the family she's shocked when her mother decides to take in paying boarders so they can meet the mortgage payments. Now, Kit loses her room to Stirling and his mother so the guest room can be rented. With supportive suggestions from Ruthie and Stirling, Kit realizes the attic to which she's been consigned can be transformed to suit her every interest so she creates a newspaper office in one alcove, a baseball nook in another, a reading corner and a "tree house" space for her bed. (69 pages)

Where it's reviewed:
Booklist, September 1, 2000, page 119
Horn Book Guide, Spring 2001, page 67
School Library Journal, December 2000, page 126

Other books by the same author:
Kit Learns a Lesson: A School Story, 2000 (American Girls, Kit Kittredge, Book 2)
Meet Josefina: An American Girl, 1997 (American Girls)
Felicity Saves the Day: A Summer Story, 1992 (American Girls)

Other books you might like:
David A. Adler, *The Babe & I*, 1999
In 1932 a young boy spots his father selling apples on the street corner and decides to sell newspapers to help support his family.
C. Coco De Young, *A Letter to Mrs. Roosevelt*, 1999
Margo uses a class assignment in letter writing to request that Eleanor Roosevelt help save her family's home.
Zilpha Keatley Snyder, *The Velvet Room*, 1965
Economic conditions during the Depression force Robin and her family to stay on the move in search of work and a place to live.

990

MAXINE TROTTIER
STELLA EAST, Illustrator

Dreamstones

(New York. Stoddart Kids, 2000)

Subject(s): Winter; Cultures and Customs; Voyages and Travels
Age range(s): Grades 1-3
Major character(s): David, Child, Son; Unnamed Character, Sea Captain, Father
Time period(s): Indeterminate Past
Locale(s): Arctic; *Lily*, At Sea

Summary: The sailing vessel *Lily* arrives in the far north just as the brief Arctic summer begins. David explores the area near the ship's anchorage while his father sketches the unique wildlife. David's father explains that the lichen-covered stone markers that remind David of the fur-wrapped Inuktitut people are called *Inukshuks* and are intended to guide people home. A sudden winter storm traps the *Lily* in a sea of ice forcing David, his father and the ship's crew to survive the long dark winter in a land where even the stones dream. Awakened one night by the sound of foxes, David leaves the ship and follows the Arctic animals until he becomes lost in the snow-covered hills. A native provides fire and a fur wrap to protect David until he's found, sleeping in front of an *Inukshuk*, by a search party from the ship in a title originally published in Canada in 1999. (24 pages)

Where it's reviewed:
Booklist, July 2000, page 2044
Children's Bookwatch, September 2000, page 5
Quill & Quire, September 1999, page 68
Resource Links, April 2000, page 7
School Library Journal, August 2000, page 166

Other books by the same author:
Little Dog Moon, 2000
Prairie Willow, 1998
Alison's House, 1996
The Tiny Kite of Eddie Wing, 1996

Other books you might like:
Lydia Dabcovich, *The Polar Bear Son: An Inuit Tale*, 1997
An elderly Inuit woman adopts an orphaned polar bear cub to hunt and fish for her.
Jean Craighead George, *Arctic Son*, 1997
At his birth Luke receives an Inuit name from the village leader who also teaches him the Inuit appreciation for nature and community.
Virginia Kroll, *The Seasons and Someone*, 1994
A young Inuit girl describes the seasonal changes in a life closely linked to time's natural cycle.
Carolyn Lesser, *Great Crystal Bear*, 1996
A poetic yet factually accurate description of a year in the life of a polar bear is complemented by illustrations.
Howard Norman, *The Girl Who Dreamed Only Geese and Other Tales of the Far North*, 1997
Ten tales drawn from the oral tradition portray the culture and customs of the Inuit.

991

GRACE TSENG
JEAN TSENG, Illustrator
MOU-SIEN TSENG, Illustrator

White Tiger, Blue Serpent
(New York: Lothrop, Lee & Shepard Books, 1999)

Subject(s): Fairy Tales; Mothers and Sons; Folk Tales
Age range(s): Grades 1-4
Major character(s): Kai, Child, Son; Mother, Single Mother; Qin, Diety
Time period(s): Indeterminate Past
Locale(s): China

Summary: While Mother weaves for a thousand days and a thousand nights to produce a special brocade just for her son, Kai labors to provide the food and firewood the family is unable to buy if they have no brocade to sell. Kai's efforts make him strong, quick and keen-sighted so he is able to pursue the completed brocade when a wind steals it and carries it across the river into the land of the goddess Qin. As Kai follows the brocade he must use the skill he's developed to overpower a huge white tiger and to outwit a ferocious blue sea serpent. Finally he confronts Qin who laughs greedily at him as she refuses the release the brocade she has stolen. The whirlwind Qin creates not only repels Kai and sends him back to his home but also causes all the images on the brocade to be swept up and sent with Kai to transform his barren homeland into a scene as beautiful as the brocade as the author's first book concludes. (32 pages)

Where it's reviewed:
Booklist, August 1999, page 2067
Horn Book Guide, Fall 1999, page 328
Kirkus Reviews, May 1, 1999, page 729
Publishers Weekly, June 7, 1999, page 83
School Library Journal, July 1999, page 81

Awards the book has won:
Notable Social Studies Trade Books for Young People, 2000

Other books you might like:
Marilee Heyer, *The Weaving of a Dream: A Chinese Folktale*, 1989
    A widow's youngest son succeeds in retrieving his mother's stolen brocade.
Robert D. San Souci, *The Enchanted Tapestry: A Chinese Folktale*, 1987
    Three sons attempt to find and return their ill mother's tapestry, but only the youngest succeeds.
Ruth Sanderson, *The Crystal Mountain*, 1999
    The wind carries a just-completed brocade to the fairies' enchanted mountain where it is found and recovered by the weaver's son.

992

MARGARET HOLLOWAY TSUBAKIYAMA
CORNELIUS VAN WRIGHT, Illustrator
YING-HWA HU, Illustrator

Mei-Mei Loves the Morning
(Morton Grove, IL: Albert Whitman & Company, 1999)

Subject(s): Grandfathers; Bicycles and Bicycling; City and Town Life
Age range(s): Grades K-2
Major character(s): Mei-Mei, Child; Grandpa, Grandfather; Bai-Ling, Bird
Time period(s): 1990s (1999)
Locale(s): China

Summary: Mei-Mei and Grandpa awaken before Mei-Mei's parents to eat a simple breakfast and feed Bai-Ling. Mei-Mei loves the morning activities she shares with Grandpa. As soon as they finish breakfast they hang Bai-Ling's cage on the handlebars of Grandpa's bike and together ride to the park. There they hang Bai-Ling's cage in a tree with other birds and meet friends for tai chi. When the graceful morning exercises conclude Grandpa and Mei-Mei return home through the crowded streets in the author's first picture book. (32 pages)

Where it's reviewed:
Booklist, March 15, 1999, page 1336
Horn Book Guide, Fall 1999, page 269
Kirkus Reviews, March 1, 1999, page 383
Publishers Weekly, April 5, 1999, page 240
School Library Journal, May 1999, page 99

Other books by the same author:
Lice Are Lousy!: All about Headlice, 1999 (nonfiction)

Other books you might like:
Judith Caseley, *Grandpa's Garden Lunch*, 1990
    Sarah's reward for helping Grandpa in his garden is a delicious lunch made from homegrown vegetables.
Niki Daly, *Not So Fast, Songololo*, 1986
    Malusi and his grandmother travel to the city to buy sneakers.
Jessie Haas, *Mowing*, 1994
    Early one morning, while Gramp and Nora mow the hay field they find a fawn and a bird's nest.
William Low, *Chinatown*, 1997
    Daily, a young boy walks with Grandma through the crowded streets of Chinatown, passing a tai chi class and greeting the street cobbler.
Sally Noll, *Lucky Morning*, 1994
    Nora and Granddaddy enjoy an early morning fishing trip while vacationing in Montana.
Eileen Spinelli, *It You Want to Find Golden*, 1993
    An early morning walk in the city allows a young boy and his mother to explore the changing, colorful effects of sunlight.

993

MICHAEL O. TUNNELL
KEVIN O'MALLEY, Illustrator

Halloween Pie

(New York: Lothrop, Lee & Shepard Books, 1999)

Subject(s): Witches and Witchcraft; Halloween; Monsters
Age range(s): Grades K-3
Major character(s): Old Witch, Witch
Time period(s): Indeterminate
Locale(s): Fictional Country

Summary: Old Witch sets her freshly baked Halloween pie on the windowsill to cool, protecting it with a magic spell. Then she takes off on her broom. The wind wafts the delicious odor of the pie over the graveyard, awakening a ghost, a ghoul, a vampire, a banshee, a zombie and a skeleton. The monsters descend on the witch's pie, devour every crumb and fall asleep in Old Witch's house. When Old Witch returns, her pie is gone, but her spell is complete for each monster is now a pie ingredient. Old Witch gathers the pumpkin, eggs, spices, sugar and cream and makes another pie. As the baked pie sits on the windowsill cooling, the odors wafting up contain the spirits of the monsters who drift back to their graveyard homes. (24 pages)

Where it's reviewed:
Booklist, September 15, 1999, page 270
Bulletin of the Center for Children's Books, September 1999, page 35
Children's Book Review Service, October 1999, page 185
Publishers Weekly, September 27, 1999, page 47
School Library Journal, September 1999, page 208

Other books by the same author:
Mailing May, 1997 (ALA Notable Books for Children)
Beauty and the Beastly Children, 1993
Chinook!, 1993

Other books you might like:
Charlotte Huck, *A Creepy Countdown*, 1998
Halloween symbols appear in a rhyming tale that uses the numbers one to ten and back again.
Bill Martin Jr., *Old Devil Wind*, 1993
A ghost begins the Halloween night's noise-making that concludes with the wind whooshing through the old haunted house.
Judy Sierra, *The House That Drac Built*, 1995
A rhyming cumulative tale introduces such unusual creatures as a manticore and the fiend of Bloodygore living in the house that Drac built.

994

ANN TURNER
DENNIS NOLAN, Illustrator

Red Flower Goes West

(New York: Hyperion Books for Children, 1999)

Subject(s): Voyages and Travels; Frontier and Pioneer Life; Family
Age range(s): Grades K-3
Major character(s): James, Son, Brother (older); Jenny, Daughter, Sister; Red Flower, Plant (geranium)
Time period(s): Indeterminate Past
Locale(s): United States

Summary: Gold fever and the promise of free land convinces James and Jenny's father to sell their belongings, buy oxen and a wagon and head west. Their mother insists on bringing a plant she digs from the garden that to Jenny and James soon becomes a symbol of their fortitude. Through the many hardships on the trail the children are sure that as long as Red Flower survives their family will be all right. While crossing the desert they share their meager water supply with Red Flower and someone holds the plant's box during rough river crossings. Eventually the family does reach California and Red Flower is planted in the ground as a testament to the family's survival. (32 pages)

Where it's reviewed:
Booklist, May 1, 1999, page 1602
Horn Book, September 1999, page 602
Kirkus Reviews, June 15, 1999, page 971
Publishers Weekly, June 14, 1999, page 69
School Library Journal, June 1999, page 108

Other books by the same author:
Dust for Dinner, 1995
Apple Valley Year, 1993
Nettie's Trip South, 1987

Other books you might like:
Eve Bunting, *Dandelions*, 1995
Dandelions found growing beside a prairie trail come to symbolize a pioneer family's resilience.
Roy Gerrard, *Wagons West!*, 1996
In a rhyming tale a family joins a wagon train heading west.
Jean Van Leeuwen, *A Fourth of July on the Plains*, 1997
Jessie is grateful that the wagon train stops for one day to allow all the families to celebrate Independence Day.
David Williams, *Grandma Essie's Covered Wagon*, 1993
As a child Essie traveled by covered wagon across the vast prairies.

U

995

CAROLINE UFF, Author/Illustrator

Hello, Lulu

(New York: Walker and Company, 1999)

Subject(s): Family; Pets; Brothers and Sisters
Age range(s): Preschool
Major character(s): Lulu, Child, Sister
Time period(s): 1990s (1999)
Locale(s): England

Summary: In the author's first book, Lulu cheerfully introduces her family members, pets and friend. Lulu proudly shows off new shoes in her favorite color—red! The three pets belonging to Lulu's family are a dog, a rabbit and a goldfish. Lulu enjoys blowing bubbles with her friend and eating snack at her grandmother's house. More than anything else, Lulu is happy for the love within her family. (24 pages)

Where it's reviewed:
Booklist, September 1, 1999, page 144
Children's Book Review Service, October 1999, page 186
Publishers Weekly, August 23, 1999, page 56
School Library Journal, September 1999, page 208
Smithsonian, November 1999, page 46

Awards the book has won:
Smithsonian's Notable Books for Children, 1999

Other books by the same author:
Happy Birthday, Lulu!, 2000
Lulu's Busy Day, 2000

Other books you might like:
Trish Cooke, *So Much*, 1994
 A baby is surrounded by loving relatives who want to hug and squeeze and play with the baby SO MUCH!
Anne Rockwell, *Long Ago Yesterday*, 1999
 Ten brief stories describe everyday family activities that are important to young children.
Vera B. Williams, *Lucky Song*, 1997
 At bedtime, after a busy day, Evie's father sings a song to her about her lucky day.

996

CAROLINE UFF, Author/Illustrator

Lulu's Busy Day

(New York: Walker & Company, 2000)

Subject(s): Playing; Friendship; Bedtime
Age range(s): Preschool
Major character(s): Lulu, Child
Time period(s): 2000s (2000)
Locale(s): England

Summary: Lulu stays busy all day drawing pictures, playing ball, and going to the park to swing. When the rain starts falling Lulu goes home to eat dinner and build castles with blocks. After Lulu cleans up her toys she has a bubble bath and brushes her teddy bear's teeth. Now they're both ready for a story and good night's sleep. (24 pages)

Where it's reviewed:
Booklist, March 1, 2000, page 1253
Horn Book Guide, Fall 2000, page 257
Publishers Weekly, February 14, 2000, page 203
School Library Journal, May 2000, page 156
Smithsonian, November 2000, page 62

Awards the book has won:
Smithsonian's Notable Books for Children, 2000

Other books by the same author:
Happy Birthday, Lulu!, 2000
Hello, Lulu, 1999

Other books you might like:
Lucy Cousins, *Maisy Takes a Bath*, 2000
 Bath time is fun for a playful young mouse.
Barbro Lindgren, *Sam's Teddy Bear*, 1982
 Sam's dog helps recover his special teddy bear.
Amy Schwartz, *Some Babies*, 2000
 A bedtime ritual for Baby is hearing Mommy's recitation of the varied activities of some babies at the park.

997

MYRON UHLBERG
GERALD FITZGERALD, Illustrator

Flying Over Brooklyn

(Atlanta: Peachtree Publishers, Ltd., 1999)

Subject(s): Winter; Dreams and Nightmares; City and Town Life
Age range(s): Grades K-3
Major character(s): Unnamed Character, Child, Son
Time period(s): 1940s (1947)
Locale(s): New York, New York (Brooklyn)

Summary: A young boy with a strong desire to fly does so one night in his dreams. He soars over the snow-covered landmarks of his community—Ebbets Field, Coney Island, Prospect Park and the Brooklyn Bridge. The dream comes to an end when his mother wakes him to show him the real wonderland outside his window—a record snowfall. A concluding note to the author's first book gives the historical inspiration for the story. (32 pages)

Where it's reviewed:
Booklist, December 1, 1999, page 707
Children's Book Review Service, October 1999, page 186
Horn Book Guide, Spring 2000, page 58
Publishers Weekly, October 4, 1999, page 74
School Library Journal, December 1999, page 114

Other books by the same author:
Mad Dog McGraw, 2000

Other books you might like:
Mark Karlins, *Music Over Manhattan*, 1998
With instruction from Uncle Louie, Bernie learns to play the trumpet so well that the music floats over Manhattan.
Ezra Jack Keats, *The Snowy Day*, 196
The Caldecott Medal winner expresses a young boy's joy with the first snowfall.
Faith Ringgold, *Tar Beach*, 1991
In an award-winning book Cassie Lightfoot soars over the rooftops of Harlem, viewing familiar sites from a new perspective.
Uri Shulevitz, *Snow*, 1998
A Caldecott Honor book celebrates the wonder of snow that falls one flake at a time to quietly cover an entire town.

998

MYRON UHLBERG
LYDIA MONKS, Illustrator

Mad Dog McGraw

(New York: G.P. Putnam's Sons, 2000)

Subject(s): Animals/Dogs; Problem Solving; Fear
Age range(s): Grades K-3
Major character(s): Mad Dog McGraw, Dog; Bait, Cat; Unnamed Character, Child, Son
Time period(s): 2000s (2000)
Locale(s): United States

Summary: Mad Dog is such a mean and ferocious dog that a young boy in the neighborhood tries to avoid the beast because he has no interest in learning if Mad Dog's bark will be followed by a bite. To protect himself from Mad Dog the child first tries stilts, but he falls and Mad Dog chases him home; then he tries to fly over the dog using an umbrella, but the wind dies and he sinks. Bait is the third plan, but Bait has no fear of the dog and the two animals sit sweetly together. Observing that behavior gives the boy an idea and he tries kindness toward Mad Dog rather than avoidance, a technique that works well. (32 pages)

Where it's reviewed:
Booklist, August 2000, page 2150
Bulletin for the Center for Children's Books, July 2000, page 417
Horn Book Guide, Spring 2001, page 52
Kirkus Reviews, June 1, 2000, page 804
School Library Journal, August 2000, page 166

Other books by the same author:
Lemuel the Fool, 2001
Flying Over Brooklyn, 1999

Other books you might like:
Carla Golembe, *Dog Magic*, 1997
Molly is afraid of the dogs in her neighborhood until she receives a pair of magic shoes that give her confidence.
Diana Hendry, *Dog Donovan*, 1995
The anxious Donovan family acquires a dog so timid that soon all the family members forget their own fears while caring for the dog.
Karen Hesse, *Lester's Dog*, 1993
Lester's dog has a reputation for meanness that suggests he is mistreated or neglected.

V

999

VLADIMIR VAGIN, Author/Illustrator

Peter and the Wolf

(New York: Scholastic Press, 2000)

Subject(s): Fairy Tales; Animals; Courage
Age range(s): Grades K-3
Major character(s): Peter, Child; Grandpapa, Grandfather
Time period(s): Indeterminate Past
Locale(s): Russia

Summary: Grandpapa warns Peter of a wolf sighting in the nearby forest and tells Peter to stay within the enclosed garden. The day is so beautiful that Peter soon forgets Grandpapa's warning. As Peter follows a bird in the meadow a duck escapes from the garden to follow Peter. A cat stalks the arguing bird and duck but Peter sees and warns the bird. Peter doesn't see the wolf until the duck's been swallowed and the wolf begins pacing beneath the tree where the bird and cat are. Clever Peter has a plan that captures the wolf so that the hunters can simply walk him to the zoo with Peter leading the way. Information about Prokofiev, composer of the symphony on which the story is based, concludes the book. (32 pages)

Where it's reviewed:
Booklist, November 15, 2000, page 644
Publishers Weekly, November 27, 2000, page 78
School Library Journal, November 2000, page 149

Other books by the same author:
The Enormous Carrot, 1998
The Nutcracker Ballet, 1995

Other books you might like:
Ian Beck, *Peter and the Wolf*, 1995
   An illustrated rendition of the story based on Prokofiev's symphony shows how Peter captures the wolf.
Michele Lemieux, *Peter and the Wolf*, 1991
   Ignoring grandfather's warnings about a wolf sighting in the area, Peter instead captures the wolf.

Colin McNaughton, *Oops!*, 1996
   Preston Pig does not try to capture the wolf but he does stay one step ahead of the wily critter.

1000

CHRIS VAN DUSEN, Author/Illustrator

Down to the Sea with Mr. Magee

(San Francisco: Chronicle Books, 2000)

Subject(s): Animals/Whales; Stories in Rhyme; Boats and Boating
Age range(s): Grades K-2
Major character(s): Mr. Magee, Sailor; Dee, Dog
Time period(s): Indeterminate Past
Locale(s): United States

Summary: It's a lovely day for a boat ride so Mr. Magee packs a lunch, loads Dee in the Studebaker and drives to the dock. The anticipated quiet day on the water turns out to be anything but when a playful young whale spouts a fountain of spray that lifts the boat into the air and strands Mr. Magee and Dee high in a spruce tree on a small island. The other whales in the pond come to the rescue with a synchronized slapping of tails that sends a huge splash of water high enough to dislodge the boat, allowing Dee and Mr. Magee to sail home and conclude the author/illustrator's first book. (32 pages)

Where it's reviewed:
Booklist, June 1, 2000, page 1911
Bulletin of the Center for Children's Books, May 2000, page 336
Children's Book Review Service, May 2000, page 113
Publishers Weekly, March 6, 2000, page 110
School Library Journal, May 2000, page 156

Other books you might like:
Cynthia Rylant, *Mr. Putter and Tabby Row the Boat*, 1997
   A boat trip on the pond on a hot summer day fails to help cither Mr. Putter or his cat feel any cooler.
Judy Sierra, *Counting Crocodiles*, 1997
   A folktale told in rhyme explains how a monkey travels

from one island to another without being eaten by crocodiles.

Chad Stuart, *The Ballymara Flood*, 1996
Stuck faucets turn a simple bath into a flood that quickly covers the town in a humorous rhyming story.

1001

NANCY VAN LAAN
AMY RUSCH, Illustrator

Moose Tales

(Boston: Houghton Mifflin Company, 1999)

Subject(s): Animals/Moose; Animals; Friendship
Age range(s): Grades 1-3
Major character(s): Moose, Moose, Friend; Beaver, Beaver, Friend
Time period(s): Indeterminate
Locale(s): Fictional Country

Summary: Three brief stories for beginning readers describe Moose's activities with his friends. On a beautiful sunny day Moose wants to go for a walk, but he's unable to find a friend to walk with him. By the time he's walked up and down the hills making inquiries of different friends, his legs are so tired that only wants to rest. In the second story Moose's nap near a tree that Beaver is gnawing on creates problems when he wakes up, bumps the tree and it topples onto Beaver. Moose calls all their friends to help get Beaver free. The final story takes place on a snowy day. Moose and Beaver join others to create a perfect snow creature with big teeth like Beaver, whiskers like the mouse, long ears like the rabbit, a bushy tail like the squirrel and antlers like Moose. (48 pages)

Where it's reviewed:
Booklist, October 15, 1999, page 446
Children's Book Review Service, September 1999, page 177
Kirkus Reviews, September 1, 1999, page 1423
Publishers Weekly, August 23, 1999, page 58
School Library Journal, December 1999, page 114

Other books by the same author:
A Tree for Me, 2000
So Say the Little Monkeys, 1998
Little Baby Bobby, 1997
Shingebiss: An Ojibwe Legend, 1997

Other books you might like:
Jim Latimer, *Moose and Friends*, 1993
The adventures of Moose continue in this tale of Moose and his animal friends.
Arnold Lobel, *Frog and Toad Together*, 1972
The Newbery Honor book is one of four titles describing the adventures and misadventures of loyal friends Frog and Toad.
James Marshall, *George and Martha*, 1972
The first book in a series about George and Martha uses several brief, humorous stories to describe the antics of two hippo buddies.
Cynthia Rylant, *Poppleton Forever*, 1998
Three glimpses of Poppleton's life show the efforts of his supportive friends to help him with different problems.

James Stevenson, *Mud Flat April Fool*, 1998
In ten brief chapters the animal residents of Mud Flat have fun trying to trick one another with April Fool's Day jokes.
Bernard Wiseman, *Morris and Boris at the Circus*, 1988
Pals Morris the Moose and Boris the Bear attend the circus together.

1002

NANCY VAN LAAN
SUSAN GABER, Illustrator

When Winter Comes

(New York: An Anne Schwartz Book/Atheneum Books for Young Readers, 2000)

Subject(s): Winter; Animals; Stories in Rhyme
Age range(s): Grades K-2
Time period(s): 2000s (2000)
Locale(s): United States

Summary: As snow begins to fall a family walks through the remnants of fallen leaves wondering where they go during winter. The child looks at dying flowers and thinks of the seeds hiding for the winter, but wonders where caterpillars go until spring. To each of the child's questions about birds, mice or fish, the parents offer a simple explanation. The snow is deeper by the time the walk concludes, the child too tired to walk. And where do tired children go in winter? They're tucked into bed, snug and warm. (32 pages)

Where it's reviewed:
Horn Book Guide, Spring 2001, page 25
Kirkus Reviews, October 1, 2000, page 1435
Publishers Weekly, October 23, 2000, page 74
Riverbank Review, Winter 2000-2001, page 33
School Library Journal, November 2000, page 136

Awards the book has won:
Charlotte Zolotow Highly Commended Book, 2001

Other books by the same author:
So Say the Little Monkeys, 1998 (School Library Journal Best Book)
Little Baby Bobby, 1997
Mama Rocks, Papa Sings, 1995

Other books you might like:
Jean Craighead George, *Dear Rebecca, Winter Is Here*, 1993
On the day of the winter solstice, a grandmother writes to her granddaughter describing the changes that indicate winter's arrival.
Bruce Hiscock, *When Will It Snow?*, 1995
A child awaits the answer to his question while animals simply prepare for the season's first snowfall.
Seymour Simon, *Winter Across America*, 1994
A factual photographic journey across America portrays the changes in nature during the winter season.

1003

JEAN VAN LEEUWEN
DONNA DIAMOND, Illustrator

Hannah's Helping Hands

(New York: Phyllis Fogelman Books/Penguin Putnam, 1999)

Series: Pioneer Daughters
Subject(s): Revolutionary War; Historical; Family Life
Age range(s): Grades 3-5
Major character(s): Hannah Perley, 10-Year-Old, Sister; Rebecca Perley, Sister, Teenager; Ben Perley, Brother (oldest), Military Personnel
Time period(s): 1770s (1779)
Locale(s): Fairfield, Connecticut

Summary: Though the war for independence has been raging for four years and their older brother has been fighting in it for two years, daily life at the Perley home has changed little. Hannah and Rebecca help their mother with spring cleaning and laundry while their brothers help in the fields or in their father's clock shop. With Ben away, Hannah's lucky to be able to help with sheep shearing and her helping hands heal an injured ram. When Ben comes home on leave he warns the family to be vigilant because the British have increased their nightly raids. Indeed, Fairfield is attacked during one such raid and, though the Perley home is burned, the helping hands of the Perley family save the animals and help to rebuild the house. (88 pages)

Where it's reviewed:
Booklist, September 15, 1999, page 262
Horn Book Guide, Spring 2000, page 71
Kirkus Reviews, August 15, 1999, page 1316
School Library Journal, November 1999, page 131

Other books by the same author:
Hannah's Winter of Hope, 2000 (Pioneer Daughters)
Oliver and Albert, Friends Forever, 2000
Hannah of Fairfield, 1999 (Pioneer Daughters)

Other books you might like:
Lisa Banim, *A Spy in the King's Colony*, 1994
  For Emily and Maggie, during the British occupation of Boston, everyone is suspected of being a possible Loyalist spy.
Kristiana Gregory, *The Winter of Red Snow: The Revolutionary War Diary of Abigail Jane Stewart*, 1996
  A "Dear America" series title presents daily events during the army's winter at Valley Forge through the diary of 11-year-old Abby.
Elizabeth Massie, *Patsy's Discovery*, 1997
  In 1776 Philadelphia, Patsy and Barbara use their little free time to form a club, the "Daughters of Liberty," that is dedicated to doing good deeds.
Valerie Tripp, *Felicity Saves the Day: A Summer Story*, 1992
  Felicity must choose between responsibility to her father and a desire to help his apprentice, Ben, who wants to run away and join Washington's army.

1004

JEAN VAN LEEUWEN
ANN SCHWENINGER, Illustrator

Oliver and Albert, Friends Forever

(New York: Phyllis Fogelman Books, 2000)

Series: Dial Easy-to-Read
Subject(s): Animals/Pigs; Friendship; Schools
Age range(s): Grades 1-2
Major character(s): Oliver, Pig, Friend; Albert, Pig, Friend
Time period(s): Indeterminate
Locale(s): Fictional Country

Summary: By the time recess concludes on Albert's first day in Oliver's class everyone knows that Albert can read but he can't run, catch or play kickball. Oliver knows that too and he also knows that he's found a friend in this tall new student who shares his love of bugs. Oliver helps Albert improve his kickball skills and Albert helps Oliver learn to read. Together they contribute to the bug collection on the classroom's science table because helping each other is what friends do best. (48 pages)

Where it's reviewed:
Booklist, December 1, 2000, page 727
Horn Book Guide, Spring 2001, page 58
Horn Book, September 2000, page 584
Kirkus Reviews, August 15, 2000, page 1205
School Library Journal, November 2000, page 136

Other books by the same author:
Amanda Pig and Her Best Friend Lollipop, 1998
Oliver and Amanda and the Big Snow, 1995
Oliver and Amanda's Halloween, 1992

Other books you might like:
Tony Johnston, *Sparky and Eddie: Wild, Wild Rodeo!*, 1998
  Sparky is disappointed his class does not beat Eddie's class in the school rodeo, but he's happy to still have his friendship with Eddie.
Stephen Krensky, *Lionel and His Friends*, 1996
  Four brief stories continue the adventures of Lionel and his friends at school and at play.
Harriet Ziefert, *Mike and Tony: Best Friends*, 1987
  Until they have an argument, Mike and Tony are inseparable; now they have to find a way to get together again.

1005

JULIA VAN NUTT
ROBERT VAN NUTT, Illustrator

The Mystery of Mineral Gorge: A Cobtown Story from the Diaries of Lucky Hart

(New York: Doubleday Book for Young Readers, 1999)

Subject(s): Diaries; Ghosts; Fear
Age range(s): Grades 2-4
Major character(s): Lucky Hart, 10-Year-Old; Heddy Peggler, Aunt; Jasper Payne, Child, Friend (Lucky's); Fliberty Jibbert, Civil Servant (town elder)
Time period(s): 1840s (1845)
Locale(s): Cobtown

Summary: Loud screams emanating nightly from Mineral Gorge have most of the townspeople quaking with fear. Aunt Heddy Peggler dismisses the talk of ghosts and suggests organizing a search party. Although many agree with the idea, only Jasper and Fliberty join Aunt Heddy and Lucky at the meeting point and venture into Mineral Gorge. The screams seem to be growing weaker, but the group locates the cave entrance from which they come and bravely enter to confront the mystery. (48 pages)

Where it's reviewed:
Booklist, August 1999, page 2060
Children's Bookwatch, July 1999, page 3
Horn Book Guide, Fall 1999, page 286
Publishers Weekly, June 21, 1999, page 70
School Library Journal, July 1999, page 82

Other books by the same author:
Pignapped!: A Cobtown Story from the Diaries of Lucky Hart, 2000
The Monster in the Shadows, 2000
Pumpkins from the Sky?: A Cobtown Story from the Diaries of Lucky Hart, 1999

Other books you might like:
Betsy Byars, *The Golly Sister Go West*, 1986
Six stories trace the amusing travels of two comical sisters on the frontier.
Janice Del Negro, *Lucy Dove*, 1998
Lucy Dove bravely accepts a challenge to sit in a graveyard and sew a pair of trousers by the light of a full moon.
Gery Greer, *Billy the Ghost and Me*, 1997
Sarah tries to redirect Billy's pranks so they will benefit the town in a beginning chapter book. Bob Ruddick, co-author

1006

VIVIAN VANDE VELDE

There's a Dead Person Following My Sister Around

(San Diego: Harcourt Brace & Company, 1999)

Subject(s): Ghosts; Slavery; Underground Railroad
Age range(s): Grades 4-7
Major character(s): Ted Beatson, 11-Year-Old, Brother (older); Vicki Beatson, Kindergartner, Sister; Marella, Spirit (ghost)
Time period(s): 1990s (1999)
Locale(s): Rochester, New York

Summary: Some little sisters have imaginary friends, but the one that Vicki talks about is a ghost named Marella. Ted thinks that Marella and the "bad lady" with her are somehow connected to the history of his family's home. Research into the lives of the builders, Ted's great-great grandparents, leads Ted to a journal in the attic. From his great-great grandmother's entries he learns that the house was sometimes used to shelter runaway slaves and two of them drowned in the canal behind the house. Marella wants to return to life by taking over the body of a living child her age. She has tried with other five-year-old residents and finally she succeeds with Vicki. Now, how does Ted get rid of Marella and get Vicki back? (143 pages)

Where it's reviewed:
Booklist, September 1, 1999, page 124
Bulletin of the Center for Children's Books, October 1999, page 72
Kirkus Reviews, September 15, 1999, page 1507
Publishers Weekly, August 30, 1999, page 85
School Library Journal, September 1999, page 229

Other books by the same author:
Never Trust a Dead Man, 1999
Ghost of a Hanged Man, 1998
Curses, Inc. and Other Stories, 1997

Other books you might like:
Avi, *Something Upstairs: A Tale of Ghosts*, 1988
When Kenny moves into an old home in Rhode Island, he finds it haunted by the ghost of a murdered slave.
Bruce Coville, *Bruce Coville's Book of Ghosts: Tales to Haunt You*, 1994
A compilation of thirteen ghost stories ranges from frightening to funny.
Betty Ren Wright, *A Ghost in the Family*, 1998
Chad accompanies a friend on a two-week stay at her aunt's boarding house and discovers a ghost haunting his room.
Jane Yolen, *The Haunted House: A Collection of Original Stories*, 1995
A succession of families rent "The Close," a ramshackle house with a past waiting to be told. Martin Greenburg, co-editor.

1007

MARCIA VAUGHAN
BILL FARNSWORTH, Illustrator

Abbie Against the Storm: The True Story of a Young Heroine and a Lighthouse

(Hillsboro, OR: Beyond Words Publishing, Inc., 1999)

Subject(s): Lighthouses; Weather; Courage
Age range(s): Grades 2-4
Major character(s): Abbie Burgess, Teenager, Daughter; Papa, Father, Lighthouse Keeper; Mahala Burgess, Sister (younger)
Time period(s): 1850s (1856)
Locale(s): Mantinicus, Maine

Summary: When Papa moves his family to the stone house on Mantinicus Rock where he is to be the keeper of the twin lighthouses Abbie takes an immediate interest in his job. She becomes his unofficial assistant and Papa confidently places the lights in her hands when he makes an overnight trip to the mainland for supplies. After Papa departs a winter storm begins to rage and Abbie, with help only from inexperienced Mahala, must keep the lights burning not just overnight but for four weeks before Papa is able to return. An Epilogue tells of Abbie's life after the events of the story. (32 pages)

Where it's reviewed:
Booklist, April 1, 2000, page 1478
Horn Book Guide, Spring 2000, page 72
Publishers Weekly, February 7, 2000, page 85
School Library Journal, July 2000, page 89

Other books by the same author:
Whistling Dixie, 1995
The Sea-Breeze Hotel, 1992
Wombat Stew, 1985

Other books you might like:
Deborah Hopkinson, *Birdie's Lighthouse*, 1997
  When her father is ill 10-year-old Birdie tends the lighthouse alone during a northeaster.

Arielle North Olson, *The Lighthouse Keeper's Daughter*, 1987
  During her father's absence, Miranda tends the lamps so the Lighthouse beacons continue to shine brightly.
Peter Roop, *Keep the Lights Burning, Abbie*, 1985
  A fictionalized biography tells how Abbie tends two lighthouses when storms prevent her father's return from the mainland. Connie Roop, co-author.

W

1008

BERNARD WABER, Author/Illustrator

The Mouse That Snored

(Boston: Houghton Mifflin Company, 2000)

Subject(s): Animals/Mice; Conduct of Life; Stories in Rhyme
Age range(s): Grades K-2
Major character(s): Will, Parrot; Mose, Cat; Unnamed Character, Mouse
Time period(s): Indeterminate Past
Locale(s): Fictional Country

Summary: A very quiet couple and their pets Mose and Will abide so quietly in their home that they eat only soft foods (nothing crunchy), dine without speaking and whisper good night to one another. Their subdued routine changes on a stormy night when a cold wet mouse sneaks into the sleeping house, raids the pantry and then settles down for a good night's sleep. The snores that soon emanate from the mouse are so loud that the home's tired occupants are soon in the pantry wondering why the mouse is here. Mose, Will and the puzzled couple listen sympathetically to the mouse's tale, invite him to stay and teach him how to live quietly within the house. The mouse's snoring is uncontrollable so everyone learns to sleep with earplugs. (32 pages)

Where it's reviewed:
Booklist, August 2000, page 2150
Horn Book, November 2000, page 750
Publishers Weekly, August 7, 2000, page 94
School Library Journal, October 2000, page 140

Other books by the same author:
Lyle at Christmas, 1998
Bearsie Bear and the Surprise Sleepover Party, 1997 (Charlotte Zolotow, Highly Commended)
A Lion Named Shirley Williamson, 1996
Do You See a Mouse?, 1995

Other books you might like:
Ann McGovern, *Too Much Noise*, 1967
An old man complains that his noisy house interferes with his sleep; the advice of the village wise man helps him find the quiet he seeks.
Bernard Most, *Z-Z-Zoink!*, 1999
A little pig with a loud snore tries sleeping in many areas on the farm before finding a location that doesn't disturb others.
Teri Sloat, *The Thing That Bothered Farmer Brown*, 1995
A buzzing mosquito keeps Farmer Brown from sleeping.

1009

MARTIN WADDELL
BARBARA FIRTH, Illustrator

Good Job, Little Bear

(Cambridge, MA: Candlewick Press, 1999)

Subject(s): Animals/Bears; Self-Reliance; Independence
Age range(s): Preschool
Major character(s): Little Bear, Bear; Big Bear, Bear
Time period(s): Indeterminate
Locale(s): Fictional Country

Summary: Little Bear proudly shows Big Bear all he can do as the two bears explore the woods. Little Bear climbs a rock and jumps off it into the arms of watchful Big Bear. After climbing onto the bouncy branch of a tree Little Bear bounces so much he bounces off—into the arms of Big Bear who rushes to catch Little Bear. Stepping stones across a stream are the next challenge Little Bear tackles but this time Little Bear slips and splashes into the water. Big Bear wades in, pulls Little Bear to safety and then takes the lead as they explore their way back to the cave where Big Bear wraps Little Bear in a warm blanket and promises to always be near when Little Bear needs him. (32 pages)

Where it's reviewed:
Booklist, August 1999, page 2067
Children's Bookwatch, July 1999, page 3
Horn Book, March 1999, page 203
Publishers Weekly, April 5, 1999, page 243
School Library Journal, May 1999, page 100

Awards the book has won:
IRA/CBC Children's Choices, 2000

Other books by the same author:
Tom Rabbit, 2001
Small Bear Lost, 1996
You and Me, Little Bear, 1996
Let's Go Home, Little Bear, 1993
Can't You Sleep, Little Bear?, 1992

Other books you might like:
Debi Gliori, *Mr. Bear's New Baby*, 1999
It takes a big brother to understand how to soothe a crying baby bear so everyone can get some sleep.
Hiawyn Oram, *Kiss It Better*, 2000
Anytime Little Bear is feeling blue Big Bear is nearby to offer comfort. One day it is Big Bear who needs hugs and kisses from Little Bear.
Ursel Scheffler, *Who Has Time for Little Bear?*, 1998
Mama and Papa are too busy to play with Little Bear so he goes walking in the woods until he meets another bear cub that's eager to play.
Rosemary Wells, *Edward's Overwhelming Overnight*, 1995
In one of a series about Edward's forays into independence, the young bear's first attempt at a sleepover reveals that he's not quite ready.

1010

MARTIN WADDELL
SALLEY MAVOR, Illustrator

The Hollyhock Wall

(Cambridge, MA: Candlewick Press, 1999)

Subject(s): Gardens and Gardening; Dreams and Nightmares; Imagination
Age range(s): Grades K-2
Major character(s): Mary, Child, Daughter; Tom, Friend
Time period(s): Indeterminate Past
Locale(s): Fictional Country

Summary: Responding to Mary's wish for a garden, her mother suggests creating one in an old pot. As the seeds grow, Mary enhances the space with a ribbon stream, matchbox bridge and painted hollyhock wall. Then she creates a clay boy and wheelbarrow and gives Tom a fishing rod so he'll have something to do. While Mary is sleeping she dreams she is in the garden with Tom and the next day a clay girl who looks remarkably like Mary appears in the pot. Before Mary can make sense of these strange occurrences she visits her grandmother's new home and discovers a hollyhock wall just beyond the garden and, on the other side, a boy named Tom who is eager to play. (32 pages)

Where it's reviewed:
Booklist, August 1999, page 2067
ForeWord, August 1999, page 76
Kirkus Reviews, June 1, 1999, page 890
Publishers Weekly, June 28, 1999, page 78
School Library Journal, July 1999, page 82

Other books by the same author:
John Joe and the Big Hen, 1995
Once There Were Giants, 1995

The Big, Big Sea, 1994

Other books you might like:
Vivian French, *The Thistle Princess*, 1998
A thistle in the royal garden changes into a baby for a lonely king and queen who, unfortunately, stifle their princess with overly protective love.
Kathryn Lasky, *Sophie and Rose*, 1998
Sophie finds a very old doll that once belonged to her mother and grandmother and that quickly becomes her companion and playmate.
Elizabeth Spurr, *The Gumdrop Tree*, 1994
A little girl plants her gumdrops in her garden with surprising results.

1011

MARTIN WADDELL
CAMILLA ASHWORTH, Illustrator

Who Do You Love?

(Cambridge, MA: Candlewick Press, 1999)

Subject(s): Parent and Child; Love; Bedtime
Age range(s): Grades K-2
Major character(s): Holly, Cat, Daughter; Mama, Cat, Mother
Time period(s): Indeterminate Past
Locale(s): Fictional Country

Summary: When Mama asks Holly to get ready for bed, Holly responds by requesting her favorite game while getting ready. Mama relents and asks, ''Who do you love, Holly?'' Each time the question is asked Holly responds with a different family member and the reasons why she loves that individual. By the time her bedtime ritual is complete Holly has described her love for everyone except Mama. She's saved her for last so the game can end with their mutual expression of love. (32 pages)

Where it's reviewed:
Booklist, June 1999, page 1845
Horn Book Guide, Fall 1999, page 242
Kirkus Reviews, March 15, 1999, page 458
Publishers Weekly, April 26, 1999, page 80
School Library Journal, June 1999, page 108

Other books by the same author:
Good Job, Little Bear, 1999 (IRA/CBC Children's Choices)
Yum, Yum, Yummy!, 1998
Mimi and the Dream House, 1995
Rosie's Babies, 1990

Other books you might like:
Barbara M. Joosse, *I Love You the Purplest*, 1996
Mama's responses to her sons' many questions affirm her love for each of them.
Sam McBratney, *Guess How Much I Love You*, 1995
Little Nutbrown Hare enjoys playing a game with his father in which each professes the magnitude of his love for the other.
Lisa McCourt, *I Love You, Stinky Face*, 1997
In replying to her child's questions, Mama is ready with tender, loving words of reassurance and never-ending love.

Susan L. Roth, *My Love for You*, 1997

Love is quantified in comparison to animals and their attributes until the pinnacle of being "loftier than ten lovebirds soaring. . ." is reached.

1012

JAN WAHL
BOB DOUCET, Illustrator

The Field Mouse and the Dinosaur Named Sue

(New York: Cartwheel Books/Scholastic Inc., 2000)

Subject(s): Dinosaurs; Animals/Mice; Paleontology
Age range(s): Grades K-2
Major character(s): Field Mouse, Mouse; Sue, Dinosaur (skeleton)
Time period(s): 1990s
Locale(s): South Dakota; Chicago, Illinois (The Field Museum)

Summary: When paleontologists take the bone that serves as the roof of Field Mouse's comfortable home burrowed into a dry hillside he goes in search of it. Thus, Field Mouse is inadvertently closed up in one of the scientists' packing crates and transported far from the South Dakota hills. By day Field Mouse hides in the large building where the boxes were unloaded, listening to workers talk about "Sue" and wondering what that is. By night Field Mouse searches the many dinosaur skeletons in the museum trying to find his bone. When the assembly of Sue is complete Field Mouse explores her skeleton too until, finally, he finds his bone in the middle of her foot. At last, Field Mouse can make a nest and sleep in his own home again. Factual information about the discovery of Sue, the largest and most complete tyrannosaurus rex skeleton ever found is appended. (32 pages)

Where it's reviewed:
Booklist, May 15, 2000, page 150
Horn Book Guide, Fall 2000, page 284
Publishers Weekly, May 8, 2000, page 223
School Library Journal, August 2000, page 167

Other books by the same author:
I Met a Dinosaur, 1997
Little Gray One, 1993
My Cat Ginger, 1992

Other books you might like:
Paulette Bourgeois, *Franklin's Class Trip*, 1999
Franklin is relieved to discover that the "real" dinosaurs at the museum are actually skeletons not living creatures. Sharon Jennings, co-author.
Wolfram Hanel, *Lila's Little Dinosaur*, 1994
A rainbow-striped dinosaur follows Lila home from the Museum of Natural History.
Pat Relf, *A Dinosaur Named Sue: The Story of the Colossal Fossil*, 2000
A nonfiction work tells the story of the discovery and reconstruction of the most complete T. rex fossil ever found.

Joanne Ryder, *Tyrannosaurus Time*, 1999
This entry in the "Just for a Day" series invites readers to imagine life as a tyrannosaurus for one day.

1013

NEIL WALDMAN, Author/Illustrator

The Starry Night

(Honesdale, PA: Boyds Mills Press, 1999)

Subject(s): Artists and Art; Museums; Fantasy
Age range(s): Grades 1-4
Major character(s): Bernard, Child; Vincent van Gogh, Artist
Time period(s): 1990s (1999)
Locale(s): New York, New York

Summary: One day while in Central Park, Bernard runs into an old man who is painting. The man introduces himself as Vincent, and says he has come to paint the city so Bernard offers to show him around. Vincent and Bernard travel all over the city, finally ending up at the Museum of Modern Art where Vincent shows Bernard a painting entitled "The Starry Night." Bernard is so inspired he tries to sketch his own version of "The Starry Night." (32 pages)

Where it's reviewed:
Booklist, November 11, 1999, page 541
Five Owls, November 1999, page 43
School Library Journal, October 1999, page 129

Other books by the same author:
Masada, 1998
The Neverending Greenness, 1997
The Two Brothers: A Legend of Jerusalem, 1997

Other books you might like:
Laurence Anholt, *Camille and the Sunflowers: A Story about Vincent Van Gogh*, 1994
Camille befriends the much ridiculed Vincent van Gogh when he comes to live in his village.
Michael Dionetti, *Painting the Wind*, 1996
When Vincent van Gogh comes to live in Claudine's house, she defends him against her neighbors.
Joan Shaddox Isom, *The First Starry Night*, 1998
Jacques sees past the rough exterior of his "brother of the heart," Vincent van Gogh.

1014

BARBARA BROOKS WALLACE

Ghosts in the Gallery

(New York: A Jean Karl Book/Atheneum Books for Young Readers, 2000)

Subject(s): Orphans; Grandfathers; Mystery
Age range(s): Grades 4-6
Major character(s): Jenny Bekins, 11-Year-Old, Orphan; Winston Graymark, Handicapped, Businessman; Jingle, 11-Year-Old, Servant; Madame Dupray, Care Giver; Violet, Care Giver
Time period(s): Indeterminate Past
Locale(s): East Coast (Graymark House)

Summary: Having traveled all the way from China after the death of her stepfather and mother Jenny expects to be welcomed when she arrives at her grandfather's home. Alas, no one is expecting and, in fact, Winston Graymark doubts her story that she is a family relative but, at the urging of Madame Dupray, he allows her to stay on as a servant in the household. Sad, confused Jenny trusts Madame Dupray and her assistant Violet but fears Mr. Graymark. Jingle sometimes assists her with chores, invites her on errands in the village and introduces her to puppies out in the stable. Together Jingle and Jenny sneak a puppy into the room of Winston's father, the man Jenny thinks is her grandfather. Unwittingly, they help to unravel the mystery of Winston's poor health, Violet's sour disposition and Jenny's true identity. (136 pages)

Where it's reviewed:
Booklist, April 1, 2000, page 1475
Horn Book Guide, Fall 2000, page 314
Horn Book, July 2000, page 469
Kirkus Reviews, June 1, 2000, page 805
School Library Journal, July 2000, page 112

Other books by the same author:
Sparrows in the Scullery, 1997 (Edgar Allan Poe Award for Best Children's Mystery)
Cousins in the Castle, 1996
The Twin in the Tavern, 1994 (Edgar Allan Poe Award for Best Children's Mystery)
The Barrel in the Basement, 1985

Other books you might like:
Franny Billingsley, *The Folk Keeper*, 1999
When Corin is taken from a foundling home to work as a folk keeper of an estate she discovers that her true identity as Corinna threatens her life.
Frances Hodgson Burnett, *The Secret Garden*, 1911
Orphaned Mary is sent to live on the Yorkshire Moors where she unlocks the secret to an overgrown garden and an invalid cousin's health.
L.M. Montgomery, *Anne of Green Gables*, 1935
A lonely brother and sister ask an orphanage to send a boy to help with the farm work but 11-year-old Anne arrives instead.

1015

IAN WALLACE, Author/Illustrator

Boy of the Deeps

(New York: DK Ink/DK Publishing, Inc., 1999)

Subject(s): Miners and Mining; Fathers and Sons; Work
Age range(s): Grades 2-4
Major character(s): James, Son, Miner; Da, Father, Miner
Time period(s): Indeterminate Past
Locale(s): Cape Breton, Nova Scotia, Canada

Summary: James is proud that he is now old enough to begin working underground beside Da, an experienced coal miner. With only their oil lamps for illumination James, Da and the other miners descend into the intense, damp darkness of the mine. By the time they reach the wall of coal on which they are to work, they are far beneath the Atlantic Ocean. With only pick ax, shovel and gunpowder Da and James labor to extract the coal and shovel it into the carts hauled by the pit ponies. After a lunch break, just as they prepare to return to work they are trapped by a cave-in. With their tools and their hands James and Da create a small tunnel through which they crawl to safety. Though they can look forward to a warm dinner they also know they will return to the deeps for such is the life of a miner at the turn of the century. The author's memory of the stories told by his grandfather about his experiences as a miner inspires the story. (32 pages)

Where it's reviewed:
Booklist, March 15, 1999, page 1336
Hungry Mind Review, Spring 1999, page 37
Kirkus Reviews, March 15, 1999, page 458
Publishers Weekly, April 26, 1999, page 83
School Library Journal, July 1999, page 82

Awards the book has won:
Smithsonian's Notable Books for Children, 1999
Notable Social Studies Trade Books for Young People, 2000

Other books by the same author:
A Winter's Tale, 1997
Morgan the Magnificent, 1988
The Sparrow's Song, 1987
Chin Chiang and the Dragon's Dance, 1984

Other books you might like:
Susan Campbell Bartoletti, *Growing Up in Coal Country*, 1996
A photoessay documents the life of child laborers in the coalmines of Pennsylvania at the turn of the century.
Elisa Bartone, *Peppe the Lamplighter*, 1993
In a Caldecott Honor book Peppe helps to support his immigrant family by lighting the city's street lamps.
George Ella Lyon, *Mama Is a Miner*, 1994
A child reflects on her mother's job deep underground in a coal mine.

1016

JOHN WALLACE, Author/Illustrator

Tiny Rabbit Goes to a Birthday Party

(New York: Holiday House, 2000)

Subject(s): Birthdays; Animals/Rabbits; Animals
Age range(s): Grades K-1
Major character(s): Tiny Rabbit, Rabbit; Blue Mouse, Mouse; Striped Cat, Cat
Time period(s): Indeterminate
Locale(s): Fictional Country

Summary: Tiny Rabbit is thrilled to receive an invitation to Blue Mouse's birthday party. He carefully selects a big empty cardboard box to wrap for a present. At the last minute shy Tiny Rabbit's anxiety over attending his first party threatens to overpower his excitement. At first Tiny Rabbit just watches the others having fun, but Blue Mouse greets him and is so happy with the present that Tiny Rabbit begins to feel more confident. When Striped Cat reaches out a paw in friendship Tiny Rabbit is finally able to join in the games with the other partygoers. All in all the party is so much fun that Tiny Rabbit begins planning one for his birthday as soon as he returns home. (32 pages)

Where it's reviewed:
Booklist, February 1, 2000, page 1030
Horn Book Guide, Fall 2000, page 258
Kirkus Reviews, January 15, 2000, page 125
Publishers Weekly, February 14, 2000, page 197
School Library Journal, April 2000, page 116

Other books by the same author:
Building a House with Mr. Bumble, 1997
Little Bean's Friend, 1997
Little Bean, 1996

Other books you might like:
Nancy White Carlstrom, *Happy Birthday, Jesse Bear!*, 1994
From the first preparations to the party fun Jesse Bear excitedly describes his fourth birthday.
Lee Davis, *P.B. Bear's Birthday Party*, 1994
Stuffed-animal friends gather to help P.B. Bear celebrate his birthday.
Pat Hutchins, *Titch and Daisy*, 1996
While attending a party shy Titch hides until he finds his friend Daisy and then they enjoy the party together.
Emily Arnold McCully, *Speak Up, Blanche!*, 1991
Shy Blanche finds a way to participate in the Farm Theater as a set designer.

1017

KAREN WALLACE
LYDIA MONKS, Illustrator

City Pig

(New York: Orchard Books, 2000)

Subject(s): Animals/Pigs; Conduct of Life; Self-Awareness
Age range(s): Grades K-1
Major character(s): Dolores, Pig, Worker
Time period(s): 1990s
Locale(s): Fictional Country

Summary: Dolores is a pig that has it all—a penthouse apartment, a fast car, an important job—but still Dolores is not happy. She tries various hobbies, but none are satisfying. When her work begins to suffer her boss sends her on a much-needed vacation and Dolores visits the country for the first time. There, she discovers other pigs and is amazed at the carefree life they live. Realizing she's found what she's been missing Dolores calls her boss and quits her job. Originally published in Great Britain in 1999. (32 pages)

Where it's reviewed:
Booklist, February 15, 2000, page 1123
Horn Book Guide, Fall 2000, page 285
Kirkus Reviews, March 1, 2000, page 309
Publishers Weekly, February 7, 2000, page 84
School Library Journal, March 2000, page 219

Other books by the same author:
Imagine You Are a Tiger, 1996
Bears in the Forest, 1994
Red Fox, 1994

Other books you might like:
Jill Kastner, *Barnyard Big Top*, 1997
Uncle Julius visits the farm with his circus inspiring Clar-

ence ("such a ham") to develop an acrobatic act and join the show.
Karla Kuskin, *City Dog*, 1994
Rhyming text describes the excitement a city dog feels to be free to roam in a country environment with no boundaries.
Danny Shanahan, *Buckledown the Workhound*, 1993
As president of a large corporation, Buckledown is "dog tired" so he plans a vacation at Shirttail Wagon Farm where he learns to lead a dog's life.

1018

KAREN WALLACE
JON BERKELEY, Illustrator

Scarlette Beane

(New York: Dial Books for Young Readers, 2000)

Subject(s): Gardens and Gardening; Food; Talent
Age range(s): Grades K-2
Major character(s): Scarlette Beane, Child, Daughter; Grandfather Beane, Grandfather, Gardener; Mrs. Beane, Mother, Gardener
Time period(s): Indeterminate
Locale(s): Fictional Country

Summary: The sight of newborn Scarlette's red face and green fingers gives Mrs. Beane assurance that this child is destined for something special. On her fifth birthday Grandfather Beane gives her a vegetable garden, her mother gives her tools and her father builds a fence around the garden. The night after Scarlette plants the garden her green fingers glow as she sleeps and in the morning her garden is full of huge vegetables. All the neighbors help with the harvest, cutting the parsley with chain saws and digging the carrots with bulldozers. Mrs. Beane makes soup in a cement mixer and everyone dines outside. That night after dreaming of something wonderful Scarlette slips outside to plant more seeds by the light of the moon. In the morning she shows her parents the vegetable castle that grew overnight—something wonderful for her family. Originally published in Great Britain in 1999. (32 pages)

Where it's reviewed:
Booklist, January 1, 2000, page 938
Bulletin of the Center for Children's Books, March 2000, page 258
Horn Book Guide, Fall 2000, page 285
Publishers Weekly, February 28, 2000, page 79
School Library Journal, March 2000, page 219

Other books by the same author:
Imagine You Are a Tiger, 1996
Bears in the Forest, 1994
My Hen Is Dancing, 1994

Other books you might like:
Eve Bunting, *Sunflower House*, 1996
A young boy plants his sunflower seeds in a circle and creates a summer play "house" to share with friends.
Mordicai Gerstein, *Daisy's Garden*, 1995
Daisy cheerfully shares the work and the crop in her garden with bugs, birds and animals.

Ruth Krauss, *The Carrot Seed*, 1945

This little boy's family has doubts that the seeds he plants will grow, but they do.

David Wiesner, *June 29, 1999*, 1992

A science experiment yields unexpected results when enormous vegetables begin falling from the sky.

Harriet Ziefert, *The Turnip*, 1996

The Russian folktale about the turnip that is so big it requires a cooperative effort to harvest is retold as an easy reader.

1019

NANCY ELIZABETH WALLACE, Author/Illustrator

Apples, Apples, Apples

(New York: Winslow Press, 2000)

Subject(s): Food; Animals/Rabbits; Nature
Age range(s): Grades K-2
Major character(s): Minna, Rabbit, Sister; Pip, Rabbit, Brother; Mr. Miller, Rabbit, Farmer
Time period(s): 2000s (2000)
Locale(s): Long Hill Orchard, Fictional Country

Summary: A family outing to Mr. Miller's orchard gives Pip a chance to pick snack apples while Minna goes for a variety to use in a surprise. Mr. Miller informs the family of the types of apples in his orchard and offers Minna and Pip information about how the trees are grown. After returning home with many bags of apples, Minna gets out her book and leads the family in creating an apple snack. The recipe for Minna's surprise is included as well as instructions for making apple prints. (40 pages)

Where it's reviewed:
Booklist, October 15, 2000, page 448
Horn Book Guide, Spring 2001, page 52
Kirkus Reviews, July 15, 2000, page 1048
Publishers Weekly, July 26, 2000, page 74
School Library Journal, September 2000, page 211

Other books by the same author:
Paperwhite, 2000
Tell-a-Bunny, 2000
Rabbit's Bedtime, 1999

Other books you might like:
Betty G. Birney, *Pie's in the Oven*, 1996

A young boy and his grandfather pick apples for Grandma to make into a pie that smells so delicious it attracts the neighbors.

Gail Gibbons, *The Seasons of Arnold's Apple Tree*, 1984

Arnold enjoys his apple tree's spring blossoms, summer shade, fall apples and bare branches in winter to hang treats for the birds.

Marjorie Priceman, *How to Make an Apple Pie and See the World*, 1994

A young baker imagines traveling to all the countries where the ingredients for an apple pie originate.

Anne Rockwell, *Apples & Pumpkins*, 1989

A family picks apples and pumpkins from a nearby farm to use on Halloween night.

Michelle Benoit Slawson, *Apple Picking Time*, 1994

Annually, residents of all ages in an apple-growing area take time from their usual activities to help bring in the apple harvest.

Ann Turner, *Apple Valley Year*, 1993

In an apple orchard the work responsibilities for members of a farm family vary with the season of the year.

1020

NANCY ELIZABETH WALLACE, Author/Illustrator

Tell-a-Bunny

(Delray Beach, FL: Winslow Press, 2000)

Subject(s): Communication; Birthdays; Animals/Rabbits
Age range(s): Grades K-1
Major character(s): Sunny, Rabbit, Sister; Earl, Rabbit, Brother; Gloria, Rabbit, Friend
Time period(s): 2000s
Locale(s): Fictional Country

Summary: In order to keep the surprise in her plans for Earl's birthday party Sunny depends on her friends to help with the preparations. First she creates a list and then calls Gloria to ask her to notify everyone. Sunny whispers into the phone so Earl will not hear the plans and thus begins a string of telephoned miscommunications. By the time word of Sunny's plans for a picnic at 6 o'clock have been passed through four more friends the party turns out to be a surprise for everyone, including Gloria, when the doorbell rings at 6 in the morning. (32 pages)

Where it's reviewed:
Booklist, May 15, 2000, page 1750
Children's Book Review Service, May 2000, page 113
Horn Book Guide, Fall 2000, page 258
School Library Journal, May 2000, page 156

Other books by the same author:
Paperwhite, 2000
Rabbit's Bedtime, 1999
Snow, 1995

Other books you might like:
Alma Flor Ada, *Dear Peter Rabbit*, 1994

Goldilocks' written communication to her friends assures that everyone understands the party plans.

Kristina Thermaenius McLarey, *When You Take a Pig to a Party*, 2000

Pet pigs at parties don't follow the plans as Adelaide learns when her pig Sherman forgets his manners and enjoys himself.

John Wallace, *Tiny Rabbit Goes to a Birthday Party*, 2000

Tiny Rabbit's excitement about attending Blue Mouse's party changes briefly to apprehension until the party starts and the fun begins.

1021

ELLEN STOLL WALSH, Author/Illustrator

Mouse Magic

(San Diego: Harcourt, Inc., 2000)

Subject(s): Magic; Wizards; Animals/Mice
Age range(s): Grades K-1
Major character(s): Wizard, Crow; Kit, Mouse
Time period(s): Indeterminate
Locale(s): Fictional Country

Summary: Kit shows Wizard his three favorite colors, red, yellow and blue. Wizard tells Kit these colors are magic. Kit is skeptical but follows Wizard's directions and picks two colors for Wizard to use in his first trick. Wizard continues mixing two colors and then pairing the new color with the remaining original color to make a pattern that seems to move. Wizard will not let Kit try to do the magic because he's not trained. However, when Wizard takes a nap Kit continues playing with colors. Kit learns that the magic in this instance is in the color not the wizard. A concluding author's note explains the color wheel and complementary colors. (32 pages)

Where it's reviewed:
Horn Book Guide, Spring 2001, page 258
Kirkus Reviews, March 1, 2000, page 309
Publishers Weekly, January 31, 2000, page 105
School Library Journal, April 2000, page 116

Other books by the same author:
Samantha, 1996
Pip's Magic, 1994
Mouse Count, 1991
Mouse Paint, 1989

Other books you might like:
Eric Carle, *Hello, Red Fox*, 1998
  Multi-colored guests at Little Frog's birthday party show off their complementary colors.
Denise Fleming, *Lunch*, 1992
  By the time a very hungry mouse finishes eating it's devoured foods of every color.
Leo Lionni, *Little Blue and Little Yellow: A Story for Pippo and Other Children*, 1959
  Best friends Little Blue and Little Yellow hug and become green.

1022

MILDRED PITTS WALTER
TERESA FLAVIN, Illustrator

Suitcase

(New York: Lothrop, Lee & Shepard Books, 1999)

Subject(s): Self-Perception; Fathers and Sons; Artists and Art
Age range(s): Grades 3-6
Major character(s): Alexander "Xander" Bingham, 11-Year-Old; Jeff, Coach; Aaron Bingham, Father
Time period(s): 1990s (1999)
Locale(s): United States

Summary: Tall for his age with feet that suggest even more growth ahead, Xander is sensitive to the teasing nicknames from his classmates. Because of his size he's expected to be good at basketball, but instead he's uncoordinated and miserable on the court. Xander's real talent is drawing, but his father does not see value in artistic pursuits and wants to see his son develop athletic skills. When Aaron is asked to assist with the basketball program at the local community center he insists that Xander come along and join the team. There, Xander meets Jeff who helps him improve his coordination and gradually his skill in the game. Xander still does not enjoy basketball, but he likes drawing the players in action. When Jeff notices Xander's art, he suggests that Xander's eye-hand coordination could be an asset in baseball. By the time baseball season begins, Xander's pitching talent earns him a place on the school team and his artistic ability wins first place in a citywide contest. At last, Xander thinks he's accomplished something to make his father feel proud of him. (107 pages)

Where it's reviewed:
Booklist, September 15, 1999, page 262
Horn Book, November 1999, page 745
Kirkus Reviews, October 15, 1999, page 1653
Publishers Weekly, November 29, 1999, page 71
School Library Journal, September 1999, page 230

Other books by the same author:
Mariah Keeps Cools, 1990
Have a Happy..., 1989
Justin and the Best Biscuits in the World, 1986

Other books you might like:
Ilene Cooper, *Choosing Sides*, 1990
  The fear of disappointing his father complicates Jonathan's desire to leave the basketball team.
Dean Hughes, *The Trophy*, 1994
  Danny pressures himself to improve his basketball game in order to please his father.
Barbara O'Connor, *Beethoven in Paradise*, 1997
  Martin's father wants him to play baseball, but talented Martin's real love is music.

1023

CATHERINE WALTERS, Author/Illustrator

Are You There, Baby Bear?

(New York: Dutton Children's Books, 1999)

Subject(s): Animals/Bears; Animals; Babies
Age range(s): Grades K-1
Major character(s): Alfie, Bear, Son; Mother Bear, Bear, Mother; Father Bear, Bear, Father
Time period(s): 1990s
Locale(s): Earth

Summary: Alfie has been waiting patiently for a new baby brother or sister to arrive, but the time comes for the bears' winter sleep and still the baby is nowhere to be seen. While Mother Bear sleeps Alfie sneaks out of the cave to find his baby sibling. Each time Alfie thinks he's spotted a baby bear closer inspection reveals a different young animal—a beaver, a bison, a mountain lion. Finally, Father Bear finds his tired, cold son and carries him back to the cave where Mother Bear is waiting to introduce him to his siblings. First published in Great Britain in 1999. (26 pages)

Where it's reviewed:
Booklist, October 15, 1999, page 457
Horn Book Guide, Spring 2000, page 58
Kirkus Reviews, November 15, 1999, page 1817
Publishers Weekly, December 13, 1999, page 85
School Library Journal, December 1999, page 114

Other books by the same author:
When Will It Be Spring?, 1997
Max & Minnie, 1994

Other books you might like:
P.D. Eastman, *Are You My Mother?*, 1960
   A lost baby bird questions many different animals while searching for its mother.
Jonathan London, *Honey Paw and Lightfoot*, 1995
   A fictionalized account of the life cycle of a brown bear realistically portrays one year in the life of Honeybear and her cub.
Brigitte Weninger, *Will You Mind the Baby, Davy?*, 1997
   After his baby sister is born Davy realizes she needs his experience as the former youngest rabbit in the large family.

1024

VIRGINIA WALTERS
S.D. SCHINDLER, Illustrator

Are We There Yet, Daddy?

(New York: Viking, 1999)

Subject(s): Automobiles; Fathers and Sons; Stories in Rhyme
Age range(s): Grades K-3
Major character(s): Daddy, Father, Driver; Son, Son, Child; Bitsy, Dog
Time period(s): 1990s (1999)
Locale(s): United States

Summary: Daddy, Bitsy and Son climb into the car for a one hundred mile trip to grandma's house. Son is in charge of the map, but that doesn't stop him from asking Daddy every ten miles if they've arrived and just how much farther they have to travel. After hearing "No" as an answer to his repeated question, just as it begins to get dark, Son finally hears Dad say "Yes" and soon he's leaping from the car to greet his grandmother. (32 pages)

Where it's reviewed:
Booklist, September 15, 1999, page 270
Bulletin of the Center for Children's Books, December 1999, page 152
Horn Book Guide, Spring 2000, page 58
Kirkus Reviews, August 1, 1999, page 1233
School Library Journal, October 1999, page 129

Other books you might like:
Jim Aylesworth, *Through the Night*, 1998
   Eager to return home to his family a father drives through the night until he reaches his destination.

John Coy, *Night Driving*, 1996
   Dad and his son drive all night to reach their camping spot near the mountains.
Jonathan London, *Old Salt, Young Salt*, 1996
   Time and distance don't matter to this father and son as they enjoy a day of fishing in their boat.

1025

SALLY WARNER
JACQUELINE ROGERS, Illustrator

Accidental Lily

(New York: Alfred A. Knopf, 1999)

Subject(s): Dreams and Nightmares; Moving, Household; Brothers and Sisters
Age range(s): Grades 2-3
Major character(s): Lily Hill, 1st Grader, Sister (younger); Casey "Case" Hill, 12-Year-Old, Brother; Mommy, Single Mother
Time period(s): 1990s (1999)
Locale(s): Philadelphia, Pennsylvania

Summary: Lily never had this embarrassing "problem" when she lived in New Jersey and she blames Mommy for making them move to Philadelphia. Now Lily has bad dreams that make her wet the bed—not every night, but much too often. Case doesn't agree that the dreams are the problem; he thinks Lily drinks too much water at night. For the first time, Lily is invited to a sleepover and she's afraid to go because she's sure she will embarrass herself at her friend's house. Case and Mommy encourage Lily to attend and Case even helps her with a plan to solve the problem so no one will know if an accident happens. (90 pages)

Where it's reviewed:
Booklist, March 15, 1999, page 330
Horn Book Guide, Fall 1999, page 286
Kirkus Reviews, May 1, 1999, page 730
Publishers Weekly, June 7, 1999, page 85
School Library Journal, July 1999, page 82

Other books by the same author:
Leftover Lily, 1999
Private Lily, 1998
Sweet and Sour Lily, 1998
Dog Years, 1995

Other books you might like:
Beverly Cleary, *The Ramona Series*, 1952-1999
   Irrepressible Ramona and her family endure school problems and sibling squabbles with love and a sense of humor.
Johanna Hurwitz, *Ever-Clever Elisa*, 1997
   First grader Elisa has unique ideas about how to have a successful year.
Barbara Park, *Junie B. Jones and Some Sneaky Peeky Spying*, 1994
   Impetuous Junie B. means well, but her impulsive exercise of her ideas could make a teacher consider finding other work.

1026

SALLY WARNER
JACQUELINE ROGERS, Illustrator

Leftover Lily
(New York: Alfred A. Knopf, 1999)

Subject(s): Friendship; Schools; Single Parent Families
Age range(s): Grades 2-3
Major character(s): Lily Hill, 6-Year-Old, Friend; Hilary Mitchell, 1st Grader, Friend; Daisy Greenough, 1st Grader, Friend
Time period(s): 1990s (1999)
Locale(s): Philadelphia, Pennsylvania

Summary: Lily misunderstands Daisy's request for a private moment with a mutual friend and thinks bossy Daisy is trying to exclude Lily from the friendship. Feeling hurt and angry, Lily decides to find a new friend. Being assigned as a partner to shy Hilary for a math lesson gives Lily the idea of using her as a friend. Lily even tries out some of Daisy's bossy behavior, but Hilary, though shy, has a mind of her own and isn't interested in all of Lily's ideas. Lily even turns to her older brother for advice on solving the problems she's having making and keeping friends because she wonders if she's put herself in the position of being left without any friends on Valentine's Day. (122 pages)

Where it's reviewed:
Booklist, July 1999, page 1947
Children's Bookwatch, November 1999, page 3
Horn Book Guide, Spring 2000, page 72
Publishers Weekly, June 7, 1999, page 85
School Library Journal, July 1999, page 83

Other books by the same author:
Totally Confidential, 2000
Accidental Lily, 1999
Private Lily, 1998
Sweet and Sour Lily, 1998
Ellie and the Bunheads, 1997

Other books you might like:
Patricia Reilly Giff, *Dance with Rosie*, 1996
   Rosie has troubles! Tommy's angry with her and new friends are hard to find.
Suzanne Williams, *Emily at School*, 1996
   As the school year begins, Emily learns that second grade has some unexpected challenges, including new student Alex.
Susan Wojciechowski, *Beany (Not Beanhead) and the Magic Crystal*, 1997
   Beany keeps her magic crystal a secret from her bossy friend Carol Ann and makes her own plans about how to use it.

1027

DONNA WASHINGTON
JACQUELINE ROGERS, Illustrator

A Big Spooky House
(New York: Jump at the Sun/Hyperion Books for Children, 2000)

Subject(s): Folklore; Self-Confidence; Haunted Houses
Age range(s): Grades 1-5
Major character(s): Unnamed Character, Traveler
Time period(s): Indeterminate Past
Locale(s): United States

Summary: A big, strong man with an overly confident attitude sets out by foot to join the army. He refuses an offer of a cart ride and another to stay overnight at an inn rather than walk into an approaching storm. As the rain begins to fall the big, strong man is not happy to also be a wet man so he seeks shelter in a large, but spooky house he passes. Inside the elegant home the big, strong, certainly-not-frightened man enters a room with a blazing fire and table set with a delicious meal. The big, strong, hungry man gobbles up the food and falls asleep in his chair before the fire. At the stroke of midnight the chiming clock wakens him to face a black cat sitting in the fire and asking if the man will still be here when John arrives. Twice more the same scenario wakens him with the cat growing larger each time. By the third visit the cat that appears is so huge that the big strong man is also a frightened man and one who is gone! (32 pages)

Where it's reviewed:
Booklist, September 15, 2000, page 251
Children's Book Review Service, August 2000, page 160
Horn Book Guide, Spring 2001, page 103
Kirkus Reviews, August 1, 2000, page 1126
School Library Journal, September 2000, page 224

Other books by the same author:
The Story of Kwanzaa, 1996

Other books you might like:
Cynthia DeFelice, *Cold Feet*, 2000
   In this retelling a bagpiper with newly found boots is surprised by a knock at the door from a corpse seeking the return of his feet.
Diane Goode, *Diane Goode's Book of Scary Stories and Songs*, 1994
   The not-too-terrifying collection of scary stories also includes songs and poems.
Angela Shelf Medearis, *The Ghost of Sifty Sifty Sam*, 1997
   A ghost that haunts an old house responds to Dan's kindness and becomes a helpful worker in Dan's restaurant.
Nicole Rubel, *The Ghost Meets Its Match*, 1992
   For 100 years a family of ghosts frightens away all potential tenants of a haunted house; the current residents have tricks of their own.

1028

BERNADETTE WATTS, Author/Illustrator

Harvey Hare's Christmas

(New York: North-South Books, 1999)

Subject(s): Animals/Rabbits; Christmas; Problem Solving
Age range(s): Grades K-2
Major character(s): Harvey Hare, Rabbit, Postal Worker
Time period(s): Indeterminate
Locale(s): Fictional Country

Summary: 'Tis the season when Harvey Hare has more mail than his satchel can hold. His helpful friends weave a large basket that works for one day, but the next day there's too much mail for the basket so the woodland animals make a cart for Harvey. Then snow begins to fall and Harvey has an accident that breaks the cart so his friends make a big sled, load the huge pile of letters and packages into it and help push it up a hill. Unfortunately the sled's contents begin falling out and rolling downhill. As Harvey's friends scramble to pick up the letters and packages each one notices that the item belongs to someone in the group. Rather than continue with Harvey's deliveries, they simply agree to gather their own mail and celebrate Christmas on the hillside. (32 pages)

Where it's reviewed:
Booklist, September 1, 1999, page 151
Children's Bookwatch, November 1999, page 7
Horn Book Guide, Spring 2000, page 58
Publishers Weekly, September 27, 1999, page 63
School Library Journal, October 1999, page 71

Other books by the same author:
Happy Birthday, Harvey Hare!, 1998
Harvey Hare, Postman Extraordinaire, 1997
The Christmas Bird, 1996
Tattercoats, 1988

Other books you might like:
Katharine Holabird, *Angelina's Christmas*, 2000
  When Angelina notices Mr. Bell, the former mailman, is alone for Christmas she comes up with an idea to cheer him.
Dee Lillegard, *Tortoise Brings the Mail*, 1997
  The delivery of mail may be slow when Tortoise handles the job, but the animals soon learn the importance of his reliability.
James Stevenson, *Christmas at Mud Flat*, 2000
  The animal residents of Mud Flat busily prepare for their communal holiday celebration.

1029

SARAH WEEKS
JANE MANNING, Illustrator

Drip, Drop

(New York: HarperCollins Publishers, 2000)

Series: I Can Read Book
Subject(s): Animals/Mice; Weather; Sleep
Age range(s): Grades 1-2
Major character(s): Pip Squeak, Mouse
Time period(s): 2000s (2000)
Locale(s): Fictional Country

Summary: First his head and then his feet feel the dampness of water dripping through a leaky roof. As the rain continues, leaks seem to spring up everywhere and Pip Squeak places so many cups, pail and buckets on his bed that he's unable to find anyplace to sleep. Pip Squeak's house is beginning to flood when the rain stops, the sun peaks out and his friends arrive to invite him to jump in puddles. The only place Pip Squeak wants to jump is back into bed and so he does. (32 pages)

Where it's reviewed:
Booklist, July 2000, page 2046
Horn Book Guide, Spring 2001, page 58
Kirkus Reviews, July 1, 2000, page 968
School Library Journal, September 2000, page 211

Other books by the same author:
Piece of Jungle, 1999
Splish, Splash!, 1999 (My First I Can Read Book)
Mrs. McNosh Hangs Up Her Wash, 1998
Follow the Moon, 1995

Other books you might like:
Deborah Eaton, *The Rainy Day Grump*, 1998
  Rain cancels his plans to play ball and makes Clay so grumpy he refuses to play with his sister in this beginning reader.
Sharon Gordon, *Drip, Drop*, 1989
  A group of wide-awake children plan how to dress for a day outside in the rain.
Edith Thacher Hurd, *Johnny Lion's Rubber Boots*, 2001
  In an "I Can Read Book" Johnny feels miserable stuck inside on a rainy day until his father brings him some new boots.
Maryann Kovalski, *Rain Rain*, 1999
  Although weather cancels a planned trip to the beach, Grandma creates a day of fun for her disappointed grandchildren.

1030

SARAH WEEKS
NADINE BERNARD WESTCOTT, Illustrator

Mrs. McNosh and the Great Big Squash

(New York: Laura Geringer/Harper Festival, 2000)

Series: Harper Growing Tree
Subject(s): Gardens and Gardening; Problem Solving; Stories in Rhyme
Age range(s): Grades K-1
Major character(s): Nelly McNosh, Gardener
Time period(s): Indeterminate
Locale(s): Fictional Country

Summary: As soon as Mrs. McNosh pushes a squash seed into the ground it begins to grow and produce a squash that rapidly becomes enormous. The large yellow vegetable flattens the cat and scares the pants off two elderly neighbors before Mrs. McNosh decides the only way to stop the runaway vine is to pick the squash. Now, she tackles the next problem—what to do with a vegetable this large. All night Mrs. McNosh works and by morning she's snuggled up asleep inside her large yellow squash home. (24 pages)

Where it's reviewed:
Booklist, October 1, 2000, page 350
Horn Book Guide, Spring 2001, page 25
School Library Journal, December 2000, page 127

Other books by the same author:
Mrs. McNosh Hangs Up Her Wash, 1998
Noodles, 1996
Crocodile Smile, 1994

Other books you might like:
Aubrey Davis, *The Enormous Potato*, 1998
  The rapid growth of a potato to an astounding size requires a community effort to harvest and eat the huge vegetable.
Steven Kroll, *The Biggest Pumpkin Ever*, 1984
  Two mice, intent on growing the biggest pumpkin, independently apply their secret gardening techniques to the same pumpkin with astounding results.
Walter Lyon Krudop, *Something Is Growing*, 1995
  Unnoticed, a young boy plants a seed in an urban neighborhood with results that get everyone's attention.
Margaret Mahy, *The Pumpkin Man and the Crafty Creeper*, 1990
  Mr. Parkin, caretaker of quiet pumpkins, has his life changed by a plant with an attitude.

1031

SARAH WEEKS

Regular Guy

(New York: A Laura Geringer Book/HarperCollins Publishers, 1999)

Subject(s): Parent and Child; Identity; Behavior
Age range(s): Grades 4-6
Major character(s): Guy Strang, 11-Year-Old, Son; Buzz, 11-Year-Old, Friend (Guy's); Robert "Bob-o" Smith, 11-Year-Old, Classmate
Time period(s): 1990s (1997)
Locale(s): Cedar Springs

Summary: There is no question in Guy's mind that the people with whom he lives could not possibly be his parents. Guy sees himself as a normal, regular guy, but his parents are certifiably weird and definitely embarrassing. Guy is sure that he was switched at birth and with help from Buzz he sneaks into the school records to find a boy who was born about the same time he was. His research yields an exact match in Bob-o, the absolutely weirdest guy in school who shares Guy's birthday. Guy and Buzz plan a fictitious school project that will allow the boys to change homes for a weekend. Guy figures that both sets of parents will recognize the mistake and he'll be rid of strange parents forever. Guy's experience at the home of his "real" parents gives him more appreciation for his own parents and for the sad, though seemingly normal life, that Bob-o leads. (120 pages)

Where it's reviewed:
Booklist, September 1, 1999, page 134
Horn Book, May 1999, page 340
Kirkus Reviews, May 1, 1999, page 730
Publishers Weekly, June 21, 1999, page 68

School Library Journal, June 1999, page 138

Other books by the same author:
Guy Time, 2000

Other books you might like:
Lynn Cullen, *The Three Lives of Harris Harper*, 1996
  Harris wishes his parents were not a major embarrassment and his home was more like the neatly organized one of the little boy he baby-sits.
Amy Goldman Koss, *The Ashwater Experiment*, 1999
  Frequent moves necessitated by her parents' follow-the-craft-shows' lifestyle have Hillary wondering who or what is real.
A. LaFaye, *Strawberry Hill*, 1999
  Twelve-year-old Raleia feels as if she's an outsider in her own family.

1032

SARAH WEEKS
ASHLEY WOLFF, Illustrator

Splish, Splash!

(New York: HarperCollins Publishers, 1999)

Series: My First I Can Read Book
Subject(s): Animals; Stories in Rhyme
Age range(s): Grades K-1
Major character(s): Chub, Fish
Time period(s): Indeterminate
Locale(s): Fictional Country

Summary: Rub-a-dub-dub Chub's in the tub and he's too polite to refuse any animal that wants to jump in with him. None are too fat, too tall, too short or too thin according to Chub who's "the more the merrier" attitude soon has the tub full to overflowing. All together the animals splish, splash and cheer for Chub. (32 pages)

Where it's reviewed:
Booklist, March 15, 1999, page 1339
Children's Bookwatch, February 1999, page 7
Horn Book Guide, Fall 1999, page 274
School Library Journal, February 1999, page 90

Other books by the same author:
Drip, Drop, 2000 (I Can Read Book)
Mrs. McNosh Hangs Up Her Wash, 1998
Follow the Moon, 1995

Other books you might like:
Jan Brett, *The Mitten: A Ukranian Folktale*, 1989
  In an award-winning adaptation of a folktale animals seeking warmth crowd into a lost mitten.
Alyssa Satin Capucilli, *Bathtime for Biscuit*, 1998
  Biscuit would never join Chub in the tub; this puppy prefers digging in the yard.
Bernard Waber, *Bearsie Bear and the Surprise Sleepover Party*, 1997
  On a cold winter night, Bearsie Bear's friends come knocking at the door asking to share his warm bed.

1033

ROSEMARY WELLS, Author/Illustrator

Emily's First 100 Days of School

(New York: Hyperion Books for Children, 2000)

Subject(s): Schools; Mathematics; Learning
Age range(s): Grades K-2
Major character(s): Emily, Rabbit, Student—Elementary School; Miss Cribbage, Teacher, Guinea Pig; Angela, Koala Bear, Student—Elementary School
Time period(s): 2000s (2000)
Locale(s): Fictional Country (North Pleasant Valley By-the-Sea)

Summary: Emily's excitement on the first day of school is quickly dampened by Miss Cribbage's announcement that the class will learn a new number friend every day and have a party when they reach day 100 of the school year. One hundred seems like an overwhelmingly high number to Emily but, by recording the numbers one at a time along with an event or anecdote to go with each number, Emily reaches the goal and makes a friend when Angela joins the class from Eighty-Mile Beach in Australia. (60 pages)

Where it's reviewed:
Booklist, May 15, 2000, page 1750
Horn Book, March 2000, page 190
Kirkus Reviews, May 15, 2000, page 724
Publishers Weekly, May 29, 2000, page 81
School Library Journal, May 2000, page 157

Awards the book has won:
Bulletin of the Center for Children's Books Blue Ribbon, 2000

Other books by the same author:
Yoko, 1998 (Booklist Editors' Choice)
Bunny Money, 1997
McDuff and the Baby, 1997 (Publishers Weekly Best Children's Books)

Other books you might like:
Margery Cuyler, *100th Day Worries*, 1999
  Jessica frets about the collection of one hundred things she's required to bring to school on the hundredth day.
Trudy Harris, *100 Days of School*, 1999
  In a rhyming tale a variety of objects and number combine to equal one hundred.
Angela Shelf Medearis, *The 100th Day of School*, 1996
  This Level 2 entry in the Hello Reader series celebrates the completion of one hundred days in the school year.
Joseph Slate, *Miss Bindergarten Celebrates the 100th Day of Kindergarten*, 1998
  Rhyming text describes the preparations of Miss Bindergarten and her students to celebrate one hundred days of school.

1034

ROSEMARY WELLS, Author/Illustrator

Max Cleans Up

(New York: Viking, 2000)

Subject(s): Cleanliness; Brothers and Sisters; Animals/Rabbits
Age range(s): Preschool
Major character(s): Max, Rabbit, Brother (younger); Ruby, Rabbit, Sister (older)
Time period(s): 2000s (2000)
Locale(s): Fictional Country

Summary: Ruby directs the clean up of Max's messy room as Max quietly asserts himself. Ruby says the dump truck with its load of sands needs to go back to the sand box; Max dumps the sand in the pocket of his bib overalls. Ruby notes that Max's ants have escaped and must be returned to the ant farm; Max puts them in his pocket. Each time Ruby finds something that belongs in the trash, Max silently adds it to his pocket. Ruby efficiently puts the toys in the toy chest, the shoes in the closet and organizes the room. When the job is done Ruby asks Max what is in his bulging pocket and he shows her by emptying his pocket onto the no-longer clean floor. (32 pages)

Where it's reviewed:
Booklist, February 1, 2001, page 1059
Kirkus Reviews, October 1, 2000, page 1435
Publishers Weekly, October 23, 2000, page 77
School Library Journal, December 2000, page 127

Other books by the same author:
Read to Your Bunny, 1998
Bunny Cakes, 1997
Bunny Money, 1997
Max's Dragon Shirt, 1991
Max's Chocolate Chicken, 1989

Other books you might like:
Eileen Christelow, *Five Little Monkeys with Nothing to Do*, 1996
  Five bored monkeys help Mama prepare for Grandma's visit; unfortunately, by the time they finish their chores, the house looks just as dirty.
Elise Petersen, *Tracy's Mess*, 1995
  Tracy appears to be fastidious but wait until you see what's behind her bedroom door!
Mark Teague, *Pigsty*, 1994
  After Wendell's mother declares his room a pigsty playful pigs arrive and thwart his attempt to complete the mandatory clean up.

1035

BRIGITTE WENINGER
EVE THARLET, Illustrator

Happy Birthday, Davy!

(New York: A Michael Neugebauer Book/North-South Books, 2000)

Subject(s): Animals/Rabbits; Birthdays; Gifts
Age range(s): Grades K-2
Major character(s): Davy, Rabbit, Brother; Grandpa, Grandfather, Rabbit; Granny, Grandmother, Rabbit

Time period(s): Indeterminate
Locale(s): Fictional Country

Summary: As Davy counts the days until his birthday he also wishes for someone to have more time to read to him, to teach him games and to just have time for him. On his birthday Davy's surprised not to see wrapped presents. His parents explain that they overheard his wishes and planned a present in response that is too big to be wrapped. Davy searches his home and finds Granny and Grandpa hiding with a book full of stories, lots of games and all the time he wants. Davy thinks this is his best birthday ever and he promises Granny and Grandpa that if they make the right wish, he'll be their birthday present too. Originally published in Switzerland. (32 pages)

Where it's reviewed:
Booklist, December 15, 2000, page 829
Horn Book Guide, Spring 2001, page 53
Kirkus Reviews, October 1, 2000, page 1436
School Library Journal, December 2000, page 127

Other books by the same author:
Merry Christmas, Davy!, 1998
Will You Mind the Baby, Davy?, 1997 (Notable Children's Trade Book in the Field of Social Studies)
What Have You Done, Davy?, 1996
Where Have You Gone, Davy?, 1996

Other books you might like:
Nancy White Carlstrom, *Happy Birthday, Jesse Bear!*, 1994
 From the first preparations through the party fun to the last good night kiss, Jesse Bear excitedly describes his fourth birthday.
Lee Davis, *P.B. Bear's Birthday Party*, 1994
 Stuffed-animal friends gather to help P.B. Bear celebrate his birthday.
Helen Oxenbury, *It's My Birthday*, 1993
 Animals friends bring the ingredients a young girl needs to make a birthday cake, help with the cooking and then enjoy the finished product with her.

1036

BRIGITTE WENINGER
ANNE MOLLER, Illustrator
SIBYLLE KAZEROID, Translator

A Letter to Santa Claus

(New York: A Michael Neugebauer Book/North-South Books, 2000)

Subject(s): Christmas; Letters; Wishes
Age range(s): Grades K-3
Major character(s): Oliver, Child, Son; Nicholas, Aged Person, Widow(er); Unnamed Character, Single Mother, Seamstress
Time period(s): Indeterminate Past
Locale(s): Brierley, Switzerland

Summary: Living an isolated life of poverty in a small mountain village could explain why Oliver has never received a gift from Santa Claus. His mother thinks that Santa brings what children wish for so perhaps Santa's failure to visit is because Oliver's never wished for anything. Oliver is not sure how to communicate with Santa until a friend gives him a bright red

helium balloon. To the balloon Oliver attaches his carefully written letter requesting a new lamp for his mother and boots and mittens for himself. The balloon finds its way to the garden of a grumpy, lonely old man. The selfless tone of the letter nags at Nicholas and lifts him out of his melancholy. In a few days Oliver receives even more than he wishes for thanks to the balloon that carried his letter to Nicholas. (32 pages)

Where it's reviewed:
Booklist, September 1, 2000, page 135
Horn Book Guide, Spring 2001, page 53
Publishers Weekly, September 25, 2000, page 72
School Library Journal, October 2000, page 63

Other books by the same author:
Why Are You Fighting, Davy?, 1999
Merry Christmas, Davy!, 1998
Lumina: A Story for the Dark Time of the Year, 1997
What Have You Done, Davy?, 1996

Other books you might like:
John Burningham, *Harvey Slumfenburger's Christmas Present*, 1993
 Weary Santa uses a variety of alternate transportation methods to deliver an overlooked present.
Dorothea Lachner, *The Gift from Saint Nicholas*, 1995
 In a snowbound village, St. Nicholas answers a wish that the snow blow away so the villagers can visit on Christmas morning.
Tom Paxton, *The Story of Santa Claus*, 1995
 An overlooked woodcarver moves to the North Pole to get assistance from elves with his toy production.

1037

BRIGITTE WENINGER
ALEXANDER REICHSTEIN, Illustrator
J. ALISON JAMES, Translator

Special Delivery

(New York: A Michael Neugebauer Book/North-South Books, 2000)

Subject(s): Surprises; Mothers; Parent and Child
Age range(s): Grades K-1
Major character(s): Mother, Mother
Time period(s): 2000s (2000)
Locale(s): Earth

Summary: Mother is happy when the vacuum cleaner she's ordered arrives one morning. She immediately unpacks the box and begins to vacuum the house. That afternoon the doorbell rings again and when Mother opens it, another large box is on the doorstep. This one is decorated and addressed simply to Mother. The box is so heavy Mother tries to guess what could be inside—rocks or treasure? Using other clues Mother guesses a large stuffed animal, a big rubber ball, and a kitten. Finally, she just opens the box, one flap at a time and out of the box jumps—her child! (32 pages)

Where it's reviewed:
Horn Book Guide, Spring 2001, page 26
Publishers Weekly, November 13, 2000, page 103
School Library Journal, December 2000, page 128

Other books by the same author:
The Elf's Hat, 2000
Ragged Bear, 1996
Good-bye, Daddy!, 1995

Other books you might like:
Shirley Isherwood, *Something for James*, 1996
What could be in the brown paper bag left on the doorstep with the tag addressed to James?
Elizabeth Spurr, *The Long, Long Letter*, 1996
A letter is so long it's shipped in a box that is broken by a tornado, raining pages of the letter on Aunt Hetta's home and town.
Janice May Udry, *Is Susan Here?*, 1993
Imaginative Susan "disappears" one day, but stays near her parents disguised as various animals before surprising them by returning at bedtime.

1038

BRIGITTE WENINGER
EVE THARLET, Illustrator
ROSEMARY LANNING, Translator

What's the Matter, Davy?

(New York: North-South Books, 1998)

Subject(s): Animals/Rabbits; Toys; Lost and Found Possessions
Age range(s): Grades K-1
Major character(s): Davy, Rabbit, Brother; Nicky, Stuffed Animal; Dinah, Baby, Sister (Davy's)
Time period(s): Indeterminate Past
Locale(s): Fictional Country

Summary: Because Nicky is Davy's special and constant companion, Davy is sad when Nicky is lost outside. Although one of his brothers helps search for Nicky and a sister loans Davy her doll so he can sleep, nothing can replace Nicky. Davy's mother sews a new stuffed animal that looks similar to the way Nicky looked when he was new, but still Davy wants to locate Nicky. After a few more days of searching, Davy spots Nicky stuck in a tree, carefully retrieves him and hurries home to give the new stuffed animal to Dinah. (32 pages)

Where it's reviewed:
Booklist, March 15, 1998, page 1253
Bulletin of the Center for Children's Books, June 1998, page 378
Horn Book Guide, Fall 1998, page 310
School Librarian, Autumn 1998, page 134
School Library Journal, August 1998, page 147

Other books by the same author:
Merry Christmas, Davy!, 1998
Will You Mind the Baby, Davy?, 1997
Where Have You Gone, Davy?, 1996

Other books you might like:
Jez Alborough, *Where's My Teddy?*, 1992
Oh no! After a walk in the forest, Eddie can't find his special teddy bear.
Catherine Bancroft, *Felix's Hat*, 1993
Felix loses his beloved orange baseball cap on a trip to the

pond and even his caring siblings can't make up for his loss.
Paulette Bourgeois, *Franklin's Blanket*, 1997
Franklin the Turtle loses his favorite blanket and can't sleep without it.
Jules Feiffer, *I Lost My Bear*, 1998
A young girl who loses her favorite bear gets very little help from her family with her search for it.
Selina Young, *Ned*, 1993
Emily and Ned, a green cloth donkey, are inseparable until Ned is lost and then found again.

1039

BRIGITTE WENINGER
EVE THARLET, Illustrator
ROSEMARY LANNING, Translator

Why Are You Fighting, Davy?

(New York: North-South Books/Michael Neugebauer Book, 1999)

Subject(s): Animals/Rabbits; Friendship; Playing
Age range(s): Grades K-2
Major character(s): Davy, Rabbit, Friend; Nicky, Stuffed Animal, Rabbit; Eddie, Rabbit, Friend
Time period(s): Indeterminate
Locale(s): Fictional Country

Summary: Best friends Eddie and Davy are playing near a brook on a hot summer day when they decide to construct a dam and float boats. Each tackles the job at which they feel most skilled, but when Eddie's dam breaks and Davy's boat is swept away by the current, Davy blames Eddie and angry words end their friendship. Davy goes home to play with Nicky, because none of his siblings are available. Growing bored, Davy returns to the brook to teach Nicky how to build a dam and discovers the job is more difficult than he realized. When Davy discovers Eddie futilely trying to make boats the two playmates share tips on making dams and boat construction while rebuilding their friendship. (32 pages)

Where it's reviewed:
Booklist, November 1, 1999, page 541
Children's Bookwatch, November 1999, page 7
Horn Book Guide, Spring 2000, page 59
Publishers Weekly, October 11, 1999, page 77
School Library Journal, November 1999, page 132

Other books by the same author:
Merry Christmas, Davy!, 1998
What's the Matter, Davy?, 1997
Will You Mind the Baby, Davy?, 1997 (Notable Social Studies Trade Books for Children)
What Have You Done, Davy?, 1996
Where Have You Gone, Davy?, 1996

Other books you might like:
Patience Brewster, *Two Bushy Badgers*, 1995
Arthur and Ollie learn to value their friendship, put aside their anger and resolve their differences.
Patricia Lee Gauch, *Christina Katerina and Fats: And the Great Neighborhood War*, 1997
Anger springing from an argument grows into a "war" that threatens friendships.

Juanita Havill, *Jamaica and Brianna*, 1993
> Insults temporarily sidetrack the friendship of two girls who face their feelings and find a way to work together cooperatively.

Lynn Reiser, *Best Friends Think Alike*, 1997
> While playing at the park Ruby and Beryl have a brief disagreement before realizing they'd prefer to play together.

Harriet Ziefert, *Mike and Tony: Best Friends*, 1987
> Until they have an argument, Mike and Tony are inseparable; now they have to find a way to work out their differences.

1040

CAROL WESTON

The Diary of Melanie Martin
(New York: Alfred A. Knopf, 2000)

Subject(s): Vacations; Family Life; Diaries
Age range(s): Grades 3-6
Major character(s): Melanie Martin, 10-Year-Old, Tourist; Matt Martin, 6-Year-Old, Brother
Time period(s): 2000s (2000)
Locale(s): New York, New York; Italy

Summary: A family trip to Italy sounds exciting but six hours on a plane next to Matt followed by a four hour car trip is not a recipe for fun. Melanie is alternately thrilled or annoyed with her role as a tourist in a foreign country. Melanie and Matt are hungry for familiar food, but their parents insist on native cuisine—sometimes too authentic when their insufficient mastery of the language brings Melanie an octopus as an appetizer. The memories of the eventful trip also include a trip to the emergency room for stitches, a lost wallet, searching for Matt when he becomes lost in the Vatican and a greater appreciation for her family. This is the first novel for this writer of nonfiction. (144 pages)

Where it's reviewed:
Booklist, May 1, 2000, page 1671
Horn Book Guide, Fall 2000, page 314
Publishers Weekly, May 8, 2000, page 221
School Library Journal, June 2000, page 155

Other books by the same author:
Private and Personal: Questions and Answers for Girls Only, 2000
For Girls Only: Wise Words, Good Advice, 1998
Girltalk: All the Stuff Your Sister Never Told You, 1992

Other books you might like:
Anni Axworthy, *Anni's Diary of France*, 1994
> In her travel diary Anni records her experiences at the different sites she visits with her parents.

Christina Bjork, *Vendela in Venice*, 1999
> Traveling with her father in Venice, Vendala visits palaces, travels by gondola and appreciates the city's beauty.

Pat Brisson, *Your Best Friend, Kate*, 1989
> During a family trip Kate sends her friend Lucy letters and postcards describing their travels.

1041

MARTHA WESTON, Author/Illustrator

Space Guys!
(New York: Holiday House, 2000)

Series: Holiday House Reader. Level 1
Subject(s): Aliens; Space Travel; Stories in Rhyme
Age range(s): Grades K-1
Major character(s): Mom, Mother; Dad, Father; Unnamed Character, Child, Son
Time period(s): 2000s (2000)
Locale(s): United States

Summary: The sound of beeping awakens a young boy who looks out his window and sees a spaceship landing in his yard. He hurries to tell Mom and Dad who think he's dreaming and send him back to bed. By the time the boy returns to his room space guys are jumping on the bed and playing in his dresser drawers. The three aliens rapidly tour (and demolish) the house—eating the bathroom soap and scattering cereal about the kitchen. The boy tries to quiet them in front of the television and takes a picture before they have to go. Finally, the young boy gets some sleep until Mom and Dad awaken and see the mess in the house. (32 pages)

Where it's reviewed:
Booklist, April 15, 2000, page 1556
Horn Book Guide, Spring 2000, page 290
Kirkus Reviews, March 15, 2000, page 392
School Library Journal, May 2000, page 158

Other books by the same author:
Cats Are Like That, 1999
Bad Baby Brother, 1997
Tuck in the Pool, 1995

Other books you might like:
Martha Alexander, *You're a Genius, Blackboard Bear*, 1995
> With help from Blackboard Bear, Anthony builds a spaceship to the moon.

Colin McNaughton, *Here Come the Aliens!*, 1995
> An orbiting picture of a group of 4-year-olds halts an invasion of creatures from outer space in this humorous rhyming story.

David McPhail, *Tinker and Tom and the Star Baby*, 1998
> Tinker repairs a spaceship that lands in his yard while the alien Star Baby eats the cat's food and levitates kitchen objects.

Daniel Pinkwater, *Guys from Outer Space*, 1989
> A boy who travels to another planet with some space guys discovers talking rocks and other amazing things.

1042

BRUCE WHATLEY, Author/Illustrator
ROSIE SMITH, Co-Author

Captain Pajamas: Defender of the Universe
(New York: HarperCollins Publishers, 2000)

Subject(s): Heroes and Heroines; Aliens; Imagination
Age range(s): Grades 1-3

Major character(s): Brian "Captain Pajamas", Brother (younger), Child; Jessie, Sister (older), Child; Shadow, Dog
Time period(s): Indeterminate
Locale(s): United States

Summary: The light on Brian's "Remote-Control, Techno-Robotic Alien Communicator" indicates that there is an alien nearby. Brian leaps from bed, dons his Captain Pajamas costume and awakens Jessie in order to save her. Jessie prefers sleeping to being saved, but she lets her brother drag her toward the source of various strange noises in the house. Each time they find Shadow up to some mischief but sporting an innocent, yet befuddled expression. Captain Pajamas knows that Shadow is fending off the alien, but Jessie is sure that Shadow is creating his own problems. Finally, everyone goes back to bed, but not to sleep—for now it's Jessie's turn to call to Brian when she suspects Shadow is in her bed—or is he? (32 pages)

Where it's reviewed:
Booklist, May 15, 2000, page 1750
Horn Book Guide, February 2000, page 285
Publishers Weekly, June 19, 2000, page 78
School Library Journal, June 2000, page 126

Other books by the same author:
Detective Donut and the Wild Goose Chase, 1997
Whatley's Quest, 1995
Looking for Crabs, 1992

Other books you might like:
G. Brian Karas, *Bebe's Bad Dream*, 2000
    Bebe's family and friends may think her aliens are part of a bad dream but Bebe knows the aliens she sees are really after her.
Neal Layton, *Smile If You're Human*, 1999
    An alien family comes to Earth to photograph a human but they land in a zoo and have difficulty determining which creature is a human.
Michael Rosen, *Mission Ziffoid*, 1999
    A young boy gives a humorous description of his brother's visit to the planet Ziffoid.
Arthur Yorinks, *Company's Coming*, 2000
    In a reissue of a 1988 title Moe and Shirley have surprise visitors—friendly aliens—on the very day they are expecting relatives for dinner.

1043

LINDA ARMS WHITE
TOM CURRY, Illustrator

Comes a Wind

(New York: DK Ink/Dorling Kindersley Publishing, Inc., 2000)

Subject(s): Brothers; Sibling Rivalry; Tall Tales
Age range(s): Grades K-3
Major character(s): Mama, Mother; Clement, Brother, Cowboy; Clyde, Brother, Cowboy
Time period(s): Indeterminate Past
Locale(s): Texas

Summary: In her letter extending an invitation to Clyde and Clement to a quiet celebration of her birthday Mama has one request of her sons—no quarrelling. Clement and Clyde have

played one-upmanship for so long they don't know how to communicate civilly so they sit in silence until they hear the squeak of the windmill turning. Then, they begin to boast about the winds they have endured. The stories become more and more preposterous until a real wind, like nothing either has ever seen, comes up and blows Mama right into the sky. When the wind stops and Mama floats back down she becomes snagged on the weather vane and her sons cooperate in order to rescue her, making Mama's birthday wish come true before they have time to cut the cake. (32 pages)

Where it's reviewed:
Booklist, March 15, 2000, page 1390
Bulletin of the Center for Children's Books, March 2000, page 258
Kirkus Reviews, March 15, 2000, page 393
Publishers Weekly, February 21, 2000, page 86
School Library Journal, May 2000, page 158

Other books by the same author:
Too Many Pumpkins, 1996

Other books you might like:
Mary Calhoun, *Jack and the Whoopee Wind*, 1987
    With friends in Whoopee, Wyoming Jack tries to tame a wind that is capable of blowing the feathers off a chicken.
Pat Hutchins, *The Wind Blew*, 1974
    A rhyming story describes the cumulative effect of a wind that blows away many objects.
Steven Kellogg, *Pecos Bill: A Tall Tale*, 1986
    The origin of some unique features of the American West are explained in a retelling of a tall tale about a legendary folk hero.
Helen Ketteman, *The Year of No More Corn*, 1993
    Old Grampa tells Beanie how he saved the 1928 corn crop by planting whittled corn kernels that grew into corn trees.

1044

IAN WHYBROW
CHRISTIAN BIRMINGHAM, Illustrator

A Baby for Grace

(New York: Kingfisher, 1998)

Subject(s): Babies; Brothers and Sisters; Parent and Child
Age range(s): Grades K-1
Major character(s): Grace, Sister
Time period(s): 1990s (1998)
Locale(s): England

Summary: Grace is excited that her mother and the new baby are coming home from the hospital, but disappointed when no one will let her do anything. Her father won't let her pour her own milk at breakfast; her grandmother won't let her open the package she brought. When Grace gets to hold the baby, everyone says she is doing it wrong. After a morning of constant refrains of "No, Grace," she finally hears a "Yes, Grace" when she gives the baby a bouquet. (32 pages)

Where it's reviewed:
Booklist, October 1, 1998, page 337
Children's Bookwatch, September 1998, page 4
Parents Magazine, February 1999, page 175
Publishers Weekly, October 26, 1998, page 64

School Library Journal, January 1999, page 108

Other books by the same author:
Jump In!, 1999
Harry and the Snow King, 1998
Parcel for Stanley, 1998

Other books you might like:
Denys Cazet, Dancing, 1995
   To assure new big brother, Alex, that the family has enough love for two children, Dad sings a song about the moon sharing the sky with the stars.
Debi Gliori, Mr. Bear's New Baby, 1999
   When Baby Bear won't stop crying it's his big sister who knows what to do.
Russell Hoban, A Baby Sister for Frances, 1976
   Frances is not sure how she will fit into the family now that baby Gloria is here.
Marisabina Russo, Hannah's Baby Sister, 1998
   Hannah looks forward to a new baby in the family.
Clara Vulliamy, Ellen and Penguin and the New Baby, 1996
   Ellen and Penguin are not sure they like Ellen's baby brother.

1045

IAN WHYBROW
TONY ROSS, Illustrator

Little Wolf's Book of Badness

(Minneapolis: Carolrhoda Books, Inc., 2000)

Subject(s): Animals/Wolves; Letters; Travel
Age range(s): Grades 2-4
Major character(s): Little Wolf, Wolf, Nephew; Bigbad Wolf, Uncle, Wolf
Time period(s): Indeterminate
Locale(s): Fictional Country (Cunning College for Brute Beasts)

Summary: In letters to his parents Little Wolf alternately describes his forced journey to Cunning College and pleas to be allowed to return home. He assures his parents that those few times he brushed his teeth and fur were actually intended as jokes and he truly is capable of being bad. After a harrowing trip, timid Little Wolf arrives at Cunning College and bravely faces dreaded Uncle Bigbad who must teach him the nine rules of badness. Little Wolf knows his parents will allow him to return home as soon as he earns his "Bad Badge" so he is a most diligent pupil although self-centered Uncle Bigbad is not much of a teacher. Little Wolf complies with Uncle Bigbad's gruff directions, but even his attempts to be mean are colored by his sensitive nature. However, it is Little Wolf who finds success and Uncle Bigbad who pays the price for his greediness. Little Wolf's a winner though perhaps not in quite the way his parents expected. Originally published in England. (130 pages)

Where it's reviewed:
Horn Book Guide, Spring 2000, page 90
Horn Book, January 2000, page 86
Kirkus Reviews, October 1, 1999, page 1585
Publishers Weekly, November 15, 1999, page 67
School Library Journal, November 1999, page 132

Other books by the same author:
Little Wolf's Diary of Daring Deeds, 2000
Little Wolf's Haunted Hall for Small Horrors, 2000
Harry and the Snow King, 1998

Other books you might like:
Alma Flor Ada, Yours Truly, Goldilocks, 1998
   Fer O'Cious intercepts an invitation to a housewarming party for three little pigs and makes plans to ambush the departing guests.
James Marshall, Rats on the Range and Other Stories, 1993
   Eight stories feature animals in humorous and unusual situations.
Jon Scieszka, The Stinky Cheese Man: And Other Fairly Stupid Tales, 1992
   In the Caldecott Honor book classic fairy tales take on a new look in these humorous retellings.
Jon Scieszka, The True Story of the Three Little Pigs, 1989
   Misunderstood A. Wolf presents his side of the story about just what happened between him and those three pigs.
Vivian Vande Velde, Tales From the Brothers Grimm and the Sisters Weird, 1995
   Thirteen traditional fairy tales are rewritten with some humorous modifications.
Nancy Willard, The Magic Cornfield, 1997
   Postcards to cousin Bottom document Tottem's travels from New York to Minneapolis through a magic cornfield.

1046

IAN WHYBROW
ADRIAN REYNOLDS, Illustrator

Sammy and the Dinosaurs

(New York: Orchard Books, 1999)

Subject(s): Dinosaurs; Toys; Imagination
Age range(s): Grades K-2
Major character(s): Sammy, Child; Gran, Grandmother
Time period(s): 1990s (1999)
Locale(s): England

Summary: Helpful Sammy finds a box of toy dinosaurs while cleaning the attic with Gran. He scrubs off the dirt, repairs the broken parts and carries them to the library in a bucket. After finding the dinosaurs' names in a book he begins using the names when playing with them and the dinosaurs respond quietly and appreciatively. Sammy and the dinosaurs are inseparable until Sammy rides the train with Gran and, in his excitement, gets off without his dinosaurs. When Sammy and Gran visit the Lost and Found, Sammy's ability to call the dinosaurs by name enables him to prove that they belong to him. (32 pages)

Where it's reviewed:
Bulletin of the Center for Children's Books, September 1999, page 36
Horn Book, September 1999, page 602
Kirkus Reviews, July 1, 1999, page 1061
School Library Journal, September 1999, page 209
Smithsonian, November 1999, page 46

Awards the book has won:
Smithsonian's Notable Books for Children, 1999

Other books by the same author:
Little Wolf's Book of Badness, 1999
A Baby for Grace, 1998
Quacky Quack-quack, 1991

Other books you might like:
James Mayhew, *Katie and the Dinosaurs*, 1992
  When Katie visits a natural history museum, she finds herself surrounded by real dinosaurs.
Martin Waddell, *Small Bear Lost*, 1996
  After Small Bear is forgotten on a train he manages to find his way home to the little girl who lost him.
Mark Alan Weatherby, *My Dinosaur*, 1997
  A little girl imagines her stuffed green dinosaur becomes real and takes her for a moonlit ride.

1047

DAVID WIESNER, Author/Illustrator

Sector 7

(New York: Clarion Books, 1999)

Subject(s): Fantasy; Change; Weather
Age range(s): Grades 1-4
Major character(s): Unnamed Character, Student—Elementary School, Artist
Time period(s): 1990s
Locale(s): New York, New York (Empire State Building); Sector 7, Fictional Country

Summary: With his classmates and teacher a young boy, whose pockets are stuffed with paper and pencils, gets off the elevator at the 86th floor of the Empire State Building and climbs the stairs to the observatory. The cloudy day soon envelops the boy in mist and he loses his cap, scarf and mittens to a playful cloud that materializes in the fog. As the sky clears, the cloud and the boy float away to Sector 7, a terminal with an interior reminiscent of Grand Central Station. The clouds awaiting assignment to their destinations greet the boy excitedly, but express disappointment in the monotony of their shape choices. The boy draws fish and other sea creatures to amuse them and soon Sector 7 looks like an undersea world. The human dispatchers are not amused and banish the boy from the facility. He returns to the Empire State Building just in time to rejoin his group and view the many unique cloud shapes floating overhead. (48 pages)

Where it's reviewed:
Booklist, September 15, 1999, page 270
Five Owls, March 2000, page 96
Horn Book, September 1999, page 603
Publishers Weekly, August 30, 1999, page 83
School Library Journal, September 1999, page 209

Awards the book has won:
ALA Notable Children's Books, 2000
School Library Journal Best Books, 1999

Other books by the same author:
June 29, 1999, 1992
Tuesday, 1991 (Caldecott Medal)
Free Fall, 1988 (Caldecott Honor Book)

Other books you might like:
Eric Carle, *Little Cloud*, 1996
  Solitary Little Cloud drifts independently of the other clouds forming his own shapes in the sky.
Pat Cummings, *C.L.O.U.D.S.*, 1986
  Chuku, the angel, grows to like his assignment as the skypainter for New York City.
Thomas Locker, *Cloud Dance*, 2000
  Expressive paintings and simple text describe clouds in various seasons and weather conditions.
Michael Lustig, *Willy Whyner, Cloud Designer*, 1994
  Willy creates a cloud-making machine and goes into business manufacturing clouds to order. Esther Lustig, co-author.
Dalia Hardoff Renberg, *Hello, Clouds!*, 1985
  While watching clouds overhead a child imagines the many objects they could be.

1048

MARGARET WILD
DAVID LEGGE, Illustrator

Tom Goes to Kindergarten

(Morton Grove, IL: Albert Whitman & Company, 2000)

Subject(s): Animals/Bears; Schools; Family
Age range(s): Grades K-1
Major character(s): Tom, Panda, Kindergartner; Baby, Panda, Baby; Mrs. Polar Bear, Teacher, Bear
Time period(s): 1990s (1999)
Locale(s): Fictional Country

Summary: With busy parents who never seem to have time for play, Tom tries to involve Baby in his imaginative activities while eagerly awaiting the first day of kindergarten. When the day arrives, separation jitters grip Tom and he holds onto his parents' legs. Astute Mrs. Polar Bear invites Tom's family to stay and the parents have so much fun during their daylong return to childhood that they are disappointed the next morning when Tom is able to go into class without them. It takes a gentle reminder from Mrs. Polar Bear that work awaits the parents before they reluctantly leave. The illustrations reveal that they manage to include a little kindergarten fun in their workday. This title was originally published in Australia in 1999. (32 pages)

Where it's reviewed:
Booklist, May 1, 2000, page 1680
Horn Book Guide, Fall 2000, page 259
Publishers Weekly, May 1, 2000, page 70
School Library Journal, April 2000, page 117

Other books by the same author:
Big Cat Dreaming, 1997
Old Pig, 1996
Our Granny, 1994

Other books you might like:
Jutta Langreutter, *Little Bear Goes to Kindergarten*, 1997
  Although Little Bear enjoys everything about his first day in kindergarten he still doesn't want his mother to leave.

Jonathan London, *Froggy Goes to School*, 1996

Worries about the first day of school have Froggy dreaming that he's gone to school in his underwear.

Mary Serfozo, *Benjamin Bigfoot*, 1993

By the time school begins Benjamin decides that he doesn't need his dad's big shoes to feel big enough to go to kindergarten.

1049

NANCY WILLARD
DAVID DIAZ, Illustrator

Shadow Story

(San Diego: Harcourt Brace & Company, 1999)

Subject(s): Good and Evil; Problem Solving; Fantasy
Age range(s): Grades 1-3
Major character(s): Holly Go Lolly, Child, Daughter; Ooboo, Monster, Villain; Mama, Mother
Time period(s): Indeterminate Past
Locale(s): Mount Ooboo, Fictional Country

Summary: Holly Go Lolly is born on the Night When Shadows Linger, an event that happens only once in fifteen years and receives a blessing to never be afraid of the dark from the shadow of a fairy godmother. Unfortunately, on the night of Holly Go Lolly's birth the hungry Ooboo eats her father, plunging the already poor household into greater poverty. Because Mama cannot afford toys, Holly Go Lolly learns to entertain herself by making shadow pictures on the wall. After Ooboo eats her mother too the shadowy fairy godmother returns to tell Holly Go Lolly she must catch the Ooboo or become his dinner some day. Holly Go Lolly follows the instructions carefully and on the night of her fifteenth birthday, the Night When Shadows Linger, she bravely climbs Mount Ooboo to confront the evil ogre. (32 pages)

Where it's reviewed:
Booklist, November 15, 1999, page 639
Horn Book, November 1999, page 731
Kirkus Reviews, October 15, 1999, page 1653
Publishers Weekly, November 22, 1999, page 55
School Library Journal, November 1999, page 132

Other books by the same author:
The Magic Cornfield, 1997
An Alphabet of Angels, 1994
A Starlit Somersault Downhill, 1993
The High Rise Glorious Skittle Skat Roarious Sky Pie Angel Food Cake, 1990

Other books you might like:
Janice Del Negro, *Lucy Dove*, 1998
Courage and determination to win a sack of gold enable Lucy Dove to complete a challenge to sew a pair of trousers in a haunted graveyard.
Mercer Mayer, *Liza Lou and the Yeller Belly Swamp*, 1976
Liza Lou outwits all the witches, haunts and spooks in the Yeller Belly Swamp.
Phyllis Root, *Aunt Nancy and Old Man Trouble*, 1996
Aunt Nancy turns her troubles into triumphs, confounding Old Man Trouble and sending him on his way to bother someone less clever.

1050

NANCY WILLARD
DAVID CHRISTIANA, Illustrator

The Tale I Told Sasha

(Boston: Little, Brown and Company, 1999)

Subject(s): Lost and Found Possessions; Imagination; Stories in Rhyme
Age range(s): Grades 1-3
Major character(s): Mother, Mother; Unnamed Character, Daughter
Time period(s): Indeterminate
Locale(s): Fictional Country

Summary: On a dark, damp day Mother hands a yellow ball to her daughter. Following the ball as it bounces away leads the girl into bright rooms, unseen before, across a Bridge of Butterflies. A golden fish says her ball was planted in hopes of growing golden flowers to attract unusual creatures to the garden. The gatherer of all lost things hoards the many objects that have vanished in the house—a needle, a card, coins and bread crusts. When the girl arrives, the ball is thrown into her living room, bringing the girl's imaginary journey to an end and leaving her to marvel at the adventures held within her small, plain house. (32 pages)

Where it's reviewed:
Booklist, June 1999, page 1826
Horn Book Guide, Fall 1999, page 286
Kirkus Reviews, April 1, 1999, page 539
Publishers Weekly, April 26, 1999, page 82
School Library Journal, June 1999, page 108

Other books by the same author:
The Magic Cornfield, 1997
A Starlit Somersault Downhill, 1993
The Sorcerer's Apprentice, 1993
Beauty and the Beast, 1992
The High Rise Glorious Skittle Skat Roarious Sky Pie Angel Food Cake, 1990

Other books you might like:
Jennifer Armstrong, *Pockets*, 1998
Embroidered scenes inside the pockets of her work clothes transport a seamstress to imaginary places each time she puts her hands in the pockets.
Ruth Brown, *Mad Summer Night's Dream*, 1999
Fantastic illustrations interpret the nonsense of a childish rhyme in which nothing is as it should be.
Berlie Doherty, *The Midnight Man*, 1998
Lyrical text describes the Midnight Man who is seen by Harry and his dog as he throws the stars into the night sky.
Arthur Geisert, *The Etcher's Studio*, 1997
While helping his grandfather prepare prints of his etchings a young boy imagines himself in each of the scenes.
Lisa Maizlish, *The Ring*, 1996
A yellow plastic ring found by a young boy in the park seems to have magical properties or perhaps the boy has an active imagination.
Julian Scheer, *Rain Makes Applesauce*, 1964
The whimsical illustrations in this Caldecott Honor book support the ''silly talk'' of the story.

Mark Teague, *The Lost and Found*, 1998

As Wendell and Floyd help Mona search for her lost hat the students tumble through the box into an underground lost and found cavern.

Audrey Wood, *The Flying Dragon Room*, 1996

Using Mrs. Jenkins special tools and his imagination, Patrick creates an amazing underground space.

1051

LAURA E. WILLIAMS
FABRICIO VANDEN BROECK, Illustrator

Torch Fishing with the Sun

(Honesdale, PA: Boyds Mill Press, 1999)

Subject(s): Fishing; Grandparents; Folklore
Age range(s): Grades K-3
Major character(s): Makoa, Child
Time period(s): Indeterminate Past
Locale(s): Hawaii

Summary: Every evening, Makoa's grandfather goes torch fishing with the sun, capturing the sun in his net so that the sun will go down and the other villagers can torch fish along the shore. When another village boy questions the grandfather's activities, Makoa confronts his grandfather who tells him that sometimes you have to believe things that you cannot see. When his grandfather passes away, the sun no longer sets, and Makoa must assume the job of torch fishing with the sun. (32 pages)

Where it's reviewed:
Booklist, March 15, 1999, page 1336
Horn Book Guide, Fall 1999, page 286
Publishers Weekly, February 15, 1999, page 107
School Library Journal, June 1999, page 108

Other books by the same author:
The Spider's Web, 1999
Behind the Bedroom Wall, 1996
The Long Silk String: A Grandmother's Legacy to Her Granddaughter, 1995

Other books you might like:
Brenda Lena Fazio, *Grandfather's Story*, 1996

In a dream the cormorant and sea turtle remind a grandfather of all that he has yet to teach his grandson about the sea.

Rebecca Nevers Fellows, *A Lei for Tutu*, 1998

Nahoa is looking forward to winning the Most Beautiful Lei Contest, until her grandmother falls ill.

Tony Johnston, *Fishing Sunday*, 1996

A young boy learns to appreciate some of Grandfather's unusual ways of doing things while on a fishing trip with him.

James Rumford, *The Island-Below-the-Star*, 1998

Five Polynesian brothers set off on a great adventure in which they discover Hawaii.

Julie Stewart Williams, *Maui Goes Fishing*, 1991

The demigod Maui pulls the Hawaiian Islands out of the water with a giant fishing hook.

1052

GINA WILLNER-PARDO

Figuring Out Frances

(New York: Clarion Books, 1999)

Subject(s): Friendship; Grandmothers; Problem Solving
Age range(s): Grades 4-6
Major character(s): Abigail Van Fossen, 10-Year-Old, Friend; Travis Mooney, 5th Grader, Friend; Grandma, Grandmother, Aged Person
Time period(s): 1990s (1999)
Locale(s): San Francisco, California (bay area)

Summary: For eight years Travis and Abigail have been very best friends every other weekend when Travis visits his mother and stepfather in their home next door to Abigail's. Then, just before school starts, Travis comes to live with his mother for a year while his father works in Saudi Arabia. At first Abigail thinks it will be wonderful to have Travis near all the time, but she quickly learns that she doesn't know him as well as she thinks she does. At school Travis ignores her, and even joins the other fifth grade boys in making fun of her grandmother. At home he visits and gives her some good ideas for solving a school-project mystery. Abigail is trying to figure out why Grandma, who has Alzheimer's, calls her ''Frances.'' As Abigail unravels the clues, she begins to find pieces of the puzzle that may explain her shattered friendship with Travis. (144 pages)

Where it's reviewed:
Booklist, September 15, 1999, page 262
Bulletin of the Center for Children's Books, October 1999, page 74
Children's Book Review Service, November 1999, page 36
Kirkus Reviews, August 1, 1999, page 1233
School Library Journal, September 1999, page 230

Awards the book has won:
Joseet Frank Award, 1999

Other books by the same author:
Daphne Eloise Slater, Who's Tall for Her Age, 1997
Hunting Grandma's Treasures, 1996
Jason and the Losers, 1995
When Jane-Marie Told My Secret, 1995

Other books you might like:
David A. Adler, *Andy and Tamika*, 1999

Fourth-grade friends Tamika and Andy prepare to become family when Tamika loses her foster family and moves into the Russell's home.

Elisa Carbone, *Starting School with an Enemy*, 1998

Sarah is not adjusting well to her family's move only three weeks before school opens.

Paula Danziger, *Amber Brown Is Not a Crayon*, 1994

Amber cannot imagine anything worse than her parents' divorce until her best friend Justin announces that he will soon move.

Sheila Greenwald, *Rosy Cole: She Grows and Graduates*, 1997

Rosy's friend Donald helps her realize that self-discovery and friendships are more important than admission to a prestigious private school.

Claudia Mills, *Losers, Inc.*, 1997

Ethan wonders if the price of self-improvement will be his friendship with Julius and his position with their Losers, Inc. club.

1053

GINA WILLNER-PARDO
HEIDI CHANG, Illustrator

Jumping into Nothing
(New York: Clarion Books, 1999)

Subject(s): Fear; Friendship; Summer
Age range(s): Grades 2-4
Major character(s): Sophie, 9-Year-Old, Child of Divorced Parents; Annalise, Friend (Sophie's); Dad, Single Father
Time period(s): 1990s (1999)
Locale(s): United States

Summary: Sophie looks forward to summers at the community swimming pool with her best friend Annalise. This summer a challenge from two popular girls to join them in a game on the high dive threatens Sophie's friendship with Annalise. Too fearful to jump from the high dive into "nothing," Sophie is immediately branded "chicken." Annalise enjoys the game on the diving board so Sophie devises a plan to increase her level of bravery gradually by sleeping without a nightlight, eating ants and riding her bike with no hands. When Sophie still is unable to conquer her fear of heights she turns to Dad for help. With his support she is able to enjoy the waning days of summer with Annalise from high atop the diving board. (58 pages)

Where it's reviewed:
Booklist, March 15, 1999, page 1330
Horn Book, May 1999, page 340
Kirkus Reviews, April 15, 1999, page 637
Publishers Weekly, March 15, 1999, page 59
School Library Journal, May 1999, page 100

Other books by the same author:
Daphne Eloise Slater, Who's Tall for Her Age, 1997
Hunting Grandma's Treasures, 1996
When Jane-Marie Told My Secret, 1995

Other books you might like:
Ann Cameron, *The Stories Julian Tells*, 1981
Six episodes of happy family interaction are told from the perspective of Julian in the first award-winning book about his family.
Betsy Duffey, *Virtual Cody*, 1997
Cody fears that, when he gives his school report, classmates will laugh to learn he's named after a dog and not the famous Buffalo Bill Cody.
Suzy Kline, *Mary Marony Hides Out*, 1993
Embarrassed by her tendency to stutter, Mary tries to avoid meeting an author visiting her school.
Nancy Hope Wilson, *Old People, Frogs, and Albert*, 1997
Albert overcomes his fears and visits former school volunteer Mr. Spear in a nursing home where he's recovering from a stroke.

1054

GINA WILLNER-PARDO
NICK SHARRATT, Illustrator

Spider Storch's Desperate Deal
(Morton Grove, IL: Albert Whitman & Company, 1999)

Subject(s): Weddings; Friendship; Humor
Age range(s): Grades 2-3
Major character(s): Joey "Spider" Storch, 3rd Grader; Mary Grace Brennerman, 3rd Grader
Time period(s): 1990s (1999)
Locale(s): United States

Summary: Spider is in a bind and Mary Grace is taking every advantage of his fear that his friends will learn that he's to be the ring bearer in her mother's wedding. Mary Grace will be the flower girl and Spider doesn't know what he'll do if anyone at school learns that he'll be stuck being nice to his worst enemy. In exchange for her silence, Mary Grace makes demands of Spider, using the shared secret to manipulate him into choosing her for the team at PE or enlisting his friends to participate in a play at recess. Finally, Spider refuses to go along with Mary Grace's demands and simply tells his friends the truth. Spider is relieved that they react with humor to the image of their friend stuck with Mary Grace during the wedding. (69 pages)

Where it's reviewed:
Booklist, January 1, 2000, page 930
Bulletin of the Center for Children's Books, December 1999, page 153
Horn Book Guide, Spring 2000, page 72
School Library Journal, January 2000, page 114

Other books by the same author:
Jumping into Nothing, 1999
Spider Storch's Fumbled Field Trip, 1998
Spider Storch's Music Mess, 1998
Spider Storch's Carpool Catastrophe, 1997
Spider Storch's Teacher Torture, 1997
When Jane-Marie Told My Secret, 1995

Other books you might like:
Betsy Duffey, *Spotlight on Cody*, 1998
Cody tries a lot of ideas for the 3rd grade talent show before discovering the one that can put him in the spotlight.
P.J. Petersen, *I Hate Weddings*, 2000
Dan's father is marrying a woman with two children—all strangers to Dan.
Eileen Spinelli, *Lizzie Logan Gets Married*, 1997
Lizzie's mom is the bride but Lizzie thinks her presence in the wedding is equally important.

1055

JACQUELINE WILSON
NICK SHARRATT, Illustrator

The Lottie Project
(New York: Delacorte Press, 1999)

Subject(s): Mothers and Daughters; Single Parent Families; Schools

Age range(s): Grades 4-6

Major character(s): Charlotte "Charlie" Enright, Student, 11-Year-Old; Lottie, Servant (imaginary); Jo Enright, Single Mother

Time period(s): 1990s (1997)

Locale(s): England

Summary: The school year that Charlie knows will be "easy-peasy, simple-pimple" begins, instead, disastrously. First, her new teacher is a strict, older woman who assigns seats alphabetically and Charlie is stuck next to an obnoxious "perfect" classmate and not near her friends. Then, Jo loses her job when her company closes and all the employees are laid off. Charlie is so worried that she's unable to keep her mind on her schoolwork until she becomes engrossed in a required project on the Victorian era. Charlie invents Lottie, a girl her age who is forced to leave school and take a job as a domestic servant to support her widowed mother and many siblings. Through the Lottie project, Charlie explores in fiction many problems similar to those she's experiencing in her life and wins her teacher's respect for a job well done. The title was originally published in the United Kingdom in 1997. (214 pages)

Where it's reviewed:
Booklist, October 1, 1999, page 360
Horn Book, November 1999, page 746
Kirkus Reviews, October 1, 1999, page 1585
Publishers Weekly, November 29, 1999, page 72
School Library Journal, November 1999, page 166

Other books by the same author:
Double Act, 1998
The Suitcase Kid, 1997
Elsa, Star of the Shelter!, 1996

Other books you might like:
Barbara Dugan, *Good-Bye, Hello*, 1994
  Sixth grade should be fun, but for Bobbie Jean, stuck in tough Sister Alice's class—what could be worse!
Yvonne MacGrory, *The Secret of the Ruby Ring*, 1994
  Using a wish granted by a magical family ring, Lucy travels back in time to Langley Castle where she is treated as a servant.
Eileen Walsh Strauch, *Hey You, Sister Rose*, 1993
  Outspoken Arlene struggles to meet strict Sister Rose's expectations of a 6th grader and learns about herself in the process.

1056

JOHN WINCH, Author/Illustrator

Keeping Up with Grandma
(New York: Holiday House, 2000)

Subject(s): Grandmothers; Grandfathers; Change

Age range(s): Grades K-3

Major character(s): Grandpa, Grandfather, Artist; Grandma, Grandmother, Cook; Unnamed Character, Child, Narrator

Time period(s): 2000s (2000)

Locale(s): Australia

Summary: The routine of painting and baking becomes a little too mundane for Grandma who decides that she and Grandpa need a little more adventure in their lives. Grandpa is not sure about Grandma's ideas, but he tries each of her suggestions from mountain climbing to fishing to bronco busting although he does so a bit reluctantly. Even dancing, canoeing and spelunking don't appeal to Grandpa and he finally pleads to stay home. This time Grandma uses the paints and Grandpa bakes the cake, but both make a mess, so their grandchild suggests they just go back to what they were doing before and that plan works just fine. (32 pages)

Where it's reviewed:
Booklist, November 15, 2000, page 651
Five Owls, January 2001, page 67
Horn Book Guide, Spring 2001, page 53
Kirkus Reviews, July 1, 2000, page 968
School Library Journal, November 2000, page 138

Other books by the same author:
The Old Woman Who Loved to Read, 1997
The Old Man Who Loved to Sing, 1996

Other books you might like:
Nancy Carlson, *A Visit to Grandma's*, 1991
  Tina and her parents are surprised to learn how Grandma has changed since she moved into a Florida condominium!
Rod Clement, *Grandpa's Teeth*, 1998
  Grandpa has the entire town searching for the thief who took his false teeth while he was sleeping.
Margaret Mahy, *A Busy Day for a Good Grandmother*, 1993
  Mrs. Oberon, grandmother extraordinaire, overcomes unusual obstacles to reach and soothe her teething grandson.
Laura Joffe Numeroff, *What Grandmas Do Best, What Grandpas Do Best*, 2000
  Grandmas and Grandpas each have unique ways to share their love with their grandchildren.
Tres Seymour, *Too Quiet for These Old Bones*, 1997
  Mother expects the children to be quiet while visiting their Granny, but Granny prefers some noise and excitement.

1057

TIM WINTON
KAREN LOUISE, Illustrator

The Deep
(Berkeley, CA: Tricycle Press, 2000)

Subject(s): Fear; Family; Animals/Dolphins

Age range(s): Grades K-2

Major character(s): Alice, Child, Sister (younger); Jesse, Brother (older); Harry, Brother (older)
Time period(s): 1990s (1998)
Locale(s): Australia

Summary: Alice's family lives near the sea so swimming is a daily activity. Harry and Jesse leap from the dock and swim with their parents in the deep water. Alice stays in the shallows because she is afraid of the beautiful deep, dark water. The dolphins fascinate Alice and she's attracted to the fun her family has together while swimming, but she just can't overcome her fears. While playing in the sand one day, Alice notices dolphins in the shallow water and wades out to meet them. As they swim away Alice follows and, before she realizes what she's done, she's swimming in the deep, dark blue water too. The title is modified from the book originally published in Australia in 1998. (32 pages)

Where it's reviewed:
Booklist, May 15, 2000, page 1750
Children's Bookwatch, June 2000, page 3
Horn Book Guide, Fall 2000, page 286
School Library Journal, July 2000, page 90

Other books you might like:
Louise Borden, *Albie the Lifeguard*, 1993
   Albie gains confidence ''guarding'' the backyard wading pool and, by summer's end, is able to join his friends at the town pool.
Betsy Jay, *Swimming Lessons*, 1998
   Fearful Jane ignores Mom's logical reasons for learning how to swim but Jimmy's teasing finally gets her to jump into the pool.
Rosemary Wells, *Edward in Deep Water*, 1995
   Edward discovers that he is not ready for birthday pool parties with big bears.
Martha Weston, *Tuck in the Pool*, 1995
   Tuck's need to rescue his lucky spider from the pool bottom helps the reluctant swimmer gain confidence.

1058

FRIEDA WISHINSKY
H. WERNER ZIMMERMAN, Illustrator

Each One Special

(Custer, WA: Orca Book Publishers, 1999)

Subject(s): Cooks and Cooking; Friendship; Old Age
Age range(s): Grades K-3
Major character(s): Ben, Child, Friend; Harry, Aged Person, Baker
Time period(s): 1990s (1999)
Locale(s): United States

Summary: Ben's friend, Harry, is a marvelous cake decorator. The varied decorations he can make include flowers, clowns, ballerinas and, on a particularly memorable birthday cake, a mocha cowboy swinging a butterscotch lasso. Sadly, when Harry's bakery is bought out, Harry finds himself out of work. Harry is lost without his work, and Ben searches for a new career for Harry until he finds one—modeling clay. (32 pages)

Where it's reviewed:
Booklist, January 1, 1999, page 892
ForeWord Magazine, April 1999, page 60
Publishers Weekly, December 14, 1998, page 74
Resource Links, December 1998, page 5
School Library Journal, July 1999, page 83

Other books by the same author:
No Frogs for Dinner, 1999
Oonga Boonga, 1999
The Man Who Made Parks: The Story of Parkbuilder Frederick Law Olmsted, 1999

Other books you might like:
Marsha Diane Arnold, *The Chicken Salad Club*, 1998
   Nathaniel Hopkins tries to find a way to lift the spirits of his great-grandfather who is a wonderful storyteller.
Peter Grosz, *The Special Gifts*, 1998
   In this Christmas tale, three retired craftsmen find a renewed purpose making gifts for others.
Judith Byron Schachner, *The Grannyman*, 1999
   An aged Siamese cat gains a new purpose in life teaching a kitten the ropes.

1059

FRIEDA WISHINSKY
NEAL LAYTON, Illustrator

Nothing Scares Us

(Minneapolis: Carolrhoda Books, Inc., 2000)

Subject(s): Fear; Friendship; Imagination
Age range(s): Grades K-2
Major character(s): Lucy, Child, Friend; Lenny, Child, Friend
Time period(s): 2000s
Locale(s): Earth

Summary: Playing as the Fearless Two, Lucy and Lenny feel invincible. They chase aliens, battle monsters and fight pirates. Playing together is great fun until Lenny finds a new television program starring a scary green creature. Lenny's eager to see the program again, but Lucy has nightmares about the show. She's afraid Lenny will tease her if she admits to being afraid of a TV character and she can't think of an excuse not to play with Lenny. When the show begins, Lucy closes her eyes until she hears someone scream. Then she opens them to see Lenny standing on the couch pointing to a small spider. Lucy's not afraid of spiders but learning of Lenny's fear helps her tell him how she feels about the TV program so Lenny turns off the TV and the Fearless Two go outside to tackle the twelve-headed snake in the apple tree instead. (32 pages)

Where it's reviewed:
Bulletin of the Center for Children's Books, October 2000, page 88
Horn Book Guide, Spring 2001, page 26
Publishers Weekly, November 6, 2000, page 90
School Library Journal, November 2000, page 138

Other books by the same author:
No Frogs for Dinner, 2000
So Long Stinky Queen, 2000
Each One Special, 1999

Oonga Boonga, 1990

Other books you might like:

Ray Bradbury, *Switch on the Night*, 1993
A new friend helps a lonely little boy overcome his fear of the dark.
Marc Brown, *Arthur's First Sleepover*, 1994
Arthur and two friends pitch his new tent in the backyard and try not to admit to any fears about sleeping outside.
Helen Cooper, *The Bear under the Stairs*, 1993
Fearful William keeps the bear under the stairs fed well so he will not come out and eat William.
Cynthia Zarin, *Rose and Sebastian*, 1997
Rose feels a little afraid of the noises from the upstairs apartment until her mother takes her to meet Sebastian who is noisily at play in his apartment.

1060

DAVID WISNIEWSKI, Author/Illustrator

Tough Cookie

(New York: Lothrop, Lee & Shepard Books, 1999)

Subject(s): Food; Humor; Crime and Criminals
Age range(s): Grades 1-4
Major character(s): Tough Cookie, Detective—Private, Hero; Pecan Sandy, Girlfriend (former), Heroine; Fingers, Criminal
Time period(s): Indeterminate Past
Locale(s): Fictional Country

Summary: Pecan Sandy brings Tough Cookie the news that his former partner's been hurt—bad. Same old story—Fingers got him. Just like Fingers got Tough Cookie's parents back in the days when the family lived at the Top of the Jar. No more hiding, Tough Cookie's got to put an end to Fingers once and for all. If the police won't do it (and they won't) then he'll do it. He arrives at the Top of the Jar just before Fingers makes another appearance sending the crowd into a panic. It looks as if the end is near for our hero but friends from the Bottom of Jar rush to his assistance and Fingers is left with nothing but crumbs. (32 pages)

Where it's reviewed:
Booklist, November 1, 1999, page 541
Kirkus Reviews, August 15, 1999, page 1318
New York Times Book Review, November 21. 1999, page 61
Publishers Weekly, August 9, 1999, page 352
School Library Journal, September 1999, page 210

Awards the book has won:
Parents' Choice Gold Award, 1999

Other books by the same author:
The Secret Knowledge of Grown-Ups, 1998
Golem, 1996 (Caldecott Medal)
The Wave of the Sea Wolf, 1994 (New York Times Best Illustrated Book)

Other books you might like:
Bruce Glassman, *The Midnight Fridge*, 1998
In a darkened kitchen within the refrigerator a food fight rages until a hero sandwich intervenes.
Bonnie Lass, *Who Took the Cookies from the Cookie Jar*, 2000

When the cookie jar is found empty Skunk tries to solve the mystery of who is responsible. Philomen Sturges, co-author.
Bruce Whatley, *Detective Donut and the Wild Goose Chase*, 1997
Fortunately for dimwit Detective Donut his partner Mouse is clever enough to retrieve the Maltese Dodo from the nefarious Goose.

1061

SUSAN WOJCIECHOWSKI
SUSANNA NATTI, Illustrator

Beany and the Dreaded Wedding

(Cambridge, MA: Candlewick Press, 2000)

Subject(s): Weddings; Cousins; Family
Age range(s): Grades 2-4
Major character(s): Beatrice Lorraine "Beany" Sherwin-Hendricks, Cousin, Sister (younger); Amy, Cousin, Bride; Carol Ann, Friend (Beany's), Neighbor
Time period(s): 2000s (2000)
Locale(s): United States

Summary: When Amy asks Beany to be the flower girl and ring bearer in her wedding Beany feels excited and a little nervous. Carol Ann, with her previous experience as a flower girl, offers information, misinformation and a too small, ugly dress that causes worrywart Beany to view the wedding experience with terror. Sure that she will be the sole cause of a wedding disaster, Beany wants to refuse Amy's request, but her supportive family helps her see how important she is to Amy and she agrees to participate worries and all. Understanding Amy does everything she can to make the day comfortable for Beany so finally, despite her worries, her shaky legs, and her imagined fears, Beany completes her task on an absolutely perfect day. (128 pages)

Where it's reviewed:
Booklist, November 15, 2000, page 643
Horn Book Guide, Spring 2001, page 68
Kirkus Reviews, September 1, 2000, page 1294
School Library Journal, October 2000, page 142

Other books by the same author:
The Best Halloween of All, 1998
Beany (Not Beanhead) and the Magic Crystal, 1997
Don't Call Me Beanhead!, 1994

Other books you might like:
Beverly Cleary, *The Ramona Series*, 1952-1999
Irrepressible Ramona and her family endure school problems and sibling squabbles with love and a sense of humor.
Gail Herman, *Flower Girl*, 1996
A little girl depends on her lucky ring to assure her perfect behavior during her sister's wedding.
Kathleen Leverich, *Violet*, 1997
When Violet's punk cousin asks her to be a flower girl Violet fears her dream is coming true in a wedding that will be a nightmare.

1062

ASHLEY WOLFF, Author/Illustrator

Stella & Roy Go Camping

(New York: Dutton Children's Books, 1999)

Subject(s): Brothers and Sisters; Animals/Bears; Camps and Camping
Age range(s): Grades K-2
Major character(s): Stella, Sister (older), Camper; Roy, Brother (younger), Camper; Mother, Mother, Camper
Time period(s): 1990s (1999)
Locale(s): Lone Pine Lake, California

Summary: Mother bears the load of a full pack as she leads Stella and Roy along the trail to the campsite. Roy hopes to see a bear and each time he spots an animal print Stella uses her book of animal tracks to correct his wrong impression that he's seeing a bear print. Before they reach Lone Pine Lake they've noticed the tracks of raccoon, marmot, coyote, bobcat, skunk, deer and porcupine, but no bear. That night as Mother and Stella sleep, the many sounds Roy hears outside keep him awake. When Roy peeks out of the tent he sees a brown bear and his camping experience is complete. (40 pages)

Where it's reviewed:
Booklist, July 1999, page 1956
Horn Book Guide, Fall 1999, page 271
Horn Book, May 1999, page 325
Publishers Weekly, May 24, 1999, page 81
School Library Journal, June 1999, page 109

Other books by the same author:
Only the Cat Saw, 1996
Stella and Roy, 1993 (School Library Journal Best Book)
Come With Me, 1990

Other books you might like:
Jim Arnosky, *I See Animals Hiding*, 1995
    A nonfiction title describes animals' use of camouflage to protect themselves.
Marion Dane Bauer, *When I Go Camping with Grandma*, 1995
    A loving relationship between a child and her grandmother is shared on a camping trip.
Lindsay Barrett George, *Around the Pond: Who's Been Here?*, 1996
    As three children walk along a lake path in search of blueberries they notice signs of animal life and successfully identify eight animals.
Cynthia Rylant, *Henry and Mudge and the Starry Night*, 1998
    A family camping trip includes hiking, singing around the campfire and quiet times with Henry's dog Mudge.

1063

JANET S. WONG
MARGARET CHODOS-IRVINE, Illustrator

Buzz

(San Diego: Harcourt, Inc., 2000)

Subject(s): Animals/Bees; Family Life; Parent and Child

Age range(s): Preschool
Major character(s): Unnamed Character, Child, Son; Daddy, Father, Spouse; Mommy, Mother, Spouse
Time period(s): 2000s (2000)
Locale(s): United States

Summary: A young boy awakens before the buzz from his parents' alarm clock to watch a bee buzz past his window and settle on a flower. The sound of buzzing accompanies Daddy's razor as he shaves and Mommy's blender as she prepares a banana shake. The buzz repeats as the garage door goes up to let Daddy's car out and Mommy grinds beans for coffee. When the doorbell buzzes the little boy knows his grandmother has arrived to care for him while Mommy hurries away to work—just like a busy bee. (32 pages)

Where it's reviewed:
Booklist, July 2000, page 2044
Horn Book, May 2000, page 304
Riverbank Review, Fall 2000, page 27
School Library Journal, May 2000, page 158

Awards the book has won:
School Library Journal Best Books, 2000

Other books you might like:
Arlene Alda, *Pig, Horse, or Cow, Don't Wake Me Now*, 1994
    A peacock's call awakens one animal after another, but Scott is reluctant to rise and face a new day.
Byron Barton, *Buzz Buzz Buzz*, 1973
    When a bee stings a bull, a chain of events begins that affects everyone on the farm.
Jonathan London, *Like Butter on Pancakes*, 1995
    Morning sounds on a farm awaken Mama, Papa and their son to begin another active day.

1064

JANET S. WONG
YANGSOOK CHOI, Illustrator

This Next New Year

(New York: Frances Foster Books/Farrar Straus Giroux, 2000)

Subject(s): Holidays; Asian Americans; Traditions
Age range(s): Grades K-3
Major character(s): Unnamed Character, Child, Son
Time period(s): 2000s (2000)
Locale(s): United States

Summary: A young boy eagerly anticipates the lunar new year, the day of the first new moon, when his family eats Korean new year soup. This year he feels the good luck beginning already and he promises not to be afraid of firecrackers or the dragon in the parade. He helps clean the house thoroughly knowing that all of last year's bad luck is being thrown out with the trash. He takes a bath to get extra clean and even flosses his teeth. While he has no new clothes he puts on the cleanest clothes he has, confident that luck will bring him new clothes soon. The Chinese New Year's Day gives him a chance to start anew to make his many dreams come true. (32 pages)

Where it's reviewed:
Booklist, September 15, 2000, page 251

Bulletin of the Center for Children's Books, September 2000, page 42

Horn Book, November 2000, page 751

Kirkus Reviews, September 1, 2000, page 1294

School Library Journal, October 2000, page 142

Other books by the same author:

Buzz, 2000 (School Library Journal Best Book)

The Rainbow Hand: Poems about Mothers and Children, 1999

Other books you might like:

Dave Bouchard, *The Dragon New Year: A Chinese Legend*, 1999

The noise of the Chinese New Year's celebration frightens a young girl who is comforted by her grandmother's story.

Karen Chinn, *Sam and the Lucky Money*, 1995

Sam receives money for the Chinese New Year and wonders how to spend it.

William Low, *Chinatown*, 1997

With his grandmother a young boy enjoys Chinatown's celebration of the New Year.

1065

JANET S. WONG
BO JIA, Illustrator

The Trip Back Home

(San Diego: Harcourt, Inc., 2000)

Subject(s): Family Life; Korean Americans; Cultures and Customs

Age range(s): Grades K-3

Major character(s): Mother, Mother, Daughter; Haraboji, Grandfather, Farmer; Halmoni, Grandmother; Unnamed Character, Daughter, Niece

Time period(s): Indeterminate Past

Locale(s): United States; Republic of Korea

Summary: A lengthy plane trip brings Mother and her young daughter to visit relatives in rural Korea. Upon arrival they present gifts from America and receive hugs in return. The little girl shops with Halmoni at the market and gathers pine branches for the kitchen fire. She watches Haraboji place persimmons on the roof for storage and listens to his stories in the evenings. With her aunt she reads from the American picture book they brought to help her learn English. When it is time to go the relatives give them gifts representative of their stay in Korea and in return they give hugs. (32 pages)

Where it's reviewed:

Booklist, November 15, 2000, page 651

Horn Book Guide, Spring 2001, page 54

Riverbank Review, Spring 2001, page 36

School Library Journal, December 2000, page 128

Other books by the same author:

Buzz, 2000

This Next New Year, 2000

The Rainbow Hand: Poems about Mothers and Children, 1999

Good Luck Gold and Other Poems, 1994

Other books you might like:

Eve Bunting, *I Have an Olive Tree*, 1999

Sophia learns about her ancestral roots when she visits an olive tree planted on the small Greek island that is her mother's birthplace.

Sook Nyul Choi, *Yunmi and Halmoni's Trip*, 1997

Yunmi and Halmoni travel to Seoul to visit family and celebrate her deceased grandfather's birthday according to Korean custom.

Yumi Heo, *Father's Rubber Shoes*, 1995

As a recent immigrant, Yungsu feels lonely for his friends in Korea and hopeful of adjusting to a new country.

1066

AUDREY WOOD
DON WOOD, Illustrator

Jubal's Wish

(New York: The Blue Sky Press/Scholastic Inc., 2000)

Subject(s): Animals/Frogs and Toads; Wishes; Friendship

Age range(s): Grades K-1

Major character(s): Jubal Bullfrog, Frog, Friend; Gerdy Toad, Toad, Mother; Dalbert Lizard, Lizard, Sea Captain

Time period(s): Indeterminate

Locale(s): Fictional Country

Summary: Jubal's sunny mood on a picnic-perfect day is quashed by the grumpy, over-worked Gerdy and the depressed, aging Captain Lizard. When Jubal wishes that he could do something to make his friends happy a wizard appears and gives him a wish. When Jubal hurries to visit his friends again to see if his wish worked he's disappointed that his friends seem to feel worse. Jubal goes home to sit on his toadstool and cry as a rainstorm begins. Just as Jubal is in danger of being swept away by floodwaters a boat sails into view and Captain Lizard rescues him. Gerdy and her children are already aboard the boat, the sun comes out and they all sail happily away on an adventure. (32 pages)

Where it's reviewed:

Booklist, December 1, 2000, page 724

Horn Book Guide, Spring 2001, page 1438

Kirkus Reviews, October 1, 2000, page 1438

Publishers Weekly, September 25, 2000, page 115

School Library Journal, October 2000, page 143

Other books by the same author:

Sweet Dream Pie, 1998

The Flying Dragon Room, 1996

The Red Racer, 1996

Other books you might like:

Keiko Kasza, *Grandpa Toad's Last Secret*, 1995

Little Toad saves Grandpa Toad just in time to learn the last of his three secrets for survival.

Jonathan London, *Let's Go, Froggy!*, 1994

On a beautiful, sunny day Froggy's father suggests they go on a bike ride and enjoy a picnic lunch.

Ellen Stoll Walsh, *Jack's Tale*, 1997

Jack agrees to walk through a tale for an author only because it's a nice day. In the end he marries the princess and lives happily ever after.

1067

DOUGLAS WOOD
DOUG CUSHMAN, Illustrator

What Dads Can't Do

(New York: Simon & Schuster Books for Young Readers, 2000)

Subject(s): Fathers; Parent and Child; Love
Age range(s): Grades K-2
Major character(s): Unnamed Character, Reptile, Son; Unnamed Character, Single Father, Reptile
Time period(s): 2000s (2000)
Locale(s): Fictional Country

Summary: A youngster observes that "regular" people can do many things such as cross the street without holding hands or hit a baseball really far, but dads can't do those things. From interacting with his father he also deduces that dads are unable to win at checkers, find their sons while playing hide and seek, or set up a tent without help. Dads also can't read alone, go to sleep without lots of kisses or ever stop loving their children. (32 pages)

Where it's reviewed:
Horn Book Guide, Fall 2000, page 286
Kirkus Reviews, May 15, 2000, page 115
Publishers Weekly, May 15, 2000, page 115
School Library Journal, May 2000, page 159

Other books by the same author:
Rabbit and the Moon, 1998
Northwoods Cradle Song, 1996
Old Turtle, 1991

Other books you might like:
Margaret Park Bridges, *If I Were Your Father*, 1999
    While sharing activities with his father a little boy imagines himself in the role.
Mercer Mayer, *Just Me and My Dad*, 1977
    The illustrations depict what actually happens during a father and son camping adventure.
Laura Joffe Numeroff, *What Mommies Do Best, What Daddies Do Best*, 1998
    Everyday in simple ways, parents' actions speak of the love they feel for their child.
Bethany Roberts, *Waiting-for-Papa Stories*, 1990
    Mama Rabbit distracts her anxious children with funny anecdotes about Papa as the family awaits his return.
Charlotte Zolotow, *A Father Like That*, 1971
    To his mom a young boy offers a description of the ideal father.

1068

ELVIRA WOODRUFF
ELAINE CLAYTON, Illustrator

The Ghost of Lizard Light

(New York: Alfred A. Knopf, 1999)

Subject(s): Ghosts; Moving, Household; Fathers and Sons
Age range(s): Grades 3-5
Major character(s): Jack Carlton, 10-Year-Old, Son; Nathaniel Witherspoon, Spirit; Mr. Carlton, Father, Principal

Time period(s): 1990s (1999)
Locale(s): Ames, Iowa; Minty, Maine (Lizard Light)

Summary: The unexpected news that Mr. Carlton has taken a job in Maine and the family is moving to a small town on the coast makes Jack both sad and angry. Jack leaves his best friend behind and his overly critical father fills his summer with math worksheets and complaints about Jack's poor performance. Having Nathaniel appear literally out of nowhere gives Jack a friend, someone to talk to and someone from whom to learn about the lighthouse, the rental cottage and the sea. Nathaniel is lonely too but also he seeks someone to set right a 150-year-old injustice done to his father, the former lighthouse keeper. He sees Jack as just the adventurous sort of boy he needs for the job. Jack uses the boating skills Nathaniel teaches him to save his mother, sister and uncle from drowning when their sailboat capsizes. The experience helps to heal the rift with his father so the move truly can become a fresh start for both of them. (176 pages)

Where it's reviewed:
Children's Book Review Service, November 1999, page 36
Children's Bookwatch, December 1999, page 5
Horn Book Guide, Spring 2000, page 91
School Library Journal, January 2000, page 136

Other books by the same author:
The Orphan of Ellis Island: A Time-Travel Adventure, 1997
Dear Levi: Letters from the Overland Trail, 1994
Ghosts Don't Get Goosebumps, 1993

Other books you might like:
Eileen Dunlop, *The Ghost by the Sea*, 1996
    Two cousins try to solve the mysterious drowning of an ancestor so Milly's spirit can finally rest and stop haunting their grandparent's home.
Hilary McKay, *The Amber Cat*, 1997
    While recovering from chicken pox, two friends meet Harriet, a ghost who returns from time to time to visit them.
Betty Ren Wright, *The Ghost of Popcorn Hill*, 1993
    To rid themselves of a lonely ghost's nightly visits Martin and Peter match him up with a ghost dog that's been visiting them too.

1069

ELVIRA WOODRUFF
MICHAEL DOOLING, Illustrator

The Memory Coat

(New York: Scholastic Press, 1999)

Subject(s): Emigration and Immigration; Jews; Cousins
Age range(s): Grades 1-4
Major character(s): Rachel, Child, Cousin; Grisha, Child, Cousin
Time period(s): Indeterminate Past
Locale(s): Russia; New York, New York (Ellis Island)

Summary: Since the death of his parents, Grisha has lived with Rachel in her shetl. In his grief, Grisha takes comfort in the coat his mother made before she died. After the tzar's cossacks terrorize their shetl, Rachel and Grisha, with her family, flee to America. After arriving at Ellis Island, while playing a game with Rachel, Grisha falls and cuts his eye. The doctor marks Grisha's coat indicating that he must go back to Russia, but Rachel just turns his coat inside out so the marks are not visible. Grisha then goes to a doctor who understands Yiddish and he is allowed to stay in America. (32 pages)

Where it's reviewed:
Booklist, January 1, 1999, page 892
Kirkus Reviews, January 1, 1999, page 73
Publishers Weekly, January 18, 1999, page 339
School Library Journal, March 1999, page 188
Smithsonian Magazine, November 1999, page 52

Awards the book has won:
Smithsonian's Notable Books for Children, 1999
Notable Social Studies Trade Books for Young People, 2000

Other books by the same author:
Mrs. McCloskey's Monkeys, 1991
The Wing Shop, 1991
Show and Tell, 1991

Other books you might like:
Amy Hest, *When Jessie Came Across the Sea*, 1997
   Jessie immigrates to America from an Eastern European shetl.
Patricia Polacco, *The Keeping Quilt*, 1988
   A quilt made in Russia connects four generations of a Jewish immigrant family.
Simms Taback, *Joseph Had a Little Overcoat*, 1999
   The newly illustrated version of Taback's book about Joseph's versatile coat won the Caldecott Medal.
Edith Tarbescu, *Annushka's Voyage*, 1998
   Annushka travels with her little sister from Russia through Ellis Island to join their father in New York.

1070

CHRISTOPHER WORMELL, Author/Illustrator

Blue Rabbit and Friends

(New York: Phyllis Fogelman Books, 2000)

Subject(s): Animals/Rabbits; Animals; Dwellings
Age range(s): Preschool
Major character(s): Blue Rabbit, Rabbit, Toy; Bear, Bear, Toy; Goose, Goose, Toy
Time period(s): Indeterminate
Locale(s): Fictional Country

Summary: Blue Rabbit abandons his unsatisfactory home and searches for something he considers more suitable. He asks each animal he meets if they know of a good dwelling place. Blue Rabbit's question seems to prompt reflection for each animal soon recognizes that they're not satisfied with their living quarters either. Bear thinks his home is a little too wet and Goose thinks her house is too dry and enclosed. Soon, Bear, Goose and Blue Rabbit find a more suitable occupant for Goose's dry home that smells of old bones. Then Goose moves into Bear's former "too wet" home; Bear happily accepts Blue Rabbit's too big and dark cave. Blue Rabbit, meanwhile, gives up on the search and decides to travel. Originally published in the United Kingdom in 1999. (32 pages)

Where it's reviewed:
Booklist, January 1, 2000, page 938
Horn Book Guide, Fall 2000, page 259
Publishers Weekly, January 17, 2000, page 55
Riverbank Review, Fall 2000, page 27
School Library Journal, February 2000, page 106

Awards the book has won:
School Library Journal Best Books, 2000

Other books by the same author:
Blue Rabbit and the Runaway Wheel, 2001
Puff-Puff, Chugga-Chugga, 2001
An Alphabet of Animals, 1996
What I Eat, 1996
Where I Live, 1996

Other books you might like:
Shirley Isherwood, *Something for James*, 1996
   The shy "something" James receives finally leaves the security of its brown paper bag to snuggle with James and his stuffed animal friends in bed.
Betsy Lewin, *Chubbo's Pool*, 1996
   Chubbo the hippo refuses to share his perfect home until a drought dries up his pool, elephants help him refill it and Chubbo learns to be generous.
Sam McBratney, *Just You and Me*, 1998
   Little Goosey and Big Gander Goose seek shelter from the rain in a spot that they don't have to share with any other animals.
A.A. Milne, *Winnie the Pooh*, 1926
   Christopher Robin and his stuffed bear, Winnie the Pooh, share humorous adventures and daring feats in the Hundred Acre Wood.

1071

MARY WORMELL, Author/Illustrator

Why Not?

(New York: Farrar Straus Giroux, 2000)

Subject(s): Animals/Cats; Mothers and Sons; Animals
Age range(s): Preschool
Major character(s): Barnaby, Cat (kitten)
Time period(s): 1990s (1999)
Locale(s): Scotland

Summary: As Barnaby's mom calls him to supper she also warns him not to chase the chickens, scare the birds, annoy the sheep or frighten the foal along the way. To each warning, Barnaby responds, "Why not?" and the adult animal of the species answers protectively. At last Barnaby meanders as far as the hay bales and, ignoring his mother again, becomes stuck when he squeezes into the pile. The adult farm animals offer to help, but independent Barnaby says no and answers their question, "Why not?" by freeing himself. (32 pages)

Where it's reviewed:
Bulletin of the Center for Children's Books, March 2000, page 259
Children's Book Review Service, April 2000, page 100
Kirkus Reviews, January 15, 2000, page 126
Publishers Weekly, January 10, 2000, page 66
School Library Journal, March 2000, page 220

Other books by the same author:
Hilda Hen's Scary Night, 1996
Hilda Hen's Happy Birthday, 1995
Hilda Hen's Search, 1994

Other books you might like:
Tomie DePaola, *Kit and Kat*, 1994
    Three brief stories in a beginning reader describe the activities of sibling cats.

Denise Fleming, *Mama Cat Has Three Kittens*, 1998
    Two of Mama Cat's three kittens follow directions while the other one, Boris, has a mind of his own.
Pat Hutchins, *Little Pink Pig*, 1994
    The other animals help Little Pink Pig's mother search the farm for her lost offspring who stays one step behind calling, ''Wait for me!''

Y

1072

DAN YACCARINO, Author/Illustrator

Deep in the Jungle

(New York: Anne Schwartz Book/Atheneum Books for Young Readers, 2000)

Subject(s): Animals; Animals/Lions; Circus
Age range(s): Grades K-3
Major character(s): Unnamed Character, Lion; Unnamed Character, Animal Trainer
Time period(s): Indeterminate
Locale(s): Fictional Country

Summary: Arrogant lion expects the other jungle animals to attend to his every need or risk becoming his next meal. The jungle animals are happy to see the pompous lion's pride convince him to take up an offer to be in show business. Too late the lion discovers that the show is the circus and he must live in a cage, respond to a whip, never roar and listen to the lion tamer get all the applause, When he's had about all he can take of the arrangement, the lion swallows the lion tamer with one gulp and follows the railroad tracks back to the jungle. He arrives just in time to demonstrate his trick again and free the other animals from cages before they can be taken away. Lion learns his lesson and treats the other jungle animals with more respect. (40 pages)

Where it's reviewed:
Booklist, March 1, 2000, page 1253
Horn Book, March 2000, page 191
Kirkus Reviews, February 15, 2000, page 246
Publishers Weekly, January 3, 2000, page 75
School Library Journal, February 2000, page 106

Other books by the same author:
First Day on a Strange New Planet, 2000
Five Little Pumpkins, 1998
An Octopus Followed Me Home, 1997
Good Night, Mr. Night, 1997
Zoom! Zoom! Zoom! I'm Off to the Moon!, 1997
If I Had a Robot, 1996 (IRA/CBC Children's Choices)

Other books you might like:
Andrew Clements, *Circus Family Dog*, 2000
   Grumps, an old dog with one trick, fears being upstaged by Sparks, a new dog with a varied repertoire.
Dr. Seuss, *If I Ran the Circus*, 1956
   Morris McGurk has grand plans for Circus McGurkus on the empty lot behind Mr. Sneelock's store.
Bernard Waber, *A Lion Named Shirley Williamson*, 2000
   The other zoo lions are jealous of the new lion with a fancy name until they're given new names too.

1073

BELLE YANG, Author/Illustrator

Chili-Chili-Chin-Chin

(San Diego: Silver Whistle/Harcourt Brace & Company, 1999)

Subject(s): Animals/Donkeys; Individuality; Friendship
Age range(s): Grades K-2
Major character(s): Chili-Chili-Chin-Chin, Donkey; Unnamed Character, Child, Friend
Time period(s): Indeterminate Past
Locale(s): China

Summary: Some people try to own a small donkey but the independent critter does not want to be ridden like a horse or hitched to a plow or kept on a leash as if it were a puppy. The only one who can catch the donkey is the little boy who gives it the name Chili-Chili-Chin-Chin. The boy enjoys the activities they share even as he allows Chili-Chili-Chin-Chin the freedom to be true to himself. What a good friend! This is the first children's book for an author of two adult titles. (32 pages)

Where it's reviewed:
Booklist, July 1999, page 1956
Horn Book Guide, Fall 1999, page 271
Kirkus Reviews, May 15, 1999, page 807
Publishers Weekly, April 26, 1999, page 81
School Library Journal, June 1999, page 110

Other books you might like:

Nancy White Carlstrom, *The Way to Wyatt's House*, 2000
    After a quiet walk to Wyatt's farm siblings play noisily with their friend and his farm animals.

Bob Graham, *Queenie*, 1997
    Caitlin's family returns Queenie to the farm but the independent hen reappears daily in their home to lay an egg in Bruno's dog bed.

Sam McBratney, *Just You and Me*, 1998
    Little Goosey refuses to share shelter from a storm with anyone but Big Gander Goose.

1074

BRENDA SHANNON YEE
THEA KLIROS, Illustrator

Sand Castle

(New York: Greenwillow Books, 1999)

Subject(s): Sandcastles; Beaches; Summer
Age range(s): Grades K-2
Major character(s): Jen, Child
Time period(s): 1990s (1999)
Locale(s): United States

Summary: As Jen sits quietly on the beach building a sand castle one uninvited child after another joins her to expand the project. No one interferes with what another child is doing; each adds another dimension and all work cooperatively. The first boy begins a moat, then a girl digs a path to the lake to bring water to the moat and another boy builds a wall while a girl decides a road is needed. Just as the children complete their work, they hear parents calling them and they are concerned about what will happen to their castle. Jen knows just what to do and everyone happily joins in to help her smash the creation as the author's first picture book concludes. (24 pages)

Where it's reviewed:

Children's Book Review Service, July 1999, page 150
Horn Book Guide, Fall 1999, page 242
Horn Book, July 1999, page 459
School Library Journal, June 1999, page 110

Other books you might like:

Marsha Hayles, *Beach Play*, 1998
    A little girl's day by the sea includes playing in the surf and building a castle of sand.

Mick Inkpen, *Sandcastle*, 1999
    After completing his sandcastle Kipper searches the beach for the perfect adornment.

Olof Landstrom, *Will Goes to the Beach*, 1995
    In the latest of Will's adventures, he enjoys a holiday swimming at the beach.

Anne F. Rockwell, *At the Beach*, 1987
    A young child enjoys a busy beach day gathering shells and making a sandcastle.

1075

WONG HERBERT YEE, Author/Illustrator

Hamburger Heaven

(Boston: Houghton Mifflin Company, 1999)

Subject(s): Food; Restaurants; Animals/Pigs
Age range(s): Grades K-2
Major character(s): Pinky Pig, Pig, Student; Chef Rhino, Rhinoceros, Cook
Time period(s): Indeterminate
Locale(s): Fictional Country

Summary: To earn the money for a new clarinet Pinky Pig works every day after school at Hamburger Heaven. Overhearing a conversation in which Chef Rhino mentions that poor business may put Pinky out of work causes Pinky some concern. Not one to worry for nothing Pinky instead puts on her thinking cap and comes up with an idea to save the restaurant. Her plan works so well that Chef Rhino gives her a raise and Pinky is finally able to buy that clarinet in the window of Moozart's store. (32 pages)

Where it's reviewed:

Children's Book Review Service, June 1999, page 126
Horn Book Guide, Fall 1999, page 271
Kirkus Reviews, March 1, 1999, page 383
Publishers Weekly, April 12, 1999, page 74
School Library Journal, May 1999, page 101

Awards the book has won:

IRA/CBC Children's Choices, 2000

Other books by the same author:

Mrs. Brown Went to Town, 1996
Fireman Small, 1994
Eek! There's a Mouse in the House, 1992

Other books you might like:

Stephanie Calmenson, *Dinner at the Panda Palace*, 1991
    A story in rhyme describes a restaurant so crowded that Mr. Panda finds innovative ways of seating his many patrons.

Maggie S. Davis, *The Rinky-Dink Cafe*, 1988
    Hungry Pig takes a restaurant's advertisement, ''Dinners Made to Order,'' to heart and stomach and keeps the cook hopping.

Tim Egan, *Friday Night at Hodges' Cafe*, 1994
    Hodges's pet duck helps to save the restaurant's patrons from three tigers that obviously have plans to dine on something that's not on the menu.

Maryann Kovalski, *Pizza for Breakfast*, 1991
    Frank and Zelda come to regret their wish for more customers at their pizza restaurant.

Daniel Pinkwater, *Blue Moose*, 1975
    One winter a talking blue moose serves as the headwaiter in a restaurant near the north woods.

1076

LAURENCE YEP

Cockroach Cooties

(New York: Hyperion Books for Children, 2000)

Subject(s): Brothers; Bullies; Animals/Insects
Age range(s): Grades 3-5
Major character(s): Bobby, 8-Year-Old, Brother; Teddy, 9-Year-Old, Brother; Arnie, Bully, 9-Year-Old
Time period(s): 1990s
Locale(s): San Francisco, California (Chinatown)

Summary: When Bobby antagonizes Arnie and Teddy tries to defend him they both become targets of a bully with a long memory. Although they try various strategies to protect themselves, they discover a secret weapon in a cockroach. Arnie is afraid of bugs! Teddy's not too fond of them either, but all forms of life fascinate Bobby. Teddy thinks his brother is a little strange for trying to look at the world from a bug's point of view, but when Bobby applies the same empathy to Arnie the brothers are able to solve the bully problem without injury to anyone. (135 pages)

Where it's reviewed:
Booklist, May 1, 2000, page 1671
Horn Book Guide, Fall 2000, page 315
Publishers Weekly, February 14, 2000, page 200
School Library Journal, May 2000, page 159

Other books by the same author:
The Journal of Wong Ming-Chung: A Chinese Miner, 2000 (My Name Is America)
The Case of the Goblin Pearls, 1997
Later, Gator, 1995

Other books you might like:
Betsy Duffey, *Alien for Rent*, 1999
Quite unintentionally J.P. and Lexie direct the powers of a small fuzzy alien against the school bully with unexpected results.
Juanita Havill, *Saving Owen's Toad*, 1994
The squabbling between Owen and his older brother almost leads to disaster when Owen's efforts to save his toad put him in the emergency room
Dyan Sheldon, *My Brother Is a Superhero*, 1996
When three bullies harass Adam and his friend they try to handle the problem but are grateful when Adam's older brother intervenes.
Elizabeth Winthrop, *Luke's Bully*, 1990
A class play gives shy Luke an opportunity to hide from a bothersome bully.

1077

LAURENCE YEP

The Journal of Wong Ming-Chung: A Chinese Miner

(New York: Scholastic Inc., 2000)

Series: My Name Is America
Subject(s): Gold Discoveries; Chinese Americans; Family Relations

Age range(s): Grades 4-6
Major character(s): Runt, Son (youngest), 12-Year-Old; Precious Stone, Uncle, Immigrant; Blessing, Brother (oldest), Teenager
Time period(s): 1850s (1851-1852)
Locale(s): Tiger Rock, China; San Francisco, California; California

Summary: News of the discovery of gold in California starts a gold fever in Uncle Stone who dreams of easy wealth. Although Runt's parents disagree with Precious Stone's plans, as the oldest son he exercises his right to sell family land to purchase his ticket to the Golden Mountain. Blessing is excited when Uncle Stone sends the family money and a demand that Blessing be sent to him. Runt's parents disobey and send their second son instead. Small and insecure, Runt has no desire to leave the family, but he obeys his parents, survives the perilous journey, makes friends and eventually finds Uncle Stone in the gold fields. Runt's literacy contributes to his ability to overcome prejudice, bullies and humiliation while his respect for family enables him to help his impulsive Uncle Stone survive and find success in the gold fields. (214 pages)

Where it's reviewed:
Booklist, April 1, 2000, page 1473
Horn Book Guide, Fall 2000, page 315
Kirkus Reviews, March 1, 2000, page 310
Kliatt, March 2000, page 12
School Library Journal, April 2000, page 143

Other books by the same author:
The Cook's Family, 1998
The Dragon Prince: A Chinese Beauty & the Beast Tale, 1997
Ribbons, 1996

Other books you might like:
Eleanor Coerr, *Chang's Paper Pony*, 1988
In San Francisco at the time of the Gold Rush, a son of Chinese immigrants wants a pony that he knows his parents cannot afford.
Barbara Diamond Goldin, *Red Means Good Fortune: A Story of San Francisco Chinatown*, 1994
In an entry in the Once Upon America Series, 12-year-old Jun Mun works in his father's laundry.
Stephen Krensky, *The Iron Dragon Never Sleeps*, 1994
Chinese laborers working on the transcontinental railroad face prejudicial treatment from construction supervisors and townspeople.

1078

LAURENCE YEP
SULING WANG, Illustrator

The Magic Paintbrush

(New York: HarperCollins Publishers, 2000)

Subject(s): Chinese Americans; Old Age; Magic
Age range(s): Grades 3-5
Major character(s): Steve, Orphan, 3rd Grader; Grandfather, Grandfather, Aged Person; Uncle Fong, Aged Person, Friend
Time period(s): 1960s; Indeterminate Past

Locale(s): San Francisco, California (Chinatown); Fictional Country

Summary: After losing his parents and his home in a fire, Steve moves to Chinatown to live in a room in a crowded, run-down building with Grandfather and Uncle Fong. Grandfather's gruff attitude makes Steve feel unwanted and afraid to tell Grandfather of his need for school supplies. When a worn-out brush causes Steve to fail an art assignment, Grandfather rummages in an old box of mementos and finds a paintbrush that has been handed down from his grandfather. The magical brush changes Steve's pictures into the actual object he paints, giving Steve an idea for transforming the dreary lives of the three lonely occupants of the room and bringing them greater understanding of themselves and each other. (96 pages)

Where it's reviewed:
Booklist, February 1, 2000, page 1024
Bulletin of the Center for Children's Books, April 2000, page 295
Kirkus Reviews, December 1, 1999, page 1893
Publishers Weekly, March 13, 2000, page 85
School Library Journal, March 2000, page 220

Other books by the same author:
The Cook's Family, 1998
The Imp that Ate My Homework, 1998
The Case of the Goblin Pearls, 1997
Ribbons, 1996

Other books you might like:
Constance Hiser, *No Bean Sprouts, Please!*, 1989
    James receives a lunch box from Uncle Wesley that seems to have the magical ability to transform his boring lunches into something more appealing.
Lensey Namioka, *Yang the Third and Her Impossible Family*, 1995
    Newly arrived from China and seeking acceptance Yingmei adopts an American name, Mary, while trying to hold on to her Chinese culture also.
Marilyn Singer, *The Painted Fan*, 1994
    A magical fan enables Bright Willow to fulfill a dangerous quest and a soothsayer's prophecy.

1079

THOMAS F. YEZERSKI, Author/Illustrator

Queen of the World

(New York: Farrar Straus Giroux, 2000)

Subject(s): Sisters; Sibling Rivalry; Family Life
Age range(s): Grades 1-3
Major character(s): Amanda, Sister (oldest), Daughter; Natalie, Sister (youngest), Daughter; Mom, Mother
Time period(s): Indeterminate Past
Locale(s): United States

Summary: Three sisters with nothing in common except the bedroom they share compete for their parents' love and attention. They see Mom's birthday as an opportunity to declare one of them the best! In anticipation of being recognized as the creator of the best birthday present they cooperatively make a crown. After the middle sister draws the shape,

Natalie cuts it out and Amanda writes "Queen of the World" in her best cursive. Then the three separate to secretly work on the gifts. The gift presentation turns into a squabble over whose gift is best. During the argument the crown is torn, Mom cries and the girls' father sends them to their room without cake. Truly remorseful, the three sisters huddle in the top bunk and plan appropriate redemption. In the morning they awaken early and secretly make Mom's favorite breakfast to serve to her in bed as they crown her "Queen of the World" forever. Despite their differences, the sisters realize that they can also agree that they love their mother "forever, with no taking back." (32 pages)

Where it's reviewed:
Booklist, September 1, 2000, page 126
Horn Book Guide, Spring 2001, page 54
Horn Book, September 2000, page 561
School Library Journal, October 2000, page 143

Other books by the same author:
Together in Pinecone Patch, 1999 (Riverbank Review Children's Books of Distinction)

Other books you might like:
Judy Blume, *The Pain and the Great One*, 1974
    A brother and sister resent each other for being the best loved in the family.
Marissa Moss, *Amelia's Notebook*, 1995
    Amelia expresses her thoughts about her older, revolting sister in a notebook decorated to illustrate her points.
Hiawyn Oram, *The Second Princess*, 1994
    Second Princess is determined to take over her sister's position as First Princess.
Jean Van Leeuwen, *Two Girls in Sister Dresses*, 1994
    As the older sister, Jennifer is alternately protective of Molly and jealous of the attention others give her.

1080

JANE YOLEN
MARK TEAGUE, Illustrator

How Do Dinosaurs Say Goodnight?

(New York: The Blue Sky Press/Scholastic Inc., 2000)

Subject(s): Dinosaurs; Bedtime; Stories in Rhyme
Age range(s): Grades K-1
Time period(s): Indeterminate
Locale(s): Fictional Country

Summary: A succession of human parents show a range of emotions as they try to coax their dinosaurs into bed. Do dinosaurs cry, mope or pout when they learn it's bedtime? Do they roar or stomp or beg to hear one more book? No, dinosaurs simply cuddle up in their beds, give one last kiss and turn out the light. (40 pages)

Where it's reviewed:
Booklist, April 1, 2000, page 1456
Five Owls, January 2000, page 65
Horn Book Guide, Fall 2000, page 259
Publishers Weekly, April 24, 2000, page 89
School Library Journal, June 2000, page 128

Awards the book has won:
Booklist Editors' Choice, 2000

School Library Journal Best Books, 2000

Other books by the same author:
Off We Go!, 2000
Nocturne, 1997
Beneath the Ghost Moon, 1994
Owl Moon, 1987 (Caldecott Medal)

Other books you might like:
Berkeley Breathed, *Goodnight Opus*, 1993
Grandma falls asleep while reading Opus's favorite bedtime story for the 210th time, so Opus carries on with his own imaginative version of the tale.
Michael Foreman, *Dad! I Can't Sleep*, 1995
Dad's going-to-sleep suggestions fail to produce the desired effect
Peggy Rathmann, *10 Minutes till Bedtime*, 1998
When a child's father announces, "10 minutes till bedtime," the hamster tour guide springs into actions with the "Bedtime Tour."

1081

JANE YOLEN
HEIDI ELISABET YOLEN STEMPLE, Co-Author
ROGER ROTH, Illustrator

The Mary Celeste: An Unsolved Mystery from History

(New York: Simon & Schuster Books for Young Readers, 1999)

Subject(s): Mystery; Ships; Abandonment
Age range(s): Grades 3-5
Major character(s): Unnamed Character, Detective—Amateur; David Reed Morehouse, Sea Captain; Mr. Deveau, Sailor (first mate)
Time period(s): 1990s (1999); 1870s (1872)
Locale(s): *Dei Gratia*, At Sea

Summary: A young girl wants to follow in her father's footsteps and become a detective. For practice she tries to solve incidents in history that seem to have no explanation. She researches all the facts she can find about the *Mary Celeste* a ship found floating crewless in the Atlantic by Captain Morehouse and his crew. Captain Morehouse sends Mr. Deveau and two of the crew to investigate the ship. They find no sign of a struggle and plenty of food and water yet the lifeboat and the ten people known to have been aboard are missing. The young amateur detective considers the facts, lists the prevalent theories and develops one of her own, but no one knows what truly happened many years ago. (32 pages)

Where it's reviewed:
Booklist, October 15, 1999, page 447
Bulletin of the Center for Children's Books, November 1999, page 111
Children's Book Review Service, December 1999, page 45
Publishers Weekly, November 22, 1999, page 56
School Library Journal, November 1999, page 133

Other books by the same author:
Meet the Monsters, 1996

Other books you might like:
Richard Berleth, *Mary Patten's Voyage*, 1994
With her tubercular husband bed-ridden and the first mate in the brig, Mary Patten takes the helm and safely brings the *Neptune Car* to port.
Odds Bodkin, *Ghost of the Southern Belle: A Sea Tale*, 1999
The *Southern Belle* sinks without a trace during a nor'easter but returns to haunt other schooners that she races to their doom.
Loretta Krupinski, *Bluewater Journal: The Voyage of the Sea Tiger*, 1995
Benjamin Slocum records the daily events of the voyage on his father's clipper ship from Boston to the Sandwich Islands.

1082

JANE YOLEN
GREG COUCH, Illustrator

Moonball

(New York: Simon & Schuster Books for Young Readers, 1999)

Subject(s): Sports/Baseball; Dreams and Nightmares; Fantasy
Age range(s): Grades 1-4
Major character(s): Danny Brower, Baseball Player, Child; Moon, Celestial Body, Pitcher
Time period(s): 1990s (1999)
Locale(s): United States; In the Air

Summary: Danny is well known for never hitting the ball and when he strikes out yet again to end a game he trudges home and goes sadly to bed. As he lies in bed staring at the moon he thinks of all the games he's played and wishes he could get just one hit. Then, as if in a dream, Danny floats out the window and into a ball game with the stars. The bases are loaded when Danny's gets his first at-bat. Moon taunts Danny, confident that he will be an easy out. The first two pitches are strikes as Danny swings and misses. For the final pitch Danny keeps his eyes open and he hits the ball for a grand slam home run! As Danny rounds the bases and dives into home he literally returns to his home and a good night's sleep. (40 pages)

Where it's reviewed:
Booklist, May 1, 1999, page 1601
Five Owls, March 2000, page 81
Publishers Weekly, March 8, 1999, page 67
Reading Teacher, May 2000, page 703
School Library Journal, March 1999, page 189

Other books by the same author:
Where Have the Unicorns Gone?, 2000
King Long Shanks, 1998 (School Library Journal Best Book)
Nocturne, 1997

Other books you might like:
Daniel Pinkwater, *Wallpaper from Space*, 1996
The space ships on Steve's new wallpaper not only glow in the dark but also carry him on an adventure to outer space.
Mindy Avra Portnoy, *Matzah Ball: A Passover Story*, 1994
Because Aaron cannot join his Gentile friends at the concession stand during Passover he's able to catch a ball hit into the stands while they're gone.

Willy Welch, *Playing Right Field*, 1995

A dejected player assigned to right field snaps out of his daydream just in time to catch a fly ball.

1083

JANE YOLEN, Adaptor
SUSAN GUEVARA, Illustrator

Not One Damsel in Distress: World Folktales for Strong Girls

(San Diego: Silver Whistle/Harcourt, Inc., 2000)

Subject(s): Folk Tales; Folklore; Women
Age range(s): Grades 3-5
Time period(s): Indeterminate Past
Locale(s): Earth

Summary: Thirteen folktales gathered from diverse traditions recount the bravery and skill of female heroes from Greece, Niger, France, Argentina and other countries. In the Chinese tale "Li Chi Slays the Serpent," Li Chi offers herself as the 10th maiden to be sacrificed to a huge serpent, asking only to be sent to face the monster with sword and snake-hunting dog and so she ends the life of the vicious serpent and saves timid maidens from death. In "Pretty Penny," a tale from the Ozarks, Old Jake's daughter Penny is not able to save her father's money from a highway robber, but she does trick the greedy thief and successfully steals his horse and saddlebags full of stolen gold and silver. Source notes and a bibliography for each tale conclude the collection. (116 pages)

Where it's reviewed:
Booklist, March 1, 2000, page 1240
Bulletin of the Center for Children's Books, April 2000, page 296
Horn Book Guide, Fall 2000, page 344
Kirkus Reviews, April 15, 2000, page 570
Publishers Weekly, May 15, 2000, page 119

Awards the book has won:
Notable Social Studies Trade Books for Young People, 2001

Other books by the same author:
Here There Be Ghosts, 1998
Here There Be Angels, 1996
Here There Be Unicorns, 1994

Other books you might like:
Alison Lurie, *Clever Gretchen and Other Forgotten Folktales*, 1980
    The fifteen tales in this collection of heroines are primarily from the European tradition.
Howard Norman, *The Girl Who Dreamed Only Geese and Other Tales of the Far North*, 1997
    An illustrated collection of ten Inuit stories records the oral history of a people and their harsh environment.
Katrin Tchana, *The Serpent Slayer*, 2000
    Eighteen folktales celebrate the strength and cleverness of heroines of diverse ages and cultures.

1084

JANE YOLEN
LAUREL MOLK, Illustrator

Off We Go!

(Boston: Little, Brown and Company, 2000)

Subject(s): Animals; Grandmothers; Stories in Rhyme
Age range(s): Preschool
Major character(s): Little Mouse, Mouse; Little Frog, Frog; Little Mole, Mole
Time period(s): 2000s
Locale(s): United States

Summary: Off hops Little Frog; off creeps Little Mole; off goes Little Mouse! Where? Off to Grandma's house, of course, the animals hurry along with a slithering snake, a crawling spider and a dashing duck, newly hatched. It doesn't matter what habitat Grandma considers home, to her grandchildren Grandma's house is the best. (32 pages)

Where it's reviewed:
Booklist, March 15, 2000, page 1390
Horn Book Guide, Fall 2000, page 259
Publishers Weekly, April 24, 2000, page 89
School Library Journal, May 2000, page 159

Other books by the same author:
King Long Shanks, 1998
Miz Berlin Walks, 1997
Nocturne, 1997
Beneath the Ghost Moon, 1994
Owl Moon, 1987 (Caldecott Medal)

Other books you might like:
Alyssa Satin Capucilli, *Good Morning, Pond*, 1994
    Early in the morning, three children observe the many animals of the pond awakening.
Lynn Plourde, *Pigs in the Mud in the Middle of the Rud*, 1997
    In this humorous story Grandma's trying to go with her family, but the Model T can't get past the animals stuck in the muddy road.
Jane Simmons, *Come Along, Daisy!*, 1998
    Mama Duck expects young Daisy to come along, but curious Daisy goes off exploring the pond until she's—lost!

1085

JANE YOLEN

The Pictish Child

(San Diego: Harcourt Brace & Company, 1999)

Series: Tartan Magic. Book 2
Subject(s): Magic; Time Travel; Brothers and Sisters
Age range(s): Grades 3-6
Major character(s): Jennifer, 13-Year-Old, Twin; Molly, 4-Year-Old, Sister; Ninia, Time Traveler (Pict), Royalty
Time period(s): 1990s (1999)
Locale(s): Fairburn, Scotland

Summary: Molly receives a talisman from one of her grandmother's friends that sets in motion a series of magical events. Jennifer, who seems to have inherited some of her grandmother's magic, feels uncomfortable about the decorated stone and soon her fears are realized when Ninia materializes in a cemetery's mist and demands the stone. More mist follows Ninia as she joins Molly, Jennifer and the others who barricade themselves in their grandmother's house using the magic of cold metal to keep out other spirits from earlier times. After learning some Pict history, they return to the nursing home and discover the true source of the power that has awakened the darkness of history. (135 pages)

Where it's reviewed:
Booklist, November 15, 1999, page 629
Horn Book Guide, Spring 2000, page 91
School Library Journal, December 1999, page 144

Other books by the same author:
The Wizard's Map, 1999 (Tartan Magic, Book 1)
Merlin, 1997 (Young Merlin Trilogy, Book 3)
Hobby, 1996 (Young Merlin Trilogy, Book 2)

Other books you might like:
Melvin Burgess, *The Earth Giant*, 1997
   When Amy finds a giant alien child trapped in the roots of a tree uprooted by a storm, she shelters it until the parents can retrieve it.
Susan Cooper, *The Boggart*, 1993
   Emily and Jessup seek a way to deal with a shape-changing, mischievous spirit that they've awakened in the Scottish castle inherited by their parents.
Dick King-Smith, *The Water Horse*, 1998
   A kelpie or Water Horse hatches from an unusual egg found on a beach and grows until it must be put someplace large—such as nearby Loch Ness.
William Mayne, *Hob and the Peddler*, 1997
   Hob, a friendly household spirit, must solve a perplexing problem lurking in the dark pond of his new home in order to keep everyone happy.

1086

ARTHUR YORINKS
MARTIN MATJE, Illustrator

Harry and Lulu

(New York: Hyperion Books for Children, 1999)

Subject(s): Animals/Dogs; Toys; Imagination
Age range(s): Grades K-2
Major character(s): Lulu, Child; Harry, Dog, Toy
Time period(s): 1990s (1999)
Locale(s): United States; Paris, France

Summary: Lulu's parents respond to her demands for a dog with a stuffed poodle named Harry. Their choice displeases temperamental Lulu so much that she throws Harry to the floor and kicks him. Later, Lulu is awakened by a squeaky bark and discovers that Harry is alive. Still angry, Lulu refuses to believe Harry's claim although she does reluctantly apologize for her mistreatment of an animal. Frustrated, Harry decides to return home to Paris and Lulu comes along for the walk. In Paris Lulu's obnoxious behavior does not improve but Harry, ever the faithful dog, willingly puts his own life at risk to save her from a speeding car. By the time the night is over, Lulu has returned the favor by rescuing Harry from the

Seine before they both return to Lulu's home for a good night's sleep. (32 pages)

Where it's reviewed:
Booklist, April 1, 1999, page 1409
Horn Book Guide, Fall 1999, page 271
Kirkus Reviews, March 15, 1999, page 459
Publishers Weekly, March 29, 1999, page 103
School Library Journal, May 1999, page 101

Other books by the same author:
The Flying Latke, 1999
The Miami Giant, 1995
Whitefish Will Rides Again, 1994
Bravo, Minski, 1988
Hey, Al, 1986 (Caldecott Medal)

Other books you might like:
Ludwig Bemelmans, *Madeline's Rescue*, 1953
   A stray dog rescues Madeleine from the Seine and then becomes her forbidden pet in this rhyming classic that won the Caldecott Medal.
John Burningham, *Courtney*, 1994
   Though their parents insist on a pedigreed dog, the children bring home a stray with so many talents, they're willing to keep it.
Wende Devlin, *The Trouble with Henriette!*, 1995
   Hay fever almost causes Jolie to lose her pet when the dog can no longer earn her keep by locating truffles.
Susan Meddaugh, *Martha Speaks*, 1992
   A bowl of alphabet soup transforms Martha from an ordinary household pet into a talking dog with a lot to say.
Cynthia Rylant, *Henry and Mudge*, 1987
   In the first book of a popular series, only-child Henry, lonely for companionship, begs his parents to allow him to have a dog.

1087

ARTHUR YORINKS
MORT DRUCKER, Illustrator

Tomatoes from Mars

(New York: Michael Di Capua Books/HarperCollins Publishers, 1999)

Subject(s): Fantasy; Humor; Problem Solving
Age range(s): Grades 1-4
Major character(s): Dr. Shtickle, Scientist, Uncle; Sally, Niece
Time period(s): 1990s
Locale(s): Minneapolis, Minnesota; Washington, District of Columbia; Earth

Summary: Attendees of the World Planetary Conference laugh at Dr. Shtickle's theory explaining the reason for the red coloration of the planet Mars. However, soon after the conference the invasion of the tomatoes begins in Minneapolis and soon the city is red. More tomatoes come, painting American landmarks crimson. Dr. Shtickle works on a plan to communicate with the tomatoes, but his initial efforts are unsuccessful. The military wants to tackle the problem, but Dr. Shtickle knows that simply means sauce all over the world. As Dr. Shtickle ponders the predicament an offer from Sally to make him a little salad with dressing gives him the inspiration for the ultimate anti-tomato weapon. The plan works, the tomatoes retreat and Dr. Shtickle receives a Red Badge of Courage award in appreciation of his solution. (32 pages)

Where it's reviewed:
Children's Book Review Service, December 1999, page 42
Horn Book Guide, Spring 2000, page 60
Kirkus Reviews, October 15, 1999, page 1654
Publishers Weekly, October 18, 1999, page 81
School Library Journal, January 2000, page 114

Awards the book has won:
IRA/CBC Children's Choices, 2000
Parents' Choice Recommendation, 1999

Other books by the same author:
Arthur Yorink's The Flying Latke, 1999
Harry and Lulu, 1999
Christmas in July, 1991
Company's Coming, 1988
Hey, Al, 1986 (Caldecott Medal)

Other books you might like:
Judi Barrett, *Pickles to Pittsburgh: The Sequel to Cloudy with a Chance of Meatballs*, 1997
All the food that falls from the sky on the beleaguered town of Chewandswallow becomes a donation to various cities around the world.
Arthur Dorros, *The Fungus That Ate My School*, 2000
While the school is closed for spring break a science experiment on mold escapes its bounds and grows until it fills the school.
Colin McNaughton, *Here Come the Aliens!*, 1995
Aliens on an invasion path to Earth beat a hasty retreat when they see an orbiting picture of a group of 4-year-olds.
David Wiesner, *June 29, 1999*, 1992
A student's science experiment has some unexpected results when enormous vegetables begin falling from the sky.

Z

1088

DEBORAH TURNEY ZAGWYN, Author/Illustrator

Apple Batter

(Berkeley, CA: Tricycle Press, 1999)

Subject(s): Success; Sports/Baseball; Gardens and Gardening
Age range(s): Grades K-3
Major character(s): Loretta, Gardener, Mother; Delmore, Son, Baseball Player
Time period(s): 1990s
Locale(s): Canada

Summary: Loretta is a capable gardener, but in five years she's not harvested an apple from her trees despite diligent care. Delmore is a great defensive baseball player who hits only foul balls when at the plate. Change begins for both of them the year that Delmore becomes eight. Loretta notices some of the many blossoms on her three trees have become fruit and five tiny apples are growing. Delmore makes a batting tee and practices his stance and his swing. A week of rain reduces Loretta's meager crop of apples to three. One by one, as Delmore's batting improves, the apple crop dwindles. The final apple takes a direct hit from Delmore's first powerfully hit line drive. Fortunately, Delmore is able to recreate that hit during his final game with a home run ball. (32 pages)

Where it's reviewed:
Booklist, January 1, 2000, page 938
Children's Book Review Service, Winter 2000, page 69
Children's Bookwatch, November 1999, page 6
Horn Book Guide, Spring 2000, page 72
School Library Journal, December 1999, page 115

Other books by the same author:
Turtle Spring, 1998
Papa's Latkes, 1994
The Pumpkin Blanket, 1990

Other books you might like:
Gail Gibbons, *The Seasons of Arnold's Apple Tree*, 1984
   Arnold finds a use for his apple tree in every season of the year.

Emily Arnold McCully, *Mouse Practice*, 1999
   Monk learns from his parents' example that diligent practice is necessary for skill development in baseball as well as music.
Lynne Rae Perkins, *Home Lovely*, 1995
   Tiffany's first attempts at gardening don't yield the flowers she expects, but a friendly letter carrier helps by giving her advice and plants.
Nancy Elizabeth Wallace, *Apples, Apples, Apples*, 2000
   The Rabbit family's trip to the orchard to pick apples is also a lesson in apple growing and use.

1089

DEBORAH TURNEY ZAGWYN, Author/Illustrator

The Winter Gift

(Berkeley, CA: Tricycle Press, 2000)

Subject(s): Grandmothers; Christmas; Moving, Household
Age range(s): Grades K-3
Major character(s): Clee, Child, Sister (older); Simon, Child, Brother (younger); Gramma, Grandmother
Time period(s): 2000s (2000)
Locale(s): Canada

Summary: Clee feels as empty as Gramma's house. How can it be Christmas if the family will not gather at Gramma's house and sing songs as Gramma plays her old upright piano? Already Gramma's belongings have been moved across town to an apartment. Gramma says her new place is too small for the piano so she's waiting to show it to a potential buyer. The grumpy man who comes looks disdainfully at the piano and at Simon creating the sound of icicles or thunder on the worn keys. Gramma sits with Simon and Clee for one last song in the old house and then tells the buyer the piano is not for sale. Christmas is at Clee's house now and though it's not the same, it does have the smell of Christmas. Under the tree, Clee and Simon find gifts and, nearby, the piano, waiting for Gramma to play a Christmas tune. (32 pages)

Where it's reviewed:
Children's Bookwatch, September 2000, page 4

Horn Book Guide, Spring 2001, page 54
Publishers Weekly, September 25, 2000, page 76
School Library Journal, October 2000, page 64

Other books by the same author:
Apple Batter, 1999
Turtle Spring, 1998
Papa's Latkes, 1994
The Pumpkin Blanket, 1990

Other books you might like:
Robin Ballard, *Good-Bye House*, 1994
After her family's belongings are loaded on a truck, a little girl walks through the empty house recalling special memories.
Barbara Bottner, *Nana Hannah's Piano*, 1996
Secretly, baseball lover Sonny practices a song on Nana's piano as a surprise to cheer her.
Mem Fox, *Wilfred Gordon McDonald Partridge*, 1985
A young boy collects items that he thinks might hold special memories for an elderly friend.
Patricia Polacco, *The Trees of the Dancing Goats*, 1996
During a scarlet fever epidemic, a kind Jewish family prepares a Christmas celebration for the sick Christian members of a community.
Joan Rothenberg, *Inside-Out Grandma*, 1995
As Rosie helps with Hanukkah preparations Grandma takes her on a memory walk of the family and traditions surrounding the holiday.

1090

HARRIET ZIEFERT
EMILY BOLAM, Illustrator

Clara Ann Cookie
(Boston: Houghton Mifflin Company, 1999)

Subject(s): Clothes; Stories in Rhyme; Mothers and Daughters
Age range(s): Preschool
Major character(s): Clara Ann Cookie, Child, Daughter; Mother, Mother
Time period(s): 1990s (1999)
Locale(s): United States

Summary: When Clara wakes up in a grumpy mood and refuses to get dressed Mother has an idea that solves the problem and leaves Clara feeling happy. Using a large mirror in Clara's room Mother has Clara make faces, beginning with angry and stubborn ones. With Clara distracted by her face-making efforts Mother gradually helps Clara get dressed. With each item of clothing, Mother's instruction about Clara's expression changes from mad or scary to more positive faces such as happy or silly and soon Clara is ready to go! (32 pages)

Where it's reviewed:
Booklist, March 1, 1999, page 1223
Horn Book Guide, Fall 1999, page 242
Publishers Weekly, April 5, 1999, page 239
School Library Journal, April 1999, page 110

Awards the book has won:
IRA/CBC Children's Choices, 2000

Other books by the same author:
Clara Ann Cookie, Go to Bed!, 2000
I Swapped My Dog, 1998
Pete's Chicken, 1994
Harry Gets Ready for School, 1991

Other books you might like:
Jennifer A. Ericsson, *The Most Beautiful Kid in the World*, 1996
Annie doesn't agree with the outfit Mama chooses so she changes into something that will make her "the most beautiful kid" for Grandma's birthday.
Mordicai Gerstein, *Stop Those Pants!*, 1998
Murray is willing to get dressed for school but his pants won't cooperate.
Marthe Jocelyn, *Hannah and the Seven Dresses*, 1999
Hannah has such a hard time deciding which dress to wear for her birthday what she tries to wear them all.
Rosemary Wells, *Max's New Suit*, 1998
Max hates his new suit and his sister Ruby's ideas about how he should wear it.

1091

HARRIET ZIEFERT
GUSTAF MILLER, Illustrator

Hats Off for the Fourth of July!
(New York: Viking, 2000)

Subject(s): Holidays; Bands; Stories in Rhyme
Age range(s): Grades K-1
Time period(s): 2000s (2000)
Locale(s): Chatham, Massachusetts (Cape Cod)

Summary: Spectators line the street waiting for the parade to begin. First come baton twirlers to the beat of the drum then cowboys, floats and a marching band pass by. Motorcycles, bicyclists and a Little League participate in the town's celebration of the Fourth of July. Hooray! (32 pages)

Where it's reviewed:
Booklist, April 15, 2000, page 1555
Bulletin of the Center for Children's Books, June 2000, page 380
Kirkus Reviews, May 1, 2000, page 642
Publishers Weekly, June 5, 2000, page 93
School Library Journal, July 2000, page 90

Other books by the same author:
Animal Music, 1999
Clara Ann Cookie, 1999 (IRA/CBC Children's Choices)
I Swapped My Dog, 1998
Rabbit and Hare Divide an Apple, 1998
Waiting for Baby, 1998

Other books you might like:
Betty Paraskevas, *On the Day the Tall Ships Sailed*, 2000
Manhattan celebrates the Fourth of July with a parade of tall ships on the Hudson River as an eagle soars overhead.
Jane Resh Thomas, *Celebration!*, 1997
Relatives gather at Maggie's house to enjoy an old-fashioned Fourth of July picnic.

Jean Van Leeuwen, *A Fourth of July on the Plains*, 1997
A wagon train heading to Oregon stops for a day so everyone can celebrate Independence Day.

1092

HARRIET ZIEFERT
DONALD DREIFUSS, Illustrator

Pumpkin Pie

(Boston: Walter Lorraine Books/Houghton Mifflin Company, 2000)

Subject(s): Animals/Goats; Contests; Fairs
Age range(s): Preschool
Major character(s): Pumpkin Pie, Goat; Donald, Farmer
Time period(s): 2000s (2000)
Locale(s): Unity, New Hampshire (Britton Hill Farm)

Summary: Pumpkin Pie knows he's the favorite of all the goats on the farm because Donald selects him to win the blue ribbon for the farm at the show in Unity. Pumpkin Pie's a normal goat—likes to eat, does not like baths. At the Fourth of July Show, Pumpkin Pie tries to wait patiently in the ring with the other goats and their handlers while the judges inspect each of them. One of the other things that Pumpkin Pie doesn't like is being inspected, but that doesn't mean he meant to kick the judge. Maybe next year Donald and Pumpkin Pie will win the blue ribbon. (32 pages)

Where it's reviewed:
Booklist, December 1, 2000, page 724
Horn Book Guide, Spring 2001, page 26
School Library Journal, October 2000, page 144

Other books by the same author:
April Fool!, 2000
Little Red Riding Hood, 2000
The Snow Child, 2000
A Dozen Dozens, 1998

Other books you might like:
Natalie Kinsey-Warnock, *The Summer of Stanley*, 1997
Stanley doesn't win any points when he eats the family's victory garden, but the goat redeems himself when he saves Tyler from drowning.
Margaret Mahy, *The Queen's Goat*, 1990
A young queen and her runaway goat receive an unexpected prize at a pet show.
Cecile Schoberle, *Esmeralda and the Pet Parade*, 1990
Juan worries that Esmeralda, his pet goat, may disrupt the pet parade with her energetic behavior.

1093

HARRIET ZIEFERT
DONALD SAAF, Illustrator

Pushkin Minds the Bundle

(New York: Anne Schwartz Book/Atheneum Books for Young Readers, 2000)

Subject(s): Animals/Dogs; Babies; Pets
Age range(s): Grades K-1
Major character(s): Pushkin, Dog; Pierre, Baby, Son
Time period(s): 2000s

Locale(s): United States

Summary: In the sequel to *Pushkin Meets the Bundle* Pushkin continues to mind "the bundle" as he calls Pierre both literally and figuratively. Pierre's parents expect Pushkin to watch over the bundle, give up his favorite position in the car to the bundle and even let the bundle have first choice of beds in the vacation cottage. Pushkin is jealous of the attention showered on the bundle but when Pierre becomes lost while berry picking it is Pushkin who locates the tot and receives lavish praise for his great "sniffer." (32 pages)

Where it's reviewed:
Booklist, September 1, 2000, page 126
Bulletin of the Center for Children's Books, May 2000, page 342
Horn Book Guide, Fall 2000, page 286
Publishers Weekly, May 1, 2000, page 73
School Library Journal, July 2000, page 91

Other books by the same author:
Animal Music, 1999
Pushkin Meets the Bundle, 1998
Baby Buggy, Buggy Baby, 1997
A Clean House for Mole and Mouse, 1988

Other books you might like:
Alexandra Day, *Afternoon in the Park*, 1991
Carl, the family's pet rottweiler, "baby sits" a puppy and a toddler while Mom visits with a friend.
Isabelle Harper, *Our New Puppy*, 1996
The arrival of Floyd, an 8-week-old puppy, is viewed with disdain by the family cat and accepted with patient tolerance by the older dog Rosie.
William Mayne, *Pandora*, 1996
When Pandora's owners arrive home with a baby the pet cat moves out temporarily until babies of her own help her be more understanding.
Rosemary Wells, *The McDuff Series*, 1997-
A West Highland terrier finds a home, adjusts to a baby's arrival and saves Santa Claus from the chimney in an award-winning series.

1094

HARRIET ZIEFERT
EMILY BOLAM, Illustrator

Talk, Baby!

(New York: Henry Holt and Company, 1999)

Subject(s): Babies; Brothers and Sisters; Growing Up
Age range(s): Grades K-2
Major character(s): Max, Child, Brother (older); Unnamed Character, Baby, Sister
Time period(s): 1990s (1999)
Locale(s): United States

Summary: Max is happy when his mother comes home from the hospital with his baby sister but disappointed because the baby only seems to sleep and cry. Max grows impatient waiting for her to be able to play with him. Each month he tries to coax the baby to talk and, though she gurgles and coos, she doesn't really talk. Finally when the baby is fourteen months old, she says her first word. Max's parents think surely her first word is mama or dada, but Max knows the word he hears is "Max." (28 pages)

Where it's reviewed:
Horn Book Guide, Spring 2000, page 60
New York Times Book Review, November 21, 1999, page 54
Publishers Weekly, September 20, 1999, page 90
School Library Journal, October 1999, page 130

Other books by the same author:
Presents for Santa, 2000
Pushkin Meets the Bundle, 1998
Waiting for Baby, 1998

Other books you might like:
Holly Keller, *Geraldine's Baby Brother*, 1994
   Annoyed to be awakened, resourceful Geraldine has a heart-to-heart talk with her screaming baby brother before reading Willie a story.
Phyllis Root, *What Baby Wants*, 1998
   The frantic relatives soon notice that only Little Brother knows what the crying baby really wants as he soothes him with a lullaby.
Carol Diggory Shields, *I Wish My Brother Was a Dog*, 1997
   A young boy imagines the improvements in his life if only Andy was his pet dog and not his little brother.
Susan Winter, *A Baby Just Like Me*, 1994
   Martha feels disappointed that her baby sister is not able to be her playmate immediately.

1095

HARRIET ZIEFERT
DONALD SAAF, Illustrator

Train Song
(New York: Orchard Books, 1999)

Subject(s): Trains; Transportation; Stories in Rhyme
Age range(s): Grades K-2
Major character(s): Unnamed Character, Child
Time period(s): Indeterminate Past
Locale(s): Bellows Falls

Summary: While playing with his toy train on a hillside, a young boy looks down at the real tracks and the freight train coming through the countryside. He counts the animals aboard, wonders what's inside the tank car and listens to the noisy song of the engine and whistle. Although the train moves out of sight with a clickety clack, the boy knows that the next morning he'll see it again. (24 pages)

Where it's reviewed:
Booklist, April 1, 2000, page 1472
Horn Book Guide, Fall 2000, page 259
Riverbank Review, Spring 2000, page 34
School Library Journal, April 2000, page 117

Other books by the same author:
Animal Music, 1999
Clara Ann Cookie, 1999
Baby Buggy, Buggy Baby, 1997

Other books you might like:
Robert Burleigh, *It's Funny Where Ben's Train Takes Him*, 1999

In Ben's imagination a real train emerges from his drawing to carry Ben and his teddy bear to the bedtime station.
Kevin Lewis, *Chugga-Chugga Choo-Choo*, 1999
   The toys load their toy train and enjoy a busy day in a rhyming picture book.
Rob Spence, *Clickety Clack*, 1999
   Noisy animal passengers drown out the sound of the train's wheels on the track until the engineer tells them to be quiet. Amy Spence, co-author.

1096

ANDREA ZIMMERMAN
DAVID CLEMESHA, Co-Author
TRUE KELLEY, Illustrator

My Dog Toby
(San Diego: Silver Whistle/Harcourt, Inc., 2000)

Subject(s): Animals/Dogs; Pets; Love
Age range(s): Grades K-2
Major character(s): Toby, Dog; Unnamed Character, Child, Sister (younger); Unnamed Character, Brother (older)
Time period(s): 2000s (2000)
Locale(s): United States

Summary: A little girl recognizes the many good traits of her beloved pet Toby but she really wants him to learn just one trick. Her friends have dogs that can shake hands, play soccer and dance, but Toby has not even learned to sit on command. Her brother says that Toby is just a dumb dog, but she knows that is not true because Toby knows when it's time to eat and how to find gophers in the yard. She tries using different languages thinking that perhaps Toby doesn't speak English but that plan also fails. Finally, after lots and lots of practice, Toby sits on command and even the girl's brother admits that Toby may be smart dog after all. (32 pages)

Where it's reviewed:
Booklist, May 1, 2000, page 1666
Bulletin of the Center for Children's Books, June 2000, page 381
Horn Book Guide, Fall 2000, page 286
Kirkus Reviews, May 1, 2000, page 642
School Library Journal, May 2000, page 159

Other books by the same author:
Trashy Town, 1999
The Cow Buzzed, 1993

Other books you might like:
Steven Kroll, *Oh, Tucker!*, 1998
   Tucker's family loves their large, exuberant and clumsy dog despite the inadvertent messes he creates in the house.
David Milgrim, *Dog Brain*, 1996
   The opinion of family members varies as to whether Sneakers is a very smart or a very dumb dog.
Cynthia Rylant, *The Henry and Mudge Series*, 1987-
   The adventures of Henry and his lovable, slobbery dog Mudge entertain beginning readers.

1097

ANDREA ZIMMERMAN
DAVID CLEMESHA, Co-Author
DAN YACCARINO, Illustrator

Trashy Town

(New York: HarperCollins Publishers, 1999)

Subject(s): Work; Cleanliness; City and Town Life
Age range(s): Grades K-1
Major character(s): Mr. Gilly, Maintenance Worker
Time period(s): 1990s (1999)
Locale(s): United States

Summary: Friendly Mr. Gilly drives the town's trash truck from the school to the pizza parlor, the park and the doctor's office. At each stop Mr. Gilly dumps the trash from the cans into his truck. He drives up and down all the streets in town until his trash truck is full and the town is clean. One last stop at the dump unloads the truck and Mr. Gilly is finished working for one day. Now he can go home and clean up in the bath. (32 pages)

Where it's reviewed:
Booklist, August 1999, page 2067
Five Owls, September 1999, page 15
Horn Book, March 1999, page 204
Riverbank Review, Summer 1999, page 31
School Library Journal, May 1999, page 102

Awards the book has won:
School Library Journal Best Books, 1999
Bulletin of the Center for Children's Books Blue Ribbon, 1999

Other books by the same author:
My Dog Toby, 2000
The Cow Buzzed, 1993

Other books you might like:
Jean Eick, *Garbage Trucks*, 1999
    A nonfiction title describes how garbage trucks work.
Linda Glaser, *Stop That Garbage Truck!*, 1993
    A garbage collector's "secret" admirer watches for the trash truck to pass by but is too shy to speak.
Daniel Kirk, *Trash Trucks!*, 1997
    In a rhyming story trash trucks travel the city streets doing their job.
Loreen Leedy, *The Great Trash Bash*, 1991
    The residents of Beaston clean up their town by reducing trash production and increasing their recycling efforts.

1098

KATHLEEN WEIDNER ZOEHFELD
PAULETTE BOGAN, Illustrator

Fossil Fever

(New York: Golden Books Publishing Co., 2000)

Series: Road to Reading. Mile 4
Subject(s): Paleontology; Dinosaurs; Vacations
Age range(s): Grades 2-3
Major character(s): Jeff, Child, Nephew; Roy, Uncle, Scientist
Time period(s): 1990s (1993)

Locale(s): United States (Wye Museum of Natural History); Sahara Desert, Africa

Summary: After the long plane ride and five days in jeep Jeff is beginning to wonder why he begged to accompany Uncle Roy on his fossil finding expedition. Once they set up camp the time continues to pass slowly because the crew's task is to search the sand for signs of dinosaur bones. Not until Jeff accidentally trips over a rock that, on closer inspection, is discovered to actually be the end of a femur bone does he realize his dream of finding an actual dinosaur bone. Careful excavation near the first fossilized bone reveals most of the skeleton that Jeff helps Uncle Roy and crew pack in paper and plaster for the trip to America for study. An author's note gives the factual basis for the story. (48 pages)

Where it's reviewed:
Booklist, May 15, 2000, page 1745
School Library Journal, November 2000, page 138

Other books by the same author:
Dinosaur Babies, 1999
Disney's Mulan, 1998
Happy New Year, Pooh!, 1997

Other books you might like:
B.B. Calhoun, *On the Right Track*, 1994
    Mysterious dinosaur tracks puzzle Fenton's paleontologist father and give Fenton a mystery to solve.
Wolfram Hanel, *Lila's Little Dinosaur*, 1994
    A rainbow-striped dinosaur follows Lila home from the Museum of Natural History.
Jurgen Lassig, *Spiny*, 1995
    An easy reader describes the frantic search dinosaur parents make to locate newly hatched Spiny before a predator finds him.
Jan Wahl, *The Field Mouse and the Dinosaur Named Sue*, 2000
    A mouse-eye view of a fossil dig follows paleontologists excavating a T. Rex skeleton that includes the "roof" to the mouse's home.

1099

CHARLOTTE ZOLOTOW
JOHN STEPTOE, Illustrator

Do You Know What I'll Do?

(New York: HarperCollins Publishers, 2000)

Subject(s): Brothers and Sisters; Growing Up; Family
Age range(s): Grades K-1
Major character(s): Unnamed Character, Child, Sister (older); Unnamed Character, Child, Brother
Time period(s): 2000s
Locale(s): United States

Summary: A loving sister answers the questions she addresses to her brother in this revised and newly illustrated version of a story originally published in 1958. The sister's gestures and responses reflect the loving relationship between the siblings. She assures her brother that she'll pick flowers to make him happy, build him a snowman when it snows and remember the songs from the movies to sing to him. If she goes to the seashore she'll bring her brother a shell and if she goes to the city she'll come home with a surprise for her little brother. When she's grown up with a baby of her own she'll visit her brother just so he can hug the baby the same way the girl is hugging her brother now. (32 pages)

Where it's reviewed:
Booklist, September 15, 2000, page 237
Horn Book Guide, Spring 2001, page 54
Kirkus Reviews, September 1, 2000, page 1294
Publishers Weekly, September 11, 2000, page 89
School Library Journal, September 2000, page 212

Other books by the same author:
The Old Dog, 1995
I Like to Be Little, 1987
But Not Billy, 1983
William's Doll, 1972
If It Weren't for You, 1966

Other books you might like:
Trish Cooke, *So Much*, 1994
    A baby is surrounded by loving relatives who want to hug, squeeze and play with the baby SO MUCH!
Angela Johnson, *Do Like Kyla*, 1990
    Kyla's younger sister follows her all day, imitating her behavior.
Jonathan London, *Puddles*, 1997
    The morning after a heavy rain siblings enjoy jumping puddles, watching frogs and slogging through mud.
Sam McBratney, *Guess How Much I Love You*, 1995
    Little Nutbrown Hare enjoys playing a game with his father in which each professes the magnitude of his love for the other.

1100

CHARLOTTE ZOLOTOW
AMANDA HARVEY, Illustrator

My Friend John

(New York: A Doubleday Book for Young Readers, 2000)

Subject(s): Friendship; Playing; Conduct of Life

Age range(s): Grades K-3
Major character(s): John, Child, Friend; Unnamed Character, Child, Friend
Time period(s): 2000s
Locale(s): United States

Summary: In a newly illustrated reissue of a 1968 title, John's best friend describes a special friendship. The boys know each other's hidden fears, secret likes and favorite hiding places. John's dad tells funnier jokes, but the narrator's mom is a better cook so the boys can choose when to be at which house. The pals help each other with academic work because one is good at spelling but needs help with math. These best friends enjoy sharing all the important things in life. (32 pages)

Where it's reviewed:
Booklist, July 2000, page 2044
Children's Bookwatch, July 2000, page 5
Horn Book Guide, Spring 2001, page 545
Publishers Weekly, May 15, 2000, page 119
School Library Journal, July 2000, page 91

Other books by the same author:
I Like to Be Little, 1987
But Not Billy, 1983
The Hating Book, 1969
Big Sister and Little Sister, 1966

Other books you might like:
Kevin Henkes, *Chester's Way*, 1988
    Although Chester and Wilson are content with their friendship Lilly's move into the neighborhood forces them to reconsider some ideas.
James Howe, *Pinky and Rex*, 1990
    Pinky and Rex begin their friendship in the first book of the series.
Arnold Lobel, *Frog and Toad Are Friends*, 1970
    The award-winning celebration of friendship shows the give-and-take necessary to make a relationship successful.
Lynn Reiser, *Best Friends Think Alike*, 1997
    Beryl and Ruby resolve a brief disagreement and continue their imaginative play knowing that best friends really do think alike.

Award Index

This index lists major awards given to books featured in the entries. Books are listed alphabetically beneath the name of the award, with author name and entry number number also indicated.

Time Period Index

This index chronologically lists the time settings in which the featured books take place. Main headings refer to a century; where no specific time is given, the headings MULTIPLE TIME PERIODS, INDETERMINATE PAST, INDETERMINATE FUTURE, and INDETERMINATE are used. The 18th through 21st centuries are broken down into decades when possible. (Note: 1800s, for example, refers to the first decade of the 19th century). Featured titles are listed alphabetically beneath time headings, with author names and entry numbers also provided.

21st CENTURY

INDETERMINATE FUTURE

INDETERMINATE

Geographic Index

This index provides access to all featured books by geographic settings—such as countries, continents, oceans, and planets. States and provinces are indicated for the United States and Canada. Also interfiled are headings for fictional place names (Spaceships, Imaginary Planets, etc.). Sections are further broken down by city or the specific name of the imaginary locale. Book titles are listed alphabetically under headings, and author names and entry numbers are also provided.

AFRICA

In the Rainfield: Who Is the Greatest? - Isaac O. Olaleye 742
Rain - Manya Stojic 961
To Dinner, for Dinner - Tololwa M. Mollel 694

Sahara Desert
Fossil Fever - Kathleen Weidner Zoehfeld 1098

AMERICAN COLONIES

Catskill Mountains
Rip Van Winkle - Washington Irving 467

KENTUCKY

Boonesborough
Adventure on the Wilderness Road, 1775 - Laurie Lawlor 561

MARYLAND

Molly Bannaky - Alice McGill 658

MASSACHUSETTS

Boston
Emma's Journal: The Story of a Colonial Girl - Marissa Moss 701

NEW ENGLAND

Squanto's Journey: The Story of the First Thanksgiving - Joseph Bruchac 117

PENNSYLVANIA

Bewildered for Three Days: As to Why Daniel Boone Never Wore His Coonskin Cap - Andrew Glass 350

TENNESSEE

Holston River
Adventure on the Wilderness Road, 1775 - Laurie Lawlor 561

VIRGINIA

Carter's Grove
Caesar's Story: 1759 - Joan Lowery Nixon 729

Williamsburg
Caesar's Story: 1759 - Joan Lowery Nixon 729

ANTARCTICA

North Pole
Auntie Claus - Elise Primavera 799

ARCTIC

The Blizzard's Robe - Robert Sabuda 858
Dreamstones - Maxine Trottier 990
The Practically Perfect Pajamas - Erik Brooks 109
Snow Bear - Jean Craighead George 343

ASIA

Basket Weaver and Catches Many Mice - Janet Gill 348
The Firework-Maker's Daughter - Philip Pullman 803

Himalayan Mountains
When Agnes Caws - Candace Fleming 321

AT SEA

Peg and the Whale - Kenneth Oppel 746

Atlanta
Hannah's Journal: The Story of an Immigrant Girl - Marissa Moss 702

Candace
Ghost of the Southern Belle: A Sea Tale - Odds Bodkin 85

Dei Gratia
The Mary Celeste: An Unsolved Mystery from History - Jane Yolen 1081

Lily
Dreamstones - Maxine Trottier 990

The Mary Ann
Captain Kate - Carolyn Reeder 815

Mongrel
The Pirate's Parrot - Lyn Rossiter McFarland 656

Monticello
Good-bye for Today: The Diary of a Young Girl at Sea - Peter Roop 828

Moon Shadow
Dolphin Freedom - Wayne Grover 385

Neptune
Abigail Takes the Wheel - Avi 42

Red Betsy
Little Bo: The Story of Bonnie Boadicea - Julie Andrews Edwards 289

SS Magnifique
Mirette & Bellini Cross Niagara Falls - Emily Arnold McCully 647

SS Nevada
Dreaming of America: An Ellis Island Story - Eve Bunting 125

AUSTRALIA

Ark in the Park - Wendy Orr 749
Celeste Sails to Spain - Alison Lester 566
The Deep - Tim Winton 1057
Henry and Amy (Right-Way-Round and Upside Down) - Stephen Michael King 522
Keeping Up with Grandma - John Winch 1056
Unknown - Colin Thompson 987
Wombat Goes Walkabout - Michael Morpurgo 697

Minyerri
Big Rain Coming - Katrina Germein 345

BAHAMAS

Dead Man Cay
Dolphin Freedom - Wayne Grover 385

BELGIUM

The Father Who Had 10 Children - Benedicte Guettier 388

CANADA

Apple Batter - Deborah Turney Zagwyn 1088
Ballerinas Don't Wear Glasses - Ainslie Manson 618
Brave Highland Heart - Heather Kellerhals-Stewart 509

CARIBBEAN

CHINA

DAHOMEY

DENMARK

EARTH

EGYPT

ENGLAND

Subject Index

This index lists subjects which are covered in the featured titles. These can include such things as family life, animals, personal and social problems, historical events, ethnic groups, and story types, e.g. Mystery and Detective Stories. Beneath each subject heading, titles are arranged alphabetically with author names and entry numbers also indicated.

Animals/Geese

Grandfather's Christmas Tree - Keith Strand 964
Louie's Goose - H.M. Ehrlich 297
My Goose Betsy - Trudi Braun 101
Waiting for Mr. Goose - Laurie Lears 564
The Way Home - Nan Parson Rossiter 839

Animals/Giraffes

The Visitor - Patrice Aggs 10

Animals/Goats

Night of the Goat Children - J. Patrick Lewis 577
Pumpkin Pie - Harriet Ziefert 1092

Animals/Hamsters

Hello, Sweetie Pie - Carl Norac 734

Animals/Hedgehogs

Hedgie's Surprise - Jan Brett 105

Animals/Horses

Cougar - Helen V. Griffith 381
The First Horse I See - Sally M. Keehn 501
O'Sullivan Stew: A Tale Cooked Up in Ireland -
   Hudson Talbott 973
Shadow Horse - Alison Hart 406

Animals/Insects

The Ant and the Grasshopper - Amy Lowry
   Poole 790
The Beautiful Butterfly: A Folktale from Spain - Judy
   Sierra 911
The Big Bug Ball - Dee Lillegard 581
Butterfly House - Eve Bunting 123
Cockroach Cooties - Laurence Yep 1076
Ed & Fred Flea - Pamela Duncan Edwards 292
Frankenfrog - Kim Kennedy 512
Gotta Go! Gotta Go! - Sam Swope 970
Inspector Hopper - Doug Cushman 218
Leo Cockroach...Toy Tester - Kevin O'Malley 745
Ma Jiang and the Orange Ants - Barbara Ann
   Porte 792
The Very Clumsy Click Beetle - Eric Carle 144

Animals/Kangaroos

The Very Boastful Kangaroo - Bernard Most 704

Animals/Leopards

To Dinner, for Dinner - Tololwa M. Mollel 694

Animals/Lions

Deep in the Jungle - Dan Yaccarino 1072

Animals/Llamas

Llama in the Library - Johanna Hurwitz 462

Animals/Marine

Crab Moon - Ruth Horowitz 447
Deadly Waters - Gloria Skurzynski 925
Dory Story - Jerry Pallotta 758

Animals/Mice

A Beasty Story - Bill Martin Jr. 625

Bravo, Livingstone Mouse! - Pamela Duncan
   Edwards 291
Cat and Mouse in the Snow - Tomek Bogacki 86
Charlie Muffin's Miracle Mouse - Dick King-
   Smith 523
Drip, Drop - Sarah Weeks 1029
The Field Mouse and the Dinosaur Named Sue - Jan
   Wahl 1012
Friend Frog - Alma Flor Ada 1
Horace and Morris but Mostly Dolores - James
   Howe 454
If You Take a Mouse to the Movies - Laura Joffe
   Numeroff 739
Mice Make Trouble - Becky Bloom 82
Monk Camps Out - Emily Arnold McCully 648
Mouse at Night - Nancy Christensen Hall 394
Mouse in Love - Robert Kraus 541
Mouse Magic - Ellen Stoll Walsh 1021
The Mouse of Amherst - Elizabeth Spires 945
Mouse Practice - Emily Arnold McCully 649
The Mouse That Snored - Bernard Waber 1008
Princess Chamomile Gets Her Way - Hiawyn
   Oram 748
Ragweed - Avi 45
Ricky Ricotta's Giant Robot: An Adventure Novel -
   Dav Pilkey 778
Shoe Town - Janet Stevens 953
Truffle's Christmas - Anna Currey 216
The Very Noisy Night - Diana Hendry 420
Wemberly Worried - Kevin Henkes 423

Animals/Moles

Mole Music - David McPhail 671

Animals/Monkeys

Ding Dong Ding Dong - Margie Palatini 756
The Hatseller and the Monkeys - Baba Wague
   Diakite 264
One Monkey Too Many - Jackie French Koller 535

Animals/Moose

Moose Tales - Nancy Van Laan 1001
Mooseltoe - Margie Palatini 757

Animals/Mules

Jake Johnson: The Story of a Mule - Tres
   Seymour 899

Animals/Penguins

Penguin Dreams - J. Otto Seibold 897
Tacky and the Emperor - Helen Lester 568
Whiteblack the Penguin Sees the World - H.A.
   Rey 817

Animals/Pigs

Albert & Lila - Rafik Schami 882
Aunt Pitty Patty's Piggy - Jim Aylesworth 46
Benny's Had Enough! - Barbro Lindgren 585
City Pig - Karen Wallace 1017
Clarence Goes Out West and Meets a Purple Horse -
   Jean Ekman Adams 3
A Day with the Bellyflops - Francine Bassede 60
Elwood and the Witch - Nicholas Heller 415
Geraldine and Mrs. Duffy - Holly Keller 506
Hamburger Heaven - Wong Herbert Yee 1075
Hogula: Dread Pig of Night - Jean Gralley 369
Isabelle and the Angel - Thierry Magnier 610
Lucille's Snowsuit - Kathryn Lasky 559
Oliver and Albert, Friends Forever - Jean Van
   Leeuwen 1004
Olivia - Ian Falconer 308

Otis - Janie Bynum 136
Pig and Crow - Kay Chorao 165
The Pig Who Ran a Red Light - Paul Brett
   Johnson 486
Poppleton Has Fun - Cynthia Rylant 854
Poppleton in Fall - Cynthia Rylant 855
Six Hogs on a Scooter - Eileen Spinelli 943
Slender Ella and Her Fairy Hogfather - Vivian
   Sathre 874
Squiggle's Tale - Andre Dahan 228
Swine Divine - Jan Carr 148
Swine Lake - James Marshall 623
The Tale of Gilbert Alexander Pig - Gael Cresp 207
Toot & Puddle: You Are My Sunshine - Holly
   Hobbie 437
When You Take a Pig to a Party - Kristina
   Thermaenius McLarey 665
Yum!: A Preston Pig Story - Colin McNaughton 668
Z-Z-Zoink! - Bernard Most 705

Animals/Rabbits

Apples, Apples, Apples - Nancy Elizabeth
   Wallace 1019
Blue Rabbit and Friends - Christopher
   Wormell 1070
Bunny and Me - Adele Aron Greenspun 375
Bunny Bungalow - Cynthia Rylant 849
Happy Birthday, Davy! - Brigitte Weninger 1035
Harvey Hare's Christmas - Bernadette Watts 1028
Little Bunny on the Move - Peter McCarty 641
Little Bunny's Easter Surprise - Jeanne Modesitt 692
Little Bunny's Sleepless Night - Carol Roth 840
Max Cleans Up - Rosemary Wells 1034
Night Rabbits - Lee Posey 793
One, Two, Three, Oops! - Michael Coleman 180
Rabbit Food - Susanna Gretz 379
Rabbit Pirates: A Tale of the Spinach Main - Judy
   Cox 200
Ruthie's Big Old Coat - Julie Lacome 549
Science Fair Bunnies - Kathryn Lasky 560
Tell-a-Bunny - Nancy Elizabeth Wallace 1020
Tiny Rabbit Goes to a Birthday Party - John
   Wallace 1016
To Dinner, for Dinner - Tololwa M. Mollel 694
Tumbleweed Stew - Susan Stevens Crummel 211
What's the Matter, Davy? - Brigitte Weninger 1038
Why Are You Fighting, Davy? - Brigitte
   Weninger 1039
Will You Be My Friend? - Nancy Tafuri 972

Animals/Rats

The Great Pet Sale - Mick Inkpen 466
Hooway for Wodney Wat - Helen Lester 567
The Most Amazing Dinosaur - James Stevenson 956

Animals/Reptiles

*The Chameleon Wore Chartreuse: From the Tattered
   Casebook of Chet Gecko, Private Eye* - Bruce
   Hale 393
I Need a Snake - Lynne Jonell 488
Lizard's Home - George Shannon 903
The Night Iguana Left Home - Megan
   McDonald 654
Turtle and Snake at Work - Kate Spohn 946

Animals/Salamanders

Creature Crossing - Betty Levin 570

Animals/Seals and Sea Lions

Selkie - Gillian McClure 643

Hiking

Henry Hikes to Fitchburg - D.B. Johnson 478

Historical

Abigail Takes the Wheel - Avi 42

Adventure on the Wilderness Road, 1775 - Laurie Lawlor 561

Anna All Year Round - Mary Downing Hahn 392

Bach's Big Adventure - Sallie Ketcham 515

A Big Cheese for the White House: The True Tale of a Tremendous Cheddar - Candace Fleming 320

Caesar's Story: 1759 - Joan Lowery Nixon 729

Captain Kate - Carolyn Reeder 815

The Drums of Noto Hanto - J. Alison James 472

Emma's Journal: The Story of a Colonial Girl - Marissa Moss 701

Hannah's Helping Hands - Jean Van Leeuwen 1003

The House of Wisdom - Florence Parry Heide 410

Iron Horses - Verla Kay 500

A Light in the Storm: The Civil War Diary of Amelia Martin - Karen Hesse 429

Molly Bannaky - Alice McGill 658

Seesaw Girl - Linda Sue Park 762

Sleds on Boston Common: A Story from the American Revoluton - Louise Borden 94

Squanto's Journey: The Story of the First Thanksgiving - Joseph Bruchac 117

The Yeoman's Daring Daughter and the Princes in the Tower - Elaine Clayton 168

Holidays

Happy Birthday, America! - Marsha Wilson Chall 158

Hats Off for the Fourth of July! - Harriet Ziefert 1091

Jake Johnson: The Story of a Mule - Tres Seymour 899

My Two Grandmothers - Effin Older 743

No Time for Mother's Day - Laurie Halse Anderson 24

The Thanksgiving Beast Feast - Karen Gray Ruelle 846

A Thanksgiving Wish - Michael J. Rosen 834

This Is the Turkey - Abby Levine 571

This Next New Year - Janet S. Wong 1064

A Valentine for Norman Noggs - Valiska Gregory 378

Holidays, Jewish

Gershon's Monster - Eric A. Kimmel 518

The Jar of Fools: Eight Hanukkah Stories from Chelm - Eric A. Kimmel 519

Latkes, Latkes Good to Eat: A Chanukah Story - Naomi Howland 455

Matzah Ball Soup - Joan Rothenberg 841

Moishe's Miracle: A Hanukkah Story - Laura Krauss Melmed 679

Our Eight Nights of Hanukkah - Michael J. Rosen 833

The Runaway Latkes - Leslie Kimmelman 521

The Very Best Hanukkah Gift - Joanne Rocklin 824

Holocaust

Good Night, Maman - Norma Fox Mazer 639

When the Soldiers Were Gone - Vera W. Propp 801

Homeless People

A Ceiling of Stars - Ann Howard Creel 206

Gowanus Dogs - Jonathan Frost 331

The Way to Schenectady - Richard Scrimger 894

Homesickness

Tea with Milk - Allen Say 876

The Very Small - Joyce Dunbar 283

Honesty

Edwurd Fudwupper Fibbed Big: Explained by Fannie Fudwupper - Berkeley Breathed 103

The Honest-to-Goodness Truth - Patricia C. McKissack 663

Lizard's Home - George Shannon 903

That's Mine, Horace - Holly Keller 508

Hospitals

Dr. White - Jane Goodall 361

Operation Ghost - Jacques Duquennoy 287

Hotels and Motels

The Elevator Family - Douglas Evans 306

Halloween Motel - Sean Diviny 269

Housing

Bunny Bungalow - Cynthia Rylant 849

George Paints His House - Francine Bassede 61

We Were Tired of Living in a House - Liesel Moak Skorpen 924

Human Behavior

Mary Louise Loses Her Manners - Diane Cuneo 214

Humor

The Absentminded Fellow - Samuel Marshak 622

Agapanthus Hum and the Eyeglasses - Joy Cowley 196

Alice's Adventures in Wonderland - Lewis Carroll 150

Aloha, Dolores - Barbara Samuels 863

Amelia Bedelia 4 Mayor - Herman Parish 760

Annabel the Actress Starring in Gorilla My Dreams - Ellen Conford 183

Annie Pitts, Burger Kid - Diane DeGroat 248

Bad Dog - Nina Laden 550

Ballerinas Don't Wear Glasses - Ainslie Manson 618

Bark, George - Jules Feiffer 311

Bedhead - Margie Palatini 755

Beezy and Funnybone - Megan McDonald 652

Benny: An Adventure Story - Bob Graham 367

The Big Bad Rumor - Jonathan Meres 680

Bigfoot Cinderrrrrella - Tony Johnston 487

Buttons - Brock Cole 179

Cajun Through and Through - Tynia Thomassie 985

Captain Underpants and the Attack of the Talking Toilets - Dav Pilkey 776

Captain Underpants and the Perilous Plot of Professor Poopypants - Dav Pilkey 777

Carlotta's Kittens and the Club of Mysteries - Phyllis Reynolds Naylor 720

A Carnival of Animals - Sid Fleischman 319

Christmas at Mud Flat - James Stevenson 954

Click, Clack, Moo: Cows That Type - Doreen Cronin 210

Club Earth - Gail Gauthier 339

Cook-a-Doodle-Doo! - Janet Stevens 952

The Day My Dogs Became Guys - Merrill Markoe 621

Ding Dong Ding Dong - Margie Palatini 756

Dog Tales - Jennifer Rae 808

Dolphin Luck - Hilary McKay 661

Don't Make Me Laugh - James Stevenson 955

Duck in the Truck - Jez Alborough 12

The Emperor's Old Clothes - Kathryn Lasky 558

The Fixits - Anne Mazer 638

Four Stupid Cupids - Gregory Maguire 611

George - Maggie Stern 950

Get That Pest! - Erin Douglas 274

The Giggler Treatment - Roddy Doyle 276

Goldilocks Returns - Lisa Campbell Ernst 304

Gus & Gertie and the Missing Pearl - Joan Lowery Nixon 730

Gypsy Rizka - Lloyd Alexander 17

Hogula: Dread Pig of Night - Jean Gralley 369

How to Catch an Elephant - Amy Schwartz 888

Howie Bowles and Uncle Sam - Kate Banks 53

The Huckabuck Family and How They Raised Popcorn in Nebraska and Quit and Came Back - Carl Sandburg 869

Huggly Takes a Bath - Tedd Arnold 35

I, Crocodile - Fred Marcellino 619

I Was a Rat! - Philip Pullman 804

I Was a Sixth Grade Alien - Bruce Coville 192

Inspector Hopper - Doug Cushman 218

It's All Greek to Me - Jon Scieszka 891

Lucky Pennies and Hot Chocolate - Carol Diggory Shields 906

The Magic Pretzel - Daniel Pinkwater 785

Marvin Redpost: Class President - Louis Sachar 859

Mary Louise Loses Her Manners - Diane Cuneo 214

Minerva Louise at the Fair - Janet Morgan Stoeke 960

Minnie and Moo and the Thanksgiving Tree - Denys Cazet 156

Mr. Persnickety and the Cat Lady - Paul Brett Johnson 484

Mr. Putter and Tabby Paint the Porch - Cynthia Rylant 853

Mud Flat Spring - James Stevenson 957

The Mystery of the Monkey's Maze - Doug Cushman 219

Nose Pickers from Outer Space - Gordon Korman 538

Old Dry Frye: A Deliciously Funny Tall Tale - Paul Brett Johnson 485

Only One Cowry: A Dahomean Tale - Phillis Gershator 346

Peril in the Bessledorf Parachute Factory - Phyllis Reynolds Naylor 721

The Pig Is in the Pantry, the Cat Is on the Shelf - Shirley Mozelle 706

The Pig Who Ran a Red Light - Paul Brett Johnson 486

The Pirate's Parrot - Lyn Rossiter McFarland 656

Poof! - John O'Brien 740

The Rain Came Down - David Shannon 902

Rainy Morning - Daniel Pinkwater 786

Raising Sweetness - Diane Stanley 947

See You Later, Gladiator - Jon Scieszka 892

Six Hogs on a Scooter - Eileen Spinelli 943

Slender Ella and Her Fairy Hogfather - Vivian Sathre 874

Spider Storch's Desperate Deal - Gina Willner-Pardo 1054

Tacky and the Emperor - Helen Lester 568

The Three Sillies - Steven Kellogg 511

Tomatoes from Mars - Arthur Yorinks 1087

Tough Cookie - David Wisniewski 1060

A Traitor Among the Boys - Phyllis Reynolds Naylor 723

The Two Sillies - Mary Ann Hoberman 439

The Very Boastful Kangaroo - Bernard Most 704

Weird Stories from the Lonesome Cafe - Judy Cox 201

What! Cried Granny: An Almost Bedtime Story - Kate Lum 603

What Is a Wise Bird Like You Doing in a Silly Tale Like This? - Uri Shulevitz 909

When Agnes Caws - Candace Fleming 321

When You Take a Pig to a Party - Kristina Thermaenius McLarey 665

Winnie Flies Again - Valerie Thomas 984

Newspapers

Obstinacy

Old Age

Orphans

Outdoor Life

Paleontology

Parent and Child

Parenthood

Peace

Pearls

Peer Pressure

Perseverance

Pets

Photography

Physically Handicapped

Pioneers

Pirates

Tall Tales

Bewildered for Three Days: As to Why Daniel Boone Never Wore His Coonskin Cap - Andrew Glass 350
Big Jabe - Jerdine Nolen 732
A Carnival of Animals - Sid Fleischman 319
Comes a Wind - Linda Arms White 1043
The Loudest, Fastest, Best Drummer in Kansas - Marguerite W. Davol 241
Peg and the Whale - Kenneth Oppel 746
Shoeshine Whittaker - Helen Ketteman 517
The Tale of Willie Monroe - Alan Schroeder 885

Teacher-Student Relationships

David Goes to School - David Shannon 901
Fourth Grade Weirdo - Martha Freeman 327
Miss Alaineus: A Vocabulary Disaster - Debra Frasier 326

Teachers

Emeline at the Circus - Marjorie Priceman 797
First Day Jitters - Julie Danneberg 235
Four Stupid Cupids - Gregory Maguire 611
Good Luck, Mrs. K.! - Louise Borden 93
Jamaica and the Substitute Teacher - Juanita Havill 407
The Landry News - Andrew Clements 172
School Trouble for Andy Russell - David A. Adler 8
Seal Island School - Susan Bartlett 59
We Share Everything! - Robert Munsch 708
The Year of Miss Agnes - Kirkpatrick Hill 434

Teasing

Dancing in the Wings - Debbie Allen 21
Hello, Sweetie Pie - Carl Norac 734
King of the Kooties! - Debbie Dadey 227
One Halloween Night - Mark Teague 979
A Traitor Among the Boys - Phyllis Reynolds Naylor 723

Television

Cody Unplugged - Betsy Duffey 279

Theater

King of Shadows - Susan Cooper 188

Time Travel

Black Belt - Matt Faulkner 309
If That Breathes Fire, We're Toast! - Jennifer J. Stewart 958
It's All Greek to Me - Jon Scieszka 891
Jackie and Me - Dan Gutman 389
Jesse's Star - Ellen Schwartz 890
King of Shadows - Susan Cooper 188
The Pictish Child - Jane Yolen 1085
Roughing It on the Oregon Trail - Diane Stanley 948
See You Later, Gladiator - Jon Scieszka 892

Toys

Chugga-Chugga Choo-Choo - Kevin Lewis 578
Cowboy Kid - Max Eilenberg 298
Elmer and the Lost Teddy - David McKee 662
Harry and Lulu - Arthur Yorinks 1086
I Love You, Blue Kangaroo! - Emma Chichester Clark 161
Jazzbo and Googy - Matt Novak 737
Leo Cockroach...Toy Tester - Kevin O'Malley 745
Lizzy and Skunk - Marie-Louise Fitzpatrick 316

Louie's Goose - H.M. Ehrlich 297
Mail for Husher Town - Mary Louise Cuneo 215
Pete and Polo's Big School Adventure - Adrian Reynolds 818
Poppy's Puppet - Patricia Lee Gauch 337
Sammy and the Dinosaurs - Ian Whybrow 1046
Three Magic Bulls - Richard Egielski 294
Too Big! - Claire Masurel 629
Trucks Trucks Trucks - Peter Sis 922
The Tub People's Christmas - Pam Conrad 185
What's the Matter, Davy? - Brigitte Weninger 1038

Traditional Stories

Aesop's Fables - Jerry Pinkney 781
Stockings of Buttermilk: American Folktales - Neil Philip 773
The Tale of the Turnip - Brian Alderson 15

Traditions

Brave Highland Heart - Heather Kellerhals-Stewart 509
Matzah Ball Soup - Joan Rothenberg 841
My Two Grandmothers - Effin Older 743
This Next New Year - Janet S. Wong 1064
While the Bear Sleeps: Winter Tales and Traditions - Caitlin Matthews 633

Trains

Chugga-Chugga Choo-Choo - Kevin Lewis 578
Clickety Clack - Rob Spence 940
It's Funny Where Ben's Train Takes Him - Robert Burleigh 131
Next Stop Grand Central - Maira Kalman 493
Train Song - Harriet Ziefert 1095

Transportation

Bus Route to Boston - Maryann Cocca-Leffler 174
How Will We Get to the Beach? - Brigitte Luciani 602
Isaac the Ice Cream Truck - Scott Santoro 872
Next Stop! - Sarah Ellis 300
Six Hogs on a Scooter - Eileen Spinelli 943
Train Song - Harriet Ziefert 1095
Trucks Trucks Trucks - Peter Sis 922
Whiteblack the Penguin Sees the World - H.A. Rey 817

Travel

Hannah and the Whistling Teakettle - Mindy Warshaw Skolsky 923
Henry Hikes to Fitchburg - D.B. Johnson 478
Little Wolf's Book of Badness - Ian Whybrow 1045
Speechless in New York - Ellen Dreyer 277
Vendela in Venice - Christina Bjork 80
The Way to Schenectady - Richard Scrimger 894

Treasure

Da Wei's Treasure: A Chinese Tale - Margaret Chang 159

Treasure, Buried

The Copper Treasure - Melvin Burgess 130
The Goose's Gold - Ron Roy 844

Trees

The Bird, the Monkey, and the Snake in the Jungle - Kate Banks 52
The Friendship Tree - Kathy Caple 142
The Grandad Tree - Trish Cooke 186

Mooseltoe - Margie Palatini 757
My Mother Talks to Trees - Doris Gove 366
Under the Lemon Moon - Edith Hope Fine 315

Trickster Tales

Bearhide and Crow - Paul Brett Johnson 483
Cold Feet - Cynthia DeFelice 246
Trickster and the Fainting Birds - Howard Norman 735
Tumbleweed Stew - Susan Stevens Crummel 211

Trust

My Big Lie - Bill Cosby 190

Twins

Be First in the Universe - Stephanie Spinner 944
The Dancing Pig - Judy Sierra 912
Mop to the Rescue - Martine Schaap 877
One-of-a-Kind Mallie - Kimberly Brubaker Bradley 98

Underground Railroad

There's a Dead Person Following My Sister Around - Vivian Vande Velde 1006

Unicorns

I Wished for a Unicorn - Robert Heidbreder 409
Nobody Rides the Unicorn - Adrian Mitchell 689
Song of the Wanderer - Bruce Coville 193

Vacations

Angel Spreads Her Wings - Judy Delton 253
Clarence Goes Out West and Meets a Purple Horse - Jean Ekman Adams 3
The Diary of Melanie Martin - Carol Weston 1040
The Elevator Family - Douglas Evans 306
Fossil Fever - Kathleen Weidner Zoehfeld 1098
The Goose's Gold - Ron Roy 844
Gus & Gertie and the Missing Pearl - Joan Lowery Nixon 730
Montezuma's Revenge - Cari Best 76
Mr. Bear's Vacation - Debi Gliori 353
Sally Goes to the Beach - Stephen Huneck 460
Squiggle's Tale - Andre Dahan 228
Strega Nona Takes a Vacation - Tomie DePaola 261
Vendela in Venice - Christina Bjork 80

Values

Reuben and the Quilt - Merle Good 360

Vampires

Bunnicula Strikes Again! - James Howe 453
Hogula: Dread Pig of Night - Jean Gralley 369
A Straw for Two - Eric Sanvoisin 873
The Vampire in My Bathtub - Brenda Seabrooke 896

Voyages and Travels

Dreaming of America: An Ellis Island Story - Eve Bunting 125
Dreamstones - Maxine Trottier 990
Hog Music - M.C. Helldorfer 411
I'm Sorry, Almira Ann - Jane Kurtz 545
Luke: 1849-On the Golden Trail - Bonnie Pryor 802
Red Flower Goes West - Ann Turner 994

Character Name Index

This index alphabetically lists the major characters in each featured title. Each character name is followed by a description of the character. Citations also provide titles of the books featuring the character—listed alphabetically if there is more than one title—author names, and entry numbers.

A

Abeyta, Armando (Indian; Grandfather)
Enchanted Runner - Kimberley Griffiths Little   590

Abuela (Grandmother; Cook)
Magda's Tortillas: Las Tortillas de Magda - Becky Chavarria-Chairez   160

Abuela (Grandmother)
Under the Lemon Moon - Edith Hope Fine   315

Addario, Ben (Child; Friend)
Creature Crossing - Betty Levin   570

Addie (Daughter; Sister)
The Promise Quilt - Candice F. Ransom   809

Addie (Child)
When Addie Was Scared - Linda Bailey   48

Addy (Slave)
Big Jabe - Jerdine Nolen   732

Adelaide (Child; Friend)
When You Take a Pig to a Party - Kristina Thermaenius McLarey   665

Agapanthus (Child; Daughter)
Agapanthus Hum and the Eyeglasses - Joy Cowley   196

al-Ma'mun (Ruler; Scholar)
The House of Wisdom - Florence Parry Heide   410

Albert (Pig; Outcast)
Albert & Lila - Rafik Schami   882

Albert (Student—Elementary School)
Angela's Top-Secret Computer Club - Holly Keller   503

Albert (Pig; Friend)
Oliver and Albert, Friends Forever - Jean Van Leeuwen   1004

Albertson, Louisa (4th Grader; Bully)
King of the Kooties! - Debbie Dadey   227

Aldine (Son; Brother)
The Promise Quilt - Candice F. Ransom   809

Aldridge, Octavia (Neighbor)
You're a Brave Man, Julius Zimmerman - Claudia Mills   688

Alex (12-Year-Old; Cousin)
Blackwater - Eve Bunting   122

Alex (Student—Elementary School)
Mr. Tanen's Ties - Maryann Cocca-Leffler   175

Alex (Son; Child)
The Night Worker - Kate Banks   55

Alfie (Bear; Son)
Are You There, Baby Bear? - Catherine Walters   1023

Alice (Child)
Alice's Adventures in Wonderland - Lewis Carroll   150

Alice (Child; Sister)
The Deep - Tim Winton   1057

Alice (Cat)
Paris Cat - Leslie Baker   50

Alice the Great (Grandmother)
One Dark and Scary Night - Bill Cosby   191

Alligator (Alligator)
Armadillo Tattletale - Helen Ketteman   516

Allison (Sister; Dancer)
Ballerinas Don't Wear Glasses - Ainslie Manson   618

Amanda (Sister; Daughter)
Queen of the World - Thomas F. Yezerski   1079

Amanda (Child; Sister)
Taking Charge - Sonia Levitin   574

Amanda (Child)
A Thanksgiving Wish - Michael J. Rosen   834

Amanda (Kindergartner)
We Share Everything! - Robert Munsch   708

Amanda Lynne (Sister; Daughter)
Angel Baby - Pat Cummings   213

Amelia (Student—Elementary School; Friend)
The All-New Amelia - Marissa Moss   698

Amelia (Daughter; Sister)
Amelia Works It Out - Marissa Moss   699

Amelia (10-Year-Old; Child of Divorced Parents)
Amelia's Family Ties - Marissa Moss   700

Amonth (Grandfather; Worker)
The Wide-Awake Princess - Katherine Paterson   765

Amos (Friend)
Dolphin Freedom - Wayne Grover   385

Amy (Cousin; Bride)
Beany and the Dreaded Wedding - Susan Wojciechowski   1061

Amy (Child; Friend)
Henry and Amy (Right-Way-Round and Upside Down) - Stephen Michael King   522

Amy (Neighbor; Child)
Yuck, a Love Story - Don Gillmor   349

Ana (4th Grader; Friend)
In the Shade of the Nispero Tree - Carmen T. Bernier-Grand   73

Anciana (Spirit)
Under the Lemon Moon - Edith Hope Fine   315

Andeg (Bird)
The Birchbark House - Louise Erdrich   303

Anderson, Tamika (4th Grader; Friend)
Andy and Tamika - David A. Adler   4

Anderson, Tamika (Friend; Niece)
Parachuting Hamsters and Andy Russell - David A. Adler   7

Andrew (Baby; Brother)
Soldier Mom - Alice Mead   672

Angel (Angel; Friend)
Isabelle and the Angel - Thierry Magnier   610

Angel, A.N. (Aged Person)
Albert and the Angels - Leslie Norris   736

Angela (Koala Bear; Student—Elementary School)
Emily's First 100 Days of School - Rosemary Wells   1033

Angelina (Cat)
The Full Belly Bowl - Jim Aylesworth   47

Angelina (Coyote; Friend)
Two Cool Coyotes - Jillian Lund   604

Ann (Insect; Friend)
What Day Is It? - Patti Trimble   988

Anna (Mother; Artisan)
The Crystal Mountain - Ruth Sanderson   870

Annabel (Child; Actress)
Annabel the Actress Starring in Gorilla My Dreams - Ellen Conford   183

Annabelle (Dog)
Annabelle's Big Move - Carla Golembe   359

Annalisa (Child; Daughter)
Kiss the Cow! - Phyllis Root   830

Annalise (Friend)
Jumping into Nothing - Gina Willner-Pardo   1053

Annie (Child; Musician)
1, 2, 3, Music! - Sylvie Auzary-Luton   41

Annie (Child)
The Missing Mitten Mystery - Steven Kellogg   510

Annie (Child)
Paris Cat - Leslie Baker   50

Anthony (Child; Son)
And My Mean Old Mother Will Be Sorry, Blackboard Bear - Martha Alexander   19

Anya (Daughter; Sister)
Shy Mama's Halloween - Anne Broyles   115

Apfel, Dustin (2nd Grader; Mentally Challenged Person)
Dustin's Big School Day - Alden R. Carter   151

April (Child; Daughter)
Different Just Like Me - Lori Mitchell   690

Arigotti, Stormy (9-Year-Old; Abuse Victim)
The Runaways - Zilpha Keatley Snyder   932

Armadillo (Armadillo; Outcast)
Armadillo Tattletale - Helen Ketteman   516

Armadillo (Armadillo; Rancher)
Tumbleweed Stew - Susan Stevens Crummel   211

Arnie (Bully; 9-Year-Old)
Cockroach Cooties - Laurence Yep   1076

Arthur (Chimpanzee; Brother)
Arthur's Birthday Party - Lillian Hoban   435

Arthur (Apprentice)
The Last Alchemist - Colin Thompson   986

Attired, Natalie (Bird; Student—Elementary School)
The Chameleon Wore Chartreuse: From the Tattered Casebook of Chet Gecko, Private Eye - Bruce Hale   393

Audrey (Cat; Friend)
A Night on the Tiles - Bruce Ingman   465

Augusta (Child; Sister)
The Fixits - Anne Mazer   638

Aunt Liza (Aunt; Aged Person)
Hog Music - M.C. Helldorfer   411

Aunt Millie (Bird)
What Is a Wise Bird Like You Doing in a Silly Tale Like This? - Uri Shulevitz   909

Auntie Claus (Aunt)
Auntie Claus - Elise Primavera   799

Aurelia (Royalty; Daughter)
King Midas and the Golden Touch - Charlotte Craft   204

Aurora (Fox)
The Practically Perfect Pajamas - Erik Brooks   109

Autumn (Child; Spirit)
Wild Child - Lynn Plourde   787

Axle Annie (Driver)
Axle Annie - Robin Pulver   805

B

Baa (Sheep; Sister)
Boo and Baa Get Wet - Olof Landstrom   554

Baba Yaga (Witch)
The Black Geese: A Baba Yaga Story from Russia - Alison Lurie   606

Babbage, Richard "Arby" (Director)
King of Shadows - Susan Cooper   188

Babcha (Grandmother)
When Addie Was Scared - Linda Bailey   48

Babe Ruth (Baseball Player)
The Babe & I - David A. Adler   5

Baby (Baby; Brother)
Baby Talk - Fred Hiatt   432

Baby (Child; Brother)
Blueberry Shoe - Ann Dixon   270

Baby (Dog)
Boomer's Big Surprise - Constance W. McGeorge   657

Baby (Baby)
Bunny and Me - Adele Aron Greenspun   375
Daisy Knows Best - Lisa Kopper   537

Baby (Dolphin)
Dolphin Freedom - Wayne Grover   385

Baby (Son)
Some Babies - Amy Schwartz   889

Baby (Panda; Baby)
Tom Goes to Kindergarten - Margaret Wild   1048

Baby Bear (Bear; Baby)
Papa's Song - Kate McMullan   666

Baby Bird (Bird; Baby)
Baby Bird's First Nest - Frank Asch   36

Baby Brother (Rabbit; Brother)
Little Bunny's Easter Surprise - Jeanne Modesitt   692

Baby Elephant (Elephant)
Elmer and the Lost Teddy - David McKee   662

Baby Rooster (Chicken)
The Bowlegged Rooster and Other Tales That Signify - Joyce Carol Thomas   982

Bach, Johann Sebastian (10-Year-Old; Musician)
Bach's Big Adventure - Sallie Ketcham   515

Bad Dog (Dog)
Bad Dog - Nina Laden   550

Badger (Badger)
Secrets of the Stone - Harriet Peck Taylor   976

Bags-Eye (Cat; Store Owner)
Princess Chamomile Gets Her Way - Hiawyn Oram   748

Bai-Ling (Bird)
Mei-Mei Loves the Morning - Margaret Holloway Tsubakiyama   992

Baila (Spouse; Housewife)
Moishe's Miracle: A Hanukkah Story - Laura Krauss Melmed   679

Bailey, Roger (Student—Elementary School; Friend)
Edwina Victorious - Susan Bonners   91

Bait (Cat)
Mad Dog McGraw - Myron Uhlberg   998

Baker, Elizabeth "Lizzy" (10-Year-Old; Sister)
Weaver's Daughter - Kimberly Brubaker Bradley   99

Baker, Hezzy (12-Year-Old; Sister)
Weaver's Daughter - Kimberly Brubaker Bradley   99

Bambolona (Assistant)
Strega Nona Takes a Vacation - Tomie DePaola   261

BaMusa (Merchant)
The Hatseller and the Monkeys - Baba Wague Diakite   264

Bandini, Margo (11-Year-Old; Daughter)
A Letter to Mrs. Roosevelt - C. Coco De Young   244

Bannaky (Slave; Farmer)
Molly Bannaky - Alice McGill   658

Bannaky, Molly (Spouse; Farmer)
Molly Bannaky - Alice McGill   658

Bao (Baby)
Ma Jiang and the Orange Ants - Barbara Ann Porte   792

Baptiste (Brother; Cousin)
Cajun Through and Through - Tynia Thomassie   985

Baring, Foster (Child; Friend)
Creature Crossing - Betty Levin   570

Barnaby (Cat)
Why Not? - Mary Wormell   1071

Barnes, Binky (Bear; Student—Elementary School)
Arthur's Underwear - Marc Brown   111

Barr (Stuffed Animal; Bear)
The Pirate's Parrot - Lyn Rossiter McFarland   656

Barrow, Frances "Frankie" (12-Year-Old; Orphan)
Nowhere to Call Home - Cynthia DeFelice   247

Bartleby (Turtle)
Bartleby of the Mighty Mississippi - Phyllis Shalant   900

Basho (Writer)
Basho and the Fox - Tim Myers   715

Basket Weaver (Artisan)
Basket Weaver and Catches Many Mice - Janet Gill   348

Bates, Abigail (Daughter; Sister)
Abigail Takes the Wheel - Avi   42

Bates, Billy (Sailor)
Little Bo: The Story of Bonnie Boadicea - Julie Andrews Edwards   289

Bates, Julian (Son; Friend)
Gloria's Way - Ann Cameron   139

Bates, Tom (Son; Brother)
Abigail Takes the Wheel - Avi   42

Baudelaire, Klaus (12-Year-Old; Brother)
The Bad Beginning - Lemony Snicket   931

Baudelaire, Sunny (Baby; Sister)
The Bad Beginning - Lemony Snicket   931

Baudelaire, Violet (14-Year-Old; Sister)
The Bad Beginning - Lemony Snicket   931

Bayliss, Murray (Traveler)
Hurry! - Emily Arnold McCully   646

Bean, Clarice (Daughter; Sister)
Clarice Bean, That's Me - Lauren Child   162

Beane, Scarlette (Child; Daughter)
Scarlette Beane - Karen Wallace   1018

Bear (Bear)
Big Brown Bear - David McPhail   669

Bear (Bear; Toy)
Blue Rabbit and Friends - Christopher Wormell   1070

Bear (Bear; Friend)
Moonbear's Dream - Frank Asch   37

Bear, Baby (Bear; Son)
Sleepy Bears - Mem Fox   324

Bear, Baxter (Bear; Son)
Sleepy Bears - Mem Fox   324

Bear, Boswell (Bear)
Boswell Wide Awake - Alexandra Day   242

Bear, Jefferson (Bear; Friend)
What Will I Do Without You? - Sally Grindley   384

Bear, Jesse (Bear; Son)
What a Scare, Jesse Bear - Nancy White Carlstrom   147

Bear, Mother (Bear; Mother)
Sleepy Bears - Mem Fox   324

Bear Noel (Bear)
Bear Noel - Olivier Dunrea   286

Beard, George (Student—Elementary School; Friend)
Captain Underpants and the Attack of the Talking Toilets - Dav Pilkey   776

Beard, George (4th Grader)
Captain Underpants and the Perilous Plot of Professor Poopypants - Dav Pilkey   777

Beatrice (Bird)
Wizzil - William Steig   949

C

Cat (Cat)
How the Cat Swallowed Thunder - Lloyd Alexander 18
Pumpkin Soup - Helen Cooper 187

Catches Many Mice (Cat)
Basket Weaver and Catches Many Mice - Janet Gill 348

Cecile (Child; Daughter)
Mama, Across the Sea - Alex Godard 356

CeeCee (Aunt; Sister)
Aunt CeeCee, Aunt Belle, and Mama's Surprise - Mary Quattlebaum 806

Celeste (Child)
Celeste Sails to Spain - Alison Lester 566

Chameleon, Shirley (4th Grader; Reptile)
The Chameleon Wore Chartreuse: From the Tattered Casebook of Chet Gecko, Private Eye - Bruce Hale 393

Chamomile (Royalty; Mouse)
Princess Chamomile Gets Her Way - Hiawyn Oram 748

Chan, Ah Pau (Grandmother)
Child Bride - Ching Yeung Russell 847

Chang (Bullied Child)
Bird Boy - Elizabeth Starr Hill 433

Charisse (Classmate)
The All-New Amelia - Marissa Moss 698

Charles (Baby; Brother)
I'd Rather Have an Iguana - Heidi Stetson Mario 620

Charlie (Golfer; Teacher)
Night Golf - William Miller 683

Charlie (Child; Son)
Too Big! - Claire Masurel 629

Charnel (Royalty)
Cinderella Skeleton - Robert D. San Souci 866

Chase (Teenager; Animal Lover)
Shadow Horse - Alison Hart 406

Chatfield, Charity (Student—Elementary School; Daughter)
No Time for Mother's Day - Laurie Halse Anderson 24

Chato (Cat; Friend)
Chato and the Party Animals - Gary Soto 936

Chef Rhino (Rhinoceros; Cook)
Hamburger Heaven - Wong Herbert Yee 1075

Cherry Sue (Llama; Friend)
Poppleton Has Fun - Cynthia Rylant 854
Poppleton in Fall - Cynthia Rylant 855

Chester (Cat)
Bunnicula Strikes Again! - James Howe 453

Cheung, Carolyn (Judge)
An American Face - Jan M. Czech 225

Chicken Chuck (Rooster)
Chicken Chuck - Bill Martin Jr. 626

Chicory (Goose)
The Way Home - Nan Parson Rossiter 839

Chief (Ruler)
Seven Spools of Thread - Angela Shelf Medearis 675

Chief Brown (Police Officer; Father)
Encyclopedia Brown and the Case of the Slippery Salamander - Donald J. Sobol 933

Chili-Chili-Chin-Chin (Donkey)
Chili-Chili-Chin-Chin - Belle Yang 1073

Chipmunk, Nigel (Chipmunk)
Thimbleberry Stories - Cynthia Rylant 857

Chongo Chingi (Penguin)
Penguin Dreams - J. Otto Seibold 897

Chrisman, Abbie (12-Year-Old; Sister)
Calling Me Home - Patricia Hermes 427

Christie, James (12-Year-Old; Brother)
Wander - Susan Hart Lindquist 587

Christie, Sary (Sister; 7-Year-Old)
Wander - Susan Hart Lindquist 587

Christopher (Brother; 6-Year-Old)
It's My Birthday, Too! - Lynne Jonell 489

Chub (Fish)
Splish, Splash! - Sarah Weeks 1032

Chulak (Friend; Servant)
The Firework-Maker's Daughter - Philip Pullman 803

Cimabue (Artist; Teacher)
A Boy Named Giotto - Paolo Guarnieri 386

Cinderella (Stepsister; Servant)
Cinderella: The Dog and Her Little Glass Slipper - Diane Goode 362

Cinderella Skeleton (Stepsister; Stepdaughter)
Cinderella Skeleton - Robert D. San Souci 866

Cindy (Mother; Spouse)
Rover - Michael Rosen 832

Cindy Ellen (Cowgirl; Stepdaughter)
Cindy Ellen: A Wild Western Cinderella - Susan Lowell 600

Claire (Child; Daughter)
Next Stop! - Sarah Ellis 300

Clara (Stepmother)
Amelia's Family Ties - Marissa Moss 700

Clara (Duck)
The Nutquacker - Mary Jane Auch 40

Clara (Horse)
Shoeshine Whittaker - Helen Ketteman 517

Clarence (Pig)
Clarence Goes Out West and Meets a Purple Horse - Jean Ekman Adams 3

Clarinda (Puppet)
Poppy's Puppet - Patricia Lee Gauch 337

Clee (Child; Sister)
The Winter Gift - Deborah Turney Zagwyn 1089

Clem (Uncle; Writer; Restaurateur)
Weird Stories from the Lonesome Cafe - Judy Cox 201

Clement (Brother; Cowboy)
Comes a Wind - Linda Arms White 1043

Cleo (Sister)
Amelia Works It Out - Marissa Moss 699

Cleopatra (Friend; Student)
Madlenka - Peter Sis 921

Clever Tortoise (Turtle)
Clever Tortoise: A Traditional African Tale - Francesca Martin 627

Clive (Child)
Celeste Sails to Spain - Alison Lester 566

Cloud, Raney (Cook; Farmer)
Old Thunder and Miss Raney - Sharon Darrow 237

Clutch (Mouse; Musician)
Ragweed - Avi 45

Clyde (Brother; Cowboy)
Comes a Wind - Linda Arms White 1043

Clyde (Rabbit; Student—Elementary School)
Science Fair Bunnies - Kathryn Lasky 560

Coates, Thurlow (Baseball Player)
Home Run Hero - Dean Hughes 456

Cocorico (Rooster)
Mouton's Impossible Dream - Anik McGrory 659

Coleman, Emma (5th Grader; Friend)
Leaving Emma - Nancy Steele Brokaw 108

Collins, Helen "Grandma" (Grandmother; Widow(er))
The Way to Schenectady - Richard Scrimger 894

Collins, Jason (Neighbor; Child)
Parachuting Hamsters and Andy Russell - David A. Adler 7

Colter, John (Explorer)
Seaman: The Dog Who Explored the West with Lewis & Clark - Gail Langer Karwoski 497

Comfort, Welcome (Foster Child)
Welcome Comfort - Patricia Polacco 789

Concha (Friend; Store Owner)
Dance of the Crystal Skull - Norma Lehr 565

Conley, Bridger (14-Year-Old; Foster Child)
Deadly Waters - Gloria Skurzynski 925

Conner, Pauline (Child; Friend)
The Man with the Black Glove - Ursel Scheffler 883

Constance (Daughter; Sister)
Kindle Me a Riddle: A Pioneer Story - Roberta Karim 496

Cookie, Clara Ann (Child; Daughter)
Clara Ann Cookie - Harriet Ziefert 1090

Cookie-Store Cat (Cat)
The Cookie-Store Cat - Cynthia Rylant 851

Cooper, Lamar (Military Personnel; 16-Year-Old)
Abraham's Battle: A Novel of Gettysburg - Sara Harrell Banks 57

Copycub (Bear)
Copy Me, Copycub - Richard Edwards 293

Cora (Dog)
Old Dog Cora and the Christmas Tree - Consie Powell 794

Cosmo (Child; Brother)
Cosmo and the Robot - Brian Pinkney 780

Cosmo (Dog)
Cosmo Zooms - Arthur Howard 449

Costos, Emerald (4th Grader; Daughter)
Stucksville - Sheila Greenwald 376

Cott, Lucas (6th Grader; Friend)
The Just Desserts Club - Johanna Hurwitz 461

Cougar (Horse; Spirit)
Cougar - Helen V. Griffith 381

Cousin Ruth (Aged Person; Widow(er))
Snowdrops for Cousin Ruth - Susan Katz 498

Cowboy Kid (Child; Son)
Cowboy Kid - Max Eilenberg 298

Coyote (Coyote)
Secrets of the Stone - Harriet Peck Taylor 976

Cozy (Cat)
Paddiwak and Cozy - Berlie Doherty 271

Crickwing (Cockroach; Artist)
Crickwing - Janell Cannon 141

Crouch, Stefan III (Handicapped; Friend)
Carolina Crow Girl - Valerie Hobbs 438

Crow (Bird; Trickster)
Pig and Crow - Kay Chorao 165

Crum, Lucretzia (Child; Daughter)
Bad Habits! - Babette Cole 178

Cur (Pirate; Sea Captain)
The Pirate's Parrot - Lyn Rossiter McFarland 656

Curbhopper, Calvin (Worker)
Messenger, Messenger - Robert Burleigh 132

Curly (Indian; Son)
Crazy Horse's Vision - Joseph Bruchac 116

Curly Dog (Dog)
Mabel Dancing - Amy Hest   430

Cushman, Sara Jane (6th Grader; Friend)
The Just Desserts Club - Johanna Hurwitz   461

D

Da (Father; Miner)
Boy of the Deeps - Ian Wallace   1015

Da Wei (Orphan)
Da Wei's Treasure: A Chinese Tale - Margaret Chang   159

Dad (Father; Camper)
All the Way to Morning - Marc Harshman   405

Dad (Father; Journalist)
Amelia's Family Ties - Marissa Moss   700

Dad (Father)
The Boy on the Beach - Niki Daly   230
Darby: The Special Order Pup - Alexandra Day   243
Happy Birthday, America! - Marsha Wilson Chall   158
Henry and Mudge and the Snowman Plan - Cynthia Rylant   852
I Am Me - Karla Kuskin   546
I Want a Pet - Lauren Child   163

Dad (Single Father)
Jumping into Nothing - Gina Willner-Pardo   1053

Dad (Mouse; Father)
Monk Camps Out - Emily Arnold McCully   648

Dad (Musician; Mouse)
Mouse Practice - Emily Arnold McCully   649

Dad (Father)
My Big Lie - Bill Cosby   190

Dad (Father; Driver)
Next Stop! - Sarah Ellis   300

Dad (Father; Jockey)
One Lucky Girl - George Ella Lyon   607

Dad (Father)
Our Eight Nights of Hanukkah - Michael J. Rosen   833
The Raft - Jim LaMarche   551

Dad (Father; Fisherman)
Rescue at Sea! - Wolfram Hanel   400

Dad (Father)
The Sand Children - Joyce Dunbar   281
Shawn and Keeper and the Birthday Party - Jonathan London   596
Space Guys! - Martha Weston   1041

Dad (Father; Cowboy)
Tall in the Saddle - Anne Carter   152

Dad (Father)
This Is the Turkey - Abby Levine   571

Dad (Father; Farmer)
The Way Home - Nan Parson Rossiter   839

Dada Segbo (Royalty)
Only One Cowry: A Dahomean Tale - Phillis Gershator   346

Daddy (Father)
Agapanthus Hum and the Eyeglasses - Joy Cowley   196

Daddy (Father; Driver)
Are We There Yet, Daddy? - Virginia Walters   1024

Daddy (Father)
Bedbugs - Megan McDonald   651

Daddy (Father; Spouse)
Buzz - Janet S. Wong   1063

Daddy (Father)
Daddy, Will You Miss Me? - Wendy McCormick   644

Daddy (Father; Nephew)
Down the Winding Road - Angela Johnson   476

Daddy (Father)
Faraway Home - Jane Kurtz   544

Daddy (Father; Spouse)
Hurricane! - Corinne Demas   255

Daddy (Father)
I Hate to Go to Bed! - Katie Davis   239
Night Shift Daddy - Eileen Spinelli   942

Daddy (Father; Musician)
Tiny's Hat - Ann Grifalconi   380

Daddy (Father; Actor)
Tree of Hope - Amy Littlesugar   591

Daddy (Father)
Vroomaloom Zoom - John Coy   203

Daisy (Duck; Sister)
Daisy and the Beastie - Jane Simmons   917

Daisy (Duck; Daughter)
Daisy and the Egg - Jane Simmons   918

Daisy (Dog; Mother)
Daisy Knows Best - Lisa Kopper   537

Daisy (Child; Friend)
Dear Daisy, Get Well Soon - Maggie Smith   930

Daisy (Child; Daughter)
Eat Your Peas - Kes Gray   370

Daisy (Dog)
The Little Green Goose - Adele Sansone   871

Daisy (Child)
Missing! - Jonathan Langley   555

Daisy (Sister; Child)
The Wedding - Angela Johnson   477

Dame Van Winkle (Spouse; Mother)
Rip Van Winkle - Washington Irving   467

Damura (Stepdaughter; Servant)
The Gift of the Crocodile: A Cinderella Story - Judy Sierra   913

Dan (Child of Divorced Parents; Stepbrother)
I Hate Weddings - P.J. Petersen   772

Daniel (7-Year-Old; Son)
Crab Moon - Ruth Horowitz   447

Danilito (Son; Immigrant)
When This World Was New - D.H. Figueredo   313

Danny (Child)
Dory Story - Jerry Pallotta   758

Darby (Dog)
Darby: The Special Order Pup - Alexandra Day   243

Darcy, Maggie (13-Year-Old; Friend)
Kat's Surrender - Theresa Martin Golding   358

Darrow, Carly (Friend)
Amelia Works It Out - Marissa Moss   699

Datt (Father)
Reuben and the Quilt - Merle Good   360

Davey (Baby; Brother)
Tadpoles - Betsy James   471

David (Student—Elementary School)
David Goes to School - David Shannon   901

David (Child; Son)
Dreamstones - Maxine Trottier   990
Island Magic - Martha Bennett Stiles   959

Davies (Orphan; Friend)
The Copper Treasure - Melvin Burgess   130

Davis, Cass (Student—Middle School; Friend)
The Ashwater Experiment - Amy Goldman Koss   539

Davis, Cory (4th Grader)
School Trouble for Andy Russell - David A. Adler   8

Davy (Rabbit; Brother)
Happy Birthday, Davy! - Brigitte Weninger   1035
What's the Matter, Davy? - Brigitte Weninger   1038

Davy (Rabbit; Friend)
Why Are You Fighting, Davy? - Brigitte Weninger   1039

Day, Merry (Animal Lover)
Charlie Muffin's Miracle Mouse - Dick King-Smith   523

Daybreak (Horse)
Granddaddy's Street Songs - Monalisa DeGross   251

De Vass, Mick (Veteran; Amputee)
The Lion and the Unicorn - Shirley Hughes   458

Dean, S. Paul "Super" (Manager)
Last Licks: A Spaldeen Story - Cari Best   75

Deane, Emma (10-Year-Old; Orphan)
The Gate in the Wall - Ellen Howard   452

Dedicate Rosethorn (Magician; Teacher)
Briar's Book - Tamora Pierce   774

Dee (Dog)
Down to the Sea with Mr. Magee - Chris Van Dusen   1000

Delarue, Marcel (Artist; Brother)
The Good Liar - Gregory Maguire   612

Delilah (Mountain Woman)
The Tale of Willie Monroe - Alan Schroeder   885

Delmore (Son; Baseball Player)
Apple Batter - Deborah Turney Zagwyn   1088

DeLucca, Joey (5th Grader; Computer Expert)
The Landry News - Andrew Clements   172

Denis, Robby (Brother; Son)
Club Earth - Gail Gauthier   339

Denis, Will (Brother; Son)
Club Earth - Gail Gauthier   339

Derrick (Child)
The Music in Derrick's Heart - Gwendolyn Battle-Lavert   63

Desert Woman (Deity)
Roadrunner's Dance - Rudolfo Anaya   23

Desta (Child; Daughter)
Faraway Home - Jane Kurtz   544

Dickens, Jedidiah "Jed" (Teenager; Brother)
My Brother's Keeper: Virginia's Diary - Mary Pope Osborne   751

Dickens, Virginia B. (9-Year-Old; Sister)
My Brother's Keeper: Virginia's Diary - Mary Pope Osborne   751

Dickinson, Emily (Historical Figure; Writer)
The Mouse of Amherst - Elizabeth Spires   945

Digger Pig (Pig; Cook)
Digger Pig and the Turnip - Caron Lee Cohen   176

Diggety (Dog)
George and Diggety - Maggie Stern   951

Dimitrii (Son; Brother)
Shy Mama's Halloween - Anne Broyles   115

Dinah (Baby; Sister)
What's the Matter, Davy? - Brigitte Weninger   1038

Dinkleschmidt (Uncle; Store Owner)
Three Magic Balls - Richard Egielski   294

Dirt Man (Monster)
Dirt Boy - Erik Jon Slangerup   926

Ditzwinkle, Dorian (Teacher)
Fourth Grade Weirdo - Martha Freeman   327

Dobbs, Phineas (Aged Person)
A Big Cheese for the White House: The True Tale of a Tremendous Cheddar - Candace Fleming 320

Dobby (Mythical Creature)
Harry Potter and the Chamber of Secrets - J.K. Rowling 842

Dr. Duck (Duck; Doctor)
Dr. Duck - H.M. Ehrlich 296

Doctor Fox (Fox)
A Pig Is Moving In! - Claudia Fries 330

Dr. Franken (Scientist)
Frankenfrog - Kim Kennedy 512

Dr. Marin (Doctor)
Hello Baby! - Lizzy Rockwell 825

Doctor Ouch (Doctor; Spirit)
Operation Ghost - Jacques Duquennoy 287

Dr. Shtickle (Scientist; Uncle)
Tomatoes from Mars - Arthur Yorinks 1087

Doctor Slythe (Villain)
Nobody Rides the Unicorn - Adrian Mitchell 689

Dr. White (Dog)
Dr. White - Jane Goodall 361

Dog (Dog)
Don't Need Friends - Carolyn Crimi 208

Doll, Annabelle (Doll; Sister)
The Doll People - Ann M. Martin 624

Dolores (Child; Sister)
Aloha, Dolores - Barbara Samuels 863

Dolores (Pig; Worker)
City Pig - Karen Wallace 1017

Dolores (Mouse; Friend)
Horace and Morris but Mostly Dolores - James Howe 454

Donald (4th Grader; Friend)
King of the Kooties! - Debbie Dadey 227

Donald (Farmer)
Pumpkin Pie - Harriet Ziefert 1092

Dora (Swan)
Swan in Love - Eve Bunting 128

Dorfman, Robert (Student—Elementary School; Friend)
Oh No, It's Robert - Barbara Seuling 898

Dorothy (Student—Elementary School)
Me Tarzan - Betsy Byars 134

Dorsatum, Erethizon "Ereth" (Porcupine)
Ereth's Birthday - Avi 43

Doug (3rd Grader; Friend)
Horrible Harry at Halloween - Suzy Kline 533

Doug (3rd Grader)
Song Lee and the "I Hate You" Notes - Suzy Kline 534

Draculink (Vampire; Uncle)
A Straw for Two - Eric Sanvoisin 873

Dream Collector (Worker)
The Dream Collector - Troon Harrison 404

Dreanne "Dreenie" (5th Grader; Friend)
Bluish - Virginia Hamilton 397

Drennan, Kendall (12-Year-Old; Runner)
Enchanted Runner - Kimberley Griffiths Little 590

Drinkwater, Lena (Daughter; Soccer Player)
The Soccer Mom from Outer Space - Barney Saltzberg 862

Drinkwater, Ruben (Father)
The Soccer Mom from Outer Space - Barney Saltzberg 862

Driver Zach (Engineer)
Clickety Clack - Rob Spence 940

Drooga (Doll)
Grandma Chickenlegs - Geraldine McCaughrean 642

Drums-Louder (Indian)
White Wolf - Henrietta Branford 100

Duck (Duck)
Cold Little Duck, Duck, Duck - Lisa Westberg Peters 771

Duck (Duck; Driver)
Duck in the Truck - Jez Alborough 12

Duck (Duck)
Pumpkin Soup - Helen Cooper 187

Duck, Baby (Duck; Student—Elementary School)
Off to School, Baby Duck! - Amy Hest 431

Duck, Dora (Duck)
Eggday - Joyce Dunbar 280

Dump, Gloria (Aged Person; Neighbor)
Because of Winn-Dixie - Kate DiCamillo 265

Duncan (Cat)
Aloha, Dolores - Barbara Samuels 863

Duncan, Donald David "Dink" (Child; Friend)
The Goose's Gold - Ron Roy 844

Dyer, Amos (Spouse; Trickster)
Bearhide and Crow - Paul Brett Johnson 483

E

Earhart, Amelia (Pilot; Historical Figure)
Amelia and Eleanor Go for a Ride - Pam Munoz Ryan 848

Earl (Rabbit; Brother)
Tell-a-Bunny - Nancy Elizabeth Wallace 1020

Earth, Germaine (Teacher)
Four Stupid Cupids - Gregory Maguire 611

Eartha (Ant)
Crickwing - Janell Cannon 141

Ebb (Dog)
Ebb and Flo and the New Friend - Jane Simmons 919

Eddie (Rabbit; Friend)
Why Are You Fighting, Davy? - Brigitte Weninger 1039

Edna (5th Grader; Friend)
Angel Spreads Her Wings - Judy Delton 253

Edward (Royalty; Child)
The Prince and the Pauper - Marianna Mayer 634

Edward (Royalty; 13-Year-Old)
The Yeoman's Daring Daughter and the Princes in the Tower - Elaine Clayton 168

Elaine (Student—Elementary School; Sister)
Vera's First Day of School - Vera Rosenberry 837

Elena (Daughter; Sister)
The Black Geese: A Baba Yaga Story from Russia - Alison Lurie 606

Elena (Child; Friend)
The Cello of Mr. O. - Jane Cutler 221

Eli (Son; Brother)
Mr. Big Brother - William H. Hooks 443

Elizabeth (Daughter; Animal Lover)
Night Rabbits - Lee Posey 793

Elizabeti (Sister)
Mama Elizabeti - Stephanie Stuve-Bodeen 969

Ella (Bird; Friend)
Poppy & Ella: 3 Stories about 2 Friends - Jef Kaminsky 494

Ella (Child)
Summerhouse - Laurence Anholt 28

Ellen (Student)
The Fungus That Ate My School - Arthur Dorros 273

Ellis, Annie (Child; Neighbor)
Last Licks: A Spaldeen Story - Cari Best 75

Elmer (Elephant; Cousin)
Elmer and the Lost Teddy - David McKee 662

Eloise (Sister)
Bertie's Picture Day - Pat Brisson 106

Elsie June (Sister)
The Bravest of Us All - Marsha Diane Arnold 34

Elson, Tom (10-Year-Old)
Hurry! - Emily Arnold McCully 646

Elvis Ann (Child)
Hogula: Dread Pig of Night - Jean Gralley 369

Elwood (Pig)
Elwood and the Witch - Nicholas Heller 415

Emeline (Student—Elementary School; 2nd Grader)
Emeline at the Circus - Marjorie Priceman 797

Emelya (Brother)
At the Wish of the Fish: A Russian Folktale - J. Patrick Lewis 576

Emily (Rabbit; Student—Elementary School)
Emily's First 100 Days of School - Rosemary Wells 1033

Emily (6-Year-Old)
The Longest Hair in the World - Lois Duncan 285

Emily (Friend; Student—Elementary School)
Louise Goes Wild - Stephen Krensky 542

Emily (10-Year-Old; Daughter)
Sky Memories - Pat Brisson 107

Emily (Cat; Sister)
Snow Valentines - Karen Gray Ruelle 845
The Thanksgiving Beast Feast - Karen Gray Ruelle 846

Emily Louise (Child; Friend)
Go Away, Shelley Boo! - Phoebe Stone 963

Emma (5th Grader; Scientist)
The Boy Trap - Nancy Matson 632

Emma (Student—Elementary School; Friend)
Emma's Magic Winter - Jean Little 589

Emmaline (Writer; Mouse)
The Mouse of Amherst - Elizabeth Spires 945

Emperor (Royalty; Father)
Basket Weaver and Catches Many Mice - Janet Gill 348

Emperor of Pickleberry (Royalty; Twin)
What Is a Wise Bird Like You Doing in a Silly Tale Like This? - Uri Shulevitz 909

Enright, Charlotte "Charlie" (Student; 11-Year-Old)
The Lottie Project - Jacqueline Wilson 1055

Enright, Jo (Single Mother)
The Lottie Project - Jacqueline Wilson 1055

Erandi (7-Year-Old; Daughter)
Erandi's Braids - Antonio Hernandez Madrigal 609

Estelita "Stella" (Daughter; Student—Elementary School)
The Rainbow Tulip - Pat Mora 696

Esther (14-Year-Old; Cousin)
Hannah's Journal: The Story of an Immigrant Girl - Marissa Moss 702

Ethan (8-Year-Old; Friend)
When You Take a Pig to a Party - Kristina Thermaenius McLarey 665

Eva (Doll)
Mama Elizabeti - Stephanie Stuve-Bodeen 969

Fuko (Mole; Friend)
To Dinner, for Dinner - Tololwa M. Mollel 694

Funcraft, Tiffany (Doll; Friend)
The Doll People - Ann M. Martin 624

Funnybone (Dog)
Beezy and Funnybone - Megan McDonald 652

G

Gaddy, Lisa (Soccer Player; Twin)
Secret Weapon - Matt Christopher 167

Gaddy, Ted (Twin; Soccer Player)
Secret Weapon - Matt Christopher 167

Gage, Thomas (Military Personnel)
Sleds on Boston Common: A Story from the American Revoluton - Louise Borden 94

Gander (Goose; Friend)
The Secret Friend - Joyce Dunbar 282

Gardner, Lizzie (3rd Grader; 8-Year-Old)
Lizard Meets Ivana the Terrible - C. Anne Scott 893

Garland, Holly (3rd Grader; Child of Divorced Parents)
The Trouble with Cats - Martha Freeman 328

Gator, Allie (Alligator; Friend)
Gator Halloween - Stephanie Calmenson 138

Gator, Amy (Alligator; Friend)
Gator Halloween - Stephanie Calmenson 138

Gecko, Chet (4th Grader; Reptile)
The Chameleon Wore Chartreuse: From the Tattered Casebook of Chet Gecko, Private Eye - Bruce Hale 393

Gennero, Alison (Neighbor)
The Vampire in My Bathtub - Brenda Seabrooke 896

George (Dog)
Bark, George - Jules Feiffer 311

George (Tiger; Friend)
Brave Horace - Holly Keller 505

George (Student—Elementary School)
George - Maggie Stern 950

George (Brother)
George and Diggety - Maggie Stern 951

George (Duck; Friend)
George Paints His House - Francine Bassede 61

George (Pig)
The Pig Who Ran a Red Light - Paul Brett Johnson 486

George (Child)
The Video Shop Sparrow - Joy Cowley 198

Geraldine (Pig; Sister)
Geraldine and Mrs. Duffy - Holly Keller 506

Gershon (Spouse; Baker)
Gershon's Monster - Eric A. Kimmel 518

Gertie (Penguin; Vacationer)
Gus & Gertie and the Missing Pearl - Joan Lowery Nixon 730

Gertrude (Cow)
The Pig Who Ran a Red Light - Paul Brett Johnson 486

Giant Baby Bear (Bear; Son)
The Very Small - Joyce Dunbar 283

Gibbs, Gloria (Student—Middle School; Baseball Player)
Play Ball! - Dean Hughes 457

Gibson, Harriet "Harry" (13-Year-Old; Orphan)
Unbroken - Jessie Haas 391

Gibson, Tessa (9-Year-Old; Twin)
Be First in the Universe - Stephanie Spinner 944

Gibson, Tod (9-Year-Old; Twin)
Be First in the Universe - Stephanie Spinner 944

Gil (Insect)
What Day Is It? - Patti Trimble 988

Gilbert (Opossum; Student—Elementary School)
Jingle Bells, Homework Smells - Diane DeGroat 250

Gingerbread Baby (Runaway)
Gingerbread Baby - Jan Brett 104

Ginny (Single Mother)
Ola's Wake - B.J. Stone 962

Giraffe (Giraffe)
The Visitor - Patrice Aggs 10

Giraux, Teresa (4th Grader; Friend)
In the Shade of the Nispero Tree - Carmen T. Bernier-Grand 73

Girl (1st Grader; Sister)
Dreams Are More Real than Bathtubs - Susan Musgrave 710

Girl (Child)
Sun & Moon: A Giant Love Story - Lisa Desimini 262

Glashka (Eskimo; Daughter)
A Symphony of Whales - Steve Schuch 886

Gloria (Rabbit; Friend)
Tell-a-Bunny - Nancy Elizabeth Wallace 1020

GninGnin (Grandmother; Worker)
Love as Strong as Ginger - Lenore Look 598

Gnormal, Norman (4th Grader)
The Magic Pretzel - Daniel Pinkwater 785

God (Deity)
Whaddayamean - John Burningham 133
What a Truly Cool World - Julius Lester 569

Goldi (Store Owner)
Goldilocks Returns - Lisa Campbell Ernst 304

Goldsnoot, Harley Joe (Pig; Bachelor)
Slender Ella and Her Fairy Hogfather - Vivian Sathre 874

Good Knight (Knight)
Good Night, Good Knight - Shelley Moore Thomas 983

Goody, Beauregard "Uncle Beau" (Businessman; Friend)
Me and Rupert Goody - Barbara O'Connor 741

Goody, Rupert B. (Mentally Challenged Person; Son)
Me and Rupert Goody - Barbara O'Connor 741

Googy (Pig)
Jazzbo and Googy - Matt Novak 737

Goose (Goose)
The Big Bad Rumor - Jonathan Meres 680

Goose (Goose; Toy)
Blue Rabbit and Friends - Christopher Wormell 1070

Goose (Bird; Friend)
Pig and Crow - Kay Chorao 165

Gorilla (Toy)
When Sophie Gets Angry—Really, Really Angry - Molly Bang 51

Graber, Hannah "Hallie" (10-Year-Old; Twin)
One-of-a-Kind Mallie - Kimberly Brubaker Bradley 98

Graber, Matilda "Mallie" (10-Year-Old; Twin)
One-of-a-Kind Mallie - Kimberly Brubaker Bradley 98

Grace (Sister)
A Baby for Grace - Ian Whybrow 1044

Grace (Child of Divorced Parents; Friend)
Starring Grace - Mary Hoffman 440

Gracie (Dog)
My Sister Gracie - Gillian Johnson 482

Gram (Grandmother; Farmer)
Hurry! - Jessie Haas 390

Gram (Grandmother)
Snow Pumpkin - Carole Lexa Schaefer 880

Gramma (Grandmother)
The Winter Gift - Deborah Turney Zagwyn 1089

Grammie (Grandmother)
Different Just Like Me - Lori Mitchell 690

Grammy Lane (Grandmother)
My Two Grandmothers - Effin Older 743

Gramp (Grandfather; Farmer)
Hurry! - Jessie Haas 390

Grampa (Duck; Grandfather)
Off to School, Baby Duck! - Amy Hest 431

Gramps "Bugsy" (Grandfather)
Brooklyn, Bugsy, and Me - Lynea Bowdish 96

Gran (Grandmother)
Beezy and Funnybone - Megan McDonald 652
Sammy and the Dinosaurs - Ian Whybrow 1046

Granda (Grandfather; Gardener)
Jody's Beans - Malachy Doyle 275

Grandad (Grandfather)
The Grandad Tree - Trish Cooke 186
Harry's Home - Laurence Anholt 26

Grandad (Grandfather; Farmer)
Island Magic - Martha Bennett Stiles 959

Granddad (Grandfather)
The First Horse I See - Sally M. Keehn 501

Granddaddy (Grandfather)
Granddaddy's Street Songs - Monalisa DeGross 251

Grandfather (Grandfather)
Butterfly House - Eve Bunting 123
I Have an Olive Tree - Eve Bunting 126

Grandfather (Grandfather; Aged Person)
The Magic Paintbrush - Laurence Yep 1078

Grandfather Beane (Grandfather; Gardener)
Scarlette Beane - Karen Wallace 1018

Grandfather Sweet-William (Grandfather; Rhinoceros)
Bud - Kevin O'Malley 744

Grandma (Grandmother)
1, 2, 3, Music! - Sylvie Auzary-Luton 41
Dear Juno - Soyung Pak 754
The Disappearing Island - Corinne Demas 254

Grandma (Grandmother; Aged Person)
Figuring Out Frances - Gina Willner-Pardo 1052

Grandma (Grandmother)
Grandma Summer - Harley Jessup 473

Grandma (Grandmother; Store Owner)
Hannah and the Whistling Teakettle - Mindy Warshaw Skolsky 923

Grandma (Grandmother; Cook)
Keeping Up with Grandma - John Winch 1056

Grandma (Grandmother; Aged Person)
Mama, Across the Sea - Alex Godard 356

Grandma (Grandmother; Cook)
Matzah Ball Soup - Joan Rothenberg 841
Our Eight Nights of Hanukkah - Michael J. Rosen 833

Grandma (Grandmother; Immigrant)
A Picnic in October - Eve Bunting 127

Grandma (Grandmother)
The Raft - Jim LaMarche 551

Roughing It on the Oregon Trail - Diane
Stanley 948
Sarah May and the New Red Dress - Andrea
Spalding 938

Grandma (Grandmother; Storyteller)
Serefina under the Circumstances - Phyllis
Theroux 980

Grandma (Grandmother)
The Storm - Kathy Henderson 419
Summerhouse - Laurence Anholt 28

Grandma "Catherine the Great" (Grandmother)
Three Cheers for Catherine the Great! - Cari
Best 77

Grandma Chickenlegs (Witch; Aged Person)
Grandma Chickenlegs - Geraldine McCaughrean 642

Grandma Fina (Grandmother; Neighbor)
Grandma Fina and Her Wonderful Umbrellas -
Benjamin Alire Saenz 861

Grandma Owl (Owl; Storyteller)
Down in the Woods at Sleepytime - Carole Lexa
Schaefer 879

Grandmother (Grandmother; Pioneer)
I'm Sorry, Almira Ann - Jane Kurtz 545

Grandmother (Grandmother; Storyteller)
Lost!: A Story in String - Paul Fleischman 317

Grandmother (Grandmother; Aged Person)
My Great-Grandmother's Gourd - Cristina
Kessler 514

Grandmother Crocodile (Crocodile)
The Gift of the Crocodile: A Cinderella Story - Judy
Sierra 913

Grandmother White Hair (Grandmother; Dancer)
Rainy's Powwow - Linda Theresa Raczek 807

Grandmother Winter (Aged Person)
Grandmother Winter - Phyllis Root 829

Grandpa (Grandfather; Musician)
1, 2, 3, Music! - Sylvie Auzary-Luton 41

Grandpa (Duck; Storyteller)
Daisy and the Beastie - Jane Simmons 917

Grandpa (Grandfather)
Everything to Spend the Night from A to Z - Ann
Whitford Paul 766
Fog Cat - Marilyn Helmer 416

Grandpa (Grandfather; Store Owner)
Grandpa's Corner Store - DyAnne DiSalvo-
Ryan 267

Grandpa (Grandfather)
Gus and Grandpa and Show-and-Tell - Claudia
Mills 686

Grandpa (Grandfather; Aged Person)
Gus and Grandpa and the Two-Wheeled Bike -
Claudia Mills 687

Grandpa (Grandfather; Store Owner)
Hannah and the Whistling Teakettle - Mindy Warshaw
Skolsky 923

Grandpa (Grandfather; Rabbit)
Happy Birthday, Davy! - Brigitte Weninger 1035

Grandpa (Grandfather)
Iris and Walter - Elissa Haden Guest 387

Grandpa (Grandfather; Artist)
Keeping Up with Grandma - John Winch 1056

Grandpa (Grandfather)
Mei-Mei Loves the Morning - Margaret Holloway
Tsubakiyama 992
Summerhouse - Laurence Anholt 28

Grandpa Sam (Grandfather; Immigrant)
Grandpa's Gamble - Richard Michelson 681

Grandpapa (Grandfather)
Peter and the Wolf - Vladimir Vagin 999
Sometimes Moon - Carole Lexa Schaefer 881

Granger, Hermione (Friend; Witch)
Harry Potter and the Prisoner of Azkaban - J.K.
Rowling 843

Granny (Grandmother; Rabbit)
Happy Birthday, Davy! - Brigitte Weninger 1035

Granny (Grandmother)
I Want a Pet - Lauren Child 163

Granny (Grandmother; Aged Person)
The Tale of Willie Monroe - Alan Schroeder 885

Granny (Grandmother)
What! Cried Granny: An Almost Bedtime Story - Kate
Lum 603

Granny Annie (Grandmother)
Hurry Granny Annie - Arlene Alda 14

Granny Ola (Grandmother)
Ola's Wake - B.J. Stone 962

Granpappy (Grandfather; Farmer)
The Rusty, Trusty Tractor - Joy Cowley 197

Gray, Josh (Brother)
Emma's Magic Winter - Jean Little 589

Gray, Sally (Neighbor; Friend)
Emma's Magic Winter - Jean Little 589

Graymark, Winston (Handicapped; Businessman)
Ghosts in the Gallery - Barbara Brooks
Wallace 1014

Green, Ivy (Student—Elementary School; Daughter)
First Day, Hooray! - Nancy Poydar 795

Green, Maureen (4th Grader; Bully)
Mean, Mean Maureen Green - Judy Cox 199

Greenough, Daisy (1st Grader; Friend)
Leftover Lily - Sally Warner 1026

Gregory (Brother)
G-Rex - Teri Daniels 234

Gretzky, Wayne (Hockey Player)
The Magic Hockey Stick - Peter Maloney 617

Grimble Grinder (Monster)
*Jimmy Zangwow's Out-of-This World Moon Pie
Adventure* - Tony DiTerlizzi 268

Griselda (Aged Person)
The Magic Kerchief - Kirby Larson 557

Grisha (Child; Cousin)
The Memory Coat - Elvira Woodruff 1069

Grouper, Austin (Child; Neighbor)
Yuck, a Love Story - Don Gillmor 349

Grover, Wayne (Diver)
Dolphin Freedom - Wayne Grover 385

Growl Bear (Bear)
A Friend for Growl Bear - Sharon A. Riley 820

Grown-too-Large (Dog)
Unknown - Colin Thompson 987

Grubbs, A.J. (Businessman)
The Blues of Flats Brown - Walter Dean Myers 716

Gruber, Solly (Aged Person; Friend)
Dave at Night - Gail Carson Levine 572

Grumps (Dog)
Circus Family Dog - Andrew Clements 170

Gus (Penguin; Vacationer)
Gus & Gertie and the Missing Pearl - Joan Lowery
Nixon 730

Gus (2nd Grader)
Gus and Grandpa and Show-and-Tell - Claudia
Mills 686

Gus (Child)
Gus and Grandpa and the Two-Wheeled Bike -
Claudia Mills 687

Gwen (Artisan; Widow(er))
The Wide-Awake Princess - Katherine Paterson 765

H

Hackemup (Cook)
Brave Potatoes - Toby Speed 939

Hahn, Diane (Foster Parent; Animal Lover)
Shadow Horse - Alison Hart 406

Hai Li Bu (Hunter)
The Hunter: A Chinese Folktale - Mary
Casanova 154

Hall, Clayton (Uncle; Farmer)
Unbroken - Jessie Haas 391

Hall, Jonathan (Doctor; Father)
Ghost Cats - Susan Shreve 908

Hall, Peter (11-Year-Old; Brother)
Ghost Cats - Susan Shreve 908

Hall, Sarah (Aunt)
Unbroken - Jessie Haas 391

Halmoni (Grandmother)
Halmoni's Day - Edna Coe Bercaw 72
The Trip Back Home - Janet S. Wong 1065

Hamlet (Elephant)
The Firework-Maker's Daughter - Philip
Pullman 803

Hamp, Quintin (Maintenance Worker; Friend)
Welcome Comfort - Patricia Polacco 789

Handy Bob (Maintenance Worker)
The Feet in the Gym - Teri Daniels 233

Hank (Mouse)
A Beasty Story - Bill Martin Jr. 625

Hank (Child; Brother)
Patrick's Dinosaurs on the Internet - Carol
Carrick 149

Hankins, Sam (Neighbor)
Bearhide and Crow - Paul Brett Johnson 483

Hannah (Child)
Fog Cat - Marilyn Helmer 416

Hannah (Child; Daughter)
Hannah and the Whistling Teakettle - Mindy Warshaw
Skolsky 923

Hannah (Child; Collector)
Hannah's Collections - Marthe Jocelyn 475

Hannah (10-Year-Old; Immigrant)
Hannah's Journal: The Story of an Immigrant Girl -
Marissa Moss 702

Hannah (Stepsister)
I Hate Weddings - P.J. Petersen 772

Happy (Dog)
Happy and Honey - Laura Godwin 357

Haraboji (Grandfather; Farmer)
The Trip Back Home - Janet S. Wong 1065

Harding, Chester (Artist)
*Bewildered for Three Days: As to Why Daniel Boone
Never Wore His Coonskin Cap* - Andrew
Glass 350

Hare, Harvey (Rabbit; Postal Worker)
Harvey Hare's Christmas - Bernadette Watts 1028

Hare, Nick (Rabbit)
A Pig Is Moving In! - Claudia Fries 330

Harmon, Gail (6th Grader; Sister)
Captain's Command - Anna Myers   711

Harmon, Ned (Uncle; Blind Person)
Captain's Command - Anna Myers   711

Harmony (Aunt; Aged Person)
Emma's Journal: The Story of a Colonial Girl -
   Marissa Moss   701

Harold (Dog; Narrator)
Bunnicula Strikes Again! - James Howe   453

Harriet (Niece; 6th Grader)
Batty Hattie - Virginia Nielsen   727

Harris, Harriet (Child; Daughter)
Harriet, You'll Drive Me Wild! - Mem Fox   323

Harry (Brother)
The Deep - Tim Winton   1057

Harry (Twin; Son)
Down the Dragon's Tongue - Margaret Mahy   613

Harry (Aged Person; Baker)
Each One Special - Frieda Wishinsky   1058

Harry (Dog; Toy)
Harry and Lulu - Arthur Yorinks   1086

Harry (Child; Son)
Harry's Home - Laurence Anholt   26

Harry (Snail)
The Most Amazing Dinosaur - James Stevenson   956

Harry (Cat; Brother)
Snow Valentines - Karen Gray Ruelle   845
The Thanksgiving Beast Feast - Karen Gray
   Ruelle   846

Harry (Child)
The Video Shop Sparrow - Joy Cowley   198

Hart, Lucky (10-Year-Old)
*The Mystery of Mineral Gorge: A Cobtown Story from
   the Diaries of Lucky Hart* - Julia Van Nutt   1005

Hartwell, Sarah Jane (Spouse; Teacher)
First Day Jitters - Julie Danneberg   235

Hastings, Almira Ann (8-Year-Old; Friend)
I'm Sorry, Almira Ann - Jane Kurtz   545

Hatford, Josh (Twin)
A Spy Among the Girls - Phyllis Reynolds
   Naylor   722

Hatford, Peter (7-Year-Old; Brother)
A Traitor Among the Boys - Phyllis Reynolds
   Naylor   723

Hawk, Ruthie (10-Year-Old; Friend)
One-of-a-Kind Mallie - Kimberly Brubaker
   Bradley   98

Hawthorne, Finian (Gentleman; Sailor)
The Folk Keeper - Franny Billingsley   78

Hazel (Monster)
It's MY Birthday! - Pat Hutchins   463

Hedgie (Hedgehog)
Hedgie's Surprise - Jan Brett   105

Helton, Jennalee (11-Year-Old)
Me and Rupert Goody - Barbara O'Connor   741

Hen (Chicken; Mother)
The Chick That Wouldn't Hatch - Claire Daniel   232

Hen, Hetty (Chicken)
Eggday - Joyce Dunbar   280

Hendon, Miles (Nobleman)
The Prince and the Pauper - Marianna Mayer   634

Henny (Hen)
Hedgie's Surprise - Jan Brett   105

Henrietta (Hen)
A Pig Is Moving In! - Claudia Fries   330

Henry (Cat)
Blue-Ribbon Henry - Mary Calhoun   137

Henry (Farmer)
The Emperor's Old Clothes - Kathryn Lasky   558

Henry (Brother)
George and Diggety - Maggie Stern   951

Henry (Child; Friend)
Go Away, Shelley Boo! - Phoebe Stone   963
Henry and Amy (Right-Way-Round and Upside Down)
   - Stephen Michael King   522

Henry (Child; Son)
Henry and Mudge and the Snowman Plan - Cynthia
   Rylant   852

Henry (Bear; Traveler)
Henry Hikes to Fitchburg - D.B. Johnson   478

Henry (Mouse; Student—Elementary School)
Look Out Kindergarten, Here I Come! - Nancy
   Carlson   146

Henry (Child; Brother)
Mice Make Trouble - Becky Bloom   82

Henry (Spirit)
Operation Ghost - Jacques Duquennoy   287

Henry (Child; Student)
Pete and Polo's Big School Adventure - Adrian
   Reynolds   818

Henry, Jack Jr. (5th Grader; Brother)
Jack on the Tracks: Four Seasons of Fifth Grade -
   Jack Gantos   333

Henry, Mike (Uncle; Scientist)
Batty Hattie - Virginia Nielsen   727

Henry, Pete (5-Year-Old; Brother)
Jack on the Tracks: Four Seasons of Fifth Grade -
   Jack Gantos   333

Herbie (Duck; Friend)
A Cake for Herbie - Petra Mathers   630

Herbie (Duck)
Lottie's New Friend - Petra Mathers   631

Herman, Chuckie (Bully; 10-Year-Old)
Alien Brain Fryout - Barbara M. Joosse   491

Herodsfoot (Adventurer)
Dangerous Games - Joan Aiken   11

Herschel (Brother)
Latkes, Latkes Good to Eat: A Chanukah Story -
   Naomi Howland   455

Hewitt, Robert Burns "Robbie" (10-Year-Old; Son)
Preacher's Boy - Katherine Paterson   764

Hilary (Mythical Creature; Friend)
A Fairy Called Hilary - Linda Leopold Strauss   966

Hill, Casey "Case" (12-Year-Old; Brother)
Accidental Lily - Sally Warner   1025

Hill, Lily (1st Grader; Sister)
Accidental Lily - Sally Warner   1025

Hill, Lily (6-Year-Old; Friend)
Leftover Lily - Sally Warner   1026

Hillerman, Seth (12-Year-Old; Stepbrother)
Captain Kate - Carolyn Reeder   815

Hobbs, Joseph (2nd Grader; Friend)
Owen Foote, Frontiersman - Stephanie Greene   373

Hobbs, Joseph (8-Year-Old; Friend)
Owen Foote, Money Man - Stephanie Greene   374

Hog, Grandma (Pig; Grandmother)
Six Hogs on a Scooter - Eileen Spinelli   943

Hog, Horace (Pig; Son)
Six Hogs on a Scooter - Eileen Spinelli   943

Hog, Penelope (Pig; Daughter)
Six Hogs on a Scooter - Eileen Spinelli   943

Hogula (Pig)
Hogula: Dread Pig of Night - Jean Gralley   369

Holly (Cat)
Holly: The True Story of a Cat - Ruth Brown   114

Holly (Cat; Daughter)
Who Do You Love? - Martin Waddell   1011

Holly Go Lolly (Child; Daughter)
Shadow Story - Nancy Willard   1049

Honey (Cat)
Happy and Honey - Laura Godwin   357

Honeybear, Lil' Honey (Child; Bear)
*Leola and the Honeybears: An African-American
   Retelling of Goldilocks and the Three Bears* -
   Melodye Benson Rosales   831

Hopper, Dwayne (Worker)
Peril in the Bessledorf Parachute Factory - Phyllis
   Reynolds Naylor   721

Hoptail (Squirrel; Friend)
What Will I Do Without You? - Sally Grindley   384

Horace (Leopard; Friend)
Brave Horace - Holly Keller   505

Horace (Mouse; Friend)
Horace and Morris but Mostly Dolores - James
   Howe   454

Horace (Leopard; Student)
That's Mine, Horace - Holly Keller   508

Howard (Friend; Student—Elementary School)
Bertie's Picture Day - Pat Brisson   106

Howard, Stirling (Child; Invalid)
Meet Kit: An American Girl - Valerie Tripp   989

Howell, Brady (6th Grader; Friend)
Batty Hattie - Virginia Nielsen   727

Howie (Dog)
Bunnicula Strikes Again! - James Howe   453

Huckabuck, Jonas Jonas (Farmer; Father)
*The Huckabuck Family and How They Raised Popcorn
   in Nebraska and Quit and Came Back* - Carl
   Sandburg   869

Huckabuck, Mama Mama (Mother; Spouse)
*The Huckabuck Family and How They Raised Popcorn
   in Nebraska and Quit and Came Back* - Carl
   Sandburg   869

Huckabuck, Pony Pony (Daughter)
*The Huckabuck Family and How They Raised Popcorn
   in Nebraska and Quit and Came Back* - Carl
   Sandburg   869

Huggly (Monster)
Huggly Takes a Bath - Tedd Arnold   35

Hughie (Brother)
Dancing in the Wings - Debbie Allen   21

Humpty Dumpty (Son)
Humpty Dumpty - Daniel Kirk   526

Hunayn (Father; Linguist)
The House of Wisdom - Florence Parry Heide   410

Hunter, Ben (12-Year-Old; Nephew)
The Birthday Room - Kevin Henkes   421

Hunter, Cara Diane (12-Year-Old)
Song of the Wanderer - Bruce Coville   193

Hunter, Devin (4th Grader)
Nose Pickers from Outer Space - Gordon
   Korman   538

Hutchins, Harold (Student—Elementary School;
   Friend)
*Captain Underpants and the Attack of the Talking
   Toilets* - Dav Pilkey   776

Hutchins, Harold (4th Grader)
*Captain Underpants and the Perilous Plot of Professor
   Poopypants* - Dav Pilkey   777

Hyperfly (Fly)
Frankenfrog - Kim Kennedy   512

I

Ian (Uncle; Artisan)
The Birthday Room - Kevin Henkes 421

Ian (Child of Divorced Parents)
Me and Mr. Mah - Andrea Spalding 937

Ian (Pig; Brother)
Olivia - Ian Falconer 308

Iguana (Iguana)
Cook-a-Doodle-Doo! - Janet Stevens 952

Iguana (Friend; Iguana)
The Night Iguana Left Home - Megan
McDonald 654

Iktomi (Indian)
Iktomi Loses His Eyes: A Plains Indian Story - Paul
Goble 355

Inspector Hopper (Detective—Private; Insect)
Inspector Hopper - Doug Cushman 218

Iris (Child; Friend)
Iris and Walter - Elissa Haden Guest 387

Irwin, Bill (Teenager)
Radio Rescue - Lynne Barasch 58

Isaac (Truck)
Isaac the Ice Cream Truck - Scott Santoro 872

Isabella (Aunt)
Paris Cat - Leslie Baker 50

Isabelle (Pig; Friend)
Isabelle and the Angel - Thierry Magnier 610

Ishaq (Son; Explorer)
The House of Wisdom - Florence Parry Heide 410

Iskander (Refugee; Child)
The Silence in the Mountains - Liz Rosenberg 835

Itilakna (Father; Indian)
*Longwalker's Journey: A Novel of the Choctaw Trail
of Tears* - Beatrice Orcutt Harrell 402

Ivan (Son)
The Language of Birds - Rafe Martin 628

Ivana the Terrible (3rd Grader; 8-Year-Old)
Lizard Meets Ivana the Terrible - C. Anne Scott 893

Ivy (Fox; Sister)
Zelda and Ivy One Christmas - Laura McGee
Kvasnosky 547

J

J.P. (3rd Grader)
Alien for Rent - Betsy Duffey 278

Jabe (Foundling; Hero)
Big Jabe - Jerdine Nolen 732

Jack (Twin; Alien)
Be First in the Universe - Stephanie Spinner 944

Jack (Dog)
A Dog Like Jack - DyAnne DiSalvo-Ryan 266

Jack (Uncle)
How to Catch an Elephant - Amy Schwartz 888

Jack (Child; Son)
Jack and the Beanstalk - Ann Keay Beneduce 70

Jack (Brother; Son)
Kindle Me a Riddle: A Pioneer Story - Roberta
Karim 496

Jack (Uncle)
Moo in the Morning - Barbara Maitland 615

Jack (Bear; Brother)
One Saturday Afternoon - Barbara Baker 49

Jackie-Joyce (Child; Friend)
Come On, Rain! - Karen Hesse 428

Jackrabbit (Rabbit)
Secrets of the Stone - Harriet Peck Taylor 976

Jackson, Ikarus (Outcast; Student)
Wings - Christopher Myers 713

Jackson, May Amelia (12-Year-Old; Sister)
Our Only May Amelia - Jennifer L. Holm 441

Jackson, Stacy Anne (4th Grader; Friend)
School Trouble for Andy Russell - David A. Adler 8

Jackson, Wilbert (13-Year-Old; Brother)
Our Only May Amelia - Jennifer L. Holm 441

Jacob (Paperboy; Friend)
The Babe & I - David A. Adler 5

Jacob (Bear; Brother)
Jacob's Tree - Holly Keller 507

Jacob (Child; Son)
Snow Family - Daniel Kirk 528

Jade (12-Year-Old; Noblewoman)
Seesaw Girl - Linda Sue Park 762

Jake (Single Father; Worker)
Soldier Mom - Alice Mead 672

Jake Johnson (Mule)
Jake Johnson: The Story of a Mule - Tres
Seymour 899

Jakob (Immigrant; Orphan)
Mirette & Bellini Cross Niagara Falls - Emily Arnold
McCully 647

Jamaica (Student—Elementary School; Friend)
Jamaica and the Substitute Teacher - Juanita
Havill 407

Jamela (Child; Daughter)
Jamela's Dress - Niki Daly 231

James (Son; Miner)
Boy of the Deeps - Ian Wallace 1015

James (Child; Golfer)
Night Golf - William Miller 683

James (Son; Brother)
Red Flower Goes West - Ann Turner 994

James (10-Year-Old; Brother)
Strong to the Hoop - John Coy 202

James, Calliope (2nd Grader; Friend)
Pa Lia's First Day - Michelle Edwards 290

James Arthur (Child; Son)
The Lizard Man of Crabtree County - Lucy
Nolan 731

Jamie (11-Year-Old; Friend)
The Copper Treasure - Melvin Burgess 130

Jane (Cat; Adventurer)
Jane on Her Own: A Catwings Tale - Ursula K. Le
Guin 563

Jane (Sorceress; Child)
The Prog Frince: A Mixed-Up Tale - C. Drew
Lamm 552

Jane (Child; Daughter)
*The Yeoman's Daring Daughter and the Princes in the
Tower* - Elaine Clayton 168

Jansen, Jennifer "Cam" (Detective—Amateur;
Friend)
Cam Jansen and the Barking Treasure Mystery -
David A. Adler 6
Young Cam Jansen and the Baseball Mystery - David
A. Adler 9

Jasper (Farmer; Prospector)
Gold Fever - Verla Kay 499

Jaylee (Servant)
The Prog Frince: A Mixed-Up Tale - C. Drew
Lamm 552

Jazzbo (Bear)
Jazzbo and Googy - Matt Novak 737

Jean, Jean Claude (Student—Boarding School; Son)
Bonaparte - Marsha Wilson Chall 157

Jeff (Child; Nephew)
Fossil Fever - Kathleen Weidner Zoehfeld 1098

Jeff (Coach)
Suitcase - Mildred Pitts Walter 1022

Jefferies, Nadene (Sister)
In My Momma's Kitchen - Jerdine Nolen 733

Jefferson, Thomas (Political Figure)
*A Big Cheese for the White House: The True Tale of a
Tremendous Cheddar* - Candace Fleming 320

Jehosephat, Willy Joe (Child; Space Explorer)
Moondogs - Daniel Kirk 527

Jellico, Josie (2nd Grader; Sister)
Josie to the Rescue - Marilyn Singer 920

Jen (Child)
Sand Castle - Brenda Shannon Yee 1074

Jennifer (Student—Elementary School; Daughter)
Halmoni's Day - Edna Coe Bercaw 72

Jennifer (Child; Friend)
Mailbox Magic - Nancy Poydar 796

Jennifer (13-Year-Old; Twin)
The Pictish Child - Jane Yolen 1085

Jenny (4th Grader)
Dear Whiskers - Ann Whitehead Nagda 717

Jenny (Daughter; Sister)
Red Flower Goes West - Ann Turner 994

Jeremiah (Aged Person; Farmer)
Jeremiah Learns to Read - Jo Ellen Bogart 88

Jeremiah (Kindergartner)
We Share Everything! - Robert Munsch 708

Jesse (Brother)
The Deep - Tim Winton 1057

Jesse (Brother; Son)
Down the Winding Road - Angela Johnson 476

Jesse (Student—Elementary School)
Jesse's Star - Ellen Schwartz 890

Jesse (Child; Friend)
Snow Pumpkin - Carole Lexa Schaefer 880

Jesse (Child; Captive)
White Wolf - Henrietta Branford 100

Jessica (1st Grader; Daughter)
100th Day Worries - Margery Cuyler 222

Jessica (12-Year-Old; Sister)
Strudel Stories - Joanne Rocklin 823

Jessie (Adoptee; Kindergartner)
An American Face - Jan M. Czech 225

Jessie (Sister; Child)
Captain Pajamas: Defender of the Universe - Bruce
Whatley 1042

Jewel (Sister)
Cosmo and the Robot - Brian Pinkney 780

Jewel (Mouse; Preschool)
Wemberly Worried - Kevin Henkes 423

Jezebel (Child; Daughter)
Jezebel's Spooky Spot - Alice Ross 838

Jibbert, Fliberty (Civil Servant)
*The Mystery of Mineral Gorge: A Cobtown Story from
the Diaries of Lucky Hart* - Julia Van Nutt 1005

Jillian (Indian; Child)
Ribbon Rescue - Robert Munsch 707

Jim (Child; Son)
The Storm - Kathy Henderson 419

Leftovers (Dog)
Nothing Wrong with a Three-Legged Dog - Graham McNamee 667

Leibush (Student; Son)
The Peddler's Gift - Maxine Rose Schur 887

Leigh (Child; Sister)
The Grandad Tree - Trish Cooke 186

Leland, John (Historical Figure; Leader)
A Big Cheese for the White House: The True Tale of a Tremendous Cheddar - Candace Fleming 320

Lenny (Child; Friend)
Nothing Scares Us - Frieda Wishinsky 1059

Lenny (Brother; Twin)
Roughing It on the Oregon Trail - Diane Stanley 948

Leo (Child; Friend)
The Cool Crazy Crickets - David Elliott 299

Leo (Cockroach)
Leo Cockroach. . .Toy Tester - Kevin O'Malley 745

Leo (Bullied Child; Musician)
The Saturday Kid - Edward Sorel 935

Leola (Child)
Leola and the Honeybears: An African-American Retelling of Goldilocks and the Three Bears - Melodye Benson Rosales 831

Leonardo (Cat)
Me and My Cat? - Satoshi Kitamura 531

Leopard (Leopard)
To Dinner, for Dinner - Tololwa M. Mollel 694

Levi, Karin (Daughter; Refugee)
Good Night, Maman - Norma Fox Mazer 639

Levi, Lenny (Child; Refugee)
The Lion and the Unicorn - Shirley Hughes 458

Levi, Marc (Brother; Refugee)
Good Night, Maman - Norma Fox Mazer 639

Levinsky, Jennie (10-Year-Old)
Strange Neighbors - Mary Labatt 548

Levy, Adam (3rd Grader; Friend)
Mean, Mean Maureen Green - Judy Cox 199

Lewis (Beaver; Classmate)
Happy Birthday to You, You Belong in a Zoo - Diane DeGroat 249

Lewis (Bear; Student—Elementary School)
Jingle Bells, Homework Smells - Diane DeGroat 250

Lewis, Carolina (11-Year-Old; Friend)
Carolina Crow Girl - Valerie Hobbs 438

Lewis, Meriwether (Explorer)
Seaman: The Dog Who Explored the West with Lewis & Clark - Gail Langer Karwoski 497

Lexie (3rd Grader)
Alien for Rent - Betsy Duffey 278

Li (Farmer)
The Greatest Treasure - Demi 256

Lian Di (Maiden; Seamstress)
Da Wei's Treasure: A Chinese Tale - Margaret Chang 159

Libby (Feminist; Cousin)
You Forgot Your Skirt, Amelia Bloomer! - Shana Corey 189

Liebowicz, Jason (Friend)
Wanna Buy an Alien? - Eve Bunting 129

Lightly, Ladysmith (10-Year-Old)
Abraham's Battle: A Novel of Gettysburg - Sara Harrell Banks 57

Lila (Hen; Outcast)
Albert & Lila - Rafik Schami 882

Lila (Daughter; Apprentice)
The Firework-Maker's Daughter - Philip Pullman 803

Lilly (Friend)
The Two Sillies - Mary Ann Hoberman 439

Lily (Child; Sister)
I Love You, Blue Kangaroo! - Emma Chichester Clark 161

Lily (Child)
Lily and Trooper's Spring - Jung-Hee Spetter 941
My Two Grandmothers - Effin Older 743

Lily (Child; Friend)
Snow Pumpkin - Carole Lexa Schaefer 880

Lily (9-Year-Old; Sister; Cousin)
Some Good News - Cynthia Rylant 856

Lily (Child; Daughter)
Why? - Lindsay Camp 140

Lincoln, A. (Historical Figure)
A. Lincoln and Me - Louise Borden 92

Ling Cho (Farmer)
Ling Cho and His Three Friends - V.J. Pacilio 753

Lionel (Lion; Stuffed Animal)
Elliot Bakes a Cake - Andrea Beck 69

Lionel (Cat; Student)
A Night on the Tiles - Bruce Ingman 465

Lit'mahn (Trickster; Mythical Creature)
The Girl Who Spun Gold - Virginia Hamilton 398

Little Badger (Badger)
Can You Do This, Old Badger? - Eve Bunting 124

Little Bear (Bear)
Big Brown Bear - David McPhail 669
Good Job, Little Bear - Martin Waddell 1009

Little Bill (Child; Son)
My Big Lie - Bill Cosby 190
One Dark and Scary Night - Bill Cosby 191

Little Brother (Child; Brother)
Jezebel's Spooky Spot - Alice Ross 838

Little Bunny (Rabbit)
Little Bunny on the Move - Peter McCarty 641

Little Bunny (Rabbit; Sister)
Little Bunny's Easter Surprise - Jeanne Modesitt 692

Little Bunny (Rabbit)
Little Bunny's Sleepless Night - Carol Roth 840

Little Cliff (Child)
Little Cliff and the Porch People - Clifton L. Taulbert 974

Little Frog (Frog)
Baby Bird's First Nest - Frank Asch 36
Off We Go! - Jane Yolen 1084

Little Frog (Frog; Friend)
Otis - Janie Bynum 136

Little Miss Spider (Spider; Child)
Little Miss Spider - David Kirk 529

Little Mole (Mole)
Off We Go! - Jane Yolen 1084

Little Monster (Monster; Child)
What If? - Frances Thomas 981

Little Mouse (Mouse)
Off We Go! - Jane Yolen 1084
The Very Noisy Night - Diana Hendry 420

Little One (Daughter; Sister)
Brave Highland Heart - Heather Kellerhals-Stewart 509

Little Piggy (Toy)
Benny's Had Enough! - Barbro Lindgren 585

Little Red Hen (Chicken; Cook)
The Little Red Hen (Makes a Pizza) - Philemon Sturges 968

Little Rose, Nannie (12-Year-Old; Indian)
My Heart Is on the Ground: The Diary of Nannie Little Rose, a Sioux Girl - Ann Rinaldi 821

Little Sister of the Sun (Maiden)
Peter and the Blue Witch Baby - Robert D. San Souci 868

Little Treasure (Dog)
Cam Jansen and the Barking Treasure Mystery - David A. Adler 6

Little Wolf (Wolf)
Big Wolf and Little Wolf - Sharon Phillips Denslow 259

Little Wolf (Wolf; Nephew)
Little Wolf's Book of Badness - Ian Whybrow 1045

Liz (Sister; Twin)
Roughing It on the Oregon Trail - Diane Stanley 948

Lizard (Lizard; Friend)
Lizard's Home - George Shannon 903

Lizard, Dalbert (Lizard; Sea Captain)
Jubal's Wish - Audrey Wood 1066

Lizzy (Child)
Lizzy and Skunk - Marie-Louise Fitzpatrick 316
Who's in the Hall: A Mystery in Four Chapters - Betsy Hearne 408

Locket (Streetperson; Friend)
A Ceiling of Stars - Ann Howard Creel 206

Locket, Lucy (Teacher; Spouse)
Raising Sweetness - Diane Stanley 947

Lola (Hamster; Student)
Hello, Sweetie Pie - Carl Norac 734

London, Dewey (10-Year-Old; Soccer Player)
The Captain Contest - Matt Christopher 166

Long, Jenny (Baseball Player; Friend)
Close Call - Todd Strasser 965

Lord Wyldon (Nobleman; Knight)
First Test - Tamora Pierce 775

Lorelei (Daughter; Maiden)
The Princess Test - Gail Carson Levine 573

Loretta (Gardener; Mother)
Apple Batter - Deborah Turney Zagwyn 1088

Lori (8-Year-Old; Sister)
Strudel Stories - Joanne Rocklin 823

Lorraine "Rainy" (Sister; Dancer)
Rainy's Powwow - Linda Theresa Raczek 807

Lottie (Hen; Friend)
A Cake for Herbie - Petra Mathers 630

Lottie (Servant)
The Lottie Project - Jacqueline Wilson 1055

Lottie (Chicken; Friend)
Lottie's New Friend - Petra Mathers 631

Lou (Bird)
What Is a Wise Bird Like You Doing in a Silly Tale Like This? - Uri Shulevitz 909

Louie (Child; Son)
Louie's Goose - H.M. Ehrlich 297

Louise (Housekeeper; Child-Care Giver)
Mama - Eleanor Schick 884

Love, Mama (Mother; Slave)
The Invisible Princess - Faith Ringgold 822

Love, Wilson (Baseball Player)
Home Run Hero - Dean Hughes 456

Lubak, Trent (Baseball Player; Friend)
Play Ball! - Dean Hughes 457

Lucas (Bullied Child)
The Ant Bully - John Nickle   726

Lucille (Dog)
Albert and the Angels - Leslie Norris   736

Lucille (Pig; Sister)
Lucille's Snowsuit - Kathryn Lasky   559

Lucille (Sister)
Twister - Darleen Bailey Beard   67

Lucille "Cat Lady" (Neighbor)
Mr. Persnickety and the Cat Lady - Paul Brett
Johnson   484

Lucy (Detective—Amateur; Friend)
Alien Brain Fryout - Barbara M. Joosse   491

Lucy (Student—Elementary School; Grocer's
Helper)
Grandpa's Corner Store - DyAnne DiSalvo-
Ryan   267

Lucy (Child; Friend)
Nothing Scares Us - Frieda Wishinsky   1059

Luella (Cow)
Kiss the Cow! - Phyllis Root   830

Luke (Farmer)
Swine Divine - Jan Carr   148

Lulu (Sister)
George and Diggety - Maggie Stern   951

Lulu (Child)
Harry and Lulu - Arthur Yorinks   1086

Lulu (Child; Sister)
Hello, Lulu - Caroline Uff   995

Lulu (Hamster; Friend)
Hello, Sweetie Pie - Carl Norac   734

Lulu (Child)
Lulu's Busy Day - Caroline Uff   996

Lupin (Cat)
Missing! - Jonathan Langley   555

Lynch, Brodie (13-Year-Old; Son)
Blackwater - Eve Bunting   122

M

Ma (Mother)
Tadpoles - Betsy James   471

Ma Jiang (Child; Daughter)
Ma Jiang and the Orange Ants - Barbara Ann
Porte   792

Mabel (Child; Daughter)
Mabel Dancing - Amy Hest   430

Mac (Restaurateur; Businessman)
The Case of the Missing Monkeys - Cynthia
Rylant   850

MacAllister, Allie (12-Year-Old; Friend)
Cherokee Sister - Debbie Dadey   226

MacDougal-MacDuff, Morgan "Morgy" (3rd
Grader)
Morgy Makes His Move - Maggie Lewis   579

MacDuff, Savanna (Aunt; Teacher)
Morgy Makes His Move - Maggie Lewis   579

Mad Dog McGraw (Dog)
Mad Dog McGraw - Myron Uhlberg   998

Madam Thunderbolt (Mother; Heroine)
Max - Bob Graham   368

Madam Yang (Dragon)
If That Breathes Fire, We're Toast! - Jennifer J.
Stewart   958

Madame Dupray (Care Giver)
Ghosts in the Gallery - Barbara Brooks
Wallace   1014

Madlenka (Child; Neighbor)
Madlenka - Peter Sis   921

Madrigal, Magda (7-Year-Old)
Magda's Tortillas: Las Tortillas de Magda - Becky
Chavarria-Chairez   160

Maggie (Friend; Child)
Annabel the Actress Starring in Gorilla My Dreams -
Ellen Conford   183

Maggie (Daughter; Musician)
The Loudest, Fastest, Best Drummer in Kansas -
Marguerite W. Davol   241

Magruder, Bernie (11-Year-Old; Brother)
Peril in the Bessledorf Parachute Factory - Phyllis
Reynolds Naylor   721

Magruder, Delores (Sister; Worker)
Peril in the Bessledorf Parachute Factory - Phyllis
Reynolds Naylor   721

Makoa (Child)
Torch Fishing with the Sun - Laura E.
Williams   1051

Malinski, Walter (15-Year-Old; Brother)
Goodbye, Walter Malinski - Helen Recorvits   814

Malinski, Wanda (5th Grader; Sister)
Goodbye, Walter Malinski - Helen Recorvits   814

Malloy, Beth (10-Year-Old; Sister)
A Spy Among the Girls - Phyllis Reynolds
Naylor   722
A Traitor Among the Boys - Phyllis Reynolds
Naylor   723

Malloy, Caroline (9-Year-Old; Sister)
A Spy Among the Girls - Phyllis Reynolds
Naylor   722

Malloy, Eddie (11-Year-Old; Sister)
A Spy Among the Girls - Phyllis Reynolds
Naylor   722

Mama (Mother)
Aunt CeeCee, Aunt Belle, and Mama's Surprise - Mary
Quattlebaum   806

Mama (Mother; Writer)
Bravo, Maurice! - Rebecca Bond   89

Mama (Widow(er); Alcoholic)
A Ceiling of Stars - Ann Howard Creel   206

Mama (Mother; Migrant Worker)
The Christmas Gift/El Regalo de Navidad - Francisco
Jimenez   474

Mama (Mother)
Comes a Wind - Linda Arms White   1043

Mama (Duck; Mother)
Daisy and the Egg - Jane Simmons   918

Mama (Mother)
Erandi's Braids - Antonio Hernandez Madrigal   609
The Honest-to-Goodness Truth - Patricia C.
McKissack   663

Mama (Mother; Cook)
How Yussel Caught the Gefilte Fish: A Shabbos Story
- Charlotte Herman   425

Mama (Mother)
I Have an Olive Tree - Eve Bunting   126
It's Time for School, Stinky Face - Lisa
McCourt   645

Mama (Bear; Mother)
Jacob's Tree - Holly Keller   507

Mama (Mother)
The Loudest, Fastest, Best Drummer in Kansas -
Marguerite W. Davol   241
Mama - Eleanor Schick   884

Mama (Widow(er); Mother)
Mama, Across the Sea - Alex Godard   356

Mama (Mother; Spouse)
Mama and Me and the Model T - Faye Gibbons   347

Mama (Mother)
Manuela's Gift - Kristyn Rehling Estes   305

Mama (Mother; Widow(er))
The Promise Quilt - Candice F. Ransom   809

Mama (Mother)
The Rainbow Tulip - Pat Mora   696
Shadow Story - Nancy Willard   1049

Mama (Immigrant; Mother)
Shy Mama's Halloween - Anne Broyles   115

Mama (Mother)
Taking Charge - Sonia Levitin   574
Three Cheers for Catherine the Great! - Cari
Best   77
Tiny's Hat - Ann Grifalconi   380
Tree of Hope - Amy Littlesugar   591

Mama (Bear; Mother)
What a Scare, Jesse Bear - Nancy White
Carlstrom   147

Mama (Mother; Immigrant)
When This World Was New - D.H. Figueredo   313

Mama (Mother; Musician)
When Uncle Took the Fiddle - Libba Moore
Gray   371

Mama (Cat; Mother)
Who Do You Love? - Martin Waddell   1011

Mama (Mother)
Wilhe'mina Miles After the Stork Night - Dorothy
Carter   153

Mama Bear (Mother; Bear)
Goldilocks Returns - Lisa Campbell Ernst   304

Mama Bear (Bear; Mother)
Papa's Song - Kate McMullan   666

Mama Bird (Bird; Mother)
Baby Bird's First Nest - Frank Asch   36

Mama Hen (Mother; Hen)
The Bowlegged Rooster and Other Tales That Signify -
Joyce Carol Thomas   982

Mama May (Mother)
Kiss the Cow! - Phyllis Root   830

Mama Pearl (Grandmother; Cook)
Little Cliff and the Porch People - Clifton L.
Taulbert   974

Mama Wolf (Wolf; Mother)
Big Wolf and Little Wolf - Sharon Phillips
Denslow   259

Maman (Mother)
The Good Liar - Gregory Maguire   612
Good Night, Maman - Norma Fox Mazer   639

Mami (Mother; Seamstress)
In the Shade of the Nispero Tree - Carmen T. Bernier-
Grand   73

Mamma (Mother; Settler)
Calling Me Home - Patricia Hermes   427

Mamma (Mother; Gardener)
Come On, Rain! - Karen Hesse   428

Man in the Stocking Cap (Streetperson)
Gowanus Dogs - Jonathan Frost   331

Manell, Vivien (12-Year-Old; Abandoned Child)
A Ceiling of Stars - Ann Howard Creel   206

Mangus (Magician; Aged Person)
Midnight Magic - Avi   44

Manuela (Child; Daughter)
Manuela's Gift - Kristyn Rehling Estes   305

Marcela, Maurice Duncan (Son)
Bravo, Maurice! - Rebecca Bond   89

Marcie (Sister; Teenager)
Clarice Bean, That's Me - Lauren Child   162

Marco (Cat; Brother)
Carlotta's Kittens and the Club of Mysteries - Phyllis Reynolds Naylor   720

Marcus (Child; Friend)
The Cool Crazy Crickets - David Elliott   299

Marcus (Basketball Player)
Strong to the Hoop - John Coy   202

Marella (Spirit)
There's a Dead Person Following My Sister Around - Vivian Vande Velde   1006

Margaret (Aunt)
Not My Dog - Colby Rodowsky   826

Margo (Child; Daughter)
Hurricane! - Corinne Demas   255

Mark (Brother)
G-Rex - Teri Daniels   234

Marquez, Robbie (Baseball Player; Friend)
Play Ball! - Dean Hughes   457

Marshall, Sarah (10-Year-Old)
Swimming with Sharks - Twig C. George   344

Martha (Child)
Brave Martha - Margot Apple   32

Martha (Dog)
Martha and Skits - Susan Meddaugh   674

Martin, Amelia (Daughter)
A Light in the Storm: The Civil War Diary of Amelia Martin - Karen Hesse   429

Martin, Ellie (8-Year-Old; Niece)
Not My Dog - Colby Rodowsky   826

Martin, Jeffrey "Jeff" (13-Year-Old; Child of Divorced Parents)
The Vampire in My Bathtub - Brenda Seabrooke   896

Martin, Matt (6-Year-Old; Brother)
The Diary of Melanie Martin - Carol Weston   1040

Martin, Melanie (10-Year-Old; Tourist)
The Diary of Melanie Martin - Carol Weston   1040

Marvin (Tiger; Brother)
Brave Horace - Holly Keller   505

Marx, Robert (10-Year-Old)
Radio Rescue - Lynne Barasch   58

Mary (Cat; Friend)
George Paints His House - Francine Bassede   61

Mary (Child; Daughter)
The Hollyhock Wall - Martin Waddell   1010
Mary and the Mystery Dog - Wolfram Hanel   399

Mary (3rd Grader)
Song Lee and the "I Hate You" Notes - Suzy Kline   534

Mary Louise (Child)
Mary Louise Loses Her Manners - Diane Cuneo   214

Mary Louise (Sister)
Mary Veronica's Egg - Mary Nethery   725

Mary Margaret (Student—Elementary School)
Bedhead - Margie Palatini   755

Mary Margaret (Sister)
Mary Veronica's Egg - Mary Nethery   725

Mary T. (Neighbor; Child)
When William Went Away - Sally J.K. Davies   238

Mary Veronica (Student—Elementary School; Sister)
Mary Veronica's Egg - Mary Nethery   725

Marya (Daughter)
At the Wish of the Fish: A Russian Folktale - J. Patrick Lewis   576

Mason, Ryan (Neighbor; Child)
Gus and Grandpa and the Two-Wheeled Bike - Claudia Mills   687

Master Min (Teacher)
The Royal Bee - Frances Park   761

Matias (Brother)
The Three Golden Oranges - Alma Flor Ada   2

Matt (10-Year-Old; Brother)
The Promise - Jackie French Koller   536

Matt (Child; Son)
Trucks Trucks Trucks - Peter Sis   922

Matthew (Student—Elementary School; Brother)
When William Went Away - Sally J.K. Davies   238

Matti (Child; Cook)
Gingerbread Baby - Jan Brett   104

Maud (Horse)
The Prairie Fire - Marilynn Reynolds   819

Max (Artist; Friend)
The Collector of Moments - Quint Buchholz   119

Max (Beaver; Friend)
Froggy's Best Christmas - Jonathan London   594

Max (Dog)
Here Come Poppy and Max - Lindsey Gardiner   336

Max (Child; Son)
Max - Bob Graham   368

Max (Rabbit; Brother)
Max Cleans Up - Rosemary Wells   1034

Max (Child; Brother)
Talk, Baby! - Harriet Ziefert   1094

Max (Son)
This Is the Turkey - Abby Levine   571

Maya (Elephant; Daughter)
All by Myself - Ivan Bates   62

Mayor Plogg (Political Figure)
The Loudest, Fastest, Best Drummer in Kansas - Marguerite W. Davol   241

Mayor Thomas (Political Figure)
Amelia Bedelia 4 Mayor - Herman Parish   760

Mbi (Orphan; Child)
The Magic Tree: A Folktale from Nigeria - T. Obinkaram Echewa   288

McAdams, Brenda (6th Grader)
Dork in Disguise - Carol Gorman   365

McBugg (Insect; Sidekick)
Inspector Hopper - Doug Cushman   218

McDoodle, Robert (6-Year-Old)
The Strange and Wonderful Tale of Robert McDoodle: The Boy Who Wanted to Be a Dog - Steven Bauer   66

McGill, Matthew (3rd Grader)
Annie Pitts, Burger Kid - Diane DeGroat   248

McGranahan, Minnie (Aunt)
Aunt Minnie McGranahan - Mary Skillings Prigger   798

McNasty, Stinky (Scientist; Inventor)
Ricky Ricotta's Giant Robot: An Adventure Novel - Dav Pilkey   778

McNosh, Nelly (Gardener)
Mrs. McNosh and the Great Big Squash - Sarah Weeks   1030

McPhee, Willie (Musician)
Cold Feet - Cynthia DeFelice   246

Meenom, Pleskit (Alien; 6th Grader)
I Was a Sixth Grade Alien - Bruce Coville   192

Megan (Friend; Student—Elementary School)
Louise Goes Wild - Stephen Krensky   542

Meglio, Rosa (Friend; 11-Year-Old)
A Letter to Mrs. Roosevelt - C. Coco De Young   244

Mehrdad (Royalty)
The Persian Cinderella - Shirley Climo   173

Mei Mei (Child; Sister)
Bird Boy - Elizabeth Starr Hill   433

Mei-Mei (Child)
Mei-Mei Loves the Morning - Margaret Holloway Tsubakiyama   992

Melinda (Student—Elementary School; Daughter)
A Difficult Day - Eugenie Fernandes   312

Mendelsohn, Yossi (Immigrant)
Jesse's Star - Ellen Schwartz   890

Mendoza, Maria (Child; Sister)
From Here to There - Margery Cuyler   224

Mentu (Child; Slave)
In the Time of the Drums - Kim L. Siegelson   910

Mercedes (Cousin; Teenager)
Annie Pitts, Burger Kid - Diane DeGroat   248

Merton, Edward (Gentleman; Nobleman)
The Folk Keeper - Franny Billingsley   78

Mflxnys, Stan (Student—Exchange; Alien)
Nose Pickers from Outer Space - Gordon Korman   538

Micah (Child)
The Rusty, Trusty Tractor - Joy Cowley   197

Michaels, Cody (9-Year-Old; Camper)
Cody Unplugged - Betsy Duffey   279

Miguel (Gentleman; Landowner)
Little Gold Star: A Spanish American Cinderella Tale - Robert D. San Souci   867

Mike (Child; Son)
A Dog Like Jack - DyAnne DiSalvo-Ryan   266

Mikie (Child; Son)
The Gift - Gabriela Keselman   513

Mikki Jo (Child; Cousin)
Blackberry Booties - Tricia Gardella   335

Miles, Wilhe'mina (Sister; 7-Year-Old)
Wilhe'mina Miles After the Stork Night - Dorothy Carter   153

Millar, Emma (10-Year-Old; Patriot)
Emma's Journal: The Story of a Colonial Girl - Marissa Moss   701

Mimmy (6-Year-Old; Sister)
Mimmy & Sophie - Miriam Cohen   177

Minal Cricket (Brother; Child)
Clarice Bean, That's Me - Lauren Child   162

Minerva Louise (Chicken)
Minerva Louise at the Fair - Janet Morgan Stoeke   960

Minho (Son; Child)
One Sunday Morning - Yumi Heo   424

Minko Ushi (10-Year-Old; Indian)
Longwalker's Journey: A Novel of the Choctaw Trail of Tears - Beatrice Orcutt Harrell   402

Minky, Finnegan (Son)
Simply Delicious! - Margaret Mahy   614

Minna (Rabbit; Sister)
Apples, Apples, Apples - Nancy Elizabeth Wallace   1019

Minnie (Cow)
Minnie and Moo and the Musk of Zorro - Denys Cazet   155

Minnie (Cow; Friend)
Minnie and Moo and the Thanksgiving Tree - Denys Cazet   156

Minshull, Aggie (Aged Person; Businesswoman)
The Gate in the Wall - Ellen Howard 452

Minty (Aunt; Aged Person)
The Lost Flower Children - Janet Taylor Lisle 588

Miranda (Child)
Annabelle's Big Move - Carla Golembe 359

Miranda (Child; Friend)
The Cool Crazy Crickets - David Elliott 299

Miranda (Twin; Daughter)
Down the Dragon's Tongue - Margaret Mahy 613

Miranda (Royalty; Daughter)
The Wide-Awake Princess - Katherine Paterson 765

Mirette (Child; Entertainer)
Mirette & Bellini Cross Niagara Falls - Emily Arnold McCully 647

Mis' Hattie (Midwife)
Wilhe'mina Miles After the Stork Night - Dorothy Carter 153

Miss Bunch (Aged Person)
The Lizard Man of Crabtree County - Lucy Nolan 731

Miss Clark (Teacher)
Daisy and the Doll - Michael Medearis 676

Miss Cribbage (Teacher; Guinea Pig)
Emily's First 100 Days of School - Rosemary Wells 1033

Miss Dobson (Teacher; Journalist)
A Letter to Mrs. Roosevelt - C. Coco De Young 244

Miss Foley (Teacher; Dancer)
Presenting Tanya, the Ugly Duckling - Patricia Lee Gauch 338

Miss Fuzzleworth (Teacher; Rodent)
Hooway for Wodney Wat - Helen Lester 567

Miss Hartwell (Aged Person; Employer)
The Piano - William Miller 684

Miss Hatchett (Teacher)
Last Licks: A Spaldeen Story - Cari Best 75

Miss Mackle (Teacher)
Horrible Harry at Halloween - Suzy Kline 533

Miss Minnie (Aged Person)
Jump Rope Magic - Afi Scruggs 895

Miss Perkins (Aged Person)
Where Is That Cat? - Carol Greene 372

Miss Posy (Duck; Teacher)
Off to School, Baby Duck! - Amy Hest 431

Miss Rosemary (Farmer)
The Pig Who Ran a Red Light - Paul Brett Johnson 486

Miss Slade (Recluse; Aged Person)
Mysterious Miss Slade - Dick King-Smith 524

Miss Viola (Neighbor; Aged Person)
Miss Viola and Uncle Ed Lee - Alice Faye Duncan 284

Miss Wheeler (Driver)
First Day, Hooray! - Nancy Poydar 795

Mistah Bear (Bear)
Callie Ann and Mistah Bear - Robert D. San Souci 865

Mister Mack (Father)
The Giggler Treatment - Roddy Doyle 276

Mitchell, Andrew (Son; Brother)
Maria's Comet - Deborah Hopkinson 446

Mitchell, Hilary (1st Grader; Friend)
Leftover Lily - Sally Warner 1026

Mitchell, Maria (Daughter; Sister)
Maria's Comet - Deborah Hopkinson 446

Miz Violet (Mother; Slave)
The Legend of Freedom Hill - Linda Jacobs Altman 22

Moishe (Milkman; Spouse)
Moishe's Miracle: A Hanukkah Story - Laura Krauss Melmed 679

Mole (Mole; Musician)
Mole Music - David McPhail 671

Molly (Child; Friend)
Missing Molly - Lisa Jahn-Clough 470

Molly (4-Year-Old; Sister)
The Pictish Child - Jane Yolen 1085

Molly (Child; Sister)
Tadpoles - Betsy James 471

Molnya (Witch)
Peter and the Blue Witch Baby - Robert D. San Souci 868

Mom (Mother)
100th Day Worries - Margery Cuyler 222
Ballerinas Don't Wear Glasses - Ainslie Manson 618
The Boy on the Beach - Niki Daly 230
Brave Highland Heart - Heather Kellerhals-Stewart 509
Bus Route to Boston - Maryann Cocca-Leffler 174
The Canning Season - Margaret Carlson 145
Darby: The Special Order Pup - Alexandra Day 243
Different Just Like Me - Lori Mitchell 690
Dirt Boy - Erik Jon Slangerup 926
A Dog Like Jack - DyAnne DiSalvo-Ryan 266
Eat Your Peas - Kes Gray 370

Mom (Mother; Daughter)
Halmoni's Day - Edna Coe Bercaw 72

Mom (Mother)
I Am Me - Karla Kuskin 546
I Want a Pet - Lauren Child 163
Island Magic - Martha Bennett Stiles 959

Mom (Mother; Mouse)
Look Out Kindergarten, Here I Come! - Nancy Carlson 146

Mom (Mother)
Lottie's Princess Dress - Doris Dorrie 272

Mom (Mouse; Mother)
Monk Camps Out - Emily Arnold McCully 648

Mom (Mother)
Moo in the Morning - Barbara Maitland 615

Mom (Musician; Mouse)
Mouse Practice - Emily Arnold McCully 649

Mom (Mother)
My Big Lie - Bill Cosby 190
My Mother Talks to Trees - Doris Gove 366
My Mother's Pearls - Catherine Myler Fruisen 332

Mom (Single Mother)
A New Room for William - Sally Grindley 383

Mom (Mother)
Next Stop! - Sarah Ellis 300
No Time for Mother's Day - Laurie Halse Anderson 24
Old Dog Cora and the Christmas Tree - Consie Powell 794
One Dark and Scary Night - Bill Cosby 191
Queen of the World - Thomas F. Yezerski 1079

Mom (Single Mother; Cancer Patient)
Sky Memories - Pat Brisson 107

Mom (Mother)
Space Guys! - Martha Weston 1041
The Storm - Kathy Henderson 419

Mom (Mother; Spouse)
The Trouble with Cats - Martha Freeman 328

Momma (Mother)
In My Momma's Kitchen - Jerdine Nolen 733
Momma, Where Are You From? - Marie Bradby 97
Silver Rain Brown - M.C. Helldorfer 414

Momma Mary (Storyteller)
Big Jabe - Jerdine Nolen 732

Mommy (Single Mother)
Accidental Lily - Sally Warner 1025

Mommy (Mother)
Agapanthus Hum and the Eyeglasses - Joy Cowley 196

Mommy (Mother; Spouse)
Buzz - Janet S. Wong 1063

Mommy (Mother)
Daisy Knows Best - Lisa Kopper 537
Hello Baby! - Lizzy Rockwell 825

Mommy (Mother; Chimpanzee)
Hug - Jez Alborough 13

Mommy (Mother; Spouse)
Hurricane! - Corinne Demas 255

Mommy (Mother)
I Hate to Go to Bed! - Katie Davis 239
I Need a Snake - Lynne Jonell 488
Some Babies - Amy Schwartz 889

Mommy (Mother; Gardener)
The Ugly Vegetables - Grace Lin 582

Mona (Child; Friend)
One Halloween Night - Mark Teague 979

Mona Lisa (Historical Figure)
Katie and the Mona Lisa - James Mayhew 636

Monique (Daughter)
The Butterfly - Patricia Polacco 788

Monk (Mouse; Son)
Monk Camps Out - Emily Arnold McCully 648

Monk (Mouse; Baseball Player)
Mouse Practice - Emily Arnold McCully 649

Monroe, Willie (Wrestler; Young Man)
The Tale of Willie Monroe - Alan Schroeder 885

Monsieur Blanc (Pirate; Rabbit)
Rabbit Pirates: A Tale of the Spinach Main - Judy Cox 200

Monsieur Lapin (Pirate; Rabbit)
Rabbit Pirates: A Tale of the Spinach Main - Judy Cox 200

Monteros, Angel (4th Grader; Neighbor)
Stucksville - Sheila Greenwald 376

Montezuma "Monty" (Dog)
Montezuma's Revenge - Cari Best 76

Montgomery, Serena (Student—Middle School; Friend)
The Ashwater Experiment - Amy Goldman Koss 539

Moo (Cow)
Minnie and Moo and the Musk of Zorro - Denys Cazet 155

Moo (Cow; Friend)
Minnie and Moo and the Thanksgiving Tree - Denys Cazet 156

Moody, Judy (3rd Grader; Sister)
Judy Moody - Megan McDonald 653

Moody, Stink (2nd Grader; Brother)
Judy Moody - Megan McDonald 653

Moon (Celestial Body; Pitcher)
Moonball - Jane Yolen 1082

Mooney, Herb (Teacher)
Me Tarzan - Betsy Byars 134

Mooney, Travis (5th Grader; Friend)
Figuring Out Frances - Gina Willner-Pardo 1052

Moore, Annie (Immigrant; Sister)
Dreaming of America: An Ellis Island Story - Eve Bunting 125

Moore, Anthony (Immigrant; Brother)
Dreaming of America: An Ellis Island Story - Eve Bunting 125

Moore, Phillip (Immigrant; Brother)
Dreaming of America: An Ellis Island Story - Eve Bunting 125

Moose (Camper; Bully)
Cody Unplugged - Betsy Duffey 279

Moose (Moose; Friend)
Moose Tales - Nancy Van Laan 1001

Moose (Moose; Father)
Mooseltoe - Margie Palatini 757

Moose, Elliott (Moose; Stuffed Animal)
Elliot Bakes a Cake - Andrea Beck 69

Mop (Dog)
Mop to the Rescue - Martine Schaap 877

Morales, Rick (11-Year-Old)
If That Breathes Fire, We're Toast! - Jennifer J. Stewart 958

Morehouse, David Reed (Sea Captain)
The Mary Celeste: An Unsolved Mystery from History - Jane Yolen 1081

Morgan (Bear)
Mud Flat Spring - James Stevenson 957

Morgan, Jim (Friend)
Summer Soldiers - Susan Hart Lindquist 586

Morgan, Lexi (2nd Grader; Friend)
Dustin's Big School Day - Alden R. Carter 151

Moriwaki, Masako "May" (Daughter; Friend)
Tea with Milk - Allen Say 876

Morris (Mouse; Friend)
Horace and Morris but Mostly Dolores - James Howe 454

Morris, Ivy (Grandmother)
Song of the Wanderer - Bruce Coville 193

Morrison, Beth (Friend)
Strange Neighbors - Mary Labatt 548

Mort (Elephant; Son)
Mort the Sport - Robert Kraus 540

Morty (Bully; Student—Elementary School)
The Saturday Kid - Edward Sorel 935

Mose (Neighbor; Farmer)
Callie Ann and Mistah Bear - Robert D. San Souci 865

Mose (Cat)
The Mouse That Snored - Bernard Waber 1008

Moses (Student—Elementary School; Deaf Person)
Moses Goes to School - Isaac Millman 685

Mother (Mother)
Clara Ann Cookie - Harriet Ziefert 1090
D.W., Go to Your Room! - Marc Brown 112

Mother (Opossum; Mother)
Happy Birthday to You, You Belong in a Zoo - Diane DeGroat 249

Mother (Mother; Widow(er))
Jack and the Beanstalk - Ann Keay Beneduce 70

Mother (Mother)
Just Like a Baby - Rebecca Bond 90

Mother (Mother; Widow(er))
Kate and the Beanstalk - Mary Pope Osborne 750

Mother (Mother)
Mary and the Mystery Dog - Wolfram Hanel 399

Mother (Patriot; Spy)
Redcoats and Petticoats - Katherine Kirkpatrick 530

Mother (Mother)
Special Delivery - Brigitte Weninger 1037

Mother (Mother; Camper)
Stella & Roy Go Camping - Ashley Wolff 1062

Mother (Mother)
The Tale I Told Sasha - Nancy Willard 1050

Mother (Mother; Daughter)
The Trip Back Home - Janet S. Wong 1065

Mother (Mother)
Vera Runs Away - Vera Rosenberry 836

Mother (Single Mother)
White Tiger, Blue Serpent - Grace Tseng 991

Mother Bear (Bear; Mother)
Are You There, Baby Bear? - Catherine Walters 1023

Mother Earth (Spirit)
Wild Child - Lynn Plourde 787

Mother Holly (Aged Person)
How the Cat Swallowed Thunder - Lloyd Alexander 18

Mother Monster (Monster; Mother)
What If? - Frances Thomas 981

Mouse (Mouse; Friend)
Cat and Mouse in the Snow - Tomek Bogacki 86

Mouse, Livingstone (Mouse; Explorer)
Bravo, Livingstone Mouse! - Pamela Duncan Edwards 291

Mouton (Sheep)
Mouton's Impossible Dream - Anik McGrory 659

Mr. Ackerby (Principal)
The Janitor's Boy - Andrew Clements 171

Mr. Apple (Administrator)
Mr. Tanen's Ties - Maryann Cocca-Leffler 175

Mr. Bates (Businessman; Father)
Gloria's Way - Ann Cameron 139

Mr. Bear (Bear; Neighbor)
Mr. Bear to the Rescue - Debi Gliori 351

Mr. Bear (Father; Bear)
Mr. Bear's New Baby - Debi Gliori 352

Mr. Bear (Bear; Father)
Mr. Bear's Vacation - Debi Gliori 353

Mr. Bellows (Sailor; Pirate)
The Pirate's Parrot - Lyn Rossiter McFarland 656

Mr. Carlton (Father; Principal)
The Ghost of Lizard Light - Elvira Woodruff 1068

Mr. Crum (Father; Scientist)
Bad Habits! - Babette Cole 178

Mr. Deveau (Sailor)
The Mary Celeste: An Unsolved Mystery from History - Jane Yolen 1081

Mr. Fentriss (Father; Monster)
Diary of a Monster's Son - Ellen Conford 184

Mr. Flotsam (Neighbor)
Yard Sale! - Mitra Modaressi 691

Mr. Ford (Businessman; Spouse)
Clever Cat - Peter Collington 182

Mr. Frimdimpny (Narrator; Reptile)
Don't Make Me Laugh - James Stevenson 955

Mr. Gilly (Maintenance Worker)
Trashy Town - Andrea Zimmerman 1097

Mr. Goodparents (Father; Spouse)
The Gift - Gabriela Keselman 513

Mr. Goose (Goose; Father)
The Little Green Goose - Adele Sansone 871

Mr. Goose (Goose)
Waiting for Mr. Goose - Laurie Lears 564

Mr. Harrison (Teacher)
The Fungus That Ate My School - Arthur Dorros 273

Mr. Hartwell (Spouse)
First Day Jitters - Julie Danneberg 235

Mr. Hill (Salesman)
The Rusty, Trusty Tractor - Joy Cowley 197

Mr. Hooper (Teacher)
Bad Dreams - Anne Fine 314

Mr. Humphrey (Neighbor)
Red Rubber Boot Day - Mary Lyn Ray 813

Mr. Jordan (Stepfather)
Just Like Mike - Gail Herman 426

Mr. Kim (Businessman)
New Cat - Yangsook Choi 164

Mr. Kleinberg (Teacher; Musician)
The Saturday Kid - Edward Sorel 935

Mr. Krebs (Blacksmith)
Hurry! - Emily Arnold McCully 646

Mr. Krupp (Principal)
Captain Underpants and the Attack of the Talking Toilets - Dav Pilkey 776

Mr. Long (Spouse; Stepfather)
Mama and Me and the Model T - Faye Gibbons 347

Mr. Magee (Sailor)
Down to the Sea with Mr. Magee - Chris Van Dusen 1000

Mr. Mah (Aged Person; Neighbor)
Me and Mr. Mah - Andrea Spalding 937

Mr. Mann (Aged Person; Neighbor)
When Night Time Comes Near - Judy Pedersen 768

Mr. Martin (Teacher)
100th Day Worries - Margery Cuyler 222

Mr. McDuffel (Farmer)
The Pig Is in the Pantry, the Cat Is on the Shelf - Shirley Mozelle 706

Mr. Miller (Rabbit; Farmer)
Apples, Apples, Apples - Nancy Elizabeth Wallace 1019

Mr. Minky (Father)
Simply Delicious! - Margaret Mahy 614

Mr. Moon (Celestial Body)
Jimmy Zangwow's Out-of-This World Moon Pie Adventure - Tony DiTerlizzi 268

Mr. Noah (Store Owner; Spouse)
Ark in the Park - Wendy Orr 749

Mr. O (Musician; Aged Person)
The Cello of Mr. O. - Jane Cutler 221

Mr. Oji (Teacher; Martial Arts Expert)
Black Belt - Matt Faulkner 309

Mr. Oysterman (Fisherman)
Selkie - Gillian McClure 643

Mr. Peebles (Neighbor)
The Robobots - Matt Novak 738

Mr. Porkpie (Photographer)
Swine Divine - Jan Carr 148

Mr. Prospero (Businessman; Father)
Down the Dragon's Tongue - Margaret Mahy 613

Mr. Putter (Aged Person; Neighbor)
Mr. Putter and Tabby Paint the Porch - Cynthia Rylant 853

Mr. Rabbit (Rabbit; Father)
One, Two, Three, Oops! - Michael Coleman 180

Mr. Rabbit-Bunn (Rabbit; Neighbor)
Mr. Bear to the Rescue - Debi Gliori 351

Mr. Rogers (Employer)
Amelia Bedelia 4 Mayor - Herman Parish 760

O

P

Robobot, M.O.M. (Mother; Robot)
The Robobots - Matt Novak   738

Robot (Robot)
Ricky Ricotta's Giant Robot: An Adventure Novel -
Dav Pilkey   778

Rocky (Friend; 3rd Grader)
Judy Moody - Megan McDonald   653

Roddy (Child)
Granddaddy's Street Songs - Monalisa DeGross   251

Rodeo Rosie (Cowgirl; Entertainer)
Sam's Wild West Christmas - Nancy Antle   29

Roger (Child)
Buster: The Very Shy Dog - Lisze Bechtold   68
I Was a Rat! - Philip Pullman   804

Roger (Child; Neighbor)
The Witch Who Was Afraid of Witches - Alice
Low   599

Roosevelt, Eleanor (Historical Figure; Friend)
Amelia and Eleanor Go for a Ride - Pam Munoz
Ryan   848

Rosabel (Child; Slave)
The Legend of Freedom Hill - Linda Jacobs
Altman   22

Rosalia (Child; Sister)
Blanca's Feather - Antonio Hernandez Madrigal   608

Rosalinda (Child)
Under the Lemon Moon - Edith Hope Fine   315

Rose (Bear; Sister)
One Saturday Afternoon - Barbara Baker   49

Rosemary (Rabbit; Student—Elementary School)
Science Fair Bunnies - Kathryn Lasky   560

Rosie (Mother)
Big Rain Coming - Katrina Germein   345

Rosie (Child)
Celeste Sails to Spain - Alison Lester   566

Rosie (Horse)
The Gate in the Wall - Ellen Howard   452

Rosie (Stuffed Animal; Goose)
Louie's Goose - H.M. Ehrlich   297

Rosie (Child; Cook)
Matzah Ball Soup - Joan Rothenberg   841

Rosie (9-Year-Old; Sister; Cousin)
Some Good News - Cynthia Rylant   856

Rosie (Pig)
Swine Divine - Jan Carr   148

Rover (Dog)
The Giggler Treatment - Roddy Doyle   276

Rover (Child; Daughter)
Rover - Michael Rosen   832

Rowan (Child; Sister)
Who's in the Hall: A Mystery in Four Chapters -
Betsy Hearne   408

Roxanne (Mother)
How Will We Get to the Beach? - Brigitte
Luciani   602

Roy (Uncle; Scientist)
Fossil Fever - Kathleen Weidner Zoehfeld   1098

Roy (Brother; Camper)
Stella & Roy Go Camping - Ashley Wolff   1062

Rrrrrella (Stepsister)
Bigfoot Cinderrrrella - Tony Johnston   487

Ruby (Rabbit; Sister)
Max Cleans Up - Rosemary Wells   1034

Ruby Jane (Sister)
The Bravest of Us All - Marsha Diane Arnold   34

Rudy (Child; Nephew)
Three Magic Balls - Richard Egielski   294

Runt (Son; 12-Year-Old)
The Journal of Wong Ming-Chung: A Chinese Miner -
Laurence Yep   1077

Rush, Johanna "Josie" (4th Grader; Sister)
Snowdrops for Cousin Ruth - Susan Katz   498

Rush, Susie (Sister; Twin)
Snowdrops for Cousin Ruth - Susan Katz   498

Russell, Andy (4th Grader; Animal Lover)
Andy and Tamika - David A. Adler   4

Russell, Andy (Friend)
Parachuting Hamsters and Andy Russell - David A.
Adler   7

Russell, Andy (4th Grader; Daydreamer)
School Trouble for Andy Russell - David A. Adler   8

Russell, Rachel (Sister)
Andy and Tamika - David A. Adler   4

Ruth Rose (Child; Friend)
The Goose's Gold - Ron Roy   844

Ruthie (Child; Fisherman)
Hurry Granny Annie - Arlene Alda   14

Ruthie (Rabbit; Friend)
Ruthie's Big Old Coat - Julie Lacome   549

Ruthie Mae (Child; Friend)
The Honest-to-Goodness Truth - Patricia C.
McKissack   663

Ryan (Child; Brother)
Who's in the Hall: A Mystery in Four Chapters -
Betsy Hearne   408

Ryan, Harvey (5th Grader; Child of Divorced
Parents)
Dear Mrs. Ryan, You're Ruining My Life - Jennifer B.
Jones   490

S

Sabu (Cook; Neighbor)
Yoshi's Feast - Kimiko Kajikawa   492

Sadie (Sister)
Latkes, Latkes Good to Eat: A Chanukah Story -
Naomi Howland   455

Sage (5th Grader)
Miss Alaineus: A Vocabulary Disaster - Debra
Frasier   326

Saliva "Sal" (Alien)
Club Earth - Gail Gauthier   339

Sally (Child)
Paddiwak and Cozy - Berlie Doherty   271

Sally (Dog; Narrator)
Sally Goes to the Beach - Stephen Huneck   460

Sally (Niece)
Tomatoes from Mars - Arthur Yorinks   1087

Sally (Aunt; Storyteller)
The Trolls - Polly Horvath   448

Sam (9-Year-Old)
Brooklyn, Bugsy, and Me - Lynea Bowdish   96

Sam (Time Traveler; Student—Elementary School)
It's All Greek to Me - Jon Scieszka   891

Sam (Child; Nephew)
The Loudness of Sam - James Proimos   800

Sam (Cowboy; Entertainer)
Sam's Wild West Christmas - Nancy Antle   29

Sam (Time Traveler; Friend)
See You Later, Gladiator - Jon Scieszka   892

Sam (Child; Brother)
Stella, Queen of the Snow - Marie-Louise Gay   340

Stella, Star of the Sea - Marie-Louise Gay   341

Sam (Dog)
Strange Neighbors - Mary Labatt   548

Sam (10-Year-Old; Nephew)
Weird Stories from the Lonesome Cafe - Judy
Cox   201

Samantha (Child)
Wherever Bears Be: A Story for Two Voices - Sue Ann
Alderson   16

Sameera (2nd Grader; Immigrant)
Dear Whiskers - Ann Whitehead Nagda   717

Sammy (Child)
Sammy and the Dinosaurs - Ian Whybrow   1046

Sammy (Milkman)
The Two Sillies - Mary Ann Hoberman   439

Samuel (Baby; Cousin)
Blackberry Booties - Tricia Gardella   335

Samuel (Orphan; Immigrant)
Hannah's Journal: The Story of an Immigrant Girl -
Marissa Moss   702

Samuel (Child; Son)
The Way Home - Nan Parson Rossiter   839

Santa (Mythical Creature; Aged Person)
Truffle's Christmas - Anna Currey   216

Santiago (Brother)
The Three Golden Oranges - Alma Flor Ada   2

Santos, Edie (Grandmother)
Swimming with Sharks - Twig C. George   344

Santos, Joseph (Grandfather; Scientist)
Swimming with Sharks - Twig C. George   344

Sara (Dog)
The Promise - Jackie French Koller   536

Sara (Child)
Three Cheers for Catherine the Great! - Cari
Best   77

Sarah (Student—Elementary School; Sister)
When Will Sarah Come? - Elizabeth Fitzgerald
Howard   451

Sarah May (Child)
Sarah May and the New Red Dress - Andrea
Spalding   938

Saruni (Child; Son)
My Rows and Piles of Coins - Tololwa M.
Mollel   693

Sassy (Dancer; Sister)
Dancing in the Wings - Debbie Allen   21

Say, Joseph (Businessman; Friend)
Tea with Milk - Allen Say   876

Scarface (Parrot)
Alien Brain Fryout - Barbara M. Joosse   491

Schuler, Jasmine "Jas" (13-Year-Old; Equestrian)
Shadow Horse - Alison Hart   406

Scrappy (Dog)
Moondogs - Daniel Kirk   527

Scratchy (Bird)
Brian's Bird - Patricia A. Davis   240

Seal (Seal; Friend)
Whiteblack the Penguin Sees the World - H.A.
Rey   817

Seaman (Dog)
*Seaman: The Dog Who Explored the West with Lewis
& Clark* - Gail Langer Karwoski   497

Searcy, Mandy (Daughter; Sister)
Mama and Me and the Model T - Faye Gibbons   347

Seezer (Alligator)
Bartleby of the Mighty Mississippi - Phyllis
Shalant   900

Character Description Index

This index alphabetically lists descriptions of the major characters in featured titles. The descriptions may be occupations (doctor, lawyer, etc.) or may describe persona (amnesiac, runaway, teenager, etc.). For each description, character names are listed alphabetically. Also provided are book titles, author names, and entry numbers.

3-YEAR-OLD

Blue, Edison
You're a Brave Man, Julius Zimmerman - Claudia Mills   688

4-YEAR-OLD

Krupnik, Sam
Zooman Sam - Lois Lowry   601

Molly
The Pictish Child - Jane Yolen   1085

Sophie
Mimmy & Sophie - Miriam Cohen   177

5-YEAR-OLD

Bloom, Amy
The Very Best Hanukkah Gift - Joanne Rocklin   824

Henry, Pete
Jack on the Tracks: Four Seasons of Fifth Grade - Jack Gantos   333

Nellie
The Lost Flower Children - Janet Taylor Lisle   588

6-YEAR-OLD

Christopher
It's My Birthday, Too! - Lynne Jonell   489

Emily
The Longest Hair in the World - Lois Duncan   285

Hill, Lily
Leftover Lily - Sally Warner   1026

Martin, Matt
The Diary of Melanie Martin - Carol Weston   1040

McDoodle, Robert
The Strange and Wonderful Tale of Robert McDoodle: The Boy Who Wanted to Be a Dog - Steven Bauer   66

Mimmy
Mimmy & Sophie - Miriam Cohen   177

Reader, Jim
Mysterious Miss Slade - Dick King-Smith   524

Shawn
Shawn and Keeper and the Birthday Party - Jonathan London   596

7-YEAR-OLD

Bunch, Junior
Plenty of Pockets - Ann Braybrooks   102

Christie, Sary
Wander - Susan Hart Lindquist   587

Daniel
Crab Moon - Ruth Horowitz   447

Erandi
Erandi's Braids - Antonio Hernandez Madrigal   609

Hatford, Peter
A Traitor Among the Boys - Phyllis Reynolds Naylor   723

Madrigal, Magda
Magda's Tortillas: Las Tortillas de Magda - Becky Chavarria-Chairez   160

Miles, Wilhe'mina
Wilhe'mina Miles After the Stork Night - Dorothy Carter   153

Omakayas
The Birchbark House - Louise Erdrich   303

Serefina
Serefina under the Circumstances - Phyllis Theroux   980

Sophie
Ark in the Park - Wendy Orr   749

William
Good-bye for Today: The Diary of a Young Girl at Sea - Peter Roop   828

8-YEAR-OLD

Benton, Sarah Eliza
I'm Sorry, Almira Ann - Jane Kurtz   545

Bloom, Daniel
The Very Best Hanukkah Gift - Joanne Rocklin   824

Bobby
Cockroach Cooties - Laurence Yep   1076

Ethan
When You Take a Pig to a Party - Kristina Thermaenius McLarey   665

Foote, Owen
Owen Foote, Money Man - Stephanie Greene   374

Gardner, Lizzie
Lizard Meets Ivana the Terrible - C. Anne Scott   893

Hastings, Almira Ann
I'm Sorry, Almira Ann - Jane Kurtz   545

Hobbs, Joseph
Owen Foote, Money Man - Stephanie Greene   374

Ivana the Terrible
Lizard Meets Ivana the Terrible - C. Anne Scott   893

Johnson, Brian
Brian's Bird - Patricia A. Davis   240

Kay
Happy Birthday, America! - Marsha Wilson Chall   158

Lori
Strudel Stories - Joanne Rocklin   823

Martin, Ellie
Not My Dog - Colby Rodowsky   826

Palmer, Kate
The Doll People - Ann M. Martin   624

Paul
Rescue at Sea! - Wolfram Hancl   400

Peregrine, Agnes
When Agnes Caws - Candace Fleming   321

Reader, Patsy
Mysterious Miss Slade - Dick King-Smith   524

Robinson, Beany
Dolphin Luck - Hilary McKay   661

Sophia
I Have an Olive Tree - Eve Bunting   126

Sophie
Sophie Skates - Rachel Isadora   468

Turner, Jessie Daisy
Daisy and the Doll - Michael Medearis   676

Van Sorg, Benjamin "Henk"
When the Soldiers Were Gone - Vera W. Propp   801

9-YEAR-OLD

Arigotti, Stormy
The Runaways - Zilpha Keatley Snyder   932

Arnie
Cockroach Cooties - Laurence Yep   1076

Burwell, Nathaniel "Nat"
Caesar's Story: 1759 - Joan Lowery Nixon   729

Caesar
Caesar's Story: 1759 - Joan Lowery Nixon   729

Poage, Elizabeth
Adventure on the Wilderness Road, 1775 - Laurie
Lawlor 561

Reed, Luke
Luke: 1849-On the Golden Trail - Bonnie Pryor 802

Smith, Robert "Bob-o"
Regular Guy - Sarah Weeks 1031

Strang, Guy
Regular Guy - Sarah Weeks 1031

Wicklow, Kathy
Dance of the Crystal Skull - Norma Lehr 565

Williams, Jasmyn "Jas"
Soldier Mom - Alice Mead 672

Yeung, Ying
Child Bride - Ching Yeung Russell 847

12-YEAR-OLD

Alex
Blackwater - Eve Bunting 122

Baker, Hezzy
Weaver's Daughter - Kimberly Brubaker Bradley 99

Barrow, Frances "Frankie"
Nowhere to Call Home - Cynthia DeFelice 247

Baudelaire, Klaus
The Bad Beginning - Lemony Snicket 931

Betts, Kate
Captain Kate - Carolyn Reeder 815

Bokko
The Year of Miss Agnes - Kirkpatrick Hill 434

Chrisman, Abbie
Calling Me Home - Patricia Hermes 427

Christie, James
Wander - Susan Hart Lindquist 587

Drennan, Kendall
Enchanted Runner - Kimberley Griffiths Little 590

Fabrizio
Midnight Magic - Avi 44

Hill, Casey "Case"
Accidental Lily - Sally Warner 1025

Hillerman, Seth
Captain Kate - Carolyn Reeder 815

Hunter, Ben
The Birthday Room - Kevin Henkes 421

Hunter, Cara Diane
Song of the Wanderer - Bruce Coville 193

Jackson, May Amelia
Our Only May Amelia - Jennifer L. Holm 441

Jade
Seesaw Girl - Linda Sue Park 762

Jessica
Strudel Stories - Joanne Rocklin 823

Kahele, Kathryn Maluhia "Kate"
Dance for the Land - Clemence McLaren 664

Landon, Jack
Deadly Waters - Gloria Skurzynski 925

Little Rose, Nannie
*My Heart Is on the Ground: The Diary of Nannie
Little Rose, a Sioux Girl* - Ann Rinaldi 821

MacAllister, Allie
Cherokee Sister - Debbie Dadey 226

Manell, Vivien
A Ceiling of Stars - Ann Howard Creel 206

O'Donnell, Danielle "Dani"
The Runaways - Zilpha Keatley Snyder 932

Peeler, Jane
The Way to Schenectady - Richard Scrimger 894

Potter, Harry
Harry Potter and the Chamber of Secrets - J.K.
Rowling 842

Runt
The Journal of Wong Ming-Chung: A Chinese Miner -
Laurence Yep 1077

Siegel, Hillary
The Ashwater Experiment - Amy Goldman Koss 539

Willow
Dance of the Crystal Skull - Norma Lehr 565

Zimmerman, Julius
You're a Brave Man, Julius Zimmerman - Claudia
Mills 688

13-YEAR-OLD

Darcy, Maggie
Kat's Surrender - Theresa Martin Golding 358

Edward
*The Yeoman's Daring Daughter and the Princes in the
Tower* - Elaine Clayton 168

Gibson, Harriet "Harry"
Unbroken - Jessie Haas 391

Jackson, Wilbert
Our Only May Amelia - Jennifer L. Holm 441

Jennifer
The Pictish Child - Jane Yolen 1085

Lynch, Brodie
Blackwater - Eve Bunting 122

Martin, Jeffrey "Jeff"
The Vampire in My Bathtub - Brenda Seabrooke 896

O'Connor, Kathryn "Kat"
Kat's Surrender - Theresa Martin Golding 358

Parnell, Roscoe
Silent Thunder: A Civil War Story - Andrea Davis
Pinkney 779

Paul
Kat's Surrender - Theresa Martin Golding 358

Schuler, Jasmine "Jas"
Shadow Horse - Alison Hart 406

Unnamed Character
Moon over Tennessee: A Boy's Civil War Journal -
Craig Crist-Evans 209

14-YEAR-OLD

Baudelaire, Violet
The Bad Beginning - Lemony Snicket 931

Bliss, Thankful
Emma's Journal: The Story of a Colonial Girl -
Marissa Moss 701

Conley, Bridger
Deadly Waters - Gloria Skurzynski 925

Esther
Hannah's Journal: The Story of an Immigrant Girl -
Marissa Moss 702

West, Libby
The Great Railroad Race: The Diary of Libby West -
Kristiana Gregory 377

15-YEAR-OLD

Malinski, Walter
Goodbye, Walter Malinski - Helen Recorvits 814

Nealan of Queenscove "Neal"
First Test - Tamora Pierce 775

Stewpot
Nowhere to Call Home - Cynthia DeFelice 247

Stonewall, Corinna "Corin"
The Folk Keeper - Franny Billingsley 78

16-YEAR-OLD

Bee
True Heart - Marissa Moss 703

Cooper, Lamar
Abraham's Battle: A Novel of Gettysburg - Sara
Harrell Banks 57

19-YEAR-OLD

Pete
The Great Railroad Race: The Diary of Libby West -
Kristiana Gregory 377

1ST GRADER

Girl
Dreams Are More Real than Bathtubs - Susan
Musgrave 710

Greenough, Daisy
Leftover Lily - Sally Warner 1026

Hill, Lily
Accidental Lily - Sally Warner 1025

Jessica
100th Day Worries - Margery Cuyler 222

Mitchell, Hilary
Leftover Lily - Sally Warner 1026

Vera
Vera Runs Away - Vera Rosenberry 836

Wilson, Bob
Surviving Brick Johnson - Laurie Myers 714

2ND GRADER

Apfel, Dustin
Dustin's Big School Day - Alden R. Carter 151

Bertie
Bertie's Picture Day - Pat Brisson 106

Emeline
Emeline at the Circus - Marjorie Priceman 797

Foote, Owen
Owen Foote, Frontiersman - Stephanie Greene 373

Fraser, Edward
'Gator Aid - Jane Cutler 220

Gus
Gus and Grandpa and Show and-Tell - Claudia
Mills 686

Hobbs, Joseph
Owen Foote, Frontiersman - Stephanie Greene 373

James, Calliope
Pa Lia's First Day - Michelle Edwards 290

Jellico, Josie
Josie to the Rescue - Marilyn Singer 920

Moody, Stink
Judy Moody - Megan McDonald 653

Morgan, Lexi
Dustin's Big School Day - Alden R. Carter 151

Sameera
Dear Whiskers - Ann Whitehead Nagda 717

Smith, Howardina "Howie"
Pa Lia's First Day - Michelle Edwards 290

Vang, Pa Lia
Pa Lia's First Day - Michelle Edwards 290

3RD GRADER

Bowles, Howie
Howie Bowles and Uncle Sam - Kate Banks 53
Howie Bowles, Secret Agent - Kate Banks 54

Brennerman, Mary Grace
Spider Storch's Desperate Deal - Gina Willner-Pardo 1054

Doug
Horrible Harry at Halloween - Suzy Kline 533
Song Lee and the "I Hate You" Notes - Suzy Kline 534

Gardner, Lizzie
Lizard Meets Ivana the Terrible - C. Anne Scott 893

Garland, Holly
The Trouble with Cats - Martha Freeman 328

Ivana the Terrible
Lizard Meets Ivana the Terrible - C. Anne Scott 893

J.P.
Alien for Rent - Betsy Duffey 278

Jordan, Michael "Mike"
Just Like Mike - Gail Herman 426

Levy, Adam
Mean, Mean Maureen Green - Judy Cox 199

Lexie
Alien for Rent - Betsy Duffey 278

MacDougal-MacDuff, Morgan "Morgy"
Morgy Makes His Move - Maggie Lewis 579

Mary
Song Lee and the "I Hate You" Notes - Suzy Kline 534

McGill, Matthew
Annie Pitts, Burger Kid - Diane DeGroat 248

Moody, Judy
Judy Moody - Megan McDonald 653

Murphy, Charlie
Anna All Year Round - Mary Downing Hahn 392

Nelson, Lilley
Mean, Mean Maureen Green - Judy Cox 199

Noonan, Byron
Morgy Makes His Move - Maggie Lewis 579

Park, Song Lee
Song Lee and the "I Hate You" Notes - Suzy Kline 534

Redpost, Marvin
Marvin Redpost: Class President - Louis Sachar 859

Rocky
Judy Moody - Megan McDonald 653

Sherwood, Anna Elizabeth
Anna All Year Round - Mary Downing Hahn 392

Spooger, Harry
Horrible Harry at Halloween - Suzy Kline 533

Stanley, Pru
Seal Island School - Susan Bartlett 59

Storch, Joey "Spider"
Spider Storch's Desperate Deal - Gina Willner-Pardo 1054

Tim
Just Like Mike - Gail Herman 426

Toby
Howie Bowles and Uncle Sam - Kate Banks 53

Zesterman, Ann
Good Luck, Mrs. K.! - Louise Borden 93

3RD GRADER

Steve
The Magic Paintbrush - Laurence Yep 1078

4TH GRADER

Albertson, Louisa
King of the Kooties! - Debbie Dadey 227

Ana
In the Shade of the Nispero Tree - Carmen T. Bernier-Grand 73

Anderson, Tamika
Andy and Tamika - David A. Adler 4

Beard, George
Captain Underpants and the Perilous Plot of Professor Poopypants - Dav Pilkey 777

Brook, Lynda
Nothing Wrong with a Three-Legged Dog - Graham McNamee 667

Brown, Amber
I, Amber Brown - Paula Danziger 236

Chameleon, Shirley
The Chameleon Wore Chartreuse: From the Tattered Casebook of Chet Gecko, Private Eye - Bruce Hale 393

Costos, Emerald
Stucksville - Sheila Greenwald 376

Davis, Cory
School Trouble for Andy Russell - David A. Adler 8

Donald
King of the Kooties! - Debbie Dadey 227

Fraser, Keath
Nothing Wrong with a Three-Legged Dog - Graham McNamee 667

Gecko, Chet
The Chameleon Wore Chartreuse: From the Tattered Casebook of Chet Gecko, Private Eye - Bruce Hale 393

Giraux, Teresa
In the Shade of the Nispero Tree - Carmen T. Bernier-Grand 73

Gnormal, Norman
The Magic Pretzel - Daniel Pinkwater 785

Green, Maureen
Mean, Mean Maureen Green - Judy Cox 199

Hunter, Devin
Nose Pickers from Outer Space - Gordon Korman 538

Hutchins, Harold
Captain Underpants and the Perilous Plot of Professor Poopypants - Dav Pilkey 777

Jackson, Stacy Anne
School Trouble for Andy Russell - David A. Adler 8

Jenny
Dear Whiskers - Ann Whitehead Nagda 717

Kidd, Daisy
Ramona's World - Beverly Cleary 169

Lansing-Ross, Nicholas
Seal Island School - Susan Bartlett 59

Lauffer, Guthry
Stucksville - Sheila Greenwald 376

Monteros, Angel
Stucksville - Sheila Greenwald 376

Nelson, Nate
King of the Kooties! - Debbie Dadey 227

Perkins, John
The Battlefield Ghost - Margery Cuyler 223

Plum, Dexter
Fourth Grade Weirdo - Martha Freeman 327

Quimby, Ramona
Ramona's World - Beverly Cleary 169

Rush, Johanna "Josie"
Snowdrops for Cousin Ruth - Susan Katz 498

Russell, Andy
Andy and Tamika - David A. Adler 4
School Trouble for Andy Russell - David A. Adler 8

Tony
Brooklyn, Bugsy, and Me - Lynea Bowdish 96

5TH GRADER

Brown, Alana
Llama in the Library - Johanna Hurwitz 462

Coleman, Emma
Leaving Emma - Nancy Steele Brokaw 108

DeLucca, Joey
The Landry News - Andrew Clements 172

Dreanne "Dreenie"
Bluish - Virginia Hamilton 397

Edna
Angel Spreads Her Wings - Judy Delton 253

Emma
The Boy Trap - Nancy Matson 632

Fine, Adam
Llama in the Library - Johanna Hurwitz 462

Fraser, Jason
'Gator Aid - Jane Cutler 220

Henry, Jack Jr.
Jack on the Tracks: Four Seasons of Fifth Grade - Jack Gantos 333

Johnson, Brick
Surviving Brick Johnson - Laurie Myers 714

Krishnan
Close Call - Todd Strasser 965

Landry, Cara
The Landry News - Andrew Clements 172

Malinski, Wanda
Goodbye, Walter Malinski - Helen Recorvits 814

Mooney, Travis
Figuring Out Frances - Gina Willner-Pardo 1052

Poppadopolis, Angel
Angel Spreads Her Wings - Judy Delton 253

Rankin, John Philip "Jack" Jr.
The Janitor's Boy - Andrew Clements 171

Rice, Justin
Llama in the Library - Johanna Hurwitz 462

Ryan, Harvey
Dear Mrs. Ryan, You're Ruining My Life - Jennifer B. Jones 490

Sage
Miss Alaineus: A Vocabulary Disaster - Debra Frasier 326

Smithson, Portia "Pixie"
The Runaways - Zilpha Keatley Snyder 932

Spicer, Cecelia "Seal"
Dear Mrs. Ryan, You're Ruining My Life - Jennifer B. Jones 490

Starr
Miss Alaineus: A Vocabulary Disaster - Debra Frasier 326

Temiyasathit, Sirat "Tem"
Leaving Emma - Nancy Steele Brokaw 108

Tulithia "Tuli"
Bluish - Virginia Hamilton 397

6TH GRADER

Welsh, Julie
My Brother Made Me Do It - Peg Kehret   502

Wilson, Alex
Surviving Brick Johnson - Laurie Myers   714

Winburn, Natalie "Bluish"
Bluish - Virginia Hamilton   397

Zarotsky, Louise
The Boy Trap - Nancy Matson   632

6TH GRADER

Cactus, Prairie
Romance of the Snob Squad - Julie Anne Peters   770

Cott, Lucas
The Just Desserts Club - Johanna Hurwitz   461

Cushman, Sara Jane
The Just Desserts Club - Johanna Hurwitz   461

Flack, Jerry
Dork in Disguise - Carol Gorman   365

Harmon, Gail
Captain's Command - Anna Myers   711

Harriet
Batty Hattie - Virginia Nielsen   727

Howell, Brady
Batty Hattie - Virginia Nielsen   727

Kaufman, Cricket
The Just Desserts Club - Johanna Hurwitz   461

McAdams, Brenda
Dork in Disguise - Carol Gorman   365

Meenom, Pleskit
I Was a Sixth Grade Alien - Bruce Coville   192

Randall, Natalie
If That Breathes Fire, We're Toast! - Jennifer J. Stewart   958

Solano, Jenny
Romance of the Snob Squad - Julie Anne Peters   770

Tompkins, Tim
I Was a Sixth Grade Alien - Bruce Coville   192

Torkerson, Hugh
Romance of the Snob Squad - Julie Anne Peters   770

Zaslow, Becky
Zink - Cherie Bennett   71

AARDVARK

Read, Arthur
Arthur's Underwear - Marc Brown   111

ABANDONED CHILD

Manell, Vivien
A Ceiling of Stars - Ann Howard Creel   206

Sparrow, John Joseph "Spider"
Spider Sparrow - Dick King-Smith   525

ABUSE VICTIM

Arigotti, Stormy
The Runaways - Zilpha Keatley Snyder   932

ACTOR

Daddy
Tree of Hope - Amy Littlesugar   591

Field, Nathan "Nat"
King of Shadows - Susan Cooper   188

Shakespeare, Will
King of Shadows - Susan Cooper   188

ACTRESS

Annabel
Annabel the Actress Starring in Gorilla My Dreams - Ellen Conford   183

Williamson, Gene
Alice-by-Accident - Lynne Reid Banks   56

ADMINISTRATOR

Mr. Apple
Mr. Tanen's Ties - Maryann Cocca-Leffler   175

ADOPTEE

Jessie
An American Face - Jan M. Czech   225

Sweetness
Raising Sweetness - Diane Stanley   947

Unnamed Character
I Love You Like Crazy Cakes - Rose Lewis   580

ADVENTURER

Herodsfoot
Dangerous Games - Joan Aiken   11

Jane
Jane on Her Own: A Catwings Tale - Ursula K. Le Guin   563

Ragweed
Ragweed - Avi   45

Reed, Eli
Luke: 1849-On the Golden Trail - Bonnie Pryor   802

Whiteblack
Whiteblack the Penguin Sees the World - H.A. Rey   817

AGED PERSON

Angel, A.N.
Albert and the Angels - Leslie Norris   736

Aunt Liza
Hog Music - M.C. Helldorfer   411

Big Joe
Basket Moon - Mary Lyn Ray   812

Block, Franny
Because of Winn-Dixie - Kate DiCamillo   265

Booker T.
The Music in Derrick's Heart - Gwendolyn Battle-Lavert   63

Cousin Ruth
Snowdrops for Cousin Ruth - Susan Katz   498

Dobbs, Phineas
A Big Cheese for the White House: The True Tale of a Tremendous Cheddar - Candace Fleming   320

Dump, Gloria
Because of Winn-Dixie - Kate DiCamillo   265

Farmer Brown
Click, Clack, Moo: Cows That Type - Doreen Cronin   210

Fish Woman
The Gift - Kristine L. Franklin   325

Frimp, DeWitt
Wizzil - William Steig   949

Grandfather
The Magic Paintbrush - Laurence Yep   1078

Grandma
Figuring Out Frances - Gina Willner-Pardo   1052
Mama, Across the Sea - Alex Godard   356

Grandma Chickenlegs
Grandma Chickenlegs - Geraldine McCaughrean   642

Grandmother
My Great-Grandmother's Gourd - Cristina Kessler   514

Grandmother Winter
Grandmother Winter - Phyllis Root   829

Grandpa
Gus and Grandpa and the Two-Wheeled Bike - Claudia Mills   687

Granny
The Tale of Willie Monroe - Alan Schroeder   885

Griselda
The Magic Kerchief - Kirby Larson   557

Gruber, Solly
Dave at Night - Gail Carson Levine   572

Harmony
Emma's Journal: The Story of a Colonial Girl - Marissa Moss   701

Harry
Each One Special - Frieda Wishinsky   1058

Jeremiah
Jeremiah Learns to Read - Jo Ellen Bogart   88

Joe
Where Does Joe Go? - Tracey Campbell Pearson   767

Juliana
Jeremiah Learns to Read - Jo Ellen Bogart   88

Mangus
Midnight Magic - Avi   44

Minshull, Aggie
The Gate in the Wall - Ellen Howard   452

Minty
The Lost Flower Children - Janet Taylor Lisle   588

Miss Bunch
The Lizard Man of Crabtree County - Lucy Nolan   731

Miss Hartwell
The Piano - William Miller   684

Miss Minnie
Jump Rope Magic - Afi Scruggs   895

Miss Perkins
Where Is That Cat? - Carol Greene   372

Miss Slade
Mysterious Miss Slade - Dick King-Smith   524

Miss Viola
Miss Viola and Uncle Ed Lee - Alice Faye Duncan   284

Mother Holly
How the Cat Swallowed Thunder - Lloyd Alexander   18

Mr. Mah
Me and Mr. Mah - Andrea Spalding   937

Mr. Mann
When Night Time Comes Near - Judy Pedersen   768

Mr. O
The Cello of Mr. O. - Jane Cutler   221

Mr. Putter
Mr. Putter and Tabby Paint the Porch - Cynthia Rylant   853

Mrs. Kaplan
My Brother Made Me Do It - Peg Kehret   502

Mrs. Teaberry
Mr. Putter and Tabby Paint the Porch - Cynthia Rylant   853

Nicholas
A Letter to Santa Claus - Brigitte Weninger   1036

Bear Noel
Bear Noel - Olivier Dunrea   286

Big Bear
Good Job, Little Bear - Martin Waddell   1009
Jazzbo and Googy - Matt Novak   737

Blackboard Bear
And My Mean Old Mother Will Be Sorry, Blackboard Bear - Martha Alexander   19

Brown Bear
Stay Awake, Bear! - Gavin Bishop   79

Copycub
Copy Me, Copycub - Richard Edwards   293

Father
Peter's Picture - Valeri Gorbachev   364

Father Bear
Are You There, Baby Bear? - Catherine Walters   1023

Giant Baby Bear
The Very Small - Joyce Dunbar   283

Growl Bear
A Friend for Growl Bear - Sharon A. Riley   820

Henry
Henry Hikes to Fitchburg - D.B. Johnson   478

Honeybear, Lil' Honey
Leola and the Honeybears: An African-American Retelling of Goldilocks and the Three Bears - Melodye Benson Rosales   831

Jack
One Saturday Afternoon - Barbara Baker   49

Jacob
Jacob's Tree - Holly Keller   507

Jazzbo
Jazzbo and Googy - Matt Novak   737

Larry
Ice Cream Larry - Daniel Pinkwater   784

Lewis
Jingle Bells, Homework Smells - Diane DeGroat   250

Little Bear
Big Brown Bear - David McPhail   669
Good Job, Little Bear - Martin Waddell   1009

Mama
Jacob's Tree - Holly Keller   507
What a Scare, Jesse Bear - Nancy White Carlstrom   147

Mama Bear
Goldilocks Returns - Lisa Campbell Ernst   304
Papa's Song - Kate McMullan   666

Mistah Bear
Callie Ann and Mistah Bear - Robert D. San Souci   865

Morgan
Mud Flat Spring - James Stevenson   957

Mother Bear
Are You There, Baby Bear? - Catherine Walters   1023

Mr. Bear
Mr. Bear to the Rescue - Debi Gliori   351
Mr. Bear's New Baby - Debi Gliori   352
Mr. Bear's Vacation - Debi Gliori   353

Mrs. Bear
Mr. Bear to the Rescue - Debi Gliori   351
Mr. Bear's New Baby - Debi Gliori   352
Mr. Bear's Vacation - Debi Gliori   353

Mrs. Polar Bear
Tom Goes to Kindergarten - Margaret Wild   1048

Old Bear
Stay Awake, Bear! - Gavin Bishop   79

Panda
The Secret Friend - Joyce Dunbar   282

Papa
Jacob's Tree - Holly Keller   507
One Saturday Afternoon - Barbara Baker   49
What a Scare, Jesse Bear - Nancy White Carlstrom   147

Papa Bear
Goldilocks Returns - Lisa Campbell Ernst   304
Papa's Song - Kate McMullan   666

Percy
The Practically Perfect Pajamas - Erik Brooks   109

Peter
Peter's Picture - Valeri Gorbachev   364

Polar Bear
Whiteblack the Penguin Sees the World - H.A. Rey   817

Polo
Pete and Polo's Big School Adventure - Adrian Reynolds   818

Rose
One Saturday Afternoon - Barbara Baker   49

Small Bear
Mr. Bear's New Baby - Debi Gliori   352
Mr. Bear's Vacation - Debi Gliori   353

Snow Bear
Snow Bear - Jean Craighead George   343

Unnamed Character
Brave Bear - Kathy Mallat   616
Drawing Lessons from a Bear - David McPhail   670
Henry Hikes to Fitchburg - D.B. Johnson   478
While the Bear Sleeps: Winter Tales and Traditions - Caitlin Matthews   633

BEAVER

Beaver
Franklin's Class Trip - Paulette Bourgeois   95
Moose Tales - Nancy Van Laan   1001

Lewis
Happy Birthday to You, You Belong in a Zoo - Diane DeGroat   249

Max
Froggy's Best Christmas - Jonathan London   594

BENEFACTOR

Unnamed Character
The Full Belly Bowl - Jim Aylesworth   47

BIRD

Andeg
The Birchbark House - Louise Erdrich   303

Attired, Natalie
The Chameleon Wore Chartreuse: From the Tattered Casebook of Chet Gecko, Private Eye - Bruce Hale   393

Aunt Millie
What Is a Wise Bird Like You Doing in a Silly Tale Like This? - Uri Shulevitz   909

Baby Bird
Baby Bird's First Nest - Frank Asch   36

Bai-Ling
Mei-Mei Loves the Morning - Margaret Holloway Tsubakiyama   992

Beatrice
Wizzil - William Steig   949

Bird
Moonbear's Dream - Frank Asch   37

Will You Be My Friend? - Nancy Tafuri   972

Bird, Baby
Oh My Baby, Little One - Kathi Appelt   31

Bird, Mama
Oh My Baby, Little One - Kathi Appelt   31

Crow
Pig and Crow - Kay Chorao   165

Ella
Poppy & Ella: 3 Stories about 2 Friends - Jef Kaminsky   494

Fledgling
Fledgling - Robert J. Blake   81

Goose
Pig and Crow - Kay Chorao   165

Kugelhopf, Dorothea "Dodo"
Lottie's New Friend - Petra Mathers   631

Lou
What Is a Wise Bird Like You Doing in a Silly Tale Like This? - Uri Shulevitz   909

Mama Bird
Baby Bird's First Nest - Frank Asch   36

Mrs. Byrd
Jingle Bells, Homework Smells - Diane DeGroat   250

Poppy
Poppy & Ella: 3 Stories about 2 Friends - Jef Kaminsky   494

Roadrunner
Roadrunner's Dance - Rudolfo Anaya   23

Scratchy
Brian's Bird - Patricia A. Davis   240

Senor Parrot
How Nanita Learned to Make Flan - Campbell Geeslin   342

Stork
The Fox and the Stork - Gerald McDermott   650

Tulip
Toot & Puddle: You Are My Sunshine - Holly Hobbie   437

Unnamed Character
Brave Bear - Kathy Mallat   616
The Ugly Duckling - Jerry Pinkney   783

BLACKSMITH

Mr. Krebs
Hurry! - Emily Arnold McCully   646

BLIND PERSON

Harmon, Ned
Captain's Command - Anna Myers   711

Johnson, Brian
Brian's Bird - Patricia A. Davis   240

Pepper, Patience
The Invisible Princess - Faith Ringgold   822

BOARDER

Bliss, Thankful
Emma's Journal: The Story of a Colonial Girl - Marissa Moss   701

BRIDE

Amy
Beany and the Dreaded Wedding - Susan Wojciechowski   1061

BULLIED CHILD

BULLY

BUSINESSMAN

Character Description Index

CELESTIAL BODY

Moon
Moonball - Jane Yolen 1082

Mr. Moon
Jimmy Zangwow's Out-of-This World Moon Pie Adventure - Tony DiTerlizzi 268

CHICKEN

Baby Rooster
The Bowlegged Rooster and Other Tales That Signify - Joyce Carol Thomas 982

Blanca
Blanca's Feather - Antonio Hernandez Madrigal 608

Hen
The Chick That Wouldn't Hatch - Claire Daniel 232

Hen, Hetty
Eggday - Joyce Dunbar 280

Little Red Hen
The Little Red Hen (Makes a Pizza) - Philemon Sturges 968

Lottie
Lottie's New Friend - Petra Mathers 631

Minerva Louise
Minerva Louise at the Fair - Janet Morgan Stoeke 960

CHILD

Addario, Ben
Creature Crossing - Betty Levin 570

Addie
When Addie Was Scared - Linda Bailey 48

Adelaide
When You Take a Pig to a Party - Kristina Thermaenius McLarey 665

Agapanthus
Agapanthus Hum and the Eyeglasses - Joy Cowley 196

Alex
The Night Worker - Kate Banks 55

Alice
Alice's Adventures in Wonderland - Lewis Carroll 150
The Deep - Tim Winton 1057

Amanda
Taking Charge - Sonia Levitin 574
A Thanksgiving Wish - Michael J. Rosen 834

Amy
Henry and Amy (Right-Way-Round and Upside Down) - Stephen Michael King 522
Yuck, a Love Story - Don Gillmor 349

Annabel
Annabel the Actress Starring in Gorilla My Dreams - Ellen Conford 183

Annalisa
Kiss the Cow! - Phyllis Root 830

Annie
1, 2, 3, Music! - Sylvie Auzary-Luton 41
The Missing Mitten Mystery - Steven Kellogg 510
Paris Cat - Leslie Baker 50

Anthony
And My Mean Old Mother Will Be Sorry, Blackboard Bear - Martha Alexander 19

April
Different Just Like Me - Lori Mitchell 690

Augusta
The Fixits - Anne Mazer 638

Autumn
Wild Child - Lynn Plourde 787

Baby
Blueberry Shoe - Ann Dixon 270

Baring, Foster
Creature Crossing - Betty Levin 570

Beane, Scarlette
Scarlette Beane - Karen Wallace 1018

Beezy
Beezy and Funnybone - Megan McDonald 652

Belinda
Wherever Bears Be: A Story for Two Voices - Sue Ann Alderson 16

Ben
Each One Special - Frieda Wishinsky 1058
Grandma Summer - Harley Jessup 473
It's Funny Where Ben's Train Takes Him - Robert Burleigh 131

Bernard
Bernard's Nap - Joan Elizabeth Goodman 363
The Starry Night - Neil Waldman 1013
The Windy Day - G. Brian Karas 495

Betsy
Happy Birthday, America! - Marsha Wilson Chall 158

Billy
Billy and the Big New School - Laurence Anholt 25

Blue, Hattie Lottie Annie Quinnie
Quinnie Blue - Dinah Johnson 479

Bobo
Hug - Jez Alborough 13

Boxer, Lowell
Annabel the Actress Starring in Gorilla My Dreams - Ellen Conford 183

Boy
Red Berry Wool - Robyn Eversole 307
Sun & Moon: A Giant Love Story - Lisa Desimini 262

Boyd, Billy
Big Mama - Tony Crunk 212

Bradley
Miss Viola and Uncle Ed Lee - Alice Faye Duncan 284

Brian "Captain Pajamas"
Captain Pajamas: Defender of the Universe - Bruce Whatley 1042

Brower, Danny
Moonball - Jane Yolen 1082

Callie Ann
Callie Ann and Mistah Bear - Robert D. San Souci 865

Canty, Tom
The Prince and the Pauper - Marianna Mayer 634

Carmela
Vroomaloom Zoom - John Coy 203

Cecile
Mama, Across the Sea - Alex Godard 356

Celeste
Celeste Sails to Spain - Alison Lester 566

Charlie
Too Big! - Claire Masurel 629

Claire
Next Stop! - Sarah Ellis 300

Clee
The Winter Gift - Deborah Turney Zagwyn 1089

Clive
Celeste Sails to Spain - Alison Lester 566

Collins, Jason
Parachuting Hamsters and Andy Russell - David A. Adler 7

Conner, Pauline
The Man with the Black Glove - Ursel Scheffler 883

Cookie, Clara Ann
Clara Ann Cookie - Harriet Ziefert 1090

Cosmo
Cosmo and the Robot - Brian Pinkney 780

Cowboy Kid
Cowboy Kid - Max Eilenberg 298

Crum, Lucretzia
Bad Habits! - Babette Cole 178

Daisy
Dear Daisy, Get Well Soon - Maggie Smith 930
Eat Your Peas - Kes Gray 370
Missing! - Jonathan Langley 555
The Wedding - Angela Johnson 477

Danny
Dory Story - Jerry Pallotta 758

David
Dreamstones - Maxine Trottier 990
Island Magic - Martha Bennett Stiles 959

Derrick
The Music in Derrick's Heart - Gwendolyn Battle-Lavert 63

Desta
Faraway Home - Jane Kurtz 544

Dolores
Aloha, Dolores - Barbara Samuels 863

Duncan, Donald David "Dink"
The Goose's Gold - Ron Roy 844

Edward
The Prince and the Pauper - Marianna Mayer 634

Elena
The Cello of Mr. O. - Jane Cutler 221

Ella
Summerhouse - Laurence Anholt 28

Ellis, Annie
Last Licks: A Spaldeen Story - Cari Best 75

Elvis Ann
Hogula: Dread Pig of Night - Jean Gralley 369

Emily Louise
Go Away, Shelley Boo! - Phoebe Stone 963

Farnello, Fister "Dirt Boy"
Dirt Boy - Erik Jon Slangerup 926

Fatima
My Great-Grandmother's Gourd - Cristina Kessler 514

Fentriss, Bradley
Diary of a Monster's Son - Ellen Conford 184

Fitzgerald, Virgie
Virgie Goes to School with Us Boys - Elizabeth Fitzgerald Howard 450

Flick
Briar's Book - Tamora Pierce 774

Flo
Ebb and Flo and the New Friend - Jane Simmons 919

Florrie
Tree of Hope - Amy Littlesugar 591

Floyd
One Halloween Night - Mark Teague 979

Frogley, Alison
The Night Iguana Left Home - Megan McDonald 654

CIVIL SERVANT

Jibbert, Fliberty
The Mystery of Mineral Gorge: A Cobtown Story from the Diaries of Lucky Hart - Julia Van Nutt 1005

CLASSMATE

Berck, Maureen
All Alone in the Universe - Lynne Rae Perkins 769

Charisse
The All-New Amelia - Marissa Moss 698

Lewis
Happy Birthday to You, You Belong in a Zoo - Diane DeGroat 249

Smith, Robert "Bob-o"
Regular Guy - Sarah Weeks 1031

Stitch, Wilhelmina
A Valentine for Norman Noggs - Valiska Gregory 378

Wiggert, Dwayne
Me Tarzan - Betsy Byars 134

CLIENT

Skeet
Inspector Hopper - Doug Cushman 218

COACH

Bradley, Don
The Captain Contest - Matt Christopher 166

Jeff
Suitcase - Mildred Pitts Walter 1022

COCKROACH

Crickwing
Crickwing - Janell Cannon 141

Leo
Leo Cockroach. . .Toy Tester - Kevin O'Malley 745

COLLECTOR

Hannah
Hannah's Collections - Marthe Jocelyn 475

COMPUTER EXPERT

DeLucca, Joey
The Landry News - Andrew Clements 172

CONSTRUCTION WORKER

Paul
An Early Winter - Marion Dane Bauer 64

COOK

Abuela
Magda's Tortillas: Las Tortillas de Magda - Becky Chavarria-Chairez 160

Big Brown Rooster
Cook-a-Doodle-Doo! - Janet Stevens 952

Bloom, Rebecca
The Runaway Latkes - Leslie Kimmelman 521

Chef Rhino
Hamburger Heaven - Wong Herbert Yee 1075

Cloud, Raney
Old Thunder and Miss Raney - Sharon Darrow 237

Digger Pig
Digger Pig and the Turnip - Caron Lee Cohen 176

Grandma
Keeping Up with Grandma - John Winch 1056
Matzah Ball Soup - Joan Rothenberg 841
Our Eight Nights of Hanukkah - Michael J. Rosen 833

Hackemup
Brave Potatoes - Toby Speed 939

Little Red Hen
The Little Red Hen (Makes a Pizza) - Philemon Sturges 968

Mama
How Yussel Caught the Gefilte Fish: A Shabbos Story - Charlotte Herman 425

Mama Pearl
Little Cliff and the Porch People - Clifton L. Taulbert 974

Matti
Gingerbread Baby - Jan Brett 104

Mrs. Farmer
Minnie and Moo and the Thanksgiving Tree - Denys Cazet 156

Pig
Pig and Crow - Kay Chorao 165

Rosie
Matzah Ball Soup - Joan Rothenberg 841

Sabu
Yoshi's Feast - Kimiko Kajikawa 492

Snake
Turtle and Snake at Work - Kate Spohn 946

Unnamed Character
The Thanksgiving Beast Feast - Karen Gray Ruelle 846

COUSIN

Alex
Blackwater - Eve Bunting 122

Amy
Beany and the Dreaded Wedding - Susan Wojciechowski 1061

Baptiste
Cajun Through and Through - Tynia Thomassie 985

Betsy
Happy Birthday, America! - Marsha Wilson Chall 158

Elmer
Elmer and the Lost Teddy - David McKee 662

Esther
Hannah's Journal: The Story of an Immigrant Girl - Marissa Moss 702

Fred
No Time for Mother's Day - Laurie Halse Anderson 24

Grisha
The Memory Coat - Elvira Woodruff 1069

Libby
You Forgot Your Skirt, Amelia Bloomer! - Shana Corey 189

Lily
Some Good News - Cynthia Rylant 856

Mercedes
Annie Pitts, Burger Kid - Diane DeGroat 248

Mikki Jo
Blackberry Booties - Tricia Gardella 335

Puddin
Squiggle's Tale - Andre Dahan 228

Rachel
The Memory Coat - Elvira Woodruff 1069

Rosie
Some Good News - Cynthia Rylant 856

Samuel
Blackberry Booties - Tricia Gardella 335

Sharp, Olivia
Nate the Great: San Francisco Detective - Marjorie Weinman Sharmat 905

Sherwin-Hendricks, Beatrice Lorraine "Beany"
Beany and the Dreaded Wedding - Susan Wojciechowski 1061

Snook
Squiggle's Tale - Andre Dahan 228

Tess
Some Good News - Cynthia Rylant 856

Ti-Boy
Cajun Through and Through - Tynia Thomassie 985

Toups, Remington Terrebonne
Cajun Through and Through - Tynia Thomassie 985

Unnamed Character
The Party - Barbara Reid 816
The Party - Barbara Reid 816

Wilbur
Elmer and the Lost Teddy - David McKee 662

Willow
Seesaw Girl - Linda Sue Park 762

COW

Gertrude
The Pig Who Ran a Red Light - Paul Brett Johnson 486

Luella
Kiss the Cow! - Phyllis Root 830

Minnie
Minnie and Moo and the Musk of Zorro - Denys Cazet 155
Minnie and Moo and the Thanksgiving Tree - Denys Cazet 156

Moo
Minnie and Moo and the Musk of Zorro - Denys Cazet 155
Minnie and Moo and the Thanksgiving Tree - Denys Cazet 156

COWBOY

Clement
Comes a Wind - Linda Arms White 1043

Clyde
Comes a Wind - Linda Arms White 1043

Dad
Tall in the Saddle - Anne Carter 152

Prince, Joe
Cindy Ellen: A Wild Western Cinderella - Susan Lowell 600

Sam
Sam's Wild West Christmas - Nancy Antle 29

Unnamed Character
Cowboy Dreams - Kathi Appelt 30

COWGIRL

Cindy Ellen
Cindy Ellen: A Wild Western Cinderella - Susan Lowell 600

DAYDREAMER

DEAF PERSON

DEITY

DETECTIVE—AMATEUR

DETECTIVE—PRIVATE

DIETY

DINOSAUR

FATHER

FROG

FRONTIERSMAN

GARDENER

GENTLEMAN

Grandma
A Picnic in October - Eve Bunting   127

Grandpa Sam
Grandpa's Gamble - Richard Michelson   681

Hannah
Hannah's Journal: The Story of an Immigrant Girl -
Marissa Moss   702

Jakob
Mirette & Bellini Cross Niagara Falls - Emily Arnold
McCully   647

Mama
Shy Mama's Halloween - Anne Broyles   115
When This World Was New - D.H. Figueredo   313

Mendelsohn, Yossi
Jesse's Star - Ellen Schwartz   890

Moore, Annie
Dreaming of America: An Ellis Island Story - Eve
Bunting   125

Moore, Anthony
Dreaming of America: An Ellis Island Story - Eve
Bunting   125

Moore, Phillip
Dreaming of America: An Ellis Island Story - Eve
Bunting   125

Papa
When This World Was New - D.H. Figueredo   313

Precious Stone
The Journal of Wong Ming-Chung: A Chinese Miner -
Laurence Yep   1077

Sameera
Dear Whiskers - Ann Whitehead Nagda   717

Samuel
Hannah's Journal: The Story of an Immigrant Girl -
Marissa Moss   702

Unnamed Character
The Little Match Girl - Jerry Pinkney   782

Yang, Yingmei "Mary"
Yang the Eldest and His Odd Jobs - Lensey
Namioka   718

Yang, Yingwu "Eldest Brother"
Yang the Eldest and His Odd Jobs - Lensey
Namioka   718

IMMORTAL

Unnamed Character
Wind Child - Shirley Rousseau Murphy   709

INDIAN

Abeyta, Armando
Enchanted Runner - Kimberley Griffiths Little   590

Curly
Crazy Horse's Vision - Joseph Bruchac   116

Drums-Louder
White Wolf - Henrietta Branford   100

Iktomi
Iktomi Loses His Eyes: A Plains Indian Story - Paul
Goble   355

Itilakna
*Longwalker's Journey: A Novel of the Choctaw Trail
of Tears* - Beatrice Orcutt Harrell   402

Jillian
Ribbon Rescue - Robert Munsch   707

Little Rose, Nannie
*My Heart Is on the Ground: The Diary of Nannie
Little Rose, a Sioux Girl* - Ann Rinaldi   821

Minko Ushi
*Longwalker's Journey: A Novel of the Choctaw Trail
of Tears* - Beatrice Orcutt Harrell   402

Old Tallow
The Birchbark House - Louise Erdrich   303

Omakayas
The Birchbark House - Louise Erdrich   303

Ramirez, Trina
Enchanted Runner - Kimberley Griffiths Little   590

Squanto
*Squanto's Journey: The Story of the First
Thanksgiving* - Joseph Bruchac   117

Sweetwater, Leaf
Cherokee Sister - Debbie Dadey   226

Tashunka Witco
Crazy Horse's Vision - Joseph Bruchac   116

Unnamed Character
The Lost Boy and the Monster - Craig Kee
Strete   967

INSECT

Ann
What Day Is It? - Patti Trimble   988

Betty
Little Miss Spider - David Kirk   529

Flea, Ed
Ed & Fred Flea - Pamela Duncan Edwards   292

Flea, Fred
Ed & Fred Flea - Pamela Duncan Edwards   292

Gil
What Day Is It? - Patti Trimble   988

Inspector Hopper
Inspector Hopper - Doug Cushman   218

McBugg
Inspector Hopper - Doug Cushman   218

Todd
What Day Is It? - Patti Trimble   988

Unnamed Character
The Ant and the Grasshopper - Amy Lowry
Poole   790
The Big Bug Ball - Dee Lillegard   581
Gotta Go! Gotta Go! - Sam Swope   970
The Very Clumsy Click Beetle - Eric Carle   144

INVALID

Howard, Stirling
Meet Kit: An American Girl - Valerie Tripp   989

INVENTOR

McNasty, Stinky
Ricky Ricotta's Giant Robot: An Adventure Novel -
Dav Pilkey   778

Muffin, Charlie
Charlie Muffin's Miracle Mouse - Dick King-
Smith   523

Wesley
Weslandia - Paul Fleischman   318

JOCKEY

Dad
One Lucky Girl - George Ella Lyon   607

JOURNALIST

Dad
Amelia's Family Ties - Marissa Moss   700

Miss Dobson
A Letter to Mrs. Roosevelt - C. Coco De Young   244

Pete
The Great Railroad Race: The Diary of Libby West -
Kristiana Gregory   377

JUDGE

Cheung, Carolyn
An American Face - Jan M. Czech   225

KANGAROO

Blue Kangaroo
I Love You, Blue Kangaroo! - Emma Chichester
Clark   161

Unnamed Character
The Very Boastful Kangaroo - Bernard Most   704
The Very Boastful Kangaroo - Bernard Most   704

KIDNAPPER

Rangsasa
The Dancing Pig - Judy Sierra   912

KINDERGARTNER

Amanda
We Share Everything! - Robert Munsch   708

Beatson, Vicki
There's a Dead Person Following My Sister Around -
Vivian Vande Velde   1006

Evan
*If You Ever Get Lost: The Adventures of Julia and
Evan* - Barbara Ann Porte   791

Jeremiah
We Share Everything! - Robert Munsch   708

Jessie
An American Face - Jan M. Czech   225

Tom
Tom Goes to Kindergarten - Margaret Wild   1048

Van Klinkenstopper, Lottie
Lottie's Princess Dress - Doris Dorrie   272

KNIGHT

Good Knight
Good Night, Good Knight - Shelley Moore
Thomas   983

Keladry of Mindelan "Kel"
First Test - Tamora Pierce   775

Lord Wyldon
First Test - Tamora Pierce   775

Nealan of Queenscove "Neal"
First Test - Tamora Pierce   775

KOALA BEAR

Angela
Emily's First 100 Days of School - Rosemary
Wells   1033

Character Description Index

Old Foot Eater
The Lost Boy and the Monster - Craig Kee Strete 967

Ooboo
Shadow Story - Nancy Willard 1049

Von Sweeney, Lance
The Magic Pretzel - Daniel Pinkwater 785

MOOSE

Moose
Moose Tales - Nancy Van Laan 1001
Mooseltoe - Margie Palatini 757

Moose, Elliott
Elliot Bakes a Cake - Andrea Beck 69

MOSQUITO

Skeet
Inspector Hopper - Doug Cushman 218

MOTHER

Anna
The Crystal Mountain - Ruth Sanderson 870

Bear, Mother
Sleepy Bears - Mem Fox 324

Betsy
My Goose Betsy - Trudi Braun 101

Bird, Mama
Oh My Baby, Little One - Kathi Appelt 31

Bunch, Henrietta
Plenty of Pockets - Ann Braybrooks 102

Bunny, Mother
Bunny Bungalow - Cynthia Rylant 849

Carlotta
Carlotta's Kittens and the Club of Mysteries - Phyllis Reynolds Naylor 720

Cindy
Rover - Michael Rosen 832

Daisy
Daisy Knows Best - Lisa Kopper 537

Dame Van Winkle
Rip Van Winkle - Washington Irving 467

Fayga
Gershon's Monster - Eric A. Kimmel 518

Hen
The Chick That Wouldn't Hatch - Claire Daniel 232

Huckabuck, Mama Mama
The Huckabuck Family and How They Raised Popcorn in Nebraska and Quit and Came Back - Carl Sandburg 869

Loretta
Apple Batter - Deborah Turney Zagwyn 1088

Love, Mama
The Invisible Princess - Faith Ringgold 822

Ma
Tadpoles - Betsy James 471

Madam Thunderbolt
Max - Bob Graham 368

Mama
Aunt CeeCee, Aunt Belle, and Mama's Surprise - Mary Quattlebaum 806
Bravo, Maurice! - Rebecca Bond 89
The Christmas Gift/El Regalo de Navidad - Francisco Jimenez 474
Comes a Wind - Linda Arms White 1043
Daisy and the Egg - Jane Simmons 918
Erandi's Braids - Antonio Hernandez Madrigal 609

The Honest-to-Goodness Truth - Patricia C. McKissack 663
How Yussel Caught the Gefilte Fish: A Shabbos Story - Charlotte Herman 425
I Have an Olive Tree - Eve Bunting 126
It's Time for School, Stinky Face - Lisa McCourt 645
Jacob's Tree - Holly Keller 507
The Loudest, Fastest, Best Drummer in Kansas - Marguerite W. Davol 241
Mama - Eleanor Schick 884
Mama, Across the Sea - Alex Godard 356
Mama and Me and the Model T - Faye Gibbons 347
Manuela's Gift - Kristyn Rehling Estes 305
The Promise Quilt - Candice F. Ransom 809
The Rainbow Tulip - Pat Mora 696
Shadow Story - Nancy Willard 1049
Shy Mama's Halloween - Anne Broyles 115
Taking Charge - Sonia Levitin 574
Three Cheers for Catherine the Great! - Cari Best 77
Tiny's Hat - Ann Grifalconi 380
Tree of Hope - Amy Littlesugar 591
What a Scare, Jesse Bear - Nancy White Carlstrom 147
When This World Was New - D.H. Figueredo 313
When Uncle Took the Fiddle - Libba Moore Gray 371
Who Do You Love? - Martin Waddell 1011
Wilhe'mina Miles After the Stork Night - Dorothy Carter 153

Mama Bear
Goldilocks Returns - Lisa Campbell Ernst 304
Papa's Song - Kate McMullan 666

Mama Bird
Baby Bird's First Nest - Frank Asch 36

Mama Hen
The Bowlegged Rooster and Other Tales That Signify - Joyce Carol Thomas 982

Mama May
Kiss the Cow! - Phyllis Root 830

Mama Wolf
Big Wolf and Little Wolf - Sharon Phillips Denslow 259

Maman
The Good Liar - Gregory Maguire 612
Good Night, Maman - Norma Fox Mazer 639

Mami
In the Shade of the Nispero Tree - Carmen T. Bernier-Grand 73

Mamma
Calling Me Home - Patricia Hermes 427
Come On, Rain! - Karen Hesse 428

Miz Violet
The Legend of Freedom Hill - Linda Jacobs Altman 22

Mom
100th Day Worries - Margery Cuyler 222
Ballerinas Don't Wear Glasses - Ainslie Manson 618
The Boy on the Beach - Niki Daly 230
Brave Highland Heart - Heather Kellerhals-Stewart 509
Bus Route to Boston - Maryann Cocca-Leffler 174
The Canning Season - Margaret Carlson 145
Darby: The Special Order Pup - Alexandra Day 243
Different Just Like Me - Lori Mitchell 690
Dirt Boy - Erik Jon Slangerup 926
A Dog Like Jack - DyAnne DiSalvo-Ryan 266
Eat Your Peas - Kes Gray 370
Halmoni's Day - Edna Coe Bercaw 72
I Am Me - Karla Kuskin 546
I Want a Pet - Lauren Child 163
Island Magic - Martha Bennett Stiles 959

Look Out Kindergarten, Here I Come! - Nancy Carlson 146
Lottie's Princess Dress - Doris Dorrie 272
Monk Camps Out - Emily Arnold McCully 648
Moo in the Morning - Barbara Maitland 615
My Big Lie - Bill Cosby 190
My Mother Talks to Trees - Doris Gove 366
My Mother's Pearls - Catherine Myler Fruisen 332
Next Stop! - Sarah Ellis 300
No Time for Mother's Day - Laurie Halse Anderson 24
Old Dog Cora and the Christmas Tree - Consie Powell 794
One Dark and Scary Night - Bill Cosby 191
Queen of the World - Thomas F. Yezerski 1079
Space Guys! - Martha Weston 1041
The Storm - Kathy Henderson 419
The Trouble with Cats - Martha Freeman 328

Momma
In My Momma's Kitchen - Jerdine Nolen 733
Momma, Where Are You From? - Marie Bradby 97
Silver Rain Brown - M.C. Helldorfer 414

Mommy
Agapanthus Hum and the Eyeglasses - Joy Cowley 196
Buzz - Janet S. Wong 1063
Daisy Knows Best - Lisa Kopper 537
Hello Baby! - Lizzy Rockwell 825
Hug - Jez Alborough 13
Hurricane! - Corinne Demas 255
I Hate to Go to Bed! - Katie Davis 239
I Need a Snake - Lynne Jonell 488
Some Babies - Amy Schwartz 889
The Ugly Vegetables - Grace Lin 582

Mother
Clara Ann Cookie - Harriet Ziefert 1090
D.W., Go to Your Room! - Marc Brown 112
Happy Birthday to You, You Belong in a Zoo - Diane DeGroat 249
Jack and the Beanstalk - Ann Keay Beneduce 70
Just Like a Baby - Rebecca Bond 90
Kate and the Beanstalk - Mary Pope Osborne 750
Mary and the Mystery Dog - Wolfram Hanel 399
Special Delivery - Brigitte Weninger 1037
Stella & Roy Go Camping - Ashley Wolff 1062
The Tale I Told Sasha - Nancy Willard 1050
The Trip Back Home - Janet S. Wong 1065
Vera Runs Away - Vera Rosenberry 836

Mother Bear
Are You There, Baby Bear? - Catherine Walters 1023

Mother Monster
What If? - Frances Thomas 981

Mrs. Beane
Scarlette Beane - Karen Wallace 1018

Mrs. Bear
Mr. Bear's New Baby - Debi Gliori 352
Mr. Bear's Vacation - Debi Gliori 353

Mrs. Bellyflop
A Day with the Bellyflops - Francine Bassede 60

Mrs. Crum
Bad Habits! - Babette Cole 178

Mrs. Fox
Moon Sandwich Mom - Jennifer Richard Jacobson 469

Mrs. Goodparents
The Gift - Gabriela Keselman 513

Mrs. Hatford
A Traitor Among the Boys - Phyllis Reynolds Naylor 723

Mrs. Rabbit
One, Two, Three, Oops! - Michael Coleman 180

O'Saurus, Mom
Trouble on Thunder Mountain - Russell Hoban 436

Peregrine, Octavia
When Agnes Caws - Candace Fleming 321

Pigza, Fran
Joey Pigza Loses Control - Jack Gantos 334

Robobot, M.O.M.
The Robobots - Matt Novak 738

Rosie
Big Rain Coming - Katrina Germein 345

Roxanne
How Will We Get to the Beach? - Brigitte Luciani 602

Solliliage, Marcel "Maman"
The Butterfly - Patricia Polacco 788

Spencer, Allie
My Mom Is My Show-and-Tell - Dolores Johnson 481

Tabby, Jane
Jane on Her Own: A Catwings Tale - Ursula K. Le Guin 563

Toad, Gerdy
Jubal's Wish - Audrey Wood 1066

Unnamed Character
All by Myself! - Aliki 20
All by Myself - Ivan Bates 62
Bark, George - Jules Feiffer 311
Crab Moon - Ruth Horowitz 447
A Difficult Day - Eugenie Fernandes 312
Harriet, You'll Drive Me Wild! - Mem Fox 323
Harry's Home - Laurence Anholt 26
Olivia - Ian Falconer 308
Shoe Town - Janet Stevens 953
The Thanksgiving Beast Feast - Karen Gray Ruelle 846

Van Sorg, Elsbeth
When the Soldiers Were Gone - Vera W. Propp 801

Wilson, Winona
The Elevator Family - Douglas Evans 306

Yeyo
My Rows and Piles of Coins - Tololwa M. Mollel 693

MOUNTAIN WOMAN

Delilah
The Tale of Willie Monroe - Alan Schroeder 885

MOUSE

Big Mouse
The Very Noisy Night - Diana Hendry 420

Blue Mouse
Tiny Rabbit Goes to a Birthday Party - John Wallace 1016

Chamomile
Princess Chamomile Gets Her Way - Hiawyn Oram 748

Clutch
Ragweed - Avi 45

Dad
Monk Camps Out - Emily Arnold McCully 648
Mouse Practice - Emily Arnold McCully 649

Dolores
Horace and Morris but Mostly Dolores - James Howe 454

Emmaline
The Mouse of Amherst - Elizabeth Spires 945

Field Mouse
The Field Mouse and the Dinosaur Named Sue - Jan Wahl 1012
Friend Frog - Alma Flor Ada 1

Hank
A Beasty Story - Bill Martin Jr. 625

Henry
Look Out Kindergarten, Here I Come! - Nancy Carlson 146

Horace
Horace and Morris but Mostly Dolores - James Howe 454

Jewel
Wemberly Worried - Kevin Henkes 423

Kit
Mouse Magic - Ellen Stoll Walsh 1021

Little Mouse
Off We Go! - Jane Yolen 1084
The Very Noisy Night - Diana Hendry 420

Mom
Look Out Kindergarten, Here I Come! - Nancy Carlson 146
Monk Camps Out - Emily Arnold McCully 648
Mouse Practice - Emily Arnold McCully 649

Monk
Monk Camps Out - Emily Arnold McCully 648
Mouse Practice - Emily Arnold McCully 649

Morris
Horace and Morris but Mostly Dolores - James Howe 454

Mouse
Cat and Mouse in the Snow - Tomek Bogacki 86

Mouse, Livingstone
Bravo, Livingstone Mouse! - Pamela Duncan Edwards 291

Muffin, Adam
Charlie Muffin's Miracle Mouse - Dick King-Smith 523

Muggs, Abbott
The Mystery of the Monkey's Maze - Doug Cushman 219

Nanny Nettle
Princess Chamomile Gets Her Way - Hiawyn Oram 748

Nick
A Beasty Story - Bill Martin Jr. 625

Pip Squeak
Drip, Drop - Sarah Weeks 1029

Poppy
Ereth's Birthday - Avi 43

Ragweed
Ragweed - Avi 45

Ricotta, Ricky
Ricky Ricotta's Giant Robot: An Adventure Novel - Dav Pilkey 778

Silly
A Beasty Story - Bill Martin Jr. 625

Truffle
Truffle's Christmas - Anna Currey 216

Unnamed Character
The Beautiful Butterfly: A Folktale from Spain - Judy Sierra 911
If You Take a Mouse to the Movies - Laura Joffe Numeroff 739
Mouse at Night - Nancy Christensen Hall 394
Mouse in Love - Robert Kraus 541
The Mouse That Snored - Bernard Waber 1008
Shoe Town - Janet Stevens 953

Watson
Mud Flat Spring - James Stevenson 957

Wemberly
Wemberly Worried - Kevin Henkes 423

MULE

Jake Johnson
Jake Johnson: The Story of a Mule - Tres Seymour 899

MUSICIAN

Annie
1, 2, 3, Music! - Sylvie Auzary-Luton 41

Bach, Johann Sebastian
Bach's Big Adventure - Sallie Ketcham 515

Booker T.
The Music in Derrick's Heart - Gwendolyn Battle-Lavert 63

Brown, Flats
The Blues of Flats Brown - Walter Dean Myers 716

Calloway, Herman E.
Bud, Not Buddy - Christopher Paul Curtis 217

Clutch
Ragweed - Avi 45

Dad
Mouse Practice - Emily Arnold McCully 649

Daddy
Tiny's Hat - Ann Grifalconi 380

Fiddlin' Sam
Fiddlin' Sam - Marianna Dengler 258

Grandpa
1, 2, 3, Music! - Sylvie Auzary-Luton 41

Leo
The Saturday Kid - Edward Sorel 935

Maggie
The Loudest, Fastest, Best Drummer in Kansas - Marguerite W. Davol 241

Mama
When Uncle Took the Fiddle - Libba Moore Gray 371

McPhee, Willie
Cold Feet - Cynthia DeFelice 246

Mole
Mole Music - David McPhail 671

Mom
Mouse Practice - Emily Arnold McCully 649

Mr. Kleinberg
The Saturday Kid - Edward Sorel 935

Mr. O
The Cello of Mr. O. - Jane Cutler 221

Pa
My Brother's Keeper: Virginia's Diary - Mary Pope Osborne 751

Perrin
The Crystal Mountain - Ruth Sanderson 870

Pig, Gilbert Alexander
The Tale of Gilbert Alexander Pig - Gael Cresp 207

Professor
The Collector of Moments - Quint Buchholz 119

Reincken, Jan Adam
Bach's Big Adventure - Sallie Ketcham 515

Uncle
When Uncle Took the Fiddle - Libba Moore Gray 371

Jeff
Fossil Fever - Kathleen Weidner Zoehfeld   1098

John
Rabbit Food - Susanna Gretz   379

Little Wolf
Little Wolf's Book of Badness - Ian Whybrow   1045

Reed, Luke
Luke: 1849-On the Golden Trail - Bonnie Pryor   802

Rudy
Three Magic Balls - Richard Egielski   294

Sam
The Loudness of Sam - James Proimos   800
Weird Stories from the Lonesome Cafe - Judy Cox   201

NIECE

Anderson, Tamika
Parachuting Hamsters and Andy Russell - David A. Adler   7

Harriet
Batty Hattie - Virginia Nielsen   727

Kringle, Sophie
Auntie Claus - Elise Primavera   799

Lauren
A Name on the Quilt: A Story of Remembrance - Jeannine Atkins   38

Martin, Ellie
Not My Dog - Colby Rodowsky   826

Nelly
Aunt Pitty Patty's Piggy - Jim Aylesworth   46

Osgood, Edwina "Eddy"
Edwina Victorious - Susan Bonners   91

Owen, Lucy
Hog Music - M.C. Helldorfer   411

Sally
Tomatoes from Mars - Arthur Yorinks   1087

Tess
Some Good News - Cynthia Rylant   856

Unnamed Character
Aunt CeeCee, Aunt Belle, and Mama's Surprise - Mary Quattlebaum   806
How to Catch an Elephant - Amy Schwartz   888
The Trip Back Home - Janet S. Wong   1065

NOBLEMAN

Hendon, Miles
The Prince and the Pauper - Marianna Mayer   634

Lord Wyldon
First Test - Tamora Pierce   775

Merton, Edward
The Folk Keeper - Franny Billingsley   78

Pang
The Greatest Treasure - Demi   256

Tiger Heart
Seesaw Girl - Linda Sue Park   762

NOBLEWOMAN

Jade
Seesaw Girl - Linda Sue Park   762

Willow
Seesaw Girl - Linda Sue Park   762

OPOSSUM

Gilbert
Jingle Bells, Homework Smells - Diane DeGroat   250

Mother
Happy Birthday to You, You Belong in a Zoo - Diane DeGroat   249

Possum
Don't Need Friends - Carolyn Crimi   208

Possum, Gilbert
Happy Birthday to You, You Belong in a Zoo - Diane DeGroat   249

ORPHAN

Barrow, Frances "Frankie"
Nowhere to Call Home - Cynthia DeFelice   247

Bee
True Heart - Marissa Moss   703

Bekins, Jenny
Ghosts in the Gallery - Barbara Brooks Wallace   1014

Boyd, Billy
Big Mama - Tony Crunk   212

Caldwell, Bud
Bud, Not Buddy - Christopher Paul Curtis   217

Caros, Dave
Dave at Night - Gail Carson Levine   572

Da Wei
Da Wei's Treasure: A Chinese Tale - Margaret Chang   159

Davies
The Copper Treasure - Melvin Burgess   130

Deane, Emma
The Gate in the Wall - Ellen Howard   452

Gibson, Harriet "Harry"
Unbroken - Jessie Haas   391

Jakob
Mirette & Bellini Cross Niagara Falls - Emily Arnold McCully   647

Mbi
The Magic Tree: A Folktale from Nigeria - T. Obinkaram Echewa   288

Mugg, Terence
Which Witch? - Eva Ibbotson   464

Phoebe
Phoebe and the River Flute - M.C. Helldorfer   413

Rizka
Gypsy Rizka - Lloyd Alexander   17

Samuel
Hannah's Journal: The Story of an Immigrant Girl - Marissa Moss   702

Steve
The Magic Paintbrush - Laurence Yep   1078

Stonewall, Corinna "Corin"
The Folk Keeper - Franny Billingsley   78

Ten Tons
The Copper Treasure - Melvin Burgess   130

Unnamed Character
The Ugly Duckling - Jerry Pinkney   783

Zoe
Nobody Rides the Unicorn - Adrian Mitchell   689

OUTCAST

Albert
Albert & Lila - Rafik Schami   882

Armadillo
Armadillo Tattletale - Helen Ketteman   516

Jackson, Ikarus
Wings - Christopher Myers   713

Lila
Albert & Lila - Rafik Schami   882

Unnamed Character
Wings - Christopher Myers   713

OUTLAW

Skald, Ubo
Night of the Goat Children - J. Patrick Lewis   577

OWL

Grandma Owl
Down in the Woods at Sleepytime - Carole Lexa Schaefer   879

Old Owl
A Friend for Growl Bear - Sharon A. Riley   820

Owl
Little Bunny's Sleepless Night - Carol Roth   840

PANDA

Baby
Tom Goes to Kindergarten - Margaret Wild   1048

Tom
Tom Goes to Kindergarten - Margaret Wild   1048

PAPERBOY

Jacob
The Babe & I - David A. Adler   5

Unnamed Character
The Babe & I - David A. Adler   5

PARENT

Large
No Matter What - Debi Gliori   354

PARROT

Scarface
Alien Brain Fryout - Barbara M. Joosse   491

Will
The Mouse That Snored - Bernard Waber   1008

PATRIOT

Father
Redcoats and Petticoats - Katherine Kirkpatrick   530

Millar, Emma
Emma's Journal: The Story of a Colonial Girl - Marissa Moss   701

Mother
Redcoats and Petticoats - Katherine Kirkpatrick   530

Strong, Thomas
Redcoats and Petticoats - Katherine Kirkpatrick   530

PEDDLER

Shimon "Shnook"
The Peddler's Gift - Maxine Rose Schur   887

PENGUIN

Chongo Chingi
Penguin Dreams - J. Otto Seibold   897

Gertie
Gus & Gertie and the Missing Pearl - Joan Lowery Nixon   730

Character Description Index

PHOTOGRAPHER

PIG

PILOT

PIONEER

PIRATE

PITCHER

PLANT

PLANTATION OWNER

POLICE OFFICER

POLITICAL FIGURE

PONY

PORCUPINE

POSTAL WORKER

Character Description Index

Dr. Shtickle
Tomatoes from Mars - Arthur Yorinks   1087

Emma
The Boy Trap - Nancy Matson   632

Henry, Mike
Batty Hattie - Virginia Nielsen   727

McNasty, Stinky
Ricky Ricotta's Giant Robot: An Adventure Novel -
   Dav Pilkey   778

Mr. Crum
Bad Habits! - Babette Cole   178

Papa
Maria's Comet - Deborah Hopkinson   446

Peregrine, Octavia
When Agnes Caws - Candace Fleming   321

Poopypants, Pippy P.
*Captain Underpants and the Perilous Plot of Professor
   Poopypants* - Dav Pilkey   777

Roy
Fossil Fever - Kathleen Weidner Zoehfeld   1098

Santos, Joseph
Swimming with Sharks - Twig C. George   344

Spinifex
The Last Alchemist - Colin Thompson   986

Tann, Irene A.
The Mystery of the Monkey's Maze - Doug
   Cushman   219

SEA CAPTAIN

Captain Bates
Abigail Takes the Wheel - Avi   42

Captain LeNoir
Ghost of the Southern Belle: A Sea Tale - Odds
   Bodkin   85

Cur
The Pirate's Parrot - Lyn Rossiter McFarland   656

Father
Ghost of the Southern Belle: A Sea Tale - Odds
   Bodkin   85

Lizard, Dalbert
Jubal's Wish - Audrey Wood   1066

Morehouse, David Reed
The Mary Celeste: An Unsolved Mystery from History
   - Jane Yolen   1081

Papa
*Good-bye for Today: The Diary of a Young Girl at
   Sea* - Peter Roop   828

Unnamed Character
Dreamstones - Maxine Trottier   990

SEAL

Seal
Whiteblack the Penguin Sees the World - H.A.
   Rey   817

Selkie
Selkie - Gillian McClure   643

SEAMSTRESS

Lian Di
Da Wei's Treasure: A Chinese Tale - Margaret
   Chang   159

Mami
In the Shade of the Nispero Tree - Carmen T. Bernier-
   Grand   73

Unnamed Character
A Letter to Santa Claus - Brigitte Weninger   1036

The Quiltmaker's Gift - Jeff Brumbeau   118

SECRETARY

Bruce
What a Truly Cool World - Julius Lester   569

SERVANT

Chulak
The Firework-Maker's Daughter - Philip
   Pullman   803

Cinderella
Cinderella: The Dog and Her Little Glass Slipper -
   Diane Goode   362

Damura
The Gift of the Crocodile: A Cinderella Story - Judy
   Sierra   913

Fabrizio
Midnight Magic - Avi   44

Jaylee
The Prog Frince: A Mixed-Up Tale - C. Drew
   Lamm   552

Jingle
Ghosts in the Gallery - Barbara Brooks
   Wallace   1014

Johnny
The Piano - William Miller   684

Lottie
The Lottie Project - Jacqueline Wilson   1055

Nelly
The Lion and the Unicorn - Shirley Hughes   458

Raisel
Raisel's Riddle - Erica Silverman   916

Walsh, Molly
Molly Bannaky - Alice McGill   658

SETTLER

Father
The Prairie Fire - Marilynn Reynolds   819

Lapp, Elisabeth
Pioneer Church - Carolyn Otto   752

Lapp, Zachary
Pioneer Church - Carolyn Otto   752

Mamma
Calling Me Home - Patricia Hermes   427

Papa
Calling Me Home - Patricia Hermes   427
Kindle Me a Riddle: A Pioneer Story - Roberta
   Karim   496

Percy
The Prairie Fire - Marilynn Reynolds   819

Unnamed Character
Grandfather's Christmas Tree - Keith Strand   964
Grandfather's Christmas Tree - Keith Strand   964

SHAPE-CHANGER

Selkie
Selkie - Gillian McClure   643

Trickster
Trickster and the Fainting Birds - Howard
   Norman   735

SHEEP

Baa
Boo and Baa Get Wet - Olof Landstrom   554

Blanche
The Friendship Tree - Kathy Caple   142

Boo
Boo and Baa Get Wet - Olof Landstrom   554

Lalo
Red Berry Wool - Robyn Eversole   307

Mouton
Mouton's Impossible Dream - Anik McGrory   659

Otis
The Friendship Tree - Kathy Caple   142

SHEPHERD

Bondone, Giotto
A Boy Named Giotto - Paolo Guarnieri   386

Boy
Red Berry Wool - Robyn Eversole   307

Sparrow, Tom
Spider Sparrow - Dick King-Smith   525

Tomas
Little Gold Star: A Spanish American Cinderella Tale
   - Robert D. San Souci   867

SIDEKICK

McBugg
Inspector Hopper - Doug Cushman   218

Muggs, Abbott
The Mystery of the Monkey's Maze - Doug
   Cushman   219

SINGER

Ribert, Mike
Speechless in New York - Ellen Dreyer   277

Roberts, Kendra
Speechless in New York - Ellen Dreyer   277

Sheppard, Ella
*A Band of Angels: A Story Inspired by the Jubilee
   Singers* - Deborah Hopkinson   445

Witt, Jessie
Speechless in New York - Ellen Dreyer   277

SINGLE FATHER

Dad
Jumping into Nothing - Gina Willner-Pardo   1053

Jake
Soldier Mom - Alice Mead   672

Unnamed Character
The Father Who Had 10 Children - Benedicte
   Guettier   388
What Dads Can't Do - Douglas Wood   1067

SINGLE MOTHER

Enright, Jo
The Lottie Project - Jacqueline Wilson   1055

Ginny
Ola's Wake - B.J. Stone   962

Mom
A New Room for William - Sally Grindley   383
Sky Memories - Pat Brisson   107

Mommy
Accidental Lily - Sally Warner   1025

Mother
White Tiger, Blue Serpent - Grace Tseng   991

Stone, Rita "Mum"
Alice-by-Accident - Lynne Reid Banks   56

SKATER

SLAVE

Mrs. Steele
Dear Whiskers - Ann Whitehead Nagda 717

Mrs. Trumble
Jeremiah Learns to Read - Jo Ellen Bogart 88

Ms. Bell
First Day, Hooray! - Nancy Poydar 795

Ms. Bradley
Look Out Kindergarten, Here I Come! - Nancy
  Carlson 146

Ms. Splinter
Emeline at the Circus - Marjorie Priceman 797

Poopypants, Pippy P.
*Captain Underpants and the Perilous Plot of Professor
  Poopypants* - Dav Pilkey 777

Sparling
Seal Island School - Susan Bartlett 59

Spencer, Allie
My Mom Is My Show-and-Tell - Dolores
  Johnson 481

Sutterfield, Agnes
The Year of Miss Agnes - Kirkpatrick Hill 434

Unnamed Character
David Goes to School - David Shannon 901
My Duck - Tanya Linch 583
We Share Everything! - Robert Munsch 708

White, George
*A Band of Angels: A Story Inspired by the Jubilee
  Singers* - Deborah Hopkinson 445

TEENAGER

Blessing
The Journal of Wong Ming-Chung: A Chinese Miner -
  Laurence Yep 1077

Burgess, Abbie
*Abbie Against the Storm: The True Story of a Young
  Heroine and a Lighthouse* - Marcia Vaughan 1007

Chase
Shadow Horse - Alison Hart 406

Dickens, Jedidiah "Jed"
My Brother's Keeper: Virginia's Diary - Mary Pope
  Osborne 751

Irwin, Bill
Radio Rescue - Lynne Barasch 58

Marcie
Clarice Bean, That's Me - Lauren Child 162

Mercedes
Annie Pitts, Burger Kid - Diane DeGroat 248

Perley, Rebecca
Hannah's Helping Hands - Jean Van Leeuwen 1003

Ribert, Mike
Speechless in New York - Ellen Dreyer 277

Roberts, Kendra
Speechless in New York - Ellen Dreyer 277

Walsh, Molly
Molly Bannaky - Alice McGill 658

Witt, Jessie
Speechless in New York - Ellen Dreyer 277

THIEF

Pittsnap, Edwin
When Agnes Caws - Candace Fleming 321

Tomten
Hedgie's Surprise - Jan Brett 105

TIGER

George
Brave Horace - Holly Keller 505

Marvin
Brave Horace - Holly Keller 505

Stripe
Stripe - Joanne Partis 763

Walter
That's Mine, Horace - Holly Keller 508

TIME TRAVELER

Field, Nathan "Nat"
King of Shadows - Susan Cooper 188

Fred
It's All Greek to Me - Jon Scieszka 891
See You Later, Gladiator - Jon Scieszka 892

Joe
It's All Greek to Me - Jon Scieszka 891
See You Later, Gladiator - Jon Scieszka 892

Ninia
The Pictish Child - Jane Yolen 1085

Sam
It's All Greek to Me - Jon Scieszka 891
See You Later, Gladiator - Jon Scieszka 892

TOAD

Toad
Lizard's Home - George Shannon 903

Toad, Gerdy
Jubal's Wish - Audrey Wood 1066

TOURIST

Martin, Melanie
The Diary of Melanie Martin - Carol Weston 1040

TOY

Bear
Blue Rabbit and Friends - Christopher
  Wormell 1070

Blue Kangaroo
I Love You, Blue Kangaroo! - Emma Chichester
  Clark 161

Blue Rabbit
Blue Rabbit and Friends - Christopher
  Wormell 1070

Goose
Blue Rabbit and Friends - Christopher
  Wormell 1070

Gorilla
When Sophie Gets Angry—Really, Really Angry -
  Molly Bang 51

Harry
Harry and Lulu - Arthur Yorinks 1086

Little Piggy
Benny's Had Enough! - Barbro Lindgren 585

Tex
Too Big! - Claire Masurel 629

Tub Child
The Tub People's Christmas - Pam Conrad 185

Tub Grandfather
The Tub People's Christmas - Pam Conrad 185

TRAVELER

Bayliss, Murray
Hurry! - Emily Arnold McCully 646

Henry
Henry Hikes to Fitchburg - D.B. Johnson 478

Unnamed Character
A Big Spooky House - Donna Washington 1027
The Magic Kerchief - Kirby Larson 557

Whittaker, Shoeshine
Shoeshine Whittaker - Helen Ketteman 517

Wilfred
The Most Amazing Dinosaur - James Stevenson 956

TRICKSTER

Crow
Pig and Crow - Kay Chorao 165

Dyer, Amos
Bearhide and Crow - Paul Brett Johnson 483

Fox
The Fox and the Stork - Gerald McDermott 650

Lit'mahn
The Girl Who Spun Gold - Virginia Hamilton 398

Rabbit, Jack
Tumbleweed Stew - Susan Stevens Crummel 211

Trickster
Trickster and the Fainting Birds - Howard
  Norman 735

Yo
Only One Cowry: A Dahomean Tale - Phillis
  Gershator 346

TRUCK

Isaac
Isaac the Ice Cream Truck - Scott Santoro 872

TURTLE

Bartleby
Bartleby of the Mighty Mississippi - Phyllis
  Shalant 900

Clever Tortoise
Clever Tortoise: A Traditional African Tale -
  Francesca Martin 627

Franklin
Franklin's Class Trip - Paulette Bourgeois 95

Turtle
Turtle and Snake at Work - Kate Spohn 946

TWIN

Emperor of Pickleberry
*What Is a Wise Bird Like You Doing in a Silly Tale
  Like This?* - Uri Shulevitz 909

Gaddy, Lisa
Secret Weapon - Matt Christopher 167

Gaddy, Ted
Secret Weapon - Matt Christopher 167

Gibson, Tessa
Be First in the Universe - Stephanie Spinner 944

Gibson, Tod
Be First in the Universe - Stephanie Spinner 944

Graber, Hannah "Hallie"
One-of-a-Kind Mallie - Kimberly Brubaker
  Bradley 98

Index entries

Rangsasa
The Dancing Pig - Judy Sierra   912

Strega Nona
Strega Nona Takes a Vacation - Tomie DePaola   261

Unnamed Character
Elwood and the Witch - Nicholas Heller   415

Wendy
The Witch Who Was Afraid of Witches - Alice Low   599

Winnie
Winnie Flies Again - Valerie Thomas   984

Wizzil
Wizzil - William Steig   949

WIZARD

Canker, Arriman
Which Witch? - Eva Ibbotson   464

Potter, Harry
Harry Potter and the Chamber of Secrets - J.K. Rowling   842
Harry Potter and the Prisoner of Azkaban - J.K. Rowling   843

Unnamed Character
Poof! - John O'Brien   740
Poof! - John O'Brien   740

Weasley, Ron
Harry Potter and the Chamber of Secrets - J.K. Rowling   842
Harry Potter and the Prisoner of Azkaban - J.K. Rowling   843

WOLF

Big Wolf
Big Wolf and Little Wolf - Sharon Phillips Denslow   259

Bigbad Wolf
Little Wolf's Book of Badness - Ian Whybrow   1045

Little Wolf
Big Wolf and Little Wolf - Sharon Phillips Denslow   259
Little Wolf's Book of Badness - Ian Whybrow   1045

Mama Wolf
Big Wolf and Little Wolf - Sharon Phillips Denslow   259

Mr. Wolf
Mr. Wolf's Pancakes - Jan Fearnley   310
Yum!: A Preston Pig Story - Colin McNaughton   668

Snowy
White Wolf - Henrietta Branford   100

Unnamed Character
The Best Place - Susan Meddaugh   673
The Big Bad Rumor - Jonathan Meres   680
Get That Pest! - Erin Douglas   274
Swine Lake - James Marshall   623

Wolf
The Tale of Gilbert Alexander Pig - Gael Cresp   207
Wolf! - Becky Bloom   83

WORKER

Amonth
The Wide-Awake Princess - Katherine Paterson   765

Bill
The Doorman - Edward Grimm   382

Curbhopper, Calvin
Messenger, Messenger - Robert Burleigh   132

Dolores
City Pig - Karen Wallace   1017

Dream Collector
The Dream Collector - Troon Harrison   404

GninGnin
Love as Strong as Ginger - Lenore Look   598

Hopper, Dwayne
Peril in the Bessledorf Parachute Factory - Phyllis Reynolds Naylor   721

Jake
Soldier Mom - Alice Mead   672

John
The Doorman - Edward Grimm   382

Jones, Joan
I Was a Rat! - Philip Pullman   804

Julian
I Like Your Buttons! - Sarah Marwil Lamstein   553

Magruder, Delores
Peril in the Bessledorf Parachute Factory - Phyllis Reynolds Naylor   721

Small, Abraham
Abraham's Battle: A Novel of Gettysburg - Sara Harrell Banks   57

Turtle
Turtle and Snake at Work - Kate Spohn   946

Woodcutter
In the Moonlight Mist: A Korean Tale - Daniel San Souci   864

WRESTLER

Monroe, Willie
The Tale of Willie Monroe - Alan Schroeder   885

WRITER

Basho
Basho and the Fox - Tim Myers   715

Clem
Weird Stories from the Lonesome Cafe - Judy Cox   201

Dickinson, Emily
The Mouse of Amherst - Elizabeth Spires   945

Emmaline
The Mouse of Amherst - Elizabeth Spires   945

Mama
Bravo, Maurice! - Rebecca Bond   89

Shakespeare, Will
King of Shadows - Susan Cooper   188

YOUNG MAN

Monroe, Willie
The Tale of Willie Monroe - Alan Schroeder   885

YOUNG WOMAN

Rani
One Grain of Rice - Demi   257

Unnamed Character
The Three Sillies - Steven Kellogg   511

ZEBRA

Zink
Zink - Cherie Bennett   71

Age Index

This index groups books according to the grade levels for which they are most appropriate. Beneath each grade range, book titles are listed alphabetically, followed by the author's name and the entry number.

GRADES 1-2

GRADES 1-3

GRADES 1-4

GRADES 1-5

GRADES 2-3

GRADES 2-4

GRADES 4-8

GRADES 5-7

GRADES 5-8

Page Count Index

This index groups books according to their page counts. Beneath each page count range, book titles are listed alphabetically, followed by the author's name, the exact page count and the entry number.

151 TO 200 PAGES

MORE THAN 200 PAGES

Illustrator Index

This index lists the illustrators of the featured titles. Illustrators are listed alphabetically, followed by the title, author, and entry number of the book or books in which the artist's work appears.

A

Adams, Jean Ekman
Clarence Goes Out West and Meets a Purple Horse - Jean Ekman Adams 3

Aggs, Patrice
The Visitor - Patrice Aggs 10

Ajhar, Brian
The Giggler Treatment - Roddy Doyle 276

Alborough, Jez
Duck in the Truck - Jez Alborough 12
Hug - Jez Alborough 13

Aldridge, Eve
Hurry Granny Annie - Arlene Alda 14

Alexander, Martha
And My Mean Old Mother Will Be Sorry, Blackboard Bear - Martha Alexander 19

Aliki
All by Myself! - Aliki 20

Allen, Jonathan
Simply Delicious! - Margaret Mahy 614

Allen, Thomas B.
Good-bye for Today: The Diary of a Young Girl at Sea - Peter Roop 828

Alley, R.W.
Hey, Little Baby! - Nola Buck 120

Allibone, Judith
Jody's Beans - Malachy Doyle 275

Andersen, Bethanne
Kindle Me a Riddle: A Pioneer Story - Roberta Karim 496

Andriani, Renee W.
Annabel the Actress Starring in Gorilla My Dreams - Ellen Conford 183

Anholt, Catherine
Billy and the Big New School - Laurence Anholt 25
Harry's Home - Laurence Anholt 26
Sophie and the New Baby - Laurence Anholt 27

Apple, Margot
Big Mama - Tony Crunk 212
Brave Martha - Margot Apple 32

Argent, Kerry
Sleepy Bears - Mem Fox 324

Arnold, Tedd
Axle Annie - Robin Pulver 805

Huggly Takes a Bath - Tedd Arnold 35

Aruego, Jose
Lizard's Home - George Shannon 903
Mouse in Love - Robert Kraus 541

Asch, Frank
Baby Bird's First Nest - Frank Asch 36
Moonbear's Dream - Frank Asch 37

Ashworth, Camilla
Who Do You Love? - Martin Waddell 1011

Atwell, Debbie
River - Debbie Atwell 39

Auch, Mary Jane
The Nutquacker - Mary Jane Auch 40

Austin, Michael
The Horned Toad Prince - Jackie Mims Hopkins 444

Auzary-Luton, Sylvie
1, 2, 3, Music! - Sylvie Auzary-Luton 41

B

Bailey, Peter
Spider Sparrow - Dick King-Smith 525

Bailey, Wendy
When Addie Was Scared - Linda Bailey 48

Baker, Leslie
Paris Cat - Leslie Baker 50

Bancroft, Bronwyn
Big Rain Coming - Katrina Germein 345

Bang, Molly
When Sophie Gets Angry—Really, Really Angry - Molly Bang 51

Barasch, Lynne
Radio Rescue - Lynne Barasch 58

Barbour, Karen
I Have an Olive Tree - Eve Bunting 126

Barron, Rex
The Big Bug Ball - Dee Lillegard 581

Bartlett, Alison
Paddiwak and Cozy - Berlie Doherty 271

Barton, Jill
Off to School, Baby Duck! - Amy Hest 431

Bassede, Francine
A Day with the Bellyflops - Francine Bassede 60
George Paints His House - Francine Bassede 61

Bates, Ivan
All by Myself - Ivan Bates 62

Bechtold, Lisze
Buster: The Very Shy Dog - Lisze Bechtold 68

Beck, Andrea
Elliot Bakes a Cake - Andrea Beck 69

Beier, Ellen
The Promise Quilt - Candice F. Ransom 809

Bendall-Brunello, John
My Goose Betsy - Trudi Braun 101

Bender, Robert
Swine Divine - Jan Carr 148

Bennett, Gary
Rainy's Powwow - Linda Theresa Raczek 807

Berkeley, Jon
Scarlette Beane - Karen Wallace 1018

Berry, Holly
The Bowlegged Rooster and Other Tales That Signify - Joyce Carol Thomas 982
Roughing It on the Oregon Trail - Diane Stanley 948

Biedrzycki, David
Dory Story - Jerry Pallotta 758

Biet, Pascal
Mice Make Trouble - Becky Bloom 82
Wolf! - Becky Bloom 83

Billin-Frye, Paige
This Is the Turkey - Abby Levine 571

Binch, Caroline
Newborn - Kathy Henderson 418
Starring Grace - Mary Hoffman 440

Birmingham, Christian
A Baby for Grace - Ian Whybrow 1044
Wombat Goes Walkabout - Michael Morpurgo 697

Bishop, Gavin
Stay Awake, Bear! - Gavin Bishop 79
The Video Shop Sparrow - Joy Cowley 198

Blake, Quentin
Trouble on Thunder Mountain - Russell Hoban 436
Wizzil - William Steig 949

Blake, Robert J.
Fledgling - Robert J. Blake 81

Illustrator Index

Y

Yaccarino, Dan
Deep in the Jungle - Dan Yaccarino 1072
Surviving Brick Johnson - Laurie Myers 714
Trashy Town - Andrea Zimmerman 1097

Yalowitz, Paul
Mary Veronica's Egg - Mary Nethery 725
The Runaway Latkes - Leslie Kimmelman 521

Yang, Belle
Chili-Chili-Chin-Chin - Belle Yang 1073

Yardley, Joanna
It's Funny Where Ben's Train Takes Him - Robert
  Burleigh 131

Yee, Wong Herbert
Get That Pest! - Erin Douglas 274
Hamburger Heaven - Wong Herbert Yee 1075

Yezerski, Thomas F.
Mimmy & Sophie - Miriam Cohen 177
Not My Dog - Colby Rodowsky 826
Queen of the World - Thomas F. Yezerski 1079

Young, Dan
Dustin's Big School Day - Alden R. Carter 151

Young, Ed
The Hunter: A Chinese Folktale - Mary
  Casanova 154

Z

Zagwyn, Deborah Turney
Apple Batter - Deborah Turney Zagwyn 1088
The Winter Gift - Deborah Turney Zagwyn 1089

Zerbetz, Evon
Blueberry Shoe - Ann Dixon 270

Zhang, Christopher Zhong-Yuan
The Royal Bee - Frances Park 761

Zimmerman, H. Werner
Each One Special - Frieda Wishinsky 1058

Zimmerman, Werner
Brave Highland Heart - Heather Kellerhals-
  Stewart 509

Author Index

This index is an alphabetical listing of the authors of books featured in entries and those listed under "Other books by the author" and "Other books you might like." For each author, the titles of books written and entry numbers are also provided. Editors and co-authors are interfiled with Author names. Bold numbers indicate a featured main entry; other numbers refer to books recommended for further reading.

A

Aardema, Verna
Bringing the Rain to Kapiti Plain: A Nandi Tale 961
How Ostrich Got Its Long Neck 18
How the Ostrich Got Its Long Neck 516
Misoso: Once Upon a Time Tales from Africa 742
Rabbit Makes a Monkey of Lion 627
Why Mosquitoes Buzz in People's Ears: A West African Tale 264

Ackerman, Karen
Bingleman's Midway 731
By the Dawn's Early Light 55, 942
The Night Crossing 639, 788, 801

Ada, Alma Flor
Dear Peter Rabbit 953, 1020
Friend Frog **1**
The Gold Coin 2, 315
Jordi's Star 1, 2
The Malachite Palace 1, 2, 413, 635
My Name Is Maria Isabel 73
The Three Golden Oranges **2**, 543
Yours Truly, Goldilocks 1, 2, 282, 304, 310, 1045

Adam, Addie
Hilda and the Mad Scientist 553

Adams, Adrienne
The Easter Egg Artists 692

Adams, Jean Ekman
Clarence Goes Out West and Meets a Purple Horse **3**

Adler, C.S.
Courtyard Cat 908
Her Blue Straw Hat 253

Adler, David A.
Andy and Tamika **4**, 7, 8, 1052
The Babe & I **5**, 975, 989
Cam Jansen and the Barking Treasure Mystery **6**
Cam Jansen and the Catnapping Mystery 6, 306
Cam Jansen and the Ghostly Mystery **6**
Cam Jansen and the Scary Snake Mystery 4, 6

The Cam Jansen Series 730, 844, 883, 905
Chanukah in Chelm 5
Hilde & Eli: Children of the Holocaust 801
Lou Gehrig: The Luckiest Man 5
Lucky Stars 5, 8
The Many Troubles of Andy Russell 4, 7, 8, 53, 220, 503, 523, 898
Parachuting Hamsters and Andy Russell **7**
A Picture Book of Thomas Jefferson 320
School Trouble for Andy Russell 4, 7, **8**
Young Cam Jansen and the Baseball Mystery **9**
Young Cam Jansen and the Ice Skate Mystery 9
Young Cam Jansen and the Lost Tooth 9
Young Cam Jansen and the Missing Cookie 9, 850, 904

Adlerman, Daniel
Africa Calling: Nighttime Falling 961

Agee, Jon
The Incredible Painting of Felix Clousseau 610

Aggs, Patrice
The Visitor **10**

Ahlberg, Allan
The Better Brown Stories 276, 314
It Was a Dark and Stormy Night 909

Ahlberg, Janet
The Jolly Christmas Postman 953
The Jolly Postman, or Other People's Letters 796

Aiken, Joan
Cold Shoulder Road **11**
Dangerous Games **11**
Is Underground 11
The Wolves of Willoughby Chase 11

Alarcon, Karen Beaumont
Louella Mae, She's Run Away! 148

Albert, Richard E.
Alejandro's Gift 514

Alberts, Nancy Markham
Elizabeth's Beauty 123

Alborough, Jez
Cuddly Dudley 12, 13
Duck in the Truck **12**
Hug **13**, 513
It's the Bear! 12, 13, 16, 343, 820
My Friend Bear 12
Watch Out! Big Bro's Coming! 12, 13, 625, 680
Where's My Teddy? 12, 13, 662, 1038

Alda, Arlene
Arlene Alda's ABC 14
Hurry Granny Annie **14**
Matthew and His Dad 14
Pig, Horse, or Cow, Don't Wake Me Now 14, 615, 1063

Alderson, Brian
Stories for Me! 15
The Swan's Stories 15
The Tale of the Turnip **15**

Alderson, Sue Ann
Bonnie McSmithers Is at It Again! 16
Hurry Up, Bonnie! 16
Ida and the Wool Smugglers 16
Wherever Bears Be: A Story for Two Voices **16**

Alexander, Lloyd
The Arcadians 17
The Fortune Tellers 18
Gypsy Rizka **17**
The House Gobbaleen 18
How the Cat Swallowed Thunder **18**, 853
The Iron Ring 11, 17, 803
The Remarkable Journey of Prince Jen 17
Time Cat: The Remarkable Journeys of Jason and Gareth 563
The Truthful Harp 18

Alexander, Martha
And My Mean Old Mother Will Be Sorry, Blackboard Bear **19**, 836
Good Night, Lily 19
Nobody Asked Me If I Wanted a Baby Sister 27, 74, 620
We're in Big Trouble, Blackboard Bear 19
Where Does the Sky End, Grandpa? 19
You're a Genius, Blackboard Bear 19, 82, 527, 1041

Alexander, Nina
Megan and the Borealis Butterfly 570

Aliki
All by Myself! **20**
Best Friends Together Again 20, 238
I'm Growing! 20
Marianthe's Story: Painted Words/ Spoken Memories 717, 835
Those Summers 20, 177, 341, 473
We Are Best Friends 604

Allard, Harry
Miss Nelson Is Back 175, 407
The Stupids Step Out 622

Allen, Debbie
Brothers of the Knight 21
Dancing in the Wings **21**, 713

Allen, Judy
Eagle 81

Alphin, Elaine Marie
Ghost Cadet 223

Altman, Linda Jacobs
Amelia's Road 22
Forever Outsiders: Jews and History from Ancient Times to August 1935 22
The Legend of Freedom Hill **22**
Small Dogs 22

Anaya, Rudolfo
Farolitos for Abuelo 23
The Farolitos of Christmas 23
Maya's Children: The Story of La Llorona 23
My Land Sings: Stories from Rio Grande 252
Roadrunner's Dance **23**

Ancona, George
Carnaval 329
The Pinata Maker 936
Powwow 807

Andersen, Hans Christian
The Fairy Tales of Hans Christian Andersen 782
Twelve Tales 573
The Ugly Duckling 338, 783

Anderson, Laurie Halse
Ndito Runs 24
No Time for Mother's Day **24**
Turkey Pox 24, 834

Bowen, Fred
Playoff Dreams 456, 457

Bowen, Gary
Stranded at Plimoth Plantation 1626 117

Bradbury, Ray
Switch on the Night 1059

Bradby, Marie
The Longest Wait 97
Momma, Where Are You From? **97**, 544
More than Anything Else 97, 450, 761

Bradley, Kimberly Brubaker
One-of-a-Kind Mallie **98**, 99, 586
Ruthie's Gift 98, 99, 392
Weaver's Daughter **99**

Bradman, Tony
This Little Baby 418
A Treasury of Pirate Stories 656

Brady, Kimberley Smith
Keeper for the Sea 325, 758

Brandenberg, Franz
A Fun Weekend 49

Brandt, Keith
Daniel Boone, Frontier Adventures 350

Branford, Henrietta
Fire, Bed and Bone 100
The Theft of Thor's Hammer 100
White Wolf **100**

Braun, Trudi
My Goose Betsy **101**

Braybrooks, Ann
Bounce Around Tigger! 102
A Hunny, Funny, Sunny Day! 102
No More Mess! 102
Plenty of Pockets **102**

Breathed, Berkeley
Edwurd Fudwupper Fibbed Big: Explained by Fannie Fudwupper 103
Goodnight Opus 103, 603, 1080
Red Ranger Came Calling 103
A Wish for Wings that Work: An Opus Christmas Story 103

Brennan, Herbie
The Mystery Machine 129

Brenner, Barbara
The Boy Who Loved to Draw: Benjamin West 670

Brett, Jan
Armadillo Rodeo 105
Christmas Trolls 105
Comet's Nine Lives 104, 401
Gingerbread Baby **104**
Goldilocks and the Three Bears 304
The Hat 104, 105
Hedgie's Surprise **105**
The Mitten: A Ukranian Folktale 104, 105, 270, 510, 1032
The Trouble with Trolls 105

Brewster, Patience
Two Bushy Badgers 208, 1039

Bridges, Margaret Park
If I Were Your Father 1067

Bridwell, Norman
Clifford and the Big Parade 677
Clifford the Small Red Puppy 678
Clifford's Birthday Party 143

Bright, Robert
Georgie 287
Georgie and the Runaway Balloon 556

Brimner, Larry Dane
Merry Christmas, Old Armadillo 954

Brink, Carol Ryrie
Caddie Woodlawn 441, 815
Magical Melons 98

Brisson, Pat
Bertie's Picture Day **106**, 755
Hot Fudge Hero 106, 107, 791
Kate on the Coast 107
Little Sister, Big Sister 106
Magic Carpet 411
Sky Memories **107**
The Summer My Father Was Ten 106, 107, 663
Wanda's Roses 87, 106, 107, 744
Your Best Friend, Kate 1040

Brokaw, Nancy Steele
Leaving Emma **108**

Brooks, Erik
The Practically Perfect Pajamas **109**

Brown, Craig McFarland
City Sounds 424

Brown, Don
Alice Ramsey's Grand Adventure 347

Brown, Ken
Mucky Pup 110
Mucky Pup's Christmas **110**
Nellie's Knot 110

Brown, Laurie Krasny
Rex and Lilly Family Time 234, 436
Rex and Lilly School Time 686

Brown, Marc
Arthur and the Popularity Test 542
Arthur and the True Francine 103
Arthur in a Pickle 250, 508
Arthur Lost and Found 111
Arthur Writes a Story 583
Arthur's Chicken Pox 930
Arthur's Family Treasury 111
Arthur's Family Vacation 353
Arthur's First Sleepover 1059
Arthur's New Puppy 243, 877
Arthur's Perfect Christmas 111
Arthur's Pet Business 466
Arthur's Underwear **111**
D.W. Flips! 112
D.W., Go to Your Room! **112**, 162
D.W. Rides Again! 112, 687
D.W.'s Lost Blankie 112
D.W. the Picky Eater 370, 379
D.W. Thinks Big 477

Brown, Marcia
Dick Whittington and His Cat 15
Stone Soup 211

Brown, Margaret Wise
Another Important Book **113**
Big Red Barn 26
Goodnight Moon 113, 641, 768
The Important Book 113
Little Donkey Close Your Eyes 65, 405, 879
The Little Scarecrow Boy 449, 637
The Noisy Book 424
The Runaway Bunny 31, 113, 354

Brown, Ruth
Copycat 114, 137, 293, 357, 695
Cry Baby 114
Holly: The True Story of a Cat **114**
Mad Summer Night's Dream 1050

The Picnic 114
Toad 114

Browne, Anthony
Bear Goes to Town 82
Changes 980
Willy and Hugh 283, 522
Willy the Dreamer 875
Willy the Wizard 593, 617

Browne, Eileen
Tick-Tock 638

Broyles, Anne
Shy Mama's Halloween **115**

Bruchac, Joseph
The Arrow Over the Door 117, 561
A Boy Called Slow 116
The Boy Who Lived with the Bears: And Other Iroquois Stories 116, 117, 355
Children of the Longhouse 117
Crazy Horse's Vision **116**
Eagle Song 590, 664
The First Strawberries: A Cherokee Story 116
Fox Song 116
Squanto's Journey: The Story of the First Thanksgiving **117**

Brumbeau, Jeff
The Man-in-the-Moon in Love 118
The Quiltmaker's Gift **118**, 543, 557

Brutschy, Jennifer
Celeste and Crabapple Sam 208

Bryan, Ashley
Beat the Story-Drum, Pum-Pum 742

Buchholz, Quint
The Collector of Moments 119
Sleep Well, Little Bear 119, 242, 666

Buck, Nola
Gotcha! 120
Hey, Little Baby! **120**
Oh, Cats! 120
Sid and Sam 120

Buckley, Helen E.
Josie and the Snow 121
Josie's Buttercup 121
Moonlight Kite 121
Someday with My Father 121
Where Did Josie Go? **121**

Buehner, Caralyn
It's a Spoon Not a Shovel 214
A Job for Wittilda 415

Bull, Emma
The Princess and the Lord of the Night 413

Bunting, Eve
Blackwater **122**, 764
Butterfly House **123**
Can You Do This, Old Badger? **124**
Cheyenne Again 125
Dandelions 994
A Day's Work 124, 125, 126, 127, 190, 663
December 126, 128, 331
Dreaming of America: An Ellis Island Story **125**
Ducky 124
Flower Garden 806
For Always 122
Going Home 125, 126, 474, 816
I Am the Mummy Heb-Nefert 128
I Have an Olive Tree 123, **126**, 747, 1065
The In-Between Days 122, 129
The Memory String 884

Night of the Gargoyles 129
Night Tree 964
On Call Back Mountain 128
Our Sixth-Grade Sugar Babies 770
A Picnic in October **127**
The Pumpkin Fair 929
Secret Place 124, 128, 712
Sharing Susan 122
Smoky Night 123, 125, 126, 128
So Far from the Sea 125, 126, 127, 128
Some Frog! 123, 129
Someday a Tree 186, 366
Spying on Miss Mueller 122
A Sudden Silence 122
Summer Wheels 132
Sunflower House 1018
Swan in Love **128**
Train to Somewhere 125, 127, 500
A Turkey for Thanksgiving 156, 571
Twinnies 124
Wanna Buy an Alien? **129**
The Wednesday Surprise 88
Your Move 129

Burgess, Melvin
An Angel for May 130
Burning Issy 130
The Copper Treasure **130**
The Earth Giant 130, 1085

Burke-Weiner, Kimberly
The Maybe Garden 966

Burleigh, Robert
Flight: The Story of Charles Lindbergh 131
Hercules 132
Home Run: The Story of Babe Ruth 131, 132
Hoops 131, 132, 202
It's Funny Where Ben's Train Takes Him **131**, 132, 710, 1095
Messenger, Messenger **132**

Burnett, Frances Hodgson
The Secret Garden 438, 458, 588, 1014

Burningham, John
Cloudland 133
Courtney 133, 367, 1086
The Friend 737
Harvey Slumfenburger's Christmas Present 602, 943, 1036
Hey! Get Off Our Train 133
Whaddayamean **133**, 569

Burns, Marilyn
Spaghetti and Meatballs for All 257

Burton, Marilee Robin
My Best Shoes 827

Burton, Virginia Lee
Katy and the Big Snow 805
The Little House 752
Mike Mulligan and His Steam Shovel 197

Bush, Timothy
Benjamin McFadden and the Robot Babysitter 506, 780

Butler, Dorothy
My Brown Bear Barney 297

Butler, Kristi T.
Rip's Secret Spot 274

Byars, Betsy
Ant Plays Bear 66, 234, 489
Beans on the Roof 134
Bingo Brown and the Language of Love 688
The Computer Nut 192

Author Index

Author Index

Author Index

Title Index

This index alphabetically lists all titles featured in entries and those listed under "Other books by the author" and "Other books you might like." Each title is followed by the author's name and the number of the entry of that title. Bold numbers indicate featured main entries; other numbers refer to books recommended for further reading.

Title Index

Title Index

Title Index

Title Index

Title Index

Title Index

Title Index

Title Index

Title Index

Title Index